MENTAL HEALTH ACT
MANUAL

MENTAL HEALTH ACT MANUAL

by

Richard M. Jones M.A. (Kent and Brunel),
Solicitor, C.Q.S.W.

Consultant, Blake Morgan, Solicitors
Honorary Professor of Law, Cardiff University

Eighteenth Edition

SWEET & MAXWELL

THOMSON REUTERS

Published in 2015 by Thomson Reuters (Professional) UK Limited trading as
Sweet & Maxwell, Friars House, 160 Blackfriars Road, London, SE1 8EZ
(Registered in England & Wales, Company No. 1679046. Registered Office and
address for service: 2nd floor, 1 Mark Square, Leonard Street,
London EC2A 4EG)

*For further information on our products and services, visit
www.sweetandmaxwell.co.uk*

Typeset in Great Britain by Hobbs the Printers Ltd, Southampton
Printed and bound by CPI Group (UK) Ltd, Croydon, CR0 4YY

*No natural forests were destroyed to make this product;
only farmed timber was used and re-planted.*

A CIP catalogue record for this book
is available from the British Library

ISBN 978-0-414-05109-6

PREFACE

The first Code of Practice on the Mental Health Act, which was published in 1990, comprised 123 pages. The latest edition of the Code comprises 459 pages. The Explanatory Memorandum on the Act, which was published in 1983, comprised 86 pages. Its successor, the Reference Guide, comprises 378 pages. This remarkable rate of inflation is to be regretted as the size of the documents might militate against them being used as working tools for busy practitioners. A less expansive approach should be encouraged as the desire to include every possible dimension can result in core messages being obscured.

A significant theme in the Code is the requirement placed on health and social care bodies to produce documents. The Code stipulates that 56 policy and procedural documents should be put in place, 25 of which are new. The need to create, monitor and review so many documents represents a significant investment of limited resources. There is a danger that this task will be seen as an end in itself; another box to be ticked rather than the creation of tools that can be used to ensure that services are delivered legally and safely. It should be remembered that the horrors of Winterbourne View Hospital occurred even though its "policy, procedures, operational practices and clinical governance . . . were impressive" (*Winterbourne View Hospital – A Serious Case Review*, p.x).

A criticism that can be levelled at the Code is that it betrays a tendency to provide guidance on the law as the authors would like it to be, rather than the law as set out in the Act. The effect of this tendency is that the Code is, in effect, attempting to legislate by the back door. For example, the authors clearly believe that the long term leave of patients in the community under s.17 of the Act should only take place in exceptional circumstances. The Code states that such leave "should normally be of short duration and not normally more than seven days" (para.27.11), and that if a longer period of leave is granted it should "be for a specific purpose or a fixed period, and not normally more than one month" (para.31.5). This guidance, which is clearly based on the authors' preference for patients to be placed on community treatment orders, bears no relation to what the Act says. Section 17 provides responsible clinicians with a straight choice as to whether to use either long term section 17 leave or community treatment orders if leave is to be granted for more than seven days. If Parliament wanted section 17 leave to be restricted in the manner suggested in the Code it could have said so. Parliament presumably left the decision in the hands of responsible clinicians because both routes have their advantages and disadvantages which need to be evaluated in the light of a patient's particular circumstances. As the case law demonstrates, patients have been successfully cared for in the community under section 17 leave for very lengthy periods.

The size of the new Code is such that it was not practicable to include all of its chapters in this edition. I have included those chapters which are directly related to the application of the Act and which offer something more than a conventional explanation of its provisions. Extensive extracts from some of the remaining chapters and from the Reference Guide are reproduced throughout the text.

The law is stated on material that was available to me on August 14, 2015.

Richard Jones
e-mail: richard.m.jones@blakemorgan.co.uk

CONTENTS

Preface   v
Table of Cases   ix

PART 1
Mental Health Act 1983   1

PART 2
Delegated Legislation
Mental Health (Care and Treatment) (Scotland) Act 2003
    (Consequential Provisions) Order 2005   637
Mental Health (Mutual Recognition) Regulations 2008   640
Mental Health (Conflicts of Interest) (England) Regulations 2008   642
Mental Health (Approved Mental Health Professionals) (Approval)
    (England) Regulations 2008   647
Mental Health (Hospital, Guardianship and Treatment) (England)
    Regulations 2008   653
Mental Health Act 1983 (Independent Mental Health Advocates)
    (England) Regulations 2008   745

PART 3
Practice and Procedure
Civil Procedure Rules 1998   749
Tribunal Procedure (First-Tier Tribunal) (Health, Education and Social
    Care Chamber) Rules 2008   753
Practice Direction—First-Tier Tribunal, Health Education and
    Social Care Chamber, Mental Health Cases   823
Practice Direction—First Tier and Upper Tribunal, Child, Vulnerable
    Adult and Sensitive Witnesses   841
Practice Statement—Delegation of functions to staff and to registrars
    on or after 27 April 2015   842

PART 4
Government Guidance
Extracts from the Code of Practice—Mental Health Act 1983   845

PART 5
Human Rights Act 1998   997

PART 6
Deprivations of Liberty—Mental Health Act 1983 or Mental
    Capacity Act 2005?   1041

APPENDIX A
Further powers to restrain and/or detain mentally disordered patients 1057

APPENDIX B
High Security Psychiatric Services (Arrangements for Visits by
    Children) Directions 2013   1061

APPENDIX C
High Security Psychiatric Services (Arrangements for Safety and
Security) Directions 2013   1067

APPENDIX D
Mental Health Act 1983—Instructions with respect to the exercise
of Approval Functions 2014   1091

APPENDIX E
Law Society Practice Note—Representation before mental
health tribunals   1103

INDEX   1117

Table of Cases

A, Re; C, Re; sub nom. A Local Authority v C; A Local Authority v A [2010] EWHC 978
(Fam); [2010] 2 F.L.R. 1363; (2010) 13 C.C.L. Rep. 404; [2010] Fam. Law 929. 6–005
A (A Mental Patient) v The Scottish Ministers. *See* Anderson v Scottish Ministers
A (A Child), Re [2015] EWHC 1709 (Fam) 1–1277
A (Children) (Conjoined Twins: Medical Treatment) (No.1), Re; sub nom. A (Children)
(Conjoined Twins: Surgical Separation), Re [2001] Fam. 147; [2001] 2 W.L.R. 480;
[2000] 4 All E.R. 961; [2001] 1 F.L.R. 1; [2000] 3 F.C.R. 577; [2000] H.R.L.R. 721;
[2001] U.K.H.R.R. 1; 9 B.H.R.C. 261; [2000] Lloyd's Rep. Med. 425; (2001) 57
B.M.L.R. 1; [2001] Crim. L.R. 400; [2001] Fam. Law 18; (2000) 150 N.L.J. 1453 CA
(Civ Div) 5–009
A (Children) (Conjoined Twins: Surgical Separation), Re. *See* A (Children) Conjoined Twins:
Medical Treatment) (No.1), Re
A (Children) (Jurisdiction: Return of Child), Re. *See* A v A (Children) (Habitual Residence)
A Local Authority v AK [2012] EWHC B29 (COP) 1–010
A Local Authority v E [2012] EWHC 1639 (COP); [2012] 2 F.C.R. 523; [2012] H.R.L.R. 29;
(2012) 15 C.C.L. Rep. 511; [2012] Med. L.R. 472; (2012) 127 B.M.L.R. 133 5–035
A Primary Care Trust v LDV. *See* LDV, Re
A v A (Children) (Habitual Residence); sub nom. A (Children) (Jurisdiction: Return of Child),
Re; ZA v NA (Abduction: Habitual Residence) [2013] UKSC 60; [2014] A.C. 1; [2013] 3
W.L.R. 761; [2014] 1 All E.R. 827; [2014] 1 F.L.R. 111; [2013] 3 F.C.R. 559; [2013]
Fam. Law 1528; (2013) 157(36) S.J.L.B. 37 1–409
A v United Kingdom (6840/74) Unreported ECHR 5–014
A v United Kingdom [1998] 2 F.L.R. 959; [1998] 3 F.C.R. 597; (1999) 27 E.H.R.R. 611; 5
B.H.R.C. 137; 1998 Fam. L.R. 118; [1998] Crim. L.R. 892; [1998] H.R.C.D. 870; [1998]
Fam. Law 733 ECHR 5–011
AA v Cheshire and Wirral Partnership NHS Foundation Trust [2009] UKUT 195 (AAC);
[2009] M.H.L.R. 308 . . . . 1–871, 1–915, , 3–068, 3–168, 3–176
AB v LB (Mental Health Patient); sub nom. B v B (Mental Health Patient) [1980] 1 W.L.R. 116;
[1979] 3 All E.R. 494; 78 L.G.R. 1; (1980) 124 S.J. 16 CA (Civ Div) 1–437, 3–005
Abdulaziz v United Kingdom (A/94); Cabales v United Kingdom (9473/81); Balkandali v
United Kingdom (9474/81) (1985) 7 E.H.R.R. 471 ECHR 5–053
AC v Partnerships in Care Ltd [2012] UKUT 450 (AAC); [2013] M.H.L.R. 52 1–945, 3–088,
3–153
ACCG v ACC [2013] EWHC 3859 (COP) 1–1147
Aerts v Belgium (2000) 29 E.H.R.R. 50; 5 B.H.R.C. 382; (2000) 53 B.M.L.R. 79; [1998]
H.R.C.D. 749 ECHR 1–524, 1–1334, 5–013, 5–022, 5–029
AF v Nottinghamshire NHS Trust [2015] UKUT 216 (AAC) 1–915, 1–1133, 3–046, 3–108
Afanasyev v Ukraine (38722/02) (2006) 42 E.H.R.R. 52 ECHR 5–011
AH v West London Mental Health Trust [2011] UKUT 74 (AAC); [2011] M.H.L.R.
85. . . . . 1–019, 3–140
AH v West London Mental Health Trust [2010] UKUT 264 (AAC); [2010] M.H.L.R. 326 . . . 3–140
AH (Sudan) v Secretary of State for the Home Department; sub nom. Secretary of State for the
Home Department v AH (Sudan) [2007] UKHL 49; [2008] 1 A.C. 678; [2007] 3 W.L.R. 832;
[2008] 4 All E.R. 190; [2008] Imm. A.R. 289; [2008] I.N.L.R. 100; (2007) 151
S.J.L.B. 1500 3–153
Al-Nashif v Bulgaria (50963/99) (2003) 36 E.H.R.R. 37 ECHR 5–039
Ali v Birmingham City Council; Tomlinson v Birmingham City Council; Ibrahim v
Birmingham City Council; Moran v Manchester City Council; R. (on the application of
Aweys) v Birmingham City Council; sub nom. Birmingham City Council v Ali [2010]
UKSC 8; [2010] 2 W.L.R. 471; [2010] P.T.S.R. 524; [2010] 2 All E.R. 175; [2010]
H.R.L.R. 18; [2010] U.K.H.R.R. 417; [2010] H.L.R. 22; [2010] B.L.G.R. 401; (2010)
154(7) S.J.L.B. 37 5–030
Aliev v Ukraine (41220/98) July 29, 2003 5–051

Table of Cases

AM v SLAM NHS Foundation Trust. *See* AM v South London & Maudsley NHS Foundation Trust

AM v South London & Maudsley NHS Foundation Trust [2013] UKUT 365 (AAC); [2014] M.H.L.R. 181 . . . . 1–034, 1–047, 1–913, 1–916, 1–919, 1–1270, 6–015, 6–021, E–012

AM v West London MH NHS Trust [2012] UKUT 382 (AAC); [2012] M.H.L.R. 399; permission to appeal refused [2013] EWCA Civ 1010 . . . . 1–915, 1–1133, 3–046, 3–112

AMA v Greater Manchester West Mental Health NHS Foundation Trust [2015] UKUT 36 (AAC) 3–012, 3–067, 3–072, 3–100

An NHS Trust v A: sub nom. A, Re [2013] EWHC 2442 (COP); [2014] 2 W.L.R. 607; [2013] Med. L.R. 561; (2014) 136 B.M.L.R. 115 . . . . 1–787, 1–788, 6–016

Anderson v Scottish Ministers; sub nom. A v Scottish Ministers; Reid v Scottish Ministers; Doherty v Scottish Ministers [2001] UKPC D 5; [2003] 2 A.C. 602; [2002] 3 W.L.R. 1460; 2002 S.C. (P.C.) 63; 2001 S.L.T. 1331; [2002] H.R.L.R. 6; [2002] U.K.H.R.R. 1; [2001] M.H.L.R. 192; 2001 G.W.D. 33–1312 . . . . 1–573, 5–019

Anufrijeva v Southwark LBC; sub nom. R. (on the application of Anufrijeva) v Southwark LBC; R. (on the application of M) v Secretary of State for the Home Department; R. (on the application of N) v Secretary of State for the Home Department [2003] EWCA Civ 1406; [2004] Q.B. 1124; [2004] 2 W.L.R. 603; [2004] 1 All E.R. 833; [2004] 1 F.L.R. 8; [2003] 3 F.C.R. 673; [2004] H.R.L.R. 1; [2004] U.K.H.R.R. 1; 15 B.H.R.C. 526; [2004] H.L.R. 22; [2004] B.L.G.R. 184; (2003) 6 C.C.L. Rep. 415; [2004] Fam. Law 12; (2003) 100(44) L.S.G. 30 . . . . 5–033, 5–034, 5–035, 5–040

Application for Judicial Review, Re [2008] NIQB 75 3–011

AR v Bronglais Hospital Pembrokeshire and Derwen NHS Trust [2001] EWHC Admin 792; [2001] M.H.L.R. 175 . . . . 1–168, 1–1157

AS v First-tier Tribunal, Upper Tribunal Case No.JR/3048/2012 . . . . 1–865, 3–153

Ashingdane v Secretary of State for Social Services Unreported February 18, 1990 CA (Civ Div) 1–1355

Ashingdane v United Kingdom (A/93); sub nom. Ashingdane v United Kingdom (8225/78) (1985) 7 E.H.R.R. 528 ECHR 1–059, 5–019, 5–022, 5–024, 5–030

Ashworth Hospital Authority v MGN Ltd; sub nom. Ashworth Security Hospital v MGN Ltd [2002] UKHL 29; [2002] 1 W.L.R. 2033; [2002] 4 All E.R. 193; [2002] C.P.L.R. 712; [2002] E.M.L.R. 36; [2002] H.R.L.R. 41; [2002] U.K.H.R.R. 1263; 12 B.H.R.C. 443; [2003] F.S.R. 17; (2002) 67 B.M.L.R. 175; (2002) 99(30) L.S.G. 37; (2002) 146 S.J.L.B. 168 . . . 5–037, 5–047

Assenov v Bulgaria (24760/94) (1999) 28 E.H.R.R. 652; [1998] H.R.C.D. 986 ECHR 5–011

Associated Provincial Picture Houses Ltd v Wednesbury Corp [1948] 1 K.B. 223; [1947] 2 All E.R. 680; (1947) 63 T.L.R. 623; (1948) 112 J.P. 55; 45 L.G.R. 635; [1948] L.J.R. 190; (1947) 177 L.T. 641; (1948) 92 S.J. 26 CA 1–729, 5–0415–009

Aswat v United Kingdom (2014) 58 E.H.R.R. 1; 34 B.H.R.C. 656; 2014] M.H.L.R. 130 ECHR. 5–015

Attia v British Gas Plc [1988] Q.B. 304; [1987] 3 W.L.R. 1101; [1987] 3 All E.R. 455; (1987) 84 L.S.G. 2360; (1987) 137 N.L.J. 661; (1987) 131 S.J. 1248 CA (Civ Div) 1–029

Attorney General's Reference (No.3 of 1994) [1998] A.C. 245; [1997] 3 W.L.R. 421; [1997] 3 All E.R. 936; [1998] 1 Cr. App. R. 91; [1997] Crim. L.R. 829; (1997) 94(36) L.S.G. 44; (1997) 147 N.L.J. 1185; (1997) 141 S.J.L.B. 189 1–048

Attorney General's Reference (No.54 of 2011), Re [2011] EWCA Crim 2276; [2012] 1 Cr. App. R. (S.) 106; [2012] Crim. L.R. 144 . . . . 1–514, 1–612

Attorney General's Reference (No.27 of 2013); R. v P (Anthony); R. v Ahmad (Goran Kamal); R. v Hanson (John); R. v Donegan (David); R. v Smith (Paul Simon); R. v Mathews (Michael Richard); R. v C; sub nom. R. v Burinskas (Gintas) [2014] EWCA Crim 334; [2014] 1 W.L.R. 4209; [2015] 1 All E.R. 93; [2014] 2 Cr. App. R. (S.) 45 1-514

Austin v Commissioner of Police of the Metropolis [2009] UKHL 5; [2009] 1 A.C. 564; [2009] 2 W.L.R. 372; [2009] H.R.L.R. 16; (2009) 153(4) S.J.L.B. 29 . . . . 6–003, 6–012

Austin v United Kingdom (39692/09) [2012] Crim. L.R. 544 . . . . 6–003, 6–012

AVS v An NHS Foundation Trust [2011] EWCA Civ 7; [2011] 2 F.L.R. 1; [2011] Fam. Law 363. 1–705

Azam v Secretary of State for the Home Department; sub nom. R. v Governor of Pentonville Prison Ex p. Azam; R. v Secretary of State for Home Department Ex p. Azam; R. v Secretary of State for Home Department Ex p. Khera; R. v Governor of Winson Green Prison Ex p. Khera; R. v Secretary of State for Home Department Ex p. Sidhu; Khera v Secretary of State for the Home Department; Sidhu v Secretary of State for the Home Department [1974] A.C. 18; [1973] 2 W.L.R. 1058; [1973] 2 All E.R. 765; [1973] Crim. L.R. 512; (1973) 117 S.J. 546 HL. 1–1352

B (A) v B(L). *See* AB v LB (Mental Health Patient); sub nom. B v B (Mental Health Patient)

Table of Cases

B (Disclosure to Other Parties), Re [2001] 2 F.L.R. 1017; [2002] 2 F.C.R. 32; [2001] Fam. Law 798 Fam Div 5–030
B v Auckland District Law Society; sub nom. Russell McVeagh McKenzie Bartleet & Co v Auckland District Law Society [2003] UKPC 38; [2003] 2 A.C. 736; [2003] 3 W.L.R. 859; [2004] 4 All E.R. 269; (2003) 100(26) L.S.G. 38; (2003) 147 S.J.L.B. 627 .... E–016
B v B (Mental Health Patient). See AB v LB (Mental Health Patient)
B v Croydon HA; sub nom. LB v Croydon HA [1995] Fam. 133; [1995] 2 W.L.R. 294; [1995] 1 All E.R. 683; [1995] 1 F.L.R. 470; [1995] 1 F.C.R. 662; [1995] P.I.Q.R. P145; [1995] Fam. Law 244; (1994) 144 N.L.J. 1696 CA (Civ Div).... 1–031, 1–260, 1–736, 1–739, 1–786, 1–787, 1–798, 1–1379
B v Cygnet Healthcare [2008] EWHC 1259 (Admin); 2008] M.H.L.R. 106 1–158
B v Mental Health Review Tribunal. See R. (on the application of B) v Mental Health Review Tribunal
B v Secretary of State for Work and Pensions [2005] EWCA Civ 929; [2005] 1 W.L.R. 3796. 5–053
B v United Kingdom (36337/97); P v United Kingdom (35974/97) [2001] 2 F.L.R. 261; [2001] 2 F.C.R. 221; (2002) 34 E.H.R.R. 19; 11 B.H.R.C. 667; [2001] Fam. Law 506 ECHR 3–140
Baker v Crown Prosecution Service [2009] EWHC 299 (Admin); (2009) 173 J.P. 215 1–1322
Balogun v United Kingdom (60286/09) (2013) 56 E.H.R.R. 3; [2012] Imm. A.R. 779 5–015
Barge v British Gas Corp (1982) 81 L.G.R. 53 DC................................. 1–1215
Barnet LBC v Robin (1999) 2 C.C.L. Rep. 454 CA (Civ Div) 1–431
Bartram v Southend Magistrates' Court [2004] EWHC 2691 (QB); [2004] M.H.L.R. 319. .... 1–492, 1–530
Bath and North East Somerset Council v AJC [1999] M.H.L.R. 184................... 3–152
BB v South London and Maudsley NHS Trust [2009] UKUT 157 (AAC); [2009] M.H.L.R. 302. .... 3–088, 3–176
Benham v United Kingdom (19380/92) (1996) 22 E.H.R.R. 293 ECHR 5–022
Benjamin v United Kingdom (28212/95) (2003) 36 E.H.R.R. 1; 13 B.H.R.C. 287; [2003] M.H.L.R. 124; [2003] Prison L.R. 1 ECHR 1–663, 1–949, 5–025
Bensaid v United Kingdom (44599/98) (2001) 33 E.H.R.R. 10; 11 B.H.R.C. 297; [2001] I.N.L.R. 325; [2001] M.H.L.R. 287 ECHR 5–035
Bezicheri v Italy (A/164) (1990) 12 E.H.R.R. 210 ECHR 5–025
Black v Forsey, 1987 S.L.T. 681...A–002
Bolam v Friern Hospital Management Committee [1957] 1 W.L.R. 582; [1957] 2 All E.R. 118; [1955–95] P.N.L.R. 7; (1957) 101 S.J. 357 QBD.................... 1–738, 1–785, 5–012
Bolitho (Deceased) v City and Hackney HA [1998] A.C. 232; [1997] 3W.L.R. 1151; [1997] 4 All E.R. 771; [1998] P.I.Q.R. P10; [1998] Lloyd's Rep. Med. 26; (1998) 39 B.M.L.R. 1; [1998] P.N.L.R. 1; (1997) 94(47) L.S.G. 30; (1997) 141 S.J.L.B. 238 HL 1–785
Bone v Mental Health Review Tribunal [1985] 3 All E.R. 330 QBD 3–153
Bostridge v Oxleas NHS Foundation Trust [2015] EWCA Civ 79; (2015) 18 C.C.L. Rep. 144; [2015] Med. L.R. 113. 1-100
Botta v Italy (21439/93) (1998) 26 E.H.R.R. 241; 4 B.H.R.C. 81; (1999) 2 C.C.L. Rep. 53; [1998] H.R.C.D. 302 ECHR 5–033, 5–035, 5–053
Bouamar v Belgium (A/129) (1989) 11 E.H.R.R. 1 ECHR 5–022
Boughanemi v France (1996) 22 E.H.R.R. 228 ECHR 5–039
Brady (Ian), Re December 11, 2013 .... 1–067, 1–1379
Brand v Netherlands (C49902/99) [2001] M.H.L.R. 275 ECHR 1–524, 1–637, 5–013
Briscoe, Re [1998] EWHC 771 (Admin); [1998] C.O.D. 402 QBD..................... 1–158
Broadmoor Special Hospital Authority v R; sub nom. Broadmoor Special HA v R [2000] Q.B. 775; [2000] 1 W.L.R. 1590; [2000] 2 All E.R. 727; [2000] E.M.L.R. 245; [2000] Lloyd's Rep. Med. 65; (2000) 52 B.M.L.R. 137; (2000) 97(3) L.S.G. 36; (2000) 144 S.J.L.B. 48 CA (Civ Div) 1–007, 1–1302, 1–1354
Buchholz v Germany (A/42) (1981) 3 E.H.R.R. 597................................ 1–128
Buck v Nottinghamshire Healthcare NHS Trust [2006] EWCA Civ 1576; (2007) 93 B.M.L.R. 28; [2006] M.H.L.R. 351; (2006) 103(47) L.S.G. 28; (2006) 150 S.J.L.B. 1568. .... C–001
Bures v Czech Republic [2013] M.H.L.R. 126 5–013
Burnip v Birmingham City Council; Trengove v Walsall MBC; Gorry v Wiltshire CC [2012] EWCA Civ 629; [2013] P.T.S.R. 117; [2012] H.R.L.R. 20; [2012] Eq. L.R. 701; [2013] H.L.R. 1; [2012] B.L.G.R. 954 1–019
Buxton v Jayne [1960] 1 W.L.R. 783; [1960] 2 All E.R. 688; (1960) 124 J.P. 380; 58 L.G.R. 274; (1960) 104 S.J. 602. .... 1–166, 1–193

Table of Cases

Buxton v Mills–Owens. *See* Richard Buxton Solicitors v Mills–Owens
C (A Minor) (Detention for Medical Treatment), Re. *See* C (A Minor) (Medical Treatment: Court's Jurisdiction), Re
C (A Minor) (Medical Treatment: Court's Jurisdiction), Re; sub nom. C (A Minor) (Detention for Medical Treatment), Re [1997] 2 F.L.R. 180; [1997] 3 F.C.R. 49; [1997] Fam. Law 474; (1997) 94(13) L.S.G. 29; (1997) 141 S.J.L.B. 72 Fam Div 1–1277, 1–1278
C (Adult: Refusal of Medical Treatment), Re [1994] 1 W.L.R. 290; [1994] 1 All E.R. 819; [1994] 1 F.L.R. 31; [1994] 2 F.C.R. 151 Fam Div 1–740, 1–788
C v A local Authority; A Local Authority v C [2011] EWHC 1539 (Admin); (2011) 14 C.C.L. Rep. 471; [2011] Med. L.R. 415; [2011] A.C.D. 105 1–1157
C v Birmingham and Solihull Mental Health NHS Trust; K v (1) St Andrews Healthcare (2) Secretary of State for Justice. *See* EC v Birmingham and Solihull Mental Health NHS Trust
C v Blackburn with Darwen BC [2011] EWHC 3321 (Fam); (2012) 15 C.C.L. Rep. 251; [2012] M.H.L.R. 202 . . . . 1–114, 1–129, 1–131, 1–132, 6–022
C v S (Minors) (Abduction: Illegitimate Child). *See* J (A Minor) (Abduction: Custody Rights), Re
C v South London and Maudsley Hospital NHS Trust [2001] M.H.L.R. 269 QBD . . 1–038, 1–1356
Cakici v Turkey (23657/94) (2001) 31 E.H.R.R. 5 ECHR 5–006
Cambridgeshire CC v R (An Adult) [1995] 1 F.L.R. 50; [1994] 2 F.C.R. 973; [1995] Fam. Law 12 Fam Div 1–132
Camenzind v Switzerland (21353/93) (1999) 28 E.H.R.R. 458; [1998] H.R.C.D. 180 ECHR 1–1323, 5–038
Campbell and Cosans v United Kingdom (A/48) (1982) 4 E.H.R.R. 293 ECHR 5–011, 5–035
Carter v Commissioner of Police of the Metropolis [1975] 1 W.L.R. 507; [1975] 2 All E.R. 33; (1975) 119 S.J. 237 CA (Civ Div) 1–1336, 1–1356
CB v Suffolk CC [2010] UKUT 413 (AAC) 3–097
Centre for Legal Resources on behalf of Valentin Campeanu v Romania (47848/08) 5–003
Chapman v United Kingdom (27238/95) (2001) 33 E.H.R.R. 18; 10 B.H.R.C. 48 ECHR 5–040
Cheshire West and Chester Council v P; Surrey CC v P; sub nom. P v Surrey CC; P v Cheshire West and Chester Council [2014] UKSC 19; [2014] 2 W.L.R. 642; [2014] 2 All E.R. 585; [2014] P.T.S.R. 460; [2014] 2 F.C.R. 71; [2014] C.O.P.L.R. 313; [2014] H.R.L.R. 13; (2014) 17 C.C.L. Rep. 5; (2014) 158(13) S.J.L.B. 37 . . . . . . 1–129, 1–916, 4–088, 4–094, 6–003, 6–004, 6–009, 6–021, 6–022
Chosta v Ukraine (35807/05) January 14, 2014 6–007
Ciliz v Netherlands (29192/95) [2000] 2 F.L.R. 469; [2000] Fam. Law 799 ECHR 5–034
Ciorap v Moldova (12066/02) Unreported June 19, 2007 5–016
Clunis v Camden and Islington HA [1998] Q.B. 978; [1998] 2 W.L.R. 902; [1998] 3 All E.R. 180; (1997–98) 1 C.C.L. Rep. 215; (1998) 40 B.M.L.R. 181; [1998] P.N.L.R. 262; (1998) 95(2) L.S.G. 23; (1998) 142 S.J.L.B. 38 CA (Civ Div) 1–163, 1–166, 1–1136, 1–1333
Clunis v United Kingdom (C45049/98) [2001] M.H.L.R. 162 ECHR 1–1126
CM, Re [2013] CSOH 143 5–036
CM v Derbyshire Healthcare NHS Foundation Trust [2011] UKUT 129 (AAC); [2011] M.H.L.R. 153 . . . . 1–031, 1–918
CNWL NHS Foundation Trust v H-JH [2012] UKUT 210 (AAC); [2012] M.H.L.R. 305 . . . . 1–927, 3–168
Connor v Chief Constable of Merseyside [2006] EWCA Civ 1549; [2007] H.R.L.R. 6; [2007] U.K.H.R.R. 621; [2006] Po. L.R. 281; (2006) 103(47) L.S.G. 29 1–1321
Cooke v DPP. *See* R. (on the application of Cooke) v DPP
Coombs v Dorset NHS Primary Care Trust; sub nom. North Dorset NHS Primary Care Trust v Coombs [2013] EWCA Civ 471; [2014] 1 W.L.R. 111; [2013] 4 All E.R. 429; (2013) 16 C.C.L. Rep. 376; [2013] P.I.Q.R. P16; [2013] M.H.L.R. 194 1–012
Costello–Roberts v United Kingdom (13134/87) [1994] 1 F.C.R. 65; (1995) 19 E.H.R.R. 112 ECHR 5–015, 5–034
Cottenham v United Kingdom (36509/97) [1999] M.H.L.R. 97 ECHR 5–026
Couchman's Will Trusts, Re; sub nom. Couchman v Eccles [1952] Ch. 391; [1952] 1 All E.R. 439; [1952] 1 T.L.R. 437; (1952) 96 S.J. 104 Ch D 1–1378
Cream Holdings Ltd v Banerjee [2004] UKHL 44; [2005] 1 A.C. 253; [2004] 3 W.L.R. 918; [2004] 4 All E.R. 617; [2005] E.M.L.R. 1; [2004] H.R.L.R. 39; [2004] U.K.H.R.R. 1071; 17 B.H.R.C. 464; (2005) 28(2) I.P.D. 28001; (2004) 101(42) L.S.G. 29; (2004) 154 N.L.J. 1589; (2004) 148 S.J.L.B. 1215 1–397

Table of Cases

Crown Prosecution Service v P; sub nom. DPP v P [2007] EWHC 946 (Admin); [2008] 1 W.L.R. 1005; [2007] 4 All E.R. 628; (2007) 171 J.P. 349; [2008] Crim. L.R. 165; (2007) 171 J.P.N. 659 .... 1–524, 1–530

CX v S Local Authority [2011] EWHC 1918 (Admin); [2011] M.H.L.R. 339; [2012] A.C.D. 14.. 1–157, 1–158

D, Re; sub nom. Life Sentence Review Commissioners v D; R. (on the application of D) v Life Sentence Review Commissioners; CD's Application for Judicial Review, Re [2008] UKHL 33; [2008] 1 W.L.R. 1499; [2008] 4 All E.R. 992; [2008] N.I. 292; [2009] 1 F.L.R. 700; [2009] Fam. Law 192; (2008) 105(29) L.S.G. 36; (2008) 152(25) S.J.L.B. 32 1–916

D (A Child) (Deprivation of Liberty), Re; sub nom. Trust A v X (A Child) [2015] EWHC 922 (Fam); [2015] C.O.P.L.R. 209; [2015] Fam. Law 636 .... 1–1271, 1–1276, 6–005

D (Mental Patient: Habeas Corpus), Re. See D v Barnet Health Care NHS Trust

D v Barnet Health Care NHS Trust [2000] 2 F.L.R. 848; [2001] 1 F.C.R. 218; (2001) 4 C.C.L. Rep. 239; [2000] M.H.L.R. 50; [2000] Fam. Law 805 CA (Civ Div)............ 1–159, 1–409

D v Commissioner of Police of the Metropolis; V v Commissioner of Police of the Metropolis; sub nom. NBV v Commissioner of Police of the Metropolis; DSD v Commissioner of Police of the Metropolis [2014] EWHC 2493 (QB); [2015] 1 W.L.R. 1833; [2015] 2 All E.R. 272... 1–100

D v Secretary of State for the Home Department and the National Assembly for Wales; sub nom. R. (on the application of D) v Secretary of State for the Home Department [2004] EWHC 2857 (Admin); [2005] M.H.L.R. 17 . . 1–633, 1–637, 1–639, 1–642, 1–643, 1–648, 1–653

D v South Tyneside Health Care NHS Trust [2003] EWCA Civ 878; [2004] P.I.Q.R. P12; [2004] M.H.L.R. 74 1–278

D v United Kingdom (30240/96) (1997) 24 E.H.R.R. 423; 2 B.H.R.C. 273; (1998) 42 B.M.L.R. 149 ECHR 1–1068, 5–013, 5–014, 5–015

DC v Nottinghamshire Healthcare NHS Trust [2012] UKUT 92 (Acc); (2012) 15 C.C.L. Rep. 537; [2012] M.H.L.R. 238 .... 1–937, 1–939, 1–941, 3–046

DCC v KH (2009) COP, Case No. 11729380 6–022

DD v Durham CC [2013] EWCA Civ 96; [2013] M.H.L.R. 85 ..... 1–188, 1–193, 1–195, 1–352, 1–1381

DD v Lithuania (13469/06) [2012] M.H.L.R. 209 1–1271

De Maroussem v Commissioner of Income Tax; sub nom. Maroussem v Income Tax Commissioner [2004] UKPC 43; [2004] 1 W.L.R. 2865; [2005] S.T.C. 125; [2004] B.T.C. 402; [2004] S.T.I. 2118 PC.. 1–1206

De Wilde v Belgium (No.1) (A/12) (1979–80) 1 E.H.R.R. 373 ECHR 1–376, 5–025, 5–026

Del Sol v France (46800/99) (2002) 35 E.H.R.R. 38 ECHR 5–030

Derbyshire CC v Maude Unreported July 5, 1999 CA (Civ Div)....................... 1–431

Devon v Hawkins [1967] 2 Q.B. 26; [1967] 2 W.L.R. 285; [1967] 1 All E.R. 235; 65 L.G.R. 123; (1966) 110 S.J. 893 DC... 1–057

Dhoest v Belgium (10448/83) (1990) 12 E.H.R.R. CD135 Eur Comm HR 5–014

Dickson v United Kingdom (44362/04) [2008] 1 F.L.R. 1315; [2007] 3 F.C.R. 877; (2008) 46 E.H.R.R. 41; 24 B.H.R.C. 19; [2008] Prison L.R. 334; [2008] Fam. Law 211; (2007) 157 N.L.J. 1766 ECHR 5–034

DL-H v Devon Partnership NHS Trust [2010] UKHT 102 (AAC); [2010] M.H.L.R. 162... 1–029, 1–915

DL-H v Partnerships in Care and the Secretary of State [2013] UKUT 500 (AAC); [2014] M.H.L.R. 241... 1–067

Dlodlo v South Thames Mental Health Review Tribunal; sub nom. R. v Secretary of State for the Home Department Ex p. D; Dlodlo, Re (1997) 36 B.M.L.R. 145; [1997] C.O.D. 40 ... 1–589

DN v Northumberland Tyne & Wear NHS Foundation Trust [2011] UKUT 327 (AAC); [2011] M.H.L.R. 249....................................... 1–913, 1–917, 6–021

DN v Switzerland (C27154/95) (2003) 37 E.H.R.R. 21; (2002) 63 B.M.L.R. 221; [2001] M.H.L.R. 117 ECHR 3–123, 5–026

Dodov v Bulgaria (59548/00) (2008) 47 E.H.R.R. 41 ECHR 5–006

Domenichini v Italy (15943/90) (2001) 32 E.H.R.R. 4 ECHR...................... 5–040

Doorson v Netherlands (1996) 22 E.H.R.R. 330 ECHR 5–030

Dordevic v Croatia (41526/10) 34 B.H.R.C. 392; (2012) 15 C.C.L. Rep. 657; [2013] M.H.L.R. 89... 5–011

Dorset Healthcare NHS Foundation Trust v MH [2009] UKUT 4 (AAC); [2009] M.H.L.R. 102............................. 1–866, 3–031, 3–042, 3–080, 3–083, 3–168, E–017

Dougoz v Greece (40907/98) (2002) 34 E.H.R.R. 61; 10 B.H.R.C. 306; [2001] Prison L.R. 136
  ECHR 5–013
Douiyeb v Netherlands (2000) 30 E.H.R.R. 790 ECHR 5–024
DP v Hywel DDA Health Board [2011] UKUT 381 (AAC); [2011] M.H.L.R. 394 1–872
DP v South Tyneside District Council Unreported July 14, 2011 1–159
DPP v Meaden [2003] EWHC 3005 (Admin); [2004] 1 W.L.R. 945; [2004] 4 All E.R. 75;
  [2004] Po. L.R. 8; [2004] Crim. L.R. 587 . . . 1–1321DPP v P *See* Crown Prosecution Service v P
Drew v United Kingdom (Admissibility) (35679/03) [2006] M.H.L.R. 203; (2006) 43 E.H.R.R.
  SE2 . . . . 1–524, 5–013
DSD and NBV v Commissioner of Police for the Metropolis. *See* D v Commissioner of Police
  of the Metropolis
D'souza v DPP; sub nom. R. v D'souza (Clarissa); R. v D'souza (Edwin) [1992] 1 W.L.R. 1073;
  [1992] 4 All E.R. 545; (1993) 96 Cr. App. R. 278; (1992) 142 N.L.J. 1540 HL . . . 1–109, 1–1322
Dudgeon v United Kingdom (A/45) (1982) 4 E.H.R.R. 149 ECHR 5–036, 5–041
Dunn v South Tyneside Health Care NHS Trust. *See* D v South Tyneside Health Care NHS
  Trust
Dunnage v Randall [2015] EWCA Civ 673 1–1355
Dybeku v Albania Unreported December 18, 2007 ECHR 5–013
Dzhurayev v Russia (71386/10) (2013) 57 E.H.R.R. 22 ECHR 5–026
E (Mental Health: Habeas Corpus), Re Unreported December 10, 1966 . . . . . . 1–137, 1–204, 2–131
E v Norway (A/181–A) (1994) 17 E.H.R.R. 30 ECHR 5–025, 5–026
E v United Kingdom (33218/96) [2003] 1 F.L.R. 348; [2002] 3 F.C.R. 700; (2003) 36 E.H.R.R.
  31; [2003] Fam. Law 157 ECHR 5–011
EC v Birmingham and Solihull Mental Health NHS Trust; K v (1) St Andrews Healthcare (2)
  Secretary of State for Justice [2013] EWCA Civ 701; [2014] M.H.L.R. 23 . . . . 1–927, 1–934,
    1–1379
Edgington v Fitzmaurice (1885) L.R. 29 Ch. D. 459 CA 1–029
Edwards v United Kingdom (46477/99) (2002) 35 E.H.R.R. 19; 12 B.H.R.C. 190; [2002]
  M.H.L.R. 220; [2002] Po. L.R. 161 5–008
English v Emery Reimbold & Strick Ltd [2002] EWCA Civ 605; [2002] 1 W.L.R. 2409; [2002]
  3 All E.R. 385; [2002] C.P.L.R. 520; [2003] I.R.L.R. 710; [2002] U.K.H.R.R. 957; (2002)
  99(22) L.S.G. 34; (2002) 152 N.L.J. 758; (2002) 146 S.J.L.B. 123 3–153
Equilibrium Health Care v AK [2013] UKUT 0543 (AAC) 3–014
Everett v Griffiths (No.1) [1921] 1 A.C. 631 HL 1–166
F (A Child) (Mental Health Act: Guardianship), Re; sub nom. F (A Child) (Care Order: Sexual
  Abuse), Re [2000] 1 F.L.R. 192; [2000] 1 F.C.R. 11; (1999) 2 C.C.L. Rep. 445; (2000) 51
  B.M.L.R. 128; [2000] Fam. Law 18; (1999) 96(39) L.S.G. 38 CA (Civ Div) 1–030, 1–115,
    1–131
Flannery v Halifax Estate Agencies Ltd (t/a Colleys Professional Services) [2000] 1 W.L.R.
  377; [2000] 1 All E.R. 373; [2000] C.P. Rep. 18; [1999] B.L.R. 107; (1999) 11 Admin.
  L.R. 465; (1999) 15 Const. L.J. 313; (1999) 96(13) L.S.G. 32; (1999) 149 N.L.J. 284;
  [1999] N.P.C. 22 CA (Civ Div) 3–153
Foulkes v Chief Constable of Merseyside [1998] 3 All E.R. 705; [1998] 2 F.L.R. 789; [1999] 1
  F.C.R. 98; [1998] Fam. Law 661 CA (Civ Div) A–002
Francis v DPP [1997] R.T.R. 113; (1997) 36 B.M.L.R. 180 1–1333
Freeman v Home Office [1984] Q.B. 524; [1984] 2 W.L.R. 802; [1984] 1 All E.R. 1036; (1984)
  81 L.S.G. 1045; (1984) 128 S.J. 298 CA (Civ Div) 1–721
G v Central & North West London Mental Health NHS Trust [2007] EWHC 3086 (QB); [2008]
  M.H.L.R. 24 1–214
G v E [2010] EWCA Civ 822; [2012] Fam. 78; [2011] 3 W.L.R. 652; [2010] 4 All E.R. 579;
  [2011] P.T.S.R. 1574; [2011] 1 F.L.R. 239; [2010] 2 F.C.R. 601; (2010) 13 C.C.L. Rep.
  384; [2010] Med.L.R. 392; (2010) 116 B.M.L.R. 162; [2010] M.H.L.R. 395; [2010] Fam.
  Law 1066 5–022
G v United Kingdom (Children: Right of Contact) (32346/96) [2001] 1 F.L.R. 153; [2000] 3
  F.C.R. 193; (2001) 33 E.H.R.R. 1; 2001 Fam. L.R. 103; [2000] Fam. Law 880 ECHR 5–033
GA v Betsi Cadwaladr University LHB [2013] 280 (AAC); [2014] M.H.L.R. 27 . . . . 1–915, 1–922,
    3–010
Gaskin v United Kingdom (A/160); sub nom. Gaskin v United Kingdom (10454/83) [1990] 1
  F.L.R. 167; (1990) 12 E.H.R.R. 36 ECHR 5–033, 5–036, 5–037
GC v Managers of the Kingswood Centre of Central and North West London NHS Foundation
  Trust (CO/7784/2008) 1–030

Table of Cases

GD v Edgware Community Hospital and Barnet LBC [2008] EWHC 3572 (Admin); [2008]
M.H.L.R. 282 . . . . .1–157, 1–158, 1–159
Gillick v West Norfolk and Wisbech AHA [1986] A.C. 112; [1985] 3 W.L.R. 830; [1985] 3 All
E.R. 402; [1986] Crim. L.R. 113; (1985) 82 L.S.G. 3531; (1985) 135 N.L.J. 1055; (1985) 129
S.J. 738 HL 4–090, 4–092, 4–093
GJ v Foundation Trust [2009] EWHC 2972 (Fam); [2010] 1 F.L.R. 1251; (2009) 12 C.C.L. Rep.
600; [2010] Med. L.R. 167; [2010] Fam. Law 139 .1–195, 6–015, 6–020
GK (Patient: Habeas Corpus), Re [1999] M.H.L.R. 128 2–052
Glaser v United Kingdom. *See* G v United Kingdom (Children: Right of Contact)
Glass v United Kingdom (61827/00) [2004] 1 F.L.R. 1019; [2004] 1 F.C.R. 553; (2004) 39
E.H.R.R. 15; (2005) 8 C.C.L. Rep. 16; (2004) 77 B.M.L.R. 120; [2004] Fam. Law 410
ECHR 1–1195, 5–034, 5–036
Glor v Switzerland (13444/04) April 30, 2009 5–053
GM, Re (Patient: Consultation) [2000] M.H.L.R. 41 QBD 1–053, 1–075, 1–155, 1–157, 1–195
Golder v United Kingdom (A/18) (1979–80) 1 E.H.R.R. 524 ECHR. 5–030
Gomez v Spain. *See* Moreno Gomez v Spain 5–040
Goodwin v United Kingdom (28957/95) [2002] I.R.L.R. 664; [2002] 2 F.L.R. 487; [2002] 2
F.C.R. 577; (2002) 35 E.H.R.R. 18; 13 B.H.R.C. 120; (2002) 67 B.M.L.R. 199; [2002]
Fam. Law 738; (2002) 152 N.L.J. 1171 ECHR 5–036, 5–051
Govell v United Kingdom (27237/95) Unreported ECHR 5–038
Grant v Mental Health Review Tribunal; R. v Mersey Mental Health Review Tribunal Ex p.
O Hara *Times*, April 26, 1986 QBD 1–934
Grare v France (18835/91) (1993) 15 E.H.R.R. CD100 Eur Comm HR. 5–013
Great Western Hospitals NHS Foundation Trust v AA [2014] 2 F.L.R. 1209; [2015] 1 F.C.R.
277; [2014] Fam. Law 412 . . . . 1–087, 1–787
Green v DPP (1991) 155 J.P. 816; [1991] Crim. L.R. 782; (1991) 155 J.P.N. 474 DC 1–1215
Green v Moore [1982] Q.B. 1044; [1982] 2 W.L.R. 671; [1982] 1 All E.R. 428; (1982) 74 Cr.
App. R. 250; [1982] Crim. L.R. 233; (1982) 126 S.J. 79 DC. .1–1215
Grove v Eastern Gas Board [1952] 1 K.B. 77; [1951] 2 All E.R. 1051; [1951] 2 T.L.R. 1128;
(1952) 116 J.P. 15; (1951) 95 S.J. 789 CA 1–1114
GS (India) v Secretary of State for the Home Department; BA (Ghana) v Secretary of State for
the Home Department; PL (Jamaica) v Secretary of State for the Home Department; GM
(India) v Secretary of State for the Home Department; EO (Ghana) v Secretary of State
for the Home Department; KK (DRC) v Secretary of State for the Home Department
[2015] EWCA Civ 40; [2015] 1 W.L.R. 3312; [2015] Imm. A.R. 608; (2015) 143
B.M.L.R. 79 5–015
Guerra v Italy (1998) 26 E.H.R.R. 357; 4 B.H.R.C. 63; [1998] H.R.C.D. 277 ECHR 5–036
Guzzardi v Italy (A/39) (1981) 3 E.H.R.R. 333 ECHR 6–005, 6–007
H v East Sussex CC [2009] EWCA Civ 249; [2009] E.L.R. 161; (2009) 153(13) S.J.L.B. 27 . 3–153
Haas v Switzerland (31322/07) (2011) 53 E.H.R.R. 33 . . . . 5–006, 5–035
Hajduova v Slovakia (2660/03) [2011] 1 F.L.R. 1247; (2011) 53 E.H.R.R. 8; [2011] Fam. Law
230 5–020
Hall v Semple (1862) 3 F. & F. 337 1–167
Hamer v United Kingdom (7114/75) (1982) 4 E.H.R.R. 139 Eur Comm HR. 5–051
Harnett v Fisher [1927] A.C. 573 HL 1–166
Harriot v DPP [2005] EWHC 965 (Admin); (2006) 170 J.P. 494; [2006] Crim. L.R. 440; (2006)
170 J.P.N. 856 1–1336
Harris v Harris (acting by his Guardian ad Litem, the Official Solicitor) Unreported April 22,
1999 CA (Civ Div) 1–008
Hasan v Bulgaria (30985/96) (2002) 34 E.H.R.R. 55; 10 B.H.R.C. 646 ECHR 5–041
Health Service Executive of Ireland v PA. *See* PA, Re
Heart of England NHS Foundation Trust v JB [2014] EWHC 342 (COP); (2014) 137 B.M.L.R.
232. 1–1270
Hellig v Germany (20999/05) (2012) 55 E.H.R.R. 3 ECHR 5–014
Helow v Advocate General for Scotland; sub nom. Helow v Secretary of State for the Home
Department [2008] UKHL 62; [2008] 1 W.L.R. 2416; [2009] 2 All E.R. 1031; 2009 S.C.
(H.L.) 1; 2008 S.L.T. 967; 2008 S.C.L.R. 830; (2008) 152(41) S.J.L.B. 29; 2008 G.W.D.
35-520 3–014
Herczegfalvy v Austria (A/242–B) (1993) 15 E.H.R.R. 437 ECHR. 1–730, 1–731, 1–786,
1–1303, 1–1354, 5–012, 5–013, 5–036
Herczegfalvy v Austria (A/244) September 24, 1992 5–022

Hereford and Worcester CC v S [1993] 2 F.L.R. 360; [1993] 1 F.C.R. 653; [1993] Fam. Law
573; (1993) 157 J.P.N. 329 1–1277
Hewer v Bryant [1970] 1 Q.B. 357; [1969] 3 W.L.R. 425; [1969] 3 All E.R. 578; (1969) 113 S.J.
525. 4–093
Hicks v Commissioner of the Metropolitan Police. *See* R. (on the application of Hicks) v
Commissioner of Police of the Metropolis
Hinchcliffe v Sheldon [1955] 1W.L.R. 1207; [1955] 3 All E.R. 406; (1956) 120 J.P. 13; (1955)
99 S.J. 797 DC 1–1215
Hirst v United Kingdom (74025/01) (2006) 42 E.H.R.R. 41; 19 B.H.R.C. 546; [2006] 1 Prison
L.R. 220; (2005) 155 N.L.J. 1551 ECHR 1–009, 5–034, 5–060
HK v Llanarth Court Hospital [2014] UKUT 410 (AAC); [2015] M.H.L.R. 88 3–153
HL v United Kingdom (45508/99); sub nom. L v United Kingdom (45508/99) (2005) 40
E.H.R.R. 32; 17 B.H.R.C. 418; (2004) 7 C.C.L. Rep. 498; [2005] Lloyd's Rep. Med. 169;
(2005) 81 B.M.L.R. 131; [2004] M.H.L.R. 236 ECHR 1–034, 6–001, 6–002, 6–006, 6–013
Hokkanen v Finland (A/299–A); sub nom. K v Finland (19823/92) [1996] 1 F.L.R. 289; [1995]
2 F.C.R. 320; (1995) 19 E.H.R.R. 139; [1996] Fam. Law 22 ECHR 5–033
HSE Ireland v SF (A Child) [2012] EWHC 1640 (Fam); [2012] 2 F.L.R. 1131; [2012] Fam. Law
1087. 1–1272
Hutchison Reid v United Kingdom (50272/99); sub nom. Reid v United Kingdom (50272/99)
(2003) 37 E.H.R.R. 9; 14 B.H.R.C. 41 ECHR 1–059, 1–066, 5–022, 5–025
IM (Nigeria) v Secretary of State for the Home Department [2013] EWCA Civ 1561 1–1378
Incal v Turkey (2000) 29 E.H.R.R. 449; 4 B.H.R.C. 476; [1998] H.R.C.D. 650 ECHR 5–030
Iovchev v Bulgaria (41211/98) February 2, 2006 5–011
Ireland v United Kingdom (A/25) (1979–80) 2 E.H.R.R. 25 ECHR 5–015
IT v Secretary of State for Justice. *See* T v Secretary of State for Justice
J (A Minor) (Abduction: Custody Rights), Re; sub nom. C v S (Minors) (Abduction:
Illegitimate Child) [1990] 2 A.C. 562; [1990] 3 W.L.R. 492; [1990] 2 All E.R. 961;
[1990] 2 F.L.R. 442; [1991] F.C.R. 129; [1991] Fam. Law 57; (1990) 154 J.P.N. 674;
(1990) 87(35) L.S.G. 39; (1990) 140 N.L.J. 1191; (1990) 134 S.J. 1039 HL 1–410
J v Devon CC [2001] EWHC Admin 958 3–153
J v Secretary of State for the Home Department [2005] EWCA Civ 629; [2005] Imm. A.R.
409. 5–015
Jalloh v Germany (54810/00) § 68, ECHR 2006-IX 5–011
Jehovah's Witnesses of Moscow v Russia (302/02) (2011) 53 E.H.R.R. 4 5–036
Jendrowiak v Germany (30060/04) April 14, 2011 5–022
JLG v Managers of Llanarth Court & SOS for Justice [2011] UKUT 62 (AAC) [2011] M.H.L.R.
74. . . . . 3–153, 3–168
Johnson v United Kingdom (1999) 27 E.H.R.R. 296; (1998) 40 B.M.L.R. 1; [1998] H.R.C.D.
41 ECHR 1–376, 1–587, 1–927, 1–935, 1–936, 1–937, 1–941, 5–022, 5–025
Johnston v Chief Constable of Merseyside [2009] EWHC 2969 (QB); [2009] M.H.L.R. 343 1–1352
Jordan v United Kingdom (24746/94) (2003) 37 E.H.R.R. 2; 11 B.H.R.C. 1; [2001] Inquest
L.R. 101 ECHR 5–008
JP v South London and Maudsley NHS Foundation Trust [2012] UKUT 486 (AAC); [2013]
M.H.L.R. 148. . . . . 1–047, 1–916, 5–045
JR45, Re [2011] NIQB 17; [2014] M.H.L.R. 17 1–397
JR49 Application for Judicial Review, Re [2011] NIQB 41. 1–1026
JT v United Kingdom (26494/95) [2000] 1 F.L.R. 909; [2000] M.H.L.R. 254; [2000] Fam. Law
533; (2000) 30 E.H.R.R. CD77 ECHR 1–439
K (A Child) v BBC; sub nom. BBC v K (A Child); K (A Child), Re [2001] Fam. 59; [2001] 2
W.L.R. 253; [2001] 1 All E.R. 323; [2001] 1 F.L.R. 197; [2000] 3 F.C.R. 509; [2000] Fam.
Law 886; (2000) 97(39) L.S.G. 41; (2000) 150 N.L.J. 1538; (2000) 144 S.J.L.B. 250 Fam
Div. 5–048
K (A Child (Secure Accommodation Order: Right to Liberty), Re, 2001. Fam 377 4–088
K v Central and North West London Mental Health NHS Trust [2008] EWHC 1217 (QB);
(2008) 11 C.C.L. Rep. 543; [2008] P.I.Q.R. P19; [2008] LS Law Medical 428; [2008]
M.H.L.R. 168. 1–1136
K v Finland (25702/94) (No.1); T v Finland (25702/94) (No.1) [2000] 2 F.L.R. 79; [2000] 3
F.C.R. 248; (2001) 31 E.H.R.R. 18; [2000] Fam. Law 534 ECHR 5–039
K v Hospital Managers of the Kingswood Centre [2014] EWCA Civ 1332; [2015] P.T.S.R. 287;
[2014] Med. L.R. 497. . . . . 1–397, 2–052

K v Kingswood Centre Hospital Managers [2014] EWCA Civ 1332; [2015] P.T.S.R. 287;
 [2014] Med. L.R. 497... 1–394, 1–397
Kalashnikov v Russia (47095/99) (2003) 36 E.H.R.R. 34; [2002] Prison L.R. 334
 ECHR 5–011, 5–013
Kay v United Kingdom (1998) 40 B.M.L.R. 20 Eur Comm HR 1–225, 1–281, 1–588
KB, Re [1997] 2 F.L.R. 180... 1–787
KD v A BC [2015] UKUT 251 (AAC).................... 1–129, 1–132, 1–929, 6–022
Keegan v Ireland (16969/90) [1994] 3 F.C.R. 165; (1994) 18 E.H.R.R. 342 ECHR......... 5–033
Keenan v United Kingdom (27229/95) (2001) 33 E.H.R.R. 38; 10 B.H.R.C. 319; [2001] Inquest
 L.R. 8; [2001] Prison L.R. 180 ECHR 1–634, 5–007, 5–012, 5–013, 5–016, 5–036
Kehayov v Bulgaria (41035/98) January 18, 2005.............................. 5–011
Kelly v BBC. *See* K (A Child) v BBC
KF v Birmingham and Solihull Mental Health NHS Foundation Trust [2010] UKUT 185
 (AAC) 1–871, 1–881, 1–915, 3–101, 3–172, 3–176
KH v Slovakia (32881/04) (2009) 49 E.H.R.R. 34; 27 B.H.R.C. 373.................... 5–037
Khan v United Kingdom (35394/97) (2001) 31 E.H.R.R. 45; 8 B.H.R.C. 310; [2000] Po. L.R.
 156; [2000] Crim. L.R. 684 ECHR....................................... 5–038
Kiernan v Harrow Crown Court [2003] EWCA Crim 1052; [2005] M.H.L.R. 1 ..... 1–528, 1–596
Kimber v Kimber; sub nom. K v K (Enforcement) [2000] 1 F.L.R. 383; [2000] Fam. Law 317
 Fam Div.. 1–411
Kiss v Hungary (38832/06) [2010] M.H.L.R. 245............................... 3–140
Kjeldsen v Denmark (A/23); Busk Madsen v Denmark; Pedersen v Denmark (1979–80) 1
 E.H.R.R. 711 ECHR.. 5–053
KL v Somerset Partnership NHS Foundation Trust [2011] UKUT 233 (AAC); [2011] M.H.L.R.
 194...1–223, 1–318, 1–1379
Klass v Germany (A/28) (1979–80) 2 E.H.R.R. 214 ECHR 5–040
Knox v Anderton (1983) 76 Cr. App. R. 156; (1983) 147 J.P. 340; [1983] Crim. L.R. 114
 QBD... 1–1336
KO v A Borough Council [2015] UKUT 251 (AAC)............................. 1–939
Koendjbiharie v Netherlands (A/185–B); sub nom. Koendjbiharie v Netherlands (11487/85)
 (1991) 13 E.H.R.R. 820 ECHR... 5–026
Kolanis v United Kingdom (517/02) (2006) 42 E.H.R.R. 12; (2006) 9 C.C.L. Rep. 297; (2005)
 84 B.M.L.R. 102; [2005] M.H.L.R. 238 ....1–935, 1–937, 1–941, 5–022, 5–025
Koniarska v United Kingdom (Admissibility) (33670/96); sub nom. Koniarski v United
 Kingdom (Admissibility) (33670/96) (2000) 30 E.H.R.R. CD139 ECHR 1–066
Koskinen v Finland (20560/92) (1994) 18 E.H.R.R. CD146 Eur Comm HR 5–014
Krastanov v Bulgaria (50222/99) (2005) 41 E.H.R.R. 50 ECHR..................... 5–013
Kucheruk v Ukraine (2570/04) (2011) 52 E.H.R.R. 28; [2008] M.H.L.R. 1............... 5–011
Kudla v Poland (30210/96) (2002) 35 E.H.R.R. 11; 10 B.H.R.C. 269; [2000] Prison L.R. 380
 ECHR 5–013
KY v DD (Without Notice Applications) [2011] EWHC 1277 (Fam); [2012] 2 F.L.R. 200;
 (2011) 14 C.C.L. Rep. 648; [2011] Fam. Law 797 1–426
Kynaston v Secretary of State for Home Affairs (1981) 73 Cr. App. R. 281; [1982] Crim. L.R.
 117 CA (Civ Div).. 1–587
L (A Child) (Care: Threshold Criteria), Re [2007] 1 F.L.R. 2050; [2007] Fam. Law 297 Fam
 Div... 5–041
L (An Infant), Re (1962) 106 S.J. 611 CA 1–437
L v Devon CC. *See* J v Devon CC
L v Sweden (10801/84) Unreported ECHR..................... 1–218, 1–232 1–935, 5–030
L v Sweden, 45 D. & R. 181 5–043
Labita v Italy (26772/95) (2008) 46 E.H.R.R. 50; [2000] Prison L.R. 337............... 5–011
Lacki v Poland [2012] EWHC 1747 (Admin)................................... 5–015
Lambert v France (2000) 30 E.H.R.R. 346; [1998] H.R.C.D. 806 ECHR 1–218
Lashin v Russia (33117/02), January 22, 2013 5–036
Lawal v Northern Spirit Ltd [2003] UKHL 35; [2004] 1All E.R. 187; [2003] I.C.R. 856; [2003]
 I.R.L.R. 538; [2003] H.R.L.R. 29; [2003] U.K.H.R.R. 1024; (2003) 100(28) L.S.G. 30;
 (2003) 153 N.L.J. 1005; (2003) 147 S.J.L.B. 783 .... 3–123, 5–030
LC v DHIC [2010] UKUT 319 (AAC); [2010] M.H.L.R. 337.................. 1–941, 3–153
LDV, Re; sub nom. A Primary Care Trust v LDV [2013] EWHC 272 (Fam)....... 1–1270, 6–005
Le Brocq v Le Brocq [1964] 1 W.L.R. 1085; [1964] 3 All E.R. 464; (1964) 108 S.J. 501
 CA.. 1–410

Table of Cases

Le Compte v Belgium (A/43); Van Leuven v Belgium (A/43); De Meyere v Belgium (A/43) [1982] E.C.C. 240; (1982) 4 E.H.R.R. 1 ECHR 1–128

Lebrooy v Hammersmith and Fulham LBC [2006] EWHC 1976 (QB); [2006] M.H.L.R. 253. . . . . 1–13152 1–1355

Lewis v Cox [1985] Q.B. 509; [1984] 3 W.L.R. 875; [1984] 3 All E.R. 672; (1985) 80 Cr. App. R. 1; (1984) 148 J.P. 601; [1984] Crim. L.R. 756; (1984) 81 L.S.G. 2538; (1984) 128 S.J. 596 DC. 1–1215

Lewis v Gibson [2005] EWCA Civ 587; [2005] 2 F.C.R. 241; (2005) 8 C.C.L. Rep. 399; (2006) 87 B.M.L.R. 93; [2005] M.H.L.R. 309 . . . . 1–030, 1–127, 1–425, 1–437, 1–438, 3–004

Liberty v United Kingdom (58243/00) (2009) 48 E.H.R.R. 1 ECHR. 5–041

Litwa v Poland (26629/95) (2001) 33 E.H.R.R. 53; (2002) 63 B.M.L.R. 199; [2000] M.H.L.R. 226 ECHR 1–059, 1–190, 1–195, 5–022

LN v Surrey NHS Primary Care Trust [2011] UKUT 76 (AAC) 3–093

Locabail (UK) Ltd v Bayfield Properties Ltd (Leave to Appeal); R. v Bristol Betting and Gaming Licensing Committee Ex p. O'Callaghan; Williams v Inspector of Taxes; Timmins v Gormley; Locabail (UK) Ltd v Waldorf Investment Corp (Leave to Appeal) [2000] Q.B. 451; [2000] 2 W.L.R. 870; [2000] 1 All E.R. 65; [2000] I.R.L.R.96; [2000] H.R.L.R. 290; [2000] U.K.H.R.R. 300; 7 B.H.R.C. 583; (1999) 149 N.L.J. 1793; [1999] N.P.C. 143 3–014

London and Globe Finance Corp (Winding Up), Re [1903] 1 Ch. 728 Ch D. 1–1201

Lopez Ostra v Spain (A/303–C) (1995) 20 E.H.R.R. 277 ECHR. 5–036

LS v Lambeth LBC [2010] UKUT 461 (AAC). 1–865, 3–168

Luberti v Italy (9019/80) (1984) 6 E.H.R.R. 440 ECHR 5–025

M, Re [2009] M.H.L.R. 154. 1–157

M (A Minor) v Newham LBC. *See* X (Minors) v Bedfordshire CC

M, Petitioner; sub nom. W, Petitioner; WM, Petitioner; In the matter of WM (Application for Judicial Review) 2002; M v Cook, 2003 S.C. 52; 2003 S.L.T. 219; 2002 S.C.L.R. 1001; [2002] M.H.L.R. 367; 2002 G.W.D. 25–843 OH. 1–736

M v Secretary of State for Work and Pensions; sub nom. Secretary of State for Work and Pensions v M; Langley v Bradford MDC [2006] UKHL 11; [2006] 2 A.C. 91; [2006] 2 W.L.R. 637; [2006] 4 All E.R. 929; [2006] 2 F.L.R. 56; [2006] 1 F.C.R. 497; [2006] H.R.L.R. 19; [2006] U.K.H.R.R. 799; 21 B.H.R.C. 254; [2006] Fam. Law 524; (2006) 150 S.J.L.B. 363. 5–053

M v South West London & St. George's Mental Health NHS Trust; sub nom. M v Queen Mary's Hospital Managers [2008] EWCA Civ 1112; [2008] M.H.L.R. 306. . 1–111, 1–167, 1–195, 1–730

M v Ukraine (2452/04) [2013] M.H.L.R. 255 ECHR 1–474, 1–707, 1–721, 1–1270

M'Naghten Case [1843–60] All E.R. 229 . . . . A–001

MA v Secretary of State for Health [2012] UKUT 474 (AAC); [2013] M.H.L.R. 56 . . 1–376, 1–404, 1–427, 1–872

Magalhaes Pereira v Portugal (44872/98) (2003) 36 E.H.R.R. 49 ECHR. 5–024

Makin, Re. *See* GM, Re

Marc Rich & Co Holding GmbH v Krasner [1999] EWCA Civ 581 1–426

Marckx v Belgium (A/31) (1979–80) 2 E.H.R.R. 330 ECHR 5–039

Marzari v Italy (Admissibility) (36448/97) (2000) 30 E.H.R.R. CD218. 5–040

Maslov v Austria (1638/03) [2007] 1 F.C.R. 707; (2008) 47 E.H.R.R. 20 ECHR. 1–1068, 5–015, 5–039

Massie v H [2011] EWCA Civ 115; [2011] M.H.L.R. 288 . . . . 1–428, 1–431

Masterman–Lister v Brutton & Co [2002] EWCA Civ 1889; [2003] 1 W.L.R. 1511; [2003] 3 All E.R. 162; [2003] C.P. Rep. 29; (2004) 7 C.C.L. Rep. 5; [2003] P.I.Q.R. P20; [2003] Lloyd's Rep. Med. 244; (2003) 73 B.M.L.R. 1; [2003] M.H.L.R. 166; [2003] W.T.L.R. 259; (2003) 147 S.J.L.B. 60 . . . . E–011

Mathew v Netherlands (24919/03) (2006) 43 E.H.R.R. 23 ECHR. 5–011

Matter v Slovakia (2001) 31 E.H.R.R. 32 ECHR 5–036, 5–042

Matthews v Ministry of Defence [2003] UKHL 4; [2003] 1 A.C. 1163; [2003] 2 W.L.R. 435; [2003] 1 All E.R. 689; [2004] I.C.R. 247; [2004] H.R.L.R. 2; [2003] U.K.H.R.R. 453; 14 B.H.R.C. 585; [2003] P.I.Q.R. P24; [2003] A.C.D. 42; (2003) 100(13) L.S.G. 26; (2003) 153 N.L.J. 261; (2003) 147 S.J.L.B. 235. 5–029

May v DPP [2005] EWHC 1280 (Admin). 1–1336

MB v BEH NHST [2011] UKUT 328 (AAC); [2011] M.H.L.R. 246. . . . . 3–011, 3–100

McCann v United Kingdom (A/324) (1996) 21 E.H.R.R. 97 ECHR 5–006, 5–008

xviii

Table of Cases

McConnell v Chief Constable of Greater Manchester [1990] 1 W.L.R. 364; [1990] 1 All E.R.
    423; (1990) 91 Cr. App. R. 88; (1990) 154 J.P.N. 62; (1990) 87(6) L.S.G. 41; (1990) 134 S.J.
    457 CA (Civ Div)...A–002
McDougall v Sefton Area Health Authority Unreported April 9, 1987 1–086
McGee, Re [2007] NICA 38; [2008] M.H.L.R. 216 1–087
McGrady's Application for Judicial Review, Re [2003] NIQB 15; [2003] N.I. 250 QBD
    (NI) 3–081
McKay v United Kingdom (543/03) (2007) 44 E.H.R.R. 41; 24 B.H.R.C. 471 ECHR.......5–019
McKerr v United Kingdom (28883/95) (2002) 34 E.H.R.R. 20; [2001] Inquest L.R. 170
    ECHR 5–010
McLeod v Commissioner of Police of the Metropolis [1994] 4 All E.R. 553 CA (Civ Div). . 1–1322
McLeod v United Kingdom (24755/94) [1998] 2 F.L.R. 1048; [1999] 1 F.C.R. 193; (1999) 27
    E.H.R.R. 493; 5 B.H.R.C. 364; [1999] Crim. L.R. 155; [1998] H.R.C.D. 878; [1998] Fam.
    Law 734 ECHR 1–1323
McMichael v United Kingdom (16424/90); sub nom. McMichael v United Kingdom (A/308)
    [1995] 2 F.C.R. 718; (1995) 20 E.H.R.R. 205; [1995] Fam. Law 478 ECHR............5–030
McMillan v Crown Prosecution Service [2008] EWHC 1457 (Admin); (2008) 172 J.P. 485;
    (2008) 172 J.P.N. 646; (2008) 172 J.P.N. 694 1–1336
MD v Mersey Care NHS Trust [2013] UKUT 127 (AAC); [2013] M.H.L.R. 164 .... 1–067, 1–917
MD v Nottinghamshire Health Care NHS Trust [2010] UKUT 59 (AAC); [2010]
    M.H.L.R. 93................................... 1–067, 1–1383, 3–022, 3–033, 3–123
Meek v Birmingham DC; sub nom. Meek v Birmingham City Council [1987] I.R.L.R. 250 CA
    (Civ Div) 3–153
Meggary v Chief Adjudication Officer Times, November 11, 1999 1–032
Megyeri v Germany (A/237A) (1993) 15 E.H.R.R. 584 ECHR.................. 5–024, E–002
Mental Health Review Tribunal v Hempstock (1998) 39 B.M.L.R. 123; [1997] C.O.D. 443
    QBD...1–927
Messina v Italy (No.2) (25498/94) Unreported September 28, 2000 ECHR..............5–020
MG v United Kingdom (39393/98) [2002] 3 F.C.R. 289; (2003) 36 E.H.R.R. 3; 13 B.H.R.C.
    179; (2002) 5 C.C.L. Rep. 525 ECHR...5–037
MH v Mental Health Review Tribunal for Northern Ireland [2014] NIQB 87 1–915
MH v United Kingdom (11577/06) (2014) 58 E.H.R.R. 35; (2014) 136 B.M.L.R. 17; [2014]
    M.H.L.R. 249 ECHR 1–040, 1–427, 1–882, 5–025
Milborrow, Applicant, 1996 S.C.L.R. 315 Sh Ct.....................1–089, 1–317, 1–360
Millar (David Cameron) v Dickson; Marshall v Ritchie; Tracey v Heywood; Payne v Heywood;
    Stewart v Heywood [2001] UKPC D 4; [2002] 1 W.L.R. 1615; [2002] 3 All E.R. 1041; 2002
    S.C. (P.C.) 30; 2001 S.L.T. 988; 2001 S.C.C.R. 741; [2001] H.R.L.R. 59; [2001] U.K.H.R.R.
    999; 2001 G.W.D. 26-1015..5–033
MJ (Angola) v Secretary of State for the Home Department [2010] EWCA Civ 557.......1–1063
MM v Nottinghamshire Healthcare NHS Trust [2013] UKUT 107 (AAC); [2013] M.H.L.R.
    161..3–090, 3–091
MN, Re [2010] EWHC 1926 (Fam); [2010] W.T.L.R. 1355 1–1273
MN v Kent County Council [2015] UKUT 125 (AAC)..............................1–929
Mocarska v Poland (26917/05) [2008] M.H.L.R. 228 ECHR 1–637, 5–022
Montgomery v Lanarkshire Health Board; sub nom. NM v Lanarkshire Health Board [2015]
    UKSC 11; [2015] 2 W.L.R. 768; [2015] 2 All E.R. 1031; 2015 S.L.T. 189; 2015 S.C.L.R.
    315; [2015] P.I.Q.R. P13; [2015] Med. L.R. 149; (2015) 143 B.M.L.R. 47; 2015 G.W.D.
    10-179 1-722
Moore v Commissioner of Police of the Metropolis; sub nom. Moore v West Park Hospital,
    Epsom, Surrey [1968] 1 Q.B. 26; [1967] 3 W.L.R. 572; [1967] 2 All E.R. 827; (1967) 111
    S.J. 35 CA (Civ Div) 1–1356
Mooren v Germany (11364/03) (2010) 50 E.H.R.R. 23 ECHR 1–102, 1–474, 5–022
Moreno Gomez v Spain (4143/02) (2005) 41 E.H.R.R. 40 ECHR......................5–040
Morley v United Kingdom (Admissibility) (16084/03) [2005] M.H.L.R. 174; (2005) 40
    E.H.R.R. SE8 ECHR 1–637, 1–670
Morsink v Netherlands (48865/99) [2005] 2 Prison L.R. 72; [2005] M.H.L.R. 161 ECHR ... 1–637
Mouisel v France (67263/01) (2004) 38 E.H.R.R. 34 ECHR..........................5–015
MP v Mersey Care NHS Trust [2011] UKUT 107 (AAC); [2011] M.H.L.R. 146..... 1–927, 1–928
MP v Nottinghamshire Healthcare NHS Trust [2003] EWHC 1782 (Admin); [2003] M.H.L.R.
    381; [2003] A.C.D. 99 .... 1–927, 1–934
MS v Croatia (No.2), February 19, 2015.............................5–011, 5–013, 5–024

Table of Cases

MS v North East London Foundation Trust [2013] UKUT 92 (AAC); [2013] M.H.L.R.
158. . . . . 1–038, 3–153
MS v United Kingdom (24527/08), May 3, 2012 . . . . 1–1334, 1–1337
Mummery v Mummery [1942] P. 107 PDAD 1–411
Munjaz v United Kingdom (2913/06) [2012] M.H.L.R. 351 ECHR 1–102, 1–1157, 1–1354,
 5–019, 5–022, 5–034, 5–036, 5–041
Musial v Poland (24557/94) (2001) 31 E.H.R.R. 29 ECHR. 5–025
N v United Kingdom (26565/05) (2008) 47 E.H.R.R. 39; 25 B.H.R.C. 258; [2008] Imm. A.R.
 657; [2008] I.N.L.R. 335 ECHR 1–1068, 5–014, 5–015
N McM v Secretary of State for Work and Pensions (DLA) [2014] UKUT 312. 1–032
Nakach v Netherlands (5379/02) [2006] M.H.L.R. 22 ECHR 5–020
Narey v Customs and Excise Commissioners [2005] EWHC 784 (Admin); [2005] M.H.L.R.
 194; [2005] A.C.D. 85 1–573
Naumenko v Ukraine Unreported February 10, 2004 ECHR 5–012
Nevmerzhitsky v Ukraine (54825/00) (2006) 43 E.H.R.R. 32; 19 B.H.R.C. 177; [2006] 1 Prison
 L.R. 119 ECHR 5–012, 5–016
Newham LBC v Mr BS and S (an Adult Represented by her Litigation Friend, the Official
 Solicitor) [2003] EWHC 1909 (Fam) 1–030
NHS Trust Av M; NHS Trust B v H [2001] Fam. 348; [2001] 2 W.L.R. 942; [2001] 1 All E.R.
 801; [2001] 2 F.L.R. 367; [2001] 1 F.C.R. 406; [2001] H.R.L.R. 12; [2001] Lloyd's Rep.
 Med. 28; (2001) 58 B.M.L.R. 87; [2001] Fam. Law 501 Fam Div. 5–016
Niedbala v Poland (27915/95) (2001) 33 E.H.R.R. 48; [2000] Prison L.R. 361 ECHR 5–027
Nielsen v Denmark (A/144); sub nom. Nielsen v Denmark (10929/84) (1989) 11 E.H.R.R. 175
 ECHR 1–1271, 4–093, 5–020, 6–009
Niemietz v Germany (A/251–B) (1993) 16 E.H.R.R. 97 ECHR 5–035
Nikolova v Bulgaria (31195/96) (2001) 31 E.H.R.R. 3 ECHR. 3–081, 5–025
NL v Hampshire County Council [2014] UKUT 475 (AAC), UT 1–129, 1–929, 3–012
Norfolk and Norwich Healthcare NHS Trust v W [1996] 2 F.L.R. 613; [1997] 1 F.C.R. 269;
 (1997) 34 B.M.L.R. 16; [1997] Fam. Law 17 Fam Div 1–1278
Northamptonshire Healthcare NHS Foundation Trust v ML [2014] EWCOP 2 . . . . . . 1–915, 3–003
Nottingham City Council v UNISON [2004] EWHC 893 (QB). 1–193, 1–1137
Nottinghamshire Healthcare NHS Trust v RC [2014] EWCOP 1317 (COP); [2014] Med. L.R.
 260. . . . . 1–785, 1–787
NR's Application for Judicial Review, Re [2015] NIQB 35. 3–080
O'Reilly v Moroney Unreported November 16, 1993 1-167
O'Rourke v United Kingdom Unreported June 26, 2001 ECHR 5–011
Osman v United Kingdom (23452/94) [1999] 1 F.L.R. 193; (2000) 29 E.H.R.R. 245; 5
 B.H.R.C. 293; (1999) 1 L.G.L.R. 431; (1999) 11 Admin. L.R. 200; [2000] Inquest L.R.
 101; [1999] Crim. L.R. 82; [1998] H.R.C.D. 966; [1999] Fam. Law 86; (1999) 163 J.P.N.
 297 ECHR 1–150, 5–006, 5–007, 5–033
P, Re. See W NHS Trust v P
P v Cheshire West and Chester Council. See Cheshire West and Chester Council v P
P v Mental Health Review Tribunal and Rampton Hospital. See R. (on the application of P) v
 Mental Health Review Tribunal and Rampton Hospital
P v P (Contempt of Court: Mental Capacity) [1999] 2 F.L.R. 897; [1999] 3 F.C.R. 547; [1999]
 Fam. Law 690 CA (Civ Div) 1–008
P v United Kingdom (56547/00) [2002] 2 F.L.R. 631; [2002] 3 F.C.R. 1; (2002) 35 E.H.R.R. 31;
 12 B.H.R.C. 615; [2002] Fam. Law 811 ECHR. 5–030, 5–039
PA, Re; PC, Re; PB, Re; sub nom. Health Service of Ireland v PC; Health Service of Ireland v
 PB; Health Service of Ireland v PA [2015] EWCOP 38. 1–1273
Pankiewicz v Poland (34151/04) [2008] M.H.L.R. 233 ECHR 1–637, 5–022
Parascineti v Romania (32060/05), March 13, 2012 5–013
Passannante v Italy (32647/96) (Admissibility (2002) 5 C.C.L. Rep. 340; (1998) 26 E.H.R.R.
 CD153 Eur Comm HR 1–059, 5–033
Peck v United Kingdom (44647/98) [2003] E.M.L.R. 15; (2003) 36 E.H.R.R. 41; 13 B.H.R.C.
 669; [2003] Info. T.L.R. 221 ECHR 5–037
Peers v Greece (28524/95) (2001) 33 E.H.R.R. 51; 10 B.H.R.C. 364; [2001] Prison L.R.
 245. 5–011
Percy v DPP [1995] 1 W.L.R. 1382; [1995] 3 All E.R. 124; (1995) 159 J.P. 337; [1995] Crim.
 L.R. 714; (1995) 159 J.P.N. 228; (1995) 92(9) L.S.G. 38; (1995) 139 S.J.L.B. 34 . . . . .A–001
Pereira v Portugal. See Magalhaes Pereira v Portugal

Table of Cases

Perkins v Bath District Health Authority; R. v Wessex Health Review Tribunal ex p. Wiltshire CC, 4 B.M.L.R. 145 . . . . 1–913, 1–927

Perry v United Kingdom (63737/00) (2004) 39 E.H.R.R. 3; [2003] Info. T.L.R. 372; [2003] Po. L.R. 355 ECHR 5–035, 5–038

Pickering v Liverpool Daily Post and Echo; sub nom. P v Liverpool Daily Post and Echo [1991] 2A.C. 370; [1991] 2 W.L.R. 513; [1991] 1 All E.R. 622; (1991) 3 Admin. L.R. 397; [1991] 2 Med. L.R. 240; (1991) 141 N.L.J. 166; (1991) 135 S.J.L.B. 166 HL 1–425, 1–453, 3–017, 3–140

Piersack v Belgium (A/53) (1983) 5 E.H.R.R. 169 ECHR. 5–030

Pleso v Hungary (41242/08) [2014] M.H.L.R. 72 . . . . 1–048, 1–059

Poltoratskiy v Ukraine (38812/97) (2004) 39 E.H.R.R. 43; [2006] 1 Prison L.R. 33 5–011

Porter v Magill; Phillips v Magill; England v Magill; Hartley v Magill; Weeks v Magill; sub nom. Magill v Porter; Magill v Weeks [2001] UKHL 67; [2002] 2 A.C. 357; [2002] 2 W.L.R. 37; [2002] 1 All E.R. 465; [2002] H.R.L.R. 16; [2002] H.L.R. 16; [2002] B.L.G.R. 51; (2001) 151 N.L.J. 1886; [2001] N.P.C. 184 3–014

Pountney v Griffiths; sub nom. R.v Bracknell Justices Ex p. Griffiths [1976] A.C. 314; [1975] 3 W.L.R. 140; [1975] 2 All E.R. 881; [1975] Crim. L.R. 702; (1975) 119 S.J. 493 HL 1–1354, A–003

Powell v United Kingdom (Admissibility) (45305/99) [2000] Inquest L.R. 19; (2000) 30 E.H.R.R. CD362 ECHR 5–006, 5–007

Practice Direction (Sup Ct: Upper Tribunal: Judicial Review Jurisdiction) [2009] 1W.L.R. 327; [2009] P.T.S.R. 95 . . . . 1–865, 3–176

Pretty v United Kingdom (2346/02); sub nom. R. (on the application of Pretty) v DPP (2346/02) [2002] 2 F.L.R. 45; [2002] 2 F.C.R. 97; (2002) 35 E.H.R.R. 1; 12 B.H.R.C. 149; (2002) 66 B.M.L.R. 147; [2002] Fam. Law 588; (2002) 152 N.L.J. 707 ECHR 1–732, 5–002, 5–006, 5–011, 5–015, 5–035, 5–036, 5–053

Proshkin v Russia (App.No.28869/03), February 7, 2012 . . . . 5–021, 5–022

PS v Camden and Islington NHS Foundation Trust [2011] UKUT 143 (AAC); [2011] M.H.L.R. 159. . . . . 1–881, 1–885

Pullar v United Kingdom (22399/93) 1996 S.C.C.R. 755; (1996) 22 E.H.R.R. 391 ECHR . . . 5–030

Quinn v France (A/311) (1996) 21 E.H.R.R. 529 ECHR. 5–020

R. v Ahluwalia (Kiranjit) [1992] 4 All E.R. 889; (1993) 96 Cr. App. R. 133; [1993] Crim. L.R. 63; (1992) 142 N.L.J. 1159. 1–518

R. v Ahmed [2013] EWCA Crim 99; [2013] M.H.L.R. 65 1–528

R. v Antoine (Pierre Harrison) [2001] 1 A.C. 340; [2000] 2 W.L.R. 703; [2000] 2 All E.R. 208; [2000] 2 Cr. App. R. 94; (2000) 54 B.M.L.R. 147; [2000] M.H.L.R. 28; [2000] Crim. L.R. 621; (2000) 97(18) L.S.G. 36; (2000) 144 S.J.L.B. 212 HL. 1–530

R. v Avbunudje (Tobora) [1999] 2 Cr. App. R. (S.) 189; [1999] Crim. L.R. 336 CA (Crim Div) 1–573

R. v Barking Havering and Brentwood Community Healthcare NHS Trust Ex p. B; sub nom. B, Re [1999] 1 F.L.R. 106; (1999) 2 C.C.L. Rep. 5; [1999] Lloyd's Rep. Med. 101; (1999) 47 B.M.L.R. 112 CA (Civ Div) 1–053, 1–064, 1–312, 1–318, 1–320, 1–867, 1–916, 1–918

R. v Barnet LBC Ex p. Shah [1983] 2 A.C. 309; [1983] 2 W.L.R. 16; [1983] 1 All E.R. 226; 81 L.G.R. 305; (1983) 133 N.L.J. 61; (1983) 127 S.J. 36. 1–409

R. v Beatty (David William) [2006] EWCA Crim 2359; (2006) 92 B.M.L.R. 22; [2006] M.H.L.R. 333. . . . . 1–518, 1–663

R. v Beaumont (98/02694 Y2) Unreported July 28, 1998 CA (Crim Div) 1–573

R. v Bennett (David Joseph) [1968] 1 W.L.R. 988; [1968] 2 All E.R. 753; (1968) 52 Cr. App. R. 514; (1968) 132 J.P. 365; (1968) 112 S.J. 418. 1–518

R. v Birch (Beulah) (1990) 90 Cr. App. R. 78; (1989) 11 Cr. App. R. (S.) 202; [1990] 2 Med. L.R. 77; [1989] Crim. L.R. 757 CA (Crim Div) 1–514, 1–519, 1–529, 1–566, 1–573, 1–574, 1–656

R. v Birmingham Mental Health Trust Ex p. Phillips Unreported May 25, 1995 . . . . . 1–086, 1–155, 1–207, 1–431

R. v Blackwood (David George) (1974) 59 Cr. App. R. 170; [1974] Crim. L.R. 437 CA (Crim Div) 1–514, 1–528, 1–567, 1–174

R. v Board of Control Ex p. Rutty; sub nom. Rutty, Re [1956] 2 Q.B. 109; [1956] 2 W.L.R. 822; [1956] 1 All E.R. 769; (1956) 120 J.P. 153; 54 L.G.R. 276; (1956) 100 S.J. 263 DC. 1–868

R. v Bournewood Community and Mental Health NHS Trust Ex p. L; sub nom. L, Re [1999] 1 A.C. 458; [1998] 3 W.L.R. 107; [1998] 3 All E.R. 289; [1998] 2 F.L.R. 550; [1998] 2 F.C.R. 501; (1997–98) 1 C.C.L. Rep. 390; (1998) 44 B.M.L.R. 1; [1998] C.O.D. 312; [1998] Fam.

Law 592; (1998) 95(29) L.S.G. 27; (1998) 148 N.L.J. 1014; (1998) 142 S.J.L.B. 195
HL 1–041, 1–1127, 1–1270, A–002
R. v Broadmoor Special Hospital Authority Ex p. S [1998] C.O.D. 199; (1998) 95(8) L.S.G. 32;
(1998) 142 S.J.L.B. 76 . . . . .1–1343, 1–1354, 5–037
R. v C (Dean) (A Juvenile) [2001] EWCA Crim 57; [2001] M.H.L.R. 2 1–539
R. v C (Michael) [2002] EWCA Crim 785; [2002] M.H.L.R. 144 1–573
R. v Canons Park Mental Health Review Tribunal Ex p. Martins (1995) 26 B.M.L.R. 134;
[1996] C.O.D. 41 QBD. 1–957
R. v Castro (Jorge Enrique) (1985) 81 Cr. App. R. 212; (1985) 7 Cr. App. R. (S.) 68; [1985]
Crim. L.R. 527 1–514
R. v Catchpole (Scott Jamie) [2014] EWCA Crim 1037; [2014] 2 Cr. App. R. (S.) 66 1–488
R. v Central London County Court Ex p. London [1999] Q.B. 1260; [1999] 3 W.L.R. 1; [1999]
3 All E.R. 991; [2000] C.P. Rep. 75; [1999] 2 F.L.R. 161; (1999) 2 C.C.L. Rep. 256; [1999]
C.O.D. 196; [1999] Fam. Law 452; (1999) 96(15) L.S.G. 30. . . . . .1–098, 1–425, 1–426
R. v Chalk (Joseph) [2002] EWCA Crim 2435; [2002] M.H.L.R. 430. 1–574
R. v Chan–Fook (Mike) [1994]1W.L.R. 689; [1994]2 All E.R. 552; (1994) 99 Cr. App. R.
147. 1–029
R. v Chippenham Magistrates' Court Ex p. Thompson (1996) 160 J.P. 207; (1996) 32 B.M.L.R.
69; [1996] C.O.D. 195 DC 1–530
R. v Chowdhury (Taher Ahmed) [2011] EWCA Crim 936; [2011] M.H.L.R. 157 1–534
R. v Clarke (May) [1972] 1 All E.R. 219; (1972) 56 Cr. App. R. 225; (1971) 116 S.J. 56 CA
(Crim Div) A–001
R. v Cockburn (John James) [1968] 1 W.L.R. 281; [1968] 1 All E.R. 466; (1968) 52 Cr. App. R.
134; (1968) 132 J.P. 166; (1967) 112 S.J. 91 1–514
R. v Collins Ex p. Ian Stewart Brady [2000] Lloyd's Rep. Med. 355; (2001) 58 B.M.L.R. 173;
[2000] M.H.L.R. 17 QBD. 1–787
R. v Cooper (Benjamin Alan) [2010] EWCA Crim 2335; [2010] M.H.L.R. 240 1–612
R. v Cooper (Jordan Richard) [2009] EWCA Crim 2646 1–573
R. v Cooper. *See* R. v C (Dean) (A Juvenile)
R. v Courtney (Joseph) (1987) 9 Cr. App. R. (S.) 404; [1988] Crim. L.R. 130 CA (Crim
Div) 1–566
R. v Cox [1999] M.H.L.R. 30 CA (Crim Div). 1–573
R. v Criminal Injuries Compensation Board Ex p. Lawton [1972] 1W.L.R. 1589; [1972] 3 All
E.R. 582; [1972] Crim. L.R. 702; (1972) 116 S.J. 901 DC 1–278
R. v Criminal Injuries Compensation Board Ex p. P; sub nom. R. v Secretary of State for the
Home Department Ex p. P; R. v Secretary of State for the Home Department Ex p. G [1995] 1
W.L.R. 845; [1995]1 All E.R. 870; [1994] 2 F.L.R. 861; [1995] 2 F.C.R. 553; [1994] C.O.D.
507; [1994] Fam. Law 670; (1994) 144 N.L.J. 674 CA (Civ Div) 5–042
R. v Crookes [1999] M.H.L.R. 45. 1–574
R. v Crozier (Peter Michael) (1990–91) 12 Cr. App. R. (S.) 206; [1991] Crim. L.R. 138 CA
(Crim Div) 1–518, 1–528
R. v Czarnota. *See* R. v C (Michael)
R. v D [2006] EWCA Crim 1139; [2006] 2 Cr. App. R. 24; [2006] Crim. L.R. 923. 1–029
R. v Daniels (Jade Louise) [2014] EWCA Crim 2009. 1-518
R. v Davies (Grace); R. v Poolton (Janet Marie) [2000] Crim. L.R. 297 CA (Crim) Div)1–1206,
1–1379
R. v De Silva (Charles) (1994) 15 Cr. App. R. (S.) 296. 1–518
R. v Deighton (Richard) [2005] EWCA Crim 3131. 1–029
R. v Deputy Governor of Parkhurst Prison Ex p. Hague; sub nom. Hague v Deputy Governor of
Parkhurst Prison; Weldon v Home Office [1992] 1 A.C. 58; [1991] 3 W.L.R. 340; [1991] 3
All E.R. 733; (1993) 5 Admin. L.R. 425; [1992] C.O.D. 69; (1991) 135 S.J.L.B. 102
HL A–003
R. v Derby Magistrates Court Ex p. B [1996] A.C. 487; [1995] 3 W.L.R. 681; [1995] 4 All E.R.
526; [1996] 1 Cr. App. R. 385; (1995) 159 J.P. 785; [1996] 1 F.L.R. 513; [1996] Fam. Law
210; (1995) 159 J.P.N. 778; (1995) 145 N.L.J. 1575; (1995) 139 S.J.L.B. 219 HL. E–016
R. v Drew (Anthony James) [2003] UKHL 25; [2003] 1 W.L.R. 1213; [2003] 4 All E.R. 557;
[2003] 2 Cr. App. R. 24; [2004] 1 Cr. App. R. (S.) 8; (2004) 75 B.M.L.R. 34; [2003]
M.H.L.R. 282; (2003) 100(26) L.S.G. 35; (2003) 153 N.L.J. 749; (2003) 147 S.J.L.B.
597. . . . . 1–381, 1–514, 1–519, 1–529, 1–561, 1–567, 1–634, 1–637
R. v Dunne (William Gerard) (1998) 162 J.P. 399 CA (Crim Div) 1–1211

R. v Ealing DHA Ex p. Fox [1993]1W.L.R. 373; [1993] 3 All E.R. 170; (1993) 5 Admin. L.R. 596; [1993] 4 Med. L.R. 101; [1993] C.O.D. 478; (1992) 136 S.J.L.B. 220 QBD 1–1122, 1–1123

R. v East London and the City Mental Health NHS Trust Ex p. von Brandenburg. *See* R. (on the application of von Brandenburg) v East London and the City Mental Health NHS Trust

R. v Edwards (Llewellyn); R. v Roberts (Eric) (1978) 67 Cr. App. R. 228; [1978] Crim. L.R. 564 CA (Crim Div). 1–1336

R. v Erskine (Kenneth) R. v Williams (Ryan) [2009] EWCA Crim 1425; [2010] 1 W.L.R. 183; [2010] 1 All E.R. 1196; [2009] 2 Cr. App. R. 29; [2009] M.H.L.R. 215; [2010] Crim. L.R. 48; (2009) 153(28) S.J.L.B. 30 1–518

R. v Farooqi (Munir Ahmed); R. v Malik (Israr Hussain); R. v Newton (Matthew) [2013] EWCA Crim 1649; [2014] 1 Cr. App. R. 8; [2014] Crim. L.R. 239. . . . . .E–011

R. v Fort (Jamie Daniel) [2013] EWCA Crim 2332; [2014] 2 Cr. App. R. (S.) 24; [2014] M.H.L.R. 334. . . . . 1–518, 1–612, 1–704

R. v Franey Ex p. Warren [1998] EWHC 5. 1–1302

R. v G; R. v R [2003] UKHL 50; [2004] 1 A.C. 1034; [2003] 3 W.L.R. 1060; [2003] 4 All E.R. 765; [2004] 1 Cr. App. R. 21; (2003) 167 J.P. 621; [2004] Crim. L.R. 369; (2003) 167 J.P.N. 955; (2003) 100(43) L.S.G. 31 1–1206

R. v Galfetti (Plinio) [2002] EWCA Crim 1916; [2002] M.H.L.R. 418 . . . . . . .1–514, 1–537, 1–545

R. v Gardiner (Alistair George Cecil) [1967] 1 W.L.R. 464; [1967] 1 All E.R. 895; (1967) 51 Cr. App. R. 187; (1967) 131 J.P. 273; (1967) 111 S.J. 93 CA (Crim Div) 1–566

R. v Ghulam (Habib) [2009] EWCA Crim 2285; [2010]1W.L.R. 891; [2010] 1 Cr. App. R. 12. 1–695

R. v Golding (Ronald Lonford) [2006] EWCA Crim 1965; [2007] 1 Cr. App. R. (S.) 79; [2006] M.H.L.R. 272; [2007] Crim. L.R. 170. 1–573

R. v Goode (Peter) [2002] EWCA Crim 1698; [2002] M.H.L.R. 337 1–567

R. v Goucher (Tania Louise) [2011] EWCA Crim 2473; [2012] M.H.L.R. 107 1-518

R. v Governor of Pentonville Prison Ex p. Azam. *See* Azam v Secretary of State for the Home Department

R. v Griffith [2002] EWCA Crim 1838; [2002] M.H.L.R. 427 1–518

R. v Griffiths (Stephen) [2002] EWCA Crim 1762; [2002] M.H.L.R. 405. 1–683

R. v Haile (Tesfalem) [2009] EWCA Crim 1996. 1–574

R. v Hall (John Hamilton) (1988) 86 Cr. App. R. 159 CA (Crim Div). 1–032

R. v Hallstrom Ex p. W (No.1). *See* Waldron, Re

R. v Hallstrom Ex p. W (No.2) [1986] Q.B. 1090; [1986] 2 W.L.R. 883; [1986] 2 All E.R. 306; (1986) 83 L.S.G. 786; (1985) 130 S.J. 204 QBD. . . . 1–005, 1–045, 1–053, 1–062, 1–104, 1–132, 1–225, 1–312, 1–318, 1–918, 1–1356

R. v Haynes (Anthony William) (1981) 3 Cr. App. R. (S.) 330; [1982] Crim. L.R. 245 CA (Crim Div). 1–566

R. v Hempston [2006] EWCA Crim 2869; [2011] M.H.L.R. 99 1–518

R. v Hendy (Jason Geoffrey) [2006] EWCA Crim 819; [2006] 2 Cr. App. R. 33; [2006] M.H.L.R. 244; [2006] Crim. L.R. 927. 1–518

R. v Hennessy (Andrew Michael) [1989]1W.L.R. 287; [1989]2 All E.R. 9; (1989) 89 Cr. App. R. 10; [1989] R.T.R. 153; [1989] Crim. L.R. 356; (1989) 133 S.J. 263 CA (Crim Div) A–001

R. v HM Coroner for North Humberside and Scunthorpe Ex p. Jamieson [1995] Q.B. 1; [1994] 3 W.L.R. 82; [1994] 3 All E.R. 972; (1994) 158 J.P. 1011; [1994] 5 Med. L.R. 217; [1994] C.O.D. 455 CA (Civ Div). 1–1206

R. v Holmes [1979] Crim. L.R. 52. 1–1206

R. v Horseferry Road Magistrates Court Ex p. K [1997] Q.B. 23; [1996]3W.L.R. 68; [1996] 3 All E.R. 719; [1996] 2 Cr. App. R. 574; (1996) 160 J.P. 441; (1997) 33 B.M.L.R. 28; [1997] Crim. L.R. 129; (1996) 160 J.P.N. 482; (1996) 93(11) L.S.G. 29; (1996) 140 S.J.L.B. 64 QBD. 1–597

R. v Howell (Seymour Joseph) (1985) 7 Cr. App. R. (S.) 360 CA (Crim Div). 1–514

R. v Humberside and Scunthorpe Coroner Ex p. Jamieson. *See* R. v HM Coroner for North Humberside and Scunthorpe Ex p. Jamieson

R. v Hurst (Ian Douglas) [2007] EWCA Crim 3436; [2008] M.H.L.R. 43 1–574

R. v Ireland (Robert Matthew); R. v Burstow (Anthony Christopher) [1998] A.C. 147; [1997] 3 W.L.R. 534; [1997] 4 All E.R. 225; [1998] 1 Cr. App. R. 177; (1997) 161 J.P. 569; [1998] 1 F.L.R. 105; [1997] Crim. L.R. 810; [1998] Fam. Law 137; (1997) 161 J.P.N. 816; (1997) 147 N.L.J. 1273; (1997) 141 S.J.L.B. 205 HL 1–029

Table of Cases

R. v Jenkin (Shane William) [2012] EWCA Crim 2557; [2013] 2 Cr. App. R. (S.) 15; [2013] M.H.L.R. 61; [2013] Crim. L.R. 246. ... 1–612

R. v Jones (Michelle Louise) [2000] M.H.L.R. 12 CA (Crim Div) ... 1–573

R. v K (James) [2000] M.H.L.R. 9 CA (Crim Div) ... 1–573

R. v Kamara. See R. v K (James)

R. v Kemp (Albert) [1957] 1 Q.B. 399; [1956]3W.L.R. 724; [1956] 3 All E.R. 249; (1956) 40 Cr. App. R. 121; (1956) 120 J.P. 457; (1956) 100 S.J. 768 Assizes ... 1–029, A–001

R. v Kent CC Ex p. Marston Unreported, July 9, 1997 QBD. ... 1–129, 1–131

R. v Kingston Crown Court Ex p. Mason Unreported July 27, 1998 CA (Civ Div) ... 1–683

R. v Kirklees MBC Ex p. C (A Minor) [1993] 2 F.L.R. 187; [1993] 2 F.C.R. 381; [1993] Fam. Law 455 CA (Civ Div). ... 1–047, 1–1270, 1–1277

R. v Lavender (Jennifer) [2012] EWCA Crim 1179 ... 11–518

R. v Lincoln (Kesteven) Magistrates Court Ex p. O Connor [1983]1W.L.R. 335; [1983]1 All E.R. 901; (1983) 147 J.P. 97; [1983] Crim. L.R. 621; (1983) 127 S.J. 121 DC. ... 1–530

R. v Liverpool City Council Ex p. F Unreported April 16, 1997 QBD ... 1–409

R. v Logan (Sharon) [2012] EWCA Crim 2542 ... 1–518

R. v Lomey (John); sub nom. R.v Lomey (John) (also known as Andrews (John Dennis)) [2004] EWCA Crim 3014; [2004] M.H.L.R. 316. ... 1–518

R. v London South West Region Mental Health Review Tribunal Ex p. Moyle [1999] M.H.L.R. 195. ... 1–915, 1–917, 1–918

R. v Lord Kylsant [1932] 1 K.B. 442; (1932) 23 Cr. App. R. 83 CCA. ... 1–1200

R. v Macrow (Richard Vernon) [2004] EWCA Crim 1159 ... 1–573

R. v Managers of South Western Hospital Ex p. M; sub nom. R. v South Western Hospital Managers Ex p. M; Mulcahy (Eleanor), Re [1993] Q.B. 683; [1993] 3 W.L.R. 376; [1994] 1 All E.R. 161; (1994) 6 Admin. L.R. 229 QBD 1–098, 1–154, 1–155, 1–158, 1–159, 1–160, 1–204, 1–207, 1–867

R. v Manchester City Council Ex p. Stennett. See R. (on the application of Stennett) v Manchester City Council

R. v Marsden (June) [1968] 1 W.L.R. 785; [1968] 2 All E.R. 341; (1968) 52 Cr. App. R. 301; (1968) 132 J.P. 347; (1968) 112 S.J. 331 CA (Civ Div). ... 1–514

R. v McDonagh (Patrick) [2008] NICA 6; [2008] M.H.L.R. 219. ... 1–032

R. v Melbourne (Paul Anthony) [2000] M.H.L.R. 2 CA (Crim Div) ... 1–573

R. v Mental Health Act Commission Ex p. Smith (1997–98) 1 C.C.L. Rep. 451; (1998) 43 B.M.L.R. 174; (1998) 142 S.J.L.B. 182 QBD ... 1–1173

R. v Mental Health Act Commission Ex p. X (1988) 9 B.M.L.R. 77. ... 1–720, 1–721, 1–740

R. v Mental Health Review Tribunal Ex p. Booth [1998] C.O.D. 203 QBD ... 3–153

R. v Mental Health Review Tribunal Ex p. Clatworthy [1985] 3 All E.R. 699 QBD ... 3–124

R. v Mental Health Review Tribunal Ex p. Cleveland CO/819/88 Unreported, 1989. ... 3–046

R. v Mental Health Review Tribunal Ex p. Cooper Unreported February 14, 1990 ... 1–937

R. v Mental Health Review Tribunal Ex p. Hall [2000] 1 W.L.R. 1323; [1999] 4 All E.R. 883; (1999) 2 C.C.L. Rep. 383; [1999] Lloyd's Rep. Med. 417; (2000) 51 B.M.L.R. 117; [1999] C.O.D. 429; (1999) 96(33) L.S.G. 31; (1999) 149 N.L.J. 1368 CA (Civ Div)... 1–1122, 1–1123

R. v Mental Health Review Tribunal Ex p. Manns [1999] M.H.L.R. 101 ... 3–088

R. v Mental Health Review Tribunal Ex p. Pierce (1997) 36 B.M.L.R. 137; [1996] C.O.D. 467 QBD. ... 1–927

R. v Mental Health Review Tribunal for South Thames Region Ex p. Smith [1998] EWHC 832 (Admin) (1999) 47 B.M.L.R. 104; [1999] C.O.D. 148 QBD ... 1–057, 1–064, 1–918

R. v Mental Health Tribunal Ex p. Pickering [1986] 1 All E.R. 99 QBD. ... 1–917, 3–153

R. v Mersey Care National Health Service Trust Ex p. Munjaz. See R. (on the application of Munjaz) v Mersey Care NHS Trust

R. v Mersey Mental Health Review Tribunal Ex p. Dillon Times, April 13, 1987 DC ... 1–1379

R. v Merseyside Mental Health Review Tribunal Ex p. K [1990] 1 All E.R. 694 CA (Civ Div). ... 1–567, 1–587, 1–936, 1–953, 1–1379

R. v Merseyside Mental Health Review Tribunal Ex p. Kelly (1998) 39 B.M.L.R. 114 QBD. ... 1–955

R. v Morrell (Karen Victoria) [2002] EWCA Crim 2547. ... 1–1206

R. v MR [2002] EWCA Crim 165; [2002] M.H.L.R. 129 ... 1–574

R. v Newington (Susan) (1990) 91 Cr. App. R. 247; [1990] Crim. L.R. 593; (1990) 87(12) L.S.G. 40; (1990) 134 S.J. 785 ... 1–1204, 1–1206, 1–1207

R. v North and East Devon HA Ex p. Coughlan [2001] Q.B. 213; [2000] 2 W.L.R. 622; [2000] 3 All E.R. 850; (2000) 2 L.G.L.R. 1; [1999] B.L.G.R. 703; (1999) 2 C.C.L. Rep. 285; [1999]

Lloyd's Rep. Med. 306; (2000) 51 B.M.L.R. 1; [1999] C.O.D. 340; (1999) 96(31) L.S.G. 39; (1999) 143 S.J.L.B. 213 CA (Civ Div) 5–040

R. v North West London Mental Health NHS Trust Ex p. S [1998] Q.B. 628; [1998] 2 W.L.R. 189; [1997] 4 All E.R. 871; (1998) 39 B.M.L.R. 105 CA (Civ Div) 1–048, 1–483, 1–531, 1–576, 1–584, 1–589, 1–648, 1–872

R. v North West London Mental Health NHS Trust Ex p. Stewart. *See* R. v North West London Mental Health NHS Trust Ex p. S

R. v Northampton Juvenile Court Ex p. Hammersmith and Fulham LBC [1985] Fam. Law 124; [1985] F.L.R. 193 1–1277

R. v Nottingham Mental Health Review Tribunal Ex p. Secretary of State for the Home Department; R. v Trent Mental Health Review Tribunal Ex p. Secretary of State for the Home Department [1989] C.O.D. 221; *Times*, October 12, 1988 CA (Civ Div) 1–897, 1–934, 3–046

R. v O [2011] EWCA Crim 376; [2011] M.H.L.R. 99. 1–518

R. v Osker (Donna) [2010] EWCA Crim 955; [2010] M.H.L.R. 115. 1–573

R. v Oxford Mental Health Authority Review Tribunal Ex p. Smith Unreported January 25, 1995 CA (Civ Div). 1–927, 1–934

R. v Oxford Regional Mental Health Tribunal Ex p. Mackman *Times* June 2, 1986. 3–015

R. v Oxford Regional Mental Health Tribunal Ex p. Secretary of State for the Home Department; sub nom. Campbell v Secretary of State for the Home Department; Secretary of State for the Home Department v Oxford Regional Mental Health Review Tribunal; R. v Yorkshire Mental Health Review Tribunal Ex p. Secretary of State for the Home Department [1988] A.C. 120; [1987] 3 W.L.R. 522; [1987] 3 All E.R. 8; (1987) 84 L.S.G. 2690; (1987) 137 N.L.J. 735; (1987) 131 S.J. 1086 HL..... 1–927, 1–935, 1–941, 1–941, 3–011, 3–112

R. v Parole Board Ex p. Bradley [1991] 1 W.L.R. 134; [1990] 3 All E.R. 828; [1990] C.O.D. 375 DC... 1–586, 1–919

R. v Petrolini (Jamie) [2012] EWCA Crim 2055; [2012] M.H.L.R. 308 1–518

R. v Poole (Matthew Jason) [2014] EWCA Crim 1641; [2015] 1 W.L.R. 522; [2015] 1 Cr. App. R. (S.) 2 .... 1-612, 1-620

R. v Preston (Mark Andrew) [2003] EWCA Crim 2086; [2004] M.H.L.R. 277 1–528

R. v Ramsgate Justices Ex p. Kazmarek (1985) 80 Cr. App. R. 366; (1985) 149 J.P. 16 DC .. 1–530

R. v Reid (Sherwin Delroy) [2005] EWCA Crim 392; [2006] M.H.L.R. 180. 1–574

R. v Richmond LBC Ex p. W; R. v Redcar & Cleveland BC Ex p. A; R. v Manchester City Council Ex p. S; R. v Harrow LBC Ex p. C [2000] M.H.L.R. 155 CA (Civ Div). 1–1135

R. v Ristic. *See* R. v MR

R. v Riverside Mental Health Trust Ex p. Huzzey (1998) 43 B.M.L.R. 167 QBD 1–317, 1–380, 1–394

R. v Roberts (Dean Terrence) [2003] EWCA Crim 858 1–574

R. v Roberts (Leroy Lloyd) [2003] EWCA Crim 2753; [2004]1W.L.R. 181; [2004] 1 Cr. App. R. 16; (2003) 167 J.P. 675; [2004] Crim. L.R. 141; (2004) 168 J.P.N. 517; (2003) 100(44) L.S.G. 30 1–1336

R. v Rogerson (Daniel Lee) [2004] EWCA Crim 2099; [2006] M.H.L.R. 175. 1–534

R. v Rosso (Rosario) [2003] EWCA Crim 3242; [2003] M.H.L.R. 404; [2004] Po. L.R. 1 . .1–1113, 1–1319, 1–1342

R. v Royse (Irene Olive) (1981) 3 Cr. App. R. (S.) 58; [1981] Crim. L.R. 426 CA (Civ Div) . 1–574

R. v Ruby (Ian) [2013] EWCA Crim 1653 1–518

R. v Runighian [1977] Crim. L.R. 361 Crown Ct 1–1352

R. v S [2012] EWCA Crim 92; [2012] M.H.L.R. 58 1–612

R. v Salisu (Musedig) [2009] EWCA Crim 2702; [2010] M.H.L.R. 58 1–1206

R. v Searles (Ashley) [2012] EWCA Crim 2685. 1–518

R. v Secretary of State for Health Ex p. Pfizer Ltd [1999] 3 C.M.L.R. 875; (1999)2 C.C.L. Rep. 270; [1999] Lloyd's Rep. Med. 289; (2000) 51 B.M.L.R. 189 QBD 1–1157

R. v Secretary of State for the Home Department Ex p. Cheblak [1991]1W.L.R. 890; [1991] 2 All E.R. 319; (1992) 4Admin. L.R. 353; [1991] C.O.D. 394; (1991) 141 N.L.J. 201 CA (Civ Div) 1–867

R. v Secretary of State for the Home Department Ex p. Daly. *See* R. (on the application of Daly) v Secretary of State for the Home Department

R. v Secretary of State for the Home Department Ex p. Didlick [1993] C.O.D. 412; (1993) 16 B.M.L.R. 71 DC. 1–583

R. v Secretary of State for the Home Department Ex p. Gilkes [1999] EWHC 47 (Admin);
  [1999] M.H.L.R. 7 1–639
R. v Secretary of State for the Home Department Ex p. H (No.1); sub nom. R. v Secretary of
  State for the Home Department Ex p. T; R. v Secretary of State for the Home Department Ex
  p. Hickey (No.1) [1995] Q.B. 43; [1994] 3 W.L.R. 1110; [1995] 1 All E.R. 479; [1994] 138
  S.J.L.B. 237 CA (Civ Div) 1–645, 1–669, 1–673
R. v Secretary of State for the Home Department Ex p. Harry [1998] 1 W.L.R. 1737; [1998] 3
  All E.R. 360; (1998) 43 B.M.L.R. 155; (1998) 95(22) L.S.G. 29 QBD 1–577
R. v Secretary of State for the Home Department Ex p. Hickey (No.1). *See* R. v Secretary of
  State for the Home Department Ex p. H (No.1)
R. v Secretary of State for the Home Department Ex p. K [1991] 1 Q.B. 270; [1990] 3 W.L.R.
  755; [1990] 3 All E.R. 562; [1990] 2 Med. L.R. 53; [1991] C.O.D. 63; (1990) 134 S.J. 1106
  CA (Civ Div) 1–004, 1–567
R. v Secretary of State for the Home Department Ex p. Simms; sub nom. R. v Secretary of State
  for the Home Department Ex p. Main; R. v Governor of Whitemoor Prison Ex p. Main; R. v
  Secretary of State for the Home Department Ex p. O Brien [2000] 2 A.C. 115; [1999] 3
  W.L.R. 328; [1999] 3 All E.R. 400; [1999] E.M.L.R. 689; 7 B.H.R.C. 411; (1999) 11
  Admin. L.R. 961; [1999] Prison L.R. 82; [1999] C.O.D. 520; (1999) 96(30) L.S.G. 28;
  (1999) 149 N.L.J. 1073; (1999) 143 S.J.L.B. 212 HL 1–939
R. v Secretary of State for the Home Department Ex p. Stroud [1993] C.O.D. 75 1–673
R. v Secretary of State for the Home Department Ex p. Williams Unreported June 21, 1994. . 1–663
R. v Shah (Safdar Haider) [2011] EWCA Crim 2333; [2012] M.H.L.R. 92 1–518
R. v Sheppard (James Martin); R. v Sheppard (Jennifer Christine) [1981] A.C. 394; [1980] 3
  W.L.R. 960; [1980] 3 All E.R. 899; (1981) 72 Cr. App. R. 82; [1981] Crim. L.R. 171;
  (1980) 124 S.J. 864 HL 1–1206
R. v Skelton [1983] Crim. L.R. 686 CA (Crim Div) 1–519
R. v Smith [2001] EWCA Crim 743; [2001] M.H.L.R. 46 1–528
R. v Solihull MBC Housing Benefit Review Board Ex p. Simpson; sub nom. Solihull MBC
  Housing Benefits Review Board v Simpson [1995] 1 F.L.R. 140; [1995] 2 F.C.R. 424;
  (1995) 27 H.L.R. 41; 92 L.G.R. 719; [1995] Fam. Law 17 CA (Civ Div) 3–153
R. v Soneji [2005] UKHL; [2005] 4 All E.R. 321 1–204
R. v South Thames Mental Health Review Tribunal Ex p. M [1998] C.O.D. 38 QBD 1–871,
  1–872
R. v South West Thames Mental Health Review Tribunal Ex p. Demetri (No.1) [1997] C.O.D.
  44 CA (Civ Div). 3–152
R. v South Western Hospital Managers Ex p. M. *See* R. v Managers of South Western Hospital
  Ex p. M
R. v Staines (Paula) [2006] EWCA Crim 15; [2006] 2 Cr. App. R. (S.) 61; [2006] M.H.L.R. 184;
  [2006] Crim. L.R. 455; (2006) 150 S.J.L.B. 167 1–612
R. v Stead. *See* R. v S
R. v Sullivan (Patrick Joseph) [1984] A.C. 156; [1983] 3 W.L.R. 123; [1983] 2 All E.R. 673;
  (1983) 77 Cr. App. R. 176; (1984) 148 J.P. 207; [1983] Crim. L.R. 740; (1983) 127 S.J. 460
  HL 1–029, A–001
R. v Teasdale (Paul John) [2012] EWCA Crim 2071; [2012] M.H.L.R. 387 1–514
R. v Thames Magistrates Court Ex p. Ramadan [1999] 1 Cr. App. R. 386; (1999) 163 J.P. 428;
  (2000) 53 B.M.L.R. 49; [1999] Crim. L.R. 498; [1999] C.O.D. 19; (1999) 163 J.P.N. 212
  DC 1–530, 1–531
R. v Thornley (William James) (1981) 72 Cr. App. R. 302; [1981] Crim. L.R. 637 CA (Crim
  Div) 1–1113
R. v Trent Mental Health Review Tribunal Ex p. Ryan [1992] C.O.D. 157 DC 1–030, 3–123
R. v Trent RHA Ex p. Somaratne (No.1) (1994) 31 B.M.L.R. 140 CA (Civ Div) 1–168
R. v Tudor (Shaun Edward) [2012] EWCA Crim 1507; [2012] M.H.L.R. 300. 1–528
R. v Uxbridge County Court Ex p Binns [2000] M.H.L.R. 179 QBD 1–426
R. v Vowles (Lucinda); R. v McDougall (Gordon); R. v Irving (David Stuart); R. v Odiowei
  (Justin Obuza); R. v Coleman (Danielle); R. v Barnes (Carl); sub nom. R. (on the application
  of Vowles) v Secretary of State for Justice [2015] EWCA Crim 45; [2015] 2 Cr. App. R. (S.)
  6; [2015] Crim. L.R. 542 . . . . 1–514, 1–519, 1–527, 1–529, 1–537, 1–566, 1–612, 1–673, 1–919,
  1–947
R. v Wang (Lin) [2005] EWCA Crim 3238; [2006] M.H.L.R. 109 1–518
R. v Warlingham Park Hospital Managers Ex p. B; sub nom. B, Re [1996] C.O.D. 224; (1994)
  22 B.M.L.R. 1CA (Civ Div) 1–313, 1–317

Table of Cases

R. v Welsh (Colin Christopher) [2011] EWCA Crim 73; (2011) 119 B.M.L.R. 21; [2011] Crim.
L.R. 421; [2011] M.H.L.R. 71. 1–567
R. v Wilson Ex p. Williamson [1996] C.O.D. 42 QBD 1–038, 1–041, 1–050, 1–086, 1–156,
1–1327, 1–1338
R. v Windle (Francis Wilfred) [1952] 2 Q.B. 826; [1952] 2 All E.R. 1; [1952] 1 T.L.R. 1344;
(1952) 36 Cr. App. R. 85; (1952) 116 J.P. 365; (1952) 96 S.J. 379 CCA A–001
R. v Wood (Clive) [2009] EWCA Crim 651; [2010] 1 Cr. App. R. (S.) 2; [2009] Crim. L.R.
543. 1–567
R. v Yusuf [2013] EWCA Crim 2077 1–518
R. (on the application of A) v East Sussex CC (No.2) [2003] EWHC 167 (Admin); (2003) 6
C.C.L. Rep. 194 1–019
R. (on the application of A) v Harrow Crown Court [2003] EWHC 2020 (Admin); [2003]
M.H.L.R. 393. . . . . .1–098, 1–474, 5–022
R. (on the application of A) v Partnerships in Care Ltd [2002] EWHC 529 (Admin); [2002] 1
W.L.R. 2610; (2002) 5 C.C.L. Rep. 330; [2002] M.H.L.R. 298; (2002) 99(20) L.S.G. 32;
(2002) 146 S.J.L.B. 117 . . . . .1–465, 1–1378, 5–004
R. (on the application of A) v Secretary of State for the Home Department; sub nom. R. (on the
application of RA) v Secretary of State for the Home Department [2002] EWHC 1618
(Admin); [2003] 1 W.L.R. 330; [2003] M.H.L.R. 54; [2003] A.C.D. 7 . . . . 1–221, 1–577, 1–934,
1–941
R. (on the application of A) v Secretary of State for the Home Department [2003] EWHC 2846
(Admin); [2004] H.R.L.R. 12; [2004] U.K.H.R.R. 413; [2004] M.H.L.R. 98; [2004] Prison
L.R. 231; [2004] A.C.D. 7 . . . . 1–466, 5–048
R. (on the application of A) v Secretary of State for the Home Department and Mental Health
Review Tribunal [2003] EWHC 270 (Admin); [2005] M.H.L.R. 144 1–941
R. (on the application of Abu–Rideh) v Mental Health Review Tribunal [2004] EWHC 1999
(Admin); [2004] M.H.L.R. 308. . . . . 1–945, 1–946
R. (on the application of Afework) v The Mayor and Burgesses of the London Borough of
Camden [2013] EWHC 1637 (Admin); [2014] M.H.L.R. 32. 1–1119
R. (on the application of Ahmadi) v Secretary of State for the Home Department [2005] EWCA
Civ 1721; [2006] I.N.L.R. 318 5–039
R. (on the application of AM) v Central and North West London Mental Health NHS Trust
Unreported February 1, 2007 1–736
R. (on the application of Anderson) v HM Coroner for Inner North Greater London [2004]
EWHC 2729 (Admin); [2004] Inquest L.R. 155; [2004] M.H.L.R. 324; [2005] A.C.D.
68. 1–1333
R. (on the application of Antoniou) v Central and North West London NHS Foundation Trust
[2013] EWHC 3055 (Admin); [2013] Med. L.R. 536; (2014) 135 B.M.L.R. 89; [2014]
A.C.D. 44; [2014] M.H.L.R. 212 5–008
R. (on the application of Ashworth Hospital Authority) v Mental Health Review Tribunal for
West Midlands and North West Region. See R. (on the application of H) v Ashworth Hospital
Authority
R. (on the application of Axon) v Secretary of State for Health [2006] EWHC 37 (Admin);
[2006] Q.B. 539; [2006] 2 W.L.R. 1130; [2006] 2 F.L.R. 206; [2006] 1 F.C.R. 175; [2006]
H.R.L.R. 12; (2006) 88 B.M.L.R. 96; [2006] A.C.D. 58; [2006] Fam. Law 272; (2006)
103(8) L.S.G. 25. . . . . 4–092, 4–093
R. (on the application of B) v Camden LBC [2005] EWHC 1366 (Admin); [2006] B.L.G.R. 19;
(2005) 8 C.C.L. Rep. 422; (2005) 85 B.M.L.R. 28; [2005] M.H.L.R. 258; [2006] A.C.D.
31. 1–1124
R. (on the application of B) v Dr SS (Responsible Medical Officer). See R. (on the application
of B) v S (Responsible Medical Officer, Broadmoor Hospital)
R. (on the application of B) v Haddock (Responsible Medical Officer) [2006] EWCA Civ 961;
[2006] H.R.L.R. 40; [2006] Lloyd's Rep. Med. 433; (2007) 93 B.M.L.R. 52; [2006]
M.H.L.R. 306. . . . . 1–730, 1–731, 1–741, 1–742, 1–743, 1–785
R. (on the application of B) v Mental Health Review Tribunal [2002] EWHC 1553 (Admin);
[2003] M.H.L.R. 19 . . . . .1–588, 3–042, 3–046
R. (on the application of B) v Mental Health Tribunal [2003] EWHC 815 (Admin); [2003]
M.H.L.R. 218. . . . . 1–921, 1–927
R. (on the application of B) v S (Responsible Medical Officer, Broadmoor Hospital) [2006]
EWCA Civ 28; [2006] 1 W.L.R. 810; [2006] H.R.L.R. 14; [2006] U.K.H.R.R. 432;
(2006) 9 C.C.L. Rep. 280; (2006) 90 B.M.L.R. 1; [2006] M.H.L.R. 131; (2006) 103(7)

L.S.G. 24; (2006) 150 S.J.L.B. 163 . . . . 1–731, 1–733, 1–740, 1–742, 3–010

R. (on the application of B) v Secretary of State for Health. *See* R. (on the application of B) v SS

R. (on the application of B) v South Region Mental Health Review Tribunal [2008] EWHC
2356 (Admin); [2008] M.H.L.R. 312; [2008] A.C.D. 91; (2008) 105(33) L.S.G. 24 3–1342

R. (on the application of B) v SS [2005] EWHC 86 (Admin); [2005] M.H.L.R. 96; [2005]
A.C.D. 55; [2005] A.C.D. 91 . . . . .1–730, 1–732, 1–733

R. (on the application of B) v Stafford Combined Court; sub nom. R. (on the application of TB)
v Stafford Crown Court [2006] EWHC 1645 (Admin); [2007] 1 W.L.R. 1524; [2007] 1 All
E.R. 102; [2006] 2 Cr. App. R. 34. 3–080

R. (on the application of BA) v Secretary of State for the Home Department [2011] EWHC
2748 (Admin). 1–653

R. (on the application of Bernard) v Enfield LBC [2002] EWHC 2282 (Admin); [2003]
H.R.L.R. 4; [2003] U.K.H.R.R. 148; [2003] H.L.R. 27; [2003] B.L.G.R. 423; (2002) 5
C.C.L. Rep. 577; [2003] A.C.D. 26; (2002) 99(48) L.S.G. 27 5–040

R. (on the application of Bitcon) v West Allerdale Magistrates Court [2003] EWHC 2460
(Admin); [2003] M.H.L.R. 399 1–494

R. (on the application of Blouet) v Bath & Wansdyke Magistrates Court [2009] EWHC 759
(Admin); [2009] M.H.L.R. 71. 1–530

R. (on the application of Brooks) v Parole Board for England and Wales [2004] EWCA Civ 80;
[2004] Prison L.R. 324; (2004) 148 S.J.L.B. 233. 1-919

R. (on the application of Bukowicki) v Northamptonshire CC; sub nom. R. (on the application
of Buckowicki) v Northamptonshire CC [2007] EWHC 310 (Admin); [2007] M.H.L.R.
121. 1–533

R. (on the application of Burke) v General Medical Council [2005] EWCA Civ 1003; [2006]
Q.B. 273; [2005] 3 W.L.R. 1132; [2005] 2 F.L.R. 1223; [2005] 3 F.C.R. 169; [2005] H.R.L.R.
35; [2006] U.K.H.R.R. 509; (2005) 8 C.C.L. Rep. 463; [2005] Lloyd's Rep. Med. 403;
(2005) 85 B.M.L.R. 1; [2006] A.C.D. 27; [2005] Fam. Law 776; (2005) 155 N.L.J.
1457. . . . . 1–705, 5–016

R. (on the application of C) v Mental Health Review Tribunal; sub nom. R. (on the application
of C) v London South and South West Region Mental Health Review Tribunal [2001] EWCA
Civ 1110; [2002] 1 W.L.R. 176; [2002] 2 F.C.R. 181; (2001) 4 C.C.L. Rep. 284; [2001]
Lloyd's Rep. Med. 450; [2001] M.H.L.R. 110; (2001) 98(29) L.S.G. 39; (2001) 145
S.J.L.B. 167 . . . . .1–381, 3–136, 5–026

R. (on the application of C) v Mental Health Review Tribunal; sub nom. R. (on the application
of SC) v Mental Health Review Tribunal [2005] EWHC 17 (Admin); [2005] M.H.L.R. 31;
[2005] A.C.D. 102; [2005] A.C.D. 89; (2005) 102(9) L.S.G. 30 . . . . 1–019, 1–954, 1–958

R. (on the application of C) v Secretary of State for the Home Department [2002] EWCA Civ
647; [2002] M.H.L.R. 105; (2002) 99(25) L.S.G. 35; (2002) 146 S.J.L.B. 162 . . . . 1–901, 1–941

R. (on the application of Care Principles Ltd) v Mental Health Review Tribunal [2006] EWHC
3194 (Admin); (2007) 94 B.M.L.R. 145; [2006] M.H.L.R. 365; [2007] A.C.D. 47 1–056,
1–110

R. (on the application of Carson) v Secretary of State for Work and Pensions; sub nom. Carson v
Secretary of State for Work and Pension; R. (on the application of Reynolds) v Secretary of
State for Work and Pensions [2005] UKHL 37; [2006] 1 A.C. 173; [2005] 2 W.L.R. 1369;
[2005] 4 All E.R. 545; [2005] H.R.L.R. 23; [2005] U.K.H.R.R. 1185; 18 B.H.R.C. 677 . . . 5–053

R. (on the application of Cart) v Upper Tribunal [2011] UKSC 28; [2011] M.H.L.R. 196; [2011]
3 W.L.R. 107; [2011] S.T.I. 1943; (2011) 161 N.L.J. 916;. 1–865

R. (on the application of Central and North West London Mental Health NHS Trust) v Mental
Health Review Tribunal (Southern Region) [2005] EWHC 337 (Admin); [2005] M.H.L.R.
183. 1–921

R. (on the application of Condliff) v North Staffordshire [2011] EWCA Civ 910; [2012] 1 All
E.R. 689; [2012] P.T.S.R. 460; [2011] H.R.L.R. 38; (2011) 14 C.C.L. Rep. 656; [2011] Med.
L.R. 572; (2011) 121 B.M.L.R. 192; [2011] A.C.D. 113; (2011) 155(30) S.J.L.B. 31 CA (Civ
Div) 5–033

R. (on the application of Cooke) v DPP; sub nom. Cooke v DPP [2008] EWHC 2703 (Admin);
(2008) 172 J.P. 596; [2008] M.H.L.R. 348 1–008

R. (on the application of Cornwall Council) v Secretary of State for Health; R. (on the application of Cornwall Council) v Somerset CC [2015] UKSC 46; [2015] 3 W.L.R. 213. 1–409,
1–412

R. (on the application of Countryside Alliance) v Attorney General; R. (on the application of
Derwin) v Attorney General; R. (on the application of Friend) v Attorney General [2007]

UKHL 52; [2008] 1 A.C. 719; [2007] 3 W.L.R. 922; [2008] 2 All E.R. 95; [2008] Eu. L.R.
359; [2008] H.R.L.R. 10; [2008] U.K.H.R.R. 1; (2007) 104(48) L.S.G. 23; (2007) 157 N.L.J.
1730; (2007) 151 S.J.L.B. 1564; [2007] N.P.C. 127. 5–033
R. (on the application of Craven) v Secretary of State for the Home Department [2001] EWHC
Admin 850; [2002] Po. L.R. 18. . . . . 1–584, 5–043
R. (on the application of CS) v Mental Health Review Tribunal [2004] EWHC 2958 (Admin);
[2004] M.H.L.R. 355; [2005] A.C.D. 54 . . . . 1–223, 1–318, 1–914, 1–915, 1–918
R. (on the application of D) v Secretary of State for the Home Department; sub nom. D v
Secretary of State for the Home Department [2002] EWHC 2805 (Admin); [2003] 1
W.L.R. 1315; [2003] U.K.H.R.R. 221; [2003] M.H.L.R. 193; [2003] Prison L.R. 178;
[2003] A.C.D. 84 . . . . 1–671, 1–674
R. (on the application of D) v Secretary of State for the Home Office [2003] EWHC 2529
(Admin). 1–634
R. (on the application of Daly) v Secretary of State for the Home Department; sub nom. R. v
Secretary of State for the Home Department Ex p. Daly [2001] UKHL 26; [2001] 2 A.C. 532;
[2001] 2 W.L.R. 1622; [2001] 3 All E.R. 433; [2001] H.R.L.R. 49; [2001] U.K.H.R.R. 887;
[2001] Prison L.R. 322; [2001] A.C.D. 79; (2001) 98(26) L.S.G. 43; (2001) 145 S.J.L.B. 156
HL 1–868
R. (on the application of DB) v Nottinghamshire Healthcare NHS Trust. *See* X v NHS Trust
R. (on the application of DB) v Secretary of State for the Home Department [2006] EWHC 659
(Admin); [2006] M.H.L.R. 158. 5–011
R. (on the application of DJ) v Mental Health Review Tribunal. *See* R. (on the application of N)
v Mental Health Review Tribunal (Northern Region)
R. (on the application of DK) v Secretary of State for Justice [2010] EWHC 82 (Admin); (2010)
112 B.M.L.R. 116; [2010] M.H.L.R. 64 . . . . 1–633, 1–639
R. (on the application of Donaldson) v Secretary of State for the Home Department [2006]
EWHC 1107 (Admin); [2006] M.H.L.R. 100 1–663
R. (on the application of DR) v Mersey Care NHS Trust; sub nom. R. (on the application of R) v
Mersey Care NHS Trust [2002] EWHC 1810 (Admin); [2002] M.H.L.R. 386. . . . . 1–053, 1–064,
1–087, 1–223, 1–225, 1–260, 1–317, 1–318, 1–319, 1–918
R. (on the application of E) v Ashworth Hospital Authority [2001] EWHC Admin 1089; [2002]
M.H.L.R. 150; [2002] A.C.D. 23 . . . . 1–1354, 5–037
R. (on the application of Epsom & St Helier NHS Trust) v Mental Health Review Tribunal
[2001] EWHC Admin 101; [2001] M.H.L.R. 8 . . . . 1–318, 1–918, 1–1379, 3–153
R. (on the application of F) v Oxfordshire Mental Healthcare NHS Trust [2001] EWHC Admin
535; [2001] M.H.L.R. 140 . . . . , 1–006, 1–1379
R. (on the application of F) v Secretary of State for the Home Department; sub nom. R. (on the
application of TF) v Secretary of State for Justice [2008] EWCA Civ 1457; (2009) 12 C.C.L.
Rep. 245; (2009) 106 B.M.L.R. 54; [2008] M.H.L.R. 370. . . . . 1–634, 1–639
R. (on the application of Faizovas) v Secretary of State for Justice [2009] EWCA Civ 373;
Times, May 25, 2009 5–015
R. (on the application of Faulkner) v Secretary of State for Justice. *See* R. (on the application of
Sturnham) v Parole Board
R. (on the application of Faulkner) v Secretary of State for Justice [2013] UKSC 23; [2013] 2
W.L.R. 1157; [2013] 2 All E.R. 1013; [2013] H.R.L.R. 24; (2013) 157(18) S.J.L.B.
31. . . . . 1–100, 5–027
R. (on the application of G) v Ealing LBC (No.3) [2002] EWHC 1112 (Admin). 1–157
R. (on the application of G) v Nottinghamshire Healthcare NHS Trust; R. (on the application of
B) v Nottinghamshire Healthcare NHS Trust; R. (on the application of N) v Secretary of
State for Health; sub nom. R. (on the application of E) v Nottinghamshire Healthcare
NHS Trust [2009] EWCA Civ 795; [2010] P.T.S.R. 674; [2009] H.R.L.R. 31; [2009]
U.K.H.R.R. 1442; (2009) 110 B.M.L.R. 87. . . . . 5–036, 5–040, 5–053
R. (on the application of Gillan) v Commissioner of Police of the Metropolis; R. (on the appli-
cation of Quinton) v Commissioner of Police of the Metropolis [2006] UKHL 12; [2006] 2
A.C. 307; [2006] 2 W.L.R. 537; [2006] 4 All E.R. 1041; [2006] 2 Cr. App. R. 36; [2006]
H.R.L.R. 18; [2006] U.K.H.R.R. 740; 21 B.H.R.C. 202; [2006] Po. L.R. 26; [2006] Crim.
L.R. 752; (2006) 150 S.J.L.B. 366 . . . . 5–020, 5–038, 6–010
R. (on the application of GP) v Derby City Council [2012] EWHC 1451 (Admin); [2012]
M.H.L.R. 252. . . . . 1–156, 1–159
R. (on the application of Greenfield) v Secretary of State for the Home Department [2005]
UKHL 14; [2005] 1 W.L.R. 673; [2005] 2 All E.R. 240; [2005] H.R.L.R. 13; [2005]

U.K.H.R.R. 323; 18 B.H.R.C. 252; [2005] 2 Prison L.R. 129; (2005) 102(16) L.S.G. 30; (2005) 155 N.L.J. 298. . . . . 1–100, 5–027
H and L v A city Council. *See* R. (on the application of H) v A City Council
R. (on the application of H) v A City Council; sub nom. H v X City Council [2011] EWCA Civ 403; [2011] U.K.H.R.R. 599; [2011] B.L.G.R. 590; (2011) 14 C.C.L. Rep. 381; [2011] A.C.D. 76; (2011) 108(17) L.S.G. 13; (2011) 155(16) S.J.L.B. 31. 5–034
R. (on the application of H) v Ashworth Hospital Authority [2001] EWHC Admin 872; [2002] 1 F.C.R. 206; (2002) 64 B.M.L.R. 124; [2001] M.H.L.R. 241; [2002] A.C.D. 19. 5–036
R. (on the application of H) v Ashworth Hospital Authority; R. (on the application of Ashworth Hospital Authority) v Mental Health Review Tribunal for West Midlands and North West Region [2002] EWCA Civ 923; [2003] 1 W.L.R. 127; (2002) 5 C.C.L. Rep. 390; (2003) 70 B.M.L.R. 40; [2002] M.H.L.R. 314; [2002] A.C.D. 102; (2002) 99(34) L.S.G. 29; (2002) 146 S.J.L.B. 198 . . . . 1–056, 1–278, 1–915, 1–917, 1–927, 1–1124, 3–015, 3–046, 3–124, 3–153
R. (on the application of H) v Mental Health Review Tribunal [2007] EWHC 884 (Admin); (2007) 10 C.C.L. Rep. 306 . . . . .1–587, 1–936, 1–939
R. (on the application of H) v Mental Health Review Tribunal for North and East London Region; sub nom. R. (on the application of H) v London North and East Region Mental Health Review Tribunal; R. (on the application of H) v North and East London Regional Mental Health Review Tribunal [2001] EWCA Civ 415; [2002] Q.B. 1; [2001] 3 W.L.R. 512; [2001] H.R.L.R. 36; [2001] U.K.H.R.R. 717; (2001) 4 C.C.L. Rep. 119; [2001] Lloyd's Rep. Med. 302; (2001) 61 B.M.L.R. 163; [2001] M.H.L.R. 48; [2001] A.C.D. 78; (2001) 98(21) L.S.G. 40; (2001) 145 S.J.L.B. 108. . . . . .1–059, 1–914, 1–915, 1–918, 1–927, 1–929, 5–022
R. (on the application of H) v Oxfordshire Mental Healthcare NHS Trust [2002] EWHC 465 (Admin); [2002] M.H.L.R. 282. . . . . .1–056, 1–163, 2–131
R. (on the application of H) v Secretary of State for Health; sub nom. H v Secretary of State for Health; R. (on the application of MH) v Secretary of State for Health [2005] UKHL 60; [2006] 1 A.C. 441; [2005] 3 W.L.R. 867; [2005] 4 All E.R. 1311; [2006] H.R.L.R. 1; [2006] Lloyd's Rep. Med. 48; (2005) 86 B.M.L.R. 71; [2005] M.H.L.R. 60 . . . . . . 1–427, 1–440, 1–871, 1–915, 3–007, 3–110
R. (on the application of H) v Secretary of State for the Home Department; sub nom. R. (on the application of IH) v Nottinghamshire Healthcare NHS Trust; R. (on the application of IH) v Secretary of State for the Home Department [2003] UKHL 59; [2004] 2 A.C. 253; [2003] 3 W.L.R. 1278; [2004] 1 All E.R. 412; [2004] H.R.L.R. 5; [2004] U.K.H.R.R. 115; 15 B.H.R.C. 571; (2004) 7 C.C.L. Rep. 147; (2004) 76 B.M.L.R. 179; [2004] M.H.L.R. 51; (2004) 101(2) L.S.G. 30; (2003) 147 S.J.L.B. 1365. . 1–901, 1–935, 1–937, 1–939, 1–941, 1–941, 1–1123, 1–1126
R. (on the application of HA (Nigeria)) v Secretary of State for the Home Department [2012] EWHC 979. 1–653
R. (on the application of Hertfordshire C.C.) v Hammersmith and Fulham LBC. *See* R. (on the application of M) v Hammersmith and Fulham LBC
R. (on the application of Hicks) v Commissioner of Police of the Metropolis; R. (on the application of Middleton) v Bromley Magistrates Court; R. (on the application of Pearce) v Commissioner of Police of the Metropolis; R. (on the application of M) v Commissioner of Police of the Metropolis [2014] EWCA Civ 3; [2014] 1 W.L.R. 2152; [2014] 2 Cr. App. R. 4; [2014] H.R.L.R. 11; [2014] Crim. L.R. 681 1–1336
R. (on the application of Holloway) v Oxfordshire CC [2007] EWHC 776 (Admin); [2007] B.L.G.R. 891; (2007) 10 C.C.L. Rep. 264. . . . . 1–426, 3–004
R. (on the application of Hurlock) v Dr Page and the Secretary of State for the Home Department [2001] EWHC Admin. 380 1–577
R. (on the application of IH) v Secretary of State for the Home Department. *See* R. (on the application of H) v Secretary of State for the Home Department
R. (on the application of IR) v Shetty [2003] EWHC 3022 (Admin); [2004] M.H.L.R.111 . . 1–663, 1–670, 1–671
R. (on the application of JB) v Haddock. *See* R. (on the application of B) v Haddock
R. (on the application of Johnson (Deceased)) v Secretary of State for Health [2006] EWHC 288 (Admin). 1–128
R. (on the application of Jones) v Isleworth Crown Court; sub nom. Jones v Isleworth Crown Court [2005] EWHC 662 (QB); [2005] M.H.L.R. 93 1–573

R. (on the application of K) v Camden and Islington HA; sub nom. R. v Camden and Islington
   HA Ex p. K [2001] EWCA Civ 240; [2002] Q.B. 198; [2001] 3 W.L.R. 553; [2001]
   U.K.H.R.R. 1378; (2001) 4 C.C.L. Rep. 170; [2001] Lloyd's Rep. Med. 152; (2001) 61
   B.M.L.R. 173; [2001] M.H.L.R. 24; (2001) 98(16) L.S.G. 34; (2001) 145 S.J.L.B. 69. . . . 1–935,
                                                                        1–937, 1–1123, 1–1147
R. (on the application of K) v West London Mental Health NHS Trust [2006] EWCA Civ 118;
   [2006] 1 W.L.R. 1865; (2006) 9 C.C.L. Rep. 319; (2006) 90 B.M.L.R. 214; [2006] M.H.L.R.
   89; (2006) 103(11) L.S.G. 26 . . . . 1–006, 1–214, 3–088
R. (on the application of KB) v Mental Health Review Tribunal; sub nom. R. (on the application
   of K) v Mental Health Review Tribunal; R. (on the application of TB) v Mental Health
   Review Tribunal; R. (on the application of PD) v Mental Health Review Tribunal; R. (on
   the application of LB) v Mental Health Review Tribunal; R. (on the application of GM) v
   Mental Health Review Tribunal; R. (on the application of JR) v Mental Health Review
   Tribunal; R. (on the application of MK) v Mental Health Review Tribunal [2002] EWHC
   639 (Admin); (2002) 5 C.C.L. Rep. 458; [2003] M.H.L.R. 1; [2002] A.C.D. 85; (2002)
   152 N.L.J. 672 3–136
R. (on the application of Kenneally) v Snaresbrook Crown Court; R. (on the application of
   Kenneally) v Rampton Hospital Authority [2001] EWHC Admin 968; [2002] Q.B. 1169;
   [2002] 2 W.L.R. 1430; [2002] M.H.L.R. 53; [2002] A.C.D. 46 . . . . 1–683, 1–684
R. (on the application of Khela) v Brandon Mental Health Unit [2010] EWHC 3313 (Admin). 1–029
R. (on the application of Kimani) v Lambeth LBC [2003] EWCA Civ 1150; [2004] 1 W.L.R.
   272; [2003] 2 F.L.R. 1217; [2003] 3 F.C.R. 222; [2004] H.L.R. 15; (2003)6 C.C.L. Rep. 484;
   [2003] Fam. Law 811; (2003) 100(37) L.S.G. 32 5–039
R. (on the application of King) v Secretary of State for Justice; R. (on the application of
   Bourgass) v Secretary of State for Justice [2012] EWCA Civ 376; [2012] H.R.L.R. 17. . . . 5–030
R. (on the application of KW) v Avon and Wiltshire Mental Health Partnership NHS Trust
   [2003] EWHC 919 (Admin); [2003] M.H.L.R. 315. 3–124
R. (on the application of L) v Secretary of State for Health; sub nom. R. (on the application of
   ML) v Secretary of State for Health; R. v Secretary of State for Health Ex p. L (M) [2001] 1
   F.L.R. 406; [2001] 1 F.C.R. 326; (2001) 4 C.C.L. Rep. 59; (2001) 58 B.M.L.R. 101; [2000]
   M.H.L.R. 191; [2001] Fam. Law 101 . . . . 5–039, B–001
R. (on the application of L) v West London Mental Health NHS Trust [2014] EWCA Civ 47;
   [2014] 1 W.L.R. 3103; (2014) 137 B.M.L.R. 76; [2014] A.C.D. 79; (2014) 158(6) S.J.L.B.
   37. . . . . 1–293, 1–294, 1–295, 1–587, 1–927
R. (on the application of L (A Child)) v Manchester City Council; R. (on the application of R (A
   Child)) v Manchester City Council [2001] EWHC Admin 707; [2002] 1 F.L.R. 43; (2002) 5
   C.C.L. Rep. 268; [2002] A.C.D. 45; [2002] Fam. Law 13. 5–053
R. (on the application of Laporte) v Chief Constable of Gloucestershire [2006] UKHL 55;
   [2007] 2 A.C. 105; [2007] 2 W.L.R. 46; [2007] 2 All E.R. 529; [2007] H.R.L.R. 13;
   [2007] U.K.H.R.R. 400; 22 B.H.R.C. 38; [2006] Po. L.R. 309; [2007] Crim. L.R. 576;
   [2007] A.C.D. 25; (2007) 151 S.J.L.B. 26. . . . . A–001
R. (on the application of Lee-Hirons) v Secretary of State for Justice [2014] EWCA Civ 553;
   [2015] Q.B. 385; [2015] 2 W.L.R. 256; (2014) 138 B.M.L.R. 44. . . . . 1–588, 1–743
R. (on the application of LH) v Mental Health Review Tribunal [2002] EWHC 170 (Admin);
   [2002] M.H.L.R. 130 1–927
R. (on the application of LH) v Mental Health Review Tribunal [2002] EWHC 1522 (Admin);
   [2002] M.H.L.R. 362 . . . . 1–914, 1–927
R. (on the application of Li) v Mental Health Review Tribunal [2004] EWHC 51 (Admin);
   [2004] M.H.L.R. 150; [2004] A.C.D. 74 1–919
R. (on the application of Lord) v Secretary of State for the Home Department [2003] EWHC
   2073 (Admin); [2004] Prison L.R. 65 3–083
R. (on the application of LS) v Brent Magistrates Court [2009] EWHC 2704
   Admin). 1–474, 1–537
R. (on the application of LV) v Secretary of State for Justice [2014] EWHC 1495
   (Admin) 1–673, 1–945
R. (on the application of M) v Hammersmith and Fulham LBC; R. (on the application of
   Hertfordshire CC) v Hammersmith and Fulham LBC [2011] EWCA Civ 77; [2011]
   P.T.S.R. 1623; [2011] B.L.G.R. 536; (2011) 14 C.C.L. Rep. 224; [2011] Med. L.R. 181;
   (2011) 119 B.M.L.R. 27; [2011] M.H.L.R. 76; [2011] A.C.D. 60 1–1142
R. (on the application of M) v Homerton University Hospital [2008] EWCA Civ 197; [2008]
   M.H.L.R. 92. . . . . 1–426, 1–440, 1–483

R. (on the application of M) v Kingston Crown Court; M v Wells Unit West London Mental Health Trust [2014] EWHC 2702 (Admin); [2015] 1 Cr. App. R. 3; (2014) 178 J.P. 438; [2015] Crim. L.R. 436; (2014) 158(31) S.J.L.B. 37 1–483

R. (on the application of M) v Mental Health Review Tribunal [2005] EWHC 2791 (Admin); (2006) 90 B.M.L.R. 65; [2006] M.H.L.R. 46. 3–014

R. (on the application of M) v Nottinghamshire Healthcare NHS Trust; sub nom. R. (on the application of M) v Nottinghamshire Health Care NHS Trust [2002] EWCA Civ 1728; [2003] 1 All E.R. 784; [2003] M.H.L.R. 101; (2002) 146 S.J.L.B. 274 . . . . 1–670, 1–671

R. (on the application of M) v Queen Mary's Hospital Managers. *See* M v South West London & St. George's Mental Health NHS Trust

R. (on the application of M) v Secretary of State for Health [2003] EWHC 1094 (Admin); [2003] U.K.H.R.R. 746; [2003] M.H.L.R. 348; [2003] A.C.D. 95 1–402

R. (on the application of M) v Secretary of State for the Home Department; sub nom. R. (on the application of MM) v Secretary of State for the Home Department [2007] EWCA Civ 687; [2007] M.H.L.R. 304; (2007) 98 B.M.L.R. 130; [2007] A.C.D. 98; (2007) 151 S.J.L.B. 927. . . . . 1–064, 1–588

R. (on the application of M) v Secretary of State for Work and Pensions [2008] UKHL 63; [2009] 1 A.C. 311; [2008] 3 W.L.R. 1023; [2009] 2 All E.R. 556; [2009] P.T.S.R. 336; [2009] H.R.L.R. 5; [2009] U.K.H.R.R. 117; 26 B.H.R.C. 587 5–053

R. (on the application of MacDonald) v Mental Health Review Tribunal [2001] EWHC Admin 1032. 3–022

R. (on the application of Mahmood) v Secretary of State for the Home Department; sub nom. R. v Secretary of State for the Home Department Ex p. Mahmood (Amjad); Mahmood (Amjad) v Secretary of State for the Home Department [2001] 1 W.L.R. 840; [2001] 1 F.L.R. 756; [2001] 2 F.C.R. 63; [2001] H.R.L.R. 14; [2001] U.K.H.R.R. 307; [2001] Imm. A.R. 229; [2001] I.N.L.R. 1; (2001) 3 L.G.L.R. 23; [2001] A.C.D. 38; [2001] Fam. Law 257 CA (Civ Div) 5–039

R. (on the application of Mellor) v Secretary of State for the Home Department; sub nom. R. v Secretary of State for the Home Department Ex p. Mellor [2001] EWCA Civ 472; [2002] Q.B. 13; [2001] 3 W.L.R. 533; [2001] 2 F.L.R. 1158; [2001] 2 F.C.R. 153; [2001] H.R.L.R. 38; (2001) 59 B.M.L.R. 1; [2001] Prison L.R. 219; [2001] Fam. Law 736; (2001) 98(22) L.S.G. 35; (2001) 145 S.J.L.B. 117 5–051

R. (on the application of Mersey Care NHS Trust) v Mental Health Review Tribunal [2003] EWHC 1182 (Admin); [2003] M.H.L.R. 354 . . . . 3–067, 3–143

R. (on the application of Mersey Care NHS Trust) v Mental Health Review Tribunal [2004] EWHC 1749 (Admin); [2005] 1 W.L.R. 2469; [2005] 2 All E.R. 820; (2005) 83 B.M.L.R. 1; [2004] M.H.L.R. 284 3–140

R. (on the application of MH) v Secretary of State for Health. *See* R. (on the application of H) v Secretary of State for Health

R. (on the application of Miah) v Secretary of State for the Home Department [2004] EWHC 2569 (Admin); [2004] M.H.L.R. 302; [2005] A.C.D. 33 . . . . .1–534, 1–633, 1–644, 1–676

R. (on the application of MM) v Secretary of State for the Home Department. *See* R. (on the application of M) v Secretary of State for the Home Department

R. (on the application of MN) v Mental Health Review Tribunal [2008] EWHC 3383 (Admin). 1–897

R. (on the application of Modaresi) v Secretary of State for Health [2013 UKSC 53; [2013] 4 All E.R. 318 . . . . 1–874, 1–877

R. (on the application of Morley) v Nottinghamshire Healthcare NHS Trust. *See* R. (on the application of M) v Nottinghamshire Healthcare NHS Trust

R. (on the application of Morton) v Governor of Long Lartin Prison; sub nom. Morton v Governor of Long Lartin Prison [2003] EWCA Civ 644; [2004] Prison L.R. 206 5–048

R. (on the application of MP) v First-tier Tribunal [2012] UKUT 231 (AAC) 3–176

R. (on the application of Munday) v Secretary of State for the Home Department [2009] EWHC 3638 (Admin). 1–588, 1–919, 1–955

R. (on the application of Munjaz) v Mersey Care NHS Trust; sub nom. Munjaz v Mersey Care NHS Trust; S v Airedale NHS Trust; R. (on the application of Colonel M) v Ashworth Hospital Authority (now Mersey Care NHS Trust); R. (on the application of Munjaz) v Ashworth Hospital Authority (now Mersey Care NHS Trust); R. (on the application of S) v Airedale NHS Trust (Appeal [2005] UKHL 58; [2006] 2 A.C. 148; [2005] 3 W.L.R. 793; [2006] 4 All E.R. 736; [2005] H.R.L.R. 42; [2006] Lloyd's Rep. Med. 1; (2005) 86 B.M.L.R. 84; [2005] M.H.L.R. 276. . . . . .1–1157, 1–1159, 1–1164, 1–1204, 1–1379, A–l001

R. (on the application of Mwanza) v Greenwich LBC [2010] EWHC 1462 (Admin); [2010]
B.L.G.R. 868; (2010) 13 C.C.L. Rep. 454; [2010] M.H.L.R. 226; [2010] A.C.D. 86 1–1137
R. (on the application of N) v Ashworth Mental Health Review Tribunal [2001] EWHC Admin
1133; [2002] M.H.L.R. 70 1–919
R. (on the application of N) v Ashworth Special Hospital Authority; sub nom. R. v Ashworth
Special Hospital Authority Ex p. N [2001] EWHC Admin 339; [2001] H.R.L.R. 46; [2001]
M.H.L.R. 77. . . . . 5–041, C–040
R. (on the application of N) v M [2002] EWCA Civ 1789; [2003]1 W.L.R. 562; [2003] 1 F.L.R.
667; [2003] 1 F.C.R. 124; [2003] Lloyd's Rep. Med. 81; (2003) 72 B.M.L.R. 81; [2003]
M.H.L.R. 157; [2003] Fam. Law 160; (2003) 100(8) L.S.G. 29. . . . . 1–729, 1–730, 1–732, 5–012
R. (on the application of N) v Mental Health Review Tribunal (Northern Region); sub nom. R.
(on the application of AN) v Mental Health Review Tribunal (Northern Region); R. (on the
application of DJ) v Mental Health Review Tribunal [2005] EWCA Civ 1605; [2006] Q.B.
468; [2006] 2 W.L.R. 850; [2006] 4 All E.R. 194; (2006) 88 B.M.L.R. 59; [2006] M.H.L.R.
59. . . . . .1–916, 1–958, 3–093
R. (on the application of N) v Secretary of State for Health. *See* R. (on the application of G) v
Nottinghamshire Healthcare NHS Trust
R. (on the application of Noorkoiv) v Secretary of State for the Home Department (No.2)
[2002] EWCA Civ 770; [2002] 1 W.L.R. 3284; [2002] 4 All E.R. 515; [2002] H.R.L.R.
36; [2002] Prison L.R. 311; [2002] A.C.D. 66; (2002) 99(27) L.S.G. 34; (2002) 146
S.J.L.B. 145 CA (Civ Div) 5–025
R. (on the application of Nottingham Healthcare NHS Trust) v Mental Health Review Tribunal
[2008] EWHC 2445 (Admin); [2008] M.H.L.R. 326. 3–088
R. (on the application of O'Reilly) v Blenheim Healthcare Ltd [2005] EWHC 241
Admin. 1–1379, 5–037
R. (on the application of O) v Mental Health Review Tribunal [2006] EWHC 2659 (Admin);
(2007) 93 B.M.L.R. 110; [2006] M.H.L.R. 326; [2007] A.C.D. 16; [2007] A.C.D. 59 1–927,
3–101, 3–102
R. (on the application of O) v West London Mental Health NHS Trust [2005] EWHC 604
(Admin); [2005] M.H.L.R. 188. 1–381
R. (on the application of OS) v Secretary of State for the Home Department [2006] EWHC1903
(Admin); [2006] M.H.L.R. 275. 1–577
R. (on the application of P (A Juvenile)) v Barking Youth Court [2002] EWHC 734 (Admin);
[2002] 2 Cr. App. R. 19; (2002) 166 J.P. 641; [2002] M.H.L.R. 304; [2002] Crim. L.R. 657;
(2002) 166 J.P.N. 778 1–530
R. (on the application of P) v Mental Health Review Tribunal and Rampton Hospital [2001]
EWHC Admin 876; [2002] M.H.L.R. 250. 1–030
R. (on the application of P) v Mental Health Review Tribunal for the East Midlands and North
East Regions [2002] EWCA Civ 697; [2002] M.H.L.R. 253 1-030
R. (on the application of P) v Mersey Care NHS Trust [2003] EWHC 994 (Admin); [2004]
M.H.L.R. 107. 1–934
R. (on the application of P) v Secretary of State for Justice [2009] EWHC 2464 (Admin). . . . 1–577
R. (on the application of P) v Secretary of State for the Home Department [2003] EWHC 2953
(Admin); [2004] M.H.L.R. 64; [2004] Prison L.R. 195 1–673
R. (on the application of PD) v West Midlands and North West Mental Health Review Tribunal
[2004] EWCA Civ 311; [2004] M.H.L.R. 174; (2004) 148 S.J.L.B. 384 . . . 2–051, 3–014, 3–123,
5–030
R. (on the application of Pendlebury) v Secretary of State for Justice [2013] EWHC 3613
(Admin)' [2014] M.H.L.R. 234. 1–669
R. (on the application of Phillips) v Walsall MBC [2001] EWHC Admin 789; (2002) 5 C.C.L.
Rep. 383. 5–042
R. (on the application of Pretty) v DPP [2001] UKHL 61; [2002] 1 A.C. 800; [2001] 3 W.L.R.
1598; [2002] 1 All E.R. 1; [2002] 2 Cr. App. R. 1; [2002] 1 F.L.R. 268; [2002] 1 F.C.R. 1;
[2002] H.R.L.R. 10; [2002] U.K.H.R.R. 97; 11 B.H.R.C. 589; (2002) 63 B.M.L.R. 1; [2002]
A.C.D. 41; [2002] Fam. Law 170; (2001) 151 N.L.J. 1819 HL 5–016, 5–053
R. (on the application of PS) v G (Responsible Medical Officer) [2003] EWHC 2335 (Admin);
[2004] M.H.L.R. 1 . . . . 1–732, 1–733
R. (on the application of R) v Secretary of State for the Home Department; sub nom. R. (on the
application of IR) v Shetty [2003] EWHC 3152 (Admin); [2004] M.H.L.R. 131 1–663
R. (on the application of RA) v Secretary of State for the Home Department. *See* R. (on the
application of A) v Secretary of State for the Home Department

R. (on the application of Rayner) v Secretary of State for the Home Department; sub nom.
Rayner v Secretary of State for the Home Department; Secretary of State for Justice v
Rayner; R. (on the application of Rayner) v Secretary of State for Justice [2008] EWCA
Civ 176; [2009] 1 W.L.R. 310; [2008] U.K.H.R.R. 847; (2008) 101 B.M.L.R. 83; [2008]
M.H.L.R. 115; (2008) 105(12) L.S.G. 19 . . . . 1–954, 1–955, 5–025
R. (on the application of Razgar) v Secretary of State for the Home Department (No.2); sub
nom. Secretary of State for the Home Department v Razgar; R. (on the application of
Soumahoro) v Secretary of State for the Home Department; R. (on the application of
Nadarajah) v Secretary of State for the Home Department [2004] UKHL 27; [2004] 2
A.C. 368; [2004] 3 W.L.R. 58; [2004] 3 All E.R. 821; [2004] H.R.L.R. 32; [2004] Imm.
A.R. 381; [2004] I.N.L.R. 349; [2004] M.H.L.R. 218; [2004] A.C.D. 83; (2004) 101(28)
L.S.G. 33; (2004) 154 N.L.J. 986; (2004) 148 S.J.L.B. 761 . . . . .5–015, 5–034, 5–043
R. (on the application of RB) v First–Tier Tribunal (Review) [2010] UKUT 160 (AAC). 3–176
R. (on the application of RD) v Mental Health Review Tribunal [2007] EWHC 781 (Admin);
(2007) 104(18) L.S.G. 29; (2007) 151 S.J.L.B. 506. 3–123
R. (on the application of Roberts) v Secretary of State for Justice [2009] EWHC 2321
(Admin) 1–1378
R. (on the application of Robinson) v Hospital Managers of Park Royal Hospital Unreported
November 26, 2007 1–411
R. (on the application of RW) v Secretary of State for Justice [2012] EWHC 2082 (Admin);
[2012] M.H.L.R. 288 1–671
R. (on the application of S) v Mental Health Review Tribunal [2002] EWHC 2522 (Admin);
[2003] M.H.L.R. 118; (2003) 100(4) L.S.G. 32. . . . . 3–123, 3–124
R. (on the application of S) v Plymouth City Council [2002] EWCA Civ 388; [2002]1W.L.R.
2583; [2002] 1 F.L.R. 1177; [2002] B.L.G.R. 565; (2002) 5 C.C.L. Rep. 251; (2002) 5 C.C.L.
Rep. 560; [2002] M.H.L.R. 118; [2002] Fam. Law 513; (2002) 146 S.J.L.B. 115 . . 1–127, 1–381,
1–402, 1–425, 1–431, 3–005, 3–045
R. (on the application of S) v Secretary of State for the Home Department [2003] EWCA Civ
426; [2003] M.H.L.R. 264; [2003] Prison L.R. 112; (2003) 100(25) L.S.G. 46; (2003) 147
S.J.L.B. 506 . . . . 1–053, 1–676
R. (on the application of S) v Secretary of State for the Home Department [2011] EWHC 2120
(Admin); (2011) 108(35) L.S.G. 20. 5–011
R. (on the application of SC) v Mental Health Review Tribunal. *See* R. (on the application of C)
v Mental Health Review Tribunal
R. (on the application of Secretary of State for the Home Department) v Mental Health Review
Tribunal [2002] EWHC Admin 1128; [2002] M.H.L.R. 241 . . . . .1–916, 1–918, 1–939
R. (on the application of Secretary of State for the Home Department) v Mental Health Review
Tribunal [2002] EWHC 2043 (Admin); [2002] M.H.L.R. 381. 1–941
R. (on the application of Secretary of State for the Home Department) v Mental Health Review
Tribunal [2003] EWHC 2864 (Admin); [2004] M.H.L.R. 91. 1–918
R. (on the application of Secretary of State for the Home Department) v Mental Health Review
Tribunal [2004] EWHC 1029 (Admin); [2004] M.H.L.R. 184. . . . . 1–936, 1–941
R. (on the application of Secretary of State for the Home Department) v Mental Health Review
Tribunal and CH [2005] EWHC 746 (Admin); [2005] M.H.L.R. 199 . . . . 1–918, 3–153
R. (on the application of Secretary of State for the Home Department) v Mental Health Review
Tribunal [2007] EWHC 2224 (Admin); [2008] M.H.L.R. 212. 1–939
R. (on the application of Secretary of State for the Home Department) v Mental Health Review
Tribunal (Adjournments); sub nom. R. v Mental Health Review Tribunal for North East
Thames Region Ex p. Secretary of State for the Home Department (2002) 63 B.M.L.R.
181; [2000] M.H.L.R. 209; [2001] A.C.D. 62 . . . . 1–927, 3–046
R. (on the application of Secretary of State for the Home Department) v Mental Health Review
Tribunal (Interim Relief); sub nom. BR v Mental Health Review Tribunal [2005] EWCA Civ
1616; [2006] M.H.L.R. 172 . . . . 1–868, 1–936
R. (on the application of Sessay) v South London and Maudsley NHS Foundation Trust [2011]
EWHC 2617 (QB); [2012] 2 W.L.R. 1071; [2012] P.T.S.R. 742; [2012] Med. L.R. 123. . . 1–038,
1–053, 1–072, 1–104, 1–1319, 1–1333, 1–1336, 1–1338, A–003
R. (on the application of SH) v Mental Health Review Tribunal. *See* R. (on the application of H)
v Mental Health Review Tribunal
R. (on the application of Sim) v Parole Board for England and Wales; sub nom. R. (on the appli-
cation of Sim) v Secretary of State for the Home Department; Secretary of State for the
Home Department v Sim [2003] EWCA Civ 1845; [2004] Q.B. 1288; [2004] 2 W.L.R.

1170; [2004] H.R.L.R. 15; [2004] Prison L.R. 44; (2004) 101(5) L.S.G. 29; (2004) 148 S.J.L.B. 60 1–919

R. (on the application of Singh) v Stratford Magistrates Court [2007] EWHC 1582 (Admin); [2007] 1 W.L.R. 3119; [2007] 4 All E.R. 407; [2008] 1 Cr. App. R. 2; (2007) 171 J.P. 557; [2007] A.C.D. 72; (2008) 172 J.P.N. 69. 1–530

R. (on the application of South West Yorkshire Mental Health NHS Trust) v Bradford Crown Court; sub nom. South West Yorkshire Mental Health NHS Trust v Bradford Crown Court [2003] EWCA Civ 1857; [2004] 1 W.L.R. 1664; [2004] 1 All E.R. 1311; [2004] M.H.L.R. 142; (2004) 148 S.J.L.B. 61 . . . . 1–098, 1–474

R. (on the application of SP) v Secretary of State for Justice [2010] EWCA Civ 1590; [2011] M.H.L.R. 65. . . . . 1–312, 1–639, 1–1379, 2–131

R. (on the application of SR) v Huntercombe Maidenhead Hospital; sub nom. R. (on the application of R) v Hackney LBC; R. (on the application of SR) v Hackney LBC [2005] EWHC 2361 (Admin); [2005] M.H.L.R. 379; [2006] A.C.D. 17; (2005) 102(39) L.S.G. 31. 1–380, 1–394

R. (on the application of SR) v Mental Health Review Tribunal; sub nom. R. (on the application of R) v Mental Health Review Tribunal [2005] EWHC 2923 (Admin); (2006) 87 B.M.L.R. 132; [2006] M.H.L.R. 121 . . . . 1–871, 1–872

R. (on the application of Stennett) v Manchester City Council; sub nom. R. v Richmond LBC Ex p. Watson; R. v Manchester City Council Ex p. Stennett; R. v Harrow LBC Ex p. Cobham; R. v Redcar and Cleveland BC Ex p. Armstrong; R. (on the application of Armstrong) v Redcar and Cleveland BC; R. (on the application of Cobham) v Harrow LBC [2002] UKHL 34; [2002] 2 A.C. 1127; [2002] 3 W.L.R. 584; [2002] 4 All E.R. 124; [2002] B.L.G.R. 557; (2002) 5 C.C.L. Rep. 500; (2002) 68 B.M.L.R. 247; [2002] M.H.L.R. 377; (2002) 99(40) L.S.G. 33; (2002) 146 S.J.L.B. 202. . . . . 1–1122, 1–1127, 1–1147

R. (on the application of Stone) v South East Coast Strategic Health Authority. *See* Stone v South East Coast SHA (formerly Kent and Medway SHA)

R. (on the application of Sturnham) v Parole Board; R. (on the application of Faulkner) v Secretary of State for Justice; sub nom. R. (on the application of Sturnham) v Secretary of State for Justice [2013] UKSC 23; [2013] 2 A.C. 254; [2013] 2 W.L.R. 1157; [2013] 2 All E.R. 1013; [2013] H.R.L.R. 24; 35 B.H.R.C. 378; (2013) 157(18) S.J.L.B. 31 1–100

R. (on the application of Sunderland City Council) v South Tyneside Council [2012] EWCA Civ 1232; [2013] 1 All E.R. 394; [2013] P.T.S.R. 549; [2013] B.L.G.R. 51; (2012) 15 C.C.L. Rep. 701; [2012] M.H.L.R. 404. . . . . 1–124, 1–192, 1–409

R. (on the application of T) v Nottinghamshire Healthcare NHS Trust [2006] EWHC 800 (Admin); [2006] M.H.L.R. 103. 1-293

R. (on the application of T) v Secretary of State for the Home Department [2003] EWHC 538 (Admin); [2003] M.H.L.R. 239. . . . . 1–633, 1–656

R. (on the application of Tagoe-Thompson) v Central and North West London Mental Health NHS Trust; sub nom. R. (on the application of T-T) v Royal Park Centre Hospital Managers [2003] EWCA Civ 330; [2003] 1 W.L.R. 1272; [2003] M.H.L.R. 326. 1–384

R. (on the application of Taylor) v Haydn–Smith; R. (on the application of Taylor) v Gallimore [2005] EWHC 1668 (Admin); [2005] M.H.L.R. 327. 1–730

R. (on the application of TF) v Secretary of State for Justice. *See* R. (on the application of F) v Secretary of State for Justice R. (on the application of T–T) v Royal Park Centre Hospital Managers.

R. (on the application of the Howard League for Penal Reform) v Secretary of State for the Home Department (No.2) [2002] EWHC 2497 (Admin); [2003] 1 F.L.R. 484; (2003) 6 C.C.L. Rep. 47; [2003] Prison L.R. 128; [2003] Fam. Law 149; (2003) 100(3) L.S.G. 30; (2003) 147 S.J.L.B. 61 1–369

R. (on the application of the Secretary of State for the Home Department) v Mental Health Review Tribunal [2001] EWHC Admin 849; [2002] M.H.L.R. 260. 1–936

R. (on the application of the Secretary of State for the Home Department) v Mental Health Review Tribunal [2004] EWHC 650 (Admin); [2004] M.H.L.R. 170 3–112

R. (on the application of V) v South London and Maudsley NHS Foundation Trust [2010] EWHC 742 (Admin); (2010) 13 C.C.L. Rep. 181; [2010] M.H.L.R. 83. . . . . 1–158, 1–159

R. (on the application of von Brandenburg) v East London and the City Mental Health NHS Trust; sub nom. R. v East London and the City Mental Health NHS Trust Ex p. von Brandenburg; R. v Tower Hamlets Healthcare NHS Trust Ex p. von Brandenburg [2003] UKHL 58; [2004] 2 A.C. 280; [2003] 3 W.L.R. 1265; [2004] 1 All E.R. 400; [2004] H.R.L.R. 6; (2004) 7 C.C.L. Rep. 121; [2004] Lloyd's Rep. Med. 228; (2004) 76 B.M.L.R. 168; [2004] M.H.L.R. 44; (2004) 101(5) L.S.G. 28; (2003) 147 S.J.L.B. 1366. . 1–038,

1–041, 1–055, 1–056, 1–163, 1–188, 1–193, 1–588, 1–913, 1–915, 1–916, 1–927, 3–010, 3–046, 3–153, 6–020, 6–021

R. (on the application of W) v Doncaster MBC; sub nom. W v Doncaster MBC [2004] EWCA Civ 378; [2004] B.L.G.R. 743; [2004] M.H.L.R. 201; (2004) 101(22) L.S.G. 32; (2004) 148 S.J.L.B. 572 . . . 1–937, 1–939, 1–941, 1–1122, 1–1123, 1–1124, 1–1126, 1–1136, 1–1355, 3–042

R. (on the application of W) v Larkin and the Secretary of State for Justice [2012] EWHC 556 (Admin); [2012] M.H.L.R. 161. 1–671

R. (on the application of W) v Mental Health Review Tribunal [2004] EWHC 3266 (Admin); [2005] M.H.L.R. 134 . . . . 1–921, 3–153

R. (on the application of WC) v South London & Maudsley NHS Trust [2001] EWHC Admin 1025; [2001] M.H.L.R. 187 1–159

R. (on the application of Wilkinson) v Broadmoor Hospital; sub nom. R. (on the application of Wilkinson) v Responsible Medical Officer Broadmoor Hospital; R. (on the application of Wilkinson) v Broadmoor Special Hospital Authority [2001] EWCA Civ 1545; [2002] 1 W.L.R. 419; [2002] U.K.H.R.R. 390; (2002) 5 C.C.L. Rep. 121; [2002] Lloyd's Rep. Med. 41; (2002) 65 B.M.L.R. 15; [2001] M.H.L.R. 224; [2002] A.C.D. 47; (2001) 98(44) L.S.G. 36; (2001) 145 S.J.L.B. 247. . .1–165, 1–166, 1–705, 1–724, 1–728, 1–729, 1–730, 1–732, 1–740, 1–741, 1–785, 1–786, 1–788, 1–1097, 1–1355, 1–1355, 5–030

R. (on the application of Wilkinson) v Responsible Medical Officer Broadmoor Hospital. *See* R. (on the application of Wilkinson) v Broadmoor Hospital

R. (on the application of Wirral HA) v Mental Health Review Tribunal; R. (on the application of Wirral HA) v Finnegan [2001] EWCA Civ 1901; [2002] M.H.L.R. 34; (2002) 99(2) L.S.G. 27; (2001) 145 S.J.L.B. 270 . . . . 1–381, 1–868

R. (on the application of Wooder) v Feggetter [2002] EWCA Civ 554; [2003] Q.B. 219; [2002] 3W.L.R. 591; [2002] M.H.L.R. 178; [2002] A.C.D. 94; (2002) 99(22) L.S.G. 33; (2002) 146 S.J.L.B. 125 . . . . .1–742, 1–743, 1–1285

R. (on the application of Wright) v Secretary of State for Health; R. (on the application of Gambier) v Secretary of State for Health; R. (on the application of Quinn) v Secretary of State for Health; R. (on the application of Jummun) v Secretary of State for Health [2009] UKHL 3; [2009] 2 W.L.R. 267; [2009] 2 All E.R. 129; [2009] H.R.L.R. 13; 26 B.H.R.C. 269; (2009) 12 C.C.L. Rep. 181; (2009) 106 B.M.L.R. 71; (2009) 106(5) L.S.G. 15; (2009) 153(4) S.J.L.B. 30 5–033

R. (on the application of Wright) v Secretary of State for the Home Department [2006] EWCA Civ 67; [2006] H.R.L.R. 23; [2005] 2 Prison L.R. 226; (2006) 103(10) L.S.G. 26. 5–027

R. (on the application of X) v Mental Health Review Tribunal [2003] EWHC 1272 (Admin); [2003] M.H.L.R. 299 . . . . 3–015, 3–046

R. (on the application of X) v Secretary of State for Justice [2009] EWHC 2465 (Admin) . . . 1–577

R. (on the application of X) v Secretary of State for the Home Department; sub nom. R. v Immigration Officer Ex p. X; X v Secretary of State for the Home Department; R. v Secretary of State for the Home Department Ex p. X [2001] 1 W.L.R. 740; [2001] I.N.L.R. 205; (2001) 4 C.C.L. Rep. 92; [2000] M.H.L.R. 67; (2001) 98(8) L.S.G. 44 CA (Civ Div) 1–1063

R. (on the application of Zhang) v Whittington Hospital [2013] EWHC 358 (Admin); [2014] M.H.L.R. 127. 1–381

R (A Minor) (Wardship: Consent to Treatment), Re [1992] Fam. 11; [1991] 3 W.L.R. 592; [1991] 4 All E.R. 177; [1992] 1 F.L.R. 190; [1992] 2 F.C.R. 229; [1992] 3 Med. L.R. 342; [1992] Fam. Law 67. 4–092

Rabone v Pennine Care NHS Trust [2012] UKSC 2; [2012] 2 W.L.R. 381; [2012] P.T.S.R. 497; [2012] 2 All E.R. 381; [2012] H.R.L.R. 10; (2012) 15 C.C.L. Rep. 13; [2012] Med. L.R. 221; (2012) 124 B.M.L.R. 148; (2012) 162 N.L.J. 261; (2012) 156(6) S.J.L.B. 31 5–007

R (A Minor) (Wardship: Medical Treatment), Re [1991] 4 All E.R. 177 CA (Civ Div) 1–721

Rakevich v Russia (58973/00) [2004] M.H.L.R. 37 ECHR 1–397, 5–025

Raninen v Finland (20972/92) (1998) 26 E.H.R.R. 563; [1998] H.R.C.D. 170 ECHR 5–036

Rantzen v Mirror Group Newspapers (1986) Ltd [1994] Q.B. 670; [1993] 3 W.L.R. 953; [1993] 4 All E.R. 975; (1993) 143 N.L.J. 507 5–048

Raymond v Honey [1983] 1 A.C. 1; [1982] 2 W.L.R. 465; [1982] 1 All E.R. 756; (1982) 75 Cr. App. R. 16 HL 1–033

RB v Nottinghamshire Healthcare NHS Trust [2011] UKUT 135 (AAC); [2011] M.H.L.R. 299. 3–063

RB v Nottinghamshire Healthcare NHS Trust [2011] UKUT 73 (AAC); [2011] M.H.L.R. 296. 1–927

RC v NHS Islington [2013] UKUT 167 (AAC) 3–046
Reid v Secretary of State for Scotland [1999] 2 A.C. 512; [1999] 2 W.L.R. 28; [1999] 1 All E.R.
    481; 1999 S.C. (H.L.) 17; 1999 S.L.T. 279; 1999 S.C.L.R. 74; (1999) 96(4) L.S.G. 37; 1998
    G.W.D. 40–2075 HL..1–065, 1–915, 1–919
Reid v United Kingdom. *See* Hutchison Reid v United Kingdom
Renolde v France (5608/05) (2009) 48 E.H.R.R. 42; [2008] M.H.L.R. 331; [2008] Inquest L.R.
    159; [2009] M.H.L.R. 25; [2010] 1 Prison L.R. 78 ....5–007, 5–013
RH v South London and Maudsley NHS Foundation Trust [2010] EWCA Civ 1273; [2011]
    Med. L.R. 270; (2011) 117 B.M.L.R. 47; [2010] M.H.L.R. 341.... 1–865, 1–935, 1–958, 3–152,
                                                                                  3–153, 3–168
Rice v Connolly [1966] 2 Q.B. 414; [1966] 3 W.L.R. 17; [1966] 2 All E.R. 649; (1966) 130 J.P.
    322; (1966) 110 S.J. 371 DC....................................... 1–1214, 1–1215
Richard Buxton Solicitors v Mills–Owens [2010] EWCA Civ 122; [2010] 1 W.L.R. 1997;
    [2010] 4 All E.R. 405; [2010] C.P. Rep. 26; [2010] 3 Costs L.R. 421; [2010] 2 E.G.L.R.
    73; [2010] 17 E.G. 96; [2010] 9 E.G. 166 (C.S.); (2010) 107(10) L.S.G. 15; (2010) 154(8)
    S.J.L.B. 29; [2010] N.P.C. 21 ....E–011
Richardson v London CC [1957] 1 W.L.R. 751; [1957] 2 All E.R. 330; (1957) 121 J.P. 355;
    (1957) 101 S.J. 429 CA 1–1355
RIVAS v France April 1, 2004 5–011
Riviere v France (33834/03) Unreported ECHR 1–637, 1–1378
RK v BCC [2011] EWCA Civ 1305................................1–1276, 4–093, 4–094
RM v St Andrew's Healthcare [2010] UKUT 119 (AAC); [2010] M.H.L.R. 176.....3–083,
                                                                     3–176, E–014, E–017
RN v Curo Care [2011] UKUT 263 (AAC); [2011] M.H.L.R. 337 .... 1–927, 1–928
Roberts v Nottinghamshire Healthcare NHS Trust [2008] EWHC 1934 (QB); [2009] F.S.R. 4;
    (2009) 12 C.C.L. Rep. 110; [2008] LS Law Medical 586; [2008] M.H.L.R. 294 ... 3–081, 3–083
Roberts v Secretary of State for Justice. *See* R. (on the application of Roberts) v Secretary of
    State for Justice
Roux v United Kingdom (1986) 48 D. & R. 263 ECHR 5–024
RP v United Kingdom (38245/08) [2013] 1 F.L.R. 744; [2013] 2 F.C.R. 77; (2013) 16 C.C.L.
    Rep. 135; (2013) 130 B.M.L.R. 1; [2013] Fam. Law 30 ECHR...............3–068, 5–029
RS's Application for Judicial Review [2015] NICA 30 .... 1–163, 2–131
S (Children) (Care Order: Implementation of Care Plan), Re; sub nom. W and B (Children)
    (Care Plan), Re; W (Children) (Care Plan), Re; W (Children) (Care Order: Adequacy of
    Care Plan), Re [2002] UKHL 10; [2002] 2 A.C. 291; [2002] 2 W.L.R. 720; [2002] 2 All
    E.R. 192; [2002] 1 F.L.R. 815; [2002] 1 F.C.R. 577; [2002] H.R.L.R. 26; [2002]
    U.K.H.R.R. 652; [2002] B.L.G.R. 251; [2002] Fam. Law 413; (2002) 99(17) L.S.G. 34;
    (2002) 146 S.J.L.B. 85 .... 1–914, 5–043
S v Estonia (17779/08) [2011] M.H.L.R. 396 5–022
S v United Kingdom (30562/04); Marper v United Kingdom (30566/04) (2009) 48 E.H.R.R.
    50; 25 B.H.R.C. 557; [2008] Po. L.R. 403; [2009] Crim. L.R. 355; (2008) 158 N.L.J.
    1755...5–041
S-C (Mental Patient: Habeas Corpus), Re [1996] Q.B. 599; [1996] 2 W.L.R. 146; [1996] 1 All
    E.R. 532; [1996] 1 F.L.R. 548; [1996] 2 F.C.R. 692; (1996) 29 B.M.L.R. 138; [1996] Fam.
    Law 210 CA (Civ Div).......1–033, 1–098, 1–099, 1–101, 1–102, 1–204 1–207, 1–317, 1–867
Saadi v United Kingdom (13229/03) (2008) 47 E.H.R.R. 17; [2008] Imm. A.R. 368; [2008]
    I.N.L.R. 436...5–022
Salgueiro da Silva Mouta v Portugal (33290/96) [2001] 1 F.C.R. 653; (2001) 31 E.H.R.R. 47;
    2001 Fam. L.R. 2 5–053
Salontaji–Drobnjak v Serbia (36500/05) October 13,2009.......................1–11353
Samuda v Secretary of State for Work and Pensions [2014] EWCA Civ 1; [2014] 3 All E.R.
    201; [2014] C.P. Rep. 18; [2014] 2 F.C.R. 425 1–865
Sanchez–Reisse v Switzerland (A/107) (1987) 9 E.H.R.R. 71 ECHR 5–025
Saoud v France (9375/02) Unreported October 9, 2007 ECHR 5–010
Sarjantson v Chief Constable of Humberside [2013] EWCA Civ 1252; [2014] Q.B. 411; [2013]
    3 W.L.R. 1540; [2014] 1 All E.R. 960; [2014] Med. L.R. 63.......................5–006
Savage v South Essex Partnership NHS Foundation Trust [2008] UKHL 74; [2009] 1 A.C. 681;
    [2009] 2 W.L.R. 115; [2009] P.T.S.R. 469; [2009] 1 All E.R. 1053; [2009] H.R.L.R. 12;
    [2009] U.K.H.R.R. 480; 27 B.H.R.C. 57; (2009) 12 C.C.L. Rep. 125; [2009] LS Law
    Medical 40; (2009) 105 B.M.L.R. 180; [2008] Inquest L.R. 126; [2009] M.H.L.R. 41;
    (2009) 153(1) S.J.L.B. 34 5–007

Schenkel v Netherlands (62015/00) (2006) 43 E.H.R.R. 31; [2006] M.H.L.R. 27 ECHR 5–020
Schuurs v Netherlands 41 D. 7 R. 186 Eur Comm HR 1–165, 5–022
Sciacca v Italy (50774/99) (2006) 43 E.H.R.R. 20 ECHR 5–035
Seal v Chief Constable of South Wales [2007] UKHL 31; [2007] 1 W.L.R. 1910; [2007] 4 All
    E.R. 177; [2007] H.R.L.R. 37; 22 B.H.R.C. 769; [2007] B.P.I.R. 1396; (2007) 10 C.C.L. Rep.
    695; (2007) 97 B.M.L.R. 172; (2007) 104(29) L.S.G. 25; (2007) 151 S.J.L.B. 927 1–1336,
                                                                            1–1352, 1–1356
Seal v United Kingdom (50330/07) December 7, 2010 1–1353
Secretary of State for Justice v KC [2015] UKUT 376 (AAC) 1–916, 1–917, 1–939
Secretary of State for Justice v MP [2013] UKUT 25 (AAC); [2013] M.H.L.R. 154 . . 1–031, 1–939
Secretary of State for Justice v Rayner. *See* R. (on the application of Rayner) v Secretary of
    State for the Home Department
Secretary of State for Justice v RB [2011] EWCA Civ 1608; [2012] M.H.L.R. 131; [2012] 1
    W.L.R. 2043; (2012) 124 B.M.L.R. 13 . . . . 1–004, 1–865, 1–939, 1–1379, 5–053
Secretary of State for Justice v SB [2013] UKUT 320 (AAC); [2014] M.H.L.R. 46 1–939
Secretary of State for the Home Department v F; E v Secretary of State for the Home
    Department; Secretary of State for the Home Department v N [2009] UKHL 28; [2009] 3
    W.L.R. 74; [2009] 3 All E.R. 643; [2009] H.R.L.R. 26; [2009] U.K.H.R.R. 1177; 26
    B.H.R.C. 738; (2009) 106(25) L.S.G. 14 3–083
Secretary of State for the Home Department v JJ; sub nom. JJ, Re; Secretary of State for the
    Home Department v KK; Secretary of State for the Home Department v GG; Secretary of
    State for the Home Department v HH; Secretary of State for the Home Department v NN;
    Secretary of State for the Home Department v LL [2007] UKHL 45; [2008] 1 A.C. 385;
    [2007] 3 W.L.R. 642; [2008] 1 All E.R. 613; [2008] H.R.L.R. 5; [2008] U.K.H.R.R. 80;
    24 B.H.R.C. 531; [2008] Crim. L.R. 489; (2007) 157 N.L.J. 1576; (2007) 151 S.J.L.B.
    1432 . . . . 6–003, 6–022
Secretary of State for the Home Department v Mental Health Review Tribunal. *See* R. (on the
    application of Secretary of State for the Home Department) v Mental Health Review
    Tribunal
Secretary of State for the Home Department v Mental Health Review Tribunal for the Mersey
    RHA; Secretary of State for the Home Department v Mental Health Review Tribunal for
    Wales [1986] 1 W.L.R. 1170; [1986] 3 All E.R. 233; (1986) 83 L.S.G. 3001; (1986) 130
    S.J. 697 QBD 1–941, 1–957
Secretary of State for the Home Department v Oxford Regional Mental Health Review
    Tribunal. *See* R. v Oxford Regional Mental Health Review Tribunal Ex p. Secretary of State for
    the Home Department
Secretary of State for Work and Pensions v SS [2010] UKHT 384 (AAC) 3–152
Sekfali v DPP; Banamira v DPP; Ouham v DPP [2006] EWHC 894 (Admin); (2006) 170 J.P.
    393; (2006) 170 J.P.N. 736 1–1215
Selmouni v France (25803/94) (2000) 29 E.H.R.R. 403; 7 B.H.R.C. 1 ECHR 5–011
Sentges v Netherlands (Admissibility) (27677/02) (2004) 7 C.C.L. Rep. 400 ECHR 5–033
SH v Cornwall Partnership NHS Trust [2012] UKUT 290 (AAC); [2012] M.H.L.R. 383 . . . 1–067,
                                                                            1–913, 3–010
Shearon, Re [1996] C.O.D. 223 DC 1–053, 1–157
Sheffield (Kristina) v United Kingdom (22985/93); Horsham v United Kingdom (23390/94)
    [1998] 2 F.L.R. 928; [1998] 3 F.C.R. 141; (1999) 27 E.H.R.R. 163; 5 B.H.R.C. 83; [1998]
    H.R.C.D. 758; [1998] Fam. Law 731 ECHR 5–035
Shtukaturov v Russia (44009/05) (2012) 54 E.H.R.R. 27; (2008) 11 C.C.L. Rep. 440; [2008]
    M.H.L.R. 238 ECHR 1–019, 5–022, 5–029, 5–030, 5–034
Silver v United Kingdom (A/161) (1983) 5 E.H.R.R. 347 ECHR 5–041
SL v Ludlow Street Healthcare [2015] UKUT 398 (AAC) 1–918
Slade v Guscott Unreported July 28, 1981 1–1113
Smirek v Williams [2000] M.H.L.R. 38 CA (Civ Div) 1–057, 1–064, 1–437, 1–918
Smith v Smith; sub nom. Smith v Secretary of State for Work and Pensions [2006] UKHL 35;
    [2006] 1 W.L.R. 2024; [2006] 3 All E.R. 907; [2007] 1 F.L.R. 166; [2006] 2 F.C.R. 487;
    [2006] Fam. Law 834; (2006) 103(30) L.S.G. 31; (2006) 150 S.J.L.B. 986 1–018
Smith v United Kingdom (33985/96); Grady v United Kingdom (33986/96) [1999] I.R.L.R.
    734; (2000) 29 E.H.R.R. 493; (1999) 11 Admin. L.R. 879 ECHR 5–041
Societe Colas Est v France (37971/97) (2004) 39 E.H.R.R. 17 ECHR 5–041
South Glamorgan CC v B; sub nom. South Glamorgan CC v Wand B [1993] 1 F.C.R. 626;
    [1993] Fam. Law 398; [1993] 1 F.L.R. 574 1–1277

South West London St George's Mental Health NHS Trust v W [2002] EWHC Admin 1770;
[2002] M.H.L.R. 392 . . . . .1–380, 1–641, 1–642
South West Yorkshire Mental Health NHS Trust v Bradford Crown Court. *See* R. (on the appli-
cation of South West Yorkshire Mental Health NHS Trust) v Bradford Crown Court
St George's Healthcare NHS Trust v S; R. v Collins Ex p. S (No.1) [1998] 3 W.L.R. 936; [1998]
3 All E.R. 673; [1998] 2 F.L.R. 728; [1998] 2 F.C.R. 685; (1997–98) 1 C.C.L. Rep. 410;
(1998) 44 B.M.L.R. 160; [1998] C.O.D. 396; [1998] Fam. Law 526; (1998) 95(22) L.S.G.
29; (1998) 148 N.L.J. 693; (1998) 142 S.J.L.B. 164 . . . . . . .1–005, 1–029, 1–033, 1–047, 1–048,
1–059, 1–193, 1–195, 1–746, 1–787
Stanev v Bulgaria (2012) 55 E.H.R.R. 22 [2012] M.H.L.R. 23 . 5–011, 5–015, 5–016, 5–022, 6–005
Stephens v Malta (33740/06) (2010) 50 E.H.R.R. 8 ECHR. 5–024
Stewart v Chapman [1951] 2 K.B. 792; [1951] 2 All E.R. 613; [1951] 2 T.L.R. 640; (1951) 35
Cr. App. R. 102; (1951) 115 J.P. 473; 49 L.G.R. 816; (1951) 95 S.J. 641 DC 1–955
Stojanovski v Former Yugoslav Republic of Macedonia 1431/03 (2009) ECHR 1615 1–584
Stone v South East Coast SHA (formerly Kent and Medway SHA) [2006] EWHC 1668
(Admin); [2007] U.K.H.R.R. 137; [2006] M.H.L.R. 288. 5–037
Storck v Germany (61603/00) (2006) 43 E.H.R.R. 6; [2005] M.H.L.R. 211 ECHR . . .5–019, 5–034,
5–035, 6–006
Sunday Times v United Kingdom (A/30) (1979-80) 2 E.H.R.R. 245; (1979) 76 L.S.G. 328. . .5–048
Sunday Times v United Kingdom (13166/87) (1992) 14 E.H.R.R. 229 ECHR. 5–048
Surrey County Council Social Services v McMurray November 11, 1994 CA. 1–425, 1–438
Syed v DPP [2010] EWHC 81 (Admin); [2010] 1 Cr. App. R. 34; (2010) 174 J.P. 97; (2010)
107(4) L.S.G. 14. 1–1322
T v Chase Farm Hospital; sub nom. Doreen T, Re [2000] M.H.L.R. 53 QBD 1–868
T v Secretary of State for Justice [2008] EWHC 1707 (Admin); [2008] M.H.L.R. 290 1–588
T v T. *See* T, Re
T, Re (a child: murdered parent) [2011] EWHC B4 (Fam); [2011] M.H.L.R. 133 1–939
T, Re; sub nom. T v T [1988] Fam. 52; [1988] 2 W.L.R. 189; [1988] 1 All E.R. 613; [1988] 1
F.L.R. 400; [1988] Fam. Law 126; (1987) 84 L.S.G. 2456; (1987) 131 S.J. 1286 Fam
Div. 1–133
Tameside and Glossop Acute Services NHS Trustv CH (A Patient) [1996] 1 F.L.R. 762; [1996]
1 F.C.R. 753; (1996) 31 B.M.L.R. 93; [1996] Fam. Law 353 Fam Div 1–787, 1–788
Tanko v Finland (23634/94) Unreported ECHR 5–013
Taylor v United Kingdom (Admissibility) (23412/94) (1994) 18 E.H.R.R. CD215 5–008
TF v Secretary of State for Justice. *See* R. (on the application of F) v Secretary of State for the
Home Department
Townley v Rushworth, 62 L.G.R. 95; [1964] Crim. L.R. 590; (1963) 107 S.J. 1004 DC 1–104
TR v Ludlow Street Healthcare Ltd and TR [2011] UKUT (AAC); [2011] M.H.L.R. 190. . . .3–045
Trew (Doreen), Re. *See* T v Chase Farm Hospital
Trust A v X (A Child). *See* D (A Child) (Deprivation of Liberty), Re
Tsirlis v Greece (19233/91) (1998) 25 E.H.R.R. 198 ECHR 1–190
TTM v Hackney LBC; sub nom, R. (on the application of M) v Hackney LBC [2011] EWCA
Civ 4; [2011] 1 W.L.R. 2873; [2011] P.T.S.R. 1419; [2011] 3 All E.R. 529; [2011] H.R.L.R.
14; [2011] U.K.H.R.R. 346; (2011) 14 C.C.L. Rep. 154; [2011] Med. L.R. 38; [2011]
M.H.L.R. 171; [2011] A.C.D. 54 . . . .1–098, 1–099, 1–110, 1–157, 1–163, 1–166, 1–168, 1–188,
1–193, 1–394, 1–1096, 1–1352, 1–1353, 1–1355, 1–1355
TV v Finland (21780/93) (1994) 18 E.H.R.R. CD179 Eur Comm HR. 5–043
TW v Enfield LBC [2014] EWCA Civ 362; [2014] M.H.L.R. 415; (2014) 17 C.C.L. Rep. 264;
(2014) 164(7602) N.L.J. 20; (2014) 158(14) S.J.L.B. 37 . . . . 1–155, 1–159, 1–12591 1–1353,
1–1355, 4–057
Uner v Netherlands (46410/99) [2006] 3 F.C.R. 340; (2007) 45 E.H.R.R. 14; [2007] Imm. A.R.
303; [2007] I.N.L.R. 273 5–042
Union of Construction, Allied Trades and Technicians v Brain [1981] I.C.R. 542; [1981]
I.R.L.R. 224 CA (Civ Div). 3–153
Unyan v Turkey, January 8, 2009 5–015
Valle v Finland (28808/95) [2000] M.H.L.R. 255; (2000) 30 E.H.R.R. CD59 ECHR. 1–1306,
5–022
Valsamis v Greece (1997) 24 E.H.R.R. 294; [1998] E.L.R. 430 ECHR 5–035
Van der Leer v Netherlands (A/170); sub nom. Van der Leer v Netherlands (11509/85) (1990)
12 E.H.R.R. 567 ECHR 5–025
Van Droogenbroeck v Belgium (A/50) (1982) 4 E.H.R.R. 443 ECHR. 1–663

Table of Cases

Varbanov v Bulgaria (C31365/96) [2000] M.H.L.R. 263 ECHR 1–165, 1–313, 1–639, 1–1334, 5–022

Vo v France (53924/00) [2004] 2 F.C.R. 577; (2005) 40 E.H.R.R. 12; 17 B.H.R.C. 1; (2004) 79 B.M.L.R. 71; [2005] Inquest L.R. 129 ECHR 1–059

VS (Adult: Mental Disorder), Re (1995) 3 Med.L.Rev. 292 1–787

W, Re [1999] M.H.L.R. 1 1–440

W (A Minor) (Medical Treatment: Court's Jurisdiction), Re; sub nom. J (A Minor) (Consent to Medical Treatment), Re [1993] Fam. 64; [1992] 3W.L.R. 758; [1992] 4 All E.R. 627; [1992] 3 Med. L.R. 317; (1992) 142 N.L.J. 1124 CA (Civ Div) 1–1278, 4–090

W (An Infant), Re [1971] A.C. 682; [1971] 2 W.L.R. 1011; [1971] 2 All E.R. 49; (1971) 115S.J. 286 HL 1–437

W and B (Children) (Care Plan), Re. See S (Children) (Care Order: Implementation of Care Plan), Re

W v Doncaster MBC. See R. (on the application of W) v Doncaster MBC

W v Egdell [1990] Ch. 359; [1990] 2 W.L.R. 471; [1990] 1 All E.R. 835; (1990) 87(12) L.S.G. 41; (1990) 134 S.J. 286 CA (Civ Div) 1–528, 1–962, 3–015

W v L [1974] Q.B. 711; [1973] 3 W.L.R. 859; [1973] 3 All E.R. 884; 72 L.G.R. 36; (1973) 4 Fam. Law 134; (1973) 117 S.J. 775 1–437

W City Council v L [2015] EWCOP 20; [2015] C.O.P.L.R. 337; (2015) 18 C.C.L. Rep. 350; [2015] P.T.S.R. D26 . . . . .6–005, 6–006, 6–009

W NHS Trust v P [2014] EWHC 119 (COP) 6–017

Wainwright v United Kingdom (12350/04) (2007) 44 E.H.R.R. 40; 22 B.H.R.C. 287; (2006) 156 N.L.J. 1524 ECHR 1–1354, 5–014, 5–038

Waite v United Kingdom (53236/99) (2003) 36 E.H.R.R. 54; [2003] Prison L.R. 160 ECHR 5–024, E–012

Waldron, Re; sub nom. R. v Hallstrom Ex p. W (No.1) [1986] Q.B. 824; [1985] 3 W.L.R. 1090; [1985] 3 All E.R. 775; (1986) 83 L.S.G. 199; (1985) 129 S.J. 892 CA (Civ Div) 1–1352

Ward v Commissioner of Police of the Metropolis [2005] UKHL 32; [2006] 1 A.C. 23; [2005] 2 W.L.R. 1114; [2005] 3All E.R. 1013; (2005) 84 B.M.L.R. 185; [2005] M.H.L.R. 128; [2005] Po. L.R. 170; (2005) 102(24) L.S.G. 35; (2005) 155 N.L.J. 747 . . . . . . .1–1319, 1–1320, 1–1325

Wassink v Netherlands (A/185–A,) September 27, 1990 . . . . .5–024, 5–027

Watson v Nottinghamshire NHS Trust September 26, 2008 Lincoln County Court C–001

Webley v St George's Hospital NHS Trust [2014] EWHC 299 (QB); (2014) 138 B.M.L.R. 190 . . . . .1–106, 1–1336, 1–1342

Weltham v DPP [1961] A.C. 103; [1960] 2 W.L.R. 669; [1960] 1 All E.R. 805; (1960) 44 Cr. App. R. 124; (1960) 124 J.P. 280; (1960) 104 S.J. 308 1–1201

Whitbread (Habeas Corpus: Compulsory Admission), Re; sub nom. Whitbread v Kingston and District NHS Trust; AW, Re; Whitbread (Mental Patient: Habeas Corpus), Re (1998) 39 B.M.L.R. 94; (1997) 94(27) L.S.G. 23; (1997) 141 S.J.L.B. 152 CA (Civ Div) 1–157, 1–158, 1–159, 1–195

Whitbread (Habeas Corpus: Continued Detention), Re [1999] C.O.D. 370 QBD 1–397

Wilkinson v United Kingdom (31145/96) (1998) 26 E.H.R.R. CD131 Eur Comm HR 5–011

Wilkinson v United Kingdom (C14659/02) [2006] M.H.L.R. 142 ECHR 1–729, 5–036

Williams v Williams [2001] EWCA Civ 197; [2001] M.H.L.R. 4 1–545

Williamson v Chief Constable of the West Midlands [2003] EWCA Civ 337; [2004] 1 W.L.R. 14; (2003) 167 J.P. 181; [2003] Po. L.R. 102; (2003) 167 J.P.N. 333; (2003) 100(17) L.S.G. 28 1–1336

Winch v Jones; Winch v Hayward [1986] Q.B. 296; [1985] 3 W.L.R. 729; [1985] 3 All E.R. 97; (1985) 129 S.J. 669 CA (Civ Div) 1–166, 1–1352

Winterwerp v Netherlands (A/33) (1979–80) 2 E.H.R.R. 387 . . . . 1–029, 1–059, 1–084, 1–313, 1–376, 1–587, 1–937, 1–1273, 1–1334, 3–081, 5–019, 5–022, 5–024, 5–025, A–003

Winzar v Chief Constable of Kent, Times, March 28, 1983 1–1336

WM, Petitioner. See M, Petitioner

A Metropolitan Borough Council v DB. See Wolverhampton MBC v DB (A Minor)

Wolverhampton MBC v DB (A Minor); sub nom. B (A Minor) (Treatment and Secure Accommodation), Re; A MBC v DB [1997] 1 F.L.R. 767; [1997] 1 F.C.R. 618; (1997) 37 B.M.L.R. 172; [1997] Fam. Law 400; (1997) 161 J.P.N. 413 Fam Div 1–1277

Wookey v Wookey; S (A Minor) (Injunction to Restrain), Re [1991] Fam. 121; [1991] 3 W.L.R. 135; [1991] 3 All E.R. 365; [1991] 2 F.L.R. 319; [1991] F.C.R. 811 CA (Civ Div) 1–008

X v A, B and C and the Mental Health Act Commission (1991) 9 B.M.L.R. 91 . . . . .1–718, 1–721, 1–740, 1–743, 1–1352, 1–1355

xl

Table of Cases

X v Belgium and Netherlands (1975) D.R. 75. 5–039
X v Denmark (1983) 32 D.R. 282 ECHR 5–012, 5–013
X v Finland (34806/04) [2012] M.H.L.R. 318 ECHR 1–729, 1–736, 1–786, 1–914, 5–036
X v Germany (1980) 20 D. & R. 193 ECHR. 5–037
X v Germany (1984) 7 E.H.R.R. 152 Eur Comm HR 5–007, 5–016
X v Germany 6 D. & R. 182 Eur Comm HR. 5–022
X v Netherlands (A/91); sub nom. X and Y v Netherlands (8978/80); Y v Netherlands (A/91)
    (1986) 8 E.H.R.R. 235 . . . . .1–150, 5–033, 5–036
X v NHS Trust [2008] EWCA Civ 1354; [2009] 2 All E.R. 792; [2008] M.H.L.R. 376; [2009]
    A.C.D. 40 1–514, 1–531, 1–532, 1–544, 1–558, 1–621
X v United Kingdom (5229/71) Unreported October 5, 1972 Eur Comm HR 1–529
X v United Kingdom (A/46); sub nom. X v United Kingdom (6998/75) (1982) 4 E.H.R.R. 188
    ECHR 1–334, 5–021, 5–023, 5–024, 5–025, 5–026, 6–006, A–003
X and Y v Netherlands (1983) 6 E.H.R.R. CD 311 Eur Comm HR 5–034
X and Y v Netherlands. *See* X v Netherlands
X and Y v Switzerland (1978) 13 D. 7 R. 105. 5–051
X (Minors) v Bedfordshire CC; M (A Minor) v Newham LBC; E (A Minor) v Dorset CC
    (Appeal); Christmas v Hampshire CC (Duty of Care); Keating v Bromley LBC (No.2)
    [1995] 2 A.C. 633; [1995] 3 W.L.R. 152; [1995] 3 All E.R. 353; [1995] 2 F.L.R. 276;
    [1995] 3 F.C.R. 337; 94 L.G.R. 313; (1995) 7 Admin. L.R. 705; [1995] Fam. Law 537;
    (1996) 160 L.G. Rev. 103; (1996) 160 L.G. Rev. 123; (1995) 145 N.L.J. 993 HL 1–166
X, Y and Z v Switzerland (6916/76) 6 D. & R. 107, 112, March 12 1976 5–029
X's Application for Judicial Review, Re [2009] NIQB 2; [2009] N.I. 224; [2009] M.H.L.R.
    109. 1–927
Y (Sri Lanka) v Secretary of State for the Home Department; Z (Sri Lanka) v Secretary of State
    for the Home Department [2009] EWCA Civ 362; *Times*, May 5, 2009 5–015
YA v Central and North West London NHS Trust [2015] UKUT 37 (AAC) 3–068, 3–073
Yousef v Netherlands (33711/96) [2003] 1 F.L.R. 210; [2002] 3 F.C.R. 577; (2003) 36 E.H.R.R.
    20; [2003] Fam. Law 89 ECHR 5–039
YZ v NHS Trust [2015] EWHC 2296 (Admin). 1–705
Z and E v Austria (1986) 49 D. & R. 67. 5–039
Z v Finland (1998) 25 E.H.R.R. 371; (1999) 45 B.M.L.R. 107 ECHR. 5–037
Z v United Kingdom (29392/95) [2001] 2 F.L.R. 612; [2001] 2 F.C.R. 246; (2002) 34 E.H.R.R.
    3; 10 B.H.R.C. 384; (2001) 3 L.G.L.R. 51; (2001) 4 C.C.L. Rep. 310; [2001] Fam. Law 583
    ECHR 5–011
Zehnalova v Czech Republic (38621/97) Unreported May 14, 2002 ECHR. 5–035
ZH v Commissioner of Police of the Metropolis; sub nom. Commissioner of Police of the
    Metropolis v ZH; H v Commissioner of Police of the Metropolis [2013] EWCA Civ 69;
    [2013] 1 W.L.R. 3021; [2013] 3 All E.R. 113; [2013] H.R.L.R. 18; [2013] Eq. L.R. 363;
    (2013) 16 C.C.L. Rep. 109; [2013] P.I.Q.R. P11; [2013] M.H.L.R. 69. . . . . 5–008, 5–011, 6–006
ZH v Hungary [2014] M.H.L.R. 1 5–011
Zoan v Rouamba [2000] 1W.L.R. 1509; [2000] 2 All E.R. 620; [2000] C.C.L.R. 18; (2000) 150
    N.L.J. 99 CA (Civ Div) 1–050, 1–107, 1–135, 1–207, 1–287, 1–316, 1–330, 1–351, 1–372,
        1–494, 1–508, 1–531, 1–544, 1–622, 1–643, 1–874, 1–883, 1–897, 1–947, 1–957

PART 1

MENTAL HEALTH ACT 1983

(1983 c.20)

ARRANGEMENT OF SECTIONS

SECTION

PART I

APPLICATION OF ACT

1. Application of Act: "mental disorder."

PART II

COMPULSORY ADMISSION TO HOSPITAL AND GUARDIANSHIP

Procedure for hospital admission

2. Admission for assessment.
3. Admission for treatment.
4. Admission for assessment in cases of emergency.
5. Application in respect of patient already in hospital.
6. Effect of application for admission.

Guardianship

7. Application for guardianship.
8. Effect of guardianship application, etc.
9. Regulations as to guardianship.
10. Transfer of guardianship in case of death, incapacity, etc. of guardian.

General provisions as to applications and recommendations

11. General provisions as to applications.
12. General provisions as to medical recommendations.
[12ZA. Agreement for exercise of approval function: England.
12ZB. Requirement to exercise approval functions: England.
12ZC. Provision of information for the purposes of section 12ZA or 12ZB.]
[12A. Conflicts of interest.]
13. [Duty of approved mental health professionals to make applications for admission or guardianship.]
14. Social reports.
15. Rectification of applications and recommendations.

Position of patients subject to detention or guardianship

SECTION
16. [. . .]
17. Leave of absence from hospital.
[17A. Community treatment orders, etc.
17B. Conditions.
17C. Duration of community treatment order.
17D. Effect of community treatment order.
17E. Power to recall to hospital.
17F. Powers in respect of recalled patients.
17G. Effect of revoking community treatment order.]
18. Return and readmission of patients absent without leave.
19. Regulations as to transfer of patients.
[19A. Regulations as to assignment of responsibility for community patients.]

Duration of detention or guardianship and discharge

20. Duration of authority.
[20A. Community treatment period.
20B. Effect of expiry of community treatment order.]
21. Special provisions as to patients absent without leave.
[21A. Patients who are taken into custody or return within 28 days.
21B. Patients who are taken into custody or return after more than 28 days].
[22. Special provisions as to patients sentenced to imprisonment, etc.]
23. Discharge of patients.
24. Visiting and examination of patients.
25. Restrictions on discharge by nearest relative.
[25A to 25J. [. . .]]

Functions of relatives of patients

26. Definition of "relative" and "nearest relative".
27. Children and young persons in care.
28. Nearest relative of minor under guardianship, etc.
29. Appointment by court of acting nearest relative.
30. Discharge and variation of orders under section 29.

Supplemental

31. Procedure on applications to county court.
32. Regulations for purposes of Part II.
33. Special provisions as to wards of court.
34. Interpretation of Part II.

PART III

PATIENTS CONCERNED IN CRIMINAL PROCEEDINGS OR UNDER SENTENCE

Remands to hospital

35. Remand to hospital for report on accused's mental condition.
36. Remand of accused person to hospital for treatment.

Hospital and guardianship orders

SECTION
37. Powers of courts to order hospital admission or guardianship.
38. Interim hospital orders.
39. Information as to hospitals.
[39A. Information to facilitate guardianship orders].
40. Effect of hospital orders, guardianship orders and interim hospital orders.

Restriction orders

41. Power of higher courts to restrict discharge from hospital.
42. Powers of Secretary of State in respect of patients subject to restriction orders.
43. Power of magistrates' courts to commit for restriction order.
44. Committal to hospital under section 43.
45. Appeals from magistrates' courts.
[45A. Power of higher courts to direct hospital admission.
45B. Effect of hospital and limitation directions.]

Detention during Her Majesty's pleasure

46. Persons ordered to be kept in custody during Her Majesty's pleasure.

Transfer to hospital of prisoners, etc.

47. Removal to hospital of persons serving sentences of imprisonment, etc.
48. Removal to hospital of other prisoners.
49. Restriction on discharge of prisoners removed to hospital.
50. Further provisions as to prisoners under sentence.
51. Further provisions as to detained persons.
52. Further provisions as to persons remanded by magistrates' courts.
53. Further provisions as to civil prisoners and persons detained under the Immigration Act 1971.

Supplemental

54. Requirements as to medical evidence.
[54A. Reduction of period for making hospital orders].
55. Interpretation of Part III.

PART IV

CONSENT TO TREATMENT

[56. Patients to whom Part 4 applies.]
57. Treatment requiring consent and a second opinion.
58. Treatment requiring consent or a second opinion.
[58A. Electro-convulsive therapy, etc.]
59. Plans of treatment.
60. Withdrawal of consent.
61. Review of treatment.
62. Urgent treatment.
[62A. Treatment on recall of community patient or revocation of order.]
63. Treatment not requiring consent.
64. Supplementary provisions for Part IV.

[PART 4A

Treatment of community patients not recalled to hospital

SECTION
64A. Meaning of "relevant treatment".
64B. Adult community patients.
64C. Section 64B: Supplementary.
64D. Adult community patients lacking capacity.
64E. Child community patients.
64F. Child community patients lacking competence.
[64FA. Withdrawal of consent.]
64G. Emergency treatment for patients lacking capacity or competence.
64H. Certificates: supplementary provisions.
64I. Liability for negligence.
64J. Factors to be considered in determining whether patient objects to treatment.
64K. Interpretation of Part 4A.]

PART V

MENTAL HEALTH REVIEW TRIBUNALS

Constitution, etc.

65. Mental Health Review Tribunals.

Applications and references concerning Part II patients

66. Applications to tribunals.
67. References to tribunals by Secretary of State concerning Part II patients.
[68. Duty of managers of hospitals to refer cases to tribunal.]
[68A. Power to reduce periods under section 68.]

Applications and references concerning Part III patients

69. Applications to tribunals concerning patients subject to hospital and guardianship orders.
70. Applications to tribunals concerning restricted patients.
71. References by Secretary of State concerning restricted patients.

Discharge of patients

72. Powers of tribunals.
73. Power to discharge restricted patients.
74. Restricted patients subject to restriction directions.
75. Applications and references concerning conditionally discharged restricted patients.

General

76. Visiting and examination of patients.
77. General provisions concerning tribunal applications.
78. Procedure of tribunals.
79. Interpretation of Part V.

PART VI

REMOVAL AND RETURN OF PATIENTS WITHIN UNITED KINGDOM, ETC.

Removal to Scotland

SECTION
80. Removal of patients to Scotland.
[80ZA. Transfer of responsibility for community patients to Scotland.]
[80A. Transfer of responsibility for conditionally discharged patients to Scotland.]
[80B. Removal of detained patients from Scotland.
80C. Removal of patients subject to compulsion in the community from Scotland.
80D. Transfer of conditionally discharged patients from Scotland.]

Removal to and from Northern Ireland

81. Removal of patients to Northern Ireland.
[81ZA. Removal of community patients to Northern Ireland.]
[81A. Transfer of responsibility for patients to Northern Ireland.]
82. Removal to England and Wales of patients from Northern Ireland.
[82A. Transfer of responsibility for conditionally discharged patients to England and Wales from Northern Ireland.]

Removal to and from Channel Islands and Isle of Man

83. Removal of patients to Channel Islands or Isle of Man.
[83ZA. Removal or transfer of community patients to Channel Islands or Isle of Man.]
[83A. Transfer of responsibility for conditionally discharged patients to Channel Islands or Isle of Man.]
84. Removal to England and Wales of offenders found insane in Channel Islands and Isle of Man.
85. Patients removed from Channel Islands or Isle of Man.
[85ZA. Responsibility for community patients transferred from Channel Islands or Isle of Man.]
[85A. Responsibility for patients transferred from Channel Islands or Isle of Man.]

Removal of aliens

86. Removal of alien patients.

Return of patients absent without leave

87. Patients absent from hospitals in Northern Ireland.
88. Patients absent from hospitals in England and Wales.
89. Patients absent from hospitals in the Channel Islands or Isle of Man.

General

90. Regulations for purposes of Part VI.
91. General provisions as to patients removed from England and Wales.
92. Interpretation of Part VI.

PART VII

MANAGEMENT OF PROPERTY AND AFFAIRS OF PATIENTS

SECTION
93–113. [. . .]

PART VIII

MISCELLANEOUS FUNCTIONS OF LOCAL AUTHORITIES AND THE SECRETARY OF STATE

[Approved Mental Health Professionals]

[114. Approval by local social services authority.]
[114ZA. Approval of courses: England.]
[114A. [Approval of courses: Wales.]]
[115. Powers of entry and inspection.]

Visiting patients

116. Welfare of certain hospital patients.

After-care

117. After-care.
[117A. After-care: preference for particular accommodation.]
[117B. After-care: exception for provision of nursing care.]

Functions of the Secretary of State

118. Code of practice.
119. Practitioners approved for purposes of Part IV and section 118.
[120. General protection of relevant patients.]
[120A. Investigation reports.]
[120B. Action statements.]
[120C. Provision of information.]
[120D. Annual reports.]
121. [. . .]
122. Provision of pocket money for in-patients in hospital.
123. [. . .]
124. [. . .]
125. [. . .]

PART IX

OFFENCES

126. Forgery, false statements, etc.
127. Ill-treatment of patients.
128. Assisting patients to absent themselves without leave, etc.
129. Obstruction.
130. Prosecutions by local authorities.

PART X

MISCELLANEOUS AND SUPPLEMENTARY

Miscellaneous provisions

SECTION

[130A. Independent mental health advocates.

130B. Arrangements under section 130A.

130C. Section 130A; supplemental.

130D. Duty to give information about independent mental health advocates.]

[130E. Independent mental health advocates: Wales.

130F. Arrangements under section 130E for Welsh qualifying compulsory patients.

130G. Arrangements under section 130E for Welsh qualifying informal patients.

130H. Independent mental health advocates for Wales; supplementary powers and duties.

130I. Welsh qualifying compulsory patients.

130J. Welsh qualifying informal patients.

130K. Duty to give information about independent mental health advocates to Welsh qualifying compulsory patients.

130L. Duty to give information about independent mental health advocates to Welsh qualifying informal patients.]

131. Informal admission of patients.

[131A. Accommodation, etc. for children.]

132. Duty of managers of hospitals to give information to detained patients.

[132A. Duty of managers of hospitals to give information to community patients.]

133. Duty of managers of hospitals to inform nearest relatives of discharge.

134. Correspondence of patients.

[134A. Review of decisions to withhold correspondence.]

135. Warrant to search for and remove patients.

136. Mentally disordered persons found in public places.

137. Provisions as to custody, conveyance and detention.

138. Retaking of patients escaping from custody.

139. Protection for acts done in pursuance of this Act.

140. Notification of hospitals having arrangements for reception of urgent cases.

141. [. . .]

142. Pay, pensions, etc. of mentally disordered persons.

[142A. Regulations as to approvals in relation to England and Wales.]

[142B. Delegation of powers of managers of NHS foundation trusts.]

Supplemental

143. General provisions as to regulations, orders and rules.

144. Power to amend local acts.

145. Interpretation.

146. Application to Scotland.

147. Application to Northern Ireland.

148. Consequential and transitional provisions and repeals.

149. Short title, commencement and application to Scilly Isles.

SCHEDULES

1. Application of certain provisions to patients subject to hospital and guardianship orders.

2. Mental Health Review Tribunals.

3. [. . .]

4. Consequential amendments.

5. Transitional and saving provisions.
6. Repeals.

An Act to consolidate the law relating to mentally disordered persons.

[May 9, 1983]

GENERAL NOTE

1–001   The origins of modern mental health legislation lie with the Mental Health Act 1959 which repealed all existing legislation dealing with mental illness and mental deficiency. It was based on the Report of the Royal Commission on the Law Relating to Mental Illness (Cmnd. 169) and incorporated the principles that no one should be admitted to hospital if care in the community would be more appropriate, and that where admission to hospital required compulsion, which was to be a medical instead of a judicial matter, this should if possible be avoided. In January 1975, the Labour Government announced its intention to review the 1959 Act in the light of the many changes which had taken place in treatment and care, in the patterns of services for the mentally disordered, and in public attitudes. An interdepartmental committee of civil servants was set up to undertake the review and it considered a number of suggestions for amending the Act including comprehensive reviews which had been carried out by the Royal College of Psychiatrists and by MIND in Vol. 1 of its publication, *A Human Condition*. It also considered that part of the "Report of the Committee on Mentally Abnormal Offenders" (Cmnd. 6244) (The Butler Report) which reviewed Pt V of the 1959 Act which is concerned with offender patients. The interdepartmental committee's suggestions were set out in a consultative document, "A Review of the Mental Health Act 1959" (HMSO, 1976), and comments were invited from interested bodies and individuals. Following the publication of the consultative document, two further major contributions to the debate came in the form of the second volume of MIND's, *A Human Condition*, on offender patients and the British Association of Social Workers' document, "Mental Health Crisis Services—A New Philosophy".

In 1978, the Government published its response to this consultative exercise in a White Paper, "The Review of the Mental Health Act 1959" (Cmnd. 7320). Some of the proposals in the White Paper were set out in a tentative form because they were either not put forward in the consultative document or were not fully developed at that time. Comments on these proposals were invited but before the Government could translate its proposals into an amending Bill a change of government took place. Further consultations then took place and the Conservative Government's conclusions were embodied in a Bill which was published in November 1981, together with an accompanying White Paper, "Reform of Mental Health Legislation" (Cmnd. 8405). The Bill, which was scrutinised by a Special Standing Committee of the House of Commons, was enacted in October 1982 as the Mental Health (Amendment) Act 1982. It made substantial amendments to the 1959 Act as well as introducing new powers relating to the treatment and discharge of mentally disordered patients. In Cmnd. 8405, the Government announced its intention to introduce a consolidation measure soon after the Royal Assent had been given to the 1982 Act and a Consolidation Bill was introduced in the House of Lords on January 20, 1983. This was referred to the Joint Committee on Consolidation Bills which reported on February 9, 1983 (HL 81, HC 193). The Bill was enacted as the Mental Health Act 1983 on May 9, 1983.

1–002   In October 1998, the Labour Government appointed a group of experts (the "Expert Committee") to advise on the degree to which the 1983 Act needed updating "to support effective delivery of modern patterns of clinical and social care for people with mental disorder and to ensure that there is a proper balance between safety (both of individuals and the wider community) and the rights of individual patients" (*Review of the Mental Health Act 1983*, 1999, App.A). The Parliamentary Under-Secretary of State made it clear to the Committee at its first meeting that the Government would not accept any recommendation that would enable a patient who was subject to compulsory powers to be non-compliant with medication when "appropriate care in appropriate settings is in place" (*Review of the Mental Health Act 1983*, 1999, App.C, para.11). The Expert Committee published its report in November 1999. Fundamental to the Committee's approach was a desire for new legislation to promote the principle of non-discrimination on the grounds of mental health. This inevitably led the Committee to emphasise the notion of patient autonomy. As the Committee stated, "in the context of physical health a patient with capacity is free to choose whether or not to accept treatment: his or her autonomy is respected". However, the Committee adopted a pragmatic approach in its recommendations. Although the Committee accepted that the safety of the public must be allowed to outweigh the individual autonomy of a capacitated mentally disordered person "where the risk is great", it provided no adequate explanation as to why the principle of patient autonomy should not lead to such a person being dealt with through the criminal justice system. The Committee divided on whether a capacitated mentally disordered person should have the same "right" as a capacitated physically disordered person to self-harm or whether such patients should be protected from themselves through mental health legislation. The Committee concluded that the choice between the two approaches was a "moral" one that should be taken by politicians and not the Committee.

Given the nature of the Committee's approach to patient autonomy, it was hardly surprising that when the Government published its response to the Committee's proposals in the form of a Green Paper (*Reform of the Mental Health Act 1983: Proposals for Consultation*, Cm. 4480) it rejected the introduction of a notion of capacity into the criteria for compulsory intervention. The Government's view was that it "is the *degree of risk* that patients with mental disorders pose, to themselves or others, that is crucial to [the decision on whether a patient should be made subject to a compulsory order]. In the presence of such risk, questions of capacity—while still relevant to the plan of care and treatment—may be largely irrelevant to the question of whether or not a compulsory order should be made" (p.32).

The Green Paper was followed in December 2000 by a White Paper, "Reforming the Mental Health Act" (Cm. 5016). This confirmed the Government's emphasis on risk: "Concerns of risk will always take precedence, but care and treatment provided under formal powers should otherwise reflect the best interests of the patient" (para.2.16). The theme of risk was further emphasised by the Government's concern that existing legislation had "failed to provide adequate public protection from those whose risk to others arises from severe personality disorder" (Foreword, p.1).

A Draft Bill was published in June 2002 (Cm. 5538). The Bill was scrutinised by the Joint Committee of the Houses of Commons and Lords on Human Rights, which reported in November 2002 (HL Paper 181; HC 1294). The Draft Bill did not cover everything that was intended to be in the final version of the Bill to be introduced in Parliament but was accompanied by a consultation document seeking views about a number of policy areas. Following the consultation process, the Government published a new version of the Bill in September 2004 (Cm. 6305). The revised draft Bill was subject to pre-legislative scrutiny from a Joint Committee of the House of Commons and House of Lords. Having considered a great deal of evidence, much of it hostile to the Government's proposals, the Committee reached the view that "the Government should proceed with the Bill, but only with significant amendments, as proposed in our report" (HL Paper 79-1; HC 95-1, p.5). The Government published its response to the Joint Committee's report in July 2005 (Cm. 6624). On March 23, 2006, the Secretary of State for Health announced that the Government had abandoned its plans to proceed with the draft Bill and would instead proceed to "introduce a shorter, streamlined Bill that amends the [1983] Act".

The Mental Health Bill, which was given its first reading in the House of Lords on November 16, 2006, was scrutinised by the Joint Committee on Human Rights which published its report in February 2007 (HL Paper 40; HC 288). A progress report was published by the Joint Committee in June 2007 (HL Paper 112; HC 555). The Parliamentary debates on the Bill, especially those in the House of Lords, largely focused on the Government's response to amendments proposed by Conservatives, Liberal Democrats and cross-benchers who were advocating on behalf of the Mental Health Alliance, an organisation which stated that it "is a coalition of 79 organisations working together to secure humane and effective mental health legislation" (the Alliance lost five of its members in May 2007 over the issue of which professional groups should have the power to renew the detention and supervised community treatment of patients). Opinions regarding both the alleged inadequacy of the current state of the law and the Government's proposals were forcibly expressed. A disinterested observer would have been surprised to learn that although the 1983 Act was clearly in need of reform, it was generally thought to have provided a legislative structure which worked reasonably well in practice by striking an appropriate balance between the interests of patients and the public. The main innovation in the Bill was the introduction of community treatment orders. The Mental Health Act 2007 received the Royal Assent on July 19, 2007.

For fuller accounts of the convoluted process that led to the passing of the 2007 Act, see Paul Bowen, *Blackstone's Guide to the Mental Health Act 2007* (2007), pp.6–18 and Phil Fennell, *Mental Health: the New Law* (2007) pp.2–12. The history of mental health legislation up to and including the 1983 Act is considered by Paul Unsworth in *The Politics of Mental Health Legislation* (1987) and by Phil Fennell in Ch.1 of *Principles of Mental Health Law and Policy* (2010).

The Mental Health Act in Wales

1–003   Subject to a number of exceptions that are noted in the annotations to the relevant sections, the functions of the Secretary of State under the Act were transferred to the National Assembly for Wales by the National Assembly for Wales (Transfer of Functions) Order 1999 (SI 1999/672, art.2 Sch.1) (as amended by SI 2000/253, art.4 Sch.3). These functions are now exercised by the Welsh Ministers by virtue of the Government of Wales Act 2006 s.162, Sch.11 para.30. References to regulations that have been made under the Act by the Welsh Ministers are made throughout this work. The Mental Health (Wales) Measure 2010, a Measure of the National Assembly of Wales, received Royal Approval on December 15, 2010. Amongst its provisions is the enactment of ss.130E to 130L of the Act which are concerned with the provision of independent mental health advocacy services for Welsh qualifying patients. Wales has its own mental Health Review Tribunal: see s.65. A second edition of a *Code of Practice for Wales* was published by the Wales Assembly Government in 2015.

Policy of the Act

1–004   According to the Court of Appeal, the "policy and objects" of the Act (prior to its amendment by the 2007 Act) are "to regulate the circumstances in which the liberty of persons who are mentally disordered may be restricted and, where there is conflict, to balance their interests against those of public policy" (*R. v Secretary of State for the Home Department Ex p. K* [1990] 3 All E.R. 562, 570, per McCowan L.J.). In *Secretary of State for Justice v RB* [2011] EWCA Civ 1608; [2012] M.H.L.R. 131, paras 25, 26, the court said that the policy of the Act is treatment not containment.

Judicial interpretation

1–005   In *R. v Hallstrom Ex p. W (No.2)* [1986] 2 All E.R. 306 at 314, McCullough J. said:

"There is . . . no canon of construction which presumes that Parliament intended that people should, against their will, be subjected to treatment which others, however professionally competent, perceive, however sincerely and however correctly, to be in their best interests. What there is is a canon of construction that Parliament is presumed not to enact legislation which interferes with the liberty of the subject without making it clear that this was its intention. It goes without saying that, unless clear statutory authority to the contrary exists, no one is to be detained in hospital or to undergo medical treatment or even to submit himself to a medical examination without his consent. That is as true of a mentally disordered person as of anyone else".

This passage was cited with approval by the Court of Appeal in *St George's Healthcare NHS Trust v S* [1998] 3 All E.R. 673 at 692–693.

Allocation of resources to detained patients

The fact that a patient is detained under the Act does not provide the patient's responsible **1–006** clinician (RC) with the power to demand that the NHS gives priority to the care of that patient: see *R. (on the application of F) v Oxfordshire Mental Health Healthcare NHS Trust and Oxfordshire NHS Health Authority* [2001] EWHC Admin 535; [2001] M.H.L.R 140 where Sullivan J. said at paras 64, 66:

"Treatment is provided to all patients in the real world where the availability of facilities is constrained by resources. By way of example, the [RC] may well consider that it would be beneficial for a particular Part II or Part III patient if he/she was given better facilities whilst in hospital: more privacy, more spacious accommodation, access to particular therapy, more attention by the nursing staff, etc. There is nothing in the 1983 Act to suggest that the Health Authority must then provide those facilities. In so far as the 1983 Act confers additional powers on the [RCs], it does so vis-à-vis the [RC's] patient, not the Health Authority . . . In simple terms, since resources are limited, there is bound to be a queue of patients seeking treatment. I do not accept the proposition that the [RC's] position under the 1983 Act is such as to propel his or her Part II or III patients to the head of the queue."

In *R. (on the application of K) v West London Mental Health NHS Trust* [2006] EWCA Civ 118; [2006] M.H.L.R. 89, the question before the Court of Appeal was whether the NHS Trust was obliged to pay the costs of a detained patient's treatment in an independent hospital where leave of absence under s.17 had been granted by the patient's RC for the purpose of enabling the patient to be admitted to that hospital. In answering the question in the negative, the court held that:

1. The decision whether or not any particular services should be provided under s.3 of the National Health Service Act 1977 is one for the Secretary of State (or his delegate) and not one for the RC. Section 3, so far as is material, provides: "It is the Secretary of State's duty to provide throughout England and Wales, to such extent as he considers necessary to meet all reasonable requirements—(a) hospital accommodation . . ." (now see s.3 of the National Health Service Act 2006).

2. When performing his functions under s.3, the Secretary of State (or his delegate) is not bound to accept and act on the clinical judgment of the RC. A decision as to whether to devote resources to a particular treatment depended on many considerations, including the seriousness of the condition, the likely success of the proposed treatment, the cost of the treatment and the competing needs of other patients.

3. A RC has no power to give directions as to how others are to discharge their functions and s.17 cannot be construed as conferring such a power.

4. The Secretary of State (or his delegate) is not obliged to use his best endeavours to give effect to a decision of a RC under s.17.

The Court further held that *F*, above, had been correctly decided.

Injunctions to support an authority's performance of its duties under the Act

1–007   In *Broadmoor Hospital Authority v R*. [2000] 2 All E.R. 727, the issue before the Court of Appeal was whether a statutory body is entitled to be granted an injunction in civil proceedings to support its performance of its statutory duties. It was held that:

(i) if a public body is given a statutory responsibility which it is required to perform in the public interest, then, in the absence of an implication to the contrary in the statute, it has standing to apply to the court for an injunction to prevent interference with its performance of its public responsibilities and the court should grant such an application when it appears to the court to be just and convenient to do so; and

(ii) conduct outside a hospital can affect what happens within the hospital and if this is so jurisdiction exists in the court to provide protection by injunction. However there would need to be a substantial risk to the hospital's powers being prejudiced for the court to exercise its discretion to issue an injunction. Lord Woolf said at 736:

"If for example an individual was causing interference with the discipline of a [high security] hospital by writing letters to the patients then notwithstanding the ability of the authority to censor correspondence, in the appropriate situation an injunction against the individual could be granted to reduce the risk of discipline being undermined and treatment interfered with."

Court orders granted against mentally incapable persons

1–008   In *Wookey v Wookey* [1991] 3 All E.R. 365, the Court of Appeal held that an injunction ought not to be granted against a person who is incapable of understanding what he is doing or that it is wrong, because such a person is incapable of complying with it. The appropriate way of dealing with the problem behaviour of a mentally incapable person is the use of the powers under the Mental Health Act. However, an interlocutory injunction might be appropriate if the court considers that the mental condition of the person against whom the injunction is sought should be investigated. In such cases the Official Solicitor should be approached for advice as to whether or not he would wish to act for the person who was liable to have an injunction made against him. *Wookey* was considered in *Cooke v Director of Public Prosecutions* [2008] EWHC 2703 (Admin); [2008] M.H.L.R. 348, where the Divisional Court held that an anti-social behaviour order (ASBO) should not be made under s.1C of the Crime and Disorder Act 1998 against a person who, by reason of mental ill health, would not have the capacity to understand or comply with the order.

If, in a borderline case, the judge concludes that the person concerned possesses the required level of capacity to enable an order to be made against him, the person's legal advisers should monitor the situation and if the position deteriorates return to the court with an application to discontinue the order (*Harris v Harris*, CA, April 22, 1999).

The degree of capacity which an individual must have in order to be subject to the contempt jurisdiction was considered by the Court of Appeal in *P v P (Contempt of Court: Mental Capacity)* [1999] 2 F.L.R. 897 where it was held that it was not necessary for the person to comprehend the meaning or significance of courts or of the legal process. What was required was that a potential contemnor should understand that an order has been made forbidding him to do certain things and that if he did them he may very well be punished.

Voting

1–009   The law relating to the right of patients in psychiatric hospitals to vote was amended by the Representation of the People Act 2000. Section 3A of the Representation of the People Act 1983 (as inserted by s.2 of the 2000 Act) essentially excludes those patients who have been detained in psychiatric hospitals as a consequence of criminal activity from voting in parliamentary and local government elections. Other patients, both detained and informal, will be entitled to be registered to vote pursuant to either s.7 of the 1983 Act (as inserted by s.4 of the 2000 Act) or to s.7A of the 1983 Act (as inserted by s.5 of the 2000 Act). Section

35 of the Electoral Administration Act 2006 amends Sch.4 to the 2000 Act so that mental health patients who are detained under Pt II of the Act are no longer prevented from voting in person if they are granted leave of absence under s.17. The amended Sch.4 also enables such patients to vote by post or by proxy if registered to do so.

Section 73(1) of the 2006 Act abolished any "rule of the common law which provides that a person is subject to a legal incapacity to vote by reason of his mental state". It is therefore the case that a person cannot be prevented from voting on capacity related grounds. Paragraph 5.3 of "Guidance from the Electoral Commission" (2010) confirms this:

"A lack of mental capacity is not a legal incapacity to vote: persons who meet the other registration qualifications are eligible for registration regardless of their mental capacity or lack thereof. Electoral Registration Officers should therefore ensure that persons with learning difficulties or mental health conditions are included in the register of electors."

Paragraphs 5.7 and 5.8 of the guidance deal with the registration of detained patients:

"For a person who is detained as a patient in a mental hospital or an establishment for the reception and treatment of persons in mental distress, the question of where they are resident will depend on the circumstances and on the length of time they are present at the hospital. They are, however, entitled to register, unless they are a detained offender.

If the length of their stay at the hospital is, or is likely to be, sufficient they may be regarded as resident at the hospital for the purposes of their entitlement to register. Such patients may also register by means of their residence at some place other than the hospital. A patient who is not qualified by virtue of residence at any place other than the hospital may choose to register by means of a declaration of local connection in respect of the address where they would be living if they were not a patient or an address where they used to live before they were a patient."

Registering a hospital patient to vote has no impact on identifying the responsible after-care bodies under s.117 because under s.7(2) of the Representation of the People Act 1983, a patient is regarded as being resident in the hospital only for the purposes of entitlement to be registered to vote.

Section 29 of the Mental Capacity Act 2005 prevents a person from voting on behalf of a mentally incapacitated person.

The blanket disenfranchisement of patients who are subject to orders made by a court under Pt III of the Act breaches art.3 of Protocol No.1 to the European Convention on Human Rights: see *Hirst v United Kingdom (No.2)* (2006) 42 E.H.R.R. 41, and the note on Protocol No.1 in Pt 5. Legislation to respond to this ruling has not been enacted.

Voting rights are considered in *Principles of Mental Health Law and Policy* (2010) at paras 25.25 to 25.34 and by Brenda Hale in *Mental Health Law* (2010), pp.312 and 313.

Marriage

The marriage of patients detained under the Act is provided for under s.1 of the Marriage **1–010** Act 1983. Guidance on the relevant procedure is contained in paras 5 to 7 DHSS Circular No. LAC (84)9:

"The Marriage Act also permits the marriages of patients detained in hospital under the Mental Health Act 1983 to take place in hospital. It does, however, exclude from these provisions those detained under the shorter-term provisions, i.e. sections 2, 4, 5, 35, 36, or 136 of the Mental Health Act 1983.

When a detained person wishes to be married in hospital the notice of marriage required by section 27 of the Marriage Act 1949 must be accompanied by a statement made in the prescribed form by the hospital managers not more than 21 days before the date on which notice of the marriage is given:

    i. identifying the establishment where the person is detained; and

    ii. stating that the hospital managers have no objection to that establishment being specified in the notice of marriage as the place where that marriage is to be solemnised.

A copy of this form is at Annex B. Further copies are obtainable from the local Superintendent Registrar.

Hospitals will wish to arrange careful counselling for any detained patient who wishes to marry, and possibly for their prospective spouses, so that both parties may consider the matter fully."

Anyone, including the doctor in charge of the patient's treatment, who does not believe that the patient is capable of giving a valid consent to the marriage, may enter a caveat with the Superintendent Registrar before the ceremony. The caveat can be in the form of a letter which sets out the grounds for contending that the patient lacks the required capacity. A patient is capable of entering into a marriage if he is capable of understanding the nature of the contract of marriage, which includes an understanding of the nature of sexual intercourse and its foreseeable consequences: see *A Local Authority v AK* [2012] EWHC B29 (COP) where Bodey J. made the following comment on the role of Registrars at para.53:

"This case has thrown up the role of Registrars and of the registration service when a borderline-incapacitated individual presents wanting to marry. It is not a Registrar's job to assess mental capacity and plainly he or she would be wholly unqualified to do so. If there is doubt in the Registrar's mind when an individual responds to the standard questions put at the notice-attestation meeting, then the procedure is for the doubt to be referred upwards, first to the local Superintendent Registrar and thereafter, if necessary, to the Office of the Registrar General. In a really tricky case, this could end up with a decision to call for a psychiatric report into capacity. That said, the standard handbook provided to Registrars presently says nothing about the need for mental capacity to contract a marriage and does not mention the Mental Capacity Act 2005."

The Superintendent Registrar will give the person who gave notice of marriage an opportunity to answer the objection and to produce evidence in rebuttal of the grounds alleged. If the Superintendent Registrar is in doubt whether or not the caveat ought to obstruct the issue of a certificate for marriage, he may refer the matter to the Registrar General. There is a right of appeal to the Registrar General against a Superintendent Registrar's refusal to issue his certificate for marriage by reason of a caveat.

The impact of the Human Rights Act 1998 on the marital rights of detained patients is considered in the note on art.12 of the European Convention on Human Rights: see Part 5.

Civil Partnerships

1–011   Under s.13 of the Civil Partnership Act 2004, any person may object to a proposed civil partnership. The notice of objection, which must be sent to the registration authority, has to state the objector's place of residence and the ground of objection. If the registration authority refuses to register the civil partnership because of the objection, either of the proposed civil partners may appeal to the Registrar General (Civil Partnership Act 2004 s.15).

If two people wish to register as civil partners of each other at the place where one of them is detained under the Act (otherwise than by virtue of s.2, 4, 5, 35, 36, or 136), the notice of the proposed civil partnership must be accompanied by a supporting statement made by the hospital managers which (a) identifies the hospital where the person is detained, and (b) states that the managers have no objection to that hospital being specified in a notice of proposed civil partnership as the place at which the person is to register as a

civil partner (Civil Partnership Act 2004 s.19). The statement must be in the form prescribed by the Civil Partnership (Registration Provisions) Regulations 2005 (SI 2005/
3176) reg.4(2).

Among the grounds set out in s.50 of the 2004 Act under which a civil partnership is
voidable are:

(i) either partner did not validly consent to its formation as a result of unsoundness of
mind, and

(ii) at the time of its formation either of the partners, although capable of giving a valid
consent, was suffering (whether continuously or intermittently) from mental disorder of such a kind or to such an extent as to be unfitted for civil partnership.

The right of a detained patient to pay for treatment

In *Coombs v Dorset NHS Primary Care Trust* [2013] EWCA Civ 471, the Court of **1–012**
Appeal held that a patient who is detained under the Act can pay for his care or treatment
as long as this does not conflict with recommendations made by his responsible clinician.
Rix L.J. said at para.34:

"[T]here is nothing inherent in the structure or wording of the Mental Health Act 1983 or
the [National Health Service Act 2006], and nothing by way of public policy, to exclude
absolutely the possibilities of detained patients (or their family or others holding
responsibility for looking after their assets) paying for or contributing in part to the
cost of their treatment or care. Presumably, private patients detained in a private hospital
do exactly that. Detained patients who are being looked after by an NHS authority will
have most, if not all, of their costs funded by the state: but even in their case, it may be
possible, as in the case of any patient within the NHS system, to purchase private accommodation or other top-up care facilities available within the applicable Guidance. Of
course, it will not be possible to provide for care or treatment which is in conflict
with the recommendations of the responsible clinician. Nor may it always or perhaps
even often be possible within the NHS system to purchase additional care or treatment
facilities without running into the principle of free provision and the limitations upon the
exceptions to that principle. However, the cases cited above show that responsible clinicians may recommend treatment or care which the NHS is not under a duty to provide,
because it goes beyond its statutory duty. There seems to me no reason in statute or public
policy why there should be an absolute bar on the provision of facilities, recommended
by or consistent with the recommendations of the responsible clinician, which may be
available at a price, within or without the NHS system."

Part 8 of the National Health Service Commissioning Board and Clinical Commissioning
Groups (Responsibilities and Standing Rules) Regulations 2012 (SI 2012/2996), which is
concerned with the right of patients to have a choice of health service provider, does not
apply to patients who are detained under the Act (reg.41).

The rights of victims of serious violent and sexual offences

This topic is considered in Ch.40 of the *Code of Practice*. Also see the General Note to **1–013**
the Tribunal Rules under the heading "victims".

Risks to prominent people or locations

Regulation 13 of the NHS Commissioning Board and Clinical Commissioning Groups **1–014**
(Responsibilities and Standing Rules) Regulations 2012 (SI 2012/2996), which is headed
"Fixated threat assessment services", states:

"(1) The [NHS Commissioning] Board must arrange, to such extent as it considers
necessary to meet all reasonable requirements, for the provision as part of the health

service of specialised clinical risk assessment and management services for people with mental health problems who may present a risk to prominent people or locations.

(2) The arrangements to be made by the Board under paragraph (1) must include—

    (a) the provision of funding for mental health staff to provide the services referred to in paragraph (1); and

    (b) such provision for partnership working with other persons or health services as is considered necessary to facilitate the effective delivery of those services."

The Fixated Threat Assessment Centre (FTAC) was established in 2006. Its role is described on its website:

"The [FTAC] is a joint partnership between the Home Office, the Department of Health and the Metropolitan Police Service. It is an innovative project developing a service that is unique and is the first joint mental health/police unit in the United Kingdom. The unit comprises police officers, in the role of caseworker / investigators, working alongside clinical psychiatric nurses with access to psychiatrists and psychologists.

FTAC's purpose is to assess and manage the risks posed by people who engage in inappropriate or threatening forms of contact towards prominent people in public life. Fixated persons are individuals who are abnormally preoccupied with certain ideas or persons. They can be clinically psychotic, pathological and obsessive about an idea or cause. Such individuals can pose a risk to their targets, to the public and to themselves, particularly in environments where there are armed police officers."

Diplomatic immunity

1–015   By virtue of the Diplomatic Privileges Act 1964 s.2, Sch.1 art.29, "the person of a diplomatic agent shall be inviolable. He shall not be liable to any form of arrest or detention. The receiving State shall treat him with due respect and shall take all appropriate steps to prevent any attack on his person, freedom or dignity". Article 1(e) defines a "diplomatic agent" as "the head of the mission or a member of the diplomatic staff of the mission" and art.37 extends the provisions of art.29 to "the members of the family of a diplomatic agent forming part of his household" who are not nationals of the receiving state. Diplomats and their families should not therefore be made subject to the provisions of the Act unless the inviolability afforded by the 1964 Act has been lifted.

According to Dr David Pariente, the legal department of the Foreign and Commonwealth Office has advised that such inviolability:

"can only be lifted by the State which the diplomat represents; in normal circumstances the State's consent must be obtained from the appropriate Head of Mission, usually an Ambassador, with whose agreement the provisions of the Mental Health Act can then be exercised. Irreversible and hazardous treatments would require his consent. In cases of extreme emergency, where immediate detention of the diplomat is the only way to protect human safety, such action would be justifiable on the basis of the inherent right of self-defence, or the duty to protect human life. In such a case the Foreign and Commonwealth Office should be informed immediately."

Dr Pariente further reports that the Medical Defence Union has "advised that the consent of the Head of Mission should be sought in writing; and that the issue of breach of confidentiality should not present a problem to a doctor who was clearly acting in the best interests of the patient" ("Diplomatic immunity and the Mental Health Act 1983" (1991) *Psychiatric Bulletin* 15 at 207–209).

An approved mental health professional faced with the possibility of making an application in respect of a person who is covered by the 1964 Act should contact the Foreign and Commonwealth Office—Diplomatic Missions and International Organisations Unit,

Protocol Directorate who will be able to confirm the person's diplomatic status and, if necessary, request the relevant Head of Mission to provide the necessary consent. At the time of publication the contact number is 020 7008 1012.

Foreign travel

Apart from the provisions noted under *Extent*, below, the reach of the Act is limited to **1–016** England and Wales. The Foreign and Commonwealth Office has published "Foreign travel advice for people with mental health issues" (2013) which can be accessed at: *www.gov.uk/ foreign-travel-advice-for-people-with-mental-health-issues*.

Mental Capacity Act 2005

Paragraph 7.8 of the *Code of Practice* states: **1–017**

"It is good practice, where practicable, for clinicians and others involved in the assessment or treatment of patients under the Act to try to find out whether the person has an attorney or deputy and to establish effective means of communication to ensure that the attorney or deputy is informed and, where relevant, consulted about the patient's care. Information regarding the appointment of any registered LPA, attorney or deputy can be obtained through a search of the registers maintained by the Office of the Public Guardian."

The effect of certain decisions taken by donees of LPAs and deputies is considered at para.7.6 of the *Code*:

"In certain cases, conditions can be imposed on patients subject to the Act in relation to leave of absence from hospital, community treatment orders (CTOs) or conditional discharge. If an attorney or deputy takes a decision on the patient's behalf which goes against one of these conditions, the patient will be taken to have gone against the condition. In CTO and conditional discharge cases, this might result in the patient's recall to hospital being considered."

International

International human rights law is built on the fundamental principle that all people **1–018** should be protected equally under the law. Article 1 of the Universal Declaration of Human Rights (UDHR), adopted by the United Nations in 1948, provides that "all people are free and equal in rights and dignity". The UN subsequently drafted two binding international human rights conventions to promote the implementation of, and expand upon the rights established in the UDHR. They are the International Covenant on Civil and Political Rights (ICCPR) and the International Covenant on Economic, Social, and Cultural Rights (ICESR). Both conventions entered into force in 1976. Together with the UDHR and the UN Charter, they make up what is known as the "International Bill of Human Rights". The UK has ratified both conventions and is therefore under an obligation, under international law, to ensure that its policies do not conflict with the rights established therein. The ICCPR is particularly relevant to patients who are subject to compulsory powers under the Act and a number of its articles are mirrored in the European Convention on Human Rights (EHCR). In 1991, the UK ratified the Convention on the Rights of the Child (CRC) which is relevant to patients who are under 18. Although the rights under the ICCPR and the CRC are not directly enforceable in England and Wales, they can be used as an aid to interpreting the rights under the ECHR. In *Smith v Secretary of State for Work and Pensions* [2006] UKHL 35; [2006] All E.R. 907, para.78, Baroness Hale cited the CRC, and said obiter:

"Even if an international treaty has not been incorporated into domestic law, our domestic legislation has to be construed so far as possible so as to comply with the international obligations which we have undertaken."

1–019 The ECHR is not the only relevant human rights instrument emanating from Europe. The Charter of Fundamental Rights of the European Union was proclaimed at Nice in December 2000. The rights set out in the Charter, which are partly based on the rights recognised by the ECHR, are divided into six sections: dignity, freedoms, equality, solidarity, citizen's rights and justice. Article 3(2) is of particular relevance to the Act:

> "In the fields of medicine and biology, the following must be respected in particular:—the free and informed consent of the person concerned according to the procedure laid down by law."

The status of the Charter was explained by Munby J. in *R. (on the application of A,B,X and Y) v East Sussex County Council (No.2)* [2003] EWHC 167 (Admin); (2003) 6 C.C.L.R. 194 at para.73:

> "The Charter is not at present legally binding in our domestic law and is therefore not a source of law in the strict sense. But it can, in my judgment, properly be consulted insofar as it proclaims, reaffirms, or elucidates the content of those human rights that are generally recognised throughout the European family of nations, in particular the nature and scope of those fundamental rights that are guaranteed by the [ECHR]."

On February 23, 1999, the Committee of Ministers of the Council of Europe adopted "Principles concerning the legal protection of incapable adults", Recommendation R (99) 4. The European Court of Human Rights has said that although "these principles have no force in law for this Court, they may define a common European standard in this area" (*Shtukaturov v Russia* (2012) 54 E.H.R.R. 27; [2008] M.H.L.R. 238, para.95).

The United Nations Convention on the Rights of Persons with Disabilities (CRPD) was adopted by the General Assembly on December 13, 2006 and was ratified by the UK Government on June 8, 2009. The European Union ratified the Convention on December 23, 2010. Although as an unincorporated international treaty the Convention does not have direct effect in UK law, in *AH v West London MHT* [2011] UKUT 74 (AAC) the Upper Tribunal, presided over by Carnwath L.J., said at para.16:

> "The CRPD provides the framework for Member States to address the rights of persons with disabilities. It is a legally binding international treaty that comprehensively clarifies the human rights of persons with disabilities as well as corresponding obligations on state parties. By ratifying a Convention, a state undertakes that wherever possible its laws will conform to the norms and values that the Convention enshrines."

This approach was approved by the Court of Appeal in *Burnip v Birmingham City Council* [2012] EWCA Civ 629, where Maurice Kay L.J. said that the Convention has "the potential to illuminate our approach to both discrimination and justification" (para.22).

Among those covered by the CRPD are people "who have long term . . . mental [or] intellectual . . . impairments which in interaction with various barriers may hinder their full and effective participation in society on an equal basis with others" (art.1). Article 14 of the Convention, which is headed "Liberty and security of the person", states:

> "1. States Parties shall ensure that persons with disabilities, on an equal basis with others:
>
> > (a) Enjoy the right to liberty and security of person;
> > (b) Are not deprived of their liberty unlawfully or arbitrarily, and that any deprivation of liberty is in conformity with the law, and that the existence of a disability shall in no case justify a deprivation of liberty.
>
> 2. States Parties shall ensure that if persons with disabilities are deprived of their liberty through any process, they are, on an equal basis with others, entitled to guarantees in

accordance with international human rights law and shall be treated in compliance with the objectives and principles of this Convention, including by provision of reasonable accommodation."

The implications of the final phrase of para.1(b) are profound in that, unless it could be argued that the phrase should be interpreted as meaning that the existence of a disability should not be the sole ground for justifying a deprivation of liberty, the Act contravenes the Convention. It is noteworthy that the United Nations High Commissioner for Human Rights in his 2009 *Thematic study — on the enhancing awareness and understanding of the Convention on the Rights of Persons with Disabilities* states, at para.48, that proposals made during the drafting of the Convention to limit the prohibition of detention to cases "solely" determined by disability were rejected. And in a "Statement on article 14 of the Convention on the Rights of Persons with Disabilities" made by the Committee on the Rights of Persons with Disabilities in September 2014 it is said that legislation "in which persons may be detained on the grounds of their actual or perceived disability, provided there are other reasons for their detention, including that they are dangerous to themselves or to others" is incompatible with art.14. It follows that, in order to be compliant with the Convention, legislation that allows for the detention of persons must be delinked from the disability so as to apply to all persons on an equal basis. This approach is impossible to reconcile with art.5(1)(e) of the ECHR which permits detention on the ground of unsoundness of mind. It is therefore not possible for the UK Government, which has incorporated the ECHR into domestic law through the Human Rights Act 1998, to legislate to implement art.14. The Convention is considered by Phil Fennell and Urfan Khaliq in "Conflicting or complementary obligations? The UN Disability Rights Convention on Human Rights and English Law", E.H.R.L.R. 2011, 6, 662–674 and by Peter Bartlett in "The United Nations Convention on the Rights of Persons with Disabilities and Mental Health Law", (2012) 75(5) M.L.R. 752–778.

The only international instrument against which UK mental health law can be judicially tested is the ECHR. The rights set out in the Convention are derived essentially from the UDHR. The Human Rights Act 1998 incorporates articles from the ECHR into UK law. Four of the articles incorporated are particularly relevant to the operation of mental health legislation: arts 3, 5, 6 and 8. In *R. (on the application of SC) v Mental Health Review Tribunal* [2005] EWHC 17 (Admin); [2005] M.H.L.R. 31 at para.54, Munby J. said that the exercise by state authorities of compulsory powers in relation to persons suffering from mental disorder calls for increased vigilance in reviewing whether the ECHR has been complied with. A note on the 1998 Act can be found in Pt 5.

International human rights law applicable to those who suffer from a mental disorder has been extensively reviewed by Lawrence O. Gostin and Lance Gable in "The human rights of persons with mental disabilities: a global perspective on the application of human rights principles to mental health" (2004) 10 Maryland Law Review 1, 20–121 and by Kris Gledhill in Ch.27 of *Principles of Mental Health Law and Policy* (2010).

Most of the materials mentioned above can be accessed on the website of the Human Rights Library of the University of Minnesota (*www1.umn.edu/humanrts/*).

Transitional provisions

Detailed transitional provisions are set out in Sch.5. Transitional provisions that relate to **1–020** the implementation of the Mental Health Act 2007 are contained in Sch.10 to that Act. They stipulate the extent to which an amendment to the Act by the 2007 Act applies to or has an impact on a patient who is subject to the Act when the amendments come into force. Further transitional provisions are contained in the Mental Health Act 2007 (Commencement No.6 and After-care under Supervision: Savings, Modifications and Transitional Provisions) Order 2008 (SI 2008/1210); the Mental Health Act 2007 (Commencement No.7 and Transitional Provisions) Order 2008 (SI 2008/1900); and the Mental Health Act (Commencement No.8 and Transitional Provisions) Order 2008 (SI 2008/2561). The

Department of Health published "Implementation of the Mental Health Act 2007: Transitional Arrangements" (July 31, 2008).

Extent

1–021   The Act applies to Scotland and Northern Ireland only to the extent provided for in ss.146 and 147, respectively. The whole of the Act was extended to the Isles of Scilly on March 12, 1985, by the Isles of Scilly (Mental Health) Order 1985 (SI 1985/149) with the modification that the expression "local social services authority" in the Act shall, in relation to the Isles, mean the Council of the Isles constituted under the Isles of Scilly Order 1978 (SI 1978/1844).

Abbreviations

1–022   In the annotations, the following abbreviations are used:

Aarvold Committee: Report on the Review of Procedures for the Discharge and Supervision of Psychiatric Patients subject to Special Restrictions (Cmnd. 5191).

Butler Committee: Report of the Committee on Mentally Abnormal Offenders (Cmnd. 6244).

Code of Practice: The *Code of Practice* published under s.118(4) of this Act.

Joint Committee: House of Lords and House of Commons Joint Committee on Human Rights.

Mental Health Bill: the Mental Health Bill introduced to Parliament on November 16, 2006.

Public Bill Committee: Public Bill Committee—Mental Health Bill (Lords).

The Reed Committee: Review of Health and Social Services for Mentally Disordered Offenders and others requiring similar services, Chairman: Dr John Reed, HMSO, 1992.

Reference Guide: Reference Guide to the Mental Health Act 1983 (2015).

Royal Commission: Report of the Royal Commission on the Law Relating to Mental Illness and Mental Deficiency 1954–1957, Chairman—Lord Percy (Cmnd. 169).

Special Standing Committee: The special Standing Committee which considered the Mental Health (Amendment) Bill.

the Tribunal Rules: the Tribunal Procedure (First-tier Tribunal) (Health, Education and Social Care Chamber) Rules 2008 (SI 2008/2699).

the 1982 Act: the Mental Health (Amendment) Act 1982.

the 2007 Act: the Mental Health Act 2007.

tribunal: the First-tier Tribunal (Mental Health) or the Mental Health Review Tribunal for Wales.

the English Regulations: Mental Health (Hospital, Guardianship and Treatment) (England) Regulations 2008 (SI 2008/1184).

the Welsh Regulations: the Mental Health (Hospital, Guardianship, Community Treatment and Consent to Treatment) (Wales) Regulations 2008 (SI 2008/2439) (W.212).

the Welsh Rules: the Mental Health Review Tribunal for Wales Rules 2008 (SI 2008/2705) (L.17).

PART I

APPLICATION OF ACT

Application of Act: "mental disorder"

1–023   **1.**—(1) The provisions of this Act shall have effect with respect to the reception, care and treatment of mentally disordered patients, the management of their property and other related matters.

(2) In this Act—

["mental disorder" means any disorder or disability of the mind;

and

"mentally disordered" shall be construed accordingly;] [. . .]

and other expressions shall have the meanings assigned to them in section 145 below.

[(2A) But a person with learning disability shall not be considered by reason of that disability to be—

(a) suffering from mental disorder for the purposes of the provisions mentioned in subsection (2B) below; or

(b) requiring treatment in hospital for mental disorder for the purposes of sections 17E and 50 to 53 below,

unless that disability is associated with abnormally aggressive or seriously irresponsible conduct on his part.

(2B) The provisions are—

(a) sections 3, 7, 17A, 20 and 20A below;

(b) sections 35 to 38, 45A, 47, 48 and 51 below; and

(c) section 72(1)(b) and (c) and (4) below.]

[(3) Dependence on alcohol or drugs is not considered to be a disorder or disability of the mind for the purposes of subsection (2) above.]

[(4) In subsection (2A) above, "learning disability" means a state of arrested or incomplete development of the mind which includes significant impairment of intelligence and social functioning.]

AMENDMENTS

The amendments to this section were made by the Mental Health Act 2007 ss.1, 55, Sch.11, Pt 1.

DEFINITION

   patient: s.145(1).

   hospital: s.145(1).

1–024

GENERAL NOTE

Apart from indicating the extent of the Act, this section defines the term "mental disorder", excludes dependence on alcohol or drugs from the definition, and makes special provision for patients who have a learning disability.

1–025

Code of Practice

Guidance on the definition of mental disorder for the purposes of the Act is contained in Ch.2. Issues of particular relevance to patients with learning disabilities and autistic spectrum disorders are considered in Ch.20. Chapter 21 considers issues relating to patients with personality disorders.

1–026

Paragraph 2.4 of the *Code* states that relevant professionals "should determine whether a patient has a disorder or disability of the mind in accordance with good clinical practice and accepted standards of what constitutes such a disorder or disability".

The *Code*, at para.2.5, provides the following non-exhaustive list of "recognised conditions" which could fall within the definition:

● Affective disorders, such as depression and bipolar disorder

● Schizophrenia and delusional disorders

● Neurotic, stress-related and somatoform disorders, such as anxiety, phobic disorders, obsessive compulsive disorders, post-traumatic stress disorder and hypochondriacal disorders

- Organic mental disorders such as dementia and delirium (however caused)

- Personality and behavioural changes caused by brain injury or damage (however acquired)

- Personality disorders

- Mental and behavioural disorders caused by psychoactive substance use

- Eating disorders, non-organic sleep disorders and non-organic sexual disorders

- Learning disabilities

- Autistic spectrum disorders (including Asperger's syndrome)

- Behavioural and emotional disorders of children and young people

The definition also includes some disorders of "sexual preference" such as "paraphilias like fetishism or paedophilia" (Explanatory Notes to the 2007 Act, para.24). Paragraph 2.8 of the *Code* states:

"Difference should not be confused with disorder. No-one may be considered to be mentally disordered solely because of their political, religious or cultural beliefs, values or opinions, unless there are proper clinical grounds to believe that they are the symptoms or manifestations of a disability or disorder of the mind. The same is true of a person"s involvement, or likely involvement, in illegal, anti-social or 'immoral' behaviour. Beliefs, behaviours or actions which do not result from a disorder or disability of the mind are not a basis for compulsory measures under the Act, even if they appear unusual or cause other people alarm, distress or danger."

Human Rights Act 1998
1–027   See the cases cited in Pt 5 under "Persons of unsound mind" in art.5(1)

Subsection (1)
1–028   MANAGEMENT OF THEIR PROPERTY.   Given the repeal of Pt VII of the Act by the Mental Capacity Act 2005, this phrase is otiose.

Subsection (2)
1–029   MENTAL DISORDER.   In *R. (on the application of Khela) v Brandon Mental Health Unit* [2010] EWHC 3313 (Admin), Judge Thornton QC said that there is no remedy currently available that "enables the court to order that the diagnosis of [the responsible clinician] should be changed and corrected" (para.6).
The Mental Health Act 2007 abolished the four categories of mental disorder previously used in the Act, namely mental illness, mental impairment, psychopathic disorder and severe mental impairment. The Minister of State explained the rationale for this change:

"At present, a patient being treated under the Act often needs to be assigned to one of four separate categories of mental disorder. We wish to replace these with a simpler single definition of mental disorder under which a patient's needs and risks, not the label that happens to be applied to a person's mental disorder, determine when action is taken. This simple single definition will also make the Act easier for clinicians to use and for others to understand. This will not alter the way in which the Act deals with learning disability" (*Hansard,* HL Vol.687, col.657).

The definition of mental disorder, as substituted by the 2007 Act, is consistent with the interpretation that the European Court of Human Rights has given to the phrase "persons of unsound mind" in art.5(1)(e) of the European Convention on Human Rights (ECHR). In *Winterwerp v Netherlands* (1979) E.H.R.R. 387, para.37, the Court held that this phrase is:

"not one that can be given a definitive interpretation . . . . it is a term whose meaning is constantly evolving as research in psychiatry progresses, an increasing flexibility in treatment is developing and society's attitude to mental illness changes, in particular so that a greater understanding of the problems of mental patients is becoming wide-spread. In any event, Art.5(1)(e) obviously cannot be taken as permitting the detention of a person simply because his views or behaviour deviate from the norms prevailing in a particular society."

The definition, which is used throughout the Act, provides clinicians with a very wide discretion in identifying which conditions come within its scope. This is, perhaps, worrying given the propensity of some in the psychiatric profession to medicalise normality: see, for example, A. Horwitz and J. Wakefield, *The Loss of Sadness: How Psychiatry Transformed Normal Sorrow into Depressive Disorder* (2007) and the remarks of Longmore L.J. in *R. v Deighton*, below.

Although the two internationally recognised diagnostic manuals which are widely used by British psychiatrists, the ICD-10 (World Health Organisation) and the DSM-V (American Psychiatric Association), provide classifications of mental disorder, it "cannot be said that something that is not in any classification is not a mental disorder" (Public Bill Committee, col.16, per the Minister of State UT Judge Jacobs made reference to the use of the diagnostic manuals in *DL-H Devon Partnership NHS Trust* [2010] UKHT 102 (AAC) at para.24:

"It is important to understand the purpose for which the criteria were devised. The specific criteria in ICD-10 are labelled as diagnostic criteria *for research* and the introduction to . . . DSM-IV (4th edition) contains this warning:

'. . . In most situations, the clinical diagnosis of a DSM-IV mental disorder is not sufficient to establish the existence for legal purposes of a "mental disorder", "mental disability", "mental disease" or "mental defect".'

That leaves open the question of how a patient's mental state is to be clarified for the purposes of the Mental Health Act. The answer cannot depend on the manual that happens to be used. This is an issue that will have to be considered by the Upper Tribunal in an appropriate case. There must be an answer that provides protection for patients from vague or differing definitions while ensuring that those who present a danger are not left free to harm themselves or others for failing to meet over-prescriptive criteria."

The Explanatory Notes to the 2007 Act state at para.17:

"Disorders or disabilities of the brain are not regarded as mental disorders unless (and only to the extent that) they give rise to a disability or disorder of the mind as well."

Patients who are being treated in a general hospital can suffer from a mental disorder which requires their detention under the Act, but which does not come within the clinical experience of most psychiatrists. Dr Eleanor Feldman describes how she:

"encountered a situation where a patient had an acute and severe but reversible brain disorder, in this case limbic encephalitis, and its treatment involved steroids and other very toxic drugs used in immunotherapy. The patient was grossly disorientated and lacked mental capacity to make a decision about his treatment or the need to remain in hospital. Moreover, his behaviour was very disturbed requiring strong and prolonged measures over a matter of up to two weeks to restrain and sedate him, to administer treatment and keep him on the neurology unit." ("The use of the Mental Health Act and common law in non-consenting patients in the general hospital" (2006) Psychiatry 5(3): 107–9).

In *St George's Healthcare NHS Trust v S* [1998] 3 All E.R. 673, 696, Judge L.J. said that the court did not doubt "that reactive depression (not merely a transient sense of being 'a little down' or 'fed up with everything') is capable of amounting to a mental disorder". His Lordship also said, at 957, that a person cannot be characterised as being mentally disordered "merely because her thinking process is unusual, even apparently bizarre and irrational, and contrary to the views of the overwhelming majority of the community at large".

The difficulties of drawing a distinction between mental distress and symptoms amounting to a recognisable psychiatric illness were identified by Judge P. in *R v D* [2006] EWCA Crim 1139 at para.30:

"As the Law Commission reports [in *Liability for Psychiatric Illness,* No.249 (1998) HC 525], the distinction 'is not clear', quoting one medical consultee who suggested that the 'overlap between mental health and illness is so large a grey area that it is not suitable for the legal purpose to which the diagnosis is being put'. The classification in DSM-IV and ICD-10 were not themselves always sufficient 'to distinguish those with the greatest impairment of functioning', and several of the consultees commented that it would be unjust to relay on the criteria in these classifications to distinguish psychiatric illness from 'mere mental distress'. It was suggested that some did not 'reflect the complexities of the psychological impact of trauma', and current categorisation might exclude some diagnoses which were generally acceptable. Observations like these confirm that current understanding of the workings of the mind is less than complete".

Also of relevance in this context are Hobhouse L.J.'s observations in *R. v Chan-Fook* [1994] 2 All E.R. 552 at 559 on the decision of the Court of Appeal in *Attia v British Gas* [1988] Q.B. 304 regarding the position at civil law:

"[T]he Court of Appeal discussed whether the borderline should be drawn between on the one hand the emotions and distress and grief, and on the other hand some actual psychiatric illness such as anxiety neurosis or a reactive depression. The authorities recognise that there is a line to be drawn and whether any given case falls on one side or the other is a matter for expert evidence."

A similar approach was taken by the House of Lords in *R. v Ireland; R. v Burstow* [1997] 4 All E.R. 225 at 231, a case under the Offences against the Person Act 1861, where Lord Steyn said that neuroses "must be distinguished from simple states of fear, or problems in coping with everyday life. Where the line is to be drawn must be a matter of psychiatric judgment".

In the context of a criminal trial where the appellant claimed that he failed to appreciate what he was doing was wrong because he was suffering from "avoidant personality disorder", the Court of Appeal said that the courts should "resist the temptation to medicalise normality" (*R. v Deighton* [2005] EWCA Crim 3131 para.14 per Longmore L.J.).

In earlier times, Bowen L.J. said that "the state of a man's mind is as much a fact as the state of his digestion" (*Edgington v Fitzmaurice* (1885) 29 Ch.D 459 at 483).

MIND.   In the context of the *McNaghten* rules, which set out the test for insanity, Devlin J. said that the term "mind" should be "used in the ordinary sense of the mental faculties of reason, memory and understanding" (*R. v Kemp* [1957] 1 Q.B. 399 at 407). This statement was approved by Lord Diplock in *R. v Sullivan* [1983] 2 All E.R. 673 HL at 677. Lord Diplock's judgment in *Sullivan* suggests that if a disorder severely impairs these faculties it can be categorised as a disorder of mind, irrespective of the aetiology of the disorder.

Subsections (2A), (2B)

These subsections (which do not apply to autistic spectrum disorders (*Code of Practice*, **1–030** para.2.17)), together with subs.(4), preserve the way the Act works with regard to people with a learning disability. They provide that for certain purposes of the Act a person may not be considered to be suffering from a mental disorder simply as a result of having a learning disability: the disability must be "associated with abnormally aggressive or seriously irresponsible conduct" on the part of the person concerned. This is a matter for recommending doctors to determine.

The preservation of the status quo by the 2007 Act, which has little to commend it, serves as a monument to the effectiveness of the learning disability lobby. The Minister of State responded to an expression of puzzlement about the rationale for the approach adopted by explaining that "there has been a historic attachment to saying that learning disability should be included in the Bill in this way, and I am afraid that there is no getting away from that" (Public Bill Committee, col.43).

IS ASSOCIATED WITH.   This phrase denotes an association which may not be the result of causation (*P v Mental Health Review Tribunal and Rampton Hospital* [2001] EWHC Admin 876; [2002] M.H.L.R. 250 para.26). The association must be with the learning disability and not with an unrelated physical disorder or condition. Lord Adebowale gave the following example of a case where an association with learning disability was absent:

"Mr S, who has a severe learning difficulty, autism and communication difficulties, lives in a residential setting. He was detained under the 1983 Act because he was becoming increasingly agitated and exhibited aggressive behaviour, banging his head against a wall. It was later discovered—this is shocking but true—that Mr S had a small twig in his ear, which was causing him distress, as it would most people, and which he expressed in his agitated behaviour. This scenario shows how the distress of a person with a learning disability can be automatically attributed to a mental disorder without paying sufficient attention to physical factors. This is about not just lazy diagnosis but making false assumptions" (*Hansard,* HL Vol.668, col.66).

The *Code of Practice* states:

"20.10 It is important to establish whether a person's learning disability is associated with conduct that could be categorised as abnormally aggressive, not simply aggressive. Relevant factors when assessing this include:

- when such aggressive behaviour has been observed, and how persistent and severe it has been

- whether it has occurred without a specific trigger or seemed disproportionate to the circumstances that triggered it

- whether, and to what degree, it has resulted in harm or distress to other people, or actual damage to property

- how likely it is to recur, and

- how common similar behaviour is in the population generally.

20.11 Similarly, in assessing whether a person's learning disability is associated with conduct that is not only irresponsible but seriously irresponsible, relevant factors may include:

- whether behaviour has been observed that suggests a disregard or an inadequate regard for its serious or dangerous consequences

- how recently such behaviour has been observed and, when it has been observed, how persistent it has been

- how seriously detrimental to the individual, or to other people, the consequences of the behaviour were or might have been

- whether, and to what degree, the behaviour has actually resulted in harm to the person or the person's interests, or in harm to other people or to damage to property, and

- how likely it is to recur."

ABNORMALLY AGGRESSIVE OR SERIOUSLY IRRESPONSIBLE CONDUCT. Paragraph 20.9 of the *Code of Practice* states:

"Neither term is defined in the Act, and it is not possible to define exactly what kind of behaviour would fall into either category. Inevitably, it will depend on the nature of the behaviour and the circumstances in which it is exhibited, and also on the extent to which it gives rise to a serious risk to the health or safety of the person or others, or both."

The origin of this phrase, which is taken from the definition of psychopathy in the Mental Health Act 1959, was recounted by Lord Rix:

"These words are very familiar to me because they arrived in the 1983 Act after a long three-way process of negotiation on the telephone between the then Minister, the noble Lord Elton, myself, then in the capacity as secretary general of Mencap, and a copy of *Roget's Thesaurus*. It was the best compromise we could then reach between the Government's position that people with a learning disability should come under the scope of the Act, and my position that people with a learning disability are not ill and should not be treated as if they were" (*Hansard*, HL Vol.687, col.662).

What is "abnormally aggressive" or "irresponsible conduct" must, to a certain extent, depend upon the cultural and social context within which the behaviour occurs. The terms must mean more than merely bizarre or unusual behaviour (*Code of Practice*, para.20.12). In *R. v Trent Mental Health Review Tribunal Ex p. Ryan* [1992] C.O.D. 157, Nolan L.J. said:

"No doubt whether the conduct is the result of the disorder . . . is a medical question. Whether it amounts to seriously irresponsible or abnormally aggressive behaviour seems to me . . . to raise questions other than of a purely clinical nature".

In *Re F (Mental Health Act: Guardianship)* [2000] 1 F.L.R. 192, the Court of Appeal adopted a restrictive construction of the phrase "seriously irresponsible conduct" by holding that a 17-year-old patient's natural desires to return home, albeit to an inadequate home where she had been exposed to chronic neglect and possible sexual exploitation, could not be categorised as irresponsible conduct. Thorpe L.J. said at 198:

"The urge to return [home] is almost universal . . . The deficiencies of the home are more apparent to other adults than to the young who have known no other. Furthermore, any measure of irresponsibility must depend on an evaluation of the consequences of return . . . Clearly each case must depend on its particular facts and we would not wish to be taken as offering any general guideline."

Although his Lordship emphasised that the court had reached its conclusions "on the special facts of a difficult and unusual case", the court's finding is significant because the urge to return home is not the only "almost universal" urge that might affect a patient. The desire to be member of a family group would also fall into this category. When determining whether a person's conduct falls into the category of "seriously irresponsible conduct", the clinician should pay special attention to the consequences of the conduct (or potential conduct) for the person and/or others. The clinician should refrain from categorising conduct as being seriously irresponsible in the absence of a clear opinion based on reliable evidence that the conduct is either likely to result or pose a significant risk to the person's health or safety or to the health or safety of others. It is doubtful whether the term "conduct" covers the passive endurance by a patient of the irresponsible behaviour of others.

In *Newham LBC v BS* [2003] EWHC 1909 (Fam), Wall J. applied *Re F* and held, rather surprisingly, that a person's total lack of road sense and a tendency to rush into the road without looking did not amount to "seriously irresponsible conduct". However, in *GC v Managers of the Kingswood Centre of Central and North West London NHS Foundation Trust* (CO/7784/2008) King J. said that it is not arguable that the *Newham* decision sets down a general proposition of law that a tendency to rush into the road could never amount to seriously irresponsible conduct. This case concerned a patient with obsessive compulsive disorder which manifested itself as a compulsion to pick up litter, even if that litter was in the road. The patient had been knocked down by vehicles but considered himself invincible. His Lordship held that the hospital managers were entitled to conclude that such conduct could be categorised as being "seriously irresponsible". I am grateful to Alexander Ruck Keene, barrister, for drawing my attention to this case.

There is no requirement for the person to be *currently* engaging in abnormally aggressive or seriously irresponsible conduct. It is enough that the learning disability caused such conduct in the past and that there is a real risk that, if treatment in hospital is discontinued, it will do so in the future: see *Lewis v Gibson* [2005] EWCA Civ 587; [2005] M.H.L.R. 309, where Thorpe L.J. said at para.31:

"To make a balanced assessment of the patient's present state some regard must be had to the past history and the future propensity. A conclusion based only on the recent past, which might represent a transient phase of quiescence, would be superficial."

The conduct need not have occurred in the recent past: see *R. (on the application of P) v Mental Health Review Tribunal for the East Midlands and North East Regions* [2002] EWCA Civ 697, a case where the conduct had not been exhibited by the patient for several years. Although this case involved a patient who was suffering from a psychopathic disorder, the same terminology that appears in this provision was considered by the court.

Subsection (3)

This provision prevents a dependence on alcohol or drugs alone from being treated as a **1–031** mental disorder for the purposes of the Act. In some respects this is an odd exclusion because alcohol and drug dependency are treatable mental disorders, and such dependency may be a ground for detention under art.5(1)(e) of the ECHR. The rationale for the exclusion as contained in the Mental Health (Amendment) Act 1982 was explained by the Government in Cmnd 7320 at para.1.29:

"Government advisory bodies have . . . pointed out that that it is incompatible with current thinking on the nature of drug dependence and drinking problems to regard them as mental disorders. These conditions are increasingly seen as social and behavioural problems, manifested in varying degrees of habit and dependency. However it is recognised that alcohol or drug dependency can be associated with certain forms of mental disorder."

The exclusion does not prevent a person being categorised as mentally disordered if, as well as being dependent on alcohol or drugs, he is suffering from:

(i) an unrelated mental disorder, or

(ii) a mental disorder which arises from, or is suspected to arise from, alcohol or drug dependence or from the withdrawal of alcohol or drugs (*Secretary of State for Justice v MP* [2013] UKUT 025 (AAC) at para.15).

Therefore a person who is suffering from a drug or alcohol induced psychosis or from delirium associated with alcohol withdrawal would not be excluded by this provision. It is also the case that a person's alcohol or drug dependency could be treated under the authority of s.63 if the dependency is categorised as being a consequence of the patient's diagnosed mental disorder, is interfering with the treatment of the disorder, or is exacerbating the symptoms of the disorder (*B v Croydon Health Authority* [1995] 1 All E.R. 683 CA). However, detention is not lawful if its sole purpose is to address the patient's drug taking and chaotic lifestyle (*CM v Derbyshire Healthcare NHS Foundation Trust* [2011] UKUT 129 (AAC); [2011] M.H.L.R. 153). A person who is not dependent on alcohol or drugs but who is acutely intoxicated following the administration of alcohol or drugs would not be excluded from the definition of mental disorder by this provision.

In his "Review of Homicides by Patients with Severe Mental Illness" (March 2006), Professor Tony Maden states at p.63:

"Substance misuse in the context of serious mental illness and violence may greatly increase risk, yet there is little sign within [the cases studied] of it being considered as an indication for use of compulsory powers. The 1983 Act does not allow detention for substance use alone but it is an important indicator of the nature and extent of mental illness, and the associated risk to others, so it should be included in any assessment for possible detention."

DRUGS. This term includes medicines and illicit drugs and "may be taken to include solvents and similar substances with a psychoactive effect" (*Code of Practice*, para.2.10).

Subsection (4)

1–032   This provision defines "learning disability" for the purposes of subs.(2A). The definition requires an impairment of both intelligence *and* social functioning (*R. v McDonagh* [2008] NICA 6; [2008] M.H.L.R. 219 (CA, Northern Ireland)). Guidance on the definition is given in Ch.20 of the *Code of Practice*.

ARRESTED OR INCOMPLETE DEVELOPMENT OF MIND.   This phrase excludes persons whose learning disability derives from accident, injury or illness occurring after the mind has fully developed. Although examining the relationship between the mind and the brain is beyond the scope of this Manual, it is instructive to note that in *N McM v Secretary of State for Work and Pensions (DLA)* [2014] UKUT 0312, UT Judge Wikeley, on interpreting the phrase "a state of arrested development or incomplete physical development of the brain" for the purposes of the social security legislation, accepted the evidence of Professor Sarah-Jayne Blakemore that neuroscience research carried out in the past 15 years "indicates that the human brain undergoes protracted development until at least the third decade of life" and that "the brain will have ceased developing, in terms of experience-expectant changes in grey matter and white matter, by the thirties or early forties in most people" (para.31). Professor Blakemore also advised that "the phrase 'arrested development' is 'arguably unhelpful and misleading' and so is not commonly used either clinically or in neuroscience these days, as it implies that no recovery of function can take place" (para.48).

INCLUDES.   What follows is not an exclusive list of attributes associated with the disability.

SIGNIFICANT IMPAIRMENT.   Whether the impairment is considered to be "significant" is a matter for clinical judgment. In *Meggary v Chief Adjudications Officer, The Times,* November 11, 1999, the Court of Appeal held that a high IQ was not conclusive in determining the existence of a "severe impairment of intelligence and social functioning" for the purposes of determining an autistic child's entitlement to disability living allowance. Simon Brown L.J. said:

"In most cases, no doubt, the measurement of IQ will be the best available method of measuring intelligence. But among the dictionary definitions of intelligence one finds the reference not merely to the functions of understanding and intellect but also to the qualities of insight and sagacity. It seems to me that in the case if an autistic child those qualities may well be lacking and to the extent that they are there will be a functional impairment which overlaps both limbs of the regulation, i.e. both intelligence and social functioning".

The significance of the impairment must be measured against the standard of normal persons, not other people with learning disabilities (*R. v Hall (John Hamilton)* (1998) 86 Cr. App. R. 159).

PART II

COMPULSORY ADMISSION TO HOSPITAL AND GUARDIANSHIP

GENERAL NOTE

The principles that underpin this Part were identified by Sir Thomas Bingham M.R. in **1–033** the following extract from his judgment in *Re S-C (Mental Patient: Habeas Corpus)* [1996] 1 All E.R. 532 CA at 534, 535:

"[N]o adult citizen of the United Kingdom is liable to be confined in any institution against his will, save by the authority of law. That is a fundamental constitutional principle, traceable back to Ch.29 of Magna Carta 1297 (25 Edw. 1 c. 1), and before that to Ch.39 of Magna Carta (1215). There are, of course, situations in which the law sanctions detention. The most obvious is in the case of those suspected or convicted of crime. Powers then exist to arrest and detain. But the conditions in which those powers may be exercised are very closely prescribed by statute and the common law.... [Mental patients] present a special problem since they may be liable, as a result of mental illness, to cause injury either to themselves or to others. But the very illness which is the source of the danger may deprive the sufferer of the insight necessary to ensure access to proper medical care, whether the proper medical care consists of assessment or treatment, and, if treatment, whether in-patient or out-patient treatment.

Powers therefore exist to ensure that those who suffer from mental illness may, in appropriate circumstances, be involuntarily admitted to mental hospitals and detained. But, and it is a very important but, the circumstances in which the mentally ill may be detained are very carefully prescribed by statute. Action may only be taken if there is clear evidence that the medical condition of a patient justifies such action, and there are detailed rules prescribing the classes of person who may apply to a hospital to admit and detain a mentally disordered person. The legislation recognises that action may be necessary at short notice and also recognises that it will be impracticable for a hospital to investigate the background facts to ensure that all the requirements of the Act are satisfied if they appear to be so. Thus we find in the statute a panoply of powers combined with detailed safeguards for the protection of the patient."

In *St George's Healthcare NHS Trust v S* [1998] 3 All E.R. 673, the Court of Appeal held that the Act cannot be deployed to achieve the detention of individuals against their will merely because their thinking process is unusual, even apparently bizarre and irrational, and contrary to the views of the overwhelming majority of the community at large. It could only be used to justify the detention of a mentally disordered person who fell within the prescribed conditions.

A patient who is detained under the Act retains all civil rights which are not taken away expressly or by necessary implication by his detention (*Raymond v Honey* [1982] 1 All E.R. 756 HL).

A child can be detained under this Part. Section 25 of the Children Act 1989, which sets restrictions on the use of secure accommodation for children, does not apply to a child who is detained under any provision of the Act (Children (Secure Accommodation) Regulations 1991 (SI 1991/1505) reg.5).

In the "Report by the Committee for Privileges on Parliamentary Privilege and the Mental Health Act" June 18, 1984, HL (254), the Committee for Privileges was of the view that the provisions of the Act override any previously existing privilege of Parliament or peerage so far as it conflicts with the liability of mentally disordered peers to compulsory detention in hospital under ss.2 to 6.

Powers, other than those contained in the Act, that are available to individuals to control and detain patients are set out in Appendix A.

The detention of compliant mentally incapable patients

1–034   The *Code of Practice* is incorrect when it states that a "person with a learning disability or autism cannot be informally admitted [to hospital] if they do not have capacity to consent to or refuse that admission and treatment" (para.20.30). The correct legal position is that the informal admission to hospital and the subsequent medical treatment of any compliant mentally incapacitated patient can be provided under the Mental Capacity Act 2005 (MCA) if he is not being deprived of his liberty in the hospital. An assessment should be undertaken if it is thought that a patient is being deprived of his liberty because a failure either to detain the patient under this Act or to authorise the deprivation under Sch.A1 of the MCA if the patient is being deprived of his liberty would violate the patient's right under art.5 of the European Convention on Human Rights (*HL v United Kingdom* (2005) 40 E.H.R.R. 32; [2004] M.H.L.R. 236). The nature of a deprivation of liberty is considered in Part 6.

In *AM v South London & Maudsley NHS Foundation Trust* [2013] UKUT 365 (AAC); [2014] M.H.L.R. 181, para.34, Charles J. held that with regard to a compliant mentally incapacitated patient who needs to be detained in hospital, decision-makers have to consider whether the patient should be detained under this Act, or whether the assessment or treatment in the proposed circumstances should be founded on the MCA and any deprivation of liberty it involves should be authorised under the deprivation of liberty safeguards (DOLS). His Lordship said that to do that, the decision-makers have to consider whether the MCA and DOLS alternative are applicable and available and, if so, whether and when they should be used. In making their decision, the decision-makers have to consider which alternative best achieves the objective of ensuring the patient's assessment or treatment in the least restrictive way. *AM* is further considered in Part 6.

The *Code of Practice* offers guidance on the choice of legal regime at paras 13.58 and 13.59. Although the *Code* states that decision-makers "should not . . . proceed on the basis that one regime generally provides greater safeguards than the other", it advises decision-makers "to exercise their professional judgement in determining which safeguards are more likely to best protect the interests of the patient in the particular circumstances of each individual case". This guidance is not particularly helpful given that the safeguards contained in the two regimes apply to all patients who are subject to the regime in question regardless of the "particular circumstances" of the case. It is therefore difficult to identify from the *Code* which criteria decision-makers should adopt when deciding between the two regimes. Decision-makers could address the question of the choice of regime as follows:

1. As both detention under this Act and an authorisation under the DOL safeguards have the same effect of sanctioning the deprivation of a person's liberty, it is not possible to claim that one regime is less restrictive than the other.

2. From the patient's perspective, the restrictions placed on him by the care plan will be of particular importance. Those restrictions will be the same whichever statutory regime is being used to implement the restrictions.

3. The only variable is the safeguards that are provided under both regimes. Decision-makers are likely to consider that the safeguards provided to the patient by this Act, in particular access to a tribunal and the consent to treatment provisions, offer far greater protection to the patient than those provided by the DOL regime.

Although such an approach is consistent with the statement in the *Code* that decision-makers should take into account "which safeguards are more likely to best protect the interests of the patient" (para.13.59), it is unlikely to have been in the minds of either Charles J. or the authors of the *Code* as it would inevitably lead to the decision-makers opting to use this Act. Having said that, it is difficult to identify an alternative principled approach that decision-makers could use to identify the "the least restrictive way" in the particular circumstances of each individual case. Perhaps all that can be said is that decision-makers should exercise their professional judgment in a pragmatic manner which takes into account: (i) the patient's best interests; (ii) the comparative impact of the two regimes on the patient; (iii) whether the patient's capacity is fluctuating; and (iv) the likelihood of the patient's continuing compliance: see *AM* at para.73.

The *Code's* guidance on "Detention under the Act or deprivation of liberty under a DoLS authorisation?" is reproduced in Part 4. Paragraph 13.69 of the *Code* states:

"In the rare cases where neither the Act nor a DoLS authorisation nor a Court of Protection order is appropriate, then to avoid an unlawful deprivation of liberty it may be necessary to make an application to the High Court to use its inherent jurisdiction to authorise the deprivation of liberty."

The power to control the activities of detained patients
See the notes on s.139 under this heading.   **1–035**

Procedure for Hospital Admission

Admission for assessment

    2.—(1) A patient may be admitted to a hospital and detained there for the period **1–036** allowed by subsection (4) below in pursuance of an application (in this Act referred to as "an application for admission for assessment") made in accordance with subsections (2) and (3) below.

    (2) An application for admission for assessment may be made in respect of a patient on the grounds that—

    (a) he is suffering from mental disorder of a nature or degree which warrants the detention of the patient in a hospital for assessment (or for assessment followed by medical treatment) for at least a limited period; and

    (b) he ought to be so detained in the interests of his own health or safety or with a view to the protection of other persons.

    (3) An application for admission for assessment shall be founded on the written recommendations in the prescribed form of two registered medical practitioners, including in each case a statement that in the opinion of the practitioner the conditions set out in subsection (2) above are complied with.

    (4) Subject to the provisions of section 29(4) below, a patient admitted to hospital in pursuance of an application for admission for assessment may be detained for a period not exceeding 28 days beginning with the day on which he is admitted, but shall not be detained after the expiration of that period unless before it has

expired he has become liable to be detained by virtue of a subsequent application, order or direction under the following provisions of this Act.

DEFINITIONS
1–037   patient: s.145(1).
hospital: ss.34(2), 145(1).
mental disorder: ss.1, 145(1).
medical treatment: s.145(1), (4).

GENERAL NOTE
1–038   This section authorises the compulsory admission of a patient to hospital for assessment (or for assessment followed by medical treatment), and for detention for this purpose for up to 28 days. Contrary to the assumption made by UT Judge Jacobs in *MS v North East London Foundation Trust* [2013] UKUT 92 (AAC); [2013] M.H.L.R. 158, at para.9, its effect is not confined to proving professionals with a power to assess the patient. Given the very wide definition of "medical treatment" in s.145(1), the treatment of the patient, which need not be confined to treatment which is an inherent part of the assessment process, will commence on his admission. If, after 28 days have elapsed the patient is to remain in hospital, he must do so either as an informal patient or be detained for treatment under s.3 if the conditions of that section are satisfied. It is not possible to use the holding powers contained in s.5 to extend the 28 day period (see the *Williamson* case, below). Patients detained under this section are subject to the consent to treatment provisions contained in Pt IV (s.56(3)). Admission under this section is unlawful if the patient is immediately granted leave of absence under s.17: see the note on "detained there" in subs.(1).

In *R. (on the application of Sessay) v South London and Maudsley NHS Foundation Trust)* [2011] EWHC 2617 (QB); [2012] M.H.L.R. 94, the Divisional Court held that the Act provides a complete statutory code for the detention on non-compliant mentally incapacitated patients and that the common law doctrine of necessity does not apply during the period when a patient is being assessed for detention under the Act. However, the court said at para.57:

"[I]n our view it is unlikely in the ordinary case that there will be a false imprisonment at common law or deprivation of liberty for the purposes of Article 5(1) [of the European Convention on Human Rights] if there is no undue delay during the processing of an application under ss.2 or 4 MHA for admission."

It is therefore the case that if, following an assessment of the patient, the potential applicant and recommending doctors agree that an application to detain the patient should be made, the common law provides authority to use restraint on the patient during the time that it takes to process the application as long as the process is not unduly delayed. Common law powers are discussed in Appendix A.

In *R. v Wilson Ex p. Williamson* [1996] C.O.D. 42, Tucker J. held that an application made under this section:

"is only intended to be of short duration for a limited purpose—assessment of the patient's condition with a view to ascertaining whether it is a case which would respond to treatment, and whether an [application] under s.3 would be appropriate. It was intended that the assessment should take place within 28 days, without any extension of time unless it was necessary for the purpose of replacing the nearest relative. Although there is nothing to suggest that s.2 is a once and for all procedure, there is nothing in the Act which justifies successive or back to back, applications under this section. . . . The powers under s.2 can only be used for the limited purpose for which they were intended, and cannot be utilised for the purpose of further detaining a patient for the purposes of assessment beyond the 28-day period, or used as a stop-gap procedure."

The *Williamson* case provides authority for the proposition that an application under s.2 cannot be used for an improper purpose. Tucker J. identified two examples of such a purpose: (1) using a second application under s.2 in order to extend the 28-day assessment period (subs.(4) prevents a second application being made under this section during the currency of an existing section); and (2) using an application under s.2 as a "stop-gap" procedure in circumstances where it is not possible to proceed with a s.3 application because of a nearest relative objection (see s.11(4)). The fact that a second use of s.2 was involved in the *Williamson* case is not relevant to (2) as the rationale for finding the use of the section to be improper is that those who had made the decision to use s.3 must have reached the conclusion that the patient does not require detention for assessment. In *C v South London and Maudsley Hospital National Health Service Trust* [2001] M.H.L.R. 269, McCombe J., on refusing an application for leave under s.139, said that an application under this section could be made "where at least one of the doctors may have thought informally that s.3 admission might in the long run be desirable". In this case, a preliminary decision was made to admit the patient under s.3 but this was aborted when the approved social worker (now the approved mental health professional (AMHP)) reported that the patient's nearest relative would object to the application. An application under this section was made three days later by a different approved social worker, who "may well have known" that an application under s.3 would not be possible. This application was supported by a medical recommendation from one of the doctors who had made the original decision to proceed under s.3. It is clear from the judgment in this case that the McCombe J. considered that the fact that medical recommendations had not been made to support a possible application under s.3 was of particular significance: also see the note on "Section 2 or section 3 as the initial detaining section?", below.

An application for a second s.2 can be made if a significant change in the patient's situation can be said to justify the need for a reassessment. For example, a patient is detained under s.2 in city A, is discharged, and then moves to city B where his mental health deteriorates to the extent that he is subject to a second application under s.2. In these circumstances the second s.2 could be in close proximity to the first s.2.

An application under this section should be the usual method of detaining a patient who requires to be assessed. An emergency application under s.4 should only be used where the need for the patient's admission is so urgent that it is not practicable to obtain the second medical recommendation that is required for an admission under this section.

An order for the patient's discharge from this section can be made at any time prior to the expiration of the 28-day period by his responsible clinician, the hospital managers or, subject to s.25, his nearest relative (s.23(2)(a)). A discharge cannot be effected by implication, e.g. by an assessment for detention under s.3 concluding that the patient should not be detained under that section.

An AMHP may not lawfully apply for the admission of a patient whose discharge has been ordered by the decision of the First-tier Tribunal or the Mental Health Review for Wales of which the AMHP is aware unless the AMHP has formed a reasonable and bona fide opinion that she has information not known to the tribunal which puts a significantly different complexion on the case as compared with that which was before the tribunal: see *R. v East London and City Mental Health NHS Trust Ex p. Brandenburg* [2003] UKHL 58; [2004] 1 All E.R. 400, which is considered in the General Note to s.3 under the heading "The detention of a patient subsequent to a discharge by the First-tier Tribunal (Mental Health) or the Mental Health Review Tribunal for Wales".

There is nothing to prevent a patient who has been detained under this section from being arrested in respect of a criminal offence.

The detention of compliant mentally incapable patients

1–039   The question of whether such patients should be detained under this Act or be made the subject of a deprivation of liberty authorisation under the Mental Capacity Act 2005 is considered in the General Note to this Part under this heading.

Human Rights Act 1998

1–040   See the note on s.3 under this heading.

In *MH v United Kingdom* (2014) 58 E.H.R.R. 965, the European Court of Human Rights held that the failure to provide the means for a mentally incapacitated patient to bring proceedings to challenge a detention under this section constituted a violation of art.5(4) of the European Convention on Human Rights: see the General Note to s.68 under this heading.

Section 2 or section 3 as the initial detaining section?

1–041   The responsibility for deciding which section to use is that of the applicant: "It is the [AMHP] who makes the application, not the doctors" (*R. v East London and the City Mental Health Trust Ex p. Brandenburg* [2003] UKHL 58, per Lord Bingham at para.12). The role of the recommending doctors is to support the application which is "founded" on the recommendations (s.11(7)).

The advice contained in the 1999 edition of the *Code of Practice* was frequently interpreted as requiring s.3 to be used as the initial detaining section for patients who are "well known" to the mental health service and who have a care plan. This interpretation was reinforced by concern expressed by the Mental Health Commission over the "misuse" of s.2 where s.3 would have been more appropriate to admit such patients (see, for example, para.3.1 of the MHAC's Sixth Biennial Report, 1993–1995) and the widely held, but totally erroneous view expressed by some practitioners that treatment under Pt IV cannot be given to patients detained under s.2. The MHAC subsequently modified its view on this issue and became supportive of the approach adopted here: see para.4.39 of the MHAC's *Twelfth Biennial Report*, 2005–2007. The question of whether s.2 or s.3 should be used to admit a patient is considered in the current edition of the *Code of Practice* at paras 14.26–14.29.

This Part of the Act provides two routes which can be used to detain and treat patients: s.2 which provides for the assessment and treatment of patients for a non-renewable period of up to 28 days, and s.3 which provides for the patient's detention and treatment for a potentially unlimited period. A patient whose current mental health and circumstances require him to be subject to the very significant procedure of compulsory detention surely needs to be assessed however well known he might be to the mental health service. Something has happened in that patient's life to justify intervention under the Act and it is the factors that precipitated the detention and their impact on the patient that need to be assessed. The extent of any prior knowledge that might exist about the patient does not deflect from the need to assess the patient's *current* situation. When a patient is admitted to hospital for treatment for a physical disorder, he is subject to an assessment on admission even if he has had multiple previous admissions. Why should a patient who is admitted for treatment for a mental disorder be treated differently? This strongly suggests that the intention of Parliament was for s.2 to be used as the initial section to detain patients because that section specifically provides for the patient's assessment, and that an application under s.3 be made if the assessment leads the clinical team to conclude that the patient needs a further period of treatment whilst being detained. In any event, practitioners' choice of section should be guided by the "least restrictive option and maximising independence" principle which is set out at paras.1.2–1.6 of the *Code of Practice*. Other factors which support the approach advocated here are:

> (i)   the fact that s.3(2)(c) states that an application under s.3 should be made if the necessary treatment can *only* be provided under that section suggests that such an application should not be made unless the patient has been assessed under s.2 as needing treatment under detained powers for a period longer than 28 days. This is because both sections provide clinicians with identical powers to treat the patient;

(ii) the finding of Tucker J. in *R. v Wilson Ex p. Williamson*, above, that one of the purposes of s.2 is to ascertain whether an application under s.3 would be appropriate;

(iii) dicta in a number of cases where the judges have assumed that s.2 can be used to admit a well known patient; see for example, *R. v Bournewood Community and Mental Health NHS Trust Ex p. L* [1998] 1 All E.R. 634,641, CA, where Lord Woolf M.R. said that it would have been possible to use s.2 to admit the patient who had been in very close contact with the mental health services for most of his life, and *R. v East London and City Mental Health NHS Trust Ex p. Brandenburg,* above, where the Court of Appeal assumed that it could be appropriate to detain a patient under s.2 subsequent to his discharge by a tribunal;

(iv) section 29(4) allows for the extension of the patient's detention under s.2 if a displacement application is made to the county court before the s.2 expires on the ground that the patient's nearest relative has "unreasonably objected" to a s.3 application being made. This provision, and the absence of any equivalent remedy to an applicant who uses s.3 as an initial detaining section and is then faced with an objection from the nearest relative, is a clear indication that the Act was drafted on the assumption that an application under s.2 would precede an application under s.3; and

(v) the fact that it is not possible to convert an application under s.4 into an application under s.3 in respect of a well known patient (see s.4(4)).

Those who advocate the use of s.3 as the initial detaining section for patients who are already well known to the mental health service fail to identify the action that an AMHP applicant should take when faced with a s.11(4) objection made by the nearest relative of a patient who has been assessed as being either actively suicidal, as posing an immediate and serious risk to the safety of others, or at risk of a serious and imminent deterioraton of his mental health. An application under s.2 cannot be made in these circumstances (see the *Williamson* case, above) and although the AMHP would have the option of applying to the county court under s.29 for an interim order displacing the nearest relative on the ground that the objection was unreasonable, the granting of the order may be too late to avoid catastrophic consequences for the patient and/or others. The *Code of Practice* does not offer any guidance on how an AMHP should act in such a situation.

The deteriorating patient
See the note under this heading in the General Note to s.3.   **1–042**

Applications to the First-tier Tribunal (Mental Health) or the Mental Health Review Tribunal for Wales
The patient may make an application within 14 days of his admission under this section **1–043** (s.66(1)(a), (2)(a)). Also see the note on the Human Rights Act 1998, above.
If a nearest relative's discharge of the patient from detention under this section is barred by the patient's responsible clinician by using her power under s.25, the nearest relative does not acquire a right to apply to the tribunal.

Code of Practice
The roles of mental health professionals when undertaking assessments that might lead **1–044** to an application for admission to hospital and the criteria for detention under this section are considered in Ch.14. Conflicts of interests that might arise in the assessment process are considered in Ch.39. Guidance on the transport of patients can be found in Ch.17.

Subsection (1)
An application under this section can be made by either the patient's nearest relative or **1–045** by an AMHP (s.11(1)). The applicant must use Form AI (for NRs) or Form A2 (for AMHPS) (in Wales, Form H01 (for NRs) or Form H02 (for AMPS)): see reg.4(1) of the

English and Welsh Regulations. The application will be addressed to the managers of the hospital to which admission is sought (s.11(2)). If the applicant is an AMHP, she must inform the patient's nearest relative that the application either is to be or has been made (s.11(3)). The nearest relative cannot prevent an AMHP making an application. In deciding whether to make an application, an AMHP is required to have regard to any wishes expressed by relatives of the patient (s.13(1)). This does not mean that the AMHP is placed under a legal obligation to consult with the patient's relatives before she makes an application. The applicant must have seen the patient within the previous 14 days (s.11(5)) and an AMHP applicant must interview the patient before the application is made (s.13(2)). The patient has to be admitted to hospital within 14 days of the time when he was last medically examined prior to the recommendations required by subs.(3) being made (s.6(1)(a)). It is possible to make an application in respect of a person who is already receiving hospital treatment as an in-patient on an informal basis (s.5(1)). An application for the admission of a ward of court cannot be made without the leave of the High Court (s.33(1)).

The effect of an application for admission for assessment is set out in s.6. The hospital named in the application is not placed under a legal obligation to admit the patient: see the note on "to hospital" in s.6(1).

DETAINED THERE. The patient can be granted leave of absence from the detaining hospital under s.17, but only after the patient has received a period of in-patient treatment at that hospital: see the *Hallstrom* case noted in the General Note to s.3. Making an application in respect of a patient where the intention is to grant the patient immediate leave of absence to enable the patient to be treated at another hospital is unlawful because the application provides authority for the patient to be detained in the hospital named in the application (see s.6(2)), which is where the initial assessment must take place. Also note the use of the term "there" in this provision.

Subsection (2)

1–046   Although informal admission should be the preferred mode of admission, compulsion should be used on a patient who is willing to be admitted informally if its absence would place the patient's safety and/or the safety of others at risk: see the General Note to s.131.

Paragraph (a)

1–047   IS SUFFERING.   A patient whose symptoms of mental disorder are being controlled by medication still suffers from that disorder: see the note on "The deteriorating patient" in the General Note to s.3.

In *R. v Kirklees MBC Ex p. C* [1993] 2 F.L.R. 187 CA, Lloyd L.J., speaking obiter, said at 190 that:

"having regard to the definition of patient in s.145 there is, in my view, power to admit a patient for assessment under s.2, if he or she appears to be suffering from mental disorder, on the ground that he or she is so suffering, even though it turns out on assessment that [he or] she is not. Any other construction would unnecessarily emasculate the beneficial power under s.2 and confine asessment to choice of treatment."

This approach was confirmed in *St George's Healthcare NHS Trust v S* [1998] 3 All E.R. 673, where the Court of Appeal held that the identification of the presence of mental disorder for the purposes of this section cannot be a final concluded diagnosis; the final diagnosis may or may not confirm that provisional view.

MENTAL DISORDER.   There is no requirement for a diagnosis of the nature of the patient's mental disorder to have been made (*JP v South London and Maudsley NHS Foundation Trust* [2012] UKUT 486 (AAC); [2013] M.H.L.R. 148, para.13).

Unlike the position under s.3, it is possible for a learning disabled person whose condition is not associated with "abnormally aggressive or seriously irresponsible conduct" to be the subject of an application under this section.

NATURE OR DEGREE.   The meaning of this phrase is considered in the note on s.3(2)(a).

WHICH WARRANTS THE DETENTION OF THE PATIENT IN A HOSPITAL.   This requirement assumes that an initial assessment has concluded that the patient's need for assessment and treatment cannot be met without recourse to this section: see further para.14.7 of the *Code of Practice* and *AM v South London & Maudsley NHS Foundation Trust*, which is noted in the General Note to this Part. The patient must need a period of detention as a hospital *in-patient*: see the note on "detained there", above. The detention must be related to or linked with the patient's mental disorder; the patient's need for treatment for an unrelated physical disorder does not provide the necessary warrant (*St George's Healthcare NHS Trust v S*, above). In the *St George's* case, the Court of Appeal declared an admission under this section to be unlawful because the grounds prescribed in this paragraph were not established. Judge L.J. said at 697:

"The contemporaneous documents themselves demonstrate that those involved in the decision to make an application for admission failed to maintain the distinction between the urgent need of [the patient] for treatment arising from her pregnancy, and the separate question whether her mental disorder (in the form of depression) warranted her detention in hospital. From the reasoning to be found in them, the conclusion that the detention was believed to be warranted in order that adequate provision could be made to deal with [the patient's] pregnancy and the safety of her unborn child is unavoidable."

ASSESSMENT.   The patient's detention under this section does not automatically lapse on the completion of the assessment because: (1) the authority to detain can only end either on the expiration of the 28-day period, an order of discharge being made by a tribunal, or an order for discharge being made under s.23; and (2) this section authorises the detention of the patient for assessment "or for assessment followed by medical treatment".

Paragraph (b)
There is no requirement for the two recommending doctors to agree on the nature of the **1–048** risk justifying detention under this section.

HEALTH.   See para.14.9 of the *Code of Practice*. The patient's mental as well as physical health is covered by this term. This interpretation was adopted by the Mental Health Act Commission in its *Second Biennial Report*, 1985–1987, at para.11.3. The opinion that is sometimes heard from practitioners that an application under this section can only be made if the patient is either a danger to himself or others or is engaging in seriously disruptive behaviour is incorrect. Also see the note on "the deteriorating patient" in the General Note to s.3.
In *Pleso v Hungary* [2014] M.H.L. 72, para.66, the European Court of Human Rights said:

"The Court is of the view that where, as in this case, the issue is not whether there is an imminent danger to the person's health but rather whether medical treatment would improve his condition or the absence of such treatment would lead to a deterioration in that condition, it is incumbent on the authorities to strike a fair balance between the competing interests emanating, on the one hand, from society's responsibility to secure the best possible health care for those with diminished faculties (for example, because of lack of insight into their condition) and, on the other hand, from the individual's inalienable right to self-determination (including the right to refusal of hospitalisation or medical treatment, that is, his or her 'right to be ill'). In other words, it is imperative to apply the principle of proportionality inherent in the structure of the provisions enshrining those Convention rights that are susceptible to restrictions."

SAFETY.   See para.14.9 of the *Code of Practice*. With the patient being exposed to the risk of being harmed, either through his own acts or omissions or through the acts or omissions of others.

Predicting risk of suicide is extremely problematic, even for patients who are considered to be at high risk of suicide: see the research examined by M. Rahman and N. Wolferstan in "A human right to be detained? Mental healthcare after 'Savage' and 'Rabone'", *The Psychiatrist* (2013), 37, 294–296.

PROTECTION OF OTHER PERSONS.   See para.14.10 of the *Code of Practice* and the note on s.72(1)(b)(ii) under this heading.

In *R. v North West London Mental Health NHS Trust Ex p. Stewart* (1996) 39 B.M.L.R. 105, Harrison J. said:

"The protection of 'other persons' does not necessarily mean the public at large because it could simply relate to an individual person or persons rather than to the public at large, nor is there the requirement that such persons should be protected 'from serious harm.'"

Although the matter is not free from doubt, it is likely that this phrase covers both protection from physical harm and protection from serious emotional harm. The *Code of Practice*, at para.14.10, states that harm includes psychological harm. The protection of the mental health of the main carer of the patient could therefore be the predominant trigger for "sectioning" the patient.

Even though this provision does not make explicit reference to the protection of a person's property, actual or threatened damage to a person's property could cause that person serious emotional harm.

Although an unborn child is not a "person" in need of protection (*The Attorney General's Reference (No.3 of 1994)* [1998] A.C. 245 at p.254), the "health or safety" of the potential mother can be assessed on the basis that she is heavily pregnant: see *St George's Healthcare NHS Trust v S*, above, where Judge L.J. said at 696:

"Those responsible have to deal in realities, and [the patient] was dangerously ill [with pre-eclampsia]. Although the risks were caused by her pregnancy, the potential damage could have fallen within s.2(2)(b)."

It is therefore permissible to detain a pregnant patient whose mental disorder requires assessment in circumstances where a major concern is the likely impact on the mother's physical and/or mental health of an unsupervised birth. Also see the note on "Human Rights Act 1998" in s.3.

Subsection (3)

1–049   FOUNDED ON.   The medical recommendations, which may be made either separately or jointly, should be perused by the applicant before the application is signed. They must comply with the provisions of s.12 and the regulations made under s.12A. A medical recommendation which is signed after the date of the application is invalid; also see the note on "on or before the date of the application" in s.12(1)).

The fact that an application has had to be aborted because, for example, the offer of a bed at the hospital named in the application has been withdrawn does not effect the validity of the medical recommendations that were made in support of the application. As long as the time limit set out in s.6(1)(a) is not contravened, the medical recommendations can be used to support a fresh application addressed to a different hospital.

Subsection (4)

NOT EXCEEDING 28 DAYS.   The 28-day period can be extended if an application is made **1–050**
to the county court on specified grounds for an acting nearest relative to be appointed
(s.29(4)) or if the patient has gone absent without leave and has been returned to the hospital before the section expires (see the note on "a patient" in s.21(1)).

BEGINNING WITH.   The day on which the patient was admitted is counted as the first day
when calculating the 28 day period (*Zoan v Rouamba* [2000] 2 All E.R. 620 CA). The authority to detain the patient will expire at midnight on the twenty-eighth day.

THE DAY ON WHICH HE IS ADMITTED.   This is either the day on which the patient was
admitted to the hospital from the community whilst subject to an application under this section, or the day on which the patient who was in hospital informally was made subject to
such an application. In both cases, admission only takes effect for the purposes of this provision when the application has been accepted by a person who has been authorised by the
hospital managers to accept it: see reg.3(2) of the English and Welsh Regulations.

UNDER THE FOLLOWING PROVISIONS OF THIS ACT.   The use of the term "following" prohibits a further application under this section being made during the currency of an existing
s.2 application (*R. v Wilson Ex p. Williamson* [1996] C.O.D. 42).

Admission for treatment

3.—(1) A patient may be admitted to a hospital and detained there for the period **1–051**
allowed by the following provisions of this Act in pursuance of an application (in
this Act referred to as "an application for admission for treatment") made in
accordance with this section.

(2) An application for admission for treatment may be made in respect of a
patient on the grounds that—

    (a) he is suffering from [mental disorder] of a nature or degree which makes it
        appropriate for him to receive medical treatment in a hospital; and

    (b) [. . .]

    (c) it is necessary for the health or safety of the patient or for the protection of
        other persons that he should receive such treatment and it cannot be pro-
        vided unless he is detained under this section[; and

    (d) appropriate medical treatment is available for him.]

(3) An application for admission for treatment shall be founded on the written
recommendations in the prescribed form of two registered medical practitioners,
including in each case a statement that in the opinion of the practitioner the conditions set out in subsection (2) above are complied with; and each such
recommendation shall include—

    (a) such particulars as may be prescribed of the grounds for that opinion so far
        as it relates to the conditions set out in paragraphs (a) and [(d)] of that sub-
        section; and

    (b) a statement of the reasons for that opinion so far as it relates to the con-
        ditions set out in paragraph (c) of that subsection, specifying whether
        other methods of dealing with the patient are available and, if so, why
        they are not appropriate.

[(4) In this Act, references to appropriate medical treatment, in relation to a person suffering from mental disorder, are references to medical treatment which is
appropriate in his case, taking into account the nature and degree of the mental
disorder and all other circumstances of his case.]

AMENDMENTS

The amendments to this section were made by the Mental Health Act 2007 ss.1(4), 4(2), (3), 55, Sch.11, Pt 2.

DEFINITIONS

1–052   patient: s.145(1).
hospital: ss.34(2), 145(1).
mental disorder: ss.1, 145(1).
medical treatment: s.145(1), (4).

GENERAL NOTE

1–053   This section provides for the compulsory admission of a patient to hospital for treatment and for his subsequent detention, which can last for an initial period of up to six months (s.20(1)). The authority to detain a patient under this section can be renewed (s.20(2)). Patients admitted under this section are subject to the consent to treatment provisions contained in Pt IV (s.56(3)). There is no legal rule which prevents: (a) an application under this section from being made subsequent to the patient's admission under s.4 (*Re Makin* [2000] M.H.L.R. 41), or (b) a patient who has been detained under this section from being subsequently detained under s.2: see further the General Note to s.2 under the heading "Section 2 or section 3 as the initial detaining section?".

For the power to restrain the patient if, following an assessment, the potential applicant and recommending doctors agree that an application under this section should be made, see *R. (on the application of Sessay v South London and Maudsley NHS Foundation Trust* which is considered in the General Note to s.2.

In *R. v Hallstrom Ex p. W* [1986] 2 All E.R. 306, McCullough J. held that admission under this section only covered those whose mental condition was believed to require a period of in-patient treatment in the hospital named in the application. (This finding was approved by the Court of Appeal in *R. v Barking Havering and Brentwood Community Healthcare NHS Trust* [1999] 1 F.L.R. 106.) His Lordship said at 315:

"In my judgment, the key to the construction of section 3 lies in the phrase 'admission for treatment'. It stretches the concept of 'admission for treatment' too far to say that it covers admission for only so long as it is necessary to enable leave of absence to be granted [under section 17], after which the necessary treatment will begin. 'Admission for treatment' under section 3 is intended for those whose condition is believed to require a period of treatment as an in-patient. It may be that such patients will also be thought to require a period of out-patient treatment thereafter, but the concept of 'admission for treatment' has no applicability to those whom it is intended to admit and detain for a purely nominal period during which no necessary treatment will be given.

The phrase 'and his mental disorder . . . makes it appropriate for him to receive treatment in a hospital' in section 3(2)(a) also leads to the conclusion that the section is concerned with those whose mental condition requires in-patient treatment. Treatment in a hospital does not mean treatment *at* a hospital as [leading counsel for the defendants], in effect contends. If his construction were correct there would be a distinction between the patient who could appropriately be treated at home and the patient who could appropriately treated at the out-patients' department of a hospital. Such a distinction would be without reason. When it is remembered that the section authorises compulsory detention in a hospital it is at once clear why a distinction should be made between those whom it is appropriate to treat *in* a hospital (i.e. as in-patients) and those whom it is appropriate to treat otherwise (whether at the out-patient department of the hospital or at home or elsewhere)."

These remarks, which equate "treatment in a hospital" with "in-patient treatment", were described as being obiter and were rejected by Wilson J. in *R. (on the application of DR) v*

Mersey Care NHS Trust [2002] EWHC 1810 (Admin); [2002] M.H.L.R. 386, which is considered in the note on s.20(4)(c). His Lordship held that the phrase "medical treatment in a hospital" in s.20(4)(a) incorporated treatment *at* a hospital and that the lawfulness of the renewal of the patient's detention did not depend upon a plan to put the patient at times in a hospital bed. His Lordship concluded his judgment as follows:

"Unless and until [the reform of the Mental Health Act] is enacted, the law will remain (if my interpretation of it be sound) that the compulsory administration of medication to a patient can be secured only by making him liable to be detained or renewing such liability; that such may be achieved only if a significant component of the plan is for treatment in hospital; and that, in such an enquiry, the difference between in-patient and out-patient treatment is irrelevant" (para.34).

Although his Lordship was correct in equating the tests in ss.3(2)(a) and 20(4)(a), his judgment in so far as it relates to s.3(2)(a) is obiter and therefore not binding as a precedent. The following factors suggest that it should not be applied to applications for the initial detention of a patient:

1. The sub-heading to ss.2 to 6 of the Act is "Procedure for hospital admission". In order to be admitted to a hospital, a person must become an in-patient of that hospital.

2. The effect of a duly completed application is to provide authority for the patient to be conveyed to the named hospital, to be admitted to that hospital (s.6(1)(2)) and to be detained there (s.3(1)).

3. An approved mental health professional (AMHP) can only make an application if she is satisfied that "detention in a hospital" is the most appropriate way of providing for the patient's mental health needs (s.13(2)). In *Hallstrom* McCullough J. said at 316: "Parliament must have been directing the social worker's attention to the patient's need for in-patient treatment".

4. On an application under s.3, the recommending doctors are required to state why "other methods of treatment or care" such as "out-patient treatment" are not appropriate (see Forms A7 and A8).

It is submitted that the correct interpretation of this section is that an application can only be made if the patient is assessed as requiring a period of hospital in-patient treatment for his mental disorder.

The "nominal period" in *Hallstrom* was an overnight admission. In *Re Shearon* [1996] C.O.D. 223, the Divisional Court held that whilst an admission for one week is a relatively small part of the initial six-month period of detention authorised by this section, there was no possible reason for stigmatising a genuine initial one week's intended in-patient treatment as "a purely nominal period during which no necessary treatment will be given". The court further held that the fact that the application was made simultaneously with the institution of a parallel Care Plan did not invalidate the admission and render it unlawful.

Where a patient is admitted to hospital under this section, any previous application that had been made in respect of him under this Part (i.e. an application under s.2 or 4 or a guardianship application under s.7) is automatically cancelled (s.6(4)).

A patient who had been detained under this section after having been released from prison on licence part way through a sentence should not, upon absconding from the detaining hospital, have been returned to prison by the Home Secretary (now the Secretary of State for Justice) using his recall power without reference to or consultation with the hospital doctors. Normally the s.3 would take precedence over a recall (*R. (on the application of S) v Secretary of State for the Home Department* [2002] EWHC Admin 2424; [2003] M.H.L.R. 114).

An order for the patient's discharge from this section can be made by his responsible clinician, the hospital managers or, subject to s.25, his nearest relative (s.23(2)(a)).

There is nothing to prevent a patient who has been detained under this section from being arrested in respect of a criminal offence. If the patient is subsequently remanded into custody or sentenced under the criminal law, the provisions of s.22 will apply.

Where a patient who has been detained under this section ceases to be so detained and leaves hospital, he has an entitlement to after-care services (s.117).

The detention of compliant mentally incapable patients

1–054   The question of whether such patients should be detained under this Act or be made the subject of a deprivation of liberty authorisation under the Mental Capacity Act 2005 is considered in the General Note to this Part under this heading.

The re-sectioning of a patient subsequent to a discharge by the First-tier Tribunal (Mental Health) or the Mental Health Review Tribunal for Wales

1–055   In *R. v East London and The City Mental Health Trust Ex p. Brandenburg* [2003] UKHL 58; [2004] 1 All E.R. 400, the House of Lords considered the following question: when a tribunal has ordered the discharge of a patient, is it lawful to re-admit him under s.2 or s.3 of the Mental Health Act when it cannot be demonstrated that there has been a relevant change of circumstances?

The only speech of substance was given by Lord Bingham who identified the following "overriding principles":

1. The common law respects and protects the personal freedom of the individual, which may not be curtailed save for a reason and in circumstances sanctioned by the law of the land. This principle is reflected in, but does not depend on, art.5(1) of the European Convention on Human Rights (ECHR). It can be traced back to Chapter 29 of Magna Carta 1297 and before that to Chapter 39 of Magna Carta 1215.

2. The law may properly provide for the compulsory detention in hospital of those who suffer from mental disorder if detention is judged to be necessary for the health or safety of the patient or for the protection of others. The necessity for such detention in appropriate cases is recognised by art.5(1)(e) of the ECHR and has long been given effect in domestic law.

3. A person compulsorily detained on mental health grounds should have the right to take proceedings by which the lawfulness of his detention may be decided by a court and his release ordered if the detention is not lawful. This right is expressed in art.5(4) of the ECHR.

4. The rule of law requires that effect should be loyally given to the decisions of legally constituted tribunals in accordance with what is decided. It follows that no one may knowingly act in a way which has the object of nullifying or setting at nought the decision of a tribunal. It is not therefore open to the nearest relative of a patient or an AMHP to apply for the admission of the patient, even with the support of the required medical recommendations, simply because he or she or they disagree with a tribunal's decision to discharge. That would make a mockery of the decision.

Lord Bingham continued by stating that in applying these principles, account must be taken of certain important considerations:

1. While doctors may be expected to exercise their best professional judgment in diagnosing the condition and assessing the cases of those suffering from mental disorder,

and prescribing treatment, their conclusions will rarely be capable of scientific verification. There will often be room for bona fide differences of professional opinion.

2. The condition of many of those suffering from mental disorder will not be static. Episodes of acute illness may be followed by episodes of remission. Thus it does not follow that a tribunal decision, however sound when made, will remain so. Other things being equal, the longer the period since the decision was made the greater the chance that the patient's mental condition may have altered whether for better or worse.

3. The focus of the tribunal's inquiry into the mental health of the patient is on whether he is "then suffering" from mental disorder. "Then" refers to the time of the tribunal's review and the tribunal has no power to consider the validity of the admission that gave rise to the liability to be detained. Although the tribunal cannot ignore the foreseeable future consequences of discharge, it is not called upon to make an assessment which will remain accurate indefinitely or for any given period of time.

4. A conscientious doctor whose opinion has not been accepted by the tribunal will doubtless ask himself whether the tribunal's view is to be preferred and whether his own opinion should be revised. But if, having done so, he adheres to his original opinion he cannot be obliged to suppress or alter it. His professional duty to his patient, and his wider duty to the public, requires him to form, and if called upon express, the best professional judgment he can, whether or not that coincides with the judgment of the tribunal.

5. It is plainly of importance that the AMHP is subject to the statutory duty under s.13 to apply for the admission of a patient where he is satisfied that such an application ought to be made and is of the opinion specified in that section.

Lord Bingham, in applying the principles set out above, rejected a change of circumstances test and held that an AMHP may not lawfully apply for the admission of a patient whose discharge has been ordered by the decision of a tribunal of which the AMHP is aware unless the AMHP has formed a reasonable and bona fide opinion that he has information not known to the tribunal which puts a significantly different complexion on the case as compared with that which was before the tribunal. His Lordship gave three hypothetical examples to illustrate the situations where re-sectioning the patient would be justified:

(a) The issue at the tribunal is whether the patient, if discharged, might cause harm to himself. The tribunal, on the evidence presented, discounts that possibility and directs the discharge of the patient. After the hearing, the AMHP learns of a fact previously unknown to him, the doctors attending the patient and the tribunal: that the patient had at an earlier date made a determined attempt on his life. Having taken medical advice, the AMHP judges that this information significantly alters the risk as assessed by the tribunal.

(b) At the tribunal hearing the patient's mental condition is said to have been stabilised by the taking of appropriate medication. The continuing stability of the patient's mental condition is said to depend on his willingness to take that medication. The patient assures the tribunal of his willingness to continue to take the medication and, on the basis of that assurance the tribunal directs the discharge of the patient. Before or after discharge the patient refuses to take the medication or communicates his intention to refuse. Having taken medical advice, the AMHP perceives a real risk to the patient or others if the medication is not taken.

(c) After the tribunal hearing, and whether before or after discharge, the patient's mental condition significantly deteriorates so as to present a degree of risk or treatment or supervision not evident at the hearing.

1–056   The following findings were also made:

1. The position of the patient's nearest relative does not in principle differ from that of the AMHP, although the nearest relative could not in many cases be expected to be familiar with the evidence or appreciate the grounds on which the tribunal had based its decision.

2. An AMHP may well learn of the existence of an earlier tribunal hearing when performing his functions under s.13(2) and will then wish to know the reasons for it. However, if no such information comes to light the law does not place on the AMHP (or a nearest relative applicant) a duty to make reasonable enquiries to establish whether any decision has been made by any tribunal and, if so, the grounds upon which it was based.

3. If an AMHP makes an application to section the patient subsequent to a decision of the tribunal to discharge him, he should be informed why the decision of the tribunal to discharge him is not thought to govern his case if the application is inconsistent in effect with that decision. As the disclosure of such reasons could be potentially harmful to the patient or to others, it may be necessary for the AMHP to give them in very general terms.

4. In terms of there being a duty to give reasons for taking a different view from the tribunal, while it would doubtless be helpful if a medical recommendation identified any new information on which it was based, a recommending doctor is not required to do more than express her best professional opinion.

The AMHP who is considering making an application might not have attended the tribunal hearing which led to the discharge of the patient. In such a situation, the AMHP should use her best endeavours to establish the factual basis upon which the tribunal reached its decision. Where it is practical, this could include an examination of the written reports that were submitted to the tribunal, contacting those who gave evidence to the tribunal and a consideration of the written reasons that the tribunal gave for its decision.

In *R. (on the application of Care Principles Ltd) v Mental Health Review Tribunal* [2006] EWHC 3194 (Admin); [2006] M.H.L.R. 365, Collins J. held that:

1. The "new information" test established in *Brandenburg* covers not only what might have happened subsequent to the tribunal's decision, but also material which had not been taken into account by the tribunal, if such material were discovered (para.43).

2. Section 6(3) enables the hospital managers to act on an application that appears to be "duly made". The extent of their obligations under that provision must depend on the facts of a particular case. If they are aware of the existence of a previous tribunal decision ordering the discharge of the patient, it requires a critical consideration of the justification for the detention in the light of that decision. It is not "sufficient for them simply to say: we were satisfied that the [AMHP] had properly considered it and discussed it, although it is not specifically explained in the application" (para.45).

With regard to point 2, if the hospital managers are aware of the existence of a decision of a tribunal to discharge the patient they should only accept the application if they are satisfied that the "new information" test has been met. The applicant should inform the managers of the existence of a tribunal discharge known to her.

The effect of the *Brandenburg* judgment is that if there is simply a disagreement between the tribunal and the mental health professionals about the interpretation of the evidence presented to the tribunal, the decision of the tribunal, assuming that it is lawful (see the *Ashworth Hospital Authority* case, below), must be allowed to stand.

In *R. (on the application of H) v Oxfordshire Mental Healthcare NHS Trust* [2002] EWHC Admin 465; [2002] M.H.L.R. 282, a case which was decided before *Brandenburg*, Sullivan J. upheld the re-detention of the patient subsequent to his deferred discharge by a tribunal in circumstances where:

(i) the patient had refused to co-operate with the arrangements that were being made for his discharge from the hospital;

(ii) where, in any event, no suitable arrangements had been identified;

(iii) the patient was, in consequence, "becoming increasingly agitated, stressed and disturbed as the prospect of release drew closer, to the extent of refusing to discuss the matter with his social workers and doctors and, indeed, throwing a table at the social workers" (para.65); and

(iv) those involved in the re-sectioning had given "careful thought" to the decision of the tribunal (para.63).

His Lordship said that in directing discharge "the tribunal could not have proceeded upon the basis that the [patient's] symptoms would deteriorate to such a marked degree as has in fact occurred" (para.67). This decision is consistent with the principle established in *Brandenburg*.

If an application cannot be made in respect of a mentally incapacitated patient who has been discharged by the tribunal by virtue of the ruling in *Brandenburg*, the patient would be eligible for an authorisation made under the deprivation of liberty procedures set out in Schs A1 and 1A of the Mental Capacity Act 2005. This is because an application under s.2 or 3 could not be made in respect of him for the purposes of para.12 of Sch.1A to the 2005 Act. Therefore, a mentally incapacitated patient who has been discharged from detention under the 1983 Act could continue to be detained in the hospital under the 2005 Act.

In *R. (on the application of H) v Ashworth Hospital Authority* [2002] EWCA Civ 923; [2001] M.H.L.R. 314, the Court of Appeal addressed the question of what steps are open to mental health professionals and the hospital managers if they are faced with a tribunal decision for discharge which they honestly and reasonably believe is perverse or arguably perverse. The Court held that:

1. In the absence of material circumstances of which the tribunal is not aware when it orders discharge, it is not open to the professionals to re-section the patient even if they have been legally advised that there are substantial grounds for saying that the tribunal's decision is arguable unlawful. [N.B. the change of circumstances test was rejected by the House of Lords in the *Brandenburg* case, above.]

2. The appropriate action for the authorities to take in this situation is to apply to the Administrative Court for a stay of the tribunal's decision where there was a grant of permission to apply for judicial review. This is the case even if the decision of the tribunal has been fully implemented by the patient being released from the hospital. The effect of a stay is to suspend the tribunal's order, and temporarily to treat it as being of no effect. The grant of an injunction under s.37 of the Senior Courts Act 1981 would be inappropriate in these circumstances.

3. The grant of permission to apply for judicial review is not a sufficient condition of a stay. The court should usually refuse to grant a stay unless satisfied that there is a strong, and not merely an arguable, case that the tribunal's decision was unlawful. Even in such a case, the court should not grant a stay in the absence of cogent evidence of risk and dangerousness.

4. In a case where a stay is ordered, it is essential that the validity of the tribunal's decision be determined by the court in a judicial review with the degree of speed

that is appropriate and usual where a detained person seeks *habeas corpus* (i.e. if at all possible, within days of the order of stay).

5. If the patient refuses to return to the hospital following the grant of a stay, the machinery of the Act can be mobilised to see that he does.

In *R. (on the application of Care Principles Ltd) v Mental Health Review Tribunal*, above, paras 38–40, Collins J. said that:

1. Where an application is made for a stay, the claimant should always, unless there are very exceptional circumstances, give notice both to the patient's solicitors or representatives and to the tribunal.

2. The necessary basis for the grant of any stay must be drawn to the judge's attention. Normally it would be wrong, as the Court of Appeal held in *H*, above, to grant a stay unless there is cogent evidence that, if the patient is released, he will be a danger to himself or the public.

3. The judge must be informed of all the relevant criteria which must be applied in deciding on a stay.

Rather than making an application to the Administrative Court for a stay, an applicant should now apply to the tribunal itself to stay the proceedings or to suspend the effect of its own decision pending a determination by the tribunal or the Upper Tribunal of an application for permission to appeal against that decision: see r.5(3)(j)(l) of the Tribunal Rules and r.5(2)(g)(h) of the Welsh Rules.

The deteriorating patient

1–057   The "Committee of Inquiry into the events leading up to and surrounding the fatal incident at the Edith Morgan Centre, Torbay, on September 1, 1993" examined the issue of the "sectionability" of a patient whose mental health is likely to deteriorate: see *The Falling Shadow: One Patient's Mental Health Care 1978–1993*, 1995, pp.153–169. The Committee disagreed with the view expressed by the *Internal Review of Legal Powers on the Care of Mentally Ill People in Community* that a patient could not be admitted under compulsory powers "simply on the grounds that his or her past medical history suggests that he or she will relapse in the future" (Department of Health, 1993, para.3.2). The conclusion that the Committee reached was that "there is probably no legal impediment to the readmission of a ['revolving door'] patient . . . at the point of loss of insight when he refuse[s] further medication" (p.160). In fact this conclusion does not conflict with the statement made by the *Internal Review* as a patient who has lost insight would not be detained "simply" on the ground of his medical history.

The Committee found the case of *Devon CC v Hawkins* [1967] 2 Q.B. 26, to be "highly pertinent" to the issue. The question before the court was whether a person who was taking drugs which successfully controlled his epilepsy could be said to be "suffering from" that disease. The answer given by the Lord Chief Justice, Lord Parker, was in the affirmative. His Lordship said that "so long as drugs are necessary to prevent the manifestation of disease, the disease in my judgment remains". In other words, so the Committee stated, what the patient "was 'suffering from' rested on a prognosis of what would occur in the future if medication was withdrawn" (p.155).

Although it might be the case that a person with a history of mental disorder who is being successfully medicated for that disorder can be said to be "suffering from" that disorder, it does not follow that merely because that person stops taking his medication the disorder becomes one of a "nature or degree which makes it appropriate for him to receive medical treatment in a hospital" (s.3(2)(a)) or one of a "nature or degree which warrants the detention of the patient in a hospital for assessment" (s.2(2)(a)). While a patient whose symptoms are being well controlled by medication cannot be said to be suffering from a "degree" of mental disorder sufficient to justify detention, can that patient be detained because of the "nature" of his disorder? This question was considered by Popplewell J. in *R. v The Mental Health Review, Tribunal for the South Thames Region Ex p. Smith*, which is noted under subs.(2)(a).

The course of a patient's mental disorder is never entirely predictable and the Act requires the professionals involved in assessing a patient for possible compulsory admission to exercise their judgment to determine whether the patient's condition and situation at the time of the assessment meet the statutory criteria for admission. If it is the case that a mere failure to continue with medication would be sufficient to satisfy the statutory criteria with respect to a patient who has a history of admissions subsequent to previous failures to continue with medication, this would result in the personal examination of the patient by the recommending doctors under s.12(2) and the interviewing of the patient by the AMHP under s.13(2) being sterile exercises. One of the objectives of the examinations and interview of such a patient would be to identify whether there is any evidence (apart from the cessation of medication) to suggest that it is likely that history will repeat itself in that the symptoms of the patient's mental disorder will reappear. If there is such evidence, the "nature" of the patient's mental disorder could lead professionals to conclude that detention in hospital is either "appropriate" or "warranted" even though there is either no current manifestation of the disorder (the "degree") or if the symptoms of the mental disorder are not yet acute.

It is suggested that the following approach should be taken by those involved in the assessment of a "revolving door" patient who has ceased to take medication for his mental disorder:

(i) a withdrawal from medication is a significant, but not a determining factor in the assessment;

(ii) the role of the professionals involved in the assessment is to assess the patient's response to the withdrawal and to identify the reasons for the decision to cease taking medication;

(iii) the "nature" test can be satisfied even though there is no evidence that the patient's mental health has begun to deteriorate: see *Smirek v Williams*, which is noted under "of a nature or degree" in subs.(2)(a); and

(iv) although it would not be possible to determine that the provisions of either ss.2(2)(a) or 3(2)(a) are satisfied solely on the ground that the patient has ceased to take medication, an evaluation of the patient's history and, in particular, of his reaction to withdrawal from medication in the past, could lead to a decision that the "nature" of the mental disorder justifies an application being made.

Section 2 or section 3 as the initial detaining section?
  The question whether it is appropriate to detain a patient under this section or under s.2 is **1–058** considered in the General Note to s.2 under this heading.

Human Rights Act 1998
  In *Winterwerp v Netherlands* (1979) 2 E.H.R.R. 387, the European Court of Human **1–059** Rights (ECtHR) held, inter alia, that in order for the detention of a person of unsound mind to be lawful the mental disorder from which the patient is suffering must be of a kind or degree warranting compulsory confinement. This finding is reflected in the phrase "nature or degree" in subs.(2)(a). *Winterwerp* also confirmed that in order to achieve compliance with art.5 of the European Convention on Human Rights (ECHR), detention under the Act must be a necessary and proportionate response to the patient's situation. Also see the decision of the European Court of Human Rights in *Pleso v Hungary* which is noted in s.2(2)(b) under "Health". The requirement of proportionality is reflected in the terms of subs.(2)(c). Other less severe measures must have been considered and found to be

insufficient to safeguard the individual or public interest, leaving no alternative to detention (*Withold Litwa v Poland* (2001) 33 E.H.R.R. 53).

The question whether the continued detention of an asymptomatic patient contravenes art.5 was considered by the Court of Appeal in *R. (on the application of H) v Mental Health Review Tribunal, North and North East London Region* [2001] EWCA Civ 415; [2001] M.H.L.R. 48, where Lord Phillips M.R. said at para.33:

"The circumstances of the present case . . . are not uncommon. A patient is detained who is unquestionably suffering from schizophrenia. While in the controlled environment of the hospital he is taking medication, and as a result of the medication is in remission. So long as he continues to take the medication he will pose no danger to himself or to others. The nature of the illness is such, however, that if he ceases to take the medication he will relapse and pose a danger to himself or to others. The professionals may be uncertain whether, if he is discharged into the community, he will continue to take the medication. We do not believe that Article 5 requires that the patient must always be discharged in such circumstances. The appropriate response should depend upon the result of weighing the interests of the patient against those of the public having regard to the particular facts. Continued detention can be justified if, but only if, it is a proportionate response having regard to the risks that would be involved in discharge".

The ECtHR has confirmed that the detention of a patient under art.5 may be justified on the ground of protecting the public (*Witold Litwa v Poland,* above) in a situation where the patient needs control and supervision rather than clinical treatment (*Reid v United Kingdom* (2003) 37 E.H.R.R. 9, para.51).

The finding of the Court of Appeal in *St George's Healthcare NHS Trust v S* [1998] 3 All E.R. 673, that a unborn child is not a "person" in need of protection for the purposes of ss.2(2)(b) and 3(2)(c) could possibly be challenged on the ground that a failure to protect the unborn child constitutes a violation of the child's right to life under art.2 of the ECHR. Although the ECtHR has found in the context of abortion and fertility treatment that an unborn child does not have a right to life and is not a "person" within the meaning of art.2, it has not ruled out that, in certain circumstances, safeguards may be extended to the unborn child (*Vo v France* (2005) 40 E.H.R.R. 12, para.80).

Although art.5 is not concerned with the suitability of the treatment that the detained patient receives or the conditions of his detention, subject to the requirement that he be detained in a hospital, clinic or other appropriate institution (*Ashingdane v United Kingdom* (1985) 7 E.H.R.R. 528 para.44), the medical treatment of a patient can constitute "inhuman or degrading treatment" under art.3 of the ECHR if it reaches a minimum level of severity.

If a patient has been assessed as either needing a particular treatment or requiring a specialist opinion, an excessive delay in providing that treatment or opinion could give rise to a claim under art.8(1) of the ECHR if the delay has a serious impact on the patient's health (*Passannante v Italy* (1998) 26 E.H.R.R. CD 153).

A failure or refusal to provide treatment that is discriminatory will be unlawful, either under art.14 of the ECHR or the Equality Act 2010.

Applications to the First-tier Tribunal (Mental Health) or the Mental Health Review Tribunal for Wales

1–060   The patient may make an application within six months of admission (s.66(1)(b), (2)(b)) and during each subsequent renewal period (ss.66(1)(f), (2)(f), 20(2)). Section 66(2A) disapplies s.66(1)(b) for recalled community patients. A reference to the tribunal will be made in the circumstances set out in s.68. The patient's nearest relative may make an application within 28 days of receiving notification that an order for discharge has been barred under s.25 (s.66(1)(g), (2)(d)).

Code of Practice

The roles of mental health professionals when undertaking assessments that might lead **1–061**
to an application for admission to hospital and the criteria for detention under this section
are considered in Ch.14. Guidance on the application of the "appropriate treatment" test
set out in subs.(3)(d) can be found in Ch.23. Conflicts of interests that might arise in the
assessment process are considered in Ch.39. Guidance on the transport of patients can
be found in Ch.17.

Subsection (1)

An application under this section can be made by either the patient's nearest relative or **1–062**
by an AMHP (s.11(1)). The applicant must use Form A5 (for NRs) or Form A6 (for
AMHPs) (in Wales, Form H05 (for NRs) or Form H06 (for AMPS)): see reg.4(1) of the
English and Welsh Regulations. The application will be addressed to the managers of
the hospital to which admission is sought (s.11(2)). If an AMHP makes the application,
she must consult with the patient's nearest relative if this is practicable and the application
cannot proceed if the nearest relative objects (s.11(4)). The positive consent of the nearest
relative to the application is not required. The applicant must have seen the patient within
the previous 14 days (s.11(5)) and an AMHP applicant must interview the patient before the
application is made (s.13(2)). The patient must be admitted to hospital within 14 days of the
time when he was last medically examined prior to the recommendations required by
subs.(3) being made (s.6(1)(a)). It is possible to make an application in respect of a person
who is already receiving hospital treatment as an in-patient on an informal basis (s.5(1)).
An application for the admission of a ward of court cannot be made without the leave of
the High Court (s.33(1)).

The effect of an application made under this section is set out in s.6. The hospital named
in the application is not placed under a legal obligation to admit the patient: see the note on
"to hospital" in s.6(1).

DETAINED THERE.   The patient can be granted leave of absence from the detaining hospital under s.17, but only after the patient has received a period of in-patient treatment at
that hospital (*R. v Hallstrom Ex p.W* [1986] 2 All E.R. 41). Making an application in respect
of a patient where the intention is to grant the patient immediate leave of absence to enable
the patient to be treated at another hospital is unlawful because the application provides
authority for the patient to be detained in the hospital named in the application (see
s.6(2)), which is where the initial in-patient treatment must take place. Also note the use
of the term "there" in this provision. It would also be unlawful for an application to be
made under this section if the motive for making the application was to enable an application for a community treatment order to be made in respect of a patient who did not
require in-patient treatment.

THE PERIOD ALLOWED.   The patient may be detained for an initial period of six months
renewable for a further six months and thereafter renewable at yearly intervals (s.20(1),
(2)).

Subsection (2)

Although informal admission should be the preferred mode of admission, compulsion **1–063**
should be used on a patient who is willing to be admitted informally if its absence
would place the patient's safety and/or the safety of others at risk: see the General Note
to s.131.

Paragraph (a)

SUFFERING FROM.   A patient whose symptoms of mental disorder are being controlled **1–064**
by medication still suffers from that disorder: see the note on "The deteriorating patient",
above.

MENTAL DISORDER.   A patient with a learning disability who suffers from no other form of mental disorder can only be made subject to an application under this section if the disability is associated with abnormally aggressive or seriously irresponsible conduct on his part (s.1(2A), (2B)).

OF A NATURE OR DEGREE.   The meaning of this phrase is also considered in the note on s.72(1)(b)(i). In *R. v Mental Health Review Tribunal for the South Thames Region Ex p. Smith* (1999) 47 B.M.L.R. 104 Popplewell J. held that:

(i)   although the wording of this phrase is disjunctive, in very many cases the nature and degree of the patient's mental disorder will be inevitably bound up so that it matters not whether the issue is dealt with under nature or degree;

(ii) the word "nature" refers to the particular mental disorder from which the patient suffers, its chronicity, its prognosis, and the patient's previous response to receiving treatment for the disorder. In making this finding, his Lordship rejected a submission made by counsel for the patient that the "nature" of a patient's mental disorder is a static condition; and

(iii) the word "degree" refers to the current manifestation of the patient's disorder.

This criterion can therefore be satisfied in respect of a well-known asymptomatic patient who has ceased to take medication for his mental disorder and who has a history of a significant deterioration in his mental health after ceasing to take such medication. This interpretation is supported by the following comment made by Hale L.J. in *Smirek v Williams* [2000] M.H.L.R. 38 at para.19:

"There are, of course, mental illnesses which come and go, but where there is a chronic condition, where there is evidence that it will soon deteriorate if medication is not taken, I find it impossible to accept that that is not a mental illness of a nature or degree which makes it appropriate for the patient to be liable to be detained in hospital for medical treatment if the evidence is that, without being detained in hospital, the patient will not take that treatment".

And in *R. (on the application of MM) v Home Secretary* [2007] EWCA Civ 687; [2007] M.H.L.R. 304, Toulson L.J. said at para.48:

"I can see no reason in law why it could not be appropriate for a person in MM's position to be detained for treatment before reaching the stage stipulated by [MM's counsel] (that is, when psychotic symptoms either had recurred or were certain to be on the point of recurring); but determining the point at which the risks are such as to make detention for treatment appropriate may involve a difficult judgment on the facts of a particular case."

Although it might be lawful to make an application in respect of a patient before the reappearance of the symptoms of mental disorder, whether it will be clinically and ethically right to do so is a separate question. It is submitted that the crucial factor in determining whether an application should be made in respect of an asymptomatic patient is the assessment of the risk to the patient and/or others following the cessation of medication. This issue is considered in the note on "The deteriorating patient", above.

APPROPRIATE FOR HIM TO RECEIVE MEDICAL TREATMENT IN A HOSPITAL.   It is submitted that this provision can only be satisfied if the patient requires treatment for his mental disorder as a hospital in-patient: see the comment on *R. (on the application of DR) v Mersey Care NHS Trust* in the General Note to this section.

An assessment of the patient's response to being treated can be a part of the medical treatment that the patient receives (*B v Barking Havering and Brentwood Community Healthcare NHS Trust* [1999] 1 F.L.R. 106 CA).

Paragraph (c)
There is no requirement for the two recommending doctors to agree on the nature of the   **1–065**
risk which justifies detention under this section.

NECESSARY.   "Necessary" is a stronger term than "ought" in s.2(2)(b). The necessity must relate to both compulsion and treatment. In *Reid v Secretary of State for Scotland* [1999] 1 All E.R. 481, 504, Lord Clyde said that the test is "one of necessity, not desirability".

HEALTH.   See the note on s.2(2).

SAFETY.   See the note on s.2(2).

PROTECTION OF OTHER PERSONS.   See the note on s.2(2) and on s.72(1)(b)(ii) under this heading.

AND THAT IT CANNOT BE PROVIDED.   By, for example, an informal admission.

UNLESS HE IS DETAINED UNDER THIS SECTION.   See the General Note to s.2 under the heading "Section 2 or section 3 as the initial detaining section?".

Paragraph (d)
This paragraph, which should be read with subs.(4) and s.145(4), replaces the require-   **1–066**
ment that the treatment of certain categories of patients detained under this section must be "likely to alleviate or prevent a deterioration of his condition" (the "treatability test") with a requirement that "appropriate treatment" be available to all patients. The 10th edition of this work stated, at para.1–051, that the interpretation in case law of the treatability test was so broad that "it is difficult to imagine the circumstances that would cause a patient to fail it". A similar comment can be made of the appropriate treatment test, given that it will almost always be appropriate to provide the patient with either specialist nursing or care for the purpose of either alleviating or preventing a worsening of the patient's mental disorder or one or more of its symptoms or manifestations so as to satisfy the terms of s.145(4). The *Code of Practice* recognises, at para.23.17, that there "may be patients whose particular circumstances mean that treatment may be appropriate even though it consists only of nursing and specialist day-to-day care under the clinical supervision of an approved clinician in a safe and secure therapeutic environment with a structured regime". With regard to patients with a personality disorder, the *Code* states at para.21.11:

"People with personality disorders may take time to engage and develop motivation for such longer-term treatment. But even patients who are not engaged in that kind of treatment may need other forms of treatment, including nurse and specialist care, to manage the continuing risks posed by their disorders, and this may constitute appropriate medical treatment."

Those who opposed the change brought about by the 2007 Act were concerned that the new test provides for the possibility of a person being detained simply for preventive purposes without any medical benefit. One of the proponents of this argument, Lord Carlile, called in aid the following extract from the evidence that Professor Nigel Eastman gave to Joint Committee on the Draft Mental Health Bill:

"Therapeutic benefit to the individual is of crucial importance in terms of protecting the boundary of what is the business of mental health professionals. I am not at all against protecting the public, of course not, but it must be in conjunction with some benefit to the individual that goes beyond simply stopping them offending. If you adopt a definition of treatability which is simply the reduction of risk or the avoidance of offending, that means that locking somebody up is treating them" (*Hansard*, HL Vol.688, col.304).

As medicine is the "science and art concerned with the cure, alleviation and prevention of disease, and with the restoration and preservation of health" (Shorter Oxford English Dictionary), it is difficult to see how medical treatment could ever be described as being "appropriate" for the patient if a view had been taken that there was no possibility of the patient ever gaining any therapeutic benefit from it, apart than the benefit that arises from preventing offending in the community. Further, it is unlikely that a doctor could be said to be acting ethically if she was involved in the admission of a patient to hospital in the knowledge that the patient would receive no therapeutic benefit from the treatment that was going to be provided. In any event, the concern about the absence of any reference to therapeutic benefit has been partly allayed by the inclusion of s.145(4) by the 2007 Act.

Although it was claimed in Parliament that the new test might not be compliant with the European Convention on Human Rights, the Joint Committee considered that "in terms of the Convention, there would appear to be no obstacle to replacing 'treatability' with 'availability of appropriate treatment' as a condition of detention" (para.20). This conclusion was reached because art.5(1)(e) of the ECHR imposes no requirement that detention in a hospital be conditional on the illness or condition being of a nature or degree amenable to medical treatment (*Koniarska v United Kingdom*, App. No. 33670/96, December 10, 2000). In *Reid v United Kingdom* (2003) 37 E.H.R.R. 9 para.51, the European Court of Human Rights held that confinement under art.5(1)(e) "may be necessary not only where a person needs therapy, medication of other clinical treatment to cure or alleviate his condition, but also where the person needs control and supervision to prevent him, for example, causing harm to himself and other persons".

1–067   APPROPRIATE.   See the definition in subs.(4). In *Re Ian Brady*, December 11, 2013, the First-tier Tribunal (Mental Health) accepted as being helpful the evidence of one of the witnesses, Professor Eastman, who "had divided the treatment of patients with mental health problems into three different forms, which had been referred to during the case as limbs one, two and three" (para.227). The tribunal went on to describe these "limbs":

"Limb one is treatment of the patient's core disorder; limb two is seeking to give the patient the skills necessary to cope with situations that they had previously found difficult or stressful but without attempting to change the core disorder; limb three is management focused on managing the patient's environment so that conflict in situations is minimised. This includes management in the hospital when the patient is on leave from the hospital and when the patient is in the community; 'this neither alters the core disorder nor gives skills to the patient'" (para.228).

The treatment, which must be actually available to the patient (*Code of Practice*, para.23.14), need not necessarily be the most appropriate treatment that could be provided, although "wherever possible" this should be provided (*Code of Practice*, para.23.13). What constitutes appropriate treatment for the patient, which is a matter of clinical judgment, may change over time. Paragraph 23.16 of the *Code of Practice* states:

"Medical treatment which aims merely to prevent a disorder worsening is unlikely, in general, to be appropriate in cases where normal treatment approaches would aim (and be expected) to alleviate the patient's condition significantly. However, for some patients with persistent and severe mental disorders, management of the undesirable effects of their disorder may be the most that can realistically be hoped for."

In *SH v Cornwall Partnership NHS Trust* [2012] UKUT 290 (AAC); [2012] M.H.L.R. 383, UT Judge Jacobs said at para.14:

> "The delivery of treatment, and the related issue of consent, is practically and conceptually distinct from the issue whether it is appropriate and available. Treatment may be appropriate, whether or not the patient consents. And it may be available, whether or not the patient is willing to receive it. Appropriateness and availability are issues that arise prior to the decision whether to give the treatment. It is only at that later stage that the patient's consent arises."

The risk that the patient poses can be relevant to the satisfaction of the appropriate treatment test. In *MD v Mersey Care NHS Trust* [2013] UKUT 0127 (AAC), Judge Jacobs said at para.9:

> "The treatment that is appropriate for a particular patient is determined by the patient's medical condition and the risk a patient presents is a consequence or feature of that condition. Risk is as relevant to treatment as any other feature of the disorder."

In this case Judge Jacobs approved of the approach that had been taken by the First-tier Tribunal to risk and to the patient's lack of engagement in treatment. In its reasons for its decision not to discharge the patient the tribunal said:

> "In our view, when assessing how long it is reasonable or appropriate to wait for a patient to engage with treatment, or to what extent relatively small indications of progress along the road to eventual motivation or engagement are sufficient to overcome the argument that continued detention amounts to mere containment, the likelihood of harm occurring and the potential severity of the harm, especially when taken together, will be highly relevant factors to consider, along with the patient's ability to weigh up their options and the likely outcomes for themselves and for others, and their potential ability to choose to engage at some point in the future."

Judge Jacobs returned to the issue of a patient's engagement with treatment in *DL-H v Partnerships in Care and the Secretary of State* [2013] UKUT 500 (AAC); [2014] M.H.L.R. 241, where it was held that:

1. A patient's refusal to engage with therapy, especially for a patient with a personality disorder, is not decisive, although it is potentially a relevant factor that has to be taken into consideration.

2. Treatment that is otherwise available and appropriate does not cease to be so merely because the patient refuses to engage or cooperate with it.

3. Although s.145 defines treatment widely, there is a common thread that runs through all the elements: its purpose must be to confer some benefit on the patient, if only to the extent of preventing the patient's condition getting worse. However the definition is so broad that it may not be difficult to identify something that will, at the least, prevent a worsening. However, the minimal nature and effect of that treatment may be relevant to the issue of appropriateness.

4. The tribunal is required to make a finding on the particular treatment that is available to the particular patient rather than resorting to general statements.

5. If the tribunal finds that the patient is not prepared to engage and will never be brought to engage, that will not necessarily be decisive. This is because the definition of treatment is so broad that it includes much that does not require the patient's engagement in formal therapy.

The *Code of Practice* considers patient engagement at para 23.19 and 23.20.

In *MD v Nottinghamshire Health Care NHS Trust* [2010] UKUT 59 (AAC); [2010] M.H.L.R. 93, para.31, Judge Jacobs said: "It may be that medical treatment is still available for a patient but, because of the circumstances of a particular case, it is no longer appropriate". In this case, the Upper Tribunal rejected a submission that detention without the possibility of reduction of the risk posed by the patient was containment not treatment ("treatment has to be appropriate, but need not reduce the risk" (para.34)) and confirmed the decision of the First-tier Tribunal that appropriate medical treatment was available because there was the *potential* for milieu therapy to benefit the patient (para.35). The latter finding begs the question of how to distinguish milieu therapy from mere detention: see further, J. Phull and P. Bartlett, "'Appropriate' medical treatment: what's in a word?", Med Sci Law 2012: 1–4.

In *Re Ian Brady*, above, the tribunal, on rejecting a submission that the way in which Ashworth Hospital was providing for the patient amounted to no more than containment, said at para.280:

"The Care Team has tailored a carefully considered environment in which it seeks to maintain the level of stability in Mr Brady's mental disorder which enables him to cope with its symptoms."

Even if the treatment is both "appropriate" and "available", it must also satisfy the necessity test set out in para.(c).

The recommending doctors must state on either Form A7 or A8 in which hospital(s) the appropriate treatment will be available to the patient. If the hospital named by both doctors is not the hospital that accepts the application, the application is fundamentally defective and incapable of rectification under s.15.

Subsection (3)

1–068   See the notes to s.2(3).

WRITTEN RECOMMENDATIONS.   If an application to hospital A is not accepted due to the lack of a hospital bed, the recommendations can be used to support an application to hospital B as long as the recommendations state that appropriate treatment for the patient is available at that hospital.

Subsection (4)

1–069   Note the circularity of the definition contained in this provision. The final phrase indicates that social factors can be taken into account.

ALL OTHER CIRCUMSTANCES.   "All the patient's circumstances must be looked at, including their age and gender, where they live, where their family and social contacts are, and their cultural background" (*Hansard*, HL Vol.688, col.320, per the Minister of State).

Admission for assessment in cases of emergency

1–070   **4.**—(1) In any case of urgent necessity, an application for admission for assessment may be made in respect of a patient in accordance with the following provisions of this section, and any application so made is in this Act referred to as "an emergency application".

(2) An emergency application may be made either by an [approved mental health professional] or by the nearest relative of the patient; and every such application shall include a statement that it is of urgent necessity for the patient to be admitted and detained under section 2 above, and that compliance with the

provisions of this Part of this Act relating to applications under that section would involve undesirable delay.

(3) An emergency application shall be sufficient in the first instance if founded on one of the medical recommendations required by section 2 above, given, if practicable, by a practitioner who has previous acquaintance with the patient and otherwise complying with the requirements of section 12 below so far as applicable to a single recommendation, and verifying the statement referred to in subsection (2) above.

(4) An emergency application shall cease to have effect on the expiration of a period of 72 hours from the time when the patient is admitted to the hospital unless—

(a) the second medical recommendation required by section 2 above is given and received by the managers within that period; and

(b) that recommendation and the recommendation referred to in subsection (3) above together comply with all the requirements of section 12 below (other than the requirement as to the time of signature of the second recommendation).

(5) In relation to an emergency application, section 11 below shall have effect as if in subsection (5) of that section for the words "the period of 14 days ending with the date of the application" there were substituted the words "the previous 24 hours".

AMENDMENT

The words in square brackets in subs.(1) were substituted by the Mental Health Act 2007 s.21, Sch.2 para.2.

DEFINITIONS   **1–071**

application for admission for assessment: ss.2, 145(1).
patient: s.145(1).
approved mental health professional: s.145(1) (1AC).
nearest relative: ss.26(3), 145(1).
the managers, s.145(1).
hospital: ss.34(2), 145(1).

GENERAL NOTE

This section provides for the compulsory admission of a person to hospital for assess- **1–072**
ment for a period of up to 72 hours based on the medical recommendation of one doctor
who, if practicable, should have previous acquaintance with the patient. The grounds for
detention under this section are the same as for s.2, with the addition that both the applicant
and the recommending doctor must certify that "it is of urgent necessity for the patient to be
admitted and detained under section 2" and that "compliance with the provisions . . . relating to applications under that section would involve undesirable delay".

Paragraph 15.8 of the *Code of Practice* states:

"An emergency may arise where the patient's mental state or behaviour presents problems which those involved cannot reasonably be expected to manage while waiting for a
second doctor. To be satisfied that an emergency has arisen, the person making the application and the doctor making the supporting recommendation should have evidence of:

● an immediate and significant risk of mental or physical harm to the patient or to others

● danger of serious harm to property, or

● a need for the use of restrictive interventions on a patient (see chapter 26)."

Under the Mental Health Act 1959, the equivalent procedure was misused and became the most widely used form of compulsory admission. Subsequent to the implementation of the Act, pressure from the Mental Health Act Commission was largely responsible for a decrease in both the number and proportion of applications made under this section. Such pressure has, on occasions, led to situations where applications under this section have not been made in circumstances where the criteria set out in subs.(2) have been satisfied. Paragraph 15.7 of the *Code of Practice* states:

"Section 4 should never be used for administrative convenience. So, for example, patients should not be admitted under section 4 merely because it is more convenient for the second doctor to examine the patient in, rather than outside, hospital."

If AMHPs consider that they are being forced to make inappropriate use of this section because of difficulties in obtaining the second medical recommendation required by s.2, they should try to resolve the difficulty at local level or, if this turns out to be unproductive, inform the Care Quality Commission or Health Inspectorate Wales who are required to keep this Act under review (s.120(1)); also see para.15.10 of the *Code of Practice*.

In *R. (on the application of Sessay) v South London and Maudsley NHS Foundation Trust)* [2011] EWHC 2617 (QB); [2012] M.H.L.R. 94, the Divisional Court held that the Act provides a complete statutory code for the detention on non-compliant mentally incapacitated patients and that the common law doctrine of necessity does not apply during the period when a patient is being assessed for detention under the Act. However, the court said at para.57:

"[I]n our view it is unlikely in the ordinary case that there will be a false imprisonment at common law or deprivation of liberty for the purposes of Article 5(1) [European Convention on Human Rights] if there is no undue delay during the processing of an application under ss.2 or 4 MHA for admission."

It is therefore the case that if, following an assessment of the patient, the potential applicant and recommending doctor agree that an application to detain the patient should be made, the common law provides authority to use restraint on the patient during the time that it takes to process the application as long as the process is not unduly delayed. Common law powers are discussed in Appendix A.

An application under this section cannot be renewed at the end of the 72 hour period. If compulsory detention is to be continued the application must either be "converted" into a s.2 application under the provisions of subs.(4), in which case the patient can be detained for 28 days beginning with the date of his admission under this section, or an application for treatment should be made under s.3. The Act does not contain a procedure under which a s.4 application can be converted into a s.3 application by the addition of a second medical recommendation.

An application under this section can be made if a patient who has been detained in a general hospital under s.5(2) needs to be transferred to a psychiatric hospital urgently.

As, under s.25, the nearest relative of a detained patient has to give not less than 72 hours' notice of his or her intention to discharge the patient, only the responsible clinician (RC) and the hospital managers have the power to order the discharge of a patient detained under this section (see s.23).

Patients admitted under this section are *not* subject to the consent to treatment provisions contained in Pt IV (s.56(3)(a)). If the patient is mentally capable of making a decision about treatment, the common law enables him to refuse to be treated for either a physical or mental disorder. However, if the patient is assessed as being mentally incapable of making a decision about treatment, the treatment can be provided under the Mental Capacity Act 2005 if it is deemed to be in his best interests.

Applications to the First-tier Tribunal (Mental Health) or the Mental Health Review Tribunal for Wales
The patient may make an application, but if the second medical recommendation pro- **1–073** vided for in subs.(4) is not forthcoming it will lapse (s.66(1)(a), (2)(a)).

Code of Practice
Guidance on the making of applications under this section is contained in Ch.15. **1–074**

Subsection (1)
APPLICATION. An application under this section can be made by either the patient's **1–075** nearest relative or by an AMHP (s.11(1)). Paragraph 15.4 of the *Code of Practice* states:

"If the application is made by an AMHP, the nearest relative should be informed at the same time, or within a reasonable time afterwards, unless the patient requests otherwise (or does not have a nearest relative). The circumstances detailed in paragraph 14.62 should be considered in deciding whether to inform the nearest relative against the patient's wishes." The applicant must use Form A9 (for NRs) or Form A10 (for AMHPs) (in Wales, Form HO9 (for NRs) or Form HO10 (for AMHPs)): see reg.4(1) of the English and Welsh Regulations. The applicant must have seen the patient within the previous 24 hours (s.11(5)) and the patient must be admitted to hospital within 24 hours beginning from the time when he was medically examined or when the application was made, whichever is the earlier (s.6(1)(b)). These time limits were introduced by the 1982 Act to help "to prevent [this section] being used for cases other than those of real emergency" (Cmnd. 7320, para.2.6). The duty of the AMHP under s.11(3) to inform the nearest relative of an application under s.2 is triggered if the application is "converted" to a s.2 applies to an application made under this section (*Re GM* [2000] M.H.L.R. 41, para.28).

An application for the admission of a ward of court cannot be made without the leave of the High Court (s.33(1)).
The effect of an application made under this section is set out in s.6. The hospital named in the application is not placed under a legal obligation to admit the patient: see the note on "to hospital" in s.6(1).

Subsection (2)
APPROVED MENTAL HEALTH PROFESSIONAL. An AMHP applicant must comply with the **1–076** requirements of s.13.

URGENT NECESSITY ... UNDESIRABLE DELAY. The use of this section should be confined to cases of real emergency where the delay that would be caused by waiting for a second medical opinion would be undesirable because of the patient's urgent need for medical treatment in a hospital. It is difficult to envisage a nearest relative applicant being aware of the distinction between an application made under this section and an application made under s.2.

Subsection (3)
ONE OF THE MEDICAL RECOMMENDATIONS. Which must be completed on Form A11 (in **1–077** Wales, Form HO11): see reg.4(1) of the English and Welsh Regulations. A medical recommendation provided under this section cannot be used to support a subsequent application made under s.3. There is no requirement for the recommending doctor to be approved under s.12.

Subsection (4)

1–078   PERIOD OF 72 HOURS.   If the application is "converted" into a s.2 application under this subsection, the 28 days period provided for in s.2 will run from the time of the patient's admission to hospital under this section. An AMHP or a nearest relative applicant should not complete an application form for an admission under s.2 if a "conversion" is effected.

SECOND MEDICAL RECOMMENDATION . . . IS GIVEN.   A second doctor who, bearing in mind the status of the first recommending doctor, complies with the provisions of s.12 should examine the patient as soon as possible after admission to decide whether the patient should be detained under s.2: see para.15.13 of the *Code of Practice*. If a second medical recommendation is given, a record should be made in Part 2 of Form H3 (in Wales, Form HO14). If it is decided that the patient should not be detained under s.2, this does not have the effect of automatically discharging the section as a discharge prior to the expiration of the 72 hours can only be effected by a decision to discharge being made by either the patient's responsible clinician or the hospital managers under s.23.

HOSPITAL.   Local social services authorities must be informed of those hospitals where arrangements are in force for the reception, in cases of special urgency, of patients requiring treatment for mental disorder (s.140).

Application in respect of patient already in hospital

1–079   **5.**—(1) An application for the admission of a patient to a hospital may be made under this Part of this Act notwithstanding that the patient is already an in-patient in that hospital or, in the case of an application for admission for treatment that the patient is for the time being liable to be detained in the hospital in pursuance of an application for admission for assessment; and where an application is so made the patient shall be treated for the purposes of this Part of this Act as if he had been admitted to the hospital at the time when that application was received by the managers.

(2) If, in the case of a patient who is an in-patient in a hospital, it appears to the registered medical practitioner [or approved clinician] in charge of the treatment of the patient that an application ought to be made under this Part of this Act for the admission of the patient to hospital, he may furnish to the managers a report in writing to that effect; and in any such case the patient may be detained in the hospital for a period of 72 hours from the time when the report is so furnished.

[(3) The registered medical practitioner or approved clinician in charge of the treatment of a patient in a hospital may nominate one (but not more than one) person to act for him under subsection (2) above in his absence.

(3A) For the purposes of subsection (3) above—

(a)   the registered medical practitioner may nominate another registered medical practitioner, or an approved clinician, on the staff of the hospital; and

(b)   the approved clinician may nominate another approved clinician, or a registered medical practitioner, on the staff of the hospital.]

(4) If, in the case of a patient who is receiving treatment for mental disorder as an in-patient in a hospital, it appears to a nurse of the prescribed class—

(a)   that the patient is suffering from mental disorder to such a degree that it is necessary for his health or safety or for the protection of others for him to be immediately restrained from leaving the hospital; and

(b)   that it is not practicable to secure the immediate attendance of a practitioner [or clinician] for the purpose of furnishing a report under subsection (2) above, the nurse may record that fact in writing; and in that event the patient may be detained in the hospital for a period of six hours from the time when that fact is so recorded or until the earlier arrival at the place where the patient is detained of a practitioner [or clinician] having power to furnish a report under that subsection.

(5) A record made under subsection (4) above shall be delivered by the nurse (or by a person authorised by the nurse in that behalf) to the managers of the hospital as soon as possible after it is made; and where a record is made under that subsection the period mentioned in subsection (2) above shall begin at the time when it is made.

(6) The reference in subsection (1) above to an in-patient does not include an in-patient who is liable to be detained in pursuance of an application under this Part of this Act [or a community patient] and the references in subsections (2) and (4) above do not include an in-patient who is liable to be detained in a hospital under this Part of this Act [or a community patient].

(7) In subsection (4) above "prescribed" means prescribed by an order made by the Secretary of State.

AMENDMENTS
The amendments to this section were made by the Mental Health Act 2007 ss.9(2), 32, Sch.3 para.2.

DEFINITIONS   **1–080**
    patient: s.145(1).
    hospital: ss.34(2), 145(1).
    application for admission for treatment: ss.3, 145(1).
    application for admission for assessment: ss.2, 145(1).
    the managers: s.145(1).
    mental disorder: s.145(1).
    approved clinician: s.145(1).
    community patient: ss.17A(7), 145(1).

GENERAL NOTE
    This section provides for applications for compulsory detention under s.2 or 3 to be made **1–081** in respect of mentally disordered patients who are already receiving treatment in hospital as informal patients. It also sets out the procedures, the "holding powers", that can be used if it is considered that an informal patient might leave the hospital before there is time to complete an application under either s.2 or s.3. The holding powers, one for doctors and approved clinicians (subs.(2)) and the other for nurses (subs.(4)), cannot be used to prolong the detention of a patient whose section is about to expire or in respect of a community patient (subs.(6)). Although detention under subss.(2) or (4) cannot be renewed, "that does not prevent it being used again on a future occasion if necessary" (*Code of Practice*, para.18.38). Hospital managers must ensure that patients detained under this section are given information about their position and their rights as required by s.132.

Patients who are detained under the provisions of subs.(2) or (4) are not subject to the consent to treatment provisions contained in Pt IV (s.56(3)(b)). If the patient is mentally capable of making a decision about treatment, the common law enables him to refuse to be treated for either a physical or mental disorder. However, if the patient is assessed as being mentally incapable of making a decision about treatment, the treatment can be provided under the Mental Capacity Act 2005 if it is deemed to be in his best interests.

A person who has been detained under either subs.(2) or subs.(4) may be retaken if he absents himself from the hospital without leave as long as the 72 hour (for subs.(2)) or six-hour (for subs.(4)) period has not expired (s.18(5)).

An account of further powers that are available to restrain and/or detain mentally disordered persons is contained in Appendix A.

Transfers to other hospitals

1–082   A patient who is detained under this section cannot be transferred to another hospital under reg.7 of the English Regulations and reg.23 of the Welsh Regulations because such a person is not "liable to be detained in a hospital by virtue of an application" under this Part (see s.19(1)(a), (2)(a)).

If a mentally capable patient who has been detained by subs.(2) needs to be taken to another hospital (the "receiving hospital") for urgent treatment or for security reasons, the transfer can be made if the patient consents to it. However, the s.5(2) will automatically lapse when the patient is moved from the hospital named on the Form H1 because the holding power only provides authority for the patient to be detained in "the hospital", i.e. the hospital that was providing in-patient treatment to the patient at the time when the Form was signed. It is submitted that the Form H1 would be reactivated if the patient returned to that hospital with his consent within the 72-hour period. Consideration would have to be given to invoking either subs.(2) or subs.(4) if the patient made an attempt to leave the receiving hospital. If the patient either does not consent to the transfer, or is mentally incapable and is resisting being transferred, and the urgency of the situation is such that there is not sufficient time to comply with the formalities of an application under s.2, an application under s.4 can be made and the transfer effected under s.19. Alternatively, the application under s.4 could be made out to the receiving hospital. If the patient is mentally incapable and is not resisting being transferred, the transfer can be effected under the Mental Capacity Act 2005 if the transfer is assessed as being in his best interests: also see paras 18.42–18.45 of the *Code of Practice*.

Code of Practice

1–083   Guidance on the use of the "holding powers" is contained in Ch.18.

Human Rights Act 1998

1–084   The powers contained in subss.(2) and (4) do not violate the European Convention on Human Rights (ECHR) because the procedural safeguards established under Convention case law do not apply to emergency situations (*Winterwerp v Netherlands* (1979) 2 E.H.R.R. 387, para.39). The use by staff of common law powers to detain and control patients in emergency situations whilst awaiting the presence of either a doctor or a specialist nurse who has the power to act under either subs.(2) or (4) is also allowable under the ECHR: see Appendix A. However, such powers should only be used as a "safety net" to cover situations were it is not possible to immediately invoke the statutory powers. In other words, to be consistent with the ECHR, common law powers should not be used as an alternative to the powers contained in the Act.

Doctors and nurses who use the holding powers are exercising "functions of a public nature" and are therefore "public authorities" for the purposes of s.6 of the Human Rights Act (s.6(3)(b)).

Subsection (1)

1–085   IN-PATIENT.   The combined effect of this subsection and subs.(6) is that:

(i)   an application for compulsory admission to hospital can be made in respect of an informal patient notwithstanding that he is already an in-patient in hospital;

(ii)   an application for compulsory admission cannot be made in respect of community patients or patients who are already in hospital under compulsory powers except that an application under s.3 can be made in respect of a patient detained under s.2;

(iii)   where an application is made in respect of a patient who is already in hospital, it is treated for the purposes of this Part of the Act as if the patient were admitted to the hospital at the time when that application was received by the managers; and

(iv)   the holding powers contained in subss.(2) and (4) cannot be used in respect of either a detained or a community patient.

Subsection (2)

This subsection enables an informal patient, including a patient who is subject to a depri-   **1–086**
vation of liberty authorisation under the Mental Capacity Act 2005 but excluding a community patient (subs.(6)), to be detained for up to 72 hours if the doctor or approved clinician (AC) who is in charge of the patient's treatment reports that an application under s.2 or 3 ought to be made. The power can be exercised in any hospital and the doctor or AC need not be a psychiatrist. The power cannot be used to prolong the detention of a patient whose section is about to expire (subs.(6)) or to provide time for an application to be made to the county court pursuant to s.29(4) to displace a nearest relative after the expiration of the 28-day period of detention provided for under s.2 (*McDougall v Sefton Area Health Authority*, April 9, 1987, McNeill J., cited in L. Gostin, *Mental Health Services—Law and Practice*, 1986, at para.10.04). The Mental Health Act Commission (MHAC) reported that it advised a NHS trust "that consecutive applications of s.5(2) are uncommon and hardly every necessary if assessments are carried out promptly" (*Seventh Biennial Report*, 1995–1997, para.3.2). It is submitted that, following the decision in *R. v Wilson Ex p. Williamson* [1996] C.O.D. 42, noted in the General Note to s.2, this practice is unlawful.

The purpose of the power is to prevent a patient from discharging himself from hospital before there is time to arrange for an application under s.2 or s.3 to be made. The patient need not have been admitted to the hospital for treatment for a mental disorder. As soon as the power is invoked, arrangements should be made for the patient to be assessed by a potential applicant and potential recommending doctors. Paragraph 18.8 of the *Code of Practice* states that patients "should not be admitted informally with the sole intention of then using the holding power".

The "Inquiry into the Care and Treatment of Gilbert Kopernik-Steckel" recommended that the MHAC should produce advice on the use of statements in a patient's file such as "For section 5(2) if he tries to leave". Although statements which fetter the discretion of the section 5(2) clinician should be avoided, there is nothing objectionable in the doctor or AC who is in charge of the patient's treatment making a record to the effect that "section 5(2) should be considered if the patient makes an attempt to leave". Paragraph 18.18 of the *Code of Practice* states:

> "Doctors and approved clinicians may leave instructions with ward staff to contact them (or their nominated deputy) if a particular patient wants or tries to leave. But they may not leave instructions for their nominated deputy to use section 5, nor may they complete a section 5 report in advance to be used in their absence. The deputy must exercise their own professional judgment."

In *R. v Wilson Ex p. Williamson* [1996] C.O.D. 42, the court declared that the patient's detention under s.2 was unlawful. Counsel for the hospital managers argued that this provision would not be available following the court's decision because it was "designed for the patient who had been a voluntary patient" and that to use the provision in respect of a patient who had been detained in the hospital unlawfuly would be to "take advantage of unlawful status" and would make the hospital managers vulnerable to judicial review on the ground that they were "using it for improper purposes". Although counsel's points have some substance, the correctness of his opinion must be doubted because a patient who has been unlawfuly detained is clearly an "in-patient", and it surely cannot be "improper" for the patient's consultant to utilise the only provision that is available to her to prevent a patient, who might have been diagnosed as being either dangerous or suicidal, from being discharged from the hospital. In *R. v Birmingham Mental Health Trust Ex p. Phillips*, May 25, 1995, the fact that the patient had been made the subject of this provision immediately after it was discovered that the application under s.2 that had been made in respect of her was invalid was accepted by Tucker J. without comment. However, the use of s.5(2) in this situation would only be lawful if the invalid section had been discharged by either the hospital managers or the patient's RC: see subs.(6).

There is no procedure for discharging the patient from the holding power. The power will automatically lapse if:

(i)   the result of the assessment is a decision not to make an application under s.2 or 3; or

(ii)   the power is invoked by a doctor or an AC who has been nominated under subs.(3) and the clinician in charge of the patient's treatment subsequently decides that no assessment for possible detention needs to be carried out, or

(iii)   an application under s.2 or 3 is made.

Where this power has been invoked by the doctor or AC nominated under subs.(3), there is no need to involve a potential applicant in the assessment if the clinician in charge of the patient's treatment subsequently examines the patient and concludes that an application should not be made.

If an approved mental health professional concludes at the assessment that an application in respect of the patient is not required and the assessing doctor holds a contrary view, there is nothing in this provision that prevents the assessment from being prolonged to enable the patient's nearest relative to consider whether he or she wishes to make an application.

The MHAC:

"found instances where section 5(2) appears either to be used simply as a three day holding power, or lasts three days by default because the clinician in charge of the patient's treatment has not informed the records officer as soon as a decision is taken not to proceed with assessment for compulsory detention or because the assessment process is not begun as soon as the section 5(2) is implemented."

This finding led the MHAC to recommend that "a record be kept of the date and time of both beginning and end of the holding power under section 5(2)" (*Fifth Biennial Report* 1991–1993, para.3.5(e)).

This power should not be used merely to justify the intervention of staff in an emergency to respond to an informal patient's disturbed behaviour as such intervention can be justified under the powers outlined in Appendix A.

1–087   IN-PATIENT IN A HOSPITAL.   The patient could be receiving treatment in a general hospital for a physical condition. In *Great Western Hospitals NHS Foundation Trust v AA* [2014] EWHC 132 (Fam) this provision was invoked in respect of a pregnant patient who was being treated in a labour suite. The patient's caesarean section and the potential use of restraint on her were authorised under the court's inherent jurisdiction: see the notes on s.63. A patient who is being treated in an out-patient department, in a day hospital or as a day patient cannot be detained under this provision. The second edition of the *Code of Practice* at para.8.4 offered the following definition of "in-patient": "one who has understood and accepted the offer of a bed, and who has freely appeared on the ward and who has co-operated in the admission procedure". In *R. (on the application of DR) v Mersey Care NHS Trust* [2002] EWHC 1810 (Admin); [2002] M.H.L.R. 386 para.27, Wilson J. said that the word in-patient "suggests the allocation and use of a hospital bed". His Lordship made no reference in his judgment to the *Code of Practice* definition. A suggested definition of a mentally incapable informal in-patient is: a compliant patient who has arrived at the ward and who has not provided any evidence of resistance (either verbal or physical) to the admission procedure. In both cases, the availability of a bed for the patient is a pre-condition to attaining in-patient status. The current edition of the *Code of Practice* merely states that, in the context of this section, "a hospital in-patient means any person who is receiving in-patient treatment in a hospital" (para.18.7).

As the power contained in this subsection only applies if the patient is an informal in-patient, it is necessary to identify how a patient can divest himself of his in-patient status. Can, for example, an in-patient avoid being held under this provision by the simple expedient of saying to the clinician who is about to invoke the power, "I discharge myself?". It is highly unlikely that the courts would find that a patient could end his in-patient status in this manner as such a finding would have the effect of totally subverting Parliament's intention in enacting this provision. It is submitted that a patient does not lose his in-patient status until he has physically removed himself from the hospital. This approach was endorsed by the Court of Appeal, Northern Ireland in *Re McGee* [2007] NICA 38; [2008] M.H.L.R. 216, where it was held that a patient did not cease to be an in-patient for the purposes of the equivalent provision in the Northern Irish legislation when he expressed his desire to leave the hospital an hour after being told of the decision of the tribunal to discharge him from detention. Girvan L.J. said at para.12: "He did not physically remove himself from the hospital [and his] bed was still available to him".

MEDICAL PRACTITIONER OR APPROVED CLINICIAN IN CHARGE. Determining the person "in **1–088** charge" of the patient's medical treatment is a question of fact.

The *Code of Practice* states:

"18.4 The identity of the person in charge of a patient's medical treatment at any time will depend on the particular circumstances. A professional who is treating the patient under the direction of another professional should not be considered to be in charge.

18.5 There may be more than one person who could reasonably be said to be in charge of a patient's treatment, eg where a patient is already receiving treatment for both a physical and a mental disorder. In a case of that kind, the psychiatrist or approved clinician in charge of the patient's treatment for the mental disorder is the preferred person to use the power in section 5, if necessary."

The person in charge should only exercise the power after having personally examined the patient (*Code of Practice*, para.18.10). Surprisingly, the Act does not require the patient to be examined.

Paragraph 18.11 of the *Code of Practice* states:

"Sometimes a report under section 5(2) may be made in relation to a patient who is not at the time under the care of a psychiatrist or an approved clinician. In such cases, the doctor invoking the power should make immediate contact with a psychiatrist or an approved clinician to obtain confirmation of their opinion that the patient needs to be detained so that an application can be made. If possible, the doctor should seek such advice before using the power."

AN APPLICATION OUGHT TO BE MADE. Although the most frequent circumstance leading to the use of this power is an attempt by the patient to leave the hospital, this ground enables a patient to be detained in the absence of such behaviour. For example, the patient could be detained in a situation where he had recently returned to the hospital after having left contrary to professional advice and the clinician in charge of the patient's treatment believed that it was likely that the patient would absent himself again in the near future.

If an application is made during the 72-hour period, the application will commence from the time when it was accepted by the hospital managers and not from the time when this provision was invoked. The responsibility for deciding whether to make an application under s.2 or s.3 is that of the applicant, not the recommending doctors. The application need not be addressed to the hospital which is holding the patient under this provison.

REPORT.   Using Form H1 (in Wales, Form HO12): see reg.4(1) of the English and Welsh Regulations.

1–089   DETAINED IN THE HOSPITAL.   Although this provision is silent on the point, it is submitted that the patient is detained by the hospital managers. If the patient is an in-patient of a hospital which is managed by more than one set of hospital managers, the patient can be detained in any part of the hospital that is managed by the hospital managers of the ward where the patient is an in-patient. There is, it is submitted, no authority to detain the patient in a part of the hospital that is managed by different hospital managers.

72 HOURS.   This is the maximum period during which a patient can be detained. The authority to detain under this provision is not renewable. However, circumstances could arise where a change in the patient's situation could lead to a second use of this provision being contemplated soon after its first use.

If a patient who has been detained under this provision absconds, he cannot be retaken once the 72-hour period has expired (s.18(5)).

TIME WHEN THE REPORT IS . . . FURNISHED.   In the Scottish case of *Milborrow, Applicant*, 1996 S.C.L.R. 315 Sh. Ct, it was held that a report is "furnished" to the hospital managers when it is committed to the internal mail system operated by those managers. The period of detention therefore starts at that point or when the report is handed over to a member of staff who is authorised to receive it: see Form H1 (or HO12) and para.18.6 of the *Code of Practice*.

If the patient is intent on leaving the hospital immediately, the powers outlined in Appendix A will provide authority for the patient to be detained for the short period that is required to complete Form H1. Once Form H1 has been completed and committed to the hospital's internal mail system or handed to the authorised member of staff, the patient can be detained even though he might have left the ward area. However, if the patient has left the hospital before the completion of Form H1, the hospital managers cannot subsequently detain him and return him to hospital on the authority of that form. This is because by leaving hospital the patient relinquishes his in-patient status which is an essential pre-condition to the use of this subsection. As a patient who is not "liable to be detained", he could not be returned to hospital under the auspices of s.18.

Subsection (3)

1–090   This subsection, which should be read with subs.(3A), is aimed at lessening pressure on clinicians to contravene the provisions of subs.(2) by, for example, allowing persons other than the "medical practitioner or approved clinician in charge" to sign Form H1 or by blank forms being signed for use when emergencies occur.

MAY NOMINATE.   The nominated clinician, who could be a junior doctor in a general hospital should exercise her own judgment when exercising the power under subs.(2). She can be advised, but not required to consult with a senior colleague before exercising the power.

Good practice dictates that the nomination should be put in writing and conveyed to all relevant staff. It is the doctor or AC in charge of the patient's treatment and not the hospital managers who must make the nomination. The nominee should be a doctor or AC who has been assessed as having the knowledge and experience that qualifies her to perform the onerous task of deciding whether patients should be deprived of their liberty.

Paragraph 18.14 of the *Code of Practice* states:

"Doctors should not be nominated as a deputy unless they are competent to perform the role. If nominated deputies are not approved clinicians (or doctors approved under section 12 of the Act), they should wherever possible seek advice from the person for whom they are deputising, or from someone else who is an approved clinician or section 12 approved doctor, before using section 5(2). Hospital managers should see that arrangements are in place to allow nominated deputies to do this."

The doctor or AC in charge of the patient's treatment should only nominate a class of doctors, such as "the duty doctor", if "there is only one nominated deputy for any patient at any time and it can be determined with certainty who that nominated deputy is" (*Code of Practice*, para.18.16). The nominated doctor or AC cannot delegate to another because of the legal principle *delegatus non potest delegare*.

Only one doctor or AC may be nominated to act during any particular period. A nomination "to Dr A or, in Dr A's absence, to Dr B" would be unlawful.

ON THE STAFF OF THAT HOSPITAL. The doctor or AC must be employed or contracted to undertake clinical responsibilities at the hospital. A medical practitioner nominee must be a fully registered person within the meaning of the Medical Act 1983 (Interpretation Act 1978, Sch.1).

Subsection (3A)

For the purpose of making a nomination under subs.(3), a doctor who is in charge of the **1–091** patient's treatment can nominate either another doctor or an AC (who need not be a doctor), while an AC who is in charge of the patient's treatment can nominate either another AC or a doctor. The nominee has to be "on the staff" of the relevant hospital.

Subsection (4)

This subsection provides for nurses of a prescribed class (see subs.(7)) to invoke a "hold- **1–092** ing power" in respect of an informal patient, including a patient who is subject to a deprivation of liberty authorisation under the Mental Capacity Act 2005 but excluding a community patient (subs.(6)), for a period of not more than six hours. During this period the "medical practitioner or approved clinician in charge" or her nominated deputy should examine the patient with a view to making a report under subs.(2). The power to detain the patient takes effect at the time when the nurse makes her report. It can only be used if the patient is indicating either verbally or otherwise that he wishes to leave the hospital. Where a patient requires restraint but is not showing any inclination to leave the hospital, nurses have to rely on the powers outlined in Appendix A. The nurse who makes the report does not have to detain the patient personally (Reference Guide, para.8.84). A nurse invoking this provision is entitled to use the minimum force necessary to prevent the patient from leaving hospital.

This power can only be used in respect of patients who are receiving hospital treatment for mental disorder; it is not sufficient for the patient to be merely suffering from a mental disorder. Although the power can be invoked in any hospital where the patient is receiving treatment for mental disorder, it is unlikely that a non-psychiatric ward will be staffed with nurses of the "prescribed class". In an emergency, a nurse who is not of the prescribed class may use the powers set out in Appendix A to restrain a patient who might be a danger to self or others from leaving hospital until a practitioner who has the power to invoke either this provision or subs.(2) attends.

Exercising the holding power is the personal decision of the nurse who cannot be instructed to exercise it by anyone else.

DEGREE. The patient cannot be made subject to this power if he is not exhibiting any manifestations of mental disorder: see the note on "of a nature or degree" in s.3(2)(a).

IMMEDIATE ATTENDANCE OF A PRACTITIONER.   It is submitted that the nurses' holding power need not be invoked if either the clinician who is in charge of the patient's treatment or her nominee is in the hospital building and can attend at the ward within a few minutes of the crises occurring. A combination of the powers outlined in Appendix A and the legal maxim *de minimis non curat lex* (the error is too trivial to be of any consequence) would enable the patient to be held during this brief period. Paragraph 18.29 of the *Code of Practice* states that, before using this power "nurses should assess:

- the likely arrival time of the doctor or approved clinician, as against the likely intention of the patient to leave. It may be possible to persuade the patient to wait until a doctor or approved clinician arrives to discuss it further, and

- the consequences of a patient leaving the hospital before the doctor or approved clinician arrives – in other words, the harm that might occur to the patient or others."

SIX HOURS.   This is the maximum and non-renewable period during which a patient can be detained. If a patient who has been detained under this provision absconds, he cannot be retaken once the six hour period has elapsed (s.18(5)).

FROM THE TIME WHEN THAT FACT IS SO RECORDED.   On Form H2 or, in Wales, HO13. Although neither Form requires the nurse to give reasons for invoking the power, the *Code of Practice*, at para.18.33, states that these should be recorded in the patient's notes. The record should be made immediately after the nurse has decided to exercise the power. The power will end six hours later or on the earlier arrival of one of the clinicians entitled to make a report under subs.(2). If a decision is made not to exercise the powers under subs.(2), the patient can either leave the hospital or remain as an informal patient.

Subsection (5)

1–093   This subsection provides that where the "holding power" provided for in subs.(4) is followed by a report made under subs.(2), the period of 72 hours provided for in subs.(2) runs from the time when the record required by subs.(4) is made.

Subsection (7)

1–094   PRESCRIBED.   Regulation 2 of the Mental Health (Nurses) (England) Order 2008 (SI 2008/1207) states:

"(1) For the purposes of section 5(4) of the Mental Health Act 1983 (power to detain patient in hospital for maximum of 6 hours) a nurse of the prescribed class is a nurse registered in either Sub-Part 1 or 2 of the register maintained under article 5 of the Nursing and Midwifery Order 2001, whose registration includes an entry specified in paragraph (2).

(2) An entry in the register referred to in paragraph (1) is an entry indicating that the nurse's field of practice is either—

(a) mental health nursing, or
(b) learning disabilities nursing."

A nurse of the prescribed class can invoke the holding power with regard to both mentally disordered and learning disabled patients.

SECRETARY OF STATE.   The functions of the Minister, so far as exercisable in relation to Wales, are exercised by the Welsh Ministers (see the General Note to the Act) who have made a similar order: see SI 2008/2441 (W.214).

Effect of application for admission

6.—(1) An application for the admission of a patient to a hospital under this **1–095** Part of this Act, duly completed in accordance with the provisions of this Part of this Act, shall be sufficient authority for the applicant, or any person authorised by the applicant, to take the patient and convey him to the hospital at any time within the following period, that is to say—

(a) in the case of an application other than an emergency application, the period of 14 days beginning with the date on which the patient was last examined by a registered medical practitioner before giving a medical recommendation for the purposes of the application;

(b) in the case of an emergency application, the period of 24 hours beginning at the time when the patient was examined by the practitioner giving the medical recommendation which is referred to in s.4(3) above, or at the time when the application is made, whichever is the earlier.

(2) Where a patient is admitted within the said period to the hospital specified in such an application as is mentioned in subs.(1) above, or, being within that hospital, is treated by virtue of s.5 above as if he had been so admitted, the application shall be sufficient authority for the managers to detain the patient in the hospital in accordance with the provisions of this Act.

(3) Any application for the admission of a patient under this Part of this Act which appears to be duly made and to be founded on the necessary medical recommendations may be acted upon without further proof of the signature or qualification of the person by whom the application or any such medical recommendation is made or given or of any matter of fact or opinion stated in it.

(4) Where a patient is admitted to a hospital in pursuance of an application for admission for treatment, any previous application under this Part of this Act by virtue of which he was liable to be detained in a hospital or subject to guardianship shall cease to have effect.

DEFINITIONS

    patient: s.145(1).   **1–096**

    hospital: ss.34(2), 145(1).

    the managers: s.145(1).

    application for admission for treatment: ss.3, 145(1).

GENERAL NOTE

    This section authorises (1) the applicant for the patient's detention or anyone authorised **1–097** by her to take and convey the patient to the hospital named in the application within specified periods (subs.(1)), and (2) the hospital managers to detain the patient once he has been admitted to that hospital (subs.(2)). It also enables the hospital managers to act on statutory documents that appear to be valid (subs.(3)) and provides for the termination of existing applications subsequent to a patient's admission for treatment under s.3 (subs.(4)). The courts have held that the power to detain necessarily carries with it a power of control: see the note on "to detain the patient" in subs.(2).

The legality of the patient's detention

    The legality of a patient's detention in circumstances where the requirements of the Act **1–098** relating to applications have not been fulfilled was considered in the following passage from the judgment of Laws J. in *R. v Managers of South Western Hospital Ex p. M* [1994] 1 All E.R. 161 at 176:

"Section 6(1) and (2) confer authority to convey or detain the patient in hospital where the application is 'duly completed in accordance with the provisions of this Part of this Act.' In my judgment this is an objective requirement and means that the application must not only *state* that the relevant provisions (which include the requirements of section 11(4)) have been fulfilled, but also that it be the case that they have actually been fulfilled. Here they were not; section 11(4) was not complied with. It follows, in my judgment, that the managers were not authorised to detain the applicant unless they were entitled to act upon [the approved mental health professional's] application by virtue of section 6(3). The contrast between section 6(1) and section 6(3) is of course between the words 'duly completed' and 'appears to be made.' In my judgment, where an application on its face sets out all the facts which, if true, constitute compliance with the relevant provisions of Part 2 of the Act (again, including section 11(4)) it is an application which 'appears to be duly made' within section 6(3). If any of the facts thus stated are not true, then although the application *appears* to be duly made, it is not duly completed for the purposes of section 6(1) and 6(2). Here, [the approved mental health professional's] application did state all the facts which, if true, constituted compliance with the relevant statutory provisions. Accordingly it was an application which appeared to be duly made. It follows that, although the managers were not authorised to detain the patient by section 6(2) standing alone, they were entitled to act upon the application, and thus to detain the patient, by virtue of section 6(3). Accordingly, the applicant's detention is not unlawful."

In *Re S-C (Mental Patient: Habeas Corpus)* [1996] 1 All E.R. 532, CA, Sir Thomas Bingham M.R. said, at 542, 543, that he:

"would accept almost everything in [the passage quoted above] as correct with the exception of the last sentence. The judge goes straight from a finding that the hospital managers were entitled to act upon an apparently valid application to the conclusion that the applicant's detention was therefore not unlawful. That is, in my judgment, a non sequitur. It is perfectly possible that the hospital managers were entitled to act on an apparently valid application, but that the detention was in fact unlawful. If that were not so the implications would, in my judgment, be horrifying. It would mean that an application which appeared to be in order would render the detention of a citizen lawful even though it was shown or admitted that the [approved mental health professional] purporting to make the application was not an [approved mental health professional], that the registered medical practitioners whose recommendations founded the application were not registered medical practitioners or had not signed the recommendations, and that the [approved mental health professional] had not consulted the patient's nearest relative or had consulted the patient's nearest relative and that relative had objected. In other words, it would mean that the detention was lawful even though every statutory safeguard built into the procedure was shown to have been ignored or violated. Bearing in mind what is at stake, I find that conclusion wholly unacceptable."

The other members of the Court of Appeal agreed with this finding. It should be noted that the decision in *Re S-C* applies to an administrative decision and not to an order of the court (*R. (on the application of A Claimant) v Harrow Crown Court* [2003] EWHC 2020 (Admin), para.24). An irregular order of the court made under the Act is effective and must be obeyed until set aside by the High Court (*South West Yorkshire Mental Health NHS Trust v Bradford Crown Court* [2003] EWHC 640 (Admin)).

In *R. v Central London County Court Ex p. London* [1999] 3 All E.R. 991 CA para.32, Stuart-Smith L.J., in giving the leading judgment, said, obiter, that he understood the Court of Appeal in *Re S-C* to have interpreted the phrase used by Laws J. which they had criticised as meaning that the patient's *continued* detention is not unlawful, rather than the original detention was not unlawful. These observations were not followed by the Court of

Appeal in *TTM v London Borough of Hackney* [2011] EWCA Civ 4; [2011] 3 All E.R. 529 which confirmed that the decision in *Re S-C* was that the detention was unlawful from the point when the patient was admitted under the defective application.

The following propositions can be said to represent the law on this issue: **1–099**

(1) An application for admission made by an approved mental health professional (AMHP) or a nearest relative setting out all the relevant facts which, if true, constituted compliance with the relevant provisions of this Part of the Act, is an application which "appears to be duly made" for the purposes of subs.(3).

(2) After having carefully checked (per Neill L.J. in *Re S-C* at 544 and see para. 35.9 of the *Code of Practice*) the documentation for obvious errors, the hospital managers are entitled to act on the application without further proof of the facts stated therein. In *Re S-C* Sir Thomas Bingham M.R. said at 537:

> "[Section 6] provides protection for a hospital to which a patient is admitted or in which a patient is detained. Such a hospital is not at risk of liability for false imprisonment if it turns out that the [approved mental health professional] does not meet the definition in section 145(1), or if the recommendations which purport to be signed by registered medical practitioners are in truth not signed by such, although appearing to be so. That is obviously good sense. A mental hospital is not obliged to act like a private detective; it can take documents at face value. Provided they appear to conform with the requirements of the statute, the hospital is entitled to act on them."

(3) If, subsequent to having accepted an application, the hospital managers discover that the application is fundamentally defective (e.g. a s.3 application which was made despite the fact that the patient's nearest relative objected to it), this has the effect of rendering the detention of the patient unlawful. In these circumstances the hospital managers should:

    (a) inform the patient of the situation and of the need for him to obtain legal advice;

    (b) make an appropriate note on the patient's file; and

    (c) if the patient is not re-detained under s.3 (which has the effect of discharging any previous application (subs.(4)), the managers should exercise their power under s.23 to discharge the patient from his liability to be detained if the patient's responsible clinician (RC) has not already exercised her power of discharge. That the detention should be "brought to an end" was confirmed by Collins J. in *TTM* at first instance: see the note to subs.(3). If the patient is not discharged from detention, *habeas corpus* and/or judicial review proceedings could be brought. In the example given, the patient could issue a claim for false imprisonment and/or compensation under art.5 of the European Convention on Human Rights (ECHR) against the local authority for the period starting with the date of his initial detention. This would be the case even if the AMHP had acted in good faith (*TTM v London Borough of Hackney*, above).

(4) A decision to re-detain the patient could be preceded by the use of the holding powers contained in s.5 if the relevant criteria are satisfied: see the Reference Guide at para.31.21.

The advice set out in (3) and (4) is confirmed in the *Code of Practice* which states at para.35.13:

"If admission documents reveal a defect which fundamentally invalidates the application and which cannot, therefore, be rectified under section 15 of the Act, the patient can no longer be detained on the basis of the application. Authority for the patient's detention can be obtained only through a new application (or, in the interim, by the use of the holding powers under section 5 if the patient has already been admitted to the hospital). Unless that authority is to be sought, the hospital managers should use their power under section 23 to discharge the patient. The patient should be informed both orally and in writing, and in an accessible format for the patient."

Damages for an unlawful detention

1–100   In *Bostridge v Oxleas NHS Foundation Trust* [2015] EWCA Civ 79, the patient had been unlawfully detained for 442 days because he had been recalled to hospital on the basis of an invalid community treatment order (CTO). His case was reviewed twice by a tribunal, where no-one identified the illegality, and on both occasions the tribunal found that his condition warranted continued detention in the hospital. The single issue before the Court of Appeal was whether the patient "is entitled to substantial damages instead of the nominal damages awarded by the judge, in circumstances where he would anyway have been detained lawfully had the defendant NHS trust been aware of the unlawfulness" (para.1). Vos L.J. said at para.20 that the "tort of false imprisonment is compensated in the same way as other torts such as to put the claimant in the position he would have been in had the tort not been committed. Thus if the position is that, had the tort not been committed, the claimant would in fact have been in exactly the same position, he will not normally be entitled to anything more than nominal damages". As the patient had suffered no loss because he would have been lawfully detained under s.3 throughout the period concerned had the lack of authority to make a CTO been drawn to the Trust's attention, the Court held that patient was only entitled to nominal damages. Substantial damages were not required "either to reflect the loss of liberty or the loss of the procedural and substantive protections afforded by a lawful detention" (para.30). At first instance, the judge anticipated that the award of damages would be £1.

Guidance on the amount of compensation to be awarded in a case where a prisoner had suffered loss by being unlawfully detained contrary to art.5(4) of the European Convention on Human Rights was given by the Supreme Court in *R. (on the application of Faulkner) v Secretary of State for Justice* [2013] UKSC 23. The Court held that at the present stage of the development of the remedy of damages under s.8 of the Human Rights Act 1998, courts should be guided, following *R. (Greenfield) v Secretary of State for the Home Department* [2005] 1 W.L.R. 673, primarily by any clear and consistent practice of the European court. In particular, the quantum of awards under s.8 should broadly reflect the level of awards made by the European court in comparable cases brought by applicants from the UK or other countries with a similar cost of living. The court awarded compensation of £6,500 for an unlawful detention that lasted 10 months. Case law on the awarding of damages under s.8 was reviewed by Green J. in *DSD and NBV v Commissioner of Police for the Metropolis* [2014] EWHC 2493 (QB).

Disputes regarding compliance with the Act

1–101   If there is a genuine dispute about whether a provision of the Act has been complied with (e.g. the patient's nearest relative disputes the AMHP's assertion on the application form that the consultation required by s.11(4) took place), the hospital managers should not attempt to resolve the dispute but should leave the patient to consider challenging the detention. In *Re S-C*, above, Turner J., speaking at first instance, said: "There is, in my judgment, no means by which managers can investigate the truth or otherwise of assertions that the form has not been duly made, let alone is there any guidance as to the manner in which they should adjudicate on such issue and come to a conclusion contrary to that which appears on the face of the application form" ([1996] C.O.D. 221). These comments are consistent with the judgments delivered in the Court of Appeal.

Human Rights Act 1998

1–102   The approach adopted in *Re S-C* to defective applications was implicitly endorsed by the European Court of Human Rights in *Mooren v Germany* (2010) 50 E.H.R.R. 23, where it was held that defects in a detention order did not necessarily render the underlying detention unlawful for the purposes of art.5(1) of the ECHR unless they amounted to "a gross and obvious irregularity".

In *Munjaz v United Kingdom* [2012] M.H.L.R. 351, the European Court of Human Rights held that in certain circumstances the seclusion of a detained patient could amount to a further deprivation of his liberty under art.5 of the ECHR: see the note on "detention" under art.5(1)(e) in Part 5.

Code of Practice
The transport of patients is covered in Ch.17.   **1–103**

Subsection (1)
AN APPLICATION.   Comprises the application form and the medical recommendation   **1–104**
form(s).

DULY COMPLETED.   This is an objective requirement. Until the application is duly completed, the patient is not subject to the Act's powers. However, in *R. (on the application of Sessay) v South London and Maudsley NHS Foundation Trust)* [2011] EWHC 2617 (QB); [2012] M.H.L.R. 94, the Divisional Court said at para.57:

> "[I]n our view it is unlikely in the ordinary case that there will be a false imprisonment at common law or deprivation of liberty for the purposes of Article 5(1) [of the ECHR] if there is no undue delay during the processing of an application under ss.2 or 4 MHA for admission."

It is therefore the case that if, following an assessment of the patient, the potential applicant and recommending doctor(s) agree that an application to detain the patient should be made, the common law provides authority to use restraint on the patient during the time that it takes to process the application as long as the process is not unduly delayed. Common law powers are discussed in Appendix A.

If those who are assessing the patient are asked to leave the patient's home before an application is completed they would be trespassers if they remained and the householder would be entitled to use reasonable force in ejecting them (*Townley v Rushworth*, 62 L.G.R. 95, DC). The professionals would not become trespassers if one co-owner gave them permission to stay, despite the fact that the other co-owner requested that they leave: see the note on "enter and inspect" in s.115.

A duly completed application does not provide authority for the applicant to force entry into the patient's home. If force is required to gain entry after the application has been completed, an application should be made for a warrant under s.135(2). If the AMHP or the person authorised under this subsection have access to the patient in his home after the application has been completed, there is no requirement for a warrant to be obtained as this section provides sufficient legal authority for an objecting patient to be conveyed to hospital.

If, having signed the application form, an AMHP applicant discovers a minor and rectifiable error on one of the medical recommendations and it is not possible to contact the relevant doctor to right the error, it is permissible for the patient to be conveyed to the hospital on the authority of the application and for the error to be rectified within the 14-day period permitted by s.15.

APPLICANT.   Who will be either the patient's nearest relative or an AMHP (ss.4(2), 11(1)). Where the AMHP is the applicant, she has a professional responsibility for ensuring that all the necessary arrangements are made for the patient to be conveyed to hospital (*Code of Practice*, para.17.9).

ANY PERSON AUTHORISED BY THE APPLICANT.   Such as the police or a member of the ambulance service. The AMHP should provide written authority to the authorised person if the patient is likely to be unwilling to be moved (*Code of Practice*, para.17.13). The AMHP is not provided with a power to *direct* another person to convey the patient. Where delegation takes place, the AMHP retains ultimate responsibility to ensure that the patient is conveyed in a lawful and humane manner (*Code of Practice*, para.17.18).

If it is not practicable for the AMHP to attend at the hospital named in the application, or where "the applicant is not travelling in the same vehicle as the patient, the application form and medical recommendations should be given to the person authorised to transport the patient, with instructions for them to be presented to the member of hospital staff receiving the patient" (*Code of Practice*, para.17.21).

CONVEY HIM.   The power to convey is only triggered when the application is "duly completed". The exercise of the power can either be delayed (subs.(1)) or not exercised at all if, subsequent to the application being completed, the AMHP forms the opinion that there is no need to use it.

Either the applicant or the person delegated by the applicant (including ambulance staff) can use such force as is reasonably necessary to achieve the objective of conveying the patient to the hospital named in the application (s.137(2); also see para.17.18 of the *Code of Practice*). If the patient is likely to be violent, police assistance should be requested (*Code of Practice*, para.17.14). A patient who is being conveyed to hospital is deemed to be in legal custody (s.137(1)) and if he escapes he may be retaken within 14 days after the last medical examination for the purposes of a medical recommendation for s.2 or 3 patients, or within 24 hours from the medical examination or the time when the application was made, whichever is the earlier for a s.4 patient (s.138).

If a mentally incapable patient requires emergency hospital treatment for a physical disorder prior to being taken to the psychiatric hospital named in the application and such treatment is deemed to be in the patient's best interests, ss.5 and 6 of the Mental Capacity Act 2005 provide authority for ambulance personnel to use reasonable force to overcome the patient's resistance to being taken to a general hospital for treatment. If the patient requires admission to the general hospital, the application should be addressed to that hospital: see further the note on "Treatment in an A and E department en route to the hospital named in the application", below.

TO HOSPITAL.   Which will be the hospital named on the application. It is unlawful to convey a patient to hospital on the authority of an application which does not state the name of the potential admitting hospital. It is also unlawful to take the patient to a hospital that is not the hospital named on the application even though the two hospitals come under the control of the same hospital managers. Although the named hospital is not under a legal obligation to admit the patient, it should only refuse to admit the patient on reasonable grounds, e.g. a suitable bed is not available or there are good clinical reasons to refuse admission. As the duly completed application does not provide authority to convey the patient to another hospital, it is essential for a recommending doctor to have confirmed to the applicant that a bed is available for the patient in the named hospital.

In its *Eighth Biennial Report*, 1997–1999, para.4.45, the Mental Health Act Commission suggested that if a patient cannot be admitted to hospital in an emergency for want of a bed "the [AMHP] should complete the application, making it out to a hospital specified to the relevant health authority in the notice required to be given under s.140 of the Act, and convey the patient to that hospital". This advice is subject to the criticism that the managers of the hospital specified in the s.140 notice are not legally obliged to admit the patient and, in any event, it might be clinically inappropriate for the patient to be admitted to that hospital. The MHAC returned to this theme in its *Ninth Biennial Report*, 1999–2001 where a "Good Practice Example" is set out at para.2.50. The example states that if no bed is available at the hospital named in the application, the patient can be formally admitted to the hospital by being held in a "holding area" and that if it proves impossible to identify a bed within the hospital, the patient should be granted leave of absence under s.17 to a "temporary bed" in another hospital. While it is perfectly lawful for a patient to be kept in a "waiting" or "holding" area for the short period that is required to prepare a bed that has been allocated to the patient, the practice commended by the MHAC of "admitting" the patient in a situation where no bed has been identified for him is both potentially dangerous and of doubtful legality. Holding a patient who might be acutely ill in a non-clinical area of a hospital for what might turn out to be a considerable amount of time can be neither in the interests of the patient nor of staff. Assuming that an approved clinician has been found who is willing to become the patient's responsible clinician (RC), it is at the very least extremely bad practice for the risk assessment that must precede a s.17 leave to be conducted in such an environment. It is also difficult to see how the hospital managers can adequately comply with their duties under s.132 in these circumstances.

The purpose of both ss.2 and 3 is for the patient to be admitted to the hospital named in the application and for him to be "detained there" (ss.2(1), 3(1)), i.e. at the hospital named in the application. To secure this aim one of the responsibilities of the recommending doctor is to ensure that, where there is to be an application for admission, a hospital bed will be available for the patient unless it has been agreed locally that AMHPs will do that (*Code of Practice*, para.14.77). It is arguably unlawful for an AMHP to make an application to detain a patient if it is known that there is no bed available for that patient in the hospital named in the application. In such a situation, can it be said that the patient has been "admitted" to the hospital for the purposes of s.6(2) if there is no bed to admit him to? If the patient has not been legally "admitted", the hospital managers have no power to detain him and he cannot be granted leave of absence. If a patient can be said to have been "admitted" merely by virtue of being held within the hospital building, he will, by definition, have become an in-patient. This interpretation conflicts with the point at which it is generally considered that a patient achieves in-patient status for the purposes of s.5(2). The 1993 edition of the *Code of Practice* stated, at para.8.4, that such status can only be achieved if the patient appears on the hospital ward to accept an offer of a bed. Even if it could be successfully argued that the patient who is being kept in a "holding area" has been admitted to the hospital, McCullough J. said in *R. v Hallstrom Ex p. W* [1986] Q.B. 1090 that the term "detention" in s.13 "cannot realistically include a purely nominal period before leave of absence is given, after which the treatment which the patient stands in need is to begin". Although the decision in *Hallstrom* was made in the context of a patient who had been granted leave of absence into the community, the finding of McCullough J. is equally applicable to a patient who has been granted immediate leave of absence to another hospital. In both cases, the detention at the hospital named in the application would be a sham.

The *Code of Practice* at para.14.91, states that patients who have been made subject to an application should not be moved unless it is known that the hospital named in the application is willing to accept them and, at para.14.99, considers the action to be taken if, on arrival at the hospital named in the application, a bed is no longer available for the patient. The guidance given in the *Code of Practice* on this issue should be followed.

If there is a significant delay in finding a hospital bed for the patient and, due to that delay, the patient remains at his home until a bed is found, responsibility for providing professional support to the patient at his home is that of the local mental health service.

In her speech to the Royal College of Psychiatrist's Annual Meeting at Glasgow in July 2006, the Parliamentary and Health Service Ombudsman, Ann Abraham, spoke of a complaint that her office had investigated which involved the non-availability of a bed for a sectioned patient. The patient, who had been provided with a limited amount of out-patient care, was sectioned at her home but, despite this, her family were told that there were no beds available for her. Faced with this situation, the family agreed to pay for a bed in a private hospital some distance away and the patient was admitted there under s.2. A bed was eventually found in the local psychiatric unit, but it was left for the family to organise a taxi and two private nurses for the transfer. The Ombudsman's investigation found that medical staff had, in fact considered that the patient needed a bed much earlier, but had felt there was little prospect of a bed becoming available and decided to manage her care at home. The complaint was upheld and a recommendation was made that the family be reimbursed.

Treatment in a general hospital

1–105   If a detained patient requires a period of in-patient treatment for a physical injury or disorder, it is unlawful for the patient to be admitted directly to the general hospital after having been given a "notional" leave of absence from the psychiatric hospital named in the application. If the patient is mentally competent, he could be admitted directly to the general hospital with his agreement and then taken to the psychiatric hospital before the expiry of the 14-day period provided for in para.(a). If the patient is unwilling to be admitted to the general hospital, he could be admitted to that hospital under the Act although any treatment for his physical condition could only proceed with his consent if he had the required mental capacity. In this situation, the general hospital would be the hospital named in the application and the patient's RC would be the psychiatrist who is in charge of the treatment of the patient's mental disorder at that hospital. To cater for this situation, it would be advisable for the psychiatric hospital to enter into a service level agreement with the general hospital for the provision of psychiatric treatment and Mental Health Act administration services at that hospital. To enable the managers of the general hospital to deal appropriately with any application for discharge that the patient might make, it is suggested that the managers should attempt to appoint the committee that has been established by the managers of the psychiatric hospital to hear such applications on their behalf.

Treatment in an A and E department en route to the hospital named in the application

1–106   If a patient who has been made the subject of an application requires emergency treatment for a physical injury or disorder he could be taken to and treated in an A and E department under common law powers or, if he was mentally incapacitated, under the Mental Capacity Act 2005 before being transported to the hospital named in the application: see the note on "Convey him", above.

In *Webley v St George's Hospital NHS Trust* [2014] EWHC 299 (QB), an AMHP applicant had delegated to the police the power to convey the patient to the hospital named in the application. Before he could be admitted, the patient's physical health deteriorated and he was taken to another hospital's A and E department for treatment. Bean J. held that the police owed a common law duty of care to the patient which "involved a duty to take reasonable steps to ensure that he did not come to physical harm while in their custody; a duty to take reasonable care only to release him into a safe environment; and a duty to provide relevant information to those into whose care he was transferred" (para.41). The "relevant information" included the fact that the patient had been assessed as being at risk of absconding. It was further held that the staff of the A and E department also owed a duty of care to the patient which included the duty to take reasonable steps to ensure his safety. A point that was not taken in this case was whether the patient, when he was being treated at the A and E department, was still in the process of being conveyed to the hospital named in the application and, if he was, whether the security staff at the department had been authorised to convey him and, therefore, to keep him in custody (see s.137(2)). It is suggested that: (1) a court would find that the patient was still involved in an, albeit interrupted, conveyance to the hospital; and (2) the doctrine of *delegatus non potest delegare* would prevent the police from further delegating their power of conveyance to the security staff.

Paragraph (a)

1–107   14 DAYS.   This period may be used to test out whether detention is the most appropriate option for the patient: see para.14.87 of the *Code of Practice*.

BEGINNING WITH THE DATE.   Including the date on which the patient was last examined (*Zoan v Rouamba* [2000] 2 All E.R. 620 CA).

LAST EXAMINED BY A REGISTERED MEDICAL PRACTITIONER.   The relevant date is that of the last medical examination, not the day on which the medical recommendation form was signed by the doctor. If the medical practitioners examined the patient separately, not more than five days must have elapsed between the respective examinations (s.12(1)).

Paragraph (b)
TIME WHEN THE PATIENT WAS EXAMINED.   Which may not be the same as the time when   **1–108**
the doctor signed the Form A11.

WHICHEVER IS THE EARLIER.   As an emergency application must be "founded on" the medical recommendation (s.4(3); also see Form A10), it should not be signed until the medical recommendation has been received by the applicant.

Subsection (2)
In *D'Souza v Director of Public Prosecutions* [1992] 4 All E.R. 545 at 553–554, Lord   **1–109**
Lowry said:

> "A person who is detained in hospital under section 6(2) is lawfully detained. If he goes absent without leave, he is then at large ..., and, since he ought not to be at large and is, by virtue of section 18(1), liable to be taken into custody and returned to the hospital, he would inevitably appear to be *unlawfully* at large [within section 17(1)(d) of the Police and Criminal Evidence Act 1984] until he is taken into custody".

The *D'Souza* case is considered in the General Note to s.135.

SUFFICIENT AUTHORITY FOR THE MANAGERS.   The application will be served by delivering it to an officer of the managers who will usually be the nurse in charge of the relevant ward: see reg.3(2) of the English and Welsh Regulations. That officer will check the documents for obvious errors and decide whether or not to accept the application. The application should only be accepted if it "appears to be duly made" and is "founded on the necessary medical recommendations"(subs.(3)). If the application is accepted, the documents should be passed to an officer who has been authorised under reg.4(3) of the English Regulations (reg.4(2) of the Welsh Regulations) to scrutinise them for the purposes of possible rectification under s.15.

Even if the application has been properly completed, there is no obligation placed on the managers by the Act to accept the application and detain the patient. There is nothing objectionable in the managers making enquiries as to the circumstances of the application to enable the appropriate officer to be put in a position to make an informed decision on whether to accept the application.

If the application is accepted, a record of admission shall be made by the managers in the form set out in Form H3: see reg.4(4) of the English Regulations (Form HO14 in Wales: see reg 4(3) of the Welsh Regulations). The date of the application for the purposes of calculation of time is the date when the patient is said to have been "formally detained" on the Form H3.

TO DETAIN THE PATIENT.   The courts have held that the express power to detain a patient for treatment necessarily implies a power to control that patient which includes the power to place him in seclusion: see the notes on s.139 under the heading "The power to control the activities of detained patients".

Subsection (3)
The effect of this provision is explained in the Reference Guide:

> "8.91 The managers do not have to seek further proof that the signatories are who they say they are or that they have the qualification to make the application which they have

signed to say they have. Nor do they need to seek further proof for any factual statement or opinion contained in the document.

8.92 For example, the managers do not need to check that signatories who state they are registered medical practitioners are in fact, registered, or seek independent verification of the time when the patient was last examined or that there was sufficient urgency to justify the making of an emergency application."

1–110 In *TTM v London Borough of Hackney* [2011] EWCA Civ 4; [2011] 3 All E.R. 529, the Court of Appeal confirmed that this provision does not have the effect of making lawful an application for admission which is fundamentally defective. Toulson L.J. made the following observations on the purpose of this provision at para.37:

"It is intended to enable hospital managers, possibly at short notice, to admit for treatment someone who they have reasonable cause to believe is in immediate need of such admission for the health and safety of himself or for the protection of the public, and, with this end in view, Parliament has considered it reasonable for the hospital managers to be able to rely on an application which appears to have been completed in accordance with the requirements of the Act. Since the section empowers hospital managers to admit a patient in respect of whom an application for his admission appears to have been duly made, it follows that they have a defence against any claim which might otherwise have been made against them for acting on an invalid application."

His Lordship further stated at para.68:

"It is in the public interest that a hospital trust should act promptly on receipt of an application for admission which appears to be in proper form, and that it should not think it necessary for its own legal protection to incur time and expense in checking the accuracy of the various matters which s 6(3) entitles it to accept as correct."

At first instance ([2010] EWHC 1349 (Admin), para.29), Collins J. made reference to para.13.9 of the 2008 edition of the *Code of Practice* and said that it was apparent from that paragraph "that the obligation to scrutinise arises after the admission based check that the documents appear to amount to an application that has been duly made. If, following such scrutiny, it is apparent that there was a defect which cannot be rectified under s.15 because it is fundamental, the detention should be brought to an end": also see the General Note to this section.

In *R. (on the application of Care Principles Ltd) v Mental Health Review Tribunal* [2006] EWHC 3194 (Admin); [2006] M.H.L.R. 365, Collins J. held that the extent of the hospital managers obligations to scrutinise the application must depend on the facts of a particular case. If they are aware of the existence of a previous tribunal decision ordering the discharge of the patient, it requires a critical consideration of the justification for the detention in the light of that decision; see the note on this case under the heading "The re-sectioning of a patient subsequent to a discharge made by the First-tier Tribunal (Mental Health) or the Mental Health Review Tribunal for Wales" in the General Note to s.3.

Subsection (4)

The Reference Guide states at para.8.98:

"Because an application for admission for treatment automatically ends any previous application for admission, it would also bring to an end a patient's CTO, if before going onto the CTO, the patient had been detained under section 3. In that case, a new CTO would have to be made for the patient when they no longer needed to be detained in hospital."

In *R. (on the application of M) v Hospital Managers of Queen Mary's Hospital* [2008] **1–111**
EWHC 1959 (Admin) para.18, Underhill J. considered this provision and said, without
deciding the point, that an ineffective application under s.3 which is subsequently found
to be unlawful would not undermine the s.2 application that preceded it, and that the s.2
application would remain in force, or be revived, until it expired.

A similar provision relating to the making of a hospital order or a guardianship order by a
court under s.37 can be found in s.40(5). For the effect that reception into guardianship has
on existing applications, see s.8(5).

APPLICATION FOR ADMISSION FOR TREATMENT.   But not an application for assessment
under s.2.

Guardianship

Application for guardianship
7.—(1) A patient who has attained the age of 16 years may be received into **1–112**
guardianship, for the period allowed by the following provisions of this Act, in
pursuance of an application (in this Act referred to as "a guardianship application") made in accordance with this section.

(2) A guardianship application may be made in respect of a patient on the
grounds that—
  (a) he is suffering from mental disorder [. . .] of a nature or degree which war-
      rants his reception into guardianship under this section; and
  (b) it is necessary in the interests of the welfare of the patient or for the protec-
      tion of other persons that the patient should be so received.

(3) A guardianship application shall be founded on the written recommendations in the prescribed form of two registered medical practitioners,
including in each case a statement that in the opinion of the practitioner the conditions set out in subsection (2) above are complied with; and each such
recommendation shall include—
  (a) such particulars as may be prescribed of the grounds for that opinion so far
      as it relates to the conditions set out in paragraph (a) of that subsection; and
  (b) a statement of the reasons for that opinion so far as it relates to the con-
      ditions set out in paragraph (b) of that subsection.

(4) A guardianship application shall state the age of the patient or, if his exact
age is not known to the applicant, shall state (if it be the fact) that the patient is
believed to have attained the age of 16 years.

(5) The person named as guardian in a guardianship application may be either a
local social services authority or any other person (including the applicant himself); but a guardianship application in which a person other than a local social
services authority is named as guardian shall be of no effect unless it is accepted
on behalf of that person by the local social services authority for the area in which
he resides, and shall be accompanied by a statement in writing by that person that
he is willing to act as guardian.

AMENDMENT
  In subs.(2)(a), the words omitted were repealed by the Mental Health Act 2007 s.55,
Sch.11 Pt 1.

DEFINITIONS
  patient: s.145(1).   **1–113**

mental disorder: ss.1, 145(1).
local social services authority: s.145(1).

GENERAL NOTE

1–114   The White Paper that preceded the Act stated that guardianship powers are needed for "a very small number of mentally disordered people who do not require treatment in hospital, either formally or informally, [but who] nevertheless need close supervision and some control in the community as a consequence of their mental disorder. These include people who are able to cope provided that they take their medication regularly, but who fail to do so, and those who neglect themselves to the point of seriously endangering their health" (Cmnd. 8405, para.43).

According to the *Code of Practice* the "purpose of guardianship is to enable patients to receive care outside hospital when it cannot be provided without the use of compulsory powers. Such care may, or may not, include specialist medical treatment for mental disorder" (para.30.2). It "provides an authoritative framework for working with a patient, with a minimum of constraint, to achieve as independent a life as possible within the community. Where it is used, it should be part of the patient's overall care plan" (para.30.4). Guardianship is used infrequently; less than 1000 cases are open in England at any one time.

Sections 5 and 6 of the Mental Capacity Act 2005 provide social care professionals who are caring for mentally incapacitated persons with protection against civil and criminal liability for certain acts done in connection with the care of such persons. The powers that staff have under that Act, which include the power to use restraint which does not constitute a deprivation of liberty, will usually be sufficient to ensure that the best interests of a mentally incapacitated person are satisfied. However, the Code of Practice on the 2005 Act, at para.13.20, provides the following examples of situations where staff might feel that a guardianship application would be appropriate:

- "they think it important that one person or authority should be in charge of making decisions about where the person should live (for example, where there have been long-running or difficult disagreements about where the person should live);

- they think the person will probably respond well to the authority and attention of a guardian, and so be more prepared to accept treatment for the mental disorder (whether they are able to consent to it or it is being provided for them under the Mental Capacity Act); or

- they need authority to return the person to the place they are to live (for example, a care home) if they were to go absent."

The reception of a patient into guardianship does not carry with it resource implications for the local authority (apart from associated administrative costs) because the fact that a patient is subject to guardianship does not provide that patient with an entitlement to receive services under the Care Act 2014. Guardianship patients are subject to the Care Programme Approach (*Reforming the Care Programme Approach: Policy and Positive Practice Guidance*, March 2008, p.14).

In cases where there is a significant dispute between the local authority and a mentally incapacitated patient and/or his carers about how best to meet the patient's needs, an application to the Court of Protection might be a more appropriate option than guardianship: see *C v Blackburn and Darwen Borough Council* which is noted under s.8(1)(a).

This section specifies the circumstances whereby a patient aged 16 or over may be received into the guardianship of a local social services authority or a person who is acceptable to the authority. A patient shall cease to be subject to guardianship if an order for his discharge is made by his responsible clinician (RC), by the responsible local social services authority or by his nearest relative (s.23(2)(b)). A discharge by the nearest relative cannot be barred by anyone.

The powers of the guardian are set out in s.8. A local social services authority (LSSA) has a duty to ensure that patients received into guardianship are visited: see reg.23 of the English Regulations and reg.10 of the Welsh Regulations. If the patient is hospitalised, the local authority has duties placed upon it by s.116. As a patient under guardianship is not "liable to be detained" for the purposes of s.56(3), he is not subject to the consent to treatment provisions contained in Pt IV.

Upon a patient being received into guardianship, the LSSA must take such steps as are practicable to inform the patient and the patient's nearest relative (unless the patient has requested otherwise) of the rights set out in reg.26(3), (4) of the English Regulations and reg.15 of the Welsh Regulations. The LSSA must also take steps to have a patient and the patient's nearest relative (unless the patient has requested otherwise) informed about independent mental health advocacy (s.130D). There is also a duty placed on the LSSA to inform a patient when his guardianship is renewed (s.20(6); also see reg.26(1)(n) of the English Regulations and reg.15(4) of the Welsh Regulations).

If a patient who has been made the subject of an application under this section is remanded into custody or sentenced under the criminal law, the provisions of s.22 will apply.

Under s.19 and regs 7, 8, and 11 of the English Regulations and regs 23, 24 and 27 of the Welsh Regulations detained patients and patients who are subject to guardianship may be transferred between hospitals and guardians or between detention in hospital and guardianship: see the notes to s.19.

It is an offence under the Act to neglect or ill-treat a patient who is under guardianship (s.127(2)).

Children

An application for guardianship cannot be made in respect of a person who is either aged **1–115** under 16 (subs.(1)) or a ward of court (s.33(3)). In *Re F (Mental Health Act: Guardianship)* [2000] 1 F.L.R. 192, the Court of Appeal held that wardship should not have been rejected by the judge as a more appropriate remedy than guardianship for a seventeen year old patient. An immediate consequence of wardship would have been the appointment of the Official Solicitor as her guardian ad litem, thereby securing the benefit of separate representation for the child. Thorpe L.J. said at 199: "[Guardianship] is not a child-centred Jurisdiction and the child lacks the benefit of independent representation".

Proceedings under s.31 and Sch.3, para.5 of the Children Act 1989 could be brought in respect of a child under 16 who requires supervision and control in the community as a consequence of mental disorder. A child is not a privately fostered child for the purposes of Pt IX of the 1989 Act while he is subject to guardianship (Children Act 1989 Sch.8, para.4).

The use of guardianship to authorise the deprivation of a person's liberty

See the note under this heading in s.8. **1–116**

Applications to the First-tier Tribunal (Mental Health) or the Mental Health Review Tribunal for Wales

The patient may make an application within six months his reception into guardianship **1–117** (s.66(1)(c), (2)(c)) and during each period of renewal (ss.66(1)(f), (2)(f), 20(2)). There is no automatic reference of guardianship cases to the tribunal.

Code of Practice

Guidance on guardianship is contained in Ch.30. Advice on deciding between guardian- **1–118** ship, leave of absence and supervised community treatment can be found in Ch.31.

With regard to the provision of information for guardianship patients, the *Code* states at para.4.52:

"Responsible local authorities are required to take steps to ensure that guardianship patients understand their rights to apply to a Tribunal and the rights of their nearest relatives. The same information also must normally be given to nearest relatives. More generally, local authorities (and private guardians) should do what they can to ensure that patients understand why they are subject to guardianship and what it means for them."

Dealing with domestic squalor and/or dangerous premises

1–119   People who live in domestic squalor may be suffering from either Diogenes syndrome or hoarding disorder. The action that a local authority can take when satisfied that premises are either (a) in such a filthy or unwholesome condition as to be prejudicial to health, or (b) are verminous is set out in ss.83 to 85 of the Public Health Act 1936. Part III of the Environmental Protection Act 1990 provides powers for local authorities to require the abatement of a range of problems including "any premises in such a state as to be prejudicial to health or a nuisance" and "any accumulation or deposit" which meets the same test. "Premises" includes open land such as a garden. These powers are considered in *Professional Practice Note: Hoarding and how to approach it – guidance for Environmental Heath Officers and others*, Chartered Institute of Environmental Health, May 2009.

If the person concerned is mentally incapacitated, it might be possible to take action under the Mental Capacity Act 2005. In "When protection matters", N.L.J., 15&22 April 2011, pp.537, 538, Robert Eckford describes how the Court of Protection made orders to allow a local authority to undertake works on a property for the sole purpose of allowing the tenant (P) to maintain his tenancy. P was suffering from a paranoid delusional disorder which led him to refuse permission to the local authority landlord to undertake annual gas inspections, thus placing himself, his neighbours and the property at risk. The order made by the court authorised contractors to enter the property and to undertake works, required P to reside at a care home for seven days, and permitted the local authority to use reasonable and proportionate force, if necessary, to effect P's removal to the care home. Similar use of the court's power could be used in a situation where P is living in domestic squalor. It would also be possible to use the power in s.8(1)(a) to require a guardianship patient to take up temporary residence in a care home while necessary works were carried out at the patient's residence.

Subsection (1)

1–120   An application for guardianship, which may be made by either the patient's nearest relative or by an AMHP (s.11(1)), must be in the form set out in Form G1 (for a nearest relative applicant) or Form G2 (for an approved mental health professional (AMHP) applicant) (in Wales, Form GU1 (for a NR applicant) or Form GU2 (for an AMHP applicant)): see reg.5 of the English Regulations and reg.9 of the Welsh Regulations. The application must either be sent to the LSSA named as guardian or to the LSSA for the area in which the individual named as guardian resides (s.11(2)). It has to be supported by two medical recommendations (subs.(3)) and it must be received by the LSSA within 14 days of the second medical examination (s.8(2)). There is no time limit within which an application must be accepted and there is no requirement for the patient to consent to the application being made. The applicant must have personally seen the patient within 14 days of making the application (s.11(5)). An AMHP, who is subject to the duty set out in s.13(1A), cannot make an application if the nearest relative objects (s.11(4)). The power of the nearest relative to object to a guardianship application can cause difficulty as:

"often social workers are concerned not that the patient may act irresponsibly, but that the relatives may act irresponsibly towards the patient. Where there is a caring relative, guardianship may not be needed. It is where there is a nearest relative who is neglectful, exploitive, or unable to care, that guardianship may well be required, but the relative has a power of veto which can only be overridden by the county court in the limited circumstances [set out in section 29]" (Phil Fennell, "The Beverley Lewis Case: was the law to blame" *New Law Journal*, November 17, 1989, pp.1557–1558).

ATTAINED THE AGE. At the commencement of his sixteenth birthday (Family Law Reform Act 1969 s.9(1)). Where on September 30, 1983, a person who was not then 16 years old was subject to guardianship, the authority for guardianship terminated on that day (s.148(1), Sch.5 para.8(1)).

PERIOD ALLOWED. A patient may be kept under guardianship for an initial period of up to six months from the day on which the application was accepted (s.20(1)). The authority for guardianship may be renewed for a further period of six months, and then for yearly periods (s.20(2)).

Paragraph (a)
MENTAL DISORDER. There is no requirement for the patient to be mentally incapaci- **1–121** tated. A patient with a learning disability who suffers from no other form of mental disorder can only be made subject to an application under this section if the disability is associated with abnormally aggressive or seriously irresponsible conduct on his part: see the notes on s.1(2A), (2B).

NATURE OR DEGREE. The meaning of this phrase is considered in the note on s.3(2)(a).

Paragraph (b)
It is difficult to see how the requirement contained in this paragraph will be met if the **1–122** powers that the guardian would enjoy under s.8 are already being exercised responsibly in respect of a mentally incapacitated patient by the donee of a lasting power of attorney of a deputy appointed by the Court of Protection.

INTERESTS OF THE WELFARE OF THE PATIENT. All factors which might affect the well-being of the patient are covered by this phrase, including the need to be protected from exploitation. The wording is wide enough to encompass the need to prevent the patient's welfare being prejudiced at some time in the future. If the concern relates to possible future harm, the recommending doctors would need to be satisfied that there is a real risk of such an eventuality occurring, e.g. an attempt by a relative to remove a mentally incompetent patient from a care setting to accommodation where the patient's welfare might be seriously prejudiced.

PROTECTION OF OTHER PERSONS. It is submitted that "protection" is not limited to protection from physical harm, but could include protection from serious emotional harm: see the notes on s.2(2)(b).

Subsection (3)
WRITTEN RECOMMENDATIONS. Made either separately or jointly (s.11(7)) using either **1–123** Form G3 (joint recommendation) or G4 (in Wales, Form GU3 (joint recommendation) or Form GU4): see reg.5(1)(c) of the English Regulations and reg.9(1)(c) of the Welsh Regulations.

TWO REGISTERED MEDICAL PRACTITIONERS. Complying with the provisions of s.12 and the regulations made under s.12A.

Subsection (5)
This subsection provides for the guardian to be either a LSSA or a person who is accepted **1–124** by the LSSA to act in that capacity. Neither the authority nor the individual is placed under any legal obligation to accept the duties of guardian. The guardian owes a common law duty of care to the patient. In the overwhelming majority of cases, the guardian is a local authority.

LOCAL SOCIAL SERVICES AUTHORITY.   This does not have to be the authority for the area where the patient lives. If the application is accepted, the authority will become "the responsible local social services authority" (s.34(3)). Although a local authority may decline any guardianship proposal, there is a requirement to take over the role of guardian where a private guardianship arrangement has broken down in the circumstances set out in s.10.

Although the relevant social services authority will be named as the guardian, the authority's scheme of delegation will identify an officer who will formally undertake the guardian's legal functions. This officer will usually be the Director of Adult Social Services. She will then identify an employee, invariably a social worker, who will perform casework functions in relation to the patient. It is this person who should represent the authority at tribunal hearings. The only function that cannot be delegated to an officer is the power to discharge the patient from guardianship: see s.23(2), (4).

OR ANY OTHER PERSON.   The local social services authority should consider the suitability of any proposed guardian before accepting the application: see para.30.24 of the *Code of Practice*.

If an AMHP considers that a private guardian has performed his or her functions negligently or in any manner contrary to the interests of the welfare of the patient, an application can be made to the county court under s.10(3) for the guardianship to be transferred to another person or to the LSSA.

A private guardian does not have the power to discharge the patient from guardianship.

ACCEPTED.   The time limits for accepting an application for a patient's admission to hospital set out in s.6 do not apply to guardianship applications. The acceptance should be recorded on Form G5 (in Wales, Form GU5): see reg.5(2) of the English Regulations and reg.9(3) of the Welsh Regulations.

THE AREA.   i.e. the area where the person named as guardian resides.

RESIDES.   In *R. (on the application of Sunderland City Council) v South Tyneside Council* [2012] EWCA Civ 1232, para.25, Lloyd L.J. said that "in general, when considering any case in which there is doubt as to the place of person's residence, the question is not only that of physical presence, and that it may be relevant to consider why the person is where he or she is, and to what extent his or her presence there is voluntary. Thus, if a person has a home, the fact that he or she is not there on a given date or for a particular period does not mean that he or she is not still resident there, if the absence is accounted for by, for example, a holiday, a business trip, or having to spend time in hospital, whether following an injury, an operation or some other form of treatment, possibly over a prolonged period, or, for that matter, a period of imprisonment following a criminal conviction".

WILLING TO ACT AS GUARDIAN.   The statement that the person is willing to act as guardian must be in the form set out in either Form G1 or G2 (in Wales, Form GU1 or GU2). The duties of private guardians are set out in reg.22 of the English Regulations and reg.11 of the Welsh Regulations.

Effect of guardianship application, etc.

1–125   **8.**—(1) Where a guardianship application, duly made under the provisions of this Part of this Act and forwarded to the local social services authority within the period allowed by subsection (2) below is accepted by that authority, the application shall, subject to regulations made by the Secretary of State, confer on the authority or person named in the application as guardian, to the exclusion of any other person—

(a) the power to require the patient to reside at a place specified by the authority or person named as guardian;

(b) the power to require the patient to attend at places and times so specified for the purpose of medical treatment, occupation, education or training;

(c) the power to require access to the patient to be given, at any place where the patient is residing, to any registered medical practitioner, [approved mental health professional] or other person so specified.

(2) The period within which a guardianship application is required for the purposes of this section to be forwarded to the local social services authority is the period of 14 days beginning with the date on which the patient was last examined by a registered medical practitioner before giving a medical recommendation for the purposes of the application.

(3) A guardianship application which appears to be duly made and to be founded on the necessary medical recommendations may be acted upon without further proof of the signature or qualification of the person by whom the application or any such medical recommendation is made or given, or of any matter of fact or opinion stated in the application.

(4) If within the period of 14 days beginning with the day on which a guardianship application has been accepted by the local social services authority the application, or any medical recommendation given for the purposes of the application, is found to be in any respect incorrect or defective, the application or recommendation may, within that period and with the consent of that authority, be amended by the person by whom it was signed; and upon such amendment being made the application or recommendation shall have effect and shall be deemed to have had effect as if it had been originally made as so amended.

(5) Where a patient is received into guardianship in pursuance of a guardianship application, any previous application under this Part of this Act by virtue of which he was subject to guardianship or liable to be detained in a hospital shall cease to have effect.

AMENDMENT
The words in square brackets in subs.(1)(c) were substituted by the Mental Health Act 2007 s.21, Sch.2 para.2.

DEFINITIONS   **1–126**
local social services authority: s.145(1).
medical treatment: s.145(1).
patient: s.145(1).
approved mental health professional: s.145(1), (1AC).
hospital: ss.34(2), 145(1).

GENERAL NOTE
The Mental Health Act 1959 gave the guardian the power that a father has over a child of **1–127** 14. These powers were therefore very wide, as well as being somewhat ill-defined, and it was felt that they were out of keeping, in their paternalistic approach, with modern attitudes to the care of the mentally disordered. Subsection (1) replaced these general powers with specific powers limited to interfering with the autonomy of the person under guardianship only to the extent necessary to ensure that various forms of treatment, social support, training, education or occupation are undertaken. This section also specifies that the guardianship application must be forwarded to the local authority within 14 days of the date when the patient was last medically examined for the purpose of the application (subs.(2)), confirms that an application which appears to be duly made and to be founded

on the necessary medical recommendations can be acted upon (subs.(3)), provides for the rectification of the statutory documents within 14 days of the acceptance of the application (subs.(4)) and states that the reception of the patient into guardianship automatically ends any previous application made in respect of the patient (subs.(5)).

The patient's guardian, who is subject to the duties laid down in Pt III of the English and Welsh Regulations, does not have any power to use or dispose of the patient's property or to carry out any financial transactions on the patient's behalf.

In *R. (on the application of S) v Plymouth City Council and C* [2002] EWCA Civ 388; [2002] 1 W.L.R. 2583, the Court of Appeal was concerned with how the interest of a guardianship patient in preserving the confidentiality of personal information about himself is to be reconciled with his mother's interest, as his nearest relative, in having access to enough information about him to exercise her statutory functions under the Act. The Court held that:

1. Both at common law and under the Human Rights Act 1998, a balance must be struck between the public and private interests in maintaining the confidentiality of information about the patient and the public and private interests in permitting, indeed requiring, its disclosure for certain purposes.

2. Striking the balance would not lead in every case to the disclosure of all the information a nearest relative might possibly want, still less to a fishing exercise amongst the local authority's files. But in most cases it would lead to the disclosure of the basic statutory guardianship documentation. In this case it would also lead to the disclosure of relevant social services records. Hale L.J. said at para.50:

   "There is no suggestion of any risk to [the patient's] health and welfare arising from this. The mother and her advisers have sought access to the information which her own psychiatric and social work experts need in order properly to advise her. That limits both the context and the content of dislosure in a way which strikes a proper balance between the competing interests."

If a local authority concludes that the powers set out in this section are insufficient to enable it to manage the case of a mentally incapacitated person appropriately, it should consider making an application under the Mental Capacity Act 2005 to the Court of Protection for an appropriate order (*Lewis v Gibson* [2005] EWCA Civ 587; [2005] M.H.L.R. 309 para.29).

Human Rights Act 1998

1–128   Guardianship proceedings must comply with the standards of art.6(1) of the ECHR because such proceedings involve the determination of a civil right. The fact that the initial determination of the guardianship application is made by an administrative body (the local authority) does not contravene art.6(1) provided that there is a right of appeal to a court (the First-tier Tribunal (Mental Health) or the Mental Health Review Tribunal for Wales) which provides the guarantees of that article (see for example, *Le Compte, Van Leuven and De Meyer v Belgium* (1981) 4 E.H.R.R. 1 para.51). The state must ensure that the appeal is heard within a reasonable time (*Buchholz v Germany* (1981) 3 E.H.R.R. 1 para.50).

As the patient's guardian is likely to exercise powers which will involve an interference with the patient's right to respect for private and family life under art.8(1) of the ECHR, a justification for the interference, which must be a proportionate response to the identified risk, will need to be found in art.8(2). In order to justify the proportionality of the power exercised, the guardian should have identified and assessed the potential effectiveness of alternatives to the use of that power.

It has been argued that the charging of those subject to guardianship who are required to reside in accommodation provided by a local authority breaches art.8: see *R. (on the application of Johnson) v Secretary of State for Health* [2006] EWHC 288 (Admin). Judicial comments made in this case suggest that it is unlikely that such an argument would succeed if the issue proceeded to trial.

The patient's private or local authority guardian is exercising functions of a public nature in respect of the patient and is therefore a "public authority" for the purposes of s.6 of the 1998 Act.

The use of guardianship to authorise the deprivation of a person's liberty

In *NL v Hampshire County Council* [2014] UKUT 475 (AAC), UT Judge Jacobs, in **1–129** applying the decision of the Supreme Court in *P v Cheshire West and Chester Council* [2014] UKSC 19, said that it "is possible for guardianship to be set up in a way that does involve a deprivation, but guardianship of itself does not necessarily involve a deprivation of liberty", and that he found "it difficult to imagine a case that could realistically arise in which [the] basic powers [set out in subs.(1)(a) to (c)] could be used in a way that would satisfy the conditions for deprivation of liberty" (para.16). He further stated at para.17:

> "[An] application for guardianship should be accompanied by a comprehensive care plan . . . . It is in the details of that plan that the potential for restriction, supervision and control sufficient to amount to a deprivation of liberty lies".

Judge Jacobs did not identify the legal source of the power to restrict, supervise and control guardianship patients. It is submitted that the source must be the implied powers that the guardian has under guardianship. That the guardian enjoys such powers was confirmed in the *Marston* case which is considered below. Whether the implied powers would include the power to subject the patient to continuous supervision and control for the purposes of the "acid test" for a deprivation of liberty identified in the *Cheshire West* case is undecided, although, given the obiter comments of Peter Jackson J. in *C v Blackburn and Darwen Borough Council* [2011] EWHC 3321; [2012] M.H.L.R. 202 at para.30, it is likely that a court would find that they do not. *Cheshire West* and the "acid test" are considered in Part 6.

The powers that can be exercised over a guardianship patient, which are not confined to those set out subs.(1), include:

1. A power to take the patient to the place specified by the guardian, using force if necessary (subs.(1) and ss.18(3), (7) and 137).

2. A power to require the patient to reside at the specified place (subs.(1)(a)).

3. A power to prevent the patient from leaving the specified place without the leave of the guardian (subs.(1) and s.18(3)).

4. A power to return the patient to the specified place if he leaves without having obtained leave, using force if necessary (ss.18(3) and 137).

It follows that a patient who is subject to such powers can be forced to leave his home to go to a place where he does not want to go, can be required to remain there, and can be returned to that place if he leaves without being given permission to do so. Although the patient might not satisfy the "acid test" for a deprivation of liberty in that he is not the subject of continuous supervision and control at the place where he is required to reside, surely nobody using ordinary language would describe a patient who is the subject of such powers as being someone who is not deprived of his liberty?

If a mentally incapacitated patient who is required under guardianship to reside at a specified place does satisfy the "acid test", a deprivation of liberty authorisation (if the patient resides in a care home) or an order of the Court of Protection (if the patient resides elsewhere) under the Mental Capacity Act 2005 should be sought (*KD v A Borough Council* [2015] UKUT 251 (AAC), para.39). In the absence of a judicial finding which clarifies the position regarding the implied powers of the guardian, if the patient is mentally capable of making a decision as to where he should live, the safe option would be not to subject him to a care plan which involves continuous supervision and control. The Government's view that guardianship cannot be used to deprive a person of his liberty is evidenced by the fact that Parliament did not reverse the burden of proof in guardianship cases when it enacted the Mental Health Act 1983 (Remedial Order) 2001 (SI 2001/3712) (see the note on s.72(4)) and by para.30.31 of the *Code of Practice* which reads:

> "The power to require patients to reside in a particular place may not be used to require them to live in a situation in which they are deprived of liberty. Guardianship will not be appropriate for a person who has the capacity to decide where to live and will not reside in the place they are required to live by their guardian, unless they were to be deprived of their liberty under the Act."

Admission to hospital of patients under guardianship

1–130   If a patient under guardianship is admitted to hospital for psychiatric treatment as an informal patient he will remain subject to guardianship unless he is discharged from it (s.23) or transferred to hospital under the procedure set out in reg.8 of the English Regulations or reg.24 of the Welsh Regulations. The guardianship will also remain in force if the patient is admitted for assessment under ss.2 or 4, but it will cease to have effect if the patient is admitted for treatment under s.3 (s.6(4)). If the patient is admitted informally he could be made subject to the holding powers provided for in s.5(2) and (4).

Subsection (1)

1–131   The guardian may exercise powers over the patient in addition to the specific powers contained in this provision. In *R. v Kent County Council Ex p. Marston* (CO/1819/96), July 9, 1997, Owen J. said that he could "find no difficulty in accepting that section 7 of necessity implies a statutory duty to act for the welfare of the patient". His Lordship further stated that:

> "the extent and consequences of that duty are not so clear. An example, of no relevance here, would be seen if a patient were to be given a sexually provocative magazine. I would have no difficulty in accepting that the guardian would have a duty to monitor the effects and if necessary to remove the magazine."

This finding was endorsed by Simon Brown L.J. who said, in refusing leave to appeal on September 5, 1997, that it is implicit in s.7:

> "that the guardian is entitled in certain respects to act so as to promote the welfare of the patient. Owen J. recognised, as I would too, that the precise extent and consequence of such an implicit duty to act for the welfare of the patient is not clear. I envisage that that may well need clarification at some future date. For example, if there were good reason to suppose that an authority was acting in some totalitarian fashion or was not properly having regard to the interests of its patients, then it seems to me clear that someone would have the standing, would have a sufficient interest to bring the case before the court so that the matter could be properly investigated and the true extent of the authority's discretion be clarified".

In *Marston*, Owen J. upheld the decision of the local authority, acting as the patient's guardian, to refuse to disclose to the patient's former foster brother where the patient was living. The foster brother was ultimately intent on taking over the care of the patient and the local authority had received medical advice that this would be contrary to the patient's interests. The patient, who was mentally incapable, had expressed no interest in seeing his former foster brother. His Lordship also said that as the patient needed protection, the guardian had a right to see letters addressed to him by the foster brother and that whether "the guardian would be entitled to censor them would depend what was in them". However, as the patient was unable to read, the right to see the letters would not have to be exercised.

Marston was not cited in *Re F (Mental Health Act: Guardianship)* [2000] 1 F.L.R. 192 where Thorpe L.J. stated, obiter, that he doubted the legality of the restrictions that the local authority, acting as guardian, has placed on the patient's contact with her parents.

A local authority guardian may delegate its functions under this provision to any committee, officer or other body or person to whom they can normally delegate functions under the Local Government Act 1972 (or the Local Government Act 2000, if relevant): see reg.21 of the English Regulations and the note thereto.

SECRETARY OF STATE. The functions of the Minister, so far as exercisable in relation to Wales, are exercised by the Welsh Ministers (see the General Note to the Act).

TO THE EXCLUSION OF ANY OTHER PERSON. This provision prevents a person from taking a decision, including a decision made under the Mental Capacity Act 2005, on the matters covered by paras (a) to (c) which conflicts with a decision made by the guardian. The prohibition covers a deputy appointed by the Court of Protection, the donee of a lasting power of attorney, and a lay or professional carer purporting to act under the protection granted by s.5 of the 2005 Act. In *C v Blackburn and Darwen Borough Council* [2011] EWHC 3321 (COP); [2012] M.H.L.R. 202, at para.39, Peter Jackson J. held that the prohibition contained in this provision applies to public bodies, including the Court of Protection.

Paragraph (a)

REQUIRE THE PATIENT TO RESIDE AT A PLACE. Which, for example, could be a care home, **1–132** supported accommodation or private residence. There is no power to require that the patient resides with a particular person. Guardianship has been used to require the patient to reside in his own home in a situation where the power to require the patient to provide access to health and social care professions was needed in order to provide support to the patient. The designated place of residence and other requirements should be recorded in the patient's care plan and communicated to the patient both orally and in writing.

The power to take the patient to the place specified by the guardian is contained in s.18(7). The person taking the patient can use force if this is required (s.137). If the patient leaves the place where he is required to reside without his guardian's consent, he can be taken into custody and returned to that place (s.18(3)) within the period specified in s.18(4). An application could be made to a magistrate under s.135(2) if it is not possible to obtain access to the place where the patient is staying. Anyone obstructing a person authorised by s.18(3) to return the patient would be guilty of an offence under s.129. It is an offence under s.128 to induce or knowingly to assist a person under guardianship to absent himself without leave of the guardian.

The *Code of Practice* states at para.30.30:

"The power to take or return patients to the place they are required to live may be used, eg to discourage them from:

- living somewhere the guardian considers unsuitable
- breaking off contact with services
- leaving the area before proper arrangements can be made, and
- sleeping rough.

But it may not be used to restrict their freedom to come and go so much that they are effectively being detained."

In *KD v A Borough Council* [2015] UKUT 251 (AAC), Charles J. said that the power of the guardian to return the person to his place of residence under s.18(3) "has the effect of a requirement or an injunction preventing [that person] from leaving"(para.30) and that the power is a "more readily available, effective and sensible means" of ensuring that the person lives in a particular place than an injunction against that person from the Court of Protection (para.31).

In *C v Blackburn and Darwen Borough Council* [2011] EWHC 3321 (COP), para.39, Peter Jackson J. held that the Court of Protection lacks jurisdiction to determine the place of residence of a mentally incapacitated person who is subject to guardianship while a residence requirement made under this provision remains in effect: also see the note on "to the exclusion of any other person", above and *KD v A Borough Council*, above, at paras 45–54. However, his Lordship said at para.37:

> "[I]t is not in my view appropriate for genuinely contested issues about the place of residence of a resisting incapacitated person to be determined either under the guardianship regime or by means of a standard authorisation under the DOLS regime. Substantial decisions of that kind ought properly to be made by the Court of Protection, using its power to make welfare decisions under s.16 [of the Mental Capacity Act]."

There no prohibition on charging a person who is subject to guardianship for the accommodation in which he is required to reside, as long as the accommodation is not being provided as an after-care service under s.117.

The person in control of the premises where the patient is required to reside has the power "under general law . . . to control who is allowed to be there and in what circumstances"; per Hale J. in *Cambridgeshire County Council v R (an Adult)* [1995] 1 F.L.R. 50 at 55. Any restrictions placed on a person having access to the patient would need to be justified under art.8(2) of the ECHR.

Although McCullough J. made the obiter comment in *R. v Hallstrom Ex p. W* [1986] 2 All E.R. 306, 312 that "there is nothing in [the Mental Health Act 1983] which appears to prevent a guardian from requiring his patient to reside in a hospital", this practice is contrary to the intention of the Act if the patient is likely to require long term hospital care: see the General Note to s.7. Also see para.30.35 of the *Code of Practice*.

There is nothing to prevent a patient who is subject to guardianship from being admitted to hospital for treatment for either a physical or a psychiatric disorder. In the event of such an admission taking place a local authority acting as the guardian of a patient is required to comply with s.116. See the note on "Admission to hospital of patients under guardianship", above, for the legal consequences of a patient being admitted to hospital for psychiatric treatment under compulsory powers.

Paragraph (b)

1–133   REQUIRE THE PATIENT TO ATTEND.   If the patient refuses to attend, guardianship does not provide authority for force to be used to secure attendance (*Code of Practice*, para.30.3).

FOR THE PURPOSES OF MEDICAL TREATMENT.   Neither the guardian, the patient's nearest relative nor any other adult, can consent to treatment on the patient's behalf. In *T v T* [1988] 1 All E.R. 613 at 617, Wood J. said:

> "The wording of section 8 will be seen to be much more restricted than the wider powers of the guardian under section 34 of the [Mental Health Act 1959]. One important effect is to remove the guardian's implicit power to consent to treatment on behalf of the patient. In my judgment there is no power to consent to [abortion] to be found in section 8 . . ., and indeed, on a construction of the statute as a whole I am satisfied that medical treatment means psychiatric treatment."

A patient under guardianship is not subject to the consent to treatment provisions contained in Pt IV (s.56(3)). If the patient is mentally capable of making a decision about medical treatment, the common law enables him to refuse to be treated for either a physical or mental disorder. However, if the patient is assessed as being mentally incapable of making a decision about treatment, the treatment can be provided under the Mental Capacity Act

2005 if it is deemed to be in his best interests. If a patient's psychiatric condition is deteriorating because a refusal to accept treatment, consideration should be given to admitting the patient to hospital under s.2 (with the guardianship order remaining in force) or to transferring the patient to hospital under reg.8 of the English Regulations and reg.24 of the Welsh Regulations (with the guardianship order ceasing to have effect).

Although guardianship does not provide authority for a mentally capable patient to be treated in the absence of his consent, the existence of guardianship can have the effect of influencing the patient to co-operate with treatment. For an example, see L. Blom-Cooper et al., *The Falling Shadow*, 1995, p.90.

The responsible social services authority must arrange for an approved clinician or a s.12 doctor to visit the patient at least once a year: see reg.23 of the English Regulations and reg.10 of the Welsh Regulations.

Paragraph (c)

REQUIRE ACCESS TO THE PATIENT.   This provision, which could be used to ensure that the **1–134** patient did not neglect himself, does not include a power to force entry if this is denied. If entry is denied consideration should be given to utilising the procedure set out in s.135(1). A refusal to permit an authorised person to have access to the patient is an offence under s.129.

Subsection (2)

The application must be sent to the LSSA within the 14 day period specified in this pro- **1–135** vision. There is no timescale within which the LSSA must accept the application.

BEGINNING WITH.   Including the date on which the patient was last examined by a medical practitioner (*Zoan v Rouamba* [2000] 2 All E.R. 620 CA).

Subsection (3)

APPEARS TO BE DULY MADE.   An incorrect or defective application can be amended **1–136** under subs.(4).

Subsection (4)

This provision provides a means of righting accidental mistakes that were made when the **1–137** statutory documentation was completed; it is not a device for overcoming a fundamental defect in the application: see the notes to s.15. The amended application must comply with the requirements for making an application. The Reference Guide states:

"28.61 An application or recommendation which is found to be incorrect or defective may be amended by the person who signed it, with the consent of the local authority. In practice, if the local authority is content for the document to be amended, it should be returned to the person who signed it for amendment. Consent to the amendment should then formally be given by the local authority. The consent should be recorded in writing and can take the form of an endorsement on the document itself. If this is all done within a period of 14 days starting with the day on which the application was accepted the documents are deemed to have had effect as though originally made as amended.

28.62 If more than 14 days have elapsed from the day the application was accepted a minor mistake would not invalidate an application (a 'de minimis' mistake). If there is a fundamental error, the application should be discharged and, if appropriate, a new application made.

28.63 Unlike applications for admission to hospital, there is no procedure for obtaining a new medical recommendation if the ones that come with the application originally prove insufficient. In that case, a new application would have to be made."

For minor mistakes, see *Re E (Mental Health: Habeas Corpus)* which is noted in the General Note to Sch.1 of the English Regulations. An application which contains a fundamentally defective error should be discharged under s.23 as soon as the error is discovered.

ACCEPTED BY THE LOCAL SOCIAL SERVICES AUTHORITY. The authority may authorise an officer or class of officer to consent to any amendment of a guardianship application which it has accepted or any medical recommendation given for the purposes of that application: see reg.21 of the English Regulations and reg.37 of the Welsh Regulations.

INCORRECT OR DEFECTIVE. The meaning of these terms is considered in the notes on s.15.

BY WHOM IT WAS SIGNED. i.e. the applicant or the recommending doctor. An unsigned application or medical recommendation cannot be remedied under this provision.

Subsection (5)
As the patient's reception into guardianship has the effect of ending any pre-existing s.3 application, it also automatically brings to an end any community treatment order that had been made in respect of the patient (s.17C(c)).

Regulations as to guardianship

1–138   **9.**—(1) Subject to the provisions of this Part of this Act, the Secretary of State may make regulations—

(a) for regulating the exercise by the guardians of patients received into guardianship under this Part of the Act of their powers as such; and

(b) for imposing on such guardians, and upon local social services authorities in the case of patients under the guardianship of persons other than local social services authorities, such duties as he considers necessary or expedient in the interest of the patients.

(2) Regulations under this section may in particular make provision for requiring the patients to be visited, on such occasions or at such intervals as may be prescribed by the regulations, on behalf of such local social services authorities as may be so prescribed, and shall provide for the appointment, in the case of every patient subject to the guardianship of a person other than a local social services authority, of a registered medical practitioner to act as the nominated medical attendant of the patient.

DEFINITIONS
1–139   patients: s.145(1).
local social services authority: s.145(1).
nominated medical assistant: s.34(1).

GENERAL NOTE
1–140   This section, which gives power to the Secretary of State (or, in relation to Wales, the Welsh Ministers: see the General Note to the Act) to make regulations for regulating guardianship, applies to patients who have been placed on a guardianship order made by a court under s.37 (Sch.1, Pt I, para.1).

The Mental Health (Hospital, Guardianship and Treatment) (England) Regulations 2008 (SI 2008/1184) and the Mental Health (Hospital, Guardianship, Community Treatment and Consent to Treatment) (Wales) Regulations 2008 (SI 2008/2439) (W.212) have been made under this section.

Transfer of guardianship in case of death, incapacity, etc. of guardian

10.—(1) If any person (other than a local social services authority) who is the **1–141**
guardian of a patient received into guardianship under this Part of this Act—

(a) dies; or

(b) gives notice in writing to the local social services authority that he desires to
relinquish the functions of guardian,

the guardianship of the patient shall thereupon vest in the local social services
authority, but without prejudice to any power to transfer the patient into the guardianship of another person in pursuance of regulations under section 19 below.

(2) If any such person, not having given notice under subsection (1)(b) above, is
incapacitated by illness or any other cause from performing the functions of
guardian of the patient, those functions may, during his incapacity, be performed
on his behalf by the local social services authority or by any other person approved
for the purposes by that authority.

(3) If it appears to the county court, upon application made by an [approved
mental health professional acting on behalf of the local social services authority],
that any person other than a local social services authority having the guardianship
of a patient received into guardianship under this Part of this Act has performed
his functions negligently or in a manner contrary to the interests of the welfare of
the patient, the court may order that the guardianship of the patient be transferred
to the local social services authority or to any other person approved for the purpose by that authority.

(4) Where the guardianship of a patient is transferred to a local social services
authority or other person by or under this section, subsection (2)(c) of section 19
below shall apply as if the patient had been transferred into the guardianship of
that authority or person in pursuance of regulations under that section.

[(5) In this section "the local social services authority", in relation to a person
(other than a local social services authority) who is the guardian of a patient,
means the local social services authority for the area in which that person resides
(or resided immediately before his death).]

AMENDMENTS
The amendments to this section were made by the Mental Health Act 2007 s.21, Sch.2
para.3.

DEFINITIONS
local social services authority: s.145(1) and subs.(5) of this section.   **1–142**
patient: s.145(1).
approved mental health professional: s.145(1), (1AC).

GENERAL NOTE
This section provides for the transfer of guardianship in circumstances where the private **1–143**
guardian of a patient dies, becomes incapacitated, wishes to relinquish his functions, or is
found to be performing his functions negligently. It applies to patients who have been
placed on guardianship orders made by a court under s.37 (Sch.1 Pt I para.1).
For the responsibility to inform the patient's nearest relative of a transfer of guardianship
under this section, see reg.26(1)(k) of the English Regulations and reg.31 of the Welsh
Regulations.
It is also possible for a patient to be transferred from one guardian to another under s.19.

Subsection (1)

1–144   This subsection provides for the automatic transfer of guardianship from a private guardian to a local social services authority if the guardian either dies or gives a notice of relinquishment to the authority. The authority, as identified in subs.(5), cannot resist a notice of relinquishment. Guardianship could subsequently be transferred to another local social services authority or to a person under reg.8 of the English Regulations or reg.4(2) of the Welsh Regulations.

Subsection (2)

1–145   This subsection allows the local social services authority, or a person authorised by the authority, to act temporarily on behalf of a guardian who is ill or is otherwise incapacitated. The Reference Guide states at para.28.134:

"The authority or person temporarily acting as guardian in these cases acts as an agent for the permanent guardian and may not go against any wishes or instructions the permanent guardian may express."

Subsection (3)

1–146   This subsection empowers an approved mental health professional to apply to the county court for an order transferring the guardianship of the patient to a local social services authority or to a person approved by that authority.

General Provisions as to Applications and Recommendations

General provisions as to applications

1–147   **11.**—(1) Subject to the provisions of this section, an application for admission for assessment, an application for admission for treatment and a guardianship application may be made either by the nearest relative of the patient or by an [approved mental health professional]; and every such application shall specify the qualification of the applicant to make the application.

[(1A) No application mentioned in subsection (1) above shall be made by an approved mental health professional if the circumstances are such that there would be a potential conflict of interest for the purposes of regulations under section 12A below.]

(2) Every application for admission shall be addressed to the managers of the hospital to which admission is sought and every guardianship application shall be forwarded to the local social services authority named in the application as guardian, or, as the case may be, to the local social services authority for the area in which the person so named resides.

(3) Before or within a reasonable time after an application for the admission of a patient for assessment is made by an [approved mental health professional, that professional] shall take such steps as are practicable to inform the person (if any) appearing to be the nearest relative of the patient that the application is to be or has been made and of the power of the nearest relative under section 23(2)(a) below.

[(4) An approved mental health professional may not make an application for admission for treatment or a guardianship application in respect of a patient in either of the following cases—

(a) the nearest relative of the patient has notified that professional, or the local social services authority on whose behalf the professional is acting, that he objects to the application being made; or

(b) that professional has not consulted the person (if any) appearing to be the nearest relative of the patient, but the requirement to consult that person does not apply if it appears to the professional that in the circumstances such consultation is not reasonably practicable or would involve unreasonable delay.]

(5) None of the applications mentioned in subsection (1) above shall be made by any person in respect of a patient unless that person has personally seen the patient within the period of 14 days ending with the date of the application.

(6) [. . .]

(7) Each of the applications mentioned in subsection (1) above shall be sufficient if the recommendations on which it is founded are given either as separate recommendations, each signed by a registered medical practitioner, or as a joint recommendation signed by two such practitioners.

AMENDMENTS

The amendments to this section were made by the Mental Health Act 2007 ss.21, 22(2), 55, Sch.2 para.4, Sch.11 Pt 1.

DEFINITIONS

    application for admission for assessment: s.145(1). **1–148**
    application for admission for treatment: s.145(1).
    nearest relative: ss.26(3), 145(1).
    approved mental health professional: s.145(1), (1AC).
    the managers: s.145(1).
    hospital: ss.34(2), 145(1).
    local social services authority: s.145(1).
    patient: s.145(1).
    mental disorder: ss.1, 145(1).

GENERAL NOTE

This section contains general provisions relating to applications for admission for assess- **1–149** ment, applications for admission for treatment, and guardianship applications.

Although primary responsibility for checking that the statutory forms have been completed correctly rests with the applicant, hospital managers and local social services authorities should each designate an officer to scrutinise the documents as soon as they have been received and to take any necessary action if they have been improperly completed: see reg.4(3) of the English Regulations and reg.4(2) of the Welsh Regulations.

Human Rights Act 1998

The European Court of Human Rights has held that there are positive obligations that are **1–150** placed on public authorities which are inherent in an effective respect for family life under art.8(1) of the European Convention on Human Rights (ECHR) (*Osman v United Kingdom* (2000) 29 E.H.R.R. 245). In particular, the European Commission of Human Rights recognised that public authorities might have to take particular steps to protect the mentally disordered in order to fulfil their obligations under that article (*X & Y v Netherlands* (8978/80): *Y v Netherlands* (A91) (1986) 8 E.H.R.R.). If a mentally disordered person is denied the care and treatment that he is assessed as needing by virtue of a nearest relative exercising the right to object to an application under subs.(4), it is arguable that the State is failing in its positive obligation under art.8 to protect that person if an application is not made under s.29(3)(c) to displace the relative.

Code of Practice

Guidance on "Applications for detention in hospital" is provided in Ch.14. **1–151**

Subsection (1)

If it has not been possible to identify the name of the patient by the time the application is made, it is suggested that the phrase "the patient known by the name of John [or Mary] Smith" be entered in the patient name space on the application form. A note of the real name of the patient should be attached to the application as soon as it is discovered. A similar note should be made if it is discovered that the patient gave a false name at the time of his admission. If the address of the patient is unknown, or if the patient is homeless, the current location of the patient should be entered in the address space of the application form.

1–152 APPLICATION. By virtue of reg.4(1) of the English Regulations, the following forms must be used: applications for assessment—Form A1 (for NRs) or A2 (for AMHPs); applications for treatment—Form A5 (for NRs) or A6 (for AMHPs); emergency applications—Form A9 (for NRs) or Form A10 (for AMHPs); and for guardianship application—Form G1 (for NRs) or G2 for AMHPs). Applications to hospitals in Wales must use the forms set out in the Welsh Regulations which are: applications for assessment—Form HO1 (for NRs) or HO2 (for AMHPs); applications for treatment—Form HO5 (for NRs) or HO6 (for AMHPs); emergency applications—Form HO9 (for NRs) or Form HO10 (for AMHPs) and for guardianship application—Form GUI (for NRs) or GU2 (for AMHPs).

An application in respect of a ward of court cannot be made without the leave of the High Court (s.33(1)).

MAY BE MADE EITHER BY. The approved mental health professional (AMHP) acting on behalf of a local authority is "usually a more appropriate applicant than the patient's nearest relative" (*Code of Practice*, para.14.30). The Royal Commission considered the nearest relative to be a more appropriate applicant than a social worker: "Ideally, in our view, the application should be made by a relative of the patient on medical recommendation, with a mental welfare officer available to explain the procedure and provide the application form and to transport the patient to hospital if necessary" (para.403). In practice, applications by nearest relatives are rare. Neither the AMHP nor the nearest relative can prevent the other from making an application. An application which is signed by a person who is neither an AMHP nor the patient's nearest relative is invalid and incapable of being rectified under s.15.

NEAREST RELATIVE. Or an acting nearest relative appointed by the court under s.29. It is possible for a nearest relative to authorise some other person to act for him under reg.24 of the English Regulations or reg.33 of the Welsh Regulations.

Subsection (1A)

1–153 REGULATIONS UNDER SECTION 12A. See the Mental Health (Conflicts of Interest) (England) Regulations 2008 which are reproduced in Pt 2. The equivalent Welsh Regulations are SI 2008/2440 (W.213).

Subsection (2)

1–154 THE MANAGERS. Who are the detaining authority (*R. v South Western Hospital Managers Ex p. M* [1994] 1 All E.R. 161). The application shall be served by delivering it to an officer of the managers of the hospital to which it is proposed that the patient shall be admitted: see reg.3(2) of the English and Welsh Regulations. Hospital managers are not obliged to admit patients in respect of whom applications under Pt II have been made. In Volume 2 of his *A Human Condition* (1977) at pp.53, 59, Larry Gostin refers to the opinion that Sir Geoffrey Howe QC, M.P. gave to the North West Thames Regional Health Authority in 1974 on the role of hospital managers in respect of hospital admissions. Sir Geoffrey concluded that a hospital consultant had no right to admit a patient, except with the authority of the hospital managers.

HOSPITAL. As the application does not authorise the applicant to take the patient to any hospital other than the hospital specified in the application, the name of the hospital should not be written on the application form until a recommending doctor has confirmed that a hospital bed has been arranged for the patient. The Mental Health Act Commission suggested that if a patient cannot be admitted to hospital in an emergency for want of a bed, the AMHP should complete an application, making it out to the hospital which has been the subject of a notification under s.140, and convey the patient to that hospital. For a criticism of this approach, see the note on "to hospital" in s.6(1).

LOCAL SOCIAL SERVICES AUTHORITY. A guardianship application does not take effect until it is accepted by the authority. If it is accepted, the authority will become the "responsible local social services authority" (s.34(3)).

RESIDES. See the note on this term in s.7(5).

Subsection (3)
This subsection, which applies to both s.2 and s.4 (*Re GM* [2000] M.H.L.R. 41, para.28), **1–155** requires an AMHP who makes an application for admission for assessment under s.2 to take such steps as are practicable to inform the patient's nearest relative that the application is either about to be or has been made and of his or her power to discharge the patient. The information could be given either orally or in writing.

If the AMHP considers that it might not be practicable to inform the nearest relative of the application on the ground that knowledge that the nearest relative had been contacted might cause the patient significant emotional distress, the AMHP should adopt the approach identified in *TW v Enfield Borough Council* [2014] EWCA Civ 362; [2014] M.H.L.R. 415 in order to reach a decision: see the notes to "not reasonably practicable" in subs.(4).

WITHIN A REASONABLE TIME. Given that an application deprives patients of their liberty, it is unlikely that a court would consider a delay of more than 24 hours to be reasonable in the absence of circumstances that make contacting the nearest relative problematic.

SUCH STEPS AS ARE PRACTICABLE. The steps taken could include telephoning to inform a nearest relative who resides at some distance from the admitting hospital or asking a social worker from the area where the nearest relative resides to inform him or her of the application. The actual giving of the information need not necessarily be undertaken by the AMHP who made the application (*R. v Managers of South Western Hospital Ex p. M* [1994] 1 All E.R. 161).

APPEARING TO BE THE NEAREST RELATIVE. This section does not impose a duty of reasonable enquiry on the AMHP in deciding who is the patient's nearest relative: see the note under this heading in subs.(4). If the AMHP makes a genuine mistake and informs a person who is not the patient's nearest relative, that mistake does not have the effect of invalidating the s.2 application: see *R. v Birmingham Mental Health Trust Ex p. Phillips* (CO/1501/95), May 25, 1995, where Tucker J. refused applications for *habeas corpus* and judicial review that had been made on behalf of a patient who had been detained under s.2 in circumstances where the patient's mother had been incorrectly identified as the patient's nearest relative. His Lordship said that a subsequent application that had been made to the county court under s.29 of the Act had also not been invalidated by the mistake. As soon as the mistake is discovered, the AMHP should comply with this provision at the earliest opportunity.

THE POWER . . . UNDER SECTION 23(2)(*a*).   Of the nearest relative to order the patients discharge from hospital. It is suggested that the AMHP should also inform the nearest relative of the power of the patient's responsible clinician to prevent the discharge from taking place: see s.25(1).

Subsection (4)

1–156   This subsection, which does not apply to a ward of court (s.33(1)), provides that: (1) an application by an AMHP for admission for treatment under s.3 or for guardianship under s.7 must be preceded by a consultation with the person appearing to be the patient's nearest relative unless this is impracticable or would involve unreasonable delay, and (2) the application cannot proceed if the patient's nearest relative objects to the application being made.

In *R. (on the application of GP) v Derby City Council* [2012] EWHC 1451 (Admin); [2012] M.H.L.R. 252, para.36, H.H. Judge Pelling, sitting as a judge of the High Court, said that this section "provides constitutional protection for those that are faced with detention under the Mental Health Act. Compliance with the requirements of section 11(4) is therefore the price which is paid for the ability of those charged with the treatment of those with mental illnesses and disabilities to detain people without immediate recourse to a court and in a way which is compliant with Article 5 [of the ECHR]. Thus there is a heavy duty on those who carry out these tasks to ensure that those statutory provisions are complied with".

If the nearest relative of a patient who is detained under s.2 objects to an application being made under s.3, the patient can continue to be detained beyond the 28-day period provided for in s.2 if an AMHP applies during the currency of the s.2 to the county court for the nearest relative to be displaced under ground (c) or (d) of s.29(3) (s.29(4)). Once formal steps have been taken to make an application under s.3, it is not possible for an AMHP to overcome a nearest relative's objection by making an application under s.2 in respect of the patient (*R. v Wilson Ex p. Williamson*, noted in the General Note to s.2).

Paragraph (a)

1–157   OBJECTS.   For the state's positive obligation if an objection is made, see the *Human Rights Act 1998*, above.

In *TTM v London Borough of Hackney* [2011] EWCA Civ 4; [2011] 3 All E.R. 529, the Court of Appeal held that:

1. If an AMHP acts in contravention of this section by signing an application despite the fact that the patient's nearest relative has objected to it, the patient's detention would be unlawful from the outset, both as a matter of domestic law and within art.5 of the ECHR. Toulson L.J. said at para.54, that the fact the hospital managers acted lawfully under s.6(3) in accepting the application "did not clothe the conduct of the AMHP with lawfulness".

2. Article 5(5) provided the patient with an enforceable right to compensation against the local authority on whose behalf the AMHP acted.

3. Despite the fact that the local authority which arranged for the AMHP to undertake the patient's assessment was not the detaining authority, the patient could also sue that authority under domestic law for false imprisonment as it had "directly caused" the detention.

The objection does not have to be made in any particular form. At an earlier hearing of the *TTM* case, it was held that AMHP must have formed an objectively reasonable belief that there was an objection to the application. In forming an opinion on this issue, the AMHP must consider whether the nearest relative had previously objected to the patient's detention by, for example, exercising his or her power to discharge the patient from detention. The nearer in time the previous events are, the more relevant they become, particularly if they show a state of mind of the nearest relative which is unlikely to be changed (*Re*

M [2009] M.H.L.R. 154). However, the lawfulness of detention does not depend on whether the AMHP reasonably believes that there is no objection but on whether in fact there was no objection (*TTM v London Borough of Hackney*, above). In *GD v Edgware Community Hospital* [2008] M.H.L.R. 282 para.27, it was accepted that objection was something that might be gleaned from the totality of what was said, including the way in which it was said. In this case, Burnett J. confirmed that the objection does not have to be either reasonable or sensible. The AMHP should provide the nearest relative with sufficient information to enable him or her to form an opinion (*Re Whitbread* (*Mental Patient: Habeas Corpus*) (1998) 38 B.M.L.R. 94). The AMHP can proceed if the relative either does not object to the application or "perhaps wishes to sit on the fence" (*R. (on the application of G) v Ealing LBC* [2002] EWHC Admin. 1112, para.10, per Scott Baker J.).

It is not necessary for the AMHP to ask the nearest relative the specific question of whether there is an objection to the application being made (*Re GM (Patient: Consultation)* [2000] M.H.L.R. 41). However, in cases where the AMHP is unsure whether the nearest relative is objecting, the specific question should be asked (*Re M*, above). In order to avoid confusion, it is suggested that in all cases the AMHP should ask the nearest relative whether he or she objects to the application being made. The nearest relative is not placed under any obligation to consent to the application being made.

If a nearest relative objects to an application being made but subsequently withdraws that objection, it is advisable for the AMHP to obtain a signed written statement to that effect (*Re Shearon* [1996] C.O.D. 223 DC). A withdrawal of an objection must be full and effective and it will be vitiated by the AMHP providing the nearest relative with incorrect and misleading advice, such as informing the nearest relative that she would have to be represented by a solicitor at a displacement hearing. The provision of such advice would render the withdrawal ineffective: see *CX v A Local Authority* which is considered under "Consulted", below.

In *GD v Edgware Community Hospital*, above, para.33, Burnett J. said, obiter, that as an application under s.3 is "not made until it is given to the hospital staff", the nearest relative has a right to signify an objection up to that point. A counter argument, which is consistent with the remarks of Phillips L.J. in *Re Whitbread* and the terms of s.6(1), is that as an application is "duly completed" under s.6 when it is signed by the applicant, the nearest relative's right to object under this provision ends at that point.

Unreasonable objection by a nearest relative to an application is one of the grounds in s.29(3) which enables a county court to transfer the powers of the nearest relative to an "acting nearest relative".

Paragraph (b)

CONSULTED. In his "Report on an investigation into Complaint No. 97/B/2696 against **1–158** Suffolk County Council" the Local Government Ombudsman said that there is a statutory duty placed upon an AMHP to consult with the patient's nearest relative "before deciding whether to apply for a Section 3 admission" (para.58). Given the explanation of the purpose of the consultation given by Phillips L.J. in *Re Whitbread*, below, this statement is correct. It is therefore the case that the consultation can precede the obtaining of the medical recommendations. The process of consultation might involve the AMHP in divulging confidential information about the patient to the nearest relative. In order to comply with art.8 of the ECHR, the transmission of such information should only be to the extent necessary to provide the nearest relative with a genuine opportunity to object to the application.

The AMHP cannot avoid consulting the nearest relative because of a belief that the nearest relative would not object to the application (*R. (on the application of V) v South London and Maudsley NHS Foundation Trust* [2010] EWHC 742 (Admin); [2010] M.H.L.R. 83). In *B v Cygnet Healthcare* [2008] EWHC 1259 (Admin); [2008] M.H.L.R. 106, King J. held that:

1. The burden of showing that proper consultation has taken place falls on the AMHP.

2. As a matter of law, there is no obligation for the nearest relative to expressly lodge an objection under this provision. An intermediary who had been nominated by the nearest relative could be used if an appropriate consultation is undertaken with that person: see *R. v Managers of South Western Hospital* [1994] 1 All E.R. 161, noted below.

In the *Cygnet* case the patient's father, as his nearest relative, told the AMHP to talk to the patient's sister because of his difficulties with English. It is not good practice to consult via an intermediary who will be neither neutral nor disinterested as the AMHP will have no means of knowing whether the views being expressed are actually those of the nearest relative.

In *Re Whitbread (Mental Patient: Habeas Corpus)* (1998) 39 B.M.L.R. 94, the Court of Appeal held that the consultation with the nearest relative can take place before the applicant has seen the patient in accordance with subs.(5). Phillips L.J. said:

"No express provision is made as to when [the] consultation should take place. Counsel for the respondents conceded that a nexus must exist between the consultation and the application that is subsequently made. The consultation must relate to that application. It must place the nearest relative in a position, if so minded, to object to that application . . . Provided that the [AMHP] explains to the nearest relative that he or she is considering making an application and why, the nearest relative will be afforded the opportunity for objecting to the application that the Act requires."

His Lordship also said: "The consultation will have two objectives. The first will be to provide information to the [AMPH] to assist with the decision of whether to apply for admission. The second will be to put the nearest relative in a position to object to an application". Merely informing the nearest relative of the proposed application will not suffice (*Re Briscoe* [1998] EWHC 771 (Admin)).

In order for there to be a sufficiently informed consultation, the AMHP must inform the nearest relative of his or her rights under the Act in accordance with para.14.64 of the *Code of Practice*. Such information would include the right to stop the application by saying "I object", the right to challenge a displacement application made under s.29 by, if necessary, being represented in court, the procedure under s.29(4) for extending the length of a s.2 application if this is relevant, and the right of discharge under s.23: see *CX v A Local Authority* [2011] EWHC 1918 (Admin); [2011] M.H.L.R. 339 where Spencer J. said that it would have been advisable for the AMHP to have made a contemporaneous record of her consultation with the nearest relative and for her to have been able to provide the nearest relative with a leaflet explaining his or her rights and the nature of a displacement application.

In *GD v Edgware Community Hospital* [2008] M.H.L.R. 282, consultation was held by Burnett J. not to have taken place where the [AMHP] and the other professionals involved in the patient's assessment did no more than nod in the direction of consultation by setting in motion:

"a course of events which was designed to leave consultation with [the nearest relative] to the very last moment, and thus seriously inhibit the chances of his having any effective input into the process and the chances of his having an opportunity to make an objection. In those circumstances, what in my judgment they contemplated, could not properly be considered consultation at all" (para.52).

In *R. v Managers of South Western Hospital*, above, Laws J. said at 175, 176, that the AMHP is not prevented in suitable circumstances from carrying out the duty to consult through the medium of another. He developed this point by stating:

"[O]rdinarily, it will clearly be desirable for the consultation to be carried out directly by the [AMHP]. But there may be circumstances in which that will be difficult, or even well-nigh impossible. What is important is that the consultation be full and effective, to ensure that the nearest relative has the opportunity to play his full part in the process. . . . I do not suggest that an [AMHP] has a wholly free hand to appoint, as it were, a delegate for the purposes of consultation. It remains throughout the [AMHP's] responsibility".

As an AMHP will have the knowledge and experience to engage in a "full and effective" consultation with the nearest relative, an attempt should be made to consult through the medium of another AMHP.

Although there appears to be no legal reason to prevent an AMHP undertaking the consultation through correspondence, this practice is unlikely to result in the "full and effective" consultation advocated by Laws J.

(IF ANY). The application can proceed without consultation having taken place if it appears to the AMHP that the patient has no nearest relative. Reasonable steps must be taken by the AMHP in an attempt to ascertain the identity of the patient's nearest relative.

APPEARING TO BE THE NEAREST RELATIVE. These words "cannot in my judgment, **1–159** embrace a situation where, on the facts known to the [AMHP], the person in question is legally incapable of being the statutory nearest relative having regard to the terms of section 26" (*R. v Managers of South Western Hospital*, above, per Laws J. at 175).

This section does not impose a duty of reasonable inquiry on the AMHP applicant when identifying the patient's nearest relative; there is no requirement for the AMHP "to don the mantle of Sherlock Holmes" (see *WC*, below, para.28). The test is subjective. A court cannot inquire into the reasonableness of the AMHP's decision, it can only inquire into the honesty of his assertion that it appeared that that relative was the nearest relative (*Re D (Mental Patient: Habeas Corpus)* [2000] 2 F.L.R. 848 CA). *Re D* was cited by Scott Baker J. in *R. (on the application of WC) v South London & Maudsley NHS Trust* [2001] EWHC Admin 1025; [2001] M.H.L.R. 187, para.27, where his Lordship said that the court will not interfere with the AMHP's conclusion under this provision unless she failed to apply the test in s.26 or acted in bad faith, or in some way reached a conclusion that was plainly wrong. *WC* was applied in *GD v Edgware Community Hospital* [2008] M.H.L.R. 282 where it was held that an additional ground for interfering with the decision of an AMHP is misuse of power. A consequence of cases cited above is that the legality of the patient's detention will not be invalidated if, subsequent to the application being accepted by the hospital managers, the AMHP learns of the existence of a previously unknown relative who is the patient's actual nearest relative. This relative should be informed of the application and of his or her power of discharge under s.23: see also the note on s.15(1).

In the absence of action being taken under s.29 to displace the nearest relative or of the nearest relative agreeing to transfer his or her functions to another under reg.24 of the English Regulations or reg.33 of the Welsh Regulations, the AMHP should consult with the person who she has identified as being the patient's nearest relative using the formula set out in s.26, even though, from a professional perspective, it might be inappropriate for that person to be consulted. However, the consultation need not take place if the AMHP considers that it is not "reasonably practicable" to undertake the consultation: see below.

APPEARS TO THE PROFESSIONAL THAT IN THE CIRCUMSTANCES. The "circumstances" are those known to the AMHP or believed by her to exist (*R.(on the application of V) v South London and Maudsley NHS Foundation Trust* [2010] EWHC 742 (Admin); [2010] M.H.L.R. 83 para.33). The court will not interfere with this subjective decision, save on well-recognised public law grounds (*GD*, above, para.42).

NOT REASONABLY PRACTICABLE. See paras 14.60–14.65 of the *Code of Practice*. It would clearly not be practicable for an AMHP to consult with a nearest relative if, having made suitable enquiries, it is not possible for the AMHP to identify who the patient's nearest relative is. Neither would it be practicable to consult if the nearest relative is either mentally or physically incapable of being consulted, or is implacably opposed to being consulted.

The correct construction of this phrase was considered by the Court of Appeal in *TW v Enfield Borough Council* [2014] EWCA Civ 362; [2014] M.H.L.R. 415. The court held that there are two aspects to the construction: the domestic law aspect and the Human Rights Act aspect. With regard to the former, the court held, at para.45, that:

(i) the word "practicable" means more than whether it is physically "possible" to consult the nearest relative;

(ii) in considering what is "reasonably practicable", it is legitimate to look at what might be the result of the proposed action; and

(iii) the word "practicable" must have sufficient elasticity to take account of the circumstances in which the powers of the mental health professionals have to be exercised.

With regard to the Human Rights Act aspect, the court held that when an AMHP is considering whether it is "reasonably practicable" to consult the nearest relative before making an application to admit a patient, the section imposes on the AMHP an obligation to strike a balance between the patient's art.5 right not to be detained unless that is done by a procedure that is in accordance with the law, which includes the duty under this provision, and the patient's art.8(1) right to respect for her private life, which includes her right to confidentiality (para.50). In other words, the AMHP has to decide which ECHR right of the patient should take priority.

Article 8(1) is a qualified right in that an interference with the right can be justified on the grounds set out in art.8(2): see the notes to art.8 in Part 5. Aikens L.J., who gave the lead judgment, said at para.49:

"The basic reason for justifying an interference with the art.8(1) rights of a patient to maintain confidentiality in her medical condition and to prevent the possibility of that breach of confidence causing the patient further distress and ill-health, would be to ensure that the patient's other ECHR right under art.5, not to be unlawfully detained 'except in accordance with the law' is also upheld. In my view that objective would, as a matter of law, be capable of being a legitimate public aim for the purposes justifying an interference with the patient's art.8(1) rights."

In a case where an AMHP's statutory obligation to consult the nearest relative under this provision would constitute an interference with the patient's art.8(1) rights, the decision of an AMHP as to whether it is "reasonably practicable" to consult the nearest relative will depend on whether that is justified and proportionate to do so in the particular circumstances of the case. Normally, proportionality is not assessed by reference simply to the subjective conclusion of the person making the judgment. However, a court will accord a decision-maker a wide margin of judgment as to what is proportional in a particular case (para.51). This finding is significant given that the AMHP's responsibility to strike a balance between the patient's art.5 and art.8 rights will, in some circumstances, be a difficult exercise (para.52). The court held, at para.52, that as a matter of construction of this provision:

(i) a patient's assertion, even if founded on fact and even if reasonable, that consultation with the nearest relative would lead to an infringement of her art.8(1) rights cannot, as a matter of law, lead automatically to the conclusion that it is "not reasonably practicable" to consult;

(ii) an AMHP's conclusion that such consultation would lead to an infringement of the patient's art.8(1) rights is not enough, in law, to lead to the decision that there should be no such consultation; and

(iii) it is wrong in law for an AMHP to conclude that because consultation with the patient's nearest relative would require disclosure of details of the patient's case and that would therefore constitute an interference with the patient's art.8(1) rights, that must necessarily lead to the conclusion that it was "not reasonably practicable" to consult.

AMHPs should fully record their reasons for concluding that their decision regarding consultation was "justified and proportionate" in the circumstances of the case.

In *DP v South Tyneside District Council*, July 14, 2011, unreported, the patient had made allegations that her family, including her father, had tried to force her to marry against her will and that she had been at risk of being killed. She subsequently went to live in a women's refuge, and had not had recent contact with her father who was her nearest relative. When making an application under s.3, the AMHP decided not to consult with the patient's nearest relative under this provision, as he was concerned that if he disclosed the patient's whereabouts her father might compromise her safety and wellbeing. Mitting J. held that it was unrealistic, in the context in which the obligation to consult was set, that the AMHP could have had a frank consultation with the father without disclosing the patient's whereabouts. If the father had objected to the application and an application for displacement was made, the father would then have discovered the patient's whereabouts. Faced with a difficult dilemma, the AMHP had reached the reasonable conclusion that it was not practicable to consult the father.

If, subsequent to the patient's detention, the nearest relative disputes the decision of the AMHP applicant that it had not been practicable to consult, the hospital managers should not attempt to resolve the dispute: see the General Note to s.6. The appropriate remedy would be for the nearest relative to seek to challenge the legality of the patient's detention by making an application for judicial review.

UNDESIRABLE DELAY.   Given the circumstances of most guardianship applications and applications for treatment, it is unlikely that this situation would often obtain. It could occur if tracing the whereabouts of the nearest relative would involve an excessive amount of investigative work on the part of the AMHP.

In *R. (on the application of V) v South London and Maudsley NHS Foundation Trust*, above, at paras 36, 37, Wyn Williams J. held that, on the facts of the case, the AMHP had been "plainly wrong" to conclude that consulting with the nearest relative would involve an unreasonable delay in a situation where she thought that the patient's detention under s.5(2) would not expire for another seven hours. A similar conclusion was reached by H.H. Judge Pelling in *R. (on the application of GP) v Derby City Council* [2012] EWHC 1451 (Admin); [2012] M.H.L.R. 252, a case where a s.3 application was made without a consultation taking place even though the s.2 application had over seven hours to run and the AMHP, who had failed to reach the nearest relative on her mobile phone, had the time to contact her at her home.

Subsection (5)

PERSONALLY SEEN.   The applicant cannot use an intermediary (*R. v Managers of South* **1–160** *Western Hospital*, above).

The relationship between this provision and s.13(2), which requires an AMHP to interview the patient before making an application, was examined in the following passage of Phillips L.J.'s judgment in *Re Whitbread (Mental Patient: Habeas Corpus)* (1998) 39 B.M.L.R. 94:

"In my judgment section 11(5) and section 13(2) do not necessarily refer to the same event. The precondition to an application imposed by s.11(5) applies whether the application is made by the nearest relative or by the [AMHP] and thus must be appropriate to either. It seems to me that the object of section 11(5) is to ensure that the view of an applicant that an application is desirable is informed by recent face to face contact with the patient. So far as the [AMHP] is concerned, this may or may not be the occasion upon which the interview required by section 13(2) takes place. I consider that the Act permits an application to follow from an interview that takes place more than 14 days before the application, provided that the [AMHP] has confirmed his conclusion that an application is desirable by face to face contact with the patient within 14 days of the application."

14 DAYS ENDING WITH THE DATE OF THE APPLICATION. With the exception of an emergency application, once an application has been completed the patient must be taken to the hospital named in the application within 14 days of the second medical examination of the patient being made (s.6(1)(a)).

General provisions as to medical recommendations

1–161   **12.**—(1) The recommendations required for the purposes of an application for the admission of a patient under this Part of this Act [or a guardianship application] (in this Act referred to as "medical recommendations") shall be signed on or before the date of the application, and shall be given by practitioners who have personally examined the patient either together or separately, but where they have examined the patient separately not more than five days must have elapsed between the days on which the separate examinations took place.

(2) Of the medical recommendations given for the purposes of any such application, one shall be given by a practitioner approved for the purposes of this section by the Secretary of State as having special experience in the diagnosis or treatment of mental disorder; and unless that practitioner has previous acquaintance with the patient, the other such recommendation shall, if practicable, be given by a registered medical practitioner who has such previous acquaintance.

[(2A) A registered medical practitioner who is an approved clinician shall be treated as also approved for the purposes of this section under subsection (2) above as having special experience as mentioned there.]

[(3) No medical recommendation shall be given for the purposes of an application mentioned in subsection (1) above if the circumstances are such that there would be a potential conflict of interest for the purposes of regulations under section 12A below.]

AMENDMENTS
The amendments to this section were made by the Mental Health Act 2007 ss.16, 22(3), (4).

DEFINITIONS
1–162   patient: s.145(1).
mental disorder: ss.1, 145(1).
approved clinician: s.145(1).

GENERAL NOTE
1–163   This section specifies the requirements that apply to medical recommendations which are made to support applications for the detention of patients and guardianship applications. A recommendation may not be given if a potential conflict of interest arises

(subs.(3)). A doctor who makes a recommendation under this section must be a fully registered person within the meaning of the Medical Act 1983 (Interpretation Act 1978 s.5, Sch.1).

If a doctor who has been approached with a view to making a medical recommendation decides not to do so on the ground that the statutory criteria are not satisfied, there is nothing to prevent an AMHP from taking steps to see whether another doctor might be willing to provide the recommendation (*TTM v London Borough of Hackney* [2011] EWCA Civ 4; [2011] 3 All E.R. 529, para.79).

A doctor who completes a medical recommendation on a form prescribed by the English or Welsh Regulations is acting in a clinical capacity, often in circumstances of considerable stress and urgency. The doctor is not "obliged to do any more than complete the form according to his or her professional judgment in the prescribed manner". It would be "wholly inappropriate" to treat that part of the form which requires the doctor to state the reasons why detention is required in the same way as a reasoned determination following a tribunal hearing (*R. (on the application of H) v Oxfordshire Mental Healthcare NHS Trust* [2002] EWHC Admin 465; [2002] M.H.L.R. 282, paras 70, 71, per Sullivan J.). In *Re RS's Application for Judicial Review* [2015] NICA 30, the Court of Appeal in Northern Ireland said that the *Oxfordshire* decision is authority for the proposition that the "statutory prescribed forms envisage the provision of summary reasons" (para.36).

A conscientious doctor whose opinion has not been accepted by a tribunal will doubtless ask herself whether the tribunal's view is to be preferred and whether her own opinion should be revised. But if, having done so, she adheres to her original opinion she cannot be obliged to suppress or alter it. Her professional duty to her patient, and her wider duty to the public, requires her to form, and if called upon express, the best professional judgment she can, whether or not that coincides with the judgment of the tribunal (*R. v East London and The City Mental Health Trust Ex p. Brandenburg*, HL, which is noted in the General Note to s.3).

There is no provision in the Act which allows for the withdrawal of a valid medical recommendation after it has been provided to a potential applicant. In a case known to the author, a request for the return of a recommendation was made subsequent to the recommending doctor being subjected to pressure from members of the patient's family. An attempt to withdraw a recommendation would be a factor that the potential applicant would take into account when making a decision about the appropriateness of making an application.

Mental Health (Approval Functions) Act 2012

In 2012, it was discovered that four Strategic Health Authorities had unlawfully delega- **1–164** ted their function of approving doctors under subs.(2) of this section, and clinicians under s.145(1), to other bodies. This error meant that there was a legal doubt about the legal validity of the detention of patients where doctors who had not been properly approved had provided medical recommendations to support the detention. In order to respond to this situation, the Government decided to introduce emergency retrospective legislation to remove any doubt about the legality of the detentions. Section 1 of the 2012 Act validates retrospectively any approval of a doctor or an approved clinician given before the Bill received Royal Assent on October 31, 2012. This means that approvals given by bodies which had no power to perform such a function are treated as if they had always been legally granted. The Act extends to the whole of the United Kingdom.

Human Rights Act 1998

A doctor who makes medical recommendations under the Act is exercising "functions of **1–165** a public nature" and is therefore a "public authority" for the purposes of the 1998 Act: see ibid., s.6(3)(b) and *R. (on the application of Wilkinson) v The Responsible Medical Officer Broadmoor Hospital* [2001] EWCA Civ 1545; [2002] 1 W.L.R. 419, per Hale L.J. speaking obiter at para.61. The effect of this is that it is unlawful for a recommending doctor to act in a way which is incompatible with a patient's rights under the European Convention on

Human Rights (Human Rights Act 1998 s.6(1)). The recommending doctor can be a general practitioner rather than a psychiatrist (*Schuurs v the Netherlands* 41 D. & R. 186, 188–189).

The medical assessment must be based on the actual state of mental health of the person concerned and not solely on past events (*Varbanov v Bulgaria* [2000] M.H.L.R. 263 para.47).

Duty of care owed by recommending doctors

1–166   In *M (A Minor) v Newham LBC* [1995] 3 All E.R. 353, HL, the local authority, in exercising functions under the child care legislation, arranged for a child whom they suspected was being sexually abused to be interviewed by a social worker and a child psychiatrist. The House of Lords held that the social worker and the psychiatrist:

> "did not, by accepting the instructions of the local authority, assume any general professional duty of care to the [child]. The professionals were employed or retained to advise the local authority in relation to the well-being of the [child] but not to advise or treat [the child]"; per Lord Browne-Wilkinson at 384.

As reference was made in both the Court of Appeal and in the House of Lords to *Everett v Griffiths* [1920] 3 K.B. 163 CA; [1921] 1 A.C. 631, a case decided under the Lunacy Act 1890 where the House of Lords assumed, without deciding the point, that a recommending doctor owed a duty of care to the patient, it could be argued that the decision in the *Newham* case determines the liability of doctors and approved mental health professionals (AMHPs) undertaking assessments under the Act. The legal position of professionals performing functions under the child care legislation and under the Act is, however, quite different.

The question whether there is a duty of care at common law must be profoundly influenced by the statutory framework within which the acts complained of were done (*X (Minors) v Bedfordshire CC* [1995] 2 A.C. 633 at 739 per Lord Browne-Wilkinson). AMHPs and doctors who undertake assessments under the Act are not involved in either reporting to or advising their employer or any other body. The AMHP is undertaking an independent legal function when determining whether to make an application and the role of the recommending doctors is to examine the patient and support the application if it is considered that the statutory criteria are satisfied. It is submitted that the assumption made by the House of Lords in *Everett v Griffiths*, an assumption shared by Lord Atkinson in *Harnett v Fisher* [1927] A.C. 573 at 596 where the House of Lords left the matter open, is correct and that the AMHP and the recommending doctors have assumed personal responsibility towards the patient to take reasonable care to avoid an inappropriate and/or unlawful detention. It follows that an action for negligence could be brought where the professional fails to exercise such care. It was assumed by the Court of Appeal in *TTM v London Borough of Hackney* [2011] EWCA Civ 4; [2011] 3 All E.R. 529, at para.97, that an AMHP owes a duty of care to the patient when completing an application for detention. Leave for negligence actions to be pursued was given in *Winch v Jones* [1986] Q.B. 296 and *Buxton v Jayne* [1960] 1 W.L.R. 783. As Atkin L.J. pointed out in the Court of Appeal in *Everett* at 212, s.330 of the Lunacy Act 1890 (now to be found in an amended form in s.139 of this Act) assumes that professionals performing functions under the Act consider themselves bound to exercise reasonable care.

Atkin L.J.'s judgment in *Everett* included the following noteworthy passages:

> "Grievous as is the wrong of unjust imprisonment of an alleged criminal, I apprehend that its colours pale beside the catastrophe of unjust imprisonment on an unfounded finding of insanity. Modern organisation has no doubt done much to remove the horrors that were associated with Bedlam in the days when the victims were subject to public exhibition. Probably even now the insane ward or reception ward is not without its revolting incidents. But it is the effect on the mind sane, even if feeble, that knows itself wrongly adjudged unsound that produces the most poignant suffering" (at 211).

"[I]t is just as it is convenient that the law should impose a duty to take reasonable care that such persons, if sane, should not suffer the unspeakable torment of having their sanity condemned and their liberty restricted; and I am glad to record my opinion, ineffectual though it may be, that for such an injury the English law provides a remedy" (at 233).

At the House of Lords, Lord Haldane described Atkin L.J.'s judgment as a "powerful piece of reasoning displaying anxiety to guard against a possible miscarriage of justice" ([1921] 1 A.C. 631 at 652).

In *Clunis v Camden and Islington Health Authority* [1998] 3 All E.R. 180, 192, the Court of Appeal said that "the question whether a doctor owes a duty of care to a patient in certifying that a patient is fit to be detained under the Mental Health Act was left undecided in *Everett v Griffiths* and still remains open for decision in an appropriate case".

Approved Clinicians owe a duty of care to the patient whenever they propose or administer treatment under the Act (*R. (on the application of Wilkinson) v Responsible Medical Officer Broadmoor Hospital* [2001] EWCA 1545; [2002] 1 W.L.R. 419 para.68).

Subsection (1)

This subsection provides that medical recommendations must be signed on or before the **1–167** date of the application by doctors who have personally examined the patient and that where the two doctors examine the patient separately not more than five days must have elapsed between the days on which the separate examinations took place. A joint medical recommendation form may be completed by both doctors if they wish to provide a joint opinion. There is no requirement that such a form can only be completed where the doctors have examined the patient at the same time.

The detention of a patient under either s.2 or s.3 can take place within 14 days of the date of the second medical examination of the patient (s.6(1)(a)). Although the medical recommendations remain valid during this period, good practice suggests that fresh examinations of the patient should take place if there has been a significant change in the patient's circumstances subsequent to the date of the original examinations. Section 6 does not apply to guardianship applications.

RECOMMENDATIONS. Incorrect or defective recommendations (apart from joint recommendations) can be rectified under s.15. Recommendations must be in the forms prescribed by reg.4(1) of the English Regulations, i.e. Form A3 (joint recommendation) or A4 for applications under s.2, Form A7 (joint application) or A8 for applications under s.3 and Form A11 for applications under s.4. The equivalent forms under reg.4(1) of the Welsh Regulations are: Form HO3 (joint recommendation) or HO4 for applications under s.2, Form HO7 (joint applications) or HO8 for applications under s.3 and Form HO11 for applications under s.4.

Paragraph 8.63 of the Reference Guide states:

"If doctors making recommendations have examined the patient in Wales they must use the equivalent Welsh form on which to make their recommendations. If doctors are making a joint recommendation, and one of them examined the patient in England and one in Wales, then they may use either the English or Welsh form": also see reg.4(2) of the English Regulations.

ON OR BEFORE THE DATE OF THE APPLICATION. An applicant should not sign an application and then try to obtain the medical recommendation to support it.

PERSONALLY EXAMINED. The medical examination of the patient is considered in the *Code of Practice* at para.14.71. The examination should be accompanied by such further enquiries as are necessary (*Hall v Semple* (1862) 3 F. & F. 337 at 354 per Crompton J.).

A personal examination of the patient must always precede the making of a medical recommendation, even though the patient might be well known to the doctor. A doctor can examine a patient for the purposes of this provision by observing his conduct over a sufficient period of time, even if he refuses, for example, to answer questions or to submit to a physical examination or is otherwise hostile and unco-operative (*M. v South West London & St George's Mental Health NHS Trust* [2008] EWHC 1959 (Admin); [2008] M.H.L.R. 303 para.12; approved by the Court of Appeal at [2008] EWCA Civ 1112; [2008] M.H.L.R. 306 para.25 where it was said, at para.26, that there is no set time that must be taken for an examination to qualify under this provision; what is required is a matter for the professional judgment of the doctor). Also of relevance are the following observations of Egan J. delivering the majority judgment of the Irish Supreme Court in *O'Reilly v Moroney*, unreported, November 16, 1993:

"There is no definition of the word 'examine' . . . and the fact that Dr. Moroney himself agreed that there was no physical examination or interview does not conclude the matter. Here was a case where the doctor had evidence which he considered to be reliable to the effect that the plaintiff had threatened suicide and needed treatment so urgently that it might be unsafe to leave it until the following day. This was followed by what he actually saw outside the plaintiff's house where she was shouting and screaming, kicking out at her husband. This observation having regard to what he had been told constituted a form of 'examination' in my opinion and justified the doctor in pursuing the course which he did."

There would appear to be no reason to prevent an examination being conducted via a video link as this would enable to examining doctor be both observe and attempt to interview the patient: see further, P. Yellowlees, (1997) "The use of telemedicine to perform psychiatric assessments under the Mental Health Act", *Journal of Telemedicine and Telecare*, 3(4), 224–226.

An examination of an unconscious or highly intoxicated patient would not enable the doctor to ascertain whether the criteria for admission under the Act were established. Such a patient could be admitted to hospital and treated under the authority of the Mental Capacity Act 2005.

FIVE DAYS. i.e. five clear days between the days on which the medical examinations took place. Therefore if, for example, the first examination took place on January 1 the second can take place no later than January 7. The relevant dates are the dates when the examinations took place and not the dates when the medical recommendations were signed.

Subsection (2)

1–168 This subsection requires the approval by the Secretary of State or the Welsh Ministers of one of the doctors who provides a recommendation in support of an application for the admission of a patient to hospital or a guardianship application. If that doctor does not have previous acquaintance with the patient, the other recommending doctor shall, if practicable, have such previous acquaintance. The Care Quality Commission is incorrect when it states that the Act "contains an expectation that the two doctors making . . . recommendations will be s.12 approved unless one of them has 'previous acquaintance' with the patient" (*Monitoring the use of the Mental Health Act in 2009/10*, p.31).

A doctor can be approved under this provision without having been approved as an approved clinician (AC). A doctor who is an AC is automatically treated as being approved under this provision (subs.(2A)). See s.142A for the mutual recognition of approvals in England and Wales.

SECRETARY OF STATE. The Secretary of State's "Instructions with respect to the exercise of Approval Functions 2014", which establish the criteria for approval of doctors under this provision, are reproduced at Appendix D. Section 12ZA enables the Secretary of State to enter into an agreement with another person or body under which an approval function is to be exercised by that person or body. For these purposes "approval function" is defined as the function of approving doctors under this provision and that of approving approved clinicians. An agreement can cover one or both functions.

The functions of the Minister, so far as exercisable in relation to Wales, are exercised by the Welsh Ministers: see the General Note to the Act. The Welsh Ministers have transferred this function to Local Health Boards (SI 2003/150 and SI 2003/813). The Mental Health (Mutual Recognition) Regulations 2008 (SI 2008/1204), which are reproduced in Part 2, provide that doctors approved in Wales for these purposes are treated as if approved in England as well (and vice versa).

SPECIAL EXPERIENCE IN THE DIAGNOSIS OR TREATMENT OF MENTAL DISORDER. In *R. v Trent Regional Health Authority Ex p. Somaratne (No.1)* (1994) 31 B.M.L.R. 140, the Court of Appeal held that "special experience" is the sole criterion for approving a doctor and that having "special experience" requires examination of the doctor's current knowledge and skills in the diagnosis and treatment of mental disorder. The approval body has to consider the doctor's qualifications and experience and not her overall suitability for appointment. Following this decision the doctor in question made a fresh application for approval to the approval body and this application was refused. An application for a judicial review of the decision was made and judgment was given by Latham J. ([1996] C.O.D. 138). In dismissing the application, his Lordship held that:

1. The approval body was entitled to take into account the doctor's age because that issue was only considered in the context of the length of the approval that might be granted.

2. The approval body was entitled to issue guidance to members of its Mental Health Approval Panel taking into account the number of psychiatrists in any given area and adjusting the standard to be applied in considering "special experience", provided that this was applied generally and that the adjustment was directed to consideration of experience only. In this case there was no shortage of approved doctors in the relevant areas which would justify departing from what would otherwise be considered an appropriate standard of experience.

THE OTHER SUCH RECOMMENDATION. The recipients of a survey undertaken by E. K. Ung questioned the "independence" of the second medical opinion ("Who should act as the second medical recommendation for sections 2 and 3 of the Mental Health Act", *Psychiatric Bulletin* (1993), 17, 466–468). If the doctor who provides the second opinion is neither approved under this provision nor knows the patient, it is difficult to identify the added value that such an opinion brings to the assessment.

SHALL, IF PRACTICABLE. In *TTM v London Borough of Hackney* [2011] EWCA Civ 4; [2011] 3 All E.R. 529, para.81, Toulson L.J. said:

"I do not think that it would be wise for the court to attempt to give a comprehensive definition of the word 'practicable' in the present context. However, Parliament must have foreseen that decisions about making applications for admission under s.3 may have to be made in circumstances of urgency. And it must have intended that the professionals involved in the process would discharge their responsibilities in a professional way with proper regard for the interests of the patient and of society. The word 'practicable' must have sufficient elasticity to accommodate these considerations, consistently with the intention of Parliament."

The Court of Appeal upheld the decision of Collins J. at first instance ([2010] EWHC 1349 (Admin)) where there had been a disagreement between the psychiatrists who had been treating the patient as to whether he satisfied the criteria for detention. In those circumstances, the hospital trust decided that it would be fairer to approach two forensic psychiatrists both of whom were approved under s.12 and neither of whom had previous acquaintance with the patient. One was from within, the other from outside the trust. Collins J., on holding that this arrangement did not breech this provision, said at para.33:

> "Thus I think that the decision to use two professionals who came afresh and who, of course, had access to all hospital notes and could question nurses or other doctors was reasonable and a proper exercise of judgment of what was in the [patient's] best interests."

At the Court of Appeal, Toulson L.J. said at para.95, without deciding the point, that he would "be surprised if the application had been invalid merely because it was not supported by a written recommendation in prescribed form by a clinician who had previous acquaintance with [the patient], when his responsible clinician (who had such acquaintance) had expressed his opinion that M's admission was necessary. In these circumstances there was no breach of the underlying purpose behind s.12(2), even if there was a failure to comply with the letter of the law. In referring to the underlying purpose, I find it hard to think that Parliament would have intended in such circumstances to have discouraged the AMHP from obtaining fresh medical assessments, when the responsible clinicians believed this to be in the interests of the patient and the public".

Judgments about practicability might also have to be made in the following situations:

(i) is it practicable to involve a doctor with previous acquaintance with the patient given the time that it will take for that doctor to attend upon the patient; and

(ii) is it practicable to involve such a doctor given the patient's need for a specialist assessment (e.g. the AMHP might conclude that the patient's disturbed behaviour and violent fantasies require an assessment from both a general and a forensic psychiatrist, neither of whom were previously acquainted with the patient.)

If it is not possible to obtain a recommendation from a doctor who has had previous acquaintance with the patient, the applicant must explain on the relevant application form why this was the case. The *Code of Practice* states, at para.14.74, that it is preferable that a doctor who does not have previous acquaintance with the patient be approved under this section. As the key purpose of the medical recommendations is to confirm that the statutory grounds for either detention or guardianship are present and as there is no absolute requirement for one of the medical recommendations to be given by a doctor who has had previous acquaintance with the patient, it is submitted that a failure by the applicant to provide an explanation would not constitute a fundamental defect which would render the application unlawful. In the *TTM* case, above, Collins J. said, at para.24, that that the relevant passages in the forms were misleading as they suggested that the test was one of possibility rather than practicability.

PREVIOUS ACQUAINTANCE. In *AR v Bronglais Hospital and Pembrokeshire and Derwen NHS Trust* [2001] EWHC Admin. 792; [2001] M.H.L.R. 175, Scott Baker J. held that this phrase did not require the doctor to have had a previous *personal* acquaintance with the patient. His Lordship said, at para.11, that the requirement is for the doctor to:

> "have some previous knowledge of the patient and must not be coming to him or her cold, as it were. There is no indication as to the extent of the previous acquaintance that is necessary, and in my judgment the words 'previous acquaintance' are ordinary English words which have to be interpreted according to the circumstances of the particular case".

In this case, his Lordship held that a doctor who (1) had attended a case conference where she learnt a good deal about the background circumstances of the patient; (2) saw the patient for the first time for about five minutes subsequent to that meeting; and (3) had scanned the patient's recently received medical notes immediately before she made her medical recommendation, did have "previous acquaintance" with the patient. A doctor who had provided a medical recommendation in respect of the patient on a previous occasion would come within this category. Also see para.14.73 of the *Code of Practice* which states that it "is sufficient for the doctor [with previous acquaintance] to have had some previous knowledge of the patient's case"].

In circumstances where general practitioners have organised themselves into large rotas or co-operatives to provide emergency out-of-hours services, the Department of Health advised the Mental Health Act Commission that the deputising doctor cannot be considered "to have prior knowledge of the patient simply because he has access to the patient's records" and that the G.P.s deputising/answering service should contact the actual G.P. if it appears from the telephone call that a mental health assessment is likely (MHAC, *Sixth Biennial Report*, 1993–1995, para.8.1).

Subsection (2A)

This provides that a doctor who has been approved as an AC is automatically approved **1–169** for the purposes of this section.

Subsection (3)

See the notes on s.12A and the Mental Health (Conflicts of Interest) (England) **1–170** Regulations 2008 (SI 2008/1205) which are reproduced in Part 2. Only one medical recommmendation in support of an application for admission to an independent hospital may be made by a doctor on the staff of that hospital (English Regulations, reg.4(2)). In Wales, neither recommendation may be given by such a doctor (Welsh Regulations, reg.4(3)).

[Agreement for exercise of approval function: England

12ZA.—(1) The Secretary of State may enter into an agreement with another **1–171** person for an approval function of the Secretary of State to be exercisable by the Secretary of State concurrently—

(a) with that other person, and

(b) if a requirement under section 12ZB has effect, with the other person by whom the function is exercisable under that requirement.

(2) In this section and sections 12ZB and 12ZC, "approval function" means—

(a) the function under section 12(2), or

(b) the function of approving persons as approved clinicians.

(3) An agreement under this section may, in particular, provide for an approval function to be exercisable by the other party—

(a) in all circumstances or only in specified circumstances;

(b) in all areas or only in specified areas.

(4) An agreement under this section may provide for an approval function to be exercisable by the other party—

(a) for a period specified in the agreement, or

(b) for a period determined in accordance with the agreement.

(5) The other party to an agreement under this section must comply with such instructions as the Secretary of State may give with respect to the exercise of the approval function.

(6) An instruction under subsection (5) may require the other party to cease to exercise the function to such extent as the instruction specifies.

(7) The agreement may provide for the Secretary of State to pay compensation to the other party in the event of an instruction such as is mentioned in subsection (6) being given.

(8) An instruction under subsection (5) may be given in such form as the Secretary of State may determine.

(9) The Secretary of State must publish instructions under subsection (5) in such form as the Secretary of State may determine; but that does not apply to an instruction such as is mentioned in subsection (6).

(10) An agreement under this section may provide for the Secretary of State to make payments to the other party; and the Secretary of State may make payments to other persons in connection with the exercise of an approval function by virtue of this section.]

AMENDMENT
This section was inserted by the Health and Social Care Act 2012 s.38(1).

DEFINITION
1–172   approved clinician: s.145(1).

GENERAL NOTE
1–173   The effect of this section, and ss.12ZB and 12ZC is explained at paras 431 to 440 of the Explanatory Notes to the Health and Social Care Act 2012:

"New section 12ZA allows the Secretary of State to arrange for one or both of the approval functions [relating to s.12 doctors and approved clinicians] to be exercised by anyone else who is willing to enter into an agreement to do so. Such an agreement may cover the approval function in general, or only to a more limited extent. For example, there may be agreements with different people in relation to different parts of the country, or (for approved clinicians) in relation to the approval of people from different professions.

An agreement may be for a fixed period, or may specify how decisions about the termination of the agreement will be made. However, it will not be possible for the agreement to give the other party a contractual right to go on exercising the approval function against the Secretary of State's wishes. The Secretary of State may at any time to issue an instruction requiring the other party to stop approving people (either at all, or to a specified extent). The agreement may include provision for the Secretary of State to pay the other party compensation if this were to happen.

The other party has to comply with other instructions given by the Secretary of State. It is for the Secretary of State to decide how these other instructions should be given, but they have to be published. In practice, at least for approved clinicians, these instructions may include rules about things such as the professions from which approved clinicians may be drawn, the competencies they must possess, and the training they must undertake before being approved. Previously, these matters were dealt with in directions to SHAs.

Agreements under the new section 12ZA may include arrangements for Secretary of State to make payments to the other party. The Secretary of State may also make payments to other people in connection with the exercise of approval functions under the agreement. For example, the Secretary of State may agree to meet the costs of another body exercising the approval function, but also directly pay a third party to give expert advice to that body.

While the new section 12ZA allows for other people to exercise the approval functions by agreement, the new section 12ZB enables the Secretary of State to require the NHS

Commissioning Board or any Special Health Authority to exercise those functions. The Secretary of State may require the NHS Commissioning Board or a Special Health Authority to exercise one or both of the approval functions, and (as in section 12ZA) that may apply to the function generally, or to a more limited extent.

It is also possible for approval functions to be exercised concurrently both by the NHS Commissioning Board or a Special Health Authority under section 12ZB and by another person under section 12ZA.

Like a party to an agreement under section 12ZA, the NHS Commissioning Board or Special Health Authority will have to comply with instructions given by the Secretary of State. The Secretary of State will have to publish those instructions. The Secretary of State will be able to end (or vary) the requirement on the NHS Commissioning Board or Special Health Authority at any time, which would in turn end (or vary) the Board or authority's power to approve people.

Where the Secretary of State requires the NHS Commissioning Board or a Special Health Authority to exercise an approval function, that function will be treated as a function under the NHS Act. That means, for example, that the Secretary of State will have to take that function into account when allocating funding to the NHS Commissioning Board or the authority. As in section 12ZA, the Secretary of State may also make payments to a third party in connection with the exercise of the approval function by the NHS Commissioning Board or a Special Health Authority.

New section 12ZC gives the Secretary of State and people exercising approval functions under sections 12ZA and 12ZB the power to disclose information in connection with those functions, whether or not they would otherwise have a power to do so. In addition, it allows information to be shared between those people (although not with third parties) even if that would not normally be allowed under the common law of confidentiality. Provided other legal requirements (such as data protection legislation) were complied with, this may, for example, allow one approving body to pass on to another approving body information it has received from, or about, an applicant, without having to obtain that applicant's consent.

Although sections 12ZA and 12ZB give the Secretary of State new ways in which to arrange for these approval functions to be exercised, there is nothing to prevent the Secretary of State deciding to exercise them directly through the Department of Health."

Subsection (1)
PERSON.   Or a corporate body (Interpretation Act 1978 s.5, Sch.1).   **1–174**

Subsection (5)
INSTRUCTIONS.   See the "Mental Health Act 1983—Instructions with respect to the **1–175** exercise of Approval Functions 2014" which are reproduced at Appendix D.

[Requirement to exercise approval functions: England

12ZB.—(1) The Secretary of State may impose a requirement on the National **1–176** Health Service Commissioning Board ("the Board") or a Special Health Authority for an approval function of the Secretary of State to be exercisable by the Secretary of State concurrently—

  (a) with the Board or (as the case may be) Special Health Authority, and

  (b) if an agreement under section 12ZA has effect, with the other person by whom the function is exercisable under that agreement.

  (2) The Secretary of State may, in particular, require the body concerned to exercise an approval function—

  (a) in all circumstances or only in specified circumstances;

(b) in all areas or only in specified areas.

(3) The Secretary of State may require the body concerned to exercise an approval function—

(a) for a period specified in the requirement, or

(b) for a period determined in accordance with the requirement.

(4) Where a requirement under subsection (1) is imposed, the Board or (as the case may be) Special Health Authority must comply with such instructions as the Secretary of State may give with respect to the exercise of the approval function.

(5) An instruction under subsection (4) may be given in such form as the Secretary of State may determine.

(6) The Secretary of State must publish instructions under subsection (4) in such form as the Secretary of State may determine.

(7) Where the Board or a Special Health Authority has an approval function by virtue of this section, the function is to be treated for the purposes of the National Health Service Act 2006 as a function that it has under that Act.

(8) The Secretary of State may make payments in connection with the exercise of an approval function by virtue of this section.]

AMENDMENT

This section was inserted by the Health and Social Care Act 2012 s.38(1).

DEFINITIONS

1–177   Special Health Authority: s.145(1).
approval function: s.12ZA(2).

GENERAL NOTE

1–178   See the General Note to s.12ZA.

[Provision of information for the purposes of section 12ZA or 12ZB

1–179   **12ZC.**— (1) A relevant person may provide another person with such information as the relevant person considers necessary or appropriate for or in connection with—

(a) the exercise of an approval function; or

(b) the exercise by the Secretary of State of the power—

(i) to enter into an agreement under section 12ZA;

(ii) to impose a requirement under section 12ZB; or

(iii) to give an instruction under section 12ZA(5) or 12ZB(4).

(2) The relevant persons are—

(a) the Secretary of State;

(b) a person who is a party to an agreement under section 12ZA; or

(c) if the Secretary of State imposes a requirement under section 12ZB on the National Health Service Commissioning Board or a Special Health Authority, the Board or (as the case may be) Special Health Authority.

(3) This section, in so far as it authorises the provision of information by one relevant person to another relevant person, has effect notwithstanding any rule of common law which would otherwise prohibit or restrict the provision.

(4) In this section, "information" includes documents and records.]

AMENDMENT

This section was inserted by the Health and Social Care Act 2012 s.38(1).

DEFINITIONS
Special Health Authority: s.145(1).
approval function: s.12ZA(2).

1–180

GENERAL NOTE
See the General Note to s.12ZA.

1–181

[Conflicts of interest

12A.—(1) The appropriate national authority may make regulations as to the **1–182** circumstances in which there would be a potential conflict of interest such that—
(a) an approved mental health professional shall not make an application mentioned in section 11(1) above;
(b) a registered medical practitioner shall not give a recommendation for the purposes of an application mentioned in section 12(1) above.
(2) Regulations under subsection (1) above may make—
(a) provision for the prohibitions in paragraphs (a) and (b) of that subsection to be subject to specified exceptions;
(b) different provision for different cases; and
(c) transitional, consequential, incidental or supplemental provision.
(3) In subsection (1) above, "the appropriate national authority" means—
(a) in relation to applications in which admission is sought to a hospital in England or to guardianship applications in respect of which the area of the relevant local social services authority is in England, the Secretary of State;
(b) in relation to applications in which admission is sought to a hospital in Wales or to guardianship applications in respect of which the area of the relevant local social services authority is in Wales, the Welsh Ministers.
(4) References in this section to the relevant local social services authority, in relation to a guardianship application, are references to the local social services authority named in the application as guardian or (as the case may be) the local social services authority for the area in which the person so named resides.]

AMENDMENT
This section was inserted by the Mental Health Act 2007 s.22(5).

DEFINITIONS
approved mental health professional: s.145(1), (1AC).
hospital: s.145(1).
local social services authority: s.145(1).

1–183

GENERAL NOTE
The Mental Health Act 2007 repealed s.12(3) to (7) of the Act which set out the circum- **1–184** stances under which a medical practitioner was disqualified from making a medical recommendation in support of an application. The Government accepted that the subsections were "complex provisions and that placing them in secondary legislation would allow more flexibility to ensure provision keeps pace with changes in practice over time" (*Hansard*, HL Vol.688, col.539, per Baroness Royall). This section therefore introduces a power to enable regulations to be made by the Secretary of State (in respect of England) and the Welsh Ministers (in respect of Wales) setting out when, because of a conflict of interest:

(i) an AMHP may not make an application for admission or a guardianship application; and

(ii) a medical practitioner may not provide a medical recommendation supporting such an application.

The Mental Health (Conflicts of Interest) (England) Regulations 2008 (SI 2008/1205), which are reproduced in Part 2, have been made under this section. Regulations in respect of Wales have been made by the Welsh Ministers: see SI 2008/2440 (W.213). It is submitted that an application that is completed in breach of these Regulations is fundamentally defective and is therefore incapable of rectification under s.15.

This section does not apply to the renewal of a patient's detention or guardianship.

Code of Practice

1–185   The circumstances in which applications by AMHPs or the provision of medical recommendations by doctors should not be made because of conflicts of interest are examined in Ch.39.

[Duty of approved mental health professionals to make applications for admission or guardianship]

1–186   **13.**—[(1) If a local social services authority have reason to think that an application for admission to hospital or a guardianship application may need to be made in respect of a patient within their area, they shall make arrangements for an approved mental health professional to consider the patient's case on their behalf.

(1A) If that professional is—

(a) satisfied that such an application ought to be made in respect of the patient; and

(b) of the opinion, having regard to any wishes expressed by relatives of the patient or any other relevant circumstances, that it is necessary or proper for the application to be made by him, he shall make the application.

(1B) Subsection (1C) below applies where—

(a) a local social services authority makes arrangements under subsection (1) above in respect of a patient;

(b) an application for admission for assessment is made under subsection (1A) above in respect of the patient;

(c) while the patient is liable to be detained in pursuance of that application, the authority have reason to think that an application for admission for treatment may need to be made in respect of the patient; and

(d) the patient is not within the area of the authority.

(1C) Where this subsection applies, subsection (1) above shall be construed as requiring the authority to make arrangements under that subsection in place of the authority mentioned there.]

(2) Before making an application for the admission of a patient to hospital an [approved mental health professional] shall interview the patient in a suitable manner and satisfy himself that detention in a hospital is in all the circumstances of the case the most appropriate way of providing the care and medical treatment of which the patient stands in need.

[(3) An application under subsection (1A) above may be made outside the area of the local social services authority on whose behalf the approved mental health professional is considering the patient's case.]

(4) It shall be the duty of a local social services authority, if so required by the nearest relative of a patient residing in their area, to [make arrangements under subsection (1) above for an approved mental health professional to consider the patient's case] with a view to making an application for his admission to hospital; and if in any such case [that professional] decides not to make an application he shall inform the nearest relative of his reasons in writing.

(5) Nothing in this section shall be construed as authorising or requiring an application to be made by an [approved mental health professional] in contravention of the provisions of section 11(4) above [or of regulations under section 12A above], or as restricting the power of [a local social services authority to make arrangements with an approved mental health professional to consider a patient's case or of] an [approved mental health professional] to make any application under this Act.

AMENDMENTS

The amendments to this section were made by the Mental Health Act 2007 ss.21, 22(6), Sch.2 para.5.

DEFINITIONS

    approved mental health professional: s.145(1), (1AC).   **1–187**

    hospital: ss.34(2), 145(1).

    patient: s.145(1).

    local social services authority: s.145(1), (4).

    relatives: s.26(1).

    medical treatment: s.145(1).

    nearest relative: ss.26(3), 145(1).

GENERAL NOTE

This section, which does not apply to applications made by nearest relatives, places a **1–188** local social services authority (LASSA) under a duty to arrange for an approved mental health professional (AMHP) to consider a patient's case on their behalf if:

  (i) the authority has reason to think that an application for admission to hospital or a guardianship application may need to be made in respect of the patient; and

  (ii) the patient is within their area (subs.(1)).

If a patient has been detained for assessment under s.2, and the LASSA that arranged for an AMHP to consider that admission under subs.(1) has reason to think that an application for treatment under s.3 may be needed, subss.(1B) and (1C) place a duty on that LSSA (rather than the one for the area in which the patient is, or where the patient lives) to arrange for an AMHP to consider the patient's case on their behalf. This duty does not arise if the s.2 lapses before the assessment for a possible s.3 application is commenced. The duties under subss.(1), (1B) and (1C) do not prevent another LSSA from exercising its power to arrange for an AMHP to consider a patient's case if this is felt by both of the authorities to be appropriate (subs.(5) and see para.14.37 of the *Code of Practice*).

The AMHP is placed under a duty to make an application in respect of the patient if she considers that an application ought to be made and, having considered any wishes expressed by relatives of the patient or any other relevant circumstances, that it is both necessary and proper for the application to made by her (subs.(1A)). This is the case even if the application is made outside the area of the LSSA on whose behalf the AMHP is considering the patient's case (subs.(3)). The role of the AMHP is to "arrange and co-ordinate the assessment, taking into account all factors to determine if detention in hospital is the best option for the patient or if there is a less restrictive alternative" (Explanatory

Notes, para.71). It is submitted that an AMHP owes a duty of care to those who are assessed for possible admissions under the Act: see the note on "Duty of care owed by recommending doctors" in the General Note to s.12. Obstructing an AMHP in the exercise of her duties under this section could constitute an offence under either s.129(1)(b) or (d).

It is not the AMHP's role to locate a bed for the patient. Eady J. said in *DD v Durham County Council* [2012] EWHC 1053 (QB), at para.12:

"It is for the medical practitioners to decide on clinical grounds whether the person concerned requires clinical assessment in a hospital environment and/or treatment. If so, it is for them also to determine whether there is a suitable bed available: see the *Code of Practice*, at paragraph 4.75 [now see para.14.77 of the 2015 edition of the *Code*]."

If a doctor who has been approached with a view to making a medical recommendation decides not to do so on the ground that the statutory criteria are not satisfied, there is nothing to prevent an AMHP from taking steps to see whether another doctor might be willing to provide the recommendation (*TTM v London Borough of Hackney* [2011] EWCA Civ 4; [2011] 3 All E.R. 529, para.79).

There is no legal obligation placed upon an AMHP to inform the patient's nearest relative of his or her right to make an application if the AMHP has concluded that the compulsory admission of the patient is not justified. As the imparting of information about the patient's situation to the nearest relative, or any other person, without the patient's consent would be a breach of the patient's right to respect for his private life under art.8(1) of the European Convention on Human Rights (ECHR), as well as being a breach of the patient's common law right to confidentiality, a justification for taking such action must be found in art.8(2).

There is no requirement for an AMHP to identify a change in the patient's circumstances before proceeding to make an application under ss.2 or 3 in respect of a patient who has been discharged by a tribunal. However, an AMHP may not lawfully apply for the admission of a patient whose discharge has been ordered by the decision of a tribunal of which the AMHP is aware unless the AMHP has formed a reasonable and bona fide opinion that he has information not known to the tribunal which puts a significantly different complexion on the case as compared with that which was before the tribunal. An AMHP may well learn of the existence of a decision of the tribunal to discharge the patient when performing her functions under this section and will then wish to know the reasons for it. However, if no such information comes to light the law does not place on the AMHP (or a nearest relative applicant) a duty to make reasonable enquiries to establish whether any decision has been made by any tribunal and, if so, the grounds upon which it was based (*R. v East London and The City Mental Health Trust Ex p. Brandenburg*, HL, noted in the General Note to s.3).

When making a decision about making an application, the AMHP should consider whether a potential conflict of interest arises under the Mental Health (Conflict of Interest) (England) Regulations 2008 (SI 2008/1205) from her involvement.

For the approval of AMHPs by LSSAs, see s.114.

Use of statutory documentation in England and Wales

1–189   Applications to hospitals in Wales must be made in accordance with the Welsh Regulations i.e. a Welsh application form must be used (Welsh Regulations, reg.4(1)). Welsh medical recommendation forms must be used if the patient is examined in Wales, even if the patient is admitted to a hospital in England (English Regulations, reg.4(2)). If the patient is medically examined in Wales and admitted to a hospital in England, an English application form must be used (English Regulations, reg.4(1)).

As the English and Welsh statutory forms reproduce the relevant statutory criteria in identical terms, it is submitted the completion of the wrong form would not constitute a fundamental defect that would render the application unlawful.

Human Rights Act 1998

An AMHP who is performing functions under the Act is exercising "functions of a pub- **1–190** lic nature" and is therefore a "public authority" for the purposes of the 1998 Act (s.6(3)(b)). The effect of this is that it is unlawful for an AMHP to act in a way which is incompatible with a patient's rights under the ECHR (Human Rights Act 1998 s.6(1)).

If an AMHP acts in an arbitrary fashion by, for example, resorting to making an application for detention in bad faith or making an application in circumstances where such action is a disproportionate response to the patient's situation, she will have violated art.5(1) of the ECHR: see *Tsirlis and Kouloumpas v Greece* (1997) 25 E.H.R.R. 198 para.56. In *Litwa v Poland* (2001) 33 E.H.R.R. 53 para.78 the European Court of Human Rights, in reiterating that a necessary element of the "lawfulness" of a detention within the meaning of art.5(1)(e) is the absence of arbitrariness, said that "the detention of an individual is such a serious measure that it is only justified where other, less severe measures have been considered and found to be insufficient to safeguard the individual or public interest which might require that the person concerned be detained. That means that it does not suffice that the deprivation of liberty is executed in conformity with national law but it must also be necessary in the circumstances". The requirement for the patient's detention to be a proportionate response to the circumstances is reflected in duty placed on the AMHP by subs.(2).

The giving of "reasons" to a nearest relative for a decision not to make an application in respect of the patient (see subs.(4)) could constitute an interference with the patient's right to respect for his private life under art.8(1) of the ECHR if the reasons contained information that was confidential to the patient. Either the reasons should be drafted in a manner which would not constitute such a violation or a justification for the violation must be found in art.8(2).

Code of Practice

Guidance on "Applications for detention in hospital" is contained in Ch.14. For the **1–191** assessment of a child or young person for detention under the Act, see paras 19.73 and 19.74. Paragraph 39.18 of the *Code* states:

"The Act requires an AMHP to take an independent decision about whether or not to make an application under the Act. If an AMHP believes that they are being placed under undue pressure to make, or not make, an application, they should raise this through the appropriate channels. Local arrangements should be in place to deal with such circumstances."

The circumstances in which applications by AMHPs should not be made because of a conflict of interest are examined in Ch.39.

Subsection (1)

This provision places an obligation on a LSSA to arrange for an AMHP to "consider the **1–192** patient's case on their behalf" if the authority has reason to think that a mentally disordered person who is in their area might need to be made subject to an application for detention or guardianship. It does not matter whether the person lives in that area. Although the AMHP is acting on behalf of the LSSA, she acts independently when performing functions under the Act: see the note on subs.(1A). As an AMHP may be approved by one LSSA but may be authorised to act on behalf of others (see the General Note to s.114), this duty can be performed either by an AMHP approved by the LASSA that has the duty under this provision and who has been authorised by that authority to act on its behalf, or by another AMHP if that AMHP has been authorised to act on its behalf by that LSSA. Subsection (5) enables (but does not oblige) another LSSA to perform the function under this provision if that is felt to be appropriate.

PATIENT WITHIN THEIR AREA. In *R. (on the application of Sunderland City Council) v South Tyneside Council* [2012] EWCA Civ 1232, para.25, Lloyd L.J. said that the test in this provision "is one of physical presence, which may be temporary or even fortuitous. It is not at all the same as residence". It follows that if a patient who resides in the area of LSSA A is admitted to a hospital as an informal patient in the area of LSSA B and then requires assessment under the Act, LSSA B has the obligation to arrange the AMHP assessment.

Subsection (1A)

1–193   The responsibilities under this provision are placed on the AMHP and not on the employing authority (*Nottingham City Council v Unison* [2004] EWHC 893 para.18). However, as an AMHP acts on behalf of the local authority (s.145(1AC)), that authority will be vicariously liable for any lack of care or bad faith on behalf of the AMHP (*TTM v London Borough of Hackney* [2010] EWHC 1349 (Admin), para.35; affirmed by the Court of Appeal at [2011] EWCA Civ 4), even though the authority might not be the AMHP's employer (*DD v Durham County Council* [2012] EWHC 1053 (QB); [2012] M.H.L.R. 245, para.21). The AMHP should exercise her own judgment, based upon social and medical evidence, and not act at the behest of her employer, medical practitioners or other persons who might be involved with the patient's care: also see para.14.52 of the *Code of Practice* and the note on s.114(10). In *St George's Healthcare NHS Trust v S* [1998] 3 All E.R. 673 at 694 CA, Judge L.J. said:

> "[The provisions of s.13] make clear that the social worker must exercise her own independent judgment on the basis of all the available material, including her interview and assessment of the 'patient', and personally make the appropriate decision. When doing so she is required to take account of the recommendations made by the medical practitioners".

Speaking of the role of the AMHP's precursor, Devlin L.J., said: "It is the business of the duly authorised officer, rather than that of the doctor, to see that statutory powers are not used for the purpose [of hospital treatment] unless the circumstances warrant it" (*Buxton v Jayne* [1960] 1 W.L.R. 783 at 784).

The duty placed on the AMHP by this section does not affect the provisions as to consultation with nearest relatives set out in s.11(4) (subs.(5)).

AN APPLICATION. If the AMHP makes an application, the reasons for taking such action should be recorded. This was the approach taken by the Local Ombudsman in his investigation into complaint 87/B/1308 where a failure by AMHPs to make adequate records of the circumstances of the compulsory admission of a patient was sufficient for the Ombudsman to find that the employing local authority was guilty of maladministration. There is a legal obligation placed on the AMHP to give reasons to the patient if the application is inconsistent in effect with a decision of the tribunal to discharge him (*R. v East London and The City Mental Health Trust Ex p. Brandenburg* HL, above).

The AMHP is obliged, as far as she is able, to ensure that the medical recommendations upon which the application is founded comply with the provisions of s.12 and the regulations made under s.12A. The AMHP should not make an application and then look for the medical recommendations to support it because the application is "founded" on the medical recommendations (s.11(7)). It is for the AMHP to determine which section of the Act to invoke: "It is the [AMHP] who makes the application, not the doctors" (*R. v East London and the City Mental Health Trust Ex p. Brandenburg* [2003] UKHL 58; [2004] 1 All E.R. 400, per Lord Bingham at para.12).

OUGHT TO BE MADE. In the case of an application for admission to hospital, the AMHP can only be satisfied that an application ought to be made if the requirements of subs.(2) have been met.

The AMHP should not challenge the diagnosis set out in the medical recommendations but, because mental disorder alone does not render a person liable to detention or guardianship, she is entitled to take the view that it is not appropriate to make an application. The view of the *Royal Commission*, at para.390, was that "medical and non-medical opinions should supplement each other; each person should be expected to contribute to the final decision only what is appropriate to his own knowledge or experience or to his relationship with the patient".

HAVING REGARD TO.   For a dramatic illustration of the need for AMHPs and other professionals to listen to, and to take account of, the views of family members and others with close knowledge of the patient, see Ch.17 of L. Blom-Cooper et al., *The Falling Shadow*, 1995. The patient's nearest relative will usually be involved in applications under s.2 (see s.11(3)) and s.3 (see s.11(4)) and with guardianship applications (see s.11(4)).

NECESSARY OR PROPER.   Generally speaking, it would not be "necessary or proper" to make an application in respect of a patient who is willing to be admitted informally: see the General note to s.131. Neither would it be "necessary or proper" for an AMHP to make an application in respect of a mentally incapable patient who is compliant to being in hospital if the patient is not being deprived of his liberty (see the note on "The detention of compliant mentally incapable patients" in the General Note to Pt II).

In *St George's Healthcare NHS Trust v S*, above, Judge L.J. said at 695: "In deciding whether it is 'necessary or proper' to make an application under section 2, the AMHP has to approach the individual 'patient' as she is, or at any rate as on the best analysis she can make at the time, the patient appears to be". In this case the Court of Appeal held that the fact that the patient was heavily pregnant and adamantly refusing treatment for her pre-eclampsia were, at least potentially, of compelling importance to the AMHP who had to make an informed judgment under this provision. To require the AMHP to make such a judgment by ignoring the reality of the patient's situation "would be absurd". However, the patient's illness associated with her pregnancy was not sufficient on its own to bring the provisions of this section into play.

If the AMHP decides not to make an application, it would be improper for that decision to be reviewed by another AMHP in the absence of any change in circumstances, fresh evidence or concern that the AMHP had acted unprofessionally. However, if the decision not to make an application was made by an AMHP with little knowledge of the patient, there should be no objection to that decision being reviewed by an AMHP who has an extensive knowledge of the patient's history and current situation. A procedure which allowed for the automatic review of a decision of an AMHP not to make an application would undermine the independent nature of the AMHP's role. For a contrary view, see "Disagreements between psychiatrists and social workers over compulsory admissions under the Mental Health Act", R. G. Sammut and H. Sergeant, *Psychiatric Bulletin* (1993), 17, 462–465.

BY HIM.   The use of the phrase "necessary or proper for the application to be made *by him*" enables the AMHP to conclude that although an application ought to be made, it would be more appropriate for the application to be made by another AMHP.

Subsections (1B), (1C)
See the General Note to this section.   **1–194**

Subsection (2)
It is possible to have a single interview under this provision doubling as a s.4/2 interview **1–195** in the first instance, followed without further interview by a s.3 application: see *Re GM (Patient: Consultation)* [2000] M.H.L.R. 41, where Burton J. said at paras 69, 70:

"It seems to me entirely possible, provided that a necessary and suitable interview is carried out, for the [AMHP] to have acquired the necessary knowledge, either retaining it in her memory or if necessary reflecting back on any notes, so that there is sufficient to justify an initial section 2 or 4 application, but subsequently, when it comes to a section 3 application, for her to be able to draw on that same knowledge when she comes to consider section 3 . . . In those circumstances there is nothing which prevents the use, for the purposes of a subsequent section 3 admission, of any proper information available on an earlier section 2/4 admission, just as there is no prohibition upon the [AMHP] using acquired knowledge prior to the interview for the purposes of the interview itself . . ."

In this case, the patient was the subject of an application under s.3 whilst he was being detained under s.4. A fresh interview would be required if the patient attained informal status subsequent to the expiry or discharge of the initial detaining section and before the need for a further period of detention arose. This is because the attaining of informal status should trigger a fresh enquiry, via an interview, as to the appropriateness of a further period of detention.

During the interview, there is no need for the AMHP to indicate under which section of the Act she is operating. What is required is for the role of the AMHP and the purpose the visit to be explained to the patient (*Re GM*, above, para.71).

Where a person requests an AMHP to undertake a mental health assessment in respect of a member of that person's family, and the AMHP concludes that an assessment for possible admission under the Act is required, the person who made the request should be informed as to the possible outcomes of the assessment: see the report of the Local Government Ombudsman into complaint No.97/A/2239. In his report into complaint No.97/A/1082, the Ombudsman found maladministration in a case where: (1) a family had been given inadequate notice of a planned assessment of a patient for possible admission under this Act; and (2) no less than three home care staff were present when the assessment took place.

BEFORE MAKING AN APPLICATION.   The interview required by this provision can take place more than 14 days before the application, provided that the AMHP has confirmed that an application is necessary by having face to face contact with the patient within 14 days of the application as required by s.11(5): see *Re Whitbread (Mental Patient: Habeas Corpus)* 39 B.M.L.R. 94 (1977) CA, which is considered in the notes to s.11(4)(5).

HOSPITAL.   This subsection does not apply to guardianship applications. A recommending doctor has responsibility for ensuring that a hospital bed is available for the patient (*Code of Practice*, para.14.77).

INTERVIEW.   The AMHP should explain the purpose of the interview to the patient who should ordinarily be given the opportunity of speaking to the AMHP alone (*Code of Practice*, para.14.54). It is submitted that, in the context of the Act, an attempt by an AMHP to communicate with a patient would be sufficient to constitute an interview and that this would be the case even if the patient was either unable or unwilling to respond. This opinion received judicial endorsement by Underhill J. in *M. v South West London & St George's Mental Health NHC Trust* [2008] EWHC 1959 (Admin); [2008] M.H.L.R. 303 para.14, who said that the purpose of the interview is "achieved in [a] case where the [AMHP] attempts to communicate with the patient but she fails to respond, or responds inappropriately, in a manner suggesting that she does indeed require treatment." His Lordship's statement that the requirement that the interview be conducted in a "suitable" manner gave a degree of flexibility to those involved was approved by the Court of Appeal at [2008] EWCA Civ 1112; [2008] M.H.L.R. 306 para.25. Richards L.J. said, at para.26, that there is no set time that must be taken for an interview to qualify under this provision; what is required is a matter for the professional judgment of the AMHP. If a patient has been admitted to hospital informally and has subsequently been heavily tranquilised following a violent incident, it is submitted that an attempt to interview the patient would be sufficient and that there would be no need for the AMHP to wait for the effect of the tranquilliser to wear off, with the patient becoming potentially violent again: see further the *Code of Practice* at para.14.56.

An interview cannot take place with a highly intoxicated patient. In these circumstances the doctor could use the powers contained in the Mental Capacity Act 2005 to treat the patient, with the AMHP intervening only when the patient is capable of being interviewed. If an unconscious patient requires immediate hospital treatment, he could be taken to hospital under the authority of the 2005 Act.

If the AMHP is unable to gain access to premises in order to interview the person, she cannot force entry but should consider making an application to a magistrate under s.135(1).

SUITABLE MANNER. These words were added to this section as a result of an amendment moved at the Special Standing Committee by Mr Tom Benyon MP who stressed the need for those who are involved in the management of deaf psychiatric patients having either the use of an interpreter or a fluency in British Sign Language. He drew the Committee's attention to a number of cases where patients had been compulsorily detained under the 1959 Act in circumstances where a lack of speech had been mistakenly attributed to mental disorder. Other MPs were concerned that applicants should be sensitive to the difficulties faced by members of ethnic minorities who might not speak English or who might not speak it well. The words "suitable manner" should direct the AMHP's attention to the particular needs of all groups, including children, who might have difficulties in communicating effectively.

ALL THE CIRCUMSTANCES OF THE CASE. In practice, these "might include the past history of the patient's mental disorder, the patient's present condition and the social, familial, and personal factors bearing on it, the other options available for supporting the patient, the wishes of the patient and the patient's relatives and carers, and the opinion of other professionals involved in caring for the patient" (Reference Guide, para.8.32). This phrase also includes "medical considerations" such as the "immediate and catastrophic consequences of self neglect" (*GJ v Foundation Trust* [2009] EWHC 2972 (Fam), para.117(a)).

The duty to consider "all the circumstances of the case" does not place the AMHP under an obligation to investigate the proposed place of detention, the location where the patient will be kept while there and the regime to which he will be subject, or to go back and research the views expressed by other psychiatrists who had been in the past involved with the patient's care. It is not for the AMHP to second guess the current medical advice (*DD v Durham County Council* [2012] EWHC 1053 (QB); [2012] M.H.L.R. 245, per Eady J. speaking obiter at paras 14, 15).

THE MOST APPROPRIATE WAY. The AMHP is placed under an obligation to be satisfied as to the appropriateness of detention in the light of her knowledge of the alternative forms of intervention that would be available for the patient: see the note on "All the circumstances of the case", above. This provision reflects the requirement under art.5(1) of the ECHR that detention must be a proportionate response to the circumstances: see *Litwa v Poland*, which is noted under "Human Rights Act 1998", above. AMHPs are not placed under an obligation to actively seek out alternatives before making an application.

A comprehensive knowledge of local resources available for the mentally disordered is essential if an informed judgment is to be made. The AMHP's view as to why there was no alternative to compulsory hospitalisation should be recorded in the client's case notes: see the Local Ombudsman's investigation into Complaint 87/B/1308, noted under subs.(1), above.

CARE AND MEDICAL TREATMENT. This means care and medical treatment for the patient's mental disorder, and not for a medical disorder which is unconnected with her mental condition (*St George's Healthcare NHS Trust v S* [1998] 3 All E.R. 673 CA). It is therefore unlawful for an application to be made in circumstances where there is no intention either to assess or treat the patient's mental disorder. Despite the confirmation of the legal position given in the *St George's* case, it is the author's experience that the Act has been used to "authorise" the removal of mentally incompetent non-compliant patients from their homes where the sole cause of concern is the patient's need for hospitalisation to treat a physical disorder.

Subsection (3)

1–196   Although an AMHP can only be approved by one LSSA, she can perform AMHP functions in the area of another LSSA (or LSSAs) if that authority has authorised the AMHP to perform such functions.

Subsection (4)

1–197   This provision, which does not apply to a nearest relative who wants a guardianship application to be made, does not require the AMHP to inform the nearest relative that he or she has the power to make an application under the Act. However the transmission of such information by the AMHP might be considered to be good practice.

The requirement "to consider the patient's case" does not necessarily mean that the AMHP undertakes an assessment of the patient or even interviews the patient. The effect of a nearest relative's request under this provision is to require an AMHP to consider whether an application should be made in respect of the patient. The extent and nature of the inquiries made by the AMHP would depend upon the knowledge that the local mental health service has about the patient. If the patient has been the subject of a recent mental health assessment, the AMHP's obligation would be confined to identifying whether there has been a change in the patient's situation that would justify a reassessment. If the patient is not known, the patient's general practitioner should be contacted to ascertain whether the patient is mentally disordered as the obligation under this section only arises if this is the case: see the note on "patient", below. It could be that the nearest relative is the mentally disordered member of the "patient's" family.

The communication from the nearest relative can be either written or verbal. It might not always be clear whether a communication from a nearest relative amounts to a request to a local authority to act under the provisions of this subsection. It is submitted that if a nearest relative indicates concern about the patient by saying, for example, that the patient "ought to be in hospital" or that "something ought to be done" about the patient, the nearest relative should be informed of the power under this subsection and asked whether he or she wishes to exercise it.

NEAREST RELATIVE.   Or acting nearest relative appointed by the court under s.29. It is submitted that this provision should apply if the approach to the local authority is made by someone acting on behalf of the nearest relative, e.g. a general practitioner.

PATIENT.   The patient could be receiving hospital treatment for a mental disorder as an informal patient. If the LSSA considers that the person concerned is not "a person suffering or appearing to be suffering from mental disorder," which is the definition of "patient" in s.145(1), this subsection will not apply.

INFORM THE NEAREST RELATIVE.   The AMHP should write to the nearest relative immediately after the decision not to make an application has been made. Note that it is the AMHP, and not the LSSA who has to inform the nearest relative. If the AMHP decides not to make an application, the nearest relative could proceed to make an application him or herself if the required medical recommendation(s) had been made. If the nearest relative's application is made under either s.2 or 3, an AMHP would be required to provide the hospital managers with a social circumstances report under s.14.

REASONS. Giving reasons need not necessarily involve the AMHP in revealing a significant degree of confidential information because statements of a general nature such as "I took medical advice and was informed that Mr X is not mentally disordered within the meaning of the Mental Health Act 1983", or "Mr X agreed to enter hospital as an informal patient", or "in my opinion it is appropriate for Mr X to continue to receive treatment at home", would constitute a reason for the purposes of this subsection. Also see the note on "The Human Rights Act", above.

Subsection (5)
This provision confirms that nothing in this section (i) effects an AMHP's obligations **1–198** under s.11(4) and the regulations made under s.12A; (ii) prevents a LSSA other than the LSSA that has duties under subss.(1), (1B) and (1C) from arranging for an AMHP to assess the patient; or (iii) can be construed as restricting an AMHP's power to make an application.

Social reports
14. Where a patient is admitted to a hospital in pursuance of an application **1–199** (other than an emergency application) made under this Part of this Act by his nearest relative, the managers of the hospital shall as soon as practicable give notice of that fact to the local social services authority for the area in which the patient resided immediately before his admission; and that authority shall as soon as practicable arrange for [an approved mental health professional] [. . .] to interview the patient and provide the managers with a report on his social circumstances.

AMENDMENTS
The words in square brackets were substituted by the Mental Health Act 2007 s.21, Sch.2, para.6. The words omitted were repealed by the Children Act 2004 s.64, Sch.5 Pt 4.

DEFINITIONS
    patient: s.145(1).   **1–200**
    hospital: ss.34(2), 145(1).
    emergency application: s.4(1).
    nearest relative: ss.26(3), 145(1).
    the managers: s.145(1).
    local social services authority: s.145(1).
    approved mental health professional: s.145(1), (1AC).

GENERAL NOTE
This section places a duty on social services authorities to provide hospital managers **1–201** with a report on a patient's social circumstances if the patient has been admitted to an NHS or private hospital pursuant to an application made by his nearest relative, or acting nearest relative appointed by a county court under s.29, under either s.2 or 3. It is presumably assumed that an AMHP applicant would automatically provide the hospital with the information that would be contained in a social circumstances report. The social circumstances report could include an account of the patient's family and social relationships (including the attitude of carers), history of mental disorder, previous contact with the local authority, access to community resources, employment record, financial situation and accommodation. The report should also contain an account of the circumstances of the admission. If the nearest relatives' application was made after an AMHP had refused to make one, it is suggested that the AMHP's report should include an account of the reasons for her decision.

A refusal to grant the AMHP access to the patient would constitute an offence under s.129(1)(b).

OTHER THAN AN EMERGENCY APPLICATION.   It is unclear whether this section requires a social circumstances report to be made where an emergency application has been converted into a 28-day detention by the addition of the second medical recommendation required by s.2 (s.4(4)). Good practice suggests that it should be.

AREA IN WHICH THE PATIENT RESIDED.   This need not necessarily be the place where the patient was staying immediately prior to his admission, as temporary absences from the place where a person lives does not affect residence, as long as there is an intention to return: see the note on "resides" in s.7(5).

Rectification of applications and recommendations

1–202   **15.**—(1) If within the period of 14 days beginning with the day on which a patient has been admitted to a hospital in pursuance of an application for admission for assessment or for treatment the application, or any medical recommendation given for the purposes of the application, is found to be in any respect incorrect or defective, the application or recommendation may, within that period and with the consent of the managers of the hospital, be amended by the person by whom it was signed; and upon such amendment being made the application or recommendation shall have effect and shall be deemed to have had effect as if it had been originally made as so amended.

(2) Without prejudice to subsection (1) above, if within the period mentioned in that subsection it appears to the managers of the hospital that one of the two medical recommendations on which an application for the admission of a patient is founded is insufficient to warrant the detention of the patient in pursuance of the application, they may, within that period, give notice in writing to that effect to the applicant; and where any such notice is given in respect of a medical recommendation, that recommendation shall be disregarded, but the application shall be, and shall be deemed always to have been, sufficient if—

(a) a fresh medical recommendation complying with the relevant provisions of this Part of this Act (other than the provisions relating to the time of signature and the interval between examinations) is furnished to the managers within that period; and

(b) that recommendation, and the other recommendation on which the application is founded, together comply with those provisions.

(3) Where the medical recommendations upon which an application for admission is founded are, taken together, insufficient to warrant the detention of the patient in pursuance of the application, a notice under subsection (2) above may be given in respect of either of those recommendations [. . .]

(4) Nothing in this section shall be construed as authorising the giving of notice in respect of an application made as an emergency application, or the detention of a patient admitted in pursuance of such an application, after the period of 72 hours referred to in section 4(4) above, unless the conditions set out in paragraphs (a) and (b) of that section are complied with or would be complied with apart from any error or defect to which this section applies.

AMENDMENT
    In subs.(3), the words omitted were repealed by the Mental Health Act 2007 s.55, Sch.11 Pt 1.

DEFINITIONS
1–203   patient: s.145(1).

hospital: ss.34(2), 145(1).
application for admission for assessment: ss.2, 145(1).
application for admission for treatment: ss.3, 145(1).
the managers: s.145(1).
emergency application: s.4(1).

GENERAL NOTE

This section, which does not apply to documents issued by a court, to documents given in **1–204** support of a patient's transfer under s.19, the renewal of the patient's detention under s.20, the use of the "holding powers" contained in s.5(2) and (4), or to documents relating to guardianship or community treatment orders, provides for admission documents which are found to be incorrect or defective to be rectified within 14 days of the patient's admission. Similar provision in respect of guardianship applications is made in s.8(4). A rectified document is treated as if it had been correctly completed at the time when it was signed.

If a document which contains a minor error is not rectified under subs.(1), the application is not invalidated by virtue of the de minimis principle, i.e. the error is too trivial to be of any consequence: see *Re E (Mental Health: Habeas Corpus),* noted in the General Note to Sch.1 to the English Regulations. Also note that in *R. v Soneji* [2005] UKHL 49; [2005] 4 All E.R. 321, the House of Lords held, in a different context, that in deciding what was the legal effect of a failure to comply with a statutory requirement, a court should examine the consequences of the failure and ask whether Parliament intended that the failure should invalidate the act.

Rectification is primarily concerned with dealing with inaccurate recording. It cannot be used to enable "a fundamentally defective application to be retrospectively validated" (per Sir Thomas Bingham M.R. in *Re S-C (Mental Patient: Habeas Corpus)* [1996] 1 All E.R. 532 at 537, CA) or to "cure a defect which arises because a necessary event in the procedural chain leading to the detention has simply not taken place at all. It is essentially concerned with correction of errors on the face of the document" (per Laws J. in *R. v South Western Hospital Managers Ex p. M* [1994] 1 All E.R. 161 at 177). If an admission document reveals a fundamental breach of law or procedure which is incapable of rectification under this section, either the hospital managers or the patient's responsible clinician should exercise their power under s.23 to discharge the patient from the section. This action is required because, once an application has been accepted by the hospital managers, only the courts can adjudicate upon the lawfulness of the application. If the patient is discharged, he could be made the subject of a report under either s.5(2) or (4) and prevented from leaving hospital if it was considered that the appropriate requirements were satisfied: see the note on "in-patient in a hospital" in s.5(2). This advice is reproduced in an extended form in the General Note to s.6. If an application is found to be fundamentally defective, authority for the patient's detention can only be obtained through a fresh application: see para.35.13 of the *Code of Practice.*

The Care Quality Commission published guidance on "Scrutinising and Rectifying Statutory Forms for Admission under the Mental Health Act". Paragraph 5 of this document states that because "the lawfulness of an application or order is a matter for the courts, Mental Health Act Commissioners must be cautious about expressing an opinion as to the validity of an application. In particular, they may not suggest that a particular patient is entitled to be released forthwith, even if there has been a clear and fundamental breach".

The hospital managers should nominate an officer to undertake the task of scrutinising admission documents when the patient is admitted or, if the patient is already in hospital, as soon as practicable after the documents have been received: see reg.4(3) of the English Regulations and reg.4(2) of the Welsh Regulations. The *Code of Practice*, at para.35.7, distinguishes between receiving documents and scrutinising them:

"[R]eceipt involves physically receiving documents and checking that they appear to amount to an application that has been duly made (since that is sufficient to give the managers the power to detain the patient). Scrutiny involves more detailed checking for omissions, errors and other defects and, where permitted, taking action to have the documents rectified after they have already been acted on."

As to the use of obsolete or defective forms, see the General Note to Sch.1 to the English Regulations.

A person who wilfully makes a false entry or statement in an application commits an offence under s.126(4).

Defective Court Orders

1–205   See the note under this heading in the General Note to Part III.

Code of Practice

1–206   Guidance on the receipt and scrutiny of documents prescribed under this Act is contained in Ch.35.

Subsection (1)

1–207   It is submitted that:

(1)   The naming of a person who is not the patient's nearest relative on an application form is an error that can be rectified under this section if, on the information available to her, and after having made the appropriate enquiries, the approved mental health professional (AMHP) made an honest mistake, for example, the AMHP was not aware of the existence of a close relative of the patient. The error would not be rectifiable if, on the information available to her, the person identified could not have been the patient's nearest relative. In other words, the AMHP made an error of law by misinterpreting s.26: see *Re S-C* and *R. v South Western Hospital Managers Ex p. M*, above, and *R. v Birmingham Mental Health Trust Ex p. Phillips*, noted under s.11(3), above. It is further submitted that an honest mistake made by the AMHP regarding the identification of the patient's nearest relative which is discovered after the rectification period has expired will not render the application unlawful if the actual nearest relative is informed of his or her status and powers at the earliest opportunity.

(2)   An application that is made in breach of the regulations made under s.12A is fundamentally defective and is not capable of being rectified.

Paragraph 31.26 of the Reference Guide states:

"In practice, any document found to contain [an error which is rectifiable under subs.(1)] should be returned to the person who signed it for amendment. When the amended document is returned to the hospital it should again be scrutinised to check that it is now in the proper form, following which consent can be given by the hospital managers (managers may authorise officers to consent to amendments on their behalf). The consent should be recorded in writing and can take the form of an endorsement on the document itself."

Beginning with.   Including the day on which the patient was admitted to hospital (*Zoan v Rouamba* [2000] 2 All E.R. 620 CA).

Incorrect.   In that, had the facts been correctly stated, the admission would have been justified, e.g. mis-stating dates, names or places. Rectification can only be used to ensure that the relevant form reflects the factual situation that obtained when the form was completed.

DEFECTIVE. Probably means that incomplete information has been provided, e.g. leaving a space blank, omitting to insert a date or failing to delete one or more alternatives in places where only one can be correct. It does not mean that a completed form which accurately reflects the factual situation can be altered to provide legal justification for detention.

BY WHOM IT WAS SIGNED. It is submitted that an unsigned application or medical recommendation cannot be remedied under this section and that an application or medical recommendation which is signed by a person who is not empowered to do so under this Act is also incapable of rectification. A check therefore needs to be made to confirm that the application is signed by someone who appears to be an AMHP, a nearest relative or an acting nearest relative and that the medical recommendations are signed by practitioners who are not excluded by s.12 or the regulations made under s.12A. When performing this task the scrutinising officer can take certain statements at face value: see the note on reg.3(8) of the English and Welsh Regulations.

Subsection (2)

This subsection provides a remedy if *one* of the medical recommendations required **1–208** under s.2 or 3 is found to be insufficient to warrant the detention of the patient. It could be used if, for example, a doctor who gives a medical recommendation for admission for treatment on Form A8 fails to convince the scrutineer that she has considered other methods of care or treatment. The hospital managers must notify the applicant in writing and if a fresh medical recommendation, not necessarily by the same doctor, is received within 14 days of the patient's admission, the application is treated as if it had been validly made from the date when it was completed. The requirement in s.12(1) that no more than five days must elapse between the two medical examinations made by the recommending doctors does not apply if a fresh medical recommendation is made under this provision. A copy of the notification to the applicant should be placed with the detention papers.

ONE OF THE TWO MEDICAL RECOMMENDATIONS. As Eldergill has pointed out, it seems that neither this subsection nor subs.(3) allows for the remedying of a defective joint medical recommendation (A. Eldergill, *Mental Health Review Tribunals* (1997), p.269).

INSUFFICIENT. The Reference Guide, at para.31.30, states that a "medical recommendation may be insufficient because:

- it has been signed after the date on which the application was made, or
- the doctor's reasons in the form do not appear to be sufficient to support the conclusions stated in it (but do not suggest that the conclusions are wrong or have no proper basis)"

As a document that is signed by a person who is disqualified from making a recommendation by reason of s.12 or the regulations made under s.12A does not constitute a "recommendation", it is submitted that it cannot be rectified under this provision.

THE APPLICANT. And not to the doctor who signed the recommendation. The Reference Guide, at para.31.33, recommends that the doctor should be informed of the action taken.

Subsection (3)

This subsection allows for the procedure set out in subs.(2) to be used when both rec- **1–209** ommendations are good in themselves but taken together are insufficient.

INSUFFICIENT. If, for example, neither recommending doctor is "approved", under s.12 or if the examinations were too far apart. The fresh recommendation and the old one taken together must comply with all the requirements of the Act (subs.(2)(b)), except the requirements about the interval between recommendations and the time of the signature (subs.(2)(a)).

Subsection (4)

1–210 This subsection provides that this section cannot be used to rectify an emergency application after it has expired unless it has been "converted" under the provisions of s.4(4).

Position of patients subject to detention or guardianship

Reclassification of patients
1–211 **16.** [*Repealed by the Mental Health Act 2007 s.55, Sch.11, Pt 1*]

Leave of absence from hospital
1–212 **17.**—(1) The [responsible clinician] may grant to any patient who is for the time being liable to be detained in a hospital under this Part of this Act leave to be absent from the hospital subject to such conditions (if any) as [that clinician] considers necessary in the interests of the patient or for the protection of other persons.

(2) Leave of absence may be granted to a patient under this section either indefinitely or on specified occasions or for any specified period; and where leave is so granted for a specified period, that period may be extended by further leave granted in the absence of the patient.

[(2A) But longer-term leave may not be granted to a patient unless the responsible clinician first considers whether the patient should be dealt with under section 17A instead.

(2B) For these purposes, longer-term leave is granted to a patient if—
- (a) leave of absence is granted to him under this section either indefinitely or for a specified period of more than seven consecutive days; or
- (b) a specified period is extended under this section such that the total period for which leave of absence will have been granted to him under this section exceeds seven consecutive days.]

(3) Where it appears to the [responsible clinician] that it is necessary so to do in the interests of the patient or for the protection of other persons, he may, upon granting leave of absence under this section, direct that the patient remain in custody during his absence; and where leave of absence is so granted the patient may be kept in the custody of any officer on the staff of the hospital, or of any other person authorised in writing by the managers of the hospital or, if the patient is required in accordance with conditions imposed on the grant of leave of absence to reside in another hospital, of any officer on the staff of that other hospital.

(4) In any case where a patient is absent from a hospital in pursuance of leave of absence granted under this section, and it appears to the [responsible clinician] that it is necessary so to do in the interests of the patient's health or safety or for the protection of other persons, [that clinician] may, subject to subsection (5) below, by notice in writing given to the patient or to the person for the time being in charge of the patient, revoke the leave of absence and recall the patient to the hospital.

(5) A patient to whom leave of absence is granted under this section shall not be recalled under subsection (4) above after he has ceased to be liable to be detained under this Part of this Act; [...].

[(6) Subsection (7) below applies to a person who is granted leave by or by virtue of a provision—

(a) in force in Scotland, Northern Ireland, any of the Channel Islands or the Isle of Man; and

(b) corresponding to subsection (1) above.

(7) For the purpose of giving effect to a direction or condition imposed by virtue of a provision corresponding to subsection (3) above, the person may be conveyed to a place in, or kept in custody or detained at a place of safety in, England and Wales by a person authorised in that behalf by the direction or condition.]

AMENDMENTS

The amendments to this section were made by the Mental Health Act 2007 ss.9(3), 33(2), 39(1) and the Mental Health (Patients in the Community) Act 1995 s.3(1).

DEFINITIONS   **1–213**
    patient: s.145(1).
    hospital: ss.34(2), 145(1).
    absent without leave: ss.18(6), 145(1).
    responsible clinician: s.34(1).
    the managers: s.145(1).

GENERAL NOTE

This section provides for the responsible clinician (RC) of a patient to grant that patient **1–214** leave of absence from the hospital in which he is liable to be detained for a specified or for an indefinite period and subject to such conditions as are considered to be necessary. The period of leave may be extended without the patient having to return to hospital. Longer-term leave of absence (i.e. leave for more than seven consecutive days) can only be granted if the patient's RC first considers whether the patient should be made subject to a community treatment order (CTO) (subss.(2A), (2B)). The RC should weigh up and record the potential benefits and risks before making a decision about leave of absence (*G v Central and North West London Mental Health NHS Trust* [2007] EWHC 3086 (QB); [2008] M.H.L.R. 24, para.152). There is no legal obligation to obtain the patient's consent to the leave, and a combination of ss.18(7) and 137 provides authority for the use of force to ensure that the patient is taken to the place where he is required to be. The RC has no power to grant leave of absence to patients who have been remanded to hospital by a court under ss.35 or 36, or who are subject to an interim hospital made under s.38.

Paragraph 27.22 of the *Code of Practice* states:

"Hospital managers should establish a standardised system by which responsible clinicians can record the leave they authorise and specify the conditions attached to it. Copies of the authorisation should be given to the patient and to any carers, professionals and other people in the community who need to know. A copy should also be kept in the patient's notes. In case they fail to return from leave, an up-to-date description of the patient should be available in their notes. A photograph of the patient should also be included in their notes, if necessary with the patient's consent (or if the patient lacks capacity to decide whether to consent, a photograph is taken in accordance with the Mental Capacity Act (MCA))."

A patient who has been granted leave of absence under this section continues to be "liable to be detained" and is therefore subject to the consent to treatment provisions in Pt IV (s.56(3)). Although there is nothing in the Act that prevents staff from using force to ensure that a patient on s.17 leave in a non-clinical setting receives medication provided under the authority of Pt IV, this practice could be unsafe for both patient and staff and, in the absence of an emergency, it would be better for the forcible administration of medication to take place after the patient has been recalled to hospital (cf. *Code of Practice*, para.27.25). A patient can be recalled to the detaining hospital from leave of absence if the RC considers it necessary to do so in the interests of the patient's health or safety or for the protection of others (subs.(4)).

A s.3 patient who has been granted leave under this section can have his detention renewed under s.20 if the patient's RC considers that hospital treatment constitutes a significant part of the patient's treatment plan: see the note on s.20(4)(c)).

If a mentally incapacitated patient is granted leave of absence either to receive care in a care home or to receive treatment for a physical health problem in a general hospital, the leave can be combined with a deprivation of liberty authorisation granted under Sch.A1 of the Mental Capacity Act 2005. An authorisation can only be granted if there is no conflict between it and a condition of the patient's leave. Any patient who is granted leave of absence can kept in custody under the procedure set out in subs.(3).

In *R. (on the application of K) v West London Mental Health NHS Trust* [2006] EWCA Civ 118; [2006] M.H.L.R. 89, the Court of appeal held that:

1. A RC has no power to give directions as to how others are to discharge their functions and this section cannot be construed as conferring such a power.

2. The Secretary of State (or his delegate) is not obliged to use his best endeavours to give effect to a decision of a RC under this section.

This case is considered in the General Note to the Act under *Allocation of resources to detained patients.*

Further provisions relating to ground access, leave of absence and the escorting of patients from high security hospitals can be found at Appendix C.

A patient who has been granted leave of absence to reside in the community has been discharged *from the hospital* for the purposes of the social security legislation, although he has not been discharged *from the section* that provides the authority for his continued liability to be detained. There is no requirement for the hospital to keep a bed open for the patient while he is on long-term leave of absence.

The duty to provide aftercare services applies to a s.3 patient on leave of absence (see the note on "cease to be detained" in s.117(1)).

It is an offence to induce or help a patient absent himself without leave or to harbour or prevent a patient being returned to hospital (s.128).

This section applies without modification to patients who have been made subject to hospital or guardianship orders by a court under s.37 (Sch.1 Pt 1 para.1). It also applies, with subss.(1), (4) and (5) modified as set out below and subss.(2A) and (2B) omitted, to restricted patients (Sch.1 Pt II paras 2, 3):

"(1) The [responsible clinician] may [with the consent of the Secretary of State] grant to any patient who is for the time being liable to be detained in a hospital under this Part of this Act leave to be absent from the hospital subject to such conditions (if any) as [that clinician] considers necessary in the interests of the patient or for the protection of other persons."

"(4) In any case where a patient is absent from a hospital in pursuance of leave of absence granted under this section, and it appears to the [the responsible clinician] [or the Secretary of State] that it is necessary so to do in the interests of the patient's health or safety or for the protection of other persons, [that clinician] [or the Secretary of State] may, subject to subsection (5) below, by notice in writing given to the patient or to the person for the time being in charge of the patient, revoke the leave of absence and recall the patient to the hospital."

"(5) A patient to whom leave of absence is granted under this section shall not be recalled [by the [responsible clinician]] under subs.(4) above after [the expiration of the period of [12] months beginning with the first day of his absence on leave]."

Leave of absence for restricted patients
See above and the notes to s.41(3)(c).   **1–215**

Leave of absence to another hospital
It is lawful to use this section to grant a patient "trial leave" to a hospital other than the   **1–216**
one in which he is formally detained and for the patient to be kept in the custody of the staff of that hospital (subs.(3)). The hospital to which the patient is sent on leave need not be registered under the Health and Social Care Act 2008 to admit detained patients (Health and Social Care Act 2008 (Regulated Activities) Regulations 2010 (SI 2010/781) reg.3, Sch.1, para.6). Such leave can be useful step in a patient's rehabilitation programme. In these circumstances, the approved clinician (AC) who is in charge of the patient's treatment at the base hospital continues to be the patient's RC. Although day-to-day functions relating to the care of the patient can be delegated to an AC at the second hospital, the responsibilities of the RC to renew the patient's detention and to issue certificates under Pt IV cannot be delegated. If the trial leave is successful, the patient could then be transferred to the second hospital under s.19.

If the patient has been granted leave of absence to be a patient at another hospital, the conditions of the leave could enable: (i) the patient to have periods of leave for specified purposes from that hospital; and (ii) the patient's AC at the other hospital to have discretion to determine when such leave should be taken.

Leave of absence to Scotland, Northern Ireland, the Channel Islands or the Isle of Man
A patient who is granted escorted leave of absence to travel to Scotland will be subject to   **1–217**
the Mental Health (Cross-border Visits) (Scotland) Regulations 2008 (SSI 2008/181) which provide that where patients have been granted leave of absence to travel to Scotland, they may be kept in charge of a person who is authorised for that purpose in relation to the leave. In addition, the Regulations make provision for such escorts to have the power to restrain and retake such patients in the event that they abscond.

Paragraph 25.7 of the Reference Guide states:

"Escorted leave to Scotland, Northern Ireland, the Channel Islands or the Isle of Man can only be granted if the law in the jurisdiction in question allows the patient to be kept in custody once there. At the time of publication, this applies only in Scotland."

Under s.88, a detained patient from England and Wales who is absent without leave in Northern Ireland may be taken into custody there and returned to England and Wales.

Human Rights Act 1998
A patient who has been granted leave of absence under this section continues to be   **1–218**
"detained" for the purposes of art.5 of the Convention on Human Rights (ECHR): see *L v Sweden*, App.No.10801/84, noted under the heading "detention" in the note on art.5(1)(e). In this case, the Commission held that the granting of leave of absence with a condition that the patient accepts medication will not contravene the ECHR if one of the grounds in art.8(2) is satisfied. In order to satisfy one of the grounds in art.8(2) to justify the violation, the patient must be informed of both the nature of the conditions and the likely consequence of breaching the conditions (*Lambert v France* (2000) 30 E.H.R.R. 346). Also see the note on "conditions" in subs.(1).

Applications to the First-tier Tribunal (Mental Health) or the Mental Health Review Tribunal for Wales

1–219   Patients on leave of absence may make an application to a tribunal as if they were still detained in hospital.

Code of Practice

1–220   Guidance on the use of this section is contained in Ch.27. Advice on deciding between guardianship, leave of absence and supervised community treatment can be found in Ch.31.

Subsection (1)

1–221   THE RESPONSIBLE CLINICIAN MAY GRANT.   The permission of the Secretary of State for Justice is required for restricted patients: see s.41(3)(c). It is lawful for the Secretary of State to decline permission unless suitable conditions are imposed by the RC (*R. (on the application of RA) v Secretary of State for the Home Department* [2002] EWHC Admin 1618; [2003] M.H.L.R. 54, para.41).

The RC can grant a patient leave of absence over the telephone in urgent cases. The RC does not have the power to delegate functions under this section (although the power can be exercised by another AC acting as RC in the absence of the patient's usual RC): also see the note on "Leave of absence to another hospital", above. Paragraph 27.14 of the *Code of Practice* states:

> "Hospital managers cannot overrule a responsible clinician's decision to grant leave. The fact that a responsible clinician grants leave subject to certain conditions, eg residence at a hostel, does not oblige the hospital managers, or anyone else, to arrange or fund the particular placement or services the clinician has in mind. Responsible clinicians should not grant leave on such a basis without first taking steps to establish that the necessary services or accommodation (or both) are available and will be funded."

RCs "may decide to authorise short-term local leave, which may be managed by other staff. For example, patients may be given leave for a shopping trip of two hours every week to a specific destination, with the decision on which particular two hours to be left to the discretion of the responsible nursing staff" (*Code of Practice*, para.27.15). The MHAC said that the patient's RC "may instruct nursing staff not to implement any authorised leave on medical grounds at their discretion" (MHAC, *Sixth Biennial Report*, para.9.4).

If a detained patient needs to be moved to a general hospital as a matter of urgency for treatment for a physical disorder or injury, legal authority for the move is present if either (1) leave of absence for such a move has been granted by the RC in anticipation of such an eventuality occurring; or (2) the RC has granted leave of absence over the telephone at the time of the emergency. Authority for treating the patient for the disorder or injury must be found in the common law or the Mental Capacity Act 2005 if the disorder or injury is not related to the patient's mental disorder: see the note on "medical treatment . . . for the mental disorder" in s.63. If the urgency of the situation is such that there is no time to contact the RC and anticipatory leave has not been granted, the 2005 Act will provide authority for a mentally incapacitated patient to be moved to the general hospital. A mentally capable patient can be moved to the hospital with his consent. In both cases, the RC should grant the patient leave of absence under this section at the earliest opportunity as the patient is technically absent without leave. Given that an urgent need for a patient to be transferred to a general hospital for treatment is unpredictable, anticipatory leave to cover such a situation should be granted as a matter of routine.

ANY PATIENT WHO IS . . . LIABLE TO BE DETAINED.   Including a patient who has been detained under s.2. In order to be granted leave of absence, the patient must have become an in-patient of the hospital named in the application (see the note on "in-patient" in s.5(2)) and the hospital must have accepted the application (see the note on "sufficient authority for the Managers" in s.6(2)).

A patient who has been detained under s.5(2) cannot be granted leave of absence because such a patient does not have a RC: see the definition of RC in s.34(1).

FROM THE HOSPITAL.   Which is the hospital named in the application or order which provides authority for the patient's detention. Every absence from hospital, however brief, requires leave to be given under this section. With the exception of a restricted patient who is detained in a named hospital unit (see the General Note to s.41) and a patient who moves between high security psychiatric services and other services provided at the same hospital (s.145(1AA)), leave is not required for the patient to move from one hospital building to another or to have access to the grounds of the hospital. A decision to allow the patient to leave the ward area, but not the hospital, is a clinical decision that should be made following a risk assessment.

A particular difficulty has arisen where a single hospital site contains a psychiatric and a general facility and the two facilities are administered by different NHS Trusts. In this situation, should a detained patient who needs treatment for a physical disorder at the general facility be sent to that facility under the authority of s.17 leave? Paragraph 27.7 of the *Code of Practice* answers this question by confirming that leave of absence under this section should be granted:

"What constitutes a particular hospital for the purpose of leave is a matter of fact which can be determined only in the light of the particular case. Where one building, or set of buildings, includes accommodation under the management of different bodies (eg two different NHS trusts), the accommodation used by each body should be treated as forming separate hospitals. Facilities and grounds shared by both can be regarded as part of both hospitals."

CONDITIONS.   There are no mandatory conditions that must be imposed by the RC. Conditions could, for example, require the patient to live with a particular person or at a specified place, to be a patient at another hospital, to maintain contact with the care co-ordinator, to abstain from substance misuse or to accept prescribed medication. Conditions of this nature constitute interferences with the patient's right to respect for family life under art.8(1) of the ECHR and a justification for the interference would have to be found in art.8(2): see the note on "Human Rights Act 1998", above.

Authority for conveying the patient to a hospital or other place specified in the leave of absence is contained in s.18(7).

Subsection (2)
SPECIFIED OCCASIONS.   Such as visits to the patient's home or shopping expeditions. The **1–222** RC should consider whether a condition that the patient be escorted should be attached to such leave (*Code of Practice*, para.27.27).

Subsections (2A), 2(B)
These subsections do not apply to restricted patients: see the General Note, above. **1–223** The *Code of Practice* states:

"27.11 Leave should normally be of short duration and not normally more than seven days. When considering whether to grant leave of absence for more than seven consecutive days, or extending leave so that the total period is more than seven consecutive days, responsible clinicians should also consider whether the patient should go onto a community treatment order (CTO) instead and, if required, consult any local agencies concerned with public protection. This does not apply to restricted patients, nor, in practice, to patients detained for assessment under section 2 of the Act, as they are not eligible to be placed on a CTO.

27.12 The option of using a CTO does not mean that the responsible clinician cannot use longer-term leave if that is the more suitable option, but the responsible clinician will need to be able to show that both options have been duly considered. Decisions should be explained to the patient and fully documented, including why the patient is not considered suitable for a CTO, and also guardianship or discharge."

Paragraph 31.5 of the *Code* contains the following guidance:

"Leave of absence may be useful in the longer term (more than seven consecutive days) where the clinical team wish to see how the patient manages outside hospital before making the decision to discharge. Leave for a longer period should also be for a specific purpose or a fixed period, and not normally more than one month. For most patients who are able to live in the community, a CTO should be considered a better option than longer-term leave for the ongoing management of their care."

The guidance that leave should not normally be more than seven days (para.27.11) or a month (para.31.5) is unduly restrictive. Patients have been successfully granted lengthy periods of s.17 leave, in some cases for a number of years, because such leave is considered to be a more suitable option than a CTO (see below).

Placing the patient on a CTO is an alternative to the practice of providing the patient with extended s.17 leave. Extended s.17 leave allows for the detention of a patient who has been placed in the community on leave of absence to be renewed under s.20 if a significant component of the patient's care plan is treatment at a hospital: see *R. (on the application of DR) v Mersey Care NHS Trust* [2002] EWHC 1810 (Admin); [2002] M.H.L.R. 386 and *R. (on the application of CS) v Mental Health Review Tribunal* [2004] EWHC 2958 (Admin); [2004] M.H.R.R. 355 which are noted under s.20(4)(c). Although these cases pre-date the introduction of CTOs, they continue to have effect (*KL v Somerset Partnership NHS Foundation Trust* [2011] UKUT 233 (AAC); [2011] M.H.L.R. 194, para.11).

Subsection (2A) uses the term "considers" without qualification. It does not state that the RC should consider a CTO and go down that route unless she has good reason not to do so. The RC is therefore obliged to examine the respective merits of a CTO and extended s.17 leave and reach a conclusion as to which is the better option for a particular patient. The Act does not provide any guidance to the RC on the criteria that should be used when coming to such a decision. RCs might prefer to use the leave option if, for example, there is a need to test out the patient's response to being on leave of absence for a period of longer than seven days before moving on to a CTO, if the patient needs to be detained in his placement (see subs.(3)), if it is anticipated that the patient might need to be recalled to hospital for more than the 72 hour period provided for in s.17F(6) or if the patient's needs could be better met by the greater flexibility provided for by s.17. A patient's antagonism to being on a CTO might also be a factor in favour of using the s.17 regime. Both options provide the RC with a power of recall.

Subsection (3)

1–224 This subsection states that the RC may direct that the patient must remain in custody during his leave if it is necessary in the interest of the patient or for the protection of other persons. Patients may be kept in the custody of any officer on the staff of the hospital or any person authorised in writing by the hospital managers. If the patient is sent on leave to a care home or other non-hospital setting, the staff there must be given written authorisation by the hospital managers if they are to keep the patient in custody. Such a patient is in "legal custody" for the purposes of s.137. The purpose of this provision is to provide those who are caring for a patient during a period of leave with an immediate power to restrain the patient should he make an attempt to abscond. Its effect is that the patient may be detained in the named hospital or care home during the period of leave and he may be escorted at all times. This power can be used to put in place security measures for patients who pose a risk to themselves or to others and to patients whose mental disorder requires that significant restrictions be placed on their movements.

If a patient who lacks the mental capacity to understand the conditions of the leave is being detained in a care home, the care home must trigger the deprivation of liberty procedure set out in Sch.A1 of the Mental Capacity Act 2005 if the patient meets the qualifying requirements (Mental Capacity Act 2005 Sch.A1, para.24). If an authorisation is granted, the staff of the care home will be authorised to detain the patient without the need to obtain written authorisation from the hospital managers of the detaining hospital. A deprivation of liberty authorisation might also be required if a mentally incapacitated patient is granted leave of absence to a hospital for treatment of a physical disorder and is detained there. The rationale for having to invoke the deprivation of liberty procedure while a patient is being kept in custody under this provision is difficult to identify as the patient's rights under art.5 of the ECHR are protected by virtue of the patient being liable to be detained under the Act.

A patient who escapes from custody can be re-captured immediately using the power contained in s.18; there is no need to wait for him to fail to return to the "base" hospital or for the leave to be revoked under subs.(4). For provisions relating to the powers of the person having custody of the patient, see ss.137 and 138.

Paragraph 27.28 of the *Code of Practice* states:

"Escorted leave to Northern Ireland is permitted under the Act – patients may be held in lawful custody by a constable or a person authorised in writing by the managers of the hospital. In Scotland, the Isle of Man or any of the Channel Islands escorted leave can only be granted if the local legislation allows such patients to be kept in custody while in that jurisdiction. If this is contemplated for a restricted patient seek advice from the Mental Health Casework Section of the Ministry of Justice."

AUTHORISED IN WRITING BY THE MANAGERS OF THE HOSPITAL.   See reg.19 of the English Regulations and reg.35 of the Welsh Regulations.

OFFICER ON THE STAFF OF THE HOSPITAL.   "Officer" is not defined in the Act and could include an employee who is neither a nurse nor a doctor. If the patient is to be escorted by a friend or relative, see para.27.29 of the *Code of Practice* which states:

"While it may often be appropriate to authorise leave subject to the condition that a patient is accompanied by a friend or relative (eg on a pre-arranged day out from the hospital), responsible clinicians should specify that the patient is to be in the legal custody of a friend or relative only if it is appropriate for that person to be legally responsible for the patient, and if that person understands and accepts the consequent responsibility."

Subsection (4)

This subsection provides for the revocation of leave of absence and the return of the **1–225** patient to the hospital where he is liable to be detained. Paragraph 27.32 of the *Code of Practice* states that a "refusal to take medication would not on its own be a reason for revocation, although it would almost always be a reason to consider revocation". It is submitted that the patient can be returned as an outpatient. Paragraph 29.59 of the *Code* allows for this option for CTO patients; also see the decision in *R. (on the application of DR) v Mersey Care NHS Trust* [2002] M.H.L.R. 386 which is supportive of such an approach. Before issuing a recall notice the RC should "consider what effect being recalled would have on the patient" (*Code of Practice*, para.27.32). Leave of absence may only be revoked when it is necessary in the interests of the patient's health or safety or for the protection of other persons that he again becomes an in-patient. It is therefore unlawful to recall a patient to hospital merely to facilitate the renewal of the patient's detention under s.20 (*R. v Hallstrom Ex p. W* [1986] 2 All E.R. 306). There is no mechanism in the Act that provides for the review of a decision to recall.

Paragraph 4.18 of the *Code of Practice* states that where a patient is to be recalled to hospital, "the responsible clinician should give (or arrange for the patient to be given) oral reasons for the decision before the recall. The patient may nominate another person who they wish to be notified of the decision".

In the absence of an emergency, a patient's leave of absence should not be revoked without up to date medical evidence to demonstrate that he remains mentally disordered (*Kay v United Kingdom* (1998) 40 B.M.L.R. 20 ECtHR).

A patient who refuses to return to the hospital becomes a patient absent without leave (s.18(1)(b)) and may be taken into custody and returned to the hospital by the categories of persons set out in s.18(1).

NOTICE IN WRITING. Paragraph 27.33 of the *Code of Practice* states:

"The responsible clinician must arrange for a notice in writing revoking the leave to be served on the patient or on the person who is for the time being in charge of the patient. Hospitals should always know the address of patients who are on leave of absence and of anyone with responsibility for them whilst on leave."

The Mental Welfare Commission for Scotland made the following comment on an equivalent provision in the Mental Health (Scotland) Act 1984: "In practical terms, particularly in emergency situations where the patient's condition has rapidly deteriorated, the staff who are returning the patient may have to deliver the letter of recall at the time they are taking him into custody" (Annual Report 1999–2000, p.23).

Subsection (5)

1–226   This subsection provides that an unrestricted patient cannot be recalled once the power to detain him has lapsed. A restriction order patient can be recalled by his RC at any time up to 12 months from the first day of his absence on leave. The Secretary of State can recall such a patient at any time (see the General Note to this section).

Subsections (6), (7)

1–227   The effect of these provisions is explained in the Reference Guide:

"11.21 A patient can be kept in custody, conveyed to a particular place or detained in a place of safety in England or Wales, if that is a condition of leave of absence from hospital granted under equivalent legislation in Scotland, Northern Ireland, the Isle of Man or any of the Channel Islands.

11.22 In each case, section 137 means they are deemed to be in legal custody while being escorted, conveyed or detained in England and Wales. As a result, if they abscond while in England or Wales, they may be retaken, under section 138, by the person authorised to keep the patient in custody in England, by a police officer, or other constable, or by an AMHP, for as long as they could be retaken under the legislation in the jurisdiction from which they are on leave."

[Community treatment orders

1–228   **17A.**—(1) The responsible clinician may by order in writing discharge a detained patient from hospital subject to his being liable to recall in accordance with section 17E below.

(2) A detained patient is a patient who is liable to be detained in a hospital in pursuance of an application for admission for treatment.

(3) An order under subsection (1) above is referred to in this Act as a "community treatment order".

(4) The responsible clinician may not make a community treatment order unless—

(a) in his opinion, the relevant criteria are met; and

(b) an approved mental health professional states in writing—

    (i) that he agrees with that opinion; and

    (ii) that it is appropriate to make the order.

(5) The relevant criteria are—

(a) the patient is suffering from mental disorder of a nature or degree which makes it appropriate for him to receive medical treatment;

(b) it is necessary for his health or safety or for the protection of other persons that he should receive such treatment;

(c) subject to his being liable to be recalled as mentioned in paragraph (d) below, such treatment can be provided without his continuing to be detained in a hospital;

(d) it is necessary that the responsible clinician should be able to exercise the power under section 17E(1) below to recall the patient to hospital; and

(e) appropriate medical treatment is available for him.

(6) In determining whether the criterion in subsection (5)(d) above is met, the responsible clinician shall, in particular, consider, having regard to the patient's history of mental disorder and any other relevant factors, what risk there would be of a deterioration of the patient's condition if he were not detained in a hospital (as a result, for example, of his refusing or neglecting to receive the medical treatment he requires for his mental disorder).

(7) In this Act—

    "community patient" means a patient in respect of whom a community treatment order is in force;

    "the community treatment order", in relation to such a patient, means the community treatment order in force in respect of him; and

    "the responsible hospital", in relation to such a patient, means the hospital in which he was liable to be detained immediately before the community treatment order was made, subject to section 19A below.]

AMENDMENT

This section was inserted by the Mental Health Act 2007 s.32(2).

DEFINITIONS

    responsible clinician: s.34(1).   **1–229**

    patient: s.145(1).

    application for admission for treatment: s.145(1).

    approved mental health professional: s.145(1), (1AC).

    mental disorder: ss.1, 145(1).

    medical treatment: s.145(1).

    hospital: s.145(1).

GENERAL NOTE

An overview of supervised community treatment, a term that is not to be found in the **1–230** Act, is set out at para.107 of the Explanatory Notes to the 2007 Act:

"The supervised community treatment (SCT) provisions will allow some patients with a mental disorder to live in the community whilst still being subject to powers under the 1983 Act. Only those patients who are detained in hospital for treatment will be eligible to be considered for SCT. In order for a patient to be placed on SCT, various criteria need to be met. An AMHP also needs to agree that SCT is appropriate. Patients who are on SCT will be subject to conditions whilst living in the community. Most conditions will depend on individual circumstances but must be for the purpose of ensuring the patient receives medical treatment, or to prevent risk of harm to the patient or others. Such conditions will form part of the patient's community treatment order (CTO) which is made by the RC. Patients on SCT may be recalled to hospital for treatment should this become necessary. Afterwards they may then resume living in the community or, if they need to be treated as an in-patient again, their RC may revoke the CTO and the patient will remain in hospital for the time being."

The purpose of a CTO is set out at para.29.5 of the *Code of Practice*:

"The purpose of a CTO is to allow suitable patients to be safely treated in the community rather than under detention in hospital, and to provide a way to help prevent relapse and any harm – to the patient or to others – that this might cause. It is intended to help patients to maintain stable mental health outside hospital and to promote recovery. The principles, in particular, treating patients using the least restrictive option and maximising their independence; and purpose and effectiveness should always be considered when considering CTOs."

During the passage of the 2007 Act through Parliament, an amendment that tried to restrict CTOs to people who had been detained more than once was not made. It is therefore the case that the use of CTOs is not restricted to patients who have a history of non-compliance with medication, i.e. "revolving door patients".

A patient who is subject to a CTO is referred to throughout the Act as a community patient (s.17A(7)). The patient will be subject to the after-care provisions of s.117 as long as he is a community patient (s.117(2)). Part IVA provides for the regulation of treatment for the patient's mental disorder whilst in the community. Unlike guardianship, a CTO is not limited to patients who are over the age of 16.

Making a patient subject to a CTO is an alternative to granting the patient long-term leave of absence under s.17 and before an RC places a patient on such leave, she must "consider" whether the patient should be dealt with under this section: see the note on s.17(2A), (2B). Research has shown that, when compared with patients who are placed on s.17 leave, the imposition of CTOs does not reduce the rate of readmission to hospital of psychotic patients (T. Burns et al, "Community treatment orders for patients with psychosis (OCTET): a randomised controlled trial", *The Lancet* Vol.381, No.9878, pp.1627–1633. Guidance on deciding between leave of absence, a CTO or guardianship is given in Ch.31 of the *Code of Practice*.

This section enables a CTO to be made by the patient's RC if she is satisfied that all of the criteria set out in subs.(5) are satisfied (subs.(4)(a)), and an AMHP agrees that the criteria are met and that an order is appropriate (subs.(4)(b)). The AMHP and the RC could be members of the same clinical team. There are no time limits that regulate the lapse of time that may take place between the AMHP stating agreement with the RC's view that a CTO and any imposed conditions are appropriate and the signing of Form CTO 1 by the RC. It is submitted that the RC has an implied power to cancel a CTO before the date and time when it is stated to come into effect: see Part 3 of Form CTO1. Patients can only be placed on a CTO if they have been either detained under s.3 or made subject to an order under Pt III without restrictions (or is treated as such after transfer from another jurisdiction): see the note to subs.(2). It is not possible for a CTO patient also to be subject to guardianship: see ss.6(4) and 8(5). The CTO must be made subject to certain conditions (s.17B) and the RC is empowered to order the patient's recall to hospital (s.17E). The duration of the CTO is specified in s.17C. Responsibility for a community patient may be assigned to another hospital under reg.17 of the English Regulations or reg.25 of the Welsh Regulations.

Although the patient's consent to the making of a CTO is not a legal requirement, "in practice patients will need to be involved in decisions about the treatment to be provided in the community and how and where it is to be given, and be prepared to co-operate with treatment" (*Code of Practice*, para.29.17). Although the patient's nearest relative cannot prevent a CTO being made, he or she can discharge the order (s.23(2)(c)).

Section 132A requires the relevant hospital managers to give information to community patients and, unless the patient objects, their nearest relatives about the effect of the CTO and their right to make an application to a tribunal. For the responsibility to inform the patient's nearest relative of the assignment of the patient to another hospital, see reg.26(1)(h) of the English Regulations and reg.32(b) of the Welsh Regulations.

Under s.130D, the:

"managers of the responsible hospital must take steps to give CTO patients information about the availability of independent mental health advocates (IMHA). Unless the patient requests otherwise, or does not have a nearest relative, the managers must also take whatever steps are practicable to give this information to the person they think is the patient's nearest relative. This must be done as soon as practicable after the CTO is made" (Reference Guide, para.26.30).

Although there is no provision in the Act for the documents relating to CTOs to be rectified, appropriate arrangements should be put in place to check that such documents have been properly completed (*Code of Practice*, paras 35.16–35.17). Minor errors and or slips of the pen may be corrected and initialled without affecting the validity of the CTO.

This section applies without modification to patients who have been made subject to hospital or guardianship orders by a court under s.37 (Sch.1 Pt 1 para.1).

Domestic Violence, Crime and Victims Act 2004
In order that hospital managers can meet their obligations under the 2004 Act to invite **1–231** representations from victims, RCs must tell the managers if they are considering discharging the following categories of patients by making a CTO:

"[P]atients subject to unrestricted hospital orders, hospital directions whose associated limitation direction is no longer in force, and unrestricted transfer directions (including hospital orders and transfer directions which were originally restricted, but where the restriction order or direction has since ended or been lifted)" ("Guidance on the extension of victims' rights under the Domestic Violence, Crime and Victims Act 2004", Department of Health, 2008, para.1.10).

Human Rights Act 1998
If a CTO is made in the interests of the patient's health or to protect the rights and free- **1–232** doms of others, there would be no interference with the patient's rights under art.8 of the European Convention on Human Rights provided that the making of the order is necessary in a democratic society and is done in accordance with the law (*L v Sweden,* App.No.10801/84). Similar considerations would apply to art.11 which provides for a right "to freedom of association with others".

Applications to the First-tier Tribunal (Mental Health) or the Mental Health Review Tribunal for Wales
Paragraphs 147 and 148 of the Explanatory Notes state: **1–233**

"A community patient may apply to the [First-tier Tribunal (Mental Health) or the Mental Health Review Tribunal for Wales], under amended s.66 . . . , when a CTO is made, when it is revoked, when it is extended after six months or a year (as appropriate) and when an order is extended after the patient has been absent without leave for more than 28 days. A NR may also apply to the [tribunal under s.66] if the NR makes a discharge order which is not put into effect because the RC reports that the patient would be likely to act in a dangerous manner if discharged; or if he or she is displaced by a court order as allowed under s.29(1)(c) or (d) . . . . The hospital managers must refer a patient to the [tribunal] if a CTO is revoked [or if an application to the tribunal has not been made within the relevant period: see s.68(7)].

In the case of community patients who were under a hospital order before being made subject to a CTO, the power under s.66 . . . to apply to a Tribunal when a CTO is made or revoked cannot be exercised until six months after the date of the hospital order. The NR of such a patient may apply to the [tribunal] whenever the patient has a right to apply [(s.69(1)(a))]. The Secretary of State can refer a case of a community patient to the [tribunal], in the same way as for detained patients [: see s.67(1)]."

The rights of community patients and their nearest relatives to make tribunal applications are also set out in figures 21 and 22 of Ch.6 of the *Reference Guide*.

The power of the tribunal to discharge a community patient is set out in s.72(1)(c),(1A). The tribunal also has the power to recommend that a detained patient be discharged subject to a CTO (s.72(3A)). There is no power for the tribunal to vary or discharge the conditions of a CTO.

Code of Practice

1–234   Guidance on CTOs is contained in Ch.29. Advice on deciding between guardianship, leave of absence and CTOs can be found in Ch.31.

Subsection (1)

1–235   BY ORDER IN WRITING.   The order, which is Form CTO1 (see reg.6(1)(a) of the English Regulations), is called a "Community Treatment Order" (subs.(3)). In Wales, the form is Form CP1: see reg.16 of the Welsh Regulations.

It is submitted that Part 3 of Form CTO1 should not be signed until Parts 1 and 2 have been completed. The CQC considers that Parts 1 and 3 of the Form can be completed by different responsible clinicians if there has been a change in the identity of the responsible clinician since the completion of Part 1 ("Monitoring the Mental Health Act in 2011/12", p.80).

A DETAINED PATIENT.   Of any age. If a child patient is a ward of court, see s.33(4).

Subsection (2)

1–236   LIABLE TO BE DETAINED.   A CTO can be made in respect of a patient who has been granted leave of absence under s.17.

APPLICATION FOR ADMISSION FOR TREATMENT.   Which is suspended during the currency of the CTO (s.17D(2)(a)), apart from when the patient is recalled to hospital when it is reinstated (s.17E(6)). A CTO can also be made in respect of patients who are subject to hospital orders (without a restriction order) and transfer directions (without a restriction direction): see Sch.1, Pt 1 and s.47(3). If the application, order or direction ceases to have effect, the CTO automatically ends (s.17C).

Subsection (4)

1–237   AN APPROVED MENTAL HEALTH PROFESSIONAL . . . AGREES.   Paragraph 29.24 of the *Code of Practice* states:

"The Act does not specify who this AMHP should be. It may (but need not) be an AMHP who is already involved in the patient's care and treatment as part of the multi-disciplinary team. It can be an AMHP acting on behalf of any willing local authority, and local authorities may agree with each other and with hospital managers the arrangements that are likely to be most convenient and best for patients. But if no other local authority is willing, responsibility for ensuring that an AMHP considers the case should lie with the local authority which would become responsible under section 117 for the patient's after-care if the patient were discharged."

Depending on the circumstances, it might be more appropriate for the default position to be for an AMHP of the local authority for the area where the patient is currently located to perform the role. This approach would be consistent with the duty placed on local authorities by s.13(1).

Contrary to what is stated at p.45 of the Care Quality Commission's "Monitoring the Mental Health Act in 2012/13", there is no requirement placed on the AMHP to state the reasoning for her decision. There is no obligation placed on the AMHP either to interview the patient or to consult the patient's nearest relative prior to signing the statement. Although the *Code of Practice*, at para.29.25, states that if the agreement of the AMHP is not forthcoming the RC "should not approach another AMHP for an alternative view", such an approach would not be unlawful. Indeed, it could be argued that the RC has a professional duty to make such an approach in an attempt to achieve an objective that she believes is in the patient's best interests. In any event, if the RC fails to obtain the agreement of an AMHP she could discharge the patient on leave of absence under s.17.

Subsection (5)

These criteria essentially state that the patient continues to be detainable under s.3 **1–238** (including the requirement that a patient's learning disability continues to be associated with abnormally aggressive or seriously irresponsible conduct), but can be treated in the community if he is subject to a power of recall. When determining whether the RC should be able to exercise the power of recall, the factors set out in subs.(6) should be considered.

Paragraphs (a), (b), (e)

See the notes to s.3(2)(a),(c) and (d). **1–239**

Subsection (6)

This provision requires the RC to "in particular" consider the risk of the patient's con- **1–240** dition deteriorating in the community when deciding whether it is necessary to be able to exercise the power to recall the patient to hospital. Apart from considering the patient's history of mental disorder, it "is important that a clinician can consider all relevant factors, an obvious example being the patient's current mental state. Other relevant factors might include the degree of recovery of symptoms, any suicidal ideas or feelings of hopelessness, which will be important predictors of likely risk. In addition, a patient's insight and attitude to their treatment, and the protective circumstances into which a patient would be discharged, might be relevant" (per the Parliamentary Under-Secretary of State, *Hansard,* HL Vol.693, cols 847, 848). The *Code of Practice* considers the sharing of information to manage risk at paras 10.15–10.17.

[Conditions

17B.—(1) A community treatment order shall specify conditions to which the **1–241** patient is to be subject while the order remains in force.

(2) But, subject to subsection (3) below, the order may specify conditions only if the responsible clinician, with the agreement of the approved mental health professional mentioned in section 17A(4)(b) above, thinks them necessary or appropriate for one or more of the following purposes—

(a) ensuring that the patient receives medical treatment;

(b) preventing risk of harm to the patient's health or safety;

(c) protecting other persons.

(3) The order shall specify—

(a) a condition that the patient make himself available for examination under section 20A below; and

(b) a condition that, if it is proposed to give a certificate under Part 4A of this Act [that falls within section 64C(4) below] in his case, he make himself available for examination so as to enable the certificate to be given.

(4) The responsible clinician may from time to time by order in writing vary the conditions specified in a community treatment order.

(5) He may also suspend any conditions specified in a community treatment order.

(6) If a community patient fails to comply with a condition specified in the community treatment order by virtue of subsection (2) above, that fact may be taken into account for the purposes of exercising the power of recall under section 17E(1) below.

(7) But nothing in this section restricts the exercise of that power to cases where there is such a failure.]

AMENDMENTS

This section was inserted by the Mental Health Act 2007 s.32(2). The words in square brackets in subs.(3)(b) were inserted by the Health and Social Care Act 2012 s.299(6).

DEFINITIONS

1–242   community treatment order: ss.17A(7), 145(1).
community patient: ss.17A(7), 145(1).
responsible clinician: s.34(1).
approved mental health professional: s.145(1), (1AC).
medical treatment: s.145(1), (4).

GENERAL NOTE

1–243   This section requires that a CTO specifies the conditions to which a community patient will be subject. There is no requirement that the patient consents to the conditions. It is not possible for a CTO not to have any conditions attached to it (subs.(1)). Although the RC and the AMHP must agree the conditions (subs.(2)), only the RC has the power to vary or suspend them (subss.(4),(5)). The mandatory conditions set out in subs.(3) are directly enforceable by recall to hospital (s.17E(2)). If the patient (or a donee or deputy taking a decision on a mentally incapacitated patient's behalf; see para.7.6 of the *Code of Practice*) fails to comply with any other condition, the RC may take that into account when considering whether it is necessary to exercise the power of recall under s.17E (subs.(6)). However, if the criteria for recall are met, the power can be exercised even if the patient is complying with the conditions (subs.(7)).

A patient has no right to seek the review of the conditions imposed on a CTO before a tribunal; conditions can only be challenged by judicial review. The Government's view is that for SCT to work, a patient must accept and be ready to co-operate with the conditions of a CTO; see, for example, *Hansard,* HL Vol.693, col.848 and para.29.33 of the *Code of Practice*.

This section applies without modification to patients who have been made subject to hospital orders by a court under s.37 (Sch.1 Pt 1 para.1).

Domestic Violence, Crime and Victims Act 2004

1–244   Before an AMHP agrees to the imposition of a condition or an RC either decides to impose or vary a condition, they must consider any representations from victims and the RC must inform the hospital managers if the patient comes within the scope of the 2004 Act: see the General Note to s.17A under this heading and "Guidance on the extension of victims' rights under the Domestic Violence, Crime and Victims Act 2004", Department of Health, 2008, paras 3.1 to 3.8.

Code of Practice
Guidance on this section is contained in Ch.29 at para.29.27 et seq.   1–245

Subsections (2), (3)
Subsection (3) does not contain an exhaustive list of conditions that can be attached to 1–246
the CTO. The RC, with the agreement of the AMHP, may agree to specify other conditions as long as they are "necessary or appropriate" for one or more of the purposes set out in subs.(2). This gives a considerable amount of discretion to the RC regarding the nature of the conditions that can be imposed. They could include conditions that the patient resides at a particular place, accepts medication as prescribed, attends at a specified place for the purposes of receiving medical or psychological treatment, or conditions concerning the "avoidance of known risk factors or high-risk situations relevant to the patient's mental disorder" (*Code of Practice*, para.29.32). A patient should be recalled to hospital under s.17E if he refuses to accept medical treatment for his mental disorder and he satisfies the criteria in subs.(1) of that section. It is not possible for a condition to be used to compel a patient to receive such treatment.

With regard to the mandatory condition contained in subs.(3) for the patient to make himself available for examination by a SOAD it should be noted that there is no legal requirement for a SOAD to examine the patient prior to issuing a certificate under Part IVA.

In the Government's opinion, it would be inappropriate to impose a conditions that amounts to a deprivation of liberty for the purposes of art.5 of the European Convention on Human Rights (Joint Committee, Appendix 3, para.38). As one of the effects of a CTO is to suspend the authority of the hospital managers to detain the patient (s.17D(2)(a)), it is submitted that such a condition would be unlawful. The Reference Guide states that the "conditions of a CTO must not deprive a person of their liberty" (para.26.20). If the patient is mentally incapacitated, the deprivation of his liberty could be authorised under Sch.A1 of the Mental Capacity Act 2005 if there is no conflict between the requirements of the authorisation and the conditions of the CTO (Mental Capacity Act Sch.1A, para.2, Case B).

There is no power to take an objecting community patient to the place where he is required to be as a condition of the CTO: see the notes on s.18(7).

Subsections (4), (5)
The power to vary or suspend a condition enables the RC to respond to changes in the 1–247
patient's circumstances. It could be exercised as a result of a request made by the patient or the patient's carer. The agreement of an AMHP to the variation or suspension is not required.

An order varying a condition must be made on Form CTO2: see reg.6(2)(b) of the English Regulations (in Wales, Form CP2: see reg.16(2) of the Welsh Regulations).

[Duration of community treatment order

17C. A community treatment order shall remain in force until—   1–248
  (a) the period mentioned in section 20A(1) below (as extended under any provision of this Act) expires, but this is subject to sections 21 and 22 below;
  (b) the patient is discharged in pursuance of an order under section 23 below or a direction under section 72 below;
  (c) the application for admission for treatment in respect of the patient otherwise ceases to have effect; or
  (d) the order is revoked under section 17F below, whichever occurs first.]

AMENDMENT
This section was inserted by the Mental Health Act 2007 s.32(2).

DEFINITIONS
1–249 community treatment order: ss.17A(7), 145(1).
application for admission for treatment: s.145(1).

GENERAL NOTE
1–250 This section specifies that a CTO will end:

1. When the period of the CTO runs out and the CTO is not extended under the provisions contained in s.20A (s.20B).

2. If the patient is discharged from the powers of the Act by virtue of an order made under s.23 by the RC, the hospital managers or the patient's nearest relative (for Pt II patients), or a direction made by a tribunal under s.72. The patient is also discharged if the application under s.3 (or order under Part III) otherwise ceases to have effect.

3. If the RC revokes the CTO following the patients recall to hospital under s.17F. Revocation does not end the underlying liability to detention (s.17G).

The CTO, and the underlying liability to detention, will also end if the patient is received into guardianship (s.8(5)), on the patient being detained under s.3 if the patient was subject to s.3 before going onto SCT, but not if the patient was subject to an order or direction made under Pt III at that time (see s.6(4) and para.26.136 of the Reference Guide), and if the patient has been "detained in custody" for more than six months (s.22).
The CTO will not end if the patient is admitted to a hospital either informally or subject to s.2, is detained under s.135 or 136, or is arrested and charged for a criminal offence.
This section applies without modification to patients who have been made subject to hospital orders (Sch.1, Pt 1, para.1).

Domestic Violence, Crime and Victims Act 2004
1–251 If the RC decides not to renew the CTO, she must inform the hospital managers if the patient comes within the scope of the 2004 Act: see the General Note to s.17A under this heading and "Guidance on the extension of victims' rights under the Domestic Violence, Crime and Victims Act 2004", Department of Health, 2008, paras 3.1 to 3.7.

Paragraph (b)
1–252 If the patient is made subject to a CTO during a period of deferred discharge granted by the tribunal under s.72(3), the CTO will end on the discharge taking effect. Placing the patient on a CTO in this situation would therefore be a pointless exercise.

[Effect of community treatment order

1–253 **17D.**—(1) The application for admission for treatment in respect of a patient shall not cease to have effect by virtue of his becoming a community patient.
(2) But while he remains a community patient—
(a) the authority of the managers to detain him under section 6(2) above in pursuance of that application shall be suspended; and
(b) reference (however expressed) in this or any other Act, or in any subordinate legislation (within the meaning of the Interpretation Act 1978), to patients liable to be detained, or detained, under this Act shall not include him.

(3) And section 20 below shall not apply to him while he remains a community patient.

(4) Accordingly, authority for his detention shall not expire during any period in which that authority is suspended by virtue of subsection (2)(a) above.]

AMENDMENT

This section was inserted by the Mental Health Act 2007 s.32(2).

DEFINITIONS   **1–254**

  application for admission for treatment: s.145(1).
  community patient: ss.17A(7), 145(1).
  the managers: s.145(1).

GENERAL NOTE

This section sets out the effect of a CTO on certain provisions of the Act. They are: **1–255**

1. Although the application for admission for treatment (or its equivalent: see the note on s.17A(2)) that was made in respect of the patient remains in force during the currency of the CTO, the hospital managers' authority to detain the patient under s.6(2) is suspended.

2. Where the Act, any other Act or any subordinate legislation, refers to patients who are "detained" or "liable to be detained", this does not include community patients. One of the effects of this is that the authority to treat the patient under Pt IV is suspended, although the three month period provided for in s.58(1)(b) continues to run.

3. The renewal provisions contained in s.20 do not apply to the patient while he is a community patient. This means that the authority to detain the patient does not expire during the time when that authority is suspended.

The CTO will come into effect from the date and time specified in Pt 3 of Form CTO 1 (or, in Wales, Form CP1). The patient does not have to leave hospital immediately after the CTO comes into effect; he could remain in hospital as an informal patient: see para.26.22 of the Reference Guide. This option could be used if the patient is awaiting suitable accommodation.

The provisions of s.133 apply to a patient who is to be discharged from hospital subject to a CTO (s.133(1A)).

See s.22 for the effect of the patient's imprisonment on the CTO.

This section applies to patients who have been made subject to hospital orders with the modification set out in para.2A of Sch.1 (Sch.1, Pt 1, para.2).

[Power to recall to hospital

17E.—(1) The responsible clinician may recall a community patient to hospital **1–256** if in his opinion—

  (a) the patient requires medical treatment in hospital for his mental disorder; and

  (b) there would be a risk of harm to the health or safety of the patient or to other persons if the patient were not recalled to hospital for that purpose.

(2) The responsible clinician may also recall a community patient to hospital if the patient fails to comply with a condition specified under section 17B(3) above.

(3) The hospital to which a patient is recalled need not be the responsible hospital.

(4) Nothing in this section prevents a patient from being recalled to a hospital even though he is already in the hospital at the time when the power of recall is exercised; references to recalling him shall be construed accordingly.

(5) The power of recall under subsections (1) and (2) above shall be exercisable by notice in writing to the patient.

(6) A notice under this section recalling a patient to hospital shall be sufficient authority for the managers of that hospital to detain the patient there in accordance with the provisions of this Act.]

AMENDMENT
This section was inserted by the Mental Health Act 2007 s.32(2).

DEFINITIONS

1–257   responsible clinician: s.34(1).
community patient; ss.17A(7), 145(1).
medical treatment: s.145(1), (4).
hospital: ss.34(2), 145(1).
responsible hospital; ss.17A(7), 145(1).
the managers: s.145(1).
mental disorder: ss.1, 135(1).

GENERAL NOTE

1–258   This section gives an exclusive power to the patient's RC to recall a community patient to hospital in the following circumstances:

1. Where the RC decides that the patient needs to receive treatment for his mental disorder in hospital and that, without such treatment, there would be a risk of harm to the health or safety of the patient, or to other people (subs.(1)). It is submitted that the risk of harm need not be immediate in the sense that the patient is exhibiting symptoms of relapse, and that a recall can be triggered if there was concern about a predicted relapse in the near future (cf s.17A(6)). While a patient can be recalled even though he is complying with the conditions of the CTO imposed under s.17B, a patient's refusal of medical treatment for mental disorder is not in itself sufficient ground to trigger a recall. Paragraph 25.26 of the *Code of Practice* states:

   "Refusal to consent to treatment in itself does not justify a recall to hospital and fuller consideration of the patient's presentation and circumstances is required when considering whether a recall to hospital is warranted (see chapter 29)."

2. Where the patient fails to comply with the mandatory conditions imposed under s.17B(3) (subs.(2)).

A RC need not examine the patient before issuing a notice of recall; she can act on reports received which provide an account of the patient's current behaviour and situation: see para.29.45 of the *Code of Practice*. Unless locally it has been agreed otherwise, the RC has responsibility for co-ordinating the recall process (*Code of Practice*, para.29.52). A patient's recall must be effected by notifying the patient in writing (subs.(5)). The task of delivering the notice of recall is usually that of the patient's care co-ordinator. The patient need not be recalled to the hospital where he had been detained immediately before the CTO was made (subs.(3)). If the patient is recalled to a different hospital, a formal transfer could subsequently be made under s.17F(2). Patients should not be recalled to a particular hospital unless it has been established that the hospital will accept the patient as hospitals are not obliged to admit patients just because a recall notice has been issued. A copy of the notice of recall, which provides the authority to detain the patient, should be sent to the managers of the hospital to which the patient is being recalled (*Code of Practice*, para.29.60). If the patient refuses to accept the recall notice or if the patient cannot be found, the notice should be delivered to the patient's usual or last known address (*Code of Practice*, para.29.53). A recall notice reinstates the power of the hospital managers to detain the patient (subs.(6)) and, if the patient has been served with the notice (or it is considered served), he may be taken into custody and returned to hospital (s.18(2A)). A patient who fails to respond to a recall notice becomes a patient who is absent from the hospital without leave and the provisions of ss.18, 21, 21A and 21B will apply. If access to the patient is denied, an application for a warrant under s.135(2) could be made once the recall notice is considered served. The 72 hour period referred to in s.17F(6) starts on the patient's arrival at the hospital. The powers which apply to the patient on recall are set out in s.17F.

A CTO patient can agree to being admitted informally to a hospital without a recall procedure being used. The treatment of the mental disorder of such patients is governed by Part IVA. The holding powers set out in s.5 cannot be used in respect of a community patient (s.5(6)). However, a recall notice may be issued even if the patient is in hospital informally at that time (subs.(4)). This would cover the situation of a hospitalised patient who, by refusing treatment, places themselves or others at risk.

If a child community patient is a ward of court, the usual rule relating to the need to act in conformity with any order made by the court in the exercise of its wardship jurisdiction does not apply during a period of recall under this section (s.33(4)).

The hospital managers must take steps to inform the patient of the effect of the recall: see reg.6(7) of the English Regulations and reg.22(1) of the Welsh Regulations.

This section applies without modification to patients who have been made subject to hospital orders (Sch.1, Pt 1, para.1).

Code of Practice
Guidance on the recall of patients is given in Ch.29 at paras 29.45 et seq. **1–259**

Subsection (1)(a)
IN HOSPITAL.   The recall could be to a hospital out-patient department: see para.29.59 of **1–260** the *Code of Practice* and *R. (on the application of DR) v Mersey Care NHS Trust* [2002] M.H.L.R. 386. A recall to a general hospital would be appropriate if the patient was to receive treatment for a physical condition which constituted an ancillary treatment for the patient's mental disorder: see *B v Croydon Health Authority*, which is noted under s.63. The patient can be transferred to units within the hospital named in Form CTO3 during the recall period.

As a community patient who has been recalled to hospital is not "liable to be detained" (s.17D(2)(b)), he cannot be granted leave of absence under s.17.

Subsection (2)
The power to recall a community patient for examination with a view to a Pt IVA cer- **1–261** tificate being given only applies to a SOAD certificate.

Subsection (3)
If this provision applies, the patient's RC will be "the approved clinician with overall **1–262** responsibility for the patient's case": see s.34(1) and the note thereto.

Subsection (5)
NOTICE IN WRITING.   Using Form CTO3: see reg.6(3)(a) of the English Regulations (in **1–263** Wales, Form CP5: see reg.19(1)(a) of the Welsh Regulations). For service of the notice of recall, see reg.6(5),(6) (reg.19(4),(5) of the Welsh Regulations). A notice of recall, properly completed by the RC and served on the patient in accordance with regulations, provides the authority to transport a patient subject to a CTO to hospital compulsorily, if necessary

(*Code of Practice*, para.17.33). The hospital managers must record the time and date of the patient's detention pursuant to such notice on Form CTO4 (reg.6(3)(d)) (in Wales, Form CP6: see reg.19(1)(d) of the Welsh Regulations).

The Reference Guide states at para.26.39:

"If the patient's responsible hospital is in Wales, recall must be done in accordance with the equivalent Welsh regulations, even if the patient is to be recalled to a hospital in England. That will involve using a Welsh statutory form, rather than CTO3, to give the patient notice of the recall".

Subsection (6)

1–264   As the notice provides the authority to detain the patient, a copy should be sent to the hospital to which the patient is being recalled.

[Powers in respect of recalled patients

1–265   **17F.**—(1) This section applies to a community patient who is detained in a hospital by virtue of a notice recalling him there under section 17E above.

(2) The patient may be transferred to another hospital in such circumstances and subject to such conditions as may be prescribed in regulations made by the Secretary of State (if the hospital in which the patient is detained is in England) or the Welsh Ministers (if that hospital is in Wales).

(3) If he is so transferred to another hospital, he shall be treated for the purposes of this section (and section 17E above) as if the notice under that section were a notice recalling him to that other hospital and as if he had been detained there from the time when his detention in hospital by virtue of the notice first began.

(4) The responsible clinician may by order in writing revoke the community treatment order if—

  (a) in his opinion, the conditions mentioned in section 3(2) above are satisfied in respect of the patient; and

  (b) an approved mental health professional states in writing—

     (i) that he agrees with that opinion; and

     (ii) that it is appropriate to revoke the order.

(5) The responsible clinician may at any time release the patient under this section, but not after the community treatment order has been revoked.

(6) If the patient has not been released, nor the community treatment order revoked, by the end of the period of 72 hours, he shall then be released.

(7) But a patient who is released under this section remains subject to the community treatment order.

(8) In this section—

  (a) "the period of 72 hours" means the period of 72 hours beginning with the time when the patient's detention in hospital by virtue of the notice under section 17E above begins; and

  (b) references to being released shall be construed as references to being released from that detention (and accordingly from being recalled to hospital).]

AMENDMENT

This section was inserted by the Mental Health Act 2007 s.32(2).

DEFINITIONS

1–266   community patient: ss.17A(7), 145(1).

hospital: s.145(1).
responsible clinician: s.34(1).
community treatment order: ss.17A(7), 145(1).
approved mental health professional: s.145(1), (1AC).

GENERAL NOTE

This section identifies the powers that apply to a community patient who has been **1–267** recalled to hospital for a maximum period of 72 hours (subs.(6)) under s.17E. They are:

1. The patient may be transferred to another hospital under reg.9 of the English Regulations or reg.26 of the Welsh Regulations (s.19A) by a person specified in reg.12 (for England) or reg.27 (for Wales). If such a transfer takes place, the patient is to be treated as if he had been recalled to, and detained in, that other hospital (subss.(2),(3)). A transfer between hospitals while a patient is recalled does not change the identity of the responsible hospital. Such a change can be effected under reg.17 of the English Regulations or reg.25 of the Welsh Regulations.

2. If the RC decides that the patient meets the criteria for detention as set out in s.3(2) and requires inpatient treatment for longer than 72 hours, the RC may, subject to an AMHP's agreement, revoke the CTO (subs.(4)). The requirement to obtain the agreement of an AMHP is unfortunate because, in the absence of such agreement, the patient will continue to be subject to a CTO which the RC no longer considers to be an appropriate response to the patient's situation. Although the *Code of Practice*, at para.29.67, states that if the agreement of the AMHP is not forthcoming it "would not be appropriate" for the RC to approach another AMHP for an alternative view, such an approach would not be unlawful. Indeed, it could be argued that the RC has a professional duty to make such an approach in an attempt to achieve an objective that she considers is in the patient's best interests. The effect of a revocation is set out in s.17G.

3. The RC may release the patient from detention within the period of 72 hours of the patient's recall to hospital, provided that the CTO has not been revoked (subss.(5),(8)). If by the end of the 72 hour period the patient has not been released, nor the CTO revoked, he shall then be released (subs.(6)). On release, the patient continues to be subject to the CTO (subs.(7)). Release means release from detention (subs.(8)(b)); there is nothing to prevent the released patient from remaining in hospital informally.

4. The patient's RC also has the option of using her power under s.23 to discharge the patient from the CTO. This has the automatic effect of also discharging the underlying application for treatment.

By virtue of s.17D(2)(b), an RC does not have the power to grant a recalled patient leave of absence under s.17.

A recalled patient can be treated for his mental disorder without consent subject to the safeguards set out in either Part IV or Part IVA: see s.62A.

A recalled patient who absconds is absent without leave and the provisions of ss.18, 21, 21A and 21B will apply. In particular, if a patient is absent without leave on the day when the 72-hour period would expire, the period will start again on the patient's return to the hospital either voluntarily or under compulsion: see s.21(4).

This section applies without modification to patients who have been made subject to hospital orders (Sch.1, Pt 1, para.1).

Domestic Violence, Crime and Victims Act 2004

If the RC decides to revoke the CTO, she must inform the hospital managers if the patient **1–268** comes within the scope of the 2004 Act: see the General Note to s.17A under this heading and "Guidance on the extension of victims' rights under the Domestic Violence, Crime and Victims Act 2004", Department of Health, 2008, paras 3.1 to 3.7.

Code of Practice

1–269   Guidance on revoking the CTO is given in Ch.29 at paras 29.63 et seq.

Subsection (2)

1–270   PRESCRIBED IN REGULATIONS.   Form CTO6 provides authority for the patient's transfer: see reg.9 of the English Regulations. The managers of the new hospital should be given a copy of Form CTO 4 or, in Wales, Form CP6 (see the note to subs.(6)). Transfers from hospitals in Wales to hospitals in England must be done in accordance with the equivalent Welsh regulations using Welsh Form TC 6: see reg.26 of the Welsh Regulations.

For the responsibility to inform the patient's nearest relative of the assignment of the patient to another hospital which assumes responsibility for that patient as a community patient, see reg.26(1)(h) of the English Regulations and reg.32(b) of the Welsh Regulations.

Subsection (4)

1–271   A CTO can only be revoked when the patient is detained in hospital as a result of recall under this section.

ORDER IN WRITING.   On Form CTO5: see reg.6(8)(a) of the English Regulations (in Wales, Form CP7: see reg.20 of the Welsh Regulations).

APPROVED MENTAL HEALTH PROFESSIONAL.   The Act does not specify which local authority is responsible for ensuring that an AMHP is made available to consider the possible revocation of the CTO. Paragraph 29.66 of the *Code of Practice* states:

"As before, the AMHP carrying out this role may (but need not) be already involved in the patient's care and treatment, or can be an AMHP acting on behalf of any willing local authority. If no other local authority is willing, responsibility for ensuring that an AMHP considers the case should lie with the local authority which has been responsible for the patient's after-care."

Depending on the circumstances, it might be more appropriate for the default position to be for an AMHP of the local authority for the area where the patient is currently located to perform the role. This approach would be consistent with the duty placed on local authorities by s.13(1).

The AMHP is not required to interview the patient before reaching her decision.

Subsection (6)

1–272   BY THE END OF THE PERIOD OF 72 HOURS.   The start of this period must be recorded on Form CTO 4 (in Wales, Form CP6). The 72-hour period starts from the time when the patient is admitted to the hospital as a result of the recall notice and not from the time when the recall notice was issued. If the patient is absent without leave at the end of that period, see the General Note, above.

Once 72 hours have elapsed, the patient must be allowed to leave if the RC has not revoked the CTO. On leaving hospital the patient will remain on the CTO as before: see para.29.61 of the *Code of Practice*. The 72-hour period cannot be extended by use of the holding powers contained in s.5(2), (4), or by the issue of a second recall notice.

[Effect of revoking community treatment order

1–273   **17G.**—(1) This section applies if a community treatment order is revoked under section 17F above in respect of a patient.

(2) Section 6(2) above shall have effect as if the patient had never been discharged from hospital by virtue of the community treatment order.

(3) The provisions of this or any other Act relating to patients liable to be detained (or detained) in pursuance of an application for admission for treatment shall apply to the patient as they did before the community treatment order was made, unless otherwise provided.

(4) If, when the order is revoked, the patient is being detained in a hospital other than the responsible hospital, the provisions of this Part of this Act shall have effect as if—

(a) the application for admission for treatment in respect of him were an application for admission to that other hospital; and

(b) he had been admitted to that other hospital at the time when he was originally admitted in pursuance of the application.

(5) But, in any case, section 20 below shall have effect as if the patient had been admitted to hospital in pursuance of the application for admission for treatment on the day on which the order is revoked.]

AMENDMENT
This section was inserted by the Mental Health Act 2007 s.32(2).

DEFINITIONS **1–274**
    community treatment order: ss.17A(7), 145(1).
    hospital: s.145(1).
    application for admission for treatment: s.145(1).
    responsible hospital: ss.17A(7), 145(1).

GENERAL NOTE
This section provides that if a patient's CTO is revoked, the authority to detain the patient **1–275** under s.6(2) applies as if the patient had never been a community patient (subs.(2)). In addition, all of the provisions of the Act relating to patients who are liable to be detained (or detained) under s.3 apply to the patient as they did before the CTO was made, unless the Act provides otherwise (subs.(3)). If, at the time when the CTO is revoked, the patient is detained in a hospital other than the one where he was detained when the CTO was made, the Act will apply as if he had been detained in that other hospital at the time when the CTO was made (subs.(4)). The "hospital managers of the new hospital must send a copy of the revocation form to the managers of the original hospital" (*Code of Practice*, para.29.71). For the purposes of calculating the renewal periods under s.20 and for applications to a tribunal, the patient is to be treated as if he had been admitted under s.3 on the day when the CTO is revoked (subs.(5)). The revocation does not effect the calculation of the three month period set out in s.58(1)(b) (s.62A(2)), i.e. the three month period does not start afresh.

Hospital managers must refer the cases of patients whose CTOs are revoked to the tribunal as soon as possible after the revocation (s.68(7)). This duty rests on the hospital managers of the hospital in which the patient is now detained, even if it was not previously the patient's responsible hospital. The tribunal does not have the power to discharge the patient during the 72-hour recall period.

This section applies to patients who have been made subject to hospital orders with the modification set out in para.2B of Sch.1 (Sch.1, Pt 1, para.2).

Return and readmission of patients absent without leave

18.—(1) Where a patient who is for the time being liable to be detained under **1–276** this Part of this Act in a hospital—

   (a) absents himself from the hospital without leave granted under section 17 above; or

   (b) fails to return to the hospital on any occasion on which, or at the expiration of any period for which, leave of absence was granted to him under that section, or upon being recalled under that section; or

   (c) absents himself without permission from any place where he is required to reside in accordance with conditions imposed on the grant of leave of absence under that section,

he may, subject to the provisions of this section, be taken into custody and returned to the hospital or place by any [approved mental health professional], by any officer on the staff of the hospital, by any constable, or by any person authorised in writing by the managers of the hospital.

(2) Where the place referred to in paragraph (c) of subsection (1) above is a hospital other than the one in which the patient is for the time being liable to be detained, the references in that subsection to an officer on the staff of the hospital and the managers of the hospital shall respectively include references to an officer on the staff of the first-mentioned hospital and the managers of that hospital.

[(2A) Where a community patient is at any time absent from a hospital to which he is recalled under section 17E above, he may, subject to the provisions of this section, be taken into custody and returned to the hospital by any approved mental health professional, by any officer on the staff of the hospital, by any constable, or by any person authorised in writing by the responsible clinician or the managers of the hospital.]

(3) Where a patient who is for the time being subject to guardianship under this Part of this Act absents himself without the leave of the guardian from the place at which he is required by the guardian to reside, he may, subject to the provisions of this section, be taken into custody and returned to that place by any officer on the staff of a local social services authority, by any constable, or by any person authorised in writing by the guardian or a local social services authority.

[(4) A patient shall not be taken into custody under this section after the later of—

   (a) the end of the period of six months beginning with the first day of his absence without leave; and

   (b) the end of the period for which (apart from section 21 below) he is liable to be detained or subject to guardianship [or, in the case of a community patient, the community treatment order is in force] [. . .]].

[(4A) In determining for the purposes of subsection (4)(b) above or any other provision of this Act whether a person who is or has been absent without leave is at any time liable to be detained or subject to guardianship, a report furnished under section 20 or 21B below before the first day of his absence without leave shall not be taken to have renewed the authority for his detention or guardianship unless the period of renewal began before that day.

(4B) Similarly, in determining for those purposes whether a community treatment order is at any time in force in respect of a person who is or has been absent without leave, a report furnished under section 20A or 21B below before the first day of his absence without leave shall not be taken to have extended the community treatment period unless the extension began before that day.]

(5) A patient shall not be taken into custody under this section if the period for which he is liable to be detained is that specified in section 2(4), 4(4) or 5(2) or (4) above and that period has expired.

(6) In this Act "absent without leave" means absent from any hospital or other place and liable to be taken into custody and returned under this section, and related expressions shall be construed accordingly.

[(7) In relation to a patient who has yet to comply with a requirement imposed by virtue of this Act to be in a hospital or place, references in this Act to his liability to be returned to the hospital or place shall include his liability to be taken to that hospital or place; and related expressions shall be construed accordingly.]

AMENDMENTS

The amendments to this section were made by the Mental Health (Patients in the Community) Act 1995 s.2(1) and the Mental Health Act 2007 ss.21, 32(4), 55, Sch.2 para.7, Sch.3 para.3, Sch.11 Pt 5.

DEFINITIONS

1–277

    patient: s.145(1).
    hospital: ss.34(2), 145(1).
    approved mental health professional: s.145(1) (1AC).
    the managers: s.145(1).
    local social services authority: s.145(1).
    responsible clinician: s.34(1).
    community patient: s.17A(7), 145(1).
    community treatment order: ss.17A(7), 145(1).

GENERAL NOTE

1–278

This section, which should be read with ss.21, 21A and 21B, identifies the action that can be taken when a detained patient, a community patient or a patient subject to guardianship absents himself without leave. It applies to patients who are absent from England and who are found in Wales, and vice versa. Provisions relating to the removal and return of patients elsewhere within the UK are contained in Pt VI. There is no power under the Act to require the return of a patient who has left the UK without authority.

By virtue of the Care Quality Commission (Registration) Regulations 2009 (SI 2009/3112), reg.17 (as amended by SI 2012/921, reg.4), the Care Quality Commission requires all service providers to notify it of any absence without leave of a person who is either detained or liable to be detained under the Act in an English NHS establishment providing secure psychiatric services and also of the return of that person. A form that must be used for this purpose may be downloaded from the Commission's website (*www.cqc.org.uk*). There is no such requirement if the patient is subject to guardianship.

A patient who has been admitted for treatment under s.3 or received into guardianship under s.7 can be taken into custody at any time up to six months from the date on which he absconded or, if later, the end of the existing authority for detention in hospital or guardianship. A community patient cannot be taken into custody after the community treatment order (CTO) ceases to be in force, or six months have elapsed since the patient was first absent without leave, whichever is the later (subs.4). A patient who has been detained under one of the short term provisions of the Act cannot be taken into custody after the authority to detain has expired (subs.(5)).

Subsection (1)(a) of this section can be used to return a patient to the detaining hospital following the granting of a stay in proceedings to appeal the lawfulness of the decision of a tribunal to discharge the patient (*R. (on the application of H) v Ashworth Hospital Authority* [2002] EWCA Civ 923; [2002] M.H.L.R. 314, noted in the General Note to s.3 under the heading "The re-sectioning of a patient subsequent to a discharge by the First-tier Tribunal (Mental Health) or the Mental Health Review Tribunal for Wales").

Those persons who have the power under subs.(1) to return the absconder to hospital are not provided with a power to force entry onto premises where the absconder is staying. If a power of entry is needed, an application should be made under s.135(2) for a warrant authorising a policeman to enter the premises to remove the patient or, alternatively, the police might be able to use their powers under s.17(1) of the Police and Criminal Evidence Act 1984: see the General Note to s.135. The *Code of Practice* states that whenever "the police are asked for help in returning a patient, they must be informed of the time limit for taking them into custody" (para.28.17). It is sensible for a hospital's absconsion policy not to require that a request for police assistance be made where this is not necessary (*Dunn v South Tyneside Health Care NHS Trust* [2003] EWCA Civ 878; [2004] M.H.L.R. 74, para.71).

It is an offence for a person to induce or knowingly to assist a detained patient to absent himself without leave, knowingly to harbour the patient whilst he is at large, or to help the patient to avoid being retaken (s.128). A patient who is absent without leave does not thereby commit an offence (*R. v Criminal Injuries Compensation Board Ex p. Lawton* [1972] 3 All E.R. 582 at 584).

This section applies to patients who have been placed under hospital or guardianship orders by a court under s.37 with the modification that subs.(5) shall be omitted (Sch.1, Pt 1, paras 2, 4). For restricted patients subss.(3), (4) and (5) shall be omitted and in subs.(1) the words "subject to the provisions of this section" shall be omitted (Sch.1, Pt II, paras 2, 4). The effect of this is that restricted patients may be retaken at any time while their restrictions remain in force. This section also applies to patients who have been sentenced and who remain liable to be detained by virtue of s.22 (s.22(2)(b)).

A hospital order patient, with or without restrictions, who is absent without leave may be arrested if a warrant for his arrest had been obtained from a magistrate (Criminal Justice Act 1967 s.72).

The National Mental Health Development Unit has published "Strategies to Reduce Missing Patients: A Practical Workbook" (2009).

Patients who abscond to Scotland

1–279   The Mental Health (Absconding Patients From Other Jurisdictions) (Scotland) Regulations 2008 (SSI 2008/333) make provision for the taking into custody of a person who is subject to compulsory measures (including community-based orders) under mental health legislation in England and Wales and who is found in Scotland, as a result of their having absconded, or otherwise having failed to comply with the requirements of the order or other measure to which they are subject. It makes such provision by applying to such persons (with some appropriate modification), the sections of the Mental Health (Care and Treatment) (Scotland) Act 2003 (ss.301 to 303) which provide for the taking into custody of absconding patients who are subject to civil compulsory mental health measures in Scotland. These Regulations, along with the Mental Health (Cross-border Visits) (Scotland) Regulations 2008 (SSI 2008/181) (which is noted under s.17), are intended to bring provision dealing with persons in Scotland who abscond or otherwise fail to comply with requirements imposed under mental health measures applicable in England and Wales within the scope of the Scottish mental health legislation.

Patients who abscond from Scotland

1–280   A patient who absconds from hospital whilst being detained under the Mental Health (Care and Treatment) (Scotland) Act 2003 may be taken into custody in England or Wales and returned to Scotland: see art.8 of the Mental Health (Care and Treatment) (Scotland) Act 2003 (Consequential Provisions) Order 2005 (SI 2005/2078). As the patient will not be liable to be detained under this Act, he will not be subject to the consent to treatment provisions contained in Part 4. If compulsory treatment may be required before the patient's return can be effected, consideration should be given to making an application under Part 2.

Human Rights Act 1998

1–281   Although it could be argued that, apart from emergency cases or cases where the patient is returned to hospital within a short period of the unauthorised absence, the return of an absconding patient to hospital would constitute a violation of art.5(1) of the European Convention of Human Rights in the absence of an up to date medical report which confirmed that he was suffering from a mental disorder (see *Kay v United Kingdom* (1998) 40 B.M.L.R. 20, noted under s.42(3)), it is likely that the procedure for the return of such patients is Convention compliant by virtue of the provisions contained in s.21B.

Code of Practice

Guidance on this section is contained in Ch.28. The transport of patients is considered in Ch.17. **1–282**

Subsection (1)

This subsection and subs.(2) identify the action that can be taken when a detained patient **1–283** goes absent without leave. Reasonable force may be used to secure the return of the patient to the hospital or the place where he is required to reside (s.137). Although there is no power to take the patient to any other place, he can initially be taken to another hospital and detained there with the written authority of the detaining hospital while arrangements are made to the patient's return: see para.28.6 of the *Code of Practice* which states that in "these (and similar) cases people may take a faxed or scanned copy of a written authorisation as evidence that they have the necessary authority without waiting for the original".

The patient may be taken into custody in, and returned to England or Wales from Northern Ireland (s.88).

OFFICER ON THE STAFF OF THE HOSPITAL.   See the notes on s.17(3).

ANY CONSTABLE.   The power to arrest under this section was specifically preserved by s.26 and Sch.2 of the Police and Criminal Evidence Act 1984 (PACE). This means that the arresting policeman has a power under s.32 of PACE to search the patient at a place other than a police station.

Subsection (2)

This subsection provides that if a patient has been granted leave of absence on condition **1–284** that he resides in a hospital other than the one in which he is formally liable to be detained, he can be taken into custody by an officer on the staff of the hospital where he is on leave, or by a person authorised by the managers of that hospital.

Subsection (2A)

This provision identifies the action that can be taken when a community patient fails to **1–285** respond to a recall notice or absconds from the hospital after having been recalled. If access to the patient is denied, consideration will have to be given to obtaining a warrant under s.135(2).

Subsection (3)

This provision identifies the action that can be taken when a patient who is subject to **1–286** guardianship absents himself from the place where he is required to reside by the guardian. If access to the patient is denied, consideration will have to be given to obtaining a warrant under s.135(2).

Subsection (4)

This subsection, which is subject to subss.(4A) and (4B), establishes the time limit within **1–287** which patients who do not come within the scope of subs.(5) and who are absent without leave can be returned to the relevant hospital or place of residence. Its effect is that the authority to take the patient into custody will last until at least six months after the first day of absence. A patient who is subject to restrictions can be retaken at any time: see the General Note to this section.

BEGINNING WITH THE FIRST DAY OF HIS ABSENCE WITHOUT LEAVE. Including the first day of the patient's absence without leave (*Zoan v Rouamba* [2000] 2 All E.R. 620 CA).

Subsections (4A), (4B)

1–288   These subsections provide that if a patient's section, guardianship or CTO is renewed or extended before the first day of the patient's absence without leave, the renewal or extension is deemed not to have taken effect unless the period of renewal or extension began before that day. This means that the period during which the patient can be taken into custody is not extended by the renewal or extension.

Subsection (5)

1–289   This subsection provides that a patient cannot be taken into custody under this section if the period of his detention under one of the following powers has expired: admission for assessment (s.2(4)), emergency admission (s.4(4)), or the detention of an in-patient by a doctor or AC (s.5(2)) or nurse (s.5(4)).

Subsection (7)

1–290   This subsection provides a power to take a patient who is subject to guardianship or a detained patient who has been granted leave of absence under s.17 to the hospital or place where he is required to be. Reasonable force may be used to ensure that the patient is taken to that hospital or place (s.137).

Although there is a power in subs.(2A) to take a community patient to the hospital to which he has been recalled, there is no power to take such a patient to a place where he is required to be as a condition of the CTO because there is no power to return the patient to that place.

Regulations as to transfer of patients

1–291   **19.**—(1) In such circumstances and subject to such conditions as may be prescribed by regulations made by the Secretary of State—

    (a) a patient who is for the time being liable to be detained in a hospital by virtue of an application under this Part of this Act may be transferred to another hospital or into the guardianship of a local social services authority or of any person approved by such an authority;

    (b) a patient who is for the time being subject to the guardianship of a local social services authority or other person by virtue of an application under this Part of this Act may be transferred into the guardianship of another local social services authority or person, or be transferred to a hospital.

(2) Where a patient is transferred in pursuance of regulations under this section, the provisions of this Part of this Act (including this subsection) shall apply to him as follows, that is to say—

    (a) in the case of a patient who is liable to be detained in a hospital by virtue of an application for admission for assessment or for treatment and is transferred to another hospital, as if the application were an application for admission to that other hospital and as if the patient had been admitted to that other hospital at the time when he was originally admitted in pursuance of the application;

    (b) in the case of a patient who is liable to be detained in a hospital by virtue of such an application and is transferred into guardianship, as if the application were a guardianship application duly accepted at the said time;

    (c) in the case of a patient who is subject to guardianship by virtue of a guardianship application and is transferred into the guardianship of another authority or person, as if the application were for his reception into the guardianship of that authority or person and had been accepted at the time when it was originally accepted;

(d) in the case of a patient who is subject to guardianship by virtue of a guardianship application and is transferred to a hospital, as if the guardianship application were an application for admission to that hospital for treatment and as if the patient had been admitted to the hospital at the time when the application was originally accepted.

(3) Without prejudice to subsections (1) and (2) above, any patient, who is for the time being liable to be detained under this Part of this Act in a hospital vested in the Secretary of State for the purposes of his functions under the [National Health Service Act 2006, in a hospital vested in the Welsh Ministers for the purposes of their functions under the National Health Service (Wales) Act 2006, in any accommodation used under either of those Acts] by the managers of such a hospital [or in a hospital vested in a National Health Service trust][, NHS foundation trust or] [, Local Health Board] [. . .], may at any time be removed to any other such hospital or accommodation [which is managed by the managers of, or is vested in the National Health Service trust[, NHS foundation trust or] [, Local Health Board] [. . .] for, the first-mentioned hospital]; and paragraph (a) of subsection (2) above shall apply in relation to a patient so removed as it applies in relation to a patient transferred in pursuance of regulations made under this section.

(4) Regulations made under this section may make provision for regulating the conveyance to their destination of patients authorised to be transferred or removed in pursuance of the regulations or under subsection (3) above.

AMENDMENTS

In subs.(3) the words in square brackets were inserted and substituted by the National Health Service and Community Care Act 1990 s.66(1), Sch.9 para.24(2), the Health and Social Care (Community Health and Standards) Act 2003 s.34, Sch.4 para.52, the Health Act 1999 (Supplementary, Consequential, etc., Provisions) Order 2000 (SI 2000/90) Sch.1 para.16(3), the National Health Service (Consequential Provisions) Act 2006 s.2, Sch.1 para.64, the Mental Health Act 2007 s.46(2) and the Health and Social Care Act 2012 Sch.5, para.25.

DEFINITIONS

    patient: s.145(1).   **1–292**
    hospital: ss.34(2), 145(1).
    local social services authority: s.145(1).
    application for admission for assessment: ss.2, 145(1).
    application for admission for treatment: ss.3, 145(1).
    guardianship application: s.7(1).
    Local Health Board: s.145(1).
    the managers: s.145(1).

GENERAL NOTE

This section empowers the Secretary of State (or, in relation to Wales, the Welsh **1–293** Ministers) to regulate the circumstances in which detained patients and patients who are subject to guardianship may be transferred between hospitals or guardians or between detention in hospital and guardianship. It only applies to transfers within England and Wales. The Mental Health (Hospital, Guardianship and Treatment) (England) Regulations 2008 (SI 2008/1184) and the Mental Health (Hospital, Guardianship,

Community Treatment and Consent to treatment) (Wales) Regulations 2008 (SI 2008/2439 (W.212)) have been made under this section.

In *R. (on the application of L) v West London Mental Health NHS Trust* [2014] EWCA Civ 47; [2014] M.H.L.R. 361, the Court of Appeal held that the requirements of the common law principles of procedural fairness applied to cases where a detained patient is being considered for transfer from conditions of medium security to conditions of high security. The court further held that:

1. Where, as in this case, the decision in question is largely a clinically-based decision with an added rationing aspect because of the scarcity of high security beds, there is a need for circumspection as to what procedure is required (para.8).

2. Procedural fairness can be satisfied by the "gist" of the letter of reference to the high security hospital by the hospital that wishes to transfer the patient and the assessment by the clinician from the high security hospital being provided to the patient and/or his or her representative. This procedure need not be followed in cases of urgency, where there is a clinical reason precluding such notification, or where there is some other reason such as the exposure of other patients or staff to the risk of harm (para.99).

3. The "gist" can be provided by enclosing them with a largely pro forma communication informing the patient and/or his representatives that, if they disagree with the factual or clinical triggers for the reference or assessment, they can make submissions in writing which will be considered by the admissions panel of the high security hospital. This does not preclude the hospital providing copies of the letter of reference and the assessment rather than the "gist" of those documents, but that is not a requirement of fairness in this context (para.99).

4. It is not necessary for the patient to be given an opportunity to make representations to the putative transferring hospital before the reference is made (para.100).

The guidance given by the Court of Appeal in this case is reflected in the *Code of Practice* at para.37.22.

In order to comply with the empowerment and involvement principle set out at paras 1.7 et seq of the *Code of Practice* and the requirements of art.8 of the European Convention of Human Rights (ECHR), patients should be involved, as far as is both practicable and proportionate, in the process leading to all transfer decisions.

In *(R. (on the application of T) v Chief Executive of Nottinghamshire Healthcare NHS Trust* [2006] EWHC 800 (Admin); [2006] M.H.L.R. 103, the patient failed in his attempt to challenge his transfer from one high security hospital to another, which was based on a policy decision of the Department of Health that, if certain criteria are met, patients should be transferred to the high security hospital closest to their postal address.

For the responsibility to inform the patient's nearest relative of a transfer under this section, see reg.26(1)(a)or (i) of the English Regulations and reg.30 of the Welsh Regulations.

This section applies to patients who are subject to hospital or guardianship orders made by a court under s.37, with the modification that subs.(2) shall read as follows:

"(2) Where a patient is transferred in pursuance of regulations under this section, the provisions of this Part of this Act (including this subsection) shall apply to him [as if the order or direction under Part III of this Act by virtue of which he was liable to be detained or subject to guardianship before being transferred were an order or direction for his admission or removal to the hospital to which he is transferred, or placing him under the guardianship of the authority or person into whose guardianship he is transferred, as the case may be]." (Sch.1, Pt 1, paras 2, 5.)

For restricted patients subs.(1), (2) and (3) shall read as follows:

"(1) In such circumstances and subject to such conditions as may be prescribed by regulations made by the Secretary of State—

(a) a patient who is for the time being liable to be detained in a hospital by virtue of an application under this Part of this Act may [with the consent of the Secretary of State] be transferred to another hospital [. . .]

(2) Where a patient is transferred in pursuance of regulations under this section, the provisions of this Part of this Act (including this sub-section) shall apply to him [as if the order or direction under Part III of this Act by virtue of which he was liable to be detained before being transferred were an order or direction for his admission or removal to the hospital to which he is transferred].

(3) Without prejudice to subsections (1) and (2) above, any patient, who is for the time being liable to be detained under this Part of this Act in a hospital vested in the Secretary of State for the purposes of his functions under the [National Health Service Act 2006, in a hospital vested in the Welsh Ministers for the purposes of their functions under the National Health Service (Wales) Act 2006, in any accommodation used under either of those Acts] by the managers of such a hospital [or in a hospital vested in a National Health Service trust][, NHS foundation trust or][Local Health Board] [. . .], may at any time [, with the consent of the Secretary of State,] be removed to any other such hospital or accommodation [which is managed by the managers of, or is vested in the National Health Service trust[, NHS foundation trust or][Local Health Board] which is managed by the managers of, or is vested in the National Health Service Trust [. . .] for, the first-mentioned hospital]; and para.(a) of subs.(2) above shall apply in relation to a patient so removed as it applies in relation to a patient transferred in pursuance of regulations made under this section." (Sch.1, Pt II, paras 2, 5.)

The effect of these provisions is that any transfer of a restricted patient between hospitals, even where the hospitals are administered by the same managers, is subject to the agreement of the Secretary of State.

Human Rights Act 1998
While art.8 contains no explicit procedural requirements, the decision-making process **1–294** leading to measures of interference must be fair and such as to afford due respect to the interests safeguarded by that article: see *R. (on the application of L) v West London Mental Health NHS Trust*, above, at para.77. Also see para.37.18 of the *Code of Practice*.

Applications to the First-tier Tribunal (Mental Health) or the Mental Health Review Tribunal for Wales
The patient may make an application within 6 months of a transfer from guardianship to **1–295** hospital (s.66(1)(e), (2)(e)) and once in every period for which the detention is renewed. If this right is not exercised within six months of the transfer, the hospital managers will refer the case to the tribunal (s.68(1)). A patient who is transferred from hospital to guardianship has the same right to make an application as a guardianship patient who is made subject to a guardianship application on the day that the transfer takes effect (subs.(2)(b)).
In *R. (on the application of L) v West London Mental Health NHS Trust* [2012] EWHC 3200 (Admin); [2013] M.H.L.R. 297, Stadlen J. said at para.184:

"[I]f a patient . . . who has been detained pursuant to a hospital order and who has been transferred against his will from a medium security hospital to a high security hospital does not seek a direction for his discharge from detention under the 1983 Act but only a transfer back to a medium secure hospital, there is in theory nothing to stop him from applying to the Tribunal for a recommendation that he be transferred . . . ."

Code of Practice
Guidance on this section is contained in Ch.37 at para.37.16 et seq.   **1–296**

Guidance

1–297   The consent of the Secretary of State is needed to transfer any restricted patient between hospitals or named hospital units under this section (s.41(3)(c)). The Mental Health Casework Section of the Ministry of Justice has published "Transfers between Hospitals in England and Wales" (2014) which provides guidance on obtaining such consent. The guidance can be accessed at: *www.justice.gov.uk/offenders/types-of-offender/mentally-dis-ordered-offenders.*

Subsection (1)

1–298   REGULATIONS.   See regs 7, 8, 10 and 11 of the English Regulations and regs 23, 24 and 27 of the Welsh Regulations.

Paragraph (a)

1–299   PATIENT.   Including, with the consent of the Secretary of State, a restricted patient: see the General Note, above, and s.41(3)(c)(ii).

In order to be transferred under this provision, the patient must have become an in-patient of the hospital named in the application (see the phrase "originally admitted" in subs.(2)(a)) and the hospital must have accepted the application (see the note on "sufficient authority for the Managers" in s.6(2)). The patient must be admitted to the hospital to which he is being transferred: see reg.7(2)(b) of the English Regulations (reg.23(2)(b) of the Welsh Regulations). There is no need for an admission to take place if the transfer is effected under subs.(3), i.e. the hospitals concerned are managed by the same hospital managers (ibid. reg.7(1)(a) and reg.23(1)(a) respectively).

A transfer under this provision can be effected at a time when the patient has been placed on leave of absence under s.17 at the hospital to which he is being transferred in which case the transfer takes place when the managers of the new hospital complete Part 2 of Form H4 (in Wales Part 2 of Form TC2).

BY VIRTUE OF AN APPLICATION.   Including a patient who has been detained under ss.2 and 4. Patients who are detained in hospital but who have not been made subject to an application are excluded, e.g. patients detained under ss.5(2), (4), 35, 36, 38, 135 and 136 or who are detained in a place of safety under s.37(4). Patients who have been made subject to hospital orders or guardianship orders by a court are included: see the General Note, above.

TRANSFERRED TO ANOTHER HOSPITAL.   Including a high security hospital.

Paragraph (b)

1–300   TRANSFERRED INTO THE GUARDIANSHIP OF ANOTHER PERSON.   Transfer from one guardian to another can, in certain circumstances, also take place under s.10.

AT THE SAID TIME.   Which is the time when he was originally admitted in pursuance of the application: see para.(a).

Subsection (2)

Paragraph (a)

1–301   The application for the detention of a patient who is transferred to another hospital under this provision is to be treated as if it is an application for the detention of the patient at that other hospital made at the time when he was originally admitted under that application.

TRANSFERRED.   Using the procedure set out in reg.7(2) and Form H4 of the English Regulations and reg.23(1),(2),(3) and Form TC1 of the Welsh Regulations. Transfer to another hospital managed by the same managers is allowed for without formality under subs.(3).

HOSPITAL. Or registered establishment (s.34(2)). The transfer of a patient between registered establishments where both establishments are under the same management is governed by reg.7(5) of the English Regulations and reg.23(6) of the Welsh Regulations.

Paragraph (b)
The application for the detention of a patient who is transferred into guardianship under **1–302** this provision is to be treated as if the application was a guardianship application made at the time when he was admitted to hospital under the application for detention.

TRANSFERRED INTO GUARDIANSHIP. Using the procedure set out in reg.7(4) and Form G6 of the English Regulations and reg.23(4),(5) and Form TC2 of the Welsh Regulations. Restricted patients may not be transferred into guardianship: see the General Note to this section.
Paragraph 10.37 of the Reference Guide states:

"An authorisation for transfer to guardianship does not give anyone any authority to convey the patient in question anywhere. If the patient did not go to the place, if any, the new guardian requires them to live, they would be considered AWOL and so could be taken to that place in accordance with section 18."

Although the patient's nearest relative has no statutory right to object to such a transfer, he or she can discharge the patient from guardianship (s.23(2)(b)).

AS IF THE APPLICATION WERE A GUARDIANSHIP APPLICATION. The original application will have either been for assessment under s.2 or for treatment under s.3 (subs.(2)(a)). Any outstanding tribunal application must proceed using guardianship criteria set out in s.72(4).

Paragraph (c)
The guardianship application of a patient who is transferred into the guardianship of **1–303** another local authority under this provision is to be treated as if it is an application for the reception of the patient into the guardianship of that other authority made at the time when the patient was originally received into guardianship.

TRANSFERRED. Using the procedure set out in reg.8(1) and Form G7 of the English Regulations and reg.24(1),(2),(3) and Form TC3 of the Welsh Regulations.

Paragraph (d)
The guardianship application of a patient who is transferred to hospital under this pro- **1–304** vision is to be treated as if it is an application for admission for treatment of the patient made at the time when the guardianship application was accepted. The guardian should ensure that this date is communicated to the hospital managers.
If a patient is transferred under this paragraph, it would appear that the three-month period relating to the administration of medicine specified in s.58(1)(b) would commence from the first occasion when medicine was administered to the patient during the period when he was subject to guardianship.

TRANSFERRED. Using the procedure set out in reg.8(2) and Form G8 of the English Regulations and reg.24(4),(5) and Form TC4 of the Welsh Regulations.

Subsection (3)
This subsection, which applies to NHS hospitals, enables a patient to be transferred to **1–305** another hospital, or other accommodation managed by the same managers without any special procedure being followed. A similar provision for independent hospitals is contained in reg.7(5) of the English Regulations and reg.23(6) of the Welsh Regulations. A

patient who is transferred under this provision is treated as if he had been admitted to the hospital to which he has been transferred at the time of the original application.

This subsection does not apply to patients who have been detained under s.5(2) or (4). If, following the use of the holding powers, the assessment of the patient concludes that an application ought to be made in respect of him, the application can be addressed to a different hospital.

VESTED IN THE SECRETARY OF STATE. Or in the Welsh Ministers for the purposes of their functions under the National Health Service (Wales) Act 2006 (SI 2000/253, Sch.3; also see the General Note to this Act).

[Regulations as to assignment of responsibility for community patients

1–306   **19A.**—(1) Responsibility for a community patient may be assigned to another hospital in such circumstances and subject to such conditions as may be prescribed by regulations made by the Secretary of State (if the responsible hospital is in England) or the Welsh Ministers (if that hospital is in Wales).

(2) If responsibility for a community patient is assigned to another hospital—

   (a) the application for admission for treatment in respect of the patient shall have effect (subject to section 17D above) as if it had always specified that other hospital;

   (b) the patient shall be treated as if he had been admitted to that other hospital at the time when he was originally admitted in pursuance of the application (and as if he had subsequently been discharged under section 17A above from there); and

   (c) that other hospital shall become "the responsible hospital" in relation to the patient for the purposes of this Act.]

AMENDMENT

This section was inserted by the Mental Health Act 2007 s.32(4), Sch.3 para.4.

DEFINITIONS

1–307   community patient: ss.17A(7), 145(1).
responsible hospital: ss.17A(7), 145(1).
application for admission for treatment: s.145(1).

GENERAL NOTE

1–308   This section enables the Secretary of State (in respect of a hospital in England) or the Welsh Ministers (in respect of a hospital in Wales) to make regulations which transfer the responsibility for a community patient to a new responsible hospital. If responsibility is transferred, the patient is to be treated as if he had been originally admitted to the new responsible hospital.

This section applies to patients who have been made subject to hospital orders with the modification that subs.(2)(b) shall be omitted (Sch.1 Pt 1 paras 2, 5A).

Subsection (1)

1–309   PRESCRIBED BY REGULATIONS. See reg.17 of the English Regulations and reg.25 of the Welsh Regulations. Authority for the assignment must be given on Form CTO10 (in Wales, Form TC5).

[Duration of authority and discharge]

Duration of authority

20.—(1) Subject to the following provisions of this Part of this Act, a patient **1–310** admitted to hospital in pursuance of an application for admission for treatment, and a patient placed under guardianship in pursuance of a guardianship application, may be detained in a hospital or kept under guardianship for a period not exceeding six months beginning with the day on which he was so admitted, or the day on which the guardianship application was accepted, as the case may be, but shall not be so detained or kept for any longer period unless the authority for his detention or guardianship is renewed under this section.

(2) Authority for the detention or guardianship of a patient may, unless the patient has previously been discharged [under section 23 below], be renewed—

(a) from the expiration of the period referred to in subsection (1) above, for a further period of six months;

(b) from the expiration of any period of renewal under paragraph (a) above, for a further period of one year,

and so on for periods of one year at a time.

(3) Within the period of two months ending on the day on which a patient who is liable to be detained in pursuance of an application for admission for treatment would cease under this section to be so liable in default of the renewal of the authority for his detention, it shall be the duty of the [responsible clinician]—

(a) to examine the patient; and

(b) if it appears to him that the conditions set out in subsection (4) below are satisfied, to furnish to the managers of the hospital where the patient is detained a report to that effect in the prescribed form;

and where such a report is furnished in respect of a patient the managers shall, unless they discharge the patient [under section 23 below], cause him to be informed.

(4) The conditions referred to in subsection (3) above are that—

(a) the patient is suffering from [mental disorder] of a nature or degree which makes it appropriate for him to receive medical treatment in a hospital; and

(b) [. . .]

(c) it is necessary for the health or safety of the patient or for the protection of other persons that he should receive such treatment and that it cannot be provided unless he continues to be detained; [and

(d) appropriate medical treatment is available to him.]

[. . .]

(5) Before furnishing a report under subsection (3) above the [responsible clinician] shall consult one or more other persons who have been professionally concerned with the patient's medical treatment.

[(5A) But the responsible clinician may not furnish a report under subsection (3) above unless a person—

(a) who has been professionally concerned with the patient's medical treatment; but

(b) who belongs to a profession other than that to which the responsible clinician belongs, states in writing that he agrees that the conditions set out in subsection (4) above are satisfied.]

(6) Within the period of two months ending with the day on which a patient who is subject to guardianship under this Part of this Act would cease under this section

to be so liable in default of the renewal of the authority for his guardianship, it shall be the duty of the [appropriate practitioner]—

(a) to examine the patient; and

(b) if it appears to him that the conditions set out in subsection (7) below are satisfied, to furnish to the guardian and, where the guardian is a person other than a local social services authority, to the responsible local social services authority a report to that effect in the prescribed form;

and where such a report is furnished in respect of a patient, the local social services authority shall, unless they discharge the patient [under section 23 below], cause him to be informed.

(7) The conditions referred to in subsection (6) above are that—

(a) the patient is suffering from [mental disorder] of a nature or degree which warrants his reception into guardianship; and

(b) it is necessary in the interests of the welfare of the patient or for the protection of other persons that the patient should remain under guardianship.

(8) Where a report is duly furnished under subsection (3) or (6) above, the authority for the detention or guardianship of the patient shall be thereby renewed for the period prescribed in that case by subsection (2) above.

(9) [. . .]

(10) [. . .]

AMENDMENTS

The amendments to this section were made by the Mental Health Act 2007 ss.1(4), 4(4), 9(4), 32(4), 55, Sch.3 para.5, Sch.11 Pts 1, 2 and 3. The cross-heading was amended by s.32(3).

DEFINITIONS

1–311
patient: s.145(1).
hospital: ss.34(2), 145(1).
application for admission for treatment: ss.3, 145(1).
appropriate medical treatment: ss.3(4), 145(1AB).
the managers: s.145(1).
mental disorder: ss.1, 145(1).
medical treatment: s.145(1), (4).
guardianship appliation: s.7(1).
local social services authority: s.145(1).
responsible clinician: s.34(1).
appropriate clinician: s.145(1).
appropriate practitioner: s.34(1).
responsible local social services authority: s.34(1).

GENERAL NOTE

1–312
This section provides for patients who have been detained for treatment under s.3 or placed under guardianship to be detained or kept under guardianship for an initial period of up to six months. It also sets out the criteria that have to be satisfied if the authority to detain a patient or keep him in guardianship is to be renewed. Renewal, which can be for one further period of six months and subsequently for periods of one year at a time, cannot cure any illegality in the original application, order or direction (*R. (on the application of SP) v Secretary of State for Justice* [2010] EWHC 1124 (Admin), para.4).

As a restricted patient whose restriction order has ceased to have effect is treated as if he had been admitted to hospital as an unrestricted patient on the date when the restriction order ceased to have effect (s.41(5)), the start date for renewals under this section is that date.

The finding of McCullough J. in *R. v Hallstrom Ex p. W* [1986] 2 All E.R. 306, that a decision to renew the authority to detain a patient cannot be made at a time when the patient is on leave of absence was overruled by the Court of Appeal in *R. v Barking Havering and Brentwood Community Healthcare NHS Trust* [1999] 1 F.L.R. 106. A renewal can be made while the patient is on leave of absence if hospital treatment comprises a significant component of the patient's treatment plan: see the note on subs.(4).

For the responsibility to inform the patient's nearest relative of the patient's renewal of detention or guardianship under this section, see reg.26(1)(b) or (l) of the English Regulations and regs 8 and 15 of the Welsh Regulations.

This section applies to patients who are subject to an unrestricted hospital order or a guardianship order made by a court under s.37, with the modification that subs.(1) shall read as follows:

"(1) Subject to the following provisions of this Part of this Act, a patient admitted to hospital in pursuance of an application for admission for treatment, and a patient placed under guardianship in pursuance of a guardianship application, may be detained in a hospital or kept under guardianship for a period not exceeding six months beginning with the [date of the relevant order or direction under Part III of this Act] but shall not be so detained or kept for any longer period unless the authority for his detention or guardianship is renewed under this section" (Sch.1, Pt 1, para.6).

Human Rights Act 1998
The question whether the continued detention of an asymptomatic patient contravenes **1–313** art.5 of the European Convention of Human Rights (ECHR) is considered in the General Note to s.3 under this heading. A finding by a RC that the patient is no longer suffering from a mental disorder (see subs.(4)(a)) does not require the patient's immediate release from detention if that patient poses a risk to the public: see the note on s.23 under this heading.

It is has been argued that the lack of any involvement of the hospital managers as detaining authority in the decision to renew the patient's detention (see the *Warlingham Park Hospital* case, noted under subs.(3)) might constitute a violation of art.5(1) of the ECHR as interpreted by the European Court of Human Rights (ECtHR) in *Winterwerp v Netherlands* (1979) 2 E.H.R.R. 387: see Phil Fennell, "The Third Way in Mental Health Policy: Negative Rights, Positive Rights and the Convention", (1999) 26 *Journal of Law and Society,* 103–127.

Among the functions that a responsible clinician (RC) has is the decision whether to renew the detention of the patient under this section. In *Winterwerp v Netherlands,* above, the ECtHR held that that in order for a detention on the ground of unsoundness of mind to be lawful it must be established by objective medical expertise that the person concerned suffers from a true mental disorder. During the passage of the 2007 Act through Parliament, the Joint Committee argued that if initial detention must be based on medical expertise to be compatible with art.5, there is an argument, following *Winterwerp,* that the same should apply to the renewal of detention. In support of this argument, the Joint Committee relied on *Varbanov v Bulgaria* [2000] M.H.L.R. 263 where the court held that it would be a breach of art.5 if a person were detained on the basis that they were of unsound mind without first obtaining the opinion of a medical expert. The Joint Committee argued that this case made it clear that that the opinion of a medical expert who is a psychiatrist is necessary and that renewal of detention by a RC who is not a psychiatrist would contravene art.5. The Government, in not agreeing that *Varbanov* requires the necessary medical expertise to be provided every time by a psychiatrist, countered by claiming that: (a) there is no caselaw specifically on what is meant by medical expertise; (b) *Winterwerp* was not seeking to lay down which sort of qualifications available in a national system which would be acceptable and which would not; (c) the ECHR is a "living instrument" that must be interpreted in the light of present day conditions; and (d) within a modern workforce, it is appropriate for Mental Health Act functions to be allocated to those who are competent to perform them. In the light of these considerations, the Government's view is that *Winterwerp* must be broadly interpreted and that what was required is a person who is able to make a decision as to whether or not the person in question is of unsound mind. As the competencies that must be satisfied before a person can become an AC include the ability to identify the presence and severity of mental disorder, the Government argued that such a person will have the objective medical expertise required by art.5. It is likely that the ECtHR court would support the Government's contention that it is for national authorities to decide which professionals possess the required expertise to perform functions under the Act as this is a matter which is likely to come within the "margin of appreciation" that the ECtHR allows national authorities to have when applying the ECHR. This issue is considered at paras 21 to 29 of the Joint Committee's Report and at paras 24 to 34 of the Government's response to the Report, Department of Health, April 13, 2007.

Applications to the First-tier Tribunal (Mental Health) or the Mental Health Review Tribunal for Wales
1–314   The patient's right to apply to a tribunal arises from the date of the renewal of the detention or guardianship (s.66(1)(f),(2)(f)).

Code of Practice
1–315   Guidance on the renewal of a patient's detention is given in Ch.32.

Subsection (1)
1–316   Six months.   A month means a calendar month (Interpretation Act 1978 s.5, Sch.1).

Beginning with.   Including the day on which the patient was admitted to hospital or the day on which the guardianship application was accepted by the local social services authority (*Zoan v Rouamba* [2000] 2 All E.R. 620 CA). This means that if the patient was admitted on March 3, the six month period would expire at midnight on September 2.

The day on which he was so admitted.   This is either the day on which the patient was admitted to the hospital from the community whilst subject to an application under s.3, or the day on which the patient who was in hospital either informally or subject to an application made under s.2 was made subject to such an application. In both cases, admission only takes effect when the s.3 application has been accepted by a person who has been authorised by the hospital managers to accept it: see reg.3(2) of the English and Welsh Regulations.

Subsection (3)
1–317   This subsection requires the RC to examine a patient detained for treatment during the two months preceding the day on which the authority for his detention is due to expire. The period of detention can be extended if the patient is absent without leave: see s.21 et seq. If the RC considers that the conditions set out in subs.(4) are satisfied, the authority to detain the patient is renewed when Form H5 (in Wales, Form HO15) has been completed and furnished to the hospital managers: see reg.13(1),(2),(3) of the English Regulations and reg.5 of the Welsh Regulations and the note on "furnish" below. The RC's duty under this section cannot be delegated. Before furnishing the report to the hospital managers, the RC must have consulted with a professional who has been concerned with the patient's medical treatment (subs.(5)) and received confirmation from such a person (not coming from the same profession as the RC) that the conditions for renewal are satisfied (subs.(5A)).

This section does not require that the RC's report should have been considered by the managers before renewal can take place, although it is clearly good practice for this to happen. In *R. v Managers of Warlingham Park Hospital Ex p. B* (1994) 22 B.M.L.R. 1 CA Sir Thomas Bingham M.R. said at 11:

"In my judgment it is essential to distinguish between the authority to detain, which section 20 makes dependent on the due furnishing of a report, and the decision whether or not to discharge, assuming that there was a continued authority to detain, which is plainly entrusted, as section 23 makes plain, to the managers": also see para.38.14 of the *Code of Practice*.

ENDING ON THE DAY.   Given that the period of detention begins with the day on which the patient was admitted (subs.(1)), it will cease at the end of the preceding day: see the note on "beginning with" above.

TWO MONTHS.   This time limit applies to the examination of the patient by the RC, the forming of the RC's opinion and the furnishing of the report to the managers of the hospital where the patient is detained.

RESPONSIBLE CLINICIAN.   The guidance contained in para.39.17 of the *Code of Practice* that a person involved in making the decision whether to renew the detention of a patient "should not have any financial interest in the outcome of the decision" should not be followed in so far as it applies to the RC who is the only person who can trigger a renewal.

EXAMINE THE PATIENT.   If a patient refuses to be examined or is assessed as being either too ill or too disturbed to be examined, the RC's examination of the patient could comprise: (1) her observations of the patient; (2) a consideration of the patient's medical history and prognosis; and (3) an evaluation of the patient's current condition in a multi-disciplinary case conference; see further the note on "personally examined" in s.12(1).

The examination could take place on an out-patient basis if the patient is on s.17 leave: see the note on subs.(4)(c).

FURNISH.   In the Scottish case of *Milborrow, Applicant*, 1996 S.C.L.R. 315 Sh.Ct, it was held that a report is "furnished" to the hospital managers when it is committed to the internal mailing system operated by those managers. An alternative method of furnishing the report is to hand it to a member of staff authorised by the hospital managers to receive it: see Form H5 (or, for Wales, HO15).

The furnishing of the RC's report gives authority for the continued detention of the patient: see subs.(8) and *R. v Managers of Warlingham Park Hospital*, noted above, where Sir Thomas Bingham M.R. said at 11: "If the authorised period of detention expires without there being a report duly furnished ..., any detention after the expiry date will plainly be unlawful and render the managers at risk of successful action".

MANAGERS OF THE HOSPITAL WHERE THE PATIENT IS DETAINED.   If, subsequent to the furnishing of a report under this section but before the hospital managers have had an opportunity to consider it, the patient is transferred to another hospital under s.19, the managers of that hospital should consider the report (s.19(2)(a)).

A REPORT.   The report, which should be kept with the patient's admission documents, requires the hospital managers to consider whether they should exercise their power of discharge in respect of the patient.

Forms H5 and HO15 provide for the patient's RC to state her reasons why it is not appropriate for the patient to revert to informal status. The fact that a Mental Health Act Administrator might consider the reasons given by the RC to be inadequate would not effect the validity of the renewal. The purpose of the requirement to give reasons is to assist the managers in their task of considering whether they should exercise their power under s.23 to discharge the patient. Unlike an application of detention, there is no requirement for the renewal to be accepted by the managers before it comes into force.

If the patient's situation changes, it is lawful for the RC to discharge him from detention after Pt I of the Form H5 (or Form HO15) has been signed, but before the hospital managers have had an opportunity to consider whether they should exercise their power of discharge. Where this occurs, the Form should be endorsed with a statement confirming that the RC's power of discharge was exercised on the date in question.

The fact that Part 4 of Form H5 (or Form HO 15) might not be completed until after the section has expired does not invalidate the renewal as it is the Form furnished by the patient's RC that renews the section. The furnishing of the Form must take place before the section expires.

A Form H5 or Form HO15 which is defective because of a minor error or slip of the pen would not render the renewal unlawful. Such errors may be corrected and initialled even though the rectification procedure in s.15 does not apply to this section. If the form is fundamentally defective in some way, for example it was signed by a person who is not the patient's RC or it was completed after the authority for the patient's detention had expired, the renewal would be unlawful: see *Re S-C (Mental Patient: Habeas Corpus)* [1996] 1 All E.R. 532, CA.

The date of the renewal is the date on which the authority to detain was due to expire and not the date of the report.

UNLESS THEY DISCHARGE THE PATIENT. In order to consider whether they should exercise their power of discharge under s.23(2)(a), the managers must meet as a panel of at least three members (s.23(4)). It is the conditions for renewal set out in subs.(4), rather than the conditions for the initial admission for treatment set out in s.3(2), that the managers should address: per Wilson J. speaking obiter in *R. (on the application of DR) v Mersey Care NHS Trust*, below, at para.19. Even if the conditions for renewal are met, the managers have a discretion under s.23(2) to order the patient's discharge *(R. v Riverside Mental Health Trust Ex p. Huzzey* (1998) 43 B.M.L.R. 167).

Subsection (4)

1–318 This subsection specifies the conditions which have to be satisfied if the authority to detain a patient who has been admitted for treatment is to be renewed.

It is not possible to renew the detention of a patient if there is no longer a need for the patient's treatment plan to contain an element of hospital treatment. In *R. v Barking Havering and Brentwood Community Healthcare NHS Trust* [1999] 1 F.L.R. 106, the patient had been granted leave of absence under s.17. At the time of the renewal of her detention under this section the patient was on leave of absence. The patient challenged the legality of the renewal on the ground that it contravened the ruling of McCullough J. in *R. v Hallstrom Ex p. W.* [1986] 2 All E.R. 306, that a patient's detention could not be renewed whilst she was "liable to be detained" during a period of leave of absence. In overruling McCullough J. on this point, the Court of Appeal held that as long as the patient's medical treatment viewed as a whole involved treatment in a hospital, the requirements of this section could be met. The fact that the patient happened to be away from hospital at the time of renewal did not mean that she was no longer "detained" for treatment. Further, a renewal would be lawful even if the periods of hospital care could be classified as being for the purposes of assessment and the monitoring of progress, rather than actual treatment.

The *Barking* case was applied by Sullivan J. in *R. (on the application of Epsom and St Helier NHS Trust) v The Mental Health Review Tribunal* [2001] EWHC Admin 101; [2001] M.H.L.R. 8, a case where the Trust challenged the decision of the Mental Health Review Tribunal to discharge the patient. The tribunal's decision was made on the ground that as the patient, who was residing in a nursing home on s.17 leave, was not receiving hospital treatment it was not "appropriate for her to be liable to be detained in hospital for medical treatment" for the purposes of s.72(1)(b)(i). His Lordship held that it would be inconsistent with the scheme of the Act if the mere prospect, that at some unspecified future time inpatient treatment would or might be required, compelled a tribunal to reject a patient's application for discharge. This case is considered in the note on s.72(1)(b)(i).

Although Lord Woolf M.R. in *Barking* made an obiter distinction between out-patient and in-patient treatment by stating that if the treatment of the patient viewed as a whole "involves treatment as an *in-patient* the requirements of [this] section can be met" (at 113H; emphasis added), in *R. (on the application of DR) v Mersey Care NHS Trust* [2002] EWHC 1810 (Admin); [2002] M.H.L.R. 386 Wilson J. held that: (1) the test laid down in this subsection was whether the treatment plan provided for a patient to receive medical treatment in a hospital; (2) any distinction between treatment *at* a hospital and *in* a hospital was too subtle; (3) the hospital treatment must form a significant component of the patient's treatment plan, which can include specialist rehabilitation (s.145(1)); and (4) it would be an impermissible and illogical gloss on the Act to make the lawfulness of renewal dependent upon a plan to put the patient at times in a hospital bed. With regard to point (2), his Lordship did not follow the obiter remarks of McCullough J. in the *Hallstrom* case which are reproduced in the General Note to s.3. In *DR*, the treatment plan provided that the patient should attend occupational therapy at the hospital once a week, that she should receive medication for her mental disorder by injection at her home at fortnightly intervals and that she should attend the ward round at the hospital at weekly intervals. The object of the third requirement was to provide for occasions for "attempted dialogue; for monitoring; for assessment; and for review". It followed that a significant component of the patient's care plan was treatment in a hospital and that the conditions for renewal had been satisfied.

Given the definition of hospital in the National Health Service Act 2006, clinical contact with the patient could take place at a clinic or out-patient department maintained in connection with the institution such as a "local Community Mental Health Treatment Base": see *KL v Somerset Partnership NHS Foundation Trust* [2011] UKUT 233 (AAC); [2011] M.H.L.R. 194, at para.9 and the note on "hospital" in s.145(1). It is submitted that there must be a clear clinical rationale for the treatment to take place at the hospital rather than at some other location. For example, medical treatment, such an injection of anti-psychotic medication, that could be appropriately undertaken at the patient's home but is provided at the hospital solely for the convenience of staff would not qualify as "treatment in a hospital" for the purposes of this provision. However, a requirement for the patient to attend the ward round at appropriate intervals for assessment and monitoring by staff would meet the test established by this subsection if the assessment and monitoring comprised a significant component of the patient's treatment plan. In *KL v Somerset Partnership NHS Foundation Trust* at para.9, UT Judge Rowland accepted a submission that *DR* "shows that reviews may be part of a patient's 'medical treatment' . . .".

DR was applied in *R. (on the application of CS) v Mental Health Review Tribunal* [2004] EWHC 2958 (Admin); [2004] M.H.L.R. 355, where Pitchford J. upheld the decision of a Mental Health Review Tribunal not to discharge a patient from detention under s.3 where the patient had been granted leave of absence under s.17 to reside at her home subject to the condition that she attended the hospital as an outpatient for weekly sessions with a psychologist, and for ward round reviews at monthly intervals. The purpose of the ward round reviews were to: (1) discuss with the patient how her leave was progressing, how her medication was suiting her and whether any adjustments were necessary to the dose of her medication; and (2) provide the patient with supportive and motivational interviewing to help her to move out of the hospital-based model of care to community-based care under the Assertive Outreach Service. His Lordship held that viewed as a whole, the course of treatment should be seen as a continuing responsive programme, during which the need for treatment at the hospital and on leave was being constantly reassessed depending upon the circumstances, including the patient's response to the Assertive Outreach Service and the ward round. Until such time as the transition was complete, the element of treatment at hospital remained a significant part of the whole (para.44). His Lordship said at para.46:

"It is clear to me that the [RC] was engaged in a delicate balancing exercise by which she was, with as light a touch as she could, encouraging progress to discharge. Her purpose was to break the persistent historical cycle of admission, serious relapse and readmission. It may be in the closing stages of the treatment in hospital her grasp on the [patient] was gossamer thin, but to view that grasp as insignificant is, in my view, to misunderstand the evidence."

His Lordship commented, at para.48, that the patient's "knowledge of the [RC's] powers was a significant element in her willingness to accept the treatment plan".

The *Epsom, DR* and *CS* cases are also considered in the notes on s.72(1)(b)(i) under "Appropriate for him to be liable to be detained in a hospital for medical treatment".

Paragraph (a)

1–319   MENTAL DISORDER.   A patient's learning disability must be associated with abnormally aggressive or seriously irresponsible conduct (s.1(2A), (2B)).

APPROPRIATE FOR HIM TO RECEIVE MEDICAL TREATMENT IN A HOSPITAL.   See *(R. (on the application of DR) v Mersey Care Trust*, above. As this provision refers to *a* hospital rather than *the* hospital, this provision can be satisfied where the patient is receiving treatment for a mental disorder at a hospital where he is required to be as a condition of leave of absence.

Paragraph (c)

1–320   HEALTH OR SAFETY OF THE PATIENT OR FOR THE PROTECTION OF OTHER PERSONS.   See the notes on s.3(2)(c).

UNLESS HE CONTINUES TO BE DETAINED.   This term means "unless he continues to be liable to be detained" and not "unless he continues actually to be detained". This ground can therefore be satisfied in respect of a patient who has been granted leave of absence under s.17: see the *Barking* case, above.

This ground could be satisfied in relation to a potentially dangerous patient who is compliant with medication and who is willing to remain in hospital as an informal patient. This is because an essential element of the patient's treatment is his preparation for eventual discharge from the hospital. A key element of such preparation is the granting of leave of absence to the patient. Given that the patient would pose a potential risk to the public, it would not be appropriate to allow the patient to leave the hospital in the absence of a mechanism that would enable staff to require the patient to return to the hospital should he exhibit a reluctance to do so. Section 17 provides such a mechanism. This ground is therefore satisfied because an essential element of the patient's treatment programme, the testing out of his readiness for discharge, can only be put in place if he were a detained patient who could be granted leave under s.17.

Paragraph (d)

1–321   See the note on s.3(2)(d).

Subsection (5)

1–322   ONE OR MORE OTHER PERSONS.   Who could belong to the same profession as the RC.

PROFESSIONALLY CONCERNED.   In respect of a patient who is being treated in hospital, it is not sufficient for the consultee merely to be working on the ward where the patient is being treated; a particular involvement with the patient's treatment is required.

Subsection (5A)

1–323   This subsection, which is considered in the *Code of Practice* at paras 32.4 to 32.9, requires the RC who is renewing the detention of the patient to obtain a written statement from a person from another profession who has been professionally concerned with the patient's treatment that states that she agrees that the conditions of renewal are satisfied. The statement must be in the form set out in Pt 2 of Form H5: see reg.13(2) of the English Regulations (in Wales, Part 2 of Form HO15: see reg.5 of the Welsh

Regulations). Subsection (5) requires the RC to consult at least one other person from the multidisciplinary team before she furnishes the renewal report and it is likely that this person will also provide the written statement as long as she comes from a different professional group from the RC. Paragraph 32.9 of the *Code of Practice* states:

"Unless there are exceptional circumstances, the decision of the identified second professional should be accepted, even if the responsible clinician does not agree with it, and documented in the patient's notes including the reasons for the disagreement. If, in exceptional circumstances, it is decided that the agreement of a different second professional should be sought, this should be fully documented and the decision should be drawn to the attention of the hospital managers if, as a result, a renewal report is made."

This paragraph does not reflect the wording of this subsection and it is submitted that in the event of the second professional deciding that the grounds for renewal are not satisfied, the agreement of another second professional could be sought even if there are no "exceptional circumstances".

Subsection (6)

This subsection, together with subss.(7) and (8), provide for the patient's appropriate **1–324** practitioner to renew the authority for guardianship. "Appropriate practitioner" is defined in s.34(1). The period of guardianship can be extended under s.21. Paragraph 30.25 of the *Code of Practice* states:

"Regulations require private guardians to appoint a doctor as the patient's nominated medical attendant. It is the nominated medical attendant who must examine the patient during the last two months of each period of guardianship and decide whether to make a report extending the patient's guardianship. (Where the patient's guardian is the local authority itself, this is done by the responsible clinician authorised by the local authority.)"

APPROPRIATE PRACTITIONER. The guidance contained in para.39.17 of the *Code of Practice* that a person involved in making the decision whether to renew the guardianship of a patient "should not have any financial interest in the outcome of the decision" should not be followed in so far as it applies to the appropriate practitioner who is the only person who can trigger a renewal.

A REPORT. See reg.13 and Form G9 of the English Regulations and reg.12 and Form GU6 of the Welsh Regulations. Minor errors in the report can be corrected: see the note on "report" in subs.(3).

LOCAL SOCIAL SERVICES AUTHORITY. Which should give the patient a hearing to consider whether to exercise their power of discharge under s.23 unless he does not wish to contest the renewal. The local authority should require the care professional who has lead responsibility for the patient's welfare to provide a report on the patient's response to being subject to guardianship.

[Community treatment period

20A.—(1) Subject to the provisions of this Part of this Act, a community treat- **1–325** ment order shall cease to be in force on expiry of the period of six months beginning with the day on which it was made.

(2) That period is referred to in this Act as "the community treatment period".

(3) The community treatment period may, unless the order has previously ceased to be in force, be extended—

(a) from its expiration for a period of six months;

(b) from the expiration of any period of extension under paragraph (a) above for a further period of one year, and so on for periods of one year at a time.

(4) Within the period of two months ending on the day on which the order would cease to be in force in default of an extension under this section, it shall be the duty of the responsible clinician—

(a) to examine the patient; and

(b) if it appears to him that the conditions set out in subsection (6) below are satisfied and if a statement under subsection (8) below is made, to furnish to the managers of the responsible hospital a report to that effect in the pre-scribed form.

(5) Where such a report is furnished in respect of the patient, the managers shall, unless they discharge him under section 23 below, cause him to be informed.

(6) The conditions referred to in subsection (4) above are that—

(a) the patient is suffering from mental disorder of a nature or degree which makes it appropriate for him to receive medical treatment;

(b) it is necessary for his health or safety or for the protection of other persons that he should receive such treatment;

(c) subject to his continuing to be liable to be recalled as mentioned in para-graph (d) below, such treatment can be provided without his being detained in a hospital;

(d) it is necessary that the responsible clinician should continue to be able to exercise the power under section 17E(1) above to recall the patient to hos-pital; and

(e) appropriate medical treatment is available for him.

(7) In determining whether the criterion in subsection (6)(d) above is met, the responsible clinician shall, in particular, consider, having regard to the patient's history of mental disorder and any other relevant factors, what risk there would be of a deterioration of the patient's condition if he were to continue not to be detained in a hospital (as a result, for example, of his refusing or neglecting to receive the medical treatment he requires for his mental disorder).

(8) The statement referred to in subsection (4) above is a statement in writing by an approved mental health professional—

(a) that it appears to him that the conditions set out in subsection (6) above are satisfied; and

(b) that it is appropriate to extend the community treatment period.

(9) Before furnishing a report under subsection (4) above the responsible clin-ician shall consult one or more other persons who have been professionally concerned with the patient's medical treatment.

(10) Where a report is duly furnished under subsection (4) above, the com-munity treatment period shall be thereby extended for the period prescribed in that case by subsection (3) above.]

AMENDMENT
This section was inserted by the Mental Health Act 2007 s.20(3).

DEFINITIONS
1–326   community treatment order: ss.17A(7), 145(1).
responsible clinician: s.34(1).
the managers: s.145(1).

appropriate medical treatment: ss.3(4), 145(1AB).
hospital: ss.34(2), 145(1).
responsible hospital: ss.17A(7), 145(1).
mental disorder: ss.1, 145(1).
medical treatment: s.145(1), (4).
approved mental health practitioner: s.145(1), (1AC).

GENERAL NOTE

This section provides that a community treatment order (CTO) lasts for an initial period **1–327** of six months from the date when the order was made (subs.(1)). This period is referred to as "the community treatment period" (subs.(2)). The community treatment period can be extended for a further period of six months and, following that, it can be extended for further periods of one year at a time (subs.(3)). The community period is extended from the date when it would otherwise expire, and not from the date of the report furnished under subs.(4)(b). If the community treatment period is not extended, the CTO shall cease to have effect (s.20B).

In order to renew the community treatment period, the patient's responsible clinician (RC) must examine the patient in the two months preceding the expiry date, and send a report to the hospital managers confirming that the conditions set out in subs.(6) are satisfied (subs.(4)). If the patient does not attend for examination voluntarily, the RC may recall him to hospital for this purpose: see ss.17B(3)(a) and 17E(2). Prior to sending the report, the RC must obtain a written statement from an AMHP confirming that (a) the conditions set out in subs.(6) are satisfied, and (b) it is appropriate to extend the community treatment period (subs.(8)). Before the report is sent, the RC must have consulted with one or more people who have been professionally concerned with the patient's medical treatment (subs.(9)). On receiving the report, the hospital managers must consider whether they should exercise their power under s.23 to discharge the patient from the CTO. If they decide not to discharge the patient, he must be informed that the CTO has been extended for the relevant period (subs.(5)). For the responsibility to inform the patient's nearest relative if the patient's period of community treatment is extended under this section, see reg.26(1)(e) of the English Regulations and reg.22(1)(a) of the Welsh Regulations.

This section applies without modification to patients who have been made subject to hospital orders (Sch.1, Pt 1, para.1).

Applications to the First-tier Tribunal (Mental Health) or the Mental Health Review Tribunal for Wales

The patient's right to apply to a tribunal arises from the date of the renewal of the CTO **1–328** (s.66(1)(fza), (2)(fza)).

Code of Practice

Guidance on the extension of the community treatment period is contained in Ch.32 at **1–329** paras 32.11 to 32.16.

Subsection (1)

BEGINNING WITH. Means "including" (*Zoan v Rouamba* [2000] 2 All E.R. 620 CA). **1–330**

DAY ON WHICH IT WAS MADE. When the patient's RC signs and dates Part 3 of Form CTO1, the RC is asserting that she is exercising powers under s.17A to make a CTO and that the CTO will be effective from a specified date. When is the CTO "made" for the purposes of the Act? Is it the date of the RC's signature or the date when the CTO becomes effective? Although the wording of the Form does not provide a straightforward answer to this question, it is suggested that the *Code of Practice* is correct when it states, at para.29.26, that the relevant date is the date when the order becomes effective.

Subsection (4)

1–331   The RC's report provides authority for the patient's continued period on a CTO, even if the hospital managers have not yet considered the report: see para.38.14 of the *Code of Practice*.

EXAMINE THE PATIENT.   See the note on this phrase in s.20(3).

PRESCRIBED FORM.   Form CTO7: see reg.13 of the English Regulations (in Wales, Form CP3: see reg.17 of the Welsh Regulations). A Form CTO7 or Form CP3 which is defective because of a minor error or slip of the pen would not render the renewal unlawful and such errors may be corrected and initialled even though the rectification procedure in s.15 does not apply to this section. If the form is fundamentally defective in some way, for example it was signed by a person who is not the patient's RC, the renewal would be invalid and the patient would no longer be subject to the CTO.

Subsection (5)

1–332   In order to consider whether they should exercise their power of discharge under s.23(2)(a), the managers must meet as a panel of at least three members (s.23(4)).

Subsection (6)

1–333   These criteria essentially state that the patient continues to be detainable under s.3 (including the requirement that a patient's learning disability continues to be associated with abnormally aggressive or seriously irresponsible conduct), but can be treated in the community if he is subject to a power of recall. When determining whether RC should be able to exercise the power of recall, the factors set out in subs.(7) should be considered.

If during a review of the CTO, the RC concludes that the conditions for extending the CTO do not apply, the RC should use the power under s.23 to discharge the CTO.

Paragraphs (a), (b), (e)

1–334   See the notes to s.3(2)(a), (c) and (d).

Subsection (7)

1–335   See the note on s.17A(6).

Subsection (8)

1–336   Paragraph 32.19 of the *Code of Practice* states:

"[The AMHP who provides the statement] does not have to be the same AMHP who originally agreed that the patient should become a CTO patient. It may (but need not) be an AMHP who is already involved in the patient's care and treatment. It can be an AMHP acting on behalf of any willing local authority. If no other local authority is willing, responsibility for ensuring that an AMHP considers the case should lie with the local authority which is responsible under section 117 for the patient's after-care."

Depending on the circumstances, it might be more appropriate for the default position to be for an AMHP of the local authority for the area where the patient is currently located to perform the role. This approach would be consistent with the duty placed on local authorities by s.13(1).

There is no requirement for the AMHP to interview the patient prior to signing the statement which is made in Part 2 of Form CTO7 or, in Wales, Form CP3.

Subsection (9)

1–337   OTHER PERSONS.   It is submitted that the intention of Parliament is that the AMHP who provided the statement required by subs.(8) cannot be the consultee under this provision because the consultation would be a pointless exercise in that the AMHP will have already stated that the renewal is "appropriate" (subs.8(b)). In any event, the AMHP cannot be the consultee unless she has been professionally concerned with the patient's medical treatment.

[Effect of expiry of community treatment order

20B.—(1) A community patient shall be deemed to be discharged absolutely **1–338** from liability to recall under this Part of this Act, and the application for admission for treatment cease to have effect, on expiry of the community treatment order, if the order has not previously ceased to be in force.

(2) For the purposes of subsection (1) above, a community treatment order expires on expiry of the community treatment period as extended under this Part of this Act, but this is subject to sections 21 and 22 below.]

AMENDMENT
This section was inserted by the Mental Health Act 2007 s.20(3).

DEFINITIONS
application for admission for treatment: ss.3(1), 145(1).   **1–339**
community patient: ss.17A(7), 145(1).
community treatment order: ss.17A(7), 145(1).
community treatment period; ss.20A(1),(2), 145(1).

GENERAL NOTE
If a CTO expires, this section provides that: (1) the patient is no longer subject to the **1–340** power of recall; and (2) the application for admission for treatment (or its equivalent under Part III) ceases to have effect. In determining whether the CTO has expired, account must be taken of the fact that the community treatment period might have been extended by the provisions of s.21, which apply to patients who are absent without leave, or of s.22, which apply if the patient has been sentenced, or committed or remanded to custody by a court.

The hospital managers should ensure that the patient and, unless he has indicated otherwise, his nearest relative are informed of the ending of the CTO.

This section applies to patients who have been made subject to hospital orders with the modification set out in para.6A of Sch.1 (Sch.1, Pt 1, para.2).

[Special provisions as to patients absent without leave

21.—(1) Where a patient is absent without leave—   **1–341**
 (a) on the day on which (apart from this section) he would cease to be liable to be detained or subject to guardianship under this Part of this Act [or, in the case of a community patient, the community treatment order would cease to be in force]; or
 (b) within the period of one week ending with that day,
he shall not cease to be so liable or subject [, or the order shall not cease to be in force,] until the relevant time.

(2) For the purposes of subsection (1) above the relevant time—
 (a) where the patient is taken into custody under section 18 above, is the end of the period of one week beginning with the day on which he is returned to the hospital or place where he ought to be;
 (b) where the patient returns himself to the hospital or place where he ought to be within the period during which he can be taken into custody under section 18 above, is the end of the period of one week beginning with the day on which he so returns himself; and

(c) otherwise, is the end of the period during which he can be taken into custody under section 18 above.]

[(3) Where a patient is absent without leave on the day on which (apart from this section) the managers would be required under section 68 below to refer the patient's case to [the appropriate tribunal], that requirement shall not apply unless and until—

(a) the patient is taken into custody under section 18 above and returned to the hospital where he ought to be; or

(b) the patient returns himself to the hospital where he ought to be within the period during which he can be taken into custody under section 18 above.]

[(4) Where a community patient is absent without leave on the day on which (apart from this section) the 72-hour period mentioned in section 17F above would expire, that period shall not expire until the end of the period of 72 hours beginning with the time when—

(a) the patient is taken into custody under section 18 above and returned to the hospital where he ought to be; or

(b) the patient returns himself to the hospital where he ought to be within the period during which he can be taken into custody under section 18 above.

(5) Any reference in this section, or in sections 21A to 22 below, to the time when a community treatment order would cease, or would have ceased, to be in force shall be construed as a reference to the time when it would cease, or would have ceased, to be in force by reason only of the passage of time.]

AMENDMENTS

This section was substituted by the Mental Health (Patients in the Community) Act 1995 s.2(2). The amendments to it were made by the Mental Health Act 2007 ss.32(4), 37(2), Sch.3 para.6. The reference to the appropriate tribunal in subs.(3) was substituted by SI 2008/2883 art.9, Sch.3 para.40.

DEFINITIONS

1–342   patient: s.145(1).
absent without leave: ss.18(6), 145(1).
hospital: ss.34(2), 145(1).
appropriate practitioner: s.34(1).
community patient: ss.17A(7), 145(1).
community treatment order: ss.17A(7), 145(1).
the managers: s.145(1).
the appropriate tribunal: ss.66(4), 145(1).

GENERAL NOTE

1–343   This section, in subss.(1), (2) and (5), extends the authority for detention, guardianship or supervised community treatment of a patient who is absent without leave when or during the week before the detention or guardianship expires or the community treatment order (CTO) would cease to be in force. The detention or guardianship is extended, or the CTO will not cease to be in force, for up to one week after the patient's return to hospital or place where he ought to be. This period enables the patient to be examined and a renewal report made if appropriate. If the patient is returned within 28 days of absconding, s.21A applies for the purposes of a renewal. Section 21B applies if the patient is returned more than 28 days after absconding. If patients have not been taken into custody, or have not come voluntarily to the hospital or place where they ought to be, before the end of the period during which they can be taken into custody under s.18, no renewal can take place.

This section also postpones the requirement for hospital managers to refer a patient's case to the tribunal if the patient is absent without leave (subs.(3)) and extends the 72 hour period mentioned in s.17F if the patient is absent without leave at the end of that period (subs.(4)).

This section applies to patients who have been placed under hospital or guardianship orders by a court (Sch.1 para.1).

Subsection (1)

A PATIENT.   Although it has been said that this section does not apply to patients who are **1–344** detained under s.2, the wording of this subsection does not have such an effect. It is therefore the case that if a s.2 patient is absent without leave during the final week of detention, the authority to detain can be extended for a week beginning with the day of recapture if he is recaptured before the expiration of the 28 day period provided for in s.2(4).

THE COMMUNITY TREATMENT ORDER WOULD CEASE TO BE IN FORCE.   See subs.(5).

Subsection (2)

RELEVANT TIME.   This allows for the patient's appropriate practitioner to examine the **1–345** patient and decide whether she wishes to make a report renewing the detention or guardianship under s.20(3) or 20(6), or extending the CTO under s.20A(4). The making of such a report is authorised by s.21A(2) (or s.21A(4) for a CTO) and the date of the renewal is provided for in s.21A(3) (or s.21A(5) for a CTO). This provision also allows time for professionals to consider the appropriateness of making an application under s.3 in respect of a patient who has been detained under s.2.

TAKEN INTO CUSTODY UNDER SECTION 18.   Although a s.2 patient cannot be taken into custody after the section expires (s.18(5)), a s.3 or guardianship patient can be taken into custody long after the detention or guardianship has expired (s.18(4)).

Subsection (3)

If the hospital managers are due to refer the patient to a tribunal under s.68 at the time **1–346** when he is absent without leave, this provision requires the managers to postpone the referral until the patient either returns or is returned to the hospital where he ought to be.

Subsection (4)

If a CTO patient is absent without leave on the day when the 72-hour period provided for **1–347** in s.17F would expire, the period will start again on the patient's return to the hospital either voluntarily or under compulsion.

[Patients who are taken into custody or return within 28 days

21A.—(1) This section applies where a patient who is absent without leave is **1–348** taken into custody under section 18 above, or returns himself to the hospital or place where he ought to be, not later than the end of the period of 28 days beginning with the first day of his absence without leave.

(2) Where the period for which the patient is liable to be detained or subject to guardianship is extended by section 21 above, any examination and report to be made and furnished in respect of the patient under section 20(3) or (6) above may be made and furnished within the period as so extended.

(3) Where the authority for the detention or guardianship of the patient is renewed by virtue of subsection (2) above after the day on which (apart from section 21 above) that authority would have expired, the renewal shall take effect as from that day.]

[(4) In the case of a community patient, where the period for which the community treatment order is in force is extended by section 21 above, any examination and report to be made and furnished in respect of the patient under section 20A(4) above may be made and furnished within the period as so extended.

(5) Where the community treatment period is extended by virtue of subsection (4) above after the day on which (apart from section 21 above) the order would have ceased to be in force, the extension shall take effect as from that day.]

AMENDMENTS

This section was substituted by the Mental Health (Patients in the Community) Act 1995 s.2(2). Subsections (4) and (5) were inserted by the Mental Health Act 2007 s.32(4), Sch.3 para.7.

DEFINITIONS

1–349   patient: s.145(1).
absent without leave: s.18(6), 145(1).
hospital: ss.34(2), 145(1).
appropriate practitioner: s.34(1).
community patient: ss.17A(7), 145(1).
community treatment order: ss.17A(7), 145(1).
community treatment period: ss.20A(1)(2), 145(1).

GENERAL NOTE

1–350   If a s.3 or guardianship patient who has absconded returns to the hospital or place where he is required to be not more than 28 days after absconding, or is taken into custody during that period, subss.(1) to (3) enable the patient's appropriate practitioner (for detained patients, this will be the patient's responsible clinician (RC) to renew the detention or guardianship under s.20 without further formality. If the provisions of s.21 apply, the authority to detain the patient (or the authority for guardianship) is extended for up to a week from the date of his return to enable the formalities of renewal to be completed.

If a community patient who has gone absent without leave returns, or is returned, to the hospital to which he has been recalled under s.17E within 28 days of the first day of his absence, subss.(4) and (5) give the patient's RC a week after the patient's return to carry out the examination required by s.20A(4) and make her report for the extension of the CTO, if the CTO would have otherwise expired. If a patient is absent without leave on the day when the 72-hour period provided for in s.17F(6) would expire, the period will start again on the patient's return to the hospital either voluntarily or under compulsion: see s.21(4).

If the patient returns or is returned to the hospital more that 28 days after the date of the absconding, the provisions of s.21B apply.

This section applies without modification to patients who have been made subject to hospital or guardianship orders by a court under s.37 (Sch.1 Pt 1 para.1).

Subsection (1)

1–351   BEGINNING WITH.   Including the first day of his absence without leave (*Zoan v Rouamba* [2000] 2 All E.R. 620 CA).

Subsection (3)

1–352   RENEWAL.   The renewal has effect from the date when the authority for detention or guardianship would have expired if it had not been extended by s.21.

Subsection (5)

Under this provision, a CTO which has been extended under subs.(4) takes effect from **1–353** the day when it would have ceased to be in force if it has not been extended by s.21.

Ceased to be in force.   See s.21(5).

[Patients who are taken into custody or return after more than 28 days

21B.—(1) This section applies where a patient who is absent without leave is **1–354** taken into custody under section 18 above, or returns himself to the hospital or place where he ought to be, later than the end of the period of 28 days beginning with the first day of his absence without leave.

(2) It shall be the duty of the [appropriate practitioner], within the period of one week beginning with the day on which the patient is returned or returns himself to the hospital or place where he ought to be [(his "return day")]—

(a) to examine the patient; and

(b) if it appears to him that the relevant conditions are satisfied, to furnish to the appropriate body a report to that effect in the prescribed form;

and where such a report is furnished in respect of the patient the appropriate body shall cause him to be informed.

(3) Where the patient is liable to be detained [or is a community patient] (as opposed to subject to guardianship), the [appropriate practitioner] shall, before furnishing a report under subsection (2) above, consult—

(a) one or more other persons who have been professionally concerned with the patient's medical treatment; and

(b) an [approved mental health professional].

[(4) Where—

(a) the patient would (apart from any renewal of the authority for his detention or guardianship on or after his return day) be liable to be detained or subject to guardianship after the end of the period of one week beginning with that day; or

(b) in the case of a community patient, the community treatment order would (apart from any extension of the community treatment period on or after that day) be in force after the end of that period, he shall cease to be so liable or subject, or the community treatment period shall be deemed to expire, at the end of that period unless a report is duly furnished in respect of him under subsection (2) above.]

[(4A) If, in the case of a community patient, the community treatment order is revoked under section 17F above during the period of one week beginning with his return day—

(a) subsections (2) and (4) above shall not apply; and

(b) any report already furnished in respect of him under subsection (2) above shall be of no effect.]

(5) Where the patient would (apart from section 21 above) have ceased to be liable to be detained or subject to guardianship on or before the day on which a report is duly furnished in respect of him under subsection (2) above, the report shall renew the authority for his detention or guardianship for the period prescribed in that case by section 20(2) above.

(6) Where the authority for the detention or guardianship of the patient is renewed by virtue of subsection (5) above—

(a) the renewal shall take effect as from the day on which (apart from section 21 above and that subsection) the authority would have expired; and

(b) if (apart from this paragraph) the renewed authority would expire on or before the day on which the report is furnished, the report shall further renew the authority, as from the day on which it would expire, for the period prescribed in that case by section 20(2) above.

[(6A) In the case of a community patient, where the community treatment order would (apart from section 21 above) have ceased to be in force on or before the day on which a report is duly furnished in respect of him under subsection (2) above, the report shall extend the community treatment period for the period pre-scribed in that case by section 20A(3) above.

(6B) Where the community treatment period is extended by virtue of subsec-tion (6A) above—

(a) the extension shall take effect as from the day on which (apart from section 21 above and that subsection) the order would have ceased to be in force; and

(b) if (apart from this paragraph) the period as so extended would expire on or before the day on which the report is furnished, the report shall further extend that period, as from the day on which it would expire, for the period prescribed in that case by section 20A(3) above.]

(7) Where the authority for the detention or guardianship of the patient would expire within the period of two months beginning with the day on which a report is duly furnished in respect of him under subsection (2) above, the report shall, if it so provides, have effect also as a report duly furnished under section 20(3) or (6) above; and the reference in this subsection to authority includes any authority renewed under subsection (5) above by the report.

[(7A) In the case of a community patient, where the community treatment order would (taking account of any extension under subsection (6A) above) cease to be in force within the period of two months beginning with the day on which a report is duly furnished in respect of him under subsection (2) above, the report shall, if it so provides, have effect also as a report duly furnished under section 20A(4) above.]

(8) [. . .]

(9) [. . .]

(10) In this section—

[. . .]

["the appropriate body" means—

(a) in relation to a patient who is liable to be detained in a hospital, the managers of the hospital;

(b) in relation to a patient who is subject to guardianship, the responsible local social services authority;

(c) in relation to a community patient, the managers of the responsible hos-pital; and

["the relevant conditions" means—

(a) in relation to a patient who is liable to be detained in a hospital, the con-ditions set out in subsection (4) of section 20 above;

(b) in relation to a patient who is subject to guardianship, the conditions set out in subsection (7) of that section;

(c) in relation to a community patient, the conditions set out in section 20A(6) above.]]

AMENDMENTS

This section was substituted by the Mental Health (Patients in the Community) Act 1995 s.2(2). The amendments to it were made by the Mental Health Act 2007 ss.9(5), 21, 32(4), 55, Sch.2 para.7, Sch.3 para.8, Sch.11 Pts 1 and 3.

DEFINITIONS

1–355

patient: s.145(1).
absent without leave: ss.18(6), 145(1).
hospital: ss.34(2), 145(1).
community patient: ss.17A(7), 145(1).
approved mental health professional: s.145(1), (1AC).
community treatment order: ss.17A(7), 145(1).
community treatment period: ss.20A(1),(2), 145(1).
responsible hospital: ss.17A, 145(1).
responsible local social services authority: s.34(3).
local social services authority: s.145(1).
appropriate practitioner: s.34(1).

GENERAL NOTE

If patients have not been taken into custody, or have not come voluntarily to the hospital **1–356** or place where they ought to be, before the end of the period during which they can be taken into custody under s.18, no renewal can take place under this section.

If a s.3 or guardianship patient who has absconded is taken into custody, or returns to the hospital or place where he is required to be, later than 28 days after absconding, the patient's appropriate practitioner (for detained patients, this will be the patient's reponsible clinician (RC) must comply with the provisions of this section by examining the patient and reporting to the hospital or local social services authority within a week beginning with the date of the patient's return (the "return date") if the patient's detention or guardianship is to be renewed under s.20 (subss.(2)). This must be done however long remains until the patient's detention next needs to be renewed (Reference Guide, para.25.42). A failure by the practitioner to complete the relevant statutory form within that week will result in the automatic expiry of the detention or guardianship. If the provisions of s.21 apply, the authority to detain the patient (or the authority for guardianship) is extended for up to a week from the return date. The renewal takes effect from the day specified in subs.(6). If the patient's detention or guardianship would expire within two months of the subs.(2) report being furnished, the provisions of subs.(7) apply: see the notes on subss.(5) to (7).

If a community patient who has been absent without leave returns, or is returned, to the hospital to which he has been recalled under s.17E more than 28 days after the patient was first absent without leave, this section provides the patient's RC with a week after the day of patient's return (the "return date") to examine the patient, and, if the RC decides that the patient meets the criteria for a community treatment order (CTO), prepare for the hospital managers a report extending the CTO (subs.(2)). However, if the CTO is revoked under s.17F during that week, the report will have no effect (subs.(4A)). A failure by the RC to complete the relevant statutory form within a week of the patient's return will result in the automatic expiry of the CTO. If the CTO expired during the patient's absence, or had less than seven days to run on his return, s.21 extends it for up to a week from the return date. If the patient is absent without leave on the day when the 72-hour period provided for in s.17F(6) would expire, the period will start again on the patient's return to the hospital either voluntarily or under compulsion: see s.21(4).

Where the patient is liable to be detained or is a community patient, the RC must undertake the consultation process identified in subs.(3) before furnishing the report under subs.(2) to the hospital managers.

If a patient's detention or guardianship would remain in force a week after the return date, the detention or guardianship will lapse in the absence of a report being furnished under subs.(2). The same applies to a CTO which would be in force at the end of that period (subs.(4)).

Where a CTO would (apart from s.21) have expired before the day on which a report is furnished under subs.(2), the report will extend the community treatment period prescribed in s.20A(2) (subs.(6A). The extension will take effect from the day when order would have expired (subs.(6B)(a)), but if that period would have expired before the subs.(2) report is furnished, there shall be a further extension of the relevant s.20A(3) period (subs.(6B)(b)). If the CTO would expire (taking into account any extension under subs.(6A)) within two months of the furnishing of the report under subs.(2), the report shall also be treated as a s.20A(4) report (subs.(7A)). This avoids the need for two reports, one under subs.(2) and the other under s.20A(4), extending the CTO.

For the responsibility to inform the patient's nearest relative if the patient's detention or guardianship is renewed under subs.(7), or is renewed retrospectively under subss.(5) and (6), or if the patient's period of community treatment is extended under subs.(7A), or is extended retrospectively under subss.(6A) and (6B), see reg.26 of the English Regulations and regs 8, 15 and 22 of the Welsh Regulations.

This section applies without modification to patients who have been made subject to hospital or guardianship orders by a court under s.37 (Sch.1 Pt 1 para.1). It does not apply to restricted patients (ibid, Pt II).

Applications to the First-tier Tribunal (Mental Health) or the Mental Health Review Tribunal for Wales

1–357   The patient's right to apply to a tribunal arises from the date of the renewal of the detention, guardianship or the CTO (s.66(1)(fa)(faa), (2)(f)(fza)).

Human Rights Act 1998

1–358   See the note on s.18 under this heading.

Subsection (1)

1–359   BEGINNING WITH.   See the note on s.21(1).

Subsection (2)

1–360   RELEVANT CONDITIONS, APPROPRIATE BODY.   See subs.(10).

FURNISH TO THE APPROPRIATE BODY.   Even if the unexpired period of detention or guardianship is longer than the one week provided for in this subsection.

In the Scottish case of *Milborrow, Applicant*, 1996 S.C.L.R. 315, Sh. Ct, it was held that a report is "furnished" to the hospital managers when it is committed to the internal mailing system operated by those managers: see the note on s.5(2).

PRESCRIBED FORM.   Form H6 for a patient who is liable to be detained, Form G10 for a patient who is subject to guardianship and Form CTO8 for a community patient: see reg.14 of the English Regulations. In Wales, the forms are: Form CP4 for a patient who is liable to be detained, Form GU7 for a patient who is subject to guardianship and Form CP4 for a community patient: see regs 13 and 18 of the Welsh Regulations.

Subsection (3)

1–361   Although the appropriate practitioner, as defined in s.34(1), must take the views expressed by the professionals into account before making a report under subs.(2), she is not obliged to obtain their agreement to this action.

PROFESSIONAL CONCERNED WITH PATIENT'S MEDICAL TREATMENT. The professional could be concerned with the patient's medical treatment in the community.

Subsection (4A)

Although there is a period of a week within which the patient's CTO can be renewed, the **1–362** period during which the patient can be detained in the hospital is limited to the 72 hour period provided for in s.17F(6).

Subsection (5)

If a patient's liability to be detained or to be subject to guardianship would have expired **1–363** before the end of the one week period provided for in subs.(2), and a report is furnished under that provision, the period of renewal shall be the period provided for in s.20(2). The date of the renewal is established by subs.(6).

Subsection (6)

This subsection provides that where the authority for detention or guardianship of a **1–364** patient has been renewed in the circumstances set out in subs.(5), the renewal has effect from the day on which the detention or guardianship would have expired. If this renewed authority is due to expire before the day on which the report under subs.(2) is made, a further period of renewal for the prescribed period is authorised by the subs.(2) report.

Subsection (6A)

CEASED TO BE IN FORCE. See s.21(5). **1–365**

Subsection (7)

This provision avoids the need for two reports renewing a patient's detention or guar- **1–366** dianship, one under subs.(2) and the other under subs.20(3) or (6), if the authority for the patient's detention or guardianship would expire within two months of the report being made under subs.(2).

[Special provisions as to patients sentenced to imprisonment, etc.

22.—(1) If— **1–367**
    (a) a qualifying patient is detained in custody in pursuance of any sentence or order passed or made by a court in the United Kingdom (including an order committing or remanding him in custody); and
    (b) he is so detained for a period exceeding, or for successive periods exceeding in the aggregate, six months, the relevant application shall cease to have effect on expiry of that period.
  (2) A patient is a qualifying patient for the purposes of this section if—
    (a) he is liable to be detained by virtue of an application for admission for treatment;
    (b) he is subject to guardianship by virtue of a guardianship application; or
    (c) he is a community patient.
  (3) "The relevant application", in relation to a qualifying patient, means—
    (a) in the case of a patient who is subject to guardianship, the guardianship application in respect of him;
    (b) in any other case, the application for admission for treatment in respect of him.
  (4) The remaining subsections of this section shall apply if a qualifying patient is detained in custody as mentioned in subsection (1)(a) above but for a period not exceeding, or for successive periods not exceeding in the aggregate, six months.
  (5) If apart from this subsection—

(a) the patient would have ceased to be liable to be detained or subject to guardianship by virtue of the relevant application on or before the day on which he is discharged from custody; or

(b) in the case of a community patient, the community treatment order would have ceased to be in force on or before that day, he shall not cease and shall be deemed not to have ceased to be so liable or subject, or the order shall not cease and shall be deemed not to have ceased to be in force, until the end of that day.

(6) In any case (except as provided in subsection (8) below), sections 18, 21 and 21A above shall apply in relation to the patient as if he had absented himself without leave on that day.

(7) In its application by virtue of subsection (6) above section 18 above shall have effect as if—

(a) in subsection (4) for the words from "later of" to the end there were substituted "end of the period of 28 days beginning with the first day of his absence without leave"; and

(b) subsections (4A) and (4B) were omitted.

(8) In relation to a community patient who was not recalled to hospital under section 17E above at the time when his detention in custody began—

(a) section 18 above shall not apply; but

(b) sections 21 and 21A above shall apply as if he had absented himself without leave on the day on which he is discharged from custody and had returned himself as provided in those sections on the last day of the period of 28 days beginning with that day.]

AMENDMENT

This Section was substituted by the Mental Health Act 2007 s.32(4), Sch.3 para.9.

DEFINITIONS

1–368

patient: s.145(1).
application for admission for treatment: ss.3, 145(1).
guardianship application: s.7(1).
community patient: ss.17A(7), 145(1).
community treatment order: ss.17A(7), 145(1).
absent without leave: ss.18(6), 145(1).
hospital: s.145(1).

GENERAL NOTE

1–369

This section provides that if a patient who is the subject of an application for treatment, a guardianship application or a community treatment order (CTO) is sentenced, or committed or remanded to custody by a court, the application will cease to have effect if the period spent in custody lasts for more than six months. The CTO will end due to the fact that the s.3 application has ceased to have effect (s.17C(c)). If the patient is detained in custody for less than six months and would, in the ordinary course of events, have ceased to be liable to be detained for treatment or subject to guardianship or to a CTO prior to his discharge from custody, subss.(4) to (8) provide that he does not cease to be so liable or subject until end of the day on which he is discharged, and for the purposes of ss.18, 21 and 21A of the Act he will be treated as if he had absconded himself without leave on that day, i.e. the patient can be taken into custody within 28 days of his release (s.18(4), as substituted by subs.(7) of this section) and there are seven days during which the application can be renewed (s.21) if it is due for renewal at that time. Subs.(8) applies to community patients who have not been recalled to hospital. If the renewal report is furnished after the expiration of the previous period of detention, guardianship or CTO, the report is deemed to have been furnished on the final day of that period (s.21A). The patient's RC can exercise the power of discharge under s.23 while the patient is in custody.

As this section is not listed in paras (a) to (c) of s.56(3), the consent to treatment provisions contained in Pt IV will continue to apply to the patient during the period spent in custody. Although it could be argued that the use of the term "patient" in s.56 indicates that Pt IV would not apply to persons detained in custody, "patient" is defined very broadly in s.145(1) as "a person suffering or appearing to suffer from mental disorder". It is also the case that s.56 does not require the patient to be detained in a hospital in order for the provision of Pt IV to apply: it requires the patient to be "liable to be detained". An interpretation that does not exclude the operation of the Act from prisons is consistent with the decision in *R. (on the application of the Howard League for Penal Reform) v Secretary of State for the Home Department* [2002] EWHC 2497 (Admin), where Munby J. held that the powers and duties which a local authority would otherwise owe to a child under the Children Act 1989 do not cease to be owed merely because the child is currently detained in a Young Offender Institution. His Lordship further held that the exercise of a local authority's functions under the 1989 Act take effect and operate subject to the necessary requirements of imprisonment. A Young Offender Institution is subject to the Secretary of State's control under the Prison Act 1952.

This section applies to patients who have been placed under hospital or guardianship orders by a court under s.37, with the modification that for references to an application for admission or a guardianship application there shall be substituted references to the order or direction under Pt III by virtue of which the patient is liable to be detained or subject to guardianship (Sch.1 Pt I paras 2, 7). For restricted patients the section applies with the modification that subss.(1) and (5) shall be omitted (Sch.1 Pt II paras 2, 6), i.e. the restriction order will not cease if the patient is detained in custody for more than six months.

Subsection (1)
QUALIFYING PATIENT.   See subs.(2).   **1–370**

UNITED KINGDOM.   This means Great Britain and Northern Ireland (Interpretation Act 1978 s.5, Sch.1).

RELEVANT APPLICATION.   See subs.(3).

Subsection (7)
The effect of this subsection was explained by the Parliamentary Under-Secretary of **1–371** State for Health, Baroness Cumberlege, during the passage of the Mental Health (Patients in the Community) Act 1995 (*Hansard*, HL, Vol.564, col.174):

"At present, section 22 of the Mental Health Act 1983 states that when a patient who has been subject to imprisonment is released, he should be treated as though he were absent without leave under section 18 of the 1983 Act. This is a legal device to provide a period of 28 days in which such patients could be returned to detention in hospital. However, as your Lordships know, clause 2 of this Bill [now s.18(4)] extends the period of time in which an absconding patient can be returned to hospital from 28 days to at least six months. An unintentional consequence of this is to extend the period of time within which a released prisoner could be returned to detention under the 1983 Act. I am sure your Lordships will agree that this is undesirable . . . The effect of the amendment, therefore, is to retain for the purposes of section 22 the period of 28 days within which a person who has been released from prison may be returned to hospital. This is followed by a period of seven days during which the responsible medical officer must examine the patient and determine whether his liability to detention should be renewed."

Subsections (7), (8)

1–372 BEGINNING WITH. Means "including" (*Zoan v Rouamba* [2000] 2 All E.R. 620 CA).

Discharge of patients

1–373 **23.**—(1) Subject to the provisions of this section and section 25 below, a patient who is for the time being liable to be detained or subject to guardianship under this Part of this Act shall cease to be so liable or subject if an order in writing discharging him [absolutely from detention or guardianship is made in accordance with this section].

[(1A) Subject to the provisions of this section and section 25 below, a community patient shall cease to be liable to recall under this Part of this Act, and the application for admission for treatment cease to have effect, if an order in writing discharging him from such liability is made in accordance with this section.

(1B) An order under subsection (1) or (1A) above shall be referred to in this Act as "an order for discharge".]

(2) An order for discharge may be made in respect of a patient—

(a) where the patient is liable to be detained in a hospital in pursuance of an application for admission for assessment or for treatment by the [responsible clinician], by the managers or by the nearest relative of the patient;

(b) where the patient is subject to guardianship, by the [responsible clinician], by the responsible local social services authority or by the nearest relative of the patient;

[(c) where the patient is a community patient, by the responsible clinician, by the managers of the responsible hospital or by the nearest relative of the patient.]

(3) [. . .]

[(3A) [. . .]]

(4) The powers conferred by this section on any authority, [trust][, board] [(other than an NHS foundation trust)][, board] or body of persons may be exercised [subject to subsection (5) below] by any three or more members of that authority [trust][, board] or body authorised by them in that behalf or by three or more members of a committee or sub-committee of that authority [trust][, board] or body which has been authorised by them in that behalf.

[(5) The reference in subsection (4) above to the members of an authority, trust[, board] or body or the members of a committee or sub-committee of an authority, trust[, board] or body,—

(a) in the case of [a [[Local Health Board] [or Special Health Authority] [. . .] or a committee or sub-committee of [a [[Local Health Board] [or Special Health Authority] [. . .]], is a reference only to the chairman of the authority[[. . .] or board] and [such members (of the authority [. . .] board, committee or sub-committee], as the case may be) as are not also officers of the authority[[. . .] or board], within the meaning of [the National Health Service Act 2006 or the National Health Service (Wales) Act 2006]; and

(b) in the case of a National Health Service trust or a committee or sub-committee of such a trust, is a reference only to the chairman of the trust and such directors or (in the case of a committee or sub-committee) members as are not also employees of the trust.]

[(6) The powers conferred by this section on any NHS foundation trust may be exercised by any three or more [persons authorised by the board of the trust in that behalf each of whom is neither an executive director of the board nor an employee of the trust.]

AMENDMENTS

The amendments to this section were made by the National Health Service and Community Care Act 1990 s.66(1), Sch.9 para.24(3), the Health Authorities Act 1995 s.2(1), Sch.1 para.107(2), the Health Act 1999 (Supplementary, Consequential, etc. Provisions) Order 2000 (SI 2000/90) Sch.1 para.13(4), the Care Standards Act 2000 s.116, Sch.4 para.9(2), the Health and Social Care (Community Health and Standards) Act 2003 s.34, Sch.4 para.53, the National Health Service (Consequential Provisions) Act 2006 s.2, Sch.1 para.65, the Mental Health Act 2007 ss.9(6), 32(4), 45(1), Sch.3 para.10, SI 2007/961 art.3, Sch. para.13(2), the Health and Social Care Act 2012 s.39, and the Health and Social Care Act 2012 Sch.5, para.26.

DEFINITIONS

1–374

patient: s.145(1).
community patient: ss.17A(7), 145(1).
application for admission for treatment: ss.3, 145(1).
the responsible hospital: ss.17A(7), 145(1).
hospital: ss.34(2), 145(1).
application for admission for assessment: ss.2, 145(1).
the managers: s.145(1).
nearest relative: ss.26(3), 145(1).
local social services authority: s.145(1).
responsible local social services authority: s.34(3).
registered establishment: ss.34(1), 145(1).
application for admission for treatment: ss.3, 145(1).
responsible clinician: s.34(1).
Local Health Board: s.145(1).
Special Health Authority: s.145(1).

GENERAL NOTE

This section provides for the absolute discharge of detained patients, patients who are **1–375** subject to guardianship and community patients to be ordered by the patient's responsible clinician (RC), the hospital managers (or the responsible local social services authority for guardianship patients) or the patient's nearest relative. It does not apply to patients who have been remanded to hospital by a court under ss.35 or 36, or who have been made subject to an interim hospital order under s.38. The discharge must be ordered: it cannot be effected by implication. In this section, the term "discharge" means discharge from detention, guardianship or from a community treatment order (CTO), not discharge from hospital.

If subsequent to being detained a mentally incapacitated patient becomes compliant to both detention and treatment, hospital managers and RCs should consider whether the patient should be detained under the deprivation of liberty safeguards contained in the Mental Capacity Act 2005 if such detention would represent the least restrictive option for the patient: see the note "The detention of compliant mentally incapable patients" in the General Note to this Part.

Section 2(1) of the Health and Safety at Work etc Act 1974 places a duty on every employer "to ensure, so far as is reasonably practicable, the health, safety and welfare at work of all his employees". Section 3(1) of that Act places employers under a similar duty with regard to persons who are not employees. A patient should therefore not be discharged in the absence of an up to date individual risk assessment.

The provisions of s.133 apply to a patient who is to be discharged under this section.

This section applies to patients who have been placed under hospital or guardianship orders made under s.37 with the modification that subs.(2) shall read as follows:

"(2) An order for discharge may be made in respect of a patient—

(a) where the patient is liable to be detained in a hospital in pursuance of an application for admission [...] for treatment by the [responsible clinician], by the managers [...],

(b) where the patient is subject to guardianship, by the [responsible clinician], by the responsible local social services authority [...],

(c) where the patient is a community patient, by the responsible clinician, by the managers of the responsible hospital [...]" (Sch.1 Pt I, para.8).

The effect of Sch.1, Pt 1 is that both the hospital managers and the RC have the power to discharge a hospital order patient during the first six months of his detention even though the patient cannot make an application to a tribunal during that period. The patient's nearest relative, who does not have the power to discharge a hospital order, can make an application to the tribunal under s.69(1).

This section also applies to restricted patients with the modification that subss.(1) and (2) shall read as follows:

"(1) Subject to the provisions of this section and section 25 below, a patient who is for the time being liable to be detained [...] under this Part of this Act shall cease to be so liable [...] if an order in writing discharging him from detention [...] (in this Act referred to as "an order for discharge") is made [with the consent of the Secretary of State] in accordance with this section.

(2) An order for discharge may be made in respect of a patient—

(a) where the patient is liable to be detained in a hospital in pursuance of an application for admission [...] for treatment by the [responsible clinician], by the managers [...];

(b) [...]." (Sch.1, Pt II, paras 2, 7.)

The Secretary of State has his own powers to discharge restricted patients under s.42(2).

Human Rights Act 1998

1–376   In *Winterwerp v Netherlands* (1979) 2 E.H.R.R. 387, the European Court of Human Rights held that the validity of the continued confinement of a mentally disordered person depends upon the persistence of such a disorder. In a subsequent decision of the Court, it was held that it does not automatically follow that a finding by an expert authority that the mental disorder which justified a patient's compulsory confinement no longer persists compels his immediate and unconditional release into the community (*Johnson v United Kingdom* (1999) 27 E.H.R.R. 296). It is therefore the case that if a patient who is deemed to pose a risk to the public is found no longer to be mentally disordered, discharge from detention can be delayed for a limited period until such time as appropriate after-care facilities are put in place. In *Johnson* the Court said, at para.63, that the authority "should be able to retain some measure of supervision over the progress of the person once he is released into the community and to that end make his discharge subject to conditions".

The question whether a decision not to discharge a patient because of a failure to put in place appropriate after-care facilities in the community violates art.5 of the European Convention on Human Rights (ECHR) is considered in the General Note to s.117 under this heading.

The persons and bodies who have the power to discharge the patient under this provision are "public authorities" for the purposes of s.6 of the 1998 Act.

In *MA v Secretary of State for Health* [2012] UKUT 474 (AAC), UT Judge Levenson held that the right of discharge conferred on a patient's nearest relative is a civil right for the purposes of art.6 of the ECHR.

When exercising their power to review the detention of a patient, the hospital managers are not a "court" for the purposes of art.5(4) of the ECHR. This is because the managers are one of the parties to the review (*De Wilde, Ooms and Versyp v Belgium (No.1)* (1979–80) 1 E.H.R.R. 373). The tribunal is the expert body established under the Act to consider applications made by patients for their discharge. It is the right to make an application to the tribunal, not the hospital managers, that satisfies the Government's obligation under art.5(4) to enable a patient to challenge the lawfulness of his detention.

Code of Practice
Guidance on the use of the RC's power of discharge is contained in Ch.32 at paras 32.17 **1–377** to 32.19. The exercise of the hospital managers' power of discharge is considered in Ch.38.

Subsection (1)
PATIENT. Although an order for the discharge of a restricted patient may be made under **1–378** this section, the discharge can only take place if the consent of the Secretary of State has been obtained: see the General Note, above.

ORDER IN WRITING. See reg.18 of the English Regulations and reg.7 of the Welsh Regulations.

DISCHARGING HIM ABSOLUTELY. The hospital managers do not have the power to order the conditional discharge of the patient. The 2008 edition of the *Code of Practice,* at para.31.38, stated that it would be lawful to order that the patient's unconditional discharge takes effect on a specified date in the near future. The accuracy of this statement is open to doubt for two reasons:

  (i) a deferred discharge is not an absolute discharge. If a patient is discharged absolutely, he has a right to leave hospital immediately; a patient who is given a deferred discharge has no such right; and
 (ii) the tribunal is provided with a specific power to order the deferred discharge in s.72(3). If Parliament was of the opinion that hospital managers have an implied power to order such a discharge, why was it felt necessary to provide the tribunal with a specific power?

If the hospital managers are concerned about the adequacy of the after-care services that will be available to the patient on discharge, they should adjourn the hearing and reconvene to a date when the relevant information should be available. If the hospital managers decide to defer the patient's discharge to a particular date, the patient would have to be discharged on that date even though the anticipated arrangements for his discharge had not been put in place. The current edition of the *Code*, which does not reproduce para.31.38, adopts the approach advocated here at para.38.40.

Subsection (1A)
Discharging the patient from a CTO has the automatic effect of also discharging the **1–379** underlying application or order.

Subsection (2)
In *R. v Riverside Mental Health Trust Ex p. Huzzey* (1998) 43 B.M.L.R. 167, Latham J. **1–380** identified the criteria that hospital managers must use when considering the continued detention of a s.3 patient where the nearest relative's application for discharge had been subject to a "barring report" made under s.25. His Lordship said:

"[S]ection 23 provides, *inter alia*, a general discretion in the managers to discharge a patient. No criteria are set out as to what should or should not be taken into account by managers when considering decision as to whether or not to discharge. The question of what are the relevant considerations has to be answered by looking at the general scheme of the Act. Clearly the criteria set out in section 3 are of fundamental importance. If the criteria for admission no longer exist, I cannot see how any decision by managers not to discharge could be other than perverse ... Section 23 implicitly recognises that managers have a discretion to discharge even if those criteria have been met. Where ... a nearest relative has sought to obtain a discharge order but has been confronted by a barring report [made under s.25], those facts must equally be relevant and material considerations. In my view, the managers are not only entitled to, but must, consider whether or not they are persuaded by the barring report that the patient, if discharged, would be likely to act in a manner dangerous to other persons or to himself. For if they are not so persuaded, they will have reached the position that the nearest relative would have been entitled to an order for discharge if the [RC] had not come to what they have decided was an erroneous conclusion as to the danger presented by the patient. That cannot be anything other than a relevant and material consideration, and would be likely, in almost all circumstances, to mean that discharge should be ordered."

In this case Latham J. held that the failure of the managers to apply their minds to the question of the patient's dangerousness meant that their decision not to order discharge was irrational and had to be quashed. *Huzzey* was applied by Jackson J. in *R. (on the application of SR) v Huntercombe Maidenhead Hospital* [2005] EWHC 2361 (Admin); [2005] M.H.L.R. 379 at para.19, where his Lordship said that "if the managers override the [RC's] report certifying dangerousness, this is a strong pointer in favour of discharge. It is not however an inflexible rule that in every case the managers must discharge if they overturn the finding of dangerousness. Mr Justice Latham in *Huzzey* acknowledged that there may be exceptions. Furthermore, para.23.12 of the [1999 edition of the *Code of Practice*] also acknowledges that there may be exceptions". In *SR*, the ordering of the patient's discharge by the hospital managers subsequent to their decision to override the RC's report was quashed partly on the ground that the managers failed to consider whether to exercise their residual discretion not to order discharge. Hospital managers must therefore consider whether to exercise their residual power not to discharge the patient if they have decided to override the RC's certificate. It is submitted that this residual power should only be exercised if the grounds for continued detention are satisfied and there is evidence to suggest that the patient's health would be significantly compromised if he were to be discharged. The *Code of Practice*, at para.38.22, states that the residual power should be invoked if there are "exceptional reasons why the patient should not be discharged". The law on this issue contrasts with that which applies to the tribunal: see the notes on s.72(1)(b)(iii).

Although the *Huzzey* case was concerned with the power of hospital managers, the approach taken by Latham J. is equally applicable to the RC's power to order discharge. In *South West London and St George's Mental Health NHS Trust v W* [2002] EWHC Admin 1770; [2002] M.H.L.R. 392, Crane J. said at para.81: "Section 23 of the Act does not specifically guide the [RC] or the managers in exercising their power of discharge, but plainly it would appropriate for them to consider the same matters as the [tribunal]". These matters are set out at para.38.15 et seq of the *Code of Practice*. If the nearest relative's order for the patient's discharge has been confronted by a barring report, the hospital managers must, in addition to considering the admission criteria, also ask themselves whether the patient would be likely to act in a manner dangerous to other persons or to himself if he were to be discharged (*Huzzey*, noted above). This "question provides a more stringent test for continuing the detention or the CTO" (*Code of Practice*, para.38.21). With regard to both community and detained patients, managers have a discretion to order the discharge of the patient even if the relevant criteria for detention or a CTO are satisfied. Managers should therefore consider exercising their discretion to discharge in this situation: see para.38.23 of the *Code of Practice*.

Paragraph (a)

APPLICATION FOR ADMISSION FOR ASSESSMENT. This includes an emergency application **1–381**
made under s.4 because such an application is "an application for admission for assessment" (see s.4(1)) which is founded on a single medical recommendation.

RESPONSIBLE CLINICIAN. The RC has a duty to discharge a patient from detention if the
medical conditions that justified admission cease to be met (*R. v Drew* [2003] UKHL 25;
[2003] 4 All E.R. 557 para.10. If discharge is ordered, the RC must comply with the notification requirements of reg.18 of the English Regulations and reg.7 of the Welsh
Regulations. The hospital managers have no power to prevent the RC from exercising
the power of discharge. The RC, who has a continuing duty to consider whether the
admission conditions remain satisfied (*R. (on the application of C) v Mental Health
Review Tribunal London South and South West Region* [2000] M.H.L.R. 220, per Scott
Baker J., at para.20), can discharge the patient at any time. If, at any time, RCs "conclude
that the criteria which would justify renewing a patient's detention or extending the
patient's CTO (as the case may be) are not met, they should exercise their power of discharge. They should not wait until the patient's detention or CTO is due to expire"
(*Code of Practice*, para.32.18). In *R. (on the application of Wirral Health Authority and
Wirral Borough Council) v Dr Finnegan and D.E.* [2001] EWHC Admin 312; [2001]
M.H.L.R. 66, Scott Baker J. said at para.68: "There are no statutory criteria governing
the exercise of this power. Its exercise is wholly within the [RC's] discretion subject, in
my judgment, to the usual restrictions of lawfulness and so forth. [I]f it is exercised for
reasons based on error of law it is susceptible to challenge by judicial review".

In order that hospital managers can meet their obligations under the Domestic Violence,
Crime and Victims Act 2004 to invite representations from victims, RCs must tell the managers if they are considering discharging the following categories of patients:

"[P]atients subject to unrestricted hospital orders, hospital directions whose associated
limitation direction is no longer in force, and unrestricted transfer directions (including
hospital orders and transfer directions which were originally restricted, but where the
restriction order or direction has since ended or been lifted). It includes patients who
have been discharged from such an order or direction onto SCT" ("Guidance on the
extension of victims' rights under the Domestic Violence, Crime and Victims Act
2004", Department of Health, 2008, para.1.10).

THE MANAGERS. Also see Ch.38 of the *Code of Practice* and the note on "Discharging
him absolutely" in subs.(1). Chapter 38, which contains guidance on the procedure that
should be adopted by the managers when conducting reviews, provides the following
specific guidance at para.38.36:

"Unless, exceptionally, it is considered too unsafe, patients should always be offered the
opportunity of speaking to the panel alone (with or without their representative and anyone else they have asked to attend to support them at the hearing)."

When offering this opportunity to patients, the managers should explain that they cannot
provide the patient with a guarantee of confidentiality. For example, if the patient discloses
information that is relevant to the issue that the managers will be determining, the rules of
natural justice and art.6 of the ECHR require that such information be shared with the hospital's representative.

The managers can delegate their power of discharge under subs.(4). The patient's RC has
no power to prevent the managers from exercising their powers of discharge, even if she
considers that the patient is dangerous.

A patient can make an application to the managers for discharge as often as he likes during a period of detention. No formal procedure is laid down for the hearing of a patient's
application. In fact, there is no explicit requirement that a hearing should take place at

all. Having a full hearing is not always the most appropriate mechanism for managers to use when exercising their review function. A limited hearing, involving (1) a consideration of written reports from relevant professionals, and (2) interviewing the patient, could take place in the following circumstances:

1. Where a patient make frequent requests for discharge from detention in the absence of any relevant change of circumstances.

2. If the patient does not wish to contest the renewal of his detention or CTO.

3. The patient makes an application for discharge immediately after an unsuccessful application to a tribunal in the absence of any relevant change of circumstances.

If a patient makes a request for a review, and a tribunal hearing in respect of the patient is imminent, the review should be adjourned until after the hearing. The lawfulness of not convening a managers' hearing in the light of the proximity of a tribunal hearing was confirmed in *R. (on the application of Zhang) v Whittington Hospital* [2013] EWHC 358 (Admin); [2014] M.H.L.R. 127. The managers should hold a limited hearing if the patient is not discharged by the tribunal and the patient persists with his request. If a relevant change in the patient's circumstances is identified at that hearing, either a full managers' hearing could take place or the Secretary of State could be requested to make a reference to the tribunal.

In order to avoid duplication of effort, a managers' review should not take place during the currency of the patient's detention under s.2 if the patient has made an application to the tribunal. However a full hearing should take place if the patient makes an application to the managers after missing the deadline for submitting an application to the tribunal.

Although the managers have the power to order the discharge of restricted patients (including patients who have been conditionally discharged who continue to be "liable to be detained": see s.73(6)), the power is exercisable only with the consent of the Secretary of State (s.41(3)(c)(iii)). Such patients are therefore entitled to request that the managers consider conducting a review of their detention.

Subject to the exceptions noted below, it is not possible for a request for a review to be made on behalf of a patient who lacks the mental capacity to make such a request. Under the Mental Capacity Act 2005, a mentally capable person (the "donor") can execute a legal document called a lasting power of attorney (LPA) which empowers another person (the "donee") to act in his stead, either generally or for specific purposes. An act done by a donee can be treated as an act done by the donor. An LPA which confers on the donee (or donees) power to make decisions about the donor's personal welfare matters could cover the making of a request to the hospital managers for a review. A personal welfare LPA can only take effect after the donor has lost the mental capacity to make the decision in question. A donee could therefore make a request to the hospital managers on the patient's behalf if:

(i) the welfare LPA either gives a general power to the donee or the power to make such a request has been specified by the donor; and

(ii) the patient does not possess the mental capacity to make the request.

A deputy appointed by the Court of Protection under the 2005 Act to make personal welfare decisions on behalf of the patient can also make a request to the hospital managers on the patient's behalf if such a power has been conferred on the deputy by the court and the patient does not have the mental capacity to make the request.

As managers, when exercising their power under this section, are acting in a quasi-judicial capacity they must abide by the rules of natural justice which require decision makers to act fairly, in good faith and without bias and to afford each party the opportunity to adequately state his case. The managers are also placed under a common law duty to give reasons for their decision: see *R. (on the application of O) v West London Mental Health NHS Trust* [2005] EWHC 604 (Admin); [2005] M.H.L.R. 187 where Collins J. held that this duty arises at the time the decision is made. His Lordship further held that a legal defect which will arise if the original reasons were inadequate cannot be cured by the managers subsequently supplementing their reasons with a proper explanation.

Although the managers' power under this section is confined to either granting or not granting the patient's absolute discharge (subs.(1)), the managers could adjourn their consideration of the patient's case if, for example, an important piece of information about the patient had not been provided to them; also see the note on "Discharging him absolutely" in subs.(1).

NEAREST RELATIVE. Who does not have the power to order the discharge of a patient who is subject to a hospital order (with or without restrictions) or to a guardianship order made by a court under Pt III: see the General Note to this section. For service of the order of discharge, see reg.3(3) of the English and Welsh Regulations. Under the provisions of s.25, 72 hours' notice of the nearest relative's intention to order the patient's discharge must be given to the hospital managers. The patient's RC can nullify the discharge if a report is made to the managers during the 72-hour period specifying that in her opinion the patient would be dangerous if discharged (s.25(1)). A nearest relative can be displaced if he or she has exercised or is likely to exercise the power under this provision "without due regard to the welfare of the patient or the interests of the public" (s.29(3)(d)).

For the disclosure of documentation to enable the nearest relative to consider exercising the power of discharge: see *R. (on the application of S) v Plymouth City Council and C* [2002] EWCA Civ 388; [2002] M.H.L.R. 118, which is noted under s.8. A doctor may visit and examine the patient for the purpose of advising a nearest relative on the exercise of the power (s.24(1)(2)).

Although it might be considered inappropriate for a nearest relative to be provided with a power to override professional opinion by ordering the patient's discharge, there have been occasions when the opposition of the nearest relative to the almost unanimous professional opinion about how to satisfy the patient's best interests has proved to be correct: see, for example, the report of the Local Government Ombudsman into an "Investigation into Complaint No.02/C/17068 against Bolton Metropolitan Borough Council" (November 2004). Also see the study by P. Shaw et al., noted in the General Note to s.25.

Paragraph (b)
GUARDIANSHIP. Neither a private guardian nor a nominated medical attendant have the **1–382** power to discharge the patient from guardianship. The RC has no power to prevent a nearest relative obtaining the discharge of a patient who is subject to guardianship. The nearest relative could be displaced if the discharge was either contrary to the welfare of the patient or to the interests of the public (s.29(3)(d)).

RESPONSIBLE LOCAL SOCIAL SERVICES AUTHORITY. Is defined in s.34(3). Local authorities may consider discharging patients from guardianship at any time, but must consider doing so when they receive a report from the patient's nominated medical attendant or RC renewing their guardianship under s.20. The power of discharge can be exercised by the local authority itself, by three or more members of the local social services authority or by three or more members of a committee or sub-committee of the authority (subs.(4)). Where decisions are taken by three or more local authority members (or a committee or sub-committee), all three people (or at least three of them, if there are more) must agree (*Code of Practice*, para.30.18). Delegation of the power of discharge to an officer is not permitted: see reg.21(2) of the English Regulations and reg.37(2) of the Welsh Regulations.

Paragraph (c)

1–383   In Wales, the discharge of a community patient by the RC or the hospital managers must be in the form set out in Form CP8: see reg.21 of the Welsh Regulations.

Subsection (4)

1–384   Neither this subsection nor subs.(5) shall apply to the exercise by the Welsh Ministers of the powers conferred by this section (SI 2000/253 Sch.3; also see the General Note to the Act).

THREE OR MORE MEMBERS OF THAT AUTHORITY TRUST OR BODY. The reference to "three" is not only for the creation of a quorum: it is a requirement that each of the three members shall support the order for discharge. In the unlikely event of seven members being appointed to the panel and three being in favour of discharge there should be implied into this provision that the "three or more" should not be a minority of those appointed (*R. (on the application of Tagoe-Thompson) v The Hospital Managers of the Park Royal Centre* [2003] EWCA Civ 330; [2003] M.H.L.R. 326).

Subsection (5)

1–385   This subsection prevents an "officer" (i.e. an employee) of an NHS body from being a member of the body's committee that has the power to order the discharge of a detained patient under this section. There is no equivalent legislative provision that relates to independent hospitals, although guidance is given at para.38.7 of the *Code of Practice*.

The payment of fees to a member of the committee (frequently referred to as an "associate hospital manager") for attending meetings of the committee does not necessarily mean that that person is disqualified from performing functions under this section by virtue of becoming an employee (*Code of Practice*, para.38.6). There are a number of factors which are taken into account by an Employment Tribunal when determining whether an employer/employee relationship exists between two parties. In essence, these are:

1. Mutuality of obligation between the parties such that the trust would be obliged to provide work to the associate managers and those managers would be obliged to accept the work.

2. The degree of control over the associate managers and the work they perform for the trust. In other words, would the trust be entitled to discipline the managers for a failure to perform their duties?

Other factors that would need be taken into consideration include tax treatment, entitlement to holiday and sick pay and any breaks in the continuity of the work provided by the trust to the managers. Similar considerations would apply to members of a committee appointed by a local authority to consider the discharge of guardianship patients. The Employment Rights Act 1996 s.230(1) defines an employee as an individual "who has entered into or works under . . . a contract of employment".

Members of the committee are not personally liable for decisions taken to discharge a patient. Liability rests with the detaining authority as a body (NHS Management Executive letter TEL (94)2).

Subsection (6)

1–386   This provision enables the board of an NHS foundation trust to delegate its power of discharge to three or more people who are neither executive directors of the board or employees of the trust. The constitution of the trust cannot permit delegation of the power of discharge to executive directors (s.142B).

Visiting and examination of patients

24.—(1) For the purpose of advising as to the exercise by the nearest relative of **1–387** a patient who is liable to be detained or subject to guardianship under this Part of this Act[, or who is a community patient,] of any power to order his discharge, any registered medical practitioner [or approved clinician] authorised by or on behalf of the nearest relative of the patient may, at any reasonable time, visit the patient and examine him in private.

(2) Any registered medical practitioner [or approved clinician] authorised for the purposes of subsection (1) above to visit and examine a patient may require the production of and inspect any records relating to the detention or treatment of the patient in any hospital [or to any after-care services provided for the patient under section 117 below].

(3) [. . .]

(4) [. . .]

AMENDMENTS

The amendments to this section were made by the Mental Health (Patients in the Community) Act 1995 s.1(2), Sch.1 para.1, the Mental Health Act 2007 ss.9(7), 32(4), Sch.3 para.11, SI 2007/961 art.3, Sch. para.13(3), SI 2010/813 art.5 and the Health and Social Care Act 2012 s.39.

DEFINITIONS **1–388**
    nearest relative: ss.26(3), 145(1).
    patient: s.145(1).
    approved clinician: s.145(1).
    community patient: ss.17A(7), 145(1).
    hospital: ss.34(2), 145(1).

GENERAL NOTE

This section provides for the visiting and examination of patients and for the production **1–389** of documents to a doctor or approved clinician for the purpose of advising the patient's nearest relative, or acting nearest relative appointed by a county court under s.29, as to the exercise of his or her power under s.23(2) to order the discharge of a patient from detention, guardianship or a community treatment order.

A person who fails to allow the visiting, interviewing or examination of a patient or who refuses to produce any document for inspection commits an offence under s.129.

Subsection (1)

There is no power to require a social work assessment to be undertaken in respect of a **1–390** patient who is subject to guardianship.

Subsection (2)

This provision does not provide for the records of a patient who is subject to guardianship **1–391** to be made available to the doctor, unless the patient is subject to s.117 after-care.

Restrictions on discharge by nearest relative

25.—(1) An order for the discharge of a patient who is liable to be detained in a **1–392** hospital shall not be made [under section 23 above] by his nearest relative except after giving not less than 72 hours' notice in writing to the managers of the hospital; and if, within 72 hours after such notice has been given, the [responsible clinician] furnishes to the managers a report certifying that in the opinion of [that clinician] the patient, if discharged, would be likely to act in a manner dangerous to other persons or to himself—

(a) any order for the discharge of the patient made by that relative in pursuance of the notice shall be of no effect; and

(b) no further order for the discharge of the patient shall be made by that relative during the period of six months beginning with the date of the report.

[(1A) Subsection (1) above shall apply to an order for the discharge of a community patient as it applies to an order for the discharge of a patient who is liable to be detained in a hospital, but with the reference to the managers of the hospital being read as a reference to the managers of the responsible hospital.]

(2) In any case where a report under subsection (1) above is furnished in respect of a patient who is liable to be detained in pursuance of an application for admission for treatment [, or in respect of a community patient,] the managers shall cause the nearest relative of the patient to be informed.

AMENDMENTS

The words in square brackets were substituted and inserted by the Mental Health Act 2007 ss.9(8), 32(4), Sch.3 para.12.

DEFINITIONS

1–393   patient: s.145(1).
hospital: ss.34(2), 145(1).
nearest relative: ss.26(3), 145(1).
the managers: s.145(1).
application for admission for treatment: ss.3, 145(1).
responsible clinician: s.34(1).
community patient: ss.17A(7), 145(1).
the responsible hospital: ss.17A(7), 145(1).

GENERAL NOTE

1–394   This section, which does not apply to hospital order patients (see the General Note to s.23), states that a patient's nearest relative, or acting nearest relative appointed by a county court under s.29, must give 72 hours' notice to the hospital managers of his or her intention to order the discharge of the patient from detention or from a community treatment order (CTO) (but not from guardianship) and that the order for discharge, when made, will have no effect if in the meantime the responsible clinician (RC) has reported to the managers that, in her opinion, the patient, if discharged, would be likely to act in a manner dangerous to other persons or to himself. If the RC makes such a report (a "barring report"), it will have the effect of preventing the nearest relative from exercising the powers of discharge for the next six months (subs.(1)(b)). It is submitted that this prohibition would also apply to any person authorised by the nearest relative subsequent to the receipt of the barring report to perform the functions of nearest relative under reg.24 of the English Regulations or reg.33 of the Welsh Regulations as the person authorised acts on the nearest relative's behalf. If the barring order is issued in respect of a patient who is detained under s.3 or is subject to a CTO, the nearest relative must be informed (subs.(2)).

In *Re GK (Patient: Habeas Corpus)* [1999] M.H.L.R. 128, Sedley L.J. said at para.6:

"[T]he power which is vested in the nearest relative and in others is there essentially to ensure that nobody who is entitled to their discharge is prevented by bureaucracy or inertia or error in a hospital's administration from gaining their freedom. But the barring order is there to ensure that the mere desire of, in particular, a closest relative to have a patient out [of hospital] does not defeat the purpose of the Act which, both in the interests of the patient and in the interests of the public, has ultimate regard to the patient's mental state."

These observations were approved by the Court of Appeal in *K v Hospital Managers of the Kingswood Centre* [2014] EWCA Civ 1332.

The wording of subs.(1) is ambiguous as to when the nearest relative's order of discharge is actually made. It could be argued the phrase "after giving not less than 72 hours notice" implies that there are two stages in the discharge process, namely:

(i) notification of the intention by the nearest relative to order discharge; and

(ii) the ordering of the discharge in the event of the patient's RC not issuing a report barring discharge within the 72 hour period.

However, the wording of para.(a), in particular the use of the term "made", suggests that the order for discharge can be made before the RC issues a report. In order to comply with the interpretive requirement in s.3 of the Human Rights Act 1998, it is suggested that the following interpretation is compatible with the rights of both patient and nearest relative under art.8 of the European Convention on Human Rights (also see the extract from the Reference Guide, noted below):

(i) the notice of intention to discharge and the notice of discharge are subsumed into one event [NB This interpretation is endorsed by the *Code of Practice* at para.32.24 and by the Reference Guide at para.27.13: see the note on "72 hours' notice" in subs.(1)];

(ii) the implementation of the notice of discharge is postponed for 72 hours in order to provide the RC with time to consider issuing a report barring discharge; and

(iii) the nearest relative can withdraw the order of discharge within the 72 hour period in the event of the RC not issuing a barring report. It would be advisable to request the nearest relative to put his or her decision to withdraw in writing.

It follows that if the patient's RC has not issued a barring report in respect of the patient's nearest relative during the previous six months, the patient's discharge takes effect at the end of the 72-hour period if the RC does not issue a report barring discharge. This will be the case whether or not arrangements have been made for the patient's after-care. The RC can discharge the patient under s.23 during this period. Although the patient's RC could place the patient on a community treatment order during the 72-hour period, the order would cease to have effect when the period expires. This is because the s.3 application that underpins the order would then be discharged: see s.17C(c).

In *TTM v Hackney LBC* [2010] EWHC 1349 (Admin), Collins J. said that hospital managers had been correct to treat a post-admission allegation by the patient's nearest relative that, contrary to what had been stated by the approved mental health practitioner, he had objected to the patient's admission under s.3, as notice of his intention to discharge the patient.

The hospital managers should consider holding a review of the patient's detention if the RC makes a report under this provision (*Code of Practice*, para.38.12). The criteria that hospital managers must use when reviewing the detention of a patient subsequent to such a report being made were identified in *R. v Riverside Mental Health Trust Ex p. Huzzey* (1998) 43 B.M.L.R. 167 and *R. (on the application of SR) v Huntercombe Maidenhead Hospital* [2005] EWHC 2361 (Admin); [2005] M.H.L.R. 379. These cases are considered in the note on s.23(2).

Under s.29(3)(d), an application can be made to the county court to displace the patient's nearest relative on the ground that he or she "has exercised without due regard to the welfare of the patient or the interests of the public his power to discharge the patient from hospital . . . under this Part of this Act, or is likely to do so".

A study on patient discharges failed to demonstrate any significant difference in the clinical outcome of patients discharged by their nearest relative and those discharged by a psychiatrist (P. Shaw et al., "In relative danger? The outcome of patients discharged by their nearest relative from sections 2 and 3 of the Mental Health Act", *Psychiatric Bulletin* (2003), 27(2), 50–54).

Applications to the First-tier Tribunal (Mental Health) or the Mental Health Review Tribunal for Wales

1–395   In the case of a patient detained for treatment or a community patient, the patient's nearest relative has a right to apply to the tribunal within 28 days of the patient's RC issuing a report under subs.(1) (s.66(1)(g), (2)(d)).

Code of Practice

1–396   Guidance on this section can be found in Ch.32 at paras 32.20 to 32.25.

Subsection (1)

1–397   ORDER FOR THE DISCHARGE.   Under s.23(2)(a). For service of the order, see regs 3(3) of the English Regulations and Welsh Regulations. If the notice is served by handing it to a member of the hospital staff, that person must be authorised to receive it: see *K v Hospital Managers of the Kingswood Centre* which is noted under reg.3(3).

72 HOURS' NOTICE.   Paragraph 27.13 of the Reference Guide states:

"Although in theory the order should not be served until 72 hours after the notice has been given, in practice it is appropriate for hospital managers to accept a discharge order without prior notice as being both notice of intention to discharge the patient after 72 hours and the actual order to do so."

Paragraph 32.25 of the *Code of Practice* contains an illustrative standard letter of discharge for nearest relatives to use.

FURNISHES TO THE MANAGERS A REPORT.   The RC's report must be in the form set out in Pt 1 of Form M2: see 25 of the English Regulations (in Wales, Form NR1: see reg.34 of the Welsh Regulations). There is no requirement for the RC to examine the patient prior to completing the form.

LIKELY TO ACT.   In *Cream Holdings Ltd v Banerjee* [2004] UKHL 44; [2004] 4 All E.R. 617, Lord Nicholls of Birkenhead said at para.12:

"As with most ordinary English words 'likely' has several different shades of meaning. Its meaning depends upon the context in which it is being used. Even when read in context its meaning is not always precise. It is capable of encompassing different degrees of likelihood, varying from 'more likely than not' to 'may well'."

In the context of art.77 of the Mental Health (Northern Ireland) Order 1986, McCloskey J. held that a "likelihood" is a probability (*In Re JR 45* [2011] NIQB 17; [2014] M.H.L.R. 17). Also see para.32.23 of the *Code of Practice*, noted below.

DANGEROUS.   This is the sole reason for preventing discharge. In the context of a person being dangerous to others, the *Butler Committee* equated "dangerousness with a propensity to cause serious physical injury or lasting psychological harm" (para.4.10). As the danger can relate to the patient, this term encompasses the danger of self harm. There is no requirement for the risk of dangerousness to be an immediate risk. A patient with a history of becoming dangerous some time after ceasing to take medication would therefore be covered. In *Re Whitbread* [1999] C.O.D. 370, David Pannick QC, sitting as a deputy judge of the High Court, upheld the decision of hospital managers who had concluded that the dangerousness test was satisfied in a case where there was a "very high level of probability that lasting psychological harm could be caused to others if the barring order were to be lifted". It is submitted that the dangerousness test would also be satisfied if it was considered that it would be likely that the patient, if discharged, would suffer serious harm to his physical and/or mental health through self neglect or the neglect of others. Paragraph 32.23 of the *Code of Practice* states:

"[The dangerousness] question focuses on the probability of dangerous acts, such as causing serious physical injury or lasting psychological harm, not merely on the patient's general need for safety and others' general need for protection."

In *Rakevich v Russia* [2004] M.H.L.R. 37 para.32, the European Court of Human Rights said that "it is not necessary for the lawmaker exhaustively to interpret the term 'danger', as it is hardly possible to embrace in the law the whole diversity of conditions which involve psychiatric hazards". Some of the problems in defining dangerousness are identified by J. Atkinson and L. Patterson in *Review of Literature Relating to Mental Health Legislation* (2001) at para.2.11:

"Inherent in the problem of defining dangerousness is the difficulty of using the same word to describe harm to others and harm to self. This includes whether it is reasonable to describe 'self-neglect' as 'dangerous' as well as concerns about whether different levels of dangerousness should apply to the risk of the individual harming him/herself or others. Dangerousness is also usually situation-specific and may require complicated formulae to determine risk, for example when the likelihood of danger is high but in a rare situation".

DURING THE PERIOD OF SIX MONTHS. The disqualification from ordering the patient's discharge is not affected by any change in the patient's legal status. Therefore a nearest relative who has been made the subject of a RC's report under this section subsequent to ordering the discharge of a patient who has been detained under s.2 is barred from ordering the discharge of the patient for the full six month period even though the s.2 is immediately followed by an application under s.3 (although the nearest relative could object to such an application (s.11(4))) or if the patient is discharged from the hospital and the section only to be re-admitted under a fresh application shortly thereafter.

ORDER FOR THE DISCHARGE. For service of the order, see regs 3(1) and 25(2) of the English Regulations and regs 3(1) and 34(2) of the Welsh Regulations.

Subsection (2)
CAUSE THE NEAREST RELATIVE TO BE INFORMED. So that the nearest relative of a patient **1–398** who has been detained for treatment or who is a community patient could consider applying to a tribunal. The nearest relative of a patient who has been detained for assessment does not have an equivalent right.

After-Care under supervision

[*Sections 25A to 25J were repealed by the Mental Health Act 2007 s.55, Sch.11* **1–399** *Pt 5*]

Functions of relatives of patients

Definition of "relative" and "nearest relative"

1–400   **26.**—(1) In this Part of this Act "relative" means any of the following persons:—

(a) husband or wife [or civil partner];

(b) son or daughter;

(c) father or mother;

(d) brother or sister;

(e) grandparent;

(f) grandchild;

(g) uncle or aunt;

(h) nephew or niece.

(2) In deducing relationships for the purposes of this section, any relationship of the half-blood shall be treated as a relationship of the whole blood, and an illegitimate person shall be treated as the legitimate child of

[(a) his mother, and

(b) if his father has parental responsibility for him within the meaning of section 3 of the Children Act 1989, his father.]

(3) In this Part of this Act, subject to the provisions of this section and to the following provisions of this Part of this Act, the "nearest relative" means the person first described in subsection (1) above who is for the time being surviving, relatives of the whole blood being preferred to relatives of the same description of the half-blood and the elder or eldest of two or more relatives described in any paragraph of that subsection being preferred to the other or others of those relatives, regardless of sex.

(4) Subject to the provisions of this section and to the following provisions of this Part of this Act, where the patient ordinarily resides with or is cared for by one or more of his relatives (or, if he is for the time being an in-patient in a hospital, he last ordinarily resided with or was cared for by one or more of his relatives) his nearest relative shall be determined—

(a) by giving preference to that relative or those relatives over the other or others; and

(b) as between two or more such relatives, in accordance with subsection (3) above.

(5) Where the person who, under subsection (3) or (4) above, would be the nearest relative of a patient—

(a) in the case of a patient ordinarily resident in the United Kingdom, the Channel Islands or the Isle of Man, is not so resident; or

(b) is the husband or wife [or civil partner] of the patient, but is permanently separated from the patient, either by agreement or under an order of a court, or has deserted or has been deserted by the patient for a period which has not come to an end; or

(c) is a person other than the husband, wife, [civil partner,] father or mother of the patient, and is for the time being under 18 years of age;

(d) [...]

the nearest relative of the patient shall be ascertained as if that person were dead.

(6) In this section "husband" [, "wife" and "civil partner" include a person who is living with the patient as the patient's husband or wife or as if they were civil partners], as the case may be (or, if the patient is for the time being an in-

patient in a hospital, was so living until the patient was admitted), and has been or had been so living for a period of not less than six months; but a person shall not be treated by virtue of this subsection as the nearest relative of a married patient [or a patient in a civil partnership unless the husband, wife or civil partner] of the patient is disregarded by virtue of paragraph (b) of subsection (5) above.

(7) A person, other than a relative, with whom the patient ordinarily resides (or, if the patient is for the time being an in-patient in a hospital, last ordinarily resided before he was admitted), and with whom he has or had been ordinarily residing for a period of not less than five years, shall be treated for the purposes of this Part of this Act as if he were a relative but—

(a) shall be treated for the purposes of subsection (3) above as if mentioned last in subsection (1) above; and

(b) shall not be treated by virtue of this subsection as the nearest relative of a married patient [or a patient in a civil partnership unless the husband, wife or civil partner] of the patient is disregarded by virtue of paragraph (b) of subsection (5) above.

AMENDMENTS

The amendments to this section were made by the Children Act 1989 (Consequential Amendment of Enactments) Order 1991 (SI 1991/1881) art.3, the Children Act 1989 s.108(7), Sch.15, and the Mental Health Act 2007 s.26(2)–(5).

DEFINITIONS

    hospital: ss.34(2), 145(1).   **1–401**

    patient: s.145(1).

GENERAL NOTE

    This section defines "relative" and "nearest relative" for the purposes of Pt II of the Act. **1–402**
The following patients who are subject to orders and remands under Pt III do not have nearest relatives for the purposes of the Act: restricted patients (including conditionally discharged patients), patients remanded to hospital under s.35 or s.36 and patients subject to interim hospital orders under s.38. Other patients who are detained under Pt III and who are not restricted patients and patients who have been made subject to guardianship orders by a court have nearest relatives by virtue of Sch.1 Pt 1 para.1.

    The role of the nearest relative in respect of detained patients was identified by Maurice Kay J. in *R. (on the application of M) v Secretary of State for Health* [2003] EWHC 1094 (Admin); [2003] M.H.L.R. 348 at paras 4 and 5 (words in square brackets inserted by the author):

"The nearest relative plays an important part in the scheme of the Act. He may make an application for assessment (section 2), an emergency application for admission for assessment (section 4) and an application for admission for treatment (section 3). No application for admission or treatment under section 3 may be made by an [approved mental health professional (AMHP)] without first consulting with the nearest relative unless the [AMHP] considers that such consultation is not reasonably practicable or would involve unreasonable delay (section 11(4)). The manager of a psychiatric institution in which a patient is detained has to inform the nearest relative in writing about, amongst other things, the right to apply to a tribunal, the right to be discharged, the right to receive and send correspondence and the right to consent to or refuse treatment (section 132(4)). A nearest relative may order the discharge of a patient who is detained under [section 2 and] section 3 (section 23). Prior to exercising this important power the nearest relative can appoint a medical practitioner to examine the patient and the appointed practitioner can require the production of records relating to the detention or treatment of the patient (section 24). The right to order discharge under section 23 is limited when the [responsible clinician] certifies that the patient would, if released, be likely to be a danger to himself or others (section 25). Where a patient to be discharged other than by the order of the nearest relative, the detaining authority is required to notify the nearest relative of the forthcoming discharge unless the patient requests that no such information is supplied (section 133(2)).

In addition to the power to order a discharge under section 23 the nearest relative may apply to [a tribunal in certain circumstances] for the discharge of the patient pursuant to section 66 . . . Where the nearest relative is the applicant to the Tribunal he may appoint a registered medical practitioner to visit and examine the patient and that practitioner may require production of and inspect any records relating to the detention and treatment of the patient (section 76(1))."

A person who has been identified as the patient's nearest relative is not legally obliged to act as such. He or she can authorise any person (other than the patient or a person disqualified under subs.(5)) to perform the functions of the nearest relative. The authority can be revoked at any time. Both the authority and the revocation must be in writing: see reg.24 of the English Regulations and reg.33 of the Welsh Regulations. A person who has been identified as the patient's "next of kin" has no powers under the Act unless he or she is also the patient's nearest relative.

In *R. (on the application of S) v Plymouth City Council and C* [2002] EWCA Civ 388; [2002] M.H.L.R. 118, the Court of Appeal was concerned with how the interest of a mentally incapacitated guardianship patient in preserving the confidentiality of personal information about himself is to be reconciled with his mother's interest, as his nearest relative, in having access to enough information about him to exercise her statutory functions under the Act. This case is considered in the General Note to s.8 and in the note on the Civil Procedure Rules 1998 in Pt 3.

The leave of the court is required before the nearest relative of a ward of court exercises his or her functions under the Act (s.33(2)).

Mental Capacity Act 2005

1–403 As this section does not provide a patient with a right to nominate his nearest relative, a condition in a personal welfare lasting power of attorney made by the patient nominating the donee of the power to be the patient's nearest relative would be ineffective. A donee or a deputy appointed by the Court of Protection or a relevant person's representative under the deprivation of liberty safeguards may only exercise the powers of the nearest relative if they are patient's nearest relative as defined in this section, have been nominated to perform the function of the nearest relative under reg.24 or reg.33 (see above), or have been appointed as acting nearest relative under s.29.

Human Rights Act 1998

1–404 The patient's nearest relative, as a person who has the power to exercise "functions of a public nature", is a "public authority" for the purposes of s.6 of the 1998 Act (s.6(3)(b)).

In *MA v Secretary of State for Health* [2012] UKUT 474 (AAC), UT Judge Levenson held that the bundle of rights conferred on the nearest relative, in particular the right of discharge, are civil rights for the purposes of art.6 of the European Convention on Human Rights.

Code of Practice

1–405 Guidance on the identification, appointment and displacement of nearest relatives is given in Ch.5. Paragraph 5.6 states:

"Where an approved mental health professional (AMHP) discovers, when assessing a patient for possible detention or guardianship under the Act (or at any other time), that the patient appears to have no nearest relative, the AMHP should advise the patient of their right to apply to the county court for the appointment of a person to act as their nearest relative. If the patient lacks capacity to decide to apply themselves, the AMHP should apply to the county court."

It is submitted that the final phrase of this extract should read: "the AMHP should consider making an application to the county court": see the note on s.29(3)(a).

Subsection (1)

The definition of relative includes relationships established through adoption (Reference **1–406** Guide, para.2.8). For the occasions when relatives are to be disregarded for the purposes of ascertaining the patient's "nearest relative", see subs.(5). The remaining notes on this subsection are concerned with the definitions of relative as they affect the identification of the patient's nearest relative.

HUSBAND OR WIFE OR CIVIL PARTNER.   This includes the marital partner of a marriage of a same sex couple (Marriage (Same Sex Couples) Act 2013 s.11, Sch.3 para.1(c)). Changes made to the Gender Recognition Act 2004 by the 2013 Act enable couples to remain married when one or both parties obtains a full gender recognition certificate, and to remain in a civil partnership when both parties obtain a full gender recognition certificate: see SI 2015/50. A person comes within the scope of this provision even if the marital or civil partner is under the age of 18 (subs.(5)(c)). If the patient is unmarried or has not entered into a civil partnership or if the marital or civil partner can be disregarded under subs.(5)(b), a person who had been living with the patient as the patient's husband or wife or civil partner for at least six months will be treated as if he or she were the patient's husband or wife or civil partner (subs.(6)).

SON OR DAUGHTER.   An adopted child is treated as the child of the adoptive parents (Adoption and Children Act 2002 s.46(2)). Once an adoption has taken place, the child's natural parents no longer have any legal connection with the child, including when the child becomes an adult. An unmarried mother's child is treated as the child of the mother (subs.(2)) and, if he has parental responsibility for the child, his father. To become the patient's nearest relative, the child must be over the age of 18 (subs.(5)(c)). A step-child is not a relative for the purposes of this provision but could become a nearest relative under the provisions of subs.(7), by being appointed as an acting nearest relative under s.29 or by being authorised to act as such under reg.24 of the English Regulations or reg.33 of the Welsh Regulations.

Paragraph 113 of the Explanatory Notes to the Marriage (Same Sex Couples) Act 2013 refers to the position of a child of woman who is married to a person of the same sex:

"Paragraph 2 [of Schedule 4] makes clear that the common law presumption, that a child born to a woman during her marriage is also the child of her husband (often referred to as 'the presumption of legitimacy'), is not extended to marriages of same sex couples by section 11. Therefore, where two women are married to each other and one of the parties to that marriage gives birth to a child, the other party will not be presumed to be the parent of that child by virtue of the common law presumption. There may be other ways in which the party to the marriage who does not give birth to the child is treated in law as the parent (for example, if that woman is treated as a parent as a result of the amendment made by paragraph 40 of Schedule 7 to this Act to section 42 of the Human Fertilisation and Embryology Act 2008), but in all such cases it is not the common law presumption that treats her as the parent of that child."

FATHER OR MOTHER.   Even if the parent is under the age of 18 (subs.(5)(c)). A step-parent is not a relative for the purposes of this section. An unmarried father is to be disregarded unless he has parental responsibility for the child: see subs.(2) which is concerned with deducing relationships "for the purposes of this section". This state of affairs is an exception to the general rule of construction established by s.1(1) of the Family Law Reform Act 1969 which provides that "unless the contrary intention" appears in a statute, any relationship between two persons "shall be construed without regard to whether or not the father and mother of either of them . . . have or had been married to each other at any time". The "contrary intention" is contained in subs.(2).

In cases where a child is in the care of a local authority by virtue of a care order or where a guardian for the child has been appointed or where a residence order has been made in respect of the child, the local authority (s.27), guardian (s.28) or person named in the residence order (s.28) is deemed to be the child's nearest relative.

Subsection (2)

1–407 RELATIONSHIP OF THE HALF-BLOOD. In order to determine whether a relationship exists for the purposes of this section, if a patient has both a full-blood relative and a half-blood relative, they are both treated as full-blood relatives. Whole blood relatives are preferred to half-blood relatives for the purposes of determining the patient's nearest relative under subs.(3).

A person has a whole blood relationship with another if they are both descended from the same pair of ancestors, e.g. two brothers who have the same parents. A person has a half blood relationship with another if they are descended from one common ancestor only, e.g. two brothers who have the same father but different mothers.

PARENTAL RESPONSIBILITY. An unmarried father who does not have parental responsibility for his child is not a relative for the purposes of this section. This exclusion applies after the child reaches adulthood. An unmarried father without parental responsibility can only become the child's nearest relative through the operation of subs.(7) or by virtue of the operation of reg.24 of the English Regulations or reg.33 of the Welsh Regulations: see the General Note to this section.

An unmarried father can acquire parental responsibility for his child under the following provisions of the Children Act 1989: by obtaining a child arrangements order (s.12(1)); by virtue of an order of the court (s.4(1)(c)); by making a parental responsibility agreement with the mother (s.4(1)(b)); by being appointed the child's guardian by the court (s.5(1)); or by being appointed as the child's guardian by the mother or another guardian (s.5(3)(4)). The appointment as guardian will not take effect while the mother is alive (s.5(8)). By virtue of amendments made to s.4 of the 1989 Act by s.111 of the Adoption and Children Act 2002, unmarried fathers registered as such on the child's birth certificate under the terms of the Births and Deaths Registration Act 1953 will have parental responsibility for that child. Parental responsibility can only be acquired in this way in respect of births registered on or after December 1, 2003, which was the commencement date for s.111 (SI 2003/3079): see s.111(7) of the 2002 Act. An unmarried father's parental responsibility for his child can be ended by order of the court (s.4(2A),(3) of the 1986 Act). It will also end when the child reaches 18 (s.91(7),(8)) of the 1989 Act) or is adopted (s.46(2) of the 2002 Act).

If an unmarried father subsequently marries the mother of the child, both parents will from that date have parental responsibility for the child (Legitimacy Act 1976 s.2). Parents do not lose parental responsiblity if they divorce.

Subsection (3)

1–408 NEAREST RELATIVE. This subsection states that the general rule for determining the patient's nearest relative is to take whoever comes first on the list of relatives set out in subs.(1), with preference being given to relatives of the whole blood, and that if there is more than one relative coming within the same category the elder or eldest is to take priority regardless of the sex of the relative, subject to preference being given to the relative who either lives with or cares for the patient (subs.(4)).

The patient cannot choose his nearest relative who must be identified by applying subss.(3) to (6) to the patient's family and social situation. The fact that a relative is either mentally disordered, mentally incapable or detained under the Act does not disqualify him or her from being a nearest relative, although there could be grounds for removal under s.29(3)(b).

The fact that a person has been sentenced to a period of imprisonment does not disqualify that person from being a nearest relative. Either the mental state or the imprisonment of the nearest relative, or the nature of the patient's relationship with the nearest relative could lead to an AMHP concluding that it would not be "practicable" either to consult with the relative prior to making an application for admission under s.3 (see s.11(4)) or to inform the relative that an application under s.2 is to be or has been made (see s.11(3)).

It is possible for a nearest relative to authorise another person to perform the functions of nearest relative on his behalf: see the General Note to this section.

ELDER OR ELDEST.   Thus the elder or eldest wife of a polygamous marriage would normally become her husband's nearest relative.

Subsection (4)
This subsection provides that if the patient is either living with or being cared for by a **1–409** relative, that relative becomes the patient's nearest relative. If the patient either resides with more than one relative or is cared for by more than one relative, or lives with one relative and is cared for by another, the nearest relative becomes either the elder or eldest relative if both relatives come within the same category, or the relative who comes first on the list set out in subs.(1) if they do not.

ORDINARILY RESIDES.   The Government has issued guidance to assist local authorities in making decisions about ordinary residence ("Ordinary Residence: Guidance on the identification of the ordinary residence of people in need of community care services, England", Department of Health, 2013; also see Ch.19 of "Care and Support Statutory Guidance", Department of Health, 2014).

The leading modern authority on the meaning of "ordinarily resides" is *R. v Barnet LBC, Ex p. Shah* [1983] 2 A.C. 309 where Lord Scarman said in a different statutory context:

"Unless, therefore, it can be shown that the statutory framework or the legal context in which the words are used requires a different meaning, I unhesitatingly subscribe to the view that 'ordinarily resident' refers to a man's abode in a particular place or country which he has adopted voluntarily and for settled purposes as part of the regular order of his life for the time being, whether of short or of long duration" (p.343).

With regard to the need for a degree of settled purpose, his Lordship said:

"This is not to say that the [person] intends to stay where he is indefinitely; indeed his purpose, while settled, may be for a limited period. . . . All that is necessary is that the purpose of living where one does has a sufficient degree of continuity to be properly described as settled." (p.344)

In *R. (on the application of Cornwall County Council) v Secretary of State for Health* [2015] UKSC 46, Lord Carnwath, who gave the judgment of the majority, said that the meaning of the term "may be strongly influenced by the particular statutory context" (para.43). His Lordship said that if a mentally incapable person who is unable to make decisions about residence herself comes to live with her parents for a short period before being placed in residential care, the single question to be answered is "whether her period of actual residence with her parents was sufficiently 'settled' to amount to ordinary residence" (para.47). In the case before it, the Supreme Court ruled that a disabled young man's brief periods of staying with his parents at holiday times could not amount to ordinary residence.

In *R. (on the application of Sunderland City Council) v South Tyneside Council* [2012] EWCA Civ 1232; [2013] 1 All E.R. 394, Lloyd L.J. said at para.31:

> "I agree with the comment made in other cases that, in general, when considering any case in which there is doubt as to the place of a person's residence, the question is not only that of physical presence and that it may be relevant to consider why the person is where he or she is, and to what extent his or her presence there is voluntary, Thus, if a person has a home, the fact that he or she is not there on a given date or for a particular period does not mean that he or she is not resident there, if the absence is accounted for by, for example, a holiday, a business trip or having to spend time in hospital, whether following an injury, an operation or some other form of treatment, possibly over a long period, or, for that matter a period of imprisonment following a criminal conviction."

Each case has to be judged on its own facts and the fact that a person has left his home does not necessarily mean that he has established an ordinary residence elsewhere. McCullough J. examined this issue in *R. v Liverpool CC Ex p. F* (CO 2744/96) April 16, 1997, a case where the patient had left the parental home in acrimonious circumstances and had gone to live with his grandmother, as well as staying at a number of other places. His Lordship said that those who were charged with the task of identifying the identity of the patient's nearest relative should have considered:

> "not just the choice between whether he was ordinarily resident with his mother or with his grandmother. They should have considered also the possibility that he may not have been ordinarily resident anywhere and should have specifically asked themselves—bearing in mind his itinerant lifestyle, his lack of stability and the condition of his mental health—whether he really had settled down sufficiently at his grandmother's for her home to be regarded as his place of ordinary residence."

If a patient leaves home, but takes up no other place of ordinary residence and no relative is caring for him, his nearest relative can be identified by applying the general rule set out in subs.(3).

CARED FOR. A person can clearly "care about" a patient without providing "care for" that patient. In *Re D (Mental patient: habeas corpus)* [2000] 2 F.L.R. 848, the Court of Appeal held that (a) the words "ordinarily" qualifies "resided with" but not "cared for"; and (b) although the words "cared for" are not defined in the Act, they are clear and everyday words set in a context where the AMHP applicant has to act in a pragmatic and common sense manner in a situation which is fraught with emotion and difficulty. In order to justify a finding that the relative is caring for the patient, the services provided by the relative must be more than minimal and they need not have been provided over the long term. In this case, the court was asked to consider the situation of a relative who assisted the patient in managing his financial affairs, checked whether he was eating appropriately and took away and cleaned his soiled clothing and bed clothes. In finding that the relative was caring for the patient the court said that there "was more than sufficient evidence to pass the 'cared for' test, wherever one sets the threshold of services amounting to 'cared for'. In other words, the services were not merely minimal. They were services which were substantial and sustained".

The patient may be "cared for" by a relative even if they do not share a residence. In *R. v Liverpool CC*, above, McCullough J. held that the quality of regularity is important when considering whether there has been a change in the identity of the person who is to be regarded as caring for the patient. His Lordship said: "In such a case it will be necessary to take into account the duration, continuity and quality of the care afforded by the relative under consideration as having assumed the role . . . and also the intention of the patient himself".

Subsection (5)

This subsection, which disqualifies certain persons from acting as a patient's nearest **1–410** relative, is applied to persons who have been deemed to be the patient's nearest relative by virtue of s.28 (s.28(2)).

PARAGRAPH (A); ORDINARILY RESIDENT IN THE UNITED KINGDOM.   "United Kingdom" means Great Britain and Northern Ireland (Interpretation Act 1978 s.5, Sch.1). It is easier for a person to lose their ordinary/habitual residence in a country than to acquire it. In *C v S (A Minor) (Abduction)* [1990] 2 F.L.R. 442 at 454 HL Lord Brandon said:

"[T]he question whether a person is or is not habitually resident in a specified country is a question of fact to be decided by reference to all the circumstances of any particular case . . . . A person may cease to be habitually resident in country A in a single day if he or she leaves it with a settled intention not to return to it but to take up long term residence in country B instead. Such a person cannot, however, become habitually resident in country B in a single day. An appreciable period of time and a settled intention will be necessary to enable him or her to become so. During that appreciable period of time the person will have ceased to be habitually resident in country A but not yet have become habitually resident in country B."

NOT SO RESIDENT.   The effect of this provision is that:

1. If the patient is ordinarily resident in the United Kingdom, the Channel Islands or the Isle of Man and the person who would normally be identified as the patient's nearest relative is not so resident, that person cannot be the patient's nearest relative. However, if that person has gone abroad temporarily, for example on business or on holiday, he or she will be the patient's nearest relative.

2. If the patient is not ordinarily resident in the United Kingdom, the Channel Islands or the Isle of Man, the nearest relative of the patient can be a person who is also not so resident.

PARAGRAPH (B); SEPARATED.   In the absence of a court order, the spouses or civil partners must have agreed that their separation is permanent; the mere fact that the couple live at different places is not sufficient to constitute separation. If one spouse or civil partner is uncertain as to whether the separation is permanent, this provision is not satisfied.

Both separation and desertion require that the couple be factually separated. It is possible for a separation to be established in a situation where both parties continue to live in the same premises if it can be said that two separate households have been established. If there continues to be a sharing of a common life by, for example, taking meals together or sharing common living areas, the parties are not separated for the purposes of the Divorce Reform Act 1969. In *Le Brocq v Le Brocq* [1964] 1 W.L.R. 1085, the wife had excluded her husband from the matrimonial bedroom by bolting the door on the inside. There was no avoidable communication between them, but the wife continued to cook meals for her husband, although he was never allowed to take meals with her, and he paid her a weekly sum for housekeeping. The court held that the necessary factual separation had not been established: there was, as Harman L.J. put it, "separation of bedrooms, separation of hearts, separation of speaking: but one household was carried on . . .".

DESERTED.   Under matrimonial law, the main elements of desertion are the fact of separation and the intention to desert. The intention to desert involves: (a) lack of consent to the separation by the spouse who has been deserted; (b) lack of any justification for the separation; and (c) the deserting spouse having the mental capacity to form the intent: see Cretney *Principles of Family Law* (2008) paras 10–027 to 10–032. A person who has been disqualified from being a patient's nearest relative under this provision can resume that role as soon as the desertion comes to an end.

PARAGRAPH (C); UNDER 18 YEARS OF AGE. Means before the commencement of his eighteenth birthday (Family Law Reform Act 1969 s.9(1)).

Subsection (6)

1–411   LIVING WITH THE PATIENT AS THE PATIENT'S HUSBAND OR WIFE OR AS IF THEY WERE CIVIL PARTNERS.   Under this provision, an individual who has been living with the patient as the patient's husband or wife or as if they were civil partners for at least six months shall be treated as the patient's nearest relative. This rule is subject to the exception that the cohabitee of a married patient or a patient who is in a civil partnership cannot be the nearest relative of that patient unless the patient's spouse or civil partner can be disregarded under subs.(5)(b) on the ground of permanent separation or desertion.

It is not sufficient for the couple to be living together; they must be living together in a settled relationship as if they were husband or wife or civil partners. In *Mummery v Mummery* [1942] P. 107, a case on desertion, Lord Merriman P. doubted that it was possible to "give a completely exhaustive definition of cohabitation". This statement was cited in *Kimber v Kimber* [2000] 1 F.L.R. 383, where Judge Tyrer identified the following factors as being relevant to the question of determining whether a man and a woman are living together as husband and wife:

(a) are the parties living together in the same household;

(b) do they share daily tasks and duties;

(c) is there stability and a degree of permanence in the relationship;

(d) is the way in which financial matters are being handled an indication of the cohabitation;

(e) do the parties have a sexual relationship with each other;

(f) are there children of the relationship;

(g) what is the intention and motivation of the parties; and

(h) would a reasonable person of normal perceptions consider that the parties were cohabiting.

Judge Tyrer said that these factors "cannot be complete nor comprehensive".

WAS SO LIVING UNTIL THE PATIENT WAS ADMITTED.   The six-month period of cohabitation must have occurred prior to the patient's admission.

PERIOD OF NOT LESS THAN SIX MONTHS.   In the unreported case of *R. (on the application of Robinson) v The Hospital Managers of Park Royal Hospital*, November 26, 2007, the cohabiting partner of a detained patient purported to discharge him under s.23 on the ground that she, and not the patient's aunt, was the patient's nearest relative. The hospital declined to discharge him on the ground that the partner was not the patient's nearest relative as she did not qualify under this provision. In dismissing an application for *habeas corpus* and judicial review of the hospital's decision, Stanley Burnton J. said that in calculating the six-month period, a hospital should take into account periods spent apart, including time spent abroad, and/or detention in a hospital or prison (notwithstanding that such absences are under compulsion). As such periods of detention would be recorded, it would not be impracticable for a hospital to make such calculations. Although it might be difficult to identify when a period of cohabitation began, a hospital was obliged to try, as it had a duty to investigate whether a six month cohabitation period had altered the identity of the patient's nearest relative. Whether or not a period apart would bring a cohabitation period to an end for the purposes of this provision would depend on the nature and duration of the relationship when the interruption took place (This case is considered by counsel for the claimant, Laura Davidson, in "Nearest Relative Consultation and the Avoidant Approved Mental Health Professional", J.M.H.L., Spring 2009, 70–80).

With regard to the nature and duration of the relationship, the imprisonment of a patient who had been cohabiting with his partner for a number of years would be unlikely to bring the cohabitation to an end. However, if the imprisonment occurred a few days after the couple had begun to live together, it would be difficult to claim after six months that they had cohabitated.

Subsection (7)

This subsection provides that a person who has been living with the patient for five years **1–412** or more shall be treated as if he or she were a relative who came last on the hierarchy of relatives set out in subs.(1). By virtue of subs.(4), that person, as a relative who "ordinarily resides" with the patient, becomes the patient's nearest relative unless a relative who came higher in the hierarchy is either living with or caring for the patient.

There may be difficulties in identifying the patient's nearest relative in cases where the patient has been residing with a number of people who are not relatives for five years or more in a communal living situation. This could occur where, for example, the patient is a member of a religious community or if he lives in a group home. In this situation the provisions of subs.(3) would apply and the eldest person who had become a "relative" under this subsection would become the patient's nearest relative. However if the patient was being "cared for" by one of the "five year" people, that person would become the nearest relative: see subs.(4).

A particular difficulty has arisen with the identification of the nearest relative of an elderly patient who is the resident of a care home. Although the question of whether a person ordinarily resides with others is a question of fact and degree which must be determined in each case (see the note on "ordinarily resides" in subs.(4)), it would be difficult to argue that the residents of many such homes do not "ordinarily reside" with each other in that they will usually eat together, use common facilities and generally live a communal life. In other words, the residents share a common home. Such a finding would not be appropriate in a case where the residents lived in self-contained units within the home and only had occasional contact with each other for social purposes. If the patient is found to have ordinarily resided with a number of fellow residents for more than five years, the combined effect of subss.(3) and (4) is to identify the eldest of these residents as the patient's nearest relative. The fact that residents might not possess the mental capacity to consent to their admission to a care home or to them being there does not mean that they are not ordinarily resident at the home as long as they are settled there: see the *Cornwall* case noted under subs.(4). If the identified nearest relative does not wish to act in that role he or she could be asked to use the simple procedure set out in reg.24 of the English Regulations or reg.33 of the Welsh Regulations to nominate some other person to take over the responsibilities of nearest relative. If the identified nearest relative is mentally incapacitated, it will not be practicable for that person to be consulted with for the purposes of s.11(4). In this situation an application could be made to the court for an acting nearest relative to be appointed under s.29(3)(b).

If a relative or a spouse of a patient who has been living in a communal situation has had a substantial and sustained contact with the patient by, for example, taking the patient out of the institution for recreational purposes, assisting with feeding the patient or entertaining the patient at his or her home, it might be possible to argue that that person was caring for the patient for the purposes of subs.(4). In these circumstances that person would take precedence over the "five year" person by virtue of subs.(3).

This provision covers the situation where an adult mentally disordered ex-patient has been "fostered" to carers under an adult placement scheme. It seems inappropriate that carers have to wait for five years before one of them is entitled to exercise the functions of nearest relative. It also appears to cover the situation of a child who has been placed with foster parents under either Pt III or Pt IX of the Children Act 1989. If the child remains at that home on reaching adulthood, the period when the child was fostered should be included in the calculation of the five-year period.

It is submitted that a landlord and tenant can only be considered as "ordinarily residing" with each other if they live in the same accommodation and there is a substantial sharing of household facilities and functions.

ORDINARILY RESIDES.   See the note in subs.(4) under this heading. This provision does not require the patient and the person with whom he has resided for five years or more to regard each other as being married or in a civil partnership, or to be lovers, or even to be friends.

FIVE YEARS.   Temporary separations resulting, for example, from separate holidays being taken should be disregarded in calculating this period.

MARRIED PATIENT OR A PATIENT IN A CIVIL PARTNERSHIP.   The "five year" person cannot be the nearest relative of a married patient or a patient in a civil partnership unless the patient's spouse or civil partner can be disregarded because of permanent separation or desertion.

[Children and young persons in care

1–413   **27.** Where—

(a) a patient who is a child or young person is in the care of a local authority by virtue of a care order within the meaning of the Children Act 1989; or—

(b) the rights and powers of a parent of a patient who is a child or young person are vested in a local authority by virtue of section 16 of the Social Work (Scotland) Act 1968,

the authority shall be deemed to be the nearest relative of the patient in preference to any person except the patient's husband or wife [or civil partner] (if any).]

AMENDMENT

This section was substituted by the Children Act 1989 s.108(5), Sch.13, para.48(1). The words in square brackets were inserted by the Mental Health Act 2007 s.26(6).

DEFINITIONS

1–414   patient: s.145(1).

nearest relative: ss.26(3), 145(1).

GENERAL NOTE

1–415   If an unmarried child or a child who is not in a civil partnership is in the care of a local authority by virtue of a care order (in England or Wales) or if parental rights and powers in respect of a child have been vested in a local authority (in Scotland), this section identifies that authority as the child's nearest relative. It would clearly be appropriate for the local authority to delegate its functions under this provision to an officer.

This section applies to children who have been placed under hospital or guardianship orders by a court under s.37 (Sch.1 Pt 1 para.1).

CHILD.   Is defined in the Children Act 1989 as a person under the age of eighteen (s.105(1)).

CARE ORDER. A care order is defined in s.31(11) of the Children Act 1989 to include an interim care order made under s.38 of that Act.

Nearest relative of minor under guardianship, etc.

1–416

28.—[(1) Where

(a) a guardian has been appointed for a person who has not attained the age of eighteen years; or

(b) a [person is named in child arrangements] order (as defined by section 8 of the Children Act 1989) [as a person with whom a person who has not attained the age of eighteen years is to live],

the guardian (or guardians, where there is more than one) or the person [so named (or the persons so named, where there is more than one)] shall, to the exclusion of any other person, be deemed to be his nearest relative.]

(2) Subsection (5) of section 26 above shall apply in relation to a person who is, or who is one of the persons, deemed to be the nearest relative of a patient by virtue of this section as it applies in relation to a person who would be the nearest relative under subsection (3) of that section.

[(3) In this section "guardian" [includes a special guardian (within the meaning of the Children Act 1989), but] does not include a guardian under this Part of this Act.]

(4) In this section "court" includes a court in Scotland or Northern Ireland, and "enactment" includes an enactment of the Parliament of Northern Ireland, a Measure of the Northern Ireland Assembly and an Order in Council under Schedule 1 of the Northern Ireland Act 1974.

AMENDMENTS

The amendments to this section were made by the Children Act 1989 s.108(5), Sch.13 para.48, the Adoption and Children Act 2002 s.139, Sch.3 para.41 and the Children and Families Act 2014 Sch.14, Pt 2, para.46.

DEFINITION

patient: s.145(1).

1–417

GENERAL NOTE

This section provides for a person who has been appointed as a child's guardian (other **1–418** than under this Act), a child's special guardian or a person who is named in a child arrangements order which has been made in respect of a child, to be that child's nearest relative. It applies to children who have been placed under hospital or guardianship orders by a court under s.37 (Sch.1 Pt 1 para.1).

Subsection (1)

ATTAINED THE AGE. At the commencement of his or her eighteenth birthday (Family **1–419** Law Reform Act 1969 s.9(1)).

GUARDIAN. A guardian can only be appointed under s.5 of the Children Act 1989 (Family Law Reform Act 1969 s.5(13)).

GUARDIANS, WHERE THERE IS MORE THAN ONE. Thus two persons, as co-guardians, could have equal powers as the patient's nearest relative. Compare this with s.26(3) where only a sole nearest relative is contemplated.

CHILD ARRANGEMENTS ORDER. Formerly known as a residence order. If more than one person is named in the order, those named will have equal powers as the patient's nearest relative.

Subsection (2)

1–420   This provides that s.26(5), which disqualifies certain persons from acting as a patient's nearest relative, applies to the person or persons deemed to be the patient's nearest relative by virtue of subs.(1).

Subsection (3)

SPECIAL GUARDIAN.   See s.14A of the Children Act 1989.

1–421   GUARDIAN UNDER THIS PART OF THIS ACT.   Such a person could become a patient's nearest relative if, apart from guardianship responsibilities under the Act, he or she would be nearest relative by virtue of either being the person named or appointed under subs.(1) or by being identified as nearest relative under s.26.

Subsection (4)

1–422   This provision should be construed in accordance with Sch.12, paras 1 to 11 of the Northern Ireland Act 1998.

Appointment by court of acting nearest relative

1–423   **29.**—(1) The county court may, upon application made in accordance with the provisions of this section in respect of a patient, by order direct that the functions of the nearest relative of the patient under this Part of this Act and sections 66 and 69 below shall, during the continuance in force of the order, be exercisable by [the person specified in the order].

[(1A) If the court decides to make an order on an application under subsection (1) above, the following rules have effect for the purposes of specifying a person in the order—

(a) if a person is nominated in the application to act as the patient's nearest relative and that person is, in the opinion of the court, a suitable person to act as such and is willing to do so, the court shall specify that person (or, if there are two or more such persons, such one of them as the court thinks fit);

(b) otherwise, the court shall specify such person as is, in its opinion, a suitable person to act as the patient's nearest relative and is willing to do so.]

(2) An order under this section may be made on the application of—

[(za) the patient;]

(a) any relative of the patient;

(b) any other person with whom the patient is residing (or, if the patient is then an in-patient in a hospital, was last residing before he was admitted); or

(c) an [approved mental health professional];

[. . .]

(3) An application for an order under this section may be made upon any of the following grounds, that is to say—

(a) that the patient has no nearest relative within the meaning of this Act, or that it is not reasonably practicable to ascertain whether he has such a relative, or who that relative is;

(b) that the nearest relative of the patient is incapable of acting as such by reason of mental disorder or other illness;

(c) that the nearest relative of the patient unreasonably objects to the making of an application for admission for treatment or a guardianship application in respect of the patient; [. . .]

(d) that the nearest relative of the patient has exercised without due regard to the welfare of the patient or the interests of the public his power to discharge the patient [. . .] under this Part of this Act, or is likely to do so[; or

(e) that the nearest relative of the patient is otherwise not a suitable person to act as such.]

(4) If, immediately before the expiration of the period for which a patient is liable to be detained by virtue of an application for admission for assessment, an application under this section, which is an application made on the ground specified in subsection (3)(c) or (d) above, is pending in respect of the patient, that period shall be extended—

(a) in any case, until the application under this section has been finally disposed of; and

(b) if an order is made in pursuance of the application under this section, for a further period of seven days;

and for the purposes of this subsection an application under this section shall be deemed to have been finally disposed of at the expiration of the time allowed for appealing from the decision of the court or, if notice of appeal has been given within that time, when the appeal has been heard or withdrawn, and "pending" shall be construed accordingly.

(5) An order made on the ground specified in subsection [(3)(a), (b) or (e)] above may specify a period for which it is to continue in force unless previously discharged under section 30 below.

(6) While an order made under this section is in force, the provisions of this Part of this Act (other than this section and section 30 below) and sections 66, 69, 132(4) and 133 below shall apply in relation to the patient as if for any reference to the nearest relative of the patient there were substituted a reference to the person having the functions of that relative and (without prejudice to section 30 below) shall so apply notwithstanding that the person who was the patient's nearest relative when the order was made is no longer his nearest relative; but this subsection shall not apply to section 66 below in the case mentioned in paragraph (h) of subsection (1) of that section.

AMENDMENTS

The amendments to this section were made by the Mental Health Act 2007 ss.21, 23, 55, Sch.2 para.7, Sch.11 Pts 4 and 5.

DEFINITIONS

1–424

patient: s.145(1).
nearest relative: ss.26(3), 145(1).
hospital: ss.34(2), 145(1).
approved mental health professional: s.145(1), (1AC).
local social services authority: s.145(1).
mental disorder: ss.1, 145(1).
application for admission for treatment: ss.3, 145(1).
application for admission for assessment: ss.2, 145(1).
guardianship application: s.7(1).

GENERAL NOTE

1–425 The section gives the county court power to make an order directing that the functions of the patient's nearest relative (NR) shall be exercised by another person, which can include a local social services authority as under the Interpretation Act 1978, Sch.1, a "person" includes a corporation. The effect of an order is to displace the person who would otherwise be the patient's nearest relative. The applicant for the order can nominate a person to act as the patient's NR. Where the nominated person is, in the court's opinion, not "suitable" or there is no nomination, the court can appoint any suitable person to act as the patient's NR if he or she is willing to do so (subs.(1A)). An application to the court can be made concurrently with, or subsequent to, an application under s.3: see s.30(4) and *R. v Central London County Court Ex p. London* [1999] 3 All E.R. 991 CA. An applicant can only rely on the grounds set out in subs.(3). In order to succeed on an application the applicant must demonstrate that the statutory criteria are made out both at the date of the application and at the date of the hearing (*Lewis v Gibson* [2005] EWCA Civ 587; [2005] M.H.L.R. 309 para.38). If the court makes an order under this section, it has no further legal role to play in respect of any subsequent application for treatment or guardianship that is made in respect of the patient.

If the acting nearest relative dies, "no-one can exercise the rights of the nearest relative while the order remains in force, until the court discharges it, or varies it to appoint a new acting nearest relative" (Reference Guide, para.2.57).

In *Surrey County Council Social Services v McMurray*, November 11, 1994, CA, Hale J., in dismissing an appeal by a nearest relative against an order that had been made under this section, said that "the displacement of a person as nearest relative in no way takes away his legitimate interest in the welfare of his daughter, which should always be paid proper respect by the authorities in making decisions about and arrangements for her care".

In *R. (on the application of S) v Plymouth City Council and C* [2002] EWCA Civ 388; [2002] 1 W.L.R. 2582, the Court of Appeal was concerned with how the interest of a mentally incapacitated guardianship patient in preserving the confidentiality of personal information about himself is to be reconciled with his mother's interest, as his nearest relative, in having access to enough information about him to defend a possible displacement application made under this section. This case is considered in the General Note to s.8 and in the note on the Civil Procedure Rules 1998 in Pt 3.

Section 30 gives the county court power to discharge or vary an order made under this section, and also specifies the duration of such an order if the duration has not been established under subs.(5) of this section. An order made under this section does not expire on the transfer of the patient under s.19.

It is prima facie a contempt of court to publish information relating to proceedings brought under this section where the county court is sitting in private: see s.12 of the Administration of Justice Act 1960 and *Pickering v Liverpool Daily Post and Echo Newspapers Plc and others* [1991] 1 All E.R. 622 HL.

Interim and without notice orders

1–426 Section 38 of the County Court Act 1984 provides the county court with the power to make an interim order when considering an application under this section. A decision of the hospital managers to rely on such an order for the purposes of the admission and detention of a patient is lawful: see *R. v Central London County Court*, above, where Stuart-Smith L.J. said at para.24: "unless there are cogent reasons to the contrary, it is preferable that questions under s.29(3)(c) should be finally determined before an application is made under s.3, and the machinery of extension of detention under section afforded by s.29(4) should be used". This statement was considered in *R. (on the application of M) v Homerton University Hospital* [2008] EWCA Civ 197; [2008] M.H.L.R. 92, where the Court of Appeal considered the patient's claim for judicial review on the basis that, where the machinery for extended detention under subs.(4) existed, it was unlawful, in the absence of exceptional circumstances, to detain her under s.3 so that she became subject to concurrent detention regimes. In dismissing the claim, the court held that:

(i) although in might be desirable in some cases to follow the approach advocated by Stuart-Smith L.J., there was nothing in the Act or in the case law to suggest that if a hospital chooses to go down the s.29 route to try to displace the unreasonable relative, they are then bound to conclude those proceedings before taking action under s.3; and

(ii) there is no requirement that "exceptional circumstances" must exist before the s.29 and s.3 regimes may run in tandem.

In order for a s.3 application to be made in these circumstances, the court would have had to have made an interim order displacing the nearest relative. The Court of Appeal did not address the question of how a recommending doctor can certify that, given the patient is subject to an extended s.2, the requirement in s.3(2)(c) that the patient's treatment "cannot be provided unless he is detained under [s.3]" is satisfied. It is submitted that, as the powers of a patient's responsible clinician to treat the patient under s.2 and s.3 are identical, the requirement cannot be satisfied until the lapsing of the extended s.2 is imminent. The making of the s.3 will enable the patient to make an application to the tribunal.

In *R. v Uxbridge County Court Ex p. Binns* [2000] M.H.L.R. 179, the court made a without notice interim order appointing the local authority as the acting nearest relative of the patient. Two hours' notice of the application was given to the nearest relative, who was not served with any papers. The displaced nearest relative was given permission to apply to the court, after giving notice to the local authority, to vary or discharge the order. On an application for judicial review of the order Hidden J. held that:

1. Section 38 of the 1984 Act is broad enough to encompass a temporary order which was both interlocutory and conditional and was not for a specified period.

2. There is nothing in Ord.49 r.12 of the County Court Rules (now see CPR Pt 8.1(6) and Practice Direction 8A—Alternative Procedure for Claims, Section C, para.18.1) which is inconsistent with the general provisions of Pt 23 of the Civil Procedure Rules which, inter alia, entitle a person against whom an order is made without notice to apply to set aside or vary it (para.23.10(1)); require the order to contain a statement of the right to make an application to set aside or vary it (para.23.9(3)); and provide a power in the court to re-list an application where an order had been made in the absence of a respondent either at the application of that person or of the court's own motion (para.23.11(2)). His Lordship said, at para.30, that the court should be slow to conclude that a practice consistent with the Civil Procedure Rules was precluded by the terms of the 1983 Act.

3. Since the 1983 Act does not set out a complete code governing the making of orders displacing the nearest relative of a patient (for example, it does not mention interim orders), then the submission that the granting of permission to apply would necessarily be ultra vires s.30 is an incorrect one.

4. The order made by the court was proportionate.

Binns was applied in *R. (on the application of Holloway) v Oxfordshire County Council* [2007] EWHC 776 (Admin); [2007] M.H.L.R. 225, where Beatson J. upheld an interim displacement order where the nearest relative had not been given notice of the proceedings. The conduct of the local authority in not giving notice was described, at para.33, as falling "far below what is required of a public authority in the exercise of its responsibilities to persons with mental illness and the nearest relatives of such person". His Lordship held that:

1. Order 49, r.12 (now CPR Pt 8.1(6) and Practice Direction 8A) did not assist the nearest relative as the words of that provision do not preclude an application being made without notice.

2. What the principles of natural justice require at the preliminary stage of a process is different from what they require where a binding decision is to be made.

3. Applications which are not determinative, such as applications for interim relief, are not subject to the guarantees set out in art.6 of the European Convention on Human Rights (ECHR) unless they cause irreversible prejudice to a party's interests. An interim displacement does not fall into this category as there are sufficient safeguards in the Act for the patient and for his nearest relative.

4. An application for an interim order made without notice to the person affected should only be made where it is necessary to act urgently.

5. It is good practice for a judge hearing a without notice application to make enquiries as to whether it was practicable to have given notice to the nearest relative and to consider whether it would be possible to adjourn the hearing for such notice to be given. Those making the application should apprise the judge of all the relevant facts, including those that may be adverse to the application.

An applicant who makes a without notice application to the court has a duty to investigate the facts and to make a full and fair disclosure of all the crucial points for and against the application. It is no excuse for an applicant to say that he was not aware of the importance of matters he has omitted to state (*Marc Rich & Co v Krasner* [1999] EWCA Civ 581). Judicial guidance on the procedure applicable to without notice applications was considered and expanded upon by Theis J. in *KY v DD* [2011] EWHC 1277 (Fam) at paras 13 to 16. Without notice applications are governed by Pt 23.9 and 10 of the Civil Procedure Rules.

Human Rights Act 1998

1–427   In *R. (on the application of H) v Secretary of State for Health* [2005] UKHL 60; [2005] 4 All E.R. 1311, it was contended on behalf of the patient that the Act fails to comply with art.5(4) of the ECHR, which is designed to procure the speedy release of someone who should not in fact have been detained in the first place or should not be detained any longer, in that it does not provide a right of review at reasonable intervals for a patient who finds herself detained by virtue of s.29(4) and is thus deprived of the right which a patient newly detained under s.3 would have. The House of Lords held that as the system provided for by s.29(4) is *capable* of acting compatibly with art.5(4), it could not be said to be incompatible with art.5(4) although action or inaction by the authorities under it may be so. The preferable means of achieving compatibility is for the Secretary of State to use her power under s.67(1) to refer the case to the tribunal. As the Secretary of State is under a duty to act compatibly with the patient's Convention rights, she would be well advised to make such a reference as soon as the position is drawn to her attention by the patient's lawyers. Should the Secretary of State decline to exercise this power, judicial review would be swiftly available to oblige her to do so. It would also be possible for the hospital managers or the local social services authority to notify the Secretary of State whenever an application is made under s.29 so that she can consider the position. Although judicial review and/or habeas corpus may be one way of securing compliance, this would be much more satisfactorily achieved either through a speedy determination of the county court proceedings or by a Secretary of State's reference under s.67. This case was considered by the European Court of Human Rights in *MH v United Kingdom* (2014) 58 E.H.R.R. 965; [2014] M.H.L.R. 249, where the Court held that the approach adopted by the House of Lords was compatible with art.5(4). The Court declined to consider the hypothetical situation "had the applicant not had a relative willing and able, through solicitors, to bring her situation to the attention of the Secretary of State" (para.95). Also see paras 37.45 and 37.46 of the *Code of Practice*.

In *MA v Secretary of State for Health* [2012] UKUT 474 (AAC), UT Judge Levenson held that the fact that the patient's nearest relative does not have a right to make an application to a tribunal in respect of a patient who has been detained for assessment and whose detention has been extended by virtue of the operation of s.29(4), does not violate art.6 of the ECHR as the availability of judicial review to challenge the lawfulness of the patient's detention is an adequate remedy.

Appeals

By virtue of art.3 of the Access to Justice 1999 (Destination of Appeals) Order 2000 (SI **1–428** 2000/1071), an appeal against an order made under this section lays with a High Court judge, not the Court of Appeal (*Massie v H* [2001] EWCA Civ 115; [2011] M.H.L.R. 288).

Applications to the First-tier Tribunal (Mental Health) or the Mental Health Review Tribunal for Wales

A patient's nearest relative who has been supplanted by an order made under subs.(3)(c) **1–429** or (d) of this section can apply to a tribunal within 12 months or the order being made and during any subsequent 12 month period while the order is in force: see subs.(6) and s.66(1)(h),(2)(g). An acting nearest relative who has been appointed under this section has a separate power to make an application: see the note on "Nearest relative" in s.66(1).

Code of Practice

The displacement of the nearest relative is considered in Ch.5. With regard to the support **1–430** that should be provided to patients, the *Code* states:

"5.21 If the patient has any concerns that any information given to the court on their views on the suitability of the nearest relative may have implications for their own safety, an application can be made to the court seeking its permission not to make the current nearest relative a party to the proceedings. The reasons for the patient's concerns should be set out clearly in the application.

5.22 Hospital managers should provide support to detained patients to enable them to attend the court, if they wish, subject to the patient being granted leave under section 17 for this purpose.

5.23 If, exceptionally, the court decides to interview the patient (as the applicant), the court has the discretion to decide where and how this interview takes place and whether it should take place in the presence of, or separate from, other parties. The patient should be fully supported in this, including through the use of an advocate to support them."

Subsection (1)

The judge has a discretion as to whether or not to make an order displacing the nearest **1–431** relative notwithstanding that one of the grounds set out in subs.(3) has been satisfied (*Barnet LBC v Robin* (1999) 2 C.C.L.R. 454, CA).

Applications under this section are brought under Part 8 of the Civil Procedure Rules (*Massie v H*, above). They "have to be dealt with quickly" (*R. (on the application of S) v Plymouth City Council*, above, per Hale L.J. at para.39). In *Derbyshire CC v Maude*, July 5, 1999, CA (unreported), Sedley L.J. described a delay of a year for an application to come to the county court as "at lowest, alarming".

An application cannot be made in respect of a person who is not suffering from a mental disorder even if it is thought that the person would be likely to develop a mental disorder at some time in the future.

COUNTY COURT. For the procedure on an application to the county court, see s.31 and the Civil Procedure Rules 1998 (SI 1998/3132) Pt 8.1(6) and Practice Direction 8A— Alternative Procedure for Claims, Section C, para.18.1 which are reproduced in Pt 3. The court has the power to make an interim order when considering an application: see the General Note to this section.

Jurisdiction under this section can only be exercised by a circuit judge (CPR Practice Direction 2B: Allocation of Cases to Levels of Judiciary, para.11.1).

FUNCTIONS OF THE NEAREST RELATIVE.   The nearest relative retains the power of discharge under s.23 during the currency of an application. If the nearest relative has exercised the power under reg.24 of the English Regulations or reg.33 of the Welsh Regulations to delegate his or her functions to another person, action under this section must be directed against the nearest relative and not the delegate.

In *R. v Birmingham Mental Health Trust Ex p. Phillips* (CO/1501/95), May 25, 1995, Tucker J. refused applications for *habeas corpus* and judicial review that had been made in respect of a patient who had been detained under s.2 and whose nearest relative had been wrongly identified for the purposes of s.11(3). His Lordship held that an application that was subsequently made under this section to displace that relative was not invalildated by the mistake.

SECTIONS 66 AND 69.   Which are concerned with applications to the First-tier Tribunal (Mental Health) or the Mental Health Review Tribunal for Wales.

Subsection (1A)

1–432   If an order is made under this section, the patient's acting nearest relative will either be:

   (i) the person nominated in the application to perform the role if that person is willing to do so and the court considers that person to be suitable; or

  (ii) otherwise, the person that the court specifies as being suitable to perform the role if that person is willing to do so.

The person appointed need not be related to the patient or otherwise qualified to be the patient's nearest relative under s.26. With regard to (i), if the application is made by an AMHP, para.5.19 of the *Code of Practice* states:

> "AMHPs should nominate someone to become the acting nearest relative in the event that application is successful. Wherever practicable, they should first consult the patient about the patient's own preferences and any concerns they have about the person the AMHP proposes to nominate. AMHPs should also seek the agreement of the proposed nominee prior to an application being made, although this is not a legal requirement."

If a local social services authority is appointed as acting nearest relative, the authority must comply with its duties under s.116.

Subsection (2)

THE PATIENT.   Who is a person suffering or appearing to be suffering from mental disorder (s.145(1)). The patient need not be a patient who is subject to either an application or an order made under the Act.

1–433   RELATIVE OF THE PATIENT.   Is defined in s.26(1).

RESIDING.   It is not necessary for the applicant to be ordinarily residing with the patient.

APPROVED MENTAL HEALTH PROFESSIONAL.   An AMHP applicant acts in a personal capacity and is not therefore bound to follow the advice of her managers. The AMHP should receive the legal advice and support that an employer would normally provide to an employee who is involved in legal proceedings by virtue of the nature of their employment.

Paragraph 5.13 of the *Code of Practice* states that "AMHPs should bear in mind that some patients may wish to apply to displace their nearest relative but may be deterred from doing so by the need to apply to the county court". Paragraph 5.16 of the *Code* states:

"Before making an application for displacement, AMHPs should consider other ways of achieving the same end, including:

- whether the nearest relative will agree to delegate their role as the patient's nearest relative to someone else, or

- providing or arranging support to the patient (or someone else) to make an application themselves. This could include support from an independent mental health advocate (IMHA)."

Subsection (3)

There is no requirement to make an application in any of the situations specified in this **1–434** provision. The list of grounds is exhaustive.

Paragraph (a)

AMHPs should consider acting on this ground if the patient is likely to be subject to the **1–435** provisions of the Act for more than a short period, or if a suitable person comes forward who is willing to perform the functions of the nearest relative.

Paragraph (b)

If an application is being made on the ground that the nearest relative is incapable of act- **1–436** ing as nearest relative by reason of mental disorder, CPR Pt 21 applies and a litigation friend should be appointed if the individual lacks capacity within the terms of CPR r.21.1(2), i.e. a person who "lacks capacity within the meaning of the [Mental Capacity Act 2005]". Normally the Official Solicitor agrees to act as litigation friend and consents to the application on the basis of the medical evidence supplied. The Official Solicitor prefers the medical evidence to be provided by a doctor who will not be involved in the potential detention of the patient.

INCAPABLE. This ground is only available if the person concerned is unable to perform the functions of nearest relative; it does not cover the situation of a nearest relative who exercises his or her functions in an irresponsible manner.

If an AMHP concludes that it is not practicable to consult with the patient's nearest relative under s.11(4) because of that person's mental incapacity, an application under s.3 can proceed without an application being made to the court under this provision.

Paragraph (c)

UNREASONABLY OBJECTS. Both at the date of the application and at the date of hearing **1–437** (*Lewis v Gibson* [2005] EWCA Civ 587; [2005] M.H.L.R. 309). In *W v L* [1974] Q.B. 711 the Court of Appeal held that the proper test for the county court to apply is an objective one: the court should ask what an objectively reasonable person would do in all the circumstances, and not ask whether the actual nearest relative involved in the case was behaving reasonably from his or her own subjective point of view. The court stated that this test is similar to the test in adoption cases in which the House of Lords approved the following statement:

". . . in considering whether she is reasonable or unreasonable we must take into account the welfare of the child. A reasonable mother surely gives great weight to what is better for the child. Her anguish of mind is quite understandable: but still it may be unreasonable for her to withhold consent" (*Re W (An Infant)* [1971] 2 All E.R. 49 at 55 per Lord Hailsham L.C. citing Lord Denning M.R. in *Re L (An Infant)* (1962) 106 Sol. Jo. 611).

In *Re W*, the court held that two reasonable parents can perfectly reasonably come to opposite conclusions on the same set of facts without forfeiting their title to be regarded as reasonable. The question before a court hearing an application under this provision is therefore whether a nearest relative's objection comes within the band of possible reasonable decisions and not whether it is right or mistaken. Lord Hailsham said at 56:

"Not every reasonable exercise of judgment is right, and not every mistaken exercise of judgment is unreasonable. There is a band of decisions within which no court should seek to replace the individuals judgment with his own."

In *Smirek v Williams* [2000] M.H.L.R. 38 CA Hale L.J. said that, in her view,

"it cannot possibly be outside that band of reasonable decisions for the [nearest relative] to agree with, and rely upon, a recent decision of a [tribunal] unless there has since been a change in the circumstances leading to that decision."

As the nearest relative is objecting to an application being made and as an AMHP applicant is required by s.13(1A) to consider "relevant circumstances", it would seem that a reasonable nearest relative is entitled to consider all the circumstances of the case and not just the medical evidence.

The obiter comment of Lawton L.J. in *B(A) v B(L) (Mental Health Patient)* [1980] 1 W.L.R. 116, CA, that "the judge must have some evidence that compulsory admission to hospital and detention is necessary" suggests that a court hearing an application under this paragraph should consider the merits for detaining the patient by reference to the statutory criteria before moving on to considering the reasonableness of the nearest relative's decision. The judge should not be concerned to establish whether the technical requirements of the Act relating to applications for detention or guardianship have been satisfied. In the words of Lawton L.J. at 121:

"The object of an application under [this paragraph] is to enable the provisions of [s.3] to be brought into operation, and until an application has been dealt with under [this section the AMHP] is not in a position to make an application under [s.3]. It follows, so it seems to me, that if there were any defects for the purposes of [s.3] in the form of the reports tendered to the county court judge they were irrelevant for the purposes of . . . the application. The county court judge had to look at the reports for their medical content; he was not concerned with their statutory form".

Paragraph (d)

1–438   WITHOUT DUE REGARD.   The test is an objective one (*Surrey County Council Social Services v McMurray*, November 11, 1994, CA).

POWER TO DISCHARGE THE PATIENT.   From detention, guardianship or a community treatment order using the power contained in s.23. When considering an application under this paragraph, the judge should consider not only the history of the matter but also the situation with which he is faced at the date of the hearing (*Lewis v Gibson*, above).

OR IS LIKELY TO DO SO.   It is possible to make an application under this provision before the patient is made subject to the provisions of the Act.

Paragraph (e)

1–439   This paragraph, which addresses the incompatibility identified by the European Commission of Human Rights in *JT v United Kingdom* (2000) 30 E.H.R.R. C.D. 77, provides an applicant with a right to apply to the county court for an order displacing his or her NR on the ground that the NR is unsuitable to act as such. The Minister of State outlined the Government's thinking on this ground:

"We have in mind situations where a NR's occupation of that role and its powers under the Act pose a real and present danger to the health or well-being of the patient. Where a NR has abused the patient, for instance, he should not be allowed to exercise the rights of the NR. It is not important how recently the abuse took place. If the patient or others who know or are close to the patient have a genuine fear that the abuse may be repeated – or even that a relationship with a formally abusive NR may cause the patient distress – we intend that such a person should be considered unsuitable to act as the NR of the patient. These applications will be heard, as they now are, in the county court. The court will not be asked to sit in judgment of any of the past actions or deeds of the NR. Their role will be to determine whether the NR is otherwise suitable to act as such.

The opinions and views of the patient will be very important and we fully expect that they will form part of the court's deliberations. However, we do not wish the court to feel that it is prevented from displacing a NR it deems unsuitable, even where the patient would wish that person to remain as their NR. I would instance cases where the victim of an abuser actually acts to protect the abuser, either out of fear of the abuser or through a form of identification with him. We do not wish the court to feel constrained in such circumstances in displacing a NR it finds unsuitable" (*Hansard,* HL Vol.688, col.672).

The Government also (i) confirmed that the term "suitable" is intended to "include, but not be so narrow as to be limited to, NRs who have a history of abusing or potential to abuse the patient" (*Hansard*, HL Vol.689, col.1404, per Baroness Royall), and (ii) said that it "intends that a person is not suitable to be the NR where that person has no relationship with – and intends to have no further relationship with – the patient. In addition, it is intended that a person is not suitable to be the NR where the risk posed to the patient is by virtue of a third party and the NR exposes the patient to that risk" (The Government's response to the report of the Joint Committee on Human Rights, Department of Health, April 13, 2007, para.40).

Paragraph 5.14 of the *Code of Practice* states:

"It is entirely a matter for the court to decide what constitutes 'suitability' of a person to be a nearest relative. Factors which an AMHP might wish to consider when deciding whether to make an application to displace a nearest relative on those grounds, and when providing evidence in connection with an application, could include:

- any reason to think that the patient has suffered, or is suspected to have suffered, abuse at the hands of the nearest relative (or someone with whom the nearest relative is in a relationship), or is at risk of suffering such abuse

- whether the patient is afraid of the nearest relative or seriously distressed by the possibility of the nearest relative being involved in their life or their care, or

- whether the patient and nearest relative are unknown to each other, there is only a distant relationship, or their relationship has broken down irretrievably.

This is not an exhaustive list."

OTHERWISE.   An application under this ground should not be brought where the facts of the case would enable an application to be made under ground (b), (c) or (d).

Subsection (4)

This subsection provides that if the patient is detained for assessment and an application **1–440** is made to the county court on ground (c) or (d) before the 28 days provided for in s.2 expire, the period for which the patient may be detained is extended until the application is finally disposed of and, if an order is made, for a further period of seven days to enable the formalities of a s.3 application to be complied with. The provisions of Pt II, including the power to grant the patient leave of absence under s.17, will continue to apply during the extended period. An authenticated copy of the application to the court should be placed with the patient's statutory documentation as this provides the hospital managers with continued authority for the patient's detention. If a patient who has had his detention extended by virtue of this provision has not applied to a tribunal within the first 14 days of the detention, there is no opportunity for the patient to make an application to the tribunal for the s.2 to be discharged even if the extended period is lengthy. For the action that should be taken in such a situation, see *R. (on the application of H) v Secretary of State for Health*, noted under "Human Rights Act 1998", above. It is submitted that that would not be compatible with the patient's rights under art.5(4) of the ECHR for the hospital managers to delay taking action until the patient is referred to the tribunal after the expiration of the six month period provided for in s.68.

A fresh assessment of the patient under the Act should be undertaken prior to the court hearing in order to determine whether the requirements of s.3 continue to be satisfied. It is lawful to make an application under s.3 before the proceedings under this section have been resolved (*R. (on the application of M) v Homerton University Hospital* [2008] EWCA Civ 197; [2008] M.H.L.R. 92).

A nearest relative is not deprived of his or her power of discharge under s.23 during the period of the extended s.2. The patient's RC could prevent such a discharge taking effect if the provisions of s.25 apply. The hospital managers and the RC also retain their power of discharge during this period.

IMMEDIATELY BEFORE THE EXPIRATION OF THE PERIOD FOR WHICH A PATIENT IS LIABLE TO BE DETAINED. Where a tribunal has ordered the discharge of the patient from s.2 and has exercised its power under s.72(3) to delay the discharge to a specified future date, the provisions of this subsection will apply if an application under this section is made to the county court before that date (*Re W* [1999] M.H.L.R. 1).

PARAGRAPH (A); FINALLY DISPOSED OF. The detention continues during the period for lodging an appeal, and if an appeal is lodged, the time taken to determine it.

If an application has been made under para.(c) and the nearest relative subsequently withdraws his or her objection, the application will be finally disposed of when it is formally withdrawn from the court by the applicant.

Subsection (5)

1–441 This subsection provides that an order made on the grounds specified in subs.(3)(a), (b) or (e) may specify a period for which the order will remain in force, unless it is discharged. One example of a way in which a court might use this power would be to specify that the order should cease on the date when the eldest child of the patient reached 18, so that he or she could then take on the role of nearest relative. Further provision relating to the duration of orders made under these paragraphs is made in s.30(4B).

Subsection (6)

1–442 This subsection specifies the functions of an acting nearest relative. Apart from the exceptions noted, the nearest relative's functions are exercisable by the acting nearest relative during the period of the appointment. Such functions include the power to delegate the functions to another person: see the General Note to s.26. It also provides that an order made under this section remains in force notwithstanding that the person who was the patient's nearest relative when the order was made is no longer his nearest relative, for example as a result of the death of that person. If the acting nearest relative dies, no-one can exercise the rights of the nearest relative unless the order is either discharged or varied under s.30.

SHALL NOT APPLY ... IN THE CASE MENTIONED IN PARAGRAPH (H). See the note on *Applications to the First-tier Tribunal (Mental Health) or the Mental Health Review Tribunal for Wales*, above.

Discharge and variation of orders under s.29

30.—(1) An order made under section 29 above in respect of a patient may be **1–443** discharged by the county court upon application made—

(a) in any case, by [the patient or] the person having the functions of the nearest relative of the patient by virtue of the order;

(b) where the order was made on the ground specified in paragraph (a) [, (b) or (e)] of section 29(3) above, or where the person who was the nearest relative of the patient when the order was made has ceased to be his nearest relative, on the application of the nearest relative of the patient.

[(1A) But, in the case of an order made on the ground specified in paragraph (e) of section 29(3) above, an application may not be made under subsection (1)(b) above by the person who was the nearest relative of the patient when the order was made except with leave of the county court.]

(2) An order made under section 29 above in respect of a patient may be varied by the county court, on the application of the person having the functions of the nearest relative by virtue of the order or on the application of [the patient or of] an [approved mental health professional], by substituting [another person for the person having those functions].

[(2A) If the court decides to vary an order on an application under subsection (2) above, the following rules have effect for the purposes of substituting another person—

(a) if a person is nominated in the application to act as the patient's nearest relative and that person is, in the opinion of the court, a suitable person to act as such and is willing to do so, the court shall specify that person (or, if there are two or more such persons, such one of them as the court thinks fit);

(b) otherwise, the court shall specify such person as is, in its opinion, a suitable person to act as the patient's nearest relative and is willing to do so.]

(3) If the person having the functions of the nearest relative of a patient by virtue of an order under section 29 above dies—

(a) subsections (1) and (2) above shall apply as if for any reference to that person there were substituted a reference to any relative of the patient, and

(b) until the order is discharged or varied under those provisions the functions of the nearest relative under this Part of this Act and sections 66 and 69 below shall not be exercisable by any person.

(4) [An order made on the ground specified in paragraph (c) or (d) of section 29(3) above shall, unless previously discharged under subsection (1) above, cease to have effect as follows]—

[(a) if—

(i) on the date of the order the patient was liable to be detained or subject to guardianship by virtue of a relevant application, order or direction; or

(ii) he becomes so liable or subject within the period of three months beginning with that date; or

(iii) he was a community patient on the date of the order,

it shall cease to have effect when he is discharged under section 23 above or 72 below or the relevant application, order or direction otherwise ceases to have effect (except as a result of his being transferred in pursuance of regulations under section 19 above);

(b) otherwise, it shall cease to have effect at the end of the period of three months beginning with the date of the order.]

[(4A) In subsection (4) above, reference to a relevant application, order or direction is to any of the following—

(a) an application for admission for treatment;

(b) a guardianship application;

(c) an order or direction under Part 3 of this Act (other than under section 35, 36 or 38).]

[(4B) An order made on the ground specified in paragraph (a), (b) or (e) of section 29(3) above shall—

(a) if a period was specified under section 29(5) above, cease to have effect on expiry of that period, unless previously discharged under subsection (1) above;

(b) if no such period was specified, remain in force until it is discharged under subsection (1) above.]

(5) The discharge or variation under this section of an order made under section 29 above shall not affect the validity of anything previously done in pursuance of the order.

AMENDMENTS

The amendments to this section were made by the Mental Health Act 2007 ss.21, 24, 32(4), Sch.2 para.7, Sch.3 para.14.

DEFINITIONS

1–444   patient: s.145(1).

nearest relative: ss.26(3), 145(1).

approved mental health professional: s.145(1), (1AC).

application for admission for treatment: ss.3, 145(1).

community patient: ss.17A(7), 145(1).

guardianship application: s.7(1).

GENERAL NOTE

1–445   This section provides for the discharge or variation of an order made by a county court under s.29 for the appointment of an acting nearest relative. It also, in subss.(4), (4A) and (4B), specifies the duration of an order.

Subsection (1)

1–446   PARAGRAPH (A), (B) OR (E).   A nearest relative who has been displaced under s.29(3)(e) cannot make an application for the order to be discharged without leave of the county court (subs.(1A)). A nearest relative who is displaced under s.29(3)(c) or (d) cannot apply for the order to be discharged.

Subsection (2)

1–447   This subsection provides for an application to be made to the county court for the variation of the order appointing the acting nearest relative.

Subsection (3)

1–448   If the person appointed as acting nearest relative dies, this subsection provides that (i) any applications that could have been made by that person under subss.(1) and (2) can be made by any relative of the patient, and (ii) no one can exercise the functions of nearest relative until the order that appointed the acting nearest relative is discharged or varied.

Subsections (4), (4A)

1–449   These subsections determine when an order appointing an acting nearest relative has been made on the grounds specified in s.29(3)(c) or (d) ceases to have effect. Their effect is that the order will either expire: (i) after three months; or (ii) if the patient was detained or subject to guardianship at the time of the order, or within three months of it, at the time when the application, order or direction authorising the patient's detention or guardianship is either discharged or otherwise ceases to have effect. The order will not end if the patient is placed on a community treatment order or is made subject to a transfer under s.19. An application can be made under subs.(1) to discharge the order.

Subsection (4B)

This subsection determines when an order appointing an acting nearest relative has been **1–450** made on the grounds specified in s.29(3)(a), (b) or (e) ceases to have effect. Its effect is that the order will either last for the period stated in it (if any) or will last indefinitely. In both cases, the order will end if it is discharged under subs.(1).

Supplemental

Procedure on applications to county court

31. [Rules of court] which relate to applications authorised by this Part of this **1–451** Act to be made to [the county court] may make provision—

(a) for the hearing and determination of such applications otherwise than in open court;

(b) for the admission on the hearing of such applications of evidence of such descriptions as may be specified in the rules notwithstanding anything to the contrary in any enactment or rule of law relating to the admissibility of evidence:

(c) for the visiting and interviewing of patients in private by or under the directions of the court.

AMENDMENTS

The amendments to this section were made by the Crime and Courts Act 2013 Sch.9, paras 52(1)(b) and 112.

DEFINITION

patient: s.145(1). **1–452**

GENERAL NOTE

This section is applied to patients who have been placed under hospital or guardianship **1–453** orders by a court under s.37 (Sch.1 Pt I para.1).

RULES OF COURT. See the Civil Procedure Rules 1998 (SI 1998/3132) Pt 8.1(6) and Practice Direction 8A—Alternative Procedure for Claims, Section C, para.18.1 which are reproduced in Pt 3.

OTHERWISE THAN IN OPEN COURT. The publication of information relating to proceedings brought under the Act before a county court sitting in private is prima facie a contempt of court: see s.12 of the Administration of Justice Act 1960 and *Pickering v Liverpool Daily Post and Echo Newspapers Plc* [1991] 1 All E.R. 622 HL.

Regulations for purposes of Part II

32.—(1) The Secretary of State may make regulations for prescribing anything **1–454** which, under this Part of this Act, is required or authorised to be prescribed, and otherwise for carrying this Part of this Act into full effect.

(2) Regulations under this section may in particular make provision—

(a) for prescribing the form of any application, recommendation, report, order, notice or other document to be made or given under this Part of this Act;

(b) for prescribing the manner in which any such application, recommendation, report, order, notice or other document may be proved, and for regulating the service of any such application, report, order or notice;

(c) for requiring [such bodies as may be prescribed by the regulations] to keep such registers or other records as may be [so prescribed] in respect of patients liable to be detained or subject to guardianship [. . .] under super-vision] under this Part of this Act [or community patients], and to furnish or make available to those patients, and their relatives, such written statements of their rights and powers under this Act as may be so prescribed;

(d) for the determination in accordance with the regulations of the age of any person whose exact age cannot be ascertained by reference to the registers kept under the Births and Deaths Registration Act 1953; and

(e) for enabling the functions under this Part of this Act of the nearest relative of a patient to be performed, in such circumstances and subject to such con-ditions (if any) as may be prescribed by the regulations, by any person authorised in that behalf by that relative;

and for the purposes of this Part of this Act any application, report or notice the service of which is regulated under paragraph (b) above shall be deemed to have been received by or furnished to the authority or person to whom it is auth-orised or required to be furnished, addressed or given if it is duly served in accordance with the regulations.

(3) Without prejudice to subsections (1) and (2) above, but subject to section 23(4) [and (6)] above, regulations under this section may determine the manner in which functions under this Part of this Act of the managers of hospitals, local social services authorities, [[Local Health Board], Special Health Authorities [. . .][, National Health Service trusts or NHS foundation trusts] are to be exercised, and such regulations may in particular specify the circumstances in which, and the conditions subject to which, any such functions may be per-formed by officers of or other persons acting on behalf of those managers[, boards,] and [authorities and trusts].

AMENDMENTS

The amendments to this section were made by the Health Authorities Act 1995 s.2(1), Sch.1 para.107(4), the Mental Health (Patients in the Community) Act 1995 s.2(1), Sch.1 para.2, the Health Act 1999 (Supplementary, Consequential, etc. Provisions) Order 2000 (SI 2000/90) Sch.1 para.16(6), the NHS and Community Care Act 1990 s.66(1), Sch.9 para.24(5), the Health and Social Care (Community Health and Standards) Act 2003 s.34, Sch.4 para.55, the Mental Health Act 2007 ss.32(4), 45(2), 55, Sch.3 para.15, Sch.11 Pt 5, SI 2007/961 art.3, Sch. para.13(7) and the Health and Social Care Act 2012 Sch.5, para.27.

DEFINITIONS

1–455   community patient: ss.17A(7), 145(1).
the managers: s.145(1).
hospital: ss.34(2), 145(1).
local social services authority: s.145(1).
patient: s.145(1).
nearest relative: ss.26(3), 145(1).
Health Authority: s.145(1).

Local Health Board: s.145(1).
Special Health Authority: s.145(1).

GENERAL NOTE
This section applies to patients who have been placed under hospital, restriction or guar- **1–456**
dianship orders by a court under ss.37 or 41 (Sch.1 Pt I para.1, Pt II para.1).

Subsection (1)
SECRETARY OF STATE. The functions of the Minister, so far as exercisable in relation to **1–457**
Wales, are exercised by the Welsh Ministers (see the General Note to the Act and SI 1999/
672 art.2, Sch.1).

Special provisions as to wards of court

33.—(1) An application for the admission to hospital of a minor who is a ward **1–458**
of court may be made under this Part of this Act with the leave of the court; and
section 11(4) above shall not apply in relation to an application so made.

(2) Where a minor who is a ward of court is liable to be detained in a hospital by
virtue of an application for admission under this Part of this Act [or is a community patient], any power exercisable under this Part of this Act or under
section 66 below in relation to the patient by his nearest relative shall be exercisable by or with the leave of the court.

(3) Nothing in this Part of this Act shall be construed as authorising the making
of a guardianship application in respect of a minor who is a ward of court, or the
transfer into guardianship of any such minor.

[(4) Where a community treatment order has been made in respect of a minor
who is a ward of court, the provisions of this Part of this Act relating to community
treatment orders and community patients have effect in relation to the minor subject to any order which the court makes in the exercise of its wardship jurisdiction;
but this does not apply as regards any period when the minor is recalled to hospital
under section 17E above.]

AMENDMENTS
The words in square brackets in subs.(2) were inserted, and subs.(4) was substituted by
the Mental Health Act 2007 s.32(4), Sch.3 para.16.

DEFINITIONS
hospital: ss.34(2), 145(1).   **1–459**
nearest relative: ss.26(3), 145(1).
community patient: ss.17A(7), 145(1).
community treatment order: ss.17A(7), 145(1).
guardianship application: s.7(1).

GENERAL NOTE
This section provides that the leave of the court must be obtained before a ward of court **1–460**
can be compulsorily detained in hospital (subs.(1)), and before the ward's nearest relative
exercises his or her powers (subs.(2)). It also prohibits the reception or transfer of a ward of
court into guardianship (subs.(3)) and makes any power or duty exercisable in respect of a
ward who is subject to a community treatment order subject to the wardship court's jurisdiction (apart from a period when the child has been recalled to hospital) (subs.(4)).

Subsection (1)

1–461   SECTION 11(4) . . . SHALL NOT APPLY.   An AMHP should not consult the nearest relative about an application to admit a ward of court under s.3 nor may the nearest relative block the application by objecting to it.

Interpretation of Part II

1–462   **34.**—(1) In this Part of this Act—

["the appropriate practitioner" means—

(a) in the case of a patient who is subject to the guardianship of a person other than a local social services authority, the nominated medical attendant of the patient; and

(b) in any other case, the responsible clinician;]

[. . .]

"the nominated medical attendant", in relation to a patient who is subject to the guardianship of a person other than a local social services authority, means the person appointed in pursuance of regulations made under section 9(2) above to act as the medical attendant of the patient;

["registered establishment" means an establishment which would not, apart from subsection (2) below, be a hospital for the purposes of this Part and which—

(a) in England, is a hospital as defined by section 275 of the National Health Service Act 2006 that is used for the carrying on of a regulated activity, within the meaning of Part 1 of the Health and Social Care Act 2008, which relates to the assessment or medical treatment of mental disorder and in respect of which a person is registered under Chapter 2 of that Part; and

(b) in Wales, is an establishment in respect of which a person is registered under Part 2 of the Care Standards Act 2000 as an independent hospital in which treatment or nursing (or both) are provided for persons liable to be detained under this Act;]

["the responsible clinician" means—

(a) in relation to a patient liable to be detained by virtue of an application for admission for assessment or an application for admission for treatment, or a community patient, the approved clinician with overall responsibility for the patient's case;

(b) in relation to a patient subject to guardianship, the approved clinician authorised by the responsible local social services authority to act (either generally or in any particular case or for any particular purpose) as the responsible clinician;]

[. . .]

[(1A) [. . .]

(2) Except where otherwise expressly provided, this Part of this Act applies in relation to [a registered establishment], as it applies in relation to a hospital, and references in this Part of this Act to a hospital, and any reference in this Act to a hospital to which this Part of this Act applies, shall be construed accordingly.

(3) In relation to a patient who is subject to guardianship in pursuance of a guardianship application, any reference in this Part of this Act to the responsible local social services authority is a reference—

(a) where the patient is subject to the guardianship of a local social services authority, to that authority;

(b) where the patient is subject to the guardianship of a person other than a local social services authority, to the local social services authority for the area in which that person resides.

AMENDMENTS

The words in square brackets in subs.(2) were substituted, by the Care Standards Act 2000 s.116, Sch.4 para.9(4). The definition of "registered establishment was substituted by SI 2010/813, art.5(3). The definition of "appropriate practitioner" was inserted, and the definition of "responsible clinician" was substituted for the definition of responsible medical officer by the Mental Health Act 2007 s.9(9),(10). The words omitted were repealed by the Mental Health Act 2007 s.55 Sch.11 Pt 5.

DEFINITIONS

patient: s.145(1).   **1–463**

local social services authority: s.145(1).

application for admission for assessment: ss.2, 145(1).

application for admission for treatment: ss.3, 145(1).

hospital: s.145(1) and subss.2 of this section.

approved clinician: s.145(1).

community patient: ss.17A(7), 145(1).

mental disorder: ss.1, 145(1).

independent hospital: s.145(1).

GENERAL NOTE

This section, which defines key terms in Part II of the Act, applies to patients who have **1–464** been placed under hospital or guardianship orders made by a court under s.37 (Sch.1 Pt I para.1), and to restricted patients with the modification that in subs.(1) the definition of "the nominated medical attendant" and subs.(3) shall be omitted (Sch.1 Pt II paras 2, 8).

Human Rights Act 1998

The appropriate practitioner, the nominated medical attendant and the responsible clin- **1–465** ician (RC) are exercising "functions of a public nature" and are therefore public authorities for the purposes of s.6 of the 1998 Act (s.6(3)(b)).

Decisions made by a private hospital relating to the care or treatment of detained patients are decisions of a public nature. The hospital therefore becomes a public authority for the purposes of s.6 and its decisions are susceptible to judicial review (*R. (on the application of A) v Partnership in Care Ltd* [2002] EWHC 529; [2002] 1 W.L.R. 2610).

Subsection (1)

THE NOMINATED MEDICAL ATTENDANT. Is appointed by a private guardian under **1–466** reg.22(a) of the English Regulations and reg.11(a) of the Welsh Regulations. Paragraph 30.26 of the *Code of Practice* states:

"It is for private guardians themselves to decide whom to appoint as the nominated medical attendant, but they should first consult the local authority. The nominated medical attendant may be the patient's GP, if the GP agrees."

RESPONSIBLE CLINICIAN. Guidance on allocating or changing a RC is contained in Ch.36 of the *Code of Practice*. The RC must be an approved clinician (AC). It follows that if a patient is detained in a general hospital where he is receiving treatment for a physical disorder and the doctor in charge of the treatment is not an AC, an AC from a mental health facility should take responsibility for the treatment of the patient's mental disorder as such treatment must be given by or under the direction of an AC (s.63).

Although the responsibilities of the RC are not delegable, "the role may be occupied on a temporary basis in the absence of the usual [RC]" (Reference Guide, para.9.29). Hospitals should therefore have protocols to "ensure that cover arrangements are in place when the responsible clinician is not available (e.g. during nonworking hours, annual leave etc)" (*Code of Practice*, para.36.3). Any AC can be the temporary RC, irrespective of status. Determining the clinician who has "overall responsibility" for the patient is a question of fact. The selection of the appropriate RC "should be based on the individual needs of the patient concerned" (*Code of Practice*, para.36.5).

With regard to the situation where the patient is receiving a range of treatments, the *Code of Practice* states:

"36.10 There may be circumstances where the responsible clinician is qualified with respect to the patient's main assessment and treatment needs but is not appropriately qualified to be in charge of a subsidiary treatment needed by the patient (eg medication which the responsible clinician is not qualified to prescribe). In such situations, the responsible clinician will maintain their overarching responsibility for the patient's case, but another appropriately qualified professional will take responsibility for a specific treatment or intervention.

36.11 Where the person in charge of a particular treatment is not the patient's responsible clinician, the person in charge of the treatment should ensure that the responsible clinician is kept informed about the treatment and that treatment decisions are discussed with the responsible clinician in the context of the patient's overall case. Guidance should be available locally on the procedures to follow, including when to seek a second opinion, if there are unresolved differences of opinion."

Any dispute about the identification the RC of a detained or community patient would need to be resolved by the hospital management. Subsequent to a patient being granted leave of absence under s.17 or being made subject to a community treatment order, the responsibilities of the RC could be transferred to a community based AC. The responsibilities would then be transferred back to the hospital based AC on the patient's readmission to hospital. A patient has no right to determine the identity of his RC.

The powers given to the RC under the Act do not enable that clinician to require the Clinical Commissioning Group to give priority to the care of a detained patient: see the General Note to the Act under *Allocation of resources to detained parents*.

Although it will normally be the patient's RC who will decide whether a patient can be interviewed and under what conditions, she cannot be the final arbiter when issues arise in relation to national security. The detaining hospital can therefore impose conditions relating to security concerns which the RC may consider to be unnecessary (*R (on the application of A) v Home Secretary* [2003] EWCA 2846 (Admin); [2004] M.H.L.R. 98 para.26).

The RC of a guardianship patient does not have "overall responsibility for the patient's case". If a guardianship patient:

"happens to be living, or receiving medical treatment for mental disorder, in Wales, the local authority may appoint a person who is approved by the Welsh Ministers as an approved clinician in Wales, even if that person is not also approved as an approved clinician in England. Otherwise, the responsible clinician must be approved as an approved clinician in England" (Reference Guide, para.28.79; also see the Mental Health (Mutual Recognition) Regulations 2008 which are reproduced in Part 2).

Subsection (3)

1–467 RESPONSIBLE LOCAL SOCIAL SERVICES AUTHORITY.   Renewal reports must be addressed to this authority which has the power to discharge the patient from guardianship by virtue of s.23(2)(b).

RESIDES. See the note on this term in s.7(5).

PART III

PATIENTS CONCERNED IN CRIMINAL PROCEEDINGS OR UNDER SENTENCE

GENERAL NOTE

This Part deals with the circumstances in which patients may be admitted to and detained **1–468** in hospital or received into guardianship on the order of a court, or may be transferred to hospital or guardianship from penal institutions on the direction of the Secretary of State for Justice.

Home Office Circular No.66/90 (as supplemented by Home Office Circular No.12/95) draws the attention of the courts and those services responsible for dealing with mentally disordered people who come into contact with the criminal justice system to the legal powers that exist and to the desirability of ensuring effective co-operation between agencies.

The functions of the Secretary of State for Justice

The functions of the Secretary of State with regard to the management of restricted **1–469** patients are undertaken on his behalf by the:

Mental Health Casework Section
Ministry of Justice
8th Floor
Zone A
102 Petty France
London SW1H 9AJ
Tel: 020 3334 3555

In cases of emergency outside office hours: 020 7035 4848 and choose option 5. This is the switchboard of the Home Office.

The website of the Ministry of Justice setting out guidance and forms for those working with restricted patients is: *www.justice.gov.uk/offenders/types-of-offender/mentally-dis-ordered-offenders*.

The functions of the Secretary of State in relation to Wales

Through inadvertence, the functions of the Home Secretary (now the Secretary of State **1–470** for Justice) under this Part, in so far as they are exercisable in relation to Wales, were transferred to the National Assembly for Wales under the National Assembly for Wales (Transfer of Functions) Order 1999 (SI 1999/672) art.2 Sch.1. These functions (subject to a number of exceptions that are noted in the appropriate sections) were transferred back to the Home Secretary by a means of a variation to the Order by the National Assembly of Wales (Transfer of Functions) Order 2000 (SI 2000/253) art.4 Sch.3. The period between the two transfer orders was covered by arrangements being put in place under s.41 of the Government of Wales Act 1998 enabling Home Office officials to exercise the functions on behalf of the Assembly.

Medical Reports prior to disposal

1–471

The *Code of Practice* states:

"22.22 Section 157 of the Criminal Justice Act 2003 requires the court to obtain a medical report before passing a custodial sentence other than one fixed by law. Before passing such a sentence, the court must consider any information before it which relates to the

231

offender's mental condition and the likely effect of such a sentence on that condition and on any treatment which may be available for it.

22.23 It may, therefore, be appropriate to include recommendations on the disposal of the case. In making recommendations for disposal the doctor should consider the longer-term, as well as immediate, consequences. Factors to be taken into account include:

- whether the court may wish to make a hospital order subject to special restrictions

- whether, for restricted patients, the order should designate admission to a named unit within the hospital

- whether, in the event of the court concluding that a prison sentence is appropriate, the offender should initially be admitted to hospital by way of a hospital direction under section 45A and a limitation direction which will subject the patient to special restrictions, and

- whether a community order with a mental health treatment requirement may be appropriate.

22.24 Consideration of longer-term implications is especially important where the court considers the offender to be dangerous under the Criminal Justice Act 2003 and where an extended determinate sentence (EDS) or a life sentence is appropriate. The medical reports especially with respect to the offender's level of responsibility for the offence, will form an important element in the court's consideration of whether a hospital order under section 37 or a hybrid order (hospital direction and prison sentence) under section 45A is appropriate."

Transporting patients subject to Part 3 of the Act
1–472   The *Code of Practice* states:

"22.32 Patients who are detained under part 3 of the Act transported between secure units, courts or prison are the responsibility of the unit or prison sending the patient unless other arrangements negotiated. In certain circumstances (eg an emergency situation) a clinical commissioning group commissioned ambulance with appropriate escort may be required to transport the patient. Secure hospitals that hold patients under part 3 of the Act and prisons should have their own security protocols for transfer of patients subject to part 3 of the Act. All agencies involved in the transportation of patients should be mindful of the need to implement reasonable adjustments in arrangements to cater for the individual needs of the patient. Further information on the transport of patients generally is included at chapter 17.

22.33 A child or young person subject to part 3 should be transferred under local escort and bed watch policies. They should be transported in 'usual transport' (eg a car) unless in an emergency or otherwise agreed when an ambulance should be used.

22.34 It may be necessary for patients subject to part 3 of the Act to be subject to mechanical restraint for the purposes of ensuring a safe transfer (see paragraphs 26.88 – 26.90)."

The power to control the activities of detained patients
1–473   See the note on s.139 under this heading.

Defective Court Orders
1–474   The concepts of voidness and voidability have no application to an order made by a superior court of record or an order made by a court of unlimited jurisdiction. The Crown Court is a superior court of record (Courts Act 1971 s.4(1)). An order made under the Act in excess of jurisdiction is irregular and can, on such ground, be set aside. Until it has been set aside it is effective and must be obeyed (*South West Yorkshire*

Mental Health NHS Trust v Bradford Crown Court [2003] EWHC Admin 640; [2004] M.H.L.R. 137). The appropriate remedy in such a case is by way of judicial review: see *R. (on the application of A) v Harrow Crown Court* [2003] EWHC 2020 (Admin), where the court held that the detention of a patient on the authority of an order mistakenly made by the Crown Court does not involve a violation of the patients rights under art.5 of the European Convention on Human Rights.

In *M v Ukraine* [2013] M.H.L.R. 255, the European Court of Human Rights said at para.56:

> "A period of detention is, in principle, 'lawful' if it is based on a court order. For the assessment of compliance with art.5(1) of the Convention a basic distinction has to be made between *ex facie* invalid detention orders –for example, given by a court in excess of jurisdiction or where the interested party did not have proper notice of the hearing – and detention orders which are *prima facie* valid and effective unless and until they have been overturned by a higher court. A detention order must be considered as *ex facie* invalid if the flaw in the order amounted to a "gross and obvious irregularity" in the exceptional sense indicated by the Court's case-law (see *Mooren v. Germany* (2010) 50 E.H.R.R. 23 at paras 74 and 75)."

If the order announced by the judge is within the court's jurisdiction but an incorrect order is subsequently signed by the court clerk, a fresh order can be signed to correct the error.

A challenge to an order made by a magistrates' court should be made by either an appeal under s.108 of the Magistrates Court Act 1980 or to the High Court by way of case stated. In the absence of special circumstances, where there is a choice between the case stated procedure and judicial review, the former is the appropriate route of challenge: see *R. (on the application of LS) v Brent Magistrates' Court* [2009] EWHC 2704 (Admin) where Laws L.J. said in a permission hearing that "the hospital is entitled to take documents dealing with admission, including apparent orders under Section 37 or Section 38, at their face value" and that s.40(1) provides the hospital managers with sufficient authority to admit the patient. His Lordship went on to say:

> "It does seem to me to be right that it would be unreal and counter productive for the law to require the hospital managers, in effect, to take what may amount to sophisticated legal advice as to the validity of hospital orders. . . . Of course I accept that the hospital must carefully ascertain that the documentation is in order and appropriate statutory orders are in place. But it is not their role to conduct an investigation, as it were, below the surface of the validity of the order".

Criminal Procedure (Insanity) Act 1964

If an accused person is found to be either not guilty by reason of insanity or unfit to plead, **1–475** the Crown Court can make a hospital order (with or without a restriction order under s.41) under ss.5 and 5A of the 1964 Act. The other options available to the court are the making of a supervision order or an order for the absolute discharge of the accused. There is no power to make a guardianship order. The Reference Guide states:

> "22.8 Patients admitted to hospital when found unfit to be tried have not received a full criminal trial, and may be sent back for trial by the prosecuting authority if that authority is satisfied, after consulting their responsible clinician, that they can now properly be tried. The Secretary of State may also do this, if the patient concerned is still subject to a restriction order and still detained in hospital. This includes patients on leave of absence from hospital, but not those who have been conditionally discharged and not recalled to hospital. Before doing so, the Secretary of State must consult the patient's responsible clinician.

22.9 The general principle observed by the Secretary of State is that people who have been accused of an offence ought, if possible, to be brought to trial so that they may have an opportunity of having their guilt or innocence determined by a court. In practice, the Secretary of State will consult the responsible clinician about a relevant patient's fitness for trial during the first six months of their detention and regularly thereafter.

22.10 If sending patients back for trial, the Secretary of State may remit them either directly to the court or to prison to await trial. The patient's hospital order (and restriction order) ceases to apply on their arrival at the court or prison."

Also see Home Office Circular 24/2005 and the General Note to s.41 under *Fitness to plead*.

Mental Health Treatment Requirements (MHTR)

1–476   *The Code of Practice* states:

"22.14 The legislative changes introduced by Legal Aid, Sentencing and Punishment of Offenders Act 2012 (LASPO) introduces a simplified procedure for the assessment of an individual for a MHTR, this may now be undertaken by a mental health practitioner, rather than a section 12 approved registered medical practitioner. MHTRs are required to be administered under the direction of a registered medical practitioner or a chartered psychologist. Here the [liaison and diversion] service may undertake the assessment and liaise with the probation office preparing the pre-sentence report, but a registered medical practitioner (doctor) would still be required to provide direction for the administration of any order made by the court.

22.15 In cases where the doctor cannot state with confidence at the time of sentencing whether a hospital order or MHTR will be appropriate, they should consider recommending an interim hospital order under section 38 of the Act. This order provides for the person to be admitted to hospital for up to 12 weeks (which may be extended for further periods of up to 28 days to a maximum total period of 12 months) so that the court can reach a conclusion on the most appropriate and effective disposal. In this situation, the most appropriate setting for the person is a hospital, not a prison."

DNA Profiling

1–477   The Criminal Evidence (Amendment) Act 1997, which came into force on March 19, 1997, enables the police to take non-intimate samples without consent, for DNA profiling purposes, from persons who were convicted before April 10, 1995 of one of the offences listed in Sch.1 to the Act (broadly sex, violent and burglary offences) and who are serving a sentence of imprisonment, or are detained under this Part of the Act, in respect of such an offence at the time when it is sought to take a sample. The Act also enables non-intimate samples to be taken without consent from persons detained under this Part who have been acquitted on grounds of insanity or found unfit to plead. Guidance on the Act is contained in Home Office Circular 27/1997.

The Registration of Sex Offenders

1–478   The Sex Offenders Act 1997, which came into force on September 1, 1997, imposes requirements on sex offenders, including those under 18, to notify the police of their name and address and of any subsequent changes of these. The purpose is to ensure that information on sex offenders contained within the Police National Computer is fully up to date. The Act applies to people who are subject to detention in hospital or guardianship under this Part following conviction or cautioning for a relevant offence. Guidance to hospital managers and local authority social services departments on the Act is contained in Local Authority Social Services Letter LASSL (97) 17/HSG (97) 37.

The Multi-Agency Public Protection Arrangements

The multi-agency public protection arrangements (MAPPA) grew out of the closer work- **1–479** ing relationships which developed between the police and probation (and latterly other agencies) in the late 1990s. The purpose of MAPPA is to minimise the risk to the public posed by those who may reoffend, either violently or sexually. The Ministry of Justice has published "Guidance for working with MAPPA and mentally disordered offenders" (the Guidance) which can be accessed at: *www.justice.gov.uk/offenders/types-of-offender/mentally-disordered-offenders*. The Introduction to the guidance states:

"The responsibility for identifying MAPPA-eligible offenders falls to each agency that has a statutory role in their supervision or care, i.e. the police, probation service, prison service, youth offending services and mental health services. These agencies must have robust internal management procedures in place to identify all MAPPA eligible offenders under their supervision in order to facilitate the lawful exchange of information for the protection of the public.

Public protection does not rest with any single agency. MAPPA exists to promote joint working. The collaborative nature of MAPPA should not, however, undermine the role of the lead agency to manage the offender in the community, but should assist in ensuring a robust risk management plan.

Under section 325(3) of the Criminal Justice Act 2003, health services have a duty to co-operate with the MAPPA responsible authorities in assessing and managing the risk of MAPPA-eligible mentally disordered offenders. Section 327 of the Criminal Justice Act 2003 identifies offenders who are MAPPA-eligible who have a mental disorder."

Mentally disordered offenders who are MAPPA-eligible are those who are convicted of a sexual or violent offence as specified in Sch.15 to the Criminal Justice Act 2003 and sentenced to twelve months or more imprisonment, **or** detained in hospital subject to powers of the Mental Health Act 1983. Relevant extracts from the Guidance which relates to the mental health service are set out below:

"*Mental Health Service*

3.1 The MAPPA Co-ordinator needs to be aware of all MAPPA-eligible offenders who are being managed in the community. It is recommended that at the first CPA meeting where a discharge or a community treatment order is considered, a designated member of the care team should be tasked with completing the appropriate notification form at appendix A and sending it to the MAPPA Co-ordinator. This will provide the opportunity both to share clinical information with the criminal justice agencies and to request information from the police and probation services to inform risk assessment.

Communication between mental health service providers and MAPPA

4.1 For detained patients, the responsible clinician has discretion to communicate significant events to the MAPPA coordinator at each stage of care that may involve a move outside the secure perimeter e.g. leave out of the hospital grounds or transfer to a different hospital. This applies also to clinicians treating patients on trial leave away from the hospital where they are liable to be detained. It is strongly recommended that the Co-ordinator should be informed by the care team of any occasion when the patient will be unsupervised in the community."

The full version of the MAPPA guidance, "MAPPA Guidance 2012 – version 4" can be accessed at: *www.gov.uk/government/publications/multi-agency-public-protection-arrangements-mappa-2*. The *Code of Practice* considers the MAPPA arrangements at paras 22.87 to 22.92.

1–480   Guidance on this Part is contained in Ch.22.

Remands to hospital

Remand to hospital for report on accused's mental condition

1–481   **35.**—(1) Subject to the provisions of this section, the Crown Court or a magistrates' court may remand an accused person to a hospital specified by the court for a report on his mental condition.

(2) For the purposes of this section an accused person is—

(a) in relation to the Crown Court, any person who is awaiting trial before the court for an offence punishable with imprisonment or who has been arraigned before the court for such an offence and has not yet been sentenced or otherwise dealt with for the offence on which he has been arraigned;

(b) in relation to a magistrates' court, any person who has been convicted by the court of an offence punishable on summary conviction with imprisonment and any person charged with such an offence if the court is satisfied that he did the act or made the omission charged or he has consented to the exercise by the court of the powers conferred by this section.

(3) Subject to subsection (4) below, the powers conferred by this section may be exercised if—

(a) the court is satisfied, on the written or oral evidence of a registered medical practitioner, that there is reason to suspect that the accused person is suffering from [mental disorder]; and

(b) the court is of the opinion that it would be impracticable for a report on his mental condition to be made if he were remanded on bail;

but those powers shall not be exercised by the Crown Court in respect of a person who has been convicted before the court if the sentence for the offence of which he has been convicted is fixed by law.

(4) The court shall not remand an accused person to a hospital under this section unless satisfied, on the written or oral evidence of the [approved clinician] who would be responsible for making the report or of some other person representing the managers of the hospital, that arrangements have been made for his admission to that hospital and for his admission to it within the period of seven days beginning with the date of the remand; and if the court is so satisfied it may, pending his admission, give directions for his conveyance to and detention in a place of safety.

(5) Where a court has remanded an accused person under this section it may further remand him if it appears to the court, on the written or oral evidence of the [approved clinician] responsible for making the report, that a further remand is necessary for completing the assessment of the accused person's mental condition.

(6) The power of further remanding an accused person under this section may be exercised by the court without his being brought before the court if he is represented by [an authorised person who] is given an opportunity of being heard.

(7) An accused person shall not be remanded or further remanded under this section for more than 28 days at a time or for more than 12 weeks in all; and the court may at any time terminate the remand if it appears to the court that it is appropriate to do so.

(8) An accused person remanded to hospital under this section shall be entitled to obtain at his own expense an independent report on his mental condition from a registered medical practitioner [or approved clinician] chosen by him and to apply to the court on the basis of it for his remand to be terminated under subsection (7) above.

(9) Where an accused person is remanded under this section—

(a) a constable or any other person directed to do so by the court shall convey the accused person to the hospital specified by the court within the period mentioned in subsection (4) above; and

(b) the managers of the hospital shall admit him within that period and thereafter detain him in accordance with the provisions of this section.

(10) If an accused person absconds from a hospital to which he has been remanded under this section, or while being conveyed to or from that hospital, he may be arrested without warrant by any constable and shall, after being arrested, be brought as soon as practicable before the court that remanded him; and the court may thereupon terminate the remand and deal with him in any way in which it could have dealt with him if he has not been remanded under this section.

AMENDMENTS

The amendments to this section were made by the Mental Health Act 2007 ss.1(4), 10(2), Sch.1 para.5 and the Legal Services Act 2007 s.208, Sch.21, para.54.

DEFINITIONS

1–482

hospital: ss.55(5), 145(1).
mental disorder: ss.1, 145(1).
approved clinician: s.145(1).
the managers: s.145(1).
place of safety: s.55(1).
authorised person: s.55(1).

GENERAL NOTE

This section gives effect to the recommendation of the Butler Committee that courts **1–483** should have the option of remanding an accused person to hospital for the preparation of a report on his mental condition. Magistrates' courts and the Crown Court have this power if they are satisfied, on medical evidence, that there is reason to suspect that the accused person is suffering from mental disorder (subs.(2)) and that it would be impracticable for a report on his mental condition to be made if he were remanded on bail (subs.(3)). The remand, which can last for a maximum of 12 weeks (subss.(7)), cannot be made unless the court is also satisfied, on hearing evidence from an approved clinician, that arrangements have been made for the accused's admission to hospital (subs.(4)). If the accused person either absconds from the hospital to which he has been remanded, or absconds while being conveyed to and from that hospital, he may be arrested without warrant by any constable and brought back before the court that remanded him (subs.(10)) which may decide on some alternative approach to his case. The provisions in the Act relating to patients who are absent without leave do not apply to patients remanded under this section. The court may terminate the remand at any time.

The effect of subss.(3) and (4) of this section:

"is expected to be that the initiative for a remand to hospital will generally come either from the defendant's legal representative (who may already have taken steps to obtain the necessary evidence from an approved [clinician] before suggesting to the court that remand to hospital might be appropriate) or from the medical officer of the prison to which the defendant has been remanded in custody at an earlier court appearance.

Prison medical officers are being asked to explore the possibility of a remand to hospital in appropriate cases. Prison medical officers will of course continue to comply to the best of their ability with requests from the courts for medical reports on prisoners remanded in custody for that purpose. If the court itself is considering the suitability of a remand to hospital and no prior arrangements with a hospital have been made, it will generally be necessary to adjourn the case so that the necessary medical recommendation can be sought and arrangements made for the defendant to be admitted to a hospital" (Home Office Circular No. 71/1984, Annex, paras 24, 25).

A remand under this section:

"does not automatically affect any existing liability for detention for assessment or treatment on any other basis, nor bring a community treatment order (CTO) or guardianship to an end. But nor does it prevent them expiring or being discharged in the normal way" (Reference Guide, para.14.23).

The purpose of a remand under this section is to inform the court about issues relating to fitness to plead and disposal; not for the purpose of obtaining evidence relevant to an issue at trial. Such an order cannot therefore be used to enable the Crown to obtain evidence that the accused had the intention, or the capacity to form the intention, to commit an offence of grievous bodily harm (*R. (on the application of M) v Kingston Crown Court* [2014] EWHC 2702 (Admin); [2015] M.H.L.R. 79).

This section does not provide the remanding court with a power to either grant the patient leave of absence under s.17 or to transfer the patient to another hospital under s.19 (although the court could further remand the patient to a different hospital: see the note on subs.(5)). If the patient needs to leave the hospital to receive, for example, emergency medical treatment at an Accident and Emergency department, the patient should be taken there and the remanding court informed of the action that has been taken. The common law (for mentally capable consenting patients) or the Mental Capacity Act 2005 (for mentally incapacitated patients) would provide authority for the patient to be treated. Appropriate security arrangements should be put in place by the remanding hospital. The *Code of Practice* states:

"22.40 Where a patient remanded under section 35 is thought to be in need of medical treatment for mental disorder which cannot otherwise be given, the patient should be referred back to court by the clinician in charge of their care as soon as possible, with an appropriate recommendation and with an assessment of whether they are in a fit state to attend court.

22.41 If there is a delay in securing a court date, consideration should be given to whether the patient meets the criteria for detention under part 2 of the Act to enable compulsory treatment to be given. This will be concurrent with, and not a replacement for, the remand made by the court."

A person remanded under this section is not subject to the consent to treatment provisions contained in Pt IV (s.56(3)(b)). This has led to the practice of using either s.2 or s.3 to bring the patient within the scope of Pt IV. Although this practice had been regarded by legal commentators as being legally questionable, the decision in *R. v North West London Mental Health NHS Trust Ex p. Stewart* [1997] 4 All E.R. 871 CA, where the court held that the powers under Pt II and Pt III can co-exist and operate independently of each other, confirmed that either s.2 or s.3 can be used during the currency of a s.35. This was a pragmatic decision of the Court of Appeal that does not sit easily with the scheme of the Act for the reasons set out in the 14th edition of this Manual at para.1–429. It is unlikely that a claim that a patient's dual detention amounts to a disproportionate and unjustified interference with his rights under art.8 of the European Convention on Human Rights would succeed: see *R. (on the application of M) v Homerton University Hospital* [2008] EWCA Civ 197 at paras 22 and 24.

Patients who are remanded under this section do not have a nearest relative for the purposes of the Act.

Criminal Procedure (Insanity) Act 1964
In a case where s.5 of the 1964 Act applies (persons not guilty by reason of insanity or **1–484** unfit to plead) but the court have yet to make a disposal, the Crown Court can remand the accused under this section (as modified by the 1964 Act s.5A(2)(a),(c)).

Applications to the First-tier Tribunal (Mental Health) or the Mental Health Review Tribunal for Wales
A patient who has been remanded under this section has no right to apply to a tribunal. **1–485**

Orders made in other proceedings
In certain circumstances, an order under this section can be made under the Contempt of **1–486** Court Act 1981 s.14(4A), the Family Law Act 1996 ss.48 and 63L, the Housing Act 1996 s.156 (see below), the Police and Justice Act 2006 s.27 and the Armed Forces Act 2006 s.169 and Sch.4 para.3.

Housing Act 1996
If there is reason to suspect that a person who has been arrested under s.155 of the 1996 **1–487** Act for breach of an injunction is suffering from a mental disorder, the court has the power under s.156 of that Act to make an order under this section.

Variation or rescission of sentence subsequent to the court receiving information about the offender's mental health
Under s.155(1) of the Powers of Criminal Courts (Sentencing) Act 2000, a sentence **1–488** imposed by the Crown Court when dealing with an offender may be varied or rescinded by that court within the period of 56 days beginning with the day on which the sentence or other order was imposed or made. In *R. v Catchpole* [2014] EWCA Crim 1037, the Court of Appeal held that it was lawfully open to the judge to have rescinded the sentence of imprisonment that he had earlier in the day imposed, leaving the sentencing of the appellant to be carried out at a later date, either by himself or another judge, with the benefit of a psychiatric report under this section.

Transport to and from court
The *Code of Practice* states: **1–489**

"22.35 For patients remanded to hospital under sections 35 or 36 of the Act, or subject to a hospital order or an interim hospital order, the court has the power to direct who is to be responsible for transporting the defendant from the court to the receiving hospital. This direction should be based on individual need and there should be contingency planning and measurable outcomes in place to ensure that people do not have to return to the holding prison. Monitoring of this process should be logged. In practice, when remand orders are first made, patients are usually returned to the holding prison briefly using the escort provision commissioned for court to prison journeys, and arrangements are then made to admit them and make arrangements for transporting them to hospital within the statutory period. Secure hospitals that hold patients under part 3 of the Act and prisons should have their own security protocols for transfer of patients subject to part 3 of the Act.

22.36 When a patient has been admitted on remand or is subject to an interim hospital order under section 38 of the Act, it is the responsibility of the hospital to return the patient to court as required. The court should give adequate notice of hearings. The hospital should liaise with the court in plenty of time to confirm the arrangements for escorting the patient to and from the court. The hospital will be responsible for providing a suitable escort for the patient when travelling from the hospital to the court and should plan for the provision of appropriately qualified staff to do this taking into account the age of the patient and any disability. The assistance of the police may be requested, if necessary. If possible, and having regard to the needs of the patient, medical or nursing staff should remain with the patient on court premises, even though legal accountability while the patient is detained for hearings, remains with the court. For restricted patients attendance at court will require the consent of the Secretary of State for Justice. For those patients who have been transferred under section 48 of the Act, permission to attend court will be provided in writing on initial admission. For other patients who are required to attend court, prior approval must be sought.

22.37 It may be possible in some circumstances, and with permission from the Tribunal or the Court, for a patient to attend a hearing by live video link. Clinical teams should seek advice from the relevant tribunal or court to establish whether this might be available."

Subsection (1)

1–490   This subsection "provides an alternative to remanding the accused person in custody for a medical report, in circumstances where it would not be practicable to obtain the report if he were remanded on bail (for instance, if he decided to break a condition of bail that he should reside at a hospital, the hospital would be unable to prevent him from discharging himself)" (Home Office Circular No.71/1984, Annex para.1).

Section 48 has been used to secure the person's immediate return to the hospital on a subsequent remand into custody (see A. Akinkunmi and K. Murray, "Inadequacies in the Mental Health Act 1983 in relation to Mentally Disordered Remand Prisoners", *Med. Sci. Law* (1997) 37:53–57).

Subsection (2)

Paragraph (a)

1–491   OFFENCE PUNISHABLE WITH IMPRISONMENT.   This section applies to a person who has been accused, but not convicted, of murder (subs.(3)).

Paragraph (b)

1–492   MAGISTRATES' COURT.   If a person is remanded under this section by the magistrates' court and the case is subsequently committed to the Crown Court, the jurisdiction of the magistrates to make a further remand ends.

OFFENCE PUNISHABLE ON SUMMARY CONVICTION WITH IMPRISONMENT.   The offence could have been committed by a person under the age of 21 (s.55(2)).

SATISFIED THAT HE DID THE ACT.   The power to remand for reports under this section applies to someone in respect of whom s.37(3) applies (*Bartram v Southend Magistrates' Court* [2004] EWHC 2691 (Admin); [2004] M.H.L.R. 319 para.6).

CONSENTED.   The consent relates to the making of the order and not to the extension of the order under subs.(5). A withdrawal of consent is therefore not relevant to the question of renewal.

Subsection (3)

1–493   PARAGRAPH (A); EVIDENCE.   For general provisions as to medical evidence, see s.54. The court can call a doctor who has provided a written report to give oral evidence (s.54(2A)).

REGISTERED MEDICAL PRACTITIONER.   Who must have been approved by the Secretary of State or the Welsh Ministers under s.12, or by another person by virtue of s.12ZA or 12ZB (s.54(1)).

REASON TO SUSPECT.   The diagnostic threshold under this section is not high.

MENTAL DISORDER.   If the person has a learning disability, the disability must be associated with abnormally aggressive or seriously irresponsible conduct (s.1(2A), (2B)). A learning disabled person might also suffer from another form of mental disorder.

PARAGRAPH (B); IMPRACTICABLE.   This presumably refers to the impracticability of preparing a sufficiently thorough report if the accused were granted bail.

FIXED BY LAW.   Although the power to remand to hospital is not available in respect of a person who has been *convicted* of murder who must be sentenced to life imprisonment (Murder (Abolition of Death Penalty) Act 1965 s.1(1)), a remand under this section can be made in a murder trial before conviction. A person who charged with murder can be bailed to a hospital to enable psychiatric reports to be prepared (Bail Act 1976 s.3(6A)).

Subsection (4)
An order under this section which has been made without this subsection being complied **1–494** with is ultra vires. If there is doubt as to whether the hospital place would be funded, the court should adjourn for a short period to enable enquiries to be made, and if necessary, to hear evidence and/or representations from the relevant funding body (*R. (on the application of Bitcon) v West Allerdale Magistrates' Court* [2003] EWHC 2640 (Admin); [2003] M.H.L.R. 399). If, subsequent to an offer of a bed having been made, circumstances arise which prevent the hospital from admitting the patient, the case should be returned to the court as a matter of urgency.

OR OF SOME OTHER PERSON.   Who need not be an approved clinician.

SEVEN DAYS.   The court does not have the power either to renew or extend this period.

BEGINNING WITH.   Including the date of the remand (*Zoan v Rouamba* [2000] 2 All E.R. 620 CA).

Subsection (5)
See the note on "consented" in subs.(2).   **1–495**

FURTHER REMAND HIM.   The new period of remand starts from the expiry date of the previous period of remand. The total period spent on remand cannot exceed 12 weeks in all (subs.(7)). It is submitted that a further remand can only be made to a different hospital if the requirements of subs.(4) are satisfied in respect of the person's admission to that hospital.

Subsection (7)
AT ANY TIME.   "It will be open to the [responsible clinician] in every case to inform the **1–496** court if the object of the remand is achieved before the expiry of the stipulated time, so that the adjourned hearing may be brought forward accordingly or if necessary an alternative form of remand, either in custody or on bail, may be substituted" (*Butler Committee*, para.12.9). An application could also be made to terminate the order if the patient proves to be unmanageable at the hospital.

Subsection (8)

1–497   This provision was successfully moved during the passage of the Mental Heatlh (Amendment) Act 1982 against Government advice. The Government view was that it would be unlikely to be of great benefit to the accused person, firstly because he already has the right to commission his own private clinical report and, secondly, because the court is unlikely to end his remand on the basis of such a report.

Once the accused has received the private clinical report, he has the right to apply to the court to seek an end to the remand even if the reports that the court has asked for are not available.

The *Code of Practice* states under the heading "Independent medical assessment":

"22.16 A patient who is remanded to hospital for a report (section 35) or for treatment (section 36) is entitled to obtain, at their own expense, or where applicable through legal aid, an independent report on their mental condition from a doctor or other clinician of their choosing, for the purpose of applying to court for the termination of the remand. Hospital managers should help in the exercise of this right by enabling the patient to contact a suitably qualified and experienced solicitor or other legal adviser.

22.17 Where the court refers the patient for assessment or treatment under sections 35 or 36, the initial report that has been requested by the court would be remunerated from central funds and not by the legal aid agency. If, however, the patient wishes to obtain a report to challenge the report produced for the court, providing that the merits criteria are satisfied, this could be remunerated under the patient's criminal legal aid. Additionally, the patient would need to satisfy the financial eligibility criteria specified by either the magistrates' court or Crown Court. The patient's representative could also consider making an application to the legal aid agency for prior authority to commission a report to challenge the report produced by the clinical staff."

Subsection (9)

1–498   CONVEY.   See the General Note to this section under "Transport to and from court". For general provisions regarding conveyance, see s.137.

SHALL ADMIT HIM.   The hospital managers are placed under an obligation to admit the patient.

Subsection (10)

1–499   There is no time limit on a recapture under this provision or under s.36(8).

ARRESTED.   The power to arrest under this section was specifically preserved by s.26 and Sch.2 of the Police and Criminal Evidence Act 1984 (PACE). This means that the arresting policeman has a power to search the patient under s.32 of PACE at a place other than a police station.

Remand of accused person to hospital for treatment

1–500   **36.**—(1) Subject to the provisions of this section, the Crown Court may, instead of remanding an accused person in custody, remand him to a hospital specified by the court if satisfied, on the written or oral evidence of two registered medical practitioners, that,

[(a) he is suffering from mental disorder of a nature or degree which makes it appropriate for him to be detained in a hospital for medical treatment;][and

(b) the appropriate medical treatment is available for him.]

(2) For the purposes of this section an accused person is any person who is in custody awaiting trial before the Crown Court for an offence punishable with imprisonment (other than an offence the sentence for which is fixed by law) or

who at any time before sentence is in custody in the course of a trial before that court for such an offence.

(3) The court shall not remand an accused person under this section to a hospital unless it is satisfied, on the written or oral evidence of the [approved clinician who would have overall responsibility for his case] or of some other person representing the managers of the hospital, that arrangements have been made for his admission to that hospital and for his admission to it within the period of seven days beginning with the date of the remand; and if the court is so satisfied it may, pending his admission, give directions for his conveyance to and detention in a place of safety.

(4) Where a court has remanded an accused person under this section it may further remand him if it appears to the court, on the written or oral evidence of the [responsible clinician], that a further remand is warranted.

(5) The power of further remanding an accused person under this section may be exercised by the court without his being brought before the court if he is represented by [an authorised person who] is given an opportunity of being heard.

(6) An accused person shall not be remanded or further remanded under this section for more than 28 days at a time or for more than 12 weeks in all; and the court may at any time terminate the remand if it appears to the court that it is appropriate to do so.

(7) An accused person remanded to hospital under this section shall be entitled to obtain at his own expense an independent report on his mental condition from a registered medical practitioner [or approved clinician] chosen by him and to apply to the court on the basis of it for his remand to be terminated under subsection (6) above.

(8) Subsections (9) and (10) of section 35 above shall have effect in relation to a remand under this section as they have effect in relation to a remand under that section.

AMENDMENTS

The amendments to this section were made by the Mental Health Act 2007 ss.1(4), 5(2), 10(3), Sch.1 para.6 and the Legal Services Act 2007 s.208, Sch.21, para.55.

DEFINITIONS

    hospital: ss.55(5), 145(1).
    mental disorder: ss.1, 145(1).
    the managers: s.145(1).
    responsible clinician: s.55(1).
    approved clinician: s.145(1).
    place of safety: s.55(1).
    authorised person: s.55(1).
    approved medical treatment: ss.3(4), 145(1AB).
    medical treatment: s.145(3), (4).

1–501

GENERAL NOTE

This section empowers the Crown Court to remand an accused person (see subs.(2)), who **1–502** is in custody either awaiting trial or during the course of a trial and who is suffering from mental disorder, to hospital for treatment for a maximum of 12 weeks. It provides an alternative to the Secretary of State's power under s.48 to transfer unsentenced prisoners to hospital. Where the accused person is in urgent need of treatment and is not due to appear before the Crown Court in the immediate future, the procedure under s.48 is to be preferred. Paragraph 36 of Home Office Circular No.71/1984 states:

"Section 36 provides the Crown Court with an alternative to the procedure laid down by the Criminal Procedure (Insanity) Act 1964 of finding a defendant under disability ('unfit to plead'). The power in s.36 can be used in cases in which if the defendant could receive treatment in hospital for a period it might be possible to proceed with the full trial. The Crown Court may prefer in appropriate cases to proceed in this way rather than under the Criminal Procedure (Insanity) Act, under which the defendant would thereafter have to be detained as a restricted patient (which may not be appropriate in relation to the nature of the alleged offence)."

A remand under this section "does not automatically affect any existing liability for detention for assessment or treatment on any other basis, nor bring a community treatment order (CTO) or guardianship to an end. But nor does it prevent them expiring or being discharged in the normal way" (Reference Guide, para.14.23).

As the Act does not provide for the application of Pt II to a patient who has been remanded under this section, there is no power to grant the patient leave of absence under s.17 or transfer the patient to another hospital under s.19 (although the court could further remand the patient to a different hospital: see the note on subs.(4)).

A person remanded under this section as a "patient liable to be detained under this Act" is subject to the consent to treatment provisions contained in Pt IV (s.56(3)).

If the remanded person absconds, the provisions in the Act relating to patients who are absent without leave do not apply. If the accused person either absconds from the hospital to which he has been remanded, or absconds while being conveyed to and from that hospital, he may be arrested and brought back before the court that remanded him (subs.(8)).

If it is anticipated that the patient will cease to be an accused person due to the case against him collapsing, an application under Part II could be prepared by completing the statutory documentation with the exception of the signature on the application form. This could be added when the patient ceased to be an accused person.

Patients who are remanded under this section do not have a nearest relative for the purposes of the Act.

Applications to the First-tier Tribunal (Mental Health) or the Mental Health Review Tribunal for Wales

1–503   A patient who has been remanded under this section has no right to apply to a tribunal.

Orders made in other proceedings

1–504   In certain circumstances, an order under this section can be made under the Armed Forces Act 2006 s.169 and Sch.4 para.4.

Transport to and from court

1–505   See the General Note to s.35 under this heading.

Subsection (1)

1–506   CROWN COURT.   But not the magistrates' court. However, such courts have the alternative, under s.37(3), of making a hospital order in respect of a defendant charged but unconvicted.

HOSPITAL.   Or a registered establishment (ss.34(2), 55(5)).

EVIDENCE.   For general provisions relating to medical evidence, see s.54. The court can call a doctor who has provided a written report to give oral evidence (s.54(2A)).

TWO REGISTERED MEDICAL PRACTITIONERS.   At least one of whom must have been approved by the Secretary of State or the Welsh Ministers under s.12, or another person by virtue of s.12ZA or 12ZB (s.54(1)). There is no prohibition on both of the doctors being on the staff of the same hospital.

MENTAL DISORDER. If the person has a learning disability, the disability must be associated with abnormally aggressive or seriously irresponsible conduct (s.1(2A), (2B)). A learning disabled person might also suffer from another form of mental disorder.

NATURE OR DEGREE. See the note on s.3(2)(a).

APPROPRIATE MEDICAL TREATMENT. See the note on s.3(2)(d).

Subsection (2)
FIXED BY LAW. Unlike s.35, this section does not apply to a person who has been **1–507** charged with murder. If such a person is in need of urgent treatment, he could be removed to hospital under s.48 if he is awaiting trial having been remanded in custody by a magistrates' court. A person who charged with murder can be bailed to a hospital to enable psychiatric reports to be prepared (Bail Act 1976 s.3(6A)).

Subsection (3)
OR OF SOME OTHER PERSON. Who need not be a clinician. **1–508**

BEGINNING WITH. Including the date of the remand (*Zoan v Rouamba* [2000] 2 All E.R. 620 CA).

Subsection (4)
A FURTHER REMAND IS WARRANTED. Because the criteria set out in subs.(1) still apply. It **1–509** is submitted that a further remand can only be made to a different hospital if the requirements of subs.(3) are satisfied in respect of the patient's admission to that hospital.

Subsection (7)
See the notes on s.35(8). **1–510**

Hospital and Guardianship Orders

Powers of courts to order hospital admission or guardianship
37.—(1) Where a person is convicted before the Crown Court of an offence **1–511** punishable with imprisonment other than an offence the sentence for which is fixed by law, or is convicted by a magistrates' court of an offence punishable on summary conviction with imprisonment, and the conditions mentioned in subsection (2) below are satisfied, the court may by order authorise his admission to and detention in such hospital as may be specified in the order or, as the case may be, place him under the guardianship of a local social services authority or of such other person approved by a local social services authority as may be so specified.
[(1A) In the case of an offence the sentence for which would otherwise fall to be imposed—
[(za) under section 1A(5) of the Prevention of Crime Act 1953,]
(a) under section 51A(2) of the Firearms Act 1968,
[(aa) under section 139AA(7) of the Criminal Justice Act 1988,]
(b) under section 110(2) or 111(2) of the Powers of Criminal Courts (Sentencing) Act 2000, [. . .]
[(ba) under section 224A of the Criminal Justice Act 2003,]
(c) under [section 225(2) or 226(2)] of the Criminal Justice Act 2003, [or
(d) under section 29(4) or (6) of the Violent Crime Reduction Act 2006 (minimum sentences in certain cases of using someone to mind a weapon),]

nothing in those provisions shall prevent a court from making an order under subsection (1) above for the admission of the offender to a hospital.

(1B) Reference in subsection (1A) above to a sentence falling to be imposed under any of the provisions mentioned in that subsection are to be read in accordance with section 305(4) of the Criminal Justice Act 2003.]

(2) The conditions referred to in subsection (1) above are that—

(a) the court is satisfied, on the written or oral evidence of two registered medical practitioners, that the offender is suffering from [mental disorder] and that either—

    (i) the mental disorder from which the offender is suffering is of a nature or degree which makes it appropriate for him to be detained in a hospital for medical treatment and [appropriate medical treatment is available for him]; or

    (ii) in the case of an offender who has attained the age of 16 years, the mental disorder is of a nature or degree which warrants his reception into guardianship under this Act; and

(b) the court is of the opinion, having regard to all the circumstances including the nature of the offence and the character and antecedents of the offender, and to the other available methods of dealing with him, that the most suitable method of disposing of the case is by means of an order under this section.

(3) Where a person is charged before a magistrates' court with any act or omission as an offence and the court would have power, on convicting him of that offence, to make an order under subsection (1) above in his case [...], then, if the court is satisfied that the accused did the act or made the omission charged, the court may, if it thinks fit, make such an order without convicting him.

(4) An order for the admission of an offender to a hospital (in this Act referred to as "a hospital order") shall not be made under this section unless the court is satisfied on the written or oral evidence of the [approved clinician who would have overall responsibility for his case] or of some other person representing the managers of the hospital that arrangements have been made for his admission to that hospital [...], and for his admission to it within the period of 28 days beginning with the date of the making of such an order; and the court may, pending his admission within that period, give such directions as it thinks fit for his conveyance to and detention in a place of safety.

(5) If within the said period of 28 days it appears to the Secretary of State that by reason of an emergency or other special circumstances it is not practicable for the patient to be received into the hospital specified in the order, he may give directions for the admission of the patient to such other hospital as appears to be appropriate instead of the hospital so specified; and where such directions are given—

(a) the Secretary of State shall cause the person having the custody of the patient to be informed, and

(b) the hospital order shall have effect as if the hospital specified in the directions were substituted for the hospital specified in the order.

(6) An order placing an offender under the guardianship of a local social services authority or of any other person (in this Act referred to as "a guardianship order") shall not be made under this section unless the court is satisfied that that authority or person is willing to receive the offender into guardianship.

(7) [. . .]

(8) Where an order is made under this section, the court [shall not:

(a) pass sentence of imprisonment or impose a fine or make a [community order (within the meaning of Part 12 of the Criminal Justice Act 2003)] [or a youth rehabilitation order (within the meaning of Part 1 of the Criminal Justice and Immigration Act 2008] in respect of the offence,

(b) if the order under this section is a hospital order, make a referral order (within the meaning of [the Powers of Criminal Courts (Sentencing) Act 2000]) in respect of the offence, or

(c) make in respect of the offender [. . .] an order under section 105 of that Act (binding over of parent or guardian)],

but the court may make any other order which it] has power to make apart from this section; and for the purposes of this subsection "sentence of imprisonment" includes any sentence or order for detention.

AMENDMENTS

The amendments to this section were made by the Criminal Justice Act 2003 s.304, Sch.32 para.38, the Criminal Justice and Immigration Act 2008 s.148, Sch.26 para.8, the Mental Health Act 2007 ss.1(4), 4(5), 10(4), 55, Sch.1 para.7, Sch.11 Pt 1, the Violent Crime Reduction Act 2006 ss.49, 65, Sch.1 para.2, Sch.5, the Crime (Sentences) Act 1997 s.56(2), Sch.6, the Youth Justice and Criminal Evidence Act 1999 s.67, Sch.4 para.11, the Criminal Justice Act 2003 s.304, Sch.32 para.38, the Powers of Criminal Courts (Sentencing) Act 2000 s.165, Sch.9 para.90, Criminal Justice and Immigration Act 2008 ss.6, 149, Sch.4, para.30, Sch.28, Pt 1 and the Legal Aid, Sentencing and Punishment of Offenders Act 2012 ss.122, 142, Sch.19 para.1 and Sch.26 para.2.

DEFINITIONS   **1–512**
hospital: ss.55(5), 145(1).
local social services authority: s.145(1).
mental disorder: ss.1, 145(1).
approved clinician: s.145(1).
appropriate medical treatment: ss.3(4), 145(1AB).
medical treatment: s.145(1), (4).
patient: s.145(1).
the managers: s.145(1).
place of safety: s.55(1).

GENERAL NOTE

This section empowers a Crown Court or magistrates' court to make a hospital or guar- **1–513** dianship order as an alternative to a penal disposal for offenders who are found to be suffering from mental disorder at the time of sentencing such as to warrant their detention in hospital or reception into guardianship. The effect of hospital and guardianship orders are set out below and in s.40. A patient who has been placed under a hospital order is subject to the consent to treatment provisions in Pt IV (s.56(3)). An offender's nearest relative has no role to play in the making by the court of a hospital or guardianship order (s.40(4)). When a person is made subject to a hospital or guardianship order under this section, any previous application or order made in respect of that person ceases to have effect (s.40(5)).

Hospital orders

The purpose and effect of a hospital order are explained in the following passage from **1–514** the judgment of the Court of Appeal in *R. v Birch* (1989) 11 Cr. App. R.(S.) 202 at 210:

"Once the offender is admitted to hospital pursuant to a hospital order or transfer order without restriction on discharge, his position is almost exactly the same as if he were a civil patient. In effect he passes out of the penal system and into the hospital regime. Neither the court nor the Secretary of State has any say in his disposal. Thus, like any other mental patient, he may be detained only for a period of six months, unless the authority to detain is renewed, an event which cannot happen unless certain conditions, which resemble those which were satisfied when he was admitted, are fulfilled. If the authority expires without being renewed, the patient may leave. Furthermore, he may be discharged at any time by the hospital managers or the 'responsible [clinician]'.'. . . .

Another feature of the regime which affects the disordered offender and the civil patient alike is the power of the responsible [clinician] to grant leave of absence from the hospital for a particular purpose, or for a specified or indefinite period of time: subject always to a power of recall . . . .

There are certain differences between the positions of the offender and of the civil patient, relating to early access to the [tribunal] and to discharge by the patient's nearest relative, but these are of comparatively modest importance. In general the offender is dealt with in a manner which appears, and is intended to be, humane by comparison with a custodial sentence. A hospital order is not a punishment. Questions of retribution and deterrence, whether personal or general, are immaterial. The offender who has become a patient is not kept on any kind of leash by the court . . . The sole purpose of the order is to ensure that the offender receives the medical care and attention which he needs in the hope and expectation of course that the result will be to avoid the commission by the offender of further criminal acts."

In *R. v Vowles* [2015] EWCA Crim 45, Lord Thomas CJ, who gave the judgment of the Court, reviewed the jurisprudence on the sentencing of mentally disordered offenders. His Lordship referred to the following passage from Mustill L.J.'s judgment in *R. v Birch* which made clear that before the powers under this section were invoked, the judge had to consider the connection between the defendant's mental disorder and the offending conduct:

"Where the sentencer considers that, notwithstanding the offender's mental disorder, there was an element of culpability in the offence which merits punishment. This may happen where there is no connection between the mental disorder and the offence, or where the defendant's responsibility for the offence is 'diminished' but not wholly extinguished. That the imposition of a prison sentence is capable of being a proper exercise of discretion is shown by . . .

In the absence of any question of culpability and punishment, the judge should not impose a sentence of imprisonment simply to ensure that if the Review Tribunal finds that the conditions under section 73 are satisfied and is therefore constrained to order a discharge, the offender will return to prison rather than be set free: *Howell* (1985) 7 Cr.App.R. (S.) 360 and *Cockburn* (1967) 52 Cr.App.R. 134."

Lord Thomas said at para.47 that this "passage underlined the importance of the observations which Lord Lane CJ had made in *Castro* (1985) 7 Cr App R(S) 68 where he stressed that the sentence had to be looked at, not only from the point of view of the offender but also from the point of view of the public". His Lordship continued at para.48:

"More recently this court has emphasised the need to examine the issues with great care and to take into account not merely the psychiatric evidence but also broader issues such as the extent of the culpability attributable to the mental disorder, the need to protect the public and the regime on release."

Having reviewed the case law, his Lordship provided the following guidance on the approach to be adopted to sentencing (although the guidance is primarily directed to indeterminate sentences, it is also in large part applicable to all determinate sentences (para.5)):

"51. It is important to emphasise that the judge must carefully consider all the evidence in each case and not, as some of the early cases have suggested, feel circumscribed by the psychiatric opinions. A judge must therefore consider, where the conditions in s.37 (2) (a) are met, what is the appropriate disposal. In considering that wider question the matters to which a judge will invariably have to have regard to include (1) the extent to which the offender needs treatment for the mental disorder from which the offender suffers, (2) the extent to which the offending is attributable to the mental disorder, (3) the extent to which punishment is required and (4) the protection of the public including the regime for deciding release and the regime after release. There must always be sound reasons for departing from the usual course of imposing a penal sentence and the judge must set these out.

52 .As to the fourth of the considerations to which we have referred, Lord Bingham at paragraph 23 of his judgment in *Drew* [[2003] UKHL 25], which was decided prior to the amendment of s.45A, accepted that there was force in the submission of the Secretary of State that where the medical criteria were met, judges had given less than adequate weight to the conditions governing release. He was, at that time, unpersuaded that a change in practice was desirable. In the light of the amendments to s.45A, the observations of Hughes LJ [in *AG's reference No. 54 of 2011* [2012] 1 Cr App R(S) 106] which we have referred at paragraph 48(ii) and the general evidence before us, we consider that a judge when sentencing must now pay very careful attention to the different effect in each case of the conditions applicable to and after release. As is shown by the case of *Teasdale* [[2012] EWCA Crim 2071] to which we have referred at paragraph 48(iv), this consideration may be one matter leading to the imposition of a hospital order under s.37/41.

53. The fact that two psychiatrists are of the opinion that a hospital order with restrictions under s.37/41 is the right disposal is therefore never a reason on its own to make such an order. The judge must first consider all the relevant circumstances, including the four issues we have set out in the preceding paragraphs and then consider the alternatives in the order in which we set them out in the next paragraph.

54. Therefore, in the light of the arguments addressed to us and the matters to which we have referred, a court should, in a case where (1) the evidence of medical practitioners suggests that the offender is suffering from a mental disorder, (2) that the offending is wholly or in significant part attributable to that disorder, (3) treatment is available, and it considers in the light of all the circumstances to which we have referred, that a hospital order (with or without a restriction) may be an appropriate way of dealing with the case, consider the matters in the following order:

   (i) As the terms of s.45A (1) of the MHA require, before a hospital order is made under s.37/41, whether or not with a restriction order, a judge should consider whether the mental disorder can appropriately be dealt with by a hospital and limitation direction under s.45A.

   (ii) If it can, then the judge should make such a direction under s.45A(1). This consideration will not apply to a person under the age of 21 at the time of conviction as there is no power to make such an order in the case of such a person as we have set out at paragraph 19 above.

   (iii) If such a direction is not appropriate the court must then consider, before going further, whether, if the medical evidence satisfies the condition in s.37(2)(a) (that the mental disorder is such that it would be appropriate for the offender to be detained in a hospital and treatment is available), the conditions set out in s.37(2)(b) would make that the most suitable method of disposal. It is essential that a judge gives detailed consideration to all the factors encompassed within s.37(2)(b). For example, in a case where the court is considering a life sentence under the Criminal Justice Act 2003 as amended in 2012 (following the guidance given in *Attorney General's Reference (No.27 of 2013), R v Burinskas* [2014] 1 WLR 4209), if (1) the mental disorder is treatable, (2) once treated there is no evidence he would be in any way dangerous, and (3) the offending is entirely due to that mental disorder, a hospital order under s.37/41 is likely to be the correct disposal.

(iv) We have set out the general circumstances to which a court should have regard but, as the language of s.37(2)(b) makes clear, the court must also have regard to the question of whether other methods of dealing with him are available. This includes consideration of whether the powers under s.47 for transfer to prison for treatment would, taking into account all the other circumstances, be appropriate."

The commencement date of a hospital order is the date when the order was made by the court, not the date of the patient's admission to the hospital: see the note to s.40(4). A court may request information about the availability of hospital places under s.39. The offender can be admitted to a hospital which is not situated in the locality where he is normally resident (*R. v Marsden (Practice Note)* [1968] 1 W.L.R. 785).

The hospital order will cease to have effect if the offender is not admitted to the hospital named in the order within 28 days of the making of the order: see *R. (on the application of DB) v Nottinghamshire Healthcare NHS Trust*, noted under subs.(4).

In *R. v Galfetti* [2002] EWCA Crim 1916; [2002] M.H.L.R. 418, the sentencing of a mentally disordered offender had been subject to repeated adjournments whilst attempts were made to secure a hospital bed for him. A hospital order was eventually made nine months after conviction. May L.J. giving the judgment of the court said at para.51:

"Whenever a hospital place is not available within a reasonable time for an offender for whom a hospital order is the appropriate disposal, the court is disabled from affording justice in the way which Parliament has provided".

His Lordship identified, at para.52, the following possibilities which are available to the sentencing court in these circumstances, none of which is "wholly satisfactory":

1. The judge can and should make every effort to persuade the hospital authorities to find a suitable place.

2. There may come a time in an individual case when, by reason of delay, a sentence other than a hospital order should be considered. However, it could scarcely ever be satisfactory, if a court is constrained to pass a different sentence simply because an appropriate hospital place is not available.

3. The court will take delay into account in deciding the eventual disposal. His Lordship said at para.48: "[I]n so far as it is necessary to characterise the process as providing a remedy under Article 6(1) [of the European Convention on Human Rights], it lies in taking the delay and its consequences into account in determining the disposal".

His Lordship said, at para.53, that the court would "draw attention in appropriate quarters to our profound disquiet" at the situation that it had encountered and to "the possible lacuna which this case illustrates, that there may be no route by which a defendant convicted in the Crown Court can appeal an order adjourning his sentence".

The Court of Appeal has said that where a court is considering making a hospital order the defendant should, except in the rarest circumstances, be represented by counsel (*R. v Blackwood* (1974) 59 Cr. App. R. 170).

The court can make a hospital order in the case of an offender who is subject to an interim hospital order made under s.38, without his being brought before the court (s.38(2)).

Where the Crown Court makes a hospital order, it may also make an order under s.41, restricting the discharge of the offender from hospital, if it considers that it is necessary for the protection of the public from serious harm so to do.

Health Bodies and local social services authorities have a duty to provide after-care services for hospital order patients who cease to be liable to be detained and leave hospital (s.117).

Applications to the First-tier Tribunal (Mental Health) or the Mental Health Review Tribunal for Wales

Either the patient or the patient's nearest relative can apply to a tribunal in the period **1–515** between six and 12 months after the making of the hospital order and in any subsequent period of one year (ss.66(1)(f), (2)(f), 40(4), 69(1)(a), Sch.1 Pt 1 paras 2, 6, 9). References to the tribunal are governed by s.68.

Guardianship orders

Little use has been made of guardianship orders by the courts even though, in the view of **1–516** the Butler Committee, they "offer a useful form of control of some mentally disordered offenders who do not require hospital treatment [and are] particularly suited to the needs of offenders [with learning disabilities] including those inadequate offenders who require help in managing their affairs" (para.15.8).

Paragraph 8(iv)(c) of Home Office Circular No.66/90 states:

> "[T]he purpose of guardianship is primarily to ensure that the offender receives care and protection rather than medical treatment, although the guardian does have powers to require the offender to attend for medical treatment. The effect of a guardianship order is to give the guardian power to require the offender to live at a specific place (this may be used to discourage the offender from sleeping rough or living with people who may exploit or mistreat him, or ensure that he resides at a particular hostel), to attend specific places at specified times for medical treatment, occupation, education, or training, and to require access to the offender to be given at the place where the offender is living to any doctor, approved [mental health professional], or other person specified by the guardian. This power could be used, for example, to ensure the offender did not neglect himself".

The effect of a guardianship order made by a court is similar to that of civil guardianship, except that the patient's nearest relative has no power of discharge (s.40(2)(4), Sch.1, Pt I, paras 2, 8).

The offender must be over the age of 16 at the time when the order is made (subs.(2)(a)(ii)) and the guardian must be willing to receive the offender into guardianship (subs.(6)). Section 39A can be used to ascertain the attitude of a potential guardian. The powers of the guardian and the effect of the guardianship order are set out in s.40. Section 18(7) provides a power to convey the offender to the place where he is required to reside. There is no provision for returning the offender to court on any subsequent failure by the offender to comply with the provisions of the guardianship order.

The first day of the patient's guardianship is the date of the order (s.40(4)).

Applications to the First-tier Tribunal (Mental Health) or the Mental Health Review Tribunal for Wales

A patient who has been made subject to a guardianship order can apply to a tribunal **1–517** within the first six months of the order (s.69(1)(b)), and during each renewal period (ss.66(1)(f), 2(f), 40(4), Sch.1 Pt 1 paras 2, 6, 9). The patient's nearest relative can apply within the first 12 months of the order and in any subsequent 12-month period (s.69(1)(b))ii)).

Appeals

1–518   A hospital order is a form of sentence and is therefore appealable to the Court of Appeal (Criminal Appeal Act 1968, ss.9(1), 50(1)). Section 11(3) of the 1968 Act provides, inter alia, that the Court of Appeal can quash a sentence if they consider that the appellant should be sentenced differently for an offence for which he was dealt with by the court below and in place of it pass such sentence or make such order as the court below had power to pass or make when dealing with him for the offence. The subsection "is sufficiently wide to permit the court to re-sentence the appellant on information placed before it which was not put before the sentencing judge . . . Such an approach clearly allows the Court of Appeal to substitute a sentence on the basis of psychiatric and other evidence coming to light after the sentence was passed" (*R. v Beatty,* [2006] EWCA Crim 2359; [2006] M.H.L.R. 333 para.51). This power has resulted in the Court of Appeal substituting a hospital order for a prison sentence (see, for example, *R. v Logan* [2012] EWCA Crim 2542, where a hospital order with restrictions was substituted for a sentence of life imprisonment due to a change in the offender's diagnosis) and quashing a conviction for murder and substituting for it a verdict of manslaughter by reason of diminished responsibility (see, for example, *R v Petrolini* [2012] EWCA Crim 2055; [2012] M.H.L.R. 308). A hospital order can be substituted for a custodial sentence even if the medical criteria for the making of such an order were met at the time of the sentence: see *R. v O* [2011] EWCA Crim 376; [2011] M.H.L.R. 106, where the substitution was made 13 years after sentencing when a hospital bed was not available for the offender. Also see *R. v Hempston* [2006] EWCA Crim 2869; [2011] M.H.L.R. 99, where the substitution was made 28 years after sentence on the ground that the medical evidence received by the Court of Appeal confirmed that the appellant's mental disorder had reduced his culpability for his crimes to the extent that a hospital order with restrictions was the appropriate disposal.

The power of the court under s.11 of the 1968 Act must not be exercised in such a way so that an appellant is more severely dealt with on appeal than she was dealt with in the court below (*R. v Wang* [2005] EWCA Crim 3238; [2006] M.H.L.R. 109 para.17). A hospital order cannot be regarded as more severe than a sentence of imprisonment, even though it may involve detention for a longer period of time (*R. v Bennett* (1968) 52 Cr. App. R. 514), or if the term of imprisonment imposed by the sentencing court is about to expire (*R. v Searles* [2012] EWCA Crim 2685). In *R. v Lavender* [2012] EWCA Crim 1179, para.10, the court said that the cases of "*Bennett* 52 Cr.App.R 514 and . . . *Crozier* [1990] 12 Cr.App.R (S) 206, [make] it clear that where the assistance and help for the future which is the purpose of a hospital order replaces punishment, such disposal is not to be considered punitive albeit that, when analysed in terms of its potential for detention, it could be so regarded". The effect of ss.3 and 4 of the 1968 Act is to prevent the court from imposing a sentence with a direction under s.45A (*R. v Hendy* [2006] EWCA Crim 819; [2006] M.H.L.R. 244 para.53).

Fresh psychiatric evidence can be received by the court under s.23 of the Criminal Appeal Act 1968. In *R. v Fort* [2013] EWCA Crim 2332; [2014] M.H.L.R. 334 at paras 66 and 67, Aikens L.J. said:

> "In the context of conviction appeals, this court has emphasised that fresh expert evidence, (which in many cases concerns the mental state of the appellant) will not automatically be received by the court pursuant to section 23 . . . : see *R v Erskine; R v Williams* [2010] 1 WLR 183. Reception will depend on the facts and circumstances of the particular case. Whilst the court must have regard to the matters set out in section 23(2), ultimately the test is the broad one set out in section 23(1), viz. whether this court thinks it 'necessary or expedient in the interests of justice' to receive the proposed 'fresh' evidence.

> Similar flexibility must be appropriate on sentence appeals which concern the mental state of the appellant at the time of the original sentence. Thus we note that in *R v Charles de Silva* (1994) 15 Cr App R(S) 296, this court received fresh medical evidence

on the mental condition of the appellant. It was argued, successfully, that the fresh evidence demonstrated conclusively that the previous medical view that there was no connection between the appellant's mental illness and his offence, was wrong."

In *R v O* [2011] EWCA Crim 376, the court observed:

"Any case involving as it does reliance on evidence of mental condition not adduced at the time of the original court appearances must require the most careful scrutiny. . . . We are satisfied that the appellant met the section 37 criteria at the time of sentencing. Moreover, a sentence can be varied if satisfaction of those criteria only becomes apparent after sentencing: see *R v De Silva* (1994) 15 Cr App R(S) 296."

Fresh medical evidence should not be admitted where such evidence is concerned with the applicant's present condition, not her condition at the time of sentence, and does not seek to suggest that the opinions expressed by the psychiatrists at the time of sentencing were wrong (*R. v Yusuf* [2013] EWCA Crim 2077; [2014] M.H.L.R. 288).

If fresh medical evidence supports the contention that a hospital order should have been made in respect of an offender who was sentenced to a term of imprisonment, the nature of the Court of Appeal's powers under the Act are statutorily circumscribed and, in particular, a hospital order cannot be made if there is no bed available for the offender or if the offender does not then suffer from a mental disorder of a nature or degree which makes it appropriate for him to be detained in hospital (*R. v Lomey* [2004] EWCA Crim 3014; [2004] M.H.L.R. 316).

The Court of Appeal has allowed appeals against the imposition of restriction orders because it differed with the trial judge's assessment on the question of the risk of future harm: see, for example, *R. v Goucher* [2012] M.H.L.R. 107. The court has also allowed such appeals because of the progress that the patient had made at the psychiatric hospital since the trial; see, for, example, *R. v Daniels* [2014] EWCA Crim 2009; [2015] M.H.L.R. 91. However, the court has not been consistent in its approach. In *R. v Shah* [2011] EWCA Crim 23333; [2012] M.H.L.R 92 at para.12, the court said that such action will only be taken in "exceptional cases". And in *R. v Ruby* [2013] EWCA Crim 1653; [2014] M.H.L.R. 205 at para.37, Pitchford L.J. said:

"We make it plain that this court will not interfere with a sentence that was appropriate at the time it was imposed merely because the offender has made progress during his service of that sentence. We may only interfere if the sentence was unlawful, wrong in principle or manifestly excessive."

In *R. v Griffith* [2002] EWCA Crim 1838; [2002] M.H.L.R. 427, the Court of Appeal said that a submission that a medical report made subsequent to the trial indicated that the restriction order was no longer necessary would be best directed at the tribunal who would review the appellant's case and should not be the subject of a decision by the court. In this context, it should be noted that s.73 does not provide the tribunal with a power to change a patient's status from a restricted to a non-restricted patient. The Secretary of State has such a power under s.42(1).

It is fundamental to the trial process that a defendant must advance all aspects of his case at trial and a court will not admit fresh evidence to enable a defendant to run a different case if that case could have been run first time round (*R. v Ahluwalia* (1993) 96 Cr. App. R. 133).

Sentencing options

The options available to the sentencing judge where an offender who is to be sentenced is **1–519** suffering from mental disorder were identified in *R. v Vowles* [2015] EWCA Crim 45 at para.10. They are:

(i) A hospital order under s.37 with or without a restriction under s.41.

(ii) A determinate or indeterminate sentence of imprisonment and direction for admission to hospital under s.45A.

(iii) An interim order under s.38.

(iv) A determinate or indeterminate sentence allowing the Secretary of State to exercise his powers of transfer to a hospital under s.47 with or without a limitation order under s.49.

The Court said at para.12 that "the primary importance of the determination by the sentencing judge in a case where the option is either to impose an indeterminate sentence or to make a hospital order under s.37/s.41 is the release regime that will apply to the offender". The Court's general guidance on the options open to the sentencing judge is set out above.

The court's finding in *R. v Birch* (1989) 11 Cr. App. R (S.) 202 that a custodial term could be imposed on a mentally disordered defendant where a hospital order was not found to be the most suitable method of disposing of the case, was approved by the House of Lords in *R. v Drew* [2003] UKHL 25; [2003] 4 All E.R. 557 where it was held that under both national law and the jurisprudence of the European Court of Human Rights a sentence of imprisonment could be passed on a mentally disordered defendant who was criminally responsible and fit to be tried.

The court cannot defer sentence on the basis of the offender undertaking to undergo treatment at a psychiatric hospital (*R. v Skelton* [1983] Crim.L.R. 686).

Named hospital units

1–520   If a hospital order is made together with a restriction order made under s.41, the court has the power to order that the patient be admitted to and detained in a named hospital unit: see the note to s.41 under this heading.

Defective Court Orders

1–521   See the General Note to this Part.

Orders made in other proceedings

1–522   In certain circumstances, a hospital order or a guardianship order can be made under the Contempt of Court Act 1981 s.14(4),(4A) the Family Law Act 1996 s.51 and the Armed Forces Act 2006 s.169 and Sch.4 para.1. A restriction order can also be made under the 2006 Act: see Sch.4 para.2. It is also possible for such orders to be made under the terms of the Colonial Prisoners Removal Act 1884 and the Repatriation of Prisoners Act 1984.

Transport to and from court

1–523   See the General Note to s.35 under this heading.

Human Rights Act 1998

1–524   If an offender satisfies the criteria for a hospital order set out in subs.(2) but is not made the subject of such an order because of an inability to identify a hospital that would be willing to accept him (see subs.(4)), he could claim that his rights under art.5(1) of the European Convention on Human Rights (ECHR) had been breached if he was subsequently incarcerated in a non-therapeutic environment to the detriment of his mental health (*Aerts v Belgium* (2000) 29 E.H.R.R. 50; also see *Drew v United Kingdom* (2006) 43 E.H.R.R. SE2; [2006] M.H.L.R. 203, para.40).

In *Brand v Netherlands* [2001] M.H.L.R. 275, the European Court of Human Rights declared inadmissible an application that a lengthy detention of a mentally disordered person in prison pending a place being found in a secure psychiatric institution constituted a breach of art.3 of the ECHR on the ground that there was no evidence that the applicant's mental health or the possibilities of treatment had suffered on account of the time spent in prison. In *Drew v United Kingdom*, above, para.43, the Court said it did not consider that "the detention of the applicant on a prison medical wing for eight days without access to effective medication [for his mental disorder] reached the threshold of art.3".

Determining whether the accused "did the act or made the omission charged" for the purposes of subs.(3) is not a criminal trial and the accused's rights under art.6 of the ECHR are not engaged (*Director of Public Prosecutions v P* [2007] EWHC 496 (Admin); [2007] 4 All E.R. 628 paras 55, 61).

Also see note on s.3 under this heading.

Subsection (1)

CONVICTED.   Under s.51(5)(6) the court can make a hospital order (with or without a **1–525** restriction order) in respect of a mentally disordered transfer direction patient in his absence and, if he is awaiting trial, without convicting him.

FIXED BY LAW.   This section does not apply to persons who have been convicted of murder who must be sentenced to life imprisonment (Murder (Abolition of Death Penalty) Act 1965 s.1(1)).

MAGISTRATES' COURT.   Although a magistrates' court does not have the power to attach a restriction order under s.41 to a hospital order made under this section, it may, instead of making a hospital order or other disposition, commit him to the Crown Court for sentencing under s.43 with a view to a hospital order with restrictions being made.

OFFENCE PUNISHABLE ON SUMMARY CONVICTION WITH IMPRISONMENT.   For young offenders, see s.55(2).

HOSPITAL.   Or a registered establishment (ss.34(2), 55(5)).

Subsections (1A), 1(B)

These subsections, which were brought into force on April 4, 2005, do not apply to pre- **1–526** commencement offences. Their effect is that the mandatory sentencing requirements contained in the provisions listed in paras (a) to (d) of subs.(1A) do not prevent the court from making a hospital order under subs.(1).

Subsection (2)

The fact that the conditions in this subsection are satisfied does not compel the making of **1–527** a hospital order or indeed give rise to a presumption that one will be made: see *R. v Vowles* [2015] EWCA Crim 45.

Paragraph (a)

EVIDENCE.   For general requirements as to medical evidence, see s.54. The court can **1–528** call a doctor who has provided a written report to give oral evidence (s.54(2A)). The doctors should prepare an up-to-date assessment of a defendant so that the court may be satisfied as to his current mental condition at the time of sentencing, and as to his susceptibility to treatment at the time of sentencing (*R. v Preston* [2003] EWCA Crim 2086 para.6). When preparing their evidence from sources, doctors are not bound by the rules of evidence. They have to look at the whole picture. But they have to exercise judgment over material which is of first, second or even third hand hearsay as to the weight that can be attached to it (*Kiernan v Harrow Crown Court*, below, para.28).

Where there are significant differences in the evidence of the doctors giving evidence to the court, the judge should explain in his sentencing remarks why he accepted one set of evidence and rejected the other (*Kiernan v Harrow Crown Court* [2003] EWCA Crim 1052 para.19). During the course of his judgment, Scott Baker J. said, at para.25, that he could see no reason in ordinary circumstances why it would be appropriate for a doctor who was to give evidence "to begin making his own investigations by contacting the victim, or someone else in a similar situation, for his own account of events, especially if, as happened in this case, it was not possible for the applicant to give him the other side of the story".

In *R. v Tudor* [2012] EWCA Crim 1507 the Court of Appeal held that it would be rare for a judge to be found to have acted wrongly in principle in refusing to adjourn to allow the preparation of a second medical report as to whether to impose a hospital order when a full and thorough report had concluded that such a disposal was not appropriate. An example of such a course being adopted is "where the reporting expert had been provided with patently wrong or incomplete information upon which an otherwise conclusive opinion had been based" (para.15). The court agreed with counsel's concession that shopping around for a favourable medical report, particularly at public expense, is a practice which is not to be encouraged. Also note that in *R. v Ahmed* [2012] EWCA Crim 99, para.33, Elias L.J. said if "a judge has made a determination not to make a hospital order when he was empowered to do so, it plainly is not legitimate for an appellant to obtain two further reports from two further expert medical witnesses and to seek to rely on those to secure a change in the sentencing outcome".

In *R. v Crozier* (1990) 12 Cr. App. R.(S.) 206, the Court of Appeal applied *W v Egdell* [1990] 1 All E.R. 835 CA (noted under s.76) by holding that, given the particular circumstances of the case, a psychiatrist who had prepared a medical report for the defence had acted responsibly and reasonably when he handed a copy of his report to counsel for the prosecution. This was a case where the strong public interest in the disclosure of the psychiatrist's opinion overrode his duty of confidence to his client. The psychiatrist was "firmly of the view that the appellant suffers from psychopathic disorder, continues to be a danger to the public and should be kept in a secure hospital without limit of time. He held this opinion so strongly that he felt impelled to ensure that the court became aware of it" (per Watkins L.J. at 213).

TWO REGISTERED MEDICAL PRACTITIONERS. One of whom must be approved by the Secretary of State or the Welsh Ministers under s.12, or by another person by virtue of s.12ZA or 12ZB (s.54(1)). Unlike the situation that obtains when applications are made under Pt II, this section does not place any constraints on the timing of the medical examinations of the offender. As the doctors are providing evidence to the court, not medical recommendations, the Mental Health (Conflict of Interest) (England) Regulations 2008 do not apply. This means, inter alia, that both doctors could be on the staff of the admitting hospital and could have a financial interest in the matter.

The Court of Appeal has advised that the trial judge should hear evidence from the doctor who will be treating the offender (*R. v Blackwood* (1974) 59 Cr. App. R. 170).

SUFFERING FROM. The Court of Appeal has said that the offender's mental condition could have developed since the date of the offence (*R. v Smith*) [2001] EWCA Crim 743; [2001] M.H.L.R. 146.

MENTAL DISORDER. If the person has a learning disability, the disability must be associated with abnormally aggressive or seriously irresponsible conduct (s.1(2A), (2B)). A learning disabled person might also suffer from another form of mental disorder.

NATURE OR DEGREE. The meaning of this phrase is considered in the note on s.3(2)(a).

APPROPRIATE MEDICAL TREATMENT. See the note on s.3(2)(d).

ATTAINED THE AGE. At the commencement of his sixteenth birthday (Family Law Reform Act 1969 s.9(1)). Also see s.55(7).

WARRANTS HIS RECEPTION INTO GUARDIANSHIP. Compare with the criteria set out in s.7(2) for guardianship applications made under Pt II.

Paragraph (b)
NATURE OF THE OFFENCE. "Although hospital orders are frequently made in cases **1–529** involving grave offences of violence, the gravity of the offences is not an important consideration in making a hospital order (except in so far as it indicates a need for detention in secure conditions). Hospital orders have been upheld or imposed on appeal on offenders whose offences would not have justified a substantial term of imprisonment" (D.A. Thomas, *Principles of Sentencing* (2nd edn, 1979) p.299).

MOST SUITABLE METHOD OF DISPOSING OF THE CASE. Note subs.(8) and *R. v Vowles* [2015] EWCA Crim 45. In *R. v Birch* (1989) 11 Cr. App. R(S.) 202 at 215, the Court of Appeal pointed out that prison might be chosen as an alternative to hospital either because the offender was dangerous and no suitable secure hospital accommodation was available or because there was an element of culpability in the offence which merited punishment, as might happen where there was no connection between the mental disorder and the offence or where the offender's responsibility for the offence was reduced but not wholly extinguished. As was pointed out in *R. v Drew* [2003] UKHL 25; [2003] 4 All E.R. 557 at para.17, there is no divergence in this respect between national law and Strasbourg jurisprudence. In *X v United Kingdom* (App.No.5229/71, October 5, 1972) the European Commission on Human Rights rejected as manifestly inadmissible a complaint by a mentally disordered defendant that he should be held in a psychiatric hospital and not in prison.

Subsection (3)
This provision, which empowers a magistrates' court (including a youth court: see *R. (on* **1–530** *the application of P (a minor)) v Barking Youth Court* [2002] EWHC Admin 734; [2002] M.H.L.R. 304) to make a hospital or guardianship order without proceeding to conviction where the defendant is suffering from mental disorder, applies only where the court, having heard the evidence required by subs.(4), is satisfied that the defendant did the act or made the omission charged. The Butler Committee said at para.10.34: "In trivial cases the magistrates may properly have recourse to the expedient of adjourning the proceedings *sine die* or of simply not proceeding".

An order under this subsection can be made even though the court has not proceeded to trial. It can therefore be made in cases where the defendant is unable by virtue of his mental disorder to give his consent as to the mode of trial (*R. v Lincolnshire (Kesteven) Justices*, below).

In *R. v Lincolnshire (Kesteven) Justices Ex p. O'Connor* [1983] 1 W.L.R. 335 DC, the accused's mental disorder was such that he was unable to understand what it meant to consent to summary trial. The magistrates decided that as they were unable to try the case, it followed that they had no power to make a hospital order under this provision. The Divisional Court held that the magistrates could have made a hospital order without holding a trial. Lord Lane C.J. said at 338:

"In our judgment the words of [s.37(3)] are clear. It gives the justices power in an appropriate case to make a hospital order without convicting the accused. No trial is therefore called for. The circumstances in which it will be appropriate to exercise this unusual power are bound to be very rare and will usually require ... the consent of those acting for the accused if he is under a disability so that he cannot be tried".

O'Connor was considered by the Divisional Court in *R. v Ramsgate Justices Ex p. Kazmarek* (1985) 80 Cr.App.R. 366 and in *R. v Chippenham Magistrates' Court Ex p. Thompson* (1996) 32 B.M.L.R. 69. In *Kazmarek* it was held that in the case of an offence triable either summarily or on indictment where the accused elects trial by jury, this subsection can apply because the magistrates "would have power, on convicting him of that offence" to make a hospital order. *Kazmarek* was distinguished in *Thompson* where the court held that this subsection cannot apply in the case of an offence triable *only* on indictment in the Crown Court because in such a case the magistrates could not convict the offender of that offence.

In *R. (on the application of Singh) v Stratford Magistrates' Court)* [2007] EWHC 1582 (Admin); [2007] 4 All E.R. 407, the Divisional Court was concerned with the meaning and ambit of this provision when an accused in the magistrates' court contends that he is insane at the time of the events charged. It was held that:

1. Insanity can be relied upon as a common law defence to a summary charge in the magistrates' court. If established by the accused in a case to which it is relevant, it prevents conviction.

2. The accused has no right to a trial on the issue of insanity. The magistrates can either:

    (a) try the issue of insanity and pronounce its conclusions upon it, without convicting or acquitting the accused, provided that the conditions for making a hospital or guardianship order under this provision are met; or
    (b) if satisfied that there is no purpose in resolving the issue of insanity, and if an order under this provision is going to be made, the court can deal with the case without trying that issue.

    If it is clear that no order under this provision is going to be possible on the medical evidence, then in the absence of some other compelling factor the case must proceed to trial, so that if the accused was insane, he is acquitted, and if he was not, he is convicted.

3. Before embarking on a case to which this provision may be applied, magistrates should make it clear that it is a possibility and should invite submissions upon the course to be adopted. In particular, careful consideration must be given to any reason advanced why the issue of insanity should be tried. Such an application should be resolved having regard to the interests of justice, which include, but are not limited, to the justice of the accused.

The procedure for determining whether a person is fit to plead in the magistrates' court is specifically provided for by this provision when read in conjunction with s.11(1) of the Powers of Criminal Courts (Sentencing) Act 2000. Section 11(1) reads as follows:

"(1) If, on the trial by a magistrates' court of an offence punishable on summary conviction with imprisonment, the court—

(a) is satisfied that the accused did the act or made the omission charged, but

(b) is of the opinion that an inquiry ought to be made into his physical or mental condition before the method of dealing with him is determined,

the court shall adjourn the case to enable a medical examination and report to be made, and shall remand him."

Further guidance was given by Goldring L.J. in *R. (on the application of Blouet) v Bath and Wansdyke Magistrates' Court* [2009] EWHC 759 (Admin); [2009] M.H.L.R. 71, at para.9:

"The approach which the district judge should follow is this. First, there should be up-to-date—and I emphasise the words 'up-to-date'—medical evidence before him. If there is a possibility of a s37(3) order being made, he will then try the issue in accordance with s11(1) of the Act. If thereafter there arises the obligation to adjourn for further reports then that is what must happen. It may of course be that – given the up-to-date reports which he will then have – only a very short adjournment will be needed or, if everyone agrees that in the circumstances it is not, the matter can proceed under s37(3) if that be appropriate."

In *Crown Prosecution Service v P* [2007] EWHC 956 (Admin); [2007] 4 All E.R. 628, Smith L.J. said, at para.16, that s.11(1) of the 2000 Act and this provision "do not provide the solution to all of the problems which may confront a youth court before which a young person of doubtful capacity appears". The court held that:

1. Before criminal proceedings are commenced, appropriate consideration should be given to the question of whether civil proceedings under the Children Act are more appropriate.

2. If, in criminal proceedings, the defence raises an issue relating to the capacity of the young person before any evidence is heard, the court should use its inherent jurisdiction to order the stay of the proceedings if it appears that the person charged cannot, by reason of incapacity, have a fair trial in only exceptional cases.

3. In most cases, the medical evidence concerning capacity should be considered as part of the evidence in the case and not as the sole evidence in a freestanding application.

4. The court has a duty to keep under continuing review the question of whether the criminal trial ought to continue. If at any stage the court concludes that the child is unable to participate effectively in the trial, it may decide to call a halt. If the trial is halted on this ground, the court should then consider whether to switch to a consideration of whether the young person has done the acts alleged (the fact finding process), under the procedure referred to in the *Barking* case.

5. The fact that the young person cannot take an effective part in the fact finding process does not infringe his rights under art.6 of the ECHR.

Smith L.J. said at para.56:

"The decision as to whether or not to switch to fact finding is one for the discretion of the court. The court will wish to consider the possibility that (either on the basis of existing medical evidence or further medical evidence) it might be appropriate to make a hospital order. If that possibility exists, the court should usually find on the facts. But even if a hospital order seems unlikely, there may be other advantages in continuing to complete the fact-finding process. If the court finds that the child did the acts alleged, it may be appropriate to alert the local authority to the position with a view to consideration of care proceedings. Although the youth court's findings may not be binding in the context of care proceedings, the fact that those findings have been made might result in the simplification of care proceedings. I consider that proceedings should be stayed as an abuse of process before fact-finding only if no useful purpose at all could be served by the finding of facts."

DID THE ACT OR MADE THE OMISSION CHARGED. In *Singh*, above, Hughes L.J. said at para.33:

"[In] all cases where an order under s.37(3) is a possibility, the court should first determine the fact-finding exercise. That may be concluded, as here, on admissions, or it may involve hearing evidence. If the court is not satisfied that the act/omission was done/made, an unqualified acquittal must follow, whatever the anxieties may be about the accused's state of health."

This fact-finding exercise is not a criminal trial (*Director of Public Prosecution v P*, above). In determining the issue, the prosecution is only required to prove the ingredients which comprise the actus reus of the offence, not the mens rea (*R. v Antoine* [2000] 2 All E.R. 208 HL).

WITHOUT CONVICTING HIM.   The person has the same right of appeal against the order as if it had been made on his conviction (s.45). Although a person dealt with under this provision is not convicted, the order is a "conviction" for the purposes of the Rehabilitation of Offenders Act 1974 s.1(4), because it includes a finding that the person did the act or made the omission charged. A criminal records entry will therefore be made.

A person who is made subject to a hospital order under this provision is an "offender" for the purposes of s.142 of the Magistrates' Courts Act 1980. Under s.142: "A magistrates' court may vary or rescind ... [an] order ... made by it when dealing with an offender ..." There were sound practical reasons for treating a defendant, made subject to a hospital order, as an offender for the purposes of s.142. If having made a hospital order the magistrates discovered information which suggested that the defendant might not suffer from mental disorder, or might not have done the acts complained of, or, as in the present case, that arrangements could not in fact be made for his admission to hospital, it was highly desirable that there should be a procedural means by which the magistrates could rectify the error (*R. v Thames Magistrates' Court Ex p. Ramadan* 1 Cr. App. R. 386). *Ramadan* was applied in *Bartram v Southend Magistrates' Court* [2004] EWHC 2691 (Admin); [2004] M.H.L.R. 319, para.19, where Collins J. said that:

"there might be a case where it would be in the interests of the accused to have the matter reopened because whilst he was unable to give instructions and was unfit to plead, the evidence which established that he had done the act could not be challenged. When his mental state recovered sufficiently to enable him to give proper instructions, it might be that it became apparent that he did indeed have a defence to the charge which was laid against him. Thus in such a case he might want the charge to be tried because he expected that he would be acquitted of it".

Subsection (4)

1–531   In *R. (on the application of DB) v Nottinghamshire Healthcare NHS Trust* [2008] EWCA Civ 1354; [2009] 2 All E.R. 792, the Court of Appeal held that a hospital order, including a hospital order which is made subject to the restrictions contained in s.41, ceases to have effect if the offender who is the subject of the order is not admitted to the hospital named in the order within the period of 28 days from the date of the making of the order. It follows that after the 28 days have expired there is no authority either to convey the offender to the hospital or to detain him there. In this situation, "no doubt consideration can rapidly be given to the question whether the defendant can be compulsorily admitted to a hospital pursuant to Pt II of the Act rather than Pt III"; per Stanley Burnton L.J. at para.30. His Lordship said at paras 25, 26:

"It would I think be preferable for the standard form of order to specify the date when the 28 day period expires. In addition, it would be sensible for orders made under section 37 to include a direction or recommendation (for it has no statutory force) on the lines of that set out in [Circular 66/1980]. All parties should bear in mind the power of the sentencing court under section 155 of the Powers of Criminal Courts (Sentencing) Act 2000 to vary or, if necessary, to rescind an order. If an order is rescinded, a hospital order may be made subsequently; but the court should consider rescission of an order as a last resort, since the consequence will usually be to prolong a patient's detention in prison.

In the present case the orders made by the Crown Court did not make provision for the detention of the Appellant pending his transfer to hospital: the direction 'that pending admission to a hospital within the 28 day period, the defendant should be conveyed to and detained in a place of safety, namely . . .' had been, in each case, deleted. The result was that there was no lawful authority for his detention during that period. The exercise by the sentencing court of the power conferred on by the last part of section 37(4) to direct conveyance to and detention in a place of safety pending admission to hospital is not automatic or mandatory. Unless the offender is to be immediately conveyed from the court to the hospital, the court must ensure that the power is expressly exercised."

This subsection applies both to orders made following conviction under subs.(1) and to orders made under subs.(3) (*R. v Thames Magistrates' Court Ex p. Ramadan*, above).

APPROVED CLINICIAN. Who could be one of the doctors giving evidence under subs.(2)(a). "Where evidence is given that a bed will be made available within that time-scale, the hospital managers must ensure that the commitment is met" ("Mental Health Act 2007: Guidance for the courts on remand and sentencing powers for mentally disordered offenders", Ministry of Justice, March 2008, para.4.20). But see subs.(5).

SOME OTHER PERSON. Who need not be a clinician.

28 DAYS. Any time that the patient is unlawfully at large is disregarded when calculating this period (s.138(5)). The Secretary of State has been given the power to reduce this period under s.54A. In Wales, this power is exercised by the Welsh Ministers (see the General Note to the Act).

BEGINNING WITH. Including the date of the making of the order (*Zoan v Rouamba* [2000] 2 All E.R. 620 CA).

CONVEYANCE ... AND DETENTION. See the General Note to s.35 under the heading "Transport to and from court". General provisions relating to conveyance and detention are set out in s.137.

PLACE OF SAFETY. Is defined in s.55(1). A patient who is detained in a place of safety is not subject to the consent to treatment provisions contained in Pt IV (s.56(3)(b)). However, following the decision by the Court of Appeal in *R. v North West London Mental Health NHS Trust Ex p. Stewart* [1997] 4 All E.R. 871, it seems that a patient who has been detained in a place of safety which is a hospital could be brought within the scope of Pt IV if he was made the subject of an application under Part II: see the General Note to s.35. There are no provisions for discharge or leave of absence from a place of safety.

If a patient escapes from a place of safety, s.138 allows for him or her to be retaken. This power is subject to the time limits set out in s.18(4). A restriction order patient may be retaken at any time.

Subsection (5)
"This provision is intended to meet the case of a hospital which has agreed to accept the **1–532** patient being unavoidably unable to do so, e.g. because of a fire or an epidemic; but in practice it is generally easier for the patient to be returned to court for a further order to be made so as to give a further 28-day period in which a bed may become available. The Crown Court hospital order form 5034 is designed to facilitate this procedure" (Home Office Circular No. 69/1983 para.5).

If it proves impossible to find a bed for the offender, the Crown Court has power under s.155 of the Powers of Criminal Courts (Sentencing) Act 2000 to vary or rescind the sentence: see *R. (on the application of DB) v Nottinghamshire Healthcare NHS Trust*, which is noted under subs.(4). An analogous power for magistrates' courts is contained in s.142 of the Magistrates' Courts Act 1980.

Secretary of State. Or, in relation to Wales, the Welsh Ministers (see the General Note to this Act).

28 days. See the note on subs.(4) above.

Subsection (6)

1–533   This subsection provides that the court cannot make a guardianship order without the consent of the potential guardian. The consent of the offender is not required.

In *R. (on the application of Bukowicki) v Northamptonshire County Council* [2007] EWHC 310 (Admin); [2007] M.H.L.R. 121, Mole J. held that that subs.(2)(b), read with this provision, makes it clear that that the judge's judgement about the suitability of making a guardianship order must be subordinate to the willingness of the local authority to accept the guardianship. The authority has a wide discretion as to the factors that they are able to take into account in deciding if they are willing to accept an offender into guardianship. When exercising that discretion, the authority should take into account every material consideration relevant to their ability to manage him under the order. The authority should also take into account the relevant chapter of the *Code of Practice* (Ch.30) and its own policy on guardianship.

Subsection (8)

1–534   This section "clearly contemplates the ability of the court to make orders over and above the hospital order itself. It specifically precludes the making of a sentence of imprisonment or a community order, or, in relation to young people, referral orders or attempts to bind over parents or guardians. But it preserves the powers of the courts to make other orders and so thought was given as to whether there were other orders that could be made which could secure the prevention of the appellant from simply leaving the jurisdiction as and when he chose to do so" (*R. v Chowdhury* [2011] EWCA Crim 936; [2011] M.H.L.R. 157, para.17). This provision is concerned with the powers of the court in sentencing and it has no application to transfers ordered by the Secretary of State for Justice under s.47 (*R. (on the application of Miah) v Secretary of State for the Home Department* [2004] EWHC 2569 (Admin); [2004] M.H.L.R. 302 para.23).

Although it is lawful for a court to impose a custodial sentence and a hospital order on the same occasion but for different offences, it is a matter of obvious impracticability for a hospital order and a sentence of custody to be simultaneously carried out. A sentence of custody takes effect from the day on which it is passed, and that clearly, in practical terms, is inconsistent with the terms of the order which is that the defendant should be admitted to a psychiatric hospital forthwith (*R. v Rogerson* [2004] EWCA Crim 2099; [2006] M.H.L.R. 175).

Any other order. For example, a compensation order or an order disqualifying the offender from driving.

Interim hospital orders

1–535   **38.**—(1) Where a person is convicted before the Crown Court of an offence punishable with imprisonment (other than an offence the sentence for which is fixed by law) or is convicted by a magistrates' court of an offence punishable on summary conviction with imprisonment and the court before or by which he is convicted is satisfied, on the written or oral evidence of two registered medical practitioners—

> (a) that the offender is suffering from [mental disorder]; and
>
> (b) that there is reason to suppose that the mental disorder from which the offender is suffering is such that it may be appropriate for a hospital order to be made in his case,

the court may, before making a hospital order or dealing with him in some other way, make an order (in this Act referred to as "an interim hospital order") authorising his admission to such hospital as may be specified in the order and his detention there in accordance with this section.

(2) In the case of an offender who is subject to an interim hospital order the court may make a hospital order without his being brought before the court if he is represented by [an authorised person who] is given an opportunity of being heard.

(3) At least one of the registered medical practitioners whose evidence is taken into account under subsection (1) above shall be employed at the hospital which is to be specified in the order.

(4) An interim hospital order shall not be made for admission of an offender to a hospital unless the court is satisfied, on the written or oral evidence of the [approved clinician who would have overall responsibility for his case] or of some other person representing the managers of the hospital, that arrangements have been made for his admission to that hospital and for his admission to it within the period of 28 days beginning with the date of the order; and if the court is so satisfied the court may, pending his admission, give directions for his conveyance to and detention in a place of safety.

(5) An interim hospital order—

(a) shall be in force for such period, not exceeding 12 weeks; as the court may specify when making the order; but

(b) may be renewed for further periods of not more than 28 days at a time if it appears to the court, on the written or oral evidence of the [responsible clinician], that the continuation of the order is warranted;

but no such order shall continue in force for more than [twelve months] in all and the court shall terminate the order if it makes a hospital order in respect of the offender or decides after considering the written or oral evidence of the [responsible clinician] to deal with the offender in some other way.

(6) The power of renewing an interim hospital order may be exercised without the offender being brought before the court if he is represented by counsel or a solicitor and his counsel or solicitor is given an opportunity of being heard.

(7) If an offender absconds from a hospital in which he is detained in pursuance of an interim hospital order, or while being conveyed to or from such a hospital, he may be arrested without warrant by a constable and shall, after being arrested, be brought as soon as practicable before the court that made the order; and the court may thereupon terminate the order and deal with him in any way in which it could have dealt with him if no such order had been made.

AMENDMENTS

The amendments to this section were made by the Mental Health Act 2007 ss.1(4), 10(5), Sch.1 para.8, the Legal Services Act 2007 s.208, Sch.21, para.56 and the Crime (Sentences) Act 1997 s.49(1).

DEFINITIONS

mental disorder: ss.1, 145(1).   **1–536**
hospital: ss.55(5), 145(1).
hospital order: ss.37, 145(1).
the managers: s.145(1).
responsible clinician: s.55(1).
approved clinician: s.145)(1).

authorised person: s.55(1).
place of safety: s.55(1).

GENERAL NOTE

1–537   The Butler Committee "gained the impression that many doctors found it difficult to decide whether to recommend that a hospital order should be made where they have been able to examine the patient only briefly in a prison hospital under the pressure of impending court proceedings, since it was often impossible to know how he would react subsequently to the psychiatric hospital regime" (para.12.5). This section responds to this concern by empowering a Crown Court or magistrates' court to send a convicted offender to hospital for up to twelve months to enable an assessment to be made on the appropriateness of making a hospital order or direction in respect of him. An order can be made by the youth court if the offender is under 18 years of age. The court cannot make an interim hospital order in respect of an unconvicted person.

If the court makes an order under this section, "the offender's response in hospital can be evaluated without any irrevocable commitment on either side to this method of dealing with the offender if it should prove unsuitable" (Home Office Circular No.71/1984, Annex, para.15). The purpose of an interim hospital order is "not to hold the position until a place in an appropriate hospital is available for an offender for whom a hospital order is known to be appropriate" (*R. v Galfetti* [2002] EWCA Crim 1916; [2002] M.H.L.R. 418 per May L.J. at para.7).

In *R. (on the application of LS) v Brent Magistrates' Court* [2009] EWHC 2704 (Admin), the court held that an offender's presence in court is not required for the making of an order under this section by reason of the terms of subs.(2). Neither need the offender be present if the order is renewed (subs.(6)) or if the court makes a hospital order (subs.(2)).

In *R. v Vowles* [2015] EWCA Crim 45 at paras 55 and 56, Lord Thomas CJ cautioned against the use of this section "unless there is very clear evidence that such an order is necessary":

> "[A] judge should pause long and hard before making . . . an interim order. Although, as was the evidence before us, there are now a number of private providers to the NHS who have facilities at which offenders who are the subject of interim orders can now be held, the making of such an order has the consequence that as regards the victim of the crime there is no closure until the final order is made, there are significant costs to the general administration of justice in bringing a case back to court and there is acute pressure on the availability of secure beds."

An offender who is placed under an interim hospital order is subject to the consent to treatment provisions contained in Pt IV (ss.40(4), 56(3)). Otherwise, the legal position of a patient subject to such an order differs markedly from that of a patient subject to a hospital order: see the note on s.40(3).

An offender who absconds when subject to an interim hospital order may be arrested without warrant by any constable and brought before the court that made the order, which may decide on an alternative way of dealing with him.

Patients who are subject to orders made under this section do not have a nearest relative for the purposes of the Act.

Applications to the First-tier Tribunal (Mental Health) or the Mental Health Review Tribunal for Wales

1–538   The patient does not have a right to make an application to the tribunal: see the note on s.40(3). If, when the case returns to court for sentencing, the court makes a hospital order under s.37, the patient will be unable to make an application to a tribunal during the first six months of the order: see the note to s.37 under this heading.

Appeals

An interim hospital order is a form of sentence and is therefore appealable to the Court of **1–539** Appeal (Criminal Appeal) Act 1968 ss.9(1), 50(1)). Under s.11(3) of that Act, such an order may only be made by the Court of Appeal if it first quashes the trial judge's sentence. The Court of Appeal has described this state of affairs as being "obviously unsatisfactory" (*R. v Cooper* [2001] EWCA Crim 57; [2001] M.H.L.R. 2 per Hooper J. at para.18).

A court that has made an order under this section may end it and make its final sentencing decision despite the fact that an appeal against the order is outstanding: see s.11(5) of the 1968 Act.

Orders made in other proceedings

In certain circumstances, an interim hospital order may be made under the Contempt of **1–540** Court Act 1981 s.14(4),(4A), the Family Law Act 1996 s.51 and the Armed Forces Act 2006 s.169 and Sch.4 para.5.

Transport to and from court

See the note on s.35 under this heading. For general provisions relating to conveyance **1–541** and detention, see s.137.

Subsection (1)

OFFENCE PUNISHABLE WITH IMPRISONMENT.   This is construed in accordance with s.47(5) **1–542** (s.55(6)).

FIXED BY LAW.   This section does not apply to persons who have been convicted of murder.

OFFENCE PUNISHABLE ON SUMMARY CONVICTION WITH IMPRISONMENT.   See s.55(2).

EVIDENCE.   For general requirements as to medical evidence, see s.54. The court can call a doctor who has provided a written report to give oral evidence (s.54(2A)).

TWO REGISTERED MEDICAL PRACTITIONERS.   One of whom must be approved by the Secretary of State or the Welsh Ministers under s.12, or by another person by virtue of s.12ZA or 12ZB (s.54(1)). Also note subs.(3).

IS SUFFERING FROM MENTAL DISORDER.   It is not sufficient that the doctors have a mere reason to suspect that the offender is suffering from mental disorder. If the person has a learning disability, the disability must be associated with abnormally aggressive or seriously irresponsible conduct (s.1(2A), (2B)). A learning disabled person might also suffer from another form of mental disorder.

HOSPITAL ORDER.   Or a hospital direction and a limitation direction (s.45A(8)).

HOSPITAL.   Or a registered establishment (ss.34(2), 55(5)). A court may request information about the availability of hospital places under s.39.

Subsection (3)

The requirement of this provision does not apply to an order made under s.37. **1–543**

Subsection (4)

In *R. (on the application of DB) v Nottinghamshire Healthcare NHS Trust* [2008] EWCA **1–544** Civ 1354; [2009] 2 All E.R. 792, noted under s.37(4), the Court of Appeal held that a hospital order ceases to have effect if the offender who is the subject of the order is not admitted to the hospital named in the order within the period of 28 days from the date of the making of the order, as stipulated by it. It is submitted that this finding applies to an order made under this section.

APPROVED CLINICIAN.   Who could be the doctor referred to in subs.(3).

SOME OTHER PERSON.   Who need not be a clinician.

28 DAYS.   The Secretary of State and the Welsh Ministers have been given the power to reduce this period (s.54A).

BEGINNING WITH THE DATE OF THE ORDER.   Including the date of the order (*Zoan v Rouamba* [2002] 2 All E.R. 620 CA).

PLACE OF SAFETY.   See the note on s.37(4). A significant difference between a patient who is in a place of safety under s.37(4) and a patient who is in a place of safety under this provision is that the latter is subject to the consent to treatment provisions contained in Pt IV (s.56(3)).

Subsection (5)

1–545   This provides that if doubts remain as to the appropriateness of a hospital order (or a hospital direction and a limitation direction (s.45A(8)) after three months, the interim hospital order can be renewed at monthly intervals up to an overall total of 12 months.

RENEWED.   It is submitted that the order can be renewed in respect of a different hospital if the requirements of subs.(4) are satisfied in respect of the patient's admission to that hospital.

THE CONTINUATION OF THE ORDER IS WARRANTED.   The continuation of the order would not be warranted in a situation where the assessment has been completed, the assessment has concluded that a hospital order would be warranted, but there is a delay in identifying a suitable hospital that would be willing to accept the patient: see *R. v Galfetti* [2002] EWCA Crim 1916; [2002] M.H.L.R. 418.

Subsection (7)

1–546   There is no time limit on a recapture under this provision.

ARRESTED.   The power to arrest under this section was specifically preserved by s.26 and Sch.2 of the Police and Criminal Evidence Act 1984 (PACE). This means that the arresting policeman has a power to search the patient under s.32 of PACE at a place other than a police station. Section 72 of the Criminal Justice Act 1967 also provides for a power of arrest under this provision, but only if a warrant of arrest has been issued by a magistrate.

Information as to hospitals

1–547   **39.**—(1) Where a court is minded to make a hospital order or interim hospital order in respect of any person it may request—

(a) the [clinical commissioning group or] [Local Health Board] for [the area] in which that person resides or last resided; or

(b) [the National Health Service Commissioning Board or] [the National Assembly for Wales or any other] [clinical commissioning group or] [Local Health Board] that appears to the court to be appropriate,

to furnish the court with such information as [that [clinical commissioning group or] [Local Health Board] [or [the National Health Service Commissioning Board or the] National Assembly for Wales] have] or can reasonably obtain with respect to the hospital or hospitals (if any) in [their area] or elsewhere at which arrangements could be made for the admission of that person in pursuance of the order, and [that [clinical commissioning group or] [Local Health Board] [or [the National Health Service Commissioning Board or the] National Assembly for Wales] shall] comply with any such request.

[(1ZA) A request under this section to the National Health Service Commissioning Board may relate only to services or facilities the provision of which the Board arranges.]

[(1A) In relation to a person who has not attained the age of 18 years, subsection (1) above shall have effect as if the reference to the making of a hospital order included a reference to a remand under section 35 or 36 above or the making of an order under section 44 below.

(1B) Where the person concerned has not attained the age of 18 years, the information which may be requested under subsection (1) above includes, in particular, information about the availability of accommodation or facilities designed so as to be specially suitable for patients who have not attained the age of 18 years.]

(2) […]

AMENDMENTS
The amendments to this section were made by the Health Authorities Act 1995 ss.2(1), 5(1), Sch.1 para.107(5), Sch.3, the National Health Service Reform and Health Care Professions Act 2002 s.2(5), Sch.1 para.46, SI 2007/961 art.3, Sch. para.13(8), the Mental Health Act 2007 s.31(92) and the Health and Social Care Act 2012 Sch.5 para.28.

DEFINITION   **1–548**
    hospital order: ss.37, 145(1).
    interim hospital order: ss.38, 145(1).
    hospital: ss.55(5), 145(1).
    Local Health Board: s.145(1).

GENERAL NOTE
    This section provides that whenever a court is considering making a hospital order, a hos- **1–549** pital and a limitation direction (s.45A(8)) or an interim hospital order it may ask the appropriate clinical commissioning group, Local Health Board, the National Health Service Commissioning Board or the National Assembly for Wales to provide information as to the availability of suitable hospital places for the person in question (subs.(1)). It also enables the court to request information about the availability of hospital places for child offenders in respect of whom the court is considering a remand under ss.35 or 36 or, in respect of a magistrates' court, a committal to hospital under s.44 (subs.(1B)). The information that may be requested includes information about the "availability of accommodation designed so as to be specially suitable" for child patients (subs.(1C)). Paragraph 105 of the Explanatory Notes states: "The purpose of [subs.(1C)] is to ensure that courts do not place a child in a prison setting when a suitable hospital bed would be a more appropriate option".
    Local Health Boards and clinical commissioning groups are required by s.140 to notify relevant social services authorities of those hospitals where patients can be treated in cases of special urgency.

Subsection (1)

1–550   IT MAY REQUEST.   The Mental Health Act Commission reported that only limited use has been made of this power (Mental Health Act Commission, *Third Biennial Report* 1987–89, para.11.2).

RESIDES.   See the note on this term in s.7(5).

HOSPITAL.   Or registered establishment (ss.34(2), 55(5)).

[Information to facilitate guardianship orders

1–551   **39A.** Where a court is minded to make a guardianship order in respect of any offender, it may request the local social services authority for the area in which the offender resides or last resided, or any other local social services authority that appears to the court to be appropriate—

(a) to inform the court whether it or any other person approved by it is willing to receive the offender into guardianship; and

(b) if so, to give such information as it reasonably can about how it or the other person could be expected to exercise in relation to the offender the powers conferred by section 40(2) below;

and that authority shall comply with any such request.]

AMENDMENT

This section was inserted by the Criminal Justice Act 1991 s.27(1).

DEFINITIONS

1–552   local social services authority: s.145(1).
guardianship order: ss.37, 145(1).

GENERAL NOTE

1–553   This section enables the court to find out whether the relevant local social services authority or a private guardian approved by the authority is willing to receive the offender into guardianship and, if this were to happen, how the authority or guardian might exercise their guardianship powers in relation to the offender.

Code of Practice

1–554   Paragraph 22.8 of the *Code* states that local authorities "should appoint a named person to respond to requests from the courts about mental health services available in the community including under guardianship".

Effect of hospital orders, guardianship orders and interim hospital orders

1–555   **40.**—(1) A hospital order shall be sufficient authority—

(a) for a constable, an [approved mental health professional] or any other person directed to do so by the court to convey the patient to the hospital specified in the order within a period of 28 days; and

(b) for the managers of the hospital to admit him at any time within that period and thereafter detain him in accordance with the provisions of this Act.

(2) A guardianship order shall confer on the authority or person named in the order as guardian the same powers as a guardianship application made and accepted under Part II of this Act.

(3) Where an interim hospital order is made in respect of an offender—

(a) a constable or any other person directed to do so by the court shall convey the offender to the hospital specified in the order within the period mentioned in section 38(4) above; and

(b) the managers of the hospital shall admit him within that period and thereafter detain him in accordance with the provisions of section 38 above.

(4) A patient who is admitted to a hospital in pursuance of a hospital order, or placed under guardianship by a guardianship order, shall, subject to the provisions of this subsection, be treated for the purposes of the provisions of this Act mentioned in Part I of Schedule 1 to this Act as if he had been so admitted or placed on the date of the order in pursuance of an application for admission for treatment or a guardianship application, as the case may be, duly made under Part II of this Act, but subject to any modifications of those provisions specified in that Part of that Schedule.

(5) Where a patient is admitted to a hospital in pursuance of a hospital order, or placed under guardianship by a guardianship order, any previous application, hospital order or guardianship order by virtue of which he was liable to be detained in a hospital or subject to guardianship shall cease to have effect; but if the first-mentioned order, or the conviction on which it was made, is quashed on appeal, this subsection shall not apply and section 22 above shall have effect as if during any period for which the patient was liable to be detained or subject to guardianship under the order, he had been detained in custody as mentioned in that section.

[(6) Where—

(a) a patient admitted to a hospital in pursuance of a hospital order is absent without leave;

(b) a warrant to arrest him has been issued under section 72 of the Criminal Justice Act 1967; and

(c) he is held pursuant to the warrant in any country or territory other than the United Kingdom, any of the Channel Islands and the Isle of Man,

he shall be treated as having been taken into custody under section 18 above on first being so held.]

AMENDMENTS

The amendments to this section were made by the Mental Health Act 2007 s.21, Sch.2 para.7 and the Mental Health (Patients in the Community) Act 1995 s.2(4).

DEFINITIONS

1–556

hospital order: ss.37, 145(1).
approved mental health professional: s.145(1), (1AC).
the managers: s.145(1).
hospital: ss.55(5), 145(1).
hospital order: s.55(4).
guardianship order: ss.37, 55(4), 145(1).
guardian: s.55(1).
absent without leave: ss.18(6), 145(1).
interim hospital order: ss.38, 145(1).
patient: s.145(1).
application for admission for treatment: ss.3, 145(1).

GENERAL NOTE

1–557   This section provides that, with very few exceptions, a patient who is admitted to hospital under a hospital order without restrictions or placed under guardianship by a guardianship order is treated the same as a patient who has been admitted to hospital or placed under guardianship under Pt II of the Act. The necessary modifications to the provisions of Pt II are made by Pt I of Sch.I and are noted in subs.(4). The effect of an interim hospital order is set out in subs.(3).

The court documents should be carefully checked by the hospital managers: see the note on "Defective Court Orders" in the General Note to this Part.

Any reference to hospital orders and guardianship orders in subs.(2), (4) or (5) of this section shall be construed as including a reference to any order or directions under this Part having the same effect as a hospital or guardianship order (s.55(4)).

Subsection (1)

Paragraph (a)

1–558   CONSTABLE.   Means the office of constable, and not the rank of constable (Police Act 1996 s.29, Sch.4).

CONVEY THE PATIENT TO HOSPITAL.   For general provisions relating to conveyance, see s.137. Before proceeding to convey the patient to hospital, the authorised person should confirm with the hospital that it is still willing to accept the patient because this section does not give authority to convey the patient *from* hospital if admission is refused.

WITHIN A PERIOD OF 28 DAYS.   Any time that the patient is unlawfully at large is disregarded when calculating this period (s.138(5)). Once this period has expired, the hospital order ceases to provide authority for the offender's conveyance to hospital or his detention there: see *R. (on the application of DB) v Nottinghamshire Healthcare NHS Trust*, noted under s.37(4).

Subsection (2)

1–559   SAME POWERS.   As contained in s.8(1). A patient placed under a guardianship order is not subject to the consent to treatment provisions contained in Pt IV because he is not a patient who is "liable to be detained": see s.56(3).

Subsection (3)

1–560   This subsection sets out the effect of an interim hospital order made under s.38. Apart from coming within the scope of Pt IV, an interim hospital order patient is treated very differently from a hospital order patient. This is because an interim hospital order patient is not to be treated as if he had been admitted in pursuance of an application for admission for treatment; he is detained "in accordance with the provisions of s.38". The consequences of this are that neither the patient nor his nearest relative can apply to a tribunal, no-one has the right to discharge the patient, and the patient may not be granted leave of absence or be transferred to another hospital. Although applications have been made to the court for authority to either grant the patient leave of absence or to transfer the patient, the Act does not provide the court with an express power to make such orders.

CONVEY THE OFFENDER TO THE HOSPITAL.   See the General Note to s.35 under the heading "Transport to and from court". For general provisions relating to conveyance and detention, see s.137.

WITHIN THE PERIOD MENTIONED IN S.38(4).   28 days beginning with the date of the order.

SHALL ADMIT HIM. The hospital specified in an interim hospital order cannot subsequently withdraw its agreement to accept the offender. However, if circumstances arise which prevent the hospital from admitting the patient, the case should be returned to the court as a matter of urgency.

Subsection (4)

HOSPITAL ORDER. With three substantive exceptions, the effect of this subsection is to **1–561** place a patient who has been placed under a hospital order in the same legal position as a patient who has been admitted to hospital for treatment under s.3. The exceptions are: (1) the nearest relative of a hospital order patient cannot order his discharge under s.23 (Sch.1 paras 2, 8); (2) unlike a s.3 patient, the hospital order patient cannot apply to a tribunal within the first six months of his detention (Sch.1 paras 2, 9); and (3) the initial six month maximum period of detention runs from the day that the hospital order is made by the court, not the patient's admission to the hospital (Sch.1 paras 2, 6).

If the medical conditions which justified the making of the hospital order cease to be met at any time, the duty of the responsible clinician, exercising a medical judgment, is to discharge the offender from the hospital order (*R. v Drew* [2003] UKHL 25; [2003] 4 All E.R. 557 para.10).

GUARDIANSHIP ORDER. The effect of a guardianship order made under s.37 is essentially the same as if the patient had been made the subject of a guardianship application under s.7. The major difference between the two is that with a guardianship order the power of the nearest relative to discharge the patient from guardianship does not apply (Sch.1 paras 2, 8).

Subsection (5)

CEASE TO HAVE EFFECT. A previous hospital order will not cease to have effect if a **1–562** restriction order made in respect of the patient under s.41 is in force at the material time (s.41(4)). The ending of the previous order or application does not effect the continuity of the three-month period provided for in s.58(1)(b). The imposition of the subsequent order provides the patient with a fresh opportunity to make an application to a tribunal during the second six months of his detention under that order.

An interim hospital order is not specified in this provision (see s.38(1)). If the patient is subject to a s.3 application when such an order is made by the court, the application should either be discharged under s.23 or allowed to continue during the currency of the interim order, in which case it will be reinstated (if it has not expired in the meantime) once the interim order is terminated. If the court proceeds to make a hospital or guardianship order in respect of the patient, this provision will terminate the s.3.

Subsection (6)

This subsection is concerned with the taking into custody of absconding patients who **1–563** have gone abroad. Paragraph 11.20 of the Reference Guide states:

"The Act does not permit patients to be retaken outside the UK, the Isle of Man or the Channel Islands. In certain cases, under the Extradition Act 2003, patients who are convicted offenders or accused of a crime may be extradited back to England, if the necessary warrants have been issued. The effect of section 40(6) is that if a patient subject to a restricted hospital order is detained overseas under extradition arrangements, the patient is treated as having been taken into custody under section 18 when first held on the basis of the extradition warrant in the country in question, rather than when returned to the UK. If the patient's restriction order is for a fixed period (see paragraph 21.15), that may affect whether it is still in force when the patient returns to England or Wales."

Restriction Orders

Power of higher courts to restrict discharge from hospital

1–564   **41.**—(1) Where a hospital order is made in respect of an offender by the Crown Court, and it appears to the court, having regard to the nature of the offence, the antecedents of the offender and the risk of his committing further offences if set at large, that it is necessary for the protection of the public from serious harm so to do, the court may, subject to the provisions of this section, further order that the offender shall be subject to the special restrictions set out in this section, [. . .] and an order under this section shall be known as "a restriction order".

(2) A restriction order shall not be made in the case of any person unless at least one of the registered medical practitioners whose evidence is taken into account by the court under section 37(2)(a) above has given evidence orally before the court.

(3) The special restrictions applicable to a patient in respect of whom a restriction order is in force are as follows—

(a)   none of the provisions of Part II of this Act relating to the duration, renewal and expiration of authority for the detention of patients shall apply, and the patient shall continue to be liable to be detained by virtue of the relevant hospital order until he is duly discharged under the said Part II or absolutely discharged under section 42, 73, 74 or 75 below;

[(aa): none of the provisions of Part II of this Act relating to [community treatment orders and community patients] shall apply;]

(b)   no application shall be made to [the appropriate tribunal] in respect of a patient under section 66 or 69(1) below;

(c)   the following powers shall be exercisable only with the consent of the Secretary of State, namely—

(i) power to grant leave of absence to the patient under section 17 above;

(ii) power to transfer the patient in pursuance of regulations under section 19 above [or in pursuance of subsection (3) of that section]; and

(iii) power to order the discharge of the patient under section 23 above; and if leave of absence is granted under the said section 17 power to recall the patient under that section shall vest in the Secretary of State as well as the [responsible clinician]; and

(d)   the power of the Secretary of State to recall the patient under the said section 17 and power to take the patient into custody and return him under section 18 above may be exercised at any time;

and in relation to any such patient section 40(4) above shall have effect as if it referred to Part II of Schedule 1 to this Act instead of Part I of that Schedule.

(4) A hospital order shall not cease to have effect under section 40(5) above if a restriction order in respect of the patient is in force at the material time.

(5) Where a restriction order in respect of a patient ceases to have effect while the relevant hospital order continues in force, the provisions of section 40 above and Part I of Schedule 1 to this Act shall apply to the patient as if he had been admitted to the hospital in pursuance of a hospital order (without a restriction order) made on the date on which the restriction order ceased to have effect.

(6) While a person is subject to a restriction order the [responsible clinician] shall at such intervals (not exceeding one year) as the Secretary of State may direct examine and report to the Secretary of State on that person; and every report shall contain such particulars as the Secretary of State may require.

AMENDMENTS

The amendments to this section were made by the Mental Health (Patients in the Community) Act 1995 s.2(1), Sch.1 para.5, the Mental Health Act 2007 ss.10(6), 32, 55, Sch.3 para.17, Sch.11 Pt 8, the Crime (Sentences) Act 1997 s.49(2) and by SI 2008/2883 art.9, Sch.3 para.41.

DEFINITIONS

    hospital order: ss.37, 55(4), 145(1).   **1–565**

    patient: s.145(1).

    hospital: ss.55(5), 145(1).

    community treatment order: ss.17A(7), 145(1).

    community patient: ss.17A(7), 145(1).

    responsible clinician: s.55(1).

    the appropriate tribunal: ss.66(4) 145(1).

GENERAL NOTE

This section empowers the Crown Court, having made a hospital order under s.37, to **1–566** make a further order (a "restriction order") restricting the patient's discharge, transfer or leave of absence from hospital without the consent of the Secretary of State. Such a patient is a restricted patient (s.79). Paragraph 22.85 of the *Code of Practice* states:

> "In exceptional circumstances, the Secretary of State for Justice may 'direct' a restricted patient's admission into hospital, outside the NHS commissioning arrangements. This is usually where it is critical that the patient receive treatment and identifying a suitable bed is difficult."

A restriction order, which can only be made where it is necessary to protect the public from serious harm, does not require renewal to prevent it from lapsing, but remains in force until it is discharged by the patient's responsible clinician with the agreement of the Secretary of State under s.23, by the Secretary of State under s.42, or by the tribunal under s.73. The patient's nearest relative does not have the power to discharge the patient (s.40(4), Sch.1 Pt II paras 2, 7). Magistrates' courts may only commit a convicted offender to the Crown Court with a view to a restriction order being made (s.43(1)).

The nature of a restriction order was considered by the Court of Appeal in *R. v Birch* (1989) 11 Cr. App. R.(S.) 202 at 211–212:

> "A restriction order has no existence independently of the hospital order to which it relates; it is not a separate means of disposal. Nevertheless, it fundamentally affects the circumstances in which the patient is detained. No longer is the offender regarded simply as a patient whose interests are paramount. No longer is the control of him handed over unconditionally to the hospital authorities. Instead the interests of public safety are regarded by transferring the responsibility for discharge from the [responsible clinician] and the hospital to [. . .] the Secretary of State and the [tribunal]. A patient who has been subject to a restriction order is likely to be detained for much longer in hospital than one who is not, and will have fewer opportunities for leave of absence".

The court made the following observations at 213–215 on the principles to be observed in deciding whether a restriction order is appropriate:

> "[The judge] is required to choose between an order without restrictions, which may enable the author of a serious act of violence to be at liberty only a matter of months after he appears in court, and a restriction order which may lead the offender to be detained for a long time: longer in some cases than the period which he would serve if sent to prison: see *Haynes* (1981) 3 Cr. App. R. (S.) 330. It is moreover a choice which depends on a prognosis, the ultimate responsibility for which is left with the judge.

This responsibility may be hard to discharge, since the judge will often have nothing on which to base his decision, if he feels reservations about the medical evidence, apart from the considerations stated by the statute, namely the nature of the offence and the antecedents of the offender: which will often consist only of a single episode of fatal violence and a blank criminal record. Where there is a trial the judge can form an impression of [the] defendant as the case unfolds which may enable him to make his own assessment of his dangerousness. But in the more usual case where a plea of guilty to manslaughter on the grounds of diminished responsibility is accepted by the prosecution and the court, this opportunity is largely absent, and did not exist at all in the present case, where the appellant was too distressed to remain for the hearing in the Crown Court . . . .

Nevertheless, section 41(1) is there and the judge must apply it. Quite plainly the addition of the words 'from serious harm' has greatly curtailed the former jurisdiction to make a restriction order: most particularly because the word 'serious' qualifies 'harm' rather than 'risk.' Thus the court is required to assess not the seriousness of the risk that the defendant will re-offend, but the risk that if he does so the public will suffer serious harm. The harm in question need not, in our view, be limited to personal injury. Nor need it relate to the public in general, for it would in our judgment suffice if a category of persons, or even a single person, were adjudged to be at risk: although the category of persons so protected would no doubt exclude the offender himself. Nevertheless the potential harm must be serious, and a high possibility of a recurrence of minor offences will no longer be sufficient [. . .]

It would [. . .] be a mistake to equate the seriousness of the offence with the probability that a restriction order will be made. This is only one of the factors which section 41(1) requires to be taken into account. A minor offence by a man who proves to be mentally disordered and dangerous may properly leave him subject to a restriction. In theory the converse is also true. *Courtney* (1987) 9 Cr. App. R.(S.) 404 shows that a serious offence committed by someone who is adjudged to have a very low risk of re-offending may lead to an unrestricted hospital order.

Nevertheless, the court will need to be very sure of its ground in such a case, and we consider that there is nothing in the 1983 Act to derogate from the following statement of principle by Lord Parker C.J., in *Gardiner* (1967) 51 Cr. App. R. 187:

> 'Thus, for example, in the case of crimes of violence, and of the more serious sexual offences, particularly if the prisoner has a record of such offences, or if there is a history of mental disorder involving violent behaviour, it is suggested that there must be compelling reasons to explain why a restriction order should not be made.'

Finally we would make [a further point] on section 41. [The] sentencer should not impose a restriction order simply to mark the gravity of the offence (although this is an element in the assessment of risk), nor as a means of punishment: for a restriction order merely qualifies a hospital order and a hospital order is not a mode of punishment."

1–567 The current approach to the sentencing of mentally disordered offenders which takes into account the amendments made to the Act by the Mental Health Act 2007 was set out by the Court of Appeal in *R. v Vowles* [2015] EWCA Crim 45 which is considered in the General Note to s.37.

In *R. v Welsh* [2011] EWCA Crim 73; [2011] M.H.L.R. 71, the Court of Appeal considered whether it was appropriate to substitute a restriction order for a discretionary life sentence for an offender who had pleaded guilty to manslaughter on the grounds of diminished responsibility. The court referred to the relevant jurisprudence which was summarised by the Lord Chief Justice in *R. v Wood (Clive)* [2009] EWCA Crim 651, para.18:

"The mere fact that the case is one of manslaughter on the grounds of diminished responsibility does not preclude a sentence of imprisonment for life. In reality this sentence would be rare in such cases, usually reserved for particularly grave cases, where the defendant's responsibility for his actions, although diminished, remains high."

While the court accepted that any discharge of the patient would be considered under the mental health regime with rigour, it bore in mind the views of the House of Lords in *R. v Drew* [2003] UKHL 25, para.21:

"Defendants made subject to hospital orders, whether restricted or not, are entitled to release when the medical conditions justifying their original admissions cease to be met . . . Further, they are liable to recall only on medical grounds. They may be a source of danger to the public even though these medical conditions are not met."

It is the duty of a judge hearing a case who has formed a clear provisional view on the material presented to her that a restriction order should be made, to inform the parties that this is so, so that, by way of evidence and argument they will be able to deal with it (*R. v Goode* [2002] EWCA Crim 1698 at para.36). If a court is considering making an order under this section the defendant should be represented by counsel (*R. v Blackwood* (1974) 59 Cr. App. R. 170).

A restriction order remains in force even if the patient is subsequently imprisoned for an offence committed after his conditional discharge (*R. v Mersey Mental Health Review Tribunal Ex p. K* [1990] 1 All E.R. 694 CA), and the patient may be recalled to hospital on the expiry of his prison sentence (*R. v Secretary of State for the Home Department Ex p. K* [1990] 1 All E.R. 703).

In subss.(3) to (5) of this section any reference to a hospital order, a guardianship order or a restriction order are to be construed as including a reference to any order or direction under this Part having the same effect as such orders (s.55(4)).

Also see the note on "sentencing options" in the General Note to s.37 and the note on "the court may by order" in s.37(1).

Named hospital units

Section 47 of the Crime (Sentences) Act 1997 provides that where a court makes a **1–568** restriction order it has the power to order that the patient be admitted to and detained in a named hospital unit. A named hospital unit can be any part of a hospital which is treated as a separate unit. Paragraph 22.26 of the *Code of Practice* states:

"A named hospital unit can be any part of a hospital which is treated as a separate unit. The hospital managers of the hospital will define the boundaries of the hospital however it will be for the court (or the Secretary of State for Justice, as the case may be) to confirm the unit or hospital covered by the detention authority in each case where it makes use of the power. When transferring a prisoner to hospital with a restriction direction attached, the Secretary of State for Justice may direct that the patient be detained in a specific hospital unit. This will normally be to a named ward to prevent patients being moved to lower levels of security within a hospital without the Secretary of State for Justice's agreement. Admission to a named unit will mean that the consent of the Secretary of State for Justice will be required for any leave of absence or transfer from the named unit, even if the transfer is to the same level of security, or transfer is to another part of the same hospital or to another hospital. If however, the transfer involves no change to either the named unit or hospital prior agreement from the Secretary of State for Justice is not required. For example, if the detention authority covers a named hospital, to move patients between units within that hospital will not require Secretary of State for Justice permission. The mental health casework section (MHCS) should be informed of the move."

Applications to the First-tier Tribunal (Mental Health) or the Mental Health Review Tribunal for Wales

1–569   A patient who is subject to a restriction order may apply to a tribunal in the period between six and 12 months of the order and in any subsequent period of one year (s.70) and the Secretary of State may, and in some circumstances must, refer such patients to a tribunal (s.71). The patient's nearest relative has no power to apply to a tribunal. The powers of a tribunal when considering the case of a restricted patient are set out in s.73.

If the patient becomes subject to a "notional hospital order" by virtue of the restriction order ceasing to have effect (subs.(5)), the patient is given the same powers to apply to a tribunal as those enjoyed by a s.3 patient (s.69(2)). These powers are also enjoyed by the patient's nearest relative (s.69(1)).

Appeals

1–570   See the note on s.37 under this heading.

Domestic Violence, Crime and Victims Act 2004

1–571   See Ch.40 of the *Code of Practice*.

The Ministry of Justice has published "Duties to victims under the Domestic Violence, Crime and Victims Act 2004: Guidance for Clinicians" (March 2009) which is available at *www.justice.gov.uk/offenders/types-of-offender/mentally-disordered-offenders*. A letter dated April 22, 2014 from the Head of Mental Health Casework Section at the Ministry of Justice states:

> "As a result of a Ministerial commitment, as of 22 April 2014, victims of restricted mentally disordered offenders, who have opted in to the Victim Contact Scheme, will be told if permission for community leave is granted by the Secretary of State unless there are exceptional reasons why they should not be told. Exceptional reasons will include risk to the patient, so any concerns about this must be flagged up to MHCS in the application for community leave."

Fitness to plead

1–572   "Resuming a Prosecution when a patient becomes fit to plead" is guidance which explains the powers and responsibilities of the Secretary of State for Justice, the Crown Prosecution Service and Her Majesty's Courts and Tribunal Service when a restricted patient becomes fit to plead and sets out the procedure to be followed when a prosecution is resumed. Paragraph 11 of the guidance states:

> "The section 37/41 order ceases to have effect on the patient's arrival at court (section 5A(4) Criminal Procedure (Insanity) Act 1964). The patient's responsible clinician should be aware of this so that procedures for detention under the civil provisions of the Mental Health Act can be considered and commenced if the patient is still sufficiently ill as to require compulsory treatment in hospital. It may be appropriate for the relevant local social services authority (LSSA) to arrange for an approved mental health professional (AMHP) to consider making an application for admission under Part 2 of the Mental Health Act (see paragraph [22.5] Code of Practice Mental Health Act 1983 (Department of Health). Wherever possible, the case should be listed first and called on promptly to avoid delay."

The detaining hospital is responsible for securing the attendance of the patient at court (*ibid.*, para.10). The guidance can be accessed at: *www.justice.gov.uk/downloads/offenders/mentally-disordered-offenders/resuming-guidance-prosecution-fit-to-plead.pdf*. The 1964 Act is considered briefly in the General Note to this Part.

Subsection (1)

HOSPITAL ORDER IS MADE. The offender must therefore have satisfied the conditions of **1–573**
s.37(2). Although this section implies that the offender will be kept in secure accommodation, this will not be necessary in all cases. The Butler Committee, at para.14.21, gave
the following example of a restricted patient who might not need to be accommodated
in secure accommodation:

"[T]he persistent molester of small children may need the continuing supervision after
discharge which a restriction order allows, and should not be permitted simply to walk
out of hospital whenever he wishes, but is unlikely to need the secure containment of
bolts and bars".

CROWN COURT. A Crown Court has jurisdiction to make a restriction order in respect of
an offence which only became triable by that court under the provisions of s.40 of the
Criminal Justice Act 1988 (*R. v Avbunudje* [1999] 2 Cr. App. R.(S.) 189 CA). Section
40 enables a summary only offence to be included in an indictment in certain specified circumstances. Although a magistrates' court cannot make a restriction order, it does have the
power to commit the offender to the Crown Court with a view to such an order being made
by that court (s.43(1)).

ANTECEDENTS. It has been reported that this term is

"construed by the judges to include not just previous convictions, but also accounts of
previous unprosecuted dangerous behaviour made in psychiatric reports (subject to
any objection by defence counsel), and some [judges] said that evidence of failure of previous treatment might also be significant. A history of violence would cause particular
concern, especially if it appeared that the violence was escalating in seriousness" (*The
Restricted Hospital Order: From Court to Community*, Home Office Research Study
186, 1998, p.40).

THE PUBLIC. The public does not include an unborn child who, when born, could be
protected by the provisions of the Children Act 1989 (*R. v Jones* [2000] M.H.L.R. 12 CA).
    In *Anderson v Scottish Ministers* [2001] UKPC D 5; [2001] M.H.L.R. 192, para.37, Lord
Hope said:

"The word 'public' and the phrase 'in order to protect the public from serious harm' in
each of the various amendments included in section 1 of the [Mental Health (Public
Safety and Appeals) (Scotland) Act 1999] is capable of meaning either the public in general or a section of the public, as the context requires. In Doherty's case there is no
question of his coming into contact with the public in general as he would be remitted
to prison in the event of his discharge from hospital. But the persons with whom he
would be liable to come into contact in a prison may be regarded as a section of the public. They include prison officers, other inmates and a variety of persons who visit prisons
for religious, educational, social work or other purposes. Read in this way, the effect of
the amendments introduced by section 1 of the 1999 Act is to require the sheriff or the
Scottish Ministers, as the case may be, to be satisfied in Doherty's case that it is necessary for him to be detained in a hospital to protect that section of the public from serious
harm . . ."

SERIOUS HARM. The insertion of this phrase into the 1982 Act gave effect to recommendation of the Butler Committee which proposed that the equivalent section in the 1959 Act
should be revised to make it clear that the intention of a restriction order is to protect the
public from serious harm. The Committee wished to ensure that a court would not impose
restrictions on "the petty recidivist because of the virtual certainty that he will persist in
similar offences in the future" (para.14.24).

The court should expressly address the question whether the order is necessary for the protection of the public from serious harm (*R. v Czarnota* [2002] EWCA Crim 785; [2002] M.H.L.R. 144). In doing so, it must undertake an assessment of risk (*R. v Cooper* [2009] EWCA Crim 2646). The index offence itself need not be serious: see, for e.g., *R. v Kamara*, below.

"Serious harm" refers to possible serious harm to the public in the future rather than to proven serious harm to the public in the past and an offender who has no history of serious violence but who, on the medical evidence, has a potentiality for causing serious harm could be made the subject of an order under this section (*R. v Kamara* [2000] M.H.L.R. 9 CA). It is not necessary that the harm should be purely physical: a risk of serious psychological harm will suffice (*R. v Melbourne* [2000] M.H.L.R. 2 CA). A risk to one person of such harm can be sufficient (*R. v Macrow* [2004] EWCA Crim 1159 para.16), but not a risk of self-harm (*R. v Osker* [2010] EWCA Crim 955; [2010] M.H.L.R. 115). The word "serious" qualifies "harm" rather than "risk". Thus the court is required "not to assess the seriousness of the risk that the defendant will re-offend, but the risk that if he does so the public will suffer serious harm" (*R. v Birch* (1989) 11 Cr. App. R.(S.) 202). In *R. v Cox* [1999] M.H.L.R. 30 the Court of Appeal said that risk of serious harm to the public must be real, rather than fanciful or remote.

The imposition of a restriction order was confirmed in *R. v Golding* [2006] EWCA Crim 1965; [2006] M.H.L.R. 272, where the court found that the appellant, who had multiple convictions for burglary but had never acted violently, satisfied the "serious harm" criterion because his psychosis was not controlled and his predilection to drugs and alcohol could well lead him to behave violently if he was confronted by a householder. The court rejected counsel's submission that if "the evidence and material before the court in this case is sufficient to make a restriction order, it is difficult to consider any case where a defendant suffers from paranoid schizophrenia where he will not be susceptible to a section 41 order" on the ground that the decisions to be made as to such orders "are very much fact specific decisions" (paras 10, 11). *Golding* is consistent with the decisions of the Court of Appeal in *Kamara*, above, and the Divisional Court in *R. (on the application of Jones) v Isleworth Crown Court* [2005] EWHC 662 (Admin) where the court emphasised that in deciding whether an offender posed a future risk of serious harm the judge was not bound to determine that risk by reference to the nature of past violence. Moses J. said at para.19:

> "Of course the evidence as to what had happened in the past provides a guide to the future; but it does not determine the nature of the risk, particularly in the context of an escalation of violence by one who suffers from paranoid schizophrenia and hears commands to harm other people".

When making a judgment about "serious harm" the court can take into account the risk to the offender from failing to take appropriate treatment to restrain his symptoms: see *Narey v Her Majesty's Customs and Excise* [2005] EWHC 784 (Admin); [2005] M.H.L.R.194 at para.19 where the court said that the importation of kilos of cocaine inevitably leads to a risk of serious harm to those to whom it is sold for consumption. In *R. v Beaumont* (98/ 02694 Y2) July 28, 1998, CA, Moses J. said that "setting fire to premises, even if it is difficult for them to ignite successfully, is likely to cause, in our judgment serious harm to others who may be affected by [the] fire".

Subsection (2)

1–574   ONE OF THE REGISTERED MEDICAL PRACTITIONERS. Who need not necessarily be approved under s.12. In *R. v Blackwood* (1974) Cr. App. R. 170, the Court of Appeal stressed the desirability of the doctor who gives oral evidence being on the staff of the admitting hospital.

EVIDENCE. It is of the utmost importance that when medical practitioners are considering whether to recommend a restriction order, they should expressly address the question whether such an order is necessary for the protection of the public from serious harm (*R. v Chalk* [2002] EWCA Crim 2435; [2002] M.H.L.R. 430 para.34).

In *R. v Birch*, above, the Court of Appeal, at 212, gave the following answer to the question whether a Crown Court judge had jurisdiction to make a restriction order in circumstances where those doctors who expressed an opinion on the matter were unanimous that the patient was not dangerous:

"It is in our judgment quite clear that the answer is 'yes'. There is a contrast between the language of sections 37(2) and 41(1) and (2). Before a hospital order can be made, the Court must be satisfied of the stated conditions 'on the written or oral evidence of two practitioners'. But where a restriction order is in question, section 41(2) requires no more than that the Court shall hear the oral evidence of one of the medical practitioners. It need not follow the course which he recommends. Section 41(1) makes the assessment of the risk, in the light of the factors there identified, one for the court. In our judgment *R. v Blackwood* (1974) 59 Cr. App. R. 170 and *R. v Royse* (1981) 3 Cr. App. R.(S.) 58 are just as good law under the 1983 Act as they were under the earlier statute."

The finding in *Birch* was applied in *R. v Crookes* [1999] M.H.L.R. 45, where the Court of Appeal said that the judge was right to impose a restriction order in a case where the medical evidence was unanimous in recommending that such an order was not necessary. In this case, the judge felt that none of the doctors was able to explain to his satisfaction why a young man with no record of violence, and not seen as in any way to be dangerous, could suddenly react with an outburst of potentially lethal ferocity. In *R. v Ristic* [2002] EWCA Crim 165; [2002] M.H.L.R. 129 at para.10, Goldring J., in giving the judgment of the court, said that the fact that none of the doctors who had prepared reports or who had given evidence had suggested a restriction order "did not mean that the judge could not impose it, after consideration of the evidence and the requirements of the section". However, the power and discretion of the judge to impose a restriction order in these circumstances should only be exercised after careful consideration and with some caution (*R. v Roberts* [2003] EWCA Crim 858, para.12). If a judge does not accept the unanimous recommendations of psychiatrists that a restriction order is not necessary, better reasons should be given in justification than the mere citing of the levels violence exhibited by the offender in the past (*R. v Haile* [2009] EWCA Crim 1996; [2009] M.H.L.R. 300; also see *R. v Hurst* [2007] EWCA Crim 3436; [2008] M.H.L.R. 43). Where the doctors giving evidence to the court are not unanimous about the appropriateness of a hospital disposal, sentencing is a matter for the judge to resolve in the light of the evidence and all the circumstances of the case (*R. v Reid* [2005] EWCA Crim 392; [2006] M.H.L.R. 180).

Subsection (3)

This subsection specifies the restrictions that are placed upon patients who are subject to restriction orders. They are: (1) there is no periodic review of the authority to detain under s.20; (2) the patient cannot be discharged, transferred to another hospital (even if managed by the same hospital managers) or granted leave of absence without the consent of the Secretary of State; (3) the patient cannot be made subject to a community treatment order; and (4) the authority to detain lasts as long as the restriction order is in force and the patient cannot obtain his discharge under the provisions of ss.17(5) or 18(4). **1–575**

Paragraph (b)

NO APPLICATION SHALL BE MADE. This paragraph only refers to a patient in his capacity as a restricted patient detained, or liable to be detained, pursuant to the hospital order. It does not apply to the patient's detention under s.3, if such an application has been made in respect of him. A patient so detained therefore has a right to apply to a tribunal under **1–576**

s.66(1)(b) (*R. v North West London Mental Health NHS Trust Ex p. Stewart, The Times,*
August 15, 1996, per Harrison J., whose decision on the ability of Pts II and III of this
Act to coexist and operate independently of each other was affirmed by the Court of
Appeal at [1997] 4 All E.R. 871).

Paragraph (c)

1–577   On a day-to-day basis, the powers of the Secretary of State under this provision are managed by the Mental Health Casework Section (MHCS) at the Ministry of Justice: see the
General Note to this Part. With regard to "community leave", the *Code of Practice* states:

> "22.58 The Secretary of State for Justice will often consent to programmes of leave
> which give responsible clinicians discretion as to leave arrangements. The expectation
> however is that the leave will be designed and conducted in such a way as to preserve
> public safety and, where appropriate, respect the feelings and fears of victims and others
> who may have been affected by the offences.
>
> 22.59 Leave request forms are provided on the Ministry of Justice website which outlines
> the information required, however the attachment of leave plans may also be useful. In
> the event that consent for leave is given, responsible clinicians should be aware that the
> Ministry of Justice may request additional reports on the restricted patient as considered
> necessary.
>
> 22.60 Should there be any concerns or doubts about the leave being taken, it should be
> suspended and MHCS informed."

With regard to "hospital transfers", the *Code* states at para.22.63:

> "It is useful for the MHCS forms accessed via the website to be used when requesting
> that a restricted patient be transferred between hospitals. In urgent situations, it may be
> sufficient for the transferring and receiving clinicians to provide confirmation of their
> assessments and the availability of appropriate treatment in writing to MHCS.
> Situations where an urgent transfer may be required include those where there is a
> serious risk of self-harm or harm to others which cannot be safely management [sic]
> in the current hospital or unit. Where the clinical team have concerns, contact with
> the casework manager should be made in the first instance."

The principles that the Secretary of State should apply when exercising his functions under
this provision were set out by Lightman J. in *R. v Secretary of State for the Home
Department, Ex p. Harry* [1998] 3 All E.R. 360, a case where the Secretary of State had
refused to consent to the transfer of a restricted patient from Broadmoor Hospital to a
regional secure unit, as recommended by a tribunal. His Lordship said at 369:

> "In short, as it seems to me, the scheme of the 1983 Act places on the [Secretary of State]
> the responsibility in the case of a restricted patient to balance the patient's claim to lib-
> erty against the interests of everyone else to be safeguarded against the risks to which
> such liberty may give rise. For his performance of these duties the [Secretary of State]
> is politically accountable to Parliament. His obligation is fully to satisfy himself as to
> the propriety of any decision before he makes it because of the serious impact of such
> decision, and if the finding or recommendation of the tribunal leaves him in doubt, he
> is not only entitled but bound to look further afield for guidance: the finding and rec-
> ommendation of the tribunal may assist him to fulfil this obligation, but cannot dilute
> it or impede its fulfilment or obviate the need for the exercise by him of an informed
> judgment whether consent should be forthcoming."

LEAVE OF ABSENCE   *Harry* was applied by Silber J. in *R. (on the application of OS) v Secretary of State for the Home Department* [2006] EWHC 1903 (Admin); [2006] M.H.L.R. 275, where his Lordship said, at para.22, that it was common ground that the Secretary of State

"is entitled in making his assessment of risk to consider the risk that the patient will not return after being granted leave [of absence]. This is important because the [Secretary of State] will be able to take into account factors, which the [tribunal] would not or could not consider, such as the immigration status of the patient and whether this or any other factor might lead him or her not to return to their hospital after their leave has expired."

In *R. (on the application of P) v Secretary of State for Justice* [2009] EWHC 2464 (Admin); [2009] M.H.L.R. 236, para.62, Keith Lindblom QC, sitting as a Deputy Judge of the High Court, said that the Secretary of State is not bound by the opinion of professionals even if that opinion was unequivocal and unanimous, and is not required to seek a second clinical opinion to substantiate his own judgment on the question of risk. The Secretary of State "has to exercise a judgment of his own". In *R. (on the application of X) v Secretary of State for Justice* [2009] EWHC 2465 (Admin); [2009] M.H.L.R. 250, para.55, Mr Lindblom said that if the Secretary of State rejects a request for leave, he must give a rational explanation for doing so which properly bears on the protection of the public.

In *R. (on the application of RA) v Secretary of State for the Home Department* [2002] EWHC 1618; [2003] M.H.L.R. 54, Crane J. rejected a submission that conditions cannot be attached to the Secretary of State's consent to a grant of leave of absence under s.17. His Lordship said at para.41:

"It is true that neither section 17 nor section 41(3) provides in terms for such conditions to the consent. However, section 17 enables conditions to be imposed by the [RC] on the patient. I can see no reason why the Secretary of State cannot in law decline to give consent unless suitable conditions are imposed. He can obviously refuse consent to leave for a particular period. And since the Secretary of State has a power to recall under section 41(3)(c), there is every reason why he should be able to insist upon conditions that have the effect of providing the necessary information to him. The power of recall would then be no less effective than under section 42(2)".

His Lordship said that the operation of the provisions of ss.17 and 41(3)(c) should ensure that there is "no unreasonable delay to the implementation of a tribunal's decision" (para.58) and that the Secretary of State should "follow recommendations made by a tribunal in the absence of sound reasons or new circumstances" (para.59). His Lordship left open the question whether conditions, such as the provision of reports, can be imposed on the RC.

In *R. (on the application of Hurlock) v Dr Page and the Secretary of State for the Home Department)* [2001] EWHC Admin 380 at para.22, Ouseley J. said that s.17 and this provision cannot arguably be read as imposing an obligation to grant a patient unescorted leave of absence as an alternative to a conditional discharge granted by a tribunal where those conditions are not yet fulfilled.

The MHCS of the Ministry of Justice has published "Guidance—Section 17 leave" (March 2015). With regard to "ground leave", the guidance states:

"10. The responsible clinician has complete discretion to allow the restricted patient access to the grounds of the hospital or unit in which the detention authority requires his detention. The detention authority means here the hospital order, hospital direction, transfer direction, warrant of recall or letter agreeing to trial leave or transfer. That authority may name a complete hospital, a named unit within a hospital, or a specific level of security within a hospital. It is for the hospital or unit to define its own geographical boundaries. If the responsible clinician wants to allow the patient beyond the boundaries of the hospital or unit named on the detention authority, then he needs the Secretary of State's agreement. So, for example, if the responsible clinician has a patient whose order states a particular Unit as the place in which the patient is detained and the responsible clinician wants to allow access to the grounds of the Hospital, an application for section 17 leave into the community must be submitted to the Secretary of State.

11. If the responsible clinician wishes to allow the patient to access wider hospital grounds, beyond the hospital or unit named on the detention authority, MHCS may consider using section 19 to transfer him to a wider range of units. However there is often little difference in public safety terms between access to a whole hospital and to the community at large, so such requests should always be accompanied by a robust risk assessment and be carefully scrutinized.

12. Where the detention authority names an entire hospital, the responsible clinician's discretion extends to all the facilities the hospital comprises. This may include non secure step-down facilities outside the hospital perimeter."

Paragraph 27.41 of the *Code of Practice* states:

"For routine medical appointments or treatment, the Secretary of State's permission will be required. It is accepted that there will be times of acute medical emergency such as heart attack, stroke or penetrative wounds or burns where the patient requires emergency treatment. There may also be acute situations which, while not life threatening still require urgent treatment, eg fractures. In these situations, the responsible clinician may use their discretion, having due regard to the emergency or urgency being presented and the management of any risks, to have the patient taken to hospital. The Secretary of State should be informed as soon as possible that the patient has been taken to hospital, what risk management arrangements are in place, be kept informed of developments and notified when the patient has been returned to the secure hospital."

The MCHS guidance, which at Annex A contains a leave request form, can be accessed at: *www.justice.gov.uk/offenders/types-of-offender/mentally-disordered-offenders*. Further provisions relating to ground access, leave of absence and the escorting of patients from Ashworth, Broadmoor and Rampton Hospitals can be found in the High Security Psychiatric Services (Arrangements for Safety and Security) Directions 2013 which are reproduced at Appendix C.

TRANSFER THE PATIENT. It is submitted that the Secretary of State does not have the power under s.47 of the Crime (Sentences) Act 1997 to require that the patient be treated in a named hospital unit on his transfer even if one was specified by the court in the original order.

Subsection (4)

1–578   The effect of this provision is that a hospital order coupled with a restriction order continues to have effect on the making of a subsequent hospital order and that subsequent hospital orders should be disregarded for the purposes of renewal when the restriction order ceases to have effect.

If a second restriction order is made, both orders will be in force. As the existence of parallel restriction orders could cause confusion, the Secretary of State should consider exercising his power under s.42(2) to order the absolute discharge of one of the them.

Subsection (5)

1–579   This subsection provides that when a restriction order ceases to have effect, the patient is to be treated as if he had been admitted to hospital under a hospital order without restrictions made on the date on which the restriction order ceased to have effect. If the patient has been conditionally discharged from hospital before the restrictions end, he will cease to be liable to be detained (s.42(5)).

Subsection (6)

This subsection, which was enacted in response to recommendation 114 of the Butler **1–580** Committee, is aimed at preventing restricted patients being detained for unjustifiably long periods. As a patient who has been conditionally discharged from a restriction order remains subject to that order (see s.42(2)), it is submitted that this provision applies to such patients. If the Secretary of State, having considered the RC's report and having weighed all the other evidence about the patients medical condition that is available to him is satisfied that the patient is no longer suffering from mental disorder, he should discharge him: see the note to section 42(2).

Powers of Secretary of State in respect of patients subject to restriction orders

42.—(1) If the Secretary of State is satisfied that in the case of any patient a **1–581** restriction order is no longer required for the protection of the public from serious harm, he may direct that the patient shall cease to be subject to the special restrictions set out in section 41(3) above; and where the Secretary of State so directs, the restriction order shall cease to have effect, and section 41(5) above shall apply accordingly.

(2) At any time while a restriction order is in force in respect of a patient, the Secretary of State may, if he thinks fit, by warrant discharge the patient from hospital, either absolutely or subject to conditions; and where a person is absolutely discharged under this subsection, he shall thereupon cease to be liable to be detained by virtue of the relevant hospital order, and the restriction order shall cease to have effect accordingly.

(3) The Secretary of State may at any time during the continuance in force of a restriction order in respect of a patient who has been conditionally discharged under subsection (2) above by warrant recall the patient to such hospital as may be specified in the warrant.

(4) Where a patient is recalled as mentioned in subsection (3) above—

(a) if the hospital specified in the warrant is not the hospital from which the patient was conditionally discharged, the hospital order and the restriction order shall have effect as if the hospital specified in the warrant were substituted for the hospital specified in the hospital order;

(b) in any case, the patient shall be treated for the purposes of section 18 above as if he had absented himself without leave from the hospital specified in the warrant [. . .].

(5) If a restriction order in respect of a patient ceases to have effect after the patient has been conditionally discharged under this section, the patient shall, unless previously recalled under subsection (3) above, be deemed to be absolutely discharged on the date when the order ceases to have effect, and shall cease to be liable to be detained by virtue of the relevant hospital order accordingly.

(6) The Secretary of State may, if satisfied that the attendance at any place in Great Britain of a patient who is subject to a restriction order is desirable in the interests of justice or for the purposes of any public inquiry, direct him to be taken to that place; and where a patient is directed under this subsection to be taken to any place he shall, unless the Secretary of State otherwise directs, be kept in custody while being so taken, while at that place and while being taken back to the hospital in which he is liable to be detained.

AMENDMENT
The words omitted in subs.(4)(b) were repealed by the Mental Health Act 2007 s.55, Sch.11 Pt 8.

DEFINITIONS
1–582   patient: s.145.
restriction order: ss.41, 55(4), 145(1).
hospital: ss.55(5), 145(1).
hospital order: ss.37, 55(4), 145(1).
absent without leave: ss.18(6), 145(1).

GENERAL NOTE
1–583   This section empowers the Secretary of State to take the following action in respect of patients who have been placed on restriction orders: (1) to direct that the order shall cease to have effect; (2) to discharge the patient from hospital absolutely; and (3) to discharge the patient from hospital subject to conditions.

A restriction order cannot cease to have effect by inference or implication: see *R. v Secretary of State for the Home Department Ex p. Didlick* (1993) 16 B.M.L.R. 71 DC where Rougier J. said at 75:

"In my opinion subsection (1) and (2) [of section 42] indicate clearly that before a restriction order can be brought to an end, the Secretary of State must either make a declaration to that effect or must discharge the patient absolutely. Each of these is a positive act. There is no room, in my opinion, for the situation whereby a restriction order ceases to have effect by inference or implication. It follows, therefore, that, by merely allowing the conditions under which the applicant was discharged to lapse, the Secretary of State did not thereby bring to an end the operation of the restriction order."

Any reference in this section to a hospital order, a guardianship order or a restriction order shall be construed as including a reference to any other order or direction under this Part having the same effect as such orders (s.55(4)).

Human Rights Act 1998
1–584   A patient who is assessed as posing no risk to the public should not be denied a conditional discharge solely on the ground that the inhabitants of a particular locality feared that he might be dangerous if released (*Stojanovski v The Former Yugoslav Republic of Macedonia* [2010] M.H.L.R. 292, para.35).

If a condition of a patient's discharge granted under subs.(2) interferes with the patient's right to respect for his private and family life, it must be justified under art.8(2) of the European Convention on Human Rights (ECHR). In *R. (on the application of Craven) v Secretary of State for the Home Department* [2001] EWHC Admin 850, Stanley Burnton J. rejected a prisoner's claim that a condition of his parole not to enter an area of Newcastle where the family of his victim lived constituted a disproportionate and therefore unlawful interference with his art.8 rights. His Lordship held that distress to the victim's family was a consideration that could lawfully be taken into account by the Parole Board and by the Secretary of State.

The exercise by the Secretary of State of his power of recall under subs.(3) will, except in emergency cases, constitute a violation of art.5(1) of the ECHR in the absence of an up to date report on the patient's medical condition (see the notes on subs.(3) and art.5).

One of the consequences of the decision of the Court of Appeal in *R. v North West London Mental Health NHS Trust Ex p. Stewart*, noted under subs.(3), is that a conditionally discharged patient who is brought back to hospital under either s.2 or s.3, can be discharged from that section by a tribunal but be liable to be re-detained by the Secretary of State using his recall power under subs.(3). It is questionable whether it could be successfully claimed that the tribunal in such a case has the power to order the discharge of the patient as required by art.5(4) of the ECHR, if the order can be immediately overridden by the Secretary of State.

Applications to the First-tier Tribunal (Mental Health) or the Mental Health Review Tribunal for Wales

A conditionally discharged patient has a right to apply to a tribunal for an absolute dis- **1–585** charge between 12 months and two years after the conditional discharge and during each subsequent two-year period (s.75(2)).

The case of a conditionally discharged patient who has been recalled to hospital must be referred to a tribunal by the Secretary of State within a month of his return to hospital (s.75(1)(a)). The patient may apply to the tribunal between six and 12 months after the recall and during each subsequent 12-month period (ss.70, 75(1)(b)). There is no duty placed on the Secretary of State to periodically refer the case of a conditionally discharged patient to the tribunal.

Subsection (1)

This subsection enables the Secretary of State to lift the restrictions from a patient who is **1–586** subject to a restriction order if he considers that they are no longer necessary to protect the public from serious harm. If the restrictions are lifted, the patient will continue to be detained as if he had been admitted to hospital under a hospital order made without restrictions (s.41(5)). The Secretary of State, who in practice acts through the Mental Health Casework Section (MHCS) of the Ministry of Justice rarely exercises this power.

PROTECTION OF THE PUBLIC. In *R. v Parole Board Ex p. Bradley* [1990] 3 All E.R. 828 at 836, DC, Stuart-Smith L.J., on examining this provision said that "the precise level of risk is not (surely cannot be) spelt out".

Subsection (2)

This subsection enables the Secretary of State to order the absolute or conditional dis- **1–587** charge of a restricted patient. The tribunal has a similar power under s.73. Guidance for the clinical and social supervisors of conditionally discharged patients can be accessed from the website of the Ministry of Justice at: *www.justice.gov.uk/offenders/types-of-offender/mentally-disordered-offenders*.

If the Secretary of State, after having weighed all the evidence about a patient's mental condition, is satisfied that the patient is no longer suffering from mental disorder, he should discharge the patient: see the obiter observations of Lawton L.J. in *Kynaston v Secretary of State for Home Affairs* (1981) 73 Cr. App. R. 281 CA. This course of action is required by the ECHR: see art.5(1) and the decision of the European Court of Human Rights in *Winterwerp v The Netherlands* (1979) 2 E.H.R.R. 387. The patient's discharge need not be absolute (*R. v Merseyside Mental Health Review Tribunal Ex p. K* [1990] 1 All E.R. 694 CA and *Johnson v United Kingdom* (1997) 27 E.H.R.R. 296).

The Secretary of State is not bound by any statutory criteria when exercising his judgment under this provision. This contrasts with the power of the tribunal under s.73. Regular reports on the patient, prepared by his RC, will be submitted to the Secretary of State under s.41(6).

ABSOLUTELY. An absolute discharge has the effect of extinguishing both the hospital order and the restriction order. In *R. (on the application of L) v West London Mental Health NHS Trust* [2012] EWHC 3200 (Admin); [2013] M.H.L.R. 297 Stadlen J. said at para.266:

"Discharge directly from a high security hospital like Broadmoor is extremely rare. A staged discharge involving normally at least a period in a medium security hospital is much more usual. There are reasons unconnected with the severity or nature of a patient's mental disorder which make it likely that a patient who is transferred to a high security hospital will experience a longer passage of time before he is ultimately discharged than would be the case if he were not so transferred."

The MHCS stated in its Newsletter of April 29, 2010:

"MHCS is responsible, on behalf of the Secretary of State, for ensuring that restricted patients are managed in such a way as to minimise the risk to the public. Our policy is that we will not grant absolute discharge (AD) unless it is clear that the restrictions are no longer required to ensure the patient's safe management. This means that we will not grant AD where the patient still has a mental disorder, and has the potential to be a risk to others if not well supervised in future, and where future supervision is not guaranteed. In forming this view we are conscious that the Mental Health Review Tribunal is available to safeguard patient's rights."

SUBJECT TO CONDITIONS.   The *Code of Practice* states:

"22.79 Conditionally discharged restricted patients will in most cases be subject to community supervision and be monitored by a clinical supervisor and a social supervisor, both of whom are required to submit reports, generally quarterly, to the Ministry of Justice detailing the patient's progress, current presentation and any concerns. These reports should be comprehensive including defining clearly any risks being presented by the patient either to themselves or others. They should also record unusual occurrences such as interactions with the police and where necessary these events should be investigated further by the appropriate supervisor and information shared with other relevant parties. Although there is a requirement for regular reports, if at any time clinical teams become concerned over a patient's behaviour or presentation, they should investigate those concerns and contact the Ministry of Justice straightaway. Similarly these reports will be closely scrutinised by the Ministry of Justice and where necessary, concerns will be raised with the relevant parties involved. See paragraphs 22.87 – 22.92 below in respect of restricted part 3 patients convicted of serious offences.

22.80 The Ministry of Justice does not stipulate the professionals who can undertake the role of social supervisor. Social supervisors should have received adequate professional development, be resourced to be able to produce prompt, accurate reports and raise any concerns with regard to the patient's behaviour in the community. Social supervisors will be allocated by local authorities, who will determine that their agreed social supervisors have the correct knowledge, expertise and skills to undertake this role, in line with the efficiency and equity principle."

A patient who has been conditionally discharged under this provision is not subject to the consent to treatment provisions contained in Pt IV (s.56(3)(c)). Paragraph 31 of the guidance for clinical supervisors states:

"The consent to treatment provisions in Part IV of the Mental Health Act 1983 do not apply to conditionally discharged patients. The clinical supervisor has no specific legal authority to require a conditionally discharged patient to take medication without his consent. However, where medication is prescribed to relieve mental disorder which, if untreated, would be likely to lead to the patient becoming a danger to himself or others, the patient's co-operation with such medication is likely to be fundamental to his remaining in the community. If, therefore, the patient refuses medication against the clinical supervisor's advice, he may need to be recalled to hospital as a detained patient. It is crucial that any withdrawal of co-operation with medication should be reported at once to the Mental Health [Casework Section]. Sometimes the Secretary of State will make cooperation with medication at the direction of the clinical supervisor a condition specified on the warrant of discharge. Generally this is unnecessary since it adds nothing to the powers of the supervisor or the Secretary of State, but there can be circumstances in which it is helpful in the management of a particular patient."

Force cannot be used to require a patient to comply with a condition (*R (on the application of SH v Mental Health Review Tribunal* [2007] EWHC 884 (Admin); [2007] M.H.L.R. 234).

Whether the Secretary of State has the power to impose conditions that have the effect of deriving the patient of his liberty is considered in the note on "conditions" in s.73(4)(b).

The Secretary of State has the power to vary any condition imposed by the tribunal or by him and can impose a new condition subsequent to the patient's discharge (s.73(4)(b) (5)). A condition that the patient refrains from entering a particular locality (e.g. the area where the family of the patient's victim lives) could be attached to the discharge if this was felt to be a proportionate response to the circumstances of the case: see the note on "Human Rights Act 1998", above.

Paragraph 7 of the guidance for clinical supervisors states:

"The Secretary of State will usually make a restricted patient's discharge from hospital subject to certain conditions. The conditions usually imposed by the Secretary of State are those of residence at a stated address, supervision by a social worker and clinical supervision. The tribunal is also likely to make discharge directions conditional, and to impose similar conditions. If it does not, the Ministry of Justice, using powers under section 73(4) of the 1983 Act, will usually add conditions of social and clinical supervision. Supervisors must understand that conditions are designed to operate for the protection of the discharged patient and others and to enable the patient's safe management in the community. They are not measures for social control, nor even for crime prevention. Breach of conditions does not, in itself, justify recall to hospital, but it should act as a trigger for considering what action is necessary in response."

The *Butler Committee* agreed, at para.8.7, with the recommendation of the *Aarvold Committee* (Cmnd. 5191, para.48) that "supervision should be undertaken by the person who can bring most to the case in the way of knowledge, expertise and resources in the particular circumstances of the case. The arrangements may need to take particular account of the needs of public safety".

Subsection (3)

THE SECRETARY OF STATE MAY RECALL THE PATIENT.   In *R. (on the application of MM) v* **1–588** *The Secretary of State for the Home Department* [2007] EWCA Civ 687; [2007] M.H.L.R. 304, the Court of Appeal dismissed an appeal against the decision of Mitting J. to uphold the decision of the Secretary of State to recall the patient under this provision. Toulson L.J said at para.50:

"For the Secretary of State to recall a patient who has been conditionally discharged by [a tribunal], he has to believe on reasonable grounds that something has happened *since the decision of the tribunal*, or information has emerged *which was not available to the tribunal*, of sufficient significance to justify recalling the patient. As I have said, it is not in dispute that he must have up-to-date medical evidence about the patient's mental health."

[The italicised words were added to this formulation by Bean J. in *IT v Secretary of State for Justice* [2008] EWHC 1707 (Admin); [2008] M.H.L.R. 290 para.13, in order to make it consistent with the decision of the House of Lords in *R. (on the application of von Brandenburg) v East London and the City Mental Health NHS Trust* [2003] UKHL 58.]

The test established in *MM* was considered by Burnett J. in *R. (on the application of Munday) v Secretary of State for the Home Department* [2009] EWHC 3638 (Admin);

[2009] M.H.L.R. 401. His Lordship said, at para.28, that the following formulation of the test, which was made by counsel for the Secretary of State at para.44 of the judgment, is correct:

". . . the [Secretary of State] should ask himself whether there had been such a material change of circumstances since the Tribunal's previous decision that he could reasonably form the view that the detention criteria were now satisfied."

Although a breach of a condition imposed on the patient may be "powerful evidence of, for example, relapse and the need for a recall" (*Secretary of State for Justice v KC* [2015] UKUT 376 (AAC), para.53. per Charles J.), in *MM*, the court held that a beach of a condition imposed on the patient was not a free-standing ground for the patient's recall. The question is whether the breach has the effect of enabling the Secretary of State to form a proper judgment (i.e. one that was not unreasonable in the public law sense) on the medical evidence that the statutory criteria for detention were established. The court further held that the language of the first statutory criterion ("of a nature or degree which makes it appropriate for him to be detained") would be unduly circumscribed if there had to be either psychotic symptoms or the certainty of psychotic symptoms in the imminent future before detention for treatment could be considered appropriate. It is therefore the case that a recall does not require any evidence of deterioration in the patient's mental state. At first instance, Mitting J. said that in the generality of cases, it is impracticable for the Secretary of State, prior to the issue of the recall warrant, to convene an assessment at which the patient is entitled to make representations of fact ([2006] EWHC 3056 (Admin); [2006] M.H.L.R. 358 para.49). In confirming the decision of the Secretary of State to recall a patient due to concerns about deterioration of his mental health associated with illicit drug use, his Lordship said at para.47:

"The Secretary of State is entitled to have at the forefront of his mind not just the health and safety of the patient, but also the safety of members of the public, including the patient's own family. The Secretary of State is not obliged to put the interests of people at significant risk by staying his hand in circumstances where he has medical evidence that the taking of illicit drugs would be likely to cause imminently a severe deterioration in his mental condition".

In *Munday*, above, at para.30, Burnett J. said that the second statutory criterion (the "necessity" test) is concerned with risk and that although "psychiatrists or other medical health professionals or social supervisors with their knowledge of a person might be in a position to express a view about risk, it is by its nature an exercise of evaluation which does not necessarily call for expert medical input". In this case, his Lordship held that given the patient's history of arson, a mere allegation and arrest for arson was sufficient justification for recall.

In *Kay v United Kingdom* (1998) 40 B.M.L.R. 20, the European Commission of Human Rights held that, in the absence of an emergency, there had been a breach of art.5(1) of the ECHR when a patient had been recalled under this provision without up to date medical evidence to demonstrate that he was suffering from a true mental disorder of a kind or degree warranting compulsory confinement. Although in *MM* Mitting J. accepted that the Secretary of State must have before him medical evidence which justifies the decision to recall, that medical evidence "need not be a report freshly prepared upon the precise condition recently obtaining". Where, as in *MM's* case:

"there is abundant medical evidence to the effect that [he] suffers from paranoid schizophrenia and that his condition is likely to deteriorate imminently and significantly if he takes illicit drugs, then that evidence suffices to justify recall unless there is good reason for believing that it is no longer currently valid" (para.41).

In *R. (on the application of B) v Mental Health Review Tribunal* [2002] EWHC 1553 (Admin); [2003] M.H.L.R. 19 para.31, Scott Baker J. said obiter that the medical evidence must show that the criteria for detention are met.

The Reference Guide states at para.27.45:

"In urgent cases, a direction recalling a patient may be given verbally outside office hours by a duty officer of the Ministry of Justice's Mental Health Casework Section on behalf of the Secretary of State. In practice, the warrant would then normally be provided on the next working day".

The *Code of Practice* states:

"22.82 A patient will be recalled where it is necessary to protect the public from the actual or potential risk posed by that patient and that the risk is linked to the patient's mental disorder. It is not possible to specify all the circumstances when recall may be appropriate and public safety will always be the most important factor. Key points include:

- the decision on whether to recall will largely depend on the degree of danger posed by the patient, the gravity of the potential or actual risk and how imminent the risk is

- recall does not necessarily require any evidence of deterioration in the patient's mental state, but evidence is required that a 'change' has occurred since the discharge decision. This is so that the Secretary of State for Justice can be satisfied that recall is a proportionate and lawful action. Other than in an emergency, medical evidence will be required that the patient is currently mentally disordered

- recall will not be used to deal with anti-social or offending behaviour that is unconnected with the patient's mental disorder

- recall decisions always give precedence to public safety considerations. This may mean that the Secretary of State for Justice will decide to recall on public safety grounds even if the supervisors (see paragraphs 22.79 – 22.80) are of the view that recall would be counter-therapeutic for the patient

- recall will be considered to protect others from harm because of a combination of the patient's mental disorder and behaviour, including potential behaviour where there is evidence that indicates the imminent likelihood of risk behaviours

- in an emergency the Secretary of State for Justice may recall for assessment in the absence of fresh evidence as regards mental disorder

- the support for recall from the patient's social supervisor is important but not determinative and the Secretary of State for Justice can, satisfied that recall is necessary, make the decision to recall in the absence of any recommendation

- where however recall is recommended by at least one supervisor, then the expectation is that the patient should be recalled unless there are compelling reasons not to recall, and

- admission under sections 2 or 3 – if a restricted patient requires compulsory detention in hospital under the Act then recall will almost invariably be appropriate.

The only circumstances where recall may not be indicated would be where discharge was imminent (within days rather than weeks), or where the admission is solely due to self-harm or suicide issues and the admission is likely to last less than a month.

22.83 Should recall be indicated, the clinical team should initially discuss their concerns with MHCS and identify a suitable bed at an appropriate security level for the patient to be admitted to. Once the arrangements are confirmed, MHCS will issue a Secretary of State for Justice warrant for the recall of a patient to a named hospital or unit."

The policy of the MHCS on recalls is set out at para.5 of "The recall of conditionally discharged restricted patients" (2009) which can be accessed at: *www.justice.gov.uk/ offenders/types-of-offender/mentally-disordered-offenders*.

Once a decision to recall has been made, it is the responsibility of the supervisor to identify an appropriate bed and to make the practicable arrangements for admission to hospital. The consent to treatment provisions contained in Pt IV apply to the patient from the date of the recall (s.56(3)(c)).

If the patient will not return to hospital willingly on being told of the recall, then the police should be asked to assist. In non-urgent cases, the police should be provided with a copy of the recall warrant. Once recalled, and until they are readmitted to hospital, patients are treated as if they were absent without leave and can therefore be taken into custody and taken to the hospital specified in the warrant. There is no power of entry attached to a recall warrant. If it is not possible to gain access to a patient who has been recalled, an application may be made to a magistrate under s.135(2).

A three-way procedure for informing restricted patients of the reasons for their recall is set out in the Annex to Department of Health Circular No. HSG(93)20 (also see Circular LAC(93)9 addressed to local authorities in similar terms):

"*Stage 1*: The person returning the patient to hospital should inform him/her in simple terms that he/she is being recalled to hospital by the [Secretary of State] under section 42(3) of the Mental Health Act 1983 and that, to the extent that this is possible, a further explanation will be given later. The reason(s) for recalling the patient should be explained to the nearest relative, if one is available, within 72 hours.

Stage 2: An explanation should be given to the patient of the reason(s) for his/her recall as soon as possible after re-admission to hospital and in any event within 72 hours. This should be done by the [RC] or deputy, an [AMHP], or an appropriate administrator representing the hospital managers. The person giving the explanation should ensure, so far as the patient's mental condition allows, that the patient understands the reason(s).

Stage 3: A written explanation of the reason(s) for recall should be provided for the patient within 72 hours of being re-admitted to hospital. Written information on the reason(s) should also be given to the patient's nearest relative (subject to the patient's consent)."

Para.1.2 of the Annex states:

"The [RC] should inform the patient's supervising officer (social worker or probation officer) in the community, the key worker attached to the patient under the Care Programme Approach and a member of the patient's family who accepts responsibility (or a legal representative) of the reason(s) for recall. In the interests of co-ordination and longer-term care programme planning (HC(90)23), it may also be necessary to inform (or otherwise involve) other agencies who are concerned with patients care."

The references to the patient's nearest relative in stages 1 and 3 of the procedure is an error as a restricted patient does not have a nearest relative for the purposes of the Act: see s.26.

In *R. (on the application of Lee-Hirons) v Secretary of State for Justice* [2014] EWCA Civ 553; [2015] M.H.L.R. 1, the Court of Appeal held that art.5 of the ECHR required that the patient must be "promptly and adequately informed of the facts and legal authority relied on to deprive him of his liberty", but did not require that information to be given to the patient immediately when he is detained. That duty was intended to be satisfied by providing an explanation for the recall within 72 hours as stipulated in HSG (93) 20. Paragraph 4.19 of the *Code of Practice* states:

"Where a conditionally discharged patient is to be recalled to hospital, a brief verbal explanation of the Secretary of State's reasons for recall must be provided to the patient at the time of recall unless there are exceptional reasons why this is not possible, eg the patient is violent or too distressed. The Secretary of State's warrant will detail the reasons. The patient should also receive a full explanation of the reasons for his or her recall within 72 hours after admission, and both written and oral explanations should be provided."

As "recall" must be understood as authorising not only the physical recall of the patient, **1–589** but also the reinstatement of a regime of control in respect of the patient, the Secretary of State may issue a warrant for the recall of a patient to a hospital in which the patient is already detained under ss.2 or 3 (*Dlodlo v Mental Health Review Tribunal for the South Thames Region* (1996) 36 B.M.L.R. 145 CA). In *Dlodlo* a restriction order patient was transferred to a local hospital. The patient was subsequently given a conditional discharge by a tribunal, but, on becoming ill, he was re-admitted to the local hospital under s.3. The re-admission was followed by the issue of a warrant for the patients recall. The legality of using s.3 to detain a restriction order patient who had been conditionally discharged was confirmed by the Court of Appeal in *R. v North West London Mental Health NHS Trust Ex p. Stewart* [1997] 4 All E.R. 871.

Paragraph 56 of the guidance for clinical supervisors states:

"If the clinical supervisor has reason to fear for the safety of the patient or of others, he may decide to take immediate local action to admit the patient to hospital for a short period either with the patient's consent or using civil powers such as those under sections 2, 3 or 4 of the Mental Health Act 1983. Whether or not such action is taken, and even if the social supervisor does not share the clinical supervisor's concern, the clinical supervisor should report to the Ministry of Justice at once so that consideration can be given to the patient's recall to hospital."

The policy of the MHCS is to consider recall where there is any admission to a psychiatric hospital. If an informal admission is being considered, the professional dealing with the patient should contact MHCS to discuss the case (Mental Health Casework Section Newsletter, January 2011). The July 2011 issue of the MHCS Newsletter states:

"Where admission is voluntary and the patient remains co-operative with treatment in hospital, the Ministry of Justice will not normally recall if medical advice is that only a brief period of in-patient treatment is necessary for observation or stabilisation. However, it is generally inappropriate for a conditionally discharged patient to remain in hospital for more than a few weeks time voluntarily. If the use of civil powers is necessary to detain a patient or enable compulsory treatment to be given, immediate recall will almost invariably be appropriate to regularise the restricted patient's status under the Act. If a patient remains on voluntary admission, MHCS will require weekly updates."

The contact numbers of the MHCS at the Ministry of Justice are 020 3334 3335 and 020 7035 4848, option 5 (outside office hours).

HOSPITAL. Or registered establishment (s.34(2)). The recall can be to any hospital in England or Wales. The legality of recalling a patient to a hospital other than the hospital named in the restriction order was confirmed in the *Dlodlo* case, above.

In "The recall of conditionally discharged restricted patients", above, para.4, the Ministry of Justice states:

"There is no statutory requirement for the Justice Secretary to obtain the agreement of the hospital doctors to re-admit a recalled patient. The Justice Secretary is entitled to take a different view to that of the supervising psychiatrist, provided there are sufficient grounds/evidence to justify this and satisfy the Secretary of State that the criteria for detention under the Mental Health Act are met."

Subsection (4)

1–590   PARAGRAPH (B).   This paragraph provides that a recalled patient can be taken into custody and conveyed to the specified hospital by any AMHP, officer on the staff of the hospital or any other person authorised by the hospital managers.

Subsection (5)

1–591   This subsection provides that if a restriction order ceases to have effect while the patient is on conditional discharge from hospital he will cease to be liable to be detained.

Subsection (6)

1–592   GREAT BRITAIN.   England, Wales and Scotland (Union with Scotland Act 1706, preamble, art.1).

TAKEN TO THAT PLACE.   See s.137 for general provisions relating to custody, conveyance and detention.

Power of magistrates' courts to commit for restriction order

1–593   **43.**—(1) If in the case of a person of or over the age of 14 years who is convicted by a magistrates' court of an offence punishable on summary conviction with imprisonment—

(a) the conditions which under section 37(1) above are required to be satisfied for the making of a hospital order are satisfied in respect of the offender; but

(b) it appears to the court, having regard to the nature of the offence, the antecedents of the offender and the risk of his committing further offences if set at large, that if a hospital order is made a restriction order should also be made,

the court may, instead of making a hospital order or dealing with him in any other manner, commit him in custody to the Crown Court to be dealt with in respect of the offence.

(2) Where an offender is committed to the Crown Court under this section, the Crown Court shall inquire into the circumstances of the case and may—

(a) if that court would have power so to do under the foregoing provisions of this Part of this Act upon the conviction of the offender before that court of such an offence as is described in section 37(1) above, make a hospital order in his case, with or without a restriction order;

(b) if the court does not make such an order, deal with the offender in any other manner in which the magistrates' court might have dealt with him.

(3) The Crown Court shall have the same power to make orders under sections 35, 36 and 38 above in the case of a person committed to the court under this section as the Crown Court has under those sections in the case of an accused person within the meaning of section 35 or 36 above or of a person convicted before that court as mentioned in section 38 above.

[(4) The powers of a magistrates' court under section 3 or 3B of the Powers of Criminal Courts (Sentencing) Act 2000 (which enable such a court to commit an offender to the Crown Court where the court is of the opinion, or it appears to the court, as mentioned in the section in question) shall also be exercisable by a magistrates' court where it is of that opinion (or it so appears to it) unless a hospital order is made in the offender's case with a restriction order.]

(5) The power of the Crown Court to make a hospital order, with or without a restriction order, in the case of a person convicted before that court of an offence may, in the same circumstances and subject to the same conditions, be exercised by such a court in the case of a person committed to the court under section 5 of the Vagrancy Act 1824 (which provides for the committal to the Crown Court of persons who are incorrigible rogues within the meaning of that section).

AMENDMENT
Subsection 4 was substituted by s.41, Sch.3 para.55(2) to the Criminal Justice Act 2003.

DEFINITIONS
    hospital order: ss.37, 145(1).   **1–594**
    restriction order: ss.41, 145(1).

GENERAL NOTE
    A magistrates' court has no power to make a restriction order. If the court is satisfied that **1–595** the conditions exist in which it could make a hospital order, but also feels that a restriction order should be made in addition, it may commit an offender (if over 14 years of age) to the Crown Court under this section. The court does not need to be satisfied as to the "serious harm" test set out in s.41(1). The magistrates may direct that the offender be detained in a hospital, pending the hearing of the case by the Crown Court (s.44). If the Crown Court decides not to make a hospital order, it can deal with the offender in any way in which the magistrates' court could have dealt with him (subs.(2)) or it can remand him under s.35 or 36 or it can make an interim hospital order in respect of him (subs.(3)).

Appeals
    In *Kiernan v Harrow Crown Court* [2003] EWCA Crim 1052; [2005] M.H.L.R. 1, the **1–596** Court of Appeal, having considered ss.9 and 10 of the Criminal Appeal Act 1968, concluded that it had no jurisdiction to hear an appeal from a hospital order imposed by the Crown Court subsequent to a committal having been made under this section. In these circumstances, the court felt it appropriate to reconstitute itself as a Divisional Court of the Administrative Court and to consider the issue by way of a deemed application for judicial review of the decision of the Crown Court. Having quashed the decision of the Crown Court and having no power in judicial review proceedings to impose any separate penalty, the court remitted the case to a Crown Court judge.

Subsection (1)
    AGE. See s.55(7). A person attains the age of 14 at the commencement of his fourteenth **1–597** birthday (Family Law Reform Act 1969 s.9(1)).

    CONVICTED. The magistrates must have convicted the offender. In *R. v Horseferry Road Magistrates' Court Ex p. K* [1996] 3 All E.R. 719 at 735 DC, Forbes J. said:

    "[The Act] makes *no* provision for committal to the Crown Court by the magistrates for imposition of a restriction order under s.41 upon a person who has been acquitted of an offence by reason of insanity. The magistrates only have such a power to commit to the Crown Court for that purpose in the case of a person *convicted* of an imprisonable offence, whether indictable or summary only".

His Lordship said that this state of affairs represented an "obvious legislative lacuna".

    MAGISTRATES' COURT. Or youth court for those under the age of 18.

OFFENCE PUNISHABLE ON SUMMARY CONVICTION WITH IMPRISONMENT. For young offenders, see s.55(2).

COMMIT HIM IN CUSTODY. Or order him to be admitted to a hospital if the conditions of s.44 are satisfied. The Secretary of State has power to transfer a mentally disordered offender from custody to hospital under s.48(2)(b).

Subsection (2)

1–598   COMMITTED TO THE CROWN COURT UNDER THIS SECTION. Or under s.3 of the Powers of Criminal Courts (Sentencing) Act 2000 (subs.(4)).

Subsection (4)

1–599   For savings, see SI 2012/1320 art.5, SI 2012/2574 arts 3 and 4, and SI 2013/1103 arts 3 and 4.

Committal to hospital under s.43

1–600   **44.**—(1) Where an offender is committed under section 43(1) above and the magistrates' court by which he is committed is satisfied on written or oral evidence that arrangements have been made for the admission of the offender to a hospital in the event of an order being made under this section, the court may, instead of committing him in custody, by order direct him to be admitted to that hospital, specifying it, and to be detained there until the case is disposed of by the Crown Court, and may give such directions as it thinks fit for his production from the hospital to attend the Crown Court by which his case is to be dealt with.

(2) The evidence required by subsection (1) above shall be given by the [approved clinician who would have overall responsibility for the offender's case] or by some other person representing the managers of the hospital in question.

(3) The power to give directions under section 37(4) above, section 37(5) above and section 40(1) above shall apply in relation to an order under this section as they apply in relation to a hospital order, but as if references to the period of 28 days mentioned in section 40(1) above were omitted; and subject as aforesaid an order under this section shall, until the offender's case is disposed of by the Crown Court, have the same effect as a hospital order together with a restriction order [. . .].

AMENDMENTS

In subs.(1) the words in square brackets were substituted by the Mental Health Act 2007 s.10(7). The words omitted in subs.(3) were repealed by s.55, Sch.11 Pt 8.

DEFINITIONS

1–601   hospital: ss.55(5), 145(1).
hospital order: ss.37, 145(1).
restriction order: ss.41, 145(1).
approved clinician: s.145(1).
the managers: s.145(1).

GENERAL NOTE

1–602   If a magistrates' court on committing an offender to the Crown Court under s.43 is satisfied that arrangements have been made for the admission of the offender to a hospital, it may direct him to be admitted to that hospital until the case is disposed of by the Crown Court. If it is impracticable or inappropriate to bring the offender before the court, the

Crown Court may either adjourn the case or make a hospital order without convicting him and in his absence under s.51(5).

A patient who is admitted to a hospital under this section is subject to the consent to treatment provisions contained in Part IV (s.56).

Transitional provision

The repeal of the reference to restriction orders made for a specified period in subs.(3) **1–603** shall have no effect in respect of—

(a) a restriction order for a specified period made before October 1, 2007, or

(b) an order made outside England and Wales which is treated under the 1983 Act as if it were a restriction order for a specified period (Mental Health Act 2007 s.40(7) and SI 2007/2798 art.2(d)).

Subsection (1)

MAGISTRATES' COURT. Or youth court for those under the age of 18.   **1–604**

ADMITTED TO THAT HOSPITAL. Which will normally be the hospital which had already agreed to admit the patient in the event of the magistrates' court itself making a hospital order. Once the offender has been admitted to the hospital, subss.(5) and (6) of s.51 shall apply to him as if he were a person subject to a transfer direction made under s.47 (s.51(3)).

DIRECTIONS AS IT THINKS FIT FOR HIS PRODUCTION FROM THE HOSPITAL. It will be the hospital's duty to arrange for the offenders attendance at the court with an appropriate escort. It is not necessary to obtain the Secretary of State's consent to leave of absence from the hospital for this purpose.

Subsection (2)

SOME OTHER PERSON. Who need not be a clinician.   **1–605**

Subsection (3)

This subsection provides that the magistrates' court can direct that the offender be **1–606** detained in a place of safety pending his admission to hospital. It also authorises a constable, approved mental health professional or any other person directed to do so by the court to convey the offender to hospital at any time and not within the 28-day period provided for by s.40(1). Subject to this exception, an order under this section has the same effect as a restriction order.

Appeals from magistrates' courts

45.—(1) Where on the trial of an information charging a person with an offence **1–607** a magistrates' court makes a hospital order or guardianship order in respect of him without convicting him, he shall have the same right of appeal against the order as if it had been made on his conviction; and on any such appeal the Crown Court shall have the same powers as if the appeal had been against both conviction and sentence.

(2) An appeal by a child or young person with respect to whom any such order has been made, whether the appeal is against the order or against the finding upon which the order was made, may be brought by him or by his parent or guardian on his behalf.

DEFINITIONS
hospital order: ss.37, 145(1).   **1–608**
guardianship order: ss.37, 145(1).

child: s.55(1).
young person: s.55(1).
guardian: s.55(1).

GENERAL NOTE

1–609   This section provides a right of appeal for a person who has been made the subject of a hospital order or a guardianship order made by a magistrates' court under s.37(3).
Paragraph 15.22 of the Reference Guide states:

"Appeals in respect of children or young people given hospital orders by magistrates' courts without being convicted may be brought on their behalf by their parents or guardians. This applies to appeals against the order itself and against the finding that the child or young person had done the act in question."

[Hospital and Limitation Directions

Power of higher courts to direct hospital admission
1–610   **45A.**—(1) This section applies where, in the case of a person convicted before the Crown Court of an offence the sentence for which is not fixed by law—
(a) the conditions mentioned in subsection (2) below are fulfilled; and
(b) [. . .], the court considers making a hospital order in respect of him before deciding to impose a sentence of imprisonment ("the relevant sentence") in respect of the offence.
(2) The conditions referred to in subsection (1) above are that the court is satisfied, on the written or oral evidence of two registered medical practitioners—
(a) that the offender is suffering from [mental disorder];
(b) that the mental disorder from which the offender is suffering is of a nature or degree which makes it appropriate for him to be detained in a hospital for medical treatment; and
[(c) that appropriate medical treatment is available for him.]
(3) The court may give both of the following directions, namely—
(a) a direction that, instead of being removed to and detained in a prison, the offender be removed to and detained in such hospital as may be specified in the direction (in this Act referred to as a "hospital direction"); and
(b) a direction that the offender be subject to the special restrictions set out in section 41 above (in this Act referred to as a "limitation direction").
(4) A hospital direction and a limitation direction shall not be given in relation to an offender unless at least one of the medical practitioners whose evidence is taken into account by the court under subsection (2) above has given evidence orally before the court.
(5) A hospital direction and a limitation direction shall not be given in relation to an offender unless the court is satisfied on the written or oral evidence of the [approved clinician who would have overall responsibility for his case], or of some other person representing the managers of the hospital that arrangements have been made—
(a) for his admission to that hospital; and
(b) for his admission to it within the period of 28 days beginning with the day of the giving of such directions;
and the court may, pending his admission within that period, give such directions as it thinks fit for his conveyance to and detention in a place of safety.

(6) If within the said period of 28 days it appears to the Secretary of State that by reason of an emergency or other special circumstances it is not practicable for the patient to be received into the hospital specified in the hospital direction, he may give instructions for the admission of the patient to such other hospital as appears to be appropriate instead of the hospital so specified.

(7) Where such instructions are given—

(a) the Secretary of State shall cause the person having the custody of the patient to be informed, and

(b) the hospital direction shall have effect as if the hospital specified in the instructions were substituted for the hospital specified in the hospital direction.

(8) Section 38(1) and (5) and section 39 above shall have effect as if any reference to the making of a hospital order included a reference to the giving of a hospital direction and a limitation direction.

(9) A hospital direction and a limitation direction given in relation to an offender shall have effect not only as regards the relevant sentence but also (so far as applicable) as regards any other sentence of imprisonment imposed on the same or a previous occasion.

(10) [. . .]

(11) [. . .]

AMENDMENTS

This section was inserted by the Crime (Sentences) Act 1997 s.46. The amendments to it were made by the Criminal Justice Act 2003 s.332, Sch.37 Pt 7 and the Mental Health Act 2007 ss.1(4), 4(6), 10(8), 55, Sch.1 para.9, Sch.11 Pt 1.

DEFINITIONS   **1–611**
   mental disorder: ss.1, 145(1).
   hospital: ss.55(5), 145(1).
   medical treatment: s.145(1), (4).
   approved medical treatment: ss.3(4), 145(1AB).
   approved clinician: s.145(1).
   managers: s.145(1).
   place of safety: s.55.

GENERAL NOTE

   This section empowers the Crown Court, when imposing a prison sentence on a mentally **1–612** disordered offender convicted of an offence other than one of which the sentence is fixed by law, to give a direction for immediate admission to and detention in a specified hospital (a "hospital direction"), together with a direction that they be subject to the special restrictions set out in s.41 (a "limitation direction"). The offender then becomes a restricted patient (s.79). The power is designed to provide an appropriate disposal for a mentally disordered offender whose responsibility for his actions, although diminished, remains high. The court, which must have considered making a hospital order before imposing a sentence of imprisonment and attaching a hospital direction (subs.(1)(b)), cannot make a hospital direction without a limitation direction (subs.(3) and *R. v Poole* [2014] EWCA Crim 1641; [2015] M.H.L.R. 84). The effect of hospital and limitation directions is set out in s.45B. They are rarely made, which may be partly due to a failure by counsel to alert the court to the availability of this option: see, for example, *R v S* [2012] EWCA Crim 92.

   The purpose and application of the power to make a hospital direction is considered in paras 3 to 5 of Home Office Circular No.52/1997:

"The hospital direction is intended to give the courts greater flexibility in dealing with cases where they conclude that a prison sentence is the appropriate disposal in spite of evidence that the offender is mentally disordered. That will be either because the offender falls to be sentenced under the automatic life sentence provision in section 2 of the Crime (Sentences) Act 1997, or because the court is satisfied that a prison sentence with a hospital direction will be the most effective way to protect the public from further harm.

When sentencing mentally disordered offenders, the court is bound by the requirement in section 4 of the Criminal Justice Act 1991 to consider any information before it which relates to the defendant's mental condition. Except where the sentence is fixed by law, the court is required to consider the effect of a custodial sentence on the offender's mental disorder and on the treatment which may be available for it before passing such a sentence.

The hospital direction does not disturb this arrangement. Section 45A(1)(b) of the 1983 Act requires the court to consider making a hospital order in all cases (other than those where the sentence is fixed by law and offenders sentenced under section 2 of the Crime (Sentences) Act 1997) before attaching a hospital direction to a prison sentence. Existing procedures for giving medical evidence need not change, since the requirements for making a hospital direction are the same as those for making a restricted hospital order. The court will simply have the new option of directing to hospital when it concludes that a custodial sentence is appropriate."

The provisions of the Criminal Justice Act 1991 and the Crime (Sentences) Act 1997 which are referred to in the above circular have been superseded by the Powers of Criminal Courts (Sentencing) Act 2000 and the Criminal Justice Act 2003.

In *R. v Vowles* [2015] EWCA Crim 45 at para.21, Lord Thomas C.J. said that the advantage of making an order under this section "in an appropriate case is that an offender sentenced to an indeterminate or long determinate sentence can immediately be directed to have treatment in hospital, but the timing of his release is subject to the decision of the Parole Board which has to take a much wider view of the risks to the public than the FTT". His Lordship said at para.54(i) :

"[B]efore a hospital order is made under s.37/41, whether or not with a restriction order, a judge should consider whether the mental disorder can appropriately be dealt with by a hospital and limitation direction under s.45A."

The *Code of Practice* states at para.22.74:

"A hospital and limitation direction may be imposed where it is considered that the offender, although suffering from a mental disorder, can be considered to be responsible, to a degree, for the offence. Generally, courts have adopted the test that there has to be a 'significant degree' of culpability for a hospital direction to be appropriate, although this test is not always applied."

In *R. v Jenkin* [2012] EWCA Crim 2557; [2013] M.H.L.R. 61, an order was made under this section in respect of an offender who had committed an appalling act of grievous bodily harm and who the judge found must bear a significant responsibility for what happened. The order was accompanied by a sentence of life imprisonment.

In *R. v Cooper* [2010] EWCA Crim 2335; [2010] M.H.L.R. 240, an order under this section was upheld where the offender was found to have had a degree of responsibility for his crime partly because by ingesting drugs "he had voluntarily embarked upon the course of events which led to his illness" (para.22). The Court rejected the argument that the transfer of the offender to prison when the criteria for detention under the Act were no longer satisfied would lead to a deterioration of his mental health placing himself and others at risk. The Court said at para.19:

> "Assuming eligibility for parole, when detention in hospital is no longer necessary the responsible [clinician] treating such a prisoner can doubtless recommend either a return to prison or a discharge into the community, presumably in the usual course of events through mental health facilities offering decreasing security. As identified in *R. v Staines* [2006] EWCA Crim 15, the procedure is for the Mental Health Review Tribunal, if so satisfied, to make a recommendation to the Parole Board for release. The offender remains in hospital until such time as the Parole Board makes its decision."

The Court of Appeal can substitute an order under this section for a prison sentence despite the Crown Court not having been referred at the time of sentence to the possibility of such an order being made (*R. v Stead* [2012] EWCA Crim 92; [2012] M.H.L.R. 58).

As an order under this section can only be made in respect of offenders who can be sentenced to imprisonment, that is to offenders over the age of 21, an order cannot be made in respect of a person under that age at the time of conviction (*Attorney General's Reference (No.54 of 2011)* [2011] EWCA Crim 2276; [2012] M.H.L.R. 87, para.22; also see *R. v Fort* [2013] EWCA Crim 2332; [2014] M.H.L.R. 334 which is noted under s.55(6)).

Appeals

A hospital direction and a limitation direction is a form of sentence and is therefore **1–613** appealable to the Court of Appeal (Criminal Appeal Act 1968 ss.9(1), 50(1)).

Named hospital units

If a hospital and limitation direction is made, the court has the power to order that the **1–614** patient be admitted to and detained in a named hospital unit: see the note to s.41 under this heading.

Leave of absence

In October 2012, the MHCS of the Ministry of Justice published revised guidance on **1–615** s.17 community leave which includes guidance on patients who have been sentenced and directed to hospital under this section. The guidance can be accessed at: *www.justice.-gov.uk/offenders/types-of-offender/mentally-disordered-offenders*.

Applications to the First-tier Tribunal (Mental Health) or the Mental Health Review Tribunal for Wales

A patient who is subject to directions made under this section has the same right to apply **1–616** to a tribunal as a restricted patient: see the note on s.41 under this heading. The procedure to be adopted on such an application being made is set out in s.74.

Domestic Violence, Crime and Victims Act 2004

See Ch.40 of the *Code of Practice* at paras 18.18 to 18.20 and Ch.30 at paras 30.29 to **1–617** 30.31. The Department of Health has published "Mental Health Act 2007: Guidance on the extension of victims' rights under the Domestic Violence, Crime and Victims Act" (2008).

Subsection (1)

CONVICTED. The sentence of the court can be either determinate or indeterminate.

FIXED BY LAW. This section does not apply to persons who have been convicted of mur- **1–618** der who must be sentenced to life imprisonment (Murder (Abolition of Death Penalty) Act 1965 s.1).

Subsection (2)

1–619   EVIDENCE.   For general requirements as to medical evidence, see s.54. The court can call a doctor who has provided a written report to give oral evidence (s.54(2A)).

TWO REGISTERED MEDICAL PRACTITIONERS.   One of whom must be approved by the Secretary of State or the Welsh Ministers under s.12, or by another person by virtue of s.12ZA or 12ZB (s.54(1)).

MENTAL DISORDER.   If the person has a learning disability, the disability must be associated with abnormally aggressive or seriously irresponsible conduct (s.1(2A), (2B)). A learning disabled person might also suffer from another form of mental disorder.

NATURE OR DEGREE.   See the note on s.3(2)(a).

APPROPRIATE MEDICAL TREATMENT.   See the note on s.3(2)(d).

Subsection (3)

1–620   LIMITATION DIRECTION.   In *R. v Poole* [2014] EWCA Crim 1641, the court rejected counsel's argument that this subsection, in referring to the restrictions set out in s.41, must thereby incorporate into the court's consideration for making a limitation direction those conditions set out in s.41(1) as a prerequisite for the making of a restriction order. Macur L.J. said that there "is good reason to differentiate the pre-requirements for a restriction order against those required for a limitation direction" (para.26).

Subsection (5)

1–621   In *R. (on the application of DB) v Nottinghamshire Healthcare NHS Trust* [2008] EWCA Civ 1354; [2009] 2 All E.R. 792, noted under s.37(4), the Court of Appeal held that a hospital order ceases to have effect if the offender who is the subject of the order is not admitted to the hospital named in the order within the period of 28 days from the date of the making of the order, as stipulated by it. It is submitted that this finding applies to directions made under this section.

1–622   BEGINNING WITH.   Including the day on which the directions were given (*Zoan v Rouamba* [2000] 2 All E.R. 620 CA).

Subsections (6), (7)

1–623   SECRETARY OF STATE.   The functions of the Secretary of State under these provisions, so far as exercisable in relation to Wales, are exercised by the Welsh Ministers: see the General Note to the Act and SI 1999/672 art.2, Sch.1, as varied by SI 2000/253 art.4, Sch.3.

Subsection (8)

1–624   This provides that ss.38(1) and (5) and 39 apply in respect of the giving of a hospital and a limitation direction as they do to the making of a hospital order. Those sections enable respectively the making of an interim hospital order and the acquisition of information from health authorities on the availability of facilities.

Subsection (9)

1–625   This provides that where a hospital and a limitation direction are made, they apply to all existing prison sentences passed on the offender.

[Effect of hospital and limitation directions

1–626   **45B.**—(1) A hospital direction and a limitation direction shall be sufficient authority—

(a) for a constable or any other person directed to do so by the court to convey the patient to the hospital specified in the hospital direction within a period of 28 days; and

(b) for the managers of the hospital to admit him at any time within that period and thereafter detain him in accordance with the provisions of this Act.

(2) With respect to any person—

(a) a hospital direction shall have effect as a transfer direction; and

(b) a limitation direction shall have effect as a restriction direction.

(3) While a person is subject to a hospital direction and a limitation direction the [responsible clinician] shall at such intervals (not exceeding one year) as the Secretary of State may direct examine and report to the Secretary of State on that person; and every report shall contain such particulars as the Secretary of State may require.]

AMENDMENTS

This section was inserted by the Crime (Sentences) Act 1997 s.46. The words in square brackets in subs.(3) were inserted by the Mental Health Act 2007 s.10(9).

DEFINITIONS   **1–627**

hospital direction: ss.45A(3)(a), 145(1).

limitation direction: ss.45A(3)(b), 145(1).

patient: s.145(1).

hospital: ss.55(5), 145(1).

managers: s.145(1).

transfer direction: ss.47, 145(1).

restriction direction: ss.49, 145(1).

responsible clinician: s.55(1).

GENERAL NOTE

The effect of hospital and limitation directions is set out in paras 7 and 8 of the Home **1–628** Office Circular 52/1997:

"The hospital direction has the effect of ordering the offender's admission to a named hospital for treatment within 28 days, as if a hospital order had been made. Once there, the offender will be managed as if admitted under a transfer direction made under section 47 of the 1983 Act. When making a hospital direction the court must at the same time make a limitation direction. This has the same effect as a restriction direction under section 49 of the 1983 Act. The offender is made subject to the restrictions set out in section 41 of the 1983 Act.

An offender who is subject to hospital and limitation directions may serve his entire sentence in hospital if the responsible [clinician] is satisfied that he is benefiting from treatment. Alternatively he may, on the recommendation of the responsible [clinician] or [a tribunal], be transferred to prison at any time during sentence by warrant of the [Secretary of State] under section 50(1) of the 1983 Act. Transfer to prison will be considered by the [Secretary of State] on receipt of medical evidence that the patient no longer requires treatment in hospital for mental disorder, or that no other effective treatment can be given in hospital. Any subsequent transfer back to hospital would be considered under section 47 of the 1983 Act."

Although the limitation direction ends on the patient's release date, the hospital direction does not. This means that if the patient is being treated in hospital subject to the hospital direction on the release date, the patient remains in hospital as if he were subject to an unrestricted hospital order. If the patient is transferred to prison, both the hospital direction and the limitation direction end (s.50(1), (2), (3) and (5)).

If the Secretary of State is informed by the patient's RC or the tribunal that the patient no longer requires treatment in hospital or that no effective treatment can be given in the hospital to which he has been removed, he may exercise his power of direction under s.50.

A patient who is subject to an order under s.45A comes within the after-care provisions of s.117. Paragraph 16.22 of the Reference Guide states:

"In practice, the Secretary of State for Justice expects clinical staff from the hospital and prison to meet to plan the patient's future care (a 'section 117 meeting') before directing the patient's removal to prison".

Subsection (1)

1–629   CONVEY THE PATIENT. If the patient absconds, he may be retaken under s.138. Paragraph 16.18 of the Reference Guide states:

"Hospital and limitation direction patients who are absent without leave, or are otherwise liable to be taken into custody, under the Act are also treated as being unlawfully at large from custody for the purposes of section 49(2) of the Prison Act 1952. This may affect their release date."

Detention during Her Majesty's pleasure

Persons ordered to be kept in custody during Her Majesty's pleasure

1–630   **46.** [*Repealed by the Armed Forces Act 1996 s.35(2), Sch.7 Pt III.*]

Transfers to hospital of prisoners, etc.

Removal to hospital of persons serving sentences of imprisonment, etc.

1–631   **47.**—(1) If in the case of a person serving a sentence of imprisonment the Secretary of State is satisfied, by reports from at least two registered medical practitioners—

(a) that the said person is suffering from [mental disorder]; and

(b) that the mental disorder from which that person is suffering is of a nature or degree which makes it appropriate for him to be detained in a hospital for medical treatment[; and

(c) that appropriate medical treatment is available for him.]

the Secretary of State may, if he is of the opinion having regard to the public interest and all the circumstances that it is expedient so to do, by warrant direct that that person be removed to and detained in such hospital [. . .] as may be specified in the direction; and a direction under this section shall be known as "a transfer direction".

(2) A transfer direction shall cease to have effect at the expiration of the period of 14 days beginning with the date on which it is given unless within that period the person with respect to whom it was given has been received into the hospital specified in the direction.

(3) A transfer direction with respect to any person shall have the same effect as a hospital order made in his case.

(4) [. . .]

(5) References in this Part of this Act to a person serving a sentence of imprisonment include references—

(a) to a person detained in pursuance of any sentence or order for detention made by a court in criminal proceedings [or service disciplinary proceedings] (other than an order [made in consequence of a finding of insanity or unfitness to stand trial [or a sentence of service detention within the meaning of the Armed Forces Act 2006]]);

(b) to a person committed to custody under section 115(3) of the Magistrates' Courts Act 1980 (which relates to persons who fail to comply with an order to enter into recognisances to keep the peace or be of good behaviour); and

(c) to a person committed by a court to a prison or other institution to which the Prison Act 1952 applies in default of payment of any sum adjudged to be paid on his conviction.

[(6) in subsection (5)(a) "service disciplinary proceedings" means proceedings in respect of a service offence within the meaning of the Armed Forces Act 2006.]

AMENDMENTS

The amendments to this section were made by the Crime (Sentences) Act 1997 s.56(2), Sch.6, the Mental Health Act 2007 ss.1(4), 4(7), 55, Sch.1 para.10, Sch.11 Pt 1, the Domestic Violence, Crime and Victims Act 2004 s.58(1), Sch.10 para.18 and the Armed Forces Act 2006 s.378, Sch.16 para.97(2)(3).

DEFINITIONS

1–632

mental disorder: ss.1, 145(1).
hospital: ss.55(5), 145(1).
medical treatment: s.145(1), (4).
appropriate medical treatment: ss.3(4), 145(1AB).
hospital order: ss.37, 145(1).

GENERAL NOTE

This section enables the Secretary of State (in practice, the Mental Health Casework **1–633** Section at the Ministry of Justice (MHCS)) to direct that a person serving a sentence of imprisonment or other detention be removed to and detained in a hospital. Such transfers (a "transfer direction") can only be made on medical grounds. Paragraph 22.42 of the *Code of Practice* states:

"The need for inpatient treatment for a prisoner should be identified and acted upon quickly, and prison healthcare staff should make contact immediately with the NHS Commissioning Board. Responsible NHS commissioners should aim to ensure that transfers of prisoners with mental disorders are carried out within a timeframe equivalent to levels of care experienced by patients who are admitted to mental healthcare services from the community. Any unacceptable delays in transfer after identification of need should be actively monitored and investigated by the NHS Commissioning Board."

In order for the Secretary of State to make a transfer direction, the following are required:

(i) agreement on the part of two medical practitioners, expressed in their reports to the Secretary of State:

(i) that the person is mentally disordered; and
(ii) that the requirements for detention in subs.(1)(b) and (c) are satisfied;

(ii) a hospital in which the patient may be appropriately treated; and

(iii) a place at that hospital that is available within 14 days.

In *R.(on the application of DK) v Secretary of State for the Home Department* [2010] EWHC 82 (Admin); [2010] M.H.L.R. 64, Collins J. said at para.33:

"One does not want to be over pedantic in these matters, but, as I have said, the court must bear in mind that it is dealing with liberty, and that therefore it is of the utmost importance that all the necessary preconditions for transfer leading to detention are properly seen through."

A transfer direction has the same effect as a hospital order made without restrictions under s.37 (subs.(3)), subject to the exception that the patient may apply to a tribunal within six months of his transfer (s.69(2)(b)). A patient who has been made subject to a transfer direction can therefore be discharged at any time by his responsible clinician (RC) or the hospital managers, can be transferred under the provisions of s.19 and will be subject to the consent to treatment provisions contained in Pt IV (s.56(3)). Although the patient's discharge from detention in hospital can take place before the expiration of his sentence, the making of a transfer direction can result in the patient remaining in hospital under compulsory powers long after the day on which he would have been released from prison had such a direction not been made.

When giving a transfer direction the Secretary of State will in most cases also impose the restrictions provided for under s.49 (a "restriction direction") which means the patient cannot be transferred to another hospital, sent on leave or discharged by the RC without the Secretary of State's consent. In practice, the only occasion when a restriction direction will not be made is if the prisoner is very close to his earliest date of release: see below and *R. (on the application of T) v Secretary of State for the Home Department*, noted in the General Note to s.49. The Secretary of State must make a restriction direction in respect of certain prisoners: see s.49(1).

Although a person who is subject to an unrestricted order under this section cannot be recalled to prison to complete his sentence, the sentence and accordingly any licence period and conditions as would normally be imposed under the Criminal Justice Act procedure, including the prospect of recall to prison on a breach of a licence condition, continue to run notwithstanding his transfer to hospital *(R. (on the application of Miah) v Secretary of State for the Home Department* [2004] EWHC 2569 (Admin); [2004] M.H.L.R. 302).

In *R. (on the application of D) v Secretary of State for the Home Department and National Assembly for Wales* [2004] EWHC 2857 (Admin); [2005] M.H.L.R. 17 para.33, Stanley Burnton J. held that once the prison service have reasonable grounds to believe that a prisoner requires treatment in a mental hospital in which he may be detained, the Secretary of State is under a duty expeditiously to take reasonable steps to obtain appropriate medical advice, and if that advice confirms the need for transfer to a hospital, to take reasonable steps within a reasonable time to effect that transfer. In many cases, the medical advice as to the appropriateness of transfer will serve as the reports required by s.47. The steps that are reasonable will depend on the circumstances, including the apparent risk to the health of the prisoner if no transfer is effected. Inappropriate retention of a prisoner in a prison or YOI may infringe his rights under art.8 of the European Convention on Human Rights (ECHR). If the consequences for the prisoner are sufficiently severe, his inappropriate retention in a prison may go so far as to bring about a breach of art.3 of the ECHR, in which case the state is under an absolute duty to prevent or bring to an end his inhumane treatment.

His Lordship made the following comment, at para.45, on the position of a prisoner who has been remanded in custody:

"If there is good reason to believe that a psychiatric assessment is appropriate, it needs to be obtained before sentence, not after what is liable to be (on what on this hypothesis is the incomplete information available to the sentencing judge) an inappropriate sentence. If, before sentence, it becomes clear that detention in a hospital under the Mental Health Act 1983 is appropriate, although transfer under s.47 is not available, I do not see why arrangements cannot be made for a prisoner to be detained under that Act while being formally remanded on bail."

In *R. v Drew* [2003] UKHL 25; [2003] 4 All E.R. 557 HL at para.19, Lord Bingham said **1–634** that if:

"it were shown that a mentally disordered defendant was held in prison, that he was there denied medical treatment, available in hospital, which his mental condition required and that he was suffering serious consequences as a result of such denial, he would have grounds for seeking judicial review of the [Secretary of State's] failure to direct his transfer to hospital under [this section]; (*Keenan v United Kingdom* (2001) 33 E.H.R.R. 38)".

In judicial review proceedings, the High Court has jurisdiction to direct the Secretary of State to make an order under this section if the necessary medical reports had been completed (*R. (on the application of D) v Secretary of State for the Home Office* [2003] EWHC 2529 (Admin)).

A decision to transfer a prisoner to hospital at the end of his sentence heightens the scrutiny which should be applied both by the Secretary of State as to the evidence on which that decision should be taken, and heightens the scrutiny which the court must apply to the decision of the Secretary of State: see *R. (on the application of TF) v Secretary of State for Justice* [2008] EWCA Civ 1457; [2008] M.H.L.R. 370, where Waller L.J. said at para.31:

"Where section 47 is proposed to be used at the very end of the sentence, and hopefully that will only be in very exceptional cases, the onus must be on the Secretary of State to show that the mind of the decision maker has focused on each of the criteria which it is necessary to satisfy if there is to be power to issue a warrant directing transfer to a hospital."

Paragraphs 3.10 and 3.13 to 3.16 of the Department of Health "Good Practice Procedure Guide: The transfer and remission of adult prisoners under s.47 and s.48 of the Mental Health Act" (2011), which can be accessed at *www.gov.uk/government/publications/the-transfer-and-remission-of-adult-prisoners-under-s47-and-s48-of-the-mental-health-act*, state:

"The Mental Health Casework Section (MHCS) . . . advise that where a prisoner is sufficiently close to their release date that admission to hospital could be appropriately achieved using civil powers of the 1983 Mental Health Act, it is unlikely that a directing a transfer under s.47 can be justified. . . .

The Secretary of State may consider late in sentence applications if the case can be made that

- admission to hospital is an urgent necessity
- it is necessary for the prisoner's own health and/or safety and
- the urgency of need is such that it is not safe to wait until the release date for admission to hospital.

It is essential that the MHCS be involved in the process at a very early stage in these circumstances, as this will support effective decision-making regarding the most appropriate application of the Mental Health Act.

If the Secretary of State has rejected a late-in-sentence s.47 transfer application, it may be appropriate to consider admission under s.2 or s.3 on completion of sentence.

In these circumstances, the assessments and applications can be made whilst the prisoner is in custody and arrangements made for post-release admission."

Under s.117, health bodies and local social services authorities have a duty to provide after-care services for patients who cease to be liable to be detained and leave hospital after having been transferred by the Secretary of State under this section. The responsibility for holding a "section 117 meeting" applies if the prisoner is discharged back to prison. Paragraphs 5.11 to 5.14 of the Department of Health guidance, above, state:

> "Before the return to prison can be authorised by the Secretary of State, a multi-agency s117 meeting must be held to agree aftercare arrangements including a Care Plan to accompany the prisoner on their return to custody.
>
> The mental health service provider treating the transferred prisoner will convene and host the s117 meeting.
>
> The local receiving prison healthcare and custody staff are expected to attend the s117 meeting. If the prisoner has at least 6 months remaining on their sentence and fits the criteria for MAPPA involvement, a representative of the local MAPPA should also attend.
>
> MHCS will only consider remission to prison without a completed s117 meeting in exceptional circumstances. In such cases, MHSC require confirmation of the date of the planned s117 meeting before the warrant can be agreed."

For the supervision in the community of a patient who has been transferred under this section and has been made the subject of a restriction direction under s.49, see the note on s.50(1)(b).

Responsibility for prison health care was fully transferred from HM Prison Service to the NHS in April 2006: see the notes to the definition of "hospital" in s.145(1).

Emergency and out-of hours transfers

1–635 Paragraphs 4.32 to 4.35 of the Department of Health guidance, above, state:

> "Transfers for prisoners who require hospital admission can be made under the Prison Act 1952; this is usually applied to prisoners who require treatment for physical health issues but can, in some circumstances be used for mentally disordered prisoners.
>
> In extreme circumstances where for example, a prisoner is refusing fluid and hospital treatment is urgently required, prison healthcare services must alert the MHCS and arrange for a s12-approved doctor to assess the prisoner.
>
> Mental health services should not be expected to treat prisoners refusing food or fluid unless this is a direct result of a severe mental disorder. The priority in such cases is to ensure that the prisoner receives appropriate hospital treatment for their physical health needs.
>
> When an urgent transfer is required out of normal office hours the MHCS can provide a verbal authorisation for transfer, the prison Governor will also need to agree to the transfer."

Named hospital units

1–636 If the Secretary of State makes a direction under this section coupled with a restriction direction made under s.49, he has the power to order that the patient be admitted to and detained in a named hospital unit: see the note to s.41 under this heading.

Human Rights Act 1998

1–637 To subject an offender requiring admission to hospital to unnecessary suffering, humiliation, distress and deterioration of his mental condition in prison could properly be regarded as inhumane or degrading treatment or punishment contrary to art.3 of the European Convention on Human Rights (*R. v Drew* [2003] UKHL 25 para.18; also see *Riviere v France* (App.No.33834/03) and the notes on art.5 in Part 5). It could also constitute an interference with his mental and physical integrity contrary to art.8 (*R. (on the* *application of D) v Secretary of State for the Home Department and National Assembly for Wales*, above).

In *Pankiewicz v Poland* (App.No.34151/04), the European Court of Human Rights held that a delay of two months and twenty five days in transferring a mentally disordered prisoner to hospital, as recommended by two psychiatrists, violated art.5(1). The Court said at paras 44, 45:

"The Court accepts the Government's arguments that it would be unrealistic and too rigid an approach to expect the authorities to ensure that a place is immediately available in a selected psychiatric hospital. However, a reasonable balance must be struck between the competing interests involved. Having regard to the balancing of interests the Court attaches weight to the fact that the applicant was held in a regular detention centre without adequate medical facilities. The delay in admission to a psychiatric hospital and thus the beginning of the treatment was obviously harmful to the applicant, in view of the expert's opinions recommending him for psychiatric treatment. In addition, the Court notes that the Government failed to advance any detailed explanation for the delay in the applicant's admission to the hospital.

The Court cannot find that, in the circumstances of the present case, a reasonable balance was struck. The Court is of the opinion that even though the delay of two months and twenty five days in the admission of the applicant to a psychiatric hospital may not at first glance seem particularly excessive, it cannot be regarded as acceptable (see *Morsink v the Netherlands*, no. 48865/99, §§ 61–70, 11 May 2004; *Brand v the Netherlands*, no. 49902/99, §§ 58–67, 11 May 2004; and *Mocarska*, cited above, § 48). To hold otherwise would entail a serious weakening of the fundamental right to liberty to the detriment of the person concerned and thus impair the very essence of the right protected by Article 5 of the Convention."

In *Morley v United Kingdom* (2005) 40 E.H.R.R. SE8, [2005] M.H.L.R. 174, the Court declared inadmissible the applicant's complaint that art.5 required the decision to transfer a prisoner to hospital to be made by the tribunal.

Applications to the First-tier Tribunal (Mental Health) or the Mental Health Review Tribunal for Wales
By virtue of subs.(3), the patient may make an application to a tribunal within six months **1–638** of the date of the direction, once during the following six months, and at yearly intervals thereafter (s.69(2)(b)). The patient's nearest relative has similar rights to make an application (s.69(1) as applied by s.55(4)). Any application, hospital order or guardianship order that was in place prior to the making of the transfer direction will cease to have effect (s.40(5)).

Subsection (1)
SENTENCE OF IMPRISONMENT. See subs.(5). The Department of Health document **1–639** *Procedure for the Transfer from Custody of Children and Young People to and from Hospital under the Mental Health Act 1983 in England* (2011) states at p.7 that this section and s.48 apply to children and young people (under the age of 18) within the following categories of custody:

- detention and training orders—s.100, Powers of Criminal Courts (Sentencing) Act 2000;

- detention during Her Majesty's Pleasure—s.90, Powers of Criminal Courts (Sentencing) Act 2000;

- detention for life—s.91, Powers of Criminal Courts (Sentencing) Act 2000;

- determinate sentence for specified "serious" offences—s.91, Powers of Criminal Courts (Sentencing) Act 2000;

- detention for public protection—s.226, Criminal Justice Act 2003;

- extended sentence for certain violent or sexual offences—s.228, Criminal Justice Act 2003; and

- remand in custody—s.128, Magistrates' Courts Act 1980.

REPORTS.   Although this provision does not require that the report be in writing, it is obviously important that there should be a written report (*R. (on the application of DK) v Secretary of State for the Home Department* [2010] EWHC 82 (Admin); [2010] M.H.L.R. 64, para.19). In *R. v Secretary of State for the Home Office Ex p. Gilkes* [1999] EWHC 47 (Admin); [1999] M.H.L.R. 7 para.12, Dyson J. said:

"If the reports are manifestly unreliable, then the Secretary of State cannot reasonably be satisfied that the . . . conditions [of this section] are met on the basis of the reports, and a decision to rely on them in such circumstances will be capable of successful challenge by judicial review. A medical report may be unreliable for a number of reasons. It may on its face not address the relevant statutory criteria. It may be based on an assessment which is so out of date that the mere fact of a lapse of time will be sufficient to render it unreliable. It may be unreliable to rely on a report based on an assessment conducted an appreciable, but not inordinate, time before the decision to transfer where the mental disorder is a fluctuating and unstable condition and/or where there has been a change of circumstances since the assessment was made. In each case, it will be for the Secretary of State to consider whether in his judgment the medical report is one on which he can safely and properly rely so as to be satisfied that the conditions set out in paragraphs (a) and (b) . . . are met. One of the considerations that will be uppermost in his mind is whether the assessment on which the report is based is sufficiently recent to provide reliable evidence of the patient's current mental condition."

In this case, Dyson J. said that although it is incorrect to say that it can never be reasonable for the Secretary of State, when considering whether to make a transfer direction, to rely on a medical report made for the purposes of s.37, the Secretary of State should be slow to conclude that such a report can be safely relied on.

The judgment of Dyson J. in *Gilkes*, which was approved by the Court of Appeal in *TF v Secretary of State for Justice* [2008] EWCA Civ 1457, was applied by the Court of Appeal in *R. (on the application of SP) v Secretary of State for Justice* [2010] EWCA Civ 1590; [2011] M.H.L.R. 65, a case where one of the reporting doctors used an obsolete form. In upholding the legality of the transfer, Arden L.J. said at paras 23 and 27:

"Section 47 does not contain any express provision as to any particular level of reasoning. Not unnaturally, that is left to the general law but it is necessary to have regard to the context. The reports of the medical practitioners are written by those who are expert in medical practice and they are addressed to the Secretary of State and his officials, who are lay persons. The Secretary of State and his officials are not concerned to pursue medical reasoning. In my judgment, in principle the decision maker is only concerned to see whether the medical practitioners have given some reasons which they consider adequate and which, on what they have said, do not fail to take account of material issues or matters and do not conflict with the facts known to the Secretary of State or the statutory requirements. . . .

I fully accept that the Secretary of State cannot write in reasons which are not there. However, at the same time in my judgment the Secretary of State is entitled to give the reports a sensible meaning and is not required to go back to the medical practitioner to ask them to articulate in words matters which are there by necessary implication."

There is no statutory time limit between the date of the report and the date of the decision of the Secretary of State. However, to achieve compliance with art.5(1)(e) of the ECHR the medical opinion cannot be seen as sufficient to justify deprivation of liberty under that provision if a significant period has elapsed since the preparation of the report (*Varbanov v Bulgaria* [2002] M.H.L.R. 263 at para.47). The practice of the MHCS is to require the prison to provide two medical reports (not more than two months old and dated within two weeks of the examination) (Mental Health Unit Bulletin, March 2008).

TWO REGISTERED MEDICAL PRACTITIONERS. One of whom must be approved by the Secretary of State or the Welsh Ministers under s.12, or by another person by virtue of s.12ZA or s.12ZB (s.54(1)). There is no requirement for either doctor to be an approved clinician. "In practice, the [Secretary of State] will normally want at least one of the two doctors to be practicing at the hospital named in the proposed transfer direction, so as to ensure that there is agreement as to the hospital's reception of the patient and as to his diagnosis, treatability and detention", per Stanley Burnton J. in *R. (on the application of D) v Secretary of State for the Home Department and National Assembly for Wales* [2004] EWHC 2857; [2005] M.H.L.R. 17 at para.21. The Secretary of State is not "required to shop around until he finds psychiatrists prepared to sign section 47 reports: it is his duty to obtain the reliable opinions of psychiatrists as to the transfer of a prisoner to a hospital with a vacancy that can offer appropriate care" (para. 49).

It is acceptable for the doctors not to have seen the patient for some time prior to the completion of their reports if the patient's mental disorder is an enduring rather than a fluctuating condition, and the patient has refused to see them and to be examined by them for the purposes of such reports (*R. (on the application of F) v Secretary of State for the Home Department* [2008] EWHC 2912 (Admin); [2008] M.H.L.R. 361 para.30). This was described as "appropriate advice" at the Court of Appeal (*R. (on the application of TF) v Secretary of State for Justice*, above, para.29).

Paragraph (a)

MENTAL DISORDER. If the person has a learning disability, the disability must be associ- **1–640** ated with abnormally aggressive or seriously irresponsible conduct (s.1(2A), (2B)). A learning disabled person might also suffer from another form of mental disorder.

Paragraph (b)

APPROPRIATE FOR HIM TO BE DETAINED . . . FOR MEDICAL TREATMENT. In *South West* **1–641** *London and St George's Mental Health NHS Trust v W* [2002] EWHC 1770 (Admin); [2002] M.H.L.R. 392, Crane J. confirmed, at para.77, that this provision does not cover transfers for assessment, but said, at para.79, that he did "not consider that detention becomes unlawful immediately a particular form of treatment is suspended if there is a period of assessment in relation to another form of possible treatment and the process of monitoring under nursing, medical and psychological supervision continues".

In this case, a mentally disordered prisoner who had been convicted of a serious and unprovoked assault on a stranger was transferred to hospital under this section. The question before the judge was whether the transfer, which was aimed at securing the staged discharge of the patient from the hospital, was lawful. The plan devised for the patient was that he would be admitted to hospital for several months. He would be given increasing leave from the hospital linked to occupational and other therapy. An attempt would then be made to find a place for him in a hostel and there would be liaison between the hostel staff and the hospital team. The patient would gradually spend increasing periods out of hospital and then progress to overnight stays at the hostel. In holding that the transfer was lawful, Crane J. held, at para.62, that although s.47 cannot be used simply to postpone release, "transfer to hospital involving admission, nursing, medical, and here psychological supervision, and staged discharge under medical supervision, is capable of amounting to 'treatment' ...".

Paragraph (c)

1–642   APPROPRIATE MEDICAL TREATMENT.   See the note on s.3(2)(d) and *South West London and St George's Mental Health NHC Trust*, noted under para.(b).

HOSPITAL.   Or registered establishment (ss.34(2), 55(5)). In *R. (on the application of D) v Secretary of State for the Home Department and National Assembly for Wales*, above, Stanley Burnton J. suggested, at para.60, that the difficulties that are sometimes encountered in finding a suitable hospital for a potential transfer direction patient could be ameliorated by the establishment of a national database that could be maintained within the Ministry of Justice, or the Department of Health, and which might be accessible (to authorised persons only) on the internet.

Subsection (2)

1–643   14 DAYS.   After which a fresh direction will be necessary if the patient has not been admitted to the hospital.

BEGINNING WITH.   Including the day on which the transfer direction is given (*Zoan v Rouamba* [2000] 2 All E.R. 620 CA).

RECEIVED INTO THE HOSPITAL.   Although the agreement of the hospital to which the patient is to be transferred is not a pre-condition of a transfer direction, practical considerations will normally dictate that its agreement is necessary (*R. (on the application of D) v Secretary of State for the Home Department and National Assembly for Wales*, above, para.30). In *D*, the court was informed by a Home Office official that approximately six transfers take place each year without the agreement of the admitting hospital, and that about 650 transfers take place each year.

Subsection (3)

1–644   The only effect of this provision is to apply s.40 to a transfer direction (*R. (on the application of Miah) v Secretary of State for the Home Department* [2004] EWHC 2569 (Admin); [2004] M.H.L.R. 302 para.23).

SAME EFFECT AS A HOSPITAL ORDER.   The patient can therefore be discharged by his RC or by the hospital managers. For the purpose of renewal, the start date of the transfer direction is the date of the direction, not the date when the patient was admitted to hospital (s.40(4)). An application for a community treatment order can be made in respect of the patient (Sch.1 Pt.1).

Subsection (5)

1–645   ANY SENTENCE OR ORDER FOR DETENTION MADE BY A COURT IN CRIMINAL PROCEEDINGS.   These words are wide enough to cover detention during Her Majesty's pleasure (*R. v Secretary of State for the Home Department Ex p. Hickey (No.1)* [1995] 1 All E.R. 479, per Rose L.J. at 488).

Removal to hospital of other prisoners

1–646   **48.**—(1) If in the case of a person to whom this section applies the Secretary of State is satisfied by the same reports as are required for the purposes of section 47 above that—

    [(a) that person is suffering from mental disorder of a nature or degree which makes it appropriate for him to be detained in a hospital for medical treatment; and

    (b) he is in urgent need of such treatment;][and

    (c) appropriate medical treatment is available for him;]

the Secretary of State shall have the same power of giving a transfer direction in respect of him under that section as if he were serving a sentence of imprisonment.

(2) This section applies to the following persons, that is to say—

(a) persons detained in a prison or remand centre, not being persons serving a sentence of imprisonment or persons falling within the following paragraphs of this subsection;

(b) persons remanded in custody by a magistrates' court;

(c) civil prisoners, that is to say, persons committed by a court to prison for a limited term [. . .], who are not persons falling to be dealt with under section 47 above;

(d) persons detained under the Immigration Act 1971 [or under section 62 of the Nationality, Immigration and Asylum Act 2002 (detention by the Secretary of State)].

(3) Subsections (2) [and (3)] of section 47 above shall apply for the purposes of this section and of any transfer direction given by virtue of this section as they apply for the purposes of that section and of any transfer direction under that section.

AMENDMENTS

The amendments to this section were made by the Statute Law (Repeals) Act 2004 Sch.1 Pt 17 Group 8, the Nationality, Immigration and Asylum Act 2002 s.62(10) and the Mental Health Act 2007 ss.1(4), 5(3), Sch.1 para.11.

DEFINITIONS

1–647

mental disorder: ss.1, 145(1).

hospital: ss.55(5), 145(1).

medical treatment: s.145(1), (4).

appropriate medical treatment: ss.3(4), 145(1AB).

transfer direction: ss.47, 145(1).

civil prisoner: s.55(1).

GENERAL NOTE

1–648

This section empowers the Secretary of State to direct the removal from prison to hospital of certain categories of *unsentenced* mentally disordered prisoners. By virtue of subs.(3), a person removed to hospital under this section is placed in the same position as a person who has been made the subject of a transfer direction under s.47 which, among other things, means that he becomes subject to the consent to treatment provisions contained in Part IV: see the note on s.47(3). In 2011, the Department of Health published "Good Practice Procedure Guide: The transfer and remission of adult prisoners under s.47 and s.48 of the Mental Health Act" which can be accessed at: *www.gov.uk/government/ publications/the-transfer-and-remission-of-adult-prisoners-under-s47-and-s48-of-the- mental-health-act.*

A transfer direction made in respect of persons coming within categories (a) or (b) of subs.(2) *must* be made subject to the restrictions provided for in s.49 (s.49(1)). The Secretary of State has a discretion to direct that persons coming within categories (c) or (d) be made subject to such restrictions. In practice, the Secretary of State will always apply restrictions to a transfer under this section (Mental Health Unit Bulletin, March 2008).

It is submitted that the requirements placed on the Secretary of State in relation to s.47 transfers which were identified by Stanley Burnton J. in *R. (on the application of D) v Secretary of State for the Home Department and National Assembly for Wales* [2004] EWHC 2857 (Admin); [2005] M.H.L.R. 17 also apply to this section: see the General Note to s.47.

Restricted Patients Detained in Special Hospitals: Information for the Special Hospitals Service Authority, Home Office, undated, states at para.5.11: "It is important for responsible [clinicians] to bear in mind that prisoners transferred to hospital under [this section] will, in most cases, not have been tried and convicted, and consequentially they should be returned to court as soon as possible. If the responsible [clinician] believes the patient is not fit to return to court, there is provision under section 51(5) for the court to make a hospital order in the patient's absence and without convicting him".

L. Birmingham states that the

"main disadvantage of section 48 as a diversion mechanism is that if for any reason the subject ceases to be a prisoner on remand (for example, is bailed or the case collapses) the powers conveyed under section 48 cease with immediate effect. If there is a real risk of this happening a concurrent civil order (section 3 of the MHA) can be imposed" ("Diversion from custody" (2001) *Advances in Psychiatric Treatment,* 7, 198–207).

The use of a concurrent s.3 in this situation is of doubtful legality because, unlike the situation that obtained in *R. v North West Mental Health NHS Trust, Ex p. Stewart* which is noted under s.35, the application is not being made to provide professionals with powers which are immediately needed; it is being made as a contingency. The safer option would be to prepare for a possible application under s.3 by completing the statutory documentation with the exception of the signature on the application form. This could be added when the patient ceased to be a prisoner on remand.

Under s.117, health bodies and local social services authorities have a duty to provide after-care services for patients who have ceased to be liable to be detained and leave hospital after having been transferred under this section.

Code of Practice

1–649   The *Code* states:

"22.66 Section 48 empowers the Secretary of State for Justice by warrant to direct the removal to and detention in hospital for treatment of certain offenders such as those on remand, civil prisoners and immigration detainees. Restrictions may also be added under section 49. Subsequent attendance at court will require Secretary of State for Justice consent and will usually be given at the time of admission. Should the patient be subsequently acquitted by the court or the legal proceedings discontinued, the section 48/49 restricted transfer direction will cease and the responsible clinician in charge of the patient's care must either discharge or consider detention under part 2 of the Act.

22.67 Professionals should be aware that immigration detainees may be particularly vulnerable and may need additional support, including reasonable adjustments. Examples include the use of interpreters and an understanding of their culture, ethnicity or religion. Staff supporting these patients should be culturally competent.

22.68 Should a transfer request be made for a prisoner under sections 47 and 49 who is near the end of his or her sentence, the Secretary of State for Justice will apply heightened scrutiny to such a request to ensure that the criteria for transfer under the Act is satisfied and taking into account the potential lengthening of detention.

22.69 In exceptional circumstances, the Secretary of State for Justice may 'direct' a restricted patient's admission into hospital, outside of NHS commissioning arrangements. This is usually where it is critical that the patient receive treatment and identifying a suitable bed is difficult."

Leave of absence

1–650   The MHCS of the Ministry of Justice has published "Guidance—Section 17 Leave" (April 2014) which includes guidance on patients transferred under this section. The guidance can be accessed at: *www.justice.gov.uk/offenders/types-of-offender/mentally-dis-ordered-offenders*.

Applications to the First-tier Tribunal (Mental Health) or the Mental Health Review Tribunal for Wales
See subs.(3) and the note on s.47 under this heading.   **1–651**

Subsection (1)
REPORTS. See the notes on "reports" and "two registered medical practitioners" in **1–652** s.47(1).

MENTAL DISORDER. See the note on s.47(1)(a).

APPROPRIATE FOR HIM TO BE DETAINED ... FOR MEDICAL TREATMENT. But not for assessment. The Reed Committee said that "it is not always feasible for thorough assessments to be undertaken in prison: a hospital can usually offer greater flexibility and specialised expertise, especially in cases where diagnosis is problematic" (*Review of Health and Social Services for Mentally Disordered Offenders and others requiring similar services, Final Summary Report*, Cm. 2088, para.9.6 (v)).

URGENT NEED OF SUCH TREATMENT. The Home Office informed the Butler Committee that the procedure under this section is adopted only where a prisoner's condition is such that immediate removal to a hospital is necessary and that normally when he is well enough he is either produced at court from hospital or returned to prison to await trial (*ibid.*, para.3.38). The Reed Committee was "concerned ... that the requirement under section 48 that the need for treatment should be 'urgent' is often interpreted narrowly". The Committee concluded that this section "should be applied where a doctor would recommend in-patient treatment if a person were seen as an out-patient in the community" (Final Summary Report, above, para.9.6(iv). This approach has been adopted by the Government: see the "Procedure for the transfer of prisoners to and from hospital under sections 47 and 48 of the Mental Health Act (1983)" (2007) p.8.

NATURE OR DEGREE. See the note on s.3(2)(a).

APPROPRIATE MEDICAL TREATMENT. See the note on s.3(2)(d).

TRANSFER DIRECTION. Which will cease to have effect unless the prisoner is admitted to hospital within 14 days of it being given (s.47(2)).

Subsection (2)
A direction made under this section would terminate if the criminal proceedings are **1–653** dropped or if the person concerned ceases to be subject to detention by, for example, being granted bail.

PARAGRAPH (A). Persons coming within this category, who will be awaiting trial or sentence in the Crown Court, are subject to the further provisions contained in s.51.
The April 2011 edition of the Ministry of Justice Mental Health Casework Section Newsletter states:

"In the last edition we advised of concerns that a person remanded in custody by the Crown Court to a Young Offender Institution is not covered by the wording of s.48(2)(a) and that the Secretary of State therefore has no power to direct their transfer to hospital. Having taken further legal advice this is not correct.

Legally no court can remand a person 'to a YOI'. For 17-20 year olds the court can only remand to prison. However a YOI (whether as a whole or a particular cell) can be designated by NOMS as a prison. It follows that s.48(2)(a) does empower the Secretary of State to transfer to hospital a young offender remanded by the Crown Court and placed in a YOI even if it does not look like (s)he is detained in prison. This is the case only for 17-20 year olds (and certain 14-16 year old males) and only if the YOI or cell has been designated as a prison.

Except for a category of 14-16 year old males who may be remanded to prison, 10-16 year olds cannot be remanded to prison. They are remanded to local authority accommodation. If remanded by a Crown Court, the Secretary of State has no powers under s.48(2)(a) to direct their transfer to hospital. Such persons who need treatment in hospital can be remanded by the Crown Court, using its own powers, or admitted using civil powers.

Young people remanded by a magistrates' court may be transferred from wherever they are remanded to under s.48(2)(b)."

PARAGRAPH (B).   Persons coming within this category are subject to the further provisions contained in s.52.

This paragraph does *not* include children and young people remanded in local authority accommodation under section 23 of the Children and Young Persons Act 1969, regardless of whether they are placed in youth detention accommodation. These are "looked after" children, for whom care planning and placement decisions (including the decision to place a young person in youth detention accommodation) are matters for the responsible local authority, and in respect of whom arrangements for hospital admission/treatment will be made within the framework of s.22 of the Children Act 1989 and ss.2 and 3 of the 1983 Act: see para.2.1 and p.8 of *Procedure for the Transfer from Custody of Children and Young People to and from Hospital under the Mental Health Act 1983 in England*, Department of Health, 2011. Paragraph 5.9 of this document states:

"For those children and young people remanded in custody by a magistrates' court and made subject to a transfer direction under section 48(2)(b) of the Act, the transfer direction will cease to have effect at the expiry of the period of remand unless the child or young person is then committed in custody to the Crown Court. However, if the magistrates' court further remands the child or young person under section 52(3) of the Act, the direction will not expire. Alternatively, if the court is satisfied that the child or young person no longer requires treatment in hospital, it may direct that the transfer direction ceases to have effect."

PARAGRAPHS (C) AND (D).   Persons coming within these categories are subject to the further provisions contained in s.53.

PARAGRAPH (D).   Although the scope of this paragraph does not extend to those who are detained under the provisions of the UK Borders Act 2007, the principle of law identified by Stanley Burnton J. in *R. (on the application of D) v Secretary of State for the Home Department and National Assembly for Wales*, which is considered in the General Note to s.47, is equally applicable in the context of Immigration Removal Centres, including detention under the 2007 Act (*R.(on the application of HA (Nigeria) v Secretary of State for the Home Department* [2012] EWHC 979 (Admin), paras 127, 169).

In *R. (on the application of BA) v Secretary of State for the Home Department* [2011] EWHC 2748 (Admin), para.125, Elisabeth Laing QC, sitting as a Deputy Judge of the High Court, considered whether, on the expiry of his sentence, BA was simply detained pursuant to this section, or whether he was subject to "dual detention"; in other words, detention in hospital pursuant this section, and, at the same time, immigration detention under para.2(1) of Sch.3 to the Immigration Act 1971. Her Ladyship held that, "BA must have been subject to dual detention. I say this because, on the view I take of paragraph 2(1) . . ., it requires detention from the end of a prisoner's custodial term. . . . A 'hospital' as defined in the 1983 Act is one of the places in which immigration detention may occur".

Restriction on discharge of prisoners removed to hospital

49.—(1) Where a transfer direction is given in respect of any person, the **1–654** Secretary of State, if he thinks fit, may by warrant further direct that that person shall be subject to the special restrictions set out in section 41 above; and where the Secretary of State gives a transfer direction in respect of any such person as is described in paragraph (a) or (b) of section 48(2) above, he shall also give a direction under this section applying those restrictions to him.

(2) A direction under this section shall have the same effect as a restriction order made under section 41 above and shall be known as "a restriction direction".

(3) While a person is subject to a restriction direction the [responsible clinician] shall at such intervals (not exceeding one year) as the Secretary of State may direct examine and report to the Secretary of State on that person; and every report shall contain such particulars as the Secretary of State may require.

AMENDMENT
The words in square brackets in subs.(3) were inserted by the Mental Health Act 2007 s.10(9).

DEFINITIONS
transfer direction: ss.47, 145(1).   **1–655**
responsible clinician: s.55(1).

GENERAL NOTE
This section provides that the Secretary of State may, and in respect of certain prisoners **1–656** must, add an order restricting the patient's discharge from hospital (a "restriction direction") to a transfer direction made under s.47. The patient then becomes a restricted patient (s.79). The effect of a restriction direction is explained in the following passage from the judgment of the Court of Appeal in *R. v Birch* (1989) 11 Cr. App. R.(S.) 202 at 212:

"If the transfer direction under section 47 is coupled with a restriction direction by the Home Secretary under section 49 (as in practice it usually is), the offender's position is in many ways the same as if he had been sent straight to hospital with order under sections 37 and 41, but the following special provisions apply: (1) Where the offender was sentenced to a fixed term of imprisonment, the restriction will automatically lift on the expiry of his sentence (allowing for remission) [the "release date"]: section 50(2). (2) Where the responsible clinician or the [tribunal] concludes that the offender no longer requires treatment in hospital for mental disorder or that no effective treatment for his disorder can be given, the Secretary of State may: (a) release him on parole (if he is eligible), (b) return him to prison to serve out his sentence, or (c) take no action [: section 50(1)]."

A patient who ceases to be subject to a restriction direction because his sentence has expired is sometimes referred to as being subject to a "notional section 37". This term, which is not found in the Act, is used to signify that on the expiry of the sentence the patient is still subject to the s.47 transfer direction which has the same legal effect as a hospital order made under s.37. A restricted patient whose restriction order has ceased to have effect is treated as if he had been admitted to hospital as an unrestricted patient on the date when the restriction order ceased to have effect (s.41(5)). Paragraph 22.77 of the *Code of Practice* states:

> "When a transferred offender becomes unrestricted, there is still a period when, if released, they will be subject to licence conditions and management by the National Probation Service. Hospitals should remain in contact with the offender manager and victim liaison officer therefore until the end of sentence."

If the Secretary of State is informed by the patient's RC or the tribunal that the patient no longer requires treatment in hospital or that no effective treatment can be given in the hospital to which he has been removed, he may exercise his power of direction under s.50.

Paragraph 5.12 of *Procedure for the Transfer from Custody of Children and Young People to and from Hospital under the Mental Health Act 1983 in England*, Department of Health, 2011 states:

> "Restriction directions made under section 49 of the Act in the case of children or young people originally in custody for reasons other than a custodial sentence or remand (civil or immigration detainees) cease to have effect, along with the transfer direction, on the expiration of the period during which the child or young person would, but for their removal to hospital, be liable to be detained in the place from which they were transferred."

In *R. (on the application of T) v Secretary of State for the Home Department* [2003] EWHC Admin 538; [2003] M.H.L.R. 239, an official in the Mental Health Unit wrote to the patient's responsible clinician declining to lift the restriction direction that had been made in respect of the patient and referred to the policy of the Secretary of State in the following terms:

> "Our normal policy is always to make a restriction direction unless it is proposed to transfer the prisoner to hospital within days of his release date and the nature of the offence suggests that restrictions are unnecessary for the protection of the public from serious harm over that short period."

The patient's challenge to this policy on the ground that a restriction order should only be imposed where there is a need for public protection was rejected by Maurice Kay J. His Lordship said that the analogy that had been made with an order made by a court under s.37 was wrong, as when making orders under this section, the Secretary of State did not stand in the shoes of the sentencing court. Rather, the Secretary of State is concerned with a person who has already been sentenced to a term of imprisonment by a court, which has not yet been fully served. Without a restriction direction a person properly sentenced to a term of imprisonment would pass wholly into the hands of the medical authorities so far as the regaining of liberty was concerned.

Named hospital units

1–657   Section 47 of the Crime (Sentences) Act 1997 provides that where the Secretary of State makes an order under this section he has the power to order that the patient be admitted to and detained in a named hospital unit. A named hospital unit can be any part of a hospital which is treated as a separate unit. The effect of this power is considered in the General Note to s.41 under this heading.

Leave of absence

1–658   The MHCS of the Ministry of Justice has published "Guidance—Section 17 Leave" (April 2014) which includes guidance on patients who have been made subject to a restriction direction. The guidance can be accessed at: *www.justice.gov.uk/offenders/types-of-offender/mentally-disordered-offenders*.

Applications to the First-tier Tribunal (Mental Health) or the Mental Health Review Tribunal for Wales

A patient who is subject to a restriction direction may apply to a tribunal within six **1–659** months of the date of the direction, once during the following six months, and at yearly intervals thereafter (s.69(2)(b)). The tribunal has no power to direct the patient's discharge: see s.74.

Remissions to Prison

The March 2008 issue of the Mental Health Unit Bulletin contains the following **1–660** statement:

"The Secretary of State can remit to prison any patient transferred under sections 47/49 (or sections 48/49 provided he is not remanded to appear at a Magistrates' Court) to hospital if the [RC] advises that it is no longer necessary for the patient to receive treatment in hospital, or if the patient presents as untreatable. In these circumstances, the [RC] should write to the [MHCS] recommending a return to prison. The [RC] should also source the prison to which the patient should return, most often the prison from which they came. If this is not possible, however, that prison must find an alternative establishment. Once a section 117 meeting has been held and both parties (hospital and prison) have confirmed that they are content for the remission to take place, [MHCS] will issue a remission warrant.

Further details . . . can be found in Prison Service Instruction 50/2007."

Domestic Violence, Crime and Victims Act 2004

See Ch.40 of the *Code of Practice*. The Department of Health has published "Mental **1–661** Health Act 2007: Guidance on the extension of victims' rights under the Domestic Violence, Crime and Victims Act" (2008).

Human Rights Act 1998

See the note on "technical lifer", below. **1–662**

Technical lifer

A "technical lifer" is a person who, although sentenced to life imprisonment (whether **1–663** discretionary or mandatory) will in certain circumstances be treated as though he had originally been made the subject of a hospital order and a restriction order made under ss.37 and 41. "Technical lifer" is a non-statutory status, based on an administrative process entirely within the discretion of the Secretary of State. In *R. (on the application of IR) v Dr G Shetty and the Secretary of State for the Home Department* [2003] EWHC 3152 (Admin); [2004] M.H.L.R. 130, Munby J. rejected a claim that the procedure for attaining "technical lifer" status was a "sentencing exercise" which breached art.6 of the European Convention on Human Rights (ECHR). His Lordship commented, at para.10, that from the claimant's perspective "technical lifer" was "a desirable status because (a) he cannot in any circumstances be returned to prison, (b) he becomes entitled under art.5(4) of [the ECHR] to periodic reviews of the lawfulness of his detention even if his tariff period has not expired (see *Van Droogenbroeck v Belgium* (1982) 4 E.H.R.R. 443 and *Benjamin and Wilson v United Kingdom* (2003) 36 E.H.R.R. 1) and (c) (see *Benjamin and Wilson v United Kingdom*, paras 28, 30) he will be entitled to his liberty if [a tribunal] so recommends".

In *R. v Secretary of State for the Home Department Ex p. Williams*, June 21, 1994, unreported, the court said:

"The effect of being classified as a 'technical lifer' is that the patient is treated, for the purposes of discharge, as though a hospital order under section 37 and a restriction order under section 41 of the 1983 Act had been made instead of the imposition of a sentence of imprisonment. He is treated with a view to rehabilitation and eventual release direct from hospital into the community. His case will not be referred to the Parole Board and he will not be released on life licence."

In *R. v Beatty* [2006] EWCA Crim 2359, para.53, Scott Baker L.J. said that if "the decision is made that a transferred prisoner should be treated as a 'technical lifer', the Home Office [now the Ministry of Justice] guarantees:

(i) that the 'technical lifer' will not return to prison when he is well enough to leave hospital;

(ii) that his tariff date will no longer be taken into consideration in deciding whether he is entitled to be discharged into the community; and

(iii) that when he leaves hospital, [he] will go out on absolute or conditional discharge under the Mental Health Act rather than on life licence."

In *Williams*, above, the court was informed that the Home Office [now the Ministry of Justice] has an equivalent system for determinate sentence prisoners:

"... the Home Office does in fact recognise that there may be exceptional circumstances in which a determinate sentence prisoner should be rehabilitated through the hospital system and not returned to prison, even though his earliest date of release is someway ahead. This would be justifiable in cases where there was clear evidence that the sentencing Court did not dispose of the case by means of a hospital order for the kind of reason which influences the Home Office in conferring 'technical lifer' status on a transferred life sentence prisoner."

A "technical lifer" can be discharged from hospital in three possible ways. Each can be initiated only by the Secretary of State. They are:

1. A conditional or absolute discharge made under s.42(2).

2. A discharge made under s.50(1)(b).

3. Through the operation of s.74(2).

In *Benjamin and Wilson v United Kingdom* (2003) 36 E.H.R.R. 1, the European Court of Human Rights held that s.74(2) violates art.5(4) of the ECHR because the power of discharge rests with the Secretary of State rather than the tribunal. This decision prompted the Parliamentary Under-Secretary of State for the Home Department to make the following Written Ministerial Statement (House of Commons Hansard, January 24, 2005):

"From 2 April 2005, life sentence prisoners who have been transferred to psychiatric hospitals for treatment will no longer be considered for technical lifer status. All life sentence prisoners will have their future release determined by the Parole Board and be subject to life licence on release. This decision has been taken in the light of the judgment in the case of *Benjamin and Wilson v the United Kingdom*, which found that technical lifer policy was in breach of Art.5(4) of the European Convention on Human Rights. This will not affect those who have already been granted technical lifer status, or the consideration of any pending applications. No new applications, however, will be considered after 2 April 2005."

Those who were preparing to seek "technical lifer" status at the time when the above announcement was made had no entitlement to continue, nor had they a legitimate expectation to be consulted over the change of policy (*R. (on the application of Donaldson and Barker) v Home Secretary* [2006] EWHC 1107 (Admin); [2006] M.H.L.R. 100).

In *R. v Beatty,* above at para.59, the court said that the Criminal Cases Review Commission had pointed out that while the effect of a patient's "technical lifer" status may be identical to a hospital order there are potential benefits for the patient and the criminal justice system for a life sentence to be replaced with a hospital order. These are:

(i) the unequivocal placement of someone who is mentally disordered into a regime of expert medical care from which he can progress, if it becomes appropriate, into a less secure regime under proper supervision and safeguards; and

(ii) the substitution would reflect the change of approach signalled by the decision in *Benjamin and Wilson* and contained in the Home Office decision to make no further use of "technical lifer" status.

The court said, at paras 61, 62:

"Bearing in mind the criteria for granting 'technical lifer' status we think it very difficult to envisage circumstances where, 'technical lifer' status having been granted, the court would not substitute a hospital order with a restriction order for a life sentence. 'Technical lifer' status is only afforded if the prisoner is treatable.

It is obviously important, perhaps even more so now that 'technical lifer' status is no longer granted, that those who should have been the subject of a hospital order under sections 37/41 rather than life imprisonment should have the position rectified on appeal. That said, however, the court will always scrutinise with great care cases in which an appellant seeks to rely on psychiatric evidence directed to his mental state at the date of sentence that was not advanced at the time. Each case is likely to be decided on its own specific facts."

Subsection (1)
IF HE THINKS FIT.   The Secretary of State is not bound by any statutory criteria when **1–664** exercising his judgment under this provision.

Subsection (2)
While a restriction direction is in force, the transfer direction also remains in force and **1–665** does not need to be renewed. For further provisions, see s.50. The Secretary of State does not have the power to make a time limited restriction direction.

Subsection (3)
REPORT.   See the note on s.41(6).   **1–666**

Further provisions as to prisoners under sentence
50.—(1) Where a transfer direction and a restriction direction have been given **1–667** in respect of a person serving a sentence of imprisonment and before [his release date] the Secretary of State is notified by the [responsible clinician], any other [approved clinician] or [the appropriate tribunal] that that person no longer requires treatment in hospital for mental disorder or that no effective treatment for his disorder can be given in the hospital to which he has been removed, the Secretary of State may—

(a) by warrant direct that he be remitted to any prison or other institution in which he might have been detained if he had not been removed to hospital, there to be dealt with as if he had not been so removed; or

(b) exercise any power of releasing him on licence or discharging him under supervision which would have been exercisable if he had been remitted to such a prison or institution as aforesaid, and on his arrival in the prison or other institution or, as the case may be, his release or discharge as aforesaid, the transfer direction and the restriction direction shall cease to have effect.

[(2) A restriction direction in the case of a person serving a sentence of imprisonment shall cease to have effect, if it has not previously done so, on his release date.

(3) In this section, references to a person's release date are to the day (if any) on which he would be entitled to be released (whether unconditionally or on licence) from any prison or other institution in which he might have been detained if the transfer direction had not been given; and in determining that day there shall be disregarded—

(a) any powers that would be exercisable by the Parole Board if he were detained in such a prison or other institution, and

(b) any practice of the Secretary of State in relation to the early release under discretionary powers of persons detained in such a prison or other institution.]

(4) For the purposes of section 49(2) of the Prison Act 1952 (which provides for discounting from the sentences of certain prisoners periods while they are unlawfully at large) a patient who, having been transferred in pursuance of a transfer direction from any such institution as is referred to in that section, is at large in circumstances in which he is liable to be taken into custody under any provision of this Act, shall be treated as unlawfully at large and absent from that institution.

[(5) The preceding provisions of this section shall have effect as if—

(a) the reference in subsection (1) to a transfer direction and a restriction direction having been given in respect of a person serving a sentence of imprisonment included a reference to a hospital direction and a limitation direction having been given in respect of a person sentenced to imprisonment;

(b) the reference in subsection (2) to a restriction direction included a reference to a limitation direction; and

(c) references in subsections (3) and (4) to a transfer direction included references to a hospital direction.]

AMENDMENTS

The amendments to this section were made by the Criminal Justice Act 2003 s.294, the Mental Health Act 2007 s.11(2), SI 2008/2883 art.9, Sch.3 para.42 and the Crime (Sentences) Act 1997 s.55, Sch.4 para.12(4)(5).

DEFINITIONS

1–668 transfer direction: ss.47, 145(1).
restriction direction: ss.49, 145(1).
hospital: ss.55(5), 145(1).
mental disorder: ss.1, 145(1).
patient: s.145(1).
responsible clinician: s.55(1).
approved clinician: s.145(1).
the appropriate tribunal: ss.66(4), 145(1).
hospital direction: s.145(1).
limitation direction: s.145(1).

GENERAL NOTE

This section provides that if the Secretary of State is informed that a patient who has been **1–669** placed on a restriction direction or a hospital and limitation direction no longer requires treatment in hospital for mental disorder or that no effective treatment for his disorder can be given in the hospital to which he has been removed, he may either direct that the patient be returned to prison to serve the remainder of his sentence or release him from hospital on the same terms on which he could be released from prison. In both instances, the transfer direction and the restriction direction cease to have effect (subs.(1)). This section also provides for a restriction direction in the case of a person serving a sentence of imprisonment to cease to have effect on the day when he would be entitled to be released from prison (subss.(2),(3)).

If a patient subject to a restriction direction is in hospital when the restrictions cease to have effect, he will remain in hospital as a detained patient subject to a hospital order made under s.37 on the day when the restriction order ceased to have effect (s.41(5)). Such a patient is often referred to as being the subject of a "notional hospital order", a term that is not found in the Act.

In *R. (on the application of Pendlebury) v Secretary of State for Justice* [2013] EWHC 3613 (Admin); [2014] M.H.L.R. 234, Recorder Fordham QC said that the judgment of Munby J. in *IR*, below, contained "a helpful description of three key questions which arise in the context of s.50". They are firstly the "s.50(1) question: does the claimant any longer require treatment in hospital for mental disorder? Or: is there any longer effective treatment for his disorder that can be given in hospital? Question 2: does the claimant's mental condition continue to be such as to warrant his compulsory confinement in a suitable therapeutic environment other than a prison? The article 5 question. Question 3: if the claimant is remitted to prison, is it more likely than not that he will suffer treatment at the hands of the prison authorities so damaging to him as to amount to inhuman or degrading treatment within the meaning of Article 3 ? The Article 3 question". In *Pendlebury*, the patient failed in his claim that the Secretary of State has acted unlawfully when issuing a warrant under this section on being notified by the patient's responsible clinician (RC) that the statutory criteria were satisfied on the ground that she had not accepted a finding of the first-tier tribunal that it was necessary for the patient to remain in hospital and to be treated there. The claim failed because the judge found that the RC had conscientiously re-evaluated and confirmed his opinion that the patient should be remitted to prison in the light of the tribunal's determination. The Secretary of State therefore had objective justification for the conclusion that the patient no longer required treatment in hospital.

The Secretary of State "also has the power, under s.42(2), on his own motion at any time, and under s.74(2), to authorise the [tribunal] to arrange for the discharge of a prisoner who has been transferred to a mental hospital"; per Rose L.J. in *R. v Secretary of State for the Home Department Ex p. Hickey (No.1)* [1995] 1 All E.R. 479 at 483 CA.

Human Rights Act 1998

In the *Morley* case, noted under subs.(1), the applicant contended that his right to respect **1–670** for his privacy under art.8 of the European Convention on Human Rights (ECHR) had been breached by virtue of his transfer from hospital to prison. The Court of Appeal dismissed this argument for the following reason:

"In the absence of a breach of another article or articles, the convention does not render unlawful that interference with private life which inevitably follows from a lawfully imposed custodial sentence. Transfer from prison to hospital and hospital back to prison, as a part of a high-security custodial regime, cannot in present circumstances be said to be breach the article notwithstanding the differences in medical treatment which may occur" (para.49).

The patient's complaint to the European Court of Human Rights was declared inadmissible (*Morley v United Kingdom* (2005) 40 E.H.R.R. SE8; [2005] M.H.L.R. 174). The Court said at para.47:

> "Even assuming, however, that the difference in regimes between the hospital and prison could be considered by itself as affecting the applicant's private life, the Court considers such interference may be regarded as complying with the second paragraph of Art.8 namely as a measure 'in accordance with the law', pursuing the aims of the prevention of disorder and crime and protection of the rights of others, as well as being 'necessary in a democratic society' for those aims".

Any argument that there are breaches of rights under the ECHR concerned with the operation of this section should be raised against the Secretary of State rather than the patient's RC, who is exercising only a clinical judgment and cannot be challenged on Convention grounds (*R. (on the application of IR) v Dr G Shetty and the Home Secretary* [2003] EWHC 3022 (Admin); [2004] M.H.L.R. 111 para.39).

Also see the note on s.74 under this heading.

Subsection (1)

1–671   In *R. (on the application of Morley) v Nottinghamshire Health Care NHS Trust* [2002] EWCA Civ 1728; [2003] 1 All E.R. 784, the Court of Appeal held that:

1. The issue under this provision is treatability and the Secretary of State's decision necessarily turns upon a clinical judgment, that of the RC, and if that judgment was fairly and rationally made, a duty in the Secretary of State to permit and consider representations from the patient does not arise.

2. There will be cases in which circumstances, including information available to the Secretary of State, either in the documents by which the notification is given, or from other sources, create a duty in the Secretary of State to make further inquiries or take further action or both.

3. The duty upon a RC before giving a notification to the Secretary of State is to make full and fair enquiries within the hospital as to whether the treatability test is satisfied and to consider views expressed, as well as his own first hand knowledge and experience, before making a recommendation. He is not placed under a duty to disclose reports on individual components of the patient's medical regime or to present to the Secretary of State contrary views which may have been expressed by some members of the inter-disciplinary team. The extent of enquiry and of disclosure of information will depend upon the circumstances of the particular case and will normally be judged as at the moment of decision.

In *R. (on the application of W) v Larkin and the Secretary of State for Justice* [2012] EWHC 556 (Admin); [2012] M.H.L.R. 161, Ouseley J., in a permission hearing, held that the two limbs of the test for a transfer back to prison under this section are not mutually exclusive. It is therefore not unlawful for an RC to tick both the "no longer requires treatment in hospital for mental disorder" and the "no effective treatment for his disorder can be given in the hospital to which he has been removed" boxes on the proforma that is used when a notification is made to the Secretary of State. His Lordship said at para.38:

> "[I]n circumstances where it may be appropriate, but not required, for someone to receive treatment for a disorder in a hospital, notwithstanding its availability to a considerable degree in the prison state, but, where it is not available to the hospital where he is currently detained, both boxes can sensibly be ticked "no", as was done here."

Confirmation that a patient can be remitted to prison in a situation where treatment was not required within a hospital but it could be provided there was given in *R. (on the application of RW) v Secretary of State for Justice* [2012] EWHC 2082 (Admin); [2012] M.H.L.R. 288, para.20.

If the Secretary of State accepts the RC's advice that the patient no longer requires treatment in hospital for a mental disorder, he has a wide and unfettered discretion as to what to do with the patient; a discretion which entitles him to take into account a wide range of facts, some no doubt referable to the patient himself but others referable to wider considerations of the public interest and in any event extending far beyond the purely clinical (*R. (on the application of IR) v Dr G Shetty and the Home Secretary*, above, para.26).

TRANSFER DIRECTION AND A RESTRICTION DIRECTION.   See subs.(5)(a).

SERVING A SENTENCE OF IMPRISONMENT.   See s.55(6).

RELEASE DATE.   See subs.(3).

NOTIFIED BY THE RESPONSIBLE CLINICIAN.   The RC should notify the Mental Health Casework section at the Ministry of Justice at once in writing if she considers that a patient meets the criteria set out in this subsection.

ANY OTHER APPROVED CLINICIAN.   In the *Morley* case, above, Burton J., sitting at first instance, was informed by counsel for the Secretary of State that notification from this clinician is, in practice, restricted to a situation in which such a clinician "is for some reason standing in for the [RC], and if it were any other medical practitioner plainly any such recommendation would have to be looked at carefully indeed by the [Secretary of State] to see whether it was appropriate to act on it" ([2003] M.H.L.R.88 at para.29).

EFFECTIVE TREATMENT.   This probably means treatment that will benefit the patient: see s.145(4).

MAY.   It is not possible to construe this provision so as to impose a duty on the Secretary of State (*R. (on the application of D) v Secretary of State for the Home Department* [2002] EWHC Admin 2805; [2003] 1 W.L.R. 1315 at para.29).

Paragraph (a)
Once a life sentenced patient no longer requires treatment in hospital, the normal course **1–672** is for the Secretary of State to remit him to prison under this paragraph where he would be eligible for a Parole Board hearing as appropriate in the normal manner.

BY WARRANT.   There is no provision for a time limit to be attached to the warrant.

Paragraph (b)
In 1985, the Home Secretary made the following policy statement on life sentence pris- **1–673** oners in response to a Parliamentary Question:

"When life sentence prisoners transferred to hospital under the Mental Health Act 1983 are to be released, it has hitherto been the practice to discharge such persons on a warrant of conditional discharge under section 42(3) of the Act. I now intend to use the powers available to me under section 50(1)(b) of the Act, which enables me to release such persons under the same arrangements as those they would have been subject to had they remained in, or been returned to, prison. This means that, in future, such persons will normally be released on life licences under the provisions of section 61 of the Criminal Justice Act 1967 [now see section 28 of the Crime (Sentences) Act 1997] in accordance with the sentencing Courts' intention, i.e. on the recommendation of the Parole Board and after consultation with the Lord Chief Justice and, if available, the trial judge. In exceptional cases, where the Lord Chief Justice and the trial judge so recommend, I will be prepared to consider whether it would be more appropriate to authorise discharge under section 42(2) of the 1983 Act.

Under the new procedure, a life sentence prisoner who has been transferred to hospital, can be released on life licence without having to return to prison before release. Persons released on life licence under these arrangements will be subject to recall to prison under the provisions of section 62 of the 1967 Act [now see s.254 of the Criminal Justice Act 2003]. Should their mental condition be such that they are recommended for transfer to hospital this could very quickly be effected under the provisions of section 47 of the 1983 Act."

This policy was challenged in *R. v Secretary of State for the Home Department Ex p. Stroud* [1993] C.O.D. 75. The applicant stated that a life prisoner released from prison on licence remains subject to supervision for the rest of his life whereas release under ss.42(2) or 74(2) allowed for the possibility of an eventual absolute discharge either by the Secretary of State or by a tribunal. He contended that the normal rule of practice set out in the policy statement deprived life sentence prisoners of the potential benefit of absolute discharge and thus the Secretary of State had fettered his discretion unlawfully. Henry J. held, in refusing the application for judicial review, that there was no illegality in the policy which had been adopted for legitimate reasons to ensure consistency of treatment between all those sentenced to life imprisonment.

In *R. v Secretary of State for the Home Department Ex p. Hickey (No.1)* [1995] 1 All E.R. 479, the principal question before the Court of Appeal was whether a prisoner sentenced either to a discretionary life term or to be detained during Her Majesty's pleasure, transferred subsequently to a hospital by the Secretary of State under ss.47 and 49 and who has served the tariff part of his sentence, can require the Secretary of State so to act that his case is considered by the Parole Board, notwithstanding that he is still in hospital needing, and receiving, treatment. The court held that a person who had been made the subject of such a transfer was governed by the regime laid down in the Mental Health Act and had no right to have his case referred to the Parole Board.

In *R. v Vowles* [2015] EWCA Crim 45, the Court of Appeal held at paras 31 et seq that if a prisoner is sentenced to an indeterminate sentence of imprisonment and then transferred to hospital under ss.47 and 49, the ECHR did not require the lawfulness of his detention to be reviewed by a single body, exercising the functions of both tribunal and the Parole Board; also see *R. (on the application of P) v Secretary of State for the Home Department* [2003] EWHC 2953 (Admin); [2004] M.H.L.R. 64.

Life prisoners who have been transferred to hospital under the Act, and whom it is not appropriate to remit to prison even though they no longer require, or can effectively be given, hospital treatment will be referred by the Secretary of State to the Parole Board, while they remain in hospital, in the same way as if they had been remitted to prison (245 HC Official Report (6th series) written answers, col.9, 20 June 1994 and *Hickey,* above, at 485, 486).

Subsection (2)

1–674   RESTRICTION DIRECTION.   See subs.(5)(b).

CEASE TO HAVE EFFECT.   The patient is to be treated as if he had been admitted to hospital under a hospital order without restrictions on the day when the restriction direction ceased to have effect (ss.49(2), 41(5)).

Unsurprisingly, a life sentence ceases to have effect on the death of the person concerned (*D v Secretary of State for the Home Department* [2002] EWHC Admin 2805 at para.30).

Subsection (3)

TRANSFER DIRECTION. Or hospital direction (subs.(5)(c)). **1–675**

Subsection (4)

"The effect of subsection (4), and the clear intention behind it, is that if an individual **1–676** absconds from the mental hospital to which he is transferred that will be treated as him being unlawfully at large, as if the hospital were the prison from which he absconded", per Collins J. in *R. (on the application of Miah) v Secretary of State for the Home Department* [2004] EWHC 2569 (Admin); [2004] M.H.L.R. 302 at para.30.

In *R. (on the application of S) v Secretary of State for the Home Department* [2003] EWCA Civ 426; [2003] M.H.L.R. 264 at para.22, the court accepted as correct the following submission made by counsel for the Secretary of State:

"Section 50(4) of the 1983 Act places those transferred from prison to hospital under sections 47 and 48 on the same footing as those still in prison: it ensures that anyone absconding from either will be treated in the same way. But section 50(4) deals only with abscondees from hospital transferred 'from any such institution as is referred to in [section 49(2)]', that is from prisons and the like, and it dictates that they be 'treated as unlawfully at large and absent from that institution'. It says nothing about those detained in hospital otherwise than pursuant to a transfer direction (under section 47 or section 48) with the result that patients detained under other provisions of the 1983 Act, notably sections 2 and 3, are to be regarded as at large irrespective of whether they are in fact in hospital or have absconded from hospital and are liable to be taken back in custody under section 18".

The court was informed that the problem that arose in this case is unlikely to recur as the Prison Service is being instructed that when the revocation of a license is requested and the offender is already sectioned under the Act, a s.47 transfer direction (which would supersede the s.2 or s.3 (ss.40(5), 55(4))) is to be sought at the same time as the revocation request is being dealt with. This is to ensure that any revocation and transfer would operate simultaneously and so avoid the recall of an offender still subject to the s.2 or s.3 (para.32).

TRANSFER DIRECTION. Or hospital direction (subs.(5)(c)).

Further provisions as to detained persons

51.—(1) This section has effect where a transfer direction has been given in **1–677** respect of any such person as is described in paragraph (a) of section 48(2) above and that person is in this section referred to as "the detainee".

(2) The transfer direction shall cease to have effect when the detainee's case is disposed of by the court having jurisdiction to try or otherwise deal with him, but without prejudice to any power of that court to make a hospital order or other order under this Part of this Act in his case.

(3) If the Secretary of State is notified by the [responsible clinician], any other [approved clinician] or [the appropriate tribunal] at any time before the detainee's case is disposed of by that court—

(a) that the detainee no longer requires treatment in hospital for mental disorder; or

(b) that no effective treatment for his disorder can be given at the hospital to which he has been removed,

the Secretary of State may by warrant direct that he be remitted to any place where he might have been detained if he had not been removed to hospital, there to be dealt with as if he had not been so removed, and on his arrival at the place to which he is so remitted the transfer direction shall cease to have effect.

(4) If (no direction having been given under subsection (3) above) the court having jurisdiction to try or otherwise deal with the detainee is satisfied on the written or oral evidence of the [responsible clinician]—

(a) that the detainee no longer requires treatment in hospital for mental disorder; or

(b) that no effective treatment for his disorder can be given at the hospital to which he has been removed,

the court may order him to be remitted to any such place as is mentioned in subsection (3) above or[, subject to section 25 of the Criminal Justice and Public Order Act 1994,] released on bail and on his arrival at that place or, as the case may be, his release on bail the transfer direction shall cease to have effect.

(5) If (no direction or order having been given or made under subsection (3) or (4) above) it appears to the court having jurisdiction to try or otherwise deal with the detainee—

(a) that it is impracticable or inappropriate to bring the detainee before the court; and

(b) that the conditions set out in subsection (6) below are satisfied,

the court may make a hospital order (with or without a restriction order) in his case in his absence and, in the case of a person awaiting trial, without convicting him.

(6) A hospital order may be made in respect of a person under subsection (5) above if the court—

(a) is satisfied, on the written or oral evidence of at least two registered medical practitioners, that:

[(i) the detainee is suffering from mental disorder of a nature or degree which makes it appropriate for the patient to be detained in a hospital for medical treatment;][and

(ii) appropriate medical treatment is available for him; and]

(b) is of the opinion, after considering any depositions or other documents required to be sent to the proper officer of the court, that it is proper to make such an order.

(7) Where a person committed to the Crown Court to be dealt with under section 43 above is admitted to a hospital in pursuance of an order under section 44 above, subsections (5) and (6) above shall apply as if he were a person subject to a transfer direction.

AMENDMENTS

The amendments to this section were made by SI 2008/2883 art.9, Sch.3 para.43, the Criminal Justice and Public Order Act 1994 s.168(2), Sch.10 para.51 and the Mental Health Act 2007 ss.1(4), 5(4), 10(3), Sch.1 para.12.

DEFINITIONS

1–678   transfer direction: ss.47, 145(1).

hospital order: ss.37, 145(1).

responsible clinician: s.55(1).

approved clinician: s.145(1).

the appropriate tribunal: ss.66(4), 145(1).

hospital: ss.55(5), 145(1).

mental disorder: ss.1, 145(1).

appropriate medical treatment: ss.3(4), 145(1AB).

restriction order: ss.41, 145(1).

medical treatment: s.145(1), (4).

GENERAL NOTE

This section provides that a transfer direction made in respect of a person detained in a **1–679** prison or remand centre shall cease to have effect when the case has been finally dealt with by the appropriate court (subs.(2)). The linked restriction direction will also cease to have effect at that time. In the meanwhile the Secretary of State has power to direct the patient's return to prison (subs.(3)). If the Secretary of State does not exercise this power, the court can, on receiving the requisite evidence, either order the patient to be returned to prison or released on bail (subs.(4)). The transfer direction will cease to have effect if the Secretary of State or court exercise their powers under subss.(3) and (4). If the patient has not been sent back to prison or released on bail, the court can make a hospital order in respect of a mentally disordered patient in his absence and without convicting him (subss.(5), (6)).

Human Rights Act 1998

The power of the court under subss.(5) and (6) to make a hospital order in the absence of **1–680** a conviction or a finding that the person concerned "did the act or made the omission charged" (as required by, for example, s.37(3)), would appear to be a breach of art.6 of the European Convention on Human Rights in that the court has passed sentence in the absence of a trial.

Subsection (3)

NOTIFIED BY THE RESPONSIBLE CLINICIAN. See the note on s.50(1). **1–681**

NO EFFECTIVE TREATMENT. A stronger test than the "appropriate treatment" test required by s.3(2)(d).

Subsection (4)

WRITTEN OR ORAL EVIDENCE. For general requirements as to medical evidence, see **1–682** s.54.

Subsection (5)

This provision, together with subs.(6), enables the court to make a hospital order (with or **1–683** without restrictions) in respect of a mentally disordered accused person who is awaiting trial without bringing that person before the court.

In *R. (on the application of Kenneally) v Snaresbrook Crown Court* [2001] EWHC Admin. 968; [2002] M.H.L.R. 53 DC para.35, Pill L.J. said that to "pass sentence, even a sentence one of the objects of which is to assist the defendant, without first convicting him is a drastic step, one that should be taken only in exceptional circumstances". In this case, the court held that it was not clear whether the power to make an order under this provision was an exercise of the Crown Court's jurisdiction in matters relating to trial on indictment within the meaning of s.29(3) of the Senior Courts Act 1981, which precludes any jurisdiction in the High Court to quash the order. The High Court did, however, have the power to quash the order if the Crown Court made a relevant jurisdictional error. Tomlinson J. said at para.52: "[I]t seems to me anomalous that the Crown Court should have and should exercise a jurisdiction affecting the liberty of the subject which apparently admits of no direct right of appeal or review". Also see the note on "without convicting him", below.

INAPPROPRIATE. In *Kenneally*, Pill L.J. said, at para.32, that this word,

"must be construed restrictively. [Section 51(5)] must not be used as a routine and easy way of avoiding a potentially troublesome trial. To construe it as 'sparing a defendant a trial' is superficially attractive, especially when the outcome of the trial is readily predictable, but there is a public interest as well as that of the defendant himself in the resolution of issues, and especially when the failure to resolve them . . . may have difficult and long term implications. I would not necessarily restrict the word 'inappropriate' so as to mean 'physically impossible' but a high degree of disablement or relevant disorder must be present. The section does not apply in a situation in which all that is involved is possible inconvenience for the Court and inevitable distress for the defendant and others likely to be concerned in a trial, if a trial is held".

HOSPITAL ORDER (WITH OR WITHOUT A RESTRICTION ORDER).   A judge, prior to the imposition of a restriction order under s.41, following the making of a hospital order under this provision, is not obliged to resolve any factual dispute between the Crown case and the defence case before he makes a finding that the "serious harm" criterion in s.41(1) is satisfied (*R. v Kingston Crown Court Ex p. Mason*, July 27, 1998, CA).

PERSON AWAITING TRIAL.   Once the trial has commenced, any question relating to the mental fitness of the accused to be tried must be determined under s.4 of the Criminal Procedure (Insanity) Act 1964 and not under this provision (*R. v Griffiths* [2002] EWCA Crim 1762; [2002] M.H.L.R. 407). In *Griffiths*, the court made reference to the following obiter comment on the meaning of this phrase made by Tomlinson J. in *Kenneally*, at para.48: "It seems to me likely that the word 'trial' is . . . intended to refer . . . to the more immediately recognisable features of a criminal trial, beginning, broadly, with the swearing-in of the jury".

WITHOUT CONVICTING HIM.   As there has been no conviction, there is no right of appeal to the Court of Appeal (Criminal Appeal Act 1968, s.9 and *R. v Griffiths*, above).

Subsection (6)

1–684   TWO REGISTERED MEDICAL PRACTITIONERS.   One of whom must be approved by the Secretary of State or the Welsh Ministers under s.12, or by another person by virtue of s.12ZA or 12ZB (s.54(1)).

MENTAL DISORDER.   If the person has a learning disability, the disability must be associated with abnormally aggressive or seriously irresponsible conduct (s.1(2A), (2B)). A learning disabled person might also suffer from another form of mental disorder.

NATURE OR DEGREE.   See the note on s.3(2)(a).

DETAINED IN A HOSPITAL FOR MEDICAL TREATMENT.   But not for assessment.

APPROPRIATE MEDICAL TREATMENT.   See the note on s.3(2)(d).

DEPOSITIONS.   The Court is entitled to have regard to the evidence in the case in deciding whether to make an order (*Kenneally*, above, at para.34).

Further provisions as to persons remanded by magistrates' courts

1–685   **52.**—(1) This section has effect where a transfer direction has been given in respect of any such person as is described in paragraph (b) of section 48(2) above; and that person is in this section referred to as "the accused".

(2) Subject to subsection (5) below, the transfer direction shall cease to have effect on the expiration of the period of remand unless the accused is [sent] in custody to the Crown Court for trial or to be otherwise dealt with.

(3) Subject to subsection (4) below, the power of further remanding the accused under section 128 of the Magistrates' Courts Act 1980 may be exercised by the court without his being brought before the court; and if the court further remands the accused in custody (whether or not he is brought before the court) the period of remand shall, for the purposes of this section, be deemed not to have expired.

(4) The court shall not under subsection (3) above further remand the accused in his absence unless he has appeared before the court within the previous six months.

(5) If the magistrates' court is satisfied, on the written or oral evidence of the [responsible clinician]—

    (a) that the accused no longer requires treatment in hospital for mental disorder; or

    (b) that no effective treatment for his disorder can be given in the hospital to which he has been removed,

the court may direct that the transfer direction shall cease to have effect notwithstanding that the period of remand has not expired or that the accused is [sent] to the Crown Court as mentioned in subsection (2) above.

(6) If the accused is [sent] to the Crown Court as mentioned in subsection (2) above and the transfer direction has not ceased to have effect under subsection (5) above, section 51 above shall apply as if the transfer direction given in his case were a direction given in respect of a person falling within that section.

(7) The magistrates' court may, in the absence of the accused, [send him to the Crown Court for trial under section 51 or 51A of the Crime and Disorder Act 1998]

    (a) the court is satisfied, on the written or oral evidence of the [responsible clinician], that the accused is unfit to take part in the proceedings; and

    (b) [. . .], the accused is represented by [an authorised person].

AMENDMENTS

The amendments to this section were made by the Criminal Justice Act 2003 s.41, Sch.3 para.55(1),(3), the Mental Health Act 2007 s.11(4) and the Legal Services Act 2007 s.208, Sch.21, para.57.

DEFINITIONS

transfer direction: ss.47, 145(1).   **1–686**
responsible clinician: s.55(1).
hospital: ss.55(5), 145(1).
mental disorder: ss.1, 145(1).
authorised person: s.55(1).

GENERAL NOTE

This section provides that a transfer direction made in respect of a person who has been **1–687** remanded in custody by a magistrates' court ceases to have effect at the expiration of the period of remand unless the accused is then sent in custody to the Crown Court (subs.(2)). However, if the magistrates' court further remands the accused under subs.(3) the direction will not expire. Alternatively, if the court is satisfied, on receiving the requisite evidence, that the accused no longer requires treatment in hospital it may direct that the transfer direction shall cease to have effect (subs.(5)). The court also has power to send the accused to the Crown Court for trial in his absence if it is satisfied that he is unfit to take part in the proceedings (subs.(7)).

Subsection (4)

MONTHS.   Means calendar months (Interpretation Act s.5, Sch.1).   **1–688**

Subsection (5)

WRITTEN OR ORAL EVIDENCE.   See s.54.   **1–689**

Further provisions as to civil prisoners and persons detained under the [Immigration Acts]

1–690   **53.**—(1) Subject to subsection (2) below, a transfer direction given in respect of any such person as is described in paragraph (c) or (d) of section 48(2) above shall cease to have effect on the expiration of the period during which he would, but for his removal to hospital, be liable to be detained in the place from which he was removed.

(2) Where a transfer direction and a restriction direction have been given in respect of any such person as is mentioned in subsection (1) above, then, if the Secretary of State is notified by the [responsible clinician], any other [approved clinician] or [the appropriate tribunal] at any time before the expiration of the period there mentioned—

(a) that that person no longer requires treatment in hospital for mental disorder; or

(b) that no effective treatment for his disorder can be given in the hospital to which he has been removed,

the Secretary of State may by warrant direct that he be remitted to any place where he might have been detained if he had not been removed to hospital, and on his arrival at the place to which he is so remitted the transfer direction and the restriction direction shall cease to have effect.

AMENDMENTS

The amendments to this section were made by the Nationality, Immigration and Asylum Act 2002 s.62(10), the Mental Health Act 2007 s.11(5) and by SI 2008/2883 art.9, Sch.3 para.44.

DEFINITIONS

1–691   transfer direction: ss.47, 145(1).
hospital: ss.55(5), 145(1).
restriction direction: ss.49, 145(1).
responsible clinician: s.55(1).
approved clinician: s.145(1).
mental disorder: ss.1, 145(1).
the appropriate tribunal: ss.66(4), 145(1).

GENERAL NOTE

1–692   This section provides that a transfer direction made in respect of a civil prisoner or a person detained under the Immigration Acts ceases to have effect on the expiration of the period of detention that would have occurred had the removal to hospital not taken place (subs.(1)). Where a transfer direction *and* a restriction direction have been made the Secretary of State has power to direct that the patient be returned to prison, and on his arrival there both the transfer direction and the restriction direction shall cease to have effect (subs.(2)).

Supplemental

Requirements as to medical evidence

1–693   **54.**—(1) The registered medical practitioner whose evidence is taken into account under section 35(3)(a) above and at least one of the registered medical practitioners whose evidence is taken into account under sections 36(1), 37(2)(a), 38(1)[, 45A(2)] and 51(6)(a) above and whose reports are taken into account under sections 47(1) and 48(1) above shall be a practitioner approved for the purposes of section 12 above by the Secretary of State[, or by another person by virtue of section 12ZA or 12ZB above] as having special experience in the diagnosis or treatment of mental disorder.

[(2) For the purposes of any provision of this Part of this Act under which a court may act on the written evidence of any person, a report in writing purporting to be signed by that person may, subject to the provisions of this section, be received in evidence without proof of the following—

    (a) the signature of the person; or

    (b) his having the requisite qualifications or approval or authority or being of the requisite description to give the report.

(2A) But the court may require the signatory of any such report to be called to give oral evidence.]

(3) Where, in pursuance of a direction of the court, any such report is tendered in evidence otherwise than by or on behalf of the person who is the subject of the report, then—

    (a) if that person is represented by [an authorised person], a copy of the report shall be given to [that authorised person];

    (b) if that person is not so represented, the substance of the report shall be disclosed to him or, where he is a child or young person, to his parent or guardian if present in court; and

    (c) except where the report relates only to arrangements for his admission to a hospital, that person may require the signatory of the report to be called to give oral evidence, and evidence to rebut the evidence contained in the report may be called by or on behalf of that person.

AMENDMENTS

The amendments to this section were made by the Crime (Sentences) Act 1997 s.55, Sch.4 para.12(6), the Mental Health Act 2007 s.11(6), the Legal Services Act 2007 s.208, Sch.21, para.58 and the Health and Social Care Act 2012 s.38(2).

DEFINITIONS

    mental disorder: ss.1, 145(1).   **1–694**

    the managers: s.145(1).

    hospital: ss.55(5), 145(1).

    child: s.55(1).

    young person: s.55(1).

    guardian: s.55(1).

    authorised person: s.55(1).

GENERAL NOTE

This section specifies when medical evidence in proceedings under this Part of the Act **1–695** must be given by a doctor who has been approved by the Secretary of State or the Welsh Ministers under s.12, or by another person by virtue of s.12ZA or 12ZB, and provides for the circumstances when written evidence by a doctor or a person representing the managers of a hospital may be accepted by a court. There is no requirement for the doctor to be an approved clinician.

A doctor who has been approved under s.12 is also approved for the purposes of s.4 of the Criminal Procedure (Insanity) Act 1964 (*R. v Ghulam* [2009] EWCA Crim 2285, para.1.19).

The *Good Practice Guidance: Commissioning, administering and production of psychiatric reports for sentencing*, issued by HMCTS and the Ministry of Justice in 2010 drafted in conjunction with the judiciary and the Royal College of Psychiatrists provides detailed guidance on report to the court.

Code of Practice

1–696   Under the heading "Assessment by a doctor", the *Code* states:

"22.9 A doctor who is asked to provide evidence in relation to a possible admission under part 3 of the Act should bear in mind that the request is not for a general report on the defendant's condition but for advice on whether or not the patient should be diverted from prison by way of a hospital order, or a hospital direction (or a community order with a mental health treatment requirement under criminal justice legislation).

22.10 Doctors should:

- identify themselves to the person being assessed, explain who has requested the report and make clear the limits of confidentiality in relation to the report. They should explain that any information disclosed, and the medical opinion, could be relevant not only to medical disposal by the court but also to the imposition of a punitive sentence, or to its length, and

- request relevant pre-sentence reports, the inmate medical record and previous psychiatric reports, as well as relevant documentation regarding the alleged offence. If any of this information is not available, the doctor's report should say so clearly.

22.11 The doctor, or one of them if two doctors are preparing reports, should have access to a bed or take responsibility for referring the case to another clinician who does if they propose to recommend admission to hospital within the period of 28 days beginning with the date of the making of the order under section 37, section 38 or section 45A of the Act. If the court is making an order under the Criminal Procedure (Insanity) Act 1964, the Court does not need a 'bed offer' as it does for other court orders but it is good practice for any doctor providing a recommendation of a hospital disposal under Domestic Violence, Crime and Victims Act 2004 (DVCVA)2 to contact the anticipated named hospital in the order.

22.12 The doctor should, identify and access other independent sources of information about the person's previous history (including convictions). This should include information from GP records, previous psychiatric treatment and patterns of behaviour."

Subsection (3)

1–697   This subsection has been enacted because medical reports "may contain facts or comments which might cause distress not only to the accused but also to his relatives. If the accused wishes, however, he may insist that the medical practitioner should give oral evidence, and he may then call evidence in rebuttal" (Home Office Circular No. 69/1983, para.44).

[Reduction of period for making hospital orders

1–698   **54A.**—(1) The Secretary of State may by order reduce the length of the periods mentioned in sections 37(4) and (5) and 38(4) above.

(2) An order under subsection (1) above may make such consequential amendments of sections 40(1) and 44(3) above as appear to the Secretary of State to be necessary or expedient.]

AMENDMENT

This section was inserted by the Criminal Justice Act 1991 s.27(2).

This section enables the Secretary of State or the Welsh Ministers to reduce, by statutory **1–699** instrument, the time periods for the admission of mentally disordered offenders to hospital.

SECRETARY OF STATE. Or, in relation to Wales, the Welsh Ministers (see the General Note to the Act).

Interpretation of Part III

55.—(1) In this Part of this Act— **1–700**
["authorised person" means a person who, for the purposes of the Legal Services Act 2007, is an authorised person in relation to an activity which constitutes the exercise of a right of audience (within the meaning of that Act);]
"child" and "young person" have the same meaning as in the Children and Young Persons Act 1933;
"civil prisoner" has the meaning given to it by section 48(2)(c) above;
"guardian", in relation to a child or young person, has the same meaning as in the Children and Young Persons Act 1933;
"place of safety", in relation to a person who is not a child or young person, means any police station, prison or remand centre, or any hospital the managers of which are willing temporarily to receive him, and in relation to a child or young person has the same meaning as in the Children and Young Persons Act 1933;
["responsible clinician", in relation to a person liable to be detained in a hospital within the meaning of Part 2 of this Act, means the approved clinician with overall responsibility for the patient's case.]

(2) Any reference in this Part of this Act to an offence punishable on summary conviction with imprisonment shall be construed without regard to any prohibition or restriction imposed by or under any enactment relating to the imprisonment of young offenders.

(3) [. . .]

(4) Any reference to a hospital order, a guardianship order or a restriction order in section 40(2), (4) or (5), section 41(3) to (5), or section 42 above or section 69(1) below shall be construed as including a reference to any order or direction under this Part of this Act having the same effect as the first-mentioned order; and the exceptions and modifications set out in Schedule 1 to this Act in respect of the provisions of this Act described in that Schedule accordingly include those which are consequential on the provisions of this subsection.

(5) Section 34(2) above shall apply for the purposes of this Part of this Act as it applies for the purposes of Part II of this Act.

(6) References in this Part of this Act to persons serving a sentence of imprisonment shall be construed in accordance with section 47(5) above.

(7) Section 99 of the Children and Young Persons Act 1933 (which relates to the presumption and determination of age) shall apply for the purposes of this Part of this Act as it applies for the purposes of that Act.

AMENDMENTS
The amendments to this section were made by the Legal Services Act 2007 s.208, Sch.21, para.59 and the Mental Health Act 2007 ss.11(7), 55, Sch.11 Pt 1.

DEFINITIONS

1–701   approved clinician: s.145(1).
   hospital: s.145(1) and see subs.(5) of this section.
   the managers: s.145(1).
   patient: s.145(1).
   application for admission for treatment: ss.3, 145(1).
   mental disorder: ss.1, 145(1).
   hospital order: ss.37, 145(1).
   guardianship order: ss.37, 145(1).
   restriction order: ss.41, 145(1).

Subsection (1)

1–702   Under s.107(1) of the Children and Young Persons Act 1933, "child" means a person under the age of 14 years, "young person" means a person who has attained the age of 14 years and is under the age of 18 years, "guardian", in relation to a child or young person, includes any person who, in the opinion of the relevant court, has for the time being the care of the child or young person, and "place of safety" means a community home provided by a local authority or a controlled community home, any police station, or any hospital, surgery, or any other suitable place, the occupier of which is willing temporarily to receive a child or young person.

RESPONSIBLE CLINICIAN.   See the note on s.34(1).

Subsection (4)

1–703   HAVING THE SAME EFFECT.   An interim hospital order made under s.38 does not have the same effect as a hospital order made under s.37: see the note on s.40(3).

Subsection (6)

1–704   In *R. v Fort* [2013] EWCA Crim 2332; [2014] M.H.L.R. 334 at paras 82 to 83, it was held that the extension of the phrase "sentence of imprisonment" in this provision applies only to persons who are actually "serving" a sentence and that it cannot extend to the phrase "deciding to impose a sentence of imprisonment" in s.45A(1)(b) so as to include "deciding to impose a sentence of detention or custody for life".

PART IV

CONSENT TO TREATMENT

GENERAL NOTE

1–705   The extent to which the Mental Health Act 1959 gave authority to the responsible medical officer to treat a detained patient without his consent was unclear. The opinion of the Department of Health and Social Security was that where the purpose of detention was treatment, the Act gave implied authority for treatment to be imposed. During the 1970s the correctness of this opinion was questioned by a number of commentators: see paras 3.57 to 3.59 of the *Butler Committee*, Joe Jacob, "The right of the mental patient to his psychosis", Modern Law Review, 1976, vol.39, pp.221–235, and Ch.11 of Phil Fennell's *Treatment Without Consent: Law Psychiatry and the Treatment of Mentally Disordered People since 1895* (1996).

   The purpose of this Part is to clarify the extent to which treatment for mental disorder can be imposed on patients who are liable to be detained under the Act. It provides for three categories of treatment which have different legal consequences. They are (1) the most serious treatments which require the patient's consent *and* a second opinion (s.57); (2) treatments that can be given without consent subject to a second opinion (s.58); and (3) treatments that can be given only with the consent of a capable patient or to an incapable patient subject to a second opinion (s.58A). Treatments that do not come within these categories can be imposed on a patient who is liable to be detained and who understands the nature and purpose of the treatment, but expressly withholds consent (s.63). The safeguards provided for by ss.57, 58 and 58A can be overridden on a temporary basis if the treatment is required urgently (s.62).

Paragraph 24.7 of the *Code of Practice* states:

"Where reasonably practicable, treatment should be based on a strong evidence-base. Professionals should ensure that any treatment is compliant with the current guidelines and standards about what is appropriate treatment. Examples include, National Institute for Health and Care Excellence (NICE)/Social Care Institute for Excellence (SCIE) guidelines, NICE quality standards and Department of Health Care Programme Approach (CPA) guidance. In the case of medications that are used to treat mental disorder, particular care is required when prescribing medications that exceed the maximum dosage listed in the British National Formulary (BNF) or where multiple medications are used to treat a patient."

The Explanatory Notes to the Mental Health Act 2007 at para.57, explain the frequent use of the phrase "approved clinician in charge of treatment" rather that "responsible clinician" in this Part and in Pt IVA:

"In the majority of cases the AC in charge of the treatment will be the patient's RC, but where, for example, the RC is not qualified to make decisions about a particular treatment (e.g. medication if the RC is not a doctor or a nurse prescriber) then another appropriately qualified professional will be in charge of that treatment, with the RC continuing to retain overall responsibility for the patient's case."

Approved Clinicians owe a duty of care to the patient whenever they propose or administer treatment under this Part (*R. (on the application of Wilkinson) v Responsible Medical Officer Broadmoor Hospital* [2001] EWCA 1545; [2002] 1 W.L.R. 419 para.68).

A Court will not order a clinician to treat a patient contrary to her professional judgment (*AVS v A NHS Foundation Trust and A PCT* [2011] EWCA Civ 7, following *R. (on the application of Burke) v GMC* [2005] EWCA Civ 1003) and, on an application for judicial review, it is not the duty of the court to investigate requests for alternative forms of treatment or "second opinions" from patients unhappy or dissatisfied with their treatment (*YZ v NHS Trust* [2015] EWHC 2296 (Admin) at para.35).

Mental Capacity Act 2005

With the exception of the provision of electro-convulsive therapy under s.58A to a **1–706** patient who is incapable of consenting to that treatment, an advance decision refusing medical treatment for mental disorder made by the patient under s.24 of the 2005 Act is rendered ineffective if the patient comes within the scope of this Part (s.28 of the 2005 Act). However, the treating psychiatrist should not ignore the existence of the advance decision in non s.58A cases. If the patient is mentally incapacitated, the advance decision should be treated as an expression of the patient's wishes and feelings about the treatment in question which should be taken into account by the psychiatrist before a decision is made on whether to provide the patient with the treatment. Psychiatrists "should, for example, consider whether it is possible to use a different form of treatment not refused by the advance decision. If it is not, they should explain why to the patient" (*Code of Practice*, para.9.9).

Neither a donee of a lasting power of attorney nor a deputy appointed by the Court of Protection can consent to treatment coming within the scope of this Part on the patient's behalf (s.28 of the 2005 Act).

1–707   In *M v Ukraine* [2013] M.H.L.R. 255, the European Court of Human Rights said at para.76:

> "The international community has developed a set of relevant principles under which the validity of a patient's consent to psychiatric treatment can be ensured. In particular, under principle 11(2) of the UN Principles [for the Protection of Persons with Mental Illness] an agreement to psychiatric treatment implies that a patient has been provided with adequate and understandable information, in a form and language he or she understands on the diagnostic assessment; the purpose, method, likely duration and expected benefit of the proposed treatment; alternative modes of treatment, including those less intrusive; possible pain or discomfort, risks and side-effects of the proposed treatment. The [European Committee for the Prevention of Torture and Inhuman or Degrading Treatment or Punishment] has specified that consent to treatment can only be qualified as free and informed if it is based on full, accurate and comprehensible information about the patient's condition and the treatment proposed."

United Nations Convention on the Rights of Persons with Disabilities
1–708   The power to impose treatments for mental disorder on non-consenting mentally capable patients conflicts with art.25(d) of this Convention (see the General Note to the Act under "International") which requires States to:

> "Require health professionals to provide care of the same quality to persons with disabilities as to others, including on the basis of free and informed consent by, inter alia, raising awareness of the human rights, dignity, autonomy and needs of persons with disabilities through training and the promulgation of ethical standards for public and private health care".

Code of Practice
1–709   Guidance on this Part is contained in Chs 24 and 25.

[Patients to whom Part 4 applies
1–710   **56.**—(1) Section 57 and, so far as relevant to that section, sections 59 to 62 below apply to any patient.

(2) Subject to that and to subsection (5) below, this Part of this Act applies to a patient only if he falls within subsection (3) or (4) below.

(3) A patient falls within this subsection if he is liable to be detained under this Act but not if—
- (a) he is so liable by virtue of an emergency application and the second medical recommendation referred to in section 4(4)(a) above has not been given and received;
- (b) he is so liable by virtue of section 5(2) or (4) or 35 above or section 135 or 136 below or by virtue of a direction for his detention in a place of safety under section 37(4) or 45A(5) above; or
- (c) he has been conditionally discharged under section 42(2) above or section 73 or 74 below and he is not recalled to hospital.

(4) A patient falls within this subsection if—
- (a) he is a community patient; and
- (b) he is recalled to hospital under section 17E above.

(5) Section 58A and, so far as relevant to that section, sections 59 to 62 below also apply to any patient who—
- (a) does not fall within subsection (3) above;

(b) is not a community patient; and

(c) has not attained the age of 18 years.]

AMENDMENT

This section was inserted by the Mental Health Act 2007 s.34(2).

DEFINITIONS

    patient: s.145(1).   **1–711**

    emergency application: s.4(1).

    hospital: ss.64(1), 145(1).

    community patient: ss.17A(7), 145(1).

GENERAL NOTE

This section identifies the categories of patients to whom this Part applies. Treatments **1–712** provided under s.57 apply to all patients, irrespective of their legal status (subs.(1)). Subject to that, treatments provided under this Part apply to patients who are liable to be detained, with the exception of the categories set out in subs.(3). It also applies to patients who are subject to hospital orders made under s.5(2)(a) of the Criminal Procedure (Insanity) Act 1964 because such an order has the same meaning as a hospital order made under s.37 (see s.5(4) of the 1964 Act). With the exception of s.57, a community patient is not subject to this Part unless he has been recalled to hospital under s.17E (subs.(4)), in which case the provisions of s.62A will apply. The medical treatment of community patients is governed by Pt IVA. An informal child patient who is not subject to a community treatment order is subject to s.58A (subs.(5)).

There is an argument to support the contention that patients who are liable to be detained under s.3 and who are either sentenced, or are committed or remanded to custody, by a court for a period of less than six months continue to be subject to the provisions of this Part: see the General Note to s.22.

Patients who do not come within the scope of this Part can be treated for both mental and physical disorders under common law rules if they are mentally capable of consenting to the treatment, and under the Mental Capacity Act 2005 if they are mentally incapable of making a decision relating to the treatment in question and the treatment is in their best interests.

Subsection (1)

This subsection extends the protection provided by s.57 to informal patients. It was orig- **1–713** inally enacted as a result on an opposition amendment to the 1982 Act which found favour with the Minister for Health who accepted the argument that "if a course of treatment is so drastic that a detained patient's consent alone should not justify it and that there should be further safeguards, it is difficult to see why the same provisions should not apply to an informal patient" (*Hansard*, HC Vol.29, col.81).

Subsection (3)

LIABLE TO BE DETAINED. As this provision refers to a patient who is "liable to be **1–714** detained" rather than to a patient who is actually detained, the provisions of this Part are triggered when the patient has been made subject to a duly completed application made under Pt II or to an order of the court made under Pt III. It is the existence of the application or order, rather than the acceptance of the application or order by the detaining hospital, that results in the patient being "liable to be detained".

Patients who have been granted leave of absence from hospital under s.17 continue to be "liable to be detained" and are subject to the provisions of this Part. It is therefore important that during such leave of absence the patient's General Practitioner is informed of the content of any certificates given under this Part as she will be bound by them.

Patients who are subject to guardianship are not "liable to be detained" and do not come within the scope of this Part.

Paragraph (c)

1–715   A PATIENT WHO HAS BEEN CONDITIONALLY DISCHARGED. The Reference Guide, at para.23.29, states that a patient's conditional discharge constitutes a break in the continuity of the patient's detention with the result that three month period provided for in s.58(1)(b) applies when the patient is recalled to hospital.

Treatment requiring consent and a second opinion

1–716   **57.**—(1) This section applies to the following forms of medical treatment for mental disorder—

(a) any surgical operation for destroying brain tissue or for destroying the functioning of brain tissue; and

(b) such other forms of treatment as may be specified for the purposes of this section by regulations made by the Secretary of State.

(2) Subject to section 62 below, a patient shall not be given any form of treatment to which this section applies unless he has consented to it and—

(a) a registered medical practitioner appointed for the purposes of this Part of this Act by [the regulatory authority] (not being the [responsible clinician (if there is one) or the person in charge of the treatment in question]) and two other persons appointed for the purposes of this paragraph by [the regulatory authority] (not being registered medical practitioners) have certified in writing that the patient is capable of understanding the nature, purpose and likely effects of the treatment in question and has consented to it; and

(b) the registered medical practitioner referred to in paragraph (a) above has certified in writing that [it is appropriate for the treatment to be given.]

(3) Before giving a certificate under subsection (2)(b) above the registered medical practitioner concerned shall consult two other persons who have been professionally concerned with the patient's medical treatment [but, of those persons—

(a) one shall be a nurse and the other shall be neither a nurse nor a registered medical practitioner; and

(b) neither shall be the responsible clinician (if there is one) or the person in charge of the treatment in question.]

(4) Before making any regulations for the purpose of this section the Secretary of State shall consult such bodies as appear to him to be concerned.

AMENDMENTS

The amendments to this section were made by the Mental Health Act 2007 ss.6(2)(a), 12(2) and the Health and Social Care Act 2008 s.52, Sch.3 para.2.

DEFINITIONS

1–717   medical treatment: s.145(1), (4).
mental disorder: ss.1, 145(1).
patient: ss.56, 145(1).
the regulatory authority: s.145(1).
responsible clinician: s.64(1).

GENERAL NOTE

1–718   This section, which applies to all patients irrespective of their age or legal status, provides that certain of the most serious forms of medical treatment for mental disorder can only be given if the patient consents to the treatment and three independent people appointed by the Care Quality Commission (the Commission) or, in relation to Wales, the Welsh Ministers, one being a doctor, have certified that the patient understands the treatment and has consented to it. If the patient is either not capable of consenting to the treatment or does not consent to it, the treatment cannot proceed. The independent doctor must also certify that it is appropriate for the treatment to be given. Before issuing the certificate the doctor must consult with two persons, other than the patient's doctor, who have been professionally concerned with the patient's treatment. The certificate of consent and the certificate relating to the need for treatment together make up Form T1 of the English Regulations and Form CO1 of the Welsh Regulations.

As treatments provided under this section require the patient's consent, they "cannot, therefore, be given to any young person or child who does not have the competence or capacity to consent, even if a person with parental responsibility consents" (*Code of Practice*, para.19.79).

Paragraph 13.51 of the Code of Practice on the Mental Capacity Act 2005 states:

"The combined effect of section 57 of the Mental Health Act and section 28 of the Mental Capacity Act is, effectively, that a person who lacks the capacity to consent to [a section 57 treatment] may never be given it. Healthcare staff cannot use the Mental Capacity Act as an alternative way of giving these kinds of treatment. Nor can an attorney [of a lasting power of attorney] or deputy [appointed by the Court of Protection] give permission for them on a person's behalf."

In *X v A, B and C and the Mental Health Act Commission* (1991) 9 B.M.L.R. 91, Morland J. held that the only legal relationship between the three persons appointed under subs.(2)(a) and the Commission's predecessor, the Mental Health Act Commission (MHAC), is that of appointees and appointor. It is the Commission on behalf of the Secretary of State who appoints the panel. It then becomes the exclusive function of the panel to carry out their responsibilities and the Commission have no further responsibility or duty in relation to a person who is aggrieved by the actions of the panel. When carrying out their functions under subs.(2)(a) the panel had to discharge duties which had quasi-judicial hallmarks and which were in the field of public administrative law. Consequently no common law duty of care is owed by the panel in private law to the patient. His Lordship said at 96:

"It may very well be although I reach no definitive conclusion about it, that a doctor giving an opinion, which was negligent, that electro-convulsive therapy should be given, that that opinion, being in the certificate given under section 58(3)(b) [now see s.58A] could be in breach of a common law duty in private law. In my judgment the reason for that is that the doctor, *qua* doctor, is giving a medical opinion about a patient, albeit not his. Similar considerations would apply to a doctor's certificate ... given under section 57(2)(b)."

If a patient is given treatment under this section, the approved clinician in charge of the patient's treatment (AC) must provide the Commission with reports on the treatment and the patient's condition (s.61).

Code of Practice

Guidance on this section is given in Ch.25 at paras 25.7 to 25.10 (also note para.19.79). **1–719**
Paragraph 25.9 states:

"A decision to administer treatments to which section 57 applies requires particularly careful consideration, given their significance and sensitivity. Hospitals proposing to offer such treatments are strongly encouraged to agree with the CQC the procedures which will be followed to implement the requirements of section 51."

Subsection (1)

1–720   PARAGRAPH (A).   Information contained from a personal communication and from reports published by the Mental Health Act Commission and the Care Quality Commission shows that during the period 1997–2014, 68 patients were referred for neuro-surgery (sometimes called "psychosurgery"), with the operation being authorised in 51 cases. It is very rare for a detained patient to be referred.

PARAGRAPH (B); OTHER FORMS OF TREATMENT.   Regulation 27(1) of the English Regulations and reg.38(1) of the Welsh Regulations specify "the surgical implantation of hormones for the purposes of reducing male sex drive" as a form of treatment to which this section shall apply. The patient must be mentally disordered as well as having an abnormal sex drive for him to come within the scope of this section.

In *R. v Mental Health Act Commission Ex p. X* (1988) 9 B.M.L.R. 77, DC at 85, the court found that the term "hormone" included synthetically produced hormones as well as the naturally occurring substance, but did not include hormone analogues, such as Goserelin, which are separate substances well known at the time the regulations were made. It was therefore held that Goserelin, even though approximately 100 times more powerful than the naturally occurring substance, is not a hormone within the meaning of reg.16. Stuart-Smith L.J. said at 83: "If Parliament passes legislation on the control of leopards, it is not to be presumed that leopards include tigers on the basis that they are larger and fiercer". On the question whether a particular procedure comes within the scope of "surgical implant" the court held that "in the end it is . . . a question of fact and degree". The court took the view that a wide bore disposable syringe used for implanting the Goserelin was more like a conventional injection and could not be described as "surgical". It would appear that an incision must be made if an implant is to be categorised as being "surgical". The effect of this judgment is that if the administration of Goserelin is used as a treatment for mental disorder, it is governed by s.58(1)(b).

There have only been four referrals (only one of which was proceeded with) of patients for hormone implantation and there have been no referrals since 1988. "This is probably because the most widely used sexual suppressant, cyproterone acetate (Androcur), is administered by mouth" (Phil Fennell, *Treatment Without Consent: Law Psychiatry and the Treatment of Mentally Disordered People since 1845* (1996) p.188).

REGULATIONS.   See subs.(4). The *Code of Practice* can also specify treatments to which this section will apply (s.118(2)).

SECRETARY OF STATE.   The functions of the Minister under this section, so far as exer-cisable in relation to Wales, are exercised by the Welsh Ministers (see the General Note to the Act).

Subsection (2)

1–721   REGISTERED MEDICAL PRACTITIONER.   See the note on s.58(3)(a).

PERSON IN CHARGE OF THE TREATMENT.   Who need not be an approved clinician: see s.64(1A).

APPOINTED . . . BY THE SECRETARY OF STATE.   The Commission (or, in Wales, Health Inspectorate Wales) will appoint the doctor and the two other persons referred to in this paragraph (Health and Social Care Act 2008 s.52(1)(a)). Those appointed may include members or employees of the Commission (Health and Social Care Act 2008 s.52(2)). They must be allowed to interview the patient and inspect his records, and the doctor must be allowed to examine the patient: see s.119 for registered establishments and the direction of the Secretary of State, published as Annex A to DHSS Circular No.HC(83)19, for hospitals. The three appointed persons have a duty to act fairly (*R. v Mental Health Act Commission Ex p. X*, above). Having been appointed these people are not regulated by the Commission but are exercising their own independent judgment (*X v A, B and C and the Mental Health Act Commission*, above, and the Health and Social Care Act 2008 (Regulated Activities) Regulations 2010 (SI 2010/781) reg.3, Sch.1 para.6(1A)). It is therefore the case that their decisions cannot be appealed against to the Commission. As the appointed persons are discharging a public law function, their decisions can be challenged by way of a judicial review. The appointed persons are "public authorities" for the purposes of s.6 of the Human Rights Act 1998 because they "exercise functions of a public nature" (s.6(3)(b)).

CONSENTED TO IT.   See *M v Ukraine* [2013] M.H.L.R. 255, which is noted under *Human Rights Act 1998* in the General Note to this Part, and paras 19.24–19.37 of the *Code of Practice* which focus on assessing the capacity or competence of children and young persons to consent to treatment.

In *Re R (A Minor) (Wardship: Medical Treatment)* [1991] 4 All E.R. 177, 184, CA, Lord Donaldson MR said that "consent by itself creates no obligation to treat". Patients must consent themselves: consent cannot be provided by a donee of a lasting power of attorney or a deputy appointed by the Court of Protection (Mental Capacity Act 2005 s.28). "Consent" is not defined in the Act, although the *Code of Practice* provides the following definition at para.24.34:

> "Consent is the voluntary and continuing permission of a patient to be given a particular treatment, based on a sufficient knowledge of the purpose, nature, likely effects and risks of that treatment, including the likelihood of its success and any alternatives to it. Permission given under any unfair or undue pressure is not consent."

The notion of consent is problematic when detained patients are being treated and it is important that professionals do not confuse compliance with consent: see, for example, M. Larkin et al., "Making sense of 'consent' in a constrained environment", Int. J. of Law and Psychiatry, 32, (2009), 176–183. "An apparent consent will not be a true consent if it has been obtained by fraud, misrepresentation, duress or fundamental mistake"; per Stuart-Smith L.J. in *R. v Mental Health Act Commission Ex p. X*, above, at 85. Ultimately, whether there was a true consent is always a question of fact (*Freeman v Home Office (No.2)* [1984] 1 Q.B. 524). If consent is subsequently withdrawn, the treatment cannot proceed (s.60(1)). Subject to s.62, if the patient loses capacity before the completion of the treatment, the treatment cannot continue (s.60(1A), (1B)).

Both the patient's consent and the doctor's certificate may apply to a plan of treatment (s.59).

The provision of information to patients
In *Montgomery v Lanarkshire Health Board* [2015] UKSC 11, the Supreme Court com-   **1–722**
prehensively reviewed the case law on a doctor's obligation to warn a patient of the risks of treatment. The substantive judgment was given by Lords Kerr and Reed who held that the correct position is that:

> "87. . . . An adult person of sound mind is entitled to decide which, if any, of the available forms of treatment to undergo, and her consent must be obtained before treatment interfering with her bodily integrity is undertaken. The doctor is therefore under a duty to take reasonable care to ensure that the patient is aware of any material risks involved in any recommended treatment, and of any reasonable alternative or variant treatments. The test of materiality is whether, in the circumstances of the particular case, a reasonable person in the patient's position would be likely to attach significance to the risk, or the doctor is or should reasonably be aware that the particular patient would be likely to attach significance to it.

88. The doctor is however entitled to withhold from the patient information as to a risk if he reasonably considers that its disclosure would be seriously detrimental to the patient's health. The doctor is also excused from conferring with the patient in circumstances of necessity, as for example where the patient requires treatment urgently but is unconscious or otherwise unable to make a decision. It is unnecessary for the purposes of this case to consider in detail the scope of those exceptions."

Their Lordships said that three further points should be made: first, assessing the significance of a risk is fact-sensitive and cannot be reduced to percentages. Second, in order to advise, the doctor must engage in dialogue with her patient. Third, the therapeutic exception is limited, and should not be abused (paras 89–91.

The *Code of Practice* considers the provision of information at paras 24.36 to 24.39.

Paragraph (a)

1–723   CERTIFIED IN WRITING. This certificate is not a substitute for a standard consent form. The certificate must be in the form set out in Form T1: see s.64(2) and reg.27(1) of the English Regulations (Form CO1 and reg.40(1) of the Welsh Regulations). The appointed persons have to be satisfied as to the patient's capacity and to the fact of consent before a certificate can be issued. In forming a view as to whether the patient has consented to the treatment, the appointed persons would need to be satisfied that the patient had been provided with sufficient information to enable a valid consent to be given: see the note on "consented to it", above. It is the responsibility of the doctor proposing to treat the patient to ensure that sufficient information has been provided.

CAPABLE OF UNDERSTANDING. See the note on this phrase in s.58(3)(a).

NATURE, PURPOSE AND LIKELY EFFECTS OF THE TREATMENT. See the note on this phrase in s.58(3)(a).

Paragraph (b)

1–724   APPROPRIATE FOR THE TREATMENT TO BE GIVEN. See the note to s.58(3)(b).

CERTIFIED. The appointed doctor is required to reach an independent view of the desirability and propriety of the AC's proposal: *R. (on the application of Wilkinson) v The Responsible Medical Officer Broadmoor Hospital* [2001] EWCA Civ 1545; [2002] 1 W.L.R. 419, noted in s.58(3)(b) under "certified".
The Commission has the power to withdraw the authority to treat provided by the certificate by issuing a notice under s.61(3).

APPROPRIATE FOR THE TREATMENT TO BE GIVEN. See s.64(3).

Subsection (3)

1–725   See the notes on s.58(4).

Treatment requiring consent or a second opinion

1–726   **58.**—(1) This section applies to the following forms of medical treatment for mental disorder—

    (a) such forms of treatment as may be specified for the purposes of this section by regulations made by the Secretary of State;

    (b) the administration of medicine to a patient by any means (not being a form of treatment specified under paragraph (a) above or section 57 above [or section 58A(1)(b) below]) at any time during a period for which he is liable to be detained as a patient to whom this Part of this Act applies if three months or more have elapsed since the first occasion in that period when medicine was administered to him by any means for his mental disorder.

(2) The Secretary of State may by order vary the length of the period mentioned in subsection (1)(b) above.

(3) Subject to section 62 below, a patient shall not be given any form of treatment to which this section applies unless—

(a) he has consented to that treatment and either the [approved clinician in charge of it] or a registered medical practitioner appointed for the purposes of this Part of this Act by [the regulatory authority] has certified in writing that the patient is capable of understanding its nature, purpose and likely effects and has consented to it; or

(b) a registered medical practitioner appointed as aforesaid (not being the [responsible clinician or the approved clinician in charge of the treatment in question]) has certified in writing that the patient is not capable of understanding the nature, purpose and likely effects of that treatment or [being so capable] has not consented to it but that [it is appropriate for the treatment to be given.]

(4) Before giving a certificate under subsection (3)(b) above the registered medical practitioner concerned shall consult two other persons who have been professionally concerned with the patient's medical treatment, [but, of those persons—

(a) one shall be a nurse and the other shall be neither a nurse nor a registered medical practitioner; and

(b) neither shall be the responsible clinician or the approved clinician in charge of the treatment in question.]

(5) Before making any regulations for the purposes of this section the Secretary of State shall consult such bodies as appear to him to be concerned.

AMENDMENTS
The amendments to this section were made by the Mental Health Act 2007 ss.6(2)(b), 12(3), 28(2) and the Health and Social Care Act 2008 s.52, Sch.3 para.3.

DEFINITIONS   **1–727**
    medical treatment: s.145(1), (4).
    mental disorder: ss.1, 145(1).
    patient: ss.56, 145(1).
    the regulatory authority: s.145(1).
    responsible clinician: s.64(1).
    approved clinician: s.145(1).

GENERAL NOTE
This section provides that certain forms of treatment shall not be given to a patient unless **1–728** the patient consents or an independent medical practitioner appointed by the Care Quality Commission (the Commission) or, in relation to Wales the Welsh Ministers, has certified that either the patient is incapable of giving consent or that the patient should receive the treatment even though he has not consented to it. The independent doctor is usually referred to as a SOAD (second opinion appointed doctor). If the patient consents to the treatment, either the approved clinician in charge of the patient's treatment (AC) or a SOAD must certify that the consent has been properly given. If a child patient who is subject to this Part of the Act is either not consenting to, or is incapable of consenting to the proposed treatment, the provisions of this section must be satisfied before the treatment can be given. There is no provision which enables a person with parental responsibility over

such a patient to consent to the treatment on his behalf. Treatments governed by this section may be given in emergencies under s.62 prior to the involvement of a SOAD.

A SOAD certificate provides an authority to provide treatment; it is not a direction to do so. In the *Wilkinson* case, below, Hale L.J. said, at para.71, that although this section is not phrased in terms of permission to treat, the only sensible construction is that it does confer permission to treat in the two circumstances set out in subs.(3).

If a patient is given treatment under this section, the patient's AC must provide the Commission with reports on the treatment and the patient's condition (s.61).

During the period 2002–2007, only two per cent of SOAD visits resulted in a "significant" change to the patient's treatment plan (MHAC, *Twelfth Biennial Report*, 2005–2007, paras 6.7, 6.20). For some unexplained reason, this figure increased significantly in the final months of the Commission's existence (MHAC, *Thirteenth Biennial Report* 2007–2009, para.3.36). The SOAD system is presumably based on the assumption that where there is a significant disagreement between the SOAD and the patient's AC about the treatment that the patient should receive, the opinion of the SOAD is to be preferred because the patient's interests would be better served by that opinion. There is no evidence to suggest that this assumption is correct, or that patients derive any benefit from the SOAD system. On the other hand, it has been said by some psychiatrists that the knowledge that their treatment decisions will be subject to outside peer review acts as a beneficial constraint on decision making. Having reviewed research on the operation of this section, Peter Bartlett and Ralph Sandland's conclusion is that "the SOAD system has done little to protect patients from overenthusiastic treatment regimes or abuses of their legal rights" (*Mental Health Law: policy and practice*, 2007, p.332). An alternative procedure was suggested in the Preface to the 13th edition of this Manual.

Human Rights Act 1998

1–729   This section, which enables mentally capacitated patients to be treated without their consent subject to limited safeguards, does not sit easily with a principle identified by the Committee for the Prevention of Torture and Inhuman or Degrading Treatment or Punishment. In para.41 of its eighth report (1998) the Committee, which, in effect, polices art.3 of the European Convention on Human Rights (ECHR) in respect of persons deprived of their liberty on behalf of the Council of Europe, states:

> "Patients should, as a matter of principle, be placed in a position to give their free and informed consent to treatment. The admission of a person to a psychiatric establishment on an involuntary basis should not be construed as authorising treatment without his consent. It follows that every competent patient, whether voluntary or involuntary, should be given the opportunity to refuse treatment or other medical intervention. Any derogation from this fundamental principle should be based upon law and only relate to clearly and strictly defined exceptional circumstances."

The question whether the procedures set out in this section provide patients with safeguards that are sufficient to avoid a breach of art.8 of the ECHR is raised by the decision of the European Court of Human Rights in *X v Finland*; [2012] M.H.L.R. 318 which is considered in the note on s.63 under this heading.

Article 6 of the ECHR does not entitle a patient in every case to challenge a treatment plan before an independent and impartial tribunal before being subjected to it (*R. (on the application of Wilkinson) v The Responsible Medical Officer Broadmoor Hospital* [2001] EWCA Civ 1545; [2002] 1 W.L.R. 419 at para.34). In *R. (on the application of N) v Dr M* [2002] EWCA Civ 1789; [2003] M.H.L.R. 157, the Court of Appeal held that:

1. Any alleged breach of a patient's art.6 rights based on the way in which the SOAD had conducted the certification process would fall away on the judge deciding the disputed facts for himself on an application for judicial review.

2. There was no requirement under art.6 for the judge to hear oral evidence on the issue.

In *Wilkinson*, a patient with a heart condition was being forcibly treated under this section in a situation where there were disputes about whether he was mentally capable and whether the treatment was in his best interests. The court held that on an application for a judicial review of the decision to treat, it would be necessary for the court to reach its own view on the disputed issues, which required them to be determined by cross-examination of the psychiatrists who had been involved with the patient's treatment. Apart from determining the issue of capacity, the court would be required to consider whether the treatment (a) would threaten the patient's life and so be impermissible under art.2, (b) would be degrading and so be impermissible under art.3, and (c) would not be justifiable as both necessary and proportionate under art.8(2) given the extent to which it would invade the appellant's right to privacy. Simon Brown L.J. said at para.29: "The precise equivalence under section 58(3)(b) between incompetent patients and competent but non-consenting patients seems to me increasingly difficult to justify". *Wilkinson* is authority for the proposition that a court, albeit exercising a judicial review function, does so, not on a *Wednesbury* basis (see *Associated Provincial Picture House Ltd v Wednesbury Corporation* [1948] 1 K.B. 223), but by deciding the matter for itself on the merits after full consideration of the evidence whether oral, or in writing. [N.B. The patient's subsequent complaint to the European Court of Human Rights that his treatment constituted a breach of arts 3, 6 and 8 of the ECHR was declared inadmissible (*Wilkinson v United Kingdom* [2006] M.H.L.R. 142).]

Wilkinson was considered in *R. (on the application of N) v Dr M*, above, where the court **1–730** held that:

1. Contrary to what was said in *Wilkinson*, it should not often be necessary to adduce oral evidence with cross-examination where there are disputed issues of fact and opinion in cases where the need for forcible medical treatment of a patient is being challenged on human rights grounds. [In *R. (on the application of JB) v Dr A. Haddock* [2006] EWCA Civ 961; [2006] M.H.L.R. 306, the Court of Appeal did not see any conflict between *Wilkinson* and *N*. Auld L.J. said at para.65: "[T]he court in *Wilkinson*, could not have intended or contemplated that every case would require the hearing and testing of oral medical evidence, especially where, as here, none of the parties requested it". In *R (on the application of Taylor) v (1) Dr Haydn-Smith (2) Dr Gallimore* [2005] EWHC 1668 (Admin); [2005] M.H.L.R. 327, para.8, Collins J. said: "In my view it will only be in a rare case that [adducing oral evidence] will be appropriate. If the court has the relevant medical notes, the reasoned decisions by the doctors concerned, statements from the doctors and other professionals, and comments on any opposing views, it is difficult to see why oral evidence should be needed". Also see *M v South West Hospital and St George's Mental Health NHS Trust* [2008] EWCA Civ 1112 paras 22–24].

2. For a judge to be satisfied that it is appropriate to give permission for treatment where the patient does not consent to it he had to be satisfied that the proposed treatment was both in the patient's best interests and was "medically necessary" as that phrase should be understood and applied for the purposes of art.3 of the ECHR.

3. The standard of proof required is that the court should be satisfied that medical necessity has been "convincingly" shown (*Herczegfalvy v Austria* (1992) E.H.R.R. 437 at 484, para.82).

4. The answer to the question whether the proposed treatment has been convincingly shown to be medically necessary will depend on a number of factors, including (a) how certain is it that the patient does suffer from a treatable mental disorder; (b) how serious a disorder is it; (c) how serious a risk is presented to others; (d) how likely is it that, if the patient does suffer from such a disorder, the proposed

treatment will alleviate the condition; (e) how much alleviation is there likely to be; (f) how likely is it that the treatment will have adverse consequences for the patient; and (g) how severe may they be. The court rejected a submission that, in a case where there is a responsible body of opinion that a patient is not suffering from a treatable condition, that the treatment is not in the patient's best interests and is not medically necessary, then it cannot be convincingly shown that the treatment proposed is in the patient's best interests or medically necessary.

Where there is an issue as to the patient's consent or his capacity to consent under subs.(3)(b), the Court of Appeal in *R. (on the application of JB) v Dr A. Haddock,* above, identified the following three-stage process:

1. The first stage is that of the AC in seeking to initiate the treatment in question.

2. The second stage is for a SOAD to issue a certificate under subs.(3)(b) authorising the treatment on the basis of medical or therapeutic necessity. Auld L.J. said at para.34(ii): "[T]he SOAD's task is a medical one, to be undertaken on the *Bolam* principle, which is likely in almost all cases to involve consideration of the best interests of the patient, and may also take into account non-clinical factors".

3. At the third stage it is for the court to determine whether the *Herczegflavy* medical or therapeutic "necessity" for the treatment has been "convincingly" established by conducting a full merits review of the lawfulness of the SOAD's certificate.

The requirement on a court to be convinced of medical necessity in the light of the medical and other evidence is not capable of being expressed in terms of a standard of evidential proof. Auld L.J. said at para.42: "It is rather a value judgment as to the future—a forecast—to be made by a court in reliance on medical evidence according to a standard of persuasion. If it is to be expressed in forensic terms at all, it is doubtful whether it amounts to more than satisfaction of medical necessity on a balance of probabilities . . .". His Lordship also said, at para.14, that courts:

"in determining whether forcible treatment of a patient has been 'convincingly shown' to be medically necessary, should, as the Court said in *R. (on the application of B) v Dr SS (RMO)* [2005] EWHC 86 (Admin), pay particular attention to the views of those charged with his care and well-being. And, as Simon Brown L.J. . . . observed in [*Wilkinson,* above,] at para.31, courts should not be astute to overrule a treatment plan decided upon by the [AC] and certified by a SOAD following the required consultation with two others concerned with the patient's care; see also *Herczegfalvy,* at para.86".

1–731 In *R. (on the application of B) v Dr SS (Responsible Medical Officer)* [2006] EWCA Civ 28; [2006] M.H.L.R. 131, paras 66–68, the Court of Appeal said that:

1. Where the real issue is whether the patient should be detained in a mental hospital at all, that issue is one that should be referred to a tribunal in the first instance, rather than be the subject of judicial review proceedings. In such circumstances the appropriate course may well be on the application for permission to grant an interim injunction and adjourn the application pending a hearing before the tribunal.

2. Where the challenge is not to the grounds for detention but to the treatment itself, careful consideration should be given to the procedure to ensure, in so far as is possible, that there are not protracted and expensive legal proceedings requiring oral evidence from medical witnesses where there is no prima facie case that anything untoward has occurred. It is, of course, essential that the requirements of art.6 are satisfied but this does not mean that permission must be given for judicial review proceedings where the papers do not disclose any arguable grounds for this.

3. Section 58 imposes preconditions to compulsory treatment which ought to ensure that this is not imposed unless there is a convincing therapeutic case for it. They will only do so, however, if the SOAD satisfies herself that the treatment in question should be imposed. This requires a truly independent assessment, not merely approval of the AC's decision on the basis that it is not manifestly unsound. If s.58 is properly complied with then issues requiring cross-examination of medical witnesses should not often arise.

In *R. (on the application of B) v Dr SS* [2005] EWHC 1936 (Admin); [2005] M.H.L.R. 347, Charles J. said, at para.231, that when there is no distinct and separate challenge to the certificate of the SOAD in judicial review proceedings, nonetheless (a) the SOAD should be joined to obtain a binding order in respect of his certificate and to give him the opportunity to make separate representations from the AC if he so wishes, and (b) if possible at an early directions hearing the issues of permission and the further participation of the SOAD should be addressed. In a postscript to his judgment in *R. (on the application of B) v Haddock [2005]* EWHC 921 (Admin); [2005] M.H.L.R. 317 at paras 38, 39, Collins J. said that it will be rare that it is necessary for a SOAD to be represented where she has granted a certificate in a case where the decision of the AC is under attack, although it will be necessary to treat the SOAD as a defendant. In this case it was confirmed that the *Herczegfalvy* test only applies to the administration of the proposed treatment; it does not apply to the determination whether the patient suffers from a mental disorder.

R. (on the application of N) v Dr M, above, was applied in *R. (on the application of PS) v* **1–732** *G* [2003] EWHC 2335 (Admin); [2004] M.H.L.R. 1, where Silber J. held that where medical treatment is administered to a patient against his will, art.3 will be contravened if:

(i)   the treatment reaches the minimum level of severity of ill-treatment, taking into account all the circumstances, including the positive and adverse mental and physical consequences of the treatment, the nature and context of the treatment, the manner and method of its execution, its duration and, if relevant, the sex, age and health of the patient; and

(ii) the medical or therapeutic necessity for the treatment has not been convincingly shown to exist.

With regard to (i), the European Court of Human Rights has held that the minimum level of severity threshold would only be met if the treatment involved "actual physical injury or intense physical or mental suffering" (*Pretty v United Kingdom* (2002) 35 E.H.R.R. 1 at para.52).

His Lordship said, at para.123, that where the patient has capacity, his lack of consent, while an important factor in determining whether treatment engages art.3, cannot be decisive and that there is no basis for concluding that the patient's objections automatically and inevitably override all other issues except where the interests of other people would be affected if the medication was not administered.

With regard to a claim made under art.8 of the ECHR, his Lordship held that the phrase "in accordance with law" in that article means that the common law "best interests test" must be satisfied in that the treatment must be in accordance with responsible and competent professional opinion, a less invasive form of treatment which would be likely to achieve the same beneficial results for the patient is not available, and it is necessary that the treatment should be given to the patient with regard to (a) his resistance to treatment, (b) the degree to which treatment is likely to alleviate or prevent deterioration of his condition, (c) the risk that he presents to himself or to others, (d) the consequences of the treatment not being given and (e) any possible adverse affects of the treatment.

The decisions in *Wilkinson, N* and *PS* were considered by Silber J. in *R. (on the application of B) v Dr SS* [2005] EWHC 86 (Admin); [2005] M.H.L.R. 96, where the claimant asserted that subs.(3)(b) when considered with s.3 of the Human Rights Act authorises the compulsory treatment of a patient who has capacity to refuse to consent only where it is shown that (a) such treatment is necessary for the protection of the public from serious harm or (b) without such treatment serious harm is likely to result to his health, alternatively is incompatible with the requirements of art.3 and/or art.8 and/or art.14 of the ECHR. In particular, the claimant contended that the fact that the objection to the treatment by a patient with capacity is merely an important factor in determining whether a ECHR right is engaged is wrong in law. Although his Lordship found that the claim could not be pursued because of its academic nature, he held that:

1. The proposed treatment of anti-psychotic medication which was a therapeutic necessity would not amount to a breach of arts 3 or 8 merely because the patient had capacity to consent but did not consent. Treatment that was a therapeutic necessity could not be regarded as "inhuman or degrading" for the purposes of art.3. So far as art.8 was concerned, art.8(1) was engaged but treatment that was a therapeutic necessity could be justified under art.8(2) provided that it was in accordance with the law. Thus it had to satisfy both the "best interests" test at common law and the express requirements of s.58.

2. In deciding whether treatment was a therapeutic necessity, the fact that the patient did not consent to it was an important factor.

3. There was no need to "read down" s.58 and that the section was compatible with the ECHR.

His Lordship also rejected the claim that the present law amounts to unlawful discrimination in breach of art.14 against a patient with capacity for reasons which included the fact that the suggested comparators were not in an analogous position and there was an objective and reasonable justification for overriding the wishes of a patient where s.58 applied.

It became clear to his Lordship during the course of the hearing that where a SOAD's certificate has been obtained difficulties arise because the certificate only lasts for three months, but under the present arrangements, the challenge in the courts to the certificate is invariably not completed in time for the treatment to be administered within the three month period. Proposals on how to resolve this problem are set out in Appendix II to the judgment. They have been endorsed by the lead judge of the Administrative Court and the Head of the Administrative Court Office. Paragraph 12 of Appendix II states:

"The best way forward would be to ensure that when any claim is brought challenging the decision of the [AC] or the SOAD to authorise medical treatment to a patient who does not consent, there should be a speedy and automatic oral case management hearing two working days after the challenge application is brought. The Mental Health Act Commission has suggested that at that case management hearing 'one of the relevant factors to take into account when making directions at such a hearing is whether the SOAD has advised on the Form [T3] that a further second opinion be obtained, and if so, at what stage'. I agree with that suggestion. Unless an application for interim relief is made very quickly, it is unlikely that an interim order would be appropriate without at least a hearing at which other parties were represented. All parties should attend that hearing and the court could then consider a timetable for steps leading up to the hearing of the substantive claim within a timetable, which would be speedy and which would enable all parties to have sufficient time in which to present their cases. In many cases, it would be appropriate at the initial hearing to order a rolled-up hearing at which the court could consider the permission application and then proceed to deal with the substantive application."

1–733 These remarks should be read subject to the comments about procedure made by the Court of Appeal in *R. (on the application of B) v Dr SS*, above.

The cases set out above were considered by Charles J. in *R. (on the application of B) v Dr SS* [2005] EWHC 1936 (Admin); [2005] M.H.L.R. 347. His Lordship held that:

1. The capacity of the patient is relevant to an assessment under art.3 of medical necessity, to assessments under s.58 and thus to whether what is proposed is "in accordance with the law" for the purposes of art.8(2). However, whether or not a patient has capacity does not carry significant weight. The correct approach is to take account of the wishes of the patient against a background of his understanding of and approach to the issues relating to the relevant treatment and to his appreciation of whether he is being forced to accept the treatment and the effects this could have.

2. Inhuman and degrading treatment under art.3 would not be demonstrated where it was convincingly shown to the court's satisfaction that the treatment was a therapeutic necessity. The phrase "convincingly shown" introduces a high standard of proof and that the language of the English criminal and civil standards of proof should not be imported into it.

3. Article 8 was engaged whether or not the patient had capacity. The issue was justification under art.8(2). Such justification did not require that it should be convincingly shown that the treatment was a therapeutic necessity. The conventional three-fold test fell to be applied: was the treatment: (i) in accordance with the law; (ii) for a legitimate aim; and (iii) necessary in a democratic society? Treatment would be in accordance with the law if it fell within the terms of s.58. His Lordship accepted a submission on behalf of the Secretary of State that the common law should not be considered as a separate and distinct consideration in determining whether the treatment being proposed was "in accordance with the law". His Lordship said at para.91:

   "[T]he s.58 MHA test is a distinct test set by Parliament for a particular situation and purpose and when it applies it supplants or suspends the common law. In my view when applying the statutory test the courts should remember this, whilst at the same time taking appropriate guidance from the approach at common law in applying the 'best interests test' and, I add, to the right to autonomy at common law."

This decision was upheld by the Court of Appeal ([2006] EWCA Civ 28; [2006] M.H.L.R. 131). The court held that:

1. On the findings of fact made by Charles J., the imposition of proposed anti-psychotic medication will be lawful under English law and will not infringe the ECHR.

2. The judge was correct to hold that: (i) capacity is not the crucial factor in determining whether treatment can be administered without consent; and (ii) when considering the severity of treatment the fact that it is imposed by compulsion is more significant than the question of whether the patient has or has not capacity to consent to the treatment.

3. It was wrong to claim that in order to avoid infringing the ECHR treatment can only be given to a competent patient against his will if the treatment is not only a "therapeutic necessity" but is also necessary for the protection of the public or to prevent the patient from suffering serious harm. The court endorsed the acceptance by Silber J. in the *PS* case of the submission that:

   "the decision to administer anti-psychotic medication has to be considered in the context that the medication is likely to lead to the claimant being rehabilitated rather than remaining subject to long-term incarceration."

The court found that it was not necessary for it to decide whether a best interests test had to be satisfied in addition to provisions set out in s.58 in order to meet requirements of art.8(2). However, the court made a number of observations on this issue which are set out in the notes on subs.(3)(b) under the heading "Appropriate for the treatment to be given".

For the compatibility of the three-month stabilising period established by subs.(1)(b) with art.8 of the ECHR, see the notes to "three months or more" in that provision.

The Mental Capacity Act 2005
1–734   See the General Note to this Part.

The Code of Practice
Guidance on this section is given in Ch.25 at paras 25.11 to 25.18.

Subsection (1)
1–735   *Paragraph (a)*   Such forms of treatment.   No treatments have been specified under this provision.

REGULATIONS.   See subs.(5). There is no power equivalent to that contained in s.118(2) for treatments to be specified for the purposes of this section by the *Code of Practice*.

SECRETARY OF STATE.   The functions of the Minister under this section, so far as exercisable in relation to Wales, are exercised by the Welsh Ministers (see the General Note to the Act).

Paragraph (b)
1–736   This paragraph enables a course of medication to be imposed on a patient coming within the scope of this Part for up to three months without the patient's consent and without the need to obtain an independent medical opinion. The protection provided by this section does not come into play until three months have elapsed since the commencement of the treatment. Authorisation for imposing treatment on the patient during the initial three months is given by s.63.

Medication that is specified in regulations made under para.(a), above, and medication that is a s.57 or s.58A treatment does not come within the scope of this paragraph.

The approach to be taken by a court when considering an application for the judicial review of decisions made by the patient's AC and a SOAD to administer medication under this section, notwithstanding the patient's refusal to consent to that treatment, is considered in the cases noted under "Human Rights Act 1998", above.

MEDICINE.   Or any combination of medicines. Paragraph 25.18 of the *Code of Practice* states:

"Certificates under this section must clearly set out the specific forms of treatment to which they apply. All the relevant drugs should be listed, including medication to be given 'as required' (prn), either by name or by the classes described in the British National Formulary (BNF). If drugs are specified by class, the certificate should state clearly the number of drugs authorised in each class, and whether any drugs within the class are excluded. The maximum dosage and route of administration should be clearly indicated for each drug or category of drugs proposed. This can exceed the dosages listed in the BNF, but particular care is required in these cases."

Phil Fennell reports that the "most striking aspect of the medication cases [he studied] was the surprisingly high number of occasions where BNF recommended dose limits were exceeded (12 per cent of the medicines cases), and in a small number of cases the very large margin by which they were exceeded" (*Treatment Without Consent*, 1996, p.216). In May 2006, the Royal College of Psychiatrists issued a revised "Consensus statement on high-dose antipsychotic medication" which contains recommendations in relation to the decision to treat patients in excess of BNF recommended limits. The statement can be accessed at: *www.rcpsych.ac.uk/files/pdfversion/CR138.pdf.*

A medicine is identified by its chemical composition and not by its method of administration. Ordinary food in liquid form, such as would be used in the tube feeding of a patient with anorexia nervosa, is therefore not a medicine within the meaning of this section. However, it is a "medical treatment" coming within the scope of s.63 (*B v Croydon Health Authority* [1995] 1 All E.R. 683 CA). For the administration of placebo medication, see the note under subs.(3).

Only medicine that is prescribed as treatment for the patient's mental disorder is "medicine" for the purpose of this section. This can include medication which is aimed at relieving the symptoms of the patient's mental disorder or which is ancillary to the core treatment that the patient is receiving: see s.145(4) and *B v Croydon Health Authority*, above, which is considered in the note on s.63. Medicines do not come within the scope of this section merely because they have an effect on the patient's mental state.

The fact that medication administered to a patient under this section might continue to have effect after the three month period has expired or after the patient has ceased to be detained is not legally relevant.

THREE MONTHS OR MORE.   Given that most detentions last less than three months, this provision provides limited protection to patients. Month means calendar month (Interpretation Act 1978, Sch.1). The first day of treatment should be included in the calculation of this period. During the debates on the Mental Health (Amendment) Bill, the Minister of State said:

"The three-month period is considered appropriate because of the time that it allows for an optimum regime of medication to be identified—or, at least, for certain options to be ruled out before a certificate is needed. Different medications need to be tried before the most suitable one is identified" (*Hansard*, HL Vol.688, cols 494,495).

The three-month period must be continuous. The period is not broken on (1) the patient being granted leave of absence or being absent without leave; (2) the patient being transferred to another hospital whilst continuing to be detained; (3) the authority to detain the patient being renewed under s.20; (4) a change of medication; (5) the medication not being administered continuously; (6) the patient being made subject to a community treatment order or having his community treatment order revoked; and (7) the section under which the patient is detained being changed. As the medication must be given "at any time during a period for which [the patient] is liable to be detained", the three-month period will clearly be broken by the patient's discharge from detention. This situation could occur where the patient's detention is found to be unlawful, he is discharged from that detention, and is then immediately re-detained. The three-month period is also broken "if a Part 2 patient is discharged without becoming a CTO patient or if the patient is placed under guardianship, or upon the conditional discharge of a restricted patient" (*Code of Practice*, para.25.12). "A patient's move between detention and CTO does not change the date on which the three-month period expires" (*Code of Practice*, para.25.16).

In the Scottish case of *Petition of WM* [2002] M.H.L.R. 367, the Court of Session (Outer House) held that the three month period set out in Pt X of the Mental Health (Scotland) Act 1984 during which the consent of a mentally competent detained patient is not required for treatment of his mental disorder did not violate art.8 of the ECHR. Although there was a closely defined departure from the principle of personal autonomy, the requirement of proportionality was not breached. The approach taken in *WM* was followed with regard to the three month period established by subs.(1)(b) in the unreported case of *R. (on the application of AM) v Central and North West London Mental Health NHS Trust*, February 1, 2007 (see Radcliffes Le Brasseur, Mental Health Law Briefing No.116). The question whether these findings are compatible with the patient's rights under art.8 of the ECHR is raised by the decision of the European Court of Human Rights in *X v Finland* [2012] M.H.L.R. 318, which is considered in the note on s.63 under the heading "Human Rights Act 1998".

FIRST OCCASION IN THAT PERIOD. The three-month period starts from the first occasion when medicine for mental disorder is given to a patient who is detained under a section which is not excluded by s.56(3). For example, if a patient is initially detained under s.4, which is subsequently converted to a s.2, and is then detained under s.3 the three-month period will start from the first time that medicine was administered to the patient after the second medical recommendation referred to in s.4(4) was received. The period starts irrespective of whether the patient has consented to the treatment.

Subsection (3)

Concurrent use of Forms T2 and T3

1–737   If a mentally capable patient consents to some of the treatment that is being provided for him (for example, anti-depressant medication) but does not consent to the remainder of his treatment (for example, anti-psychotic medication), then both of the procedures set out in paras (a) and (b) should be followed. The position of the Mental Health Act Commission had been that if a patient consents to treatment A but does not consent to treatment B, a Form T3 issued under s.58(3)(b) should be completed and treatment A should be included on the form as part of the patient's plan of treatment as authorised by s.59: see Policy Briefing for Commissioners, Issue 3, Annex 2, p.4. This is to misinterpret the effect of s.59. If the patient consents to a treatment, s.58(3)(a) requires a statutory procedure involving the use of Form T2 to be followed: the treatment "shall not be given" unless the form is completed. If the patient does not consent to a treatment, s.58(3)(b) provides for a different procedure involving the use of Form T3 to be followed. Section 59 allows either Form to relate to a plan of treatment which would allow for variations in the treatment that the patient receives under the authority granted by the Form. Section 59 does not allow for the mandatory procedure set out in s.58(3)(a) to be disregarded on the ground that the treatment in question will be included in the patients plan of treatment under s.58(3)(b). The MHAC subsequently accepted the correctness of this opinion "where a patient genuinely consents to a part of a treatment plan but refuses to consent to the remainder" ("Guidance Note for Commissioners on consent to treatment and the Mental Health Act 1983", 2008, para.9.1). The CQC adopts the same stance: see the May 2012 revision of the Guidance Note.

Covert administration of medication

1–738   Covert medication is the administration of medication in disguised form. This usually involves disguising the medication by administering it in food or drink. As a result, the patient is unknowingly taking the medication.

In para.5.8 of its *Sixth Biennial Report*, 1993–1995, the Mental Health Act Commission made the following comments about the covert administration of medication (the references are to the 1999 edition of the *Code of Practice*):

"One of the problems associated with covert administration is that it is clearly impossible to attempt to negotiate consent to such treatment and covert administration is seemingly precluded by paragraph 16.11 in the *Code of Practice* and by section 58(3)(a) of the Act, unless it has been certified as acceptable by a Second Opinion Doctor under section 58(3)(b). In contrast, it has been argued that a doctor may be entitled to withhold information from the patient under paragraph 15.13 of the Code but must be prepared to justify that decision. However, for that to be valid, the treatment must be 'in accordance with practice accepted at the time by a responsible body of medical opinion skilled in the particular form of treatment in question' (*Code of Practice* para.15.19). It would seem appropriate therefore for this matter to be considered by the Royal College of Psychiatrists and the Royal College of Nursing. Meanwhile, professional judgment must be relied upon in making decisions on this important ethical issue."

That the MHAC gave such equivocal advice on this issue is to be regretted. The quotation reproduced by the MHAC is from the case of *Bolam v Friern Hospital Management Committee* [1957] 1 W.L.R. 582, which laid down the general approach to be adopted by the courts to questions of medical negligence. The argument that this common law test can override the clear statutory language of subs.(3)(a), where it is stated that "a patient shall not be given ... treatment to which this section applies unless ... he has consented to that treatment", is clearly erroneous and should not be followed. The MHAC's slightly modified final position on this issue was set out at paras 6.38 to 6.48 of its *Twelfth Biennial Report*, 2005–2007. The legal position is that the covert administration of medication can only be given to a detained patient under the powers contained in either s.63 (i.e. during the three-month period provided for in subs.(1)(b)) or para.(b) of this subsection. Before treatment is administered covertly, the RC should consider: (a) why it is not "practicable" to seek the patient's consent (*Code of Practice* para.24.41), and (b) whether, for the purposes of art.8(2) of the ECHR, the giving of covert medication is a proportionate response to the aim of improving the patient's health or reducing the risk posed by the patient (*Code of Practice* para.24.43). The fact that the RC has considered these issues should be recorded in the patient's notes. Although it would be lawful to administer medication provided under either s.63 or para.(b) forcibly (if that is clinically possible), the RC might consider that the alternative of administering the medication covertly would be less invasive of the patient's physical integrity. While it is the case that a certificate granted under para.(b) can authorise the covert administration of medication to a patient who is mentally capable of "understanding the nature, purpose and likely effects" of the treatment but is objecting to it, the patient will obviously be aware that the treatment is likely to be given to him at some time in the future. It is suggested that the RC discusses the possibility of the covert administration of the medication with the SOAD, and that the SOAD be invited to agree to such action and to confirm this on Form T3. If a mentally incapable patient is informal, the treatment can be given under the authority of the Mental Capacity Act 2005 if the treatment is assessed as being in the best interests of the patient.

The fact that medication is being administered covertly will almost certainly be disclosed to the patient on an application or a reference to the tribunal being made: see the note to r.14(2) of the Tribunal Procedure (First-tier Tribunal) (Health, Education and Social Care Chamber) Rules 2008.

The Mental Welfare Commission for Scotland has published guidance on covert medication which can be accessed at: *http://www.mwcscot.org.uk/media/140485/covert_medication_finalnov_13.pdf.*

Placebo medication

In its *Eighth Biennial Report*, 1997–1999, at para.6.17, the MHAC said that "as an inert **1–739** substance, a placebo does not fall within the definition of 'medicine' and, therefore, falls outside the provisions of section 58" (in its *Tenth Biennial Report* 2001–2003, para.10.52 the MHAC stated that this represented a "provisional" view). This approach fails to address the reality of the situation which is that a placebo is offered to the patient as a "medicine" which, hopefully, will lead to an improvement in his condition. The fact that any improvement in the patient's condition is triggered by a psychological, rather than a physiological reaction does not disqualify the substance from being categorised as a "medicine". It is instructive to note that the *Shorter Oxford English Dictionary* states that a placebo was first described, in 1811, as a "medicine given more to please than to benefit the patient". A more recent definition is "a pill, medicine, etc. prescribed more for psychological reasons than for any physiological effect" (*Oxford English Reference Dictionary* (1996)). Given that in *B v Croydon Health Authority* [1995] 1 All E.R. 683, the Court of Appeal held that "medical treatment" included "a range of acts ancillary to the core treatment that the patient is receiving", and that ancillary treatment would include treatment which is "concurrent with the core treatment", it would seem that the administration of placebo medication is the administration of a medicine for the medical treatment of the patient's mental disorder for the purposes of subs.(1)(b). However, in most cases the practical reality is that placebo medication cannot be given to either mentally capable or mentally incapable patients who come within the scope of this Part as in both instances the patient must be given an explanation of the nature, purpose and effect of the medication in order that his capacity to consent to the treatment can be assessed.

Paragraph (a)

1–740   This paragraph applies to a capacious patient who consents to the treatment.

Section 1(2) of the Mental Capacity Act 2005 states that a "person must be assumed to have capacity unless it is established that he lacks capacity". The CQC turns this principle on its head by stating that "where a person is in the situation of requiring specialist inpatient mental health care under the powers of the Act, the assumption of capacity should be backed up by an evidential record" (*Monitoring the Mental Health Act in 2011/12*, pp.69,70). It is not clear what should comprise the "evidential record"; presumably the CQC means that a record of a formal capacity assessment of the patient should be made, a requirement that is not to be found in the Act. It is submitted that the assumption of capacity established by s.1(2) of the 2005 Act applies to this provision, and that a formal capacity assessment is only required if the patient's diagnosis, presentation or history suggests that the assumption might be rebutted. The *Code of Practice* states at para.25.17:

> "Where approved clinicians certify the treatment of a patient who consents, they should not rely on the certificate as the only record of their reasons for believing that the patient has consented to the treatment. A record of their discussion with the patient including any capacity assessment, should be made in the patient's notes as normal."

CONSENTED.   See the note on "consented to it" in s.57(2).

APROVED CLINICIAN IN CHARGE.   Only a medically qualified AC can be "in charge" of the administration of medication to a patient.

REGISTERED MEDICAL PRACTITIONER.   A visit by a SOAD for the purposes of this paragraph should only be requested if ACs "are genuinely unable to determine for themselves whether the patient has the capacity to consent or whether the patient is in fact consenting" (*Code of Practice*, para.25.44).

APPOINTED ... BY THE SECRETARY OF STATE.   The Commission (or, in Wales, Health Inspectorate Wales) makes the appointment (Health and Social Care Act 2008 s.52(1)(b)). Both the Commission and HIW require appointees to be GMC registered and to hold a current licence to practise. Those appointed may include members or employees of the Commission (Health and Social Care Act s.52(2)). There is no requirement for the SOAD to be an AC. It is rare for a SOAD to issue a certificate under this paragraph. This could happen where, contrary to the prior opinion expressed by the patient's AC, the SOAD finds that the patient is both competent and consenting to the treatment. The SOAD has a right of access to the patient and his records: see s.119 for registered establishents and the direction of the Secretary of State, published as Annex A to DHSS Circular No.HC(83)19, for hospitals. Once appointed, the SOAD is not subject to regulation by the Commission but will exercise her own independent judgment (*X v A, B and C and the Mental Health Act Commission,* noted in the General Note to s.57, and the Health and Social Care Act 2008 (Regulated Activities) Regulations 2010 (SI 2010/781) reg.3, Sch.1 para.6(1A)). Her decision cannot therefore be appealed against to the Commission.

As a person who is exercising "functions of a public nature", the SOAD is a "public authority" for the purposes of s.6 of the Human Rights Act 1998: see s.6(3)(b) and *R.*

(on the application of Wilkinson) v The Responsible Medical Officer Broadmoor Hospital [2001] EWCA Civ 1545; [2002] 1 W.L.R. 419, where Hale L.J. said that the SOAD is "performing a statutory watchdog function on behalf of the public to protect detained persons who are in an especially vulnerable position" (para.71).

CERTIFIED. Using Form T2: see s.64(2) and reg.27(2) of the English Regulations (in Wales, Form CO2: see reg.40(2) of the Welsh Regulations). Neither the Act nor the English or Welsh Regulations provide for the renewal of the Form. The statement in para.25.83 of the *Code of Practice* that Form T2 ceases to authorise treatment where there "is a permanent change in the approved clinician in charge of the patient's treatment" is, it is submitted, incorrect as para.(a) merely states that the completion of the Form gives authority for the treatment to be provided. It would be surprising if a permanent change of AC rendered the Form ineffective, while the long term absence of the AC did not have such an effect. The wording of this section supports the contention that the authority to treat provided by the Form will only end if the patient's consent is withdrawn, the patient becomes mentally incapable of consenting to the treatment, the patient ceases to be detained, or the treatment specified in the Form changes. It would be sensible for a fresh Form to be completed where there is either a permanent change of AC or the AC is likely to be absent for a considerable time because the new or acting AC will need to review the patient's medication and completing the Form will provide evidence of the review.

CAPABLE OF UNDERSTANDING. In *R. (on the application of B) v Dr SS (Responsible Medical Officer)* [2006] EWCA Civ 28 paras 33, 34, Lord Phillips C.J. said that it was arguable that the words "capable of understanding the nature, purpose and likely effects of" the treatment do not go far enough to define capacity and that whatever "the precise test of capacity to consent to treatment, we think that it is plain that a patient will lack that capacity if he is not able to appreciate the likely effects of having or not having the treatment". The judgment in this case was delivered before the implementation of the Mental Capacity Act 2005. Despite the differences in the wording of the two tests, it is suggested that in cases where there is doubt about the patient's capacity the test set out in ss.2 and 3 of that Act should be used to determine whether the patient is capable of understanding the treatment in question. Given the obiter remarks of Hale L.J. in *R. (on the application of Wilkinson) v Responsible Medical Officer Broadmoor Hospital* [2001] EWCA Civ 1545; [2002] 1 W.L.R. 419 at paras 65, 66, it is likely that the courts would endorse this approach which has been adopted by the *Code of Practice* at para.24.31. As s.1(2) of the 2005 Act states that a person must be assumed to have capacity unless it is established that he lacks capacity, a formal assessment of capacity would only be required if there is reason to believe that the presumption could be rebutted: see the note on the CQC's report on *Monitoring the Mental Health Act in 2011/12*, above.

In *R. v Mental Health Act Commission Ex p. X* (1998) 9 B.M.L.R. 77, Stuart-Smith L.J. noted, obiter, at 85, that the words in this subsection "are 'capable of understanding' and not 'understands'. Thus the question is capacity and not actual understanding". In para.6.12 of its Fourth Biennial Report 1989–1991, the Mental Health Act Commission (MHAC) stated that the judgment in this case "appeared to suggest that consent rests not on actual understanding but simply on the patient's intellectual capacity to understand". The MHAC reported that it had "taken legal advice on this approach and advised all [Second Opinion Appointed Doctors] to continue with their approach of requiring both a capacity and adequate understanding of the treatment and its consequences". It is submitted that the MHAC's advice is correct as Stuart-Smith L.J.'s remarks do little more than distinguish the two elements of this provision, i.e. the patient's capacity and the patient's consent. In any event Stuart-Smith L.J.'s formulation, at 86, of the requirements of a valid consent—"No doubt consent has to be an informed consent in that [the patient] knows the nature and likely effect of the treatment"—is supportive of the MHAC's approach. It would also be difficult to establish whether a patient is capable of understanding particular information without, at the same time, also establishing that he actually does understand that information. However, in *R. (on the application of B) v Secretary of State for Health* [2005] EWHC 86 (Admin); [2005] M.H.L.R. 96 para.87, Silber J. said that Stuart-Smith L.J.'s comment on this phrase "might mean that a patient might be regarded as having capacity even if he does not actually understand the nature, purpose and likely effects of the treatment". This formulation is not compatible with the approach taken by the Court of Appeal in *B*, above. His Lordship endorsed the finding of Hale L.J. in *R. (on the application of Wilkinson) v The Responsible Medical Officer Broadmoor Hospital*, that the threshold for capacity is a low one and said at para.91:

"The present low threshold for capacity recognises correctly the great importance to be attached to principles of autonomy, but it also means that the case for non-consensual treatment of those with capacity is increased."

NATURE, PURPOSE AND LIKELY EFFECTS OF THE TREATMENT. Prior to the passing of the Mental Capacity Act 2005, Thorpe J. held that this formulation is declaratory of the common law position relating to information that must be given to a patient before a valid consent can be obtained (*Re C (Refusal of Medical Treatment)* [1994] 1 All E.R. 819 at 824).

Paragraph (b)

1–741   This paragraph allows for the provision of medical treatments that come within the scope of this section to mentally incapacitated patients and to mentally capable non-consenting patients if a certificate by SOAD is provided. If treatment is regulated by this section, it cannot be provided to a mentally incapable detained patient under the authority of the Mental Capacity Act 2005: see s.28 of that Act. This means that if such a patient has made a valid and applicable advance decision (AD) under the 2005 Act refusing a treatment which comes within the scope of this section, the AD is not binding on the clinician. However, clinicians should try to abide by the patient's wishes as expressed in the AD if this is practicable (*Code of Practice*, para.9.9).

The decision-making process to be followed where treatment is provided under this provision was identified by the Court of Appeal in *R. (on the application of JB) v Dr A. Haddock*, which is noted under "Human Rights Act 1998", above. This section does not place the patient's AC under an obligation to continue to provide a treatment to a patient which is specified in the statutory form after it has become clinically inappropriate to do so.

CERTIFIED. Form T3 should be used: see s.64(2) and reg.27(2) of the English Regulations (in Wales, Form CO3 and reg.40(2) of the Welsh Regulations). Although the *Code of Practice*, at para.25.48, states that the SOAD should "interview the patient in private if possible", neither interviewing the patient nor medically examining him is a legal requirement. Therefore, a SOAD can give a certificate if the patient is either unwilling or too disturbed to be interviewed.

In its "Guidance note for Commissioners on consent to treatment and the Mental Health Act 1983", the CQC states at paras 8.2 to 8.4:

"The validity of a Form T3 is unaffected by changes in approved clinician or even detaining hospital. If a patient is transferred to another hospital under s.19 the Form T3 from their original hospital remains valid.

Whilst SOADs have the right to authorise time-limited authorisations Forms T3 are not time-limited, and the Code of Practice gives no guidance on when they should be reviewed. However, the Commission has taken the general view that Forms T3 should not normally be extant for more than two years. Commissioners who encounter Forms T3 that are more than two years old should pass the details of the form to the Commission Secretariat so that further investigation can take place.

If a patient gives genuine and consistent consent to the treatment authorised on a Form T3, the Approved Clinician should complete a Form T2 to replace that authority. Where consent fluctuates, it may be appropriate to continue treating under the authority of Form T3. However, the *Code of Practice* [(25.88)] states that any certificate issued on the basis that a patient is incapable of consent will cease to authorise treatment upon that patient regaining capacity. Similarly, where T3 states that the patient is capable but refusing consent, but subsequently the patient loses capacity, that certificate must no longer be deemed to authorise treatment and a further second opinion is required. The same approach should, of course, be applied where patients cease to consent and a Form T2 is extant."

In *R. (on the application of Wilkinson) v The Responsible Medical Officer Broadmoor Hospital*, above, the Court of Appeal said that the SOAD doctor is required to reach her own independent view of the desirability and propriety of the AC's proposal. Simon Brown L.J. said at paras 32, 33:

"The evidence before us, however, suggests that his approach to the [AC's] proposal is perhaps more akin to that of a review than to forming his own primary judgment on the question. Indeed, in the advice issued by the Mental Health Act Commission to Second Opinion Appointed Doctors in April 1999 it is stated:

'The treatment authorised ... may not be in accord with the SOAD's personal practice but should be reasonable in the opinion of the SOAD, i.e. the SOAD is not offering an 'academic' second opinion or imposing a treatment plan on the RMO.'

Whilst, of course, it is proper for the SOAD to pay regard to the views of the [AC] who has, after all, the most intimate knowledge of the patient's case, that does not relieve him of the responsibility of forming his own independent judgment as to whether or not 'the treatment should be given'. And certainly, if the SOAD's certificate and evidence is to carry any real weight in cases where ... the treatment plan is challenged, it will be necessary to demonstrate a less deferential approach than appears to be the norm."

Brooke and Hale L.JJ. expressed their agreement with these obiter comments.

The question whether fairness requires a SOAD to give reasons for a decision which **1–742** sanctions the violation of the autonomy of a mentally competent adult patient was considered by the Court of Appeal in *R. (on the application of Wooder) v Feggetter* [2002] EWCA Civ 554; [2002] M.H.L.R. 178. It was held that:

(i) a SOAD owes a duty to give in writing the reasons for his opinion when certifying under this section that a mentally competent detained patient should be given medication against his will;

(ii) there is no requirement for a SOAD to dot every "i" and cross every "t" when giving his reasons. So long as he gives his reasons clearly on what he reasonably regards as the substantive points on which he formed his clinical judgment, this will suffice;

(iii) the court will only grant a patient permission to challenge the reasons if it can be shown that there is a real prospect of establishing that a SOAD has not addressed any substantive point which he should have addressed, or that there is some material error underlying the reasons that he gave;

(iv) the reasons need not be disclosed to the patient if either the SOAD or the AC considers that such disclosure would be likely to cause serious harm to the physical or mental health of the patient or any other person;

(v) the SOAD should send a statement of his reasons to the AC or to the hospital together with any opinion he may have on the desirability of withholding them from the patient on "serious harm" grounds. The AC should then make them available to the patient to read, unless it is a case in which reliance can properly be placed on the "serious harm" exception from disclosure; and

(vi) although the reasons should be prepared and disclosed to the patient as soon as practicable, it may not always be appropriate to delay treatment once the SOAD's certificate has been given.

These findings would also apply to a mentally competent child patient. Their Lordships left open the question whether fairness also requires the AC's report to the SOAD to be disclosed to the patient in order that the patient can address its contents when interviewed by the SOAD.

A consideration of the implications of this decision and the role of SOADs generally is set out at paras 25.60 to 25.71 of the *Code of Practice*. Although in *R. (on the application of Lee-Hirons) v Secretary of State for Justice* [2014] EWCA Civ 553, Sir Stanley Burnton indicated at para.27 that the decision in *Wooder* is not authority for the requirement for the SOAD's reasons to be given in writing, it is suggested that this be done and the guidance given in para.25.63 of the *Code* followed.

Although the Commission has no power to attach a time limit to a Form T3, it can withdraw the power to treat provided by the Form T3 by issuing a notice under s.61(3).

NOT CAPABLE OF UNDERSTANDING.   See the note on para.(a). If the patient regains capacity, see s.60(1C), (1D).

NOT CONSENTED TO IT.   The 1978 White Paper suggested that the following principle be adopted in cases where the patient's consent is not forthcoming: "where it is not possible to agree with the patient the form the treatment is to take and the consultant feels the imposition of treatment is essential he should, wherever there is a choice, select the method of treatment the patient finds least objectionable or which would represent the minimum interference with the patient" (Cmnd. 7320 para.6.18).

APPROPRIATE FOR THE TREATMENT TO BE GIVEN.   See s.64(3). When considering this matter (as it was prior to the amendment made by the 2007 Act), the SOAD "should have regard for the [RC's] greater experience than his of the patient", per Auld L.J. in the *Dr Haddock* case, below, at para.46. In *R. (on the application of B) v Dr SS (Responsible Medical Officer)* [2006] EWCA Civ 28 at para.62, the Court of Appeal said that the phrase "likelihood of its alleviating or preventing a deterioration of his condition", which was removed by the 2007 Act:

"should not be equated with the test of whether treatment is in the best interests of a patient. That question will depend on wider considerations than the simple question of efficacy of the treatment, such as whether an alternative and less invasive treatment will achieve the same result. The distress that will be caused to the patient if the treatment has to be imposed by force will also be a relevant consideration. English common law and medical ethics both require that medical treatment shall not be imposed without the consent of the patient unless treatment is considered to be in the best interests of the patient. Thus, while the specified criteria are obviously critical to the decision of whether the treatment should be given, they are not the only considerations relevant to that question. The SOAD has to certify that the treatment should be given and we do not see how he can properly do that unless satisfied that the treatment is in the best interests of the patient."

In *R. (on the application of JB) v Dr A. Haddock* [2006] EWCA Civ 961; [2006] M.H.L.R. 306 at para.45, Auld L.J. said that considerations such as these "underline the composite nature of the question of medical necessity. It is one to which the answer will always be one of value judgment derived from other value judgments on often difficult and complex questions of diagnosis and prognosis on which there may be some difference of medical opinion".

It is submitted that the comments made in these two cases are equally applicable to the phrase substituted by the 2007 Act.

Subsection (4)

The identification and role of the "statutory consultees" is considered at paras.25.53 to **1–743** 25.59 of the *Code of Practice*. The Act does not place an obligation on any person to act as a consultee under this provision and the SOAD is not placed under an obligation to accept the nurse or "other person" put forward by the AC as a potential consultee.

If there is a significant delay in identifying an appropriate consultee, consideration could be given to treating the patient under the authority of s.62 until the completion of the consultation process.

TWO OTHER PERSONS.   In *R. (on the application of B) v Haddock* [2005] EWHC 921 (Admin); [2005] M.H.L.R. 317 para.8, Collins J. said that the SOAD "should, if he thinks it desirable to do so, consult with others than the two statutory consultees, including (with the patient's consent) the patient's nearest relative, family, carers or advocate".

WHO HAVE BEEN PROFESSIONALLY CONCERNED WITH THE PATIENT'S MEDICAL TREATMENT.   And will therefore have some direct knowledge of the patient. A particular involvement with the patient is therefore required; it would not be sufficient for a potential consultee merely to have general responsibilities on the ward where the patient is being treated.

The fact that consultation must take place with two persons who have been concerned with the patient's medical treatment, rather than with persons who are so concerned, means that a consultation can take place with a person who has no current involvement with the patient. Such a consultation can only take place if identifying the person concerned was a reasonable action for the authorities to take given the non-availability of a person with a current involvement in the patient's treatment (*R. (on the application of W) v Feggetter* [2000] M.H.L.R. 200)).

NURSE.   Means a qualified nurse whose name appears on the register maintained by the Nursing and Midwifery Council (Nursing and Midwifery Order 2001 (SI 2002/253) art.5).

THE OTHER.   The Mental Health Act Commission in its Fifth Biennial Report 1991–1993, at para.7.16, reports that identifying the "other person" is a "major source of difficulty for SOADs when undertaking second opinion visits". While recognising that the issue has not yet been tested in the courts, the MHAC "concluded that to require the statutory 'other' consultee to be invariably professionally qualified and included in a professional register would be unnecessarily restrictive". At the same time the MHAC expressed its "grave doubts about the validity of some certificates which, for example, refer to the 'ward clerk', 'Gymnasium technician' and 'Occupational Therapy Aid'". The MHAC suggested that "the appointed doctor should endeavour to meet with somebody whose qualifications, experience and knowledge of the patient should enable them to make an effective contribution to the work of the multidisciplinary team". As Parliament has required the "other person" to be "professionally concerned" as opposed to being merely "concerned" with the patient's medical treatment, it is submitted that the other person must hold a recognised professional qualification which is directly relevant to the "medical treatment" of the patient as defined in s.145(1). Persons falling into this category could include psychologists, occupational therapists, pharmacists, psychotherapists, physiotherapists, art/music therapists and social workers. The MHAC subsequently revised its position on this issue and supported the approach advocated here: see para.9 of its Guidance Note, noted below.

In its Guidance Note "People with Nursing Qualifications and Consultation with the 'other' Professional in Second Opinions under the Mental Health Act" (2008), the MHAC stated that:

"it has decided to interpret the law as preventing someone who is registered as a nurse from being the 'other' consultee, whether or not s/he is acting as a nurse or even practicing in another profession (e.g. as a psychologist or social worker). We take this view on the basis that the Act requires the person not to 'be' a nurse, rather than specifying that the person's professional relationship with the patient must not involve a nursing role" (para.3).

Accordingly, the MHAC "asked SOADs to no longer accept professionals who are registered nurses as the 'other' consultee on their Second Opinion visits" (para.5).

SOADs, who must exercise their own independent judgment and do not act under the direction of the Commission's successor, the Care Quality Commission (*X v A B C and the Mental Health Act Commission* (1991) 9 B.M.L.R. 91), should be cautious about accepting this advice for the following reasons:

1. The "other" consultee must be "professionally concerned" with the patient's medical treatment. If, for example, the other consultee is a psychologist who is providing the patient with psychological therapies and she also happens to have a nursing qualification, that person is professionally concerned with the patient's medical treatment in her capacity as a psychologist. On this interpretation, the phrase "the other shall be neither a nurse nor a registered medical practitioner" should be interpreted as meaning "the other shall be neither a nurse nor a registered medical practitioner who is treating the patient in her professional capacity as a nurse or a registered medical practitioner."

2. It is difficult to imagine that Parliament, when enacting this provision, understood that it was placing an obligation on SOADs to ask every "other" consultee whether he or she is also registered as a nurse.

An Independent Mental Health Advocate who is assisting the patient cannot be a consultee as she is representing the patient's interests and is not involved in the patient's treatment.

In the sample studied by Phil Fennell, by far the largest category of "other persons" consulted was that of social worker. He reports that "the duty to consult the other professional is becoming seen as a tiresome formality" (*Treatment Without Consent*, 1996, p.208).

[Electro-convulsive therapy, etc.

1–744   **58A.**—(1) This section applies to the following forms of medical treatment for mental disorder—

(a) electro-convulsive therapy; and

(b) such other forms of treatment as may be specified for the purposes of this section by regulations made by the appropriate national authority.

(2) Subject to section 62 below, a patient shall be not be given any form of treatment to which this section applies unless he falls within subsection (3), (4) or (5) below.

(3) A patient falls within this subsection if—

(a) he has attained the age of 18 years;

(b) he has consented to the treatment in question; and

(c) either the approved clinician in charge of it or a registered medical practitioner appointed as mentioned in section 58(3) above has certified in writing that the patient is capable of understanding the nature, purpose and likely effects of the treatment and has consented to it.

(4) A patient falls within this subsection if—

(a) he has not attained the age of 18 years; but

(b) he has consented to the treatment in question; and

(c) a registered medical practitioner appointed as aforesaid (not being the approved clinician in charge of the treatment) has certified in writing—

(i) that the patient is capable of understanding the nature, purpose and likely effects of the treatment and has consented to it; and

(ii) that it is appropriate for the treatment to be given.

(5) A patient falls within this subsection if a registered medical practitioner appointed as aforesaid (not being the responsible clinician (if there is one) or the approved clinician in charge of the treatment in question) has certified in writing—

(a) that the patient is not capable of understanding the nature, purpose and likely effects of the treatment; but

(b) that it is appropriate for the treatment to be given; and

(c) that giving him the treatment would not conflict with—

(i) an advance decision which the registered medical practitioner concerned is satisfied is valid and applicable; or

(ii) a decision made by a donee or deputy or by the Court of Protection.

(6) Before giving a certificate under subsection (5) above the registered medical practitioner concerned shall consult two other persons who have been professionally concerned with the patient's medical treatment but, of those persons—

(a) one shall be a nurse and the other shall be neither a nurse nor a registered medical practitioner; and

(b) neither shall be the responsible clinician (if there is one) or the approved clinician in charge of the treatment in question.

(7) This section shall not by itself confer sufficient authority for a patient who falls within section 56(5) above to be given a form of treatment to which this section applies if he is not capable of understanding the nature, purpose and likely effects of the treatment (and cannot therefore consent to it).

(8) Before making any regulations for the purposes of this section, the appropriate national authority shall consult such bodies as appear to it to be concerned.

(9) In this section—

(a) a reference to an advance decision is to an advance decision (within the meaning of the Mental Capacity Act 2005) made by the patient;

(b) "valid and applicable", in relation to such a decision, means valid and applicable to the treatment in question in accordance with section 25 of that Act;

(c) a reference to a donee is to a donee of a lasting power of attorney (within the meaning of section 9 of that Act) created by the patient, where the donee is acting within the scope of his authority and in accordance with that Act; and

(d) a reference to a deputy is to a deputy appointed for the patient by the Court of Protection under section 16 of that Act, where the deputy is acting within the scope of his authority and in accordance with that Act.

(10) In this section, "the appropriate national authority" means—

(a) in a case where the treatment in question would, if given, be given in England, the Secretary of State;

(b) in a case where the treatment in question would, if given, be given in Wales, the Welsh Ministers.]

AMENDMENT
This section was inserted by the Mental Health Act 2007 s.27.

DEFINITIONS
1–745   medical treatment: s.145(1), (4).
mental disorder: ss.1, 145(1).
patient: ss.56, 124(1).
responsible clinician: s.64(1).
approved clinician: ss.64(1B), 145(1).

GENERAL NOTE
1–746   This section provides that, except in an emergency, electro-convulsive therapy (ECT) and any other treatment provided for in regulations made under this section may only be given to the patient if the patient either consents to the treatment, or a second opinion appointed doctor (SOAD) has certified that it is appropriate for the treatment to be given. It applies to adult detained patients who come within the scope of this Part, apart from those who are subject to community treatment orders (s.56(5)), and to all patients who are under the age of 18 (whether or not they are detained) (subss.(4), (7)). Consent and certification can be given for a plan of treatment involving more than one administration of ECT (s.59). If a mentally capable patient refuses to consent to the treatment, it cannot be given. The advice given to the patient by the AC should be recorded (*St George's Healthcare NHS Trust v S* [1998] 3 All E.R. 673 at 703). If the patient withdraws consent, the treatment must either not proceed or must be halted (s.60(1)). A patient who loses capacity before the completion of the treatment is treated as if he had withdrawn consent and the remaining treatment has to be considered as a separate treatment (s.60(1A),(1B)). In both situations, the treatment can continue pending compliance with this section if its discontinuance would cause serious suffering to the patient (s.62(2)).

A certificate issued by a SOAD under Pt IVA will not provide authority for treatment under this section to be given to a community patient who has capacity or competence to consent but refuses consent when recalled to hospital or when the community treatment order is revoked (s.62A(4)).

If a mentally capable patient consents to the ECT, the consent must be certified by either the approved clinician in charge of the patient's treatment (AC) or a SOAD (subs.(3)). For child patients, both detained and informal (s.56(5)), the consent and the appropriateness of the treatment must be certified by a SOAD (subs.(4)). A new SOAD certificate is not required merely because a child reaches the age of 18. If the child is informal, there must also be authority to treat the child (subs.(7)).

Where the patient lacks the capacity to consent, a SOAD must certify that the patient is "not capable of understanding the nature, purpose and likely effects of the treatment" and that it is appropriate for the treatment to be given (subs.(5)(a),(b)). Before issuing the certificate the SOAD must consult with two persons who have been professionally concerned with the patient's medical treatment; one must be a nurse and the other shall be neither a nurse nor a doctor nor the patient's responsible clinician (RC) or the AC (subs.(6)). The SOAD cannot complete a certificate under subs.(5) if to do so would conflict with:

(i) an advance decision of the patient not to receive the treatment in question, which the SOAD is satisfied is valid and applicable;

(ii) a decision made by the donee of a lasting power of attorney or a deputy appointed by the Court of Protection if the donee or deputy has the authority to refuse the treatment on behalf of the patient; or

(iii) an order of the Court of Protection.

[NB Under the terms of the Mental Capacity Act 2005, a person under the age of 18 cannot make an advance decision or execute a lasting power of attorney: see ss.24(1) and 10(1)(a) of the 2005 Act.]

The SOAD's certificate provides authority for the ECT to be given; it does not require it to be given. "In all cases, SOADs should indicate on the certificate the maximum number of administrations of ECT which it approves" (*Code of Practice*, para.25.23). If a SOAD has certified that the patient lacks the capacity to consent to the ECT, the clinician who would administer the ECT should confirm at the time when the treatment is to be given that the patient's capacity status has not changed. If the patient is refusing the ECT and the clinician assesses the patient as being mentally capable of making that decision, the ECT should not be given.

This section is subject to the emergency provisions contained in s.62 (subs.(2)). Treatment under s.62, including the administration of medicine as part of ECT (see reg.27(4) of the English Regulations and reg.38(2) of the Welsh Regulations), can be given to a mentally incapacitated patient even though the patient has made a valid and applicable advance decision refusing ECT. However, the treatment could not continue under this section if the SOAD is satisfied that the patient has made such an advance decision (subs.(5)(c)(i)). Although the rationale for invoking s.62 in respect of incapacitated patients who require treatment urgently is clear, the fact that a capacious patient can be given treatment under s.62 conflicts with the underlying purpose of this section which is to respect the wishes of such patients. Baroness Murphy, a distinguished psychiatrist, said that she could not:

"envisage a clinical situation where section 62 should ever be given to a patient who has capacity. Such treatment exists to treat profoundly depressed people who have usually stopped eating and drinking and who are seriously at risk of dehydration and death before the treatment takes effect. As the British Psychological Society has pointed out, evidence from [the] Northwick Park studies shows that if a nurse can sit with a patient day in and day out over the course of a three or four-day weekend and get liquid into him one way or another through a drip and so forth, ECT can usually be avoided. But sometimes it is necessary. Sometimes the circumstances are not right and the patient may pull out the drip and refuse treatment. But I cannot understand how such a situation could arise with a patient who had full capacity. The nature of the illness is such that it would not happen" (*Hansard*, HL Vol.689, col.978).

An informal adult incapacitated patient could be given ECT under the authority of the Mental Capacity Act 2005 if the treatment is deemed to be in the patient's best interests. Such treatment could not be provided if the patient had made a valid and applicable advance decision refusing ECT or if a donee or a deputy had refused such treatment on the patient's behalf. In 2012/13, 1 per cent of serious medical treatment decisions made under s.37 of the 2005 Act involved the administration of ECT ("The Sixth Year of the Independent Mental Capacity Advocacy (IMCA) Service: 2012/2013", p.26). Paragraph 13.65 of the *Code of Practice* states:

"If ECT is to be given to an individual who lacks capacity and is under a DoLS authorisation or Court of Protection order, consideration should be given to seeking an independent second medical opinion before treatment which could, in principle, be given under the MCA (remembering that a DoLS authorisation only authorises the deprivation of liberty, not the treatment)."

Code of Practice
Guidance on this section is given in Ch.25 at paras 25.19 to 25.25. The application of this section to patients who are under the age of 18 is considered in the *Code* at paras 19.80 to 19.88.

Subsection (1)

1–747   REGULATIONS.   Regulation 27(3) of the English Regulations and reg.38(2) of the Welsh Regulations specify the administration of medicines as part of the ECT as being a form of treatment to which this section applies. Such medicines could include anaesthetics and muscle relaxants.

APPROPRIATE NATIONAL AUTHORITY.   See subs.(10).

Subsection (3)

1–748   APPROVED CLINICIAN IN CHARGE.   See s.64(1B).

NATURE, PURPOSE AND LIKELY EFFECTS.   See the note on this phrase in s.57(2).

CERTIFIED IN WRITING.   Using Form T4: see reg.24(3) of the English Regulations (in Wales, Form CO4: see reg.40(3) of the Welsh Regulations).

CONSENTED TO IT.   See the note on this phrase in s.57(2). The problems associated with obtaining a patient's informed consent to ECT were considered by the MHAC in its *Eleventh Biennial Report*, 2003–2005, at paras 4.74, 4.75.

Subsection (4)(a)

1–749   NOT ATTAINED THE AGE OF 18 YEARS.   Such patients are entitled to an independent mental health advocate in the circumstances set out in s.130C(3)(b).

Subsection (4)(c)

1–750   CERTIFIED IN WRITING.   Using Form T5 (in Wales, Form CO5). A fresh certificate is not required just because a young person reaches the age of 18.

APPROPRIATE FOR THE TREATMENT TO BE GIVEN.   See s.64(3). This criterion does not apply to adult patients.

Subsection (5)

1–751   CERTIFIED IN WRITING.   Using Form T6 (in Wales, Form CO6).

Paragraph (c)

1–752   The legal responsibility for being satisfied that an advance decision made by the patient is both "valid and applicable" is that of the SOAD. This could cause difficulties for the SOAD if there is a dispute about either the validity or the applicability of the decision. For example, the AC might dispute the existence of an advance decision in a case where the spouse of the patient claims that the patient had made an oral advance decision refusing ECT some time ago. In this situation the SOAD could not automatically rely on the judgment of the AC; the SOAD would have to form an opinion as to which view is to be preferred in order that she can be "satisfied" that a valid and applicable advance decision is in place. It would be difficult for the SOAD to reach such an opinion without interviewing the spouse, and possibly other relatives and the patient's GP. Such enquiries could prove to be very time consuming. In this example, such interviews would not be required if the SOAD concluded that the provision of ECT to the patient constituted a "life-sustaining treatment" for the purposes of s.25 of the Mental Capacity Act 2005, in which case the advance decision must be in writing, signed and witnessed, and must contain a statement that the decision is to take effect even if life is at risk. If, after investigation, the

SOAD continued to have doubts about the validity or the applicability of an advance decision, an application would have to be made to the Court of Protection for the matter to be determined. In the meantime, the ECT could be provided if it is either life-sustaining or would prevent a serious deterioration of the patient's condition (s.26(5) of the 2005 Act).

The SOAD should also make enquiries to ascertain whether a donee or deputy has been appointed under the 2005 Act and, if so, whether the donee or deputy has the authority to make a decision to refuse ECT. The SOAD should also ascertain whether the Court of Protection has ordered that ECT should not be given to the patient. This information should be noted on the patient's medical record.

Subsection (6)
See the notes on s.58(4).   **1–753**

Subsection (7)
This subsection applies to mentally incapacitated patients who come within the scope of **1–754** s.56(5) i.e. informal patients under 18 who cannot give consent. As this section does not "by itself confer sufficient authority" for providing treatment to such patients, authority to treat must be found elsewhere. The Reference Guide states at para.23.50 that, depending on the circumstances, that authority to treat might, for example, come from "a court order, or, in the case of a young person aged 16 or 17, the provisions of the MCA". It might also come from parental consent for younger children. Accordingly, s.28 of the 2005 Act, which gives preference to Pt IV in respect of treatments that come within its scope, does not apply to treatments provided under this section if the patient comes within the scope of this sub-section: see s.28(1A) of the 2005 Act. The *Code of Practice,* at para.19.85, states that "careful consideration should be given as to whether to rely on parental consent" as such a decision is likely to be outside the "zone of parental responsibility". Rather than rely on parental consent, either an application under the Act or, if the Act is not applicable, an application to the court should be considered.

Plans of treatment
59. Any consent or certificate under section 57[, 58 or 58A] above may relate to **1–755** a plan of treatment under which the patient is to be given (whether within a speci-fied period or otherwise) one or more of the forms of treatment to which that section applies.

AMENDMENT
The words in square brackets were substituted by the Mental Health Act 2007 s.28(3).

DEFINITION
patient: s.145(1).   **1–756**

GENERAL NOTE
This section enables any consent or certificate obtained for the purposes of s.57, s.58 or **1–757** s.58A to relate to a plan of treatment which would involve one or more of the treatments specified under the same section. Such a plan would allow for variations in treatment within the context of the treatment objectives and enable the approved clinician to respond rapidly to the patient's reaction to a particular drug or dosage. The plan could include a time scale for the administration of treatments. A patient may withdraw consent to a plan of treatment under s.60(2). "Treatment plans are usually described in terms of the drug categories recor-ded in the British National Formulary" (Mental Health Act Commission, *Fifth Biennial Report* 1991–1993, para.7.7).

Code of Practice
See paras 24.45 to 24.53.   **1–758**

Withdrawal of consent

1–759   **60.**—(1) Where the consent of a patient to any treatment has been given for the purpose of section 57[, 58 or 58A] above, the patient may, subject to section 62 below, at any time before the completion of the treatment withdraw his consent, and those sections shall then apply as if the remainder of the treatment were a separate form of treatment.

[(1A) Subsection (1B) below applies where—

(a) the consent of a patient to any treatment has been given for the purposes of section 57, 58 or 58A above; but

(b) before the completion of the treatment, the patient ceases to be capable of understanding its nature, purpose and likely effects.

(1B) The patient shall, subject to section 62 below, be treated as having withdrawn his consent, and those sections shall then apply as if the remainder of the treatment were a separate form of treatment.

(1C) Subsection (1D) below applies where—

(a) a certificate has been given under section 58 or 58A above that a patient is not capable of understanding the nature, purpose and likely effects of the treatment to which the certificate applies; but

(b) before the completion of the treatment, the patient becomes capable of understanding its nature, purpose and likely effects.

(1D) The certificate shall, subject to section 62 below, cease to apply to the treatment and those sections shall then apply as if the remainder of the treatment were a separate form of treatment.]

(2) Without prejudice to the application of [subsections (1) to (1D)] above to any treatment given under the plan of treatment to which a patient has consented, a patient who has consented to such a plan may, subject to section 62 below, at any time withdraw his consent to further treatment, or to further treatment of any description, under the plan.

AMENDMENT
The words in square brackets were substituted and inserted by the Mental Health Act 2007 ss.28(4), 29(2) and (3).

DEFINITION
1–760   patient: ss.56, 145(1).

GENERAL NOTE
1–761   This section provides for a patient to withdraw his consent to treatment under ss.57, 58 or 58A or to a plan of treatment. On the withdrawal of consent, the remainder of the treatment must be considered as a separate treatment for the purposes of those sections. It is submitted that the three-month period referred to in s.58(1)(b) is not re-activated on a patient withdrawing consent to be treated by medication. A patient cannot therefore be treated for a fresh period of three months in the absence of consent before the independent medical opinion referred to in s.58(3)(b) is obtained.

Subsection (1)
1–762   WITHDRAW HIS CONSENT.   The withdrawal of consent can be made in writing, orally, or through the patient's behaviour, e.g. by physically resisting the administration of the treatment.

Subsections (1A) to (1D)
1–763   The effect of these subsections is:

1. If a mentally capable patient who has consented to a s.57, s.58 or s.58A treatment loses his capacity to consent, the patient is to be treated as having withdrawn his consent to the treatment.

2. If a s.58 or s.58A treatment is being given to a mentally incapable patient but, before the treatment has been completed, the patient becomes mentally capable of consenting to the treatment, the remainder of the treatment is to be treated as a separate form of treatment for the purposes of certification under those sections.

In both instances, the treatment that the patient is receiving can continue if the approved clinician considers that stopping it would cause serious suffering to the patient (s.62(2)).

Review of treatment

61.—(1) Where a patient is given treatment in accordance with section 57(2)[,   **1–764** 58(3)(b) or 58A(4) or (5)] above[, or by virtue of section 62A below in accordance with a Part 4A certificate (within the meaning of that section) [that falls within section 64C(4) below],] a report on the treatment and the patient's condition shall be given [by the approved clinician in charge of the treatment] to [the regulatory authority]—

(a) on the next occasion on which the [responsible clinician] furnishes a report [under section 20(3)[, 20A(4) or 21B(2) above in respect] of the patient]; and

(b) at any other time if so required by [the regulatory authority].

(2) In relation to a patient who is subject to a restriction order [, limitation direction] or restriction direction subsection (1) above shall have effect as if paragraph (a) required the report to be made—

(a) in the case of treatment in the period of six months beginning with the date of the order or direction, at the end of that period;

(b) in the case of treatment at any subsequent time, on the next occasion on which the [responsible clinician] makes a report in respect of the patient under section 41(6) [, 45B(3)] or 49(3) above.

(3) [the regulatory authority] may at any time give notice [. . .] directing that, subject to section 62 below, a certificate given in respect of a patient under section 57(2)[, 58(3)(b) or 58A(4) or (5)] above shall not apply to treatment given to him [whether in England or Wales] after a date specified in the notice and sections 57[, 58 and 58A] above shall then apply to any such treatment as if that certificate had not been given.

[(3A) The notice under subsection (3) above shall be given to the approved clinician in charge of the treatment.]

AMENDMENTS

The amendments to this section were made by the Mental Health (Patients in the Community) Act 1995 s.2(5), the Crime (Sentences) Act 1997 s.55, Sch.4 para.12(7), the Mental Health Act 2007 ss.12(4), 28(5), 34(3), the Health and Social Care Act 2008 s.52, Sch.3 para.4 and the Health and Social Care Act 2012 s.299(7).

DEFINITIONS

    the regulatory authority: s.145(1).   **1–765**
    limitation direction: s.145(1).
    patient: ss.56, 145(1).
    responsible clinician: s.64(1).
    approved clinician: s.145(1).

restriction direction: s.145(1).
restriction order: s.145(1).

GENERAL NOTE

1–766   This section provides for the periodic review by the the the Care Quality Commission (the Commission) or, in relation to Wales, the Welsh Ministers (in practice, Health Inspectorate Wales) of treatment which is being given under either s.57(2), s.58(3)(b), s.58A(4) or (5) or, following a recall from a community treatment order, under s.62A in accordance with a Pt IVA certificate. The trigger for the review is set out in paras (a) and (b) of subs.(1). A review is not required where a patient has consented to treatment being given to him under s.58(3)(a) or s.58A(3) (which does not apply to child patients) or where an approved clinician has provided a Pt IVA certificate with regard to a capacious, consenting patient.

With regard to treatment provided under s.62A, the Reference Guide states:

"24.49 [A] report must be given automatically to CQC under section 61 if treatment is given on the basis of a part 4A certificate to a CTO patient who has been recalled to hospital, including one whose CTO is then revoked, in lieu of a SOAD certificate under section 58 or 58A (see paragraphs 24.32 to 24.43). This will only apply to treatment to which the patient either did not, or could not consent.

24.50 In such cases, a report must be submitted by the approved clinician in charge of the treatment at the same time it would have to be given if the treatment had, in fact, been given on the basis of section 58 or 58A SOAD certificate (see paragraphs 23.63 – 23.65). This means the approved clinician must make a report to CQC on the next occasion that the responsible clinician submits a report under section 20 to renew the patient's detention, under section 20A to extend the patient's CTO, or under section 21B to confirm the patient's detention or CTO after absence without leave for more than 28 days."

The CQC's "Section 61–Review of Treatment Form", previously Form MHAC 1, does not relate to s.57(2) treatments. A separate form, which can be obtained from the CQC's Mental Health operations team, must be used for such treatments.

Code of Practice

1–767   The *Code* states:

"25.76 Although the Act does not require the validity of certificates to be reviewed after any particular period, it is good practice for the clinician in charge of the treatment to review them (in consultation with the responsible clinician, if different) at regular intervals.

25.77 The clinician in charge of any treatment given in accordance with a SOAD certificate must provide a written report on that treatment and the relevant patient's condition at any time if requested to do so by the CQC under sections 61 or 64H of the Act. This is in addition to the reports they are automatically required to provide periodically under those sections. Copies of reports should be given to patients.

25.78 Under sections 61 and 64H, the CQC may also, at any time, direct that a certificate is no longer to approve either some or all of the treatments specified in it from a particular date.

25.79 However, where the CQC revokes approval in that way, treatment (or a course of treatment) which is already in progress may continue, pending a new certificate, if the clinician in charge of it considers that discontinuing it would cause the patient serious suffering (section 62 (2)).

25.80 This exception only applies pending compliance with the relevant requirement to have a certificate – in other words, while steps are taken to obtain a new certificate. It cannot be used to continue treatment under section 57 or section 58A against the wishes of a patient who has the capacity to refuse the treatment, because in those cases there is no prospect of obtaining a new certificate."

Subsection (1)

REPORT ON THE TREATMENT AND THE PATIENT'S CONDITION. The approved clinician **1–768** (AC) in charge of the patient's treatment should report on the treatment and the patient's response to it. There is no requirement under paragraph (a) for the AC to report on an *informal* patient who has been treated under s.57. However, the Commission can require such a report to be made under para.(b).

APPROVED CLINICIAN IN CHARGE OF THE TREATMENT. See s.64(1A), (1B).

ON THE NEXT OCCASION. And on each subsequent occasion when such a report is made.

Subsection (2)

This subsection specifies the timing of the treatment review in respect of patients who **1–769** are subject to a restriction order, limitation direction or restriction direction.

Subsection (3)

This subsection provides that the Commission may at any time give notice to the AC that **1–770** a certificate given under ss.57(2), 58(3)(b) or s.58A(4) or (5) shall cease to apply after the date it specifies. If the AC wished to continue with the treatment specified in the notice she would need to start afresh with the procedures laid down in ss.57, 58 or s.58A, unless the criteria for urgent treatment set out in s.62(2) were satisfied.

Urgent treatment

62.—(1) Sections 57 and 58 above shall not apply to any treatment— **1–771**

(a) which is immediately necessary to save the patient's life; or

(b) which (not being irreversible) is immediately necessary to prevent a serious deterioration of his condition; or

(c) which (not being irreversible or hazardous) is immediately necessary to alleviate serious suffering by the patient; or

(d) which (not being irreversible or hazardous) is immediately necessary and represents the minimum interference necessary to prevent the patient from behaving violently or being a danger to himself or to others.

[(1A) Section 58A above, in so far as it relates to electro-convulsive therapy by virtue of subsection (1)(a) of that section, shall not apply to any treatment which falls within paragraph (a) or (b) of subsection (1) above.

(1B) Section 58A above, in so far as it relates to a form of treatment specified by virtue of subsection (1)(b) of that section, shall not apply to any treatment which falls within such of paragraphs (a) to (d) of subsection (1) above as may be specified in regulations under that section.

(1C) For the purposes of subsection (1B) above, the regulations—

(a) may make different provision for different cases (and may, in particular, make different provision for different forms of treatment);

(b) may make provision which applies subject to specified exceptions; and

(c) may include transitional, consequential, incidental or supplemental provision.]

(2) Sections 60 and 61(3) above shall not preclude the continuation of any treatment or of treatment under any plan pending compliance with section 57[, 58 or 58A] above if the [approved clinician in charge of the treatment] considers that the

discontinuance of the treatment or of treatment under the plan would cause serious suffering to the patient.

(3) For the purposes of this section treatment is irreversible if it has unfavourable irreversible physical or psychological consequences and hazardous if it entails significant physical hazard.

AMENDMENTS

The amendments to this section were made by the Mental Health Act 2007 ss.12(5), 28(6) and (7).

DEFINITIONS

1–772   patient: ss.56, 145(1).
approved clinician: s.145(1).

GENERAL NOTE

1–773   This section states that the procedural safeguards provided for in ss.57 and 58 shall not apply to the categories of urgent treatment set out in paras (a) to (d) of subs.(1). Treatments provided under this section cannot be approved retrospectively by the attendance of a second opinion appointed doctor and the issuing of a certificate. Where the treatment is ECT provided under s.58A, urgent treatment can only be given if either of the grounds set out in para.(a) or (b) are satisfied (subs.(1A)). Where the treatment is another form of s.58A treatment (to be determined by regulations made under s.58A), the Secretary of State (for England) or the Welsh Ministers (for Wales) may make regulations regarding which of the criteria in subs.(1) are to apply to that treatment (subss.(1B), (1C)). Existing treatments can continue if the "serious suffering" criterion set out in subs.(2) is satisfied.

This section is not applicable to any treatment that does not come within the remit of either ss.57, 58 or s.58A, for example patients who are detained under ss.135 or 136. As neither ss.57, 58 nor 58A govern treatments given under this section which applies irrespective of the patient's capacity status, there is no legal requirement to certify whether the patient is capable of consenting to the treatment in question. A consequence of this is that treatment under this section can be given to a mentally incapacitated patient even though the patient has made an advance decision under the Mental Capacity Act 2005 refusing a s.58A treatment.

The purpose of this section is to provide for treatment to be given as a response to an urgent situation. If it is proposed to continue with the treatment thereafter, the procedures set out under ss.57, 58 or s.58A should be observed. Paragraph 25.41 of the *Code of Practice* states:

"Urgent treatment under [this section] can continue only for as long as it remains immediately necessary. If it is no longer immediately necessary, the normal requirements for certificates apply. Although certificates are not required where treatment is immediately necessary, the other requirements of [Part 4] of the Act still apply. The treatment is not necessarily allowed just because no certificate is required."

The Mental Health Act Commission expressed its concern "about treatment given in emergency situations which fall outside the Consent to Treatment provisions of the Act. Some treatment is described as being given under the provisions of section 62 when in fact the patient is either not detained or is held under the short-term holding powers of the Act to which section 62 does not apply" (*Fifth Biennial Report* 1991–1993, para.7.12). If treatment is to be given in these circumstances, it must be justified under either the common law or the Mental Capacity Act 2005.

Although there is no statutory form to be completed when this section is invoked, the *Code of Practice*, at para.25.42 states:

"Hospital managers should monitor the use of these exceptions to the certificate requirements to ensure that they are not used inappropriately or excessively. They are advised to provide a form (or other method) by which the clinician in charge of the treatment in question can record details of:

- the proposed treatment
- why it is immediately necessity to give the treatment, and
- the length of time for which the treatment was given."

Subsection (1)

The test in this provision is not one of mere necessity; the treatment must be *immediately* **1–774** necessary. The immediacy refers to the need for treatment and not to the consequences that would flow if the treatment was not provided. It follows that depot medication can be given under this provision even though the effect of the treatment is not immediate, i.e. the treatment is immediately required to ensure that the patient's medication level does not drop below the therapeutic dose.

As treatment under this section is provided under the authority of s.63 (see the note on "shall not apply", below), it is for the approved clinician (AC) who is for the time being in charge of the patient's treatment to determine whether the criteria set out in this subsection are satisfied. Such a determination can be made over the telephone.

SECTIONS 57 AND 58.   As the treatments covered by s.57 are not emergency treatments, it is difficult to envisage the circumstances that would lead a doctor to consider invoking this section in respect of such treatments.

SHALL NOT APPLY.   Which means that the treatment can be given to a detained patient without consent by virtue of the power given to the patient's AC by s.63. As s.63 does not apply to informal patients, the AC must find a justification under the Mental Capacity Act 2005 for proceeding without the patient's consent if she plans to give a s.57 treatment to a mentally incapable informal patient in any of the circumstances set out in paras (a) to (d).

Subsections (1A) to (1C)

These subsections enable emergency ECT to be provided if either of the criteria set out in **1–775** paras (a) or (b) of subs.(1) is satisfied. There are no statutory limitations to the number of ECT treatments that can be given under this section. For an expression of doubt as to whether such treatment should be given to capacious patients, see the comments of Baroness Murphy noted in the General Note to s.58A. The administration of medicine as part of ECT may also be provided (reg.27(4) of the English Regulations and reg.38(2) of the Welsh Regulations); see further the General Note to s.58A.

Subsection (2)

This subsection provides that an existing course of treatment or a plan of treatment can **1–776** continue notwithstanding that the patient has withdrawn his consent if the AC considers that discontinuing the treatment or plan of treatment would cause the patient *serious* suffering. It also applies to patients who lose capacity to consent before the completion of the treatment (s.60(1A)) and where the Commission has given a notice under s.61(3). The treatment must cease as soon as its cessation would no longer cause the patient serious suffering.

APPROVED CLINICIAN IN CHARGE OF THE TREATMENT.   See s.64(1A), (1B).

Subsection (3)

Paragraph 6.25 of the White Paper Cmnd. 7320 contains the following definitions of **1–777** "irreversible" and "hazardous" treatments: "irreversible treatments" are "treatments

which necessitate the removal or destruction of brain tissue or are designed to effect irreversible change in cerebral or bodily functions"; "hazardous treatments" are "treatments where the risk of adverse reaction or the severity of such reaction would be disproportionate to the degree of benefit the treatment is likely to confer or the prospect of success".
ECT is not regarded as an irreversible treatment.

UNFAVOURABLE. At the Special Standing Committee the Under-Secretary of State cited the removal of a brain tumour and the removal of a diseased thyroid as examples of treatments which are irreversible and which can be reasonably expected to have favourable consequences. (Sitting of June 29, 1982.)

[Treatment on recall of community patient or revocation of order

1–778   **62A.**—(1) This section applies where—
(a) a community patient is recalled to hospital under section 17E above; or
(b) a patient is liable to be detained under this Act following the revocation of a community treatment order under section 17F above in respect of him.

(2) For the purposes of section 58(1)(b) above, the patient is to be treated as if he had remained liable to be detained since the making of the community treatment order.

(3) But section 58 above does not apply to treatment given to the patient if—
(a) the certificate requirement is met for the purposes of section 64C or 64E below; or
(b) as a result of section 64B(4) or 64E(4) below, the certificate requirement would not apply (were the patient a community patient not recalled to hospital under section 17E above).

(4) Section 58A above does not apply to treatment given to the patient if there is authority to give the treatment, and the certificate requirement is met, for the purposes of section 64C or 64E below.

(5) In a case where this section applies [and the Part 4A certificate falls within section 64C(4) below], the certificate requirement is met only in so far as—
(a) the Part 4A certificate expressly provides that it is appropriate for one or more specified forms of treatment to be given to the patient in that case (subject to such conditions as may be specified); or
(b) a notice having been given under subsection (5) of section 64H below, treatment is authorised by virtue of subsection (8) of that section.

(6) Subsection (5) above shall not preclude the continuation of any treatment, or of treatment under any plan, pending compliance with section 58 or 58A above [or 64B or 64E below] if the approved clinician in charge of the treatment considers that the discontinuance of the treatment, or of the treatment under the plan, would cause serious suffering to the patient.

[(6A) In a case where this section applies and the certificate requirement is no longer met for the purposes of section 64C(4A) below, the continuation of any treatment, or of treatment under any plan, pending compliance with section 58 or 58A above or 64B or 64E below shall not be precluded if the approved clinician in charge of the treatment considers that the discontinuance of the treatment, or of treatment under the plan, would cause serious suffering to the patient.]

(7) In a case where subsection (1)(b) above applies, subsection (3) above only applies pending compliance with section 58 above.

(8) In subsection (5) above—
"Part 4A certificate" has the meaning given in section 64H below; and

372

"specified", in relation to a Part 4A certificate, means specified in the certificate.]

AMENDMENTS
This section was inserted by the Mental Health Act 2007 s.34(4). The amendments to it were made by the Health and Social Care Act 2012 s.299(8)–(10).

DEFINITIONS

1–779

community patient: ss.17A(7), 145(1).
hospital: s.145(1).
patient: ss.56, 145(1).
community treatment order: ss.17A(7), 145(1).
approved clinician: s.145(1).

GENERAL NOTE

This complex section regulates the treatment of the mental disorders of community **1–780** patients who have either been recalled to hospital under s.17E, or who have had their community treatment order (CTO) revoked under s.17F (subs.(1)). Subject to the exceptions set out in subs.(3), the treatment of such patients cannot proceed unless it is permitted by this Part. This means that if a certificate under Pt IV was in place before the CTO was made and the certificate covers the patient's current treatment needs and consent status, the certificate remains valid and a fresh certificate will not be required. Note, however, that the *Code of Practice*, at para.25.85, states, without explanation, that it is "not good practice" to rely on such certificates even though they are "technically valid".

In the case of administration of medicine, a certificate is not required if "the patient is still within the period before which a certificate is required i.e. either one month has elapsed from the time when the CTO was made or the three month period from when medication was first given to the patient, as provided for in s.58(1)(b) has not elapsed" (Explanatory Notes, para.127). The patient can be treated with medication for his mental disorder without formality during this period. For the purpose of calculating the three-month period, patients are to be treated as if they had remained liable to be detained since the making of the CTO (subs.(2)). In other words, the three-month period does not start afresh on the patient's recall.

Patients who come within the scope of this section will *not* be subject to this Part if the Pt IVA certificate requirement set out in s.64C or 64E is met (subs.(3)(a)). Under subs.(5), the certificate requirement is met only in so far as:

(i) the certificate expressly provides that it is appropriate for the specified treatment to be given on recall, and giving the treatment would not be contrary to any condition attached to the certificate, or

(ii) although the regulatory body has given notice under s.64H(5) that the treatment must stop, the treatment can continue under s.64H(8) because its discontinuance would cause serious suffering to the patient.

By virtue of the amendment made to subs.(5) by the Health and Social Care Act 2012, a "new certificate under s.58 or 58A is not required if the treatment in question is already covered by an approved clinician's Part IVA certificate [Form CTO 12] provided that the patient continues to consent to the treatment (and still has the capacity to do so)" (Explanatory Notes to the 2012 Act, para.1531)

Unless the SOAD's Part IVA certificate specifies otherwise, it will authorise the treatment even if the patient has capacity to refuse it. However, the certificate will not provide authority for treatment under s.58A to be given to a patient who has capacity or competence to consent but refuses consent when recalled to hospital or when the CTO is revoked (subs.(4)).

Existing treatment which does not satisfy the certification requirement can be continued, pending compliance with s.58 or s.58A, if the approved clinician in charge of the patient's treatment considers that its discontinuance would cause serious suffering to the patient (subss.(6), (6A)). In addition, in cases of urgency the provisions of s.62 or 64G will apply.

If the patient's CTO is revoked, with the patient being once again detained in hospital for treatment, treatment can be given on the authority of a Pt IVA certificate only until a s.58 or s.58A certificate can be arranged (subs.(7)).

The medical treatment of a CTO patient who is admitted to hospital informally is governed by Pt IVA.

Code of Practice

1–781   See paras 25.33 to 25.35.

Subsection (6A)

1–782   Paragraph 1532 of the Explanatory Notes to the Health and Social Care Act 2012 states:

"Section 62A . . . provides that, even if the treatment has not been expressly approved by a SOAD's Part 4A certificate, it may be continued while a new SOAD certificate is sought, if the approved clinician in charge thinks stopping the treatment would cause the patient serious suffering. [Subsection (6A)] extends that to include cases where (either before or during recall) the patient withdraws consent to treatment to which an approved clinician's Part 4A certificate applies, or loses capacity to consent to it. As amended, section 62A [allows] an approved clinician to continue giving medication to a patient who has withdrawn consent if they consider that its discontinuance would cause serious suffering to the patient, but it does not allow electro-convulsive therapy to be given against such a patient's will (because it is not possible to obtain a SOAD certificate authorising electro-convulsive therapy for a detained patient who has capacity to consent, but is refusing to do so)."

Treatment not requiring consent

1–783   **63.** The consent of a patient shall not be required for any medical treatment given to him for the mental disorder from which he is suffering[, not being a form of treatment to which section 57, 58 or 58A above applies,] if the treatment is given by or under the direction of the [approved clinician in charge of the treatment].

AMENDMENT

The words in square brackets were substituted by the Mental Health Act 2007 ss.12(6), 28(8).

DEFINITIONS

1–784   patient: ss.56, 145(1).
medical treatment: s.145(1), (4).
mental disorder: ss.1, 145(1).
approved clinician: s.145(1).

GENERAL NOTE

1–785   This section provides that the consent of a patient to whom this Part applies (see s.56) is not required for treatment which does not fall within ss.57, 58 or s.58A if it is given by or under the direction of the "approved clinician in charge of the treatment". Paragraph 67 of the Explanatory Notes to the Mental Health Act 2007 explains why this phrase, rather than "responsible clinician", is used in this Part:

"In the majority of cases the AC in charge of the treatment will be the patient's RC, but where, for example, the RC is not qualified to make decisions about a particular treatment (e.g. medication if the RC is not a doctor or a nurse prescriber) then another appropriately qualified professional will be in charge of that treatment, with the RC continuing to retain overall responsibility for the patient's case."

A positive decision to impose non-consensual medical treatment pursuant to this section is a public law decision susceptible to judicial review: see *R (on the application of B) v Haddock (Responsible Medical Officer)* [2006] EWCA Civ 961; [2006] M.H.L.R. 306. In *Nottinghamshire Healthcare NHS Trust v RC* [2014] EWCOP 1317, Mostyn J. held that where the approved clinician makes a decision *not* to impose treatment under this section, and where the consequences of that decision may prove to be life-threatening, then the NHS trust in question would be well advised to apply to the High Court for declaratory relief. His Lordship said at para.21:

"The hearing will necessarily involve a 'full merits review' of the initial decision. It would be truly bizarre if such a full merits review were held where a positive decision was made under s.63, but not where there was a negative one, especially where one considers that the negative decision may have far more momentous consequences (i.e. death) than the positive one."

The principles the court should apply where it conducts a full merits review on an application for declaratory relief in circumstances where a decision has been made not to impose potentially life-saving treatment under this section were identified at para.26:

"Obviously the expressed wishes of the patient will be highly relevant. If there is an advance decision in place under ss.24 and 26 of the Mental Capacity Act then this will weigh most heavily in the scales. The Hippocratic duty to seek to save life, or the benign but paternalistic view that it is in someone's best interests to remain alive must all surely be subservient to the right to sovereignty over your own body. Beyond this, considerations such as whether the treatment would be futile will no doubt be relevant; for example, if the repair of a laceration would inevitably be followed by a new one or if the patient was suffering from another unrelated terminal disease."

In this case, his Lordship said that, notwithstanding the existence of power under this section, it would be an abuse of power "even to think about imposing a blood transfusion on [a patient who is a Jehovah's Witness] having regard to my findings that he presently has capacity to refuse blood products and, were such capacity to disappear for any reason, the advance decision [that he had made refusing a blood transfusion] would be operative. To impose a blood transfusion would be a denial of a most basic freedom" (para.42). His Lordship therefore declared that the decision of the patient's RC not to impose a blood transfusion on the patient was lawful.

The Minister for Health's response to the argument that detained patients should not be forced to receive treatment is contained in the following passage from his speech to the Special Standing Committee:

"[That argument would] lead us to conclude that those who were forcibly detained and had lost their liberty against their will ... should be kept in custody in places in which they received no treatment despite the fact that those who looked after them would have to gaze on them knowing perfectly well that some treatment could be given to alleviate their suffering and distress and enable them eventually to recover their liberty. Hospitals are places of treatment and we cannot have hospitals in which people are locked up and left to wander about without receiving treatment" (sitting of June 29, 1982).

The Government's response to the criticism that this provision might authorise a disturbingly wide range of interventions was given by Lord Elton, who emphasised that it was not intended to apply to "borderline" or "experimental" treatments, but to "things which a person in hospital for treatment ought to undergo for his own good and for the good of the running of the hospital and for the good of other patients ... perfectly routine, sensible treatment"(*Hansard* H.L. Vol.426, col.107).

This section "does not absolve the doctor of his ordinary duties of care towards his patient, judged on the usual *Bolam/Bolitho* principles" (*R. (on the application of Wilkinson) v The Responsible Medical Officer Broadmoor Hospital* [2001] EWCA Civ 1545; [2002] 1 W.L.R. 419 per Hale L.J. at para.68).

There is no statutory form for treatments given under the authority of this section.

Human Rights Act 1998

1–786   In *B v Croydon Health Authority*, below, counsel for the patient submitted that if the meaning of "medical treatment for ... mental disorder" was wide enough to include ancillary forms of treatment, this section would involve a breach of art.8 of the European Convention on Human Rights (ECHR). He referred to *Herczegfalvy v Austria* (1993) 15 E.H.R.R. 437 at 485 where the European Court of Human Rights (ECtHR) said that a measure constituting an interference with private life and therefore prima facie contrary to art.8(1) (like involuntary tube feeding) can only be justified under art.8(2) if, among the other requirements of that article, its terms are sufficiently precise to enable the individual "to foresee its consequences for him". The ECtHR confirmed that this requirement is necessary to prevent such measures from being a source of arbitrary power, contrary to the rule of law. In rejecting counsel's submission, Hoffmann L.J. said at 688: "In my judgment section 63 amply satisfies this test. There is no conceptual vagueness about the notion of treating the symptoms or consequences of a mental disorder, although naturally there will be borderline cases. But there is no question of exercise of arbitrary power".

In *X v Finland* [2012] M.H.L.R. 318, the ECtHR considered whether the procedure in the Finnish Mental Health Act which allows for the forcible administration of medication was compatible with the patient's rights under art.8. The Court said at para.220:

"The Court considers that forced administration of medication represents a serious interference with a person's physical integrity and must accordingly be based on a 'law' that guarantees proper safeguards against arbitrariness. In the present case such safeguards were missing. The decision to confine the applicant to involuntary treatment included an automatic authorisation to proceed to forced administration of medication when the applicant refused the treatment. The decision-making was solely in the hands of the treating doctors who could take even quite radical measures regardless of the applicant's will. Moreover, their decision-making was free from any kind of immediate judicial scrutiny: the applicant did not have any remedy available whereby she could require a court to rule on the lawfulness, including proportionality, of the forced administration of medication and to have it discontinued."

The Court concluded that "even if there could be said to be a general legal basis for the measures provided for in Finnish law, the absence of sufficient safeguards against forced medication by the treating doctors deprived the applicant of the minimum degree of protection to which she was entitled under the rule of law in a democratic society" (para.221). This finding raises the question of whether treatment given under this section during the three-month period provided for in s.58(1)(b), treatment which is given at the sole discretion of the patient's approved clinician and which can involve the use of force on an unwilling patient, breaches art.8 on the ground that it contains no safeguards against arbitrariness. The contention that the availability of judicial review (see the *Wilkinson* line of cases noted under s.58) provides a sufficient and practical safeguard for the patient against involuntary treatment is open to doubt.

The approach that the domestic courts adopt when determining whether the forcible medical treatment of a patient breaches either art.3 or art.8 of the ECHR is considered in the note on s.58 under this heading.

Mental Capacity Act 2005
See the General Note to this Part.

CONSENT ... SHALL NOT BE REQUIRED.   Although treatments which do not come within ss.57, 58 or 58A may be given to a patient without his consent, "in practice it is impossible to undertake many of the therapies concerned without a patient's co-operation" (Cmnd. 8405, para.37).

MEDICAL TREATMENT ... FOR THE MENTAL DISORDER.   The leading case on the meaning of this phrase is *B v Croydon Health Authority* [1995] 1 All E.R. 683, where the Court of Appeal held that:

(i) a range of acts ancillary to the core treatment that the patient is receiving fall within the term "medical treatment" as defined in s.145(1);

(ii) treatment is capable of being ancillary to the core treatment if it is nursing and care "concurrent with the core treatment or as a necessary prerequisite to such treatment or to prevent the patient from causing harm to himself or to alleviate the consequences of the disorder ... " (per Hoffmann L.J. at 687);

(iii) relieving the symptoms of the mental disorder is just as much a part of treatment as relieving its underlying cause (NB This finding is reflected in s.145(4) which was inserted by the 2007 Act.); and

(iv) treatment for a physical disorder will not amount to a treatment for a mental disorder where the treatment for the physical disorder is entirely unconnected with the pre-existing mental disorder.

In *St George's Healthcare NHS Trust v S* [1998] 3 All E.R. 673 at 693, Judge L.J. said that the *Croydon* case is authority for the proposition that this section "may apply to the treatment of any condition which is integral to the mental disorder".

In *Croydon*, the Court of Appeal held that the feeding by nasogastric tube of a patient who was suffering from borderline personality disorder was treatment which fell within the scope of this section because such treatment was aimed at treating a symptom of the disorder which was a refusal to eat in order to inflict self harm. The nasogastric feeding of a patient suffering from either anorexia nervosa or depression can also come within the scope of this section: see *Re KB* [1997] 2 F.L.R. 180 and *Re VS (Adult: Mental Disorder)* (1995) 3 Med.L.Rev. 292.

In *R. v Collins and Ashworth Hospital Authority Ex p. Brady* [2000] M.H.L.R. 17, Kay J., held that as the patient's hunger strike was a manifestation or symptom of his personality disorder, the force feeding of the patient came within this section because it constituted a form of treatment for his disorder. His Lordship said at para.44:

"On any view, and to a high degree of probability, s.63 was triggered because what arose was the need for medical treatment for the mental disorder from which the Applicant was and is suffering. The hunger strike is a manifestation or symptom of the personality disorder. The fact (if such it be) that a person without mental disorder could reach the same decision on a rational basis in similar circumstances does not avail the Applicant because he reached and persists in his decision because of his personality disorder."

The *Croydon* and *Brady* cases were distinguished in *A NHS Trust v Dr A* [2013] EWHC 2442 (COP), a case where the patient went on hunger strike in the delusional belief that this would force the UK Border agency to return his passport. Baker J. accepted the evidence of the patient's responsible clinician (RC) that she did not consider it appropriate to use this section to treat the patient as she did not consider that force feeding him in the circumstances of the case to be a medical treatment for his mental disorder, but rather for a physical disorder that arose from his decision to refuse food. In declining to make a declaration that artificial nutrition and hydration could be administered to the patient under this section, but declaring that such treatment could be provided under the authority of the inherent jurisdiction of the High Court, his Lordship said that although the patient's decision to refuse food was flawed in part because his mental disorder deprived him of the capacity to use and weigh information relevant to the decision and that this lead to the conclusion that the physical disorder is in part a consequence of his mental disorder, the disorder was "not obviously either a manifestation or a symptom of the mental disorder".

His Lordship said at para.80:

"[I]t is generally undesirable to extend the meaning of medical treatment under the MHA too far so as to bring about deprivation of liberty in respect of sectioned or sectionable patients beyond what is properly within the ambit of the MHA. I recognise the need for identifying, where possible, a clear dividing line between what is and what is not treatment for a mental disorder within the meaning of the MHA; but I venture to suggest that in medicine, as in the law, it is not always possible to discern clear dividing lines. In case of uncertainty, where there is doubt as to whether the treatment falls within s.145 and s.63, the appropriate course is for an application to be made to the court to approve the treatment. That approach ensures that the treatment given under s.63 of the MHA will be confined to that which is properly within the definition of s.145 as amended. It would help to ensure that patients with mental disorders are, so far as possible, treated informally rather than under section. Finally, it ensures compliance with Art.8 [of the ECHR] and provides the patient with a more effective remedy than would otherwise be available, namely a forensic process to determine whether the treatment is in his best interests."

The reasoning in this case was followed by Hayden J. in *Great Western Hospitals NHS Foundation Trust v AA* [2014] EWHC 132 (Fam) where a declaration was granted to enable a caesarean section to undertaken on a mentally incapacitated patient who was detained under s.2. This case can be contrasted with the *Tameside* case, noted below.

In *Nottinghamshire Healthcare NHS Trust v RC* [2014] EWHC 1317 (COP), Mostyn J. was required to determine whether a blood transfusion provided to a patient who had engaged in significant self-harm would amount to treatment of a symptom or manifestation of his underlying mental disorder. In holding that it was, his Lordship said at para.31:

"It cannot be disputed that the act of self harming, the slashing open of the brachial artery, is a symptom or manifestation of the underlying personality disorder. Therefore to treat the wound in any way is to treat the manifestation or symptom of the underlying disorder. So, indisputably, to suture the wound would be squarely within s.63. As would be the administration of a course of antibiotics to prevent infection. A consequence of bleeding from the wound is that haemoglobin levels are lowered. While it is strictly true, as Dr Latham says, that 'low haemoglobin is not wholly a manifestation or symptom of personality disorder', it is my view that to treat the low haemoglobin by a blood transfusion is just as much a treatment of a symptom or manifestation of the disorder as is to stitch up the wound or to administer antibiotics."

Although the proposed treatment came within the scope of this section, Mostyn J. held that the patient's RC was "completely correct" when she decided not to use this section to impose a blood transfusion on a mentally capable patient who was refusing the treatment for strongly held religious reasons: see further the General Note to this section.

Mostyn J.'s finding in *RC* at para 31 is consistent with the finding in the *Croydon* case that treatment under this section can includes the medical and surgical treatment for the physical consequences of self-poisoning or self-injury if the self-poisoning or self-injury can be categorised as either the consequence of or a symptom of the patient's mental disorder. In *Croydon*, Hoffmann L.J. said at 687,688:

"It would seem strange to me if a hospital could, without the patient's consent, give him treatment directed to alleviating a psychopathic disorder showing itself in suicidal tendencies, but not without such consent be able to treat the consequences of the suicide attempt".

The decision in the *Croydon* case brings the monitoring of the blood of a patient who is being treated with Clozapine within the definition of treatment for mental disorder for the purposes of this section because such monitoring is clearly ancillary to the core treatment for his mental disorder. Treatments which are given to respond to the side effects of the patient's core treatment also come within the scope of this section, e.g. antiparkinsonian agents used to alleviate the motor side effects of anti-psychotic medication.

Deep-brain stimulation (i.e. the implantation of electrodes in the brain that are activated by the patient through an external stimulator) comes within the scope of this section if the procedure is used to treat the patient's mental disorder and it does not involve an operation for the destruction of brain tissue or function, in which case it will come within the scope of s.57. The CQC has recommended that "that the Mental Health regulations should extend the safeguards of section 57 to the use of [deep-brain stimulation] as a treatment for mental disorder (CQC, "Monitoring the Mental Health Act in 2013/2014", p.60).

The fact that a remedy can be bought in the High Street does not prevent it from being a medical treatment for the purposes of this section. Such treatments would include St John's Wort prescribed for mild to moderate depression and fish oils prescribed to enhance the efficacy of anti-psychotic drugs: see further, MHAC, *Twelfth Biennial Report* 2005–2005 paras 6.49–6.54.

If a patient's refusal to pay attention to his personal hygiene or to be treated for a physical condition is assessed as being a manifestation or symptom of his mental disorder, the patient can be washed and/or treated under the authority of the *Croydon* case as both nursing and specialist care come within the definition of "medical treatment" in s.145(1). If a non-detained patient is mentally incapable of making decisions about such matters, intervention must be justified under the Mental Capacity Act 2005.

The *Croydon* case was applied by Wall J. in *Tameside and Glossop Acute Services Trust v CH* [1996] 1 F.L.R. 762, a case where a pregnant patient who was suffering from schizophrenia had been detained under s.3. She had the delusional belief that the doctors who were caring for her wished to harm her baby. The baby was not developing well and the obstetrician took the view that if the pregnancy was allowed to continue the baby might die in the womb. For that reason the obstetrician wished to induce labour and, if necessary, perform a caesarean section. The trust sought a declaration that it would be lawful to carry out such treatment without the patient's consent and to use any necessary force to restrain her in order to facilitate the treatment. Wall J. held, at 773, that there were "several strands in the evidence" which brought the proposed treatment within the scope of this section:

"First, there is the proposition that an ancillary reason for the induction and, if necessary, the birth by caesarean section is to prevent a deterioration in the [patient's] mental state. Secondly, there is the clear evidence of [the patient's psychiatrist] that in order for the treatment of her schizophrenia to be effective, it is necessary for her to give birth to a live baby. Thirdly, the overall structure of her treatment requires her to receive strong anti-psychotic medication. The administration of that treatment has been necessarily interrupted by her pregnancy and cannot be resumed until her child is born. It is not, therefore, I think stretching language unduly to say that achievement of a successful outcome of her pregnancy is a necessary part of the overall treatment of her mental disorder."

1–788   His Lordship granted the declaration sought, distinguishing *Re C* (*Adult: Refusal of Medical Treatment*) [1994] 1 All E.R. 819 where a schizophrenic patient was held to have the mental capacity to refuse treatment for gangrene which was considered to be life threatening, on the ground that "C's gangrene was not likely to affect his mental condition: the manner in which the delivery of the [patient's] child is treated is likely to have a direct effect on her mental state". As the patient's pregnancy was neither a symptom nor a consequence of her mental disorder, this finding appears to allow a doctor to claim that the treatment of a condition which has no apparent connection with the patient's mental disorder comes within the scope of this section if such treatment will either enhance, or prevent a deterioration of, the patient's mental condition. Treatment proposed in circumstances that are similar to those that were present in *Tameside* should not proceed in the absence of approval by the court: see *A NHS Trust v Dr A*, above.

One reason why a declaration was sought in the *Tameside* case was the fact that the obstetrician might have had to use force on the patient. Wall J. held that it was permissible, should the doctor deem it to be clinically necessary, to use restraint to the extent to which it may be reasonably required in order to achieve the delivery by the patient of a healthy baby. It is therefore lawful for doctors and nurses to use restraint, so far as reasonably required and clinically necessary, to administer treatment under this section. His Lordship agreed, at 774, with counsel's proposition that "in cases in which the question of restraint arose or was likely to arise, and the doctor was doubtful about the lawfulness of the application of restraint or the use of force, an application should be made to the court for a declaration that the treatment would be lawful". In *R. (on the application of Wilkinson) v The Responsible Medical Officer Broadmoor Hospital* [2001] EWCA Civ 1545; [2002] 1 W.L.R. 419, Hale L.J. said, at para.64, that where a mentally incapacitated patient is "actively opposed to a course of action, the benefits which it holds for him will have to be carefully weighed against the disadvantages of going against his wishes, especially if force is required to do this". It is submitted that these remarks, which were concerned with the application of the "best interests" test under common law, are equally applicable to the situation of a detained patient, irrespective of patient's mental capacity.

Supplementary provisions for Part IV
1–789   **64.**—(1) In this Part of this Act ["the responsible clinician" means the approved clinician with overall responsibility for the case] of the patient in question and "hospital" includes a [registered establishment].

[(1A) References in this Part of this Act to the approved clinician in charge of a patient's treatment shall, where the treatment in question is a form of treatment to which section 57 above applies, be construed as references to the person in charge of the treatment.]

[(1B) References in this Part of this Act to the approved clinician in charge of a patient's treatment shall, where the treatment in question is a form of treatment to which section 58A above applies and the patient falls within section 56(5) above, be construed as references to the person in charge of the treatment.

(1C) Regulations made by virtue of section 32(2)(d) above apply for the purposes of this Part as they apply for the purposes of Part 2 of this Act.]

(2) Any certificate for the purposes of this Part of this Act shall be in such form as may be prescribed by regulations made by the Secretary of State.

[(3) For the purposes of this Part of this Act, it is appropriate for treatment to be given to a patient if the treatment is appropriate in his case, taking into account the nature and degree of the mental disorder from which he is suffering and all other circumstances of his case.]

AMENDMENTS
The amendments to this section were made by the Care Standards Act 2000 s.116, Sch.4 para.9(2) and the Mental Health Act 2007 ss.6(3), 12(7), 28(9).

DEFINITIONS
    approved clinician: s.145(1).   **1–790**
    patient: s.145(1).
    hospital: s.145(1).
    registered establishment: ss.34(1), 145(1).

GENERAL NOTE

Subsection (1)
RESPONSIBLE CLINICIAN.   See the note on s.34(1).   **1–791**

APPROVED CLINICIAN IN CHARGE OF A PATIENT'S TREATMENT.   This clinician will not be subject to the supervision of another clinician in respect of the provision of the treatment in question. The Reference Guide states at para.23.11:

"Where a patient has a responsible clinician in overall charge of their case, the responsible clinician need not be in charge of any particular form of treatment. There may be different clinicians in charge of different forms of treatment."

Any dispute between the RC and the AC concerning the medical treatment of the patient that cannot be resolved through discussion would have to be referred to the hospital management for resolution.

Subsection (2)
SECRETARY OF STATE.   Or, in relation to Wales, the Welsh Ministers (see the General **1–792** Note to the Act and SI 1999/672 art.2, Sch.1).

SUBSECTION (3)
Note the circularity of this definition.   **1–793**

[PART 4A
TREATMENT OF COMMUNITY PATIENTS NOT RECALLED TO HOSPITAL]

GENERAL NOTE
    This Part authorises the provision of "relevant treatment" (see s.64A) to either a men- **1–794** tally capable or mentally incapable community patient who has not been recalled to hospital under s.17E. A community patient is a patient in respect of whom a community treatment order is in force (s.17A(7)). Such patients can only be given treatment if they consent or, if they lack the capacity to consent, do not actively object. Treatment can also be given in emergencies to a mentally incapable patient who resists it. The medical treatment of community patients who have been recalled to hospital is governed by s.62A.
    The requirements of this Part are of two types: authority and certification. Although there must always be authority to give the treatment, the certificate requirement does not always apply.
    There is no requirement for the treatment provided under this Part to be given in a clinical setting.

1–795   Guidance on this Part is contained in Ch.24.

[Meaning of "relevant treatment"

1–796   **64A.**—In this Part of this Act "relevant treatment", in relation to a patient, means medical treatment which—

    (a) is for the mental disorder from which the patient is suffering; and

    (b) is not a form of treatment to which section 57 above applies.]

AMENDMENT
This section was inserted by the Mental Health Act 2007 s.35(1).

DEFINITIONS
1–797   medical treatment; s.145(1), (4).
mental disorder: ss.1, 145(1).
patient: s.145(1).

GENERAL NOTE
1–798   The meaning of the phrase "medical treatment . . . for the mental disorder" was explained by the Court of Appeal in *B v Croydon Health Authority* [1995] 1 All E.R. 683 which is considered in the note on s.63.

Section 57 treatments are regulated by the requirements of that section which apply to "any patient" receiving such treatment (s.56(1)).

[Adult community patients

1–799   **64B.**—(1) This section applies to the giving of relevant treatment to a community patient who—

    (a) is not recalled to hospital under section 17E above; and

    (b) has attained the age of 16 years.

(2) The treatment may not be given to the patient unless—

    (a) there is authority to give it to him; and

    (b) if it is section 58 type treatment or section 58A type treatment, the certificate requirement is met.

(3) But the certificate requirement does not apply if—

    (a) giving the treatment to the patient is authorised in accordance with section 64G below; or

    (b) the treatment is immediately necessary and—

        (i) the patient has capacity to consent to it and does consent to it; or

        (ii) a donee or deputy or the Court of Protection consents to the treatment on the patient's behalf.

(4) Nor does the certificate requirement apply in so far as the administration of medicine to the patient at any time during the period of one month beginning with the day on which the community treatment order is made is section 58 type treatment.

(5) The reference in subsection (4) above to the administration of medicine does not include any form of treatment specified under section 58(1)(a) above.]

AMENDMENT
This section was inserted by the Mental Health Act 2007 s.35(1).

DEFINITION
1–800   community patient: ss.17A(7), 145(1).

GENERAL NOTE

This section and s.64C provide authority to treat a community patient who is over the age **1–801** of 16 if (a) there is authority to give it to him because either the patient has capacity and consents to the treatment (even the emergency treatment of such patients requires their consent), or a donee or a deputy or the Court of Protection consents to it on his behalf, or it is authorised under s.64D (treatment for patients who lack capacity) or 64G (emergency treatment for patients who lack capacity) (subs.(2)(a) and s.64C(2)) and, (b) if it is a treatment coming within the scope of s.58 or 58A, the certificate requirement is met in that a SOAD (or the approved clinician in charge of the treatment if the patient is capacious and has consented to the treatment (s.64C(4A),(4B)) has certified that the treatment (or a plan of treatment (s.64H(1)) should be given to the patient (subs.(2)(b) and s.64C(4)). The certificate requirement does *not* apply if the treatment:

(i) is emergency treatment given to a mentally incapacitated patient which is authorised under s.64G (subs.(3)(a)), or

(ii) is immediately necessary (see s.64C(5)–(7)) and either the patient has the capacity to consent to it and does consent to it or a donee or a deputy of a mentally incapacitated patient consents to the treatment on his behalf (subs.(3)(b)), or

(iii) is medication coming within the scope of s.58(1)(b) and the medication is being given to the patient within a month of the CTO being made (subss.(4), (5)) or three months from when the medication was first given to the patient (whether in the community or in hospital), whichever is later. The three month period is relevant because s.58 only applies to medicines after three months have elapsed since they were first given.

The situations set out in paras (i) and (ii) allow for treatment to continue pending a SOAD visit after the one or three-month period mentioned in para.(iii) has elapsed, as long as the relevant criteria are satisfied.

If a certificate is withdrawn by the regulatory authority, the treatment can continue pending compliance with this section if the person in charge of the treatment considers that the discontinuance of the treatment would cause serious suffering to the patient (s.64H(5)–(9)).

Where treatment has been given on the basis of a Pt IVA certificate, the person in charge of the treatment must send the regulatory authority a report on the treatment and the patient's condition if required by that authority (s.64H(4)).

Subsection (1)

RELEVANT TREATMENT.   See s.64C(3).   **1–802**

HOSPITAL.   See s.64K(7).

Subsection (2)(a)

See s.64C(2).   **1–803**

Subsection (2)(b)

The meaning of a "section 58 type treatment or section 58A type treatment" is explained **1–804** in s.64C(3).

CERTIFICATE REQUIREMENT.   See s.64C(4).

Subsection (3)(b)

IMMEDIATELY NECESSARY.   See s.64C(5) to (9) and reg.28(2) of the English Regulations **1–805** and reg.39(a) of the Welsh Regulations.

CAPACITY TO CONSENT.   See s.64K(2). The emergency treatment of patients who lack capacity or competence is governed by s.64G.

DONEE; DEPUTY.   The decision must be within the scope of the authority of the donee or deputy: see s.64K(4), (5).

Subsection (4)

1–806   PERIOD OF ONE MONTH.   The certificate requirement also does not apply during the period of three months from the date when the medication was first given to the patient: see the note on s.64C(4). The SOAD certificate is required from the later of the two periods.

[Section 64B: supplemental

1–807   **64C.**—(1) This section has effect for the purposes of section 64B above.

(2) There is authority to give treatment to a patient if—

(a) he has capacity to consent to it and does consent to it;

(b) a donee or deputy or the Court of Protection consents to it on his behalf; or

(c) giving it to him is authorised in accordance with section 64D or 64G below.

(3) Relevant treatment is section 58 type treatment or section 58A type treatment if, at the time when it is given to the patient, section 58 or 58A above (respectively) would have applied to it, had the patient remained liable to be detained at that time (rather than being a community patient).

(4) The certificate requirement is met in respect of treatment to be given to a patient if—

(a) a registered medical practitioner appointed for the purposes of Part 4 of this Act (not being the responsible clinician or the person in charge of the treatment) has certified in writing that it is appropriate for the treatment to be given or for the treatment to be given subject to such conditions as may be specified in the certificate; and

(b) if conditions are so specified, the conditions are satisfied.

[(4A) Where there is authority to give treatment by virtue of subsection (2)(a), the certificate requirement is also met in respect of the treatment if the approved clinician in charge of the treatment has certified in writing that the patient has capacity to consent to the treatment and has consented to it.

(4B) But, if the patient has not attained the age of 18, subsection (4A) does not apply to section 58A type treatment.]

(5) In a case where the treatment is section 58 type treatment, treatment is immediately necessary if—

(a) it is immediately necessary to save the patient's life; or

(b) it is immediately necessary to prevent a serious deterioration of the patient's condition and is not irreversible; or

(c) it is immediately necessary to alleviate serious suffering by the patient and is not irreversible or hazardous; or

(d) it is immediately necessary, represents the minimum interference necessary to prevent the patient from behaving violently or being a danger to himself or others and is not irreversible or hazardous.

(6) In a case where the treatment is section 58A type treatment by virtue of subsection (1)(a) of that section, treatment is immediately necessary if it falls within paragraph (a) or (b) of subsection (5) above.

(7) In a case where the treatment is section 58A type treatment by virtue of subsection (1)(b) of that section, treatment is immediately necessary if it falls within

such of paragraphs (a) to (d) of subsection (5) above as may be specified in regulations under that section.

(8) For the purposes of subsection (7) above, the regulations—

(a) may make different provision for different cases (and may, in particular, make different provision for different forms of treatment);

(b) may make provision which applies subject to specified exceptions; and

(c) may include transitional, consequential, incidental or supplemental provision.

(9) Subsection (3) of section 62 above applies for the purposes of this section as it applies for the purposes of that section.]

AMENDMENTS

This section was inserted by the Mental Health Act 2007 s.35(1). Subss.(4A) and 4(B) were inserted by the Health and Social Care Act 2012 s.299(2).

DEFINITIONS

patient: s.145(1). **1–808**
community patient: ss.17A(7), 145(1).
responsible clinician: ss.34(1), 64K(6).

GENERAL NOTE

Subsection (2)(a)

If the patient has fluctuating capacity, capacity should be regularly re-assessed. With the **1–809** exception of s.58A treatments, a mentally capable patient may only be treated without consent on being recalled to hospital (s.62A).

Subsection (2)(b)

If a valid consent has been given by a donee or deputy or the Court of Protection (i.e. the **1–810** consent is valid in that the donee or deputy have the authority to make such a decision (s.64(4),(5))) the treatment may be given despite the objections of the incapacitated patient. The donee, deputy and the court have an obligation to act in the best interests of the patient: see ss.4 and 16(3) of the Mental Capacity Act 2005.

Subsection (4)

Apart from capacious consenting patients (see subss.(4A) and (4B)), all community **1–811** patients receiving the type of treatment which falls under s.58 or 58A must have that treatment certified by a SOAD in accordance with the provisions of this Part. For treatment specified in s.58(1)(b), i.e. medication, a certificate is not required immediately, but must be in place after a certain period. This period is one month from when a patient leaves hospital or three months from when the medication was first given to the patient (whether that medication was given in the community or in hospital), whichever is later. The SOAD must certify in writing that it is appropriate for the treatment to be given.

The one month period is specified in s.64B(4). The legal rationale for the alternative period of three months from when the medication was first given is that during that period the provision of medication is not a "section 58 type treatment" (see subs.(3)) as that section would not have applied to it during that period.

A certificate for a s.58A type treatment is required immediately before the treatment is started.

CERTIFIED IN WRITING. Although the *Code of Practice*, at para.25.48, states that the SOAD should "interview the patient in private if possible", neither interviewing the patient nor medically examining him is a legal requirement. Therefore, a SOAD can give a certificate if the patient is unwilling to be interviewed. Before giving a certificate, the SOAD must undertake the consultation exercise provided for in s.64H(3). Form CTO11 must be used: see reg.28(1) of the English Regulations (in Wales, Form CO7: see reg.40(4) of the Welsh Regulations).

The SOAD's role when completing the Form is confined to considering whether it would be appropriate for the treatment to be given to the patient. In other words, the SOAD is not required to confirm the patient's consent to the treatment as the two conditions set out in s.64B(2) are not dependent on each other. This interpretation is supported by the following advice that the Mental Health Act Commission (MHAC) received from the Department of Health which is reproduced in the Commission's *Thirteenth Biennial Report* 2007–2009, at para.3.73:

> "'Appropriateness' does not include [legal] authority. The Act itself provides that treatment cannot lawfully be given unless there is authority to do so, and sets out when such authority will exist. So it is not necessary . . . for SOADs to concern themselves with the question of whether there would be authority to give the treatment. So, in effect, the SOAD is required to consider whether it would be appropriate for the treatment to be given, assuming there were legal authority to give it."

Paragraph 25.32 of the *Code of Practice* states:

> "When giving part 4A certificates, SOADs do not have to certify whether a patient has, or lacks, capacity to consent to the treatments in question, nor whether a patient with capacity is consenting or refusing. They may make it a condition of their approval that particular treatments are given only in certain circumstances. For example, they might specify that a particular treatment is to be given only with the patient's consent. Similarly, they might specify that a medication may be given up to a certain dosage if the patient lacks capacity to consent, but that a higher dosage may be given with the patient's consent."

The fact that a patient who is subject to a community treatment order does not consent to treatment that is deemed to be appropriate for him suggests that long term s.17 leave would be the more appropriate option.

CONDITIONS.   See paras 25.34 and 25.35 of the *Code of Practice*. The Explanatory Notes to the Mental Health Act 2007 state at para.134:

> "The SOAD may specify within the certificate that certain treatment can be given to the patient only if certain conditions are satisfied: so, for example, the SOAD could specify that a particular antipsychotic and dosage can only be given in the community if the patient retains capacity to consent to it. The SOAD can also specify whether and if so what treatments can be given to the patient on recall to hospital and the circumstances in which the treatment can be given. For example, the SOAD can specify, if appropriate, that an antipsychotic can be given to the patient on recall without the patient's consent."

If the certificate specifies conditions, the treatment may only be given in accordance with those conditions.

Subsection (4)(a)

1–812   APPROPRIATE FOR THE TREATMENT TO BE GIVEN.   See ss.64K(8) and 64(3).

Subsections (4A) and (4B)

1–813   These subsections provide that, if the patient consents to the treatment in question, the approved clinician in charge of the treatment will satisfy the certificate requirement by issuing their own Part IVA certificate stating that the patient consents to the treatment and has the capacity to do so. This certificate is sufficient to meet the certificate requirement so long as the patient continues to consent and has capacity to do so: see s.64FA. The subsections do not apply to electro-convulsive therapy for patients under 18. That is because, unless it is an emergency, treatments covered by section 58A may not be given to any patient under 18 (whether or not they are otherwise subject to the Act) without the approval of a SOAD.

For the position where the patient either loses capacity or withdraws his consent, see s.64FA.

APPROVED CLINICIAN IN CHARGE. Only a medically qualified AC can be "in charge" of the administration of medication to a patient.

CERTIFIED IN WRITING. Using Form CTO 12 (in Wales, Form CO8).

Subsection (5)
In this provision, the immediacy refers to the need for treatment and not to the conse- **1–814** quences that would flow if the treatment was not provided.

Subsection (6)
Treatment under this provision can be given to a mentally incapacitated patient even **1–815** though the patient has made an advance decision refusing ECT.

Subsection (9)
Section 62(3) defines "irreversible" and "hazardous". **1–816**

[Adult community patients lacking capacity

64D.—(1) A person is authorised to give relevant treatment to a patient as men- **1–817** tioned in section 64C(2)(c) above if the conditions in subsections (2) to (6) below are met.

(2) The first condition is that, before giving the treatment, the person takes reasonable steps to establish whether the patient lacks capacity to consent to the treatment.

(3) The second condition is that, when giving the treatment, he reasonably believes that the patient lacks capacity to consent to it.

(4) The third condition is that—
(a) he has no reason to believe that the patient objects to being given the treatment; or
(b) he does have reason to believe that the patient so objects, but it is not necessary to use force against the patient in order to give the treatment.

(5) The fourth condition is that—
(a) he is the person in charge of the treatment and an approved clinician; or
(b) the treatment is given under the direction of that clinician.

(6) The fifth condition is that giving the treatment does not conflict with—
(a) an advance decision which he is satisfied is valid and applicable; or
(b) a decision made by a donee or deputy or the Court of Protection.

(7) In this section—
(a) reference to an advance decision is to an advance decision (within the meaning of the Mental Capacity Act 2005) made by the patient; and
(b) "valid and applicable", in relation to such a decision, means valid and applicable to the treatment in question in accordance with section 25 of that Act.]

AMENDMENT
This section was inserted by the Mental Health Act 2007 s.35(1).

DEFINITIONS

1–818   relevant treatment: s.64A.
patient: s.145(1).
approved clinician: s.145(1).

GENERAL NOTE

1–819   This section sets out the conditions that must be satisfied before relevant treatment (see s.64A) can be provided to a community patient who lacks the capacity to consent to the treatment. It provides authority to give treatment to the patient for the purposes of ss.64B(2)(a): see 64C(2)(c). The treatment cannot be given if force would have to be used to ensure that an objecting patient received the treatment (subs.(4)), or if it conflicts with a valid and applicable advance decision made under the Mental Capacity Act 2005 (the 2005 Act) or a decision made by a donee, a deputy or the Court of Protection (subs.(6)). Note that s.64G allows for force to be used to provide treatment to a mentally incapacitated patient in an emergency.

Nothing in this section excludes a person's liabilities resulting from his or her negligence in undertaking anything authorised to be done under it (s.64I).

Subsection (2)

1–820   The capacity of the patient to consent to the treatment should be assessed using the test set out in ss.2 and 3 of the 2005 Act (s.64K(2)).

Subsection (4)

1–821   The factors to be considered in determining whether a patient objects to the treatment are set out in s.64J. If the patient does not object to the treatment, the use of force, which is not defined, is permitted under this section "in cases where, for example, the patient is suffering from tremor and physical force is needed as a practical measure to administer the treatment" (Explanatory Notes, para.130).

FORCE.   The *Code of Practice* states that "force means the actual use of physical force on the patient" (para.24.20).

Subsection (5)(b)

1–822   The patient's GP can only prescribe medication for the patient's mental disorder if it is covered by the SOAD certificate or if a donee or deputy has consented to the medication on the patient's behalf.

Subsection (6)

1–823   Under the terms of the 2005 Act a person who is under the age of 18 cannot make an advance decision or execute a lasting power of attorney.

ADVANCE DECISION.   See subs.(7).

DONEE OR DEPUTY.   The decision must be within the scope of the authority of the donee or deputy: see s.64K(4), (5).

[Child community patients

1–824   **64E.**—(1) This section applies to the giving of relevant treatment to a community patient who—

(a) is not recalled to hospital under section 17E above; and

(b) has not attained the age of 16 years.

(2) The treatment may not be given to the patient unless—

(a) there is authority to give it to him; and

(b) if it is section 58 type treatment or section 58A type treatment, the certificate requirement is met.

(3) But the certificate requirement does not apply if—

(a) giving the treatment to the patient is authorised in accordance with section 64G below; or

(b) in a case where the patient is competent to consent to the treatment and does consent to it, the treatment is immediately necessary.

(4) Nor does the certificate requirement apply in so far as the administration of medicine to the patient at any time during the period of one month beginning with the day on which the community treatment order is made is section 58 type treatment.

(5) The reference in subsection (4) above to the administration of medicine does not include any form of treatment specified under section 58(1)(a) above.

(6) For the purposes of subsection (2)(a) above, there is authority to give treatment to a patient if—

(a) he is competent to consent to it and he does consent to it; or

(b) giving it to him is authorised in accordance with section 64F or 64G below.

(7) Subsections [(3) to (4A) and (5) to (9)] of section 64C above have effect for the purposes of this section as they have effect for the purposes of section 64B above [; and for the purpose of this subsection, subsection (4A) of section 64C above has effect as if—

(a) the references to treatment were references only to section 58 type treatment,

(b) the reference to subsection (2)(a) of section 64C were a reference to subsection (6)(a) of this section, and

(c) the reference to capacity to consent were a reference to competence to consent.].

(8) Regulations made by virtue of section 32(2)(d) above apply for the purposes of this section as they apply for the purposes of Part 2 of this Act.]

AMENDMENTS

This section was inserted by the Mental Health Act 2007 s.35(1). The amendments to subs.(7) were made by the Health and Social Care Act 2012 s.299(3).

DEFINITIONS   **1–825**

relevant treatment: s.64A.

community patient: ss.17A(7), 145(1).

community treatment order: ss.17A(1), 145(1).

hospital: ss.64K(7), 145(1).

GENERAL NOTE

This section identifies when relevant treatment (see s.64A) can be provided to a com- **1–826** munity patient who is under the age of 16 and who has not been recalled to hospital under s.17E. Such treatment cannot be provided to the patient unless (a) he is competent to consent to it and does consent to it, or the giving of the treatment is authorised by s.64F (treatment for child patients lacking competence) or s.64G (emergency treatment for child patients lacking competence) (subss.(2)(a), (6)), and (b) if it is a treatment coming within the scope of s.58 or s.58A, the certificate requirement is met in that a SOAD (or the approved clinician in charge of the treatment if the patient is mentally competent and has consented to the treatment (subs.(7)) has certified that the treatment (or plan of treatment (s.64H(1)) should be given (subss.(2)(b), (7) and s.64C(4)). The certificate requirement does not apply if the treatment:

(i) is emergency treatment which is authorised under s.64G (subs.(3)(a)), or

(ii) is immediately necessary (subss.(3)(b), (7), s.64C(5), (6)), or

(iii) is medication coming within the scope of s.58(1)(b) and the medication is being given to the patient within a month of the CTO being made (subss.(4), (5)) or three months from when the medication was first given to the patient (whether in the community or in hospital), whichever is later.

A certificate for a s.58A type treatment is required immediately before the treatment is started.

If a certificate is withdrawn by the regulatory authority, the treatment can continue pending compliance with the this section if the person in charge of the treatment considers that the discontinuance of the treatment would cause serious suffering to the patient (s.64H(5)–(9)).

A parent (or another person with parental responsibility) cannot either consent to or refuse treatment for mental disorder on behalf of a child who is subject to a CTO.

Code of Practice

1–827   See paras 19.24 to 19.37 of the *Code* which are concerned with assessing the competence of children to consent to treatment. Paragraph 19.114 confirms that parents cannot consent (or refuse consent) to treatment for mental disorder on a child or young person's behalf while the child or young person is on a CTO.

Subsection (2)

1–828   The meaning of "section 58 type treatment or section 58A type treatment" is explained in s.64C(3) (subs.(7)).

Subsection (3)(b)

1–829   IMMEDIATELY NECESSARY.   See reg.28(2) of the English Regulations and reg.39(a) of the Welsh Regulations.

[Child community patients lacking competence

1–830   **64F.**—(1) A person is authorised to give relevant treatment to a patient as mentioned in section 64E(6)(b) above if the conditions in subsections (2) to (5) below are met.

(2) The first condition is that, before giving the treatment, the person takes reasonable steps to establish whether the patient is competent to consent to the treatment.

(3) The second condition is that, when giving the treatment, he reasonably believes that the patient is not competent to consent to it.

(4) The third condition is that—

(a) he has no reason to believe that the patient objects to being given the treatment; or

(b) he does have reason to believe that the patient so objects, but it is not necessary to use force against the patient in order to give the treatment.

(5) The fourth condition is that—

(a) he is the person in charge of the treatment and an approved clinician; or

(b) the treatment is given under the direction of that clinician.]

AMENDMENT
This section was inserted by the Mental Health Act 2007 s.35(1).

DEFINITION
    relevant treatment: s.64A.   **1–831**
    patient: s.145(1).
    approved clinician: s.145(1).

GENERAL NOTE
    This section sets out the conditions that must be satisfied before relevant treatment (see **1–832** s.64A) can be provided to a community patient who is under the age of 16 and who lacks the competence to consent to the treatment. Children lack competence (the equivalent to "capacity" for adults) if they do not have sufficient understanding and intelligence to enable them fully to understand what is involved in a proposed treatment: see paras 19.34 to 19.37 of the *Code of Practice*. The treatment cannot be given if force would have to be used to ensure that an objecting patient received the treatment (subs.(4)); but force can be used in an emergency (s.64G)). As is the case with capacious adults, treatment cannot be given to a child in the community who is competent to consent and does not consent to it.
    A person with parental responsibility for a child patient may not consent on the child's behalf to treatment for mental disorder (or refuse it) while the child is a community patient.
    Nothing in this section excludes a person's liabilities resulting from his or her negligence in undertaking anything authorised to be done under it (s.64I).

Code of Practice
See the note to s.64E under this heading.   **1–833**

Subsection (4)
    The factors to be considered in determining whether a patient objects to the treatment are **1–834** set out in s.64J.

[Withdrawal of consent

    64FA.—(1). Where the consent of a patient to any treatment has been given as **1–835** mentioned in section 64C(2)(a) above for the purposes of section 64B or 64E above, the patient may at any time before the completion of the treatment withdraw his consent, and those sections shall then apply as if the remainder of the treatment were a separate form of treatment.
    (2) Subsection (3) below applies where—
  (a) the consent of a patient to any treatment has been given as mentioned in section 64C(2)(a) above for the purposes of section 64B or 64E above; but
  (b) before the completion of the treatment, the patient loses capacity or (as the case may be) competence to consent to the treatment.
    (3) The patient shall be treated as having withdrawn his consent and section 64B or (as the case may be) section 64E above shall then apply as if the remainder of the treatment were a separate form of treatment.
    (4) Without prejudice to the application of subsections (1) to (3) above to any treatment given under the plan of treatment to which a patient has consented, a patient who has consented to such a plan may at any time withdraw his consent to further treatment, or to further treatment of any description, under the plan.
    (5) This section shall not preclude the continuation of any treatment, or of treatment under any plan, pending compliance with section 58, 58A, 64B or 64E above if the approved clinician in charge of the treatment considers that the

discontinuance of the treatment, or of treatment under the plan, would cause serious suffering to the patient.]

AMENDMENT
This section was inserted by the Health and Social Care Act 2012 s.299(4).

DEFINITIONS
1–836 approved clinician: s.145(1).
patient: s.145(1).

GENERAL NOTE
1–837 The section provides that a community patient who has consented to treatment may at any time withdraw that consent. It also sets out what happens if a patient who has consented to treatment subsequently loses the capacity to do so. In both cases, the patient will be treated as having withdrawn consent to the treatment in question. A consequence of this is that any approved clinician's certificate relating to the treatment would no longer be valid, and a SOAD's certificate would be required instead. However, subs.(5) provides that treatment may continue whilst a new certificate is being sought, if the approved clinician considers that stopping the treatment would cause serious suffering to the patient. Subsection (5) does not allow treatment to continue against the wishes of a patient who still has capacity to consent, unless the patient is recalled to hospital. This is because a SOAD's certificate does not provide legal authority to give the treatment to a capacious, non-consenting patient.

[Emergency treatment for patients lacking capacity or competence
1–838 **64G.**—(1) A person is also authorised to give relevant treatment to a patient as mentioned in section 64C(2)(c) or 64E(6)(b) above if the conditions in subsections (2) to (4) below are met.

(2) The first condition is that, when giving the treatment, the person reasonably believes that the patient lacks capacity to consent to it or, as the case may be, is not competent to consent to it.

(3) The second condition is that the treatment is immediately necessary.

(4) The third condition is that if it is necessary to use force against the patient in order to give the treatment—
  (a) the treatment needs to be given in order to prevent harm to the patient; and
  (b) the use of such force is a proportionate response to the likelihood of the patient's suffering harm, and to the seriousness of that harm.

(5) Subject to subsections (6) to (8) below, treatment is immediately necessary if—
  (a) it is immediately necessary to save the patient's life; or
  (b) it is immediately necessary to prevent a serious deterioration of the patient's condition and is not irreversible; or
  (c) it is immediately necessary to alleviate serious suffering by the patient and is not irreversible or hazardous; or
  (d) it is immediately necessary, represents the minimum interference necessary to prevent the patient from behaving violently or being a danger to himself or others and is not irreversible or hazardous.

(6) Where the treatment is section 58A type treatment by virtue of subsection (1)(a) of that section, treatment is immediately necessary if it falls within paragraph (a) or (b) of subsection (5) above.

(7) Where the treatment is section 58A type treatment by virtue of subsection (1)(b) of that section, treatment is immediately necessary if it falls within such of

paragraphs (a) to (d) of subsection (5) above as may be specified in regulations under section 58A above.

(8) For the purposes of subsection (7) above, the regulations—

(a) may make different provision for different cases (and may, in particular, make different provision for different forms of treatment);

(b) may make provision which applies subject to specified exceptions; and

(c) may include transitional, consequential, incidental or supplemental provision.

(9) Subsection (3) of section 62 above applies for the purposes of this section as it applies for the purposes of that section.]

AMENDMENT

This section was inserted by the Mental Health Act 2007 s.35(1).

DEFINITIONS

    relevant treatment: s.64A.   **1–839**

    patient: s.145(1).

GENERAL NOTE

This section sets out the criteria that must be satisfied before relevant treatment (see **1–840** s.64A) can be given in an emergency to adult community patients who lacks capacity or child community patients who lacks competence, and identifies in subs.(4) when force can be used in order to provide such treatment. The requirement to obtain a certificate from a SOAD does not apply to such treatment (s.64B(3)(a)). The person providing the treatment need not be acting under the direction of an approved clinician (*Code of Practice*, para.24.24).

Emergency treatment should be provided in those rare situations where it is in the best interests of the patient to be immediately treated with force in the community rather than be transported to hospital under the recall power contained in s.17E for the treatment to be provided there. Such treatment can be given even if it conflicts with an advance decision to refuse the treatment or a decision of a donee or a deputy. The provisions of subs.(5) are virtually identical to the criteria that must be satisfied before urgent treatment can be given under s.62.

The emergency circumstances in which s.58A type treatment can be given are more limited than the circumstances in which other treatments can be given in an emergency: see subss.(6) to (8).

Nothing in this section excludes a person's liabilities resulting from his or her negligence in undertaking anything authorised to be done under it (s.64I).

Code of Practice

This section is considered at paras 24.24 to 24.28.   **1–841**

Subsection (1)

TREATMENT.   Including the treatment specified in reg.28(3) of the English Regulations **1–842** and reg.39(b) of the Welsh Regulations.

Subsection (2)

LACKS CAPACITY.   See s.64K(2).   **1–843**

Subsection (3)

IMMEDIATELY NECESSARY.   See subss.(5) to (8) and the note on this phrase in s.62(1).   **1–844**

Subsection (4)

1–845   Although physical force cannot be used to provide treatment in order to prevent harm to others, treatment which is aimed at preventing harm to the patient could also have that effect. For example, treatment which is aimed at preventing the patient being aggressive to others could have the effect of preventing harm to the patient through possible retaliation.

Subsection (9)

1–846   Section 62(3) defines "irreversible" and "hazardous".

[Certificates: supplementary provisions

1–847   **64H.**—(1) A certificate under section 64B(2)(b) or 64E(2)(b) above (a "Part 4A certificate") may relate to a plan of treatment under which the patient is to be given (whether within a specified period or otherwise) one or more forms of section 58 type treatment or section 58A type treatment.

(2) A Part 4A certificate shall be in such form as may be prescribed by regulations made by the appropriate national authority [; and the regulations may make different provision for the different descriptions of Part 4A certificate].

(3) Before giving a Part 4A certificate [that falls within section 64C(4) above], the registered medical practitioner concerned shall consult two other persons who have been professionally concerned with the patient's medical treatment but, of those persons—

(a) at least one shall be a person who is not a registered medical practitioner; and

(b) neither shall be the patient's responsible clinician or the person in charge of the treatment in question.

(4) Where a patient is given treatment in accordance with a Part 4A certificate [that falls within section 64C(4) above], a report on the treatment and the patient's condition shall be given by the person in charge of the treatment to the [regulatory authority] if required by that authority.

(5) The [regulatory authority] may at any time give notice directing that a Part 4A certificate [that falls within section 64C(4) above] shall not apply to treatment given to a patient after a date specified in the notice, and the relevant section shall then apply to any such treatment as if that certificate had not been given.

(6) The relevant section is—

(a) if the patient is not recalled to hospital in accordance with section 17E above, section 64B or 64E above;

(b) if the patient is so recalled or is liable to be detained under this Act following revocation of the community treatment order under section 17F above—

  (i) section 58 above, in the case of section 58 type treatment;

  (ii) section 58A above, in the case of section 58A type treatment; (subject to section 62A(2) above).

(7) The notice under subsection (5) above shall be given to the person in charge of the treatment in question.

(8) Subsection (5) above shall not preclude the continuation of any treatment or of treatment under any plan pending compliance with the relevant section if the person in charge of the treatment considers that the discontinuance of the treatment or of treatment under the plan would cause serious suffering to the patient.

(9) In this section, "the appropriate national authority" means—

(a) in relation to community patients in respect of whom the responsible hospital is in England, the Secretary of State;

(b) in relation to community patients in respect of whom the responsible hospital is in Wales, the Welsh Ministers.]

AMENDMENTS

This section was inserted by the Mental Health Act 2007 s.35(1). The amendments to it were made by the Health and Social Care Act 2008 s.52, Sch.3 para.5 and the Health and Social Care Act 2012 s.299(5).

DEFINITIONS

    patient: s.145(1).   **1–848**

    the regulatory authority: s.145(1).

    medical treatment: s.145(1),(4).

    responsible clinician: ss.64K(6), 145(1).

    hospital: ss.64K(7), 145(1).

    community treatment order: ss.17A(3), 145(1).

    responsible hospital: ss17A(7), 145(1).

GENERAL NOTE

Subsection (2)   **1–849**

    APPROPRIATE NATIONAL AUTHORITY.   See subs.(9).

Subsection (3)

    This provision requires that any SOAD certifying that treatment is appropriate in the case **1–850** of a community patient must first have consulted with two persons who have been professionally concerned with the patient's treatment, at least one of whom shall not be a doctor, and neither of whom may be the responsible clinician or approved clinician in charge of the treatment in question. As such, there is no positive requirement to consult with a specific type of professional, in contrast to the arrangements for SOAD visits to detained patients, where one of the statutory consultees must be a nurse.

    Paragraph 24.26 of the Reference Guide states:

    "[T]he certificate would not authorise any treatment if, at the time it is proposed to give the treatment, the person who is now the patient's responsible clinician or the approved clinician in charge of the treatment in question happens to be one of the two people who were originally consulted by the SOAD before giving the certificate."

Subsection (4)

    For reviews of treatment by the CQC, see s.61 under the heading *Code of Practice*.   **1–851**

Subsections (4), (5)

    THE REGULATORY AUTHORITY.   Is the Care Quality Commission or, in relation to Wales, **1–852** the Welsh Ministers (s.145(1)).

Subsection (5)

    RELEVANT SECTION.   See subs.(6).   **1–853**

[Liability for negligence

    64I.—Nothing in section 64D, 64F or 64G above excludes a person's civil liab- **1–854** ility for loss or damage, or his criminal liability, resulting from his negligence in doing anything authorised to be done by that section.]

AMENDMENT
This section was inserted by the Mental Health Act 2007 s.35(1).

[Factors to be considered in determining whether patient objects to treatment

1–855   **64J.**—(1) In assessing for the purposes of this Part whether he has reason to believe that a patient objects to treatment, a person shall consider all the circumstances so far as they are reasonably ascertainable, including the patient's behaviour, wishes, feelings, views, beliefs and values.

(2) But circumstances from the past shall be considered only so far as it is still appropriate to consider them.]

AMENDMENT
This section was inserted by the Mental Health Act 2007 s.35(1).

DEFINITION
1–856   patient: s.145(1).

GENERAL NOTE
1–857   An objection is not rendered invalid because a view is taken that it is unreasonable.

[Interpretation of Part 4A

1–858   **64K.**—(1) This Part of this Act is to be construed as follows.

(2) References to a patient who lacks capacity are to a patient who lacks capacity within the meaning of the Mental Capacity Act 2005.

(3) References to a patient who has capacity are to be read accordingly.

(4) References to a donee are to a donee of a lasting power of attorney (within the meaning of section 9 of the Mental Capacity Act 2005) created by the patient, where the donee is acting within the scope of his authority and in accordance with that Act.

(5) References to a deputy are to a deputy appointed for the patient by the Court of Protection under section 16 of the Mental Capacity Act 2005, where the deputy is acting within the scope of his authority and in accordance with that Act.

(6) Reference to the responsible clinician shall be construed as a reference to the responsible clinician within the meaning of Part 2 of this Act.

(7) References to a hospital include a registered establishment.

(8) Section 64(3) above applies for the purposes of this Part of this Act as it applies for the purposes of Part 4 of this Act.]

AMENDMENT
This section was inserted by the Mental Health Act 2007 s.35(1).

DEFINITION
1–859   patient: s.145(1).
hospital: s.145(2).
registered establishment: ss.34(1), 145(1).

GENERAL NOTE

Subsection (6)
1–860   RESPONSIBLE CLINICIAN.   See s.34(1) and the notes thereto.

PART V

MENTAL HEALTH REVIEW TRIBUNALS

Constitution, etc.

Mental Health Review [Tribunal for Wales]

65.—[(1) There shall [be a Mental Health Review Tribunal for Wales.]   **1–861**

(1A) The purpose of [that tribunal] is to deal with applications and references by and in respect of patients under the provisions of this Act.]

(2) The provisions of Schedule 2 to this Act shall have effect with respect to the constitution of [the Mental Health Review Tribunal for Wales].

(3) Subject to the provisions of Schedule 2 to this Act, and to rules made by the Lord Chancellor under this Act, the jurisdiction of [the Mental Health Review Tribunal for Wales] may be exercised by any three or more of its members, and references in this Act to [the Mental Health Review Tribunal for Wales] shall be construed accordingly.

[(4) The Welsh Ministers may pay to the members of the Mental Health Review Tribunal for Wales such remuneration and allowances as they may determine, and defray the expenses of that tribunal to such amount as they may determine, and may provide for that tribunal such officers and servants, and such accommodation, as that tribunal may require.]

AMENDMENTS

The amendments to this section were made by the Mental Health Act 2007 s.38(2) and SI 2008/2883 art.9, Sch.3 para.45.

DEFINITION

patient: s.145(1).   **1–862**

GENERAL NOTE

Wales—The Mental Health Review Tribunal for Wales

This section, together with Sch.2, provides for the establishment of a Mental Health   **1–863** Review Tribunal for Wales. This Tribunal, which has a Chairman and covers the whole of Wales, has its office within the National Assembly for Wales administrative building in Cardiff. The equivalent tribunal in England, the First-tier Tribunal (Mental Health), was established under the Tribunals, Courts and Enforcement Act 2007 (the 2007 Act). The two tribunals have identical powers and duties to discharge patients and to make recommendations.

One curious difference between the two tribunals is that while the requirement for a practicing medical practitioner to have a licence to practice has been disapplied with respect to First-tier Tribunal medical members by SI 2008/2692, r.1(2), similar action has not been taken with respect to medical members of the Welsh tribunal.

England—The First-tier Tribunal (Mental Health)

In the report of his Review of Tribunals, *Tribunals for Users—One System, One Service*,   **1–864** published in August 2001, Sir Andrew Leggatt recommended extensive reform to the tribunals system. He recommended that tribunals should be brought together in a single system, that they should become separate from their current sponsoring departments, and that such a system be administered instead by a single Tribunals Service. The Government agreed and its response is to be found in the 2007 Act. The Act creates two new, generic tribunals, the First-tier Tribunal and the Upper Tribunal, into which existing tribunal jurisdictions have been transferred: see SI 2008/2833 art.3, Sch.1. The Upper Tribunal is primarily an appellate tribunal from the First-tier Tribunal.

The 2007 Act also provides for the establishment of "chambers" within the two tribunals which enable tribunals to be grouped appropriately. A Health, Education and Social Care Chamber has been created which, inter alia, has functions relating to "applications and references by and in respect of patients under the provisions of the Mental Health Act 1983 or paragraph 5(2) of the Schedule to the Repatriation of Prisoners Act 1984" (SI 2008/2684 art.5(h)). The tribunal within the Health, Education and Social Care Chamber that deals with mental health cases is known as the First-tier Tribunal (Mental Health) (referred to here as the "tribunal"). Each Chamber is headed by a Chamber President and the tribunals judiciary is headed by a Senior President of Tribunals. The First-tier Tribunal (Mental Health) only has jurisdiction in England.

The 2007 Act also provides for the membership of the tribunals and the making of Tribunal Procedure Rules, which can be supplemented by means of practice directions. The First-tier Tribunal (Health, Education and Social Care Chamber) Rules 2008 (SI 2008/2699) (the Tribunal Rules) and related practice directions are reproduced in Part 3.

An account of various aspects of the operation of the First-tier Tribunal (Mental Health) can be found in the General Note to the Tribunal Rules.

Appeals (Also see the notes to r.46 of the Tribunal Rules in Part 3)

1–865   A decision, apart from an "excluded decision" but including an interlocutory decision (*LS v London Borough of Lambeth* [2010] UKUT 461 (AAC)), of the First-tier Tribunal (and the Mental Health Review Tribunal for Wales: see s.78A) may be appealed to the Administrative Appeals Chamber of the Upper Tribunal (s.11 of the 2007 Act and SI 2008/2684, arts 6, 7(a)(i) and (iv)), and a decision of the Upper Tribunal may be appealed to the Court of Appeal. However, the Court of Appeal cannot grant permission to appeal from a refusal of the Upper Tribunal to review its decision to refuse permission to appeal. The only remedy of the aggrieved party is by way of judicial review, which is subject to the restrictions laid down in *Cart*, below (*Samuda v Secretary of State for Work and Pensions* [2014] EWCA Civ 1; [2014] 3 All E.R. 201). Permission to appeal to the Court of Appeal should only be granted if the appeal raises an important point of principle or practice, or there is some other compelling reason for the Court of Appeal to consider the appeal (*RH v South London and Maudsley NHS Foundation Trust* [2010] EWCA Civ 1273; [2010] M.H.L.R. 341, para.36). An appeal to the Upper Tribunal can only succeed if "the making of the decision concerned involved the making of an error on a point of law" (s.12(1) of the 2007 Act).

The rights of appeal may only be exercised with permission of the First-tier Tribunal or the Upper Tribunal itself. If the Upper Tribunal exercises its discretion to set aside the decision of the First-tier Tribunal it must either remit the case to the tribunal with directions for its reconsideration, or remake the decision: see s.12(2) of the 2007 Act. The procedure of the Upper Tribunal, which is a superior court of record (2007 Act s.3(5)) and can therefore lay down authoritative precedents, is governed by the Tribunal Procedure (Upper Tribunal) Rules 2008 (SI 2008/2698). The Upper Tribunal has a similar power to that of the First-tier Tribunal to review its own decisions, and to take similar actions following a review (2007 Act s.10). The Upper Tribunal has published a leaflet on "Appealing to the Administrative Appeals Chamber of the Upper Tribunal from the First-tier Tribunal Mental Health Decisions", a form for applying for permission to appeal (Form UT3), and a guidance note to accompany the form. The Upper Tribunal also deals with most of the judicial review cases relating to the tribunal which previously would have been dealt with by the High Court. Applications to the Upper Tribunal for judicial review may be made by virtue of ss.15 to 18 of the 2007 Act where the application does not seek a declaration of incompatibility under the Human Rights Act 1998 and it is within the scope of *Practice Direction (Upper Tribunal: Judicial Review Jurisdiction)* [2009] 1 W.L.R. 327. The Upper Tribunal is subject to the jurisdiction of the High Court by way of judicial review but only where there is an important point of principle or practice or some other compelling reason to review the case (*R. (on the application of Cart) v The Upper Tribunal* [2011] UKSC 28; [2011] 4 All E.R. 127).

The Upper Tribunal does not have any habeas corpus jurisdiction (*AS v First-tier Tribunal*, Upper Tribunal Case No.JR/3048/2012, para.3).

As it is exercising a jurisdiction of equivalent status, the Upper Tribunal is not bound by decisions of the High Court, but will follow them unless convinced they are wrong (*Secretary of State for Justice v RB* [2010] UKUT 454 (AAC); [2011] M.H.L.R. 37, para.47).

Rules of Precedence in the Upper Tribunal

The following guidelines were identified by the Upper Tribunal in *Dorset Healthcare* **1–866** *NHS Foundation Trust v MH* [2009] UKUT 4 (AAC); [2009] M.H.L.R. 102, para.37:

1. Judges of the Upper Tribunal in the Administrative Appeals Court (AAC) speak with equal authority. All their decisions may be cited to the Upper Tribunal, First-tier Tribunals and other tribunals from which appeals to the AAC come and the appropriate decision-making authorities. Where they decide questions of legal principle they must be followed by the appropriate decision-making authorities and the tribunals below in cases involving the application of that principle, unless they can be distinguished. It should be borne in mind that similarity in underlying facts does not automatically give rise to similarity in the principle to be applied and questions of fact should not be elevated into questions of legal principle.

2. If confronted with decisions which conflict, the appropriate decision-making authority and tribunals below must prefer the decision of a Three-Judge Panel of the AAC to that of a single judge.

3. In so far as the AAC is concerned, on questions of legal principle, a single judge shall follow a decision of a Three-Judge Panel of the AAC . . . unless there are compelling reasons why he should not, as, for instance, a decision of a superior court affecting the legal principles involved. A single judge in the interests of comity and to avoid confusion on questions of legal principle normally follows the decisions of other single judges. It is recognised however that a slavish adherence to this could lead to the perpetuation of error and he is not bound to do so.

Habeas Corpus and Judicial Review

If a patient considers that his detention was unlawful he can attempt to secure his release **1–867** by making an application to the High Court for a writ of habeas corpus. The writ of habeas corpus, which requires the detaining body to show lawful justification for a detention, runs to the party having the applicant in his custody (the hospital managers) and not the doctor who made medical recommendation in support of an application under Pt II (*R. v South Western Hospital, Managers Ex p. M* [1994] 1 All E.R. 161). If the writ is issued, the applicant must be released. An alternative course of action would be to make an application for the judicial review of the decision to detain him. Most cases that would in the past have resulted in applications to the High Court for the judicial review of a tribunal decision will now be dealt with as appeals on points of law to the Upper Tribunal, which also has a judicial review jurisdiction (see above). The Upper Tribunal has no jurisdiction over the decisions of hospital managers taken under s.23.

The distinction between the habeas corpus and judicial review procedures was explained by Lord Donaldson M.R. in the following extract from his judgment in *R. v Secretary of State for the Home Department Ex p. Cheblak* [1991] 2 All E.R. 319 at 322, 323, a case where the applicant was seeking to challenge his arrest and the decision to deport him:

"Although, as I have said, the two forms of relief which Mr. Cheblak seeks are interrelated on the facts of his case, they are essentially different. A writ of *habeas corpus* will issue where someone is detained without any authority or the purported authority is beyond the powers of the person authorising the detention and so is unlawful. *The remedy of judicial review* is available where the decision or action sought to be impugned is within the powers of the person taking it but, due to procedural error, a misappreciation of the law, a failure to take account of relevant matters, a taking account of irrelevant matters or the fundamental unreasonableness of the decision or action, it should never have been taken. In such a case the decision or action is lawful, unless and until it is set aside by a court of competent jurisdiction. In the case of detention, if the warrant, or the underlying decision to deport, were set aside but the detention continued, a writ of *habeas corpus* would issue."

The distinction between the two forms of proceedings was applied to the Act in *Re S-C (Mental Patient: Habeas Corpus)* [1996] 1 All E.R. 532, CA, where the patient was challenging the lawfulness of his detention on the ground that the application for his detention under s.3 was not "duly completed" as required by s.6(1) because a condition precedent relating to the application was not present in that the patient's nearest relative had not been consulted as required by s.11(4). The Court held that as the patient's challenge was not directed to an administrative decision but to the jurisdiction of the hospital managers to detain him, an application for habeas corpus was the appropriate remedy rather than proceedings for judicial review. In *B v Barking Havering and Brentwood Community Healthcare NHS Trust* [1999] 1 F.L.R. 106, CA, Lord Woolf M.R. referred to a passage in the judgment of Sir Thomas Bingham M.R. in *Re S-C* where his Lordship said that on the facts of that case "an application for habeas corpus is *an* appropriate, and possibly even *the* appropriate course to pursue". Lord Woolf expressed his disagreement with the suggestion that "possibly" an application for habeas corpus was the only procedure that was appropriate. While accepting that in *Re S-C* habeas corpus was an appropriate procedure, his Lordship suggested that judicial review was equally appropriate and would even have advantages over habeas corpus. His Lordship would discourage applications for habeas corpus unless it was clear that no other form of relief would be required. Where applications were made for both judicial review and habeas corpus, the proceedings should be harmonised if at all possible.

1–868   In *Re Doreen Trew* [2000] M.H.L.R. 53, the applicant submitted that the court considering the remedy of habeas corpus is not limited to considering whether the procedural requisites for detention are met, but can also take action where there is inadequate evidence to justify the detention. Owen J., in refusing the application, held that although there was authority to support the contention that habeas corpus is available when there is no evidence to justify the decision to detain (see *R. v Board of Control Ex p. Rutty* [1956] 2 Q.B. 109), this does not support an argument that when a case before a tribunal is strong, but no decision has been given because the tribunal adjourned the hearing, the court hearing the application can consider the evidence, sideline the tribunal, and find that the tribunal should discharge. His Lordship said that in these circumstances "it is evident that the tribunal should make the decision".

The court or Upper Tribunal considering an application for judicial review is exercising a public law jurisdiction and is not required to grant the application even if unlawfulness is established. In order to succeed in an application one of the established grounds must be made out, namely that the decision maker has acted illegally, has behaved irrationally, has abused power, or has failed to act with procedural fairness toward one of the parties. The court will also consider whether there has been a breech of the applicant's rights under the European Convention on Human Rights (*R. v Secretary of State for the Home Department, Ex p. Daly* [2001] 2 A.C. 532, HL).

If, on an application for judicial review an order quashing the decision of the tribunal to discharge the patient is made, this has the effect of treating the decision to discharge as never having been made and restoring the patient to the status of a detained patient (*R. (on the application of Wirral Health Authority and Wirral Borough Council) v Mental Health Review Tribunal and DE* [2001] EWCA Civ 1901; [2002] M.H.L.R. 34). However, the remedies afforded on judicial review are as flexible as justice requires and the need for a fresh tribunal decision does not automatically require a quashing order. In *R. (on the application of the Secretary of State for the Home Department) v Mental Health Review Tribunal and BR* [2005] EWCA Civ 1616; [2006] M.H.L.R. 172, the patient appealed against the effect of a quashing order made following a successful appeal by the Secretary of State against a decision by a tribunal that the patient be unconditionally discharged from hospital. The issue before the tribunal was whether discharge should be absolute or conditional, not whether he was entitled to be discharged at all. The effect of the quashing order was to allow the patient to be detained again, which is what happened. On allowing the appeal, the Court of Appeal made orders quashing as much of the tribunal's decision as granted the patient an absolute discharge, and declaring that pending a rehearing the patient is entitled to be treated as having been conditionally discharged. Sedley L.J. said at para.16:

"Modern public law is quite capable enough to do this if necessary, and here it was called for by the requirements both of the common law and the European Convention on Human Rights that nobody is to be deprived of his liberty except according to law."

Applications and references concerning Part II patients

Applications to tribunals

66.—(1) Where—   **1–869**

    (a) a patient is admitted to a hospital in pursuance of an application for admission for assessment; or

    (b) a patient is admitted to a hospital in pursuance of an application for admission for treatment; or

    (c) a patient is received into guardianship in pursuance of a guardianship application; or

    [(ca) a community treatment order is made in respect of a patient; or

    (cb) a community treatment order is revoked under section 17F above in respect of a patient; or]

[. . .]

    (e) a patient is transferred from guardianship to a hospital in pursuance of regulations made under section 19 above; or

    (f) a report is furnished under section 20 above in respect of a patient and the patient is not discharged [under section 23 above]; or

    [(fza) a report is furnished under section 20A above in respect of a patient and the patient is not discharged under section 23 above; or]

    [(fa) a report is furnished under subsection (2) of section 21B above in respect of a patient and subsection (5) of that section applies (or subsections (5) and (6)(b) of that section apply) in the case of the report; or

    [(faa) a report is furnished under subsection (2) of section 21B above in respect of a community patient and subsection (6A) of that section applies (or subsections (6A) and (6B)(b) of that section apply) in the case of the report; or]

    [. . .]

    (g) a report is furnished under section 25 above in respect of a patient who is detained in pursuance of an application for admission for treatment [or a community patient]; or

    [. . .]

    (h) an order is made under section 29 above [on the ground specified in paragraph (c) or (d) of subsection (3) of that section] in respect of a patient

who is or subsequently becomes liable to be detained or subject to guardianship under Part II of this Act [or who is a community patient],
an application may be made to [the appropriate tribunal] within the relevant period—
  (i) by the patient (except in the cases mentioned in paragraphs (g) and (h) above) [. . .] and
  (ii) in the cases mentioned in paragraphs (g) and (h) above, by his nearest relative.
  (2) In subsection (1) above "the relevant period" means—
  (a) in the case mentioned in paragraph (a) of that subsection, 14 days beginning with the day on which the patient is admitted as so mentioned;
  (b) in the case mentioned in paragraph (b) of that subsection, six months beginning with the day on which the patient is admitted as so mentioned;
  (c) in the [case mentioned in paragraph (c)] of that subsection, six months beginning with the day on which the application is accepted;
[(ca) in the case mentioned in paragraph (ca) of that subsection, six months beginning with the day on which the community treatment order is made;
  (cb) in the case mentioned in paragraph (cb) of that subsection, six months beginning with the day on which the community treatment order is revoked;]
  (d) [in the case mentioned in paragraph (g)] of that subsection, 28 days beginning with the day on which the applicant is informed that the report has been furnished;
  (e) in the case mentioned in paragraph (e) of that subsection, six months beginning with the day on which the patient is transferred;
  (f) in the case mentioned in paragraph (f) [or (fa) of that subsection, the period or periods] for which authority for the patient's detention or guardianship is renewed by virtue of the report;
[(fza) in the cases mentioned in paragraphs (fza) and (faa) of that subsection, the period or periods for which the community treatment period is extended by virtue of the report;]
  [. . .]
  (g) in the case mentioned in paragraph (h) of that subsection, 12 months beginning with the date of the order, and in any subsequent period of 12 months during which the order continues in force.
  [(2A) Nothing in subsection (1)(b) above entitles a community patient to make an application by virtue of that provision even if he is admitted to a hospital on being recalled there under section 17E above.]
  (3) Section 32 above shall apply for the purposes of this section as it applies for the purposes of Pt II of this Act.
  [(4) In this Act "the appropriate tribunal" means the First-tier Tribunal or the Mental Health Review Tribunal for Wales.
  (5) For provision determining to which of those tribunals applications by or in respect of a patient under this Act shall be made, see section 77(3) and (4) below.]

AMENDMENTS
  The amendments to this section were made by the Mental Health Act 2007 ss.1(4), 25, 36(3), 55, Sch.1 para.13, Sch.11 Pts 1 and 5 and SI 2008/2883 art.9, Sch.3 para.46.

DEFINITIONS

    patient: s.145(1).

    hospital: ss.79(6), 145(1).

    application for admission for assessment: ss.2, 145(1).

    application for admission for treatment: ss.3, 145(1).

    guardianship application: s.7(1).

    nearest relative: ss.26(3), 145(1).

    community treatment order: ss.17A(7), 145(1).

    community patient: ss.17A(7), 145(1).

    community treatment period: ss.20A(2), 145(1).

    the appropriate tribunal: subs.(4).

GENERAL NOTE

This section identifies the occasions on which a patient or his nearest relative may make **1–871** an application to a tribunal. By virtue of ss.132(1)(b) and 132A, hospital managers have a duty to inform patients of their right to make an application. If either the patient or the nearest relative changes his mind subsequent to making an application, the application must proceed unless it is formally withdrawn with the consent of the tribunal under r.17 the Tribunal Rules. An application lapses if the patient is no longer subject to the provisions of the Act.

Although an application has to be made in writing, it can be signed by any person authorised by the patient to do so on his behalf: see r.32(1) of the Tribunal Rules. This could be a relative, a social worker, an advocate, or a nurse, provided that the patient has sufficient capacity to authorise that person to act for him. The threshold for capacity is not a demanding one (*R. (on the application of H) v Secretary of State for Health* [2005] UKHL 60; [2005] M.H.L.R. 302, para.26).

Donees of lasting powers of attorneys and deputies appointed by the Court of Protection are able to exercise a patient's rights to apply to the tribunal for discharge from detention, guardianship or a community treatment order (CTO) if they have the relevant authority under the LPA or the order of the court appointing them and the patient concerned lacks the capacity to do so themselves. Such an application would be made "in respect of" the patient for the purposes of s.77(1): also see para.7.7 of the *Code of Practice*.

In *R. v South Thames Mental Health Review Tribunal Ex p. M* [1998] C.O.D. 38, Collins J. held that the right of a patient to make an application to a tribunal is founded on the patient's admission, which is something that happens in a moment of time, and not on his detention. Applying this ruling to the situation of a patient who is admitted and detained under s.2 and who is subsequently detained under s.3 during the currency of the s.2, his Lordship held that the following passage from para.5.3 of the *Code of Practice* (1993 edition) is correct:

> "Changing a patient's status from section 2 to section 3 will not deprive him of a Mental Health Review Tribunal hearing if the change takes place after a valid application has been made to the Tribunal but before it has been heard. The patient's right to apply for a Tribunal under section 66(1)(b) in the first period of detention after his change of status are unaffected."

His Lordship said that in these circumstances the tribunal must consider the patient's case by using the s.3 criteria set out in s.72(1)(b).

Does an application to the tribunal by a s.3 patient lapse on the patient being made subject to CTO? This question was answered in *AA v Cheshire and Wirral Partnership NHS Foundation Trust* [2009] UKUT 195 (AAC); [2009] M.H.L.R. 308 where UT Judge Rowland held that a tribunal has the power—or, if the conditions of s.72(1)(c) are satisfied, a duty—to direct that a person subject to a CTO be discharged notwithstanding that that person made the application to the tribunal while liable to be detained under s.2 or 3. Therefore, an application to the tribunal made by or on behalf of a person detained under s.2 or 3 does not lapse if a CTO is made in respect of that person before the application is determined. The tribunal will consider the case using the CTO criteria. Judge Rowland said at para.61:

"[P]arties need to co-operate sensibly with each other and the First-tier Tribunal if a patient is made the subject of a CTO while an application to the tribunal is pending. In particular, it will clearly be incumbent on any representative of the applicant to inform the tribunal as soon as possible whether or not the application is being withdrawn and it is also clearly incumbent on all parties to inform the tribunal whether or not a postponement of any hearing that has already been fixed will be required in the light of the change of circumstances."

In *KF v Birmingham and Solihull Mental Health NHS Foundation Trust* [2010] UKUT 185 (AAC); [2010] M.H.L.R. 176, a three judge panel of the Upper Tribunal (UT) was satisfied that *AA* was correctly decided. The issue of principle that was considered in this case was: what should happen where an appeal from a tribunal's substantive decision on a s.2 application is overtaken by events. Having undertaken a comprehensive analysis, the tribunal concluded that:

" . . . any movement from s.2 to s.3 or to community patient status does not affect the continuing validity of an extant and undetermined application or reference to the First-tier Tribunal. The application or reference still falls to be determined by the tribunal in accordance with the patient's status at the time of the actual hearing and subject to the relevant criteria under section 72(1)(a)–(c)" (para.59).

The use of the tribunal's case management powers to deal with the practical consequences of this finding was considered at para.60:

"The effective use of the First-tier Tribunal's case management powers should enable outstanding proceedings to be consolidated, heard and determined together. . . . [T]he position may be more complicated where there is a change in the patient's status from s.3 to a CTO. Different clinicians and other mental health professionals may become involved in the patient's care and reports provided by the professionals who were involved in the patient's care whilst he or she was an in-patient may not address the criteria which the First-tier Tribunal will have to consider at the hearing in accordance with the patient's status at that time. This is an important factor which judges dealing with case management will need to keep firmly in mind when using case management powers, to ensure that cases are dealt with in a timely fashion and that, when appropriate and possible, hearing dates already fixed are retained for the hearing of the new application or reference. Appropriate and imaginative use of the case management powers should be encouraged to ensure that the relevant professionals are able to provide the required reports in time, notwithstanding the presence of a sometimes rapidly changing landscape in respect of the patient's status".

It is not always appropriate for the tribunal to refuse permission to appeal a s.2 application on the ground that the appeal was academic because the patient had in the meantime been detained under s.3. The UT said at para.30 (also see the note to r.17 of the Tribunal Rules):

"In general, unless there is good reason why not, if the First-tier Tribunal is asked to review a tribunal decision on a s.2 application, and concludes that it involves an error of law, then the appropriate way forward is for the First-tier Tribunal to set aside the substantive decision and to re-list the case for hearing together with any existing s.3 application."

The UT rejected a submission that the discharge of the patient should inevitably result in the tribunal declining to continue with the proceedings as there "may well be circumstances in which it remains appropriate for there to be further scrutiny of the initial tribunal decision, notwithstanding the individual's subsequent discharge. There may be a danger that a future decision-maker may give inappropriate weight to a flawed decision. Moreover, there may be an urgent need for the legal principles at stake to be clarified" (para.41).

To be consistent with the finding in *R. (on the application of SR) v Mental Health Review Tribunal* [2005] EWHC 2923 (Admin) that an application to a tribunal under s.3 did not survive if the patient was discharged and made subject to "after-care under supervision" under the repealed s.25A, it is submitted that an application to a tribunal by a guardianship patient lapses if, prior to the hearing, he is detained under s.3. Unlike the position in *AA*, above, where both CTO and the s.3 applications come within s.72(1), guardianship applications are governed by s.72(4). The same argument would apply if a detained patient who has made an application to the tribunal is transferred into guardianship prior to the hearing. In both situations, the patient should make a fresh application to the tribunal.

For patients who have been placed under hospital or guardianship orders by a court under s.37, subss.(1) and (2) of this section read as follows:

"(1) Where—

[(ca) a community treatment order is made in respect of a patient; or
(cb) a community treatment order is revoked under section 17F above in respect of a patient; or]
(e) a patient is transferred from guardianship to a hospital in pursuance of regulations made under section 19 above; or
(f) a report is furnished under section 20 above in respect of a patient and the patient is not discharged; or
(fza) a report is furnished under section 20A above in respect of a patient and the patient is not discharged under section 23 above; or
(fa) a report is furnished under subsection (2) of section 21B above in respect of a patient and subsection (5) of that section applies (or subsections (5) and (6)(b) of that section apply) in the case of the report; or
(faa) a report is furnished under subsection (2) of section 21B above in respect of a community patient and subsection (6A) of that section applies (or subsections (6A) and (6B)(b) of that section apply) in the case of the report;

an application may be made to the appropriate tribunal within the relevant period by the patient.

(2) In subsection (1) above 'the relevant period' means—

(ca) in the case mentioned in paragraph (ca) of that subsection, six months beginning with the day on which the community treatment order is made;

(cb) in the case mentioned in paragraph (cb) of that subsection, six months beginning with the day on which the community treatment order is revoked;

(d) in the case mentioned in paragraph (gb) of that subsection, 28 days beginning with the day on which the applicant is informed that the report has been furnished;
(e) in the case mentioned in paragraph (e) of that subsection, six months beginning with the day on which the patient is transferred;
(f) in the case mentioned in paragraph (f) [or (fa) of that subsection, the period or periods] for which authority for the patient's detention or guardianship is renewed by virtue of the report; or
(fza) in the cases mentioned in paragraphs (fza) and (faa) of that subsection, the period or periods for which the community treatment period is extended by virtue of the report" (Sch.1, Pt 1, paras 2,9).

The effect of subss.(1)(f), (2)(f), as amended by Sch.1, is to enable a hospital order patient to make his first application to a tribunal during the *second* six months of his detention. The rationale for this is explained in the note to s.69(1). Thereafter the patient's entitlement to make applications corresponds to the entitlements accruing on renewal of the authority to detain Pt II patients.

Applications by or on behalf of hospital and guardianship order patients can also be made under s.69. Applications by restricted patients are governed by s.70.

Subsection (1)

1–872 PARAGRAPH (A); APPLICATION FOR ADMISSION FOR ASSESSMENT. If the patient's status changes to a s.3 patient, see *R. v South Thames Mental Health Review Tribunal Ex p. M*, above. Patients admitted under s.4 are not excluded as an application under that section is "an application for admission for assessment" (s.4(1)) which is founded on one medical recommendation. An application which was made immediately after the patient's admission would automatically lapse if the second medical recommendation required by s.4(4) was not forthcoming.

PARAGRAPH (B); APPLICATION FOR ADMISSION FOR TREATMENT. If the patient does not make an application within six months of his admission, including any period of detention under s.2 (s.68(5)(b)), the hospital managers will automatically refer the case to the tribunal (s.68(1)(b), (2)). A patient who is subject to a hospital order can make his first application to a tribunal during the *second* six months of his detention: see above.

A conditionally discharged patient who has been made subject to an application under s.3 has a right to make an application under this paragraph (*R. v North West London Mental Health NHS Trust Ex p. Stewart* [1997] C.O.D. 42).

PARAGRAPH (E). A patient who does not exercise his right to apply to a tribunal within six months of the transfer (subs.(2)(e)) will have his case automatically referred to a tribunal by the hospital managers (s.68(1)(e), (2)).

PARAGRAPH (G). The tribunal has no jurisdiction to deal with the application if the responsible clinician's report under s.25 has been withdrawn before the application was sent to or received by the tribunal: see *DP v Hywel Dda Health Board* [2011] UKUT 381 (AAC); [2011] M.H.L.R. 394, a case where the report was withdrawn after the hospital had received legal advice that the relative who had ordered the patient's discharge under s.23 was not the patient's nearest relative. The Upper Tribunal left open the question whether it would have jurisdiction if the report had not been withdrawn.

In *MA v Secretary of State for Health* [2012] UKUT 474 (AAC), UT Judge Levenson held that the fact that the patient's nearest relative does not have a right to make an application under this provision in respect of a patient who has been detained for assessment and whose detention has been extended by virtue of the operation of s.29(4), does not violate art.6 of the European Convention on Human Rights.

PARAGRAPH (H). Applications under this paragraph can only be made by nearest relatives who have been displaced by the court on the grounds that they have unreasonably objected to an application being made or have used (or were likely to use) their powers of discharge without due regard to the welfare of the patient or the interests of the public.

AN APPLICATION. This refers to the process for beginning the proceedings before the tribunal: see *R. (on the application of SR) v Mental Health Review Tribunal*, above, para.20, where the court held that the statutory restriction contained in s.77(2) is not on more than one application being made to a tribunal in any specified period because more than one application can be made in any period, if it is of a different kind from that made in that period (para.26).

Nearest relative. Or, except in relation to para.(h), an acting nearest relative. Where **1–873**
an acting nearest relative has been appointed under s.29 that person exercises the right of
the nearest relative to make applications to a tribunal under this section and under s.69
(s.29(1)). However, the supplanted nearest relative can make one application to a tribunal
for the patient's discharge within the periods specified in subs.(2)(g) (s.29(6)).

If the patient is a ward of court the nearest relative cannot make an application to a tribunal without the leave of the High Court (s.33(2)).

The nearest relative could consider using his or her powers of discharge under s.23(2)(a)
as an alternative to making an application to a tribunal.

Subsection (2)

14 days. The application must be received by the tribunal within the 14-day period: **1–874**
see r.32(1)(c) of the Tribunal Rules. However, if the tribunal office is closed during the
whole of the 14th day, the application will be validly received if it arrives at that office
at any time during the first succeeding day on which the office is open (i.e. the next business
day). So if the final day for receiving the application would otherwise be Christmas Day,
the application can be validly received on December 27 (unless it is a weekend, in
which case it would be the following Monday) (*R. (on the application of Modaresi) v
Secretary of State for Health* [2011] EWCA Civ 1359; [2011] M.H.L.R. 311). At the
Supreme Court hearing of this case, which was concerned with the scope of the
Secretary of State's power under s.67(1), Lady Hale said that it would be helpful if the
Code of Practice advised that the hospital should ensure that tribunal applications which
have been given to hospital staff are transmitted to the tribunal without delay ([2013]
UKSC 53, para.32).

A patient who has been detained under s.2, who has had their period of detention
extended by virtue of s.29(4) will have his case referred to the tribunal six months after
admission if the application to the county court has not been determined (s.68(1)(a), (2)).

Beginning with. Means "including" (*Zoan v Rouamba* [2000] 2 All E.R. 620, CA).

References to tribunals by Secretary of State concerning Part II patients

67.—(1) The Secretary of State may, if he thinks fit, at any time refer to [the **1–875**
appropriate tribunal] the case of any patient who is liable to be detained or subject
to guardianship [. . .] under Part II of this Act [or of any community patient].

(2) For the purpose of furnishing information for the purposes of a reference
under subsection (1) above any registered medical practitioner [or approved clin-
ician] authorised by or on behalf of the patient may, at any reasonable time, visit
the patient and examine him in private and require the production of and inspect
any records relating to the detention or treatment of the patient in any hospital [or
to any after-care services provided for the patient under section 117 below].

(3) Section 32 above shall apply for the purposes of this section as it applies for
the purposes of Part II of this Act.

AMENDMENTS

The amendments to this section were made by SI 2008/2883 art.9, Sch.3 para.47, the
Mental Health (Patients in the Community) Act 1995 s.2(1), Sch.1 para.8 and the
Mental Health Act 2007 ss.13(2)(a), 32(4), 55, Sch.3 para.19, Sch.11 Pt 5.

DEFINITIONS

the appropriate tribunal: ss.66(4), 145(1). **1–876**
community patient: ss.17A(7), 145(1).
approved clinician: s.145(1).
hospital: ss.79(6), 145(1).

patient: s.145(1).

GENERAL NOTE

1–877   This section applies to patients who have been placed under hospital or guardianship orders by a court under s.37 (Sch.1, Pt 1, para.1). It enables the Secretary of State (or, in relation to Wales, the Welsh Ministers) to refer a patient who is liable to be detained, or subject to guardianship or to a community treatment order to a tribunal at any time. It also provides for either a registered medical practitioner or an approved clinician to visit and examine the patient, including a community patient, and to inspect relevant records relating to the patient, for the purposes of gathering information for the reference. A failure to allow such a person to undertake this function could amount to an offence under s.129.

The Secretary of State for Justice has a similar power to refer the case of a restricted patient to a tribunal under s.71(1).

Anyone may request a referral. Requests for referrals with respect to patients detained in England should be sent to:

> Department of Health
> Mental Health Legislation
> Area 313A, 3rd Floor, Richmond House
> 79 Whitehall
> London
> SW1A 2NS
> Tel: 0207 210 5775
> Fax: 0115 902 3211
> E-mail:mentalhealthact2007@dh.gsi.gov.uk

The address for patients detained in Wales is:

> Head of Mental Health, Vulnerable Groups & Offenders Branch
> Welsh Assembly Government
> Cathays Park
> Cardiff CF10 3NQ

The following guidance has been published by the Department of Health (April 22, 2013):

"Information required to support the request

Your letter will need to set out clearly why a Secretary of State's reference under s.67 is being sought. You will need to read the guidance and complete the tribunal **referral** form and **not** the application form on the Tribunals Service website *http://www.justice.gov.uk/ forms/hmcts/ts-mh* when requesting a s.67 reference and attach it to your letter. Please do not sign or date the **referred** form. In addition to the information to be given in the form, please indicate in your letter the length of time the patient has been on the section of the Act.

The issues that the Secretary of State for Health will take into account when considering making a reference under section 67

The issues that the Secretary of State for Health will take into account include but are not limited to:

the reason for the request;

the length of time since the case was last considered by a Tribunal (if ever);

the length of time it may be before an application may (or a reference must) be made under other sections of the Act; and

whether any decision being sought falls within the remit of a Tribunal.

These are not, however, the only factors. Each case will be considered on its merits. The Secretary of State will not refer cases where the patient has already been discharged from their section.

If the Secretary of State makes a reference under s.67, he will ask the Tribunal Secretariat to make the necessary arrangements, and the person who made the request will be informed."

The *Code of Practice* states:

"37.45 Hospital managers should consider asking the Secretary of State to make a reference in respect of any patients whose rights under article 5(4) of the ECHR might otherwise be at risk of being violated because they are unable (for whatever reason) to have their cases considered by the Tribunal speedily following their initial detention or at reasonable intervals afterwards.

37.46 In particular, they should normally seek such a reference in any case where:

- a patient's detention under section 2 has been extended under section 29 of the Act pending the outcome of an application to the county court for the displacement of their nearest relative

- the patient lacks the capacity to request a reference, or

- either the patient's case has never been considered by the Tribunal, or a significant period has passed since it was last considered."

In *R. (on the application of Modaresi) v Secretary of State for Health* [2013] UKSC 53; [2013] 4 All E.R. 318, the Supreme Court held that the Secretary of State's discretion to make a reference under this provision is underpinned by his duty to avoid a breach of art.5(4) of the European Convention on Human Rights. There is no breach of art.5(4) if a patient who, through no fault of her own, loses her opportunity to make an application to the tribunal under s.2 and is then detained under s.3 before the s.2 expires. In these circumstances, a request to the tribunal for an urgent hearing of the patient's s.3 application should be made. The disadvantage of the patient having to use up her s.3 application at an early stage was not such as to make it unlawful for the Secretary of State to decline to use his power under this section in the expectation that she would apply under s.3. Lord Carnwath, who gave the lead judgment of the court, said at para.22:

"The position might well have been different . . . if she had continued to be detained under s.2 [due to an application having being made to displace her nearest relative], and had not acquired a separate right under s.3. In circumstances where she had lost her right of immediate access to the tribunal wholly through the fault of the trust, itself an agent of the state for these purposes, it could well be said that the Secretary of State had a positive duty to remedy the position. It is however unnecessary to decide that point, which does not arise on the facts before us."

If the reference is made, there is no deadline within which the tribunal must hear the reference.

Subsection (1)
SECRETARY OF STATE.   In practice, the Secretary of State for Health. The functions of **1–878** the Minister, so far as exercisable in relation to Wales, are exercised by the Welsh Ministers (see the General Note to the Act).

[Duty of managers of hospitals to refer cases to tribunal

68.—(1) This section applies in respect of the following patients—   **1–879**

(a) a patient who is admitted to a hospital in pursuance of an application for admission for assessment;

(b) a patient who is admitted to a hospital in pursuance of an application for admission for treatment;

(c) a community patient;

(d) a patient whose community treatment order is revoked under section 17F above;

(e) a patient who is transferred from guardianship to a hospital in pursuance of regulations made under section 19 above.

(2) On expiry of the period of six months beginning with the applicable day, the managers of the hospital shall refer the patient's case to [the appropriate tribunal].

(3) But they shall not do so if during that period—

(a) any right has been exercised by or in respect of the patient by virtue of any of paragraphs (b), (ca), (cb), (e), (g) and (h) of section 66(1) above;

(b) a reference has been made in respect of the patient under section 67(1) above, not being a reference made while the patient is or was liable to be detained in pursuance of an application for admission for assessment; or

(c) a reference has been made in respect of the patient under subsection (7) below.

(4) A person who applies to a tribunal but subsequently withdraws his application shall be treated for these purposes as not having exercised his right to apply, and if he withdraws his application on a date after expiry of the period mentioned in subsection (2) above, the managers shall refer the patient's case as soon as possible after that date.

(5) In subsection (2) above, "the applicable day" means—

(a) in the case of a patient who is admitted to a hospital in pursuance of an application for admission for assessment, the day on which the patient was so admitted;

(b) in the case of a patient who is admitted to a hospital in pursuance of an application for admission for treatment—

(i) the day on which the patient was so admitted; or

(ii) if, when he was so admitted, he was already liable to be detained in pursuance of an application for admission for assessment, the day on which he was originally admitted in pursuance of the application for admission for assessment;

(c) in the case of a community patient or a patient whose community treatment order is revoked under section 17F above, the day mentioned in subparagraph (i) or (ii), as the case may be, of paragraph (b) above;

(d) in the case of a patient who is transferred from guardianship to a hospital, the day on which he was so transferred.

(6) The managers of the hospital shall also refer the patient's case to [the appropriate tribunal] if a period of more than three years (or, if the patient has not attained the age of 18 years, one year) has elapsed since his case was last considered by such a tribunal, whether on his own application or otherwise.

(7) If, in the case of a community patient, the community treatment order is revoked under section 17F above, the managers of the hospital shall also refer the patient's case to [the appropriate tribunal] as soon as possible after the order is revoked.

(8) For the purposes of furnishing information for the purposes of a reference under this section, a registered medical practitioner or approved clinician authorised by or on behalf of the patient may at any reasonable time—

(a) visit and examine the patient in private; and

(b) require the production of and inspect any records relating to the detention or treatment of the patient in any hospital or any after-care services provided for him under section 117 below.

(9) Reference in this section to the managers of the hospital—

(a) in relation to a community patient, is to the managers of the responsible hospital;

(b) in relation to any other patient, is to the managers of the hospital in which he is liable to be detained.]

AMENDMENTS

This section was inserted by the Mental Health Act 2007 s.37(3). The references to the appropriate tribunal in subss.(2), (6) and (7) were substituted by SI 2008/2883 art.9, Sch.3 para.48.

DEFINITIONS **1–880**

application for admission for assessment: ss.2, 145(1).
application for admission for treatment: ss.3, 145(1).
the appropriate tribunal: ss.66(4), 145(1).
approved clinician: s.145(1).
community patient: ss.17A(7), 145(1).
community treatment order: ss.17A(7), 145(1).
hospital: ss.34(2), 79(6), 145(1).
the managers: s.145(1) and see subs.(9) of this section.
responsible hospital: ss.17A(7), 145(1).
patient: s.145(1).

GENERAL NOTE

This section requires the hospital managers to refer a patient to a tribunal in specified **1–881** circumstances. The purpose of the referral system is to "ensure that patients who lack the ability or initiative to make an application to a Tribunal . . . have the safeguard of an independent review of their case" (Cmnd.8405, para.24). The key provisions for patients who are subject to Part II are:

1. A requirement to make a referral to the tribunal six months from the day on which the patient was first detained, whether under s.2 for assessment (including s.2 patients whose detention has been extended by virtue of the operation of s.29(4)) or s.3 for treatment (including patients who are subsequently placed on a community treatment order (CTO)), or the day on which he was detained in hospital following a transfer from guardianship (subs.(2)). The day in question is defined as "the applicable day" (subs.(5)). A s.3 patient must be referred even though he has had a tribunal hearing while detained under s.2. In such cases, the applicable is the day on which the patient was admitted under s.2 (subs.(5)(b)(ii)). The applicable day for a patient who was detained under either s.2 or 3 is not affected by the patient being subsequently place on a CTO (subs.(5)(c)). Under s.68A, the six-month period can be reduced by order of the Secretary of State, in relation to hospitals in England, or the Welsh Ministers, in relation to hospitals in Wales.

2. The hospital managers also have a duty to make a referral if the tribunal has not considered the patient's case at a hearing in three years (or one year if the patient is under

18) (subs.(6)). The order making power under s.68A can be used to reduce the three-year and one-year periods.

3. The duty to make a referral in respect of a CTO patient rests with the hospital managers of the responsible hospital (subs.(9)(a)).

4. The hospital managers of the detaining hospital must refer the case of a community patient to the tribunal as soon as possible after the CTO is revoked (subs.(7)).

5. Either a registered medical practitioner or an approved clinician may visit and examine the patient, including a community patient, and inspect relevant records relating to the patient for the purposes of gathering information for the reference (subs.(8)). A failure to allow such a person to undertake this function could amount to an offence under s.129.

In *PS v Camden and Islington NHS Foundation Trust* [2011] UKUT 143 (AAC); [2011] M.H.L.R. 159, UT Judge Jacobs said that the difficulties encountered by the tribunal when faced with a referred CTO patient who does not wish to co-operate or even participate in the tribunal proceedings might be tackled in the following manner:

"One power that the tribunal could use is the power to stay proceedings under rule 5(3)(j) of the Tribunal Procedure (First-tier Tribunal) (Health, Education and Social Care Chamber) Rules 2008. However, it might be considered an abuse of that power if it were effectively used as a means of permanent disposal or as a means of avoiding deciding the case at all.

More appropriate, perhaps, would be for the tribunal to arrange block hearings of community treatment references on the limited information that it is able to obtain. The tribunal is only under a duty to examine the patient 'as far as practicable' (rule 34(1)) and it is not practicable if a patient will not co-operate. In those circumstances, the tribunal can hear the case in the patient's absence under rule 39. The tribunal can use its powers under rules 5 and 15 to give directions on evidence from the responsible clinician and others that is appropriate in all the circumstances, taking account of the overriding objective and, in particular, of the need to act proportionately under rule 2(2)(a)" (paras 25, 26).

For the need for hospital managers to request the Secretary of State to make a reference to the tribunal under s.67(1) in a situation where a s.2 patient has had his detention extended under s.29(4), see the note on "Human Rights Act 1998" in s.29.

Any change in the patient's legal status, for example from a s.3 to a community patient, does not affect the continuing validity of an extant and undetermined reference to the First-tier Tribunal (*KF v Birmingham and Solihull Mental Health NHS Foundation Trust* [2010] UKUT 185 (AAC)).

The fact that a reference has been made under this section does not prevent the patient from making an application under s.66(1)(f) during the period of detention when the reference takes place. Although s.77(2) prohibits the making of more than one application during a specific period of detention, a reference is not an application.

Patients who are absent without leave at the point at which they should be referred to the tribunal must be referred on their return to hospital (s.21(3)).

The start date for calculating when a reference should be made for a restricted patient whose restrictions have ended (a "notional hospital order" patient) is the date when the restrictions ceased to have effect: see ss.41(5). Otherwise the period starts from the date when the order was made or, for patients transferred from hospitals from outside England or Wales, the date of the patient's admission to hospital in England or Wales (or the date when they were treated as being subject to a CTO).

For the application of this section to Part III patients who have been made subject to hospital orders without restrictions or to guardianship orders, see Sch.1 Pt 1, paras 2, 10 which provide that:

1. Only patients who are transferred from a guardianship order to a hospital order will be referred by the hospital managers after six months. Other patients will not have their cases referred at that time because, as their initial detention will have been considered by the sentencing court, they cannot apply to the tribunal themselves during that period.

2. The duty to make a referral at three years (or one year) applies to all unrestricted Part III patients, including hospital order patients who have been placed on a CTO.

Under s.71(2), the Secretary of State for Justice must refer the case of a restricted patient whose case has not been considered by the tribunal for three years.

A referral form (T111) which has been produced by HM Courts and Tribunals Service can be accessed at *http://hmctsformfinder.justice.gov.uk/HMCTS/GetForms.do?court_forms_num=&court_forms_title= &court_forms_category=Mental+Health+Tribunal.*

Human Rights Act 1998

In *MH v United Kingdom* (2014) 58 E.H.R.R. 965; [2014] M.H.L.R. 249, the European **1–882** Court of Human Rights held, at para.87, that the failure to provide the means for a mentally incapacitated patient to bring proceedings to challenge a detention under s.2 constituted a violation of art.5(4) of the European Convention on Human Rights. The Court said at para.82:

"As the right set forth in Article 5(4) of the Convention is guaranteed to everyone, it is clear that special safeguards are called for in the case of detained mental patients who lack legal capacity to institute proceedings before judicial bodies. However, it is not for this Court to dictate what form those special safeguards should take, provided that they make the right guaranteed by Article 5(4) as nearly as possible as practical and effective for this particular category of detainees as it is for other detainees. While automatic judicial review might be one means of providing the requisite safeguard, it is not necessarily the only means."

The Government's response to this judgment can be found in the following information that was provided to the Council of Europe on February 18, 2015:

"Since the events giving rise to this case took place, the 1983 Act has been substantially amended by the Mental Health Act 2007. This has addressed the violation identified in the judgment by introducing provisions on independent mental health advocates (IMHA). An IMHA is there to offer patients advice as to how the 1983 Act applies to them and give them an idea about what rights they have. They can represent patients including by accompanying them to any meetings and consultations, speak on their behalf and contact a lawyer for them. For example, there is now a duty under section 130D of the 1983 Act for a specified person to take such steps as are practicable to ensure that a patient understands the help that is available to them from an IMHA and how to obtain that help. There is now a duty upon local authorities to make arrangements to enable an IMHA to be available to help any patient liable to be detained under the 1983 Act.

To further protect persons lacking capacity, the Government made amendments to the relevant statutory guidance which applies in England: the "Code of Practice Mental Health Act 1983". The amendments make clear that if a patient lacks capacity to decide whether to seek help from an IMHA, an IMHA should be introduced to the patient so that the IMHA can explain what help they can offer. The revised Code was laid before Parliament on 15 January 2015 and will come into force on 1 April 2015.

In Wales, the Mental Health Act Code of Practice for Wales provides guidance on all aspects of the 1983 Act. It currently specifies that hospital managers should always consider a referral to the Tribunal for someone in the applicant's circumstances, lacking capacity, and where otherwise necessary."

The Government's response can be accessed at: *https://wcd.coe.int/ViewDoc.jsp?id=2293953&Site=CM*.

Subsection (2)

1–883   BEGINNING WITH.   Means "including" (*Zoan v Rouamba* [2000] 2 All E.R. 620, CA).

MANAGERS OF THE HOSPITAL.   See subs.(9).

Subsection (3)

The purpose of this provision is to prevent duplication of proceedings.

Subsection (6)

1–884   ATTAINED THE AGE.   At the commencement of his 18th birthday (Family Law Reform Act 1969 s.9(1)).

CONSIDERED.   At a hearing.

Subsection (7)

1–885   In *PS v Camden and Islington NHS Foundation Trust* [2011] UKUT 143 (AAC); [2011] M.H.L.R. 159, the UT held that a decision of the First-tier tribunal to treat a reference made under this provision as having lapsed on the ground that the patient had been made the subject of a fresh CTO following the revocation of the previous CTO was unlawful. UT Judge Jacobs criticised the hospital managers for not making the reference until 12 days after the revocation.

[Power to reduce periods under section 68

1–886   **68A.**—(1) The appropriate national authority may from time to time by order amend subsection (2) or (6) of section 68 above so as to substitute for a period mentioned there such shorter period as is specified in the order.

(2) The order may include such transitional, consequential, incidental or supplemental provision as the appropriate national authority thinks fit.

(3) The order may, in particular, make provision for a case where—

(a) a patient in respect of whom subsection (1) of section 68 above applies is, or is about to be, transferred from England to Wales or from Wales to England; and

(b) the period by reference to which subsection (2) or (6) of that section operates for the purposes of the patient's case is not the same in one territory as it is in the other.

(4) A patient is transferred from one territory to the other if—

(a) he is transferred from a hospital, or from guardianship, in one territory to a hospital in the other in pursuance of regulations made under section 19 above;

(b) he is removed under subsection (3) of that section from a hospital or accommodation in one territory to a hospital or accommodation in the other;

(c) he is a community patient responsibility for whom is assigned from a hospital in one territory to a hospital in the other in pursuance of regulations made under section 19A above; [or]

(d) on the revocation of a community treatment order in respect of him under section 17F above he is detained in a hospital in the territory other than the one in which the responsible hospital was situated; [. . .]

(e) [. . .]

(5) Provision made by virtue of subsection (3) above may require or authorise the managers of a hospital determined in accordance with the order to refer the patient's case to [the appropriate tribunal].

(6) In so far as making provision by virtue of subsection (3) above, the order—

(a) may make different provision for different cases;

(b) may make provision which applies subject to specified exceptions.

(7) Where the appropriate national authority for one territory makes an order under subsection (1) above, the appropriate national authority for the other territory may by order make such provision in consequence of the order as it thinks fit.

(8) An order made under subsection (7) above may, in particular, make provision for a case within subsection (3) above (and subsections (4) to (6) above shall apply accordingly).

(9) In this section, "the appropriate national authority" means—

(a) in relation to a hospital in England, the Secretary of State;

(b) in relation to a hospital in Wales, the Welsh Ministers.]

AMENDMENTS

This section was inserted by the Mental Health Act 2007 s.37(3). The amendments to it were made by SI 2008/2883 art.9, Sch.3 para.49 and the Health and Social Care Act 2012 s.42(2).

DEFINITIONS

1–887

patient: s.145(1).

hospital: ss.34(2), 79(6), 145(1).

community patient: ss.17A(7), 145(1).

community treatment order: ss.17A(7), 145(1).

responsible hospital: ss.17A(7), 145(1).

the managers: s.145(1).

the appropriate tribunal: ss.66(4), 145(1).

GENERAL NOTE

1–888

This section enables the Secretary of State and the Welsh Ministers to make an order reducing the referral periods specified in s.68. It also "enables the order to include any consequential provisions that may be required to ensure that patients who are transferred from England to Wales or vice versa between the period of referral in one territory and the other do not miss out on a referral to the tribunal by virtue of the transfer" (Explanatory Notes, para.154). There is no power to lengthen the periods. At the time of writing, no orders have been made under this provision.

Subsection (1)

1–889

APPROPRIATE NATIONAL AUTHORITY. See subs.(9).

BY ORDER. See s.143(1).

Applications to tribunals concerning patients subject to hospital and guardianship orders

1–890 **69.**—(1) Without prejudice to any provision of section 66(1) above as applied by section 40(4) above, an application to [the appropriate tribunal] may also be made—

[(a) in respect of a patient liable to be detained in pursuance of a hospital order or a community patient who was so liable immediately before he became a community patient, by the nearest relative of the patient in any period in which an application may be made by the patient under any such provision as so applied;] and

(b) in respect of a patient placed under guardianship by a guardianship order—

    (i) by the patient, within the period of six months beginning with the date of the order;

    (ii) by the nearest relative of the patient, within the period of 12 months beginning with the date of the order and in any subsequent period of 12 months.

(2) Where a person detained in a hospital—

(a) is treated as subject to a hospital order [, hospital direction] or transfer direction by virtue of section 41(5) above, [or section 80B(2), 82(2) or 85(2) below.] [. . .]; or

(b) is subject to a direction having the same effect as a hospital order by virtue of section [. . .] 47(3) or 48(3) above,

then, without prejudice to any provision of Part II of this Act as applied by section 40 above, that person may make an application to [the appropriate tribunal] in the period of six months beginning with the date of the order or direction mentioned in paragraph (a) above or, as the case may be, the date of the direction mentioned in paragraph (b) above.

[(3) The provisions of section 66 above as applied by section 40(4) above are subject to subsection (4) below.

(4) If the initial detention period has not elapsed when the relevant application period begins, the right of a hospital order patient to make an application by virtue of paragraph (ca) or (cb) of section 66(1) above shall be exercisable only during whatever remains of the relevant application period after the initial detention period has elapsed.

(5) In subsection (4) above—

(a) "hospital order patient" means a patient who is subject to a hospital order, excluding a patient of a kind mentioned in paragraph (a) or (b) of subsection (2) above;

(b) "the initial detention period", in relation to a hospital order patient, means the period of six months beginning with the date of the hospital order; and

(c) "the relevant application period" means the relevant period mentioned in paragraph (ca) or (cb), as the case may be, of section 66(2) above.]

AMENDMENTS

The amendments to this section were made by the Mental Health Act 2007 ss.32(4), 39(2), 55, Sch.3 para.20, Sch.5 Pt 2 para.18, Sch.11 Pt 5, the Domestic Violence, Crime and Victims Act 2004 s.58(2), Sch.11 and SI 2008/2883 art.9, Sch.3 para.50.

DEFINITIONS

the appropriate tribunal: ss.66(4), 145(1).   **1–891**
patient: s.145(1).
hospital: ss.34(2), 79(6), 145(1).
hospital order: ss.37, 55(4), 145(1).
hospital direction: ss.45A(3)(a), 145(1).
guardianship order: s.55(4).
transfer direction: ss.47, 145(1).
nearest relative: ss.26(3), 145(1).
community patient: ss.17A(7), 145(1).

GENERAL NOTE

This section specifies when a tribunal application can be made by the nearest relative, or **1–892**
an acting nearest relative appointed by the county court (s.29(6)), of a patient who has been
placed under a hospital order made by a court under s.37 or has been subsequently placed
on a community treatment order. The right of the nearest relative to make an application can
be exercised even through the patient has made an application during the same period. This
section also enables tribunal applications to be made in respect of guardianship order
patients and provides an opportunity for certain other patients who have been transferred
from prison to hospital after having committed offences to have their cases reviewed by
a tribunal within six months of their transfer. Applications by restricted patients are governed by s.70.

Subsection (1)
PERIOD IN WHICH AN APPLICATION MAY BE MADE BY THE PATIENT.   See subss.(3) to (5).   **1–893**

Subsection (2)
This subsection affects: **1–894**

"certain categories of patient whose cases have not recently been looked at by a court but
who are, simply by reason of the way [this Act is] put together, deemed to be detained as
though subject to a fresh hospital order. [. . .] As a result of [Schedule 1, Part 1, paragraphs 2, 9], such patients, who may already have been in hospital for a substantial
period, would have a six months' gap during which they were not entitled to apply to
a Tribunal and had not just had their cases looked at by a court … [This subsection
removes] that gap. In addition, [it] seeks to meet the concern which has been expressed
… about the position of patients immediately after they have been transferred from
prison. Again, the grounds for their detention in hospital will not previously have
been considered by a court. The Government now accept that such people should
have an immediate right to a Tribunal hearing"; per Lord Belstead, *Hansard* HL,
Vol.427, col.868.

Applications to tribunals concerning restricted patients

70. A patient who is a restricted patient within the meaning of section 79 below **1–895**
and is detained in a hospital may apply to [the appropriate tribunal]—

(a) in the period between the expiration of six months and the expiration of 12
    months beginning with the date of the relevant hospital order [, hospital
    direction] or transfer direction; and
(b) in any subsequent period of 12 months.

AMENDMENTS

The amendments to this section were made by SI 2008/2883 art.9, Sch.3 and by the
Crime (Sentences) Act 1997 s.55, Sch.4 para.12(9).

DEFINITIONS

1–896   patient: s.145(1).
restricted patient: s.79(1).
hospital: ss.79(6), 145(1).
the appropriate tribunal: ss.66(4), 145(1).
the relevant hospital direction: s.79(2)–(5).
the relevant hospital order: s.79(2)–(5).
the relevant transfer direction: s.79(2)–(5).

GENERAL NOTE

1–897   This section provides for a tribunal application to be made by a restricted patient during the second six months of the duration of the hospital order or transfer direction, and at yearly intervals thereafter. Section 69(2)(b) provides patients who are made the subject of a restricted transfer direction with an additional right to make an application to the tribunal during the first six months starting with the date of the direction. The nearest relative of a restricted patient does not have a right to make an application to a tribunal.

A tribunal considering an application made by a restricted patient under this section has no power to adjourn the proceedings so as to monitor the patient's progress in the hope that a projected course of treatment would eventually permit it to discharge the patient (*R. v Nottingham Mental Health Review Tribunal Ex p. Secretary of State for the Home Department*, *The Times*, March 25, 1987).

An application made under this section ceases to have effect if the patient ceases to be a restricted patient. However, it is the practice of the tribunal to treat such an application as converted into one made under s.69(2)(a) so as to avoid the patient being placed under a disadvantage to which he would have otherwise have been placed of having to wait six months before he could make an application (*R. (on the application of MN) v Mental Health Review Tribunal*) [2008] EWHC 3383 (Admin); [2009] M.H.L.R. 98). A restricted patient whose restriction order has ceased to have effect is treated as if he had been admitted to hospital as an unrestricted patient on the date when the restriction order ceased to have effect: see s.41(5).

BEGINNING WITH.   Including the date of the hospital order or transfer direction (*Zoan v Rouamba* [2001] 2 All E.R. 620 CA).

References by Secretary of State concerning restricted patients

1–898   **71.**—(1) The Secretary of State may at any time refer the case of a restricted patient to [the appropriate tribunal].

(2) The Secretary of State shall refer to [the appropriate tribunal] the case of any restricted patient detained in a hospital whose case has not been considered by such a tribunal, whether on his own application or otherwise, within the last three years.

(3) The Secretary of State may by order vary the length of the period mentioned in subsection (2) above.

[(3A) An order under subsection (3) above may include such transitional, consequential, incidental or supplemental provision as the Secretary of State thinks fit.]

(4) Any reference under subsection (1) above in respect of a patient who has been conditionally discharged and not recalled to hospital shall be made to the tribunal for the area in which the patient resides.

(5), (6) [*Repealed by the Domestic Violence, Crime and Victims Act 2004 s.58(2), Sch.11*].

AMENDMENTS

The amendments to this section were made by the Mental Health Act 2007 s.37(4) and SI 2008/2883 art.9, Sch.3 para.52.

DEFINITIONS

restricted patient: s.79(1).

1–899

the appropriate tribunal: ss.66(4), 145(1).

hospital: ss.34(2), 79(6), 145(1).

patient: s.145(1).

GENERAL NOTE

This section provides that the Secretary of State may, and in certain circumstances must **1–900** refer the case of a restricted patient, including a conditionally discharged patient, to a tribunal.

For the duty of the Secretary of State to refer to the tribunal a conditionally discharged patient who has been recalled to hospital, see s.75(1).

Subsection (1)

The nature of the Secretary of State's discretion under this provision was examined in *R.* **1–901** *(on the application of C) v The Secretary of State for the Home Department* [2001] EWHC Admin 501; [2001] M.H.L.R. 100, where Collins J. held that:

(i) the discretion of the Secretary of State to refer a case in a situation where the tribunal has reached a decision is not untrammelled, in that the Secretary of State must pay proper respect to the decision of the tribunal. He should not use his power merely because he disagreed with the decision reached by the tribunal; and

(ii) a reference can be made: (a) where the decision of the tribunal has been ruled unlawful or stayed by the court on judicial review; (b) where the tribunal has imposed a condition that has proved impossible to put into effect; and (c) where there has been a material change of circumstances. With regard to (c), to be consistent with the patient's rights under art.5 of the European Convention on Human Rights, a reference should only be made if the Secretary of State has formed the view that it is probable that the material in question would have affected the decision of the tribunal in that it would have decided either that a more onerous condition be imposed or that a conditional discharge would not have been ordered.

This case went to appeal and point (ii)(c) of Collins J.'s judgment must be read subject to the following finding of the Court of Appeal. If a change in the patient's circumstances is brought to the Secretary of State's attention after a tribunal has made a deferred conditional discharge but before discharge has been directed, he should utilise the procedure set out in *R. (on the application of IH) v The Secretary of State for the Home Department* [2002] EWCA Civ 646, by inviting the tribunal to reconsider its decision. He should not make a referral to a fresh tribunal under this provision (*R. (on the application of C) v Secretary of State for the Home Department* [2002] EWCA Civ 647; [2002] M.H.L.R. 105). The decision of the Court of Appeal in *IH* in so far as it relates to the ability of the tribunal to reconsider its decision was affirmed by the House of Lords in *R. v Secretary of State for the Home Department Ex p. IH* [2003] UKHL 59; [2004] 1 All E.R. 412, which is noted under s.73(7).

SECRETARY OF STATE. Functions under this provision have not been transferred to Welsh Ministers (see the General Note to the Act and SI 1999/672 art.2, Sch.1).

Subsection (2)

1–902   This provision applies to a restricted patient who has received a deferred conditional discharge but three years have elapsed without the conditions being met or the tribunal reconvening to consider the case.

Subsection (3)

1–903   At the time of writing, no order has been made under this provision.

Discharge of patients

Powers of tribunals

1–904   **72.**—[(1) Where application is made to [the appropriate tribunal] by or in respect of a patient who is liable to be detained under this Act [or is a community patient], the tribunal may in any case direct that the patient be discharged, and—

(a)   the tribunal shall direct the discharge of a patient liable to be detained under section 2 above if [it is] not satisfied—
  (i)   that he is then suffering from mental disorder or from mental disorder of a nature or degree which warrants his detention in a hospital for assessment (or for assessment followed by medical treatment) for at least a limited period; or
  (ii)   that his detention as aforesaid is justified in the interests of his own health or safety or with a view to the protection of other persons;

(b)   the tribunal shall direct the discharge of a patient liable to be detained otherwise than under section 2 above if [it is] not satisfied—
  (i)   that he is then suffering from [mental disorder or from mental disorder] of a nature or degree which makes it appropriate for him to be liable to be detained in a hospital for medical treatment; or
  (ii)   that it is necessary for the health or safety of the patient or for the protection of other persons that he should receive such treatment; or
  [(iia)   that appropriate medical treatment is available for him; or]
  (iii)   in the case of an application by virtue of paragraph (g) of section 66(1) above, that the patient, if released, would be likely to act in a manner dangerous to other persons or to himself.]

[(c)   the tribunal shall direct the discharge of a community patient if [it is] not satisfied—
  (i)   that he is then suffering from mental disorder or mental disorder of a nature or degree which makes it appropriate for him to receive medical treatment; or
  (ii)   that it is necessary for his health or safety or for the protection of other persons that he should receive such treatment; or
  (iii)   that it is necessary that the responsible clinician should be able to exercise the power under section 17E(1) above to recall the patient to hospital; or
  (iv)   that appropriate medical treatment is available for him; or
  (v)   in the case of an application by virtue of paragraph (g) of section 66(1) above, that the patient, if discharged, would be likely to act in a manner dangerous to other persons or to himself.]

[(1A) In determining whether the criterion in subsection (1)(c)(iii) above is met, the tribunal shall, in particular, consider, having regard to the patient's history of mental disorder and any other relevant factors, what risk there would be of a deterioration of the patient's condition if he were to continue not to be detained in a hospital (as a result, for example, of his refusing or neglecting to receive the medical treatment he requires for his mental disorder).]

(2) [. . .]

(3) A tribunal may under subsection (1) above direct the discharge of a patient on a future date specified in the direction; and where a tribunal [does not] direct the discharge of a patient under that subsection the tribunal may—

(a) with a view to facilitating his discharge on a future date, recommend that he be granted leave of absence or transferred to another hospital or into guardianship; and

(b) further consider his case in the event of any such recommendation not being complied with.

[(3A) Subsection (1) above does not require a tribunal to direct the discharge of a patient just because [it thinks] it might be appropriate for the patient to be discharged (subject to the possibility of recall) under a community treatment order; and a tribunal—

(a) may recommend that the responsible clinician consider whether to make a community treatment order; and

(b) may (but need not) further consider the patient's case if the responsible clinician does not make an order.]

(4) Where application is made to [the appropriate tribunal] by or in respect of a patient who is subject to guardianship under this Act, the tribunal may in any case direct that the patient be discharged, and shall so direct if [it is] satisfied—

(a) that he is not then suffering from [mental disorder]; or

(b) that it is not necessary in the interests of the welfare of the patient, or for the protection of other persons, that the patient should remain under such guardianship.

[(4A) [. . .]

(5) [. . .]

(6) Subsections (1) to [(4)] above apply in relation to references to [the appropriate tribunal] as they apply in relation to applications made to [the appropriate tribunal] by or in respect of a patient.

(7) Subsection (1) above shall not apply in the case of a restricted patient except as provided in sections 73 and 74 below.

AMENDMENTS

The amendments to this section were made by the Mental Health Act 1983 (Remedial Order) Order 2001 (SI 2001/3712) art.3, the Mental Health Act 2007 ss.1(4), 2(8), 32(4), 55, Sch.1 para.14, Sch.3 para.21, Sch.11 Pts 1, 2 and 5 and SI 2008/2883 art.9, Sch.3 para.53.

DEFINITIONS

the appropriate tribunal: ss.66(4), 145(1). **1–912**
patient: s.145(1).
appropriate medical treatment: ss.3(4), 145(1).
community patient: ss.17A(7), 145(1).
mental disorder: ss.1, 145(1).
hospital: ss.34(2), 79(6), 145(1).
medical treatment: s.145(1), (4).
responsible clinician: ss.34(1), 79(6).
community treatment order: ss.17A(7), 145(1).

restricted patient: s.79(1).

GENERAL NOTE

1–913   This section empowers tribunals to discharge patients from hospital, guardianship or community treatment orders (CTOs) and directs tribunals to discharge such patients if specified criteria are satisfied. For detained and community patients, the discharge can take place at a specified future date (subs.(3)).

The tribunal's powers under this section are confined to granting or refusing relief in respect of persons who are liable to be detained or liable to be recalled; it has no power to consider either the validity of the admission which gave rise to the liability to be detained (*R. v East London and The City Mental Health trust Ex p. Brandenburg* [2003] UKHL 58; [2004] 1 All E.R. 400 para.9(3) or issues relating to a patient's consent to medical treatment: see *SH v Cornwall Partnership NHS Trust* [2012] UKUT 290 (AAC); [2012] M.H.L.R. 383 where UT Judge Jacobs said at para.15:

> "Judicial oversight *by the First-tier Tribunal* is limited to the issue whether the person should be subject to the Act. The treatment of patients under the Act is subject to judicial oversight *by the courts*, but not by the First-tier Tribunal."

When determining whether a compliant mentally incapacitated patient's detention is either warranted for the purposes of subs.(1)(a)(i) or is necessary for the purposes of sub-s.(1)(b)(ii), the tribunal must consider whether the patient should be detained under this Act, or whether the assessment or treatment in the proposed circumstances should be founded on the Mental Capacity Act (MCA) and any deprivation of liberty it involves should be authorised under the deprivation of liberty safeguards (DOLS). To do that, the tribunal has to consider whether the MCA and its DOLS alternative are applicable and available and, if so, whether and when they should be used. In making its decision, the tribunal has to consider which alternative best achieves the objective of ensuring the patient's assessment or treatment in the least restrictive way. As the tribunal has no power to compel a DOL authorisation, a decision to discharge the patient should usually be deferred to enable the relevant DOLS authorisation to be sought: see *AM v South London & Maudsley NHS Foundation Trust* [2013] UKUT 365 (AAC); [2014] M.H.L.R. 181, per Charles J. at paras 34, 74 and 75. *AM* is considered in Part 6 under the heading "The 1983 Act or the 2005 Act?" and the note on "The detention of compliant mentally incapable patients" in the General Note to Part II. It is suggested that adjourning the hearing, rather that deferring the decision, would be the appropriate option as the deferred discharge would have to take effect even if a DOL authorisation had not been obtained: also see *Perkins v Bath District Health Authority*, which is noted under subs.(3). There is no reason why the DOL safeguards cannot be applied in anticipation of the patient being discharged from detention: see Sch.A1, para.63 of the Mental Capacity Act 2005 and *DN v Northumberland Tyne and Wear NHS Foundation Trust* which is noted under subs.(1)(b).

The legality of a decision to make an application to detain a patient immediately after a decision of a tribunal to discharge him is considered in the General Note to s.3 under the heading "The re-sectioning of a patient subsequent to a discharge by the First-tier Tribunal (Mental Health) or the Mental Health Review Tribunal for Wales".

Human Rights Act 1998

1–914   In *R. (on the application of H) v Mental Health Review Tribunal* [2002] EWHC Admin 1522; [2002] M.H.L.R. 362, a declaration of incompatibility was sought on the basis that this section does not authorise a tribunal to consider and to determine questions such as whether a hospital is a particularly suitable hospital in terms of the degree of security or in terms of geographical proximity to the family of a patient. With regard to the latter point, it was claimed that as this section does not empower a tribunal to consider or to determine the rights of a patient or the members of his family under art.8 it is incompatible with the European Convention on Human Rights (ECHR). The application was rejected on the authority of *Re S (Care Plan)* [2002] UKHL 10; [2002] 2 All E.R. 192, where the House of Lords held that a lacuna in an Act, or a failure to provide an effective remedy for a violation of a Convention right, does not lead to the conclusion that the Act is incompatible with that Convention right or the provisions of the Convention in question.

The question whether the continued detention of an asymptomatic patient contravenes art.5 of the ECHR was considered by the Court of Appeal in *R. (on the application of H) v Mental Health Review Tribunal, North and North East London Region* which is noted under "nature or degree" in subs.(1)(b)(i), below.

Article 5 protects against arbitrary detention; it does not incorporate any additional requirement of proportionality. There is therefore no need for the court to consider whether this section, which sets out a test to prevent arbitrary detention, is itself a proportional response to art.5(1)(e) (*R. (on the application of CS) v Mental Health Review Tribunal* [2004] EWHC 2958 (Admin); [2004] M.H.L.R. 355). The detention itself can only be justified "where other, less severe, measures have been considered and found to be insufficient to safeguard the individual or public interest which might require that the person concerned be detained" (*X v Finland* [2012] M.H.L.R. 318, para.151).

The question whether a decision not to discharge a patient who had been granted a conditional discharge by a tribunal due to a failure to put in place appropriate after-care facilities in the community constitutes a violation of art.5 is considered in the notes on s.117 under this heading.

Subsection (1)

This provision requires a tribunal to discharge an unrestricted detained patient if it is not **1–915** satisfied as to any one of the criteria set out in (a)(i)(ii) or (b)(i)(ii)(iii). A community patient must be discharged if the tribunal is not satisfied as to any one of the criteria set out in (c)(i), (ii), (iii), (iv) or (v). When determining whether criterion (c)(iii) is met, the tribunal must consider the matters set out in subs.(1A). A tribunal is not required to discharge a patient because it considers that it might be appropriate for the patient to be made subject to a community treatment order (CTO) (subs.3A).

This provision also provides the tribunal with discretion to discharge the patient even though it considers that the relevant criteria are satisfied: see the note on "May in any case direct that the patient be discharged".

In *MH v Mental Health Review Tribunal for Northern Ireland* [2014] NIQB 87, Horner J., sitting in the High Court of Justice in Northern Ireland, said that the tribunal should have expressly dealt with a claim by the patient that if he was discharged, he would remain in the hospital as a voluntary patient.

In *DL-H v Devon Partnership NHS Trust* [2010] UKUT 102 (AAC); [2010] M.H.L.R. 162, UT Judge Jacobs rejected a submission that the tribunal had to apply a test of proportionality to the patient's detention:

"The tribunal must discharge the patient unless detention for treatment is necessary for the patient's health or safety or for the protection of others. The legislation authorises detention by reference to the twin requirements of treatment and protection, moderated by the word 'necessary'. That is a demanding test and provides ample protection for the patient without the need for any additional consideration of proportionality." (para.27)

This issue was also addressed in the *CS* case which is noted under "Human Rights Act 1998", above.

As essentially the same criteria have to be applied in relation to admission and discharge (*Reid v Secretary of State for Scotland* [1999] 1 All E.R. 481, per Lord Clyde at 503 and *R. v East London and City Mental Health NHS Trust Ex p. Brandenburg* [2001] EWCA Civ 239; [2001] M.H.L.R. 36, per Lord Phillips at para.18), reference should be made to the notes on the admission criteria under ss.2(2) and 3(2). As the patient may be on leave of absence under s.17 at the time of the tribunal hearing, reference should also be made to the notes on s.20(4) and to the notes on "appropriate for him to be liable to be detained in a hospital for medical treatment" in para.(b)(i), below. It is not fatal to a decision of a tribunal if it does not expressly consider whether the patient meets the admission criteria, so long as it considers the discharge criteria and provided that in the process it has effectively considered all the criteria that would be relevant to admission: see (*R. (on the application of H) v Mental Health Review Tribunal, North and East London Region* [2000] M.H.L.R. 242) where Crane J. said at para.52:

"Moreover, if the question is asked, namely would the admission criteria be fulfilled if this patient presented today, that question undoubtedly requires amplification in the case of a patient detained in hospital. If a doctor is considering admission criteria, he must ask himself whether there is a risk of failure to take medication in the future and of a consequent deterioration. So, similarly, if the patient is already in hospital, a similar question must be asked. If he is no longer in hospital, to what extent is there a risk of a failure to take medication and of consequent deterioration? It would plainly be too simplistic a question simply to ask, if he were as he is today, would he qualify for admission?"

A similar approach was adopted by Latham J. in *R. v London South West Region Mental Health Review Tribunal Ex p. Moyle* [1999] M.H.L.R. 195, para.34, where his Lordship said that although the discharge criteria mirror the admission criteria:

"the patient applying for discharge is *ex hypothesi* in a different situation from the person who is in the community. As a patient, he or she is receiving care and medication in the controlled environment of the hospital and not ... free to exercise his or her own wishes. In a case like the present, the assessment of risk must involve a judgment as to the extent to which release into the community will give rise to the likelihood that he or she will not comply with medication, with the consequences described by the psychiatrist".

It is therefore submitted that the patient's RC should not be asked: "Would the patient's current mental state justify making an application?". Rather, she should be asked to identify the consequences for the patient and/or the public if the tribunal decided to discharge the patient.

The question of what after-care services will be available in the community is relevant to the issue of whether the criteria in this provision are met: see *R. (on the application of Ashworth Hospital Authority) v Mental Health Review Tribunal for the West Midlands and North West Regions*, noted under para.(b). However, it is not essential for the tribunal to have specific information about aftercare in every case: see *AM v West London MH NHS Trust & Secretary of State for Justice* [2012] UKUT 382 where UT Judge Jacobs said at para.29:

"On the tribunal's findings, Mr M had not yet progressed to the point where the issue of aftercare that was actually available would arise. Without some acceptance or insight, Mr M could not progress to the point where his management in the community could even be tested by unescorted leave, let alone where he could be conditionally discharged."

On refusing permission to appeal in this case, Richards L.J. said:

"[It] seems to me . . . that it must, as a matter of principle, be open to a Tribunal to conclude in the circumstances of a particular case that information or better information of aftercare is incapable of affecting the decision, and that an adjournment to secure its provision could achieve nothing beyond additional expense and delay and would therefore be inappropriate" ([2013] EWCA Civ 1010, para.9).

Also see the obiter comments of UT Judge Wright in *AF v Nottinghamshire NHS Trust* [2015] UKUT 216 (AAC) which are reproduced in the General Note to s.117 under the heading *Applications to the First-tier Tribunal (Mental Health) and to the Hospital Managers.*

This subsection only applies to restricted patients to the extent provided for in ss.73 and 74 (subs.(7)).

APPLICATION. Or a reference made by the Secretary of State (subs.(6)).

IN RESPECT OF A PATIENT WHO IS LIABLE TO BE DETAINED UNDER THIS ACT OR IS A COMMUNITY PATIENT. In *KF v Birmingham and Solihull Mental Health NHS Foundation Trust* [2010] UKUT 185 (AAC); [2010] M.H.L.R. 176, para.57, the Upper Tribunal said:

(i) in the context of references, these words refer to the patient's status both at the date the reference is made and at the subsequent hearing of that reference;

(ii) a patient may therefore fall within this provision by being liable to be detained under the Act when the reference is made and by being a community patient at the time of the hearing; and

(iii) sub-paragraphs (a) to (c) of subs.(1) refer *only* to the patient's status as at the time of the hearing (not the date of the reference), and set out the legal tests to be applied depending on the patient's particular status at that time (see *AA v Cheshire and Wirral Partnership NHS Trust* [2009] UKUT 195 (AAC) at para.45).

MAY IN ANY CASE DIRECT THAT THE PATIENT BE DISCHARGED. The tribunal has power to discharge the patient even though the legal grounds for compulsory detention or a CTO still subsist. The discharge could take place some time after the tribunal's decision (subs.(3)). This discretion should only be exercised in "exceptional circumstances" where the tribunal is "satisfied that the identified needs [of the patient] for treatment and protection can be properly catered for". It "will almost certainly only be appropriate where discharge would be consistent with the existence of the statutory criteria in [this subsection]" (*GA v Betsi Cadwaladr University LHB* [2013] 0280 (AAC); [2014] M.H.L.R. 27, per Judge Jacobs at paras 22 and 24). *GA* was a patient on a CTO. Judge Jacobs said at para.23:

"A tribunal exercising its discretionary power must act consistently with the logic of its reasoning. Having decided that the patient does require treatment and should be subject to recall, it will have two options. One is to refuse to discharge the patient, who then remains subject to the 1983 Act and the powers of recall, leave and treatment under that Act. The other option is to discharge the patient under the discretionary power. That allows the authorities: (i) to detain the patient again under the 1983 Act; or (ii) if the patient lacks capacity to consent to treatment, to make arrangements for treatment under the Mental Capacity Act 2005. I can see no point in (i), which is a more cumbersome way to achieve the same effect as recall. As to (ii), the tribunal could only properly exercise its discretion to leave a patient to be dealt with under the 2005 Act if satisfied that the patient did lack capacity and would be treated under the powers of that Act. If the tribunal were to direct discharge without those factors being satisfied, it would act inconsistently with the logic of its reasoning that the patient required treatment. It would potentially leave the patient and the public without the protection that it had decided was required."

In a case known to the author, the tribunal exercised its discretionary power to discharge a detained patient to enable him to join his parents in the USA and to receive treatment for his mental disorder there. Also see *Northamptonshire Healthcare NHS Foundation Trust v ML* [2014] EWCOP 2 where a discretionary discharge was ordered by the tribunal in a situation where the patient's reaction to an intensive behavioural intervention programme had resulted in him being placed in seclusion on multiple occasions.

Where the discharge of a patient who has been detained under s.2 has been barred by the RC issuing a report under s.25, a tribunal is not obliged to consider the dangerousness criterion in that section when exercising its discretion to discharge even if the patient's detention under s.2 has been extended by the operation of s.29(4). Whether it does so will depend on its assessment of the facts of an individual case (*R. (on the application of MH) v Secretary of State for Health* [2004] EWHC 56 (Admin); [2004] M.H.L.R. 155).

Paragraph (a)

1–916   The tribunal must discharge the patient if it is not satisfied as to either of the criteria set out in paras (i) and (ii).

DISCHARGE.   This term has to be read in a way which is compatible with art.5(1) of the European Convention on Human Rights. Consequently a person is discharged from detention if he is no longer deprived of his liberty (*R.(on the application of Secretary of State for the Home Department) v Mental Health Review Tribunal* [2002] EWHC Admin 1128; [2002] M.H.L.R. 241). In *Secretary of State for Justice v KC* [2015] UKUT 376 (AAC), Charles J. said that this and earlier cases need "to be considered having regard to [the decision of the Supreme Court in *P v Cheshire West and Chester Council* [2014] UKSC 19] and in particular its conclusion that a wide range of circumstances and settings can give rise to the result that on an objective assessment a person is deprived of his liberty" (para.87).

SATISFIED.   The burden of proof is placed on the detaining authority to satisfy the tribunal as to the matters set out in this provision. In *R. (on the application of N) v Mental Health Review Tribunal (Northern Region)* [2005] EWCA Civ 1605; [2006] 4 All E.R. 194, the Court of Appeal held that:

1. The correct standard of proof to be applied by the tribunal under this section and s.73 is the civil standard of proof on the balance of probabilities (or preponderance of probability). Richards L.J. said at para.62:

    "Although there is a single *standard* of proof, it is flexible in its *application*. In particular, the more serious the allegation or the more serious the consequences if the allegation is proved, the stronger must be the evidence before a court will find the allegation proved on the balance of probabilities. Thus the flexibility of the standard lies not in any adjustment to the degree of probability required for an allegation to be proved (such that a more serious allegation has to be proved to a higher degree of probability), but in the strength or quality of the evidence that will in practice be required for an allegation to be proved on the balance of probabilities."

2. In relation to this section and s.73, no more than cogent evidence that was accepted as correct will be required in order to satisfy the tribunal, on the balance of probabilities, that the conditions for continuing detention are met. Demanding an especially high evidential requirement would subvert the obvious purpose of the Act which sought both to protect the interests of the individual whose ability to act in his own best interests was impaired and at the same time enable a proportionate balance to be struck between individual and public interests.

3. The findings in 1 and 2 are in full conformity with the requirements of the ECHR.

4. The standard of proof has a potential part to play in the decision-making process even in relation to issues that are the subject of judgment and evaluation. Richards L.J said at para.103:

"We . . . think it likely that the tribunal's task will be made easier if, instead of dividing up the issues into matters that are susceptible to proof to a defined standard and those that are not, it approaches the entire range of issues by reference to the standard of proof on the balance of probabilities, whilst recognising that in practice the standard of proof will have a much more important part to play in the determination of disputed issues of fact that it will generally have in matters of judgment as to appropriateness and necessity."

The finding made by Richards L.J. at point 1 was endorsed by the House of Lords in *Re D* [2008] UKHL 33 para.27, where Lord Carswell said that it "effectively states in concise terms the proper state of the law on this topic". Lord Carswell stated that he would add one small qualification to the statement made by Richard's L.J. concerning the seriousness of the anticipated consequences. His view was that this should be considered as no more than a facet of the seriousness of the allegation. The following example was given, at para.28, to illustrate the point:

"[I]f it is alleged that a bank manager has committed a minor peculation, that could entail very serious consequences for his career, so making it less likely that he would risk doing such a thing."

THEN SUFFERING. The term "then" refers to the time of the tribunal's review and the tribunal has no power to consider the validity of the admission which gave rise to the liability to detain. The tribunal will doubtless endeavour to assess a patient's condition in the round, and in considering issues of health, safety and public protection under this provision and under sub-para.(b)(ii) it cannot ignore the foreseeable future consequences of discharge, but the temporal reference of "then" is clear and the tribunal is not called upon to make an assessment which will remain accurate indefinitely or for any given period of time (*R. v East London and The City Mental Health Trust Ex p. Brandenburg* [2003] UKHL 58 para.9(3)).

MENTAL DISORDER. There is no requirement for a diagnosis of the nature of the patient's mental disorder to have been made (*JP v South London and Maudsley NHS Foundation Trust* [2012] UKUT 486 (AAC), para.13). In this case, UT Judge Lane said that the "Tribunal would be entitled to accept a report prepared by a doctor from medical notes, though it would have to be examined with care to justify the Tribunal's conclusions" (para.16).

NATURE OR DEGREE. See the note on para.(b)(i), below.

WARRANTS. See *AM v South London & Maudsley NHS Foundation Trust* [2013] UKUT 365 (AAC); [2014] M.H.L.R. 181 which is noted in the General Note to this section.

DETENTION. Or the patient's liability to be detained during a period of leave of absence granted under s.17 (*R. v Barking Havering and Brentford Community Healthcare NHS Trust* [1999] 1 F.L.R. 106).

PROTECTION OF OTHER PERSONS. See the note on para.(b)(ii), below.

Paragraph (b)
The tribunal must discharge the patient if they are not satisfied as to any one of the cri- **1–917**
teria set out in paras (i), (ii) and (iii). Where a tribunal is considering the matters specified in paras (i) or (ii) they must bear in mind the distinction between the two matters and "one must somehow be able to read from the reasons the issue to which the reasons are directed" (*R. v Mental Health Review Tribunal Ex p. Pickering* [1986] 1 All E.R. 99 at 104, per

Forbes J.). In *MD v Mersey Care NHS Trust* [2013] UKUT 0127 (AAC); [2013] M.H.L.R. 164, UT Judge Jacobs said at para.8:

"The criteria in section 72(1)(b) may be separate, but they are also related in the sense that evidence may be relevant to more than one. Similarly, the conclusion in respect of one criterion may be relevant to another. As Latham J. recognised in *R v London South and South West Region Mental Health Review Tribunal, ex parte Moyle* [1999] MHLR 195, the legal tests may be different but the facts found in relation to one test may determine the application of another."

In *MD* it was accepted that risk is relevant to both paras (i) and (ii), but it is not necessarily relevant to the issue of whether appropriate treatment is available for a patient under para.(-iia): see the notes on s.3(2)(d).

In *R. (on the application of Ashworth Hospital Authority) v Mental Health Review Tribunal for West Midlands and North West Regions* [2001] EWHC Admin 901; [2002] M.H.L.R. 13, Stanley Burnton J. said at para.64:

"[S]atisfaction of the criteria for the discharge of a patient under [this provision] may depend on the availability of suitable after-care. If no such after-care is available, it may follow that it is appropriate for the patient to be liable to be detained, or that it is necessary for him to receive treatment in a hospital".

This case was appealed and the following observations of Stanley Burnton J. were endorsed by the Court of Appeal:

"If there is uncertainty as to the putting in place of the after-care arrangements on which satisfaction of the discharge criteria depends, the tribunal should adjourn . . . to enable them to be put in place, indicating their views and giving appropriate directions" ([2002] EWCA Civ 923; [2002] M.H.L.R. 314).

In *DN v Northumberland Tyne and Wear NHS Foundation Trust* [2011] UKUT 327 (AAC); [2011] M.H.L.R. 249, UT Judge Jacobs held that there was no reason why the deprivation of liberty safeguards contained in the Mental Capacity Act 2005 cannot be applied in anticipation of the patient being discharged from detention and moving to a care home as long as he was not "within the scope of the Mental Health Act" on his discharge (see Sch.1A of the 2005 Act). This would enable suitable arrangements, in particular those relating to him accessing alcohol, to be in place on his arrival at the care home. Also see *Secretary of State for Justice v KC* [2015] UKUT 376 (AAC) noted under "Conditions" in s.73(4).

DISCHARGE. See the note on para.(a).

Sub-paragraph (i)

1–918   THEN SUFFERING. See the note on para.(a).

MENTAL DISORDER. If the person has a learning disability, the disability must be associated with abnormally aggressive or seriously irresponsible conduct (s.1(2A), (2B)).

NATURE OR DEGREE. The meaning of this phrase is considered in the note on s.3(2)(a). In *R. v The Mental Health Review Tribunal or the South Thames Region Ex p. Smith* (1999) 47 B.M.L.R. 104, the tribunal refused to discharge the patient who was suffering from paranoid schizophrenia, the symptoms of which were well controlled by medication. On refusing the patient's application to judicially review this decision, Popplewell J. said:

"[At the time of the tribunal hearing the patient] was in a stable condition and it is quite clear that the illness was not of a degree which of itself made it appropriate for him to be liable to be detained. The reason for that was because he had a chronic condition which was static. However, the nature of the condition was that it might cease to be static so that the interpretation that nature is in some way unchanging in one view may be right, but the effect of the condition is that because of its very nature it may not remain static. It seems to me that if the facts upon which the tribunal rely have shown that it may not be static, that goes to the nature of the condition. The degree in the instant case, in relation to his condition, was not relevant because it was static and stable."

His Lordship continued:

"If one had simply to look at the degree it would have been right for the discharge to take place, but the nature of the condition was such that it was clear that he should not be discharged. It may well be in a great number of cases that nature and degree involve much the same questions ... and it maybe that tribunals will be wise, if they have any doubts about it, to include them both [in their conclusions]."

Smith was followed by Latham J. in *R. v London and South West Region Mental Health Review Tribunal Ex p. Moyle* [1999] M.H.L.R. 195 where his Lordship, when considering the position of a patient with a history of relapsing, said:

"The correct analysis, in my judgment, is that the nature of the illness of a patient such as the applicant is that it is an illness which will relapse in the absence of medication. The question that then has to be asked is whether the nature of that illness is such as to make it appropriate for him to be liable to be detained in hospital for medical treatment. Whether it is appropriate or not will depend upon an assessment of the probability that he will relapse in the near future if he were free in the community."

In *CM v Derbyshire Healthcare NHS Foundation Trust* [2011] UKUT 129 (AAC); [2011] M.H.L.R. 153, at para.27, UT Judge Levenson emphasised Latham J.'s finding that the assessment of the probability of the patient's non-compliance with medication after discharge and the risk of consequent relapse must relate to "the near future".

A finding by a tribunal that the patient's "illness is of a nature to justify detention in hospital but not at present of a degree" constituted a misdirection of law because it erroneously treated "nature or degree" as conjunctive rather than disjunctive. Separate consideration of nature and degree is needed (*R. (on the application of the Home Secretary) v Mental Health Review Tribunal* [2003] EWHC 2864 (Admin); [2004] M.H.L.R. 91 para.57). In *R. (on the application of the Secretary of State for the Home Department) v Mental Health Review Tribunal and CH* [2005] EWHC 746 (Admin); [2005] M.H.L.R. 199, Stanley Burnton J. said, at para.33, that he had "some sympathy" with the difficulties faced by tribunals in addressing the statutory criteria and the distinction between "nature" and "degree", and that in many cases "the distinction is elusive, and it may not matter under which head the question is addressed".

The question whether the continued detention of an asymptomatic patient contravenes art.5 of the ECHR was considered by the Court of Appeal in *R. (on the application of H) v Mental Health Review Tribunal, North and North East London Region* [2001] EWCA Civ 415; [2001] M.H.L.R. 48, where Lord Phillips M.R. said at para.33:

"The circumstances of the present case, which are similar to those considered by Latham J. in [*Moyle*], are not uncommon. A patient is detained who is unquestionably suffering from schizophrenia. While in the controlled environment of the hospital he is taking medication, and as a result of the medication is in remission. So long as he continues to take the medication he will pose no danger to himself or to others. The nature of the illness is such, however, that if he ceases to take the medication he will relapse and pose a danger to himself or to others. The professionals may be uncertain whether, if he is discharged into the community, he will continue to take the medication. We do not believe that Article 5 requires that the patient must always be discharged in such circumstances. The appropriate response should depend upon the result of weighing the interests of the patient against those of the public having regard to the particular facts. Continued detention can be justified if, but only if, it is a proportionate response having regard to the risks that would be involved in discharge."

APPROPRIATE FOR HIM TO BE LIABLE TO BE DETAINED IN A HOSPITAL FOR MEDICAL TREATMENT. In *R. (on the application of the Secretary of State for the Home Department) v Mental Health Review Tribunal)* [2002] EWHC Admin 1128; [2002] M.H.L.R. 241 para.24, Elias J. cited the observations of Lord Phillips in *H*, above, and said:

"In determining whether it is appropriate to detain a patient in hospital, the interests of the patient have to be weighed against those of the public, and the tribunal has to determine whether the detention is proportional to the risks involved. If it is not satisfied that it is a proportional response to those risks to detain the patient, then he must be discharged."

A judgment on proportionality also has to be made with respect to the risk to the patient's health should he be discharged from detention even if there is no risk to the public. In *Smirek v Williams* [2000] M.H.L.R. 38, the Court of Appeal held that it can be appropriate for a patient to be liable to be detained in a hospital if the evidence is that, without being detained in hospital, the patient will not take the medication that is required to prevent the deterioration of a chronic mental illness.

The phrase "liable to be detained" includes patients who have been granted leave of absence from hospital under s.17 (*R. v Hallstrom Ex p. W* [1986] 2 All E.R. 306 at 312). In *R. (on the application of Epsom and St Helier NHS Trust) v Mental Health Review Tribunal* [2001] EWHC Admin 101; [2001] M.H.L.R. 8, the Trust challenged the decision of the tribunal to discharge the patient. The tribunal's decision was made on the ground that as the patient, who had been granted leave of absence under s.17 to reside in a nursing home, was not receiving in-patient treatment it was not "appropriate for her to be liable to be detained in hospital for medical treatment" for the purposes of this provision. Sullivan J. held that:

1. The decision of the Court of Appeal in *R. v Barking Havering and Brentwood Community Healthcare NHS Trust* [1999] 1 F.L.R. 106 is authority for the proposition that one has to look at the whole course of the patient's treatment. To do so, one has to look at the past, present and future.

2. It would be inconsistent with the scheme of the Act if the mere prospect, that at some unspecified future time in-patient treatment would or might be required, compelled a tribunal to reject a patient's application for discharge. His Lordship said at para.52:

   "The matter has to be looked at in the round, including the prospect of future in-patient treatment, but there will come a time when, even though it is certain that treatment will be required at some stage in the future, the timing of that treatment is so uncertain that it is no longer 'appropriate' for the patient to continue to be liable to detention. It is the tribunal's function to use its expertise to decide whether the certainty, or the possibility, of the need for in-patient treatment at some future date makes it 'appropriate' that the patient's liability to detention shall continue."

His Lordship's references to "in-patient treatment" should now be read as if they were references to "hospital treatment": see *R. (on the application of DR) v Mersey Care NHS Trust* [2002] EWHC 1810 (Admin); [2002] M.H.L.R. 386.

Subsequent to the decision in the *Epsom* case, the High Court has held that if the patient is on s.17 leave, hospital treatment, which can comprise out-patient treatment, must form a significant component of the patient's treatment plan if this provision is to be satisfied: see *R. (on the application of CS) v Mental Health Review Tribunal* [2004] EWHC 2958 (Admin); [2004] M.H.L.R. 355. The *Barking, Epsom, DR* and *CS* cases are considered in the note on s.20(4). In *SL v Ludlow Street Healthcare* [2015] UKUT 398 (AAC), UT Judge Jacobs, having accepted the *Epsom, DR* and *CS* cases as "correctly stating the law" (para.34), made the following obiter comments at para.35 under the heading "Dangers to avoid":

"There are two dangers that tribunals must bear in mind in applying the approach set out in the cases. First, the tribunal must not reason by analogy from the facts of those cases. It must apply the principles established by the cases, but their application can only be undertaken by reference to the facts and circumstances of the case before the tribunal. Even small differences may justify, or even require, a different analysis. Second, it is not sufficient merely to repeat the language of the principles. The tribunal must, of course, make sufficient findings of fact to support, and provide an explanation that justifies, its conclusion."

Sub-paragraph (ii)
NECESSARY. See *AM v South London & Maudsley NHS Foundation Trust* [2013] **1–919** UKUT 365 (AAC); [2014] M.H.L.R. 181 which is noted in the General Note to this section. The standard "is one of necessity, not desirability" (*Reid v Secretary of State for Scotland* [1999] 1 All E.R. 481 per Lord Clyde at 504).

PROTECTION OF OTHER PERSONS. The Court of Appeal in *R. v Vowles* [2015] EWCA Crim 45 at para.35(iv) said:

"The concept of burden of proof is not relevant in risk evaluation, even though the risk may be defined differently. This was determined by the courts in relation to the Parole Board: see *R (Sim) v Parole Board* [2004] QB 1288; *R (Brooks) v Parole Board* [2004] EWCA Civ 80. We agree with the submission that there is no difference in principle to the assessment of risk before the FTT."

In *R. v Parole Board Ex p. Bradley* [1990] 3 All E.R. 828 at 836 DC, Stuart-Smith L.J., on examining this provision, said that "the precise level of risk is not (surely cannot be) spelt out". In *R. (on the application of N) v Mental Health Review Tribunal* [2001] EWHC 1133 (Admin); [2002] M.H.L.R. 70, Gibbs J., having referred to *Bradley*, made the following comments on risk assessment at paras 53–54:

"It is submitted that there was a requirement on the Tribunal itself to quantify the risk in the face of Dr Gravett's expressed inability at this stage, to do so. I accept ... that there may arise a stage at which a Tribunal must reasonably be required to quantify a risk. It depends on the context. If it was clear that all available evidence was there for it to consider but that the tribunal simply walked away from its responsibility and sat on the fence, then there would be justice in the criticism. I acknowledge also that even where the medical evidence before it does not enable it to quantify the risk there must come, or may come, a point in where continuous deferment of quantification is unreasonable ... Here the context is one in which Dr Gravett is, in my judgment, clearly expressing the view that there is a substantial and unacceptable, in unquantifiable, risk. There is a project for the treatment of the [patient], partially completed, one of the purposes of which is to define that risk more closely. There is, in my judgment, nothing wrong in principle in the psychiatrist, pending the outcome of that process, defining the possible range of risk widely. Nor, in my judgment, is there anything wrong in principle with the Tribunal accepting the psychiatrist's view. It is, in my judgment, unreasonable in that context to say that the Tribunal should attempt the impossible and reach some kind of assessment of risk which would be in danger of amounting to purely arbitrary speculation."

In *R. (on the application of Munday) v Secretary of State for the Home Department* [2009] EWHC 3638 (Admin), para.30, Burnett J. said:

"Although psychiatrists or other medical health professionals or social supervisors with their knowledge of a person might be in a position to express a view about risk, it is by its nature an exercise of evaluation which does not necessarily call for expert medical input."

The fact that a patient could pose a risk to the public for reasons unconnected with his mental illness is not relevant to the tribunal's decision (*R. (on the Application of Li) v Mental Health Review Tribunal* [2004] EWHC 51 (Admin)).

THAT HE SHOULD RECEIVE SUCH TREATMENT. Compare with the criterion set out in para.(a)(ii).

Sub-paragraph (iia)

1–920 APPROPRIATE MEDICAL TREATMENT. See the notes on s.3(2)(d).

Sub-paragraph (iii)

1–921 PARAGRAPH (G) OF SECTION 66(1). Which provides for an application to a tribunal to be made by a nearest relative on the issue by the RC of a report under s.25, barring the nearest relative's discharge powers. Although the tribunal is under a duty to consider the "dangerousness" criterion where an application has been made by a nearest relative under s.66(1)(g), there is no such duty in the case of an application by the patient, although the tribunal is entitled to take it into account when deciding whether to exercise its discretionary power to discharge (*R. (on the application of W) v Mental Health Review Tribunal* [2004] EWHC 3266 (Admin); [2005] M.H.L.R. 134).

The test in para.(iii) is much narrower than that in para.(ii). It implies a likely serious psychological or physical injury to the patient or to some other person. A mere suspicion that the patient might be dangerous is not sufficient: see the notes on "likely to act" and "dangerous" in s.25(1). If they are not satisfied as to the criterion set out in this paragraph, the tribunal must discharge the patient, even if detention is still justified under paras (i) and (ii).

Section 66(1)(g) does not apply to patients who are detained under Pt III: applications made by or in respect of such patients are governed by s.69(1)(a) (*R. (on the application of Central and North West London Mental Health NHS Trust) v Mental Health Review Tribunal (Southern Region)* [2005] EWHC 337 (Admin); [2005] M.H.L.R. 183).

IF RELEASED. As this phrase does not necessarily refer to immediate release, the tribunal could make an order for the deferred discharge of the patient (*R. (on the application of B) v Mental Health Review Tribunal* [2003] EWHC 815 (Admin); [2003] M.H.L.R. 218 para.8).

Paragraph (c)

1–922 This paragraph states that if the tribunal is not satisfied as to any of the matters set out in (i) to (v) in relation to a community patient, the patient must be discharged. Sub-paragraphs (i) to (iv) replicate the criteria set out in s.17A(5)(a), (b), (d) and (e) and reference should be made to the notes thereto. The tribunal also has a general discretion to discharge the patient.

The tribunal does not have the power to vary or discharge the conditions of a CTO or to determine whether a CTO patient is the subject of a deprivation of liberty in the community. A challenge to an alleged unauthorised deprivation of liberty must be made either to the Court of Protection or the Administrative Court. A community patient can be the subject of a deprivation of liberty authorisation made under Sch.A1 of the Mental Capacity Act 2005: see Sch.1A, Case C of the 2005 Act.

In *GA v Betsi Cadwaladr University LHB* [2013] 0280 (AAC); [2014] M.H.L.R. 27, UT Judge Jacobs held that the tribunal had no jurisdiction under this provision to deal with issues of consent to treatment when a patient was on a CTO. After analysing the legislation, Judge Jacobs came to this conclusion at para.16:

> "The result is that the tribunal has the right to order the release of the patient, but no more. It does not have power to order that the patient be recalled to hospital. Nor does it have any power to direct the responsible authority to take any steps in respect of the patient's treatment, including steps to allow it to give treatment without consent. Those would be surprising limitations on the tribunal's powers, if it had jurisdiction to deal with issues of consent. The tribunal can make recommendations about treatment (as under s.72(3A)(a)), but they are powers only. It has no right to impose that recommendation on the clinical staff."

Sub-paragraph (i)
MENTAL DISORDER.   If the person has a learning disability, the disability must be associ-   **1–923**
ated with abnormally aggressive or seriously irresponsible conduct (s.1(2A), (2B)).

Sub-paragraph (iii)
See subs.(1A).   **1–924**

Sub-paragraph (v)
See the notes on para.(b)(iii), above.   **1–925**

Subsection (1A)
See the notes on s.17A(6).   **1–926**

Subsection (3)
This provision enables the tribunal to defer the patient's discharge to a future date. If the   **1–927**
tribunal decides not to exercise its power of deferment, it may make a recommendation that the patient be either granted leave of absence, or transferred to another hospital or into guardianship and may reconsider the case if the recommendation is not complied with. As a patient who is subject to a deferred discharge continues to be "liable to be detained", the RC retains the power to grant leave of absence during the period of deferment.

The power to defer discharge applies to situations where the tribunal has exercised either its mandatory or its discretionary duty to discharge (*R. v Mental Health Review Tribunal for the North Thames Region Ex p. Pierce* (1996) 36 B.M.L.R. 137). A different conclusion was reached by Stephens J., sitting in the High Court in Northern Ireland, who, on considering an equivalent provision in art.77(2) of the Mental Health (Northern Ireland) Order 1986, held that the power to defer discharge is confined to a discretionary discharge (*X's Application (No.2)* [2009] NIQB 2).

Deferral cannot be used to test whether a patient is ready for discharge: see *CNWL NHS Foundation Trust v H-JH* [2012] UKUT 210 (AAC); [2012] M.H.L.R. 305, at para.17, a case where a deferred discharge was held to be lawful where the reason for the deferral was to allow an opportunity for the patient's RC to reduce the patient's medication. The reason for this was not to make the patient ready for release, but because she had been complaining about the medication's side-effects.

If a detained patient is made subject to a CTO during a period of deferred discharge, the CTO will end on the discharge taking effect as the s.3 application upon which the CTO is based will no longer be in place. Placing the patient of a CTO in this situation would therefore be a pointless exercise. This was accepted as being the correct legal position in *MP v Mersey Care NHS Trust* [2011] UKUT 107 (AAC); [2011] M.H.L.R. 146, para.14.

In the *CNWL* case, above, UT Judge Jacobs identified the action that could be taken by a detaining authority if the condition of a CTO patient deteriorated after a deferred discharge had been made in respect of him:

"An authority's powers have to be considered at two stages: (i) before the discharge takes effect; and (ii) thereafter. As to (i), the community treatment order remains in force until the discharge takes effect. Until then, a patient remains liable to have her medication changed and to be recalled to hospital. As to (ii), it is possible to detain a patient immediately following discharge. . . . It is permissible to re-admit a patient on the basis of 'information not known to the tribunal which puts a significantly different complexion on the case as compared with that which was before the tribunal' [see *R. v East London and The City Mental Health NHS Trust Ex p. Brandenburg* which is considered in the General Note to s.3]."

The discharge on a future date of a patient who is found by the tribunal not to be suffering from a mental disorder would be in danger of violating art.5(1)(e) of the ECHR if the delay between the decision to discharge and the date of discharge was excessive: see *Johnson v United Kingdom* (1999) 27 E.H.R.R. 296, noted in art.5(1)(e) under "persons of unsound mind". Also see the note on "Human Rights Act 1998" in s.73.

Deferment can be used to enable preparations to be made to receive a patient back into the community, although there is no power for the tribunal to reconsider the deferment if circumstances show that what is required to provide after-care services to the patient cannot be put in place. In *R. (on the application of H) v Ashworth Hospital Authority* [2002] EWCA Civ 923; [2002] M.H.L.R. 362, Dyson L.J. said at para.68:

"If the tribunal had any doubt as to whether [after-care] services would be available, they should have adjourned to obtain any necessary information. I regard the alternative of a deferral [. . .] as less satisfactory . . . [I]f the tribunal is in doubt as to whether suitable after-care arrangements will be available, it is difficult to see how they can specify a particular date for discharge. In cases of doubt, the safer course is to adjourn."

The power to defer discharge may also be used in a case of an application made by a nearest relative under s.66(1)(g): see *R. (on the application of B) v Mental Health Review Tribunal* [2003] EWHC 815 (Admin); [2003] M.H.L.R. 218, where Stanley Burnton J. said at para.8:

"If a tribunal, on the evidence before it, comes to the conclusion that a patient, if released immediately, would be likely to act in a manner dangerous to other persons, or to himself or herself, but that if proper after-care arrangements are put in place that will not be the position, in my judgement, it is clear that the tribunal may make an order for a deferred discharge under section 72(3) deferring discharge to a date when it is reasonably assured that the appropriate aftercare arrangements will be in place."

In *Perkins v Bath District Health Authority; R. v Wessex Health Review Tribunal Ex p. Wiltshire CC*, 4 B.M.L.R. 145, the tribunal directed the patient's discharge from s.2 but directed that the patient's discharge be deferred "to give an adequate opportunity to those responsible to consider whether an application for treatment might be appropriate". Although counsel for the tribunal was prepared to accept that a tribunal cannot defer discharge under this provision to enable the authorities to decide whether there is some other basis for lawful detention, the Court of Appeal was not required to resolve the point. It is likely that counsel's concession would be upheld if the point was required to be resolved. The tribunal could defer discharge if it was felt that the patient would be fit for discharge at the expiration of a further short period of treatment.

DIRECT THE DISCHARGE OF A PATIENT UNDER THAT SUBSECTION. i.e. under subs.(1) which is concerned with the powers of tribunals to discharge unrestricted patients. This subsection does not therefore apply to patients who are subject to restriction orders (*R. v Oxford Mental Health Authority Review Tribunal Ex p. Smith,* January 25, 1995 CA). A submission that art.5(4) of the ECHR requires that this subsection be construed to apply to restricted patients was rejected by Collins J. in *R. (on the application of the Secretary of State for the Home Department) v Mental Health Review Tribunal* [2001] A.C.D. 62.

The power to defer does not apply to patients who are subject to guardianship because applications under subs.(1) can only be made in respect of patients who are "liable to be detained".

DATE SPECIFIED IN THE DIRECTION. It is submitted that Gostin and Fennell are correct in arguing that a tribunal "could not specify a date for discharge after that on which the authority for a patient's detention expires" (*Mental Health: Tribunal Procedure,* 1992, p.91). The date specified in the direction cannot be changed by the tribunal subsequent to the communication to the patient of the decision to defer discharge: see *Secretary of State for the Home Department v Oxford Regional Mental Health Review Tribunal* [1987] 3 All E.R. 8, noted under s.73(7).

RECOMMEND. There is no power under this provision to make a recommendation with a view to doing something other than "facilitating the discharge of the patient on a future date". For example, there is no power to make a recommendation for the transfer of the patient to another hospital more convenient for him or his family (*R. (on the application of H) v Mental Health Review Tribunal* below) or to make a recommendation which is contingent upon an event occurring, such as the patient's mental disorder being stabilised. For judicial guidance on the making of extra-statutory recommendations, see the remarks of UT Judge Rowland in *C v Birmingham and Solihull Mental Health NHS Trust* [2012] UKUT 178 (AAC) which are reproduced in the General Note to s.73.

A failure to make a recommendation is not amenable to judicial review because it is not a final decision (*R. (on the application of LH) v Mental Health Review Tribunal* [2002] EWHC 170 (Admin); [2002] M.H.L.R. 130), although a failure to give reasons for not making a recommendation might be susceptible to judicial review in circumstances where the contentions and material before the tribunal justified its consideration of such a recommendation (*R. (on the application of H) v Mental Health Review Tribunal* [2002] EWHC 1522 (Admin); [2002] M.H.L.R. 362 para.24). The appropriate procedure now would be for an application to be made to the tribunal under r.49 of the Tribunal Rules for it to review its decision. This happened in *RB v Nottinghamshire Healthcare NHS Trust* [2011] UKUT 73 (AAC); [2011] M.H.L.R. 296 where UT Judge Jacobs made the following comments on the tribunal's power to make recommendations:

"The first question is whether to make a recommendation at all. The more obvious the recommendation, the more likely it is that the authority will consider it anyway. So recommendations are likely to be made in those cases where the authority has not considered the possibility or would be unlikely to do so. If the tribunal does make a recommendation, it has to take account of the tenuous nature of its control. This makes it essential to consider very carefully the timescale and the directions that the tribunal might give in order (i) to apply its moral pressure on the authority and (ii) to be fully informed by the time it has to decide whether to reconvene. It may, for example, be appropriate for the tribunal to direct that a progress report be provided shortly before a specified date so that it can decide if there is any practical purpose in reconvening. Finally, the tribunal has to decide whether to reconvene. In making that decision, it has to decide what practical value this would serve. It has no power to enforce the recommendation and is not reconvening for that purpose. It has the power to embarrass the authority into explaining its thinking or, possibly, into compliance. But it has to make a judgment on what it can practically achieve, if anything."(para.16)

In this case, Judge Jacobs said that as the tribunal's power to make a recommendation must be exercised judicially, tempered by the reality that it has no power to coerce (para.12), it should have given reasons for its decision to make a recommendation (para.13) and for exercising its discretion not to reconvene (para.15). The tribunal should also give reasons if it is asked to make a recommendation and declines to do so (*RN v Curo Care* (2011) UKUT 263 (AAC); [2011] M.H.L.R. 337).

TRANSFERRED TO ANOTHER HOSPITAL. The lack of a power to secure the transfer of a patient to another hospital does not breech art.5 of the ECHR (*MP v Nottinghamshire Healthcare NHS Trust* [2003] EWHC 1782 (Admin); [2003] M.H.L.R. 381).

In *R. (on the application of L) v West London Mental Health NHS Trust* [2012] EWHC 3200 (Admin); [2013] M.H.L.R. 297, para.178, Stadlen J. said that it should "be noted that the Tribunal's power to recommend a transfer may only be exercised with a view to facilitating the patient's discharge. Although that may coincide with a conclusion that the patient's continued detention in a high security hospital is not necessary for the protection of himself or others it may not necessarily be so".

FURTHER CONSIDER HIS CASE. The tribunal will set a time limit at the expiration of which it will reconsider the case. It may then decide to reconvene the hearing. At such a hearing the tribunal has all the powers available that it enjoyed at the original hearing (*Mental Health Review Tribunal v Hempstock* (1998) 39 B.M.L.R. 123).

Hempstock was applied in *R. (on the application of O) v Mental Health Review Tribunal* [2006] EWHC 2659 (Admin); [2006] M.H.L.R. 326, where Collins J. held that the phrase "his case" meant the patient's application to the tribunal. Accordingly, that application and the tribunal's powers in respect of it, including the power to agree to the patient's request for his application to be withdrawn, remain extant after the tribunal has made a recommendation under this provision.

Subsection (3A)

1–928   This subsection, which is only relevant in a case where the tribunal is not under a positive duty to discharge (*MP v Mersey Care NHS Trust* [2011] UKUT 107 (AAC); [2011] M.H.L.R. 146, para.45), states that a tribunal is not required to discharge a patient because they think it might be appropriate for the patient to be made subject to a CTO. If the tribunal has formed such a view, they can recommend to the RC that she considers applying for a CTO and can reconvene in the event of the recommendation not being followed. As a recommendation can only be made where the tribunal is not under a duty to discharge the patient and as the patient would satisfy the criteria for detention under subs.(1)(b), at the reconvened hearing, the exercise by the tribunal of its discretionary power to discharge in this situation is likely to be a rare occurrence.

If the patient's representative requests the tribunal to make a recommendation under this provision and that request is denied, the tribunal should explain its reasons (*RN v Curo Care* (2011) UKUT 263 (AAC); [2011] M.H.L.R. 337).

Subsection (4)

1–929   This subsection enables the tribunal to discharge a patient under guardianship and directs the tribunal to discharge the patient if either of the criteria set out in paras (a) or (b) is satisfied. The tribunal does not have the power either to defer the patient's discharge from guardianship or to make recommendations with a view to facilitating discharge at a later date.

In *NL v Hampshire County Council* [2014] UKUT 475 (AAC), UT Judge Jacobs said at para.20:

"Given the importance of the welfare of those suffering from a mental disorder and of the need for protection of other persons, it is difficult to imagine a case in which the tribunal could properly exercise its discretion to discharge [a guardianship patient] without there being appropriate safeguards to ensure the necessary treatment and protection."

A guardianship patient can be the subject of a deprivation of liberty authorisation made under Sch.A1 of the Mental Capacity Act 2005 (DOLS): see Sch.1A, Case D of the 2005 Act and *KD v A Borough Council* [2015] UKUT 251 (AAC), para.39. In *MN v Kent County Council* [2015] UKUT 0125 (AAC), Judge Jacobs held that consideration of para.(b) may require the tribunal to consider whether it is possible for a DOL to provide sufficient protection for the person's welfare and the protection of others, in which case guardianship would not be "necessary". Where the issue arises, the tribunal should:

(i) be alert to the potential relevance of DOLS to the issue it has to decide under the Act;

(ii) take account of the practical effect of a DOL; and

(iii) be aware that there is no rule that a DOL always trumps guardianship, any more than there is a rule that guardianship inevitably trumps a DOL.

It is also important for the tribunal to bear in mind that the "Mental Capacity Act deals with the person's best interests, whereas the Mental Health Act deals with protection of the patient and the public. Each is subject to different adjudication procedures before different judicial bodies" (para.29).

In *MN*, a crucial factor in favour of guardianship was the power contained in s.18(3) to ensure the return of an absconding patient. Judge Jacobs said at para.26:

"I do not accept the argument put by Mr M's solicitors that a DOLS is sufficient protection as it allows the home to prevent Mr M leaving. That argument does not deal with the possibility that he may abscond, especially given his wish to live elsewhere and the tribunal's findings that he is devious in the pursuit of his own objectives. This is a limitation inherent in the nature of a DOLS . . . ."

MN was cited in *KD v A Borough Council*, above, where Charles J. said at para.59:

"[I]f it is satisfied that the relevant person (P) lacks capacity to consent to the proposed placement and care plan and it would create an unlawful deprivation of P's liberty a FTT should not discharge the guardianship until a lawful alternative placement is in place and so until either a DOLS standard authorisation (or a court order) authorising the deprivation of liberty is in place."

With regard to the availability of alternative placement options, his Lordship said at para.64:

"The FTT is an investigative tribunal. But this does not mean that it has to embark on an investigation of and so identify all available options and initiate the gathering of evidence about them. Rather, in my view the parties have the primary obligation of providing and advancing:

(i) evidence on the available options, including sufficient detail of their terms and availability,

(ii) evidence to support argument that an identified option is or would be the appropriate option (which may have to include evidence on other possibilities), and

(iii) argument on the application of the 'necessity test' set by [this subsection] to the identified and competing options."

At paras 68 to 72, his Lordship suggested the following check list for tribunals when an issue involving an argument that an alternative involving the application of the Mental Capacity Act is said to be the basis for a discharge of guardianship:

"*Is the proposed alternative actually available in practice? If not when will it be available?* This will involve considering:

 (i) Whether the relevant placement and care plan are agreed and defined.

 (ii) If not when will it be agreed and so defined.

(iii) The terms of the care plan and whether its application will result in a deprivation of liberty.

(iv) If the answer to (iii) is yes or maybe has an authorisation under the MCA's DOLS or an order of the Court of Protection been obtained.

 (v) If such an authorisation has not been obtained, can it be obtained and if so how and when will it be obtained. This will involve considering (a) whether P lacks capacity applying the MCA tests, (b) whether P is not ineligible (and so is eligible) to be deprived of his liberty by the MCA and (c) whether the decision makers under the MCA are likely to conclude that the proposed placement is in P's best interests.

(vi) If there is already an authorisation under the DOLS or from the Court of Protection when this will be confirmed on the basis of a change in the status of P from Case D to Case E.

These questions will enable the FTT to form a view on whether on discharge of the guardianship the proposed alternative is lawful or is likely to be made lawful.

What are the advantages and disadvantages of the rival alternatives? This will involve:

 (i) An identification of the relevant legal differences between the proposed alternatives.

 (ii) Making the findings of fact that are needed to apply those differences to the circumstances of the case and in particular to the legal criteria set by s. 72(4) MHA, which is the test they have to apply.

These questions will enable the FTT to form a view on whether the availability of a lawful alternative would satisfy the test for a direction that the patient be discharged from guardianship.

Have the parties provided sufficient evidence and argument on the above issues? This involves considering whether the parties have sufficiently complied with the approach set out in paragraph 64 above.

What issues should the FTT decide? This engages issues that inform the availability of alternatives and thus, for example, an argument that (a) the patient has capacity, or (b) the placement does not give rise to a deprivation of liberty (see paragraphs 61 and 62 above).

Should the FTT adjourn or discharge the guardianship? This is the ultimate question and will depend on the assessment of the earlier ones. The choice between adjournment and discharge will turn on the prediction as to whether and when evidence can be obtained to demonstrate the existence of a practically available alternative."

Also see the note on "The use of guardianship to authorise the deprivation of a person's liberty" in s.8.

When Parliament responded to the declaration of incompatibility made by the Court of Appeal in *R. (on the application of H) v Mental Health Review Tribunal, North and East London Region* [2001] EWCA Civ 415; [2001] M.H.L.R. 48, by approving the Mental Health Act 1983 (Remedial Order) 2001 (SI 2001/3712), it did not act to amend this subsection by requiring the tribunal to be positively satisfied that the criteria justifying guardianship continue to exist before refusing to order a patient's discharge.

Note the failure in this provision to reproduce the "nature or degree" requirement which is found in s.7(2)(a).

Paragraph (a)

MENTAL DISORDER.   If the person has a learning disability, the disability must be associ- **1–930** ated with abnormally aggressive or seriously irresponsible conduct (s.1(2A), (2B)).

Paragraph (b)

WELFARE.   See the note on s.7(2).   **1–931**

Power to discharge restricted patients

73.—[(1) Where an application to [the appropriate tribunal] is made by a **1–932** restricted patient who is subject to a restriction order, or where the case of such a patient is referred to [the appropriate tribunal], the tribunal shall direct the absolute discharge of the patient if—

(a) [the tribunal is] not satisfied as to the matters mentioned in paragraph (b)(i) [, (ii) or (iia)] of section 72(1) above; and

(b) [the tribunal is] satisfied that it is not appropriate for the patient to remain liable to be recalled to hospital for further treatment.

(2) Where in the case of any such patient as is mentioned in subsection (1) above—

(a) paragraph (a) of that subsection applies; but

(b) paragraph (b) of that subsection does not apply,

the tribunal shall direct the conditional discharge of the patient.]

(3) Where a patient is absolutely discharged under this section he shall thereupon cease to be liable to be detained by virtue of the relevant hospital order, and the restriction order shall cease to have effect accordingly.

(4) Where a patient is conditionally discharged under this section—

(a) he may be recalled by the Secretary of State under subsection (3) of section 42 above as if he had been conditionally discharged under subsection (2) of that section; and

(b) the patient shall comply with such conditions (if any) as may be imposed at the time of discharge by the Tribunal or at any subsequent time by the Secretary of State.

(5) The Secretary of State may from time to time vary any condition imposed (whether by the Tribunal or by him) under subsection (4) above.

(6) Where a restriction order in respect of a patient ceases to have effect after he has been conditionally discharged under this section the patient shall, unless previously recalled, be deemed to be absolutely discharged on the date when the order ceases to have effect and shall cease to be liable to be detained by virtue of the relevant hospital order.

(7) A Tribunal may defer a direction for the conditional discharge of a patient until such arrangements as appear to the Tribunal to be necessary for that purpose

have been made to [its satisfaction]; and where by virtue of any such deferment no direction has been given on an application or reference before the time when the patient's case comes before the Tribunal on a subsequent application or reference, the previous application or reference shall be treated as one on which no direction under this section can be given.

(8) This section is without prejudice to section 42 above.

AMENDMENTS

The amendments to this section were made by the Mental Health Act 1983 (Remedial) Order 2001 (SI 2001/3712) art.4, the Mental Health Act 2007 s.4(9) and SI 2008/2883 art.9, Sch.3 para.54.

DEFINITIONS

1–933   the appropriate tribunal: ss.66(4), 145(1).
restricted patient: s.79(1).
restriction order: ss.41, 145(1).
hospital: ss.34(2), 79(6), 145(1).
relevant hospital order: s.79(2)–(5).

GENERAL NOTE

1–934   This section requires the tribunal to order either the absolute or conditional discharge of a restricted patient if the requirements of subss.(1) or (2) are satisfied. The tribunal also has the power to attach conditions to a conditional discharge (subs.(4)) and to defer the discharge (subs.(7)). The conditions of a conditional discharge can be varied by the Secretary of State (subs.(5)). The tribunal has no general discretion to order the discharge of a restricted patient where the statutory criteria are not met and has no power to adjourn the patient's application to give an opportunity for the patient's condition to improve or to see if an improvement already made is sustained (*R. v Nottingham Mental Health Review Tribunal Ex p. Secretary of State for the Home Department, The Times*, October 12, 1988 CA).

Although the tribunal has no power under this section to make recommendations (*Grant v Mental Health Review Tribunal, The Times*, April 26, 1986; *R. v Oxford Mental Health Authority Review Tribunal Ex p. Smith*, January 25, 1995 CA), the following Written Answer was given by Mr Douglas Hogg MP, a Home Office Minister, to a question on what would happen if a tribunal which had considered the case of a restricted patient included in its decision a recommendation that the patient be granted leave of absence or be transferred to another hospital or be transferred to guardianship:

"Any such recommendation received in the Home Office [now the Ministry of Justice] is acknowledged, and any comments are offered which can usefully be made at that stage. Correspondence with the tribunal is copied to the patient's [responsible clinician] since it is for this officer to consider the recommendation in the first instance. If the [responsible clinician] submits a proposal based on a tribunal's recommendation, full account is taken of the tribunal's views. At any subsequent hearing of the case, the statement which the Home Office provides will explain the outcome of any recommendation which the tribunal had made" (*Hansard* HC Vol.121, cols 261, 262, October 28, 1987).

In *C v Birmingham and Solihull Mental Health NHS Trust* [2013] EWCA Civ 701; [2014] M.H.L.R. 23, the Court of Appeal held that the ministerial answer given by Mr Hogg did not give rise to a legitimate expectation that a patient had a right to have a request for an extra-statutory recommendation heard by the tribunal. A patient therefore has no right to challenge a decision of the tribunal to refuse to make such a recommendation. At the Upper Tribunal hearing of this case ([2012] UKUT 178 (AAC); [2012] M.H.L.R. 292), UT Judge Rowland said at para.35:

"In the absence of any formalisation, some inconsistency – even if more perceived than actual – in the approaches of the First-tier Tribunal to the making of extra-statutory recommendations seems inevitable. Courts and tribunals of all types and at all levels make comments or suggestions that are not necessary for their decisions. It is a matter of judgment when to do so and among the matters taken into consideration are likely to be whether the court or tribunal considers itself sufficiently well informed to make a useful comment or suggestion and whether doing so is likely to be seen as inappropriate interference with another body's decision making. I will not express any view as to the circumstances in which the First-tier Tribunal should or should not make extra-statutory recommendations in mental health cases, save that, if some panels are routinely spending a great deal of time considering issues not necessary for the exercise of their statutory functions for no better reason than that a party has asked them to do so, I would deprecate that practice."

A tribunal cannot use its power to adjourn an application to enable it to decide whether an extra-statutory recommendation should be made (*R. (on the application of the Secretary of State for the Home Department) v Mental Health Review Tribunal* [2000] M.H.L.R. 209).

If an extra-statutory recommendation is made, the question of risk has ultimately to be determined by the Secretary of State who is the statutory decision-maker, and not by the court or the tribunal. The court could not substitute its own decision, and would afford the decision-maker a margin of discretion, though it would scrutinise the decision and ensure that all relevant material has been taken into account. The recommendation is an important input, but it is not determinative. Article 8 of the ECHR did not alter the legal framework (*R. (on the application of P) v Mersey Care NHS Trust and others* [2003] EWHC 994 (Admin); [2004] M.H.L.R. 107). In R. *(on the application of RA) v Secretary of State for the Home Department* [2002] EWHC Admin 1618; [2003] M.H.L.R. 54, para.59, Crane J. said that the Secretary of State should (i) respond with reasonable promptness to recommendations made by the tribunal and (ii) follow them in the absence of sound reasons or new circumstances.

In *MP v Nottinghamshire Healthcare NHS Trust* [2003] EWHC 1782 (Admin); [2003] M.H.L.R. 381, Silber J. held that art.5 of the ECHR does not require the tribunal to be able to secure the transfer of a restricted patient to less secure accommodation.

The relationship between the Secretary of State and the tribunal has been described as being one of "constructive tension"; per the Parliamentary Under-Secretary of State, Department for Constitutional Affairs (*Hansard,* HL Vol.688, col.740).

The legality of a decision to make an application to detain a patient immediately after a decision of a tribunal to discharge him is considered in the General Note to s.3.

Guidance for the clinical supervisors of conditionally discharged patients was published by the Mental Health Casework Section of the Ministry of Justice in 2009. It can be accessed at the website of the Ministry of Justice (*www.justice.gov.uk/offenders/types-of-offender/mentally-disordered-offenders*).

Human Rights Act 1998

There have been a number of cases on whether the power to defer a patient's discharge **1–935** under subs. (7) is compatible with art.5 of the ECHR: see the notes on subs.(7).

In *Johnson v United Kingdom* (1997) 27 E.H.R.R. 296, the Court held that the absence of a power to ensure that the deferred conditional discharge of a patient who is found not to be suffering from mental disorder is not unreasonably delayed, is a violation of art.5; also see *Kolanis v United Kingdom* (2006) 42 E.H.R.R. 12; [2005] M.H.L.R. 238. In *R. v Camden and Islington Health Authority Ex p. K* [2001] EWCA Civ 240; [2001] 3 W.L.R. 553, the Court of Appeal said that the decision of the House of Lords in *Secretary of State for the Home Department v Oxford Regional Mental Health Review Tribunal* [1987] 3 All E.R. 8, to the effect that should it prove to be impossible to implement the conditions specified by a tribunal on a deferred conditional discharge, that tribunal could not consider whether to impose alternative conditions, may not be consistent with art.5 as interpreted by the

Court in *Johnson*. The *Oxford* case was subsequently found to be incompatible with the ECHR and was overruled by the House of Lords in *R. (on the application of H) v Secretary of State for the Home Department* [2003] UKHL 59; [2004] 1 All E.R. 412 where it was held that it was not the case that, because the tribunal lacked the power to secure compliance with its conditions, it lacked the coercive power which is one of the essential attributes of a court for the purposes of art.5. Lord Bingham said at para.26:

"What Article 5(1)(e) and (4) require is that a person of unsound mind compulsorily detained in hospital should have access to a court with power to decide whether the detention is lawful and, if not, to order his release. This power the tribunal had. Nothing in Article 5 suggests that discharge subject to conditions is impermissible in principle, and nothing in the Convention jurisprudence suggests that the power to discharge conditionally (whether there are specific conditions or a mere liability to recall), properly used, should be viewed with disfavour."

The conditional discharge regime set out in this section is therefore not incompatible with art.5. This was implicitly confirmed by the European Court of Human Rights in *Kolanis v United Kingdom*, above.

The question whether a decision not to discharge a patient because of a failure to put in place appropriate after-care facilities in the community would constitute a violation of art.5 is considered in the General Note to s.117 under this heading.

Although it was accepted by Sullivan L.J. in *RH v South London and Maudsley NHS Foundation Trust* [2010] EWCA Civ 1273; [2010] M.H.L.R. 341, para.27, that conditions imposed on a conditional discharge are capable of amounting to an interference with a patient's rights under art.8, the granting of a discharge with a condition that the patient continues to accept medication will not contravene that article if one of the grounds in art.8(2) is satisfied (*L v Sweden*, noted Part 5 under art.8(2) under "protection of health").

Subsection (1)

1–936   The effect of this subsection is that a tribunal must order the *absolute* discharge of a restricted patient if:

(i)   they are not satisfied that he is then suffering from mental disorder of a nature or degree which makes it appropriate for him to be liable to be detained in a hospital for medical treatment; *or*

(ii) they are not satisfied that it is necessary for the health and safety of the patient or for the protection of other persons that he should receive such treatment; *or*

(iii) they are not satisfied that appropriate medical treatment is available for him; *and*

(iv) they are satisfied that it is not appropriate for the patient to remain liable to be recalled to hospital for further treatment.

If an absolute discharge is ordered, the patient ceases to be liable to be detained.

RESTRICTED PATIENT.   A restricted patient who is no longer suffering from a mental disorder remains a "patient" for the purposes of this section until he is discharged absolutely (*R. v Merseyside Mental Health Review Tribunal Ex p. K* [1990] 1 All E.R. 694 CA). The relevant extract from the judgment of Butler-Sloss L.J. is reproduced in the note on "patient" in s.145(1); also see *Johnson v United Kingdom*, noted under subs.(2).

REFERRED TO SUCH A TRIBUNAL.   See the note on s.75(1).

DISCHARGE. There is no power in the tribunal to defer an absolute discharge (*R. (on the application of Secretary of State for Home Department) v Mental Health Review Tribunal* [2004] EWHC 1029 (Admin); [2004] M.H.L.R. 184).

If the High Court quashes an order of the tribunal granting a conditionally discharged patient an absolute discharge, the court can declare that pending a rehearing the patient is to be treated as if he had been conditionally discharged: see *R. (on the application of the Secretary of State for the Home Department) v Mental Health Review Tribunal and BR* [2005] EWCA Civ 1616, noted in the General Note to s.65 under the heading "Habeas Corpus and Judicial Review".

SATISFIED. See the note on s.72(1)(a).

MATTERS MENTIONED IN PARAGRAPH (B)(I), (II) OR (IIA) OF SECTION 72(1). Reference should be made to the notes thereto.

RECALLED TO HOSPITAL FOR FURTHER TREATMENT. This paragraph is relevant only to the question of whether any discharge should be conditional or absolute. The tribunal would have to be satisfied at the time of the hearing that it would not be appropriate for the patient to remain liable to be recalled to hospital to receive treatment that might be required at some time in the future. In *R. (on the application of the Secretary of State) v Mental Health Tribunal* [2001] EWHC Admin 849; [2002] M.H.L.R. 260, the Administrative Court quashed the decision of the tribunal to grant the patient an absolute discharge on the ground that the tribunal ignored this provision when giving the reasons for its decision. Pill L.J. said at para.25: "The possible consequences for the safety of member of the public and the patient, when an order of absolute discharge is made are such that the question of liability to be recalled must be dealt with expressly". This case was cited in *R. (on the application of Secretary of State for Home Department) v Mental Health Review Tribunal*, above, para.21, where Moses J. said that even where the tribunal conclude that the patient is not mentally disordered, "it is incumbent upon the tribunal in cases of restricted patients to go on to consider whether it is satisfied that it is not appropriate for the patient to remain liable to be recalled to hospital for further treatment".

Subsection (2)

The effect of this subsection is that a tribunal must direct the *conditional* discharge of a **1–937** restricted patient if:

(i) they are not satisfied that he is then suffering from mental disorder of a nature or degree which makes it appropriate for him to be liable to be detained in a hospital for medical treatment; *or*

(ii) they are not satisfied that it is necessary for the health and safety of the patient or for the protection of other persons that he should receive such treatment *or*

(iii) they are not satisfied that appropriate medical treatment is available to him.

This section does not attach, or empower the attachment of, any sanction for failure to comply with a condition. The Secretary of State has a general power of recall under subs.(4)(a), but there is nothing to make recall an automatic sanction for non-compliance with a specific condition (*R (on the application of SH) v Mental Health Review Tribunal* [2007] EWHC 884 (Admin), [2007] MHLR 234, para.26).

In *R. (on the application of H) v Secretary of State for the Home Department* [2003] UKHL 59; [2004] 1 All E.R. 412, Lord Bingham said at para.26:

"[T]he conditional discharge regime, properly used, is of great benefit to patients and the public, and conducive to the Convention object of restricting the curtailment of personal liberty to the maximum, because it enables tribunals to ensure that restricted patients compulsorily detained in hospital represent the hard core of those who suffer from mental illness, are a risk to themselves or others and cannot be effectively treated and supervised otherwise than in hospital. If there is any possibility of treating and supervising a patient in the community, the imposition of conditions permits that possibility to be explored and, it may be, tried."

A tribunal has power to direct a patient's conditional discharge even if the patient does not suffer from a mental disorder: see the note on "restricted patient" under subs.(1). The direction can be deferred under subs.(7).

In *R. (on the application of H) v Secretary of State for the Home Department* [2002] EWCA Civ 646; [2002] M.H.L.R. 87, para.98, the Court of Appeal summarised the position where a tribunal considers a conditional discharge:

1. The tribunal can, at the outset, adjourn the hearing to investigate the possibility of imposing conditions. [In *DC v Nottinghamshire Healthcare NHS Trust* [2012] UKUT 92 (AAC); [2012] M.H.L.R. 238, para.19, UT Judge Jacobs said that this must mean that the tribunal can adjourn at any time before it is under a duty to direct a discharge.]

2. The tribunal can make a provisional decision to make a conditional discharge on specified conditions, including submitting to psychiatric supervision, but defer directing a conditional discharge while the authorities responsible for after-care under s.117 make the necessary arrangements to enable the patient to meet those conditions.

3. The tribunal should meet after an appropriate interval to monitor progress in making these arrangements if they have not been put in place.

4. Once the arrangements have been made, the tribunal can direct a conditional discharge without holding a further hearing.

5. If problems arise with making arrangements to meet the conditions, the tribunal has a number of options, depending on the circumstances.

   (a) It can defer for a further period, perhaps with suggestions as to how any problems can be overcome.
   (b) It can amend or vary the proposed conditions to seek to overcome the difficulties that have been encountered.
   (c) It can order a conditional discharge without specific conditions, thereby making the patient subject to recall.
   (d) It can decide that the patient must remain detained in hospital for treatment.

6. It will not normally be appropriate for a tribunal to direct a conditional discharge on conditions with which the patient will be unable to comply because it has not proved possible to make the necessary arrangements.

The court identified a "categorical difference" between the case of a patient who had been found by the tribunal not to be mentally disordered and who did not therefore satisfy the criteria identified in *Winterwerp v Netherlands* (1979) 2 E.H.R.R. 387, and the case of a patient who did satisfy the *Winterwerp* criteria and the tribunal considered that he could be satisfactorily treated and supervised in the community. [The *Winterwerp* case determined that detention on the ground of mental disorder is only lawful under art.5 of the ECHR if (1) there is objective medical evidence that the patient suffers from mental disorder; (2) the mental disorder is of a kind or degree warranting compulsory confinement; and (3) the mental disorder persists.] In the former case, if the conditions of discharge were not met the alternative was not continued detention but discharge, either absolutely or subject only to a condition of recall. In this situation the conditional discharge must not be deferred beyond a reasonable limited period if a violation of art.5(4) is to be avoided. In the latter case, if the tribunal's conditions proved impossible to meet the alternative was continued detention.

The implications of this aspect of the decision in *H* were explained by Mance L.J. in *W v Doncaster MBC* [2004] EWCA Civ 378; [2004] M.H.L.R. 201 at paras 72, 73:

"The central question is whether the *Winterwerp* criteria for detention are satisfied. If a person is no longer suffering from any mental illness, these criteria are clearly not met. If someone is still suffering from mental illness, they may or may not be met. It may still be possible to release the person in question into the community, either unconditionally or in the expectation that he or she will receive treatment there under appropriate conditions. In the latter case, there are two alterative possibilities. Upon true analysis, the provision of the expected treatment either may or may not be regarded by the tribunal as an essential pre-requisite of discharge from detention: contrast paragraphs 91 and 96 of the Master of the Rolls judgment in [the Court of Appeal], quoted with approval in the House of Lords at . . . paragraphs 24 and 28.

If such treatment is an essential pre-requisite of discharge (as it was in *H*), but it proves impossible to provide, then continuing detention is lawful, although the impossibility of providing the treatment envisaged by the tribunal means that the matter will have to return to the tribunal for reconsideration: [2003] UKHL 59, paragraph 27. If such treatment is not an essential pre-requisite to discharge, then, although discharge may be delayed for a period while efforts are made to arrange the expected treatment, discharge cannot be unreasonably delayed, even if it proves impossible to arrange it: see *Johnson v United Kingdom* (1997) 27 E.H.R.R. 296)."

In *Kolanis v United Kingdom* (2006) 42 E.H.R.R. 12; [2005] M.H.L.R. 238, the court observed, at paras 68–70, that in *Johnson* the tribunal had found that the applicant was no longer suffering from a mental disorder, no longer had the symptoms and did not require any further medication or treatment. In the case before the court the applicant continued to suffer from mental illness and continued to require treatment and medical supervision in order to control her illness. The court was therefore unable to accept the applicant's contention that the tribunal's decision that she could be discharged subject to conditions was tantamount to a finding that the second criterion in *Winterwerp* was no longer fulfilled, i.e. that her disorder was not of a kind or degree requiring compulsory confinement. The discharge of the applicant had only been regarded as appropriate if the continued treatment or supervision necessary to protect her own health and the safety of the community was available. In the absence of that treatment, her detention continued to be necessary in line with the purposes of art.5(1)(e).

The decision of the Court of Appeal in *H*, above, that a Health Authority was not under an absolute obligation to procure compliance with the tribunal's conditions was affirmed by the House of Lords ([2003] UKHL 59; [2004] 1 All E.R. 413) where it was held that the obligation is for the authority to use its best endeavours to secure compliance. The tribunal has "no power to require any psychiatrist to act in a way which conflicted with the conscientious professional judgment of that psychiatrist" (per Lord Bingham at para.29; also see *R. v Camden and Islington Health Authority Ex p. K* [2001] EWCA Civ 240 CA, noted in the General Note to s.117). The House of Lords found it unnecessary to determine whether in this context psychiatrists were or could be a hybrid public authority within the meaning of s.6 of the Human Rights Act 1998. If such a finding were made it would have the effect of requiring a psychiatrist to supervise a patient who had been conditionally discharged by a tribunal even though the psychiatrist was professionally opposed to conditions attached to the discharge. It is unlikely that the courts would countenance such an outcome.

A conditionally discharged patient can apply to a tribunal for his absolute discharge under s.75.

PARAGRAPH (B) OF THAT SUBSECTION DOES NOT APPLY. In *R. v Mental Health Review Tribunal Ex p. Cooper*, unreported, February 14, 1990, Rose J. held that the tribunal could direct a conditional discharge, rather than an absolute discharge, solely for therapeutic reasons and that it was not the case that the maintenance of liability to recall under para.(b) of subs.(1) of this section can only be proper if the applicant poses some danger to others.

CONDITIONAL DISCHARGE. For the nature of the conditions that can be imposed, see subs.(4). A conditional discharge can be deferred under subs.(7).

Subsection (4)

Paragraph (a)

1–938 MAY BE RECALLED. And have his case referred to a tribunal under s.75(1)(a). Only the Secretary of State can recall the patient to hospital: see the note on s.42(3).

Paragraph (b)

1–939 CONDITIONS. An after-care body is not placed under an absolute obligation to satisfy the conditions imposed by the tribunal: see the note on subs.(2).

In *Secretary of State for Justice v MP* [2013] UKUT 025 (AAC), UT Judge Jacobs said at para.20:

> "It is permissible to direct a conditional discharge without imposing any further conditions, as envisaged by section 73(4)(b). A tribunal is under a duty to explain its decision, including a decision not to impose further conditions. In some cases, the circumstances alone may be sufficient to show why the tribunal did not impose conditions. This is not such a case. The tribunal found that Mr P had a drug-induced psychosis and that he had continued to use drugs. Indeed, he said that he would do if he were discharged. The tribunal found that that involved a risk of self-neglect. In those circumstances, the tribunal was under a duty to explain why it did not impose conditions."

This section does not empower the attachment of any sanction for failure to comply with a condition, but provides for a general power of recall which, except in an emergency situation, cannot be exercised without up to date medical evidence being obtained by the Secretary of State: see the notes to s.42(3).

In *Re T (A child: murdered parent)* [2011] EWHC B4 (Fam); [2011] M.H.L.R. 133, it was held that the family court (i) does not have the power to vary or discharge the conditions imposed by the tribunal, (ii) is not constrained by the conditions imposed by the tribunal, and (iii) can make orders under its jurisdiction that have the effect of supplementing the protection provided to victims by the tribunal's conditions. Judge Bellamy, sitting as a Judge of the High Court, said at para.76:

> "The problem of conflict between an order of this court and conditions imposed by the Tribunal does not arise [in this case]. The question of the approach to be taken where there may be such a conflict is, therefore, academic. That said, it seems to me that in any case in which the court is seriously considering making an order which, if complied with, would cause a patient to be in breach of conditions imposed by a Tribunal, the appropriate course would be for the court to invite the Secretary of State to set out his position to the court and, in particular, to indicate whether and if so to what extent he is prepared to vary the conditions imposed by the Tribunal in order to enable the court's order to take effect without risk of the patient being in breach of the conditions."

In *Secretary of State for Justice v RB* [2011] EWCA Civ 1608; [2012] M.H.L.R. 131, the Court of Appeal held that a tribunal could not order the conditional discharge of a patient on terms that would inevitably involve a deprivation of the patient's liberty, albeit outside hospital. The court said that this would be the case even if a mentally incapacitated patient was content with the terms of the discharge. In *Secretary of State for Justice v KC* [2015] UKUT 376 (AAC), Charles J. said at para.19 that the ratio of the RB case is that it:

"(1) prevents the First-tier Tribunal (FTT) (or the Secretary of State) from imposing or requiring conditions which when implemented would result in a deprivation of liberty that would be in breach of Article 5 and so be unlawful,

but it does not prevent

(2) the FTT (or the Secretary of State) from imposing (and so directing a conditional discharge on) conditions that when implemented will, on an objective assessment, give rise to a deprivation of liberty that is lawful because it has been authorised by the Court of Protection under the Mental Capacity Act (MCA) or pursuant to the DOLS contained in the MCA and so complies with Article 5".

Having undertaken an extensive review of the case law on this issue, his Lordship summarised his conclusions with regard to mentally incapacitated patients at para.141:

"(2) The FTT has power to impose (and so direct a conditional discharge on) conditions that when implemented will, on an objective assessment, give rise to a deprivation of liberty that is lawful because it has been authorised by the Court of Protection under the MCA or pursuant to the DOLS contained in the MCA (the MCA authorisations) and so complies with Article 5.

(3) The FTT should consider and generally should include in the protective conditions it imposes an ability to apply to it for a variation or discharge of them on the basis of a material change in circumstances (a) if a variation or discharge is refused by the Secretary of State or the FTT agrees to consider the application, and (b) if the FIT is invited to consider such an application by the Court of Protection (or a DOLS decision maker).

(4) The MCA authorisations can only be given if the relevant restricted patient lacks capacity to consent to the relevant conditions and is not ineligible to be deprived of his or her liberty by the MCA. Provided that the terms and conditions that give rise to the deprivation of liberty do not conflict with conditions the FTT have decided are necessary and have identified the restricted patient will not be ineligible and such authorisations can be given under the MCA applying the tests it sets out.

(5) Both of the MCA authorisations can be given to come into effect at a future date or on a future event but the MCA decision maker needs to know the conditions (including those that when implemented will objectively give rise to a deprivation of liberty) that the FTT considers necessary to satisfy the tests under the Mental Health Act (MHA), before the MCA decision maker can properly make the relevant MCA decision.

(6) So, the FTT needs to identify what conditions it considers need to be in place as and when the direction for the conditional discharge of the restricted patient takes effect so that the MCA decision maker knows what they are when applying the MCA tests.

(7) The FTT will need to be satisfied that the proposed placement on the relevant conditions (and so the relevant care plan) is sufficiently defined and an available option in practice and if it is not when it will be so available (see *KO v A Borough Council* [2015] UKUT 251 (AAC) at para.68).

(8) The parties will therefore need to provide the necessary evidence on this and any other factors that will need to be taken into account by the FTT.

(9) The FTT should apply the guidance given by Upper Tribunal Judge Jacobs in *DC v Nottinghamshire Healthcare NHS Trust and the Secretary of State for Justice* [2012]

UKUT 92 (AAC) on when the FTT should adjourn, make a decision under s. 73(7) of the MHA or a provisional decision in reliance on *R(H) v SSHD* [2003] QB 320 and [2004] 2 AC 253).

(10) The Court of Protection and the DOLS decision makers cannot override the conditions identified by the FTT and so can only choose between alternatives that include them."

Charles J. said at para.132 that he disagreed with the opinion expressed in RB regarding patients with capacity; an opinion which he considered was expressed obiter (para.46). In his Lordship's obiter opinion, "if real consent is given to the relevant protective conditions there will be no deprivation of liberty under or in breach of Article 5".

In *Secretary of State for Justice v SB* [2013] UKUT 320 (AAC); [2014] M.H.L.R. 46, para.29, UT Judge Levenson held that the cumulative effect of the conditions of discharge imposed by the tribunal, which were imposed largely to protect the public, "would amount to detention and to an unlawful deprivation of liberty such that it could hardly be characterised as a discharge at all". The meaning of a deprivation of liberty is considered in Part 6.

When imposing conditions the tribunal may have regard not only to considerations relating to treatment itself, but also to the question of risk, both to the patient and to the public. The proportionate response to the risk posed by the patient may be achieved by the imposition of suitable conditions on a conditional discharge rather than by continuing the patient's detention (*R. (on the application of the Secretary of State for the Home Department) v Mental Health Review Tribunal* [2002] EWHC 1128 (Admin); [2002] M.H.L.R. 241, at paras 26 and 27). A tribunal has a duty to impose such conditions of discharge of a restricted patient as it considers necessary, even if was in no position to enforce those conditions and it was apparent that it would be difficult to put in place arrangements to enable the conditions to be satisfied (*R. v Mental Health Review Tribunal, Ex p. Hall* [2000] 1 W.L.R. 1323 CA). However, only reasonable conditions can be imposed and a condition that the tribunal positively knows will be impossible or highly unlikely to be put into effect is not reasonable. If necessary, the tribunal should use its power of adjournment to ascertain whether conditions which appear attractive are achievable (*R. (on the application of H) v Secretary of State for the Home Department* [2002] EWCA Civ 646; [2002] M.H.L.R. 87). The tribunal should give reasons for its decision to impose conditions. It would be helpful in a situation where the patient continues to suffer from an underlying mental illness which can only be managed in the community provided the conditions imposed are implemented if the tribunal says so when it orders the patient's conditional discharge (*W v Doncaster MBC* [2004] EWCA Civ 378; [2004] M.H.L.R. 201).

In *R (on the application of SH) v Mental Health Review Tribunal* [2007] EWHC 884 (Admin); [2007] M.H.L.R. 234 paras 18–20, Holman J. said that a condition: (a) could not lawfully be capricious; (b) must be relevant and for a proper purpose within the scope of the Act; and (c) is subject to the principle of legality as described by Lord Hoffmann in *R. v Secretary of State for the Home Department, Ex p. Simms* [2000] 2 A.C. 115, i.e. the courts presume that even the most general words were intended to be subject to the basic rights of the individual.

The tribunal cannot lawfully impose a condition which effectively makes the conditional discharge subject to the agreement of some other body, such as the Ministry of Justice, as such a requirement is not a condition of discharge, but a pre-condition to discharge (*R (on the application of Secretary of State for the Home Department) v Mental Health Review Tribunal* [2007] EWHC 2224 (Admin); [2008] M.H.L.R. 212).

Although a condition may require that the patient attends for treatment, treatment cannot be forced upon him in the absence of his consent because conditionally discharged patients are not subject to the consent to treatment provisions contained in Pt IV (s.56(3)(c)). In *R. (on the application of SH) v Mental Health Review Tribunal,* above, Holman J. held that:

(i) a condition that the patient "shall comply" with medication prescribed by his responsible [clinician] was lawfully imposed as it did not interfere with the patient's absolute right to choose whether to accept treatment, nor did it interfere with his rights under art.8(1) the ECHR;

(ii) the condition must be read as respecting and being subject to the patient's own final choice, which must be his real or true choice; and

(iii) a tribunal should not impose such a condition unless it has a proper basis for anticipating that the patient does and will consent to the treatment in question.

His Lordship said, at para.42, that it would be preferable for a tribunal, when imposing a similar condition to add words such as the following: "subject always to his right to give or withhold consent to treatment on any given occasion".

The usual conditions relate to supervision, residence and medical treatment; see further, the notes on s.42(2) under the heading "Subject to conditions". In his "Review of Homicides by Patients with Severe Mental Illness" (March 2006), Professor Tony Maden made the following recommendation at p.63: "In patients subject to a restriction order there should always be consideration of setting conditions relating to abstinence from drugs or alcohol and the standard procedure should be immediate recall if that condition is breached".

After a conditional discharge the patient's progress in the community will be monitored **1–940** by the Ministry of Justice in the same way as that of a patient conditionally discharged by the Secretary of State, and the Secretary of State may vary conditions imposed by the tribunal (subs.(5)).

IF ANY. The tribunal is not obliged to impose conditions on a conditionally discharged patient. In practice, it is unlikely that a patient will be conditionally discharged without conditions being imposed either by the tribunal or the Secretary of State.

SECRETARY OF STATE. Functions under this provision have not been transferred to Welsh Ministers (see the General Note to the Act and SI 1999/672 art.2, Sch.1). The Secretary of State can impose conditions even though the tribunal has not.

Subsection (7)

A TRIBUNAL MAY DEFER. A deferred discharge is a mechanism that postpones the **1–941** coming into effect of a direction ordering the patient's conditional discharge until the tribunal is satisfied that suitable arrangements have been put in place to enable the conditions to be met. There is no power in the tribunal to defer an absolute discharge (*R. (on the application of the Secretary of State for the Home Department) v Mental Health Review Tribunal* [2004] EWHC 1029 (Admin)). The deferment cannot be to a fixed date (*Secretary of State for the Home Department v Oxford Regional Mental Health Review Tribunal* [1987] 3 All E.R. 8, at 13).

UT Judge Jacobs examined the operation of this provision in *DC v Nottinghamshire Healthcare NHS Trust* [2012] UKUT 92 (AAC); [2012] M.H.L.R. 238, at paras 25 and 26:

"The language of section 73(7) is important. The tribunal does not defer the patient's conditional discharge. It defers the direction for the discharge. That is what section 73(7) says and it is significant. That presupposes that there is a direction to discharge ready to take effect. Until there is, there is nothing to defer. That means that the conditions for discharge must be identified and included in the direction. The deferral allows time for the necessary arrangements to be made. That means the arrangements necessary for the conditional discharge. And it is impossible to make those arrangements without knowing what the conditions for the discharge are. Section 73(7), by its terms, operates until the tribunal is satisfied that the arrangements are in place. Once it is, there is nothing left for the tribunal to do except to lift the deferral.

In summary, the tribunal cannot exercise the power in section 73(7) unless it finds that the patient should not be detained but should be subject to recall and it formulates a direction, including conditions for discharge, that can take effect if the necessary arrangements can be made. Until then, it is free to adjourn."

Judge Jacobs considered when this provision may not be used at para.28:

"The tribunal may not bypass the detention and discharge conditions and use section 73(7) as (i) a device for gathering information that it needs. Nor may it bypass difficulties in formulating conditions for discharge and use section 73(7) to gather the information it needs to decide (ii) whether a conditional discharge would be possible or (iii) what conditions might be appropriate. The proper approach in all three circumstances is to adjourn for the information to be obtained. It is only permissible to use section 73 when (a) it is able to find, on the balance of probabilities, that the patient should not be detained but should be subject to recall, and (b) it has drafted the conditions for the discharge."

It is unlawful for a tribunal to make a "wait and see" decision to defer discharge for the purpose of seeing whether any change in the patient's circumstances might arise and thus provide material which will point to the correct decision in the application: see *R. (on the application of the Secretary of State for the Home Department) v Mental Health Review Tribunal* [2002] EWHC Admin 2043; [2002] M.H.L.R. 381, where the tribunal used its power under this provision to await the results of a therapeutic assessment of the patient. It is also unlawful for a tribunal to defer a discharge until arrangements are made to secure the patient's admission to another hospital (*Secretary of State for the Home Department v Mental Health Review Tribunal for the Mersey Regional Health Authority* [1986] 3 All E.R. 233).

In *R. (on the application of H) v Secretary of State for the Home Department* [2002] EWCA Civ 646; [2002] M.H.L.R. 87, the Court of Appeal considered the problem that can develop where a tribunal determines that a restricted patient is entitled to release on condition that he receives psychiatric supervision, but no psychiatrist can be found who is prepared to provide that supervision. In *Secretary of State for the Home Department v Oxford Regional Mental Health Review Tribunal*, above, the House of Lords had held that in this situation a tribunal cannot subsequently reconvene to reconsider its original decision that the patient be discharged. The Court of Appeal held that:

1. The decision of the House of Lords could lead to the patient finding himself "in limbo" should it prove impossible to make the necessary arrangements for him to comply with the proposed condition.

2. The period spent "in limbo" may last too long to be compatible with art.5(4) of the ECHR and may result in the patient being detained in violation of art.5(1) of the Convention: see *Johnson v United Kingdom*, noted, above.

3. Tribunals should no longer proceed on the basis that they cannot reconsider a decision to direct a conditional discharge on specified conditions where, after deferral and before directing discharge, there is a material change of circumstances. Such a change may be demonstrated by fresh material placed before or obtained by a tribunal. Such material may, for instance, show that the patient's condition has relapsed. It may show that the patient's condition has improved. It may demonstrate that it is not possible to put in place arrangements necessary to enable the conditions that the tribunal proposed to impose on the patient to be satisfied. The original decision should be treated as a provisional decision, and the tribunal should monitor progress towards implementing it so as to ensure that the patient is not left "in limbo" for an unreasonable length of time.

4. Accordingly, where a tribunal decides (i) that a restricted patient is suffering from mental disorder for which psychiatric treatment is necessary for the health or safety of the patient or for the protection of other persons and (ii) that detention in hospital is not necessary if, but only if, psychiatric treatment is provided in the community, the tribunal can properly make a provisional decision to direct a conditional discharge, but defer giving that direction to enable arrangements to be made for providing psychiatric treatment in the community. The Health Authority subject to the s.117 duty will then be bound to use its best endeavours to put in place the necessary aftercare. If it fails to use its best endeavours it will be subject to judicial review. If, despite its best endeavours, the Health Authority is unable to provide the necessary services, the tribunal must think again (see the note on this case under subs.(2)). If, as is likely in those circumstances, it concludes that it is necessary for the patient to remain detained in hospital in order to receive the treatment, it should record that decision.

The decision of the Court of Appeal was affirmed by the House of Lords in *R. (on the application of H) v Secretary of State for the Home Department* [2003] UKHL 59; [2004] 1 All E.R. 412 where their Lordships overruled *Secretary of State for the Home Department v Oxford Regional Mental Health Review Tribunal*.

If a change in the patient's circumstances or the availability of additional material relating to the patient is brought to the Secretary of State's attention after deferral but before discharge has been directed, he should utilise the procedure set out in *H* by inviting the tribunal to reconsider its decision. He should not make a referral to a fresh tribunal using his power under s.71(1) (*R. (on the application of C) v Secretary of State for the Home Department* [2002] EWCA Civ 647; [2002] M.H.L.R. 105). If the tribunal departs from its original reasoning, it must identify a material change in circumstances which may be demonstrated by fresh material placed before or obtained by the tribunal (*LC v DHIC (CHL)* [2010] UKUT 319 (AAC)).

When a deferred conditional discharge has been granted by a tribunal, leave of absence, with the consent of the Secretary of State (see s.41(3)(c)), is the normal method designed by the Act to facilitate the patient's discharge from hospital by, for example, providing for overnight stays in a hostel. The Secretary of State should only use his power under s.42(2) to grant such a patient a conditional discharge if there is some development that the tribunal is unable to deal with: see *R. (on the application of RA) v Secretary of State for the Home Department* [2002] EWHC Admin 1618; [2003] M.H.L.R. 54 where Crane J. held that an extra-statutory recommendation made by a tribunal has legal force where it is linked to the satisfaction of conditions imposed by a tribunal as part of a deferred conditional discharge: see further the General Note, above.

A deferment should not result in the patient's discharge being unreasonably delayed: see the decision of the European Court of Human Rights in *Johnson v United Kingdom* (1997) 27 E.H.R.R. 296. Subsequent to this decision the Department of Health wrote to health and social services authorities asking the authorities "to give priority to ensuring that all cases of deferred conditional discharge are implemented within six months of the [tribunal's] decision".

In *Kolanis v United Kingdom* (1987) 27 E.H.R.R. 296, the court, at para.80, confirmed that where a tribunal finds that a patient may be conditionally discharged,

"new issues of lawfulness may arise where the detention nonetheless continues due, for example, to difficulties in fulfilling the conditions. It follows that such patients are entitled under Art.5(4) to have the lawfulness of that continued detention determined by a court with requisite promptness".

However, where the treatment considered to be necessary as a condition of discharge was not available, there could be no question of interpreting art.5(1)(e) as requiring discharge without the stipulated conditions for the protection of the applicant and the public being fulfilled, or as imposing an absolute obligation on the authorities to ensure that those conditions were fulfilled (para.71).

It is desirable for there to be, as far as practicable, a continuation of the membership of a tribunal which is to monitor and continue to consider a deferred conditional discharge: see *R. (on the application of A) v Secretary of State for the Home Department and the Mental Health Review Tribunal* [2003] EWHC 270 (Admin); [2005] M.H.L.R. 144, where Stanley Burnton J. said at para.16:

> "Where a relatively short time has passed between the original decision and its reconsideration, the advantages and the fairness involved in requiring the original constitution to reconsider the matter must be greater than when a considerable time has passed."

HAVE BEEN MADE TO THEIR SATISFACTION. The wording of this provision clearly implies that the tribunal is required to formally indicate whether the arrangements that have been put in place to enable the patient to be discharged are satisfactory.

THE PREVIOUS APPLICATION OR REFERENCE. The patient cannot be discharged on the basis of the earlier deferred direction: the matter must be considered afresh.

Subsection (8)

1–942   SECTION 42. Which, inter alia, empowers the Secretary of State to discharge the patient from hospital either absolutely or subject to conditions.

Restricted patients subject to restriction directions

1–943   **74.**—(1) Where an application to [the appropriate tribunal] is made by a restricted patient who is subject to [a limitation direction or] a restriction direction, or where the case of such a patient is referred to [the appropriate tribunal], the Tribunal—

(a) shall notify the Secretary of State whether, in [its] opinion, the patient would, if subject to a restriction order, be entitled to be absolutely or conditionally discharged under section 73 above; and

(b) if [the tribunal notifies] him that the patient would be entitled to be conditionally discharged, may recommend that in the event of his not being discharged under this section he should continue to be detained in hospital.

(2) If in the case of a patient not falling within subsection (4) below—

(a) the Tribunal [notifies] the Secretary of State that the patient would be entitled to be absolutely or conditionally discharged; and

(b) within the period of 90 days beginning with the date of that notification the Secretary of State gives notice to the Tribunal that the patient may be so discharged,

the Tribunal shall direct the absolute or, as the case may be, the conditional discharge of the patient.

(3) Where a patient continues to be liable to be detained in a hospital at the end of the period referred to in subsection (2)(b) above because the Secretary of State has not given the notice there mentioned, the managers of the hospital shall, unless [the tribunal has] made a recommendation under subsection (1)(b) above, transfer the patient to a prison or other institution in which he might have been detained if he had not been removed to hospital, there to be dealt with as if he had not been so removed.

(4) If, in the case of a patient who is subject to a transfer direction under section 48 above, the Tribunal [notifies] the Secretary of State that the patient would be

entitled to be absolutely or conditionally discharged, the Secretary of State shall, unless [the tribunal has] made a recommendation under subsection (1)(b) above, by warrant direct that the patient be remitted to a prison or other institution in which he might have been detained if he had not been removed to hospital, there to be dealt with as if he had not been so removed.

(5) Where a patient is transferred or remitted under subsection (3) or (4) above [the relevant hospital direction and the limitation direction or, as the case may be,] the relevant transfer direction and the restriction direction shall cease to have effect on his arrival in the prison or other institution.

[(5A) Where [the tribunal has] made a recommendation under subsection (1)(b) above in the case of a patient who is subject to a restriction direction or a limitation direction—

(a) the fact that the restriction direction or limitation direction remains in force does not prevent the making of any application or reference to the Parole Board by or in respect of him or the exercise by him of any power to require the Secretary of State to refer his case to the Parole Board, and

(b) if the Parole Board make a direction or recommendation by virtue of which the patient would become entitled to be released (whether unconditionally or on licence) from any prison or other institution in which he might have been detained if he had not been removed to hospital, the restriction direction or limitation direction shall cease to have effect at the time when he would become entitled to be so released.]

(6) Subsections (3) to (8) of section 73 above shall have effect in relation to this section as they have effect in relation to that section, taking references to the relevant hospital order and the restriction order as references to [the hospital direction and the limitation direction or, as the case may be, to] the transfer direction and the restriction direction.

(7) This section is without prejudice to subsections 50 to 53 above in their application to patients who are not discharged under this section.

AMENDMENTS

The amendments to this section were made by the Crime (Sentences) Act 1997 s.55, Sch.4 para.12, the Criminal Justice Act 2003 s.295 and SI 2008/2883 art.9, Sch.3 para.55.

DEFINITIONS

the appropriate tribunal: ss.66(4), 145(1).　　　　　　　　　　　　　　**1–944**
restricted patient: s.79(1).
restriction direction: ss.49, 145(1).
restriction order: ss.41, 145(1).
hospital: ss.34(2), 79(6), 145(1).
hospital direction: s.145(1).
limitation direction: s.145(1).
the managers: s.145(1).
relevant hospital direction: s.79(2)–(5).
relevant hospital order: s.79(2)–(5).
relevant transfer direction: s.79(2)–(5).
transfer direction: ss.47, 145(1).

GENERAL NOTE

This section, which should be read with s.50, provides for the procedure to be adopted on **1–945** an application to a tribunal by a patient who has been transferred from prison to hospital under either s.47 or 48, subject to the special restrictions set out in s.49, or has been made the subject of hospital and limitation directions under s.45A. It also applies to references to tribunals made in respect of such patients by the Secretary of State. A patient who has been transferred subject to a restriction direction ceases to be subject to restrictions on reaching his release date had he remained in prison (s.50(2)(3)).

The reason for the distinction between the regimes for discharge set out in s.73 and in this section was explained by Irwin J. in *R. (on the application of LV) v Secretary of State for Justice* [2014] EWHC 1495 (Admin) at para.48:

"In making a hospital order and a restriction order the judge in the crown court is conducting the definitive sentencing exercise in the case. Whereas, the prisoner who is transferred to hospital and made subject of a restriction direction may very likely be suffering from a mental disorder which arose after his sentence began. The statutory provisions preserve the capacity of such a prisoner to apply to the Parole Board irrespective of – indeed as if there had never been – a transfer direction and a restriction direction. The considerations which arise for the Parole Board are different and additional to those which arise for the Tribunal, either in respect of a patient subject to a hospital order and a restriction order, or in respect of a patient subject to a transfer direction and a restriction direction."

The Reference Guide describes the effect of this section:

"6.89 As with other restricted patients, the Tribunal has no general discretion to discharge patients subject to hospital and limitation directions or restricted transfer directions.

6.90 In addition, because these patients are liable to resume serving their sentence of imprisonment, or its equivalent, if they no longer require treatment in hospital, special arrangements apply where the Tribunal believes that the criteria for discharge from detention are met.

6.91 The criteria for the discharge of patients subject to these directions are the same as those for patients subject to restricted hospital orders – see paragraphs 6.81 and 6.82.

6.92 Where the Tribunal decides that such a patient would be entitled to be discharged absolutely or conditionally if the patient were subject to a restriction order . . . it must inform the Secretary of State for Justice.

6.93 If the patient would be entitled to conditional discharge, the Tribunal may recommend that the patient continue to be detained in hospital, rather than going to prison or other custodial institution, if the patient is not, in fact, discharged.

6.94 In the case of patients who are remand prisoners or other unsentenced prisoners subject to restricted transfer directions under section 48, the Secretary of State has no discretion. If the Tribunal has decided that such a patient would be entitled to be conditionally discharged and has made a recommendation for the patient's continued detention in hospital, the patient remains detained and subject to the restriction direction or limitation direction. Otherwise, the Secretary of State must issue a warrant directing the person's return to prison, or any other place of detention in which the patient could have been detained but for being in hospital.

6.95 In the case of a sentenced prisoner subject to hospital and limitation directions or a restricted transfer direction under section 47, the Secretary of State has the discretion to agree to the patient's discharge.

6.96 In these cases, the Secretary of State has 90 days from being informed of the Tribunal's findings in which to give notice that the patient may be discharged. If the Secretary of State does not do so, the patient must be returned to prison, or its equivalent, unless the Tribunal has recommended that the patient remain in hospital if not conditionally discharged.

6.97 Where sentenced prisoners subject to hospital and limitation directions or transfer directions remain in hospital only as a result of a recommendation by the Tribunal, they have the right to apply to the Parole Board for release once they have served the minimum period set by the court (the 'tariff' period) in the same way as other prisoners. If that point has already been reached when the Tribunal recommendation is first acted on, the Secretary of State will refer their case automatically to the Parole Board."

In *R. (on the application of Abu-Rideh) v Mental Health Review Tribunal* [2004] EWHC 1999 (Admin); [2004] M.H.L.R. 308 at paras 19–22, Gage J. adopted the following summary, drafted by counsel, of the effect of this section in the case of a patient subject to a direction made under s.48 and a restriction direction made under s.49 who appears before a tribunal:

1. The tribunal must, if not satisfied *either* that the patient is suffering from a mental disorder of a nature or degree which makes it appropriate for him to be liable to be detained in a hospital for medical treatment *or* that it is necessary for the health and safety of the patient or the protection of others that he continue to receive medical treatment in hospital, make a recommendation for discharge under s.74(1)(a).

2. If the tribunal is satisfied that it is not appropriate for the patient to remain liable to be recalled to hospital, they must recommend the patient's absolute discharge; if they are not so satisfied, they must recommend the patient's conditional discharge (s.73(1)(b) and 73(2)).

3. If the tribunal recommends the patient's conditional discharge then it may also make a recommendation under s.74(1)(b) that, in the event of his not being discharged under s.74, the patient should continue to be detained in hospital. If the Secretary of State accepts the recommendation the patient remains in hospital notwithstanding he no longer satisfies the criteria for detention under the Act (or under art.5(1)(e) [of the European Convention on Human Rights]).

4. By virtue of s.74(4) a patient subject to a transfer direction under s.48 *cannot* be discharged by the Secretary of State under s.74 either absolutely or conditionally. His discharge powers under s.74(2) only apply to serving prisoners transferred under s.47. The patient will automatically be remitted back to the place of his former detention if the recommendation is for absolute discharge *or* if a recommendation for conditional discharge has been made without a recommendation under s.74(1)(b). If a recommendation has been made under s.74(1)(b) the patient is not automatically remitted back to their place of detention and he will remain detained until remitted back to prison by the Secretary of State under s.53, discharged by the Secretary of State under s.42(2) or the justification for his underlying detention expires.

In *AC v Partnerships in Care Ltd and Secretary of State for Justice* [2012] UKUT 450 (AAC); [2013] M.H.L.R., UT Judge Jacobs said at para.16:

"The tribunal in this case decided that 'conditional discharge would envisage the discharge being subject only to such conditions as the tribunal could properly impose under s.73(4).' That is precisely correct. The tribunal's jurisdiction is limited to issues of discharge. It has no power to impose conditions as to release, which is the exclusive preserve of the Parole Board. The tribunal was right to refuse to take account of the conditions that might be imposed by the Parole Board."

The policy of the Secretary of State on receiving a notification under paras (a) and (b) of subs.(1) is set out in the note on s.50(1)(b).

Subsection (1)

1–946 PATIENT.   See the note on "any such patient" in s.73(2).

SECRETARY OF STATE.   Functions under this provision have not been transferred to Welsh Ministers (see the General Note to the Act and SI 1999/672 art.2, Sch.1).

DISCHARGE.   In the context of para.(a) this term means only discharge from hospital; it does not exclude consideration of discharge back to prison (*R. (on the application of Abu-Rideh) v Mental Health Review Tribunal*, above).

Subsection (2)

1–947 In *R. v Vowles* [2015] EWCA Crim 45, Lord Thomas CJ, who gave the judgment of the Court, said that this "sub-section imposed on the Secretary of State an obligation to notify the FTT within 90 days of his decision in relation to [the patient's] discharge. It was the policy of the Secretary of State set out in Chapter 10 of the MHCS Casework Manual never to agree to a conditional discharge in such cases. The case therefore had to be referred to the Parole Board".

BEGINNING WITH.   Including the date of the notification (*Zoan v Rouamba* [2000] 2 All E.R. 620 CA).

CONDITIONAL DISCHARGE.   A patient who has been conditionally discharged under this provision is not subject to the consent to treatment provisions contained in Pt IV (s.56(3)(c)).

Subsection (5)

1–948 RELEVANT HOSPITAL DIRECTION ... RELEVANT TRANSFER DIRECTION.   See s.79(2).

Subsection (5A)

1–949 This subsection, which was inserted as a response to the decision of the European Court of Human Rights in *Benjamin and Wilson v United Kingdom* (2003) 36 E.H.R.R. 1, relates to transferred prisoners detained in hospital beyond their release date whose detention in hospital has been found by the tribunal to be no longer justified by their mental disorder, but who the tribunal has recommended should remain in hospital, rather than return to prison, in the event that the Secretary of State does not agree to discharge them from hospital. It provides that the fact that restrictions under the Act remain in force does not prevent an application or reference to the Parole Board for release. It further provides that if the Parole Board directs or recommends release, the restrictions cease to have effect at the time he is entitled to release. The effect of this is that the transferred prisoner is assured access to the Parole Board, and the possibility of release on licence, once he has reached his release date and the tribunal find he is no longer appropriately detained in hospital for medical treatment.

Subsection (6)

1–950 RELEVANT HOSPITAL ORDER.   See s.79(2).

Applications and references concerning conditionally discharged restricted patients

1–951 **75.**—(1) Where a restricted patient has been conditionally discharged under section 42(2), 73 or 74 above and is subsequently recalled to hospital—

 (a) the Secretary of State shall, within one month of the day on which the patient returns or is returned to hospital, refer his case to [the appropriate tribunal]; and

(b) section 70 above shall apply to the patient as if the relevant hospital order [, hospital direction] or transfer direction had been made on that day.

(2) Where a restricted patient has been conditionally discharged as aforesaid but has not been recalled to hospital he may apply to [the appropriate tribunal]—

(a) in the period between the expiration of 12 months and the expiration of two years beginning with the date on which he was conditionally discharged; and

(b) in any subsequent period of two years.

(3) Sections 73 and 74 above shall not apply to an application under subsection (2) above but on any such application the Tribunal may—

(a) vary any condition to which the patient is subject in connection with his discharge or impose any condition which might have been imposed in connection therewith; or

(b) direct that the restriction order [, limitation direction] or restriction direction to which he is subject shall cease to have effect;

and if the tribunal [gives] a direction under paragraph (b) above the patient shall cease to be liable to be detained by virtue of the relevant hospital order [, hospital direction] or transfer direction.

AMENDMENTS

The amendments to this section were made by the Crime (Sentences) Act 1997 s.55, Sch.4 para.12(13), the Mental Health Act 2007 s.41 and SI 2008/2883 art.9, Sch.3 para.56.

DEFINITIONS

restricted patient: s.79(1).   **1–952**
hospital: ss.34(2), 79(6), 145(1).
the appropriate tribunal: ss.66(4), 145(1).
limitation direction: s.145(1).
hospital direction: s.145(1).
the relevant hospital direction: s.79(2)–(5).
the relevant hospital order: s.79(2)–(5).
the relevant transfer direction: s.79(2)–(5).
restriction order: ss.41, 145(1).
restriction direction: ss.49, 145(1).
restricted patient: s.79(1).

GENERAL NOTE

This section directs the Secretary of State to refer the case of a conditionally discharged **1–953** restricted patient who has been recalled to hospital to a tribunal (subs.(1)). It also provides for a tribunal application to be made by a conditionally discharged restricted patient who has not been recalled to hospital (subs.(2)). On hearing such an application the tribunal has the power to vary the conditions of the discharge, to impose new conditions, or to direct that the restriction order, restriction direction or hospital direction shall cease to have effect (subs.(3)).

A restricted patient who is no longer suffering from a mental disorder remains a "patient" for the purposes of this section until discharged absolutely (*R. v Merseyside Mental Health Review Tribunal Ex p. K* [1990] 1 All E.R. 694 CA).

Human Rights Act 1998

In *Secretary of State for Justice v Rayner* [2008] EWCA Civ 176; [2008] M.H.L.R. 115, **1–954** the Court of Appeal held that this section was capable of satisfying the requirement of art.5(4) of the European Convention on Human Rights (ECHR) for the lawfulness of the patient's detention to be decided "speedily" if the Secretary of State referred the patient's case to the tribunal with reasonable dispatch, having regard to all the material circumstances. Keene L.J., who gave the only judgment of substance, said, at para.25, that one would normally expect a reference to be made within days, not weeks, of the return of the patient to hospital, and normally within a few days. The court also considered whether subs.(1)(b) of this section, which has the effect of enabling a recalled patient to make an application to a tribunal only after six months has elapsed since his return to hospital, violates the entitlement in art.5(4) for the patient to "take proceedings" to challenge the lawfulness of the detention. In concluding that it did not, Keene L.J. said at para.46:

"I conclude that while s.75 . . ., if it stood alone, might now not be regarded as sufficient to achieve the protection of Art.5(4) rights required by the ECHR and the Strasbourg jurisprudence, the combination of that statutory mechanism, the right of the patient to enforce the Secretary of State's statutory duty (as interpreted in the light of the Convention) by way of judicial review, and the right of the patient to challenge the lawfulness of his detention directly in the courts on its substantive merits by judicial review and/or *habeas corpus* does suffice to comply with Art.5(4). The patient has direct access as of right to the courts and can obtain swift redress if he is being unlawfully detained. I would only add that, as a matter of procedure, if judicial review has to be resorted to by a patient, he or she would normally find it quicker and more effective to apply for an order enforcing the Secretary of State's statutory duty rather than embark on a direct challenge in the courts to the lawfulness of the detention."

In *R. (on the application of SC) v Mental Health Review Tribunal and the Secretary of State for Health* [2005] EWHC 17 (Admin); [2005] M.H.L.R. 31, Munby J. held that subs.(3) is not incompatible with arts 6 and 8 of the ECHR as the relevant law is both sufficiently foreseeable and adequate to protect the patient from all risk of arbitrariness.

Subsection (1)

1–955   WITHIN ONE MONTH.   Disregarding the day of the patient's return to hospital (*Stewart v Chapman* [1951] 2 K.B. 792). The referral should normally be made within a few days of the patient's return to hospital (*Secretary of State for Justice v Rayner,* above). If the patient is already in the hospital as an informal patient when he is recalled, the one-month period runs from the date of the recall (*R (on the application of Rayner) v Secretary of State for the Home Department* [2007] EWHC 1028 (Admin); [2007] 1 W.L.R. 2239 para.7).

REFER HIS CASE TO THE APPROPRIATE TRIBUNAL.   The tribunal will exercise its powers under s.73. In *R. v Mental Health Review Tribunal for Merseyside Ex p. Kelly* [1998] 39 B.M.L.R. 114, Keene J. said that he could:

"see that in general terms the events leading up to a recall of a patient may not be relevant to the issues arising under s.72(1)(b)(i) and (ii) [see s.73(1)(a)] ... However, it is also true that such events prior to a patient's recall may be relevant. Diagnosis of and opinions as to such matters as are referred to in the relevant statutory paragraphs are not arrived at by ignoring events which have happened. The behaviour of the patient may well be material to such diagnosis and opinions. It will depend at least partly on how the expert witness or witnesses have arrived at their conclusions."

In this case, his Lordship declared that the decision of the tribunal was ultra vires in that it was contrary to the rules of natural justice because of a refusal by the tribunal to allow the cross-examination of the patient's responsible clinician on statements that he had made in his report to the tribunal concerning allegations that had been made about the patient's conduct prior to his recall to hospital.

Although the tribunal may consider events leading up to the recall, there is no jurisdiction to examine "the underlying circumstances of the mechanics of the recall and particularly the extent to which there had been discussion between [the patient's responsible clinician and the Mental Health Casework Section]" (*R. (on the application of Munday) v Secretary of State for the Home Department* [2009] EWHC 3638 (Admin), para.23, per Burnett J.).

Paragraph (b)
The effect of this provision is that a recalled patient may not make an application to a **1–956** tribunal until six months after his return to hospital.

Subsection (2)
CONDITIONALLY DISCHARGED.   A patient is conditionally discharged for the purposes of **1–957** calculating time under this provision, not on the date when the tribunal decided that he be discharged subject to conditions being met, but on the date when he actually leaves hospital once those conditions had been met: see *R. v Canons Park Mental Health Review Tribunal Ex p. Martins* (1995) 26 B.M.L.R. 134 where Ognall J. followed Mann J.'s finding in *Secretary of State for the Home Department v Mental Health Review Tribunal for the Mersey Regional Health Authority* [1986] 3 All E.R. 233 at 237 that:

"The word 'discharge' as employed in sections 72 to 75 of the Act of 1983 means, and in my judgment can only mean, release from hospital. The release may be absolute or it may be conditional."

NOT BEEN RECALLED TO HOSPITAL.   A conditionally discharged restricted patient who has been brought back to hospital under either s.2 or s.3 has not been "recalled to hospital" as such a recall can only be made by the Secretary of State under s.42(3).

MAY APPLY.   To the tribunal for the area in which he resides (s.77(4)).

BEGINNING WITH.   Including the date of his conditional discharge (*Zoan v Rouamba* [2000] 2 All E.R. 620 CA) which is day when he leaves hospital: see the note on "conditionally discharged" above.

Subsection (3)
Under this provision a tribunal is not "concerned so much with finding facts which are **1–958** capable of exact demonstration but rather with a process of judgment, evaluation and assessment which involves the appreciation and evaluation of inherently imprecise and often differing or conflicting psychiatric evidence" (*R. (on the application of DJ v Mental Health Review Tribunal* [2005] EWHC 587; [2005] M.H.L.R. 56, para.102, per Munby J.). These observations were followed by the Court of Appeal in *R. (on the application of N) v Mental Health Review Tribunal (Northern Region)* [2005] EWCA Civ 1605; [2006] 4 All E.R. 194, at para.98.
In *R. (on the application of SC) v Mental Health Review Tribunal and the Secretary of State for Health* [2005] EWHC 17 (Admin); [2005] M.H.L.R. 31 paras 56, 57, Munby J. said that a patient who makes an application under subs.(2) will have been convicted of an offence grave enough to merit a possible sentence of imprisonment, found to have been suffering from a mental disorder meriting detention in hospital for treatment, and to have presented a risk of re-offending such that a restriction order was necessary for the protection of the public from serious harm; and found by a tribunal to be someone who, although not requiring detention for treatment for the time being, nonetheless required to remain liable to recall. Accordingly, when exercising its powers under this provision, the tribunal:

"will need to consider such matters as the nature, gravity and circumstances of the patient's offence, the nature and gravity of his mental disorder, past present and future, the risk and likelihood of the patient re-offending, the degree of harm to which the public may be exposed if he re-offends, the risk and likelihood of a recurrence or exacerbation of any mental disorder, and the risk and likelihood of his needing to be recalled in the future for further treatment in hospital. The tribunal will also need to consider the nature of any conditions previously imposed, whether by the tribunal or by the Secretary of State, under ss.42(2), 73(4)(b) or 73(5), the reasons why they were imposed and the extent to which it is desirable to continue, vary or add to them."

His Lordship said, at para.60, that the effect of this provision:

"is not to *preclude* the tribunal from considering the kind of factors which fall for consideration under s.73. Rather . . . the effect is that the tribunal, when exercising its discretion under s.75(3), is not constrained by the mandatory terms of s.73 which bind the approach of the tribunal when considering the exercise of its powers under s.73".

His Lordship further stated, at para.59, that:

"in effect, one of the key questions that the tribunal will wish to ask is whether it is—as s.73(1)(b) puts it—'satisfied that it is not appropriate for the patient to remain liable to be recalled to hospital for further treatment.' If the tribunal is not so satisfied, then it is difficult to see that it could be appropriate for it to make an order under s.75(3)(b)".

In *RH v South London and Maudsley NHS Foundation Trust* [2010] EWCA Civ 1273; [2010] M.H.L.R. 341, para.29, the Court of Appeal held that Munby J.'s formulation of the question to be asked by the tribunal under this provision, which is set out at para.59 of his judgment and which places the burden of proof on the patient, does not violate the ECHR.

General

Visiting and examination of patients

1–959   **76.**—(1) For the purpose of advising whether an application to [the appropriate tribunal] should be made by or in respect of a patient who is liable to be detained or subject to guardianship [. . .] under Part II of this Act [or a community patient,] or of furnishing information as to the condition of a patient for the purposes of such an application, any registered medical practitioner [or approved clinician] authorised by or on behalf of the patient or other person who is entitled to make or has made the application—

(a) may at any reasonable time visit the patient and examine him in private, and

(b) may require the production of and inspect any records relating to the detention or treatment of the patient in any hospital [or to any after-care services provided for the patient under section 117 below].

(2) Section 32 above shall apply for the purposes of this section as it applies for the purposes of Part II of this Act.

AMENDMENTS

The amendments to this section were made by the Mental Health Act 2007 ss.13(2)(b), 32(4), 55, Sch.3 para.22, Sch.11 Pt 5 and SI 2008/2883 art.9, Sch.3 para.57.

DEFINITIONS

1–960   the appropriate tribunal: ss.66(4), 145(1).
community patient: s.17A(7).
approved clinician: s.145(1).
patient: s.145(1).

hospital: ss.34(2), 79(6), 145(1).

GENERAL NOTE

This section, which is applied to patients who have been placed under hospital, restric- **1–961**
tion or guardianship orders by a court under s.37 or 41 of the Act (Sch.1, Pt 1, para.1; Pt 2,
para.1), provides for a medical practitioner or approved clinician to be authorised by or on
behalf of the patient, or anyone else entitled to make an application to a tribunal, to advise
on whether an application should be made, or to provide information on the patient's condition for the purposes of an application. The authorised person may visit and examine the
patient, and inspect relevant records.

A failure to allow authorised persons to carry out their functions under this section could
amount to an obstruction under s.129.

Subsection (1)

FURNISHING INFORMATION.   In *W v Egdell* [1990] 1 All E.R. 835, the Court of Appeal **1–962**
held that where a medical practitioner is called on to examine a patient with a view to providing an independent psychiatric report to support the patient's application to a tribunal, he
owes a duty not only to his patient but also a duty to the public. His duty to the public would
enable him to place before the proper authorities the results of his examination if, in his
opinion, the public interest so required. This would be so whether or not the patient
instructed him not to do so. Bingham L.J. said at 852, 853:

> "There is one consideration [in this case] which in my judgment . . . weighs the balance
> of public interest decisively in favour of disclosure. It may be shortly put. Where a man
> has committed multiple killings under the disability of serious mental illness, decisions
> which may lead directly or indirectly to his release from hospital should not be made
> unless a responsible authority is properly able to make an informed judgment that the
> risk of repetition is so small as to be acceptable. A consultant psychiatrist who becomes
> aware, even in the course of a confidential relationship, of information which leads him,
> in the exercise of what the court considers a sound professional judgment, to fear that
> such decisions may be made on the basis of inadequate information and with a real
> risk of consequent danger to the public is entitled to take such steps as are reasonable
> in all the circumstances to communicate the grounds of his concern to the responsible
> authorities."

General provisions concerning tribunal applications

77.—(1) No application shall be made to [the appropriate tribunal by or in **1–963**
respect of a patient under this Act] except in such cases and at such times as
are expressly provided by this Act.

(2) Where under this Act any person is authorised to make an application to [the
appropriate tribunal] within a specified period, not more than one such application
shall be made by that person within that period but for that purpose there shall be
disregarded any application which is withdrawn in accordance with [Tribunal
Procedure Rules or] rules made under section 78 below.

(3) Subject to subsection (4) below an application to [a tribunal] authorised to
be made by or in respect of a patient under this Act shall be made by notice in writing addressed

[(a) in the case of a patient who is liable to be detained in a hospital, [to the First-
tier Tribunal where that hospital is in England and to the Mental Health
Review Tribunal for Wales where that hospital is in Wales];

(b) in the case of a community patient, [to the First-tier Tribunal where the
responsible hospital is in England and to the Mental Health Review
Tribunal for Wales where that hospital is in Wales];

(c) in the case of a patient subject to guardianship, [to the First-tier Tribunal where the patient resides in England and to the Mental Health Review Tribunal for Wales where the patient resides in Wales].]

(4) Any application under section 75(2) above shall be made [to the First-tier Tribunal where the patient resides in England and to the Mental Health Review Tribunal for Wales where the patient resides in Wales].

AMENDMENTS

The amendments to this section were made by the Mental Health Act 2007 s.32(4), Sch.3 para.23, SI 2008/2883 art.9, Sch.3 para.58 and SI 2009/1307 art.5, Sch.1 para.161.

DEFINITIONS

1–964   patient: s.145(1).
community patient: s.17A(7).
the appropriate tribunal: ss.66(4), 145(1).
hospital: ss.34(2), 79(6), 145(1).
responsible hospital: ss.17A(7), 145(1).

GENERAL NOTE

1–965   This section provides, in subss.(1) and (2), that there is no right to apply to a tribunal apart from those situations expressly provided for in the Act, that where the Act gives rise to a right to make an application within a specified period only one such application may be made within that period, and that where the tribunal authorises the withdrawal of an application the applicant can re-apply during the relevant period. Where a patient is transferred between England and Wales, a tribunal application made in one country counts as an application to a tribunal in the other.

Subsections (3) and (4) determine whether an application should be made to the First-tier Tribunal (Mental Health) or the Mental Health Review Tribunal for Wales.

Subsection (2)

1–966   See the note on "an application" in s.66(1).

WITHDRAWN IN ACCORDANCE WITH THE RULES.   References cannot be withdrawn.

Subsection (4)

1–967   APPLICATION UNDER SECTION 75(2).   By a restricted patient who has been conditionally discharged from hospital.

RESIDES.   See the note on this term in s.7(5).

Procedure of [Mental Health Review Tribunal for Wales]

1–968   **78.**—(1) The Lord Chancellor may make rules with respect to the making of applications to [the Mental Health Review Tribunal for Wales] and with respect to the proceedings of [that tribunal] and matters incidental to or consequential on such proceedings.

(2) Rules made under this section may in particular make provision—

(a) for enabling [the tribunal], or the chairman of [the tribunal], to postpone the consideration of any application by or in respect of a patient, or of any such application of any specified class, until the expiration of such period (not exceeding 12 months) as may be specified in the rules from the date on which an application by or in respect of the same patient was last considered and determined [under this Act by the tribunal or the First-tier Tribunal];

[(b) for the transfer of proceedings to or from the Mental Health Review Tribunal for Wales in any case where, after the making of the application, the patient is moved into or out of Wales;]

(c) for restricting the persons qualified to serve as members of [the tribunal] for the consideration of any application, or of an application of any specified class;

(d) for enabling [the tribunal] to dispose of an application without a formal hearing where such a hearing is not requested by the applicant or it appears to the tribunal that such a hearing would be detrimental to the health of the patient;

(e) for enabling [the tribunal] to exclude members of the public, or any specified class of members of the public, from any proceedings of the tribunal, or to prohibit the publication of reports of any such proceedings or the names of any persons concerned in such proceedings;

(f) for regulating the circumstances in which, and the persons by whom, applicants and patients in respect of whom applications are made to [the tribunal] may, if not desiring to conduct their own case, be represented for the purposes of those applications;

(g) for regulating the methods by which information relevant to an application may be obtained by or furnished to the tribunal, and in particular for authorising the members of [the tribunal], or any one or more of them, to visit and interview in private any patient by or in respect of whom an application has been made;

(h) for making available to any applicant, and to any patient in respect of whom an application is made to [the tribunal], copies of any documents obtained by or furnished to the tribunal in connection with the application, and a statement of the substance of any oral information so obtained or furnished except where the Tribunal considers it undesirable in the interests of the patient or for other special reasons;

(i) for requiring [the tribunal], if so requested in accordance with the rules, to furnish such statements of the reasons for any decision given by the tribunal as may be prescribed by the rules, subject to any provision made by the rules for withholding such a statement from a patient or any other person in cases where the tribunal considers that furnishing it would be undesirable in the interests of the patient or for other special reasons;

(j) for conferring on the [tribunal] such ancillary powers as the Lord Chancellor thinks necessary for the purposes of the exercise of [its] functions under this Act;

(k) for enabling any functions of [the tribunal] which relate to matters preliminary or incidental to an application to be performed by the chairman of the tribunal.

(3) Subsections (1) and (2) above apply in relation to references to [the Mental Health Review Tribunal for Wales] as they apply in relation to applications to [that tribunal] by or in respect of patients.

(4) Rules under this section may make provision as to the procedure to be adopted in cases concerning restricted patients and, in particular—

(a) for restricting the persons qualified to serve as president of [the tribunal] for the consideration of an application or reference relating to a restricted patient;

[(b) for the transfer of proceedings to or from the tribunal in any case where, after the making of a reference or application in accordance with section 71(4) or 77(4) above, the patient begins or ceases to reside in Wales.]

(5) Rules under this section may be so framed as to apply to all applications or references or to applications or references of any specified class and may make different provision in relation to different cases.

(6) Any functions conferred on the chairman of [the Mental Health Review Tribunal for Wales] by rules under this section may [. . .], be exercised by another member of that tribunal appointed by him for the purpose.

(7) [The Mental Health Review Tribunal for Wales] may pay allowances in respect of travelling expenses, subsistence and loss of earnings to any person attending the Tribunal as an applicant or witness, to the patient who is the subject of the proceedings if he attends otherwise than as the applicant or a witness and to any person (other than [an authorised person (within the meaning of Part 3)]) who attends as the representative of an applicant.

(8) [. . .]

(9) [Part I of the Arbitration Act 1996] shall not apply to any proceedings before [the Mental Health Review Tribunal for Wales] except so far as any provisions of that Act may be applied, with or without modifications, by rules made under this section.

AMENDMENTS

The amendments to this section were made by the Arbitration Act 1996 s.107(1), Sch.3 para.40, the Mental Health Act 2007 ss.38(3)(e), 55, Sch.11 Pt.6, SI 2008/2883 art.9, Sch.3 para.59 and the Legal Services Act 2007 s.208, Sch.21, para.60.

DEFINITIONS

1–969 patient: s.145(1).
restricted patient: s.79(1).

GENERAL NOTE

1–970 The Mental Health Review Tribunal for Wales Rules 2008 (SI 2008/2705 (L.17)) govern the practice and procedure to be followed in proceedings before the Mental Health Review Tribunal for Wales.

Subsection (1)

1–971 THE LORD CHANCELLOR.   Who cannot transfer his functions under this section to another person (Constitutional Reform Act 2005 s.19, Sch.7).

Subsection (2)

1–972 PARAGRAPH (A); PRESIDENT OF A TRIBUNAL.   See Sch.2 para.2.

PARAGRAPH (B); AREA OF THE TRIBUNAL.   See s.65(1).

Subsection (4)

1–973 QUALIFIED TO SERVE AS CHAIRMAN OF A TRIBUNAL.   Provision for restricting those who can act as president in cases relating to restricted patients is made in r.11(2) of the Welsh Rules. There is no equivalent provision in the Tribunal Rules.

Subsection (7)

1–974 LOSS OF EARNINGS.   This would not cover the payment of a fee for representing the client or acting as an expert witness.

ATTENDING. Expenses cannot be paid for preparatory work.

AUTHORISED PERSON. Is defined in s.55(1).

[Appeal from the Mental Health Review Tribunal for Wales to the Upper Tribunal

78A.—(1) A party to any proceedings before the Mental Health Review **1–975** Tribunal for Wales may appeal to the Upper Tribunal on any point of law arising from a decision made by the Mental Health Review Tribunal for Wales in those proceedings.

(2) An appeal may be brought under subsection (1) above only if, on an application made by the party concerned, the Mental Health Review Tribunal for Wales or the Upper Tribunal has given its permission for the appeal to be brought.

(3) Section 12 of the Tribunals, Courts and Enforcement Act 2007 (proceedings on appeal to the Upper Tribunal) applies in relation to appeals to the Upper Tribunal under this section as it applies in relation to appeals to it under section 11 of that Act, but as if references to the First-tier Tribunal were references to the Mental Health Review Tribunal for Wales.]

AMENDMENT
This section was inserted by SI 2008/2883 art.9, Sch.3 para.60.

GENERAL NOTE
As the Mental Health Review Tribunal for Wales is not administered through the Courts **1–976** and Tribunal Service, this section ensures that the onward appeal right to the Upper Tribunal which is enjoyed by the First-tier Tribunal (Mental Health) is also available in Wales.

Interpretation of Part V

79.—(1) In this Part of this Act "restricted patient" means a patient who is sub- **1–977** ject to a restriction order [, limitation direction] or restriction direction and this Part of this Act shall, subject to the provisions of this section, have effect in relation to any person who
[(a) is treated by virtue of any enactment as subject to a hospital order and a restriction order; or]
(b) [. . .]
[(c) is treated as subject to a hospital order and a restriction order, or to a hospital direction and a limitation direction, or to a transfer direction and a restriction direction, by virtue of any provision of Part 6 of this Act (except section 80D(3), 82A(2) or 85A(2) below),]
as it has effect in relation to a restricted patient.

(2) Subject to the following provisions of this section, in this Part of this Act "the relevant hospital order" [, "the relevant hospital direction"] and "the relevant transfer direction," in relation to a restricted patient, mean the hospital order [, the hospital direction] or transfer direction by virtue of which he is liable to be detained in a hospital.

(3) In the case of a person within paragraph (a) of subsection (1) above, references in this Part of this Act to the relevant hospital order or restriction order shall be construed as references to the direction referred to in that paragraph.

(4) In the case of a person within paragraph (b) of subsection (1) above, references in this Part of this Act to the relevant hospital order or restriction order shall

be construed as references to the order under the provisions mentioned in that paragraph.

(5) In the case of a person within paragraph (c) of subsection (1) above, references in this Part of this Act to the relevant hospital order, [the relevant hospital direction,] the relevant transfer direction, the restriction order [, the limitation direction] or the restriction direction or to a transfer direction under section 48 above shall be construed as references to the hospital order, [hospital direction,] transfer direction, restriction order, [limitation direction,] restriction direction or transfer direction under that section to which that person is treated as subject by virtue of the provisions mentioned in that paragraph.

[(5A) Section 75 above shall, subject to the modifications in subsection (5C) below, have effect in relation to a qualifying patient as it has effect in relation to a restricted patient who is conditionally discharged under section 42(2), 73 or 74 above.

(5B) A patient is a qualifying patient if he is treated by virtue of section 80D(3), 82A(2) or 85A(2) below as if he had been conditionally discharged and were subject to a hospital order and a restriction order, or to a hospital direction and a limitation direction, or to a transfer direction and a restriction direction.

(5C) The modifications mentioned in subsection (5A) above are—

(a) references to the relevant hospital order, hospital direction or transfer direction, or to the restriction order, limitation direction or restriction direction to which the patient is subject, shall be construed as references to the hospital order, hospital direction or transfer direction, or restriction order, limitation direction or restriction direction, to which the patient is treated as subject by virtue of section 80D(3), 82A(2) or 85A(2) below; and

(b) the reference to the date on which the patient was conditionally discharged shall be construed as a reference to the date on which he was treated as conditionally discharged by virtue of a provision mentioned in paragraph (a) above.]

(6) In this Part of this Act, unless the context otherwise requires, "hospital" means a hospital [, and "the responsible clinician" means the responsible clinician,] within the meaning of Part II of this Act.

(7) [*Repealed by SI 2008/2883 art.9, Sch.3 para.61*]

AMENDMENTS

The amendments to this section were made by the Domestic Violence, Crime and Victims Act 2004 s.58, Sch.10 para.21(a), Sch.11 of that Act, SI 2005/2078 Sch.1 para.2(3), the Crime (Sentences) Act 1997 s.55, Sch.4 para.12(14)(15) and the Mental Health Act 2007 ss.13(3), 38(4), 39(2), Sch.5 Pt 2 para.19.

DEFINITIONS

1–978   patient: s.145(1).
restriction order: ss.41, 145(1).
restriction direction: ss.49, 145(1).
hospital order: ss.37, 145(1).
transfer direction: ss.47, 145(1).
hospital direction: s.145(1).
limitation direction: s.145(1).

GENERAL NOTE
Subsection (6)
HOSPITAL.　See section 34(2).

1-979

PART VI

REMOVAL AND RETURN OF PATIENTS WITHIN UNITED KINGDOM, ETC.

GENERAL NOTE
This Part deals with the transfer between the United Kingdom jurisdictions and the **1-980**
Channel Islands or the Isle of Man of patients who are subject to certain compulsory
powers. It ensures that the patients remain in legal custody whilst in transit and that they
are liable to equivalent compulsory powers on their arrival in the receiving jurisdiction.
It also provides, in s.86, powers for moving mentally disordered patients who are neither
British citizens nor Commonwealth citizens with the right of abode in the United
Kingdom from hospitals in England and Wales to countries abroad.

The procedure to be followed on the removal of a patient to England under this Part is set
out in regs 15 and 16 of the English Regulations and reg.29 of the Welsh Regulations.

Corresponding legislative provisions
Corresponding legislative provisions relating to transfers from Scotland and Northern **1-981**
Ireland can be found in figures 88 and 90 of Ch.34 of the Reference Guide.

The Parliament of the Isle of Man, the Tynwald, has produced a helpful table which sets
out equivalent provisions from the mental health legislation of the Isle of Man, England and
Wales, Scotland, Northern Ireland and Jersey: see Schs 1, 2 and 3 to the Mental Health
(Transfer of Patients) (Equivalent Provisions of Relevant Territories) Regulations 2009
(Statutory Document 117/09).

Contact details (taken from Ch.34 of the Reference Guide)
Scotland　**1-982**
Directorate for Population Health Improvement Mental Health, St Andrews
House, Regents Road, Edinburgh, EH1 3DG
Telephone: 0131 244 5668
Email: andy.lawson2@scotland.gsi.gov.uk
For cases concerned with criminal proceedings email:
restrictedpatients@scotland.gsi.gov.uk

Northern Ireland
Mental Health Unit, Department of Health, Social Services and Public
Safety, D1.4 Castle Buildings, Stormont Estate, Belfast BT4 3SQ
Telephone: 028 9052 2562
Fax: 028 9052 2500
Email: mentalhealthunit@dhsspsni.gov.uk

States of Jersey
Community Mental Health Service, 20 La Chasse, St Helier, Jersey,
Channel Islands, JE24UE
Tel: 01534 445841
Fax: 01534 445140
Email: health@gov.je

Bailiwick of Guernsey
Corporate Headquarters, Rue Mignot, St Andrews, Guernsey, Channel

Islands, GY6 8TW
Tel: 01481 725241
Fax: 01481 235341
Email: healthandwellbeing@gov.gg

Isle of Man
Department of Health and Social Care, Mental Health Service, Cronk Coar,
Noble's Hospital, Braddan, Isle of Man, IM4 4RF
Telephone: 01624 656015
Fax: 01624 642805
Email: mentalhealthcustomerservices.dh@gov.im

[Removal to and from Scotland

Removal of patients to Scotland
1–983   **80.**—(1) If it appears to the Secretary of State, in the case of a patient who is for
the time being liable to be detained [. . .] under this Act (otherwise than by virtue
of section 35, 36 or 38 above), that it is in the interests of the patient to remove him
to Scotland, and that arrangements have been made for admitting him to a hospital
[. . .] there [or, where he is not to be admitted to a hospital, for his detention in
hospital to be authorised by virtue of the Mental Health (Care and Treatment)
(Scotland) Act 2003 or the Criminal Procedure (Scotland) Act 1995], the
Secretary of State may authorise his removal to Scotland and may give any
necessary directions for his conveyance to his destination.
(2)—(6) *[Repealed by SI 2005/2078 art.16, Sch.3]*
(7) In this section "hospital" has the same meaning as in the [Mental Health
(Care and Treatment) (Scotland) Act 2003].
[(8) Reference in this section to a patient's detention in hospital being authorised by virtue of the Mental Health (Care and Treatment) (Scotland) Act 2003 or
the Criminal Procedure (Scotland) Act 1995 shall be read as including references
to a patient in respect of whom a certificate under one of the provisions listed in
section 290(7)(a) of the Act of 2003 is in operation.]

AMENDMENTS
The amendments to this section were made by SI 2003/2078 Sch.1 para.2(4) and the
Mental Health Act 2007 s.55, Sch.11 Pt 7. The cross-heading immediately above this sec-
tion was substituted by s.39(2), Sch.5 Pt 1 para.2.

DEFINITIONS
1–984   patient: s.145(1).
hospital: subs. (7).
restriction order: ss.41, 145(1).
restriction direction: ss.49, 145(1).

GENERAL NOTE
1–985   This section enables the Secretary of State (or, for certain categories of patient, the Welsh
Ministers) to transfer a patient who is detained (otherwise than under s.35, 36 or 38) in
England or Wales to Scotland without a break in the powers of detention. The Secretary
of State (or the Welsh Ministers) must be satisfied that such a move is in the interests of
the patient.
Transfer to Scotland requires the approval of Scottish Ministers in accordance with the
Mental Health (Cross Border transfers: patients subject to detention requirements or

otherwise in hospital) (Scotland) Regulations 2005 (SSI 2005/467) which regulate both the removal of patients from Scotland as well as the reception of patients into Scotland. In terms of the reception of patients into Scotland, reg.24 sets out that the consent of Scottish Ministers is required for any patients coming into Scotland and lists the information that needs to be made available to Scottish Ministers to allow them to consider a request for transfer; this includes details of the relevant measures to which the patient is currently subject. Scottish Ministers are then required, under reg.24(5) to consider the request and give notice to the relevant hospital managers whether their consent has been given. Regulation 30(5) provides that, following reception into Scotland, the order to which a patient is now subject will be treated as if that measure was made or given on the date which the order the patient was subject to immediately preceding transfer was made or given. Given this, difficulties have arisen where a patient is received into a Scottish hospital with only a few days left to run on their order. In such cases, there is often insufficient time for the Scottish responsible medical officer to adequately discharge her responsibilities in relation to the appropriate assessment and possible re-detention of a patient. In view of this "it will now be our practice in considering requests for the consent of Scottish Ministers to the transfer of patients into Scotland to request that, where an application is made under the 2005 Regulations for a patient to transfer into Scotland, there must be a minimum of 10 days and, where possible, at least 14 days left before the expiry of their existing detention order" (Letter from the Mental Health Division of the Primary and Community Directorate, January 29, 2010). The Department of Health or the Welsh Ministers (or the Ministry of Justice for restricted patients) will seek approval directly from the Scottish Executive. When the transfer is completed, the application, order or direction on the basis of which the patient was detained in England, ceases to have effect and cannot be revived. For the patient to return to England a further transfer would be necessary, in accordance with Scottish legislation, which will require the agreement of the Scottish Ministers.

Once the transfer of a detained patient has been agreed in principle between the sending and receiving hospitals, the sending hospital should write to:

Department of Health
Wellington House
133–155 Waterloo Road
London SE1 8UG
Tel: 020 7972 2000

The Department of Health has devised a pro-forma (Gateway ref. 14651) for completion by responsible hospitals in England to request transfer of non-restricted patients to a hospital outside England and Wales. The pro-forma should be completed by or on behalf of the managers of the responsible hospital in England. The Department's e-mail address for this purpose is: mentalhealthact2007@dh.gsi.gov.uk.

For patients who are detained in Wales, the information should be sent to:

The National Assembly for Wales
Cathays Park
Cardiff CF10 3NQ
Tel: 029 20825111

Full details of the proposed transfer of a restricted patient should be sent to:

Mental Health Casework Section
Ministry of Justice
Ground Floor
Grenadier House
99-105 Horseferry Road

London SWIP 2DD
Tel: 020 3334 3555

For the effect of a transfer under this section on the existing application, see s.91.

Subsection (1)

1–986   SECRETARY OF STATE.   The functions of the Secretary of State, so far as exercisable in relation to Wales, are exercised by the Welsh Ministers (see the General Note to the Act and SI 1999/672 art.2, Sch.1, as varied by SI 2000/253 art.4, Sch.3) except in relation to a patient who is subject to one or more of the following, namely:

(a) a restriction order;

(b) a hospital direction;

(c) a limitation direction; or

(d) a restriction direction,

made under ss.41, 45A or, as the case may be, 49.

CONVEYANCE TO HIS DESTINATION.   General provisions relating to the custody, conveyance and detention of patients are contained in s.137. The Reference Guide, at para.35.13, states:

"The Scottish Ministers may also give directions about the patient's conveyance once in Scotland under Scottish regulations (or authorise the patient's intended responsible medical officer in Scotland to do so)".

[Transfer of responsibility for community patients to Scotland

1–987   80ZA.—(1) If it appears to the appropriate national authority, in the case of a community patient, that the conditions mentioned in subsection (2) below are met, the authority may authorise the transfer of responsibility for him to Scotland.

(2) The conditions are—

(a) a transfer under this section is in the patient's interests; and

(b) arrangements have been made for dealing with him under enactments in force in Scotland corresponding or similar to those relating to community patients in this Act.

(3) The appropriate national authority may not act under subsection (1) above while the patient is recalled to hospital under section 17E above.

(4) In this section, "the appropriate national authority" means—

(a) in relation to a community patient in respect of whom the responsible hospital is in England, the Secretary of State;

(b) in relation to a community patient in respect of whom the responsible hospital is in Wales, the Welsh Ministers.]

AMENDMENT

This section was inserted by the Mental Health Act 2007 s.39(2), Sch.5 Pt 1 para.3(1).

DEFINITIONS

1–988   community patient: ss.17A(7), 145(1).
patient: s.145(1).
hospital: ss.34(2), 92(1), 145(1).
responsible hospital: ss.17A(7), 145(1).

GENERAL NOTE

This section enables a community patient who has not been recalled to hospital to be **1–989** transferred to Scotland as long as the transfer is in the patient's best interests and arrangements have been made for dealing with him or her under the corresponding legislation in Scotland. In practice, this means "a CTO under the Mental Health (Care and Treatment) (Scotland) Act 2003 (or a compulsion order under the Criminal Procedure (Scotland) Act 1995), which does not authorise the patient's detention in hospital" (Reference Guide, para.35.22). The Mental Health (England and Wales Cross-border transfer: patients subject to requirements other than detention) (Scotland) Regulations 2008 (SSI 2008/356) enable the cross-border transfer of Scottish patients on community-based orders to England and Wales and allow patients on community treatment orders in England and Wales to transfer to Scotland. The arrangements for the transfer will be made by either the Secretary of State or the Welsh Ministers depending on the location of the responsible hospital. A transfer of responsibility for a community patient does not give anyone the power to convey the patient to Scotland against the patient's will.

A transfer of responsibility for a patient on a CTO does not give anyone any power to convey the patient to Scotland against the patient's will (Reference Guide, para.35.26).

The Department of Health has devised a pro-forma (Gateway ref. 14651) for completion by responsible hospitals in England to request transfer of community patients to Scotland. The pro-forma should be completed by or on behalf of the managers of the responsible hospital in England. The Department's e-mail address for this purpose is: mentalhealthact2007@dh.gsi.gov.uk.

There is no power to transfer a guardianship patient to guardianship in Scotland.

For the effect of a transfer under this section on the existing order, see s.91.

[Transfer of responsibility for conditionally discharged patients to Scotland]

80A.—(1) If it appears to the Secretary of State, in the case of a patient who— **1–990**

(a) is subject to a restriction order under section 41 above; and

(b) has been conditionally discharged under section 42 or 73 above,

that a transfer under this section would be in the interests of the patient, the Secretary of State may, with the consent of the Minister exercising corresponding functions in Scotland, transfer responsibility for the patient to that Minister.]

(2)—(3) [*Repealed by SI 2005/2078, art.16, Sch.3*]

AMENDMENTS

This section was inserted by the Crime (Sentences) Act 1997 s.48, Sch.3 para.1. The heading was substituted by the Mental Health Act 2007 s.39(2), Sch.5 Pt 1 para.4.

DEFINITIONS **1–991**

    patient: s.145(1).

    restriction order: ss.41, 145(1).

GENERAL NOTE

This section makes provision for the transfer of responsibility for conditionally dis- **1–992** charged restricted patients from England and Wales to Scotland. It enables the Secretary of State to authorise such a transfer where it appears to be in the interests of the patient, and where the relevant Scottish Minister has consented to the transfer.

For the effect of a transfer under this section on the existing order, see s.91.

Corresponding legislative provisions **1–993**

    See the General Note to this Part under this heading.

SECRETARY OF STATE. Functions under this provision have not been transferred to Welsh Ministers (see the General Note to the Act and SI 1999/672 art.2, Sch.1).

[Removal of detained patients from Scotland

1–994   **80B.**—(1) This section applies to a patient if—

(a) he is removed to England and Wales under regulations made under section 290(1)(a) of the Mental Health (Care and Treatment) (Scotland) Act 2003 ("the 2003 Act");

(b) immediately before his removal, his detention in hospital was authorised by virtue of that Act or the Criminal Procedure (Scotland) Act 1995; and

(c) on his removal, he is admitted to a hospital in England or Wales.

(2) He shall be treated as if, on the date of his admission to the hospital, he had been so admitted in pursuance of an application made, or an order or direction made or given, on that date under the enactment in force in England and Wales which most closely corresponds to the enactment by virtue of which his detention in hospital was authorised immediately before his removal.

(3) If, immediately before his removal, he was subject to a measure under any enactment in force in Scotland restricting his discharge, he shall be treated as if he were subject to an order or direction under the enactment in force in England and Wales which most closely corresponds to that enactment.

(4) If, immediately before his removal, the patient was liable to be detained under the 2003 Act by virtue of a transfer for treatment direction, given while he was serving a sentence of imprisonment (within the meaning of section 136(9) of that Act) imposed by a court in Scotland, he shall be treated as if the sentence had been imposed by a court in England and Wales.

(5) If, immediately before his removal, the patient was subject to a hospital direction or transfer for treatment direction, the restriction direction to which he is subject by virtue of subsection (3) above shall expire on the date on which that hospital direction or transfer for treatment direction (as the case may be) would have expired if he had not been so removed.

(6) If, immediately before his removal, the patient was liable to be detained under the 2003 Act by virtue of a hospital direction, he shall be treated as if any sentence of imprisonment passed at the time when that hospital direction was made had been imposed by a court in England and Wales.

(7) Any directions given by the Scottish Ministers under regulations made under section 290 of the 2003 Act as to the removal of a patient to which this section applies shall have effect as if they were given under this Act.

(8) Subsection (8) of section 80 above applies to a reference in this section as it applies to one in that section.

(9) In this section—

"hospital direction" means a direction made under section 59A of the Criminal Procedure (Scotland) Act 1995; and

"transfer for treatment direction" has the meaning given by section 136 of the 2003 Act.]

AMENDMENT
This section was inserted by the Mental Health Act 2007 s.39(2), Sch.5 Pt 1 para.4(1).

DEFINITIONS
1–995   patient: s.145(1).
hospital:ss.34(2), 92(1), 145(1).

GENERAL NOTE

This section applies to a detained patient who is transferred from Scotland to England or **1–996** Wales. The date of his hospital admission will be the date of his arrival at the hospital in England or Wales under the provision in force which most closely corresponds to the legislation that the patient was detained under in Scotland. For example, if a patient who is detained in Scotland under the equivalent of s.3 is transferred to England on August 1, he will be treated as if he had been admitted to the hospital in England on August 1 under s.3. Such a patient is therefore given the same powers to apply to a tribunal as those enjoyed by a s.3 patient (s.69(2)). These powers are also enjoyed by the patient's nearest relative (s.69(1), as applied by s.55(4)).

Paragraph 34.28 of the Reference Guide states:

"In practice, the Scottish Executive will generally ask the Department of Health (or the Ministry of Justice for restricted patients) to confirm that arrangements have been made. The Secretary of State for Justice will not, in practice, agree to the transfer of a restricted patient to England unless satisfied that the proposed arrangements will enable the patient's safe management in England."

The Mental Health (Care and Treatment) (Scotland) Act 2003 provides for the transfer of patients subject to a detention requirement or otherwise in hospital from Scotland and for patients subject to corresponding measures in England and Wales to be received in Scotland. The Mental Health (Cross-border transfer: patients subject to detention requirement or otherwise in hospital) (Scotland) Regulations 2005 (SSI 2005/467) make provision for those transfers to take place.

Requesting a transfer warrant

The Reference Guide states: **1–997**

"35.9 Requests for the transfer of restricted patients should be made to the Ministry of Justice. The Act only provides for the transfer of patients between hospitals in different jurisdictions but not the transfer between a prison in one jurisdiction and a hospital in another. If such a transfer is being contemplated, it will need to be undertaken in two stages. Either the patient will be transferred from prison to hospital and from there to a hospital in the other jurisdiction or from prison to another prison and then prison to hospital. Although this might appear complicated, it can be agreed in principle with the patient only having to move once.

35.10 For patients detained under section 2 of the Act, the Scottish authorities require there to be at least 10 days and preferably 14 days remaining on the section 2 when the transfer takes place. This means that the pro-forma for such a transfer should be completed as soon as it is known that the patient is to be transferred to Scotland and the hospital in England has been advised that there is a bed available for the patient at the receiving hospital in Scotland. The completed pro-forma should be faxed or emailed to the Department of Health by day 11 (day 14 at the very latest) and the hospital in England would need to transfer the patient by day 18 (preferably by day 14). A warrant issued for a patient detained under section 2 would not be valid beyond day 18 of the patient's detention."

Subsection (3)

MOST CLOSELY CORRESPONDS. See the table set out at figure 88 of Ch.34 of the **1–998** Reference Guide and the General Note to this Part under the heading "Corresponding legislative provisions".

[Removal of patients subject to compulsion in the community from Scotland

80C.—(1) This section applies to a patient if— **1–999**

(a) he is subject to an enactment in force in Scotland by virtue of which regulations under section 289(1) of the Mental Health (Care and Treatment) (Scotland) Act 2003 apply to him; and

(b) he is removed to England and Wales under those regulations.

(2) He shall be treated as if on the date of his arrival at the place where he is to reside in England or Wales—

(a) he had been admitted to a hospital in England or Wales in pursuance of an application or order made on that date under the corresponding enactment; and

(b) a community treatment order had then been made discharging him from the hospital.

(3) For these purposes—

(a) if the enactment to which the patient was subject in Scotland was an enactment contained in the Mental Health (Care and Treatment) (Scotland) Act 2003, the corresponding enactment is section 3 of this Act;

(b) if the enactment to which he was subject in Scotland was an enactment contained in the Criminal Procedure (Scotland) Act 1995, the corresponding enactment is section 37 of this Act.

(4) "The responsible hospital", in the case of a patient in respect of whom a community treatment order is in force by virtue of subsection (2) above, means the hospital to which he is treated as having been admitted by virtue of that subsection, subject to section 19A above.

(5) As soon as practicable after the patient's arrival at the place where he is to reside in England or Wales, the responsible clinician shall specify the conditions to which he is to be subject for the purposes of section 17B(1) above, and the conditions shall be deemed to be specified in the community treatment order.

(6) But the responsible clinician may only specify conditions under subsection (5) above which an approved mental health professional agrees should be specified.]

AMENDMENT

This section was inserted by the Mental Health Act 2007 s.39(2), Sch.5 Pt 1 para.4(1).

DEFINITIONS

1–1000 patient: s.145(1).
community treatment order: ss.17A(7), 145(1).
hospital: ss.34(2), 92(1), 145(1).
responsible clinician: ss.34(1), 145(1).
approved mental health professional: s.145(1).

GENERAL NOTE

1–1001 This section applies to a patient who is subject to compulsion in the community in Scotland who is transferred to England or Wales. On arrival at the place where he is required to reside in England or Wales, the patient will be treated as if he had been admitted to a hospital in England or Wales on that date under s.3 or s.37 and a community treatment order (CTO) had been made discharging him from that hospital. As soon as practicable after the patient's arrival, "a CTO should be made" (Explanatory Notes, para.164).

The Mental Health (England and Wales Cross-border transfer: patients subject to requirements other than detention) (Scotland) Regulations 2008 (SSI 2008/356) allow for patients who are subject to community based orders to be transferred from Scotland.

Subsection (5)
SHALL SPECIFY THE CONDITIONS. On form CTO 9; see reg.16(4) of the English **1–1002**
Regulations.

[Transfer of conditionally discharged patients from Scotland

80D.—(1) This section applies to a patient who is subject to— **1–1003**
   (a) a restriction order under section 59 of the Criminal Procedure (Scotland)
       Act 1995; and
   (b) a conditional discharge under section 193(7) of the Mental Health (Care and
       Treatment) (Scotland) Act 2003 ("the 2003 Act").

(2) A transfer of the patient to England and Wales under regulations made under
section 290 of the 2003 Act shall have effect only if the Secretary of State has consented to the transfer.

(3) If a transfer under those regulations has effect, the patient shall be treated
as if—
   (a) on the date of the transfer he had been conditionally discharged under sec-
       tion 42 or 73 above; and
   (b) he were subject to a hospital order under section 37 above and a restriction
       order under section 41 above.

(4) If the restriction order to which the patient was subject immediately before
the transfer was of limited duration, the restriction order to which he is subject by
virtue of subsection (3) above shall expire on the date on which the first-mentioned order would have expired if the transfer had not been made.]

AMENDMENT
This section was inserted by the Mental Health Act 2007 s.39(2), Sch.5 Pt 1 para.4(1).

DEFINITIONS
   patient: s.145(1). **1–1004**
   hospital order: ss.37, 145(1).
   restriction order: ss.41, 145(1).

GENERAL NOTE
This section makes provision for the transfer of a conditionally discharged patient from **1–1005**
Scotland to England or Wales. On his arrival in England or Wales the patient will be treated
as if he was a restricted patient who had been granted a conditional discharge under either
ss.42 or 73. The transfer can only take place if the Secretary of State (subs.(2)) and the
Scottish Ministers (Mental Health (Cross-border transfer: patients subject to detention
requirement or otherwise in hospital) (Scotland) Regulations 2005 (SSI 2005/467)) have
consented to it.

Removal to and from Northern Ireland

Removal of patients to Northern Ireland

81.—(1) If it appears to the Secretary of State, in the case of a patient who is for **1–1006**
the time being liable to be detained or subject to guardianship under this Act
(otherwise than by virtue of section 35, 36 or 38 above), that it is in the interests
of the patient to remove him to Northern Ireland, and that arrangements have been
made for admitting him to a hospital or, as the case may be, for receiving him into
guardianship there, the Secretary of State may authorise his removal to Northern

Ireland and may give any necessary directions for his conveyance to his destination.

(2) Subject to the provisions of subsections (4) and (5) below, where a patient liable to be detained under this Act by virtue of an application, order or direction under any enactment in force in England and Wales is removed under this section and admitted to a hospital in Northern Ireland, he shall be treated as if on the date of his admission he had been so admitted in pursuance of an application made, or [a restriction order or a restriction direction] made or given, on that date under the corresponding enactment in force in Northern Ireland, and, [where he is subject to a hospital order and a restriction order or a transfer direction and a restriction direction under any enactment in this Act, as if he were subject to a hospital order and a restriction order or a transfer direction and a restriction direction under the corresponding enactment] in force in Northern Ireland.]

(3) Where a patient subject to guardianship under this Act by virtue of an application, order or direction under any enactment in force in England and Wales is removed under this section and received into guardianship in Northern Ireland, he shall be treated as if on the date on which he arrives at the place where he is to reside he had been so received in pursuance of an application, order or direction under the corresponding enactment in force in Northern Ireland, and as if the application had been accepted or, as the case may be, the order or direction had been made or given on that date.

(4) Where a person removed under this section was immediately before his removal liable to be detained by virtue of an application for admission for assessment under this Act, he shall, on his admission to a hospital in Northern Ireland, be treated as if he had been admitted to the hospital in pursuance of an application [for assessment under Article 4 of the Mental Health (Northern Ireland) Order 1986] made on the date of his admission.

(5) Where a person removed under this section was immediately before his removal liable to be detained by virtue of an application for admission for treatment under this Act, he shall, on his admission to a hospital in Northern Ireland, be treated as if [he were detained for treatment under Part II of the Mental Health (Northern Ireland) Order 1986 by virtue of a report under Article 12(1) of that Order made on the date of his admission.]

(6) Where a person removed under this section was immediately before his removal liable to be detained under this Act by virtue of a transfer direction given while he was serving a sentence of imprisonment (within the meaning of section 47(5) above) imposed by a court in England and Wales, he shall be treated as if the sentence had been imposed by a court in Northern Ireland.

(7) Where a person removed under this section was immediately before his removal subject to a [. . .] restriction direction of limited duration, [the [. . .] restriction direction] to which he is subject by virtue of subsection (2) above shall expire on the date on which [the first mentioned [. .] restriction direction would have expired if he had not been so removed.

(8) In this section "hospital" has the same meaning as in the Mental Health [(Northern Ireland) Order 1986].

AMENDMENTS

The amendments to this section were made by the Mental Health (Northern Ireland Consequential Amendments) Order 1986 (SI 1986/596) art.2 and the Mental Health Act 2007 ss.39(2), 55, Sch.5 Pt 1 para.5, Sch.11 Pt 8.

DEFINITIONS   **1–1007**
    patient: s.145(1).
    hospital order: ss.37, 145(1).
    restriction order: ss.41, 145(1).
    restriction direction: ss.49, 145(1).
    application for admission for assessment: ss.2, 145(1).
    application for admission for treatment: ss.3, 145(1).
    transfer direction: ss.47, 92(5), 145(1).

GENERAL NOTE
    This section enables the Secretary of State (or, for certain categories of patient in relation **1–1008**
to Wales, the Welsh Ministers) to transfer a patient who is detained (otherwise than under
ss.35, 36 or 38) or subject to guardianship in England or Wales to Northern Ireland without
a break in the powers of detention or guardianship. The Secretary of State (or the Welsh
Ministers) must be satisfied that such a move is in the interests of the patient and that suitable arrangements have been made for admitting him to hospital or receiving him into
guardianship in Northern Ireland. On arrival in Northern Ireland the patient will become
subject to the equivalent Northern Irish legislation, and the application or direction
made in England or Wales will cease to have effect.
    Once the transfer of a detained patient has been agreed in principle between the sending
and receiving hospitals, the sending hospital should contact either the Department of
Health or the National Assembly for Wales. Details of the proposed transfer of a restricted
patient should be sent to the Ministry of Justice. The Department of Health has devised a
pro-forma to be used by hospitals in England for non-restricted patients: see the General
Note to s.80.
    For the effect of a transfer under this section on the existing application, see s.91.
    It is not possible to grant a patient escorted leave of absence under s.17 to Northern
Ireland because the escort would have no jurisdiction there.

Transitional provision
    The repeal of the reference to restriction orders made in subs.(7) shall have no effect in **1–1009**
respect of:

    (a) a restriction order for a specified period made before October 1, 2007, or

    (b) an order made outside England and Wales which is treated under the 1983 Act as if it
         were a restriction order for a specified period (Mental Health Act 2007 s.40(7) and
         SI 2007/2798 art.2(d)).

Subsection (1)
    SECRETARY OF STATE.   See the note on s.80(1).   **1–1010**

    GUARDIANSHIP.   Paragraph 36.23 of the Reference Guide states:

    "In practice, a request for a transfer warrant should be made by, or on behalf of, the
patient's responsible local authority in England to the Department of Health using the
same pro-forma as for detained patients. The request should explain why the transfer
would be in the patient's interests, the arrangements that have been agreed for the patient
to be received into guardianship in Northern Ireland, and whether, and if so why, the
patient needs to be kept in custody while being taken there."

    ARRANGEMENTS.   For the transmission of information about these arrangements, see
the general note to s.80.

Subsection (6)

1–1011 TRANSFER DIRECTION. See s.92(5).

Subsection (8)

1–1012 HOSPITAL. Is defined in art.2(1) and (2A) of the 1986 Order.

[Removal of community patients to Northern Ireland

1–1013 **81ZA.**—(1) Section 81 above shall apply in the case of a community patient as it applies in the case of a patient who is for the time being liable to be detained under this Act, as if the community patient were so liable.

(2) Any reference in that section to the application, order or direction by virtue of which a patient is liable to be detained under this Act shall be construed, for these purposes, as a reference to the application, order or direction under this Act in respect of the patient.]

AMENDMENT

This section was inserted by the Mental Health Act 2007 s.39(2), Sch.5 Pt 1 para.6.

DEFINITIONS

1–1014 community patient: ss.17A(7), 145(1).
patient: s.145(1).

GENERAL NOTE

1–1015 The Reference Guide states:

"36.19 At the time of publication, there is no equivalent of a CTO under Northern Ireland legislation, so responsibility for patients on a CTO may not be transferred to a hospital in Northern Ireland.

36.20 If it is in their interests, patients on a CTO may instead be transferred to detention in Northern Ireland under a transfer warrant [issued under s.81], as if (in effect) they had never become a patient on a CTO.

36.21 In practice, a request for the transfer of a patient on a CTO should be made to the Department of Health by, or on behalf of, the managers of the patient's responsible hospital."

In practice, a request for the transfer of an SCT patient should be made to the Department of Health by, or on behalf of, the managers of the patient's responsible hospital."

[Transfer of responsibility for patients to Northern Ireland

1–1016 **81A.**—(1) If it appears to the Secretary of State, in the case of a patient who—
[(a) is subject to a hospital order under section 37 above and a restriction order under section 41 above or to a transfer direction under section 47 above and a restriction direction under section 49 above;] and
(b) has been conditionally discharged under section 42 or 73 above,
that a transfer under this section would be in the interests of the patient, the Secretary of State may, with the consent of the Minister exercising corresponding functions in Northern Ireland, transfer responsibility for the patient to that Minister.

(2) Where responsibility for such a patient is transferred under this section, the patient shall be treated—
(a) as if on the date of the transfer he had been conditionally discharged under the corresponding enactment in force in Northern Ireland; and

(b) as if he were subject to [a hospital order and a restriction order, or to a transfer direction and a restriction direction,] under the corresponding enactment in force in Northern Ireland.

(3) Where a patient responsibility for whom is transferred under this section was immediately before the transfer subject to a [. . .] or restriction direction of limited duration, the [. .] or restriction direction to which he is subject by virtue of subsection (2) above shall expire on the date on which the first-mentioned [. . .] direction would have expired if the transfer had not been made.]

AMENDMENTS

The amendments to this section were made by the Crime (Sentences) Act 1997 s.48, Sch.3 para.2 and the Mental Health Act 2007 ss.39(2), 55, Sch.5 Pt 1 para.7, Sch.11 Pt 8.

DEFINITIONS

patient: s.145(1).   **1–1017**
hospital order: ss.37, 145(1).
transfer direction: ss.47, 145(1).
restriction order: ss.41, 145(1).
restriction direction: ss.49, 145(1).

GENERAL NOTE

This section makes provision for the transfer of responsibility for conditionally dis- **1–1018**
charged restricted patients from England and Wales to Northern Ireland. It is an
equivalent provision to s.80A and reference should be made to the notes on that section.

Corresponding legislative provisions

See the General Note to this Part under this heading.   **1–1019**

Transitional provision

The repeal of the reference to restriction orders in subs.(3) shall have no effect in respect **1–1020**
of:

(a) a restriction order for a specified period made before October 1, 2007, or

(b) an order made outside England and Wales which is treated under the 1983 Act as if it
were a restriction order for a specified period (Mental Health Act 2007 s.40(7) and
SI 2007/2798 art.2(d)).

Subsection (1)

SECRETARY OF STATE. Functions under this provision have not been transferred to **1–1021**
Welsh Ministers (see the General Note to the Act and SI 1999/672, art.2, Sch.1).

Removal to England and Wales of patients from Northern Ireland

82.—(1) If it appears to the responsible authority, in the case of a patient who is **1–1022**
for the time being liable to be detained or subject to guardianship under the Mental
Health [(Northern Ireland) Order 1986 (otherwise than by virtue of Article 42, 43
or 45 of that Order)], that it is in the interests of the patient to remove him to
England and Wales, and that arrangements have been made for admitting him
to a hospital or, as the case may be, for receiving him into guardianship there,
the responsible authority may authorise his removal to England and Wales and
may give any necessary directions for his conveyance to his destination.

(2) Subject to the provisions of [subsections (4) and (4A)] below, where a
patient who is liable to be detained under the [Mental Health (Northern
Ireland) Order 1986] by virtue of an application, order or direction under any

enactment in force in Northern Ireland is removed under this section and admitted to a hospital in England and Wales, he shall be treated as if on the date of his admission he had been so admitted in pursuance of an application made, or an order or direction made or given, on that date under the corresponding enactment in force in England and Wales and, [where he is subject to a hospital order and a restriction order or a transfer direction and a restriction direction under any enactment in that Order, as if he were subject to a hospital order and a restriction order or a transfer direction and a restriction direction under the corresponding enactment] in force in England and Wales].

(3) Where a patient subject to guardianship under the [Mental Health (Northern Ireland) Order 1986] by virtue of an application, order or direction under any enactment in force in Northern Ireland is removed under this section and received into guardianship in England and Wales, he shall be treated as if on the date on which he arrives at the place where he is to reside he had been so received in pursuance of an application, order or direction under the corresponding enactment in force in England and Wales and as if the application had been accepted or, as the case may be, the order or direction had been made or given on that date.

[(4) Where a person removed under this section was immediately before his removal liable to be detained for treatment by virtue of a report under Article 12(1) or 13 of the Mental Health (Northern Ireland) Order 1986, he shall be treated, on his admission to a hospital in England and Wales, as if he had been admitted to the hospital in pursuance of an application for admission for treatment made on the date of his admission.

(4A) Where a person removed under this section was immediately before his removal liable to be detained by virtue of an application for assessment under Article 4 of the Mental Health (Northern Ireland) Order 1986, he shall be treated, on his admission to a hospital in England and Wales, as if he had been admitted to the hospital in pursuance of an application for admission for assessment made on the date of his admission.]

(5) Where a patient removed under this section was immediately before his removal liable to be detained under the [Mental Health (Northern Ireland) Order 1986] by virtue of a transfer direction given while he was serving a sentence of imprisonment (within the meaning of [Article 53(5) of that Order]) imposed by a court in Northern Ireland, he shall be treated as if the sentence had been imposed by a court in England and Wales.

(6) Where a person removed under this section was immediately before his removal subject to [a restriction order or restriction direction] of limited duration, the restriction order or restriction direction to which he is subject by virtue of subsection (2) above shall expire on the date on which the [first-mentioned restriction order or restriction direction] would have expired if he had not been so removed.

(7) In this section "the responsibility authority" means the Department of Health and Social Services for Northern Ireland or, in relation to a patient who is subject to [a restriction order or restriction direction], the [Department of Justice in Northern Ireland].

AMENDMENTS

The amendments to this section were made by the Mental Health (Northern Ireland Consequential Amendments) Order 1986 (SI 1986/596) art.2, the Mental Health Act 2007 s.39(2), Sch.5 Pt 1 para.8 and SI 2010/976, Sch.14, para.28.

DEFINITIONS

    patient: s.145(1).

1–1023

    hospital: ss.34(2), 92(1), 145(1).

    application for admission for assessment: ss.2, 145(1).

    application for admission for treatment: ss.3, 145(1).

    hospital order: ss.37, 145(1).

    transfer direction: ss.47, 145(1).

    restriction order: ss.41, 145(1).

    restriction direction: ss.49, 145(1).

GENERAL NOTE

This section provides that a patient who is detained or subject to guardianship in **1–1024** Northern Ireland may be transferred to England or Wales without a break in the powers of detention or guardianship. On arrival in England or Wales the patient will become subject to detention or guardianship under the Act.

Paragraph 34.33 of the Reference Guide states:

> "In practice, the Northern Ireland authorities will generally ask the Department of Health (or the Ministry of Justice for restricted patients) to confirm that arrangements have been made for the patient to be admitted to hospital or received into guardianship in England or Wales. The Secretary of State for Justice will not, in practice, agree to the transfer of a restricted patient to England unless satisfied that the proposed arrangements will enable the patient's safe management in England."

Applications to the First-tier Tribunal (Mental Health) or the Mental Health Review Tribunal for Wales

A patient who has been transferred under this section has a right to apply to a tribunal **1–1025** within six months of his transfer (ss.66(1), 69(2)(a)). The patient's nearest relative has similar rights to make an application (s.69(1), as applied by s.55(4)).

Subsection (1)

Appears. In the Northern Ireland case *Re JR49 (Application for Judicial Review)* **1–1026** [2011] NIQB 41; [2011] M.H.L.R. 351, para.39, Treacy J. held that this term "means 'is deemed or judged to' after all appropriate investigations and assessments have been completed". His Lordship said that the "level of the investigation and assessment required will depend on the gravity of the decision involved. As we know a decision to transfer a patient to England against his family's wishes and his own ascertainable wishes is a very grave decision indeed which demands the best informed and most anxious scrutiny".

Interests of the patient. Means making a choice "which brings more benefits to the patient than any other choice that could be made, i.e. the choice of the best option" (see *Re JR49*, above, para.34).

Subsection (2)

Date of his admission. Which must be recorded on Form M1: see reg.15 of the **1–1027** English Regulations (in Wales, Form TC7: see reg.29 of the Welsh Regulations).

Corresponding enactment. See the table set out at figure 89 of Ch.34 of the Reference Guide and the General Note to this Part under the heading "Corresponding legislative provisions".

[Transfer of responsibility for [conditionally discharged] patients to England and Wales from Northern Ireland

1–1028   **82A.**—(1) If it appears to [the Department of Justice in Northern Ireland], in the case of a patient who—

    (a) is subject to a restriction order or restriction direction under Article 47(1) or 55(1) of the Mental Health (Northern Ireland) Order 1986; and

    (b) has been conditionally discharged under Article 48(2) or 78(2) of that Order,

that a transfer under this section would be in the interests of the patient, [the Department of Justice in Northern Ireland] may, with the consent of the Secretary of State, transfer responsibility for the patient to the Secretary of State.

(2) Where responsibility for such a patient is transferred under this section, the patient shall be treated—

    (a) as if on the date of the transfer he had been conditionally discharged under section 42 or 73 above; and

    [(b) as if he were subject to a hospital order under section 37 above and a restriction order under section 41 above or to a transfer direction under section 47 above and a restriction direction under section 49 above.]

(3) Where a patient responsibility for whom is transferred under this section was immediately before the transfer subject to a restriction order or restriction direction of limited duration, the restriction order or restriction direction to which he is subject by virtue of subsection (2) above shall expire on the date on which the first-mentioned order or direction would have expired if the transfer had not been made.

(4) [. . .]

AMENDMENTS

    This section was inserted by the Crime (Sentences) Act 1997 s.48, Sch.3 para.3. The amendments to it were made by SI 2010/976, Sch.14, para.28 and the Mental Health Act 2007 s.39(2), Sch.5 Pt 1 para.9.

DEFINITIONS

1–1029   patient: s.145(1).

    hospital order: ss.37, 145(1).

    restriction order: ss.41, 145(1).

    restriction direction: ss.41, 145(1).

    transfer direction: ss.47, 145(1).

GENERAL NOTE

1–1030   This section enables the Secretary of State to authorise the transfer of a conditionally discharged restricted patient from Northern Ireland to England and Wales. The expiry date of the original order or direction is not effected by the transfer.

Subsection (1)

1–1031   SECRETARY OF STATE.   Functions under this provision have not been transferred to Welsh Ministers (see the General Note to the Act and SI 1999/672 art.2, Sch.1).

Removal to and from Channel Islands and Isle of Man

Removal of patients to Channel Islands or Isle of Man

83. If it appears to the Secretary of State, in the case of a patient who is for the **1–1032**
time being liable to be detained or subject to guardianship under this Act (otherwise than by virtue of section 35, 36 or 38 above), that it is in the interests of the
patient to remove him to any of the Channel Islands or to the Isle of Man, and that
arrangements have been made for admitting him to a hospital or, as the case may
be, for receiving him into guardianship there, the Secretary of State may authorise
his removal to the island in question and may give any necessary directions for his
conveyance to his destination.

DEFINITIONS
    patient: s.145(1).   **1–1033**
    hospital: ss.34(2), 92(1), 145(1).

GENERAL NOTE
    This section provides for patients who are detained or subject to guardianship in England **1–1034**
or Wales to be transferred to the Channel Islands or the Isle of Man by the Secretary of State
(or, for certain categories of patient in relation to Wales, the Welsh Ministers) without a
break in the powers of detention or guardianship. It does not apply to patients who travel
to the Channel Islands or the Isle of Man and who are not detained in hospital or received
into guardianship on arrival there. Transfers may require the approval of the relevant island
authorities in accordance with the local legislation. The Department of Health (or the
Ministry of Justice) will seek this as necessary. The Department of Health has devised a
pro-forma to be used by hospitals in England for non-restricted patients: see the General
Note to s.80.
    For the effect of a transfer under this section on the existing application, see s.91.
    If a patient is granted escorted leave of absence under s.17 to travel to the Isle of Man or
any of the Channel Islands, the escort would have no jurisdiction on arrival there.

    SECRETARY OF STATE.   See the note on s.80(1).

    GUARDIANSHIP.   The Reference Guide states at para.37.24:

    "In practice, a request for a transfer warrant should be made by, or on behalf of, the
patient's responsible local authority in England to the Department of Health. The request
should explain why the transfer would be in the patient's interests, the arrangements that
have been agreed for the patient to be received into guardianship in the island in question, and whether, and if so why, the patient needs to be kept in custody while being taken
there. The transfer may also have to be agreed with the relevant island authorities in
accordance with local legislation."

    ARRANGEMENTS.   For the transmission of information about these arrangements, see the
General Note to s.80.

    CONVEYANCE.   General provisions relating to the custody, conveyance and detention of
patients are contained in s.137.

[Removal or transfer of community patients to Channel Islands or Isle of Man

1–1035   **83ZA.**—(1) Section 83 above shall apply in the case of a community patient as it applies in the case of a patient who is for the time being liable to be detained under this Act, as if the community patient were so liable.

(2) But if there are in force in any of the Channel Islands or the Isle of Man enactments ("relevant enactments") corresponding or similar to those relating to community patients in this Act—

(a) subsection (1) above shall not apply as regards that island;
    and
(b) subsections (3) to (6) below shall apply instead.

(3) If it appears to the appropriate national authority, in the case of a community patient, that the conditions mentioned in subsection (4) below are met, the authority may authorise the transfer of responsibility for him to the island in question.

(4) The conditions are—

(a) a transfer under subsection (3) above is in the patient's interests; and
(b) arrangements have been made for dealing with him under the relevant enactments.

(5) But the authority may not act under subsection (3) above while the patient is recalled to hospital under section 17E above.

(6) In this section, "the appropriate national authority" means—

(a) in relation to a community patient in respect of whom the responsible hospital is in England, the Secretary of State;
(b) in relation to a community patient in respect of whom the responsible hospital is in Wales, the Welsh Ministers.]

AMENDMENT
This section was inserted by the Mental Health Act 2007 s.39(2), Sch.5 Pt 1 para.10.

DEFINITION
1–1036   community patient: ss.17A(7), 145(1).
    hospital: ss.34(2), 92(1), 145(1).
    patient: s.145(1).
    responsible hospital: ss.17A(1), 145(1).

GENERAL NOTE
1–1037   This section and s.85ZA provide for community patients to be transferred from England and Wales to the Channel Islands and the Isle of Man and vice versa. The Explanatory Notes state at para.166:

"At present the Channel Islands and the Isle of Man do not have legislation enabling patients to be treated in the community under arrangements similar to Supervised Community Treatment so [these sections] would not, as things stand, have any effect in relation to the Channel Islands or the Isle of Man".

The Reference Guide states:

"37.21 If there is no equivalent of a CTO in the island in question, patients on a CTO may instead be transferred to detention in the island under a transfer warrant [made under s.83], as if (in effect) they had never become a patient on a CTO.

37.22 In practice, a request for the transfer of a patient on a CTO should be made to the Department of Health by, or on behalf of, the managers of the patient's responsible hospital. At the time of publication the Isle of Man legislation contains provision for 'After-care under supervision' (section 28 et seq). The Jersey Mental Health Act 1969 contains no provision equivalent to the CTO. The Mental Health Law 2010 of the Bailiwick of Guernsey does contain provision for CTOs (section 26 et seq)."

[Transfer of responsibility for conditionally discharged patients to Channel Islands or Isle of Man

83A. If it appears to the Secretary of State, in the case of a patient who— **1–1038**

(a) is subject to a restriction order or restriction direction under section 41 or 49 above; and

(b) has been conditionally discharged under section 42 or 73 above,

that a transfer under this section would be in the interests of the patient, the Secretary of State may, with the consent of the authority exercising corresponding functions in any of the Channel Islands or in the Isle of Man, transfer responsibility for the patient to that authority.]

AMENDMENTS

This section was inserted by the Crime (Sentences) Act 1997 s.48, Sch.3 para.4. The heading was substituted by the Mental Health Act 2007 s.39(2), Sch.5 Pt 1 para.10.

DEFINITIONS

patient: s.145(1). **1–1039**
restriction order: ss.41, 145(1).
restriction direction: ss.49, 145(1).

GENERAL NOTE

This section provides a procedure for the Secretary of State to authorise the transfer of a **1–1040** conditionally discharged restricted patient from England and Wales to the Channel Island or the Isle of Man.

For the effect of a transfer under this section on the existing order or direction, see s.91.

Corresponding legislative provisions

See the General Note to this Part under this heading. **1–1041**

SECRETARY OF STATE. Functions under this provision have not been transferred to Welsh Ministers (see the General Note to the Act and SI 1999/672, art.2, Sch.1).

Removal to England and Wales of offenders found insane in Channel Islands and Isle of Man

84.—(1) The Secretary of State may by warrant direct that any offender found **1–1042** by a court in any of the Channel Islands or in the Isle of Man to be insane or to have been insane at the time of the alleged offence, and ordered to be detained during Her Majesty's pleasure, be removed to a hospital in England and Wales.

(2) A patient removed under subsection (1) above shall, on his reception into the hospital in England and Wales, be treated as if he [were subject to a hospital order together with a restriction order [. . .]

(3) The Secretary of State may by warrant direct that any patient removed under this section from any of the Channel Islands or from the Isle of Man be returned to the island from which he was so removed, there to be dealt with according to law in all respects as if he had not been removed under this section.

AMENDMENTS
The amendments to this section were made by the Domestic Violence, Crime and Victims Act 2004 s.58(1), Sch.10 para.22 and the Mental Health Act 2007 s.55, Sch.11 Pt 8.

DEFINITIONS
1–1043   hospital: ss.34(2), 92(1), 145(1).
patient: s.145(1).
hospital order: ss.37, 145(1).
restriction order: ss.41, 145(1).

GENERAL NOTE
1–1044   This section enables the Secretary of State to transfer to a hospital in England or Wales an offender who has been found to be insane by a court in the Channel Islands or Isle of Man. On arrival at the hospital, the patient will be treated as if he were subject to a hospital order with restrictions (subs.(2)).
For procedure and tribunal rights, see the General Note to s.82.

Transitional provision
1–1045   The repeal of the reference to restriction orders made for a specified period in subs.(2) shall have no effect in respect of—

(a) a restriction order for a specified period made before October 1, 2007, or

(b) an order made outside England and Wales which is treated under the 1983 Act as if it were a restriction order for a specified period (Mental Health Act 2007 s.40(7) and SI 2007/2798 art.2(d)).

Subsection (1)
1–1046   SECRETARY OF STATE. Functions under this provision have not been transferred to Welsh Ministers (see the General Note to the Act and SI 1999/672 art.2, Sch.1).

Patients removed from Channel Islands or Isle of Man
1–1047   **85.**—(1) This section applies to any patient who is removed to England and Wales from any of the Channel Islands or the Isle of Man under a provision corresponding to section 83 above and who immediately before his removal was liable to be detained or subject to guardianship in the island in question under a provision corresponding to an enactment contained in this Act (other than section 35, 36 or 38 above).

(2) Where the patient is admitted to a hospital in England and Wales he shall be treated as if on the date of his admission he had been so admitted in pursuance of an application made, or an order or direction made or given, on that date under the corresponding enactment contained in this Act and, where he is subject to an order or direction restricting his discharge, as if he were subject [to a hospital order and a restriction order or to a hospital direction and a limitation direction or to a transfer direction and a restriction direction].

(3) Where a patient is received into guardianship in England and Wales, he shall be treated as if on the date on which he arrives at the place where he is to reside he had been so received in pursuance of an application, order or direction under the corresponding enactment contained in this Act and as if the application had been accepted or, as the case may be, the order or direction had been made or given on that date.

(4) Where the patient was immediately before his removal liable to be detained by virtue of a transfer direction given while he was serving a sentence of imprisonment imposed by a court in the island in question, he shall be treated as if the sentence had been imposed by a court in England and Wales.

(5) Where the patient was immediately before his removal subject to an order or direction restricting his discharge, being an order or direction of limited duration, the restriction order or restriction direction to which he is subject by virtue of subsection (2) above shall expire on the date on which the first-mentioned order or direction would have expired if he had not been removed.

(6) While being conveyed to the hospital referred to in subsection (2) or, as the case may be, the place referred to in subsection (3) above, the patient shall be deemed to be in legal custody, and section 138 below shall apply to him as if he were in legal custody by virtue of section 137 below.

(7) In the case of a patient removed from the Isle of Man the reference in subsection (4) above to a person serving a sentence of imprisonment includes a reference to a person detained as mentioned in section 60(6)(a) of the Mental Health Act 1974 (an Act of Tynwald).

AMENDMENT

In subs.(2) the words in square brackets were substituted by the Mental Health Act 2007 s.39(2), Sch.5 Pt 1 para.11.

DEFINITIONS

1–1048

    patient: s.145(1).
    hospital: ss.34(2), 92(1), 145(1).
    hospital order: ss.37, 145(1).
    hospital direction: ss.45A(3), 145(1).
    limitation direction: ss.45A(3), 145(1).
    restriction order: ss.41, 145(1).
    restriction direction: ss.49, 145(1).
    transfer direction: ss.47, 92(5), 145(1).

GENERAL NOTE

This section provides for a patient who is detained or subject to guardianship in the **1–1049** Channel Islands or the Isle of Man to be transferred to England or Wales without a break in the powers of detention or guardianship.

The Reference Guide states:

"34.38 Patients transferred from the Isle of Man or the Channel Islands are treated on their arrival in England or Wales as if subject to the application, order or direction which corresponds to the provisions to which they were subject in the island in question. Advice should be sought from the island authorities or from the Department of Health or the Ministry of Justice, as applicable, if there is doubt about what the relevant corresponding provision is. Patients subject to the equivalent of remand to hospital under sections 35 or 36, or an interim hospital order under section 38, cannot be transferred.

34.39 For patients transferred from the Isle of Man who become subject to the equivalent of hospital directions or restriction directions in England, detention under sections 53 and 54 of the Mental Health Act 1998, is treated, where relevant, as if it were a sentence of imprisonment which has been given by a court in England or Wales."

For the procedure to be followed when a patient is transferred to England or Wales, see reg.15 of the English Regulations and reg.29 of the Welsh Regulations.

1–1050 *Corresponding legislative provisions*

1–1050   See the General Note to this Part under this heading.

Applications to the First-tier Tribunal (Mental Health) or the Mental Health Review Tribunal for Wales

1–1051   A patient who has been transferred under this section has a right of appeal to a tribunal within six months of his transfer (ss.66(1), 69(2)(a)). The patient's nearest relative has similar rights to make an application (s.69(1), as applied by s.55(4)).

[Responsibility for community patients transferred from Channel Islands or Isle of Man

1–1052   **85ZA.**—(1) This section shall have effect if there are in force in any of the Channel Islands or the Isle of Man enactments ("relevant enactments") corresponding or similar to those relating to community patients in this Act.

(2) If responsibility for a patient is transferred to England and Wales under a provision corresponding to section 83ZA(3) above, he shall be treated as if on the date of his arrival at the place where he is to reside in England or Wales—

    (a) he had been admitted to the hospital in pursuance of an application made, or an order or direction made or given, on that date under the enactment in force in England and Wales which most closely corresponds to the relevant enactments;
    and

    (b) a community treatment order had then been made discharging him from the hospital.

(3) "The responsible hospital", in his case, means the hospital to which he is treated as having been admitted by virtue of subsection (2) above, subject to section 19A above.

(4) As soon as practicable after the patient's arrival at the place where he is to reside in England or Wales, the responsible clinician shall specify the conditions to which he is to be subject for the purposes of section 17B(1) above, and the conditions shall be deemed to be specified in the community treatment order.

(5) But the responsible clinician may only specify conditions under subsection (4) above which an approved mental health professional agrees should be specified.]

AMENDMENT
This section was inserted by the Mental Health Act 2007 s.39(2), Sch.5 Pt 1 para.12.

DEFINITIONS
1–1053   community patient: ss.17A(1), 145(1).
patient: s.145(1).
hospital: ss.34(2), 92(1), 145(1).
community treatment order: ss.17A(7), 145(1).
responsible clinician: ss.34(1), 145(1).
approved mental health professional: s.145(1).

GENERAL NOTE
1–1054   See the General Notes to ss.83ZA and 85.

Subsection (4)
1–1055   SHALL SPECIFY THE CONDITIONS.   On form CTO 9: see reg.16(4) of the English Regulations.

[Responsibility for conditionally discharged patients transferred from Channel Islands or Isle of Man

85A.—(1) This section applies to any patient responsibility for whom is trans- **1–1056** ferred to the Secretary of State by the authority exercising corresponding functions in any of the Channel Islands or the Isle of Man under a provision corresponding to section 83A above.

(2) The patient shall be treated—

(a) as if on the date of the transfer he had been conditionally discharged under section 42 or 73 above; and

[(b) as if he were subject to a hospital order under section 37 above and a restriction order under section 41 above, or to a hospital direction and a limitation direction under section 45A above, or to a transfer direction under section 47 above and a restriction direction under section 49 above.]

(3) Where the patient was immediately before the transfer subject to an order or direction restricting his discharge, being an order or direction of limited duration, the restriction order[, limitation direction] or restriction direction to which he is subject by virtue of subsection (2) above shall expire on the date on which the first-mentioned order or direction would have expired if the transfer had not been made.]

AMENDMENTS

This section was inserted by the Crime (Sentences) Act 1997 s.48, Sch.3 para.4. The amendments to it were made by the Mental Health Act 2007 s.39(2), Sch.5 Pt 1 paras 12, 13.

DEFINITIONS

    patient: s.145(1).   **1–1057**
    hospital order: ss.37, 145(1).
    hospital direction: ss.45A(3), 145(1).
    limitation direction: ss.45A(3), 145(1).
    restriction order: ss.41, 145(1).
    restriction direction: ss.49, 145(1).

GENERAL NOTE

This section states that a patient who has been transferred from the Channel Islands or the **1–1058** Isle of Man under a provision that corresponds to section 83A, shall be treated as if on the date of the transfer he was a conditionally discharged restricted patient. Also see the General Note to s.85.

Corresponding legislative provisions

See the General Note to this Part under this heading.   **1–1059**

Subsection (1)

SECRETARY OF STATE. Functions under this provision have not been transferred to **1–1060** Welsh Ministers (see the General Note to the Act and SI 1999/672 art.2, Sch.1).

Removal of Aliens

Removal of alien patients

86.—(1) This section applies to any patient who is neither a British citizen nor a **1–1061** Commonwealth citizen having the right of abode in the United Kingdom by virtue of section 2(1)(b) of the Immigration Act 1971, being a patient who is receiving treatment for [mental disorder] as an in-patient in a hospital in England and Wales or a hospital within the meaning of the Mental Health Act [(Northern Ireland) Order 1986] and is detained pursuant to—

(a) an application for admission for treatment or [a report under Article 12(1) or 13 of that Order];

(b) a hospital order under section 37 above or [Article 44 of that Order]; or

(c) an order or direction under this Act (other than under section 35, 36 or 38 above) or [under that Order (other than under Article 42, 43 or 45 of that Order] having the same effect as such a hospital order.

(2) If it appears to the Secretary of State that proper arrangements have been made for the removal of a patient to whom this section applies to a country or territory outside the United Kingdom, the Isle of Man and the Channel Islands and for his care or treatment there and that it is in the interests of the patient to remove him, the Secretary of State may, subject to subsection (3) below—

(a) by warrant authorise the removal of the patient from the place where he is receiving treatment as mentioned in subsection (1) above, and

(b) give such directions as the Secretary of State thinks fit for the conveyance of the patient to his destination in that country or territory and for his detention in any place or on board any ship or aircraft until his arrival at any specified port or place in any such country or territory.

(3) The Secretary of State shall not exercise his powers under subsection (2) above in the case of any patient except with the approval of [the appropriate tribunal] or, as the case may be, of the Mental Health Review Tribunal for Northern Ireland.

[(4) In relation to a patient receiving treatment in a hospital within the meaning of the Mental Health (Northern Ireland) Order 1986, the reference in subsection (1) above to mental disorder shall be construed in accordance with that Order [and any reference in subsection (2) or (3) to the Secretary of State shall be construed as a reference to the Department of Justice in Northern Ireland].]

AMENDMENTS

The amendments to this section were made by the Mental Health (Northern Ireland Consequential Amendments) Order 1986 (SI 1986/596) art.2, the Mental Health Act 2007 s.1(4), Sch.1 para.15, SI 2010/976, Sch.14, para.28 and SI 2008/2883 art.9, Sch.3 para.62.

DEFINITIONS

1–1062   patient: s.145(1).

mental disorder: s.145(1), and see subs.(4) of this section.

hospital: ss.34(2), 92(2), 145(1).

application for admission for treatment: ss.3, 145(1).

hospital order: ss.37, 145(1).

the appropriate tribunal: ss.66(4), 145(1).

GENERAL NOTE

1–1063   This section empowers the Secretary of State (or, for certain purposes, the Welsh Ministers) to authorise the removal to any country abroad of certain detained in-patients (see subs.(1)) who do not have a right of abode in this country and who are receiving in-patient treatment for mental disorder (subs.(2)). It does not apply to detained patients who have been granted leave of absence under s.17. Before they exercise their powers the Secretaries of State or the Welsh Ministers must have obtained the approval of the appropriate tribunal (subs.(3)).

The main purpose of this section is to "enable patients who are either irrationally opposed to their removal, or are unable to express a view, to be compulsorily removed to another country when this is judged to be in their best interests. It is also used to enable patients to be kept under escort on their journey home if this is necessary" (Cmnd. 7320, para.8.26).

Paragraph 38.2 of the Reference Guide states:

"A removal warrant under the Act is only necessary where patients are not willing to travel or need to be kept in custody on the journey. A warrant is not necessary if patients are willing to travel and it is safe for them to do so without being in legal custody."

It is not appropriate to use this section where the patient is likely to be discharged within six months ("Foreign national restricted patients: Guidance on repatriation", Ministry of Justice, March 25, 2009, p.4).

If the patient is not a restricted patient, the patient will be granted leave of absence under s.17 to travel to the port of embarkation. The Secretary of State will use his power under s.42 to conditionally discharge a restricted patient, subject to the condition that he is taken directly to the port of embarkation. In *MJ (Angola) v Secretary of State for the Home Department* [2010] EWCA Civ 557, the Court of Appeal held that it was lawful for the Secretary of State to (a) use s.42 for this purpose and (b) make a decision to deport a person who is a restricted patient.

There is nothing to prevent a patient who has been removed under this section from applying for re-admission to the UK. If the patient was subject to a hospital order with restrictions when he was removed, both the hospital order and the restriction order will remain in force (s.91(2)). Otherwise the application, order or direction will cease to have effect when the patient leaves the UK (s.91(1)).

Proposals for the removal of Pt II patients detained in English hospitals should be made to the Secretary of State for Health (Wellington House, 133–155 Waterloo Road, London SE1 8UG). Proposals for the removal of Pt III patients should be made to the Secretary of State for Justice (Mental Health Casework Section, Ground Floor, Grenadier House, 99–105 Horseferry Road, London SWIP 2DD).

Functions under this section, so far as exercisable in relation to Wales, are transferred to the Welsh Ministers except in relation to a patient who is subject to a restriction order made under s.41, a hospital direction made under s.45A(3)(a), a limitation direction made under s.45A(3)(b), or a restriction direction made under s.49 (SI 2008/1786 art.2).

The Reference Guide states at para.38.8:

"Before deciding whether to seek the agreement of the Tribunal, the Department of Health or the Ministry of Justice will need to have details of the reasons for the proposed transfer and the arrangements that have or could be made for the patient's transport (in the UK and abroad) and for the patient's subsequent care and treatment. In practice, the Departments will expect the managers of the hospital in which the patient is detained to provide this information and (if the case is referred to the Tribunal) to provide any further information which the Tribunal requires."

In *R. (on the application of X) v Secretary of State for the Home Department* [2001] W.L.R. 740; [2000] M.H.L.R. 67, the Court of Appeal held that where a person detained under the Act had no basis for remaining in the UK under the Immigration Act 1971, the Secretary of State was entitled to remove him under the provisions of that Act, and was not obliged to do so only in accordance with his power of removal under this section. Schiemann L.J. said at para.28:

"There appears to us no reason why the two regimes should not run in parallel in the case of a person who is both an immigrant and mentally ill. Clearly if the [Secretary of

State] proposes to use his Immigration Act powers in relation to a mentally ill person that illness will be a factor which he must take into account."

In *MJ (Angola) v Secretary of State for the Home Department*, above, para.28, the Court of Appeal said that when exercising powers under the 1971 Act, the Secretary of State "must have regard to the patient's mental illness and any barriers to securing proper care and treatment in the country of destination".

As an alternative to the use of this section, the voluntary repatriation of restricted patients can be considered. This process is described in "Foreign national restricted patients: Guidance on repatriation", Ministry of Justice, March 25, 2009, p.3:

"Voluntary repatriation is an arrangement whereby the Ministry of Justice conditionally discharges the patient, subject to the condition that the patient is taken directly to a port of embarkation and from there to their home country The process is largely in the hands of the RC, and allows the RC the opportunity to contact and liaise with psychiatric services abroad to ensure that suitable care would be available for the patient on his or her return home. In order for a patient to be repatriated in this way the RC needs to be satisfied that:

- The patient is willing to return;

- The authorities in his home country are prepared to accept him;

- There are acceptable arrangements for continued treatment, including detention if appropriate;

- There are suitable transport arrangements.

If all of these provisions were met, a request for repatriation should be made to the [Mental Health Casework Section]. Once he is satisfied that the conditions are met, the Justice Secretary can issue a conditional discharge under section 42 of the Mental Health Act. The patient can then be conveyed, in accordance with the conditions of the discharge, to their destination country."

A similar approach, which would not involve either the Mental Health Casework Section or the Secretary of State, can be adopted for the voluntary repatriation of consenting non-restricted patients.

Guidance

1–1064   The Ministry of Justice has published guidance on "Foreign national restricted patients: Guidance on repatriation", see above, which can be accessed at: *www.justice.gov.uk/ offenders/types-of-offender/mentally-disordered-offenders*. The guidance covers voluntary repatriation and repatriation under this section.

Repatriation of Prisoners Act 1984

1–1065   It is possible for a patient who has been made subject to a hospital order or restriction order by a court to be transferred out of the UK by a warrant issued by the Secretary of State under the Repatriation of Prisoners Act 1984.

UK Borders Act 2007

1–1066   Section 32 of the UK Borders Act 2007 makes provision for the deportation of certain categories of foreign criminals where this is conducive to the public good. Section 33 of that Act provides that if the criminal is made the subject of a hospital order, a guardianship order, a hospital direction or a transfer direction, there is not an automatic assumption that deportation is conducive to the public good.

Travel Restriction Orders

Section 33 of the Criminal Justice and Police Act 2001 gives power in some circum- **1–1067** stances to the Crown Court to make travel restriction orders in relation to offenders convicted of drug trafficking offences. Such orders prohibit the offender from leaving the UK for a specified period after release from custody. Section 37 of the Act provides that a travel restriction order made in relation to any person shall not prevent that person being removed from the UK under a prescribed removal power. The Travel Restrictions Order (Prescribed Removal Powers) Order 2002 (SI 2002/313) Sch.1, designates subs.2(a) and (b) of this section as a prescribed removal power for the purposes of s.37.

Human Rights Act 1998

The removal of a patient under this section could involve a breach of art.3 of the **1–1068** European Convention on Human Rights (ECHR) if there is a real risk of the patient being the subject of inhuman or degrading treatment in the country to which he is sent. In *D v United Kingdom* (1997) 24 E.H.R.R. 423 para.54, the European Court of Human Rights (ECtHR) said:

"[T]he court emphasises that aliens who have served their prison sentences and are subject to expulsion cannot in principle claim any entitlement to remain in the territory of a Contracting State in order to continue to benefit from the medical, social or other forms of assistance provided by the expelling State during their stay in prison".

The same principle would apply to persons who are detained under this Act: also see *N v United Kingdom* (2008) 47 E.H.R.R. 39 and the notes to art.3 in Part 5.

Article 8 of the ECHR is engaged in deportation cases. In *Maslov v Austria* (2008) E.H.R.R. 20, para.75, the ECtHR held that "for a settled migrant who has lawfully spent all or the major part of his or her childhood and youth in the host country very serious reasons are required to justify expulsion. This is all the more so where the person concerned committed the offences underlying the expulsion measure as a juvenile".

Subsection (1)

UNITED KINGDOM. Means Great Britain and Northern Ireland (Interpretation Act 1978 **1–1069** s.5, Sch.1).

Subsection (2)

BY WARRANT AUTHORISE. Paragraph 38.9 of the Reference Guide states: **1–1070**

"If the Secretary of State obtains the Tribunal's approval and decides to authorise the patient's transfer, the Secretary of State will issue a warrant which directs that the patient is taken directly to the point of embarkation and which may also include any appropriate directions to allow the patient to be conveyed, while remaining in legal custody, out of the UK. This includes being kept in custody while en route to another country, eg on a plane or ship. But the Secretary of State cannot authorise the patient being kept in custody or detained once the patient has arrived in another country – so any escort arrangements for the rest of the journey would have to be made under the law of that country, if that is allowed."

CONVEYANCE ... AND FOR HIS DETENTION. General provisions relating to the custody, **1–1071** conveyance and detention of patients are contained in s.137.

Subsection (3)

THE APPROVAL OF THE APPROPRIATE TRIBUNAL. The Secretary of State will exercise his **1–1072** power under r.32(8) of the Tribunal Procedure (First-tier Tribunal) (Health, Education and Social Care Chamber) Rules 2008 (SI 2008/2699).

Return of patients absent without leave

GENERAL NOTE

Scotland

1–1073   Authority for the retaking of patients who have absconded from hospitals or other places in Scotland is contained in art.8 of the Mental Health (Care and Treatment) (Scotland) Act 2003 (Consequential Provisions) Order 2005 (SI 2005/2078) which is reproduced in Part 2.

Channel Islands and Isle of Man

The Explanatory Notes state at para.167:

"The Channel Islands and the Isle of Man have powers of their own, which they can use to return patients from England and Wales."

Patients absent from hospitals in Northern Ireland

1–1074   **87.**—(1) Any person who—

(a) under [Article 29 or 132 of the Mental Health (Northern Ireland) Order 1986] (which provide, respectively, for the retaking of patients absent without leave and for the retaking of patients escaping from custody); or

(b) under the said [Article 29 as applied by Article 31 of the said Order] (which makes special provision as to persons sentenced to imprisonment),

may be taken into custody in Northern Ireland, may be taken into custody in, and returned to Northern Ireland from, England and Wales by an [approved mental health professional], by any constable or by any person authorised by or by virtue of the [said Order] to take him into custody.

(2) This section does not apply to any person who is subject to guardianship.

AMENDMENTS

The amendments to this section were made by the Mental Health (Northern Ireland Consequential Amendments) Order 1986 (SI 1986/596) art.2 and the Mental Health Act 2007 s.21, Sch.2 para.7.

DEFINITIONS

1–1075   patient: s.145(1).
absent without leave: ss.18(6), 145(1).
approved mental health professional: s.145(1), (1AC).

GENERAL NOTE

1–1076   This section permits a patient from Northern Ireland who has either escaped from custody or who is absent without leave from a hospital, to be taken into custody in England or Wales and returned to Northern Ireland. It does not apply to patients subject to guardianship.

Subsection (1)

1–1077   RETURNED.   For the powers of a constable or approved mental health professional on taking the patient into custody and returning him to Northern Ireland, see s.137. The period during which the patient may be returned may not be the same as it is for patients subject to similar forms of detention in England. Advice should be sought from the Northern Ireland authorities on this point.

Patients absent from hospitals in England and Wales

88.—(1) Subject to the provisions of this section, any person who, under sec- **1–1078** tion 18 above or section 138 below or under the said section 18 as applied by section 22 above, may be taken into custody in England and Wales may be taken into custody in, and returned to England and Wales from, [Northern Ireland].

[(2) For the purposes of the enactments referred to in subsection (1) above in their application by virtue of this section, the expression "constable" includes an officer or constable of the Police Service of Northern Ireland.]

(3) For the purposes of the said enactments in their application by virtue of this section [. . .], any reference to an [approved mental health professional] shall be construed as including a reference—

(a) [. . .];
(b) [. . .] to any [approved social worker within the meaning of the Mental Health (Northern Ireland) Order 1986.]

(4) This section does not apply to any person who is subject to guardianship.

AMENDMENTS

The amendments to this section were made by the Mental Health Act 2007 ss.21, 39(2), 55, Sch.2 para.7, Sch.5 Pt 1 para.14, Sch.11 Pt 7 and the Mental Health (Northern Ireland Consequential Amendments) Order 1986 (SI 1986/596) art.2.

DEFINITION

approved mental health professional s.145(1).   **1–1079**

GENERAL NOTE

This section permits patients from England or Wales who are absent without leave from **1–1080** hospital or who have escaped from custody, to be taken into custody in, and returned to England and Wales from Northern Ireland. It does not apply to patients who are subject to guardianship. The patient must be taken into custody within the time limits specified in ss.18 and 22.

For patients who have absconded to Scotland, see the General Note to s.18.

Patients absent from hospitals in the Channel Islands or Isle of Man

89.—(1) Any person who under any provision corresponding to section 18 **1–1081** above or 138 below may be taken into custody in any of the Channel Islands or the Isle of Man may be taken into custody in, and returned to the island in question from, England and Wales by an [approved mental health professional] or a constable.

(2) This section does not apply to any person who is subject to guardianship.

AMENDMENT

The words in square brackets in subs.(1) were substituted by the Mental Health Act 2007 s.21, Sch.2 para.7.

DEFINITION

approved mental health professional: s.145(1).   **1–1082**

GENERAL NOTE

The purpose of this section is to ensure that a detained patient who absconds to England **1–1083** or Wales from the Channel Islands or the Isle of Man can be apprehended and returned to the island in question. It does not apply to patients who are subject to guardianship.

RETURNED. For the powers of a constable or approved mental health professional, see s.137. The period during which the patient may be returned may not be the same as it is for patients subject to similar forms of detention in England. Advice should be sought from the relevant authority on this point.

General

Regulations for purposes of Part VI

1–1084　**90.** Section 32 above shall have effect as if references in that section to Part II of this Act included references to this Part of this Act[, so far as this Part of this Act applies to patients removed to England and Wales or for whom responsibility is transferred to England and Wales.]

AMENDMENT

In this section the words in square brackets were substituted by the Mental Health Act 2007, s.39(2), Sch.5, Pt 1, para.15.

DEFINITION

1–1085　patient: s.145(1).

General provisions as to patients removed from England and Wales

1–1086　**91.**—(1) Subject to subsection (2) below, where a patient liable to be detained or subject to guardianship by virtue of an application, order or direction under Part II or III of this Act (other than section 35, 36 or 38 above) is removed from England and Wales in pursuance of arrangements under this Part of this Act, the application, order or direction shall cease to have effect when he is duly received into a hospital or other institution, or placed under guardianship [or, where he is not received into a hospital but his detention in hospital is authorised by virtue of the Mental Health (Care and Treatment) (Scotland) Act 2003 or the Criminal Procedure (Scotland) Act 1995], in pursuance of those arrangements.

(2) Where the Secretary of State exercises his powers under section 86(2) above in respect of a patient who is detained pursuant to a hospital order under section 37 above and in respect of whom a restriction order is in force, those orders shall continue in force so as to apply to the patient if he returns to England and Wales [. . .].

[(2A) Where responsibility for a community patient is transferred to a jurisdiction outside England and Wales (or such a patient is removed outside England and Wales) in pursuance of arrangements under this Part of this Act, the application, order or direction mentioned in subsection (1) above in force in respect of him shall cease to have effect on the date on which responsibility is so transferred (or he is so removed) in pursuance of those arrangements.]

[(3) Reference in this section to a patient's detention in hospital being authorised by virtue of the Mental Health (Care and Treatment) (Scotland) Act 2003 or the Criminal Procedure (Scotland) Act 1995 shall be read as including references to a patient in respect of whom a certificate under one of the provisions listed in section 290(7)(a) of the Act of 2003 is in operation.]

AMENDMENTS

The amendments to this section were made by SI 2005/2078 Sch.1 para.2(7) and the Mental Health Act 2007 ss.39(2), 55, Sch.5 Pt 1 para.16, Sch.11 Pt 8.

1–1087
 patient: s.145(1).
 hospital: ss.34(2), 92(2), 145(1).
 hospital order: ss.37, 145(1).
 restriction order: ss.41, 145(1).
 community patient: ss.17A(7), 145(1).

GENERAL NOTE
 This section provides that, with one exception, when a patient is removed from England **1–1088** or Wales under a provision in this Part, any application, order or direction made in respect of him (other than s.35, 36 or 38) will cease to have effect on arrival at his destination (subs.(1)) or, in the case of a community patient, the date on which responsibility for the patient is transferred (subs.(2A)). The exception is that if a patient who is subject to a hospital order with restrictions is removed, both the hospital order and the restriction order will remain in force (subs.(2)).

Transitional provision
 The repeal of the reference to restriction orders made for a specified period in subs.(2) **1–1089** shall have no effect in respect of—

(a) a restriction order for a specified period made before October 1, 2007, or

(b) an order made outside England and Wales which is treated under the 1983 Act as if it were a restriction order for a specified period (Mental Health Act 2007 s.40(7) and SI 2007/2798 art.2(d)).

Interpretation of Part VI
 92.—(1) References in this Part of this Act to a hospital, being a hospital in **1–1090** England and Wales, shall be construed as references to a hospital within the meaning of Part II of this Act.

 [(1A) References in this Part of this Act to the responsible clinician shall be construed as references to the responsible clinician within the meaning of Part 2 of this Act.]

 (2) Where a patient is treated by virtue of this Part of this Act as if he had been removed to a hospital in England and Wales in pursuance of a direction under Part III of this Act, that direction shall be deemed to have been given on the date of his reception into the hospital.

 (3) [. . .]

 [(4) Sections 80 to 85A above shall have effect as if—

(a) any hospital direction under section 45A above were a transfer direction under section 47 above; and

(b) any limitation direction under section 45A above were a restriction direction under section 49 above.

 (5) Sections 80(5), 81(6) and 85(4) above shall have effect as if any reference to a transfer direction given while a patient was serving a sentence of imprisonment imposed by a court included a reference to a hospital direction given by a court after imposing a sentence of imprisonment on a patient.]

AMENDMENTS
 The amendments to this section were made by the Mental Health Act 2007 ss.39(2), 55, Sch.5 Pt 1 para.17, Sch.11 Pt 1 and the Crime (Sentences) Act 1997 s.55, Sch.4 para.16.

DEFINITIONS

1–1091   responsible clinician: ss.34(1), 145(1).
patient: s.145(1).
mental disorder: ss.1, 145(1).
hospital direction: s.145(1).
transfer direction: s.145(1).
limitation direction: s.145(1).
restriction direction: s.145(1).

Subsection (1)

1–1092   HOSPITAL. See section 34(2).

PART VII

1–1093   *[Repealed by the Mental Capacity Act 2005 s.67(2), Sch.7.]*

PART VIII

MISCELLANEOUS FUNCTIONS OF LOCAL AUTHORITIES AND THE SECRETARY OF STATE

[Approved mental health professionals

Approval by local social services authority

1–1094   **114.**—(1) A local social services authority may approve a person to act as an approved mental health professional for the purposes of this Act.

(2) But a local social services authority may not approve a registered medical practitioner to act as an approved mental health professional.

(3) Before approving a person under subsection (1) above, a local social services authority shall be satisfied that he has appropriate competence in dealing with persons who are suffering from mental disorder.

(4) The appropriate national authority may by regulations make provision in connection with the giving of approvals under subsection (1) above.

(5) The provision which may be made by regulations under subsection (4) above includes, in particular, provision as to—

(a) the period for which approvals under subsection (1) above have effect;
(b) the courses to be undertaken by persons before such approvals are to be given and during the period for which such approvals have effect;
(c) the conditions subject to which such approvals are to be given; and
(d) the factors to be taken into account in determining whether persons have appropriate competence as mentioned in subsection (3) above.

(6) Provision made by virtue of subsection (5)(b) above may relate to courses approved or provided by such person as may be specified in the regulations (as well as to courses approved under section [114ZA or] 114A below).

(7) An approval by virtue of subsection (6) above may be in respect of a course in general or in respect of a course in relation to a particular person.

(8) The power to make regulations under subsection (4) above includes power to make different provision for different cases or areas.

(9) In this section "the appropriate national authority" means—

(a) in relation to persons who are or wish to become approved to act as approved mental health professionals by a local social services authority whose area is in England, the Secretary of State;

(b) in relation to persons who are or wish to become approved to act as approved mental health professionals by a local social services authority whose area is in Wales, the Welsh Ministers.

(10) In this Act "approved mental health professional" means—

(a) in relation to acting on behalf of a local social services authority whose area is in England, a person approved under subsection (1) above by any local social services authority whose area is in England, and

(b) in relation to acting on behalf of a local social services authority whose area is in Wales, a person approved under that subsection by any local social services authority whose area is in Wales.]

AMENDMENTS

This section was substituted by the Mental Health Act 2007 s.18. The amendment to subs.(6) was made by the Health and Social Care Act 2012 s.217(3).

DEFINITIONS   **1–1095**
    local social services authority: s.145(1).
    mental disorders. ss.1, 145(1).
    approved mental health professional: s.145(1C) and see subs.(10) of this section.

GENERAL NOTE

This section provides for the approval of approved mental health professionals (AMHPs) **1–1096**
by local social services authorities. AMHPs perform key functions under the Act: see the note on "For the purposes of this Act" in subs.(1). AMHPs can be drawn from social workers; first level nurses, whose field of practice is mental health or learning disability nursing; occupational therapists; and chartered psychologists: see the Mental Health (Approved Mental Health Professionals) (Approval) (England) Regulations (SI 2008/ 1206), which are reproduced in Pt 2. The equivalent regulations for Wales are SI 2008/ 2436 (W.209). A registered medical practitioner is specifically prohibited from being approved to act as an AMHP (subs.(2)). Although all of the professionals involved in an assessment of the patient for detention may be employed by the NHS, "the skills and training required of AMHPs aim to ensure that they provide an independent social perspective" (Explanatory Notes to the Mental Health Act 2007, para.64). An AMHP acts in a personal capacity when performing functions under the Act (see the notes on subs.(10) and on "that professional" in s.13(1A)).

The *Code of Practice*, at para.14.35, states that local authorities should ensure that sufficient AMHPs are available to carry out their functions under the Act and that arrangements must be in place to provide a 24-hour service that can respond to patient's needs. The Association of Directors of Adult Social Services issued an advice note to its members in July 2008 on "Local Social Services Authorities (LSSAs) and the Approved Mental Health Professional Role". In order to meet its obligations under this section, the Association recommends that LSSAs "enter into a contractual arrangement with the individual AMHP to cover remuneration, training requirements, disciplinary procedures, access to legal advice and legal indemnity whilst carrying out duties on behalf of the LSSA" (para.5.1). LASSAs are prevented from entering into agreements under s.75 of the National Health Service Act 2006 for NHS Trusts to exercise functions under this section on their behalf: see NHS Bodies and Local Authorities Partnership Arrangements Regulations 2000 (SI 2000/617) reg.6(a)(iv). SI 2000/617 has effect as if made under s.75, by virtue of the National Health Service (Consequential Provisions) Act 2006 s.4, Sch.2 Pt 1 para.1.

The approval of an AMHP is made by the LSSA (subs.(1)) and the AMHP acts on behalf of the authority (s.145(1AC)). A person may be approved as an AMHP by only one LSSA at any time. Even though an AMHP acts as an independent statutory decision maker, as an AMHP acts on behalf of the local authority that authority will be vicariously liable for any lack of care or bad faith on behalf of the AMHP (*TTM v London Borough of Hackney* [2010] EWHC 1349 (Admin); [2010] M.H.L.R. 214, para.35). In *TTM* Collins J. said that he could see no reason in principle why an AMHP should not owe a duty of care to the patient, thus giving rise to a possible action for negligent behaviour (para.36). Both the finding on vicarious liability and the conclusion reached on the duty of care owed by an AMHP were implicitly affirmed on appeal: see [2011] EWCA Civ 4; [2011] 3 All E.R. 529 at paras 59 and 97.

Approval will only be granted if the authority is satisfied that the applicant has appropriate competence in dealing with mentally disordered people (subs.(3)) and complies with any regulations issued by the Secretary of State if the authority is located in England, or the Welsh Ministers if the authority is located in Wales (subss.(4)–(8)).

Although an AMHP can only be approved by one LSSA, she can perform AMHP functions in the area of another LSSA (or LSSAs) if that authority has authorised the AMHP to perform such functions on its behalf. Confirmation of the authorisation can be given informally, e.g. by e-mail. On such an authorisation being made, the AMHP must notify the approving LSSA (SI 2008/1206, reg.5(b)). The Reference Guide states at para.30.5:

"Being approved by a local authority to be an AMHP is not the same as being permitted by a local authority to act on its behalf. It is for each local authority to establish its own arrangements for determining which AMHPs may act as such on its behalf and when they may do so. A local authority may arrange for AMHPs to act on its behalf even though they are approved by a different local authority."

To act as an AMHP on behalf of a Welsh LSSA would require approval by a Welsh LSSA under the Mental Health (Approval of Persons to be Approved Mental Health Professionals (Wales) Regulations 2008 (SI 2008/2436 (W.209). However, there is nothing to prevent an AMHP acting on behalf of an English LSSA in Wales where necessary. Paragraph 30.31 of the Reference Guide states:

"For example, an AMHP acting on behalf of an English local authority can make applications for admission to hospitals in Wales, or apply for a warrant under section 135 of the Act to a magistrates' court in Wales. Similarly, an AMHP acting on behalf of a Welsh local authority can make applications to hospitals in England or to English magistrates' courts."

In this situation, the AMHP acting on behalf of the English LSSA would have to use the statutory forms that are applicable in Wales, and vice versa.

Schedule 1 to SI 2008/2561 requires LSSAs to treat as an AMHP a person who had been approved as an ASW by an LSSA in Wales immediately before November 3, 2008.

Human Rights Act 1998

1–1097   An AMHP who is performing functions under the Act is exercising "functions of a public nature" and is therefore a "public authority" for the purposes of the 1998 Act: see s.6(3)(b) of that Act and *R. (on the application of Wilkinson) v Responsible Medical Officer Broadmoor Hospital* [2001] EWCA Civ 1545; [2002] 1 W.L.R. 419, at para.61. The effect of this is that it is unlawful for an AMHP to act in a way which is incompatible with a patient's rights under the European Convention on Human Rights (s.6(1) of the 1998 Act).

Subsection (1)

APPROVE. An AMHP should be provided with documentary evidence of her approval **1–1098** as some sections of the Act require the production of such a document. There is no statutory form that can be used for this purpose. The document, which should be authenticated by a senior officer of the approving authority, could read as follows: "[Name] has been approved under s.114 of the Mental Health Act 1983 to perform the functions of an Approved Mental Health Professional under that Act". It would be advisable to reproduce s.115, which provides AMHPs with a power of entry and inspection, on the document.

FOR THE PURPOSES OF THIS ACT. AMHPs perform functions under the following sections of the Act: ss.4, 6, 8, 10, 11, 13, 14, 17A, 17B, 17F, 20A, 18, 21B, 29, 30, 40, 47, 87, 88, 89, 115, 130B, 145, 135, 136 and 138.

Subsection (2)

Doctors cannot be appointed as AMHPs, even if they also have a qualification listed in **1–1099** the approval regulations.

Subsection (3)

APPROPRIATE COMPETENCE. See the competencies set out in Sch.2 to SI 2008/1206. The **1–1100** approving LSSA should have a mechanism in place to enable it to be satisfied that AMHPs continue to possess "appropriate competence" after approval.

Subsection (4)

APPROPRIATE NATIONAL AUTHORITY. See subs.(9). **1–1101**

REGULATIONS. See SIs 2008/1206 and SI 2008/2436 (W.209), noted above.

Subsection (10)

ACTING ON BEHALF OF A LOCAL SOCIAL SERVICES AUTHORITY. Concern was expressed in **1–1102** Parliament that if an AMHP is said to be acting on behalf of a LSSA, the authority could in some way direct the decisions of the AMHP. The Government denied that this was the case. Baroness Royall, speaking for the Government, said:

"An AMHP is required to make an independent decision about whether to make an application. I can assure your Lordships that nothing changes this. Paragraph 5(2) of Schedule 2 [which amends s.13 of the Act] makes it clear that AMHPs must make an application only if they are personally satisfied that it is necessary and proper to do so. The decision cannot be overturned by the local social services authority for which they are acting. The AMHP acts independently and will continue to do so in their decision making.

The [Act] makes it clear [in s.145(1AC)] that an AMHP carries out their functions on behalf of the LSSA. This underlines the independence of the AMHP from the trust that may employ the doctors who also examine a patient's case for admission. It also ensures that the responsibility for providing that an AMHP service is in place clearly lies with the LSSA, whether or not it chooses to enter into arrangements with another body, such as a trust, to provide the service" (*Hansard*, HL Vol.688, cols 681,682).

As AMHPs act on behalf of the appointing LSSA, that authority should provide legal advice on AMHP responsibilities to AMHPs, including those who are not employees of the authority. It might not always be easy to determine when an AMHP is performing the functions of an AMHP and, therefore, acting on behalf of the LSSA, and when the AMHP is performing her normal professional role and being accountable to her employer, which might not be the LSSA.

[Approval of courses: England

1–1103   **114ZA.**—(1) The Health and Care Professions Council may approve courses for persons who are, or wish to become, approved to act as approved mental health professionals by a local social services authority whose area is in England.

(2) The Council must publish a list of—

(a) the courses which are approved under this section, and

(b) the courses which have been, but are no longer, approved under this section and the periods for which they were so approved.

(3) The functions of an approved mental health professional are not to be considered to be relevant social work for the purposes of Part 4 of the Care Standards Act 2000.

(4) Where the function under subsection (1) is, in accordance with the Health and Social Work Professions Order 2001, exercisable by a committee of the Council, the committee may arrange for another person to exercise the function on the Council's behalf.]

AMENDMENT

This section was inserted by the Health and Social Care Act 2012 s.217 (2).

DEFINITIONS

1–1104   approved mental health professional: s.145(1), (1AC).
local social services authority: s.145(1).

GENERAL NOTE

1–1105   This section enables the Health and Care Professions Council to approve courses for the training of English AMHPs, regardless of the trainees' profession. The Council has produced criteria that set out its expectations of education providers and individuals completing these courses: see "Approval criteria for approved mental health professional (AMHP) programmes" (2013).

[Approval of courses: Wales]

1–1106   **[114A.**—[(1) The Care Council for Wales may, in accordance with rules made by it, approve courses for persons who are, or wish to become, approved to act as approved mental health professionals by a local social services authority whose area is in Wales.]

(2) For that purpose—

(a) subsections (2) to (4)(a) and (7) of section 63 of the Care Standards Act 2000 apply as they apply to approvals given, rules made and courses approved under that section; and

(b) sections 66 and 71 of that Act apply accordingly.

(3) [. . .]

(4) The functions of an approved mental health professional shall not be considered to be relevant social work for the purposes of Part 4 of the Care Standards Act 2000.

(5) The [. . .] Care Council for Wales may also carry out, or assist other persons in carrying out, research into matters relevant to training for approved mental health professionals.]

AMENDMENTS

This section was inserted by the Mental Health Act 2007 s.19. The amendments to it were made by the Health and Social Care Act 2012 s.217(4)–(8).

approved mental health professional: s.145(1), (1AC).   **1–1107**
local social services authority: s.145(1).

GENERAL NOTE
This section enables the Care Council for Wales to approve courses for the training of **1–1108**
Welsh AMHPs, regardless of the trainees' profession.

Powers of entry and inspection

[**115.**—(1) An approved mental health professional may at all reasonable times **1–1109**
enter and inspect any premises (other than a hospital) in which a mentally disordered patient is living, if he has reasonable cause to believe that the patient is
not under proper care.

(2) The power under subsection (1) above shall be exercisable only after the
professional has produced, if asked to do so, some duly authenticated document
showing that he is an approved mental health professional.]

AMENDMENT
This section was substituted by the Mental Health Act 2007 s.21, Sch.2 para.8.

DEFINITIONS
approved mental health professional: s.145(1), (1AC).   **1–1110**
hospital: s.145(1).
mentally disordered patient: s.1(2).
patient: s.145(1).

GENERAL NOTE
This section provides approved mental health professionals (AMHPs) with a power to **1–1111**
enter and inspect premises where a mentally disordered patient is believed to be living.
It does not provide the AMHP with authority to remove the patient. The power, which is
not limited to premises within the area of the AMHP's approving authority, does not
apply to NHS hospitals.

Section 42(1) of the Care Act 2014 requires a local authority to undertake an adult safeguarding enquiry where it:

"has reasonable cause to suspect that an adult in its area (whether or not ordinarily resident there)—

(a) has needs for care and support (whether or not the authority is meeting any of those
needs),

(b) is experiencing, or is at risk of, abuse or neglect, and

(c) as a result of those needs is unable to protect himself or herself against the abuse or
neglect or the risk of it".

A visiting headquarters, as defined by art.3 of the Visiting Forces and International
Headquarters (Application of Law) Order 1999 (SI 1999/1736), is exempted from the operation of this section (art.12, Sch.5).

Wales
Section 127 of the Social Services and Well-being (Wales) Act 2014 enables applications **1–1112**
to be made to magistrates' courts for adult protection and support orders. The purpose of
such orders is to enable an authorised officer to speak in private to a person suspected of
being an adult at risk to establish whether he or she can make decisions freely, to assess

whether the person is an adult at risk and to establish whether any action should be taken, and if so, what action.

Subsection (1)

1–1113   ALL REASONABLE TIMES.   The reasonableness of the time will presumably depend upon the urgency of the situation.

ENTER AND INSPECT.   This section does not empower the AMHP to force entry on to the premises, or to override the owner's refusal to give permission to enter. The Court of Appeal has held that a wife who is the co-owner of a house may give permission for a person to enter the house, and that person shall not be a trespasser, notwithstanding that the husband purports to refuse permission: see *Slade v Guscott*, July 28, 1981, 78/0656, (unreported), noted in L. Gostin, *Mental Health Services—Law and Practice*, 1986, at para.21.13.5. There is also authority for the proposition that a co-occupier of premises can allow entry to another person: see *R. v Thornley* (1981) 72 Cr. App. R 302. Permission to enter premises may also be given by a landlord in a situation where the tenant does not enjoy an exclusive right of occupation: see *R. v Rosso* [2003] EWCA Crim 3242, noted in the General Note to s.135.

If entry is refused, the AMHP could point out to the person concerned that a refusal to allow the inspection to take place would constitute an offence under s.129. If this information fails to impress the obstructor and entry is still denied, the AMHP should consider whether the facts of the case would justify making an application to a magistrate under s.135 for a warrant authorising a policeman to enter the premises by force. The police also have powers to enter premises without a warrant under s.17(1)(e) of the Police and Criminal Evidence Act 1984 and under the common law: see the General Note to s.135.

Whether the common law doctrine of necessity would provide a defence if force is used to gain entry to private property to apprehend a dangerous mentally disordered person in cases where there is an imminent threat of serious harm either to that person or to others and action is required before the arrival of the police is doubted by Brenda Hale: see *Mental Health Law* (2010), p.114.

PREMISES.   Which could include a care home or a private dwelling.

MENTALLY DISORDERED PATIENT.   The use of this phrase rather than the term "patient" (see s.145(1)), suggests that this section can only be invoked in respect of persons who have been diagnosed as being mentally disordered.

Subsection (2)

1–1114   PRODUCED, IF ASKED TO DO SO.   The right of entry is not dependent upon someone being available to whom the document can be produced (*Grove v Eastern Gas Board* [1952] 1 K.B. 77).

DULY AUTHENTICATED DOCUMENT.   See the note on "approve" in s.114(1).

Visiting Patients

Welfare of certain hospital patients

1–1115   **116.**—(1) Where a patient to whom this section applies is admitted to a hospital [, independent hospital or care home] in England and Wales (whether for treatment for mental disorder or for any other reason) then, without prejudice to their duties in relation to the patient apart from the provisions of this section, the authority shall arrange for visits to be made to him on behalf of the authority, and shall take such other steps in relation to the patient while in the hospital [, independent hospital or care home] as would be expected to be taken by his parents.

(2) This section applies to—

[(a) a child or young person—

(i) who is in the care of a local authority by virtue of a care order within the meaning of the Children Act 1989, or

(ii) in respect of whom the rights and powers of a parent are vested in a local authority by virtue of section 16 of the Social Work (Scotland) Act 1968;]

(b) a person who is subject to the guardianship of a local social services authority under the provisions of this Act [. . .]; or

(c) a person the functions of whose nearest relative under this Act [. . .] are for the time being transferred to a local social services authority.

AMENDMENTS

The amendments to this section were made by the Care Standards Act 2000 s.116, Sch.4 para.9(5), the Courts and Legal Services Act 1990 s.116, Sch.16 para.42 and SI 2005/2078 art.16, Sch.3.

DEFINITIONS

    patient: s.145(1).   **1–1116**

    hospital: s.145(1).

    care home; s.145(1).

    independent hospital: s.145(1).

    mental disorder: ss.1, 145(1).

    local social services authority: s.145(1).

    nearest relative: ss.26(3), 145(1).

GENERAL NOTE

This section obliges local authorities to arrange for visits to be made to certain categories **1–1117** of patients who have been admitted to NHS hospitals, independent hospitals and care homes. It also requires local authorities to take other steps in relation to such patients as would be expected to be taken by patients' parents. There is no requirement that the patients concerned need to be receiving treatment for mental disorder.

Section 131A places a qualified duty on hospital managers to place mentally disordered children who are admitted to hospital, whether informally or under compulsion, in a child friendly environment.

Where a child is provided with accommodation by any Local Health Board, Special Health Authority, NHS Trust, NHS Foundation Trust or local education authority for a period of three months, s.85 of the Children Act 1989 requires that body to notify the appropriate officer of the responsible local authority who shall take steps to ensure that the child's welfare is safeguarded. Similar responsibilities are placed on the proprietors of care homes and independent hospitals by s.86 of the 1989 Act. Following a notification under s.85 or 86, the local authority must arrange for the child to be visited (Children Act 1989 s.86A). Such visits must be carried out in accordance with the Children in Long-term Residential Care Regulations 2011 (SI 2011/1010).

The Secretary of State and, in relation to Wales, the Welsh Ministers (see the General Note to the Act and SI 1999/672 art.2, Sch.1) have the power to conduct, or assist other persons in conducting, research into this section so far as it relates to children looked after by local authorities (Children Act 1989 s.83).

Subsection (1)

1–1118   SUCH OTHER STEPS.   Which could include seeking a discussion with the hospital doctors about the patient's condition, ensuring that the patient's domestic arrangements are catered for during the stay in hospital, and providing a child patient with toys and reading matter.

Subsection (2)

1–1119   PARAGRAPH (A) CHILD.   This section does not apply to children who are wards of court.

PARAGRAPH (C) FOR THE TIME BEING TRANSFERRED TO A LOCAL SOCIAL SERVICES AUTHORITY. By virtue of s.29.

After-Care

After-care

1–1120   **117.**—(1) This section applies to persons who are detained under section 3 above, or admitted to a hospital in pursuance of a hospital order made under section 37 above, or transferred to a hospital in pursuance of [a hospital direction made under section 45A above or] a transfer direction made under section 47 or 48 above, and then cease to be detained and [(whether or not immediately after so ceasing)] leave hospital.

(2) It shall be the duty of the [clinical commissioning group or] [. . .] [Local Health Board] and of the local social services authority to provide [or arrange for the provision of], in co-operation with relevant voluntary agencies, after-care services for any person to whom this section applies until such time as the [clinical commissioning group or] [. . .] [Local Health Board] and the local social services authority are satisfied that the person concerned is no longer in need of such services [; but they shall not be so satisfied in the case of a [community patient while he remains such a patient.]]

[(2A) . . .]

[(2B) Section 32 above shall apply for the purposes of this section as it applies for the purposes of Part II of this Act.]

[(2C) References in this Act to after-care services provided for a patient under this section include references to services provided for the patient—

(a)   in respect of which direct payments are made under

[(i)   sections 31 to 33 of the Care Act 2014 (as applied by Schedule 4 to that Act),

(ii)   sections 50, 51 and 53 of the Social Services and Well-being (Wales) Act 2014 (as applied by Schedule A1 to that Act), or

(iii)   regulations under] section 12A(4) of the National Health Service Act 2006, and

(b)   which would be provided under this section apart from [those sections (as so supplied) or] the regulations.]

[(2D) Subsection (2), in its application to the clinical commissioning group, has effect [as if the words "provide or" were omitted].

(2E) The Secretary of State may by regulations provide that the duty imposed on the clinical commissioning group by subsection (2) is, in the circumstances or to the extent prescribed by the regulations, to be imposed instead on another clinical commissioning group or the Health Service Commissioning Board.

(2F) Where regulations under subsection (2E) provide that the duty imposed by subsection (2) is to be imposed on the National Health Service Commissioning

Board, subsection (2D) has effect as if the reference to the clinical commissioning group were a reference to the National Health Service Commissioning Board.

(2G) Section 272(7) and (8) of the National Health Service Act 2006 applies to the power to make regulations under subsection (2E) as it applies to a power to make regulations under that Act.]

(3) In this [section "the [clinical commissioning group or] [. . .] [Local Health Board]" means the [clinical commissioning group or] [. . .] [Local Health Board], and "the local social services authority" means the local social services authority[—

(a) if, immediately before being detained, the person concerned was ordinarily resident in England, for the area in England in which he was ordinarily resident;

(b) if, immediately before being detained, the person concerned was ordinarily resident in Wales, for the area in Wales in which he was ordinarily resident; or

(c) in any other case], for the area] in which the person concerned is resident or to which he is sent on discharge by the hospital in which he was detained.

[(4) Where there is a dispute about where a person was ordinarily resident for the purposes of subsection (3) above—

(a) if the dispute is between local social services authorities in England, section 40 of the Care Act 2014 applies to the dispute as it applies to a dispute about where a person was ordinarily resident for the purposes of Part 1 of that Act;

(b) if the dispute is between local social services authorities in Wales, section 195 of the Social Services and Well-being (Wales) Act 2014 applies to the dispute as it applies to a dispute about where a person was ordinarily resident for the purposes of that Act;

(c) if the dispute is between a local social services authority in England and a local social services authority in Wales, it is to be determined by the Secretary of State or the Welsh Ministers.

(5) The Secretary of State and the Welsh Ministers shall make and publish arrangements for determining which of them is to determine a dispute under subsection (4)(c); and the arrangements may, in particular, provide for the dispute to be determined by whichever of them they agree is to do so.]

[(6) In this section, "after-care services", in relation to a person, means services which have both of the following purposes—

(a) meeting a need arising from or related to the person's mental disorder; and

(b) reducing the risk of a deterioration of the person's mental condition (and, accordingly, reducing the risk of the person requiring admission to a hospital again for treatment for mental disorder).]

AMENDMENTS

The amendments to this section were made by the Health Authorities Act 1995 s.2(1), Sch.1 para.107(8), the Mental Health (Patients in the Community) Act 1995 s.2(1), Sch.1 para.15, Crime (Sentences) Act 1997 s.55, Sch.4 para.12(17), Sch.11 Pt 5, the National Health Service Reform and Health Care Professions Act 2000 s.2(5), Sch.1 para.47, SI 2007/961 art.3, Sch. para.13(9), the Mental Health Act 2007 s.32(4), Sch.3 para.24 and the Health Act 2009, s.13, Sch.1, para.3, the Health and Social Care Act 2012 s.40 and the Care Act 2014 s.75.

TRANSITORY PROVISIONS

Transitory provisions for Wales pending the implementation of certain provisions of the Social Services and Well-being (Wales) Act 2014 are contained in SI 2015/993, art.7.

DEFINITIONS

1–1121   hospital: s.145(1).
hospital order: ss.37, 145(1).
hospital direction: s.145(1).
Local Health Board: s.145(1), and see subs.(3) of this section.
transfer direction: ss.47, 145(1).
local social services authority: s.145(1), and see subs.(3) of this section.

TRANSITIONAL PROVISION

Section 75(12) of the Care Act 2014 states:

"In the case of a person who, immediately before the commencement of subsections (3) and (4), is being provided with after-care services under section 117 of the Mental Health Act 1983, the amendments made by those subsections do not apply while those services are continuing to be provided to that person."

For the case law that applied before the commencement of subss.(3) and (4) on April 1, 2015, reference should be made to the notes on this section in the 17th edition of this Manual.

GENERAL NOTE

1–1122   This section imposes an enforceable joint duty on the relevant health and social services authorities to provide or to arrange to provide after-care services for certain categories of mentally disordered patients who have ceased to be detained and leave hospital (or prison, having spent part of their sentence detained in hospital). The duty to provide after-care services (as defined in subs.(6)) is a freestanding one i.e. the services are provided under this section alone. It is not a "gateway" provision which places a duty on the "responsible after-care bodies" to prove services under other legislation (*R. v Manchester City Council Ex p. Stennett* [2002] UKHL 34). When discharging their duties under this section, clinical commissioning groups and local authorities may provide the person with direct payments (subs.(2C)). A local authority may authorise a third party to exercise on its behalf a function under this section (Care Act 2014 s.79). Functions under this section are NHS functions for the purposes of the NHS Bodies and Local Authorities Partnership Arrangements Regulations 2000 (SI 2000/617): see "Partnership arrangements", below.

As this section does not appear in the list of provisions set out in Sch.3 to the Nationality, Immigration and Asylum Act 2002, the duty under this section applies to patients irrespective of their country of origin. Section 54 and Sch.3 to the 2002 Act have the effect of preventing local authorities from providing support under the provisions listed in the Schedule to certain categories of refugees and asylum seekers.

The nature of the obligation placed on authorities by this section was considered in *R. v Ealing District Health Authority Ex p. Fox* [1993] 3 All E.R. 170 where Otton J. held that (1) a "proper interpretation of this section to be that it is a continuing duty in respect of any patient who may be discharged and falls within s.117, although the duty to any particular patient is only triggered at the moment of discharge"; and (2) a Health Authority "acts unlawfully in failing to seek to make practical arrangements for after-care prior to [a] patient's discharge from hospital where such arrangements are required by a [tribunal] in order to enable the patient to be conditionally discharged from hospital".

In *R. v Mental Health Review Tribunal Ex p. Hall* [1999] 3 All E.R. 132, Scott Baker J. said, at 143:

"In my judgment *Ex p. Fox* supports the following propositions which I accept to be the law: (i) an authority's duty to provide after-care services includes a duty to set up the arrangements that will be required on discharge. It is not a duty that arises for the first time at the moment of discharge; (ii) an authority with a duty to provide after-care arrangements acts unlawfully by failing to seek to make arrangements for the fulfilling of conditions imposed by a [tribunal] under section 73(2); (iii) if such an authority is unable to make the necessary arrangements it must try to obtain them from another authority; (iv) if arrangements still cannot be made an impasse should not be allowed to continue; the case must be referred back to a [tribunal] through the Secretary of State."

Fox and *Hall* were considered by Stanley Burnton J. in *R. (on the application of W) v Doncaster MBC* [2003] EWHC (Admin) 192; [2004] M.H.L.R. 189. His Lordship held that:

1. Neither *Fox* nor *Hall* is authority for the proposition that in a contested case the after-care bodies are placed under a duty to put in place after-care arrangements before the decision of a tribunal because the duty under this section only arises if (i) the patient has been in hospital under one of the provisions specified in subs.(1); (ii) the patient ceases to be detained; and (iii) the patient leaves hospital. His Lordship said at para.34:

   "It would be wasteful of the limited resources of (in this case) a local social services authority for it to have to plan and make arrangements for the after-care of all patients whose applications come before [tribunals]. Most applications are contested, and a relatively small proportion of contested applications succeed".

   His Lordship noted that in *R. v Mental Health Review Tribunal Ex p. Hall* [1994] 4 All E.R. 883, 890, Kennedy L.J. said that the terms of para.27.7 of the 1999 edition of the *Code of Practice* suggest that a care plan "at least in embryo" should be available before a tribunal hearing takes place.

2. In the case of a restricted patient the bodies are normally bound before actual discharge to endeavour to put in place the arrangements required by the tribunal as conditions of a conditional discharge, or which the tribunal requires before a deferred discharge takes effect, or which the tribunal provisionally decides should be put in place.

3. With both restricted and non-restricted patients where the discharge is not contested, the bodies should if practicable plan after-care before a tribunal hearing in order for it to be able to comply with its duty under this section on the patient's discharge.

With regard to the first proposition set out by Scott Baker J. in *Hall*, above, his Lordship **1–1123** said, at para.39, that it is "confined to cases in which the tribunal has decided on the discharge of the patient, and the arrangements ... were those specified by the tribunal". In *W v Doncaster MBC* [2004] EWCA Civ 378; [2004] M.H.L.R. 201. Scott Baker L.J. said, at para.49, that Stanley Burnton J. was correct in his analysis and that the observations that had been made by Otton J. in *Fox* and by himself in *Hall* to the effect that there is a duty under this section to set up after-care arrangements prior to the patient's discharge should not be followed. His Lordship said at para.51:

"Although the section 117 duty does not bite on local authorities or health authorities until after the tribunal decision, they do not at that point start entirely from scratch. Most such authorities will be faced fairly frequently with circumstances in which they are expected to exercise their section 117 duty to help to rehabilitate mental patients within the community. It is reasonable to suppose therefore that they have procedures in place for coping with situations of this kind. Also, they certainly have the *power*, in appropriate cases, to start making plans before the tribunal sits. Kennedy L.J. in *Hall* referred to them as plans in embryo. Once the tribunal has made its decision it will be a case of tailoring their procedures to meet the needs of the particular case."

The nature of the duty imposed by this section in a case where the tribunal has ordered the conditional discharge of a restricted patient was considered in *R. v Camden and Islington Health Authority Ex p. K* [2001] EWCA Civ 240; [2001] M.H.L.R. 24, where the Court of Appeal confirmed that this section does not impose on Health Authorities an absolute obligation to satisfy any conditions that a tribunal may specify as prerequisites to the discharge of a patient. Lord Phillips M.R. said at para.29:

"[This section] imposes on Health Authorities a duty to provide after care facilities for the benefit of patients who are discharged from mental hospitals. The nature and extent of those facilities must, to a degree, fall within the discretion of the Health Authority which must have regard to other demands on its budget".

In *K,* Lord Phillips endorsed a concession that had been made by the Health Authority that a failure to use reasonable endeavours to fulfil conditions imposed by a tribunal, in the absence of strong reasons, would be likely to be an unlawful exercise of discretion. If, despite the exercise of all reasonable endeavours, it proves impossible for the after-care bodies to fulfil the tribunal's conditions, the continued detention of the patient would not violate art.5 of the European Convention on Human Rights: also see the note on "Human Rights Act 1998", below. In *R. v Secretary of State for the Home Department Ex p. IH* [2003] UKHL 59; [2004] 1 All E.R. 412, para.29, the House of Lords confirmed that the "best endeavours" principle (which is the same as the "reasonable endeavours" principle (*W v Doncaster MBC,* above, para.50)) applies whether under this section or in response to the conditions attached to a patient's discharge by the tribunal.

1–1124   In *R. (on the application of B) v Camden LBC* [2005] EWHC 1366 (Admin); [2005] M.H.L.R. 258, Stanley Burnton J. held that:

1. As the duty under subs.(2) is only owed to a person who ceases to be detained and leaves hospital, the duty could not have arisen until after the decision of the tribunal that the preconditions for B's discharge had been satisfied. However, there is a power to make preparatory after-care plans prior to the patient leaving hospital: see the obiter remarks of Scott Baker L.J. in the *Doncaster* case, above.

2. The practical effect of the concession endorsed by Lord Phillips in *K,* above, is that a s.117 authority is under a duty to use reasonable endeavours to fulfil the conditions attached by the tribunal to the conditional discharge before the discharge has taken place.

3. It is unrealistic and wrong to require s.117 authorities to act to provide residential accommodation without exploring funding issues. Resources are limited, and any authority is entitled to consider, without dragging its feet, whether a suggested placement would involve an efficient use of its resources, and therefore whether there is a possibility of that placement being funded by central government or by another authority.

4. A s.117 authority is not placed under a duty to monitor the condition of a detained patient with a view to deciding whether there is occasion to exercise their discretion to arrange for the provision of after-care services in case he is discharged. Where a patient is represented before the tribunal, the patient's solicitor should inform the s.117 authorities of the decision; and the hospital should do so too. His Lordship said, at para.72, that consideration should be given to sending the written tribunal decision to the s.117 authorities in any case where a deferred conditional discharge is ordered.

In *B*, Stanley Burnton J. said obiter, following the comments made by Scott Baker L.J. in *W v Doncaster MBC*, above, that even if the after-care bodies had been in breach of their duties to B under this section or s.47 of the National Assistance Act 1984 [now see s.9 of the Care Act 2014], and that breach had prolonged his detention, they would not have been liable for damages under ss.6 and 8 of the Human Rights Act 1998 for breaches of B's rights under arts 5 or 8 of the ECHR as it was only the detaining authority that could potentially be liable for such breaches. Permission to appeal this case was refused by Wall L.J. at an oral hearing held on February 21, 2006 ([2006] EWCA Civ 256).

If there is uncertainty as to the putting in place of the after-care arrangements in respect of a patient, a tribunal should adjourn to enable them to be put in place, indicating their views and giving appropriate directions (*R. (on the application of H) v Ashworth Hospital Authority* [2002] EWCA Civ 923; [2002] M.H.L.R. 314, per Dyson L.J. at para.68).

Wales

With regard to patients who come within the scope of Part 2 of the Mental Health (Wales) **1–1125** Measure 2010, paras 6.23 and 6.24 of the Code of Practice to Parts 2 and 3 of the Measure state:

"For those relevant patients to whom aftercare under section 117 applies, the care and treatment plan under Part 2 of the Measure may be the means to record the aftercare arrangements in terms of outcomes to be achieved and the services to be provided or actions taken.

It is recommended that meeting the requirements to regularly review aftercare under section 117 and adhering to the statutory duties to review care plans are combined to reduce the need for multiple meetings that could otherwise create duplication."

Human Rights Act 1998

Whether a decision not to discharge a patient who had been granted a conditional dis- **1–1126** charge by a tribunal due to a failure to put in place appropriate after-care facilities in the community would constitute a violation of art.5 of the European Convention on Human Rights (ECHR) was considered by the House of Lords in *R. (on the application of H) v Secretary of State for the Home Department*, and by the European Court of Human Rights (ECtHR) in *Johnson* and *Kolanis*. These cases are analysed in the notes to s.73(7).

The question whether the ECHR places a general duty on states to provide community based services to respond to the needs of mentally disordered patients was considered by the Court of Appeal in *R. (on the application of H) v The Secretary of State for the Home Department* [2002] EWCA Civ 646; [2002] M.H.L.R. 87, where Lord Phillips M.R. said at para.87:

"We are not aware of any Strasbourg jurisprudence that indicates that a Member State owes a duty under the Convention to put in place facilities for the treatment in the community of those suffering from mental disorder so as to render it unnecessary to detain them in hospital."

In *Clunis v United Kingdom* [2001] M.H.L.R. 162, ECtHR, the applicant maintained that the failure of the authorities to implement their duties under this section amounted to a breach of the Government's positive obligations under art.8 of the ECHR, having regard to the harm which he had suffered. In declaring the complaint inadmissible, the Court said at paras 82, 83:

"[T]he Court considers that in the instant case there is no direct link between the measures which, in the applicant's view, should have been taken by Camden and the prejudice caused to his psychiatric well-being attendant on the realisation of the gravity of his act, his conviction and subsequent placement in a hospital placement without limit of time. The Court acknowledges that the assumption of responsibilities by the authorities of a Contracting State for the health of an individual may in certain defined contexts engage their liability under the Convention with respect to that individual as well as respect to third parties.

However, in the Court's opinion it cannot be said that Camden's failure to discharge its statutory duty under section 117 . . . led inevitably to the fatal stabbing of Jonathan Zito. It is a matter of speculation as to whether the applicant would have consented to become an in-patient on a voluntary basis or followed a prescribed course of medication or co-operated in any other way with the authorities. In these circumstances, and without prejudice to the question as to whether Article 8 is applicable in the circumstances of this case, the Court finds that the applicant's complaint does not disclose an appearance of a violation of that Article."

In *W v Doncaster MBC* [2004] EWCA Civ 378 para.67, Scott Baker L.J. said that the ECHR places no greater obligation upon a s.117 after-care authority than domestic legislation.

Charging for local authority services provided under section 117

1–1127   In *R. v Manchester City Council Ex p. Stennett* [2002] UKHL 34; [2002] 4 All E.R. 124, the House of Lords dismissed an appeal from the Court of Appeal ([2001] 1 All E.R. 436) by holding that as this section imposes a freestanding duty to provide after-care services, and, as there is no express power to charge for services provided under it, such services must be provided free of charge.

At the first instance hearing ((1999) 2 C.C.L.R. 402), Sullivan J. held that if a charged for service is being provided to the patient prior to the patient's admission under one of the provisions set out in subs.(1), that service would have to be provided free of charge on the patient's discharge from hospital if the provision of the service was a component of the patient's after-care plan. This finding is unaffected by the decision of the House of Lords.

The decision of the House of Lords, which is now subject to the additional cost provisions of the Care and Support and After-care (Choice of Accommodation) Regulations 2014 (SI 2014/2670) noted under s.117A, leads to the following consequences:

Case 1. A 50-year-old man with pre-senile dementia is admitted informally to hospital as a compliant mentally incompetent patient. He is assessed as requiring residential care on his discharge from hospital. He will almost certainly require such accommodation for the rest of his life. He could be charged for the accommodation by virtue of s.14 of the Care Act 2014.

Case 2. A 50-year-old man with pre-senile dementia and with identical needs to the man in Case 1 is admitted to hospital under s.3 because he happened not to be compliant when the crisis in his mental health occurred. He is assessed as requiring residential care on his discharge from hospital. He will almost certainly require such accommodation for the rest of his life. He will be provided with the accommodation without charge because he comes within the scope of s.117.

In *Stennett*, counsel for the local authority described this scenario as the anomaly of the compliant and non-compliant patients in adjacent beds. Lord Steyn rejected this view as being "too simplistic". His Lordship said, at para.13, that there:

"may well be a reasonable view that generally patients compulsorily admitted under ss.3 and 37 pose greater risks upon discharge to themselves and others than compliant patients. Moreover, Parliament necessarily legislates for the generality of cases".

Nicolette Priaulx comments that the anomaly is far from "simplistic" in that it highlights "the manifest unfairness which can arise from differential treatment in circumstances where the 'need' of the patients are objectively no different at all" ("Charging for

After-care services under Section 117 of the Mental Health Act 1983—The Final Word?", *Journal of Mental Health Law* (2002), 8, 313–322, at 317; see also Phil Fennell, All E.R. Rev. 2002, paras 18.57, 18.58). In *R. v Bournewood Community and Mental Health NHS Trust Ex p. L* [1998] 3 All E.R. 298 at 309, Lord Steyn described mentally incapable compliant patients as being "diagnostically indistinguishable from compulsory patients". The decision in *Stennett* has resulted in the charging for residential care provided to the mentally disordered operating in an arbitrary manner with free care being provided for those whose clinical and financial needs may not be as great as those who are charged for such care.

For many patients who are provided with after-care services under this section, the administration of medication for their mental disorder will be a key component of their after-care plan. "Psychiatric treatment" was identified as an after-care service by Lord Steyn in *Stennett* (at para.7). By virtue of the principle established in *Stennett*, medication provided by the Health Authority as an after-care service is provided under this section and the National Health Service (Charges for Drugs and Appliances) Regulations 2000 (SI 2000/620) do not apply. The medication should therefore be provided free of charge. It has been reported that the Department of Health does not agree with this opinion (Mind's legal newsletter, Issue 7, November 2010, p.9). Regulation 5(3A) of SI 2000/620 has been amended by SI 2008/2593 to provide that patients who are subject to a community treatment order must be provided with medicines for the treatment of their mental disorder free of charge.

The three Local Government Ombudsmen, pursuant to their power under s.23(12A) of the Local Government Act 1974, produced a "Special Report" providing "advice and guidance on the funding of aftercare under s.117 of the Mental Health Act 1983" (2003). The report considers the extent to which authorities are liable for financial restitution to those who have been charged for s.117 services.

If a local authority refunds charges that were wrongly made for residential care provided under this section, the refund will be taken into account as capital by the Department of Work and Pensions in determining a claimant's entitlement to income support after the date of the repayment (Decision of the Social Security Commissioner (CIS/3760/2006), October 2007).

NHS Continuing Healthcare
Paragraphs 120 to 122 of the *National Framework for NHS Continuing Healthcare and* **1–1128**
NHS-funded Nursing Care (November 2012 (revised)) state:

"Responsibility for the provision of section 117 services lies jointly with LAs and the NHS. Where a patient is eligible for services under section 117 these should be provided under section 117 and not under NHS continuing healthcare. It is important for CCGs to be clear in each case whether the individual's needs (or in some cases which elements of the individual's needs) are being funded under section 117, NHS continuing healthcare or any other powers, irrespective of which budget is used to fund those services.

There are no powers to charge for services provided under section 117, regardless of whether they are provided by the NHS or LAs. Accordingly, the question of whether services should be 'free' NHS services (rather than potentially charged-for social services) does not arise. It is not, therefore, necessary to assess eligibility for NHS continuing healthcare if all the services in question are to be provided as after-care services under section 117.

However, a person in receipt of after-care services under section 117 may also have ongoing care/support needs that are not related to their mental disorder and that may, therefore, not fall within the scope of section 117. Also a person may be receiving services under section 117 and then develop separate physical health needs (e.g. through a stroke) which may then trigger the need to consider NHS continuing healthcare only in relation to these separate needs, bearing in mind that NHS continuing healthcare should not be used to meet section 117 needs. Where an individual in receipt of section 117 services develops physical care needs resulting in a rapidly deteriorating condition which may be entering a terminal phase, consideration should be given to the use of the Fast Track Pathway Tool."

Independent Mental Health Advocates and Care Act Advocates

1–1129 Paragraph 7.23 of "Care and Support Statutory Guidance", Department of Health, 2014, states:

"Under the Mental Health Act 1983 (MHA) certain people, known as 'qualifying patients', are entitled to the help and support from an Independent Mental Health Advocate (IMHA). Section 117 of the MHA places a duty on the NHS and local authorities to provide aftercare and this will usually involve a joint assessment (often under the Care Programme Approach) including an assessment of the person's care and support needs, a care and support or support plan and subsequent review (which may reach a decision that a person is no longer in need of aftercare). Those people who do not retain a right to an IMHA, whose care and support needs are being assessed, planned or reviewed should be considered for an advocate under the Care Act, if they have substantial difficulty in being involved and if there is no appropriate person to support their involvement (see paragraph 7.32)."

Independent Mental Capacity Advocates

1–1130 Section 39 of the Mental Capacity Act 2005 applies if a local authority intends to arrange for a patient to be provided with long-stay residential accommodation under this section, or for the accommodation to be changed, if:

(i) there is no-one apart from a professional or paid carer for the authority to consult in determining whether the placement would be in the patient's best interests; and

(ii) the patient lacks the mental capacity to make a decision about the arrangements.

In this situation, the authority is required to instruct an independent mental capacity advocate (IMCA) to represent the patient and any information given, or submissions made, by the IMCA must be taken into account when a decision is made about the placement. Such consultation need not take place if the patient is likely to stay in the accommodation for less than eight weeks or if the need for the accommodation is urgent. However, the consultation must take place after the placement has been effected if the authority subsequently believes that the accommodation will be provided for the patient for at least eight weeks. Section 39 does not apply if the accommodation is provided as a result of an obligation imposed on the patient under this Act: see further, paras 1–367 to 1–474 of the author's *Mental Capacity Act Manual* (6th edn, 2014).

Partnership arrangements

1–1131 This section is prescribed as a NHS function which may be the subject of a partnership arrangement with local authorities under s.75 of the National Health Service Act 2006 (NHS Bodies and Local Authority Partnership Arrangements Regulations 2000 (SI 2000/617) reg.5). Section 75 enables NHS bodies and local authorities to pool resources, delegate functions and transfer resources from one body to another so that there can be a single provider of services. By virtue of reg.6 of SI 2000/617, this section is a health-related function of a local authority that may be the subject of a partnership arrangement. SI 2000/617 has effect as if made under s.75, by virtue of the National Health Service (Consequential Provisions) Act 2006 s.4, Sch.2 Pt 1 para.1.

Contracting out

Provision to enable a local authority in England to authorise another person, or that per- **1–1132** son's employees, to exercise functions under this section is made by the Contracting Out (Local Authorities Social Services Functions) (England) Order 2014 (SI 2014/829) art.2, Sch.

Applications to the First-tier Tribunal (Mental Health) and to the Hospital Managers

See para.33.12 of the *Code of Practice*. **1–1133**

It is not essential for the tribunal to have specific information about aftercare in every case, in particular a case where the patient has not progressed to the point where the issue of after-care that was actually available would arise: see *AM v West London MH NHS Trust & Secretary of State for Justice* [2012] UKUT 382; [2012] M.H.L.R. 399, which is noted under s.72(1).

In *AF v Nottinghamshire NHS Trust* [2015] UKUT 216 (AAC), para.50, UT Judge Wright observed obiter that the law does not "require the social circumstances report to include details about s.117 after-care in every case. I say this because it is arguable that the terms of para.14(i) in the Practice Direction only require that the report includes details of the care pathway and s.117 after-care to be made available, so far as is known, and that may therefore absolve the report from including such information if it is not known, for example where no s.117 after-care '*is to be made available*' because the views of all those treating the patient is that he is not close to being able to be discharged".

Code of Practice

Guidance on this section is contained in Ch.33. For the application of this section to chil- **1–1134** dren, see paras 19.111 and 19.112 of the *Code*. With regard to the provision of information to patients, the *Code* states at para.4.30:

"When a detained patient or a community patient is discharged, or the authority for their detention or the CTO expires, this fact should be made clear to them. The patient should be given an explanation of what happens next, including any section 117 after-care or other services which are to be provided."

Subsection (1)

This section applies to patients of all ages, including children and young persons, who come within the scope of this provision.

HOSPITAL ORDER MADE UNDER SECTION 37. This section also applies to hospital order **1–1135** patients who have been made subject to restriction orders under s.41. A person who is admitted to a hospital in pursuance of an admission order made otherwise than under s.14A of the Criminal Appeal Act 1968 shall be treated for the purposes of this Act as if he had been admitted in pursuance of a hospital order or, if the court so directs, a restriction order (Criminal Procedure (Insanity and Unfitness to Plead) Act 1991 Sch.1 para.2(1)).

TRANSFER DIRECTION MADE UNDER SECTION 47 OR 48. This section also applies to transfer direction patients who have been made subject of restriction directions under s.49.

In 2011, the Department of Health published "Good Practice Procedure Guide: The transfer and remission of adult prisoners under s.47 and s.48 of the Mental Health Act". Paragraphs 5.11 to 5.14 of this document state:

"Before the return to prison can be authorised by the Secretary of State, a multi-agency s.117 meeting must be held to agree aftercare arrangements including a Care Plan to accompany the prisoner on their return to custody.

The mental health service provider treating the transferred prisoner will convene and host the s.117 meeting.

The local receiving prison healthcare and custody staff are expected to attend the s.117 meeting. If the prisoner has at least 6 months remaining on their sentence and fits the criteria for MAPPA involvement, a representative of the local MAPPA should also attend.

Mental Health Casework Section (MHCS) will only consider remission to prison without a completed s.117 meeting in exceptional circumstances. In such cases, MHCS require confirmation of the date of the planned s.117 meeting before the warrant can be agreed."

Paragraphs 17.6 and 17.7 of "Care and Support Statutory Guidance", Department of Health, 2014, state:

"Where prisoners have previously been detained under sections 47 and 48 of the Mental Health Act 1983 and transferred back to prison, their entitlement to section 117 aftercare should be dealt with in the same way as it would be in the community, apart from any provisions which are disapplied in custodial settings, such as direct payments and choice of accommodation, which are set out in more detail below. Section 117(3), as amended by the Care Act 2014, will apply in determining which local authority is responsible for commissioning or providing the section 117 after-care.

If the person was ordinarily resident in the area of a local authority immediately before being detained in hospital, that local authority will be responsible for the after-care while the person is in prison and upon their release from prison (see Chapter 19 for further detail on determination). However, if the person was not ordinarily resident in any area immediately before detention, the local authority responsible will be where the person is resident or where they have been discharged (i.e. the local authority responsible for the prison to which the person has been discharged). The local authority will be jointly responsible for after-care with NHS England while the person is in prison."

With regard to children returning to custody from hospital, paras 5.6 and 5.7 of *Procedure for the Transfer from Custody of Children and Young People to and from Hospital under the Mental Health Act 1983 in England*, Department of Health, 2011, state:

"In keeping with best practice and the Act, children and young people returning to custody from hospital will be accompanied by a CPA care plan indicating whether or not the child or young person requires ongoing mental health services. This is in addition to updating the child's or young person's sentence plan and Asset. An S117 meeting should be held for this purpose. Healthcare providers working in the secure estate establishment receiving the transferred patient must be invited to attend the pre-discharge planning meeting and must make best efforts to attend. Where representation from the receiving secure estate establishment is not possible, this should not delay the child or young person returning there. The meeting should include planning and preparation for both return to custody and future release from custody, including transportation requirements.

Only in exceptional, emergency circumstances (for example, where there is a severe, non-containable risk) may a child or young person be returned to custody **before** an S117 plan has been agreed. In such circumstances an S117 meeting should be organised as soon as practicable afterwards, and always within 24 hours of the transfer. This will be reinforced by the YJB and the Mental Health Casework Section which will not issue a remission warrant unless such a meeting has been held, except in wholly exceptional circumstances. The Mental Health Casework Section must be advised which secure estate establishment the YJBPS has deemed the most appropriate for the child or young person before the remission warrant can be issued."

CEASE TO BE DETAINED. The duty to provide after-care services under this section extends to patients who, having been detained under s.3, are granted leave of absence under s.17. In *R. v Richmond LBC Ex p. W* [1999] M.H.L.R. 155, Sullivan J. said at para.99:

"In my view, this section is dealing with a practical problem: what after-care is to be provided for a patient who has suffered from mental illness requiring inpatient treatment when he actually leaves hospital? A person on leave under section 17 is in just as much, if not more, need of care after he leaves hospital as a person who leaves hospital subject to guardianship or supervision. For the purposes of section 17, he has ceased to be detained, and left hospital. It would be remarkable if, in such circumstances there was no duty to provide him with after-care under section 117, even though it would almost certainly have been a condition of his being given leave that he should reside in particular accommodation."

His Lordship's reasoning on this point would also apply to a restricted patient who had been conditionally discharged from hospital. His Lordship further held that the duty under this section extends to s.3 patients who are transferred into guardianship under the provisions of s.19.

Whether patients who have been granted s.17 leave will require after-care services during such leave will "depend on the specific circumstances of the case" (Reference Guide, para.29.15).

WHETHER OR NOT IMMEDIATELY AFTER SO CEASING. This section applies to a patient who has been detained under one of the sections mentioned in this subsection and who subsequently acquires informal status prior to leaving hospital. It also applies to a patient who having been discharged from the s.3, is re-detained under another provision of the Act (e.g. under s.5(2)) prior to his discharge from hospital.

Subsection (2)

DUTY. The nature of this duty is considered in the General Note to this section. The **1–1136** duty will last until the after-care bodies are satisfied that the patient no longer needs any after-care service for his mental disorder. The patient is not legally obliged to accept the after-care services that are offered. An unwillingness to receive after-care services should not be equated with an absence of a need for such services. A patient's continued refusal to receive after-care services should be confirmed by professional inquiry at appropriate intervals.

In *Clunis v Camden and Islington Health Authority* [1998] 3 All E.R. 180 CA the Court of Appeal held that (1) the duty under this section to provide after-care services does not give rise to a private law claim for damages if it is not fulfilled; and (2) the primary method of enforcement of the duty is by complaint to the Secretary of State. The patient's complaint under art.6(1) of the ECHR that he was denied a right of access to a court to argue his case against the defendant after-care body was declared inadmissible by the European Court of Human Rights on September 11, 2001. In *K v Central and North West London Mental Health Trust* [2008] EWHC 1217 (Q.B.); [2008] M.H.L.R. 168, King J., in allowing an appeal in a striking out action, said that: (1) the proposition expounded in *Clunis* was confined to the facts of that case; and (2), in any event, subsequent legal developments, particularly arising under the ECHR meant that *Clunis* could no longer be regarded as a definitive ruling on the question of a common law duty of care in the context of functions being performed under this section.

In *R. (on the application of W) v Doncaster MBC* [2003] EWHC (Admin) 192; [2004] M.H.L.R. 189, Stanley Burnton J. held that although a breach of the duty imposed by this section does not of itself give rise to a cause of action for damages for breach of statutory duty (*Clunis*, above), an authority whose breach of its duty causes the detention (or prolongs the detention) of a patient who would otherwise be discharged will normally cause an infringement of his rights under art.5(1) of the ECHR.

CLINICAL COMMISSIONING GROUP. For the identity of the relevant CCG, see subs.(3).

OR ARRANGE FOR THE PROVISION OF. CCGs and local authorities can commission as well as provide after-care services.

1–1137 LOCAL SOCIAL SERVICES AUTHORITY. For the identity of the relevant social services authority, see subs.(3). There is no requirement for the authority's duty to be carried out by approved mental health professionals (*Nottingham City Council v Unison* [2004] EWHC 893, para.24).

AFTER-CARE SERVICES. See subs.(6).

ANY PERSON. If the person is a child, the local authority should ensure that it complies with its responsibilities under Pt III of the Children Act 1989.

1–1138 SATISFIED. The after-care must be satisfied that the patient is no longer in need of after-care services (*R. (on the applicant of Mwanza) v Greenwich LBC* [2010] EWHC 1462 (Admin); [2010] M.H.L.R. 226 para.88). The after-care bodies cannot be so satisfied if the patient is a community patient (subs.(2)). A decision that a patient no longer qualifies for services under this section can only be made if the after-care bodies have monitored the patient's progress in the community since discharge. It "is for the authority responsible for providing particular services to take the lead in deciding whether those services are no longer required. The patient, his/her carer and other agencies should always be consulted" (Local Authority Circular LAC (2000) 3, para.4). The duty to provide after care services continues until *both* authorities have come to a decision that the patient no longer needs *any* after-care service. Given the nature of after-care services, many patients will require such services for substantial periods. A patient should not be discharged from care under this section solely on the ground that: (1) he has been discharged from the care of a responsible clinician or specialist mental health services (2) an arbitrary period has elapsed since the care was first provided; (3) the provision of care is successful in that he is well settled in the community or in residential care and the continuation of after-care is needed to prevent a relapse or further deterioration in his condition (*Code of Practice*, para.33.23); (4) he is no longer subject to a community treatment order or s.17 leave; (5) he returns to hospital as an informal patient or under s.2 and subsequently leaves the hospital; (6) the diagnostic category of the patient's mental disorder changes; or (7) the patient has been made the subject of a deprivation of liberty authorisation under the Mental Capacity Act 2005. See further, the *Code of Practice* at para.33.21.

With regard to (3), responsibility under this section could end if the needs that were being addressed after the patient became settled in a care home related to the patient's age and mental frailty rather than to the patient's mental disorder: see further "A report by the Health Service Ombudsman and the Local Government Ombudsman about the provision of section 117 aftercare", HC 642, Oct 2012 which is noted under subs.(6).

If a person is assessed as no longer coming within the scope of this section, he should be formally discharged from receiving s.117 services. In the absence of a discharge, it might be difficult to establish when the obligation to charge for services arose. Paragraph 33.22 of the *Code of Practice* states that after-care services "may be reinstated if it becomes obvious that they have been withdrawn prematurely, eg where a patient's mental condition begins to deteriorate immediately after services are withdrawn".

A patient's expressed wish to be "discharged" from this section has no legal effect if he continues to have a need for after-care services: see further, the report of the Local Government Ombudsman on an investigation into complaint no. 04/B/01280 against York City Council.

Subsection (2C)

This provision brings within the scope of this section relevant services provided under **1–1139** the direct payments scheme. The *Code of Practice* considers direct payments at paras 33.17 and 33.19.

SECTIONS 31 TO 33 OF THE CARE ACT 2014. As they apply to this section, these provisions are subject to Sch.4 to the 2014 Act which makes a number of modifications to the application of certain provisions of that Act to enable direct payments to be made in respect of services provided under this section.

REGULATIONS MADE UNDER SECTION 12A: See the National Health Service (Direct Payments) Regulations 2013 (SI 2013/1617).

Subsection (2D)

This provision makes clear that the duty of a clinical commissioning group (or the NHS **1–1140** Commissioning Board) is to commission, rather than provide, after-care services.

Subsection (2E)

HEALTH SERVICE COMMISSIONING BOARD. See para.33.8 of the *Code of Practice*. **1–1141**

Subsection (3)

This provision is concerned with identifying the bodies that have a duty to provide ser- **1–1142** vices under this section.

Registering a hospital patient to vote has no impact on identifying the responsible after-care bodies under this section because under s.7(2) of the Representation of the People Act 1983, a patient is regarded as being resident in the hospital only for the purposes of entitlement to be registered to vote.

CLINICAL COMMISSIONING GROUP. The identity of the relevant CCG and the circumstances in which the duty to provide services under this section is placed on the Health Service Commissioning Board are governed by regs 14 and 15 of the NHS Commissioning Board and Clinical Commissioning Groups (Responsibilities and Standing Rules) Regulations 2012 (SI 2012/2996) which read:

"Circumstances in which duty may be imposed on another CCG

14.—(1) The duty imposed by subsection (2) of section 117 of the 1983 Act on a CCG (CCGA) to arrange for the provision of after-care services for a person (P) to whom section 117 applies is to be imposed instead on another CCG (CCG B) in the circumstances below.

(2) These circumstances are where CCG B has responsibility for P by virtue of

    (a) section 3(1A) of the [National Health Service Act 2006]; or

    (b) regulation 4 of, and sub-paragraph (c), (g), (h), (i) or (j) of paragraph 2 of Schedule 1 to these Regulations.

Circumstances in which duty may be imposed on the Board

15.—(1) The duty imposed by subsection (2) of section 117 of the 1983 Act on a CCG to arrange for the provision of after-care services for a person (P) to whom section 117 of the 1983 Act applies is to be imposed instead on the Board in the circumstances below.

(2) These circumstances are where P is receiving an after-care service under section 117 which, if it were being provided under the 2006 Act, would be a service whose provision the Board had a duty to arrange."

The effect of reg.14 is set out in "Who pays? Determining responsibility for payments to providers", NHS England (2013) (the Guidance):

> "33. If a person is detained for treatment under the Mental Health Act 1983, the responsible commissioner will be as set out in paragraph 1 [which sets out the general rule for identifying which CCG is responsible for commissioning and paying for care as follows: (a) where a patient is registered on the list of NHS patients of a GP practice, the responsible commissioner will be the CCG of which the GP practice is a member; (b) where a patient is not registered with a GP practice, the responsible commissioner will be the CCG in whose geographic area the patient is usually resident]. Every effort should be made to determine GP practice registration or establish an address where they are usually resident, but if this fails and the patient refuses to assist, then as a last resort the responsible commissioner should be determined by the location of the unit providing treatment
>
> 34. It is the duty of the CCG and local social services authority to commission after-care for those persons discharged from hospital following detention under section 117 of the Mental Health Act. The responsible CCG should be established by the usual means (see paragraph 1). If a patient who is resident in one area (CCG A) is discharged to another area (CCG B), it is then the responsibility of the CCG in the area where the patient moves (CCG B) to pay for their aftercare under section 117 of the Act as agreed with the appropriate local social services authority".

The reference the patient's usual residence is to the patient's usual residence on discharge from hospital. The criteria for assessing usual residence are set out in Annex B to the Guidance. The main criterion is the patient's perception of where they are resident in the UK (either currently, or failing that, most recently) (para.2). Where the patient gives an address, they should be treated as usually resident at that address (para.3). Where a patient cannot, or chooses not to, give either a current or recent address, and an address cannot be established by other means, they should be treated as usually resident in the place where they are present (para.7).

Regulation 15 places a duty on the NHS Commissioning Board to provide after-care services if the service required is one which it provides.

As the Regulations do not contain transitional provisions, it must be assumed that reg.14 applies to patients who were discharged from hospital on or after April 1, 2013.

The functions of a CCG exercisable under this section may, subject to such restrictions and conditions as the CCG considers appropriate, be exercised jointly with a Local Health Board. These functions can be exercised by a joint committee of the CCG and the Local Health Board (SI 2013/261 regs 13, 14, Sch. para.18).

LOCAL SOCIAL SERVICES AUTHORITY. The identity of the relevant local authority for the purposes of this section is set out in the following extract from "Care and Support Statutory Guidance", Department of Health, 2014:

> "19.43. The duty on local authorities to commission or provide mental health after-care rests with the local authority for the area in which the person concerned was ordinarily resident immediately before they were detained under the 1983 Act, even if the person becomes ordinarily resident in another area after leaving hospital.
>
> 19.44. Although any change in the patient's ordinary residence after discharge will affect the local authority responsible for their social care services, it will not affect the local authority responsible for commissioning the patient's section 117 after-care. As amended by the Care Act 2014, section 117 provides that, if a person is ordinarily resident in local authority area (A) immediately before detention under the 1983 Act, and moves on discharge to local authority area (B) and moves again to local authority area (C), local authority (A) will remain responsible for providing or commissioning their after-care. However, if the patient, having become ordinarily resident after

discharge in local authority area (B) or (C), is subsequently detained in hospital for treatment [under s.3] again, the local authority in whose area the person was ordinarily resident immediately before their subsequent admission (local authority (B) or (C)) will be responsible for their after-care when they are discharged from hospital.

19.45. If, however, the patient's ordinary residence immediately before being detained cannot be established, the local authority responsible for commissioning the patient's aftercare will be the one for the area in which the patient was resident immediately before being detained under the 1983 Act. Only if that cannot be established, either, will the responsible local authority be the one for the area to which the patient is sent on discharge. However, local authorities should only determine that a person is not resident anywhere as a last resort."

The identification of a person's ordinary residence is examined in the note on "ordinarily resides" in s.26(4). The Government has issued guidance to assist local authorities in making decisions about ordinary residence ("Ordinary Residence: Guidance on the identification of the ordinary residence of people in need of community care services, England", Department of Health, 2013. Also see Ch.19 of "Care and Support Statutory Guidance", Department of Health, 2014. Subsection (4) applies if there is a dispute between local authorities about where the person was ordinarily resident immediately before being detained.

A consequence of the incorporation of an ordinary residence test into this provision by s.39(4) of the Care Act 2014 is that the decision of the Court of Appeal in *R. (on the application of Hertfordshire C.C.) v Hammersmith and Fulham LBC* [2011] EWCA Civ 77; [2015] M.H.L.R. 41, which focused on the absence of "deeming" provisions in this Act prior to its amendment by the 2014 Act, is no longer good law.

In *R. (on the application of Hertfordshire County Council) v London Borough of Hammersmith and Fulham)* [2011] EWCA Civ 77; [2011] M.H.L.R. 76, it was held that during a period of detention under the Act the person is not "resident" for the purposes of this provision in the hospital in which he is detained. It is submitted that this finding also applies to the "ordinary residence" of the person.

The identity of the local authority which arranged for an AMHP to make an application under s.3 in respect of the person has no bearing on the question of which local authority has responsibility to provide services under this section.

Responsibility for assessing a person who is receiving services under this section for a possible re-admission under the Act is that of the LSSA for the area where the person currently is, not that of the LSSA with responsibilities under this section if different: see s.13(1).

The difference in the rules for establishing the identities of the relevant CGCs and local authorities can result in the local authority and the CGC who are responsible for providing services for a person under this section being located in different parts of England.

Subsection (4)
Paragraph (a)
Section 40 provides that where a dispute about where an adult is ordinarily resident cannot be resolved by local authorities in England, the local authorities involved may request a determination of ordinary residence to be made by the Secretary of State or a person appointed by the Secretary of State. The Care and Support (Disputes Between Local Authorities) Regulations 2014 (SI 2014/2820) set out the procedure to be followed. **1–1143**

Paragraph (b)
Section 195, which is due to come into force in April 2016, states that disputes of the nature described in para.(a) that occur between local authorities in Wales are to be determined by the Welsh Ministers or person appointed by the Welsh Ministers. **1–1144**

Paragraph (c)

1–1145 A dispute that arises under this paragraph will be determined under the arrangements provided for in subs.(5).

Subsection (5)

1–1146 Disputes between a local authority in England and a local authority in Wales are determined by the Secretary of State for Health or the Welsh Ministers under the following arrangements which were made under this provision and were published by the Department of Health and the Welsh Government in March 2015:

"1. In these arrangements—

'dispute' means a dispute between at least one local authority in England and at least one local authority in Wales about where a person was ordinarily resident for the purposes of section 117(3) of the 1983 Act; 'the 1983 Act' means the Mental Health Act 1983;

'the lead authority' is the local authority in whose area the person to whom the dispute relates was living immediately before being detained under the 1983 Act.

2. The Secretary of State will determine the dispute if the lead authority is in England.

3. The Welsh Ministers will determine the dispute if the lead authority is in Wales.

4. If there is a dispute as to where the person was living immediately before being detained under the 1983 Act, the Secretary of State and the Welsh Ministers will agree between themselves who will determine the dispute.

5. The Secretary of State and Welsh Ministers (each referred to in this paragraph as a 'responsible Minister') agree that each will –

a. notify the other responsible Minister immediately on being made aware of the dispute;

b. agree in accordance with these arrangements which responsible Minister will determine the dispute, as soon as it is known where the person to whom the dispute relates was living immediately before being detained under the 1983 Act;

c. consult the other responsible Minister and take their views into account, prior to determining the dispute; and

d. notify the other responsible Minister of the outcome of the determination, prior to notifying the local authorities which are parties to the dispute.

6. These arrangements have effect from 1 April 2015.

Where the dispute is to be referred to the Secretary of State, local authorities should contact:

Department of Health Quality and Safety Team
Social Care Policy Division
Area 313B Richmond House
79 Whitehall
London
SW1A 2NS

Where the dispute is to be referred to the Welsh Ministers, local authorities should contact:

Mental Health & Vulnerable Groups Division
Health and Social Services Directorate General
Welsh Assembly Government
Cathays Park

Cardiff
CF10 3NQ
MentalHealthandVulnerableGroups@Wales.GSI.Gov.UK."

Subsection (6)

Prior to the enactment of this provision by the Care Act 2014, after-care services were **1–1147**
not defined. Paragraph 33.4 of the *Code of Practice* states:

"CCGs and local authorities should interpret the definition of after-care services
broadly. For example, after-care can encompass healthcare, social care and employment
services, supported accommodation and services to meet the person's wider social, cultural and spiritual needs, if these services meet a need that arises directly from or is
related to the particular patient's mental disorder, and help to reduce the risk of a deterioration in the patient's mental condition."

Speaking for the Government during a debate on the definition, Earl Howe said:

"I reassure the House that the definition we are now considering is the result of extensive
consultation. In consequence, we have added a positive objective to prevent deterioration as well as preventing readmission to hospital, and have further changed the
clause to remove the definite article when referring to 'the mental disorder', for
which the noble Lord made the case in Committee. This is intended to remove any
doubt about our intention that the scope of aftercare covers more than just one form
of mental disorder, and is not necessarily limited to the specific disorder or disorders
for which a person was previously detained under the Act and which gave rise to the
right to aftercare" (*Hansard*, HL Vol.748, col.600).

Although the definition gives a considerable discretion to the after-care bodies as to the
nature and extent of the services that can be provided, the bodies "must have regard to
other demands" on their budgets (*R. v Camden and Islington Health Authority, Ex p. K*
[2001] EWCA Civ 240; [2001] M.H.L.R. 24, para.29).

In *R. (on the application of Afework) v The Mayor and Burgesses of the London Borough of
Camden* [2013] EWHC 1637 (Admin); [2014] M.H.L.R. 32, para.14, Mostyn J. said:

"After-care services . . . would normally include (1) social work; (2) support in helping
the ex-patient with problems of (a) employment, (b) accommodation or (c) family
relationships; (3) the provision of domiciliary services; and (4) the use of day centre
and residential facilities."

And in *R. v Manchester City Council ex p. Stennett* [2002] UKHL 34, Lord Steyn said that
"psychiatric treatment" (para.7) and "caring residential care" (para.15) would qualify as
after-care services. It is submitted that these observations, which were made before the
definition was enacted, have continuing relevance.

With regard to the provision of ordinary accommodation, in *Afework* Mostyn J. held that
"basic or pure or ordinary accommodation" does not come within the concept of after-care
services. This finding is consistent with the definition as the provision of ordinary accommodation meets a basic human need that applies to all individuals; it is not one which either
arises from or is related to the person's mental disorder.

The fact that a person was receiving a service, such as residential care, for his mental
health needs prior to the admission to hospital does not mean that that service cannot be
an "after-care" service for the purposes of this section. The residential care would have
been provided under the Care Act 2014 prior to the admission (apart from self-funders),
and under this section on discharge as long as the person still required the accommodation
to meet his mental health needs. The person could therefore not be charged for the

accommodation on returning to it from hospital even if he was charged for it prior to the admission. This interpretation is supported by the finding of Sullivan J. in the *Stennett* case which is noted under "Charging for local authority services under section 117", above.

The search for necessary after-care services should not be confined to those services and facilities provided directly by the health and social services authorities.

In *ACCG v ACC* [2013] EWHC 3859 (COP) at para.86(ii), Eleanor King J. confirmed that judicial review in the Administrative Court "remains the proper vehicle through which to challenge unreasonable or irrational decisions made by 'care providers' and other public authorities".

A NEED ARISING FROM OR RELATED TO THE PERSON'S MENTAL DISORDER. Determining whether a need is "related to" the person's mental disorder will not always be easy. It is submitted that there must be a clear connection between the person's need and his mental disorder for the need is to come within the definition. A need which is related to the person's general well-being would not be sufficient.

In *Afework,* above, Mostyn J. held that the patient's claim that his need for specialist accommodation came within the scope of this section failed because the need arose from a brain injury which he incurred after his discharge from hospital. This finding is consistent with the definition unless it could be argued that the circumstances that gave rise to the brain injury were directly related to the person's mental disorder.

If a person's need for residential care arises from his physical disability which requires full-time support for his daily living needs, the fact that he continues to suffer from the symptoms of mental disorder does not bring the residential care within the scope of this section: see "A report by the Health Service Ombudsman and the Local Government Ombudsman about the provision of section 117 aftercare", HC 642, Oct 2012.

REDUCING THE RISK OF A DETERIORATION OF THE PERSON'S MENTAL CONDITION. The nature of the person's mental condition might have changed since his discharge from hospital.

ADMISSION TO HOSPITAL. As either a detained or an informal patient.

[After-care: preference for particular accommodation

1–1148 **117A.**—(1) The Secretary of State may by regulations provide that where—

(a) the local social services authority under section 117 is, in discharging its duty under subsection (2) of that section, providing or arranging for the provision of accommodation for the person concerned;

(b) the person concerned expresses a preference for particular accommodation; and.

(c) any prescribed conditions are met,

the local social services authority must provide or arrange for the provision of the person's preferred accommodation.

(2) Regulations under this section may provide for the person concerned, or a person of a prescribed description, to pay for some or all of the additional cost in prescribed cases.

(3) In subsection (2), "additional cost" means the cost of providing or arranging for the provision of the person's preferred accommodation less the amount that the local social services authority would expect to be the usual cost of providing or arranging for the provision of accommodation of that kind..

(4) The power to make regulations under this section—

(a) is exercisable only in relation to local social services authorities in England;.

(b) includes power to make different provision for different cases or areas.]

AMENDMENT

This section was inserted by the Care Act 2014 s.75(6).

DEFINITION

local social services authority: s.145(1).   **1–1149**

GENERAL NOTE

This section, which does not apply to local authorities in Wales, empowers the Secretary **1–1150** of State to make regulations to place a duty on a local authority to enable a person who qualifies for accommodation under s.117 to live in accommodation of their choice, provided that conditions specified in the regulations are met. If the cost of the preferred accommodation is more expensive than the local authority would normally expect to pay, this will involve the person themselves or another person entering into a written agreement with the authority to pay some or all of the additional cost of the preferred accommodation. These additional payments are sometimes called "top-up payments".

Paragraph 45 of Annex A to "Care and Support Statutory Guidance", Department of Health, 2014, states:

"The regulations give people who receive mental health after-care broadly the same rights to choice of accommodation as someone who receives care and support under the Care Act 2014. But some differences arise because after-care is provided free of charge and, as the legislative requirement for a care and support plan under the Care Act 2014 does not apply to section 117 after-care, the care plan should instead be drawn up under guidance on the Care Programme Approach (CPA). Care planning under the CPA should, if accommodation is an issue, include identifying the type of accommodation which is suitable for the person's needs and affording them the right to choice of accommodation set out in the regulations made under section 117A. The person should be fully involved in the care planning process."

REGULATIONS

Paragraphs 4 and 5 of the Care and Support and After-care (Choice of Accommodation) **1–1151** Regulations 2014 (SI 2014/2670), which were made under subss.(1), (2) and (4) of this section, state:

"Application to after-care

4.—Where—

(a) a local authority is, in discharging its duty under section 117(2) of the 1983 Act, providing or arranging for the provision of accommodation in England for a person;

(b) the person expresses a preference for particular accommodation (identifiable by reference to its address or provider); and

(c) the conditions in paragraph (2) are met,

the local authority must provide or arrange for the provision of the preferred accommodation in accordance with these Regulations.

(2) The following conditions must be met for the provision of preferred accommodation under paragraph (1)—

(a) the person must be aged 18 or over;

(b) the accommodation which the local authority is providing or arranging must be of a specified type;

(c) the preferred accommodation must be of the same type that the local authority has decided to provide or arrange;

(d) the preferred accommodation must be suitable to meet the person's needs;

(e) the preferred accommodation must be available;

(f) where the preferred accommodation is not provided by the local authority, the provider of the accommodation must agree to provide the accommodation to the person on the local authority's terms; and

(g) where the cost to the local authority of providing or arranging for the provision of the preferred accommodation is greater than the amount that the local authority would expect to be the usual cost of providing or arranging for the provision of accommodation of that kind, the additional cost conditions in paragraph (3) must also be met.

(3) The additional cost conditions referred to in paragraph (2)(g) are that—

(a) the local authority is satisfied that the person for whom the accommodation is to be provided or another person ('the payer'), is willing and able to pay the additional cost of the preferred accommodation for the period during which the local authority expects to meet needs by providing or arranging for the provision of that accommodation; and

(b) the payer enters into a written agreement with the authority in which the payer agrees to pay the additional cost.

(4) In a case to which paragraph (3) applies, the local authority must comply with the requirements of regulation 5(2), (3)(a) and (c) to (f), and (4).

(5) For the purposes of this regulation the additional cost that is to be met by the payer may be less than the full amount of the additional cost referred to in section 117A(3) of the 1983 Act, if the local authority agrees that a lesser amount should be paid.

(6) The specified types of accommodation are those referred to in regulation 2(2) but for the purposes of this regulation any reference to 'an adult' in regulations 7 and 8 should be read as a reference to 'a person'.

The additional cost condition

5.—(1) The additional cost condition is met if—

(a) the local authority is satisfied that—

(i) a person other than the adult, or
(ii) in a case to which paragraph (5) applies, the adult, ('the payer') is able and willing to pay the additional cost of the preferred accommodation for the period during which the local authority expects to meet the adult's needs by providing or arranging for the provision of that accommodation; and

(b) the payer enters a written agreement with the local authority in which the payer agrees to pay the additional cost.

(2) The local authority must provide the payer with access to sufficient information and advice to enable the payer to understand the terms of the proposed written agreement before entering into it.

(3) The written agreement must include—

(a) the additional cost;

(b) the amount specified in the adult's personal budget in relation to the provision of accommodation;

(c) the frequency of payments;

(d) details of the person to whom the payments are to be made;

(e) provision for review of the agreement;

(f) provisions about the matters specified in paragraph (4).

(4) The specified matters are—

(a) the consequences of ceasing to make payments;

(b) the effect of increases in charges made by the provider of the preferred accommodation;

(c) the effect of changes in the payer's financial circumstances.

(5) The local authority may not agree with the adult for whom the accommodation is to be provided for that adult to pay the additional cost unless—

(a) paragraph 2 of Schedule 2 to the Care and Support (Charging and Assessment of Resources) Regulations 2014 (the 12 week property disregard) applies to that adult; or

(b) the adult and the local authority agree to enter into a deferred payment agreement in accordance with the Care and Support (Deferred Payment) Regulations 2014 in respect of the additional cost.

(6) For the purposes of this regulation the additional cost that is to be met by the payer may be less than the full amount of the additional cost referred to in section 30(3) of the Act, if the local authority agrees that a lesser amount should be paid."

[117B After-care: exception for provision of nursing care   1–1152

(1) Section 117 does not authorise or require a local social services authority in England, in or in connection with the provision of services under that section, to provide or arrange for the provision of nursing care by a registered nurse.

(2) In this section "nursing care by a registered nurse" means a service provided by a registered nurse involving—

(a) the provision of care, or

(b) the planning, supervision or delegation of the provision of care,

other than a service which, having regard to its nature and the circumstances in which it is provided, does not need to be provided by a registered nurse.]

AMENDMENT
This section was inserted by SI 2015/914, reg.2, Sch.para.28.

DEFINITION
local social services authority: s.145(1).   **1–1153**

GENERAL NOTE
This section ensures continuation of the current prohibition on the provision of registered **1–1154** nursing care as defined in subs.(2) by a local social services authority under s.117.

Functions of the Secretary of State

Code of practice

1–1155   **118.**—(1) The Secretary of State shall prepare, and from time to time revise, a code of practice—

  (a) for the guidance of registered medical practitioners[, approved clinicians], managers and staff of hospitals[, independent hospitals and care homes] and [approved mental health professionals] in relation to the admission of patients to hospitals [and registered establishments] under this Act [and to guardianship and [community patients] under this Act]; and

  (b) for the guidance of registered medical practitioners and members of other professions in relation to the medical treatment of patients suffering from mental disorder.

[(1A) The Code which must be prepared, and from time to time revised, in relation to Wales shall also be for the guidance of independent mental health advocates appointed under arrangements made under section 130E below.]

(2) The code shall, in particular, specify forms of medical treatment in addition to any specified by regulations made for the purposes of section 57 above which in the opinion of the Secretary of State give rise to special concern and which should accordingly not be given by a registered medical practitioner unless the patient has consented to the treatment (or to a plan of treatment including that treatment) and a certificate in writing as to the matters mentioned in subsection (2)(a) and (b) of that section has been given by another registered medical practitioner, being a practitioner [appointed for the purposes of this section by the regulatory authority].

[(2A) The code shall include a statement of the principles which the Secretary of State thinks should inform decisions under this Act.

(2B) In preparing the statement of principles the Secretary of State shall, in particular, ensure that each of the following matters is addressed—

  (a) respect for patients' past and present wishes and feelings,

  (b) respect for diversity generally including, in particular, diversity of religion, culture and sexual orientation (within the meaning of section 35 of the Equality Act 2006),

  (c) minimising restrictions on liberty,

  (d) involvement of patients in planning, developing and delivering care and treatment appropriate to them,

  (e) avoidance of unlawful discrimination,

  (f) effectiveness of treatment,

  (g) views of carers and other interested parties,

  (h) patient wellbeing and safety, and

  (i) public safety.

(2C) The Secretary of State shall also have regard to the desirability of ensuring—

  (a) the efficient use of resources, and

  (b) the equitable distribution of services.

(2D) In performing functions under this Act persons mentioned in subsection (1)(a) or (b) [and subsection (1A)] shall have regard to the code.]

(3) Before preparing the code or making any alteration in it the Secretary of State shall consult such bodies as appear to him to be concerned.

(4) The Secretary of State shall lay copies of the code and of any alteration in the code before Parliament; and if either House of Parliament passes a resolution requiring the code or any alteration in it to be withdrawn the Secretary of State shall withdraw the code or alteration and, where he withdraws the code, shall prepare a code in substitution for the one which is withdrawn.

(5) No resolution shall be passed by either House of Parliament under subsection (4) above in respect of a code or alteration after the expiration of the period of 40 days beginning with the day on which a copy of the code or alteration was laid before that House; but for the purposes of this subsection no account shall be taken of any time during which Parliament is dissolved or prorogued or during which both Houses are adjourned for more than four days.

(6) The Secretary of State shall publish the code as for the time being in force.

[(7) The Care Quality Commission may at any time make proposals to the Secretary of State as to the content of the code of practice which the Secretary of State must prepare, and from time to time revise, under this section in relation to England.]

AMENDMENTS

The amendments to this section were made by the Mental Health (Patients in the Community) Act 1995 s.2(1), Sch.1 para.16, the Care Standards Act 2000 s.116, Sch.4 para.9(6) and the Mental Health Act 2007 ss.8, 14(2), 21, 32(4), Sch.2 para.9, Sch.3 para.25, the Mental Health (Wales) Measure 2010 s.39 and the Health and Social Care Act 2008 s.52, Sch.3 para.6.

DEFINITIONS   **1–1156**
    approved clinician: s.145(1).
    the managers: s.145(1).
    hospital: s.145(1).
    registered establishment: ss.34(1), 145(1).
    care home: s.145(1).
    independent hospital: s.145(1).
    approved mental health professional: s.145(1), (1AC).
    patient: s.145(1).
    community patient: ss.17A(7), 145(1).
    medical treatment: s.145(1), (4).
    mental disorder: ss.1, 145(1).
    the regulatory body: s.145(1).

GENERAL NOTE   **1–1157**
    This section imposes a duty on the Secretary of State (and, in relation to Wales, the Welsh Ministers) to prepare, publish and from time to time revise, a *Code of Practice* for the guidance of those concerned with the admission, treatment, guardianship and supervised community treatment of mentally disordered patients. The *Code* can specify forms of treatment which give rise to special concern and which should not be given without the patient's consent and an independent second medical opinion (subs.(2)). The Welsh *Code of Practice* must provide guidance to independent mental health advocates appointed under s.130E (subs.(1A)).

Those who are mentioned in subss.(1) and (1A) must "have regard" to the *Code* (subs.(2D)). Those mentioned do not include members of the First-tier Tribunal (Mental Health) and members of the Mental Health Review Tribunal for Wales. A failure to have regard to the *Code* could be used in legal or disciplinary proceedings as prima facie evidence of either bad practice or unlawful behaviour, although the effect of non-compliance will largely depend upon the nature of the provision in the *Code* that has not been followed.

The following statement is made at para.XXV of the Introduction to the *Code:*

"Where the principles and guidance of the Code are not implemented, the CQC may use its regulatory powers to facilitate change and improvement in local services as a failure to apply the Act and its Code may show a breach of one of the registration requirements in the Health and Social Care Act 2008, (Regulated Activities) Regulations 2014, or Care Quality Commission (Registration) Regulations (2009)."

The legal status of the *Code* was considered by the House of Lords in *R. (on the application of Munjaz) v Mersey Care National Health Service Trust* [2005] UKHL 58; [2006] 4 All E.R. 736, where it was contended that the policy of Ashworth Hospital relating to the seclusion of patients was unlawful because it provided for less frequent medical reviews, particularly after the first week of seclusion, than that laid down in the *Code*. Ashworth had also adopted a definition of seclusion that differed from that set out in the 1999 edition of the *Code*. It was held that:

1. The *Code* does not have the binding effect which a statutory provision or a statutory instrument would have. It is what it purports to be, guidance and not instruction.

2. The guidance in the *Code* should be given great weight. Although it is not instruction, the *Code* is much more than mere advice which an addressee is free to follow or not as it chooses. In other words, it is more than something to which those to whom it is addressed must "have regard to".

3. The *Code* contains guidance which should be considered with great care, and should be followed unless there are cogent reasons for not doing so. The reason need not be confined to the facts of an individual case; it can relate to a matter of policy. The requirement that cogent reasons must be shown for any departure sets a high standard which is not easily satisfied. With regard to subsection (2) of this section, Lord Bingham said, at para.69, that "any departure would call for even stronger reasons".

4. In reviewing any departures from the *Code*, the court should scrutinise the reasons given for departure with the intensity which the importance and sensitivity of the subject matters requires.

5. There were cogent reasons for Ashworth's decision not to follow the guidance in the Code, even though there were many eminent professional experts who took a different view. The reasons were:

   (a) The *Code* was directed at the generality of mental hospitals and did not address the special problems of high security hospitals;
   (b) The *Code* did not recognise the special position of patients whom it was necessary to seclude for longer than a very few days.
   (c) The statutory scheme, while providing for the Secretary of State to give guidance, deliberately left the power and responsibility of final decision to those who bear the legal and practicable responsibility for detaining, treating, nursing and caring for patients.

6. For the purpose of determining whether Ashworth's policy on seclusion was compatible with the European Convention on Human Rights (ECHR), the *Code* is irrelevant: if the policy is incompatible, consistency with the *Code* will not save it; if it is compatible, it requires no support from the *Code*. The policy on seclusion was compatible with the ECHR because it did not expose patients to a significant risk of treatment prohibited by art.3, did not amount to a separate deprivation of liberty which engages art.5, and any possible breach of art.8(1) was proportionate, in

accordance with the law and had a purpose that fell within art.8(2). Lord Bingham said at para.34:

> "The procedure adopted by the Trust does not permit arbitrary or random decision-making. The rules are accessible, foreseeable and predictable. It cannot be said, in my opinion, that they are not in accordance with or prescribed by law."

The patient unsuccessfully claimed before the European Court of Human Rights that art.8 of the ECHR required that the *Code* should be interpreted as having the force of law which had universal application. The Court, in agreeing with the judgment of the House of Lords that Ashworth was justified in its decision to depart from the *Code's* guidance, found that there had been no violation of art.8 (*Munjaz v United Kingdom* [2012] M.H.L.R. 351).

It is suggested that the following circumstances could provide cogent reasons for not following the guidance contained in the *Code*:

1. A determination by the High Court that a particular aspect of the *Code* is not legally accurate (see, for example, *AR v Bronglais Hospital and Pembrokeshire and Derwen NHS Trust* [2001] EWHC 792 (Admin); [2001] M.H.L.R. 175, which is noted under s.12(2)).

2. A requirement of the *Code* has been made redundant by subsequent caselaw or legislation.

3. A statement in the *Code* being obviously legally incorrect e.g. the 2008 edition of the *Code of Practice for Wales* stating, at para.23.9, that, contrary to the provisions of s.25, the nearest relative of a guardianship patient has to give 72 hours notice of their intention to discharge the patient.

4. Legal advice being obtained which casts a significant doubt on the legal correctness of an aspect of the guidance.

5. Following the guidance would involve breaching the patient's rights under the ECHR.

6. A judgment is made that a particular aspect of the guidance should not be followed for safety or another cogent reason relating to the care or treatment of patients (see, for example, para.2.20.59 of the *Committee of Inquiry into the Personality Disorder Unit, Ashworth Special Hospital* (1999) where para.26.3 of the 1999 edition of the *Code* was described as being "untenable" in the context of a high security hospital).

Reasons for departing from the guidance in the *Code* "must be spelled out clearly, logically and consistently" (*Munjaz*, above, per Lord Hope at para.69).

In *R. v Secretary for State for Health Ex p. Pfizer Ltd* (1999) 2 C.C.L.R. 270, Collins J. held that Government guidance which is expressed in unqualified and mandatory language and which appeared to override the clinical judgment which a doctor was entitled to exercise in an individual case, was unlawful.

Extracts from the latest edition of the *Code* for England are reproduced in Pt 4. The full version of the *Code* can be accessed at: *www.gov.uk/government/publications/code-of-practice-mental-health-act-1983*. A separate *Code of Practice for Wales* has been published for Wales.

Reference Guide to the Act
The following statement is set out in the Introduction to the *Code*:   **1–1158**

> "XVII The Reference Guide to the Mental Health Act 1983 is intended as a source of reference for people who want to understand the main provisions of the Mental Health Act 1983 and regulations under the Act, as amended at 1 April 2015, including

by the Mental Health Act 2007, Health and Social Care Acts 2008 and 2012 and Care Act 2014.

XVIII Guidance on the way the Act should be applied in practice is given in this Code. The two documents support one another and should be read together, as well as with other material available to assist people to understand their duties, rights and responsibilities under the Act.

XIX The Reference Guide is not a definitive statement of the law. It is not a substitute for consulting the Act itself or for taking legal advice."

The Reference Guide can be accessed at: *www.gov.uk/government/publications/mental-health-act-1983-reference-guide*.

Subsection (1)

1–1159   PARAGRAPH (A): ADMISSION OF PATIENTS TO HOSPITALS.   This term is not limited to the actual admission process; it covers what happens to the patient after he has been detained (*R. v Mersey Care National Health Service Trust Ex p. Munjaz*, above, para.19).

PARAGRAPH (B).   This provision is not limited to the hospital care of patients; it also covers patients cared for in the community. In *C v A local Authority* [2011] EWHC 1539 (Admin) the *Code* was held to apply in a residential special school which used seclusion.

The term "medical treatment", as defined in s.145(1), is wide enough to cover nursing and caring for a patient in seclusion, even though seclusion cannot properly form part of a treatment programme (*Munjaz*, above, para.19).

Subsection (2)

1–1160   SPECIFY FORMS OF MEDICAL TREATMENT.   The *Code* has not added to the forms of treatment covered by s.57.

Subsections (2A) to (2C)

1–1161   During the Parliamentary passage of the 2007 Act, the Minister of State said that "the question of how the Government should express principles to inform practitioners making decisions under the Act as amended by the Bill has dominated our discussions and caused a great deal of interest" (*Hansard,* HL Vol.690, col.118). A considerable amount of Parliamentary time was spent debating whether the principles should be contained in the Act or, as the Government preferred, in the Code of Practice. A compromise was eventually reached by the Government proposing an amendment which is given legislative effect in these provisions. The purpose of the amendment was described by the Minister of State:

"Our amendment places in statute a new requirement that the Secretary of State and Welsh Ministers include a statement of principles in the respective codes of practice for England and Wales, which should inform decision-making under the 1983 Act. The amendment legally obliges the Secretary of State and the Welsh Ministers to address certain fundamental issues in preparing this statement of principles" (*Hansard*, HL Vol.690, col.119).

Guidance on the five overarching principles of "Least restrictive option and maximising independence", "Empowerment and involvement", "Respect and dignity", "Purpose and effectiveness" and "Efficiency and equity" are set out in Ch.1 of the *Code of Practice*.

Subsection (2A)

1–1162   Paragraph 1.23 of the *Code* states that all "five sets of principles are of equal importance, and should inform any decision made under the Act. The weight given to each principle in reaching a particular decision will need to be balanced in different ways according to the circumstances and nature of each particular decision".

Whether the requirement for the principles to "inform decisions" differs from the general duty of practitioners to "have regard" to the *Code* (subs.(2D)) is not clear.

Subsection (2C)

In her response to concern that had been expressed about this provision, the Minister of State said: **1–1163**

"I can also reassure hon. Members that there is nothing sinister about the wording of proposed subsection (2C). [It] was drafted to include the fundamental matters considered most important in England and Wales. The Welsh national service framework for mental health has four underpinning principles: the so-called four Es of equality, equity, efficiency and effectiveness. When drafting the clause, we wanted to ensure that the Welsh principles were incorporated, given that the legislation covers England and Wales" (Public Bill Committee, col.208).

Subsection (2D)

Although the purpose of this provision was said to be the giving of legislative effect to the decision of the House of Lords in *R. (on the application of Munjaz) v Mersey Care NHS Trust* (*Hansard*, HL Vol.690, col.118: also see the Explanatory Notes to the 2007 Act, para.45), it could be argued that it diminishes the effect of that decision in that Lord Hope, speaking with the majority, said that the Code is less than a direction but is "more than something to which those to whom it is addressed must 'have regard to'" (para.68). However, it is clear that this was not the intention of Parliament and it is therefore submitted that this provision should be interpreted in accordance with the principles set out in *Munjaz,* above. **1–1164**

Practitioners approved for Part IV and section 118

119.—(1) [The regulatory authority] may make such provision as [it] may with the approval of the Treasury determine for the payment of remuneration, allowances, pensions or gratuities to or in respect of registered medical practitioners appointed [by the authority] for the purposes of Part IV of this Act and section 118 above and to or in respect of other persons appointed for the purposes of section 57(2)(a) above. **1–1165**

(2) A registered medical practitioner or other person appointed [. . .] for the purposes of the provisions mentioned in subsection (1) above may, for the purpose of exercising his functions under those provisions [or under Part 4A of this Act], at any reasonable time—

(a) visit and interview and, in the case of a registered medical practitioner, examine in private any patient detained [in a hospital or registered establishment or any community patient in a hospital or [regulated establishment (other than a hospital)] or (if access is granted) other place]; and

(b) require the production of and inspect any records relating to the treatment of the patient [there].

[(3) In this section, "regulated establishment" means—

(a) an establishment in respect of which a person is registered under Part 2 of the Care Standards Act 2000; or

(b) premises used for the carrying on of a regulated activity, within the meaning of Part 1 of the Health and Social Care Act 2008, in respect of which a person is registered under Chapter 2 of that Part.]

AMENDMENTS
The amendments to this section were made by the Mental Health Act 2007 s.35(2), the Health and Social Care Act 2008 ss.52, 166, Sch.3 para.7, Sch.15 Pt.1 and SI 2010/813, art.5(4).

DEFINITIONS
1–1166   the regulatory authority: s.145(1).
patient: s.145(1).
residential establishment: ss.34(1), 145(1).
community patient: ss.17A(7), 145(1).
hospital: s.145(1).

GENERAL NOTE
1–1167   This section provides for the payment of medical practitioners appointed by the Care Quality Commission or, in relation to Wales, the Welsh Ministers to carry out certain functions under the Act, and for them to have access to detained and community patients and their records.

Subsection (2)
1–1168   Anyone who obstructs a person in the exercise of his functions under this section commits an offence under s.129.

[General protection of relevant patients
1–1169   **120.**—(1) The regulatory authority must keep under review and, where appropriate, investigate the exercise of the powers and the discharge of the duties conferred or imposed by this Act so far as relating to the detention of patients or their reception into guardianship or to relevant patients.

(2) Relevant patients are—
(a) patients liable to be detained under this Act,
(b) community patients, and
(c) patients subject to guardianship.

(3) The regulatory authority must make arrangements for persons authorised by it to visit and interview relevant patients in private—
(a) in the case of relevant patients detained under this Act, in the place where they are detained, and
(b) in the case of other relevant patients, in hospitals and regulated establishments and, if access is granted, other places.

(4) The regulatory authority must also make arrangements for persons authorised by it to investigate any complaint as to the exercise of the powers or the discharge of the duties conferred or imposed by this Act in respect of a patient who is or has been detained under this Act or who is or has been a relevant patient.

(5) The arrangements made under subsection (4)—
(a) may exclude matters from investigation in specified circumstances, and
(b) do not require any person exercising functions under the arrangements to undertake or continue with any investigation where the person does not consider it appropriate to do so.

(6) Where any such complaint as is mentioned in subsection (4) is made by a Member of Parliament or a member of the National Assembly for Wales, the results of the investigation must be reported to the Member of Parliament or member of the Assembly.

(7) For the purposes of a review or investigation under subsection (1) or the exercise of functions under arrangements made under this section, a person authorised by the regulatory authority may at any reasonable time—

(a) visit and interview in private any patient in a hospital or regulated establishment,

(b) if the authorised person is a registered medical practitioner or approved clinician, examine the patient in private there, and

(c) require the production of and inspect any records relating to the detention or treatment of any person who is or has been detained under this Act or who is or has been a community patient or a patient subject to guardianship.

(8) The regulatory authority may make provision for the payment of remuneration, allowances, pensions or gratuities to or in respect of persons exercising functions in relation to any review or investigation for which it is responsible under subsection (1) or functions under arrangements made by it under this section.

(9) In this section "regulated establishment" means—

(a) an establishment in respect of which a person is registered under Part 2 of the Care Standards Act 2000, or

(b) premises used for the carrying on of a regulated activity (within the meaning of Part 1 of the Health and Social Care Act 2008) in respect of which a person is registered under Chapter 2 of that Part.]

AMENDMENT

This section was substituted by the Health and Social Care Act 2008 s.52, Sch.3 para.8.

DEFINITIONS   **1–1170**

the regulatory authority: s.145(1).
patients: s.145(1)
relevant patients: subs.(2).
community patient: ss.17A(1), 145(1).
hospital: s.145(1).
regulated establishment: subs.(9).
approved clinician: s.145(1).

GENERAL NOTE

This section places a duty on the regulatory authority (i.e. the Care Quality Commission **1–1171** (CQC) or, in relation to Wales, the Welsh Ministers (s.145(1)) to review and, where appropriate, investigate the exercise of powers and the discharge of duties in relation to detention, supervised community treatment and guardianship under the Act. For the purposes of such reviews and investigations, the regulatory body can authorise persons to visit and examine patients in hospitals, and to inspect relevant records (subs.(7)). There is no right to enter private premises. For the duty to provide the regulatory body with relevant information, see s.120C. Reports of reviews and investigations may be published (s.120A). Under subs.(3), the regulatory body must make arrangements for authorised persons to visit and interview "relevant patients" as defined in subs.(2). The regulatory body must also make arrangements for authorised persons to investigate complaints concerning the exercise of powers under the Act in respect of detained or relevant patients. Such an investigation need not be either instigated or continued if this is considered not to be appropriate (subss.(4),(5)). It is an offence under s.129 to obstruct a person carrying out functions under this section.

Although the CQC does not have the power to investigate the deaths of detained patients, reg.17 of the Care Quality Commission (Registration) Regulations 2009 (SI 2009/3112) requires the registered person to notify the CQC without delay of the death of a service user who is liable to be detained under the Act (for Wales, see SI 2011/734 (W.112), reg.30). Regulation 17 also requires the notification of the unauthorised absence (and return) of a service user who is liable to be detained in an English NHS establishment providing secure psychiatric services. A person who is "liable to be detained" includes a community patient who has been recalled to hospital in accordance with s.17E, but does not include a patient who has been conditionally discharged and not recalled to hospital (para.(3)(a)). Notification forms may be downloaded from the Commission's website (*www.cqc.org.uk*).

One curious aspect of the duty imposed by this section is that the regulatory authority, as the sole provider of the second opinion appointed doctor service which operates in Pts IV and IVA, is required to review its own service provision.

The Optional Protocol to the United Nations Convention Against Torture, which the UK ratified in December 2003, requires states to establish a "national preventative mechanism" (NPM) to carry out a system of regular visits to places of detention in order to prevent torture and other cruel, inhuman or degrading treatment or punishment. The Government has designated a number of bodies to form the United Kingdom NPM, including the CQC and the Healthcare Inspectorate of Wales (*Hansard,* March 31, 2009, col.55WS).

Subsection (1)

1–1172   REGULATORY AUTHORITY.   The functions of the Welsh Ministers under this section are exercised by the Health Inspectorate Wales (HIW).

Persons authorised by the CQC may include members or employees of the Commission (Health and Social Care Act 2008 s.52(2)). When performing its functions, the Commission must have regard to:

"the need to protect and promote the rights of people who use health and social care services (including, in particular, the rights of children, of persons detained under the Mental Health Act 1983, of persons who are deprived of their liberty in accordance with the Mental Capacity Act 2005, and of other vulnerable adults)" (2008 Act, s.4(1)(d)).

The contact details of the Commission and HIW for issues relating to the Mental Health Act are:

CQC Mental Health Act
Citygate
Gallowgate
Newcastle
NE1 4PA

tel no: 03000 616161

Healthcare Inspectorate Wales
Bevan House
Caerphilly Business Park
Van Road
Caerphilly
CF83 3ED

tel no: 029 2092 8850

Subsection (4)

1–1173   The CQC has published its policy on "Complaining about the use of the Mental Health Act" (October 2012).

EXERCISE OF THE POWERS OR THE DISCHARGE OF THE DUTIES. In *R. v Mental Health Act Commission Ex p. Smith* (1998) 43 B.M.L.R. 174, complaints were made to the CQC's predecessor, the Mental Health Act Commission (MHAC), regarding a hospital patient who had committed suicide during a period when he was subject to detention under s.3 of the Act. There were four essential complaints:

(i) it was said that the patient's original detention was neither appropriate nor legal;

(ii) it was said that he was inappropriately detained in a secure unit for a period;

(iii) it was alleged that the patient was given drugs in such quantities that it was unlikely that he could have given consent, and the level of dosage was inappropriate; and

(iv) it was said that the patient was inadequately cared for during his detention, and his condition was not adequately assessed for the purposes of determining whether there was any risk of self harm.

The MHAC had always been prepared to accept jurisdiction to entertain complaint (i), was persuaded that it had jurisdiction to accept complaint (iii), but only to a limited extent, but considered that it did not have jurisdiction to entertain complaints (ii) and (iv). On a judicial review of the MHAC's decision, Latham J. held that it is too restrictive to construe this provision as referring only to the express powers and duties set down in the Act. Rights and duties which flow necessarily and by necessary implication from the patient's detention also come within its scope. It followed that any complaints arising out of the exercise of the power to detain, manage and control, and the duty to treat detained patients could be investigated by the MHAC. Accordingly, the MHAC had jurisdiction to consider complaints (ii) and (iv), and had an unrestricted jurisdiction to consider complaint (iii).

Subsection (7)
It is submitted that the power granted by para.(c) is not limited to authorised persons who **1–1174** are either registered medical practitioners or approved clinicians.

[Investigation reports
120A.—(1) The regulatory authority may publish a report of a review or inves- **1–1175** tigation carried out by it under section 120(1).

(2) The Secretary of State may by regulations make provision as to the procedure to be followed in respect of the making of representations to the Care Quality Commission before the publication of a report by the Commission under subsection (1).

(3) The Secretary of State must consult the Care Quality Commission before making any such regulations.

(4) The Welsh Ministers may by regulations make provision as to the procedure to be followed in respect of the making of representations to them before the publication of a report by them under subsection (1).]

AMENDMENT
This section was inserted by the Health and Social Care Act 2008 s.52, Sch.3 para.9.

DEFINITION
the regulatory authority: s.145(1). **1–1176**

GENERAL NOTE
Under s.84 of the Health and Social Care Act 2008, the Care Quality Commission must **1–1177** make copies of any reports published under the Act available for inspection at its offices by any person at any reasonable time and any person who requests a copy of the report is

entitled to have one on payment of such reasonable fee (if any) as the Commission considers appropriate.

Subsection (2)

1–1178   No regulations have been made under this provision.

[Action statements

1–1179   **120B.**—(1) The regulatory authority may direct a person mentioned in subsection (2) to publish a statement as to the action the person proposes to take as a result of a review or investigation under section 120(1).

(2) The persons are—

(a) the managers of a hospital within the meaning of Part 2 of this Act;

(b) a local social services authority;

(c) persons of any other description prescribed in regulations.

(3) Regulations may make further provision about the content and publication of statements under this section.

(4) "Regulations" means regulations made—

(a) by the Secretary of State, in relation to England;

(b) by the Welsh Ministers, in relation to Wales.]

AMENDMENT

This section was inserted by the Health and Social Care Act 2008 s.52, Sch.3 para.9.

DEFINITIONS

1–1180   the regulatory authority: s.145(1).

the managers: s.145(1).

hospital: s.145(1).

local social services authority: s.145(1).

GENERAL NOTE

1–1181   This section enables the regulatory authority to require hospital managers, social services departments and other prescribed people to publish a statement of the action they propose to take in response to any recommendations following a review or investigation undertaken under s.120(1). Paragraph 223 of the Explanatory Notes on the Health and Social Care Act 2008 states:

"[It] is not only hospital managers and social services authorities and their staff who exercise relevant functions under the Mental Health Act and contribute to its operation. There may, therefore, be circumstances in which reviews or investigations make recommendations that are addressed (in whole or in part) to other people. In these cases, it would make sense for the people concerned to be asked directly to publish a report of the action they propose to take as a result. This might include, for example, other NHS bodies that are responsible for providing or commissioning services for patients subject to the Mental Health Act."

[Provision of information

1–1182   **120C.**—(1) This section applies to the following persons—

(a) the managers of a hospital within the meaning of Part 2 of this Act;

(b) a local social services authority;

(c) persons of any other description prescribed in regulations.

(2) A person to whom this section applies must provide the regulatory authority with such information as the authority may reasonably request for or in connection with the exercise of its functions under section 120.

(3) A person to whom this section applies must provide a person authorised under section 120 with such information as the person so authorised may reasonably request for or in connection with the exercise of functions under arrangements made under that section.

(4) This section is in addition to the requirements of section 120(7)(c).

(5) "Information" includes documents and records.

(6) "Regulations" means regulations made—

(a) by the Secretary of State, in relation to England;

(b) by the Welsh Ministers, in relation to Wales.]

AMENDMENT

This section was inserted by the Health and Social Care Act 2008 s.52, Sch.3 para.9.

DEFINITIONS

    the managers: s.145(1).   **1–1183**

    hospital: s.145(1).

    local social services authority: s.145(1).

    the regulatory authority: s.145(1).

    information: subs.(5).

GENERAL NOTE

This section obliges hospital managers, local social services authorities and other pre- **1–1184** scribed people to provide the regulatory authority with information, including records and documents, that the authority may require in relation to its functions under s.120.

Paragraph 224 of the Explanatory Notes on the Health and Social Care Act 2008 states that examples "of the kind of information which might be requested are:

- statistical information on people subject to the formal powers under the Mental Health Act, including data relating to particular groups of patients such as children, adolescents, women, and black and ethnic minority patients;

- information on the use of particular powers, such as the granting of leave of absence;

- the number of deaths and other serious incidents;

- information on the use of seclusion in respect of patients."

[Annual reports

120D.—(1) The regulatory authority must publish an annual report on its **1–1185** activities in the exercise of its functions under this Act.

(2) The report must be published as soon as possible after the end of each financial year.

(3) The Care Quality Commission must send a copy of its annual report to the Secretary of State who must lay the copy before Parliament.

(4) The Welsh Ministers must lay a copy of their annual report before the National Assembly for Wales.

(5) In this section "financial year" means—

(a) the period beginning with the date on which section 52 of the Health and Social Care Act 2008 comes into force and ending with the next 31 March following that date, and

(b) each successive period of 12 months ending with 31 March.]

AMENDMENT
This section was inserted by the Health and Social Care Act 2008 s.52, Sch.3 para.9.

DEFINITIONS
1–1186 the regulatory authority: s.145(1).
financial year: subs.(5).

GENERAL NOTE
1–1187 Both the Care Quality Commission and the Health Inspectorate Wales have taken a relaxed attitude to the meaning of the phrase "as soon as possible" in subs.(2): see p.69 of the December 2014 issue of "Keeping up to date", MHA and MCA Law Ltd.

Mental Health Act Commission
1–1188 **121.** [*Repealed by the Health and Social Care Act 2008 s.166, Sch.15 Pt 1*]

Provision of pocket money for in-patients in hospital
1–1189 **122.**—(1) The [Welsh Ministers may (in relation to Wales)] pay to persons who are receiving treatment as in-patients (whether liable to be detained or not) in [. . .] hospitals wholly or mainly used for the treatment of persons suffering from mental disorder, such amounts as [the Welsh Ministers think fit] in respect of [those persons] occasional personal expenses where it appears to [the Welsh Ministers] that [those persons] would otherwise be without resources to meet those expenses.

(2) For the purposes of the [. . .] the National Health Service (Wales) Act 2006], the making of payments under this section to persons for whom hospital services are provided under [that Act] shall be treated as included among those services.

AMENDMENTS
The amendments to this section were made by the Health Act 1999 s.65, Sch.5, the National Health Service (Consequential Provisions) Act 2006 s.2, Sch.1 para.67 and the Health and Social Care Act 2012 s.41.

DEFINITIONS
1–1190 patient: s.145(1).
hospital: s.145(1).
mental disorder: ss.1, 145(1).

GENERAL NOTE
1–1191 This effect of this section, as amended by s.41 of the Health and Social Care Act 2012, is explained at paras 452 to 454 of the Explanatory Memorandum to the 2012 Act:

"This section abolishes the power of the Secretary of State in section 122 of the 1983 Act to make payments to in-patients in mental health hospitals in respect of their occasional personal expenses, where they cannot meet those expenses themselves. In England, this power was previously delegated to PCTs by means of regulations. It is primarily used to provide small personal allowances for patients who have been transferred from prison to hospital under section 47 of the 1983 Act and who are therefore not eligible for social security benefits.

CCGs and the NHS Commissioning Board would still be able to arrange for such payments to be made to NHS patients under the NHS Act. And the Secretary of State would be able to make regulations requiring such payments to be made, using the power to make 'standing rules' introduced in section 20.

The section also removes this power entirely in Scotland (where it has no practical significance). This change does not affect the powers of the Scottish Ministers to make pocket-money payments under Scottish mental health legislation. This section does not affect the position in Wales, where the Secretary of State's powers are exercisable by the Welsh Ministers. Indeed, it amends section 122 to confer the power directly on the Welsh Ministers."

Subsection (1)
SECRETARY OF STATE.   The functions of the Minister, so far as exercisable in relation to   **1–1192**
Wales, are exercised by the Welsh Ministers (see the General Note to the Act).

Transfers to and from special hospitals
123. [*Repealed by the Health and Social Care Act 2012 s.42(1).*]   **1–1193**

GENERAL NOTE
The repeal of this section does not affect the validity of the detention of anyone who had   **1–1194**
been transferred under it prior to its repeal, nor prevent the recapture of anyone who escaped from custody while being transferred under it: see s.42(5) of the 2012 Act.

Default powers of Secretary of State
124. [*Repealed by the National Health Service and Community Care Act 1990*   **1–1195**
s.66(2), Sch.10.]

Inquiries
125. [*Repealed by the Inquiries Act 2005 s.49, Sch.3.*]   **1–1196**

PART IX

OFFENCES

GENERAL NOTE
Part I of the Sexual Offences Act 2003 creates a number of offences "against persons   **1–1197**
with a mental disorder impeding choice". They are:

- Sexual activity with a person with a mental disorder impeding choice (s.30).

- Causing or inciting a person, with a mental disorder impeding choice, to engage in sexual activity (s.31).

- Engaging in sexual activity in the presence of a person with a mental disorder impeding choice (s.32).

- Causing a person, with a mental disorder impeding choice, to watch a sexual act (s.33).

- Inducement, threat or deception to procure sexual activity with a person with a mental disorder (s.34).

- Causing a person with a mental disorder to engage in or agree to engage in sexual activity by inducement, threat or deception (s.35).

- Engaging in sexual activity in the presence, procured for inducement, threat or deception, of a person with a mental disorder (s.36).

- Causing a person with a mental disorder to watch a sexual act by inducement, threat or deception (s.37).

The 2003 Act also introduces a number of specific offences which relate to care workers. They elevate the position of trust and responsibility enjoyed by a care worker from a simple aggravating feature of an offence to an offence in its own right. The definition of care worker in s.42 is extremely broad and includes informal carers who provide services to the mentally disordered. The offences are:

- Care workers: sexual activity with a person with a mental disorder (s.38).

- Care workers: causing or inciting sexual activity (s.39).

- Care workers: sexual activity in the presence of a person with a mental disorder (s.40).

- Care workers: causing a person with a mental disorder to watch a sexual act (s.41).

"Guidance on Part I of the Sexual Offences Act 2003", which considers the offences set out above, is attached to Home Office Circular 21/2004.

Forgery, false statements, etc.

1–1198   **126.**—(1) Any person who without lawful authority or excuse has in his custody or under his control any document to which this subsection applies, which is, and which he knows or believes to be, false within the meaning of Part I of the Forgery and Counterfeiting Act 1981, shall be guilty of an offence.

(2) Any person who without lawful authority or excuse makes or has in his custody or under his control, any document so closely resembling a document to which subsection (1) above applies as to be calculated to deceive shall be guilty of an offence.

(3) The documents to which subsection (1) above applies are any documents purporting to be—

(a) an application under Part II of this Act;

(b) a medical [or other] recommendation or report under this Act; and

(c) any other document required or authorised to be made for any of the purposes of this Act.

(4) Any person who—

(a) wilfully makes a false entry or statement in any application, recommendation, report, record or other document required or authorised to be made for any of the purposes of this Act; or

(b) with intent to deceive, makes use of any such entry or statement which he knows to be false,

shall be guilty of an offence.

(5) Any person guilty of an offence under this section shall be liable—

(a) on summary conviction, to imprisonment for a term not exceeding six months or to a fine not exceeding the statutory maximum, or to both;

(b) on conviction on indictment, to imprisonment for a term not exceeding two years or to a fine of any amount, or to both.

AMENDMENT

In subs.(3)(b) the words in square brackets were inserted by the Mental Health (Patients in the Community) Act 1995 s.2(1), Sch.1 para.17.

GENERAL NOTE

Under this section, it is an offence either to forge or make false statements in applica- **1–1199**
tions, recommendations or other documents made under the Act. Proceedings can be
instituted by a local social services authority (s.130).

Subsection (1)

ANY PERSON.   Or corporation (Interpretation Act s.5, Sch.1). **1–1200**

FALSE.   This term is defined for the purposes of the Forgery and Counterfeiting Act
1981 in s.9 of that Act. An entry or statement may be false on account of what it omits,
even though the statement or entry itself is literally true (*R. v Lord Kylsant* [1932] 1
K.B. 442).

Subsection (2)

TO DECEIVE.   "To deceive is . . . to induce a man to believe a thing to be true which is **1–1201**
false, and which the person practising the deceit knows or believes to be false", per
Buckley J. in *Re London and Globe Finance Corporation Ltd* [1903] 1 Ch. 728 at 732.
In *Weltham v DPP* [1961] A.C. 103 Lord Radcliffe extended the scope of Buckley J.'s
obiter remarks to include the inducing of a man to believe a thing to be false which is true.

Ill-treatment of patients

127.—(1) It shall be an offence for any person who is an officer on the staff of or **1–1202**
otherwise employed in, or who is one of the managers of, a hospital [, independent
hospital or care home]—

(a) to ill-treat or wilfully to neglect a patient for the time being receiving treat-
    ment for mental disorder as an in-patient in that hospital or home; or
(b) to ill-treat or wilfully to neglect, on the premises of which the hospital or
    home forms part, a patient for the time being receiving such treatment
    there as an out-patient.

(2) It shall be an offence for any individual to ill-treat or wilfully to neglect a
mentally disordered patient who is for the time being subject to his guardianship
under this Act or otherwise in his custody or care (whether by virtue of any legal or
moral obligation or otherwise).

[. . .]

(3) Any person guilty of an offence under this section shall be liable—

(a) on summary conviction, to imprisonment for a term not exceeding six
    months or to a fine not exceeding the statutory maximum, or to both;
(b) on conviction on indictment, to imprisonment for a term not exceeding [five
    years] or to a fine of any amount, or to both.

(4) No proceedings shall be instituted for an offence under this section except
by or with the consent of the Director of Public Prosecutions.

AMENDMENT

The amendments to this section were made by the Care Standards Act 2000 s.116, Sch.4
para.9(8) and the Mental Health Act 2007 ss.42, 55, Sch.11 Pt 5.

DEFINITIONS

the managers: s.145(1). **1–1203**
hospital: s.145(1).
independent hospital: s.145(1).
care home: ss.34(1), 145(1).
patient: s.145(1).

mental disorder: ss.1, 145(1).
mentally disordered: s.1(2).

GENERAL NOTE

1–1204   This section, which fortifies the common law duty of care owed by those who have custody of or treat or look after patients (*R. v Mersey Care National Health Service Trust Ex p.
Munjaz* [2005] UKHL 58; [2006] 4 All E.R. 736 para.4), creates two separate offences.
Under subs.(1) it is an offence for an employee or a manager of a hospital or care home
to ill-treat or wilfully to neglect an in-patient or out-patient of that hospital or home.
Under subs.(2) it is an offence for a guardian or some other person who has the custody
or care of a mentally disordered person who is living in the community to ill-treat or wilfully to neglect that person. It is an essential pre-requisite for each offence that the victim is
a mentally disordered person within the meaning of s.1 at the time when the offence is
committed.

In *R. v Newington* (1990) 91 Cr. App. R. 247, the Court of Appeal said that "ill-treatment" could not be equated with "wilfully to neglect". The court therefore advised the
Crown Prosecution Service that, when proceedings were brought under this section,
charges of "ill-treatment" and of "wilfully to neglect" should be put in separate counts
in the indictment.

Proceedings under this section can either be instituted by the Director of Public
Prosecutions, or by a local social services authority with the Director's consent (s.130
and subs.(4)). As s.139 does not apply to proceedings brought under this section
(s.139(3)), prosecutions may be commenced without proof of bad faith or lack of reasonable care.

Under s.44 of the Mental Capacity Act 2005, it is an offence for either a lay or professional carer, a donee of a lasting power of attorney (or of an enduring power of
attorney) or a deputy appointed by the Court of Protection to ill-treat or wilfully neglect
a person who lacks, or is believed to lack, mental capacity.

Dave Sheppard and Gemma Bensley have published a comprehensive analysis of cases
brought under this section. The document, "Offences of ill-treatment and/or wilful neglect
under the Mental Health Act 1983 and the Mental Capacity Act 2005 in England and
Wales" (March, 2014) can be obtained from Dave Sheppard at *www.mhaandmca.co.uk*.

Criminal Justice and Courts Act 2015

1–1205   Section 20 of the 2015 Act makes it an offence for an individual who has the care of
another individual by virtue of being a care worker to ill-treat or wilfully neglect that individual. A care worker is defined as an individual who is paid specifically to provide health
care for adults or, with certain exceptions, children, or to provide adult social care. "Care
worker" also includes an individual who is paid specifically to supervise or manage individuals providing such care, and a director or equivalent of an organisation providing such
care. The Explanatory Notes to the Act state that the "intention is to ensure that the individual offence can apply to any individual perpetrator, not just those on the 'front line' of
care provision. However, it will only apply where the individual supervisor, director, etc
has themselves directly committed ill-treatment or wilful neglect. They will not commit
the individual offence by virtue of the acts or omissions of others they supervise or
manage".

Section 21 creates a separate offence relating to care providers. A care provider commits
an offence if:

- an individual employed or otherwise engaged by the care provider ill-treats or wilfully neglects someone to whom they are providing health care or adult social care
  and to whom the care provider owes a relevant duty of care; and

- the way in which the care provider manages or organises its activities amounts to a
  gross breach of that duty of care; and

- if that breach had not occurred, the ill-treatment or wilful neglect would not have happened, or would have been less likely to happen.

Subsection (1)

OFFICER ON THE STAFF OF THE HOSPITAL. "Officer" is not defined. The term could **1–1206** include a person who is neither a nurse nor a doctor.

CARE HOME. Registration of such a home by the regulatory authority is not the test of whether an establishment is a care home. The fact of being a care home triggers the obligation to register, not the reverse: see *R. v Davies and Poolton* [2000] Crim.L.R. 297, CA where the Court of Appeal held that it was not a requirement of an offence under this section that the accused should be aware that the establishment where she worked was a mental nursing home (now an independent hospital or a care home) and that the victim of ill-treatment or wilful neglect was receiving treatment for mental disorder. The relevant mens rea is found in the element of ill-treatment or wilful neglect that is the gist of the offence.

ILL-TREAT. It is not necessary to establish a course of conduct as a single act, such as slapping the patient's face on one occasion, could constitute ill-treatment under this section (*R. v Holmes* [1979] Crim.L.R. 52, Bodmin Crown Court).

In *R. v Newington*, above, the Court of Appeal held that for there to be a conviction of ill-treatment under this section (the case in question was brought under subs.(2)), the Crown would have to prove: (1) deliberate conduct by the accused which could properly be described as ill-treatment irrespective of whether it damaged or threatened to damage the victim's health; (2) a guilty mind involving either an appreciation by the accused that she was inexcusably ill-treating a patient, or that she was reckless as to whether she was inexcusably acting in that way; and (3) that the victim was a mentally disordered person within the meaning of s.1. The court disapproved of a direction given by the trial judge "that violence would inevitably amount to ill-treatment" on the ground that violence necessarily used for the reasonable control of a patient would not amount to ill-treatment. As the court found that for the offence to have been committed there is no need for the prosecution to show that the treatment caused actual injury to the victim, it is clear that "ill-treatment" encompasses a wide range of conduct. M. J. Gunn has stated that the decision in *R. v Newington* suggests that an offence of ill-treatment "might deal with matters such as inadequate feeding, heating, etc., or the use of harsh words and gratuitous bullying as well as what would be ordinarily understood to be ill-treatment" (*Journal of Forensic Psychiatry* (1990) 1(3), at p.361; also see Gunn's commentary on this case at [1990] Crim. L.R. 595–597).

WILFULLY. The leading case on this term is *R. v Sheppard* [1981] A.C. 394 HL, a case brought under s.1(1) of the Children and Young Persons Act 1933 where it was held that the primary meaning of "wilful" is "deliberate", but it may also include recklessness. Lord Keith said at 418:

"It is used here to describe the mental element, which, in addition to the fact of neglect, must be proved . . . The primary meaning of 'wilful' is 'deliberate'. So a parent who knows that his child needs medical care and deliberately, that is by conscious decision, refrains from calling a doctor, is guilty under the subsection. As a matter of general principle, recklessness is to be equiparated with deliberation. A parent who fails to provide medical care which his child needs because he does not care whether it is needed or not is reckless of his child's welfare. He too is guilty of an offence. But a parent who has genuinely failed to appreciate that his child needs medical care, through personal inadequacy or stupidity or both, is not guilty."

A direction of the kind suggested by Lord Keith's reasoning, suitably tailored to the facts of the case, should be given by the trail judge hearing a case under this section: see *R. v Morrell* [2002] EWCA Crim 2547, where Poole J. said at para.45:

"We do recognise the force of Crown counsel's argument that in the [appellant's] case, that of an experienced professional, unlike the feckless parent being considered by Lord Keith, questions of inadequacy or stupidity scarcely arose. Nonetheless there is or can be room for genuine mistake, even in an experienced practitioner, and we are quite satisfied that a suitably tailored direction should have been given".

In *R. v Salisu* [2009] EWCA Crim 2702; [2010] M.H.L.R. 58, a case involving appeals against convictions under this section, Hughes L.J. said, at para.11, that in *R. v G* [2003] UKHL 50; [2003] 4 All E.R. 765, the House of Lords had "made clear that recklessness involves subjective fault and actual foresight of risk".

In *De Maroussem v Commissioner of Income Tax* [2004] UKPC 43 at para.41, the Privy Council held that the meaning to be attributed to the expression "wilful neglect" may vary according to the context but generally the expression should be taken to mean that there has been an intentional or purposive omission to do something that the person in question knows he or she has a duty to do.

NEGLECT.   In the context of a verdict of neglect made at a Coroner's inquest, Sir Thomas Bingham MR said that neglect

"means a gross failure to provide adequate nourishment or liquid, or provide or procure basic medical attention or shelter or warmth for someone in a dependent position (because of youth, age, illness or incarceration) who cannot provide it for himself. Failure to provide medical attention for a dependent person whose physical condition is such as to show that he obviously needs it may amount to neglect. So it may be if it is the dependent person's mental condition which obviously calls for medical attention (as it would, for example, if a mental nurse observed that a patient had a propensity to swallow razor blades and failed to report this propensity to a doctor, in a case where the patient had no intention to cause himself injury but did thereafter swallow razor blades with fatal results). In both cases the crucial consideration will be what the dependent person's condition, whether physical or mental, appeared to be" (*R. v Humberside and Scunthorpe Coroner Ex p. Jamieson* [1994] 3 All E.R. 972 at 990, 991).

PATIENT.   There is no requirement under this subsection for the victim to have been detained. The ill-treatment or wilful neglect of an in-patient need not have taken place on the hospital premises.

Subsection (2)

1–1207   MENTALLY DISORDERED PATIENT.   Is a person who is either suffering or appearing to be suffering from mental disorder (*R. v Newington*, above). There is no need for the victim to be receiving treatment for mental disorder, to have had a history of in-patient treatment in a hospital, or to have been a detained patient or a detained patient on leave of absence from a hospital. At the time of the offence the victim could, for example, be living in his own home, with relatives or friends, or in a care home.

OTHERWISE IN HIS CUSTODY OR CARE.   The custodians or carers could include social workers, care workers, teachers, relatives or friends. It is submitted that the use of the term "moral obligation" extends the scope of this section to include a family member, friend or volunteer who is caring for the mentally disordered person.

Assisting patients to absent themselves without leave, etc.

128.—(1) Where any person induces or knowingly assists another person who **1–1208** is liable to be detained in a hospital within the meaning of Part II of this Act or is subject to guardianship under this Act [or is a community patient] to absent himself without leave he shall be guilty of an offence.

(2) Where any person induces or knowingly assists another person who is in legal custody by virtue of section 137 below to escape from such custody he shall be guilty of an offence.

(3) Where any person knowingly harbours a patient who is absent without leave or is otherwise at large and liable to be retaken under this Act or gives him any assistance with intent to prevent, hinder or interfere with his being taken into custody or returned to the hospital or other place where he ought to be he shall be guilty of an offence.

(4) Any person guilty of an offence under this section shall be liable—
(a) on summary conviction, to imprisonment for a term not exceeding six months or to a fine not exceeding the statutory maximum, or to both;
(b) on conviction on indictment, to imprisonment for a term not exceeding two years or to a fine of any amount, or to both.

AMENDMENT

In subs.(1) the words in square brackets were inserted by the Mental Health Act 2007 s.32(4), Sch.3 para.28.

DEFINITIONS
absent without leave: ss.18(6), 145(1). **1–1209**
patient: s.145(1).
community patient: ss.17A(7), 145(1).
hospital: ss.34(2), 145(1).

GENERAL NOTE

Under this section it is an offence to induce or to help a patient escape from custody or to **1–1210** absent himself from hospital or place where he is required to be without leave, or to harbour or prevent the recapture or return of such patients. The patient does not commit an offence by absenting himself without leave. Proceedings under this section can be instituted by local social services authorities (s.130).

Subsection (1)
KNOWINGLY. The use of this term emphasises the requirement of mens rea (*R. v Dunne* **1–1211** (1998) 162 J.P. 399 CA).

Subsection (3)
OTHER PLACE WHERE HE OUGHT TO BE. Such as a specified place of residence under **1–1212** guardianship or a community treatment order.

Obstruction

129.—(1) Any person who without reasonable cause— **1–1213**
(a) refuses to allow the inspection of any premises; or
(b) refuses to allow the visiting, interviewing or examination of any person by a person authorised in that behalf by or under this Act [or to give access to any person to a person so authorised]; or
(c) refuses to produce for the inspection of any person so authorised any document or record the production of which is duly required by him; or

[(ca) fails to comply with a request under section 120C; or]

(d) otherwise obstructs any such person in the exercise of his functions,

shall be guilty of an offence.

(2) Without prejudice to the generality of subsection (1) above, any person who insists on being present when required to withdraw by a person authorised by or under this Act to interview or examine a person in private shall be guilty of an offence.

(3) Any person guilty of an offence under this section shall be liable on summary conviction to imprisonment for a term not exceeding three months or to a fine not exceeding level 4 on the standard scale or to both.

AMENDMENTS

The amendments to this section were made by the Mental Health (Patients in the Community) Act 1995 s.2(1), Sch.1 para.19 and the Health and Social Care Act 2008 s.52, Sch.3 para.10.

GENERAL NOTE

1–1214 This section specifies when a person commits the offence of obstruction under the Act. Proceedings can be instituted by a local social services authority (s.130).

A person who is suspected of committing an offence under this section could be arrested. This would enable the police to use reasonable force to prevent a continuation of the offence.

The Committee of Inquiry into Complaints about Ashworth Hospital stated that they were "inclined to the view that the right of silence is abrogated by [this section] which makes it an offence for anyone, without reasonable excuse, to obstruct an authorised investigation" (Cm. 2028, Vol.1, Ch. XIII, p.126). This opinion runs counter to the decision of the Divisional Court in *Rice v Connolly*, below.

Subsection (1)

1–1215 ANY PERSON.   Or corporation (Interpretation Act 1978 s.5, Sch.1).

OBSTRUCTS.   Cases on the offence of obstructing a policeman in the execution of his duty suggest that an offence under this section: (1) need not involve physical violence (*Hinchcliffe v Sheldon* [1955] 1 W.L.R. 1207); (2) is not committed on a mere refusal to answer questions or otherwise assist with enquiries (*Rice v Connolly* [1966] 2 Q.B. 414) or on advising a person not to answer questions (*Green v DPP* [1991] Crim. L.R. 782 DC); (3) will be committed if a person exercising powers under the Act approaches a person who she is entitled to approach and that person runs away (*Sekfali v DPP* [2006] EWHC 894 (Admin)); and (4) might be committed if a verbal warning of an impending inspection was given (*Green v Moore* [1982] 2 W.L.R. 671). There is also authority to support the contention that an offence is committed if the defendant's conduct makes it more difficult for an authorised person to carry out his duties; see the dictum of Lord Goddard C.J. in *Hinchcliffe v Sheldon*, above, at 1210 which was followed by the Divisional Court in *Lewis v Cox* [1984] 3 W.L.R. 875. In *Barge v British Gas Corporation* (1982) 81 L.G.R. 53, a case heard under the Trade Descriptions Act 1968, it was held that a refusal to co-operate will be an offence only in relation to a valid requirement which the enforcement officer is entitled to make.

During the Parliamentary passage of the 2007 Act, a Government Minister said that behaviour intended to stop a professional from making an independent decision that they are required to make under the Act could constitute the offence of obstruction (*Hansard,* HL Vol.688, col.749).

Subsection (2)

IN PRIVATE. Although an approved mental health professional (AMHP) is required to **1–1216** interview a patient "in a suitable manner" before making an application under Pt II (s.13(2)), there is no express provision authorising the interview to be in private. A person who disrupts an AMHP's interview with a patient would be guilty of an offence under subs.(1)(d).

Prosecutions by local authorities

130. A local social services authority may institute proceedings for any offence **1–1217** under this Part of this Act, but without prejudice to any provision of this Part of this Act requiring the consent of the Director of Public Prosecutions for the institution of such proceedings.

DEFINITION

local social services authority: s.145(1).   **1–1218**

GENERAL NOTE

This section empowers a local social services authority to institute proceedings for an **1–1219** offence alleged to have been committed under this Part.

Local authority staff who are charged with the duty of investigating offences under this Part must have regard to relevant provisions of the Codes of Practice issued under the Police and Criminal Evidence Act 1984 (s.67(9)). In particular, the following caution must be administered to a suspect before any questions about the offence are put to him or her: "You do not have to say anything. But it may harm your defence if you do not mention when questioned something which you later rely on in court. Anything you do say may be given in evidence" (*Code of Practice C* (2012 revision), para.10.5).

CONSENT OF THE DIRECTOR OF PUBLIC PROSECUTIONS. Is required by s.127.

PART X

MISCELLANEOUS AND SUPPLEMENTARY

Miscellaneous Provisions

[Independent mental health advocates]

[**130A.**—(1) [A local social services authority whose area is in England] shall **1–1220** make such arrangements as it considers reasonable to enable persons ("independent mental health advocates") to be available to help qualifying patients [for whom the authority is responsible for the purposes of this section].

(2) The appropriate national authority may by regulations make provision as to the appointment of persons as independent mental health advocates.

(3) The regulations may, in particular, provide—

(a) that a person may act as an independent mental health advocate only in such circumstances, or only subject to such conditions, as may be specified in the regulations;

(b) for the appointment of a person as an independent mental health advocate to be subject to approval in accordance with the regulations.

(4) In making arrangements under this section, [a local social services authority] shall have regard to the principle that any help available to a patient under the arrangements should, so far as practicable, be provided by a person

who is independent of any person who is professionally concerned with the patient's medical treatment.

(5) For the purposes of subsection (4) above, a person is not to be regarded as professionally concerned with a patient's medical treatment merely because he is representing him in accordance with arrangements—

(a) under section 35 of the Mental Capacity Act 2005; or

(b) of a description specified in regulations under this section.

(6) Arrangements under this section may include provision for payments to be made to, or in relation to, persons carrying out functions in accordance with the arrangements.

(7) Regulations under this section—

(a) may make different provision for different cases;

(b) may make provision which applies subject to specified exceptions;

(c) may include transitional, consequential, incidental or supplemental provision.]

AMENDMENTS

This section was inserted by the Mental Health Act 2007 s.30(2). The amendments to it were made by the Health and Social Care Act 2012 s.43.

WALES

This section has been amended in respect of Wales by the Mental Health (Wales) Measure 2010 s.53(1), Sch.1.

DEFINITIONS

1–1221   medical treatment: s.145(1), (4).

patient: s.145(1).

qualifying patient: s.130C(1)–(4).

GENERAL NOTE

1–1222   This section places a duty on local authorities to make arrangements for independent mental health advocates (IMHAs) to be available to help "qualifying patients". The mechanism for identifying which local authority is responsible for a qualifying patient is contained in s.130C(4A), (4B). In making arrangements under this section local authorities must have regard to the principle that any help provided under the arrangements to a qualifying patient should, as far as practicable, be provided by a person who is independent of anyone who is professionally concerned with the patient's treatment (subs.(4)). Qualifying patients are defined in s.130C(2), (3), (4). The IMHA must help the patient to obtain information about and to understand the matters set out in s.130B(1) and (2). The powers available to the IMHA are identified in s.130B(3), (4) and (7). A "responsible person", as defined in s.130D(2), has a duty to provide a qualifying patient with oral and written information about the IMHA service (s.130D(1), (4)). A qualifying patient can decline the services of an IMHA (s.130B(6)). Much of the detail of the IMHA scheme is set out in the Mental Health Act 1983 (Independent Mental Health Advocates) (England) Regulations 2008 (SI 2008/3166) which are made under subs.(2) and reproduced in Part 2 (for Wales, see SI 2008/2437 (W.210)).

Paragraph 4.11 of the Reference Guide states:

"The help which independent mental health advocacy services must provide also includes helping patients to exercise their rights, which can include representing them and speaking on their behalf. Independent mental health advocacy services are not designed to take the place of advice from, or representation by, qualified legal professionals."

However, there is nothing to prevent IMHAs from accompanying patients to tribunals and hospital managers hearings in a supportive role. Although, as Fennell states, there is no specific provision in the Tribunal Rules which entitles IMHAs to attend tribunal hearings, the tribunal is unlikely to refuse permission given that r.2(2)(c) of the Rules requires the tribunal to ensure ", so far as practicable, that the parties are able to fully participate in the proceedings" (Phil Fennell, *Mental Health: Law and Practice* (2011) para.5.22). The IMHA can act as the patient's representative at hearings if this is the patient's wish. See further r.11(1) (for representing the patient) and (5) (for attending the hearing) of the Tribunal Rules.

A concern about a perceived low take up rate by patients of the services of IMHAs has led Mental Health Commissioners of the CQC to advise that hospitals should either routinely provide the IMHA service with a list of all current detained patients or operate an "opt-out" system in that unless a patient states that he does not wish to be provided with the services of an IMHA, all detained patients should be referred to the service. Neither option is lawful as hospitals do not possess the statutory power to provide such lists or to make such referrals. In an event, the operation of such a system would involve a breach of patient confidentiality. The Health Committee of the House of Commons recommended that the IMHA service becomes an opt-out rather than an opt-in service (*Post-legislative scrutiny of the Mental Health Act 2007* (July 2013) para.45).

Hospital managers cannot withhold correspondence between patients and their IMHAs (s.134(3)(eb), (3A)).

In August 2009, the National Institute for Mental Health (England) published "Independent Mental Health Advocacy: Effective Practice Guide". The University of Central Lancashire has produced a study on the quality of IMHA services in England: "The right to be heard. Review of the quality of independent mental health advocate (IMHA) services in England" (June 2012). Also see the report of the Royal College of Psychiatrists on "Independent advocacy for people with mental disorder" (CR171, February 2012) and the British Institute of Human Rights publication "Mental Health Advocacy and Human Rights: Your Guide" (2013).

Code of Practice

Guidance on IMHAs is contained in Ch.6. Paragraph 6.3 of the *Code* states that "IMHAs **1–1223** should be independent of any person who has been professionally involved in the patient's medical treatment". Professionals "should remember that the normal rules on patient confidentiality apply to conversations with IMHAs, even when the conversation is at the patient's request. IMHAs have a right of access to patients' records in certain cases [see s.130B(4)], but otherwise professionals should be careful not to share confidential information with IMHAs, unless the patient has consented to the disclosure or the disclosure is justified on the normal grounds" (*Code*, para.6.29). With regard to patients seeking help from an IMHA, the *Code* states:

> "6.21 A qualifying patient may request the support of an IMHA at any time after they become a qualifying patient. Patients have the right to access the independent mental health advocacy service itself, rather than the services of a particular IMHA, though where possible it would normally be good practice for the same IMHA to remain involved while the person remains subject to the Act.
>
> 6.22 IMHAs must also comply with any reasonable request to visit and interview a qualifying patient, if the request is made by the patient's nearest relative, an approved mental health professional (AMHP) or the patient's responsible clinician (if they have one).
>
> 6.23 AMHPs and responsible clinicians should consider requesting an IMHA to visit a qualifying patient if they think that the patient might benefit from an IMHA's visit but is unable, or unlikely, for whatever reason to request an IMHA's help themselves. If a patient lacks capacity to decide whether to seek help from an IMHA, an IMHA should be introduced to the patient.

6.24 Before requesting an IMHA to visit a patient, they should, wherever practicable, first discuss the idea with the patient, and give the patient the opportunity to decide for themselves whether to request an IMHA's help. AMHPs and responsible clinicians should not request an IMHA to visit where they know, or strongly suspect, that the patient does not want an IMHA's help, or the help of the particular IMHA in question.

6.25 Patients may refuse to be interviewed and do not have to accept help from an IMHA if they do not want it. Equally, a patient may choose to end the support they are receiving from an IMHA at any time."

Subsection (1)

1–1224   LOCAL SOCIAL SERVICES AUTHORITY.   See s.130(4A),(4B).

Subsection (2)

1–1225   APPROPRIATE NATIONAL AUTHORITY.   See s.130C(5), (6).

Subsection (4)

1–1226   PROFESSIONALLY CONCERNED.   See subs.(5).

Subsection (5)

SECTION 35 OF THE MENTAL CAPACITY ACT 2005.   Which provides for the appointment of independent mental capacity act advocates.

SPECIFIED IN REGULATIONS.   See reg.7 of the Mental Health Act 1983 (Independent Mental Health Advocates) (England) Regulations 2008 (SI 2008/3166).

Arrangements under section 130A

1–1227   **[130B.**—(1) The help available to a qualifying patient under arrangements under section 130A above shall include help in obtaining information about and understanding—

   (a)   the provisions of this Act by virtue of which he is a qualifying patient;

   (b)   any conditions or restrictions to which he is subject by virtue of this Act;

   (c)   what (if any) medical treatment is given to him or is proposed or discussed in his case;

   (d)   why it is given, proposed or discussed;

   (e)   the authority under which it is, or would be, given; and

   (f)   the requirements of this Act which apply, or would apply, in connection with the giving of the treatment to him.

   (2) The help available under the arrangements to a qualifying patient shall also include—

   (a)   help in obtaining information about and understanding any rights which may be exercised under this Act by or in relation to him; and

   (b)   help (by way of representation or otherwise) in exercising those rights.

   (3) For the purpose of providing help to a patient in accordance with the arrangements, an independent mental health advocate may—

   (a)   visit and interview the patient in private;

   (b)   visit and interview any person who is professionally concerned with his medical treatment;

   (c)   require the production of and inspect any records relating to his detention or treatment in any hospital or registered establishment or to any after-care services provided for him under section 117 above;

   (d)   require the production of and inspect any records of, or held by, a local social services authority which relate to him.

(4) But an independent mental health advocate is not entitled to the production of, or to inspect, records in reliance on subsection (3)(c) or (d) above unless—

(a) in a case where the patient has capacity or is competent to consent, he does consent; or

(b) in any other case, the production or inspection would not conflict with a decision made by a donee or deputy or the Court of Protection and the person holding the records, having regard to such matters as may be prescribed in regulations under section 130A above, considers that—

    (i) the records may be relevant to the help to be provided by the advocate; and

    (ii) the production or inspection is appropriate.

(5) For the purpose of providing help to a patient in accordance with the arrangements, an independent mental health advocate shall comply with any reasonable request made to him by any of the following for him to visit and interview the patient—

(a) the person (if any) appearing to the advocate to be the patient's nearest relative;

(b) the responsible clinician for the purposes of this Act;

(c) an approved mental health professional.

(6) But nothing in this Act prevents the patient from declining to be provided with help under the arrangements.

(7) In subsection (4) above—

(a) the reference to a patient who has capacity is to be read in accordance with the Mental Capacity Act 2005;

(b) the reference to a donee is to a donee of a lasting power of attorney (within the meaning of section 9 of that Act) created by the patient, where the donee is acting within the scope of his authority and in accordance with that Act;

(c) the reference to a deputy is to a deputy appointed for the patient by the Court of Protection under section 16 of that Act, where the deputy is acting within the scope of his authority and in accordance with that Act.]

AMENDMENT

This section was inserted by the Mental Capacity Act 2007 s.30(2).

DEFINITIONS   **1–1228**

medical treatment: s.145(1), (4).

hospital: s.145(1).

registered establishment: s.145(1).

local social services authority: s.145(1).

nearest relative: s.145(1).

responsible clinician. ss.34(1), 145(1).

approved mental health professional: s.145(1), (1C).

GENERAL NOTE

This section identifies the help that an IMHA who is acting under s.130A should provide **1–1229** to the patient (subss.(1), (2)) and the powers of the IMHA (subss.(3), (4), (7)). It also requires the IMHA to comply with the reasonable requests of specified persons to visit and interview the patient (subs.(5)) and provides the patient with the power to decline the assistance of an IMHA (subs.(6)).

Subsections (1),(2)

Note that the IMHA is not entitled to adopt either a befriending or campaigning role. **1–1230**

Subsection (2)(b)

1–1231   Help under this provision could include providing assistance to the patient in bringing legal proceedings relating to his detention. The IMHA has no independent right to take such action.

Subsection (3)

1–1232   The normal rules of confidentiality apply to conversations between professionals and IMHAs: see para.6.29 of the *Code of Practice*.

Paragraph (d)

1–1233   Anyone who refuses, without reasonable cause, to produce records that an IMHA has a right to inspect may be guilty of the offence of obstruction under s.129.

Subsection (4)

1–1234   An IMHA's access to patients' records is considered in the following paragraphs of the *Code of Practice*:

> "6.30 Where the patient consents, IMHAs have a right to see any clinical or other records relating to the patient's detention or treatment in any hospital, or relating to any after-care services provided to the patient. An IMHA has a similar right to see any records relating to the patient held by a local authority.
>
> 6.31 Where the patient does not have the capacity (or in the case of a child, the competence) to consent to an IMHA having access to their records, the holder of the records must allow the IMHA access if they think that it is appropriate and that the records in question are relevant to the help to be provided by the IMHA.
>
> 6.32 When an IMHA seeks access to the records of a patient who does not have the capacity or the competence to consent, the person who holds the records should ask the IMHA to explain what information they think is relevant to the help they are providing to the patient and why they think it is appropriate for them to be able to see that information.
>
> 6.33 The Act does not define any further what it means by access being appropriate, so the record holder needs to consider all the facts of the case. But the starting point should always be what is in the patient's best interests and not (for example) what would be most convenient for the organisation which holds the records.
>
> 6.34 In deciding whether it is appropriate to allow the IMHA access, the holder of the records needs to consider whether disclosure of the confidential patient information contained in the records is justified.
>
> 6.35 The key consideration will therefore be whether the disclosure is in the patient's best interests. That decision should be taken in accordance with the Mental Capacity Act 2005 (MCA) (or, for children under 16, the common law).
>
> 6.36 Record holders should start from a general presumption that it is likely to be in the patient's interests to be represented by an IMHA who is knowledgeable about their case. But each decision must still be taken on its merits, and the record holder must, in particular, take into account what they know about the patient's wishes and feelings, including any written statements made in advance. (For further information on taking decisions in the best interests of people who lack capacity to make the decision themselves, please see the Code of Practice to the MCA.)
>
> 6.37 Records must not be disclosed if that would conflict with a decision made on the patient's behalf by the patient's attorney or deputy, or by the Court of Protection.

6.38 If the record holder thinks that disclosing the confidential patient information in the records to the IMHA would be in the patient's best interests, it is likely to be appropriate to allow the IMHA access to those records in all but the most exceptional cases."

Paragraph (b)
Capacity; donee; deputy.   See subs.(7).   **1–1235**

Person holding the record.   It is for this person, and not the IMHA, to determine whether to record is "relevant" and its production or inspection is "appropriate".

Subsection (7)
Capacity.   Is to be determined by using the tests set out in ss.2 and 3 of the 2005 Act. **1–1236**

Section 130A: supplemental
[**130C.**—(1) This section applies for the purposes of section 130A above.   **1–1237**
(2) A patient is a qualifying patient if he is—
(a) liable to be detained under this Act (otherwise than by virtue of section 4 or 5(2) or (4) above or section 135 or 136 below);
(b) subject to guardianship under this Act; or
(c) a community patient.
(3) A patient is also a qualifying patient if—
(a) not being a qualifying patient falling within subsection (2) above, he discusses with a registered medical practitioner or approved clinician the possibility of being given a form of treatment to which section 57 above applies; or
(b) not having attained the age of 18 years and not being a qualifying patient falling within subsection (2) above, he discusses with a registered medical practitioner or approved clinician the possibility of being given a form of treatment to which section 58A above applies.
(4) Where a patient who is a qualifying patient falling within subsection (3) above is informed that the treatment concerned is proposed in his case, he remains a qualifying patient falling within that subsection until—
(a) the proposal is withdrawn; or
(b) the treatment is completed or discontinued.
[(4A) A local social services authority is responsible for a qualifying patient if—
(a) in the case of a qualifying patient falling within subsection (2)(a) above, the hospital or registered establishment in which he is liable to be detained is situated in that authority's area;
(b) in the case of a qualifying patient falling within subsection (2)(b) above, that authority is the responsible local social services authority within the meaning of section 34(3) above;
(c) in the case of a qualifying patient falling within subsection (2)(c), the responsible hospital is situated in that authority's area;
(d) in the case of a qualifying patient falling within subsection (3)—
  (i) in a case where the patient has capacity or is competent to do so, he nominates that authority as responsible for him for the purposes of section 130A above, or
  (ii) in any other case, a donee or deputy or the Court of Protection, or a person engaged in caring for the patient or interested in his welfare, nominates that authority on his behalf as responsible for him for the purposes of that section.

(4B) In subsection (4A)(d) above—

(a) the reference to a patient who has capacity is to be read in accordance with the Mental Capacity Act 2005;

(b) the reference to a donee is to a donee of a lasting power of attorney (within the meaning of section 9 of that Act) created by the patient, where the donee is acting within the scope of his authority and in accordance with that Act;

(c) the reference to a deputy is to a deputy appointed for the patient by the Court of Protection under section 16 of that Act, where the deputy is acting within the scope of his authority and in accordance with that Act.]

(5) References to the appropriate national authority are—

(a) in relation to a qualifying patient in England, to the Secretary of State;

(b) in relation to a qualifying patient in Wales, to the Welsh Ministers.

(6) For the purposes of subsection (5) above—

(a) a qualifying patient falling within subsection (2)(a) above is to be regarded as being in the territory in which the hospital or registered establishment in which he is liable to be detained is situated;

(b) a qualifying patient falling within subsection (2)(b) above is to be regarded as being in the territory in which the area of the responsible local social services authority within the meaning of section 34(3) above is situated;

(c) a qualifying patient falling within subsection (2)(c) above is to be regarded as being in the territory in which the responsible hospital is situated;

(d) a qualifying patient falling within subsection (3) above is to be regarded as being in the territory determined in accordance with arrangements made for the purposes of this paragraph, and published, by the Secretary of State and the Welsh Ministers.]

AMENDMENTS

This section was inserted by the Mental Health Act 2007 s.30(2). The amendments to it were made by the Health and Social Care Act 2012 s.43.

WALES

This section has been amended in respect of Wales by the Mental Health (Wales) Measure 2010 s.53(1), Schs 1, 2.

DEFINITIONS

1–1238   community patient: ss.17A(7), 145(1).
approved clinician: s.145(1).
hospital: s.145(1).
registered establishment: ss.34(1), 145(1).
responsible hospital: ss.17A(7), 145(1).
local social services authority: s.145(1).

GENERAL NOTE

1–1239   This section defines a "qualifying patient" (subss.(2) to (4)) and "the appropriate national authority" (subss.(5), (6)) for the purposes of s.130A, and identifies which local authority is responsible for a qualifying patient (subss.(4A), (4B)).

A patient who lacks the capacity to decline the assistance of an IMHA (see s.130B(6)) is a qualifying patient for the purposes of this provision. Paragraph 5.3 of "Independent Mental Health Advocacy—Guidance for Commissioners", NIMH for England, Dec.2008, which is headed "Instructed and non-instructed advocacy", offers the following guidance on patients who lack the capacity to instruct an advocate:

"Wherever possible IMHAs will take instruction from the person they are supporting. An IMHA may support a person to obtain information, explore options and carry out actions, but throughout this process the IMHA will be directed by the person and act only on their behalf. IMHAs may also provide non-instructed advocacy when helping patients who are unable to express their wishes clearly, or at all, because they lack the mental capacity to instruct or have difficulties communicating. When providing non-instructed advocacy, the IMHA will represent the patient's wishes (as far as those wishes are known) and ensure the patient's rights are respected. Where a patient qualifies for both an IMHA and an Independent Mental Capacity Advocate (IMCA), the IMCA will represent the patient in line with the IMCA's statutory role. An example is a qualifying patient who lacks capacity and it is being considered for cancer treatment: in this case, the IMCA would represent the patient in the decision making process for this treatment."

By virtue of reg.4 and Sch.1, para.2(i) and (j) of the National Health Service Commissioning Board and Clinical Commissioning Groups (Responsibilities and Standing Rules) Regulations 2012 (SI 2012/2996), a Clinical Commissioning Group has a duty to commission services for the following categories of persons:

"(i) every person resident in Scotland, Wales or Northern Ireland and present in the CCG's area who is a qualifying patient within the meaning of section 130C of the 1983 Act (section 130A: supplemental), and not provided with primary medical services by a member of any CCG;

(j) every person who is a qualifying patient within the meaning of section 130C of the 1983 Act and liable to be detained under that Act in a hospital or registered establishment (within the meaning of that Act) in the CCG's area."

Subsection (2)(a)
A patient who is on s.17 leave is "liable to be detained" and is therefore included. The **1–1240** exclusions reflect the fact that the IMHA service is not intended to be an emergency response service.

Subsections (3), (4)
The Reference Guide states, at para.4.5, that informal patients who qualify because they **1–1241** are being considered for one of the treatments specified in subss.(3), "remain eligible until the treatment is finished, or stopped, or it is decided that they will not be given the treatment for the time being".

Duty to give information about independent mental health advocates

[130D.—(1) The responsible person in relation to a qualifying patient (within **1–1242** the meaning given by section 130C above) shall take such steps as are practicable to ensure that the patient understands—
  (a) that help is available to him from an independent mental health advocate; and
  (b) how he can obtain that help.
  (2) In subsection (1) above, "the responsible person" means—
  (a) in relation to a qualifying patient falling within section 130C(2)(a) above (other than one also falling within paragraph (b) below), the managers of the hospital or registered establishment in which he is liable to be detained;
  (b) in relation to a qualifying patient falling within section 130C(2)(a) above and conditionally discharged by virtue of section 42(2), 73 or 74 above, the responsible clinician;

(c) in relation to a qualifying patient falling within section 130C(2)(b) above, the responsible local social services authority within the meaning of section 34(3) above;

(d) in relation to a qualifying patient falling within section 130C(2)(c) above, the managers of the responsible hospital;

(e) in relation to a qualifying patient falling within section 130C(3) above, the registered medical practitioner or approved clinician with whom the patient first discusses the possibility of being given the treatment concerned.

(3) The steps to be taken under subsection (1) above shall be taken—

(a) where the responsible person falls within subsection (2)(a) above, as soon as practicable after the patient becomes liable to be detained;

(b) where the responsible person falls within subsection (2)(b) above, as soon as practicable after the conditional discharge;

(c) where the responsible person falls within subsection (2)(c) above, as soon as practicable after the patient becomes subject to guardianship;

(d) where the responsible person falls within subsection (2)(d) above, as soon as practicable after the patient becomes a community patient;

(e) where the responsible person falls within subsection (2)(e) above, while the discussion with the patient is taking place or as soon as practicable thereafter.

(4) The steps to be taken under subsection (1) above shall include giving the requisite information both orally and in writing.

(5) The responsible person in relation to a qualifying patient falling within section 130C(2) above (other than a patient liable to be detained by virtue of Part 3 of this Act) shall, except where the patient otherwise requests, take such steps as are practicable to furnish the person (if any) appearing to the responsible person to be the patient's nearest relative with a copy of any information given to the patient in writing under subsection (1) above.

(6) The steps to be taken under subsection (5) above shall be taken when the information concerned is given to the patient or within a reasonable time thereafter.]

AMENDMENT

This section was inserted by the Mental Health Act 2007 s.30(2).

DEFINITIONS

1–1243   the managers: s.145(1).
hospital: s.145(1).
registered establishment: s.145(1).
responsible hospital: ss.17A(7), 145(1).
local social services authority: s.145(1).
responsible clinician: ss.34(1), 145(1).
approved clinician: s.145(1).
community patient: ss.17A(7), 145(1).
nearest relative: s.145(1).

GENERAL NOTE

1–1244   This section places a duty on the "responsible person", as defined in subs.(2), to take practicable steps to ensure that a qualifying patient understands the help that an IMHA can provide and how to obtain such help (subs.(1)). The information, which has to be given both orally and in writing (subs.(4)), must be given to the patient as soon as practicable after the patient becomes a qualifying patient (subs.(3)). The nearest relative of a patient who comes within s.130C(2) (but not a Pt III patient) must be given a written copy of the information that the patient receives unless the patient objects (subss.(5), (6)).

[Independent mental health advocates: Wales

130E.—(1) The Welsh Ministers shall make such arrangements as they con- **1–1245** sider reasonable to enable persons ("independent mental health advocates") to be available to help—

(a) Welsh qualifying compulsory patients; and

(b) Welsh qualifying informal patients.

(2) The Welsh Ministers may by regulations make provision as to the appointment of persons as independent mental health advocates.

(3) The regulations may, in particular, provide—

(a) that a person may act as an independent mental health advocate only in such circumstances, or only subject to such conditions, as may be specified in the regulations;

(b) for the appointment of a person as an independent mental health advocate to be subject to approval in accordance with the regulations.

(4) In making arrangements under this section, the Welsh Ministers shall have regard to the principle that any help available to a patient under the arrangements should, so far as practicable, be provided by a person who is independent of any person who—

(a) is professionally concerned with the patient's medical treatment; or

(b) falls within a description specified in regulations made by the Welsh Ministers.

(5) For the purposes of subsection (4) above, a person is not to be regarded as professionally concerned with a patient's medical treatment merely because he is representing him in accordance with arrangements–

(a) under section 35 of the Mental Capacity Act 2005; or

(b) of a description specified in regulations under this section.

(6) Arrangements under this section may include provision for payments to be made to, or in relation to, persons carrying out functions in accordance with the arrangements.

(7) Regulations under this section and sections 130F to 130H—

(a) may make different provision for different cases;

(b) may make provision which applies subject to specified exceptions;

(c) may include transitional, consequential, incidental or supplemental provision.]

AMENDMENT

This section was inserted by the Mental Health (Wales) Measure 2010 s.31.

GENERAL NOTE

This section places a duty on the Welsh Ministers to make arrangements for help to be **1–1246** provided by IMHAs. Such help must be made available to two client groups: Welsh qualifying compulsory patients, as defined in s.130I, and Welsh qualifying informal patents, as defined in s.130J. The nature of the help to be provided is set out in s.130F, for compulsory patients, and s.130G, for informal patients.

The Mental Health (Independent Mental Health Advocates) (Wales) Regulations 2011 (SI 2011/2501 (W.273)) have been made under this section.

[Arrangements under section 130E for Welsh qualifying compulsory patients

1–1247 **130F.**—(1) The help available to a Welsh qualifying compulsory patient under arrangements under section 130E shall include help in obtaining information about and understanding—

(a) the provisions of this Act by virtue of which he is a qualifying compulsory patient;

(b) any conditions or restrictions to which he is subject by virtue of this Act;

(c) what (if any) medical treatment is given to him or is proposed or discussed in his case;

(d) why it is given, proposed or discussed;

(e) the authority under which it is, or would be, given; and

(f) the requirements of this Act which apply, or would apply, in connection with the giving of the treatment to him.

(2) The help available under the arrangements to a Welsh qualifying compulsory patient shall also include—

(a) help in obtaining information about and understanding any rights which may be exercised under this Act by or in relation to him;

(b) help (by way of representation or otherwise)—

(i) in exercising the rights referred to in paragraph (a);

(ii) for patients who wish to become involved, or more involved, in decisions made about their care or treatment, or care or treatment generally;

(iii) for patients who wish to complain about their care or treatment;

(c) the provision of information about other services which are or may be available to the patient;

(d) other help specified in regulations made by the Welsh Ministers.]

AMENDMENT
This section was inserted by the Mental Health (Wales) Measure 2010 s.32.

DEFINITION
1–1248 medical treatment: s.145(1), (4).

GENERAL NOTE
1–1249 This section sets out the nature of the help which must be made available for Welsh qualifying compulsory patients under arrangements made under s.130E.

[Arrangements under section 130E for Welsh qualifying informal patients

1–1250 **130G.**—(1) The help available to a Welsh qualifying informal patient under arrangements under section 130E shall include help in obtaining information about and understanding—

(a) what (if any) medical treatment is given to him or is proposed or discussed in his case;

(b) why it is given, proposed or discussed;

(c) the authority under which it is, or would be, given.

(2) The help available under the arrangements to a Welsh qualifying informal patient shall also include—

(a) help (by way of representation or otherwise)—

    (i) for patients who wish to become involved, or more involved, in decisions made about their care or treatment, or care or treatment generally;

    (ii) for patients who wish to complain about their care or treatment;

  (b) the provision of information about other services which are or may be available to the patient;

  (c) other help specified in regulations made by the Welsh Ministers.]

AMENDMENT

This section was inserted by the Mental Health (Wales) Measure 2010 s.33.

DEFINITION

medical treatment: s.145(1), (4).   **1–1251**

GENERAL NOTE

This section sets out the nature of the help which must be made available for Welsh **1–1252** qualifying informal patients under arrangements made under s.130E.

[Independent mental health advocates for Wales: supplementary powers and duties

    130H.—(1) For the purpose of providing help to a patient in accordance with **1–1253** arrangements made under section 130E, an independent mental health advocate may—

  (a) visit and interview the patient in private;

  (b) visit and interview–

    (i) any person who is professionally concerned with his medical treatment;

    (ii) any other person who falls within a description specified in regulations made by the Welsh Ministers;

  (c) require the production of and inspect any records relating to his detention, treatment or assessment in any hospital or registered establishment or to any after-care services provided for him under section 117 above;

  (d) require the production of and inspect any records of, or held by, a local social services authority which relate to him.

    (2) But an independent mental health advocate is not entitled to the production of, or to inspect, records in reliance on subsection (1)(c) or (d) above unless—

  (a) in a case where the patient has capacity or is competent to consent, he does consent; or

  (b) in any other case, the production or inspection would not conflict with a decision made by a donee or deputy or the Court of Protection and the person holding the records, having regard to such matters as may be prescribed in regulations under section 130E above, considers that—

    (i) the records may be relevant to the help to be provided by the advocate;

    (ii) the production or inspection is appropriate.

    (3) For the purpose of providing help to a Welsh qualifying compulsory patient in accordance with the arrangements, an independent mental health advocate shall comply with any reasonable request made to him by any of the following for him to visit and interview the patient—

  (a) the patient;

(b) the person (if any) appearing to the advocate to be the patient's nearest relative;

(c) the responsible clinician for the purposes of this Act;

(d) an approved mental health professional;

(e) a registered social worker who is professionally concerned with the patient's care, treatment or assessment;

(f) where the patient is liable to be detained in a hospital or registered establishment, the managers of the hospital or establishment or a person duly authorised on their behalf;

(g) the patient's donee or deputy.

(4) For the purpose of providing help to a Welsh qualifying informal patient in accordance with the arrangements, an independent mental health advocate shall comply with any reasonable request made to him by any of the following for him to visit and interview the patient—

(a) the patient;

(b) the managers of the hospital or establishment in which the patient is an inpatient or a person duly authorised on their behalf;

(c) any person appearing to the advocate to whom the request is made to be the patient's carer;

(d) the patient's donee or deputy;

(e) a registered social worker who is professionally concerned with the patient's care, treatment or assessment.

(5) But nothing in this Act prevents the patient from declining to be provided with help under the arrangements.

(6) In subsection (2) above the reference to a patient who has capacity is to be read in accordance with the Mental Capacity Act 2005.

(7) In subsection (4) above—

(a) "carer", in relation to a Welsh qualifying informal patient, means an individual who provides or intends to provide a substantial amount of care on a regular basis for the patient, but does not include any individual who provides, or intends to provide care by virtue of a contract of employment or other contract with any person or as a volunteer for a body (whether or not incorporated);

(b) "registered social worker" means a person included in the principal part or the visiting European part of a register maintained under section 56(1) of the Care Standards Act 2000.

(8) In subsections (2) to (4) above—

(a) the reference to a donee is to a donee of a lasting power of attorney (within the meaning of section 9 of the Mental Capacity Act 2005) created by the patient, where the donee, in making the decision referred to in subsection (2) or the request referred to in subsection (3) or (4), is acting within the scope of his authority and in accordance with that Act;

(b) the reference to a deputy is to a deputy appointed for the patient by the Court of Protection under section 16 of that Act, where the deputy, in making the decision referred to in subsection (2) or the request referred to in subsection (3) or (4), is acting within the scope of his authority and in accordance with that Act.]

AMENDMENT

This section was inserted by the Mental Health (Wales) Measure 2010 s.34.

DEFINITIONS

local social services authority: s.145(1).
hospital: s.145(1).
registered establishment: s.145(1).
patient: s.145(1).
nearest relative: s.145(1).
approved mental health professional: s.145(1), (1AC).
medical treatment: s.145(1), (4).

GENERAL NOTE

The Explanatory Notes to the Mental Health (Wales) Measure 2010 state at paras 59 to **1–1255** 63:

"[This] section . . . applies in respect of both Welsh qualifying compulsory patients and Welsh qualifying informal patients. IMHAs may meet such patients in private, and visit and interview anyone professionally concerned with the patient's medical treatment. Regulations may be made by the Welsh Ministers to specify other persons who the IMHA may visit and interview.

Where a patient has the capacity, or is competent, to consent to records being made available to an IMHA (and does consent), the IMHA may require the production of any hospital or local authority records relating to the patient. If a patient lacks the capacity or is not competent to consent to records being made available to an IMHA, the record holder can still allow access to such records. The record holder can only do this if it is appropriate and relevant to the help the advocate will provide to the patient, and such access does not conflict with a valid decision of a donee of deputy (within the meaning of the Mental Capacity Act 2005).

An IMHA must meet with a Welsh qualifying compulsory patient on the reasonable request of the patient themselves, the patient's nearest relative, the responsible clinician, an approved mental health professional (AMHP), a social worker professionally concerned with the patient, hospital managers or a person duly authorised on their behalf, or the patient's donee or deputy.

An IMHA must meet with a Welsh qualifying informal patient on the reasonable request of the patient themselves, the hospital managers or a person duly authorised on their behalf, the patient's carer, the patient's donee or deputy, or a social worker professionally concerned with the care, treatment or assessment of the patient.

A patient is not obliged to accept the help provided or offered by an IMHA."

The Mental Health (Independent Mental Health Advocates) (Wales) Regulations 2011 (SI 2011/2501 (W.273)) have been made under this section.

[Welsh qualifying compulsory patients

130I.—(1) This section applies for the purposes of section 130E above. **1–1256**

(2) A patient is a Welsh qualifying compulsory patient if he is—

(a) liable to be detained under this Act (other than under section 135 or 136 below) and the hospital or registered establishment in which he is liable to be detained is situated in Wales;

(b) subject to guardianship under this Act and the area of the responsible local social services authority within the meaning of section 34(3) above is situated in Wales; or

(c) a community patient and the responsible hospital is situated in Wales.

(3) A patient is also a Welsh qualifying compulsory patient if the patient is to be regarded as being in Wales for the purposes of this subsection and—

(a) not being a qualifying patient falling within subsection (2) above, he discusses with a registered medical practitioner or approved clinician the possibility of being given a form of treatment to which section 57 above applies; or

(b) not having attained the age of 18 years and not being a qualifying patient falling within subsection (2) above, he discusses with a registered medical practitioner or approved clinician the possibility of being given a form of treatment to which section 58A above applies.

(4) For the purposes of subsection (3), a patient is to be regarded as being in Wales if that has been determined in accordance with arrangements made for the purposes of that subsection and section 130C(3), and published, by the Secretary of State and the Welsh Ministers.

(5) Where a patient who is a Welsh qualifying compulsory patient falling within subsection (3) above is informed that the treatment concerned is proposed in his case, he remains a qualifying patient falling within that subsection until—

(a) the proposal is withdrawn; or

(b) the treatment is completed or discontinued.]

AMENDMENT
This section was inserted by the Mental Health (Wales) Measure 2010 s.35.

DEFINITIONS
1–1257   approved clinician: s.145(1).
community patient: ss.17A(7), 145(1).
hospital: s.145(1).
patient: s.145(1).
registered establishment: ss.34(1), 145(1).
the responsible hospital: ss.17A(7), 145(1).

GENERAL NOTE
1–1258   This section determines which patients are considered to be Welsh qualifying compulsory patients.

[Welsh qualifying informal patients

1–1259   130J.—(1) This section applies for the purposes of section 130E above.

(2) A patient is a Welsh qualifying informal patient if—

(a) the patient is an in-patient at a hospital or registered establishment situated in Wales;

(b) the patient is receiving treatment for, or assessment in relation to, mental disorder at the hospital or registered establishment; and

(c) no application, order, direction or report renders the patient liable to be detained under this Act.]

AMENDMENT
This section was inserted by the Mental Health (Wales) Measure 2010 s.36.

DEFINITIONS
1–1260   hospital: s.145(1).
patient: s.145(1).
registered establishment: ss.34(1), 145(1).
mental disorder: ss.1, 145(1).

GENERAL NOTE
This section determines which patients are considered to be Welsh qualifying informal **1–1261** patients.

[Duty to give information about independent mental health advocates to Welsh qualifying compulsory patients

130K.—(1) The responsible person in relation to a Welsh qualifying compul- **1–1262** sory patient (within the meaning given by section 130I above) shall take such steps as are practicable to ensure that the patient understands—

(a) that help is available to him from an independent mental health advocate; and

(b) how he can obtain that help.

(2) In subsection (1) above, the "responsible person" means—

(a) in relation to a Welsh qualifying compulsory patient falling within section 130I(2)(a) above (other than one also falling within paragraph (b) below), the managers of the hospital or registered establishment in which he is liable to be detained; or

(b) in relation to a Welsh qualifying compulsory patient falling within section 130I(2)(a) above and conditionally discharged by virtue of section 42(2), 73 or 74 above, the responsible clinician;

(c) in relation to a Welsh qualifying compulsory patient falling within section 130I(2)(b) above, the responsible local social services authority within the meaning of section 34(3) above;

(d) in relation to a Welsh qualifying compulsory patient falling within section 130I(2)(c) above, the managers of the responsible hospital;

(e) in relation to a Welsh qualifying compulsory patient falling within section 130I(3) above, the registered medical practitioner or approved clinician with whom the patient first discusses the possibility of being given the treatment concerned.

(3) The steps to be taken under subsection (1) above shall be taken—

(a) where the responsible person falls within subsection (2)(a) above, as soon as practicable after the patient becomes liable to be detained;

(b) where the responsible person falls within subsection (2)(b) above, as soon as practicable after the conditional discharge;

(c) where the responsible person falls within subsection (2)(c) above, as soon as practicable after the patient becomes subject to guardianship;

(d) where the responsible person falls within subsection (2)(d) above, as soon as practicable after the patient becomes a community patient;

(e) where the responsible person falls within subsection (2)(e) above, while the discussion with the patient is taking place or as soon as practicable thereafter.

(4) The steps to be taken under subsection (1) above shall include giving the requisite information both orally and in writing.

(5) The responsible person in relation to a Welsh qualifying compulsory patient falling within section 130I(2) above (other than a patient liable to be detained by virtue of Part 3 of this Act) shall, except where the patient otherwise requests, take such steps as are practicable to furnish any person falling within subsection (6) with a copy of any information given to the patient in writing under subsection (1) above.

(6) A person falls within this subsection if—

(a) the person appears to the responsible person to be the patient's nearest relative;

(b) the person is a donee of a lasting power of attorney (within the meaning of section 9 of the Mental Capacity Act 2005) created by the patient and the scope of the donee's authority includes matters related to the care and treatment of the patient;

(c) the person is a deputy appointed for the patient by the Court of Protection under section 16 of that Act and the scope of the deputy's authority includes matters related to the care and treatment of the patient.

(7) The steps to be taken under subsection (5) above shall be taken when the information concerned is given to the patient or within a reasonable time thereafter.]

AMENDMENT

This section was inserted by the Mental Health (Wales) Measure 2010 s.37.

DEFINITIONS

1–1263   approved clinician: s.145(1).
community patient: ss.17A(7), 145(1).
hospital: s.145(1).
patient: s.145(1).
nearest relative: s.145(1).
the managers: s.145(1)
registered establishment: ss.34(1), 145(1).
the responsible hospital: ss.17A(7), 145(1).

GENERAL NOTE

1–1264   The person(s) responsible for ensuring the patient understands that help from an IMHA is available is known as the "responsible person". Subsection (2) defines who the responsible person is in relation to the different groups of Welsh qualifying compulsory patients. The responsible person must provide written information regarding the IMHA service to the nearest relative, donee or deputy (if any) of a qualifying compulsory patient.

[Duty to give information about independent mental health advocates to Welsh qualifying informal patients

1–1265   130L.—(1) The responsible person in relation to a Welsh qualifying informal patient (within the meaning given by section 130J above) shall take such steps as are practicable to ensure that the patient understands—

(a) that help is available to him from an independent mental health advocate; and

(b) how he can obtain that help.

(2) In subsection (1) above, the "responsible person" means the managers of the hospital or registered establishment to which the patient is admitted as an in-patient.

(3) The steps to be taken under subsection (1) above shall be taken as soon as practicable after the patient becomes an in-patient.

(4) The steps to be taken under subsection (1) above shall include giving the requisite information both orally and in writing.

(5) The responsible person in relation to a Welsh qualifying informal patient shall, except where the patient otherwise requests, take such steps as are

practicable to furnish any person falling within subsection (6) with a copy of any information given to the patient in writing under subsection (1) above.

(6) A person falls within this subsection if—

(a) the person appears to the responsible person to be a carer of the patient;

(b) the person is a donee of a lasting power of attorney (within the meaning of section 9 of the Mental Capacity Act 2005) created by the patient and the scope of the donee's authority includes matters related to the care and treatment of the patient;

(c) the person is a deputy appointed for the patient by the Court of Protection under section 16 of that Act and the scope of the deputy's authority includes matters related to the care and treatment of the patient.

(7) In subsection (6), "carer", in relation to a Welsh qualifying informal patient, means an individual who provides or intends to provide a substantial amount of care on a regular basis for the patient, but does not include any individual who provides, or intends to provide care by virtue of a contract of employment or other contract with any person or as a volunteer for a body (whether or not incorporated);

(8) The steps to be taken under subsection (5) above shall be taken when the information concerned is given to the patient or within a reasonable time thereafter.]

AMENDMENT

This section was inserted by the Mental Health (Wales) Measure 2010 s.38.

DEFINITIONS

    hospital: s.145(1).   **1–1266**

    the managers: s.145(1).

    patient: s.145(1).

    registered establishment: ss.34(1), 145(1).

GENERAL NOTE

This section provides for "information-giving" arrangements in respect of Welsh quali- **1–1267** fying informal patients. It is similar to those provided for Welsh qualifying compulsory patients in s.130K.

Informal admission of patients

131.—(1) Nothing in this Act shall be construed as preventing a patient who **1–1268** requires treatment for mental disorder from being admitted to any hospital or [registered establishment] in pursuance of arrangements made in that behalf and without any application, order or direction rendering him liable to be detained under this Act, or from remaining in any hospital or [registered establishment] in pursuance of such arrangements after he has ceased to be so liable to be detained.

[(2) Subsections (3) and (4) below apply in the case of a patient aged 16 or 17 years who has capacity to consent to the making of such arrangements as are mentioned in subsection (1) above.

(3) If the patient consents to the making of the arrangements, they may be made, carried out and determined on the basis of that consent even though there are one or more persons who have parental responsibility for him.

(4) If the patient does not consent to the making of the arrangements, they may not be made, carried out or determined on the basis of the consent of a person who has parental responsibility for him.

(5) In this section—

(a) the reference to a patient who has capacity is to be read in accordance with the Mental Capacity Act 2005; and

(b) "parental responsibility" has the same meaning as in the Children Act 1989.]

AMENDMENTS

The amendments to this section were made by the Care Standards Act 2000 s.116, Sch.4 para.9(2), the Children Act 1989 s.108(5), Sch.13 para.48(5) and the Mental Health Act 2007 s.43.

DEFINITIONS

1–1269 patient: s.145(1).
mental disorder: ss.1, 145(1).
hospital: s.145(1).
registered establishment: ss.34(1), 145(1).

GENERAL NOTE

1–1270 This section, which applies to mentally capable patients who consent to their admission and to patients lacking such capacity who do not object to their admission (*R. v Bournewood NHS Trust, Ex p. L* [1998] 3 All E.R. 289), provides that a patient can either enter hospital for treatment for mental disorder on an informal basis, or remain in hospital on an informal basis once the authority for the original detention has come to an end. It also provides that in the case of patients aged 16 or 17 years who have the capacity to consent to their informal admission to hospital for treatment for their mental disorder, they may consent (or may not consent) to the admission and their decision cannot be overridden by a person with parental responsibility for them. If such a child does not consent to the admission, he could be admitted for compulsory treatment under Pt II if the relevant criteria are satisfied.

In *M v Ukraine* [2013] M.H.L.R. 255, the Court said at para.71:

"[I]f in-patient psychiatric treatment is voluntary this presupposes that the patient has the guaranteed right to stop any further treatment and to leave the hospital whenever he or she wishes to do so. This freedom of action is subject to mental health practitioners' authority to refuse to discharge the patient, provided that the relevant compulsory admission procedures are immediately applied, following which the person shall be treated as an involuntary patient."

The question of whether a person has the mental capacity to consent to admission as an informal patient "will be likely to include consideration of the person's capacity to agree (a) to the relevant admission to hospital for the relevant purpose, (b) to stay in hospital whilst its purpose is carried out and (c) to the circumstances relating to a possible deprivation of liberty that will prevail during that admission" (*AM v South London & Maudsley NHS Foundation Trust* [2013] UKUT 365 (AAC); [2014] M.H.L.R. 181, per Charles J. at para.40). An assessment of the patient's capacity would only need to be undertaken if there was reason to believe that the assumption of capacity set out in s.1(2) of the Mental Capacity Act 2005 might be rebutted. In *A Primary Care Trust v LDV* [2013] EWHC 272 (Fam), a case decided under the 2005 Act, Baker J., without "seeking to set any sort of precedent", said, at para.39, that "the clinicians and the court should ask whether [the patient] has the capacity to understand, retain and weigh the following information:

(1) that she is in hospital to receive care and treatment for a mental disorder;

(2) that the care and treatment will include varying levels of supervision (including supervision in the community), use of physical restraint and the prescription and administration of medication to control her mood;

(3) that staff at the hospital will be entitled to carry out property and personal searches;

(4) that she must seek permission of the nursing staff to leave the hospital, and, until the staff at the hospital decide otherwise, will only be allowed to leave under supervision;

(5) that if she left the hospital without permission and without supervision, the staff would take steps to find and return her, including contacting the police."

This list requires the patient to possess a very high level of capacity. Indeed, some members of the hospital staff might find it difficult to satisfy this capacity test without the assistance of written prompts. Assessors should bear in mind the note of caution expressed by Peter Jackson J. at para.26 of *Heart of England NHS Foundation Trust v JB* [2014] EWCOP 342:

"What is required here is a broad, general understanding of the kind that is expected from the population at large. JB is not required to understand every last piece of information about her situation and her options: even her doctors would not make that claim. It must also be remembered that common strategies for dealing with unpalatable dilemmas – for example indecision, avoidance or vacillation – are not to be confused with incapacity. We should not ask more of people whose capacity is questioned than of those whose capacity is undoubted."

It is suggested that a more appropriate list might be: can the patient understand etc. that he is being admitted to hospital informally and that this means that, subject to s.5, he can leave whenever he wants, that the purpose of the admission is to treat his mental disorder, that such treatment might involve the administration of medication, that during his stay in hospital he will be subject to hospital rules, and that the rules might involve placing restrictions on him.

Although informal admission should be the preferred mode of admission, there is nothing in the Act which expressly prevents an application being made in respect of a mentally capable patient who is willing to enter hospital as an informal patient. While it is true that s.5 can be invoked to prevent an informal patient from leaving hospital, circumstances can arise which justify the use of compulsion on "willing" patients. Compulsion should be used where its absence would place the patient's safety and/or the safety of others at significant risk. The *Code of Practice*, at para.14.16 suggests that compulsion should be considered for patients whose history suggests that they might have a change of mind about being admitted informally. Paragraph 14.16 (as it appeared in the previous edition of the *Code*) was endorsed by Charles J. in *AM v South London & Maudsley NHS Foundation Trust*, above, at para.20.

The *Code of Practice* is incorrect when it states that a "person with a learning disability or autism cannot be informally admitted if they do not have capacity to consent to or refuse that admission and treatment" (para.20.30). The correct legal position is that the admission to hospital of such patients can be provided under the Mental Capacity Act 2005 if they are not being deprived of their liberty in the hospital. An assessment should be undertaken if it is thought that a patient is being deprived of his liberty as a failure either to detain the patient under this Act or to authorise the deprivation under Sch.A1 of the 2005 Act would violate the patient's right under art.5 of the European Convention on Human Rights (*HL v United Kingdom* (2005) 40 E.H.R.R. 32; [2004] M.H.L.R. 236: also see the General Note to Part II under the heading "The detention of compliant mentally incapable patients"). The nature of a deprivation of liberty is considered in Part 6.

In *R. v Kirklees Metropolitan Borough Council Ex p. C* [1992] 2 F.L.R. 117, Kennedy J., on an application for the judicial review of a decision by the local authority to consent to the admission of an adolescent girl to a psychiatric hospital, held that an admission to a psychiatric hospital can be lawful even though it does not take place within the framework of the Act, which did not cover all eventualities. His Lordship found that there is no reason to conclude that the right to arrange an informal admission is limited to the terms of this section. If that were the case it would produce the surprising result that no one, adult or child, who had not been diagnosed as being mentally disordered, could ever be admitted to a psychiatric hospital for assessment. This section did not apply to the patient because there was no evidence that she required "treatment for mental disorder" (see subs.(1)). The local authority was entitled to consent on the patient's behalf because a care order had been made in respect of her and at the material time she was not "Gillick competent". On affirming this decision at [1993] 2 F.L.R. 187, the Court of Appeal confirmed that although the informal admission of a patient for assessment is not covered by this section, there is nothing to prohibit such an admission taking place under common law. The effect of this decision is merely to fill a gap in the statutory scheme, a gap which was described by Lloyd L.J., at 190, as being "odd".

J. Bindman and his colleagues found that a third of patients who had been admitted informally to a psychiatric hospital felt highly coerced at admission, and the majority were uncertain that they were free to leave the hospital ("Perceived coercion at admission to psychiatric hospital and engagement with follow up", Soc. Psychiatry Psychiatr Epidemiol (2005) 40: 160–166). Informal patients should therefore "have their legal position and rights explained to them" (*Code of Practice*, para.4.49).

Human Rights Act 1998

1–1271   Article 5 of the European Convention on Human Rights (ECHR), which as aimed at preventing unjustified deprivations of liberty, applies to children. In *Nielsen v Denmark* (1989) 11 E.H.R.R. 175, the European Court of Human Rights (ECtHR) found that no deprivation of liberty had occurred when the mother of a 12 year-old boy consented to his admission to a psychiatric hospital against his wishes and that of his father. Among the factors that were cited in support of this decision, the court emphasised at para.72:

(i)   the fact that the mother was the sole holder of parental responsibility in respect of the child. The court said that the "care and upbringing of children normally and necessarily require that the parents or an only parent decide where the child must reside and also impose, or authorise others to impose, various restrictions on the child's liberty". However, it accepted that "the rights of the holder of parental authority cannot be unlimited and that it is incumbent on the State to provide safeguards against abuse";

(ii) that the "restrictions to which the [child] was subject were no more than the normal requirements for the care of a child of 12 years of age receiving treatment in hospital"; and

(iii) its view that the child "was still of an age at which it would be normal for a decision to be made by the parent against the wishes of the child".

The court concluded by stating that it "must be possible for a child like the applicant to be admitted to hospital at the request of the holder of parental rights, a case which is clearly not covered by paragraph 1 of Article 5". This statement was made because the child, not having been diagnosed as being mentally ill, was not detained as a person of unsound mind so as to bring the case within art.5(1)(e).

It has been said that although *Nielsen* is a relatively recent decision, "there must be doubt how far, if at all, [it] will be followed in future. In considering any similar issue today, account should be taken of the Convention of the Rights of the Child 1989" (S. Grosz, J. Beatson, P. Duffy, *Human Rights: The 1998 Act and the European Convention*, (2000) p.199.) Despite this, the ECtHR has yet to confine *Nielsen* to history: see *DD v Lithuania* [2012] M.H.L.R. 209 para.148. Also see *Trust A v X* noted under *Children under the age of 16*, below.

The detention of children under Brussels II Revised

A determination by the High Court under Council Regulation (EC) No. 2201/2003 of the **1–1272** European Union concerning jurisdiction and the recognition and enforcement of judgments in matrimonial matters and the matters of parental responsibility (commonly known as "Brussels II Revised") can lead to a foreign child being compulsorily detained in a psychiatric hospital in England or Wales without being detained under this Act. The underlying principle of the Regulation is set out in Article 21(1):

"A judgment given in a Member State shall be recognised in the other Member States without any special procedure being required".

Article 28 is concerned with enforcement:

"1. A judgment on the exercise of parental responsibility in respect of a child given in a Member State which is enforceable in that Member State and has been served shall be enforced in another Member State when, on the application of any interested party, it has been declared enforceable there.

2. However, in the United Kingdom, such a judgment shall be enforced in England and Wales, in Scotland or in Northern Ireland when, on the application of any interested party, it has been registered for enforcement in that part of the United Kingdom."

The procedure in England and Wales for registering a foreign judgment on the exercise of parental responsibility (and hence obtaining a declaration of enforceability) is set down in Part 31 of the Family Procedure Rules 2010, as amplified by paras 2.1 and 3.1 of the associated Practice Direction 31A.

For an example of a case where a child was detained under Brussels II Revised, see *HSE Ireland v SF (A Minor)* [2012] EWHC 1640 (Fam) where Baker J. made the following interim declaration:

"1. SF do reside at [the English Unit] for purposes of such care and treatment as may in the opinion of the Director of [the English Unit] be necessary.

2. There be leave to the staff of [the English Unit] to detain at or return SF to [the English Unit] and to use reasonable force (if necessary) in so detaining her or returning her.

3. There be leave generally to Director of [the English Unit] and those under their direction (to include all or any of the multi-disciplinary team including clinical, care or similar professional and/or ancillary health care staff) to furnish such treatment and care as in their opinion may be necessary.

4. The above orders are made as being in the best interests of SF and are exercisable whether or not she consents thereto".

On reaching adulthood, the patient could be detained under the procedure established under Sch.3 of the Mental Capacity Act 2005.

Schedule 3 of the Mental Capacity Act 2005

Schedule 3 makes provision as to the private international law of England and Wales in **1–1273** relation to those who are over the age of 16 who, as a result of impairment or insufficiency of their personal faculties (which is not a test of lack of mental capacity), cannot protect their interests. In particular, it gives effect in England and Wales to the Convention on the International Protection of Adults (Cm.5881) which was signed at The Hague on January 13, 2000 and entered into force on January 1, 2009. It does so on a very wide basis in that the Schedule provides for the mutual recognition of "protective measures", which can include detention in a psychiatric institution, imposed by a foreign court regardless of whether that court is located in a Convention country. This means that Sch.3 comes into play whenever a cross-border "incapacity" issue arises. The aims of the Convention are set out in art.1. They are to:

- provide for the protection in international situations of adults who, by reason of impairment or insufficiency in their personal faculties, are not in a position to defend their interests

- establish rules on jurisdiction, applicable law, international recognition and enforcement of protective measures which are to be respected by all Contracting States, and co-operation between Contracting States.

- The basis of the jurisdiction is habitual residence, not best interests: (*Re MN* [2010] EWHC 1926 (Fam), para.38). The habitual residence of the person therefore determines which State authorities have jurisdiction over his person and property.

A detailed analysis of the jurisdiction of the Court of Protection to recognise and enforce foreign protective measures under Sch.3 was provided by Baker J. in *Health Service Executive of Ireland v PA* [2015] EWCOP 38. In particular, his Lordship held that:

"[W]hen considering applications to recognise and enforce compulsory psychiatric placements under Schedule 3, the limited review [undertaken by the Court] should encompass the Court being satisfied that (1) the *Winterwerp* criteria are met and (2) that the individual's right to challenge the detention under Article 5(4) is effective (i.e. that they have a right to take proceedings to challenge the detention and the right to regular reviews thereafter)" (para.96).

Schedule 3 is examined in *International Protection of Adults,* edited by Richard Frimston, Alexander Ruck Keene, Claire van Overdijk, and Adrian Ward, 2015.

Code of Practice

1–1274   Guidance on the informal admission of children and young people in contained in Ch.19. With regard to the provision of information for informal hospital patients, the *Code* states:

"4.49 Although the Act does not impose any duties to give information to informal patients, these patients should have their legal position and rights explained to them.

4.50 Informal patients should be provided with relevant information (eg about how to make a complaint and consent requirements for treatment).

4.51 Informal patients must be allowed to leave if they wish, unless they are to be detained under the Act. Both the patient and, where appropriate, their carer and advocate should be made aware of this right with information being provided in a format and language the patient understands. Local policies and arrangements about movement around the hospital and its grounds must be clearly explained to the patients concerned. Failure to do so could lead to a patient mistakenly believing that they are not allowed to leave hospital, which could result in an unlawful deprivation of their liberty and a breach of their human rights."

Subsection (2)–(5)
Children aged 16 or 17 (see paras 19.53–19.57 of the Code of Practice)

1–1275   These subsections provide that patients aged 16 or 17 who have the capacity to consent to their admission to a hospital for treatment for mental disorder can consent or not consent to such arrangements on their own behalf. If the patient consents to the making of arrangements, he can be informally admitted to hospital, and the consent cannot be over-ridden by a person with parental responsibility for him. If the patient does not consent to the making of the arrangements, he cannot be informally admitted on the basis of consent from a person with parental responsibility.

The capacity of the patient to consent to the arrangements should be assessed according to the test set out in ss.2 and 3 of the MCA. If the young person lacks the capacity to consent to the admission, para.19.57 of the *Code of Practice* states:

"Where a young person aged 16 or 17 lacks capacity it may be possible for them to be admitted informally, in accordance with the MCA, unless the admission and treatment amounts to a deprivation of liberty. In cases where the MCA cannot authorise informal admission, but the admission is thought to be necessary, consideration should be given to as whether the criteria for admission under the Act are met. If the Act is not applicable, legal advice should be sought on the need to seek authorisation from the court before further action is taken."

Children under the age of 16

Paragraph 19.65 of the *Code of Practice* states: **1–1276**

"Where a child who is Gillick competent to decide about their admission to hospital for assessment and/or treatment of their mental disorder consents to this, they may be admitted to hospital as an informal patient."

The nature of Gillick competence is identified in the *Code* at paras 19.34 to 19.37.

Paragraph 19.66 of the *Code* states:

"Where a child who is Gillick competent refuses to be admitted for treatment it may be inadvisable to rely on the consent of a person with parental responsibility (see paragraph 19.39). In such cases, consideration should be given to whether admission under the Act is necessary, and if so, whether the criteria are met. If the Act is not applicable, legal advice should be sought on the need to seek authorisation from the court before further action is taken."

In *Trust A v X* [2015] EWHC 922 (Fam), Keehan J. held that the references made by the Court of Appeal in *Re RK v BCC* [2011] EWCA Civ 1305 to the effect that an adult in the exercise of parental responsibility may not lawfully detain or authorise the deprivation of liberty of a child were made obiter and did not correctly state the legal position. His Lordship held that it was possible for parents in the proper exercise of parental responsibility, to consent to the accommodation of their mentally incapacitated child in a hospital and thus render what would otherwise be a deprivation of liberty not a deprivation of liberty. His Lordship said at para.57:

"The decisions which might be said to come within the zone of parental responsibility for a 15 year old who did not suffer from the conditions with which D has been diagnosed will be of a wholly different order from those decisions which have to be taken by parents whose 15 year old son suffers with D's disabilities. Thus a decision to keep such a 15 year old boy under constant supervision and control would undoubtedly be considered an inappropriate exercise of parental responsibility and would probably amount to ill treatment. The decision to keep an autistic 15 year old boy who has erratic, challenging and potentially harmful behaviours under constant supervision and control is a quite different matter; to do otherwise would be neglectful. In such a case I consider the decision to keep this young person under constant supervision and control is the proper exercise of parental responsibility."

At para.67, his Lordship confirmed that in the case of a young person under the age of 16, the court may, in the exercise of the inherent jurisdiction, authorise a deprivation of liberty.

Hospitals as "secure accommodation"

1–1277   If the main objective is to detain the child because of the child's behavioural disturbance rather than to hospitalise the child to provide medical treatment for the child's mental disorder, it might be appropriate to invoke s.25 of the Children Act 1989 which sets out the criteria that must be satisfied before a child can be placed in secure accommodation. It is possible to make a secure accommodation order in general terms, leaving it to the local authority to place the child in an appropriate unit as and when one is identified (*Re A* [2015] EWHC 1709 (Fam) at para.11). Regulation 5 of the Children (Secure Accommodation) Regulations 1991 (SI 1991/1505) provides that s.25 does not apply to a child who is detained under any provision of the Mental Health Act, although it will apply if the child is granted leave of absence under s.17 (*Hereford and Worcester County Council v S* [1993] 2 F.L.R. 360). Section 25 will also apply if the child is either admitted informally under this section or is admitted under the common law powers identified in *R. v Kirklees Metropolitan Borough Council Ex p. C* [1992] 2 F.L.R. 117, if the unit of the hospital where the child is being accommodated is "secure accommodation". Secure accommodation is defined as "accommodation which is provided for the purpose of restricting the liberty of children to whom section 25 [of the 1989 Act] applies" (reg.2(1) of the 1991 Regulations). Paragraph 8.10 of the *Children Act 1989: Guidance and Regulations, Vol.4, Residential Care*, HMSO, 1991, states that "it is important to recognise that any practice or measure which prevents a child from leaving a room or building of his own free will may be deemed by the court to constitute restriction of liberty". In *R. v Northampton Juvenile Court Ex p. London Borough of Hammersmith and Fulham* [1985] F.L.R. 193 an adolescent "behaviour modification unit" of an independent hospital where "the locking of the unit is part of the planned treatment regime which enables the medical staff to control, modify and eliminate aggressive and dangerous behaviour" was held to be "accommodation provided for the purpose of restricting liberty". Ewbank J. found that the purpose of the unit was to restrict the liberty of the children with a view to modifying their behaviour. A psychiatric unit which Douglas Brown J. held in *South Glamorgan County Council v W and B* [1993] 1 F.L.R. 574, to be "just short" of a secure unit was described in the following terms:

> "Although Merrifield is not a secure unit, we would endeavour to prevent [the child] from leaving the premises unaccompanied and it will be important that we have clear permission from the court to do this, otherwise it would not be possible to admit [the child] to our unit without her consent."

These cases were referred to by Wall J. in *Re C (Detention: Medical Treatment)* [1997] 2 F.L.R. 180, where his Lordship held that a psychiatric unit for the treatment of eating disorders did not constitute secure accommodation. The primary purpose of the placement of a child in the unit:

> "is to achieve treatment: the accommodation provides a structure for that treatment. The fact that such a structure includes a degree of restriction on the patient's liberty is ... an incident of the treatment programme, and the fact that steps can be taken to prevent [a child] leaving the premises does not, of itself, render the clinic secure accommodation" (at 192, 193).

In doubting the finding of Cazalet J. in *A Metropolitan Borough Council v DB* [1997] 1 F.L.R. 767, that a maternity ward to which entry and exit could only be effected by the use of a key out pass was secure accommodation, Wall J. said that the natural meaning of the words "provided for the purpose of restricting liberty" is "designed for, or having as its primary purpose" the restriction of liberty.

The power of the High Court to make declarations regarding the detention of child patients
In *Re C (Detention: Medical Treatment)*, above, a 16-year-old child needed treatment for **1–1278**
anorexia nervosa in a private psychiatric unit in circumstances where the unit would not
accept patients who were detained under this Act and where there were sound reasons
for not instituting care proceedings. Wall J. held that:

(i) the High Court has the power under the inherent jurisdiction to order the detention of
a child in a specified institution for the purpose of medical treatment being administered to the child without her agreement (see *Re W (A Minor) (Medical Treatment)*,
above);

(ii) the court has power to authorise the use of reasonable force (if necessary) to detain
the child in the institution and to ensure that any necessary treatment is received (see
Norfolk and Norwich Healthcare (NHS) Trust v W [1996] 2 F.L.R. 613);

(iii) as the clinic was not "secure accommodation" for the purposes of s.25 of the
Children Act 1989 and the attendant regulations (see above), the inherent jurisdiction was not ousted. An application under s.25 for a secure accommodation order
would have had to have been made if the clinic did constitute secure
accommodation;

(iv) although s.25 did not apply, the court should pay careful attention to the scheme laid
down by Parliament under that section, and an order should not be made under the
inherent jurisdiction unless the s.25 criteria are, by analogy to the facts of the case,
met. The rights given to a child who is the subject of a s.25 application should be
made available, and equivalent safeguards to those provided for in s.25 should be
built into the order; and

(v) although consideration should always be given to alternative avenues (for example,
under s.31 of the Children Act or the Mental Health Act) a refusal to exercise the
inherent jurisdiction on the basis that an alternative avenue was available could
lead to the child falling between several statutory stools, and not receiving the treatment that he or she needs. A primary purpose of the inherent jurisdiction is to fill
lacunae in the statutory schemes; if the court is satisfied that in the particular circumstances of the case no statutory scheme is available, it should not hesitate to use its
powers under the inherent jurisdiction.

Accommodation, etc. for children

[**131A.**—(1) This section applies in respect of any patient who has not attained **1–1279**
the age of 18 years and who—
(a) is liable to be detained in a hospital under this Act; or
(b) is admitted to, or remains in, a hospital in pursuance of such arrangements
as are mentioned in section 131(1) above.
(2) The managers of the hospital shall ensure that the patient's environment in the
hospital is suitable having regard to his age (subject to his needs).
(3) For the purpose of deciding how to fulfil the duty under subsection (2)
above, the managers shall consult a person who appears to them to have knowledge or experience of cases involving patients who have not attained the age of 18
years which makes him suitable to be consulted.
(4) In this section, "hospital" includes a registered establishment.]

AMENDMENT
This section was inserted by the Mental Health Act 2007 s.31(3).

DEFINITIONS

1–1280   patient: s.145(1).
hospital: s.145(1) and see subs.(4) of this section.
the managers: s.145(1).
registered establishment: ss.34(1), 145(1).

GENERAL NOTE

1–1281   This section places a duty on hospital managers to ensure that the hospital environment of a detained or informal mentally disordered patient who is under the age of 18 is "suitable having regard to his age (subject to his needs)" (subss.(1), (2)). The duty applies to children and young people who are detained in hospital as a place of safety under ss.135 or 136. Prior to making a decision about how to fulfil this duty, the managers must consult with a suitable person as defined in subs.(3). This person is likely to be a child and adolescent mental health services professional.

The Minister of State said:

"We have used the word 'environment' because what matters to a child or young person goes well beyond mere physical segregation from older people. . . . By using the word 'environment' we can ensure not only that children and young people have separate facilities, but that they are appropriate physical facilities, with staff who have the right training to understand and address their specific needs as children, and a hospital routine that will allow their personal, social and educational development to continue as normally as possible" (*Hansard*, HC, Vol.461, col.1144).

Paragraph 91 of "Post-legislative assessment of the Mental Health Act 2007", Cm 8408, states that "admission to an adult ward may be the most appropriate option [for young people] because of (a) overriding need when a young person needs immediate admission for their safety or that of others, and (b) atypical need when, even if a CAMHS (Child and Adolescent Mental Health Service) bed was available, an adult ward is the most appropriate clinical placement": see further, paras 19.94 et seq of the *Code of Practice*.

From April 1, 2013, a registered person must notify the Care Quality Commission where a person under the age of 18 has been admitted to an adult psychiatric unit for more than 48 hours (Care Quality Commission (Registration) Regulations 2009 (SI 2009/3112) reg.18(2)(h)). A form that must be used for this purpose may be downloaded from the Commission's website (*www.cqc.org.uk*).

Under ss.85 and 86 of the 1989 Act where a child is to be accommodated by a Local Health Board or NHS trust for a consecutive period of at least three months, or where a child is to be accommodated in a care home or independent hospital for a similar period, the accommodating authority or the person carrying on the home must notify the local authority for the area where the child is ordinarily resident. The local authority is then placed under a duty to determine whether the child's welfare is being adequately safeguarded and to consider whether it should exercise any of its functions under the 1989 Act in respect of the child.

See s.140 for the duty of health bodies to notify local authorities of the arrangements that are in force for the provision of accommodation or facilities designed to be specially suitable for mentally disorder child patients.

Article 37(c) of the United Nations *Convention on the Rights of the Child* states that "every child deprived of liberty shall be separated from adults unless it is considered in the child's best interest not to do so". The United Kingdom entered the following reservation to this aspect of the Convention:

"Where at any time there is a lack of suitable accommodation or adequate facilities for a particular individual in any institution in which young offenders are detained, or where the mixing of adults and children is deemed to be mutually beneficial, the United

Kingdom reserves the right not to apply Article 37(c) in so far as those provisions require children who are to be detained to be accommodated separately from adults."

The Royal College of Psychiatrists has developed a set of standards to identify safe and appropriate care for young people on adult wards: see "Safe and Appropriate Care for Young People on Adult Mental Health Wards", July, 2009. The risks that children face when placed in adult psychiatric wards was highlighted by the Children's Commissioner for England in his report "Pushed into the Shadows: Young People's Experience of Adult Mental Health Facilities" (2007).

Code of Practice
    This section is considered in Ch.36 at paras 19.90 to 19.104.   **1–1282**

Duty of managers of hospitals to give information to detained patients

    132.—(1) The managers of a hospital or [registered establishment] in which a **1–1283** patient is detained under this Act shall take such steps as are practicable to ensure that the patient understands—

    (a) under which of the provisions of this Act he is for the time being detained and the effect of that provision; and

    (b) what rights of applying to a [tribunal] are available to him in respect of his detention under that provision;

and those steps shall be taken as soon as practicable after the commencement of the patient's detention under the provision in question.

    (2) The managers of a hospital or [registered establishment] in which a patient is detained as aforesaid shall also take such steps as are practicable to ensure that the patient understands the effect, so far as relevant in his case, of sections 23, 25, 56 to 64, 66(1)(g), 118 and 120 above and section 134 below; and those steps shall be taken as soon as practicable after the commencement of the patient's detention in the hospital or [establishment].

    (3) The steps to be taken under subsections (1) and (2) above shall include giving the requisite information both orally and in writing.

    (4) The managers of a hospital or [registered establishment] in which a patient is detained as aforesaid shall, except where the patient otherwise requests, take such steps as are practicable to furnish the person (if any) appearing to them to be his nearest relative with a copy of any information given to him in writing under subsections (1) and (2) above; and those steps shall be taken when the information is given to the patient or within a reasonable time thereafter.

AMENDMENTS
    The amendments to this section were made by the Care Standards Act 2000 s.116, Sch.4 para.9(2), the Mental Health Act 2007 s.32 (4), Sch.3 para.29 and SI 2008/2883 art.9, Sch.3 para.63.

DEFINITIONS   **1–1284**
    the managers: s.145(1).
    patient: s.145(1).
    hospital: s.145(1).
    registered establishment: ss.34(1), 145(1).
    nearest relative: ss.26(3), 145(1).

GENERAL NOTE

1–1285   This section, requires the managers of NHS and independent hospitals to inform detained patients of their legal position and rights. It does not apply to a community patient who has been recalled to hospital unless the patient's community treatment order is revoked and the patient becomes a detained patient (see s.17G), and there is no requirement to give information to patients who are detained under the Act in places other than a hospital, e.g. a patient who is detained in a police station under s.136. Unless the patient requests otherwise, the information must also be given to the patient's nearest relative or acting nearest relative. Section 132A places a similar duty on hospital managers with respect to community patients. There is also a duty placed on hospital managers to inform patients when their detention is renewed (s.20(3); also see reg.26(1)(b) of the English Regulations and reg.8 of the Welsh Regulations). It would clearly be good practice for a detained patient to be informed when he attains informal status.

As a result of the decision in *R. (on the application of Wooder) v Feggetter and Mental Health Act Commission* [2002] EWCA Civ 554, noted under s.58(3)(b), a patient should be informed of the reasons for the imposition of treatment given without consent under s.58.

Regulation 26 of the English Regulations and regs 8, 22, 39 and 32 of the Welsh Regulations provides that the nearest relative of the patient must be informed of various statutory events concerning the patient unless the patient objects to the information being provided or providing the information would not be practicable.

Code of Practice

1–1286   Guidance on this section and on providing information to patients, nearest relatives, carers and others is given in Ch.4. Guidance on providing information to those who are detained and are under 18 is contained in paras 19.75 to 19.77 of the *Code*. In addition to the obligations set out in this section, the *Code* states:

> "4.15 Patients should also be told the essential legal and factual grounds for their detention or CTO. For the patient to be able to adequately and effectively challenge the grounds for their detention or their CTO, should they wish, they should be given the full facts rather than simply the broad reasons. This should be done promptly and clearly. They should be told they may seek legal advice, and assisted to do so if required.

> 4.16 In addition, a copy of the detention or CTO documentation should be made available to the patient as soon as practicable and as a priority, unless the hospital managers are of the opinion (based on the advice of the authors of the documents) that the information disclosed would adversely affect the health or wellbeing of the patient or others. It may be necessary to remove any personal information about third parties.

> 4.17 Where the section of the Act under which the patient is being detained changes, they must be provided with the above information to reflect the new situation. The same applies where a detained patient becomes subject to a CTO."

Information about how to make a complaint to the service commissioner, the CQC or Parliamentary and Health Ombudsmen should also be readily available (*Code*, para.4.63). Paragraph 4.28 of the *Code* states:

> "Those with responsibility for patient care should ensure that patients are reminded from time to time of their rights and the effects of the Act. It may be necessary to give the same information on a number of different occasions or in different formats and to check regularly that the patient has fully understood it. Information given to a patient who is unwell may need to be repeated when their condition has improved. It is helpful to ensure that patients are aware that an IMHA can help them to understand the information."

Leaflets

Model leaflets on patients' rights that have been designed to assist hospitals and local **1–1287**
social services authorities to meet their legal obligations under this section have been produced by the Department of Health. They can be accessed at: *http://*
webarchive.nationalarchives.gov.uk/20130107105354/http://www.dh.gov.uk/en/
Publicationsandstatistics/Publications/PublicationsPolicyAndGuidance/DH_089275.

Information about firms of solicitors who could represent patients at tribunal and
managers' hearings

This issue is best addressed by looking separately at the position of patients who lack the **1–1288**
mental capacity to instruct a solicitor and patients who possess such capacity.

Mentally Incapacitated Patients.

Hospital staff should not approach a solicitor with a request to represent a mentally incapacitated patient. Apart from a situation where either a court appointed deputy or the donee
of a lasting power of attorney instructs a solicitor to represent a mentally incapacitated
patient, solicitors are prevented by their professional Code of Conduct from acting for a
client who lacks capacity: see para.4.2 of Appendix E. Although the First-tier Tribunal
has the power under r.11 of the Tribunal Rules to appoint a solicitor to represent such
patients, hospital managers do not have an equivalent power. However, an independent
mental health advocate can represent the patient at the both tribunal and managers' hearings (s.130B(2)(b)).

Mentally Capable Patients.

Hospital staff should not recommend a particular firm of solicitors to a patient because,
as well as the clear conflict of interest issues that arise, solicitors will have a legitimate
cause for complaint if they are not recommended. If the patient does not have a solicitor
and wishes to be represented, staff should provide the patient with a list of local solicitors
who are accredited by the Law Society to represent patients at tribunal hearings.
Independent mental health advocates can assist patients with their choice of an appropriate
solicitor.

Subsection (1)

SUCH STEPS AS ARE PRACTICABLE. The steps must include giving the requisite infor- **1–1289**
mation both orally and in writing (subs.(3)). It is clearly not practicable for staff to
attempt to provide the information orally to a patient who is either too ill to understand
the information, refuses to listen to staff, or becomes significantly distressed when the
attempt is made. If the patient initially fails to understand the information or is too distressed to receive it, staff should make further attempts to provide the information if it is
considered that the patient's mental state has improved to the extent that such an attempt
would be likely to succeed. In appropriate cases, the managers should use an interpreter.

FOR THE TIME BEING DETAINED. Including patients who are detained under the "holding
powers" contained in s.5. This provision requires the patient to be provided with the relevant information when the section under which he is detained changes.

RIGHTS OF APPLYING TO A TRIBUNAL. If the patient (or his nearest relative) has missed an
opportunity to apply to a tribunal because of a failure to provide the information set out in
this provision, the patient (or his representative) should request that the Secretary of State
refers the case to the tribunal under s.67 or s.71.

Subsection (2)

Sections 23, 25 and 66(1)(a) are concerned with the powers of the responsible clinician, **1–1290**
the hospital managers and the nearest relative to discharge the patient, ss.56 to 64 contain
the consent to treatment provisions, s.118 provides for the publishing of the *Code of*

Practice, s.120 is concerned with the Care Quality Commission and the Welsh Ministers' functions relating to the general protection of patients who are subject to the Act and s.134 deals with the withholding of detained patient's correspondence.

Subsection (4)
Paragraph 4.32 of the *Code* states:

"When a patient detained under the Act or subject to a CTO is given information, they should be told that the written information will also be supplied to their nearest relative, so that they can discuss their views about sharing this information and following this discussion, raise any concerns or object to the sharing of some or all of this information. There should be discussion with the patient at the earliest possible time as to what information they are happy to share and what they would like to be kept private."

With regard to the patient's rights under the European Convention on Human Rights (ECHR), the *Code* states at para.4.36:

"In addition, occasionally there will be cases where [the duties to provide information to nearest relatives] do not apply because disclosing information about the patient to the nearest relative cannot be considered practicable, on the grounds that it would have a detrimental impact on the patient that is disproportionate to any advantage to be gained from informing the nearest relative. This would therefore be a breach of the patient's right to privacy under article 8 of the ECHR. The risk of this is greatest where the nearest relative is someone whom the patient would not have chosen themselves. Before disclosing information to nearest relatives without a patient's consent, the person concerned must consider whether the disclosure would be likely to:

- put the patient at risk of physical harm or financial or other exploitation

- cause the patient emotional distress or lead to a deterioration in their mental health, or

- have any other detrimental effect on their health or wellbeing and, if so, whether the advantages to the patient and the public interest of the disclosure outweigh the disadvantages to the patient, in the light of all the circumstances of the case."

1–1291 If the patient is mentally incapable of requesting that the information be not copied to his nearest relative, the information should be sent unless the patient, when mentally capable, had indicated that the nearest relative should not be contacted by the hospital. This opinion is subject to the note on "such steps as are practicable", below.

PATIENT OTHERWISE REQUESTS. It is submitted that the patient should be informed of the provisions of this subsection at the same time as he is given the information required by subss.(1) and (2). A nearest relative will usually be informed about an admission under s.2 (s.11(3)) and consulted about an admission under s.3 (s.11(4)).

SUCH STEPS AS ARE PRACTICABLE. If the hospital managers consider that it might not be practicable to copy the information to the nearest relative of a patient on the ground that knowledge that the nearest relative had been contacted might cause the patient's rights under art.8 of the ECHR to be violated, the managers should adopt the approach identified in *TW v Enfield Borough Council* [2014] EWCA Civ 362; [2014] M.H.L.R. 415 in order to reach a decision: see the notes to "not reasonably practicable" in s.11(4) and para.4.36 of the *Code of Practice*, above.

[Duty of managers of hospitals to give information to community patients

132A.—(1) The managers of the responsible hospital shall take such steps as **1–1292** are practicable to ensure that a community patient understands—

(a) the effect of the provisions of this Act applying to community patients; and

(b) what rights of applying to a [tribunal] are available to him in that capacity; and those steps shall be taken as soon as practicable after the patient becomes a community patient.

(2) The steps to be taken under subsection (1) above shall include giving the requisite information both orally and in writing.

(3) The managers of the responsible hospital shall, except where the community patient otherwise requests, take such steps as are practicable to furnish the person (if any) appearing to them to be his nearest relative with a copy of any information given to him in writing under subsection (1) above; and those steps shall be taken when the information is given to the patient or within a reasonable time thereafter.]

AMENDMENTS

This section was inserted by the Mental Health Act 2007 s.32(4), Sch.3 para.30. The reference to the tribunal in subs.(1)(b) was substituted by SI 2008/2883 art.9, Sch.3 para.64.

DEFINITIONS **1–1293**
the managers: s.145(1).
responsible hospital: ss.17A(7), 135(1).
community patient: ss.17A(7), 145(1).
nearest relative: s.145(1).

GENERAL NOTE

This section places a duty on the managers of the responsible hospital to inform a com- **1–1294** munity patient, both orally and in writing, of the legal effect of being a community patient and of his rights to make an application to a tribunal. Unless the patient otherwise requests, the written information must also be sent to the patient's nearest relative. This section mirrors the duty contained in s.132 and reference should be made to the notes on that section. There is also a duty placed on hospital managers to inform a patient when his CTO renewed (s.20A(5); also see reg.26(1)(g) of the English Regulations and reg.22(2) of the Welsh Regulations).

Code of Practice

Guidance on this section and on providing information to patients, nearest relatives, **1–1295** carers and others is contained in Ch.4. Reference should be made to the note to s.132 under this heading.

Duty of managers of hospitals to inform nearest relatives of discharge

133.—(1) Where a patient liable to be detained under this Act in a hospital or **1–1296** [registered establishment] is to be discharged otherwise than by virtue of an order for discharge made by his nearest relative, the managers of the hospital or [registered establishment] shall, subject to subsection (2) below, take such steps as are practicable to inform the person (if any) appearing to them to be the nearest relative of the patient; and that information shall, if practicable, be given at least seven days before the date of discharge.

[(1A) The reference in subsection (1) above to a patient who is to be discharged includes a patient who is to be discharged from hospital under section 17A above.

(1B) Subsection (1) above shall also apply in a case where a community patient is discharged under section 23 or 72 above (otherwise than by virtue of an order for discharge made by his nearest relative), but with the reference in that subsection to the managers of the hospital or registered establishment being read as a reference to the managers of the responsible hospital.]

(2) Subsection (1) above shall not apply if the patient or his nearest relative has requested that information about the patient's discharge should not be given under this section.

AMENDMENTS

The amendments to this section were made by the Care Standards Act 2000 s.116, Sch.4 para.9(2) and the Mental Health Act 2007 s.32(4), Sch.3 para.31.

DEFINITIONS

1–1297   patient: s.145(1).
hospital: s.145(1).
registered establishment: ss.34(1), 145(1).
nearest relative: ss.26(3), 145(1).
the managers: s.145(1).
community patient: ss.17A(7), 145(1).
responsible hospital: ss.17A(7), 145(1).

GENERAL NOTE

1–1298   This section places a duty on the managers of NHS and independent hospitals to inform the nearest relative of a detained patient that the patient is about to be discharged from detention (including being discharged subject to a community treatment order) or discharged from a community treatment order (other than a discharge ordered by the patient's nearest relative). The information should be given at least seven days before the date of discharge if this is practicable. The duty does not arise if either the patient or his nearest relative has requested that this information should not be given.

Restricted patients, patients remanded to hospital under s.35 or s.36 and patients subject to interim hospital orders under s.38 do not have nearest relatives for the purposes of the Act.

Subsection (1)

1–1299   SUCH STEPS AS ARE PRACTICABLE.   See the note on s.132(4).

Correspondence of patients

1–1300   **134.**—(1) A postal packet addressed to any person by a patient detained in a hospital under this Act and delivered by the patient for dispatch may be withheld from [the postal operator concerned]—

(a) if that person has requested that communications addressed to him by the patient should be withheld; or

(b) subject to subsection (3) below, if the hospital is [one at which high security psychiatric services are provided] and the managers of the hospital consider that the postal packet is likely—

   (i) to cause distress to the person to whom it is addressed or to any other person (not being a person on the staff of the hospital); or

   (ii) to cause danger to any person;

and any request for the purposes of paragraph (a) above shall be made by a notice in writing given to the managers of the hospital, [or the [approved clinician with overall responsibility for the patient's case] [. . .].

(2) Subject to subsection (3) below, a postal packet addressed to a patient detained [under this Act in a hospital at which high security psychiatric services are provided] may be withheld from the patient if, in the opinion of the managers of the hospital, it is necessary to do so in the interests of the safety of the patient or for the protection of other persons.

(3) Subsections (1)(b) and (2) above do not apply to any postal packet addressed by a patient to, or sent to a patient by or on behalf of—

(a) any Minister of the Crown [or the Scottish Ministers] or Member of either House of Parliament [or a Member of the Scottish Parliament] [or of the Northern Ireland Assembly];

[(aa) any of the Welsh Ministers, the Counsel General of the Welsh Assembly Government or a member of the National Assembly for Wales;]

[(b) any judge or officer of the Court of Protection, any of the Court of Protection Visitors or any person asked by that Court for a report under section 49 of the Mental Capacity Act 2005 concerning the patient;]

(c) the Parliamentary Commissioner for Administration, [the Scottish Public Services Ombudsman] [the Public Services Ombudsman for Wales] the Health Service Commissioner for England, [. . .] or a Local Commissioner within the meaning of Part III of the Local Government Act 1974;

[(ca) the Care Quality Commission;]

(d) [the First-tier Tribunal or the Mental Health Review Tribunal for Wales];

(e) [the National Health Service Commissioning Board, a clinical commissioning group] [. . .] [[Local Health Board] [or Special Health Authority][. . .], a local social services authority, a Community Health Council [. . .]] or a [local probation board established under section 4 of the Criminal Justice and Court Services Act 2000] [or a provider of probation services];

[(ea) a provider of a patient advocacy and liaison service for the assistance of patients at the hospital and their families and carers;

(eb) a provider of independent advocacy services for the patient;]

(f) the managers of the hospital in which the patient is detained;

(g) any legally qualified person instructed by the patient to act as his legal adviser; or

(h) the European Commission of Human Rights or the European Court of Human Rights

[and for the purposes of paragraph (d) above the reference to the First-tier Tribunal is a reference to that tribunal so far as it is acting for the purposes of any proceedings under this Act or paragraph 5(2) of the Schedule to the Repatriation of Prisoners Act 1984.]

[(3A) In subs.(3) above—

(a) "a patient advocacy and liaison service" means a service of a description prescribed by regulations made by the Secretary of State, and

[(b) "independent advocacy services" means services provided under—

(i) arrangements under section 130A [or section 130E] above;

(ii) arrangements under [section 223A of the Local Government and Public Involvement in Health Act 2007] or section 187 of the National Health Service (Wales) Act 2006; or

(iii) arrangements of a description prescribed as mentioned in paragraph (a) above.]

(4) The managers of a hospital may inspect and open any postal packet for the purposes of determining—

(a) whether it is one to which subsection (1) or (2) applies, and

(b) in the case of a postal packet to which subsection (1) or (2) above applies, whether or not it should be withheld under that subsection;

and the power to withhold a postal packet under either of those subsections includes power to withhold anything contained in it.

(5) Where a postal packet or anything contained in it is withheld under subsection (1) or (2) above the managers of the hospital shall record that fact in writing.

(6) Where a postal packet or anything contained in it is withheld under subsection (1)(b) or (2) above the managers of the hospital shall within seven days give notice of that fact to the patient and, in the case of a packet withheld under subsection (2) above, to the person (if known) by whom the postal packet was sent; and any such notice shall be given in writing and shall contain a statement of the effect of [section 134A(1) to (4)].

(7) The functions of the managers of a hospital under this section shall be discharged on their behalf by a person on the staff of the hospital appointed by them for that purpose and different persons may be appointed to discharge different functions.

(8) The Secretary of State may make regulations with respect to the exercise of the powers conferred by this section.

(9) In this section [and section 134A] "hospital" has the same meaning as in Part II of this Act, [and "postal operator" and] "postal packet" [have] the same meaning as in [Part 3 of the Postal Services Act 2011].

AMENDMENTS

The amendments to this section were made by the Scotland Act 1998 (Consequential Modifications) (No.2) Order 1999 (SI 1999/1820) art.4, Sch.2 para.71, the Northern Ireland Act 1998 s.99, Sch.13 para.5(2), the Government of Wales Act 1998 s.125, Sch.12 para.22, the Health Act 1999 s.65, Sch.4 para.68, the Mental Capacity Act 2005 s.67(1), Sch.6 para.29(2), the Mental Health Act 2007 ss.14(4),30(3), SI 2007/1388 art.3, Sch.1 para.18, the Public Services Ombudsman (Wales) Act 2005 s.39, Sch.6 para.21, Sch.7, the Health and Social Care Act 2008 s.52, Sch.3 para.11, the Health Authorities Act 1995 s.2(1), Sch.1 para.107(10), the Health Act 1999 (Supplementary, Consequential, etc., Provisions) Order 2000 (SI 2000/90) Sch.1 para.16(7), the Criminal Justice and Court Services Act 2000 s.74, Sch.7 para.74, the NHS Reform and Health Care Professions Act 2002 s.19(6), the National Health Service Reform and Health Care Professions Act 2002 (Supplementary, Consequential, etc. Provisions) Regulations 2002 (SI 2002/2469) reg.4, Sch.1, SI 2007/961 art.3, Sch. para.13(10), SI 2008/912 art.3, Sch.1 Pt 1 para.7, the Local Government and Public Involvement in Health Act 2007 s.241, Sch.18 Pt 18, the Health and Social Care Act 2001 s.67, Sch.5 para.6, SI 2008/2883 art.9, Sch.3 para.65, the Postal Services Act 2011 s.91, Sch.12, para.115, the Mental Health (Wales) Measure 2010 s.53(1), Sch.1 and the Health and Social Care Act 2012 s.44, Sch.5, para.29.

DEFINITIONS

1–1301   patient: s.145(1).

hospital: ss.34(2), 145(1).

approved clinician: s.145(1).

high security psychiatric services: s.145(1).

special managers: s.145(1).

the managers: s.145(1).

local social services authority: s.145(1).
Local Health Board: s.145(1).
Special Health Authority: s.145(1).

GENERAL NOTE

This section provides authority for the inspection and withholding of a detained patient's **1–1302**
outgoing and incoming mail. It does not apply to patients on community treatment orders.
There is no authority for the hospital managers to censor correspondence, i.e. to strike out
certain passages in a letter. However, there is power to withhold something contained in a
postal packet (subs.(4)). A patient whose mail is withheld under subs.(1)(b) or (2) can have
the decision reviewed by the Care Quality Commission (CQC) or, in relation to Wales, the
Welsh Ministers (s.134A). For the procedure to be adopted when mail is opened and inspected, see reg.29 of the English Regulations and reg.41 of the Welsh Regulations.

If either a detained or an informal patient is sent articles of potential danger, such as
weapons, explosives or matches, through the mail, s.3(1) of the Criminal Law Act 1967
and the common law provide authority for hospital staff to take reasonable measures to prevent the patient from receiving or keeping the article in his possession (see further, "A
review of the Mental Health Act 1959" D.H.S.S. (1976), para.10.28, and Appendix A).

This section does not confer on a hospital a power to require the return of a patient's mail
once it has reached its destination. In *Broadmoor Hospital Authority v R* [2000] 2 All E.R.
727, the Court of Appeal refused the hospital's application for an injunction requiring the
return of a draft manuscript of a book which had been sent by a patient to his agent. The
hospital considered that the contents of the book, if published, would be prejudicial to
the interests of the sender and would cause distress to the family of his victim. The court
held that it could, if appropriate, grant an injunction to restrain an activity outside the hospital if it could be shown that it was having a sufficiently significant impact on the security
of the hospital or the treatment of a patient; see further the General Note to the Act under the
heading "Injunctions to support an authority's performance of its duties under the Act".

Further provisions relating to items brought to hospital premises for patients, patients'
access to computer equipment and mobile phones, patients' post and patients' telephone
calls for patients at high security hospitals can be found in the High Security Psychiatric
Services (Arrangements for Safety and Security) Directions 2013 which are reproduced
at Appendix C. In *R. v Franey Ex p. Warren* [1998] EWHC 5, Turner J., in refusing
leave to bring judicial review proceedings, held that the decision of the Chief Executive
of Broadmoor Hospital to remove, inter alia, personal computers from patients' rooms
was a lawful decision which did not prevent patients from communicating with the authorities or the courts. Arrangements had been made for patients to have access to their
computers in the hospital's day areas.

The Malicious Communications Act 1988 makes provision for the prosecution of persons who send or deliver letters or other articles for the purpose of causing distress or
anxiety.

Human Rights Act 1998

A restriction on a patient's freedom to communicate with others constitutes an inter- **1–1303**
ference with the patient's right to respect for his private life under art.8(1) of the
European Convention on Human Rights (ECHR). Such an interference will contravene
art.8 unless it is "in accordance with the law", pursues one or more of the legitimate
aims referred to in art.8(2) and is "necessary in a democratic society" in order to achieve
them. It is likely that the power contained in this section does not contravene art.8, given the
interpretation that the Court has given to art.8(2) in *Herczegfalvy v Austria* (1993) 15
E.H.R.R. 437, at paras 85 to 92; also see the note on art.10(2) of the ECHR in Part 5.

Code of Practice

Paragraph 4.27 of the *Code* states: **1–1304**

"Detained patients must be told that their letters for posting may be withheld if the person to whom it is addressed asks the hospital managers to do so. Patients in high security psychiatric hospitals must be told about the other circumstances in which their correspondence may be withheld, the procedures that will be followed and of their right to ask the CQC to review the decisions taken."

Subsection (1)

1–1304 This subsection authorises a person appointed by the hospital managers (subss.(4), (7)) to withhold a detained patient's outgoing mail if the addressee has requested that the communications addressed to him or her by the patient should be withheld. The outgoing mail of patients detained in a high security psychiatric hospital can also be withheld if it is felt that the communication is likely to cause distress or danger to any person. It is intended that this power should be used to withhold, for example, threatening letters, letters to victims of crime, or letters containing dangerous objects. There is no provision equivalent to that which was contained in s.36 of the Mental Health Act 1959 which authorised the withholding of outgoing mail which would "be likely to prejudice the interests of the patient".

POSTAL PACKET.   Is defined in subs.(9).

WITHHELD.   Paragraph 5.14 of the Reference Guide states:

"In practice, because a patient can ask the CQC to review the decision within six months of receiving the notice, anything addressed to a patient which is withheld should be retained for at least six months, unless it is necessary to give it to the police or other similar body. After that – assuming the CQC is not in the process of reviewing the decision – it may be returned to the sender, if that can be done safely."

PARAGRAPH (A).   The review procedure set out in s.121(7)(8) does not apply to outgoing mail which is withheld under the provisions of this paragraph.
Contrary to what is stated in the *Code of Practice* at para.37.37, there is no obligation placed on the hospital managers to inform the patient that mail has been withheld under this paragraph. Such an obligation exists if the mail is withheld under para.(b): see subs.(6).

PARAGRAPH (B): MANAGERS OF THE HOSPITAL.   Who shall comply with their obligation under subs.(6). This function shall be discharged by a member of the hospital staff (subs.(7)).

DISTRESS.   The level of distress that has to be experienced is not identified.

APPROVED CLINICIAN.   It is submitted that the request remains valid if, subsequent to it being made, the identity of the approved clinician changes.

Subsection (2)

1–1305 This subsection authorises the withholding of the incoming mail of a patient detained in a high security hospital if it is considered that such action is necessary in the interests of the safety of the patient or for the protection of other persons. Either the patient or the sender can have the decision reviewed by the CQC or, in relation to Wales, the Welsh Ministers (s.134A). There is no power to withhold incoming mail on the ground that it would cause distress to the patient.
Paragraph 1.127 of the Mental Health Act Commission's *Thirteenth Biennial Report* 2007–2009, states:

"Legal advice received by the MHAC in 1997 suggested that the first ground under s.134(2) for withholding mail addressed to High Security Hospital patients ('necessary in the interests of the safety of the patient') should not be deemed to extend to include the patient's health or welfare. However, the second ground ('protection of others') might apply individually in these cases to the authors of the letters, or indeed to classes of persons, such as women or children, provided that the actual risk posed by the patient should he receive such material is clearly expressed. Such a risk could, in our view, be related to the patient's pathology and the treatment he is receiving for it, but a decision must be taken on the facts of any individual case."

Although there is no power to withhold the incoming mail of a patient who is detained in a hospital which is not a high security hospital, para.1.135 of the MHAC's *Thirteenth Biennial Report* states:

"Some medium secure hospital policies stipulate that, whilst it is unlawful to withhold incoming mail from a patient, or to open mail addressed to a patient without that patient's permission, if a staff member has concerns about the possible contents of a particular package or letter, it is acceptable for the patient to be advised that he or she may only open it in a controlled environment (i.e. the nurses' office) in the presence of staff. Once open, the contents may be treated like any other item of patient property and confiscated if necessary. The MHAC accepts the need for such arrangements as a last resort, but they should be carefully monitored and reviewed to ensure that they are and continue to be a justified interference with the patient's rights to privacy, and must never [be] used as a blanket measure irrespective of individual risk assessment."

THE MANAGERS.   Who shall comply with their obligation under subs.(6). This function shall be discharged by a member of the hospital staff (subs.(7)).

Subsection (3)
This subsection excludes the provisions of subss.(1)(b) and (2) in respect of certain **1–1306** bodies and individuals. Any person or body listed in this subsection can request that communications addressed to him or her by the patient be withheld (subs.(1)(a)).

Although the Criminal Cases Review Commission is not a body that is listed in this provision, it is suggested that, given the function of the Commission, letters addressed to it should not be opened unless the Commission has requested otherwise.

The Mental Health Act Commission held the view that:

"patient telephone calls to the same organisations [listed in this subsection] should attract a similar degree of privacy and that whilst any supervision of phone calls should not generally include listening into the contents of the calls (in certain circumstances this may be necessary) such listening in should never take place when the patient's phone call is with one of the specific organisations referred to above" (MHAC, *Sixth Biennial Report* 1993–1995, para.9.8).

Any policy that restricts a patient's access to a telephone must be consistent with the patient's rights under art.8 of the ECHR (*Valle v Finland* [2000] M.H.L.R. 255).

PATIENT ADVOCACY AND LIAISON SERVICE.   See the note of "Regulations" in subs.(3A).

Subsection (3A)
REGULATIONS.   For the purposes of subs.(3)(ea), above, "patient advocacy and liaison **1–1307** service" is defined in reg.31(1) of the English Regulations.

For the purposes of para.(b)(iii), the prescribed arrangements are arrangements in respect of independent mental capacity advocates: see reg.31(2) of the English Regulations and reg.42 of the Welsh Regulations.

Subsection (4)

1–1308   THE MANAGERS.   See subs.(7).

OPEN.   It will not usually be necessary to open the mail of patients who are not detained in high security hospitals, as the requirements of subs.(1)(a) can be met by looking at the addresses on patients' outgoing mail. However, it would be permissible for such mail to be opened if staff had a reasonable suspicion that a postal packet contained letters which the patient wanted the addressee to forward to people who had requested that mail be withheld. In high security psychiatric hospitals it will be necessary to open both outgoing and incoming mail if there is a reasonable suspicion that either subs.(1) or (2) applies. If, as a result of the inspection, nothing is withheld from the patient, the procedure set out in reg.29(1) of the English Regulations should be followed.

Although the issue has not been tested in the courts, it is likely that the inspection of the contents of a postal packet can include viewing the contents of a computer disc.

Subsection (5)

1–1309   RECORD.   See reg.29(2) of the English Regulations and reg.41(a) of the Welsh Regulations.

WITHHELD.   The obligation to record does not apply to the opening of mail under subs.(4).

Subsection (6)

1–1310   NOTICE.   See reg.29(3) of the English Regulations.

Subsection (7)

1–1311   SHALL BE DISCHARGED.   The hospital managers must appoint a member of staff to discharge their functions under this section. This person will need to consult with the patient's responsible clinician before a decision is made to withhold post.

Subsection (8)

1–1312   SECRETARY OF STATE.   The functions of the Minister, so far as exercisable in relation to Wales, are exercised by the Welsh Ministers (see the General Note to the Act and SI 1999/672, art.2, Sch.1).

Subsection (9)

1–1313   POSTAL OPERATOR.   By virtue of s.125(1) of the Postal Services Act 2000, the definition of this phrase is to be found in s.27(3) to (5) of the Postal Services Act 2011 which reads as follows:

"'postal operator' means a person who provides—

    (a) the service of conveying postal packets from one place to another by post, or
    (b) any of the incidental services of receiving, collecting, sorting and delivering postal packets.

(4) A person is not to be regarded as a postal operator merely as a result of receiving postal packets in the course of acting as an agent for, or otherwise on behalf of, another.

(5) The Secretary of State may make regulations prescribing circumstances in which subsection (4) is not to apply."

POSTAL PACKET.   Means "a letter, parcel, packet or other article transmitted by post": Postal Services Act 2000 s.125(1).

[Review of decisions to withhold correspondence

134A.—(1) The regulatory authority must review any decision to withhold a **1–1314** postal packet (or anything contained in it) under subsection (1)(b) or (2) of section 134 if an application for a review of the decision is made—

  (a) in a case under subsection (1)(b) of that section, by the patient; or

  (b) in a case under subsection (2) of that section, either by the patient or by the person by whom the postal packet was sent.

(2) An application under subsection (1) must be made within 6 months of receipt by the applicant of the notice referred to in section 134(6).

(3) On an application under subsection (1), the regulatory authority may direct that the postal packet (or anything contained in it) is not to be withheld.

(4) The managers of the hospital concerned must comply with any such direction.

(5) The Secretary of State may by regulations make provision in connection with the making to and determination by the Care Quality Commission of applications under subsection (1), including provision for the production to the Commission of any postal packet which is the subject of such an application.

(6) The Welsh Ministers may by regulations make provision in connection with the making to them of applications under subsection (1), including provision for the production to them of any postal packet which is the subject of such an application.]

AMENDMENT
    This section was inserted by the Health and Social Care Act 2008 s.52, Sch.3 para.12.

DEFINITIONS
    the regulatory authority: s.145(1).   **1–1315**
    postal packet: s.134(9).
    patient: s.145(1).
    the managers: s.145(1).
    hospital:ss.34(2), 145(1) (by virtue of s.134(9)).

GENERAL NOTE
    This section provides that the Care Quality Commission or, in relation to Wales, the **1–1316** Welsh Ministers must review any decision made under s.134(1)(b) or (2) to withhold a postal packet or anything contained within it if an application is made by a person specified in subs.(1)(a) or (b) within the timescale set out in subs.(2). Subsection (3) provides that such a review could result in the regulatory authority directing that the postal packet is not withheld.

    Although the CQC upholds very few appeals without qualification, it reports that a "larger number of appeals result in a compromise, for instance where elements of the postal packet are released or alternative arrangements are made that are acceptable to the sender or the intended recipient of postal packages. In 2013/14, four cases were resolved in that way" (CQC, "Monitoring the Mental Health Act in 2013/2014", p.26).

Warrant to search for and remove patients

135.—(1) If it appears to a justice of the peace, on information on oath laid by **1–1317** an [approved mental health professional], that there is reasonable cause to suspect that a person believed to be suffering from mental disorder—

  (a) has been, or is being, ill-treated, neglected or kept otherwise than under proper control, in any place within the jurisdiction of the justice, or

  (b) being unable to care for himself, is living alone in any such place, the justice may issue a warrant authorising any constable [...] to enter, if need be by force, any premises specified in the warrant in which that person is believed to be, and, if thought fit, to remove him to a place of safety with a view to the making of an application in respect of him under Part II of this Act, or of other arrangements for his treatment or care.

(2) If it appears to a justice of the peace, on information on oath laid by any constable or other person who is authorised by or under this Act or under [article 8 of the Mental Health (Care and Treatment) (Scotland) Act 2003 (Consequential Provisions) Order 2005] to take a patient to any place, or to take into custody or retake a patient who is liable under this Act or under the said [article 8] to be so taken or retaken—

(a) that there is reasonable cause to believe that the patient is to be found on premises within the jurisdiction of the justice; and

(b) that admission to the premises has been refused or that a refusal of such admission is apprehended,

the justice may issue a warrant authorising any constable [...] to enter the premises, if need be by force, and remove the patient.

(3) A patient who is removed to a place of safety in the execution of a warrant issued under this section may be detained there for a period not exceeding 72 hours.

[(3A) A constable, an approved mental health professional or a person authorised by either of them for the purposes of this subsection may, before the end of the period of 72 hours mentioned in subsection (3) above, take a person detained in a place of safety under that subsection to one or more other places of safety.

(3B) A person taken to a place of safety under subsection (3A) above may be detained there for a period ending no later than the end of the period of 72 hours mentioned in subsection (3) above.]

(4) In the execution of a warrant issued under subsection (1) above, [a constable] shall be accompanied by an [approved mental health professional] and by a registered medical practitioner, and in the execution of a warrant issued under subsection (2) above [a constable] may be accompanied—

(a) by a registered medical practitioner;

(b) by any person authorised by or under this Act or under [article 8 of the Mental Health (Care and Treatment) (Scotland) Act 2003 (Consequential Provisions) Order 2005] section 83 of the [Mental Health (Scotland) Act 1984] to take or retake the patient.

(5) It shall not be necessary in any information or warrant under subsection (1) above to name the patient concerned.

(6) In this section "place of safety" means residential accommodation provided by a local social services authority under [Part 1 of the Care Act 2014 or] Part III of the National Assistance Act 1948 [...], a hospital as defined by this Act, a police station, [an independent hospital or care home] for mentally disordered persons or any other suitable place the occupier of which is willing temporarily to receive the patient.

AMENDMENTS

The amendments to this section were made by SI 2005/2078 Sch.1 para.2(9), the Police and Criminal Evidence Act 1984 s.119, Sch.6, para.26, Sch.7, the National Health Service and Community Care Act 1990 s.66(2), Sch.10, the Care Standards Act 2000 s.116, Sch.4

para.9(9), the Mental Health Act 2007 ss.21, 44(2), Sch.2 para.10 and SI 2015/914 Sch. para.29.

DEFINITIONS
    approved mental health professional: s.145(1), (1AC).   **1–1318**
    mental disorder: ss.1, 145(1).
    patient: s.145(1).
    local social services authority: s.145(1).
    hospital: ss.34(2), 145(1).
    independent hospital: s.145(1).
    care home: s.145(1).

GENERAL NOTE
    This section provides for a magistrate to issue a warrant authorising a constable to enter **1–1319** premises, using force if necessary, for the purpose of removing a mentally disordered person to a place of safety for a period not exceeding 72 hours. It provides a means by which an entry which would otherwise be a trespass, becomes a lawful act. The existence of the warrant does not mean that it must be executed; the decision to do so is that of the constable. The warrant is executed once entry to the premises has been effected by the constable, either by force, or by invitation if the occupier is aware of the warrant. However, if the occupier of the premises allows entry without knowledge of the existence of the warrant and without the constable producing the warrant, it is submitted that the warrant has not been executed as long as the occupier's consent to the entry is not withdrawn. Any police officer can execute the warrant: see the note on "constable" in s.136(1). By virtue of Sch.1 to the Magistrates Courts Fees Order 2008 (SI 2008/1052) (as amended) a fee of £20 shall be charged for the issuing of a warrant under this section. Local authorities can use the fee account system to ensure that payment for the warrant does not become a delaying factor: see *www.justice.gov.uk/courts/fees/payment-by-account*.
    Note the distinction between warrants issued under subs.(1) and (2). Subsection (1) is used where there is concern about the well-being of a person who is not liable to be detained under the Act. Subsection (2) is used where the person concerned is either liable to be detained or is required to reside at a particular place under the terms of guardianship, a community treatment order (CTO) or under the Scottish legislation. In both instances, the person can be transferred to another place of safety during the 72-hour period (subss.(3)(A), (3)(B)) and reasonable force may be used in the transfer if this proves to be necessary (s.137).
    In *Ward v Commissioner of Police for the Metropolis* [2005] UKHL 32; [2005] 3 All E.R. 1013, the House of Lords held that when issuing a warrant under subs.(1) a magistrate has no power to impose a condition that the constable executing it should be accompanied by a *named* approved mental health professional (AMHP) and/or medical practitioner. The reasoning adopted by the House of Lords would also apply to warrants issued under subs.(2).
    Access to premises can be effected lawfully if a co-owner or, possibly, a co-occupier of the premises gives permission for the mental health professionals to enter: see the note on "enter and inspect" in s.115. If permission is granted to enter premises, such as a hotel, where members of the public can reside, a warrant under this section is not required to enter a room in the premises that the mentally disordered person is occupying if that person has no right of exclusive occupation of the room, for example, a television lounge (*R. v Rosso* [2003] EWCA Crim 3242; [2003] M.H.L.R. 404). The Court of Appeal, at para.19, determined whether the person had an exclusive right to occupy a room by asking the following questions:

1. Does the occupant have a right to exclude others from the room?
2. Does the occupant have the right to deny anybody access to the room?

As the answer to both questions was "no", no such right existed.

Sections 5 and 6 of the Mental Capacity Act 2005 do not confer on police officers authority to remove mentally incapacitated persons to hospital or other places of safety for the purposes set out in this section (*R. (on the application of Sessay) v South London and Maudsley NHS Foundation Trust*) [2011] EWHC 2617 (QB); [2012] M.H.L.R. 94).

The consent to treatment provisions contained in Part IV do not apply to a patient who is detained under this section (s.56(3)(b)). If the person is mentally capable of making a decision about treatment, the common law enables him to refuse to be treated for either a physical or mental disorder. However, if the person is assessed as being mentally incapable of making a decision about treatment, the treatment can be provided under the Mental Capacity Act 2005 if it is deemed to be in his best interests. Restraint can be used in the provision of the treatment if its use is both necessary and proportionate to prevent harm to the person (2005 Act s.6).

Where an adult who has been removed under this section is admitted to accommodation provided under ss.18 or 19 of the Care Act 2014 or to any hospital, and it appears to the local social services authority that there is a danger of loss or damage to moveable property in the local authority's area because the adult is unable (whether permanently or temporarily) to protect or deal with the property and no other suitable arrangements have been or are being made, s.47 of the 2014 Act places the authority under a duty to take reasonable steps to prevent or mitigate the loss or damage. The authority has the power to enter the person's home in order to carry out this duty if certain criteria are satisified, and to recover its reasonable expenses.

The Government's "Mental Health Crisis Care Concordat" (2014) is a national agreement between services and agencies involved in the care and support of people in crisis, including people who are detained under this section. It sets out how organisations will work together better to make sure that people get the help they need when they are having a mental health crisis. The Concordat does not extend to Wales.

The literature on this section has been reviewed by the Department of Health and the Home Office in "Review of the Operation of Sections 135 and 136 of the Mental Health Act 1983: A Literature Review" (2014).

Police and Criminal Evidence Act 1984 (PACE)

1–1320   Section 15(1) of PACE states:

> "This section and section 16 ... have effect in relation to the issue to constables under any enactment, including an enactment contained in an Act passed after this Act, of warrants to enter and search premises, and an entry on or search of premises under a warrant is unlawful unless it complies with this section and section 16 ..."

Although it would appear from the heading of this section that a warrant issued to a constable under either subs.(1) or (2) comes within the scope of ss.15 and 16 of PACE, the wording of s.15(4), which states that the "constable shall answer on oath any question that the justice of the peace ... hearing the application asks him", suggests that the two sections only relate to warrants issued on the application of a constable. However, in *Ward v Commissioner of Police for the Metropolis*, above, Baroness Hale said, at para.27, that she was "inclined to the view" that ss.15 and 16 do apply to warrants issued under this section. It is submitted that the view expressed by Baroness Hale should be followed and that the following requirements of PACE be satisfied:

1. The application for the warrant shall be made without notice and the information laid before the magistrate must be in writing (s.15(3)).

2. The warrant shall authorise an entry on one occasion only unless it specifies that it authorises multiple entries (either unlimited or limited to a specified maximum) (s.15(5), (5A)).

3. The warrant shall specify the name of the person who applies for it, the date on which it is issued, and the fact that it was issued under the Mental Health Act (s.15(6)).

4. The warrant shall identify, so far as is practicable, the person to be sought (s.15(6)).

5. Apart from a warrant that authorises multiple entries where as many copies as are reasonably required may be made, two copies shall be made of the warrant and the copies shall be clearly certified as copies (s.15(7), (8)). One copy is retained by the police and the other is handed to the occupier of the premises. It is suggested that a third copy be taken for retention by the person in charge of the place of safety to which the patient is removed.

6. Entry and search under the warrant must be within three months from the date of its issue (s.16(3)).

7. Entry and search under the warrant must be at a reasonable hour unless it appears to the constable executing it that the purpose of the search may be frustrated on an entry at a reasonable hour (s.16(4)).

8. If the occupier of the premises is present at the time when the constable seeks to execute the warrant, the constable shall (a) identify himself; (b) produce the warrant to him; and (c) supply him with a copy of it. If the occupier of the premises is not present but some other person who appears to the constable to be in charge of the premises is present, the above procedure will be followed in respect of that other person. If there is no person present who appears to the constable to be in charge of the premises, he shall leave a copy of the warrant in a prominent place on the premises (s.16(5), (6), (7)).

9. A search under the warrant may only be a search to the extent required for the purpose for which the warrant was issued (s.16(8)).

10. The constable executing the warrant shall make an endorsement on it stating whether the person sought was found (s.16(9)).

11. A warrant which has been executed, or which has not been executed within the time authorised for its execution, shall be returned to the designated officer for the local justice area in which the justice was acting who shall retain it for a period of 12 months. During this period the occupier of the premises to which the warrant relates shall be allowed to inspect the warrant (s.16(10), (10A), (11), (12)).

The powers of the Police under PACE
Under s.117 of PACE, the constable may use reasonable force, if necessary, when **1–1321** executing the warrant, which can include restricting the movement of those in occupation of the premises while the premises are being searched (*DPP v Meaden* [2003] EWHC 3005 (Admin); [2004] 4 All E.R. 75, para.32). *Meaden* was applied by the Court of Appeal in *Connor v Chief Constable of Merseyside Police* [2006] EWCA Civ 1549, where it was held, at paras 67 and 69, that the power of the police when executing a warrant extended to taking reasonable and necessary steps to detain the occupants of the premises who might otherwise put lives in danger or themselves be put in danger.

"Guidance on Responding to People with Mental Ill Health or Learning Disabilities", National Police Improvement Agency (2010), para.6.8.7, states that a warrant permits "a degree of control of others within the premises to ensure the safety of everyone present".

The power to arrest under this section was not specifically preserved by s.26 and Sch.2 of PACE. This means that the arresting policeman does not have the power under s.32 of PACE to search the patient at a place other than a police station. However, the policeman can search the premises for the person believed to be suffering from mental disorder.

Code of Practice C on the "Detention, Treatment and Questioning of Persons by Police **1–1322** Officers", which is issued under PACE, applies to a person who has been removed to a police station as a place of safety under this section (para.1.10). The implications of this requirement are set out in the General Note to s.136.

In *D'Souza v Director of Public Prosecutions* [1992] 4 All E.R. 545, the House of Lords held that the power to obtain a warrant under subs.(2) of this section is not the exclusive method of gaining access to premises in order to retake a detained patient who has absconded from hospital and that an alternative is provided for in s.17(1)(d) of PACE. Section 17(1)(d) states that a policeman "may enter and search any premises for the purpose ... of recapturing a person who is unlawfully at large and whom he is pursuing". The leading speech in the House of Lords was given by Lord Lowry who held, at 556, that the

> "verb in the clause 'whom he is pursuing' is in the *present continuous* tense and therefore, give or take a few seconds or minutes—this is a question of degree—the pursuit must be almost contemporaneous with the entry into the premises. There must, I consider, be an act of pursuit, that is a chase, however short in time or distance. It is not enough for the police to form an intention to arrest, which they put into practice by resorting to the premises where they believe that the person whom they seek may be found".

His Lordship further held, at 553, 554, that if a person who is lawfully detained in hospital under s.6(2) goes absent without leave, he is by virtue of s.18(1) liable to be taken into custody and returned to the hospital, and is therefore "unlawfully at large" for the purposes of s.17(1)(d).

Section 17(1)(e) of PACE provides the police with the power to enter and search any premises without a warrant if such action is required to save "life or limb" or to prevent "serious damage to property". In *Baker v Crown Prosecution Service* [2009] EWHC 299 (Admin), the Divisional Court held that:

1. The power enables the police to enter premises where permission has not been given if there is a reasonable belief that the requirements of s.17(1)(e) are satisfied. The requirements will not be satisfied if the police merely have a concern for the welfare of someone within the premises (*Syed v Director of Public Prosecutions* [2010] EWHC 81 (Admin)).

2. The words "saving life or limb" (a) refer to a degree of apprehended *serious* bodily injury and (b) are wide enough to cover saving a person from seriously harming himself or herself, as well as seriously harming third parties.

3. The power to search in s.17(4) is only a power to search to the extent that is reasonably required for the purpose for which the power of entry is exercised; it is not a general power to search.

Although s.17(1)(e) does not provide the police with authority to remove any person from the premises, the police could arrest the person for any offence that might have been committed. Section 17(1)(d) of PACE enables the police to enter and search premises without a warrant to effect an arrest for an indictable offence.

PACE has not removed the common law power of the police to enter private premises without a warrant to prevent a breach of the peace occurring if they reasonably believe that an imminent breach of the peace, usually an assault, is likely to occur on the premises (*McLeod v Commissioner of Police of the Metropolis* [1994] 4 All E.R. 553 CA). The nature of a breach of the peace is considered in Appendix A.

Human Rights Act 1998

1–1323   Use of this section involves an interference with the mentally disordered person's home and private life that must be justified under art.8(2) of the European Convention on Human Rights. Entry to the person's home must be a proportionate measure in all the circumstances and the reasons adduced to justify the search must be relevant and sufficient (*McLeod v*

United Kingdom (1999) 27 E.H.R.R. 493). In *Camenzind v Switzerland* (1999) 28 E.H.R.R. 458 at para.45, the European Court of Human Rights held that the State's governing legislation and practice must afford adequate and effective safeguards against abuse if the test of proportionality is to be satisfied. Although it has been argued that the failure to give formal notification to the mentally disordered person of an impending application for a warrant under this section might breach art.8, it is likely that a court would find that the adjudication of the application by a magistrate provides the safeguard required.

Code of Practice
The issuing of warrants under this section is considered in Ch.16.   **1–1324**

Subsection (1)
This subsection enables an AMHP, when acting on behalf of a local social services auth- **1–1325** ority, to make an application to a magistrate for a warrant authorising a constable to enter premises where a mentally disordered person is believed to be living for the purpose of removing that person to a place of safety if an initial assessment indicates that removal is required. The constable must be accompanied by a doctor and an AMHP when executing the warrant (subs.(4)). The power to enter the premises includes a power to search those premises in order to find the person believed to be suffering from mental disorder (*Ward v Commissioner of Police for the Metropolis*, above, para.23).

It is not a precondition for the making of an application that admission to the premises has been refused. An application could be made where consent to entry is likely to be given in circumstances where the person is thought likely to be either violent or to immediately abscond once entry has been effected. In other words, the warrant is being sought not to gain entry but to provide authority to the police to effectively manage the risks which will have been identified in the application. In the absence of a warrant, the legal powers of the police in such a situation would be limited to using their powers under either s.3 of the Criminal Law Act 1967, or to prevent a breach of the peace (see Appendix A).

Once entry to the premises has been effected, the power of the professionals is confined to assessing whether the person should be removed to a place of safety; there is no power while in the premises to subject the person to an assessment for sectioning under Pt II in the absence of the person's consent: see para.16.8 of the *Code of Practice*. It is submitted that if the doctor concludes on her initial examination that the person is not mentally disordered, the power to remove the person to a place of safety and for the professionals to remain in the premises lapses.

During the debates on the Mental Health Bill, a Government Minister said: "Under [this] provision, the ill-treatment, neglect, lack of proper control or inability to care for onself need not be linked to the existence of the mental disorder from which the person is suffering" (*Hansard*, HL Vol.688, col.663).

A warrant can be issued though the name of the mentally disordered person is not known (subs.(5)). The relevant premises must be specified in the warrant.

INFORMATION.   There is no requirement for the person who is the subject of the application to be informed of the fact that it is being made: see the note on "Human Rights Act 1998", above.

APPROVED MENTAL HEALTH PROFESSIONAL.   Only an AMHP acting on behalf of a local authority can apply for a warrant to be issued under this subsection. If the person has a care co-ordinator who is not an AMHP, he or she can accompany the AMHP applicant and provide evidence to the magistrate.

BELIEVED TO BE SUFFERING FROM MENTAL DISORDER.   But has not yet reliably been shown to be so (*Ward v Commissioner of Police for the Metropolis*, above, para.13).

KEPT OTHERWISE THAN UNDER PROPER CONTROL. This phrase encompasses not only the situation where a person is being subjected to a degree of improper control, but also the situation where a person is suffering from the absence of control.

UNABLE TO CARE FOR HIMSELF. This paragraph is aimed at a mentally disordered person who is unable to look after himself appropriately. As "care" is a broad term which encompasses matters that relate to a person's daily needs, a warrant could be applied for where the main cause of concern is the apparent failure of the person to take essential prescribed medication.

LIVING ALONE. The suggestion by the Royal College of Psychiatrists that this section should also provide for a situation where two mentally disordered people were living together and were unable to care for themselves was not adopted (Cmnd. 7320, para.2.21).

PREMISES. It is submitted that this term includes the land on which the building in question is situated. The constable would therefore have power to remove the person from the garden of the premises specified in the warrant. In *Ward v Commissioner of Police for the Metropolis*, above, the person concerned had locked herself in her car. The policeman executing the warrant gained access to the car and the person was taken to the place of safety by ambulance.

IF THOUGHT FIT. This section does not specify whose decision this is. It is suggested that the policeman's role is to gain entry to the premises and to ensure the safety of the doctor and the AMHP, whose joint role is to assess whether the patient should be removed to a place of safety for further assessment there. In *Ward v Commissioner of Police for the Metropolis*, above, Baroness Hale said that "professionals should be able to help the police officer to decide whether or not it is 'fit' to take the person concerned to a place of safety" (para.12), and that it may be "that the police officer can authorise others, such as the ambulance service or an [AMHP], to transport the person to the place of safety rather than doing it himself" (para.23).

PLACE OF SAFETY. See the note on subs.(3). The authority to detain the person at the place of safety ceases once it has been decided to take no action in respect of him. Although the action taken could include making an application under the Act, the assessment could result in other interventions which are aimed at securing the person's "treatment or care".

OTHER ARRANGEMENTS. Such as an informal admission to hospital, or the provision of community care services at the person's home.

Subsection (2)

1–1326   This subsection provides for the issue of a warrant to a policeman to enter premises, using force if necessary, for the purposes of taking or retaking a patient who is *already* liable to be detained into custody. It also applies to a patient under guardianship, a CTO or the Scottish legislation who has absconded from a place where he is required to reside. The warrant can only be issued if admission to the premises has been refused or that refusal can be anticipated. The policeman may be accompanied by a doctor or any other person, such as an AMHP, who is authorised to take or retake the patient when executing the warrant (subs.(4); also see para.16.15 of the Code of Practice). The police have the power under s.138 to retake patients who have escaped from custody. Also note the power of the police under s.17(1)(d) of the Police and Criminal Evidence Act 1984 which is considered in the General Note to this section.

PERSON AUTHORISED. The persons authorised to retake patients under s.18 (and who can therefore be applicants under this provision) are, in addition to a constable, any officer on the staff of the hospital, any AMHP or any person authorised by the hospital managers, or, in the case of a patient subject to guardianship, any officer on the staff of a local social services authority, or any person authorised by the guardian or a local social services authority. For community patients, see s.18(2A). Mental Health Act sdministrators, care co-ordinators and nurses have made applications under this provision.

REMOVE THE PATIENT. To the place where the patient is required to be.

Subsection (3)
REMOVED. For general provisions relating to the conveyance of patients from one place **1–1327** to another, see s.137.

PLACE OF SAFETY. Is defined in subs.(6). The place of safety is not obliged to accept the person. If entry to the preferred place of safety is refused, it is lawful to take the person to another place of safety. The patient can be transferred from one place of safety to another during the 72-hour period (subss.(3A), (3B)):
If a person escapes while being taken to or detained in a place of safety, he can only be retaken within the 72-hour period specified in s.138(3).

72 HOURS. This is the maximum period of detention. It starts from the time when the person arrives at the place of safety. If the place of safety is a hospital, this period cannot be continued under s.5(2) or (4) as it is Parliament's intention that the assessment be completed within the 72 hours: see *R. v Wilson Ex p. Williamson* [1996] C.O.D. 42, noted in the General Note to s.2.

Subsections (3A), (3B)
These provisions, which respond to concern that was expressed during debates on the **1–1328** 2007 Act about mentally disordered people being detained in a police cell (see for e.g. *Hansard,* HL Vol. 689, col.1467), enable a person who has been detained in a place of safety under this section to be transferred to another one before the time limit of 72 hours for detention has expired. Such a transfer does not have the effect of increasing the 72-hour limit. Guidance on transfers between places of safety is reproduced in the notes on s.136(3), (4).

Subsection (4)
APPROVED MENTAL HEALTH PROFESSIONAL. Who need not be the AMHP who made the **1–1329** application.

Subsection (6)
ANY OTHER SUITABLE PLACE. Which could be the home of a relative or friend of the **1–1330** patient.

Mentally disordered persons found in public places

136.—(1) If a constable finds in a place to which the public have access a per- **1–1331** son who appears to him to be suffering from mental disorder and to be in immediate need of care or control, the constable may, if he thinks it necessary to do so in the interests of that person or for the protection of other persons, remove that person to a place of safety within the meaning of section 135 above.

(2) A person removed to a place of safety under this section may be detained there for a period not exceeding 72 hours for the purpose of enabling him to be examined by a registered medical practitioner and to be interviewed by an

[approved mental health professional] and of making any necessary arrangements for his treatment or care.

[(3) A constable, an approved mental health professional or a person authorised by either of them for the purposes of this subsection may, before the end of the period of 72 hours mentioned in subsection (2) above, take a person detained in a place of safety under that subsection to one or more other places of safety.

(4) A person taken to a place of a safety under subsection (3) above may be detained there for a purpose mentioned in subsection (2) above for a period ending no later than the end of the period of 72 hours mentioned in that subsection.]

AMENDMENTS

In subs.(2) the words in square brackets were substituted by the Mental Health Act 2007 s.21, Sch.2 para.10. Subss.(3) and (4) were inserted by s.44(3).

DEFINITIONS

1–1332   mental disorder: ss.1, 145(1).

approved mental health professional: s.145(1), (1AC).

GENERAL NOTE

1–1333   This section empowers a constable to remove a person from a public place to a place of safety if he considers that the person is suffering from mental disorder and is in immediate need of care or control. As many people who are detained under this section could be charged with a criminal offence, it provides a key pathway into mental health care. Neither the lack of mental capacity of the person to make decisions concerning his welfare nor the person's unwillingness to attend the place of safety are pre-conditions to the exercise of the power. It is for the constable to determine whether he is detaining a person under this section; he cannot make a determination which is conditional on a subsequent confirmation by a superior officer. The person can be detained in a place of safety for up to 72 hours for the purpose of being examined by a doctor and interviewed by an approved mental health professional (AMHP) in order that suitable arrangements can be made for his treatment or care. It is therefore the case that the detention can continue after the assessment has been completed until such time, within the 72 hour limit, that the necessary arrangements have been put in place. The authority to detain under this section ends immediately if the doctor's assessment leads her to conclude that the person is not mentally disordered. The further detention of the patient in these circumstances would be unlawful: see the note on "Human Rights Act 1998", below. The detained person can be transferred to another place of safety as long as the 72-hour period has not expired (subss.(3), (4)). This section, which is not supported by any statutory forms, is usually invoked "where a person's abnormal behaviour is causing nuisance or offence" (Cmnd. 7320, para.2.2.2). There is nothing to prevent a patient who is already liable to be detained under the Act, for example, a patient on s.17 leave, from being detained under this section.

The powers contained in this section:

"inevitably require that the person concerned can be kept safe in the sense that harm to himself or others is prevented until he can be seen by a doctor and, if necessary, given some form of sedation . . . A police officer in exercising his powers under s.136 is entitled to use reasonable force. If someone is violent, he can be restrained" (*R. on the application of Anderson) v HM Coroner for Inner North Greater London* [2004] EWHC 2729 (Admin); [2004] M.H.L.R. 324 paras 8, 9, per Collins J.).

Sections 5 and 6 of the Mental Capacity Act 2005 do not confer on police officers authority to remove mentally incapacitated persons to hospital or other places of safety for the purposes set out in this section (*R. (on the application of Sessay) v South London and Maudsley NHS Foundation Trust)* [2011] EWHC 2617 (QB); [2012] M.H.L.R. 94). *Sessay* is authority for the proposition that the staff of a hospital's accident and emergency or out-patient department can hold a patient under common law powers for a brief period while awaiting the arrival of the police to exercise their power under this section if such action is necessary to prevent the patient from causing harm to himself or to another: see Appendix A.

This section does not specify who, other than the constable, might have the power to convey the patient to the place of safety. The Butler Committee, at para.9.2, had "no doubt" that the constable's power "extends to persons acting under his direction, such as the ambulance staff who are taking the disordered person to hospital". In this situation, ambulance staff would have the powers of a constable when conveying the patient: see s.137(2).

A person who is detained under this section is not subject to the consent to treatment provision contained in Pt IV (s.56(3)(b)). If the person is mentally capable of making a decision about treatment, the common law enables him to refuse to be treated for either a physical or mental disorder. However, if the person is assessed as being mentally incapable of making a decision about treatment, the treatment can be provided under the Mental Capacity Act 2005 if it is deemed to be in his best interests.

As the purpose of the section "is to allow for assessment within the shortest possible period, up to a maximum of 72 hours ... it should *not* therefore be treated, as in the case of some hospitals, as an admission section authorising 72 hours' detention" (Mental Health Act Commission, *Second Biennial Report* 1985–87, para.11.1(e)).

The power to arrest under this section was specifically preserved by s.26 and Sch.2 of PACE (the references below are to sections of PACE). Apart from providing the arresting policeman with a power to search the person concerned at a place other than a police station (see s.32 and para.16.68 of the *Code of Practice*), this means that a person who has been removed to a place of safety under this section is given the following rights: to be told that they have been arrested and the grounds for the arrest as soon as practicable (s.28), to have another person of his choice informed of his removal (s.56) and to consult a solicitor privately at any time (s.58). Although s.58 relates to a patient who is being "held in custody in a police station *or other premises*", the wording of the section suggests that it is not intended to apply where a patient is detained under this section in a hospital. Section 58 states that where a patient makes a request to consult privately with a solicitor, the time when the request was made "shall be recorded in the custody record" (s.58(2)). Under para.2.1 of *Code of Practice C* (2012 revision), a custody record is only opened in respect of "each person brought to a police station under arrest or arrested at the station having gone there voluntarily". As the mandatory requirement in s.58(2) cannot be satisfied in respect of a patient who is detained in a hospital, it would appear that s.58 does not apply in such circumstances. Paragraph 16.69 of the *Code of Practice* states that hospital managers should facilitate "access to legal advice . . . whenever it is requested". Although a person who has been detained under this section has technically been arrested, there is no requirement for a caution to be administered and this should not be done.

PACE Code of Practice C, which is concerned with the "Detention, Treatment and Questioning of Persons by Police Officers", applies to persons who have been removed to a police station under this section (para.1.10). Paragraph 3.16 of *Code C* states:

"It is imperative that a mentally disordered or otherwise mentally vulnerable person, detained under the Mental Health Act 1983, section 136, be assessed as soon as possible. A police station should only be used as a place of safety as a last resort but if that assessment is to take place at the police station, an approved mental health professional and a registered medical practitioner shall be called to the station as soon as possible to carry it out. . . . The appropriate adult has no role in the assessment process and their presence is not required. Once the detainee has been assessed and suitable arrangements made for their treatment or care, they can no longer be detained under section 136. A detainee must be immediately discharged from detention under section 136 if a registered medical practitioner, having examined them, concludes they are not mentally disordered within the meaning of the Act" also see para.16.67 of the *Code of Practice*.

The attendance of an appropriate adult is necessary if a person who, having been detained under this section, has also been arrested for a criminal offence. This happened in *Francis v Director of Public Prosecutions* (1997) 36 B.M.L.R. 180, where the Divisional Court held that detention under this section does not give rise to any legal bar to any subsequent use of the breath specimen procedure under s.7 of the Road Traffic Act 1988. The court held that the fact of detention under this section, while giving rise to obligations on the police, was not determinative of the issue of whether the procedure could be used, and that the propriety or fairness of using the procedure in such circumstances fell to be decided on the facts. If a person who has been detained under this section has also been arrested for a criminal offence, the appropriate adult should not be the AMHP who has been involved with that person's assessment. "Guidance on Responding to People with Mental Ill Health or Learning Disabilities", National Police Improvement Agency (2010), para.6.4.4.1, states that "there is nothing in law . . . to prevent police officers from using s.136 and the power of arrest for a criminal offence in the same case at the same time".

There is no statutory form that can be used to record an admission of a person to a hospital which is acting as a place of safety under this section. If such an admission takes place, the hospital should not record it on Form H3 (in Wales, Form HO14) as no application has been made in respect of that person: see reg.4(4) of the English Regulations and reg.4(3) of the Welsh Regulations.

If a person is removed to a hospital under this section, the managers of the hospital are obliged to give that person information under s.132.

A person who escapes while being taken to or detained in a place of safety can only be retaken within the period specified in s.138(3).

In *Clunis v Camden and Islington Health Authority* [1998] 3 All E.R. 180, the Court of Appeal doubted whether the wording of this section places on the constable a duty to take care which gives rise to a claim for damages at the suit of the disordered person.

The fact that a person has been detained by the police under this section could be disclosed to a potential employer as part of the criminal record disclosure process in a disclosure and barring certificate issued under s.113B(4) of the Police Act 1997 if the relevant criteria are satisfied.

The Government's "Mental Health Crisis Care Concordat" (2014) is a national agreement between services and agencies involved in the care and support of people in crisis, including people who are detained under this section. It sets out how organisations will work together better to make sure that people get the help they need when they are having a mental health crisis. The Concordat does not extend to Wales.

The Royal College of Psychiatrists has published "Standards on the use of Section 136 of the Mental Health Act 1983 (England and Wales)" (College Report 159) which considers all aspects of the process of detaining and assessing a person under this section. This has been supplemented by "Guidance for commissioners: service provisions for Section 136 of the Mental Health Act 1983", Position Statement PS2/2013, April 2013.

The literature on this section has been reviewed by the Department of Health and the Home Office in "Review of the Operation of Sections 135 and 136 of the Mental Health Act 1983: A Literature Review" (2014).

Human Rights Act 1998

1–1334   In *Winterwerp v Netherlands* (1979) 2 E.H.R.R. 387 at para.39, the European Court of Human Rights held that "except in emergency cases", an individual "should not be deprived of his liberty unless he has been reliably shown to be of 'unsound mind' ". The court has subsequently said that it cannot "be inferred from the *Winterwerp* judgment that [a medical report on the patient] must in all conceivable cases be obtained before rather than after the confinement of a person on the ground of unsoundness of mind" (*X v United Kingdom* (1981) 4 E.H.R.R. 188 at para.41; also see *Varbanov v Bulgaria* [2000] M.H.L.R. 263, para.47). As the power under this section applies to a person who appears to be in *immediate* need of care or control and lasts for a relatively brief period, it is clearly an emergency measure which complies with art.5(1)(e) of the European Convention on

Human Rights (ECHR). A medical assessment should take place promptly after the person's arrival at the place of safety. The continued detention of a person under this section subsequent to a finding by the assessing doctor that the person was not mentally disordered would contravene the ECHR as there would be no ground under art.5(1)(e) to detain him.

Although it could be argued that using a police station as a place of safety contravenes art.5(1)(e) of the ECHR because it does not provide a therapeutic environment for the medical assessment (*Aerts v Belgium* (2000) 29 E.H.R.R. 50), it is likely that the court would hold that the emergency nature of this provision would justify the use of such an environment for a limited period. However, art.3 of the ECHR could be breeched if the relevant threshold is reached. This occurred in *MS v United Kingdom* (2012) 55 E.H.R.R. 23 where a severely mentally ill person was detained under this section in a police cell for more than 72 hours in a situation where "no psychiatric treatment could be provided for him" (para.41). During his time in police custody, MS, who "was in direct need of appropriate psychiatric treatment" (para.44), banged his head against the cell wall, beat his chest, stripped naked, drank from the toilet bowl, ranted incoherently and appeared to smear himself with food or faeces. The European Court of Human Rights held that, even though there was no intention to humiliate or debase MS, the conditions which he had to endure "were an affront to human dignity and reached the thresholds of degrading treatment for the purposes of art.3" (para.45). It is submitted that there would be no breech of art.3 in a case of this nature if the detainee is transferred to a psychiatric facility without undue delay.

The death of a person who has been detained under this section following a disproportionate use of restraint or a failure to prevent the suicide of a person who was known to be a suicide risk could engage art.2 of the ECHR: see the notes on art.2 in Part 5.

Code of Practice
This section is considered in Ch.16.   **1–1335**

Subsection (1)
CONSTABLE. Means the office of constable, and not the rank of constable (Police Act **1–1336** 1964 s.18, Sch.2). Therefore, any police officer can exercise this power.

FINDS. It is submitted that if a constable arrests a person inside their home for a breach of the peace and then takes that person outside, this section cannot be invoked there because the constable has not "found" that person in a place to which the public have access. In *Seal v Chief Constable of South Wales Police* [2007] UKHL 31; [2007] 4 All E.R. 177 at para.60, Baroness Hale said obiter:

"If [Mr Seal] was 'removed' under s.136 of the 1983 Act from his mother's home, he cannot have been 'found in a place to which the public have access'. If he was arrested in her home for a breach of the peace, and then 'removed' under s.136 after they had taken him outside, can it be said that they 'found' him there?"

In *McMillan v CPS* [2008] EWHC 1457 (Admin), a police constable was held to have acted lawfully when he physically escorted a woman from a private garden to a public footpath and then arrested her for the criminal offence of being drunk and disorderly in a public place. The court noted, at para.12, that at the Magistrates' Court the Justices had "rejected any suggestion that [Ms McMillan] was being moved from a private place to a public place simply so as to justify an arrest outside the garden for an offence which had a public place requirement". It follows that although a police constable has the right to escort a person from a private place to a public place if, for example, that is necessary either to diffuse an emotionally fraught situation or to lawfully remove a trespasser (see *Winzar v Chief Constable of Kent, The Times*, March 28, 1983), it would not be lawful to remove the person solely for the purpose of bringing him or her within the scope of this section.

The practice of arresting a person in their home for a breach of the peace and then detaining him under this section when he is taken outside his home is unlawful as a person who is arrested for a breach of the peace must be taken to a police station and then brought before a justice as soon as reasonably practicable (*Williamson v Chief Constable of West Midlands Police* [2003] EWCA Civ 337, para.19; also see *Hicks v Commissioner of the Metropolitan Police* [2004] EWCA Civ 3).

PLACE TO WHICH THE PUBLIC HAVE ACCESS. This phrase is not defined. It probably includes (1) places to which members of the public have open access, e.g. the public highway; (2) places to which members of the public have access if a payment is made, e.g. a cinema or a music festival; and (3) places to which members of the public have access at certain times of day, e.g. a public house. It does not cover areas such as a private garden where members of the public have access by virtue of being visitors to private premises: see *R. v Edwards* (1978) 67 Cr. App. R. 228, where the Court of Appeal held that the fact that the public can obtain access to a private house as visitors through the front garden does not make the garden a public place for the purposes of the Public Order Act 1936. A garden is not a place to which the public have access even if a person standing in the garden could injure a passing pedestrian with a knife (*R v Roberts* [2003] EWCA Crim 2753). In *Knox v Anderton* (1983) 76 Cr. App. R. 156, a case under s.1(4) of the Prevention of Crime Act 1953, the Divisional Court held that a "public place" to which the public have access could include premises where there are no barriers or notices restricting access, such as the upper landing of a block of flats which could be entered by members of the public without hindrance. *Roberts* and *Anderton* were applied in *Harriot v Director of Public Prosecutions* [2005] EWHC 965 (Admin) where the Divisional Court held that the forecourt of a bail hostel to which access from the street was unimpeded, whether physically or by displayed notices, was not a "public place" within the meaning of s.139 of the Criminal Justice Act 1988. In this case Mitting J. rejected counsel's submission that the phrase "to which the public has access" is synonymous with "from which the public is not excluded". His Lordship said:

"A private garden, clearly delimited as such, is not a place to which the public have access merely because public access is not physically obstructed by a fence, wall or gate, or legally prohibited by a notice or by any combination of them. It remains a private not a public place unless evidence is led which proves that members of the public do in fact have access to it by going onto it in their capacity as members of the public. In the absence of such evidence, a private garden, whether of a single dwelling house, a block of flats or a hostel, is not a place to which the public have access."

A case on the Road Traffic Act 1988 suggests that the phrase would cover a private car park which was attached to premises and which did not restrict access to members of the public, even though the car park was intended for the use of customers of the premises (*May v DPP* [2005] EWHC 1280 (Admin)). In the only reported case on this section, *Carter v Metropolitan Police Commissioner* [1975] 1 W.L.R. 507, the Court of Appeal proceeded on the basis that a communal balcony in a block of flats was a "place to which the public have access". A railway line, being private property, is not such a place.

The Mental Health Act Commission (MHAC) reported that there "have been occasions when police, called to a disturbed individual in an Accident and Emergency Department, have declined to use s.136 on grounds that it is not a public place" (*Fifth Biennial Report* 1991–1993, para.10.7(a)). As a hospital Accident and Emergency Department waiting area is a place at which members of the public can attend without hindrance such a place comes within the scope of this provision. This was confirmed by the Divisional Court in *R. (on the application of Sessay) v South London and Maudsley NHS Foundation Trust)* [2011] EWHC 2617 (QB); [2012] M.H.L.R. 94, at para.39. However, a hospital ward is excluded as it is a place to which only particular members of the public can attend at the request (actual or implied) of the patient and with the permission of the hospital managers.

If there is serious concern about the safety of a person who is on private premises and the police are refused access to the premises, the police might be able to use their power under s.17(1)(e) of PACE to gain access without a warrant. Section 17(1)(e) is considered in the General Note to s.135.

A PERSON. Of any age. As an alternative to invoking this section where there is reasonable cause to believe that a person under 18 would otherwise be likely to suffer significant harm, a constable may remove that person to "suitable accommodation and keep him there" (Children Act 1989 s.46).

APPEARS TO HIM. No medical evidence is needed. All that is required is that the constable has a reasonable belief that the person is mentally disordered within the meaning of s.1.

NECESSARY TO DO SO. There is nothing to prevent the person from being escorted to hospital without this section being invoked if the person is willing to be admitted as an informal patient, is thought not likely to abscond, and the hospital is prepared to admit him.

REMOVE. Only a constable has the power to remove the person to a place of safety. A person who is being conveyed to a place of safety is deemed to be in legal custody (s.137) and, as the person has been arrested, reasonable force may be used to facilitate the removal. The constable owes a duty of care to the person being conveyed: see *Webley v St George's Hospital NHS Trust* [2014] EWHC 299 (QB) which is noted under *Treatment in an A and E department en route to the hospital named in the application* in s.6.

Subsection (2)
Contrary to an opinion that is sometimes heard, it is not unlawful for a person who has **1–1337** drunk alcohol to be assessed in a place of safety under this section. In other words, there is no need for the assessment to be delayed until person blows zero on the Intoximeter. To delay intervention until complete sobriety is achieved could put a person who is an alcoholic at physical risk.

PLACE OF SAFETY. Is defined in s.135(6)(subs.(1)). The choice of place of safety is that of the police. If the police take the person to a place that comes within the scope of s.135(6), that place becomes the place of safety for the purposes of this section if that place is willing to receive him. This is the case even though that place has not been designated as a place of safety in local protocols: see further paras 16.36 to 16.44 of the *Code of Practice*.
Paragraph 16.38 of the *Code of Practice* states that a "police station should not be used as a place of safety except in exceptional circumstances, for example it may be necessary to do so because the person's behaviour would pose an unmanageably high risk to other patients, staff or other users if the person were to be detained in a healthcare setting".
The Government's "Mental Health Crisis Care Concordat" (2014) states at p.24:

"Local protocols should set out an agreement about what constitutes a truly exceptional basis, for example seriously disturbed or aggressive behaviour. Local Mental Health Crisis Declarations should include local ambitions to reduce the use of police cells as places of safety."

Despite these exhortations, police cells are regularly used as places of safety: see "A criminal use of police cells? The use of police custody as a place of safety for people with mental health needs" (June 2013) a report of a joint inspection carried out by HM Inspectorates of Constabulary and Prisons, the Care Quality Commission and Healthcare Inspectorate Wales.
The House of Commons Health Committee reported on the use of police cells for children detained under this section:

"The Committee is concerned that there is little information regarding the outcomes of children detained by the police under s.136 of the Mental Health Act. We believe that this form of detention should be regarded as a last resort and that any commonplace use of police custody as a place of safety for children is completely inappropriate. We recognise that circumstances may arise where, for their own safety and the safety of others, police officers may have no option but to hold a child in custody. It is the responsibility of local commissioners to work with providers to ensure that places of safety with suitable child protection and safeguarding arrangements are available to the police when a child is held under s.136" ("Post-legislative scrutiny of the Mental Health Act 2007", August 2013, para.69).

If a person who is severely mentally disordered is detained in a police station as the place of safety, he should be transferred to hospital under subss.(3) and (4) at the earliest opportunity: see *MS v United Kingdom*, noted under "Human Rights Act 1998", above. People detained in police custody under this section are kept in the same style of cell as those arrested for crimes.

If the person is taken to a health based facility as the place of safety, the police officer is only legally obliged to remain there if his presence is required to ensure the safety of the patient and staff: see para.16.34 of the *Code of Practice*. The Care Quality Commission is incorrect when it states that the police officer is obliged "to wait with the person during the assessment" (*Monitoring the use of the Mental Health Act in 2009/10*, p.33). "Guidance on Responding to People with Mental Ill Health or Learning Disabilities", National Police Improvement Agency (2010) states, at para.6.4.7.3, that in general, "the police should only need to stay where, in their professional judgement, there is a medium to high risk of violence or breach of the peace".

1–1338   MAY BE DETAINED.   "The powers of detention given by section 136(2) are not conferred expressly on the police, but are given to any person who is a party to the detention of the disordered person once he has been brought to a place of safety" (Butler Committee, para.9.2).

The authority to detain under this section ends immediately if the doctor's assessment leads her to conclude that the person is not mentally disordered. The further detention of the patient in these circumstances would be unlawful: see the note on "Human Rights Act 1998", above.

In its *Second Biennial Report*, 1985–87, at para.11.1(e), the MHAC reported that it had:

"found that doubt exists when the person brought to the hospital [under this section] has been examined by the doctor but no [AMHP] is available to conduct the interview. The legal consequences of failure to provide an [AMHP] interview are open to debate. Has the person to remain in detention even though the doctor does not consider that compulsory admission is necessary, until the [AMHP] is available? Good practice would suggest that if the delay is going to be considerable (say more than four hours) then the requirements of the section shall be deemed to have been fulfilled so that detention may end. The case where the doctor decides that compulsory admission is appropriate is more controversial, since Parliament clearly intended that the [AMHP's] opinion would be of great importance both in providing a safeguard for the rights of the individual and in deciding what arrangements are most appropriate to provide the care which the person needs."

It is submitted that the wording of subs.(2) clearly envisages the person being both examined by a doctor and interviewed by an AMHP and that in both of the situations identified by the MHAC the patient will remain subject to detention under this section until the interview by the AMHP takes place and any necessary arrangements for the patient's treatment or care have been put in place. In the passage quoted, the MHAC appeared to assume that the sole purpose of being removed to a place of safety is to assess the patient for possible compulsory admission under the Act. Such an outcome is, in fact, only one of a number of options that would be considered on an assessment. The MHAC adopted a more orthodox approach to this section in its *Ninth Biennial Report* 1999–2001 at paras 4.7–4.9.

The IPCC's report on the "Investigation into West Yorkshire Police contact with Martin Middleton" (2004) states that where a police station is used as the place of safety this section "does not give a custody sergeant the discretion to release someone or refuse to authorise the detention of a person who has been detained under s.136 before an assessment has been carried out". After the assessment has been carried out, the discretion should not be exercised by the custody sergeant until the "necessary arrangements" have been put in place.

72 HOURS. This is the maximum period of detention: see para.16.26 of the *Code of Practice* which states that the "imposition of consecutive periods of detention under section 136 is unlawful". Paragraph 16.40 of the *Code* states that, wherever practicable, "detention in a police station under section 136 should not exceed a maximum period of 24 hours". The power to detain under this section will lapse as soon as the person has been examined and interviewed and it is considered that no further arrangements need be made for his treatment or care. If it is determined that such arrangements have to be made, the person can continue to be detained, subject to the 72-hour limit, while the arrangements are put in place. As the 72 hour period starts from the time when the person arrives at the place of safety, a record of the time of arrival there should be made. If the place of safety is a hospital, this period cannot be continued under s.5(2) or (4) as it is Parliament's intention that the assessment be completed within the 72 hours; see *R. v Wilson Ex p. Williamson* [1996] C.O.D. 42, noted in the General Note to s.2 and the *Code of Practice* at para.16.76. If a person escapes from the place of safety he cannot be retaken after the 72 hours have expired (s.138(3)).

If a decision is taken to admit the person to hospital under s.2, the admission should be actioned without undue delay (*R. (on the application of Sessay) v South London and Maudsley NHS Foundation Trust*) [2011] EWHC 2617 (QB); [2012] M.H.L.R. 94, para.56).

REGISTERED MEDICAL PRACTITIONER. Wherever possible, the examining doctor should **1–1339** be approved by the Secretary of State or the Welsh Ministers under s.12, or by another person by virtue of s.12ZA or 12ZB (*Code of Practice*, para.16.46).

APPROVED MENTAL HEALTH PROFESSIONAL. Although this section is silent on the issue, to be consistent with the duty placed on local authorities under s.13(1) it is submitted that the responsibility for providing an AMHP to undertake the assessment rests with the local authority for the area where the place of safety is located.

The CQC found that 61 per cent of health bases places of safety reported that "AMHPs refused to start assessments until a bed was available" (*A safer place to be*, October 2014, p.38). Such refusals are certainly inappropriate and possibly unlawful as the purpose of an assessment under this section is not confined to assessing whether the person should be detained under the Act.

NECESSARY ARRANGEMENTS. These could include detention under the Act, informal admission to hospital, or making arrangements for the person to be assessed for the possible provision of community care services.

If the patient has been assessed as requiring detention under the Act, the authority to detain under this section continues until a bed has been found for him.

If it is established that the patient is absent without leave from the detaining hospital, he can be immediately returned to that hospital under the authority of s.18. If the patient is either on leave of absence under s.17 or is subject to a community treatment order, the assessment of the patient should be completed. The patient's responsible clinician should be contacted to establish whether the patient is going to be recalled to hospital.

Subsections (3),(4)

1–1340   These provisions, which respond to concern that was expressed during debates on the 2007 Act about mentally disordered people being detained in a police cell (see, for e.g., *Hansard,* HL Vol. 689, col.1467), enable a person who has been detained in a place of safety under this section to be transferred to another one before the time limit of 72 hours for detention has expired. Such a transfer does not have the effect of increasing the 72 hour limit. The transfer can take place before the assessment has begun, while it is in progress, or after it has been completed while arrangements are being put in place for the person's treatment or care.

Before a transfer takes place, the agreement of a person in control of the new place of safety to accept the patient must be obtained. On arrival at the new place of safety, the person in control should be informed, preferably in writing, of the time when the original detention under this section started.

The transfer of a person between places of safety is considered in the *Code of Practice* at paras 16.53 to 16.58 and in Home Office Circular No.007/2008.

Provisions as to custody, conveyance and detention

1–1341   **137.**—(1) Any person required or authorised by or by virtue of this Act to be conveyed to any place or to be kept in custody or detained in a place of safety or at any place to which he is taken under section 42(6) above shall, while being so conveyed, detained or kept, as the case may be, be deemed to be in legal custody.

(2) A constable or any other person required or authorised by or by virtue of this Act to take any person into custody, or to convey or detain any person shall, for the purposes of taking him into custody or conveying or detaining him, have all the powers, authorities, protection and privileges which a constable has within the area for which he acts as constable.

(3) In this section "convey" includes any other expression denoting removal from one place to another.

GENERAL NOTE

1–1342   This section specifies the circumstances whereby a person is deemed to be in legal custody for the purposes of the Act. It also provides that a person who is required or authorised to detain or convey a person who is in legal custody shall have the powers of a constable when so acting. That person owes a duty of care to the patient: see *Webley v St George's Hospital NHS Trust* [2014] EWHC 299 (QB) which is noted under *Treatment in an A and E department en route to the hospital named in the application* in s.6(1). A person who escapes from legal custody can be retaken under s.138.

The powers contained in this section do not include the power to use force to enter premises to remove a person simply because he or she was believed to be suffering from a mental disorder or was a person liable to be taken into custody under the Act (*R. v Rosso* [2003] EWCA Crim 3242; [2003] M.H.L.R. 404 para.17). Section 135 should be used in such circumstances.

Subsection (2)

1–1343   In *R. v Broadmoor Special Hospital Authority and The Secretary of State for the Department of Health Ex p. SH and D*, February 5, 1998, Potts J. held that this subsection was concerned with the limited function of detention for the purpose of conveyance to hospital, not with detention once there. This finding was referred to without comment when this case reached the Court of Appeal: see [1998] C.O.D. 199.

POWERS . . . WHICH A CONSTABLE HAS.   Which include the powers to arrest a person who is wilfully obstructing him in the execution of his duties, to use reasonable force in effecting an arrest, to prevent a person from escaping, to secure the conveyance of the person, and to require other persons to assist him in the execution of his duties.

Retaking of patients escaping from custody

138.—(1) If any person who is in legal custody by virtue of section 137 above **1–1344** escapes, he may, subject to the provisions of this section, be retaken—

  (a) in any case, by the person who had his custody immediately before the escape, or by any constable or [approved mental health professional];

  (b) if at the time of the escape he was liable to be detained in a hospital within the meaning of Part II of this Act, or subject to guardianship under this Act, [or a community patient who was recalled to hospital under section 17E above,] by any other person who could take him into custody under section 18 above if he had absented himself without leave.

(2) A person to whom paragraph (b) of subsection (1) above applies shall not be retaken under this section after the expiration of the period within which he could be retaken under section 18 above if he had absented himself without leave on the day of the escape unless he is subject to a restriction order under Part III of this Act or an order or direction having the same effect as such an order; and subsection (4) of the said section 18 shall apply with the necessary modifications accordingly.

(3) A person who escapes while being taken to or detained in a place of safety under section 135 or 136 above shall not be retaken under this section after the expiration of the period of 72 hours beginning with the time when he escapes or the period during which he is liable to be so detained, whichever expires first.

(4) This section, so far as it relates to the escape of a person liable to be detained in a hospital within the meaning of Part II of this Act, shall apply in relation to a person who escapes—

  (a) while being taken to or from such a hospital in pursuance of regulations under section 19 above, or of any order, direction or authorisation under Part III or VI of this Act (other than under section 35, 36, 38, 53, 83 or 85) [. . .]; or

  (b) while being taken to or detained in a place of safety in pursuance of an order under Part III of this Act (other than under section 35, 36 or 38 above) pending his admission to such a hospital,

as if he were liable to be detained in that hospital and, if he had not previously been received in that hospital, as if he had been so received.

(5) In computing for the purposes of the power to give directions under section 37(4) above and for the purposes of sections 37(5) and 40(1) above the period of 28 days mentioned in those sections, no account shall be taken of any time during which the patient is at large and liable to be retaken by virtue of this section.

(6) Section 21 above shall, with any necessary modifications, apply in relation to a patient who is at large and liable to be retaken by virtue of this section as it applies in relation to a patient who is absent without leave and references in that section to section 18 above shall be construed accordingly.

AMENDMENTS
    The amendments to this section were made by the Mental Health Act 2007 ss.21, 32(4), Sch.2 para.10, Sch.3 para.32 and the Health and Social Care Act 2012 s.42(3).

DEFINITIONS
1–1345   approved mental health professional: s.145(1), (1AC).
absent without leave: ss.18(6), 145(1).
restriction order: ss.41, 145(1).
patient: s.145(1).
community patient: ss.17A(7), 145(1).
hospital: s.145(1).

GENERAL NOTE
1–1346   This section provides for the retaking of persons who have escaped from legal custody. A patient who has been made subject to an application under Pt II and who escapes whilst on the way to hospital can only be retaken if he can be apprehended within the relevant period set out in either para.(a) or para.(b) of s.6(1). A person who assists another person who is in legal custody to escape commits an offence under s.128(2).

This section does not provide authority for force to be used to enter premises where the patient is believed to be. An application to a magistrate under s.135 should be made if such action is deemed to be necessary.

The power of the police to arrest under this section was specifically preserved by s.26 and Sch.2 of the Police and Criminal Evidence Act 1984 (PACE). This means that the arresting policeman has a power under s.32 of PACE to search the patient at a place other than a police station. Section 72 of the Criminal Justice Act 1967 also provides for a power of arrest under this provision, but only if a warrant of arrest has been issued by a magistrate.

Subsections (1), (4)
1–1347   HOSPITAL WITHIN THE MEANING OF PART II.   See s.34(2).

Subsection (6)
1–1348   The effect of this subsection is that if the patient is retaken within the last week of the period during which he can be retaken, the authority to detain will end a week after the day he is retaken.

Protection for acts done in pursuance of this Act

1–1349   **139.**—(1) No person shall be liable, whether on the ground of want of jurisdiction or on any other ground, to any civil or criminal proceedings to which he would have been liable apart from this section in respect of any act purporting to be done in pursuance of this Act or any regulations or rules made under this Act, [. . .] unless the act was done in bad faith or without reasonable care.

(2) No civil proceedings shall be brought against any person in any court in respect of any such act without the leave of the High Court; and no criminal proceedings shall be brought against any person in any court in respect of any such act except by or with the consent of the Director of Public Prosecutions.

(3) This section does not apply to proceedings for an offence under this Act, being proceedings which, under any other provision of this Act, can be instituted only by or with the consent of the Director of Public Prosecutions.

(4) This section does not apply to proceedings against the Secretary of State or against [the National Health Service Commissioning Board, a clinical commissioning group,] a [. . .] [Local Health Board] [or Special Health Authority] [. . .] [or against a National Health Service trust established under [the National Health Service Act 2006 or the National Health Service (Wales) Act 2006]] [or NHS foundation trust] [or against the Department of Justice in Northern

Ireland] [or against a person who has functions under this Act by virtue of section 12ZA in so far as the proceedings relate to the exercise of those functions].

(5) In relation to Northern Ireland the reference in this section to the Director of Public Prosecutions shall be construed as a reference to the Director of Public Prosecutions for Northern Ireland.

AMENDMENTS

The amendments to this section were made by the Mental Capacity Act 2005 s.67(2), Sch.7, the National Health Service and Community Care Act 1990 s.66(1), Sch.9 para.24(7), the Health Authorities Act 1995 s.2(1), Sch.1 para.107(11), the National Health Service Reform and Health Care Professions Act 2002 (Supplementary, Consequential, etc. Provisions) Regulations 2002 (SI 2002/2469) reg.4, Sch.1, the Health and Social Care (Community Health and Standards) Act 2003 s.34, Sch.4 para.56, SI 2007/961 art.3, Sch. para.13(11), the National Health Service (Consequential Provisions) Act 2006 s.2, Sch.1 para.6, SI 2010/976 para.28 and the Health and Social Care Act 2012 s.38(3), Sch.5, para.30.

DEFINITIONS

Local Health Board: s.145(1).   **1–1350**
Special Health Authority: s.145(1).

TRANSITIONAL PROVISION

This section continues to apply to proceedings brought against a Primary Care Trust or **1–1351** Strategic Heath Authority before April 1, 2013, if those proceedings are continued after March 31, 2013 (SI 2013/160, art.10, Sch., para.3).

GENERAL NOTE

This section, which has its origins in s.330 of the Lunacy Act 1890, provides that: (1) **1–1352** apart from proceedings against the Secretary of State or a body mentioned in subs.(4) and proceedings under s.127, no civil or criminal proceedings can be brought against any person in any court in respect of an act purporting to be done under the Act without the leave of the High Court or the Director of Public Prosecutions; and (2) for such proceedings to succeed the court must be satisfied that the person proceeded against acted in bad faith or without reasonable care. Its scope does not extend to claims made under s.7 of the Human Rights Act 1998: see the decision of the Court of Appeal in *TTM v London Borough of Hackney* which is noted under "Human Rights Act 1998", below. At first instance, Collins J. said that it seemed "slightly anomalous" that the protection given by this section "is in effect removed in the case of public but not in the case of private hospitals" ([2010] EWHC 1349 (Admin), para.5).

During the passage of the 1982 Act, the Government resisted an amendment to exclude the provisions of this section for informal patients on the ground that this would remove the protection given to someone who purports to do something under the Act when he believes that the patient is a detained patient. The Minister for Health gave the following illustration in support of this argument:

"An ambulance man . . . has a patient in his charge whom he believes is a detained patient because he is told so. Therefore, he is told that he should prevent the patient escaping. If the patient attempts to go off and he takes steps to stop him escaping, he might be liable to an action thereafter, but he would be protected if we retain [this section] with its present wording" (*Hansard* HC, Vol.29, col.173).

This interpretation is consistent with the use of the term "purporting" in this provision. Although there is Crown Court authority for the contention that this section does not cover acts done in respect of informal patients (*R. v Runighian* [1977] Crim. L.R. 361),

Cox J. in *Lebrooy v Hammersmith and Fulham LBC* [2006] EWHC 1976 (QB); [2006] M.H.L.R. 253 at para.15, rejected a submission that this section "only applies to those who have been detained under [the] Act". It is submitted that the Government's approach is correct, and that although this section does not apply to every act done in respect of informal patients, it does apply to an informal patient if the individual undertaking the act genuinely believes at the relevant time that he or she is acting under a provision of the Act.

This section does not affect the right of a patient to apply to the High Court for his discharge by means of a writ of habeas corpus (*R. v Governor of Pentonville Prison Ex p. Azam* [1974] A.C. 18 at 31). *Azam* was cited in *R. v Hallstrom Ex p. W* [1985] 3 All E.R. 775 where the Court of Appeal held that leave under this section is also not required for applications for judicial review.

In *Winch v Jones*, [1985] 3 All E.R. 97, the Court of Appeal held that the test to be applied by the court when considering to grant leave under this section was whether, on the materials immediately available to the court, the applicant's complaint appeared to deserve the fuller investigation which will be possible if the intended applicant is allowed to proceed. Sir John Donaldson M.R. said, at 102, that this section:

"is intended to strike a balance between the legitimate interests of the applicant to be allowed, at his own risk as to costs, to seek the adjudication of the courts on any claim which is not frivolous, vexatious or an abuse of the process and the equally legitimate interests of the respondent to such an application not to be subjected to the undoubted exceptional risk of being harassed by baseless claims by those who have been treated under the Mental Health Acts".

In *Seal v Chief Constable of South Wales Police* [2007] UKHL 31; [2007] 4 All E.R. 177, para.20, Lord Bingham said that the judgment in *Winch v Jones* set the threshold for obtaining leave "at a very unexacting level . . . an applicant with an arguable case will be granted leave". Lord Brown said, at para.70, that "the test is now simply whether the case deserves further investigation by the court". Both remarks were made obiter. In *Johnston v Chief Constable of Merseyside Police* [2009] EWHC 2969 (QB); [2009] M.H.L.R. 343, Coulson J. considered whether the test identified by Sir John Donaldson in *Which v Jones* should be modified to take account of CPR Part 24 which introduced a new emphasis on allowing claims to go to trial only where they have a real prospect of success. His Lordship concluded, at para.15, "that a court faced with an application for permission under section 139(2) of the Act must strive to apply the test set out by Sir John Donaldson MR in *Winch v Jones* . . ., with the proviso that the court should also consider whether, in all the circumstances, the proposed claim has a real prospect of success". *Winch v Jones* and *Johnston v Chief Constable of Merseyside Police* were cited in *DD v Durham County Council* [2013] EWCA Civ 96; [2013] M.H.L.R. 85, para.23, as authority for the proposition that the threshold under this section is "a low one".

A successful application under subs.(2) of this section does not inhibit a judge on an application to strike out reaching a conclusion following fuller investigation that a statement of claim should be struck out as disclosing no reasonable cause of action (*X v A, B and C and the Mental Health Act Commission* (1991) 9 B.M.L.R. 91).

Article 12 of the Mental Health (Care and Treatment) (Scotland) Act 2003 (Consequential Provisions) Order 2005 (SI 2005/2078), which is reproduced in Pt 2, extends the protection afforded by this section to acts done in pursuance of that Order.

Human Rights Act 1998

1–1353   On rejecting a claim that subs.(2) violates art.6(1) of the European Convention on Human Rights (ECHR), the European Court on Human Rights (ECtHR) confirmed in *Seal v United Kingdom* ((2011) 54 E.H.R.R. 6) that the "right of access to court is not absolute and may be subject to limitations" (para.75) and accepted the Government's argument that subs.(2) "is aimed at providing an additional layer of protection for those exercising sensitive powers under the 1983 Act and does not assume that all those who are, or have been, subject to compulsory powers contained in the Mental Health Act 1983 are vexatious litigants" (para.77). A claim that subs.(2) would violate art.6 if it is read together with art.14 was rejected in *TW v London Borough of Enfield* [2013] EWHC 1180) (QB); [2013] M.H.L.R. 214 at para.39. The ECtHR in *Salontaji-Drobnjak v Serbia* (App.No.36500/05) Oct 13, 2009, para.133, said that limitations on a mentally disordered patient's right of access to a court must be proportionate.

This section should be "read down" under s.3 of the 1998 Act so as to permit a patient's claim under s.7 of that Act for judicial review and damages for unlawful detention to proceed without leave (*TTM v London Borough of Hackney* [2011] EWCA Civ 4; [2011] 3 All E.R. 529, para.66).

The power to control the activities of detained patients

In *Pountney v Griffiths* [1976] A.C. 314, the House of Lords quashed the conviction of a **1–1354** nurse who had been charged with assaulting a patient when ushering the patient to his ward after a visit from the patient's family on the ground that leave to prosecute had not been obtained under subs.(2) of this section. Their Lordships approved the finding of Lord Widgery C.J. in the Court of Appeal that "when a male nurse is on duty and exercising his functions of controlling the patients in the hospital, acts done in pursuance of such control are acts within the scope of [s.139] and are thus protected by the section". Although the Act provides for the detention and treatment of patients, it nowhere explicitly refers to the control of patients. The House of Lords held that:

(i)   subs.(2) extends to any act, provided that it had been carried out in purported pursuance of the Act, and that its scope is not limited to acts done or purported to be done in pursuance of functions specifically provided for in the terms of the Act; and

(ii) treating patients necessarily involves the exercise of discipline and control, and that suitable arrangements for visits to patients by family and friends was an obvious part of the patient's treatment.

In *R. (on the application of E.) v Ashworth Hospital Authority* [2001] EWHC Admin 1089; [2002] M.H.L.R. 150, Richards J., in holding that the power to control what patients wear is a necessary incident of the power to detain, said that to be lawful the implied power must be exercised:

(i)   for the purpose of detention and/or treatment rather than for some ulterior purpose;

(ii)   in accordance with *Wednesbury* principles of reasonableness; and

(iii) compatibly with the ECHR and in particular with art.8.

Pountney v Griffiths was cited by Auld L.J. in *R. v Broadmoor Special Hospital and the Secretary of State for the Department of Health Ex p. S, H, and D* [1998] C.O.D. 199, where the Court of Appeal held that the exercise of discipline and control in respect of a detained patient includes, where necessary, a power to search patients with or without cause and despite individual medical objections. To be lawful, a hospital's search policy must:

(i)   be proportionate to the level of risk posed by the patient population to the maintenance of a safe and therapeutic environment; and

(ii) take account of a patient's right to respect for private life under art.8 of the ECHR.

The application of art.8 to the searching of patients is considered in the notes on that article in Pt 5 under the heading "Private life". A strip and intimate body search could engage art.3: see *Wainwright v United Kingdom* (2007) 44 E.H.R.R. 40, paras 42, 43, noted in the General Note to art.3. The *Code of Practice* guidance on personal and other searches is contained in Ch.8.

In the *Broadmoor* case, Auld L.J. said that both the 1959 and 1983 Acts:

"leave unspoken many of the necessary incidents of control flowing from a power of detention for treatment, including: the power to restrain patients, to keep them in seclusion . . ., to deprive them of their personal possessions for their own safety and to regulate the frequency and manner of visits to them . . .".

Observations to a similar effect were made by Lord Woolf M.R. in *Broadmoor Hospital Authority v R.* [2000] 2 All E.R. 727 at para.26. In *R. v Mersey Care National Health Service Trust Ex p. Munjaz* [2005] UKHL 58; [2006] 4 All E.R. 736, Lord Bingham said at para.34:

"[T]he power to seclude a patient within a hospital is implied from the power to detain as a 'necessary ingredient flowing from a power of detention for treatment'".

In *Munjaz v United Kingdom* [2012] M.H.L.R. 351, the European Court of Human Rights held that in certain circumstances the seclusion of a detained patient could amount to a further deprivation of his liberty under art.5: see the note in "detention" under art.5(1)(e) in Part 5. The *Code of Practice* guidance on seclusion and on long-term segregation is contained in Ch.8.

The power to control includes the power to restrain patients as long as its use is necessary and proportionate. To avoid breeches of arts 5 or 8 of the ECHR the restraint must satisfy the test of "medical necessity": see *Herczegfalvy v Austria* (1992) 15 E.H.R.R. 437 and the General Note to art.3 in Part 5. A legal basis for the use of restraint can also be found in the provisions considered in Appendix A.

The Department of Health has published "Positive and Proactive Care: reducing the need for restrictive interventions" (2014) which "provides guidance on the delivery of services together with key actions that will ensure that people's quality of life is enhanced and that their needs are better met, which will reduce the need for restrictive interventions and promote recovery" (para.5).

Subsection (1)

1–1355   This "subsection does not create any cause of action and only relates to pre-existing possible liability. It creates a hurdle for a plaintiff to surmount"; per Morland J. in *X v A, B and C and the Mental Health Act Commission*, above, at 96.

PERSON.   Or corporation (Interpretation Act 1978 s.5, Sch.1).

SHALL BE LIABLE.   The question whether the protection of this section can be claimed by a health body in a situation where that body is vicariously liable for any shortcomings of a doctor employee in the performance of duties vested in him or her personally by the Act is undecided: see the conflicting opinions of Brooke and Hale L.JJ. in *R. (on the application of Wilkinson) v The Responsible Medical Officer Broadmoor Hospital* [2001] EWCA Civ 1545; [2002] 1 W.L.R. 419, at paras 42 and 58.

CIVIL OR CRIMINAL PROCEEDINGS.   The proceedings need not necessarily involve a patient.

In *Dunnage v Randall* [2015] EWCA Civ 673, the Court of Appeal held that there was no principle that requires the law to excuse from liability in negligence a defendant who fails to meet the normal standard of care partly because of a medical problem. Vos L.J. said at para.131:

"In my judgment, only defendants whose attack or medical incapacity has the effect of entirely eliminating any fault or responsibility for the injury can be excused. It is only defendants in that category that have not actually broken their undoubted duty of care.

The actions of a defendant, who is merely impaired by medical problems, whether physical or mental, cannot escape liability if he causes injury by failing to exercise reasonable care."

ACT PURPORTING TO BE DONE IN PURSUANCE OF THIS ACT.   In *TW v London Borough of Enfield* [2013] EWHC 1180) (QB), para.41, Bean J. said that it is clear from *TTM v Hackney LBC* [2011] EWCA Civ 4; [2011] 3 All E.R. 529 that in order to be compliant with the ECHR this provision is to be read as though the following words were added to this phrase "or is otherwise unlawful, for example because of a contravention of s.11(4)".

Although nearly all such acts will relate to detained patients, this section also applies to patients who are subject to guardianship and community treatment orders. Whether the protection afforded by this section applies to omissions, such as a failure to detain a person under the Act, is undecided. In *R. (on the application of W) v Doncaster M.B.C.* [2003] EWHC 192 (Admin); [2004] M.H.L.R. 189, Stanley Burnton J. said that he would have been "reluctant to accept [a] submission that s.139(1) does not apply to an omission or failure to act, and is confined to positive acts. I do not think that Parliament intended there to be any such illogical and unmeritorious distinction in the application of that section" (para.55).

In the unreported case of *Ashingdane v Secretary of State for Social Services*, February 18, 1980, the Court of Appeal held that the immunity conferred by this section is confined to an act done by a person to whom authority to do an act of that type is expressly or impliedly conferred by the Act or by regulations made under it. Applying this test the Court held that the decision of a nurses' union not to allow patients who were subject to restriction orders to be transferred to a particular hospital was a policy decision which fell outside their express or implied authority and was not, therefore, covered by this section.

This section was engaged in a case where it was alleged that the defendants had made maliciously false, defamatory allegations in medical notes made by them in conection with the management and care of the claimant when he had suffered from mental illness: see *Lebrooy v Hammersmith and Fulham LBC* [2006] EWHC 1976 (QB); [2006] M.H.L.R. 253.

ACTED IN BAD FAITH OR WITHOUT REASONABLE CARE.   In *Richardson v London County Council* [1957] 1 W.L.R. 751 it was held that: (1) whether a person has acted in bad faith or without reasonable care is a question of fact with the burden of proof lying with the applicant; and (2) this section offers protection even though the person proceeded against acted either without jurisdiction or misconstrued the Act, as long as the misconstruction was one which the Act was reasonably capable of bearing.

In *R. (on the application of Wilkinson) v The Responsible Medical Officer Broadmoor Hospital* [2001] EWCA Civ 1545; [2002] 1 W.L.R. 419, at para.57, Hale L.J., citing *Richardson*, said that it may well be that the immunity provided by this section does not relieve against "a negligent mistake of law as to the extent of the legal authority conferred by the Act".

If bad faith were established, there could be a private law claim based on misfeasance in public office (*TTM v London Borough of Hackney* [2010] EWHC 1349 (Admin), para.36).

Subsection (2)
Failure to obtain the necessary leave or consent required by this provision before the proceedings are begun renders the proceedings a nullity (*Seal v Chief Constable of South Wales Police* [2007] UKHL 31; [2007] 4 All E.R. 177).   **1–1356**

CIVIL PROCEEDINGS.   This phrase does not include proceedings for judicial review. Acts purportedly done in pursuance of the Act can therefore be reviewed even if bad faith or lack of reasonable care are not alleged (*R. v Hallstrom, Ex p. W* [1986] 2 All E.R. 306).

LEAVE. The leave of a High Court judge is required even if the case would normally be heard in the county court. An appeal lies to the Court of Appeal against a judge's decision but either the leave of the judge or of the Court of Appeal is required before the appeal can be made (*Moore v Commissioner of Metropolitan Police* [1968] 1 Q.B. 26). A Master or District Judge may not make orders or grant interim remedies in applications under this section (CPR Practice Direction 2B, Allocation of Cases to Levels of Judiciary, para.3(1)).

The onus is on the applicant to satisfy the court or the D.P.P. that the proceedings should be commenced (*Carter v Commissioner of Police for the Metropolis* [1975] 1 W.L.R. 507 CA). The "overriding objective" set out in Pt 1 of the Civil Procedure Rules 1998 has no application to an application for leave under this section (*C v South London and Maudsley Hospital National Health Service Trust* [2001] M.H.L.R. 269).

Subsection (3)

1–1357 CONSENT OF THE DIRECTOR OF PUBLIC PROSECUTIONS. Is required for proceedings under s.127.

Subsection (4)

1–1358 DOES NOT APPLY. The acts of a local social services authority performed in pursuance of the Act are protected by this section.

An approved mental health professional (AMHP) who is employed by a health body is acting on behalf of a local social services authority when performing the functions of an AMHP and is therefore protected by this section: see s.145(1AC).

SECRETARY OF STATE. Or the Welsh Ministers (see the General Note to this Act and SI 2000/253, Sch.3).

Notification of hospitals having arrangements for reception of urgent cases

1–1359 **140.** It shall be the duty of [every clinical commissioning group and of] every [Local Health Board] to give notice to every local social services authority for an area wholly or partly comprised within the [area of the [clinical commissioning group or] [Local Health Board]] specifying the hospital or hospitals administered by [or otherwise available] [to the [clinical commisioning group or] [Local Health Board]] in which arrangements are from time to time in force [—

(a) for the reception of patients in cases of special urgency;

(b) for the provision of accommodation or facilities designed so as to be specially suitable for patients who have not attained the age of 18 years.]

AMENDMENTS

The amendments to this section were made by the National Health Service and Community Care Act 1990 s.66(1), Sch.9 para.24(8), the Health Authorities Act 1995 s.2(1), Sch.1 para.107(12), the National Heath Service Reform and Health Care Professions Act 2002 s.2(5), Sch.2 para.48, the Mental Health Act 2007 s.31(4), SI 2007/961 art.3, Sch. para.13(12) and the Health and Social Care Act 2012 s.45.

DEFINITIONS

1–1360 Local Health Board: s.145(1).
local social services authority: s.145(1).
hospital: s.145(1).
patient: s.145(1).

GENERAL NOTE

1–1361 This section, which is considered in the *Code of Practice* at paras 14.77 et seq., requires relevant health bodies to notify local social services authorities within their area of the arrangements that are in force for the reception of mentally disordered patients to hospital in cases of special urgency and the provision of accommodation or facilities designed to be specially suitable for child patients who are mentally disordered. The patients may be either detained or informal. For the duty to provide suitable accommodation and facilities for children, see s.131A. Also note the duty placed by s.39 on clinical commissioning groups and Local Health Boards to provide the courts with information as to the availability of hospital places.

Paragraph 14.78 of the *Code of Practice* states:

"Clinical commissioning groups (CCGs) are responsible for commissioning mental health services to meet the needs of their areas. Under section 140 of the Act, CCGs have a duty to notify local authorities in their areas of arrangements which are in force for the reception of patients in cases of special urgency or the provision of appropriate accommodation or facilities specifically designed for patients under the age of 18. The arrangements should include details of which providers in their area can receive patients in cases of special urgency and provide accommodation or facilities designed to be specifically suitable for patients under the age of 18. CCGs should provide a list of hospitals and their specialisms to local authorities which will help inform AMHPs as to where these hospitals are. This should in turn help inform AMHPs as to where beds are available in these circumstances if they are needed."

The Mental Health Act Commission suggested that if a patient cannot be admitted to hospital in an emergency for want of a bed the approved mental health professional should complete an application, making it out to the hospital which has been the subject of a notification under this provision, and convey the patient to that hospital. For a comment on this suggestion, see the note on "to hospital" in s.6(1).

Although this section does not oblige the specified hospitals to admit patients, a refusal to admit should only be made with good reason. If a hospital bed cannot be found for a patient who requires admission, it is the responsibility of the local mental health service to provide the patient with appropriate treatment and/or care until a bed is found.

Members of Parliament suffering from mental illness

141.—[*Repealed by the Mental Health (Discrimination) Act 2013 s.1(1)*] 1–1362

GENERAL NOTE

Section 1(2) of the Mental Health (Discrimination) Act 2013 abolished any rule of the 1–1363 common law which disqualifies a person from membership of the House of Commons on grounds of mental illness.

Pay, pensions, etc. of mentally disordered persons

142.—(1) Where a periodic payment falls to be made to any person by way of 1–1364 pay or pension or otherwise in connection with the service or employment of that or any other person, and the payment falls to be made directly out of moneys provided by Parliament or the Consolidated Fund [or the Scottish Consolidated Fund], or other moneys administered by or under the control or supervision of a government department, the authority by whom the sum in question is payable, if satisfied after considering medical evidence that the person to whom it is payable (referred to in this section as "the patient") is incapable by reason of mental disorder of managing and administering his property and affairs, may, instead of paying the sum to the patient, apply it in accordance with subsection (2) below.

(2) The authority may pay the sum or such part of it as they think fit to the institution or person having the care of the patient, to be applied for his benefit and may pay the remainder (if any) or such part of the remainder as they think fit—

(a) to or for the benefit of persons who appear to the authority to be members of the patient's family or other persons for whom the patient might be expected to provide if he were not mentally disordered, or

(b) in reimbursement, with or without interest, of money applied by any person either in payment of the patient's debts (whether legally enforceable or not) or for the maintenance or other benefit of the patient or such persons as are mentioned in paragraph (a) above.

(3) In this section "government department" does not include a Northern Ireland department.

AMENDMENT

The words in square brackets in subsection (1) were inserted by the Scotland Act 1998 (Consequential Modifications) (No.2) Order 1999 (SI 1999/1820) art.4, Sch.2 para.71.

DEFINITION

1–1365   mental disorder: ss.1, 145(1).

REPEAL

1–1366   Although this section has been repealed by the Mental Capacity Act 2005 s.67(2), Sch.7 it is reproduced because of the terms of s.67(1), Sch.6 para.29(5) and (6) of that Act which state:

"(5) Sub-paragraph (6) applies where, before the [repeal of s.142 on October 1, 2007], an authority has, in respect of a person referred to in that section as 'the patient', made payments under that section—

(a) to an institution or person having the care of the patient, or
(b) in accordance with subsection (2)(a) or (b) of that section.

(6) The authority may, in respect of the patient, continue to make payments under that section to that institution or person, or in accordance with subsection (2)(a) or (b) of that section, despite the [repeal of s.142]".

GENERAL NOTE

1–1367   Under this section provision is made in the case of any pay, pension or similar payment payable by Parliament or the Government, for direct payment to the institution or person having the care of the patient. Any sums which remain can be paid to members of the patient's family, or to other persons for whom the patient might be expected to provide were he not mentally disordered, or to reimburse people who have paid his debts or helped to maintain him or his family. This section applies to any person who "is incapable by reason of mental disorder of managing and administering his property and affairs" and is not limited to either detained or hospital patients.

[Regulations as to approvals in relation to England and Wales

1–1368   **142A.**—The Secretary of State jointly with the Welsh Ministers may by regulations make provision as to the circumstances in which—

(a) a practitioner approved for the purposes of section 12 above, or
(b) a person approved to act as an approved clinician for the purposes of this Act, approved in relation to England is to be treated, by virtue of his approval, as approved in relation to Wales too, and vice versa.]

AMENDMENT

This section was inserted by the Mental Health Act 2007 s.17.

approved clinician: s.145(1).

1–1369

This section gives the Secretary of State, jointly with Welsh Ministers, the power to set 1–1370
out in regulations the circumstances in which approval in England under s.12, and approval
as an approved clinician should be considered to mean approval in Wales, and vice versa.
   The Mental Health (Mutual Recognition) Regulations 2008 (SI 2008/1204), which are
reproduced in Pt 2, have been made under this section.

[Delegation of powers of managers of NHS foundation trusts

142B.—(1) The constitution of an NHS foundation trust may not provide for a 1–1371
function under this Act to be delegated otherwise than in accordance with provisions made by or under this Act.
   (2) Paragraph 15(3) of Schedule 7 to the National Health Service Act 2006
(which provides that the powers of a public benefit corporation may be delegated
to a committee of directors or to an executive director) shall have effect subject to
this section.]

This section was inserted by the Mental Health Act 2007 s.45(3).

Schedule 7 of the National Health Service Act 2006 sets out mandatory requirements for 1–1372
the contents of the constitution of a NHS foundation trust. The effect of this section is that
the constitution may not permit the trust's functions under this Act to be delegated to executive directors or committees of directors unless that is permitted by this Act.

Supplemental

General provisions as to regulations, orders and rules

143.—(1) Any power of the Secretary of State or the Lord Chancellor to make 1–1373
regulations, orders or rules under this Act shall be exercisable by statutory
instrument.
   (2) Any Order in Council under this Act [or any order made [by the Secretary of
State] under section 54A [or 68A(7)][. . .] above] and any statutory instrument
containing regulations [made by the Secretary of State, or rules made,] under
this Act shall be subject to annulment in pursuance of a resolution of either
House of Parliament.
   (3) No order shall be made [by the Secretary of State] under section [45A(10)]
[68A(1)]) or 71(3) above unless a draft of it has been approved by a resolution of
each House of Parliament.
   [(3A) Subsections (3B) to [(3DB)] apply where power to make regulations or
an order under this Act is conferred on the Welsh Ministers (other than by or
by virtue of the Government of Wales Act 2006).
   (3B) Any power of the Welsh Ministers to make regulations or an order shall be
exercisable by statutory instrument.
   (3C) Any statutory instrument containing regulations, or an order under section
68A(7) above, made by the Welsh Ministers shall be subject to annulment in
pursuance of a resolution of the National Assembly for Wales.

(3D) No order shall be made under section 68A(1) above by the Welsh Ministers unless a draft of it has been approved by a resolution of the National Assembly for Wales.

[(3DA) Subsection (3C) does not apply to regulations to which subsection (3DB) applies.

(3DB) A statutory instrument which contains (alone or with other provisions) the first regulations to be made under any of the following provisions—

(a) section 130E(2),

(b) section 130E(4)(b),

(c) section 130E(5)(b),

(d) section 130F(2)(d),

(e) section 130G(2)(c), or

(f) section 130H(1)(b)(ii),

must not be made unless a draft of the instrument containing the regulations has been laid before, and approved by resolution of, the National Assembly for Wales.

(3E) In this section—

(a) references to the Secretary of State include the Secretary of State and the Welsh Ministers acting jointly; and

(b) references to the Welsh Ministers include the Welsh Ministers and the Secretary of State acting jointly.]

[(4) This section does not apply to rules which are, by virtue of section 108 of this Act, to be made in accordance with Part 1 of Schedule 1 to the Constitutional Reform Act 2005.]

AMENDMENTS

The amendments to this section were made by the Criminal Justice Act 1991 s.27(3), the Mental Health Act 2007 ss.37(5), 47(2),(3), 55, Sch.11 Pt 6, the Crime (Sentences) Act 1997 s.55, Sch.4 para.12(18), the Mental Health (Wales) Measure 2010 s.40 and the Constitutional Reform Act 2005 s.12, Sch.1, para.16.

GENERAL NOTE

Subsection (1)

1–1374   SECRETARY OF STATE.   Or, in relation to Wales, the Welsh Ministers (see the General Note to the Act and SI 1999/672 art.2, Sch.1).

THE LORD CHANCELLOR.   Who cannot transfer his functions under this provision to another person (Constitutional Reform Act 2005 s.19, Sch.7).

Power to amend local Acts

1–1375   **144.** Her Majesty may by Order in Council repeal or amend any local enactment so far as appears to Her Majesty to be necessary in consequence of this Act.

Interpretation

1–1376   **145.**—(1) In this Act, unless the context otherwise requires—

"absent without leave" has the meaning given to it by section 18 above and related expressions [(including expressions relating to a patient's liability to be returned to a hospital or other place)] shall be construed accordingly;

"application for admission for assessment" has the meaning given in section 2 above;

"application for admission for treatment" has the meaning given in section 3 above;

["the appropriate tribunal" has the meaning given by section 66(4) above;]

["approved clinician" means a person approved by the Secretary of State [or another person by virtue of section 12ZA or 12ZB above] (in relation to England) or by the Welsh Ministers (in relation to Wales) to act as an approved clinician for the purposes of this Act;]

["approved mental health professional" has the meaning given by section 114, above;]

["care home" has the same meaning as in the Care Standards Act 2000;]

["community patient" has the meaning given in section 17A above;]

["community treatment order" and "the community treatment order" have the meanings given in section 17A above;]

["the community treatment period" has the meaning given in section 20A above;]

[. . .]

["high security psychiatric services" has the same meaning as in [section 4 of the National Health Service Act 2006 or section 4 of the National Health Service (Wales) Act 2006]

"hospital" means—

    (a) any health service hospital within the meaning of [National Health Service Act 2006 or the National Health Service (Wales) Act 2006]; and

    (b) any accommodation provided by a local authority and used as a hospital or on behalf of the Secretary of State under [the National Health Service Act 2006, or of the Welsh Ministers under the National Health Service (Wales) Act 2006][; and

    (c) any hospital as defined by section 206 of the National Health Service (Wales) Act 2006 which is vested in a Local Health Board;]

and "hospital within the meaning of Part II of this Act" has the meaning given in section 34 above;

["hospital direction" has the meaning given in section 45A(3)(a) above;]

"hospital order" and "guardianship order" have the meanings respectively given in section 37 above;

["independent hospital"—

    (a) in relation to England, means a hospital as defined by section 275 of the National Health Service Act 2006 that is not a health service hospital as defined by that section, and

    (b) in relation to Wales, has the same meaning as in the Care Standards Act 2000;]

"interim hospital order" has the meaning given in section 38 above;

["limitation direction" has the meaning given in section 45A(3)(b) above;]

["Local Health Board" means a Local Health Board established under section 11 of the National Health Services (Wales) Act 2006;]

["local social services authority" means—

    (a) an authority in England which is a local authority for the purposes of Part 1 of the Care Act 2014, or

    (b) an authority in Wales which is a local authority for the purposes of the Social Services and Well-being (Wales) Act 2014;]

"the managers" means—

(a) in relation to a hospital vested in the Secretary of State for the purposes of his functions under [the National Health Service Act 2006, or in the Welsh Ministers for the purposes of their functions under the National Health Service (Wales) Act 2006], and in relation to any accommodation provided by a local authority and used as a hospital by or on behalf of the Secretary of State under [the National Health Service Act 2006, or of the Welsh Ministers under the National Health Service (Wales) Act 2006,] [the Secretary of State where the Secretary is responsible for the administration of the hospital or] the [. . .] [. . .] [[Local Health Board] or Special Health Authority] responsible for the administration of the hospital;

(b) [. . .];

[(bb) in relation to a hospital vested in [. . .] a National Health Service trust, [. . .] the trust;]

[(bc) in relation to a hospital vested in an NHS foundation trust, the trust;]

[(bd) in relation to a hospital vested in a Local Health Board, the Board;]

[(c) in relation to a registered establishment—

(i) if the establishment is in England, the person or persons registered as a service provider under Chapter 2 of Part 1 of the Health and Social Care Act 2008 in respect of the regulated activity (within the meaning of that Part) relating to the assessment or medical treatment of mental disorder that is carried out in the establishment, and

(ii) if the establishment is in Wales, the person or persons registered in respect of the establishment under Part 2 of the Care Standards Act 2000;]

and in this definition "hospital" means a hospital within the meaning of Part II of this Act;

"medical treatment" includes nursing, [psychological intervention and specialist mental health habilitation, rehabilitation and care (but see also subsection (4) below);]

["mental disorder" has the meaning given in section 1 above (subject to [section 86(4));]

[. . .];

"nearest relative," in relation to a patient, has the meaning given in Part II of this Act;

"patient" [. . .] means a person suffering or appearing to be suffering from mental disorder;

[. . .]

["registered establishment" has the meaning given in section 34 above;]

["the regulatory authority" means—

(a) in relation to England, the Care Quality Commission;

(b) in relation to Wales, the Welsh Ministers;]

[. . .]

["the responsible hospital" has the meaning given in section 17A above;]

"restriction direction" has the meaning given to it by section 49 above;

"restriction order" has the meaning given to it by section 41 above;

["Special Health Authority" means a Special Health Authority established under [section 28 of the National Health Service Act 2006, or section 22 of the National Health Service (Wales) Act 2006];]

[. . .]

[. . .]

[. . .]

[. . .]

"transfer direction" has the meaning given to it by section 47 above.

[(1AA) Where high security psychiatric services and other services are provided at a hospital, the part of the hospital at which high security psychiatric services are provided and the other part shall be treated as separate hospitals for the purposes of this Act.]

[(1AB) References in this Act to appropriate medical treatment shall be construed in accordance with section 3(4) above.]

[(1AC) References in this Act to an approved mental health professional shall be construed as references to an approved mental health professional acting on behalf of a local social services authority, unless the context otherwise requires.]

[(1A) . . .]

(2) [. . .]

(3) In relation to a person who is liable to be detained or subject to guardianship [or a community patient] by virtue of an order or direction under Part III of this Act (other than under section 35, 36, or 38), any reference in this Act to any enactment contained in Part II of this Act or in section 66 or 67 above shall be construed as a reference to that enactment as it applies to that person by virtue of Part III of this Act.

[(4) Any reference in this Act to medical treatment, in relation to mental disorder, shall be construed as a reference to medical treatment the purpose of which is to alleviate, or prevent a worsening of, the disorder or one or more of its symptoms or manifestations.]

AMENDMENTS

The amendments to this section were made by the National Health Service and Community Care Act 1990 s.66(1), Sch.9 para.24(9), the Health Authorities Act 1995 s.2(1), Sch.1 para.107(14), the Mental Health (Patients in the Community) Act 1995 s.1(2), Sch.1 para.20, the Health Act 1999 s.65, Sch.4 para.69, the Crime (Sentences) Act 1997 s.55, Sch.4 para.12(19), the Health Act 1999 (Supplementary, Consequential, etc. Provisions) Order 2000 (SI 2000/90) Sch.1 para.16(9), the Care Standards Act 2000 ss.116, 117(2) Sch.4 para.9(10), Sch.6, the National Health Service and Health Care Professions Act 2002 s.2(5), Sch.2 para.49, the National Health Service Reform and Health Care Professions Act 2002 (Supplementary, Consequential, etc. Provisions) Regulations 2002 (SI 2002/2469) reg.4, Sch.1, the Mental Health Act 2007 ss.1(4), 4, 7(2)(3), 14(5), 21, 32(4), 46, Sch.1 para.17, Sch.2 para.11(2)(3), Sch.3 para.34, SI 2007/961 art.3, Sch. para.13(13), SI 2008/2883 art.9, Sch.3 para.66, the Health and Social Care Act 2008 s.52, Sch.3 para.13 and SI 2010/813, art.5(5), the Mental Health Act 2007 s.55, Sch.11 Pt 5, the Statute Law (Repeals) Act 1993 s.1(1), Sch.1 Pt XIV, Group 2, the Mental Health (Amendment) Act 1994 s.1, the Mental Capacity Act 2005 s.67(2), Sch.7, the Health and Social Care (Community Health and Standards) Act 2003 s.34, Sch.4 para.57, the Health Act 1999 s.65, Sch.4 para.69, Sch.5, the National Health Service (Consequential Provisions) Act 2006 s.2, Sch.1, para.70, the Health and Social Care Act 2012 s.39(4), Sch.5, para.31, the Mental Health (Discrimination) Act 2013 s.1(1), Sch., para.1(1) and the Care Act 2014 s.75(13).

GENERAL NOTE

Subsection (1)

1–1377   APPROVED CLINICIAN.   The Secretary of State's "Instructions with respect to the exercise of Approval Functions 2014", which establish the criteria for approval as an Approved Clinician (AC), are reproduced at Appendix D. Approval is for the whole of England. Unlike s.12, no explicit test for approval of an AC is given in the Act. Doctors who are approved as ACs are automatically approved as doctors who are approved under s.12(2) (s.12(2A)). For Wales, see the Mental Health Act 1983 Approved Clinician (Wales) Directions 2008. See s.142A for the mutual recognition of approval as an AC in England and Wales.

The Mental Health (Approval Functions) Act 2012 was passed to retrospectively validate the approval of clinicians where the approval function had been unlawfully delegated: see the note on the 2012 Act in the General Note to s.12.

1–1378   HIGH SECURITY PSYCHIATRIC SERVICES.   These comprise:

> "hospital accommodation and services for persons who are—(a) liable to be detained under the Mental Health Act 1983, and (b) in the opinion of the Secretary of State require treatment under conditions of high security on account of their dangerous, violent or criminal propensities" (National Health Service Act 2006 s.4(1)).

The National Health Service Commissioning Board has been directed to perform certain functions with respect to high security psychiatric services: see the High Security Psychiatric Services (National Health Service Commissioning Board) Directions 2013.

HOSPITAL.   The definition of hospital in s.275(1) of the 2006 Act is very broad:

> "'hospital' means—
>
> (a) any institution for the reception and treatment of persons suffering from illness,
> (b) any maternity home, and
> (c) any institution for the reception and treatment of persons during convalescence or persons requiring medical rehabilitation,
>
> and includes clinics, dispensaries and out-patient departments maintained in connection with any such home or institution, and 'hospital accommodation' must be construed accordingly".

In *Re Couchman's Will Trusts* [1952] Ch. 391, Danckwerts J. considered a similar definition in s.79(1) of the National Health Service Act 1946 and held that:

1. "Reception" means taking people into a building and keeping them there. An institution that confines itself to treating patients as out-patients does not qualify.

2. The phrase "maintained in connection with" means maintained in connection with a particular hospital. It does not cover a clinic which was "maintained for the purpose of dealing with people who needed subsequent treatment, and it would have dealt with persons coming from any hospital—a hospital, perhaps in another country—or with persons who were not connected with any hospital".

The definition, which is not confined to mental hospitals (*IM (Nigeria) v Secretary of State for the Home Department* [2013] EWCA Civ 1561, para.19), does not include an independent hospital, which is brought within the scope of the Act by s.34(1)(2) and s.55(5).

By virtue of s.8(1) of the Health and Social Care Act 2008 and reg.3 and Sch.1 to SI 2014/2936, a hospital which provides for the assessment or medical treatment (other than surgical procedures) of patients detained under the Act (with the exception of s.135

or 136) must be registered for that activity by the Care Quality Commission. Such registration "is not required to provide assessment or treatment of mental disorder to patients who are detained by another authority, but admitted to the treating hospital under the powers to grant leave of absence from the place of detention under MHA 1983, section 17. This will be the case even if the detaining authority authorises that the patient remains in the custody of the treating hospital" ("Use of the Mental Health Act 1983 in general hospitals without a psychiatric unit" CQC, April 2010).

Prison healthcare centres are excluded from the definition as such facilities are provided under prison legislation. Responsibility for prison health care was fully transferred from HM Prison Service to the NHS in April 2006. The Government has stated that "prisoners should have access to the same range and quality of services appropriate to their needs as are available to the general population through the NHS" (*Changing the Outlook*, DH and MHPS, 2001, p.5). This policy was considered in *Roberts v Secretary of State for Justice* [2009] EWHC 2321, where Michael Supperstone QC said at para.20:

"In my view, if there is any restriction on the access that prisoners have to health services so that prisoners are not provided with access to the same range and quality of healthcare services as the general public receives, it is in the public interest that such restriction be published and made generally known."

In *Riviere v France* (App.No.33834/03) the European Court of Human Rights observed that Recommendation No. R (98) 7 of the Committee of Ministers of the Council of Europe concerning the ethical and organisational aspects of health care in prison provides that prisoners suffering from serious mental disturbance should be kept and cared for in a hospital facility that was adequately equipped and possessed appropriately trained staff.

THE MANAGERS.   General guidance on the functions of the hospital managers is given in Ch.37 of the *Code of Practice*. Managers are accountable for the lawfulness of each patient's detention under the Act (ss.6(2), 40(1)(b)).

The *Code of Practice* states:

"37.3 Hospital managers have the authority to detain patients under the Act. They have the primary responsibility for seeing that the requirements of the Act are followed. In particular, they must ensure that patients are detained only as the Act allows, that their treatment and care accord fully with its provisions, and that they are fully informed of, and are supported in exercising, their statutory rights.

37.4 As managers of what the Act terms 'responsible hospitals', hospital managers have equivalent responsibilities towards CTO patients, even if those patients are not actually being treated at one of their hospitals."

When a detained patient is transferred to the detention of different hospital managers, any outstanding responsibilities of the original hospital managers, such as the duty to hold a review, are transferred to the new hospital managers.

"Hospitals vested in the Secretary of State" include hospitals vested in the Welsh Ministers for the purposes of their functions under the National Health Service (Wales) Act 2006 (see the General Note to the Act and SI 2000/253, Sch.3).

The managers of an independent hospital act as a "public authority" within s.6 of the Human Rights Act 1998 when making decisions relating to the staffing and/or facilities to be provided to a detained patient (*R. (on the application of A) v Partnerships in Care* [2002] EWHC 529 (Admin); [2002] 1 W.L.R. 2610).

MEDICAL TREATMENT.   In *Secretary of State for Justice v RB* [2011] EWCA Civ 1608; **1–1379** [2012] M.H.L.R. 131, paras 25, 26, the Court of Appeal said that the policy of the Act is treatment, not containment.

This definition, which should be considered along with subs.(4), is inclusive, not exhaustive. It includes interventions that are not ordinarily considered to be "medical". The definition does not deal with the willingness of any person to accept treatment ((*R. (on the application of SP) v Secretary of State for Justice* [2010] EWCA Civ 1590; [2011] M.H.L.R. 65, para.4). Medical treatment for the purposes of the Act includes the specific treatments mentioned in Pt IV. Cases on the definition prior to its amendment by the 2007 Act confirmed that the mere fact of being cared for or nursed is sufficient to constitute medical treatment: see, for example *R. v Mersey Mental Health Review Tribunal Ex p. D*, DC, *The Times*, April 13, 1987, where the continued detention of the patient was upheld even though there was nothing other than nursing care that could be provided for him. Ward round reviews may be part of a patient's medical treatment (*KL v Somerset Partnership NHS Foundation Trust* [2011] UKUT 233 (AAC); [2011] M.H.L.R. 194, para.9). In *R. (on the application of Epsom and St Helier NHS Trust) v Mental Health Review Tribunal* [2001] EWHC 101; [2001] M.H.L.R. 8, Sullivan J. said at para.47:

> "[O]ne has to look at the whole course of treatment. To do so, one has to look at the past, present and future. It is not enough to say that a patient is not receiving treatment at a particular time."

In *Re Ian Brady*, December 11, 2013, at para.207, the First-tier Tribunal (Mental Health) "observed that this sub-section does not seek to provide a comprehensive definition. It sets out various actions which may be taken when seeking to assist a patient. There may be a degree of overlap of the nature of that assistance encompassed by the items mentioned but they must also connote some different action. Thus, in the opinion of the Tribunal whilst 'specialist care' may include 'nursing' it must also encompass other actions. Conversely, 'nursing' does not necessarily encompass 'specialist care'. This indicates the width of meaning of the term 'treatment'".

As the definition of mental disorder in s.1(2) includes "paraphilias like fetishism or paedophilia" (Explanatory Notes, para.24), medication which acts as a sexual suppressant could be medical treatment for the purposes of this provision.

In *R. (on the application of Munjaz) v Mersey Care National Health Service Trust* [2005] UKHL 58; [2005] M.H.L.R. 276, para.19, Lord Bingham said that the definition of "medical treatment" in this sub-section is "wide enough to cover the nursing and caring of a patient in seclusion, even though seclusion cannot properly form part of a treatment programme".

Enquiries made to a third party about either the patient's diagnosis or treatment are enquiries made with a view to treatment and do not themselves constitute treatment: see *R. (on the application of O'Reilly) v Blenheim Healthcare Ltd* [2005] EWHC 241 (Admin) where Stanley Burnton J. said, at para.14, that it "does not follow from [the judgment in *B v Croydon Health Authority* [1995] 1 All E.R. 683] that acts carried out for the purposes of treatment, or with a view to deciding on treatment, are themselves treatment".

Practical examples of psychological interventions include "cognitive therapy, behaviour therapy and counselling" (Explanatory Notes, para.39).

A decision to transfer a patient to another hospital can, in certain circumstances, be regarded as part of the patient's medical treatment: see *R. (on the application of F) v Oxfordshire Mental Healthcare NHS Trust* [2001] EWHC 535 (Admin); [2002] M.H.L.R. 140 where Sullivan J. said at para.68:

> "Treatment includes rehabilitation, and I can envisage cases where transfer to a particular institution because of the particular form of therapy available there would be a necessary step in the patient's rehabilitation."

Also see *C v Birmingham and Solihull Mental Health NHS Trust* [2013] EWCA Civ 701, para.15, where Laws L.J. accepted a submission that "leave of absence and transfer are, or may be, functions of a patient's treatment, sometimes an important part".

An illustration of the distinction between habilitation and rehabilitation was given by Mr Terry Davis MP at the Special Standing Committee on the Mental Health (Amendment) Bill 1982:

"'Habilitation' would cover those cases in which someone, probably a child, was so severely mentally impaired that he had never learnt certain social skills such as being able to eat or communicate in some way. The remedying of that impairment cannot be called 'rehabilitation' because that person never had those skills, so one has to use the word 'habilitation' in its technical sense" (Sitting of June 22, 1982).

PATIENT. In *R. v Davies* [2000] Crim. L.R. 297, the Court of Appeal considered a similar definition of patient found in s.22 of the Registered Homes Act 1984. The court said:

"It is obvious that a person may be receiving treatment for mental disorder, without actually suffering from it, if he or she *appears* to be suffering from it. Much medical diagnosis and treatment is based on probability, not certainty or therefore, in some cases, actuality."

In *R. v Merseyside Mental Health Review Tribunal Ex p. K* [1990] 1 All E.R. 694 CA, the appellant, a restricted patient, sought judicial review of the tribunal's decision on the ground that once it had found as a fact that he was not suffering from mental disorder he was no longer a "patient" as defined in this section and he was therefore entitled to an absolute discharge. The Court of Appeal affirmed the tribunal's decision to grant the patient a conditional discharge and held that a restricted patient remains a "patient" until he is discharged absolutely. Butler-Sloss L.J. said at 699:

"At the time the offender is detained under a hospital order he is a patient within the interpretation of section 145. By section 41(3)(a) a restricted patient continues to be liable to be detained until discharged under section 73 and, in my judgment, remains a patient until he is discharged absolutely, if at all, by the tribunal. Any other interpretation of the word 'patient' makes nonsense of the framework of the 1983 Act and the hoped-for progression to discharge of the treatable patient, treatable being a prerequisite of his original admission."

REGULATORY AUTHORITY. The regulatory functions of the Welsh Ministers under the Act are performed by Health Inspectorate Wales.

Subsection (1AA)
If a hospital contains a unit where high security services are provided, that unit is treated **1–1380** as a separate hospital for the purposes of the Act.

Subsection (1AC)
The fact that the AMHP acts on behalf of the local authority does not provide the auth- **1–1381** ority with a power to direct the AMHP to make a particular decision while performing a function under the Act: see the note on s.114(10).

In *DD v Durham County Council* [2012] EWHC 1053 (QB); [2012] M.H.L.R. 245, para.21, Eady J. said:

"It seems clear from this [provision] that the legislative purpose is to ensure that there will be a local social services authority available to stand in the shoes of any AMHP against whom a claim is made. The section is neutral as to whether there has to exist any employment or other contractual relationship between the relevant authority and the AMHP in question."

Subsection (3)

1–1382   I gratefully adopt Phil Fennell's interpretation of this obscurely drafted provision:

"For certain purposes, such as the renewal of detention, and entitlement to [tribunals hearings], parties liable to be detained under Part III are treated as if liable to be detained under section 3. What section 145(3) does is to ensure that this happens subject to the modifications specified in sections 40(4), 41(3) and (5), 55(4) and Schedule 1, Part 1. . . . The modifications relate to the powers to remand and to sentence to interim hospital orders. People who are on remand remain under the jurisdiction of the courts. They are liable to be detained, but they remain under the jurisdiction of the courts rather than the mental health system. The reason that they are expressly mentioned in section 145(3) is that they have no rights to seek discharge from a [tribunal]" ("Double Detention under the Mental Health Act 1984—A Case of Extra Parliamentary Legislation?" [1991] J.S.W.F.L. 200).

Subsection (4)

1–1383   This provision was tabled as an amendment to the Mental Health Bill by a backbencher. It received cross party support and was accepted by the Government because of the concerns that had been expressed about the absence of any reference to therapeutic benefit in the appropriate treatment test: see the notes on s.3(2)(d). The test set out here is one of an intention to bring about therapeutic benefit, rather than the likelihood of achieving such benefit. In *MD v Nottinghamshire Health Care NHS Trust* [2010] UKUT 59 (AAC) [2010] M.H.L.R. 93, para.34, UT Judge Jacobs said:

"Section 145(4) provides that it is sufficient if the treatment is for the purpose of preventing a worsening of the symptoms or manifestations. That envisages that the treatment required may not reduce risk. It is also sufficient if it will alleviate but one of the symptoms or manifestations, regardless of the impact on the risk posed by the patient."

The *Code of Practice* states:

"23.4 Purpose is not the same as likelihood. Medical treatment must be for the purpose of alleviating or preventing a worsening of mental disorder even if it cannot be shown, in advance, that a particular effect is likely to be achieved.

23.5 Symptoms and manifestations include the way a disorder is experienced by the individual concerned and the way in which the disorder manifests itself in the person's thoughts, emotions, communication, behaviour and actions. It should be remembered that not every thought or emotion or every aspect of the behaviour, of a patient suffering from mental disorder will be a manifestation of that disorder."

Baroness Royall, speaking for the Government, explained the distinction between symptoms and manifestations:

"[S]ymptoms and manifestations are intended to cover all the ways that the disorder affects the patient's functioning, in terms of how the patient thinks, feels or believes. While there is almost certainly some overlap between the two, broadly speaking we think that 'symptoms' covers the consequences of which patients themselves complain while 'manifestations' more obviously covers the evidence of the disorder as seen by other people. In the end, the important point is not the distinction between the two words but the certainty that between them they cover the whole gamut of what can be addressed by medical treatment" (*Hansard*, HL Vol.693, col.835).

Application to Scotland

146. Sections 42(6), 80, [. . .], 116, [. . .], [. . .], [. . .], 137, 139(1), [. . .], 142, **1–1384**
143 (so far as applicable to any Order in Council extending to Scotland) and 144
above shall extend to Scotland together with any amendment or repeal by this Act
or any provision of Schedule 5 to this Act relating to any enactment which so
extends; but, except as aforesaid and except so far as it relates to the interpretation
or commencement of the said provisions, this Act shall not extend to Scotland.

AMENDMENTS

The words omitted were repealed by the Mental Capacity Act 2005 s.67(2), Sch.7, the
Mental Health Act 2007 s.55, Sch.11 Pts 5 and 7, the Health and Social Care Act 2013
s.41 and the Mental Health (Discrimination) Act s.1(1), Sch., para.1(2).

DEFINITION
    patient: s.145(1).   **1–1385**

GENERAL NOTE
    This section provides for a limited application to the Act to Scotland.   **1–1386**

Application to Northern Ireland

147. Sections 81, 82, 86, 87, 88 (and so far as applied by that section sections **1–1387**
18, 22, and 138), [. . .], section 128 (except so far as it relates to patients subject to
guardianship), 137, 139, [. . .], 142, 143 (so far as applicable to any Order in
Council extending to Northern Ireland) and 144 above shall extend to Northern
Ireland together with any amendment or repeal by this Act of or any provision
of Schedule 5 to this Act relating to any enactment which so extends; but except
as aforesaid and except so far as it relates to the interpretation or commencement
of the said provisions, this Act shall not extend to Northern Ireland.

AMENDMENTS

The amendments to this section were made by the Mental Capacity Act 2005, s.67(2),
Sch.7 and the Mental Health (Discrimination) Act 2013 s.1(1), Sch., para.1(3).

DEFINITION
    patient: s.145(1).   **1–1388**

GENERAL NOTE
    This section provides for a limited application of the Act to Northern Ireland.   **1–1389**

Consequential and transitional provisions and repeals

148.—(1) Schedule 4 (consequential amendments) and Schedule 5 (transitional **1–1390**
and saving provisions) to this Act shall have effect but without prejudice to the
operation of sections 15 to 17 of the Interpretation Act 1978 (which relate to
the effect of repeals).

(2) Where any amendment in Schedule 4 to this Act affects an enactment
amended by the Mental Health (Amendment) Act 1982 the amendment in
Schedule 4 shall come into force immediately after the provision of the Act of
1982 amending that enactment.

(3) The enactments specified in Schedule 6 to this Act are hereby repealed to
the extent mentioned in the third column of that Schedule.

Short title, commencement and application to Scilly Isles

1–1391   **149.**—(1) This Act may be cited as the Mental Health Act 1983.

(2) Subject to subsection (3) below and Schedule 5 to this Act, this Act shall come into force on September 30, 1983.

(3) [*Repealed by the Statute Law (Repeals) Act 2004, Sch.1, Pt 17, Group 8.*]

(4) Section 130(4) of the National Health Service Act 1977 (which provides for the extension of that Act to the Isles of Scilly) shall have effect as if the references to that Act included references to this Act.

GENERAL NOTE

Subsection (4)

1–1392   The Isles of Scilly (Mental Health) Order 1985 (SI 1985/149) extends the Act to the Isles of Scilly from March 12, 1985, with the modification that the expression "local social services authority" in the Act shall, in relation to the Isles, mean the Council of the Isles of Scilly.

SCHEDULES

Sections 40(4),   SCHEDULE 1
41(3) and (5),
and 55(4)

APPLICATION OF CERTAIN PROVISIONS TO PATIENTS SUBJECT TO HOSPITAL AND
GUARDIANSHIP ORDERS

PART I

PATIENTS NOT SUBJECT TO SPECIAL RESTRICTIONS

1–1393   1. Sections 9, 10, 17 [to 17C, 17E, 17F, 20A], [21 to 21B], [. . .], [26] to 28, 31, 32, 34, 67 and 76 shall apply in relation to the patient without modification.

2. Sections [. . .], [17D, 17G, 18 to 20, 20B], 22, 23[, 66 and 68] shall apply in relation to the patient with the modifications specified in [paragraphs 2A][to 10] below.

[2A In section 17D(2)(a) for the reference to section 6(2) above there shall be substituted a reference to section 40(1)(b) below.

2B In section 17G—

(a) in subsection (2) for the reference to section 6(2) above there shall be substituted a reference to section 40(1)(b) below;

(b) in subsection (4) for paragraphs (a) and (b) there shall be substituted the words "the order or direction under Part 3 of this Act in respect of him were an order or direction for his admission or removal to that other hospital"; and

(c) in subsection (5) for the words from "the patient" to the end there shall be substituted the words "the date of the relevant order or direction under Part 3 of this Act were the date on which the community treatment order is revoked".]

3. [. . .]

4. In section 18 subsection (5) shall be omitted.

5. In section 19(2) for the words from "as follows" to the end of the subsection there shall be substituted the words "as if the order or direction under Part III of this Act by virtue of which he was liable to be detained or subject to guardianship before being transferred were an order or direction for his admission or removal to the hospital to which he is transferred, or placing him under the guardianship of the authority or person into whose guardianship he is transferred, as the case may be".

[5A In section 19A(2), paragraph (b) shall be omitted.]

6. In section 20—

(a) in subsection (1) for the words from "day on which he was" to "as the case may be" there shall be substituted the words "date of the relevant order or direction under Part III of this Act;" [. . .]

[6A In section 20B(1), for the reference to the application for admission for treatment there shall be substituted a reference to the order or direction under Part 3 of this Act by virtue of which the patient is liable to be detained.]

7. In section 22 for references to an application for admission or a guardianship application there shall be substituted references to the order or direction under Part III of this Act by virtue of which the patient is liable to be detained or subject to guardianship.

8. In section 23(2)—

(a) in paragraph (a) the words "for assessment or" shall be omitted; and

(b) in paragraphs (a) [to (c)] the references to the nearest relative shall be omitted.

[. . .]

9. In section 66—

(a) in subsection (1), paragraphs (a), (b), (c), (g) and (h), the words in parenthesis in paragraph (i) and paragraph (ii) shall be omitted; and

(b) in subsection (2), paragraphs (a), (b), (c) and (g) [, and in paragraph (d), "(g)", shall be omitted.]

[10. In section 68—

(a) in subsection (1) paragraph (a) shall be omitted; and

(b) subsections (2) to (5) shall apply if the patient falls within paragraph (e) of subsection (1), but not otherwise.]

AMENDMENTS

The amendments to this Part were made by the Mental Health (Patients in the Community) Act 1995 s.2(1), Sch.1, the Mental Health Act 2007 ss.32(4), 36(4), 37(6), 55, Sch.3 para.36, Sch.11 Pts 1 and 5 and the Health and Social Care Act 2012 s.39.

PART II

PATIENTS SUBJECT TO SPECIAL RESTRICTIONS

1. Sections [. . .] 32 and 76 shall apply in relation to the patient without modification.

1–1394

2. Sections [17, 18, 19], 22, 23 and 34 shall apply in relation to the patient with the modifications specified in paragraphs 3 to 8 below.

3. In section 17—

(a) in subsection (1) after the word "may" there shall be inserted the words "with the consent of the Secretary of State";

[(aa) subsections (2A) and (2B) shall be omitted;]

(b) in subsection (4) after the words ["the responsible clinician"] and after the words ["that clinician"] there shall be inserted the words "or the Secretary of State"; and

(c) in subsection (5) after the word "recalled" there shall be inserted the words ["by the responsible clinician"], and for the words from "he has ceased" to the end of the subsection there shall be substituted the words "the expiration of the period of [twelve] months beginning with the first day of his absence on leave".

4. In section 18 there shall be omitted—

(a) in subsection (1) the words "subject to the provisions of this section"; and

(b) subsections (3), (4) and (5).

5. In section 19—

(a) in subsection (1) after the word "may" in paragraph (a) there shall be inserted the words "with the consent of the Secretary of State", and the words from "or into" to the end of the subsection shall be omitted; [. . .]

(b) in subsection (2) for the words from "as follows" to the end of the subsection there shall be substituted the words "as if the order or direction under Part III of this Act by virtue of which he was liable to be detained before being transferred were an order or direction for his admission or removal to the hospital to which he is transferred" [and

(c) in subsection (3) after the words "may at any time" there shall be inserted the words ", with the consent of the Secretary of State",]

[6. In section 22, subsections (1) and (5) shall not apply.]
7. In section 23—

(a) in subsection (1) references to guardianship shall be omitted and after the word "made" there shall be inserted the words "with the consent of the Secretary of State and"

(b) in subsection (2)—

    (i) in paragraph (a) the words "for assessment or" and "or by the nearest relative of the patient" shall be omitted; and
    (ii) paragraph (b) shall be omitted.

8. In section 34, in subsection (1) the definition of "the nominated medical attendant" and subsection (3) shall be omitted.

AMENDMENTS

The amendments to this Part were made by the Mental Health Act 2007 ss.11(8), 33(4), 33(3), Sch.3 para.37, the Crime (Sentences) Act 1997 ss.49(3), 56(2), Sch.6 and the Health and Social Care Act 2012 s.39.

Section 65(2)   **SCHEDULE 2**

MENTAL HEALTH REVIEW [TRIBUNAL FOR WALES]

1–1395   1. [The Mental Health Review Tribunal for Wales] shall consist of—

(a) a number of persons (referred to in this Schedule as "the legal members") appointed by the Lord Chancellor and having such legal experience as the Lord Chancellor considers suitable;

(b) a number of persons (referred to in this Schedule as "the medical members") being registered medical practitioners appointed by the Lord Chancellor [. . .]; and

(c) a number of persons appointed by the Lord Chancellor [. . .] and having such experience in administration, such knowledge of social services or such other qualifications or experience as the Lord Chancellor considers suitable.

[1A. As part of the selection process for an appointment under paragraph 1(b) or (c) the Judicial Appointments Commission shall consult the Secretary of State.]
2. [Subject to paragraph 2A below,] the members of [the Mental Health Review Tribunal for Wales] shall hold and vacate office under the terms of the instrument under which they are appointed, but may resign office by notice in writing to the Lord Chancellor; and any such member who ceases to hold office shall be eligible for re-appointment.
[2A. A member of [the Mental Health Review Tribunal for Wales] shall vacate office on the day on which he attains the age of 70 years; but this paragraph is subject to section 26(4) to (6) of the Judicial Pensions and Retirement Act 1993 (power to authorise continuance in office up to the age of 75 years).]

[3. (1) [. . .]
(2) The Lord Chancellor shall appoint one of the legal members of the Mental Health Review Tribunal for Wales to be the President of that tribunal.]

4. Subject to rules made by the Lord Chancellor under section 78(2)(c) above, the members who are to constitute [the Mental Health Review Tribunal for Wales] for the purposes of any proceedings or class or group of proceedings under this Act shall be appointed by the chairman of the tribunal or [. . .], by another member of the tribunal appointed for the purpose by the chairman; and of the members so appointed—

(a) one or more shall be appointed from the legal members;

(b) one or more shall be appointed from the medical members; and

(c) one or more shall be appointed from the members who are neither legal nor medical members.

[5.—(1) A member of the First-tier Tribunal who is eligible to decide any matter in a case under this Act may, at the request of the President of the Mental Health Review Tribunal for Wales and with the approval of the Senior President of Tribunals, act as a member of the Mental Health Review Tribunal for Wales.

(2) Every person while acting under this paragraph may perform any of the functions of a member of the Mental Health Review Tribunal for Wales.

(3) Until section 38(7) of the Mental Health Act 2007 comes into force, the reference in sub-paragraph (1) to the President of the Mental Health Review Tribunal for Wales is to be read as a reference to the chairman of the tribunal.]

6. Subject to any rules made by the Lord Chancellor under section 78(4)(a) above, where the chairman of the tribunal is included among the persons appointed under para.4 above, he shall be President of the tribunal; and in any other case the chairman of the tribunal shall be such one of the members so appointed (being one of the legal members) as the chairman may nominate.

AMENDMENTS

The amendments to this Schedule were made by the Judicial Pensions and Retirement Act 1993 s.26, Sch.6 para.40, the Constitutional Reform Act 2005 ss.15, 146, Sch.4 para.158(3), Sch.18 Pt.2; the Mental Health Act 2007 s.38(7)(b); SI 2008/2833 art.9, Sch.3 para.67; and SI 2009/1307 art.5, Sch.1 para.162.

GENERAL NOTE

The President and members of the MHRT for Wales are subject to the selection process **1–1396** set out in ss.86 to 93 of the Constitutional Reform Act 2005 (s.85, Sch.14 Pt 3).

Paragraph 1

THE LORD CHANCELLOR. Who, in the exercise of his functions under this provision in **1–1397** relation to Wales, is required to consult with the Welsh Ministers with regard to appointments made under paragraphs (b) and (c) (see the General Note to the Act and SI 1999/ 672 art.5, Sch.2). The Lord Chancellor cannot transfer his functions under this paragraph, or under paras 2 or 3, to another person (Constitutional Reform Act 2005 s.19, Sch.7).

Paragraph 5

This allows members of the First-tier Tribunal who may hear mental health cases to sit in **1–1398** the Mental Health Review Tribunal for Wales. There is no reciprocal arrangement.

Section 113   **SCHEDULE 3**

1–1399   *[Repealed by the Mental Capacity Act 2005 s.67(2), Sch.7.]*

Section 148   **SCHEDULE 4**

CONSEQUENTIAL AMENDMENTS

1–1400   *[Not reproduced.]*

Section 148   **SCHEDULE 5**

TRANSITIONAL AND SAVING PROVISIONS

1–1401   1. Where any period of time specified in an enactment repealed by this Act is current at the commencement of this Act, this Act shall have effect as if the corresponding provision of this Act had been in force when that period began to run.

2. Nothing in this Act shall affect the interpretation of any provision of the Mental Health Act 1959 which is not repealed by this Act and accordingly sections 1 and 145(1) of this Act shall apply to any such provision as if it were contained in this Act.

3. Where, apart from this paragraph, anything done under or for the purposes of any enactment which is repealed by this Act would cease to have effect by virtue of that repeal it shall have effect as if it had been done under or for the purposes of the corresponding provisions of this Act.

4. [. . .]

5. [. . .]

6. This Act shall apply in relation to any authority for the detention or guardianship of a person who was liable to be detained or subject to guardianship under the Mental Health Act 1959 immediately before September 30, 1983 as if the provisions of this Act which derive from provisions amended by section 1 or 2 of the Mental Health (Amendment) Act 1982 and the amendments in Sch.3 to that Act which are consequential on those sections were included in this Act in the form the provisions from which they derive would take if those amendments were disregarded but this provision shall not apply to any renewal of that authority on or after that date.

7. [. . .]

8. [. . .]

9.—(1) [. . .]

(2) Section 20(2) of this Act shall have effect in relation to any authority renewed before October 1, 1983 with the substitution for the words "six months" of the words "one year" and for the words "one year" in both places they occur of the words "two years".

(3) [. . .]

10. [. . .]

11. [. . .]

12. [. . .]

13. [. . .]

14. [. . .]

15. The provisions of this Act which derive from sections 24 to 27 of the Mental Health (Amendment) Act 1982 shall have effect in relation to a transfer direction given before September 30, 1983 as well as in relation to one given later, but where, apart from this paragraph, a transfer direction given before September 30, 1983 would by virtue of the words in section 50(3) of this Act which are derived from section 24(3) of the Mental Health (Amendment) Act 1982 have ceased to have effect before that date it shall cease to have effect on that date.

16. The words in section 42(1) of this Act which derive from the amendment of section 66(1) of the Mental Health Act 1959 by section 28(1) of the Mental Health (Amendment) Act 1982 and the provisions of this Act which derive from section 28(3) of and Sch.1 to that Act have in relation to a restriction order or, as the case may be, a restriction direction made or given before September 30, 1983 as well as in relation to one made or given later, but—

(a) any reference to a tribunal under section 66(6) of the said Act of 1959 in respect of a patient shall be treated for the purposes of subsections (1) and (2) of section 77 of this Act in their application to sections 70 and 75(2) of this Act as an application made by him; and

(b) sections 71(5) and 75(1)(*a*) of this Act do not apply where the period in question has expired before September 30, 1983.

17. Section 91(2) of this Act shall not apply in relation to a patient removed from England and Wales before September 30, 1983.

18.[. . .]

19. [. . .]

20. The repeal by the Mental Health (Amendment) Act 1982 of section 77 of the Mental Health Act **1–1402** 1959 does not affect subsection (4) of that section in its application to a transfer direction given before September 30, 1983, but after the coming into force of this Act that subsection shall effect for that purpose as if for the references to subsection (6) of section 60, Part IV of that Act and the provisions of that Act there were substituted respectively references to section 37(8), Part III and the provisions of this Act.

[21. Any direction to which section 71(4) of the Mental Health Act 1959 applied immediately before the commencement of this Act shall have the same effect as a hospital order together with a restriction order, made without limitation of time.]

22. [. . .]

23. For any reference in any enactment, instrument, deed or other document to a receiver under Part VIII of the Mental Health Act 1959 there shall be substituted a reference to a receiver under Part VII of this Act.

24. Nothing in this Act shall affect the operation of the proviso to section 107(5) of the Mental Health Act 1959 in relation to a charge created before the commencement of this Act under that section.

25. Nothing in this Act shall affect the operation of subsection (6) of section 112 of the Mental Health Act 1959 in relation to a charge created before the commencement of this Act by virtue of subsection (5) of that section.

26. [. . .]

27. Nothing in this Act shall affect the operation of section 116 of the Mental Health Act 1959 in relation to orders made, directions or authorities given or other instruments issued before the commencement of this Act.

28. References to applications, recommendations, reports and other documents in section 126 of this Act shall include those to which sections 125 of the Mental Health Act 1959 applied immediately before the commencement of this Act and references in section 139 of this Act to the acts to which that section applies shall include those to which section 141 of the said Act of 1959 applied at that time.

29. The repeal by the Mental Health Act 1959 of the Mental Treatment Act 1930 shall not affect any amendment effected by section 20 of that Act in any enactment not repealed by the said Act of 1959.

30. The repeal by the Mental Health Act 1959 of the provisions of the Lunacy Act 1890 and of the Mental Deficiency Act 1913 relating to the superannuation of officers or employees shall not affect any arrangements for the payment of allowances or other benefits made in accordance with those provisions and in force on November 1, 1960.

31.—(1) Any patient who immediately before the commencement of this Act was liable to be detained in a hospital or subject to guardianship by virtue of para.9 of Sch.6 to the Mental Health Act 1959 shall unless previously discharged continue to be so liable for the remainder of the period of his treatment current on November 1, 1960.

(2) The patient may before the expiration of the period of treatment referred to in sub-paragraph (1) above apply to a Mental Health Review Tribunal.

32. Any patient who immediately before the commencement of this Act was liable to be detained or subject to guardianship by virtue of an authority which had been renewed under para.11 of Sch.6 to the Mental Health Act 1959 shall unless previously discharged continue to be so liable during the period for which that authority was so renewed.

33.—(1) This paragraph applies to patients who at the commencement of this Act are liable to be detained or subject to guardianship by virtue of para.31 or 32 above.

(2) Authority for the detention or guardianship of the patient may on the expiration of the relevant period, unless the patient has previously been discharged, be renewed for a further period of two years.

(3) Sections 20(3) to (10) and 66(1)(*f*) of this Act shall apply in relation to the renewal of authority for the detenton or guardianship of a patient under this paragraph as they apply in relation to the renewal of authority for the detention or guardianship of the patient under section 20(2).

(4) In this paragraph "the relevant period" means—

(a) in relation to a patient liable to be detained or subject to guardianship by virtue of the said paragraph 31, the period of his treatment referred to in that paragraph;

(b) in relation to a patient detained by virtue of the said paragraph 32, the period for which authority for the detention or guardianship of the patient has been renewed under paragraph 11 of Schedule 6 to the 1959 Act;

(c) in relation to a patient the authority for whose detention or guardianship has previously been renewed under this paragraph, the latest period for which it has been so renewed.

34.—(1) Any patient who is liable to be detained in a hospital or subject to guardianship by virtue of para.31 above shall (subject to the exceptions and modifications specified in the following provisions of this paragraph) be treated as if he has been admitted to the hospital in pursuance of an application for admission for treatment under Part II of this Act or had been received into guardianship in pursuance of a guardianship application under the said Part II and had been so admitted or received as a patient suffering from the form or forms of mental disorder recorded under para.7 of Sch.6 to the Mental Health Act 1959 or, if a different form or forms have been specified in a report under section 38 of the Act as applied by that paragraph, the form or forms so specified.

(2) Section 20 of this Act shall not apply in relation to the patient, but the provisions of para.33 above shall apply instead.

(3) Any patient to whom para.9(3) of Sch.6 to the Mental Health Act 1959 applied at the commencement of this Act who fell within paragraph (b) of that paragraph shall cease to be liable to be detained on attaining the age of 25 years unless, during the period of two months ending on the date when he attains that age, the responsible medical officers records his opinion under the following provisions of this Schedule that the patient is unfit for discharge.

(4) If the patient was immediately before November 1, 1960 liable to be detained by virtue of section 6, 8(1) or 9 of the Mental Deficiency Act 1913, the power of discharging him under section 23 of this Act shall not be exercisable by his nearest relative, but his nearest relative may make one application in respect of him to [the appropriate tribunal] in any period of 12 months.

35.—(1) The responsible medical officer may record for the purposes of para.34(3) above his opinion that a patient detained in a hospital is unfit for discharge if it appears to the responsible medical officer—

(a) that if that patient were released from the hospital he would be likely to act in a manner dangerous to other persons or to himself, or would be likely to resort to criminal activities; or

(b) that that patient is incapable of caring for himself and that there is no suitable hospital or other establishment into which he can be admitted and where he would be likely to remain voluntarily;

and where the responsible medical officer records his opinion as aforesaid he shall also record the grounds for his opinion.

(2) Where the responsible medical officer records his opinion under this paragraph in respect of a patient, the managers of the hospital or other persons in charge of the establishment where he is for the time being detained or liable to be detained shall cause the patient to be informed, and the patient may, at any time before the expiration of the period of 28 days beginning with the date on which he is so informed, apply to a Mental Health Review Tribunal.

(3) On any application under sub-paragraph (2) above the tribunal shall, if satisfied that none of the conditions set out in paragraphs (a) and (b) of sub-paragraph (1) above are fulfilled, direct that the patient be discharged, and subsection (1) of section 72 of this Act shall have effect in relation to the application as if paragraph (b) of that subsection were omitted.

36. Any person who immediately before the commencement of this Act was deemed to have been named as the guardian of any patient under para.14 of Sch.6 to the Mental Health Act 1959 shall be deemed for the purposes of this Act to have been named as the guardian of the patient in an application for his reception into guardianship under Part II of this Act accepted on that person's behalf by the relevant local authority.

37.—(1) This paragraph applies to patients who immediately before the commencement of this Act were transferred patients within the meaning of para.15 of Sch.6 to the Mental Health Act 1959.

(2) A transferred patient who immediately before the commencement of this Act was by virtue of sub-paragraph (2) of that paragraph treated for the purposes of that Act as if he were liable to be detained in a hospital in pursuance of a direction under section 71 of that Act shall be treated as if he were so liable in pursuance of a [hospital order together with a restriction order, made without limitation of time].

(3) A transferred patient who immediately before the commencement of this Act was by virtue of sub-paragraph (3) of that paragraph treated for the purposes of the Act as if he were liable to be detained

in a hospital by virtue of a transfer direction under section 72 of that Act and as if a direction restricting his discharge had been given under section 74 of that Act shall be treated as if he were liable by virtue of a transfer direction under section 47 of this Act and as if a restriction direction had been given under section 49 of this Act.

(4) Section 84 of this Act shall apply to a transferred patient who was treated by virtue of sub-paragraph (5) of that paragraph immediately before the commencement of this Act as if he had been removed to a hospital under section 89 of that Act as if he had been so removed under the said section 84.

(5) Any person to whom sub-paragraph (6) of that paragraph applied immediately before the commencement of this Act shall be treated for the purposes of this Act as if he were liable to be detained in a hospital in pursuance of a transfer direction given under section 48 of this Act and as if a restriction direction had been given under section 49 of this Act [. . .].

38. Any patient who immediately before the commencement of this Act was treated by virtue of sub-paragraph (1) of para.16 of Sch.6 to the Mental Health Act 1959 as if he had been conditionally discharged under section 66 of that Act shall be treated as if he had been conditionally discharged under section 42 of this Act and any such direction as is mentioned in paragraph (b) of that sub-paragraph shall be treated as if it had been given under the said section 42.

39. [. . .]

40. A person who immediately before the commencement of this Act was detained by virtue of para.19 of Sch.6 to the Mental Health Act 1959 may continue to be detained until the expiration of the period of his treatment current on November 1, 1960 or until he becomes liable to be detained or subject to guardianship under this Act, whichever occurs first, and may be so detained in any place in which he might have been detained under that paragraph.

41. Any opinion recorded by the responsible medical officer under the foregoing provisions of this Schedule shall be recorded in which form as may be prescribed by regulations made by the Secretary of State.

42.—(1) In the foregoing provisions of this Schedule—

(a) references to the period of treatment of a patient that was current on November 1, 1960 are to the period for which he would have been liable to be detained or subject to guardianship by virtue of any enactment repealed or excluded by the Mental Health Act 1959, or any enactment repealed or replaced by any such enactment as aforesaid, being a period which began but did not expire before that date; and

(b) "the responsible medical officer" means—

(i) in relation to a patient subject to guardianship, the medical officer authorised by the local social services authority to act (either generally or in any particular case or for any particular purpose) as the responsible medical officer;

(ii) in relation to any other class of patient, the registered medical practitioner in charge of the treatment of the patient.

(2) Subsection (2) of section 34 of this Act shall apply for the purposes of the foregoing provisions of this Schedule as it applies for the purposes of Part II of this Act.

(3) The sentence or other period of detention of a person who was liable to be detained or subject to guardianship immediately before November 1, 1960 by virtue of an order under section 9 of the Mental Deficiency Act 1913 shall be treated for the purposes of the foregoing provisions of this Schedule as expiring at the end of the period for which that person would have been liable to be detained in a prison or other institution if the order had not been made.

(4) For the purposes of the foregoing provisions of this Schedule, an order sending a person to an institution or placing a person under guardianship made before March 9, 1956 on a petition presented under the Mental Deficiency Act 1913 shall be deemed to be valid if it was so deemed immediately before the commencement of this Act by virtue of section 148(2) of the Mental Health Act 1959.

43. [. . .]
44. [. . .]
45. [. . .]
46. [. . .]

AMENDMENTS

The amendments to this Schedule were made by the Health Authorities Act 1995 s.5(1), Sch.3, the Statute Law (Repeals) Act 2004 Sch.1 Pt 17, the Mental Capacity Act 2005 s.67(2), Sch.7, the Mental Health Act 2007 s.55, Sch.11 Pt 1, the Domestic Violence, Crime and Victims Act 2004 s.58(1), Sch.10 para.23 and SI 2008/2833 art.9, Sch.3 para.68.

DEFINITIONS

1–1403   local social services authority: s.145(1).
approved mental health professional: s.145(1).
application for admission for treatment: ss.3, 145(1).
patient: s.145(1).
nearest relative: ss.26(3), 145(1).
hospital order: ss.37, 145(1).
transfer direction: ss.47, 145(1).
restriction order: ss.41, 145(1).
restriction direction: ss.49, 145(1).
mental disorder: ss.2, 145(1).
hospital: s.145(1).
the managers: s.145(1).
appropriate tribunal: ss.66(4), 135(1).

GENERAL NOTE

1–1404   This Schedule makes provision to cover the transition from the Mental Health Act 1959, as amended by the Mental Health (Amendment) Act 1982, to this Act. It therefore affects patients detained on or before the commencement date of this Act (September 30, 1983) and anything which was in the process of being done at that date.

Paragraph 1

1–1405   This paragraph states the general rule that any period of time specified in legislation which was in force on September 30, 1983 will be replaced by the corresponding provision in this Act, calculated from the time when the original order or application was made. This rule is subject to the important exceptions set out in para.9.

Paragraph 6

1–1406   This paragraph ensures that the changes in the definitions of mental disorder will not affect the authority to detain somebody who was detained prior to September 30, 1983. This paragraph does not apply to the renewal of authority.

Paragraph 9

1–1407   When an authority to detain a patient admitted for treatment or to subject a patient to guardianship is renewed before October 1, 1983 the duration of the authority applicable under the 1959 Act (of one or two years) will continue to apply. However, where the authority has been renewed for two years and less than 16 months has passed since the renewal by September 30, 1983, that period of detention will expire after 18 months rather than two years. If that detention is subsequently renewed the period of one year will apply.

Paragraphs 31 to 42

1–1408   Inter alia, provide authority for the continued detention or guardianship of patents whose detention or guardianship commenced before the Mental Health Act 1959 came into force.

Section 134   **SCHEDULE 6**

1–1409   *[Not reproduced.]*

DELEGATED LEGISLATION

THE MENTAL HEALTH (CARE AND TREATMENT) (SCOTLAND) ACT 2003 (CONSEQUENTIAL PROVISIONS) ORDER 2005

(SI 2005/2078)

Dated July 21, 2005 and made by the Secretary of State for Constitutional Affairs under the Scotland Act 1998 (c.46) sections 104, 112(1) and 113

GENERAL NOTE

This Order makes provision consequential on the Mental Health (Care and Treatment) **2–001** (Scotland) Act 2003. Only those articles that extend to England and Wales are reproduced.

Article 8 provides that any person who may be taken into custody in Scotland under the 2003 Act or regulations made under that Act may be taken into custody in any other part of the UK and returned to Scotland. Article 10 makes it an offence in England and Wales and in Northern Ireland to do anything in relation to a person subject to the 2003 Act that would be an offence under s.316 of the 2003 Act if done in Scotland. Section 316 makes it an offence to induce or assist patients to abscond. Article 11 provides that where patients are being conveyed to any place in England, Wales or Northern Ireland by virtue of the 2003 Act or this Order they will be in legal custody while being conveyed through those territories and that persons taking patients into custody or conveying or detaining them by virtue of the 2003 Act or this Order will have all the powers and privileges of a constable. Article 12 extends the protection afforded by s.139 of the 1983 Act to acts done in pursuance of this Order.

Citation, commencement, interpretation and extent

1.—(1) This Order may be cited as the Mental Health (Care and Treatment) **2–002** (Scotland) Act 2003 (Consequential Provisions) Order 2005 and, subject to paragraph (2), shall come into force on 5th October 2005.

(2) The entry in Schedule 3 to this Order in respect of the Mental Health (Scotland) Act 1984 shall come into force immediately after the coming into force of the entry in Schedule 5 to the 2003 Act in respect of the Mental Health (Scotland) Act 1984.

(3) In this Order, unless the context otherwise requires—

"the 1995 Act" means the Criminal Procedure (Scotland) Act 1995;

"the 2003 Act" means the Mental Health (Care and Treatment) (Scotland) Act 2003;

"hospital", except as provided in articles 2(7) and 4(8), has the meaning given in section 329(1) of the 2003 Act;

"hospital direction" means a direction made under section 59A of the 1995 Act;

"patient" has the meaning given in section 329(1) of the 2003 Act;

"restriction order" means an order made under section 59 of the 1995 Act; and "transfer for treatment direction" has the meaning given by section 136 of the 2003 Act.

(4) A reference in this Order to "a patient whose detention in hospital was authorised by virtue of the 2003 Act or the 1995 Act" shall be read as including references to a patient in respect of whom a certificate under one of the provisions listed in section 290(7)(a) of the 2003 Act is in operation.

(5) [. . .]

(6) Articles 4, 5, 6, 7 and 9 extend to Northern Ireland only.

(7) Articles 8, 10, 11 and 12(2) extend to England and Wales and Northern Ireland only.

(8) Articles 12(1), 13 and 14 extend to Scotland only.

(9) Subject to paragraph (10), the modifications in Schedules 1 and 2 and the repeals in Schedule 3 have the same extent as the provisions being modified or repealed.

(10) Those modifications and repeals do not extend to Scotland other than the modifications in paragraphs 1(4)(b), 5 and 6 of Schedule 1 and paragraph 20 of Schedule 2 and the repeal in Schedule 3 of the Mental Health (Scotland) Act 1984.

AMENDMENT

Paragraph (5) was repealed by the Mental Health Act 2007 s.55, Sch.11 Pt 7.

*　　*　　*　　*

[Patients absent from hospitals or other places in Scotland]

2–003   **8.**—(1) Subject to the provisions of this article, any person who may be taken into custody in Scotland under—

(a) sections 301 to 303 of the 2003 Act; or

(b) regulations made under section [289, 290, 309, 309A] or 310 of that Act, may be taken into custody in, and returned to Scotland from, any other part of the United Kingdom.

(2) For the purposes of the enactments referred to in paragraph (1), in their application by virtue of this article to England and Wales or Northern Ireland

(a) "constable" includes a constable in England or Wales or a constable of the Police Service of Northern Ireland, as the case may be; and

(b) "mental health officer" includes—

(i) in England and Wales, any approved [mental health professional] within the meaning of the Mental Health Act 1983; and

(ii) in Northern Ireland, any approved social worker within the meaning of the Mental Health (Northern Ireland) Order 1986.

AMENDMENTS

The amendments to this article were made by the Mental Health Act 2007 s.39(2), Sch.5 Pt 2 para.21(3) and SI 2008/2828 art.20.

*　　*　　*　　*

Assisting patients to absent themselves without leave etc.

2–004   **10.**—(1) Any person who in England and Wales or Northern Ireland does anything in relation to a person whose detention in hospital is authorised by the 2003 Act which, if done in Scotland, would make him guilty of an offence under section 316 of the 2003 Act shall be guilty of an offence.

(2) Where a person is charged with an offence under paragraph (1) as it applies to section 316(1)(b) of the 2003 Act, it shall be a defence for such person to prove that the doing of that with which the person is charged—

(a) did not obstruct the discharge by any person of a function conferred or imposed on that person by virtue of the 2003 Act or this Order; and

(b) was intended to protect the interests of the patient.

(3) Any person guilty of an offence under this article shall be liable—

(a) on summary conviction, to imprisonment for a term not exceeding 3 months or to a fine not exceeding level 5 on the standard scale;

(b) on conviction on indictment, to imprisonment for a term not exceeding 2 years or to a fine, or both.

Provisions as to custody, removal and detention

11.—(1) Any person required or authorised by or by virtue of the 2003 Act or by virtue of this Order to be moved to any place or to be kept in custody or detained in a place of safety shall, while being so moved, kept or detained, as the case may be, be deemed to be in legal custody. **2–005**

(2) A constable or any other person required or authorised by or by virtue of that Act or by virtue of this Order to take any person into custody, or to move or detain any person shall, for the purposes of taking him into custody or moving or detaining him, have all the powers, authorities, protection and privileges which a constable has—

(a) in the case of a constable, within the area for which he acts as constable; and

(b) in the case of any other person, in the area where he has taken any person into custody or is moving or detaining him.

Protection for acts done under this Order

12.—(1) No person shall be liable, whether on ground of want of jurisdiction or on any other ground, to any civil or criminal proceedings to which he would have been liable apart from this paragraph in respect of any act purporting to be done in pursuance of this Order, unless the act was done in bad faith or without reasonable care. **2–006**

(2) Section 139 of the Mental Health Act 1983 (which relates to protection for acts done in pursuance of that Act) shall apply in respect of any act purporting to be done in pursuance of articles [4 to 11] of this Order.

AMENDMENT

The amendment to para.(2) was made by the Mental Health Act 2007 s.39(2), Sch.5 Pt 2 para.21(4).

*　　*　　*　　*

THE MENTAL HEALTH (MUTUAL RECOGNITION) REGULATIONS 2008

(SI 2008/1204)

Dated April 28, 2008 and made by the Secretary of State and the Welsh Ministers acting jointly under the Mental Health Act 1983, section 142A

GENERAL NOTE

2–007   These Regulations set out the circumstances in which a practitioner approved in England for the purposes of s.12 of the Act or a person approved in relation to England to act as an approved clinician for the purposes of the Act may be treated as approved in relation to Wales by virtue of that approval, and vice versa. They apply where a patient is liable to be detained, subject to a community treatment order or subject to guardianship under the Act. This flexibility is particularly helpful in areas near the border between England and Wales, where services are accessed for patients across that border.

Citation, commencement and interpretation

2–008   **1.**—(1) These Regulations may be cited as the Mental Health (Mutual Recognition) Regulations 2008 and shall come into force on 3rd November 2008.

(2) In these Regulations, "the Act" means the Mental Health Act 1983.

Approval under section 12(2) of the Act

2–009   **2.**—(1) Any person who is approved in relation to England for the purposes of section 12(2) of the Act, or treated as approved by virtue of section 12(2A) of the Act, shall in all circumstances relevant to the purposes of section 12(2) be treated as approved in relation to Wales.

(2) Any person who is approved in relation to Wales for the purposes of section 12(2) of the Act, or treated as approved by virtue of section 12(2A) of the Act, shall in all circumstances relevant to the purposes of section 12(2) be treated as approved in relation to England.

Person approved to act as an approved clinician

2–010   **3.**—(1) The circumstances in which a person who is approved to act as an approved clinician in relation to England shall be treated, by virtue of his approval, as approved in relation to Wales too are where—

(a) the approved clinician is acting in respect of a patient who is liable to be detained in accordance with the provisions of the Act or is subject to a community treatment order,

(b) the patient is in Wales, and

(c) the patient's relevant hospital is in England.

(2) The circumstances in which a person who is approved to act as an approved clinician in relation to Wales shall be treated, by virtue of his approval, as approved in relation to England too are where—

(a) the approved clinician is acting in respect of a patient who is liable to be detained in accordance with the provisions of the Act or is subject to a community treatment order,

(b) the patient is in England, and

(c) the patient's relevant hospital is in Wales.

(3) In this regulation, "relevant hospital"—

(a) in respect of a patient liable to be detained, means the hospital in which the patient is liable to be detained in accordance with the provisions of the Act;

(b) in respect of a patient subject to a community treatment order, has the same meaning as "the responsible hospital".

Guardianship

4.—(1) In relation to a patient subject to guardianship, the circumstances in **2–011** which a responsible local social services authority in England may treat a person who is approved to act as an approved clinician in relation to Wales as approved in relation to England in order to authorise that person to be the patient's responsible clinician are where—

(a) the patient is in Wales, or

(b) the patient receives medical treatment for mental disorder in Wales.

(2) In relation to a patient subject to guardianship, the circumstances in which a responsible local social services authority in Wales may treat a person who is approved to act as an approved clinician in relation to England as approved in relation to Wales in order to authorise that person to be the patient's responsible clinician are where—

(a) the patient is in England, or

(b) the patient receives medical treatment for mental disorder in England.

(3) In relation to a patient subject to guardianship, the circumstances in which a person approved to act as an approved clinician in England shall be treated as approved to act as an approved clinician in relation to Wales are where—

(a) that approved clinician has been authorised to act as the patient's responsible clinician by the patient's responsible local social services authority in England, and

(b) that approved clinician is acting in respect of a patient who is in Wales.

(4) In relation to a patient subject to guardianship, the circumstances in which a person approved to act as an approved clinician in Wales shall be treated as approved to act as an approved clinician in relation to England are where—

(a) that approved clinician has been authorised to act as the patient's responsible clinician by the patient's responsible local social services authority in Wales, and

(b) that approved clinician is acting in respect of a patient who is in England.

(5) In this regulation, "responsible local social services authority" has the same meaning as in section 34(3) of the Act.

THE MENTAL HEALTH (CONFLICTS OF INTEREST) (ENGLAND) REGULATIONS 2008

(SI 2008/1205)

Dated April 28, 2008 and made by the Secretary of State under the Mental Health Act 1983, section 12A

GENERAL NOTE

2–012   These Regulations, which are considered in Ch.39 of the *Code of Practice*, set out the circumstances in which there is a potential conflict of interest such that an approved mental health professional (AMHP) cannot make an application mentioned in s.11(1) of the Act, or a registered medical practitioner cannot make a medical recommendation for the purposes of such an application.

An AMHP considering making such an application, or a registered medical practitioner considering giving a medical recommendation for the purposes of such an application, will have a potential conflict of interest if the reasons set out in the Regulations apply. These may be financial reasons (reg.4), business reasons (reg.5), professional reasons (reg.6) or because of a personal relationship existing between the assessor and another assessor, or between the assessor and the patient or, where the application is to be made by the patient's nearest relative, the nearest relative (reg.7).

There is provision for an AMHP or a registered medical practitioner to make an application or a medical recommendation despite a potential conflict of interest for professional reasons in specified circumstances in cases of urgent necessity where there would otherwise be a delay with a serious risk to the health or safety of the patient or to others (reg.6).

Other potential conflicts

2–013   Under this heading, the *Code of Practice* states:

> "39.15 There may be circumstances not covered by these regulations where the assessor feels, nonetheless, that there is (or could be seen to be) a potential conflict of interest. Assessors should work on the principle that in any situation where they believe that the objectivity or independence of their decision is (or could be seen to be) undermined then they should not become involved or should withdraw.
>
> 39.16 These regulations do not cover potential conflicts of interest relating to a community treatment order (CTO). The responsible clinician responsible for making the decision as to whether to place a patient on a CTO, or any decision to revoke a CTO, should not have any financial interest in the outcome of the decision. Responsible clinicians should not be considered to have a financial interest in a hospital on the sole basis that they work there. Similarly, the responsible clinician should not be a relative of the patient.
>
> 39.17 These regulations do not cover potential conflicts of interest relating to renewal of detention or guardianship. The persons involved in making the decision as to whether to renew the detention (the responsible clinician and other professionals consulted by the responsible clinician) or the guardianship (the appropriate practitioner) should not have any financial interest in the outcome of the decision."

The guidance contained in para.39.17 should not be followed in so far as it applies to the RC of a detained patient or to the appropriate practitioner of a patient who is subject to the guardianship because they are the only professionals who can trigger a renewal.

Wales

The Welsh Ministers have made separate Regulations in relation to Wales: see the 2–014
Mental Health (Conflicts of Interest) (Wales) Regulations 2008 (SI 2008/2440) (W.213).

Citation, commencement and application

1.—(1) These Regulations may be cited as the Mental Health (Conflicts of 2–015
Interest) (England) Regulations 2008 and shall come into force on 3rd
November 2008.

(2) These Regulations apply to England only.

Interpretation

2. In these Regulations—   2–016
"the Act" means the Mental Health Act 1983;
"AMHP" means an approved mental health professional;
"application" means an application mentioned in section 11(1) of the Act;
"assessor" means—
  (a) an AMHP, or
  (b) a registered medical practitioner.

General

3. Regulations 4 to 7 set out the circumstances in which there would be a poten- 2–017
tial conflict of interest within the meaning of section 12A(1) of the Act such that
an AMHP shall not make an application or a registered medical practitioner shall
not give a medical recommendation.

Potential conflict for financial reasons

4.—(1) A assessor shall have a potential conflict of interest for financial 2–018
reasons if the assessor has a financial interest in the outcome of a decision whether
or not to make an application or give a medical recommendation.

(2) Where an application for the admission of the patient to a hospital which is a
registered establishment is being considered, a registered medical practitioner
who is on the staff of that hospital shall have a potential conflict of interest for
financial reasons where the other medical recommendation is given by a registered medical practitioner who is also on the staff of that hospital.

GENERAL NOTE

Paragraph 39.6 of the *Code of Practice* states: 2–019

"An assessor will have a conflict of interest for financial reasons if the assessor stands to
make a financial benefit (or loss) for their decision. There will not be a potential conflict
of interest for financial reasons where an assessor is paid a fee for making an application
or giving a medical recommendation if it is paid regardless of the outcome of the
assessment."

Paragraph (2)

Paragraph 39.4 of the *Code of Practice* states: 2–020

"The current regulations require that where the patient is to be admitted to an independent hospital and the doctor providing one of the medical recommendations is on the
staff of that independent hospital, the other medical recommendation must be given
by a doctor who is not on the staff of that independent hospital. That is, there will be

a potential conflict if both doctors giving recommendations are on the staff of the independent hospital. It is also good practice for doctors on the staff of an NHS trust or NHS foundation trust to ensure that one of the recommendations is given by a doctor not on the staff of that trust."

The "good practice" point made in the final sentence is not a legal requirement.

Potential conflict of interest for business reasons

2–021   5.—(1) When considering making an application or considering giving a medical recommendation in respect of a patient, an assessor shall have a potential conflict of interest for business reasons if both the assessor and the patient or another assessor are closely involved in the same business venture, including being a partner, director, other office-holder or major shareholder of that venture.

(2) Where the patient's nearest relative is making an application, a registered medical practitioner who is considering giving a medical recommendation in respect of that patient shall have a potential conflict of interest for business reasons if that registered medical practitioner and the nearest relative are both closely involved in the same business venture, including being a partner, director, other office-holder or major shareholder of that venture.

GENERAL NOTE

2–022   The *Code of Practice* states:

"39.7 An assessor will have a potential conflict of interest if both that assessor and one of the other assessors, the patient or the nearest relative (if the nearest relative is the applicant) are closely involved in the same business venture. Being 'closely involved' is not defined in the regulations. Examples could include being a partner in a partnership, being a director or other office-holder of a company, or being a major shareholder in it. This will apply even if the business venture is not associated with the provision of services for the care and treatment of persons with a mental disorder.

39.8 Business ventures include any form of commercial enterprise from which the person concerned stands to profit. Such people include: directors and major investors in a company (of any size) which provides goods or services for profit; partners in a general practitioner (GP) practice; partners in a business established as a limited liability partnership. Involvement in a business venture does not include involvement in societies and similar organisations which are essentially non-commercial, and from which the people concerned do not stand to profit."

Potential conflict of interest for professional reasons

2–023   6.—(1) When considering making an application or considering giving a medical recommendation in respect of a patient, an assessor shall have a potential conflict of interest for professional reasons if the assessor—

(a) directs the work of, or employs, the patient or one of the other assessors making that consideration;

(b) except where paragraph (3) applies, is a member of a team organised to work together for clinical purposes on a routine basis and—

(i) the patient is a member of the same team, or

(ii) the other two assessors are members of the same team.

(2) Where the patient's nearest relative is making an application, a registered medical practitioner who is considering giving a medical recommendation in

respect of that patient shall have a potential conflict of interest for professional reasons if that registered medical practitioner—

(a) directs the work of, or employs, the nearest relative, or

(b) works under the direction of, or is employed by, the patient's nearest relative.

(3) Paragraph (1)(b) shall not prevent a registered medical practitioner giving a medical recommendation or an AMHP making an application if, in their opinion, it is of urgent necessity for an application to be made and a delay would involve serious risk to the health or safety of the patient or others.

GENERAL NOTE

The *Code of Practice* states: **2–024**

> "39.9 Regulations set out that a conflict of interest for professional reasons will occur where:
>
> - the assessor is in a line management or employment relationship with one of the other assessors or the patient or the nearest relative (where the nearest relative is the applicant)
>
> - the assessor is a member of the same team as the patient, or
>
> - where there are three assessors, all of them are members of the same team.
>
> 39.10 A line management relationship will exist whether an assessor manages, or is managed by, one of the other assessors, the patient or the nearest relative (where the nearest relative is the applicant). Similarly an employment relationship will exist whether the assessor employs, or is employed by, one of the other assessors, the patient or the nearest relative (where the nearest relative is the applicant).
>
> 39.11 For the purposes of the regulations a team is defined as a group of professionals who work together for clinical purposes on a routine basis. That might include a community mental health team, a crisis resolution or home treatment team, or staff on an in-patient unit (but not necessarily the staff of an entire hospital)."

Paragraph (1)

Sub-paragraphs (a) and (b) provide alternative reasons for identifying a potential conflict **2–024** of interest.

Paragraph (3)

URGENT NECESSITY.   The *Code of Practice* states:

> "39.12 If there is a case of urgent necessity all three assessors may be from the same team. However, this should happen only in a genuine emergency, where the patient's need for urgent assessment outweighs the desirability of waiting for another assessor who has no potential conflict of interest. Any decisions made to proceed despite a potential conflict of interest should be recorded, with reasons, in case notes.
>
> 39.13 In a case of urgent necessity it is preferable to proceed with three assessors, despite a potential conflict of interest, rather than make the application under section 4 of the Act with only two assessors (one doctor and one AMHP) (see paragraphs 15.6 – 15.8).
>
> 39.14 There are no other circumstances in which potential conflict of interest can be set aside because of urgent necessity."

IN THEIR OPINION.   This criterion is to be judged by adopting a subjective test.   **2–025**

Potential conflict of interest on the basis of a personal relationship

2–026   **7.**—(1) A assessor who is considering making an application or considering giving a medical recommendation in respect of a patient, shall have a potential conflict of interest on the basis of a personal relationship if that assessor is—

   (a) related to a relevant person in the first degree;
   (b) related to a relevant person in the second degree;
   (c) related to a relevant person as a half-sister or half-brother;
   (d) the spouse, ex-spouse, civil partner or ex-civil partner of a relevant person, or
   (e) living with a relevant person as if they were a spouse or a civil partner.

   (2) For the purposes of this regulation—

   (a) "relevant person" means another assessor, the patient, or, if the nearest relative is making the application, the nearest relative;
   (b) "related in the first degree" means as a parent, sister, brother, son or daughter and includes step relationships;
   (c) "related in the second degree" means as an uncle, aunt, grandparent, grandchild, first cousin, nephew, niece, parent-in-law, grandparent-in-law, grandchild-in-law, sister-in-law, brother-in-law, son-in-law, daughter-in-law and includes step relationships;
   (d) references to step relationships and in-laws in sub-paragraph (b) and (c) are to be read in accordance with section 246 of the Civil Partnership Act 2004.

THE MENTAL HEALTH (APPROVED MENTAL HEALTH PROFESSIONALS) (APPROVAL) (ENGLAND) REGULATIONS 2008

(SI 2008/1206)

Dated April 28, 2008 and made by the Secretary of State under the Mental Health Act 1983, section 114

GENERAL NOTE

These Regulations set out a number of matters in connection with the giving by local **2–027** social services authorities (LSSAs) in England of approvals to persons to act as approved mental health professionals (AMHPs) for the purposes of the Act.

Before a person can be approved (or re-approved) in England to act as an AMHP by a LSSA, the person must have appropriate competence. In deciding whether it is satisfied that the person has appropriate competence, the LSSA must take into account that the person has at least one of the professional requirements set out in Sch.1 and the matters set out in Sch.2 (reg.3).

Before a person can be approved to act as an AMHP if he or she has not been approved before, that person must have completed a course within the last five years that was approved by the Health and Care Professions Council or the Care Council for Wales. The period for which an AMHP is approved (or re-approved) is five years (reg.4). Approval (or re-approval) is subject to specified conditions (reg.5).

The approval shall be suspended for any period that the AMHP is suspended from the register or list relevant to the AMHP's professional requirements (reg.6).

The approval or re-approval of an AMHP will end when the period of approval expires or before that in specified circumstances. When the approval ends, the LSSA must inform the AMHP and any other LSSA for which it knows that AMHP has agreed to act. If one LSSA approves a person to act as an AMHP who is already approved by another, it must inform that other LSSA (reg.7).

Each LSSA is required to keep records with specified details of AMHPs for whom it is the approving LSSA (reg.8).

Wales

The Welsh Ministers have made separate regulations relating to the approval of persons **2–028** to act as AMHPs in relation to Wales: see the Mental Health (Approval of Persons to be Approved Mental Health Professionals) (Wales) Regulations 2008 (SI 2008/2436) (W.209). The Schedule to Mental Health Act 2007 (Commencement No. 8 and Transitional Provisions) Order 2008 (SI 2008/2561) requires LSSAs to treat as AMHPs a person who has been approved as an approved social worker by an LSSA in Wales immediately before November 3, 2008.

Transitional Provisions

See the Schedule to the Mental Health Act 2007 (Commencement No.7 and Transitional **2–029** Provisions) Order 2008 (SI 2008/1900).

Citation, commencement and application

1.—(1) These Regulations may be cited as the Mental Health (Approved **2–030** Mental Health Professionals) (Approval) (England) Regulations 2008 and shall come into force on 3rd November 2008.

(2) These Regulations apply to England only.

Interpretation

2. In these Regulations—   **2–031**

"the Act" means the Mental Health Act 1983;

"AMHP" means an approved mental health professional;

"approve" and "approval" include "re-approve" and "re-approval";

"approving LSSA" means the local social services authority in England that has approved the person to act as an AMHP;

[. . .];

"LSSA" means a local social services authority in England;

"professional requirements" means the requirements set out in Schedule 1.

AMENDMENT

The definition of "General Social Care Council" was repealed by SI 2012/1479, Sch.1, Pt 2, para.84.

Granting approval

2–032   **3.**—(1) An LSSA may only approve a person to act as an AMHP if it is satisfied that the person has appropriate competence in dealing with persons who are suffering from mental disorder.

(2) In determining whether it is satisfied a person has appropriate competence, the LSSA must take into account the following factors—

(a) that the person fulfils at least one of the professional requirements, and

(b) the matters set out in Schedule 2.

(3) Before an LSSA may approve a person to act as an AMHP who has not been approved, or been treated as approved, before in England and Wales, the person must have completed within the last five years a course approved by [the Health and Care Professions Council under section 114ZA of the Mental Health Act 1983 or by] the Care Council for Wales.

AMENDMENT

The amendment to para.(3) was made by SI 2012/1479, Sch.1, Pt 2, para.84.

Period of approval

2–033   **4.** An LSSA may approve a person to act as an AMHP for a period of five years.

Conditions

2–034   **5.** When any approval is granted under these Regulations, it shall be subject to the following conditions—

(a) in each year that the AMHP is approved, the AMHP shall complete at least 18 hours of training agreed with the approving LSSA as being relevant to their role as an AMHP;

(b) the AMHP shall undertake to notify the approving LSSA in writing as soon as reasonably practicable if they agree to act as an AMHP on behalf of another LSSA, and when such agreement ends;

(c) the AMHP shall undertake to cease to act as an AMHP and to notify the approving LSSA immediately if they are suspended from any of the registers or listings referred to in the professional competencies, or if any such suspension ends, and

(d) the AMHP shall undertake to cease to act as an AMHP and to notify the approving LSSA immediately if they no longer meet at least one of the professional requirements.

Suspension of approval

6.—(1) If at any time after being approved, the registration or listing required **2–035** by the professional requirements of a person approved to act as an AMHP is suspended, the approving LSSA shall suspend that AMHP's approval for as long as the AMHP's registration or listing is suspended.

(2) Where an AMHP's approval is suspended, that person may not act as an AMHP unless and until the suspension of approval is ended by the approving LSSA in accordance with subsection (3).

(3) Where the approving LSSA is notified that the suspension of the AMHP's registration or listing has ended, the approving LSSA shall, unless it is not satisfied the AMHP has appropriate competence in dealing with persons suffering from mental disorder, end the suspension of approval.

(4) Where the suspension of approval has ended, the approval shall continue to run for any unexpired period of approval, unless the approving LSSA ends it earlier in accordance with regulation 7.

End of approval

7.—(1) Except where paragraph (2) applies, a person shall cease to be approved **2–036** to act as an AMHP at the end of the day on which their period of approval expires.

(2) Except where regulation 6 applies, the approving LSSA shall end the approval of a person it has approved to act as an AMHP before their period of approval expires—

(a) in accordance with a request in writing to do so from that AMHP;

(b) if it is no longer satisfied that the AMHP has appropriate competence taking into account the matters set out in Schedule 2;

(c) immediately upon becoming aware that the AMHP—

    (i) is no longer a person who meets at least one of the professional requirements;

    (ii) is in breach of any of the conditions set out in regulation 5, or

    (iii) has been approved to act as an AMHP by another LSSA.

(3) When an approval ends, the approving LSSA shall notify the AMHP immediately that the approval has ended and give reasons for ending the approval.

(4) When an approval ends, the approving LSSA shall notify that fact to any other LSSA for whom it knows the AMHP has agreed to act as an AMHP.

(5) If an LSSA approves a person as an AMHP knowing that that AMHP is already approved by another LSSA, it shall notify the previous approving LSSA.

GENERAL NOTE
Paragraph (2)(b),(c)(i)(ii)
The AMHP has no right of appeal against the decision of the local authority. **2–037**

Records

8.—(1) The approving LSSA shall keep a record of each AMHP it approves **2–038** which shall include—

(a) the name of the AMHP;

(b) the AMHP's profession;

(c) the AMHP's date of approval;

(d) details of any period of suspension under regulation 6;

(e) details of the completion of training to comply with regulation 5(a);

(f) details of any previous approvals as an AMHP within the previous five years;

(g) the names of other LSSAs for whom the AMHP has agreed to act as an AMHP, and

(h) the date of and reason for the end of approval, if applicable.

(2) The record referred to in paragraph (1) shall be retained by the approving LSSA for a period of five years commencing with the day on which the AMHP's approval ended.

SCHEDULE 1   **Regulation 2**

PROFESSIONAL REQUIREMENTS

2–039   The professional requirements are as follows—

(a) [. . .];

(b) a first level nurse, registered in Sub-Part 1 of the Nurses' Part of the Register maintained under article 5 of the Nursing and Midwifery Order 2001, with the inclusion of an entry indicating their field of practice is mental health or learning disabilities nursing;

(c) an occupational therapist registered in Part 6 [, or a social worker registered in Part 16,] of the Register maintained under article 5 of the [Health and Social Work Professions Order 2001]; or

(d) a chartered psychologist who is listed in the British Psychological Society's Register of Chartered Psychologists and who holds a relevant practising certificate issued by that Society.

AMENDMENTS

The amendments to this Schedule were made by SI 2012/1479, Sch.1, Pt 1, para.54, Sch.1, Pt 2, para.84.

GENERAL NOTE

2–040   Paragraph 84(5) of Sch.1, Pt 2 to the Health and Social Care Act 2012 (Consequential Provision—Social Workers) Order 2012 (SI 2012/1479) reads:

"In relation to a course approved before 1st August 2012, regulations 2 and 3 of these Regulations are to be treated as continuing to have effect as if they had not been amended by sub-paragraphs (2) and (3) of this paragraph."

Regulation 3(2)   **SCHEDULE 2**

MATTERS TO BE TAKEN INTO ACCOUNT TO DETERMINE COMPETENCE

2–041 **1. Key Competence Area 1: Application of Values to the AMHP Role**

Whether the applicant has—

(a) the ability to identify, challenge and, where possible, redress discrimination and inequality in all its forms in relation to AMHP practice;

(b) an understanding of and respect for individuals' qualities, abilities and diverse backgrounds, and is able to identify and counter any decision which may be based on unlawful discrimination;

(c) the ability to promote the rights, dignity and self determination of patients consistent with their own needs and wishes, to enable them to contribute to the decisions made affecting their quality of life and liberty, and

650

(d) a sensitivity to individuals' needs for personal respect, confidentiality, choice, dignity and privacy while exercising the AMHP role.

2. Key Competence Area 2: Application of Knowledge: The Legal and Policy Framework

(1) Whether the applicant has—
(a) appropriate knowledge of and ability to apply in practice—
  (i) mental health legislation, related codes of practice and national and local policy guidance, and
  (ii) relevant parts of other legislation, codes of practice, national and local policy guidance, in particular the Children Act 1989, the Children Act 2004, the Human Rights Act 1998 and the Mental Capacity Act 2005;
(b) a knowledge and understanding of the particular needs of children and young people and their families, and an ability to apply AMHP practice in the context of those particular needs;
(c) an understanding of, and sensitivity to, race and culture in the application of knowledge of mental health legislation;
(d) an explicit awareness of the legal position and accountability of AMHPs in relation to the Act, any employing organisation and the authority on whose behalf they are acting;
(e) the ability to—
  (i) evaluate critically local and national policy to inform AMHP practice, and
  (ii) base AMHP practice on a critical evaluation of a range of research relevant to evidence-based practice, including that on the impact on persons who experience discrimination because of mental health.

(2) In paragraph (1), "relevant" means relevant to the decisions that an AMHP is likely to take when acting as an AMHP.

3. Key Competence Area 3: Application of Knowledge: Mental Disorder

Whether the applicant has a critical understanding of, and is able to apply in practice—
(a) a range of models of mental disorder, including the contribution of social, physical and development factors;
(b) the social perspective on mental disorder and mental health needs, in working with patients, their relatives, carers and other professionals;
(c) the implications of mental disorder for patients, their relatives and carers, and
(d) the implications of a range of treatments and interventions for patients, their relatives and carers.

4. Key Competence Area 4: Application of Skills: Working in Partnership

Whether the applicant has the ability to—
(a) articulate, and demonstrate in practice, the social perspective on mental disorder and mental health needs;
(b) communicate appropriately with and establish effective relationships with patients, relatives, and carers in undertaking the AMHP role;
(c) articulate the role of the AMHP in the course of contributing to effective inter-agency and inter-professional working;
(d) use networks and community groups to influence collaborative working with a range of individuals, agencies and advocates;
(e) consider the feasibility of and contribute effectively to planning and implementing options for care such as alternatives to compulsory admission, discharge and aftercare;
(f) recognise, assess and manage risk effectively in the context of the AMHP role;
(g) effectively manage difficult situations of anxiety, risk and conflict, and an understanding of how this affects the AMHP and other people concerned with the patient's care;

(h) discharge the AMHP role in such a way as to empower the patient as much as practicable;

(i) plan, negotiate and manage compulsory admission to hospital or arrangements for supervised community treatment;

(j) manage and co-ordinate effectively the relevant legal and practical processes including the involvement of other professionals as well as patients, relatives and carers, and

(k) balance and manage the competing requirements of confidentiality and effective information sharing to the benefit of the patient and other persons concerned with the patient's care.

5. Key Competence Area 5: Application of Skills: Making and Communicating Informed Decisions
Whether the applicant has the ability to—

(a) assert a social perspective and to make properly informed independent decisions;

(b) obtain, analyse and share appropriate information having due regard to confidentiality in order to manage the decision-making process including decisions about supervised community treatment;

(c) compile and complete statutory documentation, including an application for admission;

(d) provide reasoned and clear verbal and written reports to promote effective, accountable and independent AMHP decision making;

(e) present a case at a legal hearing;

(f) exercise the appropriate use of independence, authority and autonomy and use it to inform their future practice as an AMHP, together with consultation and supervision;

(g) evaluate the outcomes of interventions with patients, carers and others, including the identification of where a need has not been met;

(h) make and communicate decisions that are sensitive to the needs of the individual patient, and

(i) keep appropriate records with an awareness of legal requirements with respect to record keeping and the use and transfer of information.

THE MENTAL HEALTH (HOSPITAL, GUARDIANSHIP AND TREATMENT) (ENGLAND) REGULATIONS 2008

(SI 2008/1184)

Dated April 28, 2008 and made by the Secretary of State under the Mental Health Act 1983, sections 9, 17F(2), 19(1) and (4), 31(1), (2) and 3, 57(1)(b), 58A(1)(b), 64(2), 64H(2), 134(3A)(a) and 134(8)

GENERAL NOTE

These regulations are the principal regulations dealing with the exercise of powers in **2–042** respect of persons who are liable to be detained, or subject to a community treatment order or guardianship under the Act. They provide for certain applications, recommendations and records under the Act to be in the form set in the Forms in Sch.1.

Wales

The Welsh Ministers have made separate Regulations in relation to Wales (the "Welsh **2–043** Regulations"): see the Mental Health (Hospital, Guardianship, Community Treatment and Consent to Treatment) (Wales) Regulations 2008 (SI 2008/2439) (W.212).

Code of Practice

The receipt and scrutiny of documents is considered in Ch.35.   **2–044**

PART 1

GENERAL

Citation and commencement

1.—(1) These Regulations may be cited as the Mental Health (Hospital, **2–045** Guardianship and Treatment) (England) Regulations 2008 and shall come into force on 3rd November 2008.

(2) These Regulations apply to England only.

Interpretation

2.—(1) In these Regulations—   **2–046**

"the Act" means the Mental Health Act 1983;

"bank holiday" includes New Year's Day, Good Friday, Easter Monday, Christmas Day and Boxing Day;

"business day" means any day except Saturday, Sunday or a bank holiday;

"the Commission" means the [Care Quality Commission] referred to in section 121;

"document" means any application, recommendation, record, report, order, notice or other document;

"electronic communication" has the same meaning as in section 15(1) of the Electronic Communications Act 2000;

"guardianship patient" means a person who is subject to guardianship under the Act;

"private guardian", in relation to a patient, means a person, other than a local social services authority, who acts as guardian under the Act;

"responsible registered establishment" is a registered establishment which is a responsible hospital;

"served", in relation to a document, includes addressed, delivered, given, forwarded, furnished or sent.

(2) Unless otherwise stated, any reference in these Regulations to—

(a) a numbered section is to the section of the Act bearing that number;

(b) an alphanumeric form is a reference to the form in Schedule 1 bearing that designation.

AMENDMENT

The amendment to the definition of "the Commission" was made by SI 2009/462 art.12, Sch.5 para.25(a).

Documents

2–047 **3.**—(1) Except in a case to which paragraph (2), (3), (4) or (5) applies, or in a case to which regulation 6(3) (recall notices in respect of community patients) applies, any document required or authorised to be served upon any authority, body or person by or under Part 2 of the Act (compulsory admission to hospital, guardianship or community treatment orders) or these Regulations may be served by delivering it to—

(a) the authority, body or person upon whom it is to be served;

(b) any person authorised by that authority, body or person to receive it;

(c) by sending it by pre-paid post addressed to—

  (i) the authority or body at their registered or principal office; or

  (ii) the person upon whom it is to be served at that person's usual or last known residence, or

(d) by delivering it using an internal mail system operated by the authority, body or person upon whom it is to be served, if that authority, body or person agrees.

(2) Any application for the admission of a patient to a hospital under Part 2 of the Act shall be served by delivering the application to an officer of the managers of the hospital to which it is proposed that the patient shall be admitted, who is authorised by them to receive it.

(3) Where a patient is liable to be detained in a hospital under Part 2 of the Act—

(a) any order by the nearest relative of the patient under section 23 for the patient's discharge, and

(b) the notice of such order given under section 25(1), shall be served either by—

  (i) delivery of the order or notice at that hospital to an officer of the managers authorised by the managers to receive it, or

  (ii) sending it by pre-paid post to those managers at that hospital, or

  (iii) delivering it using an internal mail system operated by the managers upon whom it is to be served, if those managers agree.

(4) Where a patient is a community patient—

(a) any order by the nearest relative of the patient under section 23 for the patient's discharge, and

(b) the notice of such order given under section 25(1A), shall be served by—

  (i) delivery of the order or notice at the patient's responsible hospital to an officer of the managers authorised by the managers to receive it,

  (ii) sending it by pre-paid post to those managers at that hospital, or

(iii) delivering it using an internal mail system operated by the managers upon whom it is to be served, if those managers agree.

(5) Any report made under subsection (2) of section 5 (detention of patient already in hospital for 72 hours) shall be served by—

(a) delivery of the report to an officer of the managers of the hospital authorised by those managers to receive it, or

(b) delivering it using an internal mail system operated by the managers upon whom it is to be served, if those managers agree.

(6) Where a document referred to in this regulation is sent by pre-paid—

(a) first class post, service is deemed to have taken place on the second business day following the day of posting;

(b) second class post, service is deemed to have taken place on the fourth business day following posting,

unless the contrary is shown.

(7) Where a document under this regulation is delivered using an internal mail system, service is considered to have taken place immediately it is delivered into the internal mail system.

(8) Subject to sections 6(3) and 8(3) (proof of applications), any document—

(a) required or authorised by or under Part 2 of the Act or these Regulations, and

(b) purporting to be signed by a person required or authorised by or under that Part or these Regulations to do so,

shall be received in evidence and be deemed to be such a document without further proof.

(9) Where under Part 2 of the Act or these Regulations the managers of a hospital are required to make any record or report, that function may be performed by an officer authorised by those managers in that behalf.

(10) Where under these Regulations the decision to accept service by a particular method requires the agreement of the managers of a hospital, that agreement may be given by an officer authorised by those managers in that behalf.

DEFINITIONS
    document: reg.2(1).   **2–048**
    served: reg.2(1).
    the Act: reg.2(1).

GENERAL NOTE
    The regulation sets out rules on how documents required under the Act are to be served. **2–049**

Paragraph (1)
    PERSON AUTHORISED. The authorisation should be formally recorded. Hospitals should **2–050** ensure that there is a 24-hour cover from staff with good knowledge of the Act.

    PREPAID POST. See para.(6). If a notice of recall to hospital is sent to the patient's last known residence, he becomes absent without leave if there is a failure to respond to the notice.

    INTERNAL MAIL SYSTEM. See para.(7).

Paragraph (2)
    SERVED. The application documents cannot be served by post.   **2–051**

OFFICER. In *R. (on the application of PD) v West Midlands and North West Mental Health Review Tribunal* [2004] EWCA Civ 311; [2004] M.H.L.R. 174, the Court of Appeal held that the meaning of "officer" will depend upon the context in which it is used, and that in the context of a tribunal hearing an "officer" means a person holding office and taking part in the management of the authority that is detaining the patient. It is submitted that in the context of these regulations, which are largely concerned with process issues rather than decision making, the meaning of "officer" should be extended to embrace an "employee". The *Code of Practice*, at para.35.7, states that hospital managers "should formally delegate their duties to receive and scrutinise admission documents to a limited number of officers, who may include clinical staff on wards. Someone with the authority to receive admission documents should be available at all times at which patients may be admitted to the hospital."

Paragraph (3)(b)(i)

2–052 SERVED. In *Re GK (Patient: Habeas Corpus)* [1999] M.H.L.R. 128, the nearest relative of a patient who had been admitted to hospital under s.3 handed a letter to the ward receptionist requesting the patient's discharge. This took place on May 27. The nearest relative was told that the letter would be handed to the appropriate person, namely the Mental Health Act administrator. The letter was received by the administrator on June 3. On that day, as no barring report under s.25 had been issued, the nearest relative arrived on the ward, seeking the discharge of the patient. A barring report was then made. In rejecting an application for *habeas corpus,* the court held that the purpose of this provision was to ensure that an order for discharge came to the notice of the proper authorised person without delay. That being the case, the handing of the letter to the ward receptionist did not satisfy that requirement and was not good delivery. The notice was served when the letter was received by the administrator on June 3. In *K v Hospital Managers of the Kingswood Centre* [2014] EWCA Civ 1332; [2015] M.H.L.R. 75, the letter requesting discharge was faxed to the hospital by the patient's solicitor and then put into the in-tray of the authorised person who worked part-time and did not return to her desk for four days (including the weekend). The Court of Appeal, on finding that the legislative scheme had been correctly applied in *Re GK,* held that the method of delivery used by the solicitor was not prescribed by this regulation. The court agreed with the following submission made on behalf of the hospital:

"A hospital can be expected to put in place systems to deal with methods of delivery that are prescribed. That is not the circumstance here. It is submitted that they should not be expected to provide for a non-prescribed method of delivery. Delivery to a general fax number is not a prescribed form of service, the deeming provisions do not apply to it and the default prescribed method of delivery then governs service so that it is not until the authorised officer has the order delivered to her that time begins to run" (para.15).

It was therefore the case that the 72 hour notice period did not start to run from the time when the discharge order was received at the hospital's fax machine; it started to run from the time when it was received by the officer authorised by the hospital managers.

The court said that non-prescribed methods of service "might include e-mail and social networking, both of which, like attempted fax service, are regularly excluded from commercial methods of service because in the context of the purpose to be served, the risk of non-delivery is too great" (para.19).

Paragraph 3(8)

WITHOUT FURTHER PROOF. The officer checking the document may take certain state- **2–053** ments at face value. For example, there is no need to check that the doctor who states that she is a registered medical practitioner is so registered, or that the mental health professional who states that she is an approved mental health practitioner has been approved under s.114.

Paragraphs (9), (10)

OFFICER AUTHORISED. See the note on "officer" in para.2, above. **2–054**

PART 2

PROCEDURES AND RECORDS RELATING TO HOSPITAL ADMISSIONS, GUARDIANSHIP
AND COMMUNITY TREATMENT ORDERS

Procedure for and record of hospital admissions

4.—(1) Subject to paragraph (2), for the purposes of admission to hospital **2–055** under Part 2 of the Act—

(a) any application for admission for assessment under section 2 shall be in the form set out—
  (i) where made by the nearest relative, in Form A1,
  (ii) where made by an approved mental health professional, in Form A2;
(b) any medical recommendation for the purposes of section 2 shall be in the form set out—
  (i) in the case of joint recommendations, in Form A3,
  (ii) in any other case, in Form A4;
(c) any application for admission for treatment under section 3 shall be in the form set out—
  (i) where made by the nearest relative, in Form A5,
  (ii) where made by an approved mental health professional, in Form A6;
(d) any medical recommendation for the purposes of section 3 shall be in the form set out—
  (i) in the case of joint recommendations, in Form A7,
  (ii) in any other case, in Form A8;
(e) any emergency application under section 4 shall be in the form set out—
  (i) where made by the nearest relative, in Form A9,
  (ii) where made by an approved mental health professional, in Form A10;
(f) any medical recommendation for the purposes of section 4 shall be in the form set out in Form A11;
(g) any report made under subsection (2) of section 5 (detention of in-patient already in hospital for a maximum 72 hours) by—
  (i) the registered medical practitioner or approved clinician in charge of the treatment of the patient, or
  (ii) any person nominated by the registered medical practitioner or approved clinician to act for them,
  shall be in the form set out in Part 1 of Form H1 and the hospital managers shall record receipt of that report in Part 2 of that Form;
(h) any record made under subsection (4) of section 5 (power to detain an in-patient for a maximum of 6 hours) by a nurse of the class for the time

being prescribed for the purposes of that subsection shall be in the form set out in Form H2.

(2) For the purposes of any medical recommendation under sections 2, 3, 4 and 7 (admission for assessment, admission for treatment, admission for assessment in cases of emergency and application for guardianship respectively) in the case of—

(a) a single recommendation made in respect of a patient whom a doctor has examined in Wales, the medical recommendation shall be in the form required by Regulations made by the Welsh Ministers to similar effect for Wales;

(b) joint recommendations made in respect of a patient whom both doctors have examined in Wales, the medical recommendation shall be in the form required by Regulations made by the Welsh Ministers to similar effect for Wales;

(c) joint recommendations made in respect of a patient whom one doctor has examined in Wales and one doctor has examined in England, the medical recommendation shall either be in the form required by these Regulations or in the form required by Regulations made by the Welsh Ministers to similar effect for Wales.

(3) For the purposes of section 15 (rectification of applications and recommendations), the managers of the hospital to which a patient has been admitted in pursuance of an application for assessment or for treatment may authorise an officer on their behalf—

(a) to consent under subsection (1) of that section to the amendment of the application or any medical recommendation given for the purposes of the application;

(b) to consider the sufficiency of a medical recommendation and, if the recommendation is considered insufficient, to give written notice as required by subsection (2) of that section.

(4) Where a patient has been admitted to a hospital pursuant to an application under section 2, 3 or 4 (admission for assessment, admission for treatment and admission for assessment in cases of emergency respectively), a record of admission shall be made by the managers of that hospital in the form set out in Part 1 of Form H3 and shall be attached to the application.

(5) Where a patient has been admitted to a hospital pursuant to an application under section 4 (admission for assessment in cases of emergency), a record of receipt of a second medical recommendation in support of the application for admission of the patient shall be made by the managers in the form set out in Part 2 of Form H3 and shall be attached to the application.

DEFINITION

2–056   the Act: reg.2(1).

GENERAL NOTE
Paragraph (1)

2–057   SHALL BE IN THE FORM SET OUT.   See the General Note to Sch.1.

Paragraph (2)

2–058   This paragraph sets out when the equivalent Welsh forms are to be used for medical recommendations for patients who have been examined by doctors in Wales. If patients who are admitted to hospitals in Wales are medically examined in England, the medical recommendation forms set out in these Regulations must be used: see reg.(4)(4) of the

Welsh Regulations. The application to the Welsh Hospital will be made using a Welsh application form: see para.8.64 of the Reference Guide.

Paragraph (3)
AN OFFICER.   See the note on reg.3(2). This officer is unlikely to be the person who **2–059** records the patient's admission for the purposes of reg.4(4). The scrutiny of documents for the purposes of possible rectification "should happen at the same time as the documents are received or as soon as possible afterwards (and certainly no later than the next working day)" (*Code of Practice*, para.35.11). Also see the notes to s.6(3).

Paragraph (4)
FORM H3.   If an application has been "duly completed" for the purposes of s.6(1), a **2–060** failure to comply with the requirement to complete this form would not invalidate the detention of a patient made pursuant to an application because the application is "sufficient authority" to detain the patient (s.6(2)). The form should be completed retrospectively on the omission being discovered.

Procedure for and acceptance of guardianship applications

5.—(1) For the purposes of section 7 (application for guardianship)—   **2–061**
  (a) an application for guardianship shall be in the form set out—
     (i) where made by the nearest relative, in Part 1 of Form G1,
     (ii) where made by an approved mental health professional, in Part 1 of Form G2;
  (b) where a person other than a local social services authority is named as guardian, the statement of willingness of that person to act as guardian shall be in the form set out in Part 2 of Form G1 or, as the case may be, G2;
  (c) any medical recommendation shall be in the form set out—
     (i) in the case of joint recommendations, in Form G3,
     (ii) in any other case, in Form G4.
  (2) Where an application for guardianship is accepted by the responsible local social services authority, it shall record its acceptance of the application in the form set out in Form G5 (which shall be attached to the application).

Procedure for and records relating to community treatment orders

6.—(1) For the purposes of section 17A (community treatment orders)—   **2–062**
  (a) an order made by the responsible clinician shall be in the form set out in Parts 1 and 3 of Form CTO1;
  (b) the agreement of the approved mental health professional shall be in the form set out in Part 2 of Form CTO1;
  (c) as soon as reasonably practicable, the responsible clinician shall furnish the managers of the responsible hospital with that order.
  (2) For the purposes of section 17B (conditions in community treatment orders)—
  (a) the conditions to which the patient is subject whilst the order remains in force shall be in the form set out in Form CTO1;
  (b) a variation of any of those conditions by the responsible clinician shall be in the form set out in Form CTO2;
  (c) as soon as reasonably practicable, the responsible clinician shall furnish the managers of the responsible hospital with Form CTO2.
  (3) For the purposes of section 17E (power to recall a community patient to hospital)—

(a) a responsible clinician's notice recalling a patient to hospital shall be in the form set out in Form CTO3;

(b) as soon as reasonably practicable, the responsible clinician shall furnish the managers of the hospital to which the patient is recalled with a copy of the notice recalling the patient to hospital;

(c) where the patient is recalled to a hospital which is not the responsible hospital, the responsible clinician shall notify the managers of the hospital to which the patient is recalled in writing of the name and address of the responsible hospital;

(d) the managers of the hospital to which the patient is recalled shall record the time and date of the patient's detention pursuant to that notice in the form set out in Form CTO4.

(4) Where the patient's responsible hospital is in Wales, the patient's recall shall be effected in accordance with Regulations made by the Welsh Ministers to similar effect for Wales.

(5) A responsible clinician's notice recalling a patient to hospital for the purposes of section 17E (power to recall a community patient to hospital) in Form CTO3 shall be served by—

(a) delivering it by hand to the patient,

(b) delivering it by hand to the patient's usual or last known address, or

(c) sending it by pre-paid first class post addressed to the patient at the patient's usual or last known address.

(6) Notice of recall in Form CTO3 is considered served—

(a) in the case of sub-paragraph 5(a), immediately on delivery of the notice to the patient;

(b) in the case of sub-paragraph 5(b), on the day (which does not have to be a business day) after it is delivered;

(c) in the case of sub-paragraph 5(c), on the second business day after it was posted.

(7) As soon as practicable following the patient's recall, the managers of the responsible hospital shall take such steps as are reasonably practicable to—

(a) cause the patient to be informed, both orally and in writing, of the provisions of the Act under which the patient is for the time being detained and the effect of those provisions, and

(b) ensure that the patient understands the effect, so far as is relevant to the patient's case, of sections 56 to 64 (consent to treatment).

(8) For the purposes of section 17F (powers in respect of recalled patients)—

(a) an order referred to in subsection (4) (responsible clinician's order revoking a community treatment order) shall be in the form set out in Parts 1 and 3 of Form CTO5;

(b) a statement of an approved mental health professional referred to in that subsection (signifying agreement with the responsible clinician's opinion and that it is appropriate to revoke the order) shall be in the form set out in Part 2 of Form CTO5;

(c) as soon as practicable, the responsible clinician shall furnish the managers of the hospital to which the patient is recalled with that Form;

(d) where the patient is recalled to a hospital which is not the responsible hospital, the managers of that hospital shall (as soon as reasonably practicable) furnish the managers of the hospital which was the patient's responsible hospital prior to the revocation of the patient's community treatment order, with a copy of Form CTO5.

DEFINITION
    the Act: reg.2(1).
    served: reg.2(1).

2–063

GENERAL NOTE

Paragraph (4)
    Where a community patient's responsible hospital is in Wales, the patient's recall to hospital is be effected in accordance with the Welsh Regulations and the appropriate Welsh form (Form CP5) should be used (even if the patient is to be recalled to a hospital in England).   **2–064**

Paragraph (7)
    This is similar to the duty that hospital managers have under s.132 of the Act in respect of **2–065** detained patients as patients recalled from a community treatment order do not count as detained patients for the purposes of s.132.

Transfer from hospital to hospital or guardianship

7.—(1) This regulation shall apply in respect of any patient ("a hospital **2–066** patient") to whom section 19(1)(a) applies and who is not a patient transferred under—

    (a) section 19(3) (transfer between hospitals under the same managers), or

    (b) section 123(1) and (2) (transfers between and from special hospitals).

    (2) A hospital patient may be transferred to another hospital where—

    (a) an authority for transfer is given by the managers of the hospital in which the patient is liable to be detained in the form set out in Part 1 of Form H4, and

    (b) those managers are satisfied that arrangements have been made for the admission of the patient to the hospital to which the patient is being transferred within a period of 28 days beginning with the date of the authority for transfer.

    (3) Upon completion of the transfer of the patient, the managers of the hospital to which the patient is transferred shall record the patient's admission in the form set out in Part 2 of Form H4.

    (4) A hospital patient may be transferred into the guardianship of a local social services authority, or a person approved by a local social services authority, where—

    (a) an authority for transfer is given by the managers of the hospital in which the patient is detained in the form set out in Part 1 of Form G6;

    (b) the transfer has been agreed by the local social services authority, which will be the responsible local social services authority if the proposed transfer takes effect;

    (c) that local social services authority has specified the date on which the transfer shall take place;

    (d) the managers of the transferring hospital have recorded the agreement of the local social services authority referred to in paragraph (b) and the date for transfer referred to in paragraph (c), in the form set out in Part 1 of that Form;

(e) in the case of a person other than a local social services authority being named as guardian, the agreement of that person to act as guardian is recorded in the form set out in Part 2 of that Form.

(5) A hospital patient who is detained in a registered establishment—

(a) may be transferred from that registered establishment to another registered establishment where both are under the same management, and paragraph (2) shall not apply, and

(b) where such a patient is maintained under a contract with a [clinical commissioning group,] Local Health Board, [. . .], National Health Service trust, National Health Service foundation trust, a Special Health Authority [, the National Health Service Commissioning Board] or the Welsh Ministers, any authority for transfer required under paragraph (2)(a) or, as the case may be, (4)(a), and the record (where relevant) required under paragraph (4)(d), may be made or given by an officer of that [group, board, trust or authority] authorised by that [group, board, trust or authority], board or trust in that behalf, or by those Ministers, instead of by the managers.

(6) The functions of the managers referred to in this regulation may be performed by an officer authorised by them in that behalf.

AMENDMENTS
The amendments to this regulation were made by SI 2013/235 art.11, Sch.2 para.117.

GENERAL NOTE
2–067   See reg.10 for transfers between Wales and England.

Paragraph (2)
2–068   The conveyance of a patient who is transferred to another hospital is governed by reg.11.

TRANSFERRED TO ANOTHER HOSPITAL.   There must be a physical transfer of the patient within the 28 day period allowed for in para.(b).

Paragraph (4)
2–069   DATE ON WHICH THE TRANSFER TAKES.   The patient could be granted leave of absence under s.17 to take up residence in the place where he will be required to reside before that date.

Paragraph 5(b)
2–070   The effect of this provision is explained in the Reference Guide:

"10.13 If an NHS patient is detained in an independent hospital, an authorisation to transfer the patient to a hospital under different managers, but not the same managers, may also be given by an officer of the relevant NHS body who has been authorised by that body to do so.

10.14 In other words, the relevant NHS body can authorise the patient's transfer without the agreement of the managers of the independent hospital. For restricted patients, the agreement of the Secretary of State for Justice is still required."

Paragraph (6)
2–071   OFFICER.   See the note on reg.3(2).

Transfer from guardianship to guardianship or hospital

8.—(1) A guardianship patient may be transferred into the guardianship of **2–072** another local social services authority or person where—

(a) an authority for transfer is given by the guardian in the form set out in Part 1 of Form G7;

(b) that transfer has been agreed by the receiving local social services authority, which will be the responsible local social services authority if the proposed transfer takes effect;

(c) that local social services authority has specified the date on which the transfer shall take place;

(d) the guardian has recorded the agreement of the receiving local social services authority mentioned in paragraph (b) and the date for transfer mentioned in paragraph (c) in Part 1 of that Form;

(e) a person other than a local social services authority is named in the authority for transfer as proposed guardian, the statement of willingness of that person to act as guardian is recorded in the form set out in Part 2 of that Form.

(2) An authority for transfer to hospital of a guardianship patient may be given by the responsible local social services authority in the form set out in Part 1 of Form G8 where—

(a) an application for admission for treatment has been made by an approved mental health professional in the form set out in Form A6;

(b) that application is founded on medical recommendations given by two registered medical practitioners in accordance with section 12 in the form set out—

(i) in the case of joint recommendations, in Form A7;

(ii) in any other case, in Form A8;

(c) the responsible local social services authority is satisfied that arrangements have been made for the admission of the patient to that hospital within the period of 14 days beginning with the date on which the patient was last examined by a registered medical practitioner for the purposes of paragraph (b).

(3) Where paragraph (2)(a) applies, for the purposes of the application referred to in that paragraph, sections 11(4) (consultation with nearest relative) and 13 (duty of approved mental health professional) shall apply as if the proposed transfer were an application for admission for treatment.

(4) On the transfer of a guardianship patient referred to in paragraph (2), a record of admission shall be made by the managers of the hospital to which the patient is transferred in the form set out in Part 2 of Form G8 and shall be attached to the application referred to in paragraph (2)(a).

(5) Where the conditions of paragraph (2) are satisfied, the transfer of the patient must be effected within 14 days of the date on which the patient was last examined, failing which the patient will remain subject to guardianship.

(6) The functions of the managers referred to in this regulation may be performed by an officer authorised by them in that behalf.

DEFINITION
    guardianship patient: reg.2(1).   **2–073**

GENERAL NOTE

2–074   A patient who has been transferred from guardianship to hospital has a right to apply to a tribunal within six months of the day of the transfer (s.66(1)(e), (2)(e)). If the patient does not exercise this right, the hospital managers must automatically refer the case to the tribunal (s.68(1)).

Paragraph (1)(e)

2–075   PERSON OTHER THAN A LOCAL SOCIAL SERVICES AUTHORITY.   Who, after the transfer has been completed, must appoint a doctor to act as the nominated medical attendant of the patient and send relevant details to the local social services authority (reg.22).

Paragraph (2)

2–076   The provisions of s.15 of the Act concerning the rectification of applications and medical recommendations do not apply to documents given in support of a transfer. The application and recommendations should therefore be scrutinised carefully to ensure that they comply with legislative requirements before the authority for transfer is signed. Minor errors can be corrected without affecting the validity of the transfer.

   The patient must be admitted to the hospital within 14 days beginning with the date of the latter of the two medical examinations on which the medical recommendations are based (reg.11(1)(b)).

Paragraph (6)

2–077   OFFICER.   See the note on reg.3(2).

Transfer of community patients recalled to hospital

2–078   **9.**—(1) The managers of a hospital in which a community patient is detained, having been recalled to hospital, may authorise the transfer of that patient to another hospital.

   (2) Where the hospital to which the patient has been recalled and the hospital to which the patient is being transferred are not under the same management, a transfer may only take place if the requirements of paragraphs (3) to (5) are satisfied.

   (3) Those requirements are that the managers of the hospital to which the patient was recalled—

   (a) authorise the transfer of the patient in the form set out in Part 1 of Form CTO6, and

   (b) are satisfied that arrangements have been made for the admission of the patient to the hospital to which the patient is being transferred.

   (4) The managers of the hospital from which the patient is being transferred shall furnish the managers of the hospital to which the patient is being transferred with a copy of Form CTO4 (record of patient's detention in hospital after recall) before, or at the time of, the patient's transfer.

   (5) On the transfer of the patient, the managers of the hospital to which the patient is transferred shall record the patient's admission in the form set out in Part 2 of Form CTO6.

   (6) Where—

   (a) a patient has been recalled to a registered establishment, and

   (b) that patient is maintained under a contract with a [clinical commissioning group,] Local Health Board, [. . .], National Health Service trust, National Health Service foundation trust, a Special Health Authority [, the National Health Service Commissioning Board] or the Welsh Ministers, any authority for transfer required under paragraph (3)(a) may be given by an officer of that [group, board, trust or authority] authorised by that [group, board, trust or authority] in that behalf, or by those Ministers, instead of the managers.

(7) The functions of the managers referred to in this regulation may be performed by an officer authorised by them in that behalf.

AMENDMENTS
The amendments to this regulation were made by SI 2013/235 art.11, Sch.2 para.117.

GENERAL NOTE
This regulation allows community patients who have been recalled to one hospital to be   **2–079**
transferred to another, provided this is done within the 72-hour maximum period allowed
for a patient to be detained following recall: see s.17F(6). The requirements are similar to
those for the transfer of detained patients between hospitals under reg.7. In particular, no
statutory form is required when managers authorise the transfer of a patient between hospitals which are both under their own management. The conveyance of a patient who is
transferred under this provision is governed by reg.12. Assignment of responsibility for
community patients between one hospital and another is dealt with in reg.17. For the
responsibility to inform the patient's nearest relative of the assignment, see reg.26(1)(h)
(reg.32(b) of the Welsh Regulations).

If a recalled patient is to be transferred from a hospital in Wales to one in England, the
transfer must be authorised and recorded in accordance with the Welsh Regulations.
Transfers from England to Wales are to be made in accordance with these regulations.

Paragraph (7)
OFFICER.   See the note on reg.3(2).   **2–080**

Transfers from England to Wales and from Wales to England
10.—(1) Where a patient who is liable to be detained or is subject to guardian- **2–081**
ship under the Act is transferred from a hospital or guardianship in England to a
hospital or guardianship in Wales, that transfer shall be subject to the conditions in
these Regulations.

(2) Where a patient who is liable to be detained or is subject to guardianship
under the Act is transferred from a hospital or guardianship in Wales to a hospital
or guardianship in England, that transfer and the duty to record the admission of a
patient so transferred shall be subject to such conditions as may be prescribed in
Regulations made by the Welsh Ministers to similar effect for Wales.

(3) Where paragraph (2) applies and any Regulations made by the Welsh
Ministers to similar effect for Wales provide for authority to convey a patient
in Wales, those Regulations shall provide authority to convey the patient whilst
in England.

GENERAL NOTE
This regulation deals with transfers of detained and guardianship patients between **2–082**
England and Wales. Its main effect is that, if a patient is to be transferred from Wales to
England, the procedure in the Welsh Regulations is to be followed.

Conveyance to hospital on transfer from hospital or guardianship
11.—(1) Where the conditions of regulation 7(2) or 8(2) are satisfied, the auth- **2–083**
ority for transfer given in accordance with those regulations shall be sufficient
authority for the following persons to take the patient and convey the patient to

the hospital to which the patient is being transferred within the periods specified—

(a) in a case to which regulation 7(2) applies—

    (i) an officer of the managers of either hospital, or

    (ii) any person authorised by the managers of the hospital to which the patient is being transferred,

within the period of 28 days beginning with the date of the authority for transfer;

(b) in a case to which regulation 8(2) applies—

    (i) an officer of, or

    (ii) any person authorised by,

the responsible local social services authority, within the period of 14 days beginning with the date on which the patient was last examined by a medical practitioner for the purposes of regulation 8(2)(b).

(2) Paragraph (1) shall apply to a patient who—

(a) is liable to be detained under the Act and is removed to another hospital in circumstances to which section 19(3) applies, as if the authority given by the managers for that transfer were an authority for transfer given in accordance with regulation 7(2);

(b) is liable to be detained in a hospital at which high security psychiatric services are provided and who, pursuant to a direction given by the Secretary of State under section 123(1) or (2) (transfers to and from special hospitals), is removed or transferred to another hospital, as if that direction were an authority for transfer given in accordance with regulation 7(2).

(3) In a case to which regulation 7(5)(a) applies, an officer of or any other person authorised by the managers of the registered establishment may take and convey the patient to the registered establishment to which the patient is being transferred.

GENERAL NOTE

2–084   Paragraph 10.19 of the Reference Guide states:

> "In all cases [of patients being conveyed to hospital], patients are deemed to be in legal custody while being conveyed, which means that the person conveying them can take steps to stop them absconding, and retake them if they do . . . . If they abscond while being transferred, they are also treated as if they were absent without leave (AWOL) from both hospitals—which affects who may take them into custody and allows them to be returned to either hospital . . . ."

Conveyance from hospital to hospital following recall of community patients

2–085   **12.** Where the conditions of regulation 9(1) or (3) are satisfied, the authority for transfer given in accordance with that regulation shall be sufficient authority for the following persons to take the patient and convey him to the hospital to which he is being transferred—

(a) an officer of the managers of either hospital, or

(b) any person authorised by the managers of the hospital to which the patient is being transferred,

within the period of 72 hours beginning with the time of the patient's detention pursuant to the patient's recall under section 17E (power to recall to hospital).

Renewal of authority for detention or guardianship and extension of community treatment period

13.—(1) Any report for the purposes of section 20(3) (medical recommen- **2–086** dation for renewal of authority to detain) shall be in the form set out in Parts 1 and 3 of Form H5.

(2) The statement for the purposes of section 20(5A) (agreement with medical recommendation for renewal of authority to detain) shall be in the form set out in Part 2 of Form H5.

(3) The receipt of Form H5 shall be recorded by the managers of the hospital in which the patient is liable to be detained in the form set out in Part 4 of that Form.

(4) Any report for the purposes of section 20(8) (medical recommendation for renewal of guardianship) shall be in the form set out in Part 1 of Form G9.

(5) The responsible social services authority shall record receipt of Form G9 in the form set out in Part 2 of that Form.

(6) For the purposes of section 20A (community treatment period)—

(a) a report for the purposes of subsection (4) of that section (responsible clinician's report extending the community treatment period) shall be in the form set out in Parts 1 and 3 of Form CTO7;

(b) a statement for the purposes of subsection (8) of that section (approved mental health professional's statement that it is appropriate to extend the order) shall be in the form set out in Part 2 of Form CTO7.

(7) The managers of the responsible hospital shall record the receipt of Form CTO7 in the form set out in Part 4 of that Form.

Detention, guardianship or community treatment after absence without leave for more than 28 days

14.—(1) In relation to a patient who is liable to be detained— **2–087**

(a) any report for the purposes of section 21B(2) (authority for detention or guardianship of patients who are taken into custody or return after more than 28 days) shall be in the form set out in Part 1 of Form H6, and

(b) the receipt of that report shall be recorded by the managers of the hospital in which the patient is liable to be detained in the form set out in Part 2 of that Form.

(2) In relation to a patient who is subject to guardianship—

(a) any report for the purposes of section 21B(2) shall be in the form set out in Part 1 of Form G10, and

(b) the receipt of that report shall be recorded by the responsible local social services authority in the form set out in Part 2 of that Form.

(3) In relation to a community patient—

(a) any report for the purposes of section 21B(2) shall be in the form set out in Part 1 of Form CTO8, and

(b) the receipt of that report shall be recorded by the managers of the responsible hospital in the form set out in Part 2 of that Form.

Removal to England

15.—(1) This regulation shall apply to a patient who is removed from Scotland, **2–088** Northern Ireland, any of the Channel Islands or the Isle of Man to England ("a removed patient") under—

(a) section 82, 84 or 85 (as the case may be), or

(b) regulations made under section 290 of the Mental Health (Care and Treatment) (Scotland) Act 2003 (removal and return of patients within United Kingdom).

(2) Where a removed patient is liable to be detained in a hospital, the managers of the hospital shall record the date on which the patient is admitted to the hospital in the form set out in Form M1.

(3) The managers of the hospital shall take such steps as are reasonably practicable to inform the person (if any) appearing to them to be the patient's nearest relative as soon as practicable of the patient's admission to hospital.

(4) Where a removed patient is received into guardianship—

(a) the guardian shall record the date on which the patient arrives at the place at which the patient is to reside on the patient's reception into guardianship under the Act in the form set out in Form M 1;

(b) the guardian shall take such steps as are reasonably practicable to inform the person (if any) appearing to them to be the patient's nearest relative as soon as practicable that the patient has been received into guardianship under the Act;

(c) a private guardian shall notify the responsible local social services authority of the—

(i) date mentioned in sub-paragraph (a), and

(ii) particulars mentioned in regulation 22(1)(b) and (e).

DEFINITION

2–089   private guardian: reg.2(1).

GENERAL NOTE

2–090   This regulation deals with the statutory forms to be used to record the arrival in England of detained and guardianship patients from Scotland, Northern Ireland, and any of the Channel Islands or the Isle of Man.

Paragraphs (3),(4)(b)

2–091   SUCH STEPS AS ARE REASONABLY PRACTICABLE.   Paragraph 4.36 of the *Code of Practice* states:

"In addition, occasionally there will be cases where these duties do not apply because disclosing information about the patient to the nearest relative cannot be considered practicable, on the grounds that it would have a detrimental impact on the patient that is disproportionate to any advantage to be gained from informing the nearest relative. This would therefore be a breach of the patient's right to privacy under article 8 of the European Convention on Human Rights (ECHR). The risk of this is greatest where the nearest relative is someone whom the patient would not have chosen themselves. Before disclosing information to nearest relatives without a patient's consent, the person concerned must consider whether the disclosure would be likely to:

● put the patient at risk of physical harm or financial or other exploitation

● cause the patient emotional distress or lead to a deterioration in their mental health, or

● have any other detrimental effect on their health or wellbeing and, if so, whether the advantages to the patient and the public interest of the disclosure outweigh the disadvantages to the patient, in the light of all the circumstances of the case."

Removal to England of patients subject to compulsion in the community

16.—(1) This regulation shall apply to a patient who is removed from Scotland, **2–092** any of the Channel Islands or the Isle of Man to England under—

(a) section 289(1) of the Mental Health (Care and Treatment) (Scotland) Act 2003 (crossborder transfer: patients subject to requirement other than detention) in the case of Scotland; or

(b) section 85ZA (responsibility for community patients transferred from any of the Channel Islands or the Isle of Man) in the case of any of the Channel Islands or the Isle of Man.

(2) The managers of the responsible hospital shall record the date on which the patient arrived at the place where the patient is to reside in the form set out in Form M1.

(3) The managers of the hospital shall take such steps as are reasonably practicable to inform the person (if any) appearing to them to be the patient's nearest relative as soon as practicable that the patient is a community patient.

(4) The conditions specified by the responsible clinician under section 80C(5) (removal of patients subject to compulsion in the community from Scotland) or section 85ZA(4), shall be recorded by that responsible clinician in Part 1 of Form CTO9.

(5) The approved mental health professional's agreement to the conditions referred to in paragraph (4) shall be recorded by that approved mental health professional in Part 2 of Form CTO9.

GENERAL NOTE

This regulation deals with the reception of patients in England or Wales as community **2–093** patients on their transfer from Scotland, any of the Channel Islands or the Isle of Man.

Paragraph (3)

See the note on reg.15(3), (4)(b) above. **2–094**

Assignment of responsibility for community patients

17.—(1) This regulation applies to a community patient whether or not the **2–095** patient has been recalled to hospital in accordance with section 17E (power to recall to hospital).

(2) Responsibility for a patient referred to in paragraph (1) may be assigned by the managers of the responsible hospital to any other hospital whether or not that other hospital is under the same management as the responsible hospital.

(3) Responsibility for a patient shall not be assigned to a hospital which is not under the same management as the responsible hospital unless—

(a) an authority for the assignment is given by the managers of the assigning responsible hospital in the form set out in [assignment] Form CTO10;

(b) that [. . .] has been agreed by the managers of the hospital which will be the responsible hospital if the proposed [assignment] takes effect;

(c) the managers of the hospital referred to in (b) have specified the date on which the [assignment] shall take place;

(d) the managers of the assigning responsible hospital record—

(i) the agreement of the managers of the new responsible hospital to the assignment, and

(ii) the date on which the assignment is to take place,

in the form set out in that Form.

(4) The managers of the receiving hospital must notify the patient in writing of—

(a) the assignment, either before it takes place or as soon as reasonably practicable thereafter; and

(b) their name and address (irrespective of whether or not there are any changes in the managers).

(5) Where responsibility for a patient is assigned from a responsible registered establishment to another hospital which is not under the same management and the patient is maintained under a contract with a [clinical commissioning group,] Local Health Board, [. . .], National Health Service trust, National Health Service foundation trust, a Special Health Authority [, the National Health Service Commissioning Board] or the Welsh Ministers, any authority for [assignment] required under paragraph (3)(a), and the record required under paragraph (3)(b), may be given by an officer of that [group, board, trust or authority] authorised by it in that behalf, or by those Ministers, instead of by the managers.

(6) Any hospital to which a patient has been assigned may, in accordance with the provisions of this regulation, assign the patient to another hospital.

(7) The functions of the managers referred to in this regulation may be performed by an officer authorised by them in that behalf.

AMENDMENTS

The amendments to this regulation were made by SI 2008/2560 reg.2(2) and SI 2013/235 art.11, Sch.2 para.117.

GENERAL NOTE

2–096   This regulation sets out the procedure to be followed to authorise the reassignment of responsibility for a community patient from one hospital to another. No statutory form is required when managers authorise the transfer of responsibility for the patient between hospitals which are both under their management.

If responsibility is to be assigned from a hospital in Wales to one in England, the assignment must be made in accordance with the Welsh Regulations. This regulation should be followed for assignments from England to Wales.

Paragraph (5)

2–097   Paragraph 26.133 of the Reference Guide states:

"If an independent hospital is the responsible hospital for an NHS patient, an officer authorised by the relevant NHS body may also authorise the patient's transfer to another hospital under different management. The relevant NHS body is the one which has contracted with the independent hospital to act as the responsible hospital."

Paragraph (7)

2–098   OFFICER.   See the note on reg.3(2).

Discharge of patients

2–099   **18.** For the purposes of section 23 (discharge of patients) a responsible clinician's order for the discharge of—

(a) a patient liable to be detained under the Act, or a community patient, shall be sent to the managers of the hospital in which the patient is liable to be detained or the responsible hospital (as applicable) as soon as practicable after it is made;

(b) a guardianship patient, shall be sent to the guardian as soon as practicable after it is made.

guardianship patient: reg.2(1).   **2–100**

GENERAL NOTE

This regulation deals with the discharge of a patient under s.23 of the Act by the respon- **2–101** sible clinician. There is no statutory form to be used for this purpose in England; a letter to the appropriate body would suffice. In Wales, if an RC discharges a patient from detention Form HO17 must be used. This Form must also be used in Wales if the hospital managers order discharge: see reg.7 of the Welsh Regulations.

Delegation of hospital managers' functions under the Act

19. The functions of the managers of a hospital in respect of the following— **2–102**
  (a) notifying local social services authorities under section 14 (social reports) of patients detained on the basis of applications by their nearest relatives;
  (b) authorising persons under section 17(3) (leave of absence from hospital) to keep in custody patients who are on leave of absence who are subject to a condition that they remain in custody;
  (c) authorising persons under sections 18(1) and (2A) (return and readmission of patients absent without leave) to take and return detained and community patients respectively who are absent without leave,
may be performed by any person authorised by them in that behalf.

GENERAL NOTE

For the avoidance of doubt, this regulation expressly allows hospital managers to auth- **2–103** orise a person to exercise on their behalf the functions set out in paras (a), (b) and (c).

Delegation of managers' functions under the Domestic Violence, Crime and Victims Act 2004

20. The functions of the managers of a hospital under sections 35 to 44B of the **2–104** Domestic Violence, Crime and Victims Act 2004 (provision of information to victims of patients under the Act etc.) may be performed by any person authorised by them in that behalf.

GENERAL NOTE

The Explanatory Memorandum to these regulations states: **2–105**

"The Committee's attention is drawn to section 45(4) of the Domestic Violence, Crime and Victims Act 2004 which provides that a function conferred on the managers of a hospital under sections 35 to 44B of that Act is to be treated as a function of those managers under Part 3 of the 1983 Act for the purposes of section 32(3) of the 1983 Act (regulations as to delegation of managers' functions, etc). Section 32(3) of the 1983 Act, in turn, allows for the delegation of the functions of hospital managers under the 1983 Act."

Delegation by local social services authorities

21.—(1) Except as provided by paragraph (2), a local social services authority **2–106** may delegate its functions under Parts 2 and 3 of the Act and these Regulations in the same way and to the same persons as its functions referred to in the Local

Government Act 1972 may be delegated in accordance with section 101 of that Act.

(2) The function of the local social services authority under section 23 (discharge of patients) may not be delegated otherwise than in accordance with that section.

GENERAL NOTE

2–107   This regulation confirms that local social services authorities to whom s.101 of the Local Government Act 1972 applies (those authorities who do not operate executive arrangements) may delegate their functions under Pts II and III of the Act (apart from decisions made under s.23), and under these regulations, in any way and to any person to whom they could delegate them under that section. Authorities which operate executive arrangements have separate and extensive powers of delegation under the Local Government Act 2000.

PART 3

FUNCTIONS OF GUARDIANS AND NEAREST RELATIVES

Duties of private guardians

2–108   **22.**—(1) It shall be the duty of a private guardian—

  (a) to appoint a registered medical practitioner to act as the nominated medical attendant of the patient;

  (b) to notify the responsible local social services authority of the name and address of the nominated medical attendant;

  (c) in exercising the powers and duties of a private guardian conferred or imposed by the Act and these Regulations, to comply with such directions as that authority may give;

  (d) to furnish that authority with all such reports or other information with regard to the patient as the authority may from time to time require;

  (e) to notify that authority—

    (i) on the reception of the patient into guardianship, of the private guardian's address and the address of the patient,

    (ii) except in a case to which paragraph (f) applies, of any permanent change of either address, before or not later than 7 days after the change takes place;

  (f) on any permanent change of the private guardian's address, where the new address is in the area of a different local social services authority, to notify that authority—

    (i) of that address and that of the patient,

    (ii) of the particulars mentioned in paragraph (b),

    and to notify the authority which was formerly responsible of the permanent change in the private guardian's address;

  (g) in the event of the death of the patient, or the termination of the guardianship by discharge, transfer or otherwise, to notify the responsible local social services authority as soon as reasonably practicable.

(2) Any notice, reports or other information under this regulation may be given or furnished in any other way (in addition to the methods of serving documents provided for by regulation 3(1)) to which the relevant local social services authority agrees, including orally or by electronic communication.

DEFINITION
private guardian: reg.2(1). **2–109**

GENERAL NOTE
Paragraph (1)(a)
The nominated medical attendant is responsible for examining the patient for the pur- **2–110** poses of renewing guardianship (ss.20(6), 34(1)). This doctor could be the patient's general practitioner.

Visits to patients subject to guardianship

23. The responsible local social services authority shall arrange for every **2–111** patient received into guardianship under the Act to be visited at such intervals as the authority may decide, but—

(a) in any case at intervals of not more than 3 months, and

(b) at least one such visit in any year shall be made by an approved clinician or a practitioner approved by the Secretary of State for the purposes of section 12 (general provisions as to medical recommendations).

GENERAL NOTE
Paragraph (b)
The approved clinician need not be a medical practitioner. **2–112**

Performance of functions of nearest relative

24.—(1) Subject to the conditions of paragraph (7), any person other than— **2–113**

(a) the patient;

(b) a person mentioned in section 26(5) (persons deemed not to be the nearest relative), or

(c) a person in respect of whom the court has made an order on the grounds set out in section 29(3)(b) to (e) (which sets out the grounds on which an application to the court for the appointment of a person to exercise the functions of a nearest relative may be made) for so long as an order under that section is in effect,

may be authorised in accordance with paragraph (2) to act on behalf of the nearest relative in respect of the matters mentioned in paragraph (3).

(2) Subject to paragraph (8), the authorisation mentioned in paragraph (1) must be given in writing by the nearest relative.

(3) The matters referred to in paragraph (1) are the performance in respect of the patient of the functions conferred upon the nearest relative under—

(a) Part 2 of the Act (as modified by Schedule 1 to the Act as the case may be), and

(b) section 66 (applications to tribunals).

(4) An authorisation given under paragraph (1) shall take effect upon its receipt by the person authorised.

(5) Subject to the conditions of paragraph (7), the nearest relative of a patient may give notice in writing revoking that authorisation.

(6) Any revocation of such authorisation shall take effect upon the receipt of the notice by the person authorised.

(7) The conditions mentioned in paragraphs (1) and (5) are that the nearest relative shall immediately notify—

(a) the patient;

(b) in the case of a patient liable to be detained in a hospital, the managers of that hospital;

(c) in the case of a patient subject to guardianship, the responsible local social services authority and the private guardian, if any;

(d) in the case of a community patient, the managers of the responsible hospital, of the authorisation or, as the case may be, its revocation.

(8) An authorisation or notification referred to in this regulation may be transmitted by means of electronic communication if the recipient agrees.

DEFINITIONS

2–114   private guardian: reg.2(1).
electronic communication: reg.2(1).

GENERAL NOTE

2–115   This regulation enables the patient's nearest relative to delegate the functions specified in para.(3) to another person at any time. The delegate can exercise all of the functions of nearest relative with the exception that, by virtue of the legal principle delegatus non potest delegare, he or she does not have the power to further delegate such functions to another. A delegation cannot be made to the persons identified in para.(1)(a),(b) or (c). The patient, who cannot prevent the nearest relative from making a delegation, does not need to be subject to the Act's provisions at the time when the delegation is made. If this is the case, the only formality that is required is for the nearest relative to give written notice of the authorisation to the authorised person and for the patient to be notified of the authorisation.

A letter will suffice; there is no statutory form that needs to be completed. The letter, which should be signed and dated, could be written along the following lines:

"I [insert name] of [insert address] being the nearest relative of [insert patient's name and address] for the purposes of the Mental Health Act 1983, hereby delegate my powers of nearest relative to [insert name] of [insert address]. I confirm that [insert name] has consented to act as the nearest relative of [insert patient's name]"

The authorisation or notification may be given by electronic means if the recipient agrees (para.(8)). Notification to one of the bodies mentioned in para.(7) is required if the patient is subject to the Act's provisions at the time of the authorisation. However, it would be sensible for the relevant body to be notified before it becomes necessary to utilise the provisions of the Act. That body should check whether the author of the letter is in fact the patient s nearest relative and whether the delegate has agreed to the delegation. If a delegation is made, the nearest relative may revoke it at any time by notifying the authorised person in writing (para.(5)) or electronically (para.(8)).

If an approved mental health professional (AMHP) suspects that the nearest relative might not have possessed the required mental capacity at the time when the delegation was made, the AMHP should attempt to assess the nearest relative's capacity. If the assessment, together with the result of enquiries made by the AMHP, suggests that the nearest relative was likely to have been mentally incapacitated at the relevant time, an application should be made to the Court of Protection to determine the issue.

A delegation made under this provision would end on the death of the nearest relative or on the nearest relative ceasing to have that status by virtue of the operation of either s.26 or s.29 of the Act.

An acting nearest relative appointed by the court under s.29 cannot use this power but must apply to the county court under s.30 for the s.29 order to be varied if he or she no longer wishes to perform the functions of acting nearest relative.

Paragraph (1)

ANY PERSON.   The person authorised need not be a relative of the patient. Although **2–116** there is no requirement for the person concerned to have consented to the delegation, it must be assumed that such consent is a pre-condition of delegation.

Discharge by nearest relative

25.—(1) Any report given by the responsible clinician for the purposes of sec-   **2–117** tion 25 (restrictions on discharge by nearest relative)—

(a)   shall be in the form set out in Part 1 of Form M2, and

(b)   the receipt of that report by—

    (i) the managers of the hospital in which the patient is liable to be detained, or

    (ii) the managers of the responsible hospital in the case of a community patient, shall be in the form set out in Part 2 of that Form.

(2) In addition to the methods of serving documents provided for by regulation 3(1), reports under this regulation may be furnished by—

(a)   transmission by facsimile, or

(b)   the transmission in electronic form of a reproduction of the report, if the managers of the hospital agree.

GENERAL NOTE

Paragraph 32.25 of the *Code of Practice* contains an illustrative letter of discharge.   **2–118**

PART 4

PROVISION OF INFORMATION

26.—(1) Unless the patient requests otherwise, where —   **2–119**

(a)   a patient is to be or has been transferred from hospital to hospital pursuant to section 19 or section 123 (regulations as to transfer of patients and transfer to and from special hospitals respectively), the managers of the hospital to which the patient is to be or has been transferred shall take such steps as are reasonably practicable to cause the person (if any) appearing to them to be the patient's nearest relative to be informed of that transfer before it takes place or as soon as practicable thereafter;

(b)   a patient's detention is renewed pursuant to a report furnished under section 20 (duration of authority), the managers of the responsible hospital shall take such steps as are reasonably practicable to cause the person (if any) appearing to them to be the patient's nearest relative to be informed of that renewal as soon as practicable following their decision not to discharge the patient;

(c)   by virtue of section 21B(7) (patients who are taken into custody or return after more than 28 days) a patient's detention is renewed pursuant to a report furnished under section 21B(2), the managers of the responsible hospital in which the patient is liable to be detained shall take such steps as are reasonably practicable to cause the person (if any) appearing to them to be the patient's nearest relative to be informed of that renewal as soon as practicable following their decision not to discharge the patient;

(d)   by virtue of section 21B(5) and (6) (patients who are taken into custody or return after more than 28 days), a patient's detention is renewed

675

retrospectively pursuant to a report furnished under section 21B(2), the managers of the hospital in which the patient is liable to be detained shall take such steps as are reasonably practicable to cause the patient and the person (if any) appearing to them to be the patient's nearest relative to be informed of that renewal as soon as practicable following their receipt of that report;

(e) a patient's period of community treatment is extended pursuant to a report furnished under section 20A (community treatment period), the managers of the responsible hospital shall take such steps as are reasonably practicable to cause the person (if any) appearing to them to be the patient's nearest relative to be informed of that extension as soon as practicable following their decision not to discharge the patient;

(f) by virtue of section 21B(7A) (patients who are taken into custody or return after more than 28 days) a patient's period of community treatment is extended pursuant to a report furnished under section 21B(2), the managers of the responsible hospital shall take such steps as are reasonably practicable to cause the person (if any) appearing to them to be the patient's nearest relative to be informed of that extension as soon as practicable following their decision not to discharge the patient;

(g) by virtue of section 21B(6A) and (6B) (patients who are taken into custody or return after more than 28 days) a patient's period of community treatment is extended retrospectively pursuant to a report furnished under section 21B(2), the managers of the responsible hospital shall take such steps as are reasonably practicable to cause the patient and the person (if any) appearing to them to be the patient's nearest relative to be informed of that extension as soon as practicable following their receipt of that report;

(h) a patient is to be or has been assigned to another hospital which assumes responsibility for that patient as a community patient, the managers of the hospital to which the patient is to be or has been assigned shall take such steps as are reasonably practicable to cause the person (if any) appearing to them to be the patient's nearest relative to be informed of that assignment before or as soon as practicable following it taking place;

(i) a patient is to be or has been transferred from hospital to guardianship pursuant to section 19 (regulations as to transfer of patients), the responsible local social services authority shall take such steps as are reasonably practicable to cause the person appearing to it to be the patient's nearest relative to be informed of that transfer before it takes place or as soon as practicable thereafter;

(j) a patient is to be or has been transferred from the guardianship of one person to the guardianship of another person pursuant to section 19 (regulations as to transfer of patients), the new responsible local social services authority shall take such steps as are reasonably practicable to cause the person (if any) appearing to it to be the patient's nearest relative to be informed of that transfer before it takes place or as soon as practicable thereafter;

(k) a patient's guardianship becomes vested in the local social services authority or the functions of a guardian are, during the guardian's incapacity, transferred to the authority or a person approved by it under section 10 (transfer of guardianship in case of death, incapacity, etc of guardian), the responsible local social services authority shall take such steps as are reasonably practicable to cause the person (if any) appearing to it to be the patient's nearest relative to be informed of that vesting, or as the case may be, transfer before it takes place or as soon as practicable thereafter;

(l) a patient's guardianship is renewed pursuant to a report furnished under section 20 (duration of authority), the responsible local social services authority shall take such steps as are reasonably practicable to cause the person (if any) appearing to it to be the patient's nearest relative to be informed of that renewal as soon as practicable following the decision of the responsible local social services authority [not] to discharge the patient;

(m) by virtue of section 21B(7) (patients who are taken into custody or return after more than 28 days) a patient's guardianship is renewed pursuant to a report furnished under section 21B(7), the responsible local social services authority shall take such steps as are reasonably practicable to cause the person (if any) appearing to it to be the patient's nearest relative to be informed of that renewal as soon as practicable following the decision of the responsible local social services authority not to discharge the patient;

(n) by virtue of section 21B(5) and (6) (patients who are taken into custody or return after more than 28 days) a patient's guardianship is renewed retrospectively pursuant to a report furnished under section 21B(2), the responsible local social services authority shall take such steps as are reasonably practicable to cause the patient and person (if any) appearing to it to be the patient's nearest relative to be informed of that renewal as soon as practicable following the receipt by the responsible local social services authority of that report.

(2) Where paragraph (1)(m) or (n) applies, the responsible local social services authority shall, as soon as practicable inform the private guardian (if any) of its receipt of a report furnished under section 21B (patients who are taken into custody or return after more than 28 days).

(3) Upon a patient becoming subject to guardianship under the Act, the responsible local social services authority shall take such steps as are reasonably practicable to cause to be informed both the patient and the person (if any) appearing to the authority to be the patient's nearest relative of the rights referred to in paragraph (4).

(4) Those rights are—

(a) the patient's rights under section 66 (applications to tribunals),

(b) the nearest relative's right, as the case may be, to—

   (i) discharge the patient under section 23 (discharge of patients), or

   (ii) make an application under section 69 (application to tribunals concerning patients subject to hospital and guardianship orders where the patient is, or is treated as being, subject to guardianship under section 37).

(5) Where information referred to in paragraph (1)(d), (g) or (n), or in paragraph (3) is to be given to the patient, it shall be given both orally and in writing.

(6) Where information referred to in paragraph (1) [or (3)] is to be given to the person appearing to be the patient's nearest relative, it shall be given in writing.

(7) Where information referred to in paragraph (2) is to be given to the private guardian, it shall be given in writing.

(8) Information that is to be given in writing under paragraphs (6) and (7) may be transmitted by means of electronic communication if the recipient agrees.

(9) The functions of the managers referred to in this regulation may be performed by an officer authorised by them in that behalf.

AMENDMENTS
The amendments to this regulation were made by SI 2008/2560 reg.2(3).

GENERAL NOTE

2–120   This regulation sets out when hospital managers and local authorities are required to give information about various statutory events relating to the patient's detention, supervised community treatment or guardianship to the patient's nearest relative (and sometimes patients themselves and, where applicable, private guardians). This requirement is in addition to the duties placed on hospital managers by ss.132, 132A and 133 of the Act to give information to patients and their nearest relatives. The information must not be given to the nearest relative if this is the patient's wish (para.(1)) or it is not "reasonably practicable" to provide the information: see the note on reg.15(3), (4)(b), above.

PART 5

CONSENT TO TREATMENT

Consent to treatment

2–121   **27.**—(1) For the purposes of section 57 (treatment requiring consent and a second opinion)—

(a) the form of treatment to which that section shall apply, in addition to the treatment mentioned in subsection (1)(a) of that section (any surgical operation for destroying brain tissue or for destroying the functioning of brain tissue), shall be the surgical implantation of hormones for the purpose of reducing male sexual drive, and

(b) the certificates required for the purposes of subsection (2)(a) and (b) of that section shall be in the form set out in Form T 1.

(2) For the purposes of section 58 (treatment requiring consent or a second opinion) the certificates required for the purposes of subsection (3)(a) and (b) of that section shall be in the form set out in Forms T2 and T3 respectively.

(3) For the purposes of section 58A (electro-convulsive therapy, etc.)—

(a) the form of treatment to which that section shall apply, in addition to the administration of electro-convulsive therapy mentioned in subsection (1)(a) of that section, shall be the administration of medicine as part of that therapy; and

(b) the certificates required for the purposes of subsections (3), (4) and (5) of that section shall be in the form set out in Forms T4, T5 and T6 respectively.

(4) Section 58A does not apply to treatment by way of the administration of medicine as part of electro-convulsive therapy where that treatment falls within section 62(1)(a) or (b) (treatment immediately necessary to save the patient's life or to prevent a serious deterioration in the patient's condition).

GENERAL NOTE
Paragraph (1)(a)

2–122   The oral administration of hormones for the purpose of reducing the male sex drive does not come within the scope of s.57.

Paragraph (4)

2–123   This provides that administration of medicine as part of ECT (like ECT itself: see para.(3)(a)) does not require a certificate from a SOAD if it is immediately necessary to save the patient's life or to prevent a serious deterioration of his condition.

PART 6

TREATMENT OF COMMUNITY PATIENTS NOT RECALLED TO HOSPITAL

28.—(1) For the purposes of Part 4A of the Act (treatment of community **2–124** patients not recalled to hospital), the certificates required for the purposes of sections 64B(2)(b) and 64E(2)(b) (which set out when treatment under Part 4A of the Act may be given to adult and child community patients respectively) shall be in the form set out in Form CTO11 [except where paragraph (1A) applies].

[(1A) Where there is authority to give treatment to a patient by virtue of section 64C(2)(a) or section 64E(6)(a), the certificate required for the purposes of sections 64B(2)(b) and 64E(2)(b) shall be in the form set out in Form CTO12.]

(2) Treatment of a patient to whom section 64B(3)(b) or section 64E(3)(b) applies (adult and child patients for whom treatment is immediately necessary), may include treatment by way of administration of medicine as part of electro-convulsive therapy but only where that treatment falls within section 64C(5)(a) or (b) (treatment immediately necessary to save the patient's life or to prevent a serious deterioration in the patient's condition).

(3) Treatment of a patient to whom section 64G (emergency treatment for patients lacking capacity or competence) applies may include treatment by way of the administration of medicine as part of electro-convulsive therapy but only where that treatment falls within section 64G(5)(a) or (b) (treatment immediately necessary to save the patient's life or to prevent a serious deterioration in the patient's condition).

AMENDMENTS
The amendments to this rule were made by SI 2012/1118 reg.2(2).

GENERAL NOTE
This regulation makes similar provision to reg.27(2) to (4) in respect of patients who are **2–125** subject to community treatment orders and who have not been recalled to hospital.

PART 7

CORRESPONDENCE OF PATIENTS

Inspection and opening of postal packets
29.—(1) Where under section 134(4) (inspection and opening of postal packets **2–126** addressed to or by patients in hospital) any postal packet is inspected and opened, but neither the packet nor anything contained in it is withheld under section 134(1) or (2) the person appointed who inspected and opened it, shall record in writing—
  (a) that the packet had been so inspected and opened,
  (b) that nothing in the packet has been withheld, and
  (c) the name of the person appointed and the name of the hospital, and shall, before resealing the packet, place the record in that packet.

(2) Where under section 134(1) or (2) any postal packet or anything contained in it is withheld by the person appointed—
  (a) that person shall record in a register kept for the purpose—
    (i) that the packet or anything contained in it has been withheld,
    (ii) the date on which it was so withheld,

(iii) the grounds on which it was so withheld,

(iv) a description of the contents of the packet withheld or of any item withheld, and

(v) the name of the person appointed; and

(b) if anything contained in the packet is withheld, the person appointed shall record in writing—

(i) that the packet has been inspected and opened,

(ii) that an item or items contained in the packet have been withheld,

(iii) a description of any such item,

(iv) the name of the person appointed and the name of the hospital, and

(v) in any case to which section 134(1)(b) or (2) applies, the further particulars required for the purposes of section 134(6),

and shall, before resealing the packet, place the record in that packet.

(3) In a case to which section 134(1)(b) or (2) applies—

(a) the notice required for the purposes of section 134(6) shall include—

(i) a statement of the grounds on which the packet in question or anything contained in it was withheld, and

(ii) the name of the person appointed who so decided to withhold that packet or anything contained in it and the name of the hospital; and

(b) where anything contained in a packet is withheld the record required by paragraph (2)(b) shall, if the provisions of section 134(6) are otherwise satisfied, be sufficient notice to the person to whom the packet is addressed for the purposes of section 134(6).

(4) For the purposes of this regulation "the person appointed" means a person appointed under section 134(7) to perform the functions of the managers of the hospital under that section.

Review of decisions to withhold postal packets

2–127   **30.**—(1) Every application for review by the Commission under [section 134A(1) (review of decisions to withhold correspondence)] shall be—

(a) made in such manner as the Commission may accept as sufficient in the circumstances of any particular case or class of case and may be made otherwise than in writing, and

(b) made, delivered or sent to an office of the Commission.

(2) Any person making such an application shall furnish to the Commission the notice of the withholding of the postal packet or anything contained in it, given under section 134(6), or a copy of that notice.

(3) For the purpose of determining any such application the Commission may direct the production of such documents, information and evidence as it may reasonably require.

AMENDMENT

In para.(1), the words in square brackets were substituted by SI 2009/462 art.12, Sch.5 para.25(b).

DEFINITION

2–128   the Commission: reg.2(1).

Patient advocacy and liaison services and independent mental capacity advocate services

31.—(1) In section 134 (correspondence of patients), for the purposes of sub- **2–129** section (3)(ea) "patient advocacy and liaison service" means a service affording assistance in the form of advice and liaison for patients, their families and carers provided by—

(a) an NHS trust,
(b) an NHS foundation trust,
[(c) a clinical commissioning group, or
(d) the National Health Service Commissioning Board.]

(2) For the purposes of section 134(3A)(b)(iii), the prescribed arrangements are arrangements in respect of independent mental capacity advocates made under section 35 to 41 of the Mental Capacity Act 2005 (independent advocacy service).

AMENDMENT
The amendment to this regulation was made by SI 2013/235 art.11, Sch.2 para.117.

PART 8

REVOCATIONS

Revocations

32. The Regulations specified in column 1 of Schedule 2 are hereby revoked to **2–130** the extent mentioned in column 3 of that Schedule.

Regulations 4–9, 13–17, 25,   **SCHEDULE 1**
27 and 28

AMENDMENTS
The amendments to Forms A7, A9, H2, CTO8 and CTO 11 were made by SI 2008/2560 reg.2(4).

GENERAL NOTE
Health bodies and local authorities can produce their own forms as long as the wording **2–131** set out in this Schedule is reproduced. A handwritten form would suffice in an emergency if printed forms were not available. An alternative course of action would be to remove the appropriate pages from this Manual. Copies of the forms can be downloaded from the Mental Health Law Online website at: *www.mentalhealthlaw.co.uk/Mental_Health_Act_ 1983_Statutory_Forms*. Welsh forms can also be accessed from the MHLO website.

The use of a form which failed to produce the exact wording set out in these regulations would not necessarily invalidate the application or recommendation because minor departures would be regarded by the courts as being de minimis, i.e. too trivial to be of any consequence. In *Re E (Mental Health: Habeas Corpus)*, December 10, 1966, the court held that the detention of a patient was lawful in a situation where obsolete forms had been used because the differences between the two sets of forms was de minimis and were not intended by the Act to be taken account of. The Court of Appeal has confirmed the validity of a transfer direction made under s.47 of the Act where one of the reporting doctors had used an obsolete form (*R. (on the application of SP) v Secretary of State for Justice* [2010] EWCA Civ 1590; [2011] M.H.L.R. 65). It is likely that a court would find a patient's detention to be unlawful if the statutory criteria set out in the form failed to reproduce the correct wording in some material respect.

In *Re RS's Application for Judicial Review* [2015] NICA 30, the Court of Appeal in Northern Ireland said that the decision in *R. (on the application of H) v Oxfordshire Mental Healthcare NHS Trust* [2002] EWHC 465 (Admin), which is noted in the General Note to s.12, is authority for the proposition that the "statutory prescribed forms envisage the provision of summary reasons" (para.36).

Faxed forms

2–132   Although only reg.25(2)(a) provides specific authority for a form to be served by fax, it is submitted that a faxed reproduction of a completed form can be acted upon if (a) the recipient confers with the signatory by telephone to confirm that that the form was completed by the signatory; and (b) the original is delivered to the recipient at the earliest opportunity. The Mental Health Act Commission endorsed the use of faxed forms (MHAC, *Sixth Biennial Report*, 1993–1995, para.3.13).

Lost forms

2–133   If the forms that were used to provide authority for the patient's detention or guardianship are lost, the authority for the detention or guardianship no longer exists and a fresh assessment under the Act must be undertaken if it is considered that the patient has a continuing need for either detention or guardianship. However, if copies of the original forms were made there would be no need for a fresh assessment if the signatories endorsed the relevant copy as a true copy of the original form.

Scanned documents

2–134   Provided that the scanning process and procedures are compliant with the British Standards Institution's BIP:0008 Code of Practice for "Legal Admissibility and Evidential Weight of Information Stored Electronically", the paper versions of Forms used under the Act can be destroyed under confidential conditions. Information about the Code of Practice can be accessed at *www.bsigroup.com*.

Retention of statutory forms

2–135   Annex D2 of "Records management: NHS code of practice", Department of Health, April 5, 2006, states that "Mental Health Act administration records" must be kept for five years from the date of the last record. However, a 30 year time limit will apply if a medical practitioner considers that such records form part of the patient's health record. With regard to Mental Health Act records, Annex D2 states:

"There is no obligation to treat this type of mental health record as being part of a patient's health record. There may, however, be exceptions, such as where they are required to be kept as evidence in actual or expected litigation or where they are needed by a healthcare professional in order to provide healthcare. Each healthcare practitioner has discretion as to the information which s/he wishes to include as part of a patient record. If in any particular case a healthcare practitioner requires a document which forms part of the mental health act administration record to be included in a patient's record (because he or she regards it as relevant to the patient's healthcare), it should then be regarded as part of the patient's health record."

**FORMS FOR USE IN CONNECTION WITH COMPULSORY
ADMISSION TO HOSPITAL, GUARDIANSHIP AND
TREATMENT**

Form A1   *Regulation 4(1)(a)(i)*

Mental Health Act 1983 section 2—application by nearest relative for admission for assessment 2–136

To the managers of [name and address of hospital]

I [PRINT your full name and address] apply for the admission of [PRINT full name and address of patient] for assessment in accordance with Part 2 of the Mental Health Act 1983.

Complete (a) or (b) as applicable and delete the other.

  (a) To the best of my knowledge and belief I am the patient's nearest relative within the meaning of the Act

       I am the patient's [state your relationship with the patient].

  (b) I have been authorised to exercise the functions under the Act of the patient's nearest relative by a county court/the patient's nearest relative *<delete the phrase which does not apply>*, and a copy of the authority is attached to this application.

I last saw the patient on [date], which was within the period of 14 days ending on the day this application is completed.

This application is founded on two medical recommendations in the prescribed form.

If neither of the medical practitioners had previous acquaintance with the patient before making their recommendations, please explain why you could not get a recommendation from a medical practitioner who did have previous acquaintance with the patient:—

. . . .
. . . .
. . . .

If you need to continue on a separate sheet please indicate here [ ] and attach that sheet to this form]

Signed . . . .

Date . . . .

2–137 **Mental Health Act 1983 section 2—application by an approved mental health professional for admission for assessment**

To the Managers of [name and address of hospital]

I [PRINT your full name and address] apply for the admission of [PRINT full name and address of patient] for assessment in accordance with Part 2 of the Mental Health Act 1983.

I am acting on behalf of [PRINT name of local social services authority] and am approved to act as an approved mental health professional for the purposes of the Act by <*delete as appropriate*>

that authority
[name of local social services authority that approved you, if different]

Complete the following if you know who the nearest relative is.

Complete (a) or (b) as applicable and delete the other.

  (a) To the best of my knowledge and belief [PRINT full name and address] is the patient's nearest relative within the meaning of the Act.

  (b) I understand that [PRINT full name and address] has been authorised by a county court/the patient's nearest relative* to exercise the functions under the Act of the patient's nearest relative.
       <*Delete the phrase which does not apply*>

I have/have not yet* informed that person that this application is to be made and of the nearest relative's power to order the discharge of the patient. <*Delete the phrase which does not apply*>

Complete the following if you do not know who the nearest relative is.

Delete (a) or (b).

  (a) I have been unable to ascertain who is the patient's nearest relative within the meaning of the Act.

  (b) To the best of my knowledge and belief this patient has no nearest relative within the meaning of the Act.

The remainder of the form must be completed in all cases.

I last saw the patient on [date], which was within the period of 14 days ending on the day this application is completed.

I have interviewed the patient and I am satisfied that detention in a hospital is in all the circumstances of the case the most appropriate way of providing the care and medical treatment of which the patient stands in need.

This application is founded on two medical recommendations in the prescribed form.

If neither of the medical practitioners had previous acquaintance with the patient before making their recommendations, please explain why you could not get a recommendation from a medical practitioner who did have previous acquaintance with the patient—

. . . .
. . . .
. . . .

[If you need to continue on a separate sheet please indicate here [ ] and attach that sheet to this form]

Signed . . . .

Date . . . .

Form A3   *Regulation 4(1)(b)(i)*

Mental Health Act 1983 section 2—joint medical recommendation for admission for assessment **2–138**

We, registered medical practitioners, recommend that [PRINT full name and address of patient] be admitted to a hospital for assessment in accordance with Part 2 of the Mental Health Act 1983.

I [PRINT full name and address of first practitioner] last examined this patient on [date].

*I had previous acquaintance with the patient before I conducted that examination.

*I am approved under section 12 of the Act as having special experience in the diagnosis or treatment of mental disorder.

<*Delete if not applicable>

I [PRINT full name and address of second practitioner] last examined this patient on [date].

*I had previous acquaintance with the patient before I conducted that examination.

*I am approved under section 12 of the Act as having special experience in the diagnosis or treatment of mental disorder.

<*Delete if not applicable>

In our opinion

   (a) this patient is suffering from mental disorder of a nature or degree which warrants the detention of the patient in hospital for assessment (or for assessment followed by medical treatment) for at least a limited period,

AND

   (b) ought to be so detained
       (i) in the interests of the patient's own health
      (ii) in the interests of the patient's own safety
     (iii) with a view to the protection of other persons
      <*Delete the indents not applicable>

Our reasons for these opinions are:

[Your reasons should cover both (a) and (b) above. As part of them: describe the patient's symptoms and behaviour and explain how those symptoms and behaviour lead you to your opinion; explain why the patient ought to be admitted to hospital and why informal admission is not appropriate.]

. . . .
. . . .
. . . .

[If you need to continue on a separate sheet please indicate here [ ] and attach that sheet to this form]

Signed . . . .

Date . . . .

Signed . . . .

Date . . . .

NOTE: AT LEAST ONE OF THE PRACTITIONERS SIGNING THIS FORM MUST BE APPROVED UNDER SECTION 12 OF THE ACT.

2–139 **Mental Health Act 1983 section 2—medical recommendation for admission for assessment**

I [PRINT full name and address of medical practitioner], a registered medical practitioner, recommend that [PRINT full name and address of patient] be admitted to a hospital for assessment in accordance with Part 2 of the Mental Health Act 1983.

I last examined this patient on [date].

*I had previous acquaintance with the patient before I conducted that examination.

*I am approved under section 12 of the Act as having special experience in the diagnosis or treatment of mental disorder.

<*Delete if not applicable>

In my opinion,

    (a) this patient is suffering from mental disorder of a nature or degree which warrants the detention of the patient in hospital for assessment (or for assessment followed by medical treatment) for at least a limited period,

AND

    (b) ought to be so detained
        (i) in the interests of the patient's own health
       (ii) in the interests of the patient's own safety
      (iii) with a view to the protection of other persons
       <*Delete the indents not applicable>

My reasons for these opinions are:

[Your reasons should cover both (a) and (b) above. As part of them: describe the patient's symptoms and behaviour and explain how those symptoms and behaviour lead you to your opinion; explain why the patient ought to be admitted to hospital and why informal admission is not appropriate.]

. . . .
. . . .
. . . .

[If you need to continue on a separate sheet please indicate here [ ] and attach that sheet to this form]

Signed . . . .

Date . . . .

Form A5   *Regulation 4(1)(c)(i)*

Mental Health Act 1983 section 3—application by nearest relative for admission for treatment   **2–140**

To the Managers of [name and address of hospital]

I [PRINT your full name and address] apply for the admission of [PRINT full name and address of patient] for treatment in accordance with Part 2 of the Mental Health Act 1983.

Complete either (a) or (b) as applicable and delete the other

  (a) To the best of my knowledge and belief I am the patient's nearest relative within the meaning of the Act.

      I am the patient's [state relationship with the patient].

  (b) I have been authorised to exercise the functions under the Act of the patient's nearest relative by a county court/the patient's nearest relative *<delete the phrase which does not apply>*, and a copy of the authority is attached to this application.

I last saw the patient on [date], which was within the period of 14 days ending on the day this application is completed.

This application is founded on two medical recommendations in the prescribed form.

If neither of the medical practitioners had previous acquaintance with the patient before making the recommendations, please explain why you could not get a recommendation from a medical practitioner who did have previous acquaintance with the patient—

. . . .
. . . .
. . . .
. . . .
. . . .

[If you need to continue on a separate sheet please indicate here [ ] and attach that sheet to this form]

Signed . . . .

Date . . . .

2–141 **Mental Health Act 1983 section 3—application by an approved mental health professional for admission for treatment**

To the managers of [name and address of hospital]

I [PRINT your full name and address] apply for the admission of [PRINT full name and address of patient] for treatment in accordance with Part 2 of the Mental Health Act 1983.

I am acting on behalf of [name of local social services authority] and am approved to act as an approved mental health professional for the purposes of the Act by *<delete as appropriate>*

    that authority
    [name of local social services authority that approved you, if different]

Complete the following where consultation with the nearest relative has taken place.

Complete (a) or (b) and delete the other.

  (a) I have consulted [PRINT full name and address] who to the best of my knowledge and belief is the patient's nearest relative within the meaning of the Act.

  (b) I have consulted [PRINT full name and address] who I understand has been authorised by a county court/the patient's nearest relative* to exercise the functions under the Act of the patient's nearest relative.
  *<*Delete the phrase which does not apply>*

That person has not notified me or the local social services authority on whose behalf I am acting that he or she objects to this application being made

Complete the following where the nearest relative has not been consulted.

Delete whichever two of (a), (b) and (c) do not apply.

  (a) I have been unable to ascertain who is this patient's nearest relative within the meaning of the Act.

  (b) To the best of my knowledge and belief this patient has no nearest relative within the meaning the Act.

  (c) I understand that [PRINT full name and address] is

     (i) this patient's nearest relative within the meaning of the Act,
    (ii) authorised to exercise the functions of this patient's nearest relative under the Act,
     <Delete either (i) or (ii)>

but in my opinion it is not reasonably practicable/would involve unreasonable delay *<delete as appropriate>* to consult that person before making this application, because—

. . . .
. . . .
. . . .

[If you need to continue on a separate sheet please indicate here [ ] and attach that sheet to this form]

The remainder of this form must be completed in all cases.

I saw the patient on [date], which was within the period of 14 days ending on the day this application is completed.

I have interviewed the patient and I am satisfied that detention in a hospital is in all the circumstances of the case the most appropriate way of providing the care and medical treatment of which the patient stands in need.

This application is founded on two medical recommendations in the prescribed form.

If neither of the medical practitioners had previous acquaintance with the patient before making their recommendations, please explain why you could not get a recommendation from a medical practitioner who did have previous acquaintance with the patient—

. . . .
. . . .
. . . .

[If you need to continue on a separate sheet please indicate here [ ] and attach that sheet to this form]

Signed . . . .

Date . . . .

2–142 Mental Health Act 1983 section 3—joint medical recommendation for admission for treatment

We, registered medical practitioners, recommend that [PRINT full name and address of patient] be admitted to a hospital for treatment in accordance with Part 2 of the Mental Health Act 1983.

I [PRINT full name and address of first practitioner] last examined this patient on [date].

*I had previous acquaintance with the patient before I conducted that examination.

*I am approved under section 12 of the Act as having special experience in the diagnosis or treatment of mental disorder.

<*Delete if not applicable>

I [PRINT name and address of second practitioner] [last examined this patient on [date].]

*I had previous acquaintance with the patient before I conducted that examination.

*I am approved under section 12 of the Act as having special experience in the diagnosis or treatment of mental disorder.

<*Delete if not applicable>

In our opinion,

  (a) this patient is suffering from mental disorder of a nature or degree which makes it appropriate for the patient to receive medical treatment in a hospital,

AND

  (b) it is necessary
      (i) for the patient's own health
      (ii) for the patient's own safety
      (iii) for the protection of other persons
            <delete the indents not applicable>

that this patient should receive treatment in hospital, AND

  (c) such treatment cannot be provided unless the patient is detained under section 3 of the Act,

because—[Your reasons should cover (a), (b) and (c) above. As part of them: describe the patient's symptoms and behaviour and explain how those symptoms and behaviour lead you to your opinion; say whether other methods of treatment or care (eg out-patient treatment or social services) are available and, if so, why they are not appropriate; indicate why informal admission is not appropriate.]

. . . .
. . . .
. . . .

[If you need to continue on a separate sheet please indicate here [ ] and attach that sheet to this form]

. . . .

Mental Health (Hospital) (England) Regs 2008, Form A7

We are also of the opinion that, taking into account the nature and degree of the mental disorder from which the patient is suffering and all the other circumstances of the case, appropriate medical treatment is available to the patient at the following hospital (or one of the following hospitals):—

[Enter name of hospital(s). If appropriate treatment is available only in a particular part of the hospital, say which part.]

. . . .
. . . .
. . . .

Signed . . . .

Date . . . .

Signed . . . .

Date . . . .

NOTE: AT LEAST ONE OF THE PRACTITIONERS SIGNING THIS FORM MUST BE APPROVED UNDER SECTION 12 OF THE ACT.

2–143 **Mental Health Act 1983 section 3—medical recommendation for admission for treatment**

I [PRINT full name and address of practitioner], a registered medical practitioner, recommend that [PRINT full name and address of patient] be admitted to a hospital for treatment in accordance with Part 2 of the Mental Health Act 1983.

I last examined this patient on [date].

*I had previous acquaintance with the patient before I conducted that examination.

*I am approved under section 12 of the Act as having special experience in the diagnosis or treatment of mental disorder.

<*Delete if not applicable>

In my opinion,

   (a) this patient is suffering from mental disorder of a nature or degree which makes it appropriate
         for the patient to receive medical treatment in a hospital,

AND

   (b) it is necessary
         (i) for the patient's own health
         (ii) for the patient's own safety
         (iii) for the protection of other persons
               <delete the indents not applicable>

that this patient should receive treatment in hospital,

AND

   (c) such treatment cannot be provided unless the patient is detained under section 3 of the Act,

because — [Your reasons should cover (a), (b) and (c) above. As part of them: describe the patient's symptoms and behaviour and explain how those symptoms and behaviour lead you to your opinion; say whether other methods of treatment or care (eg out-patient treatment or social services) are available and, if so, why they are not appropriate; indicate why informal admission is not appropriate.]

. . . .
. . . .
. . . .

[If you need to continue on a separate sheet please indicate here [ ] and attach that sheet to this form]

I am also of the opinion that, taking into account the nature and degree of the mental disorder from which the patient is suffering and all the other circumstances of the case, appropriate medical treatment is available to the patient at the following hospital (or one of the following hospitals):—

. . . .
. . . .

[Enter name of hospital(s). If appropriate treatment is available only in a particular part of the hospital, say which part.]

Signed . . . .

Date . . . .

Form A9   *Regulation 4(1)(e)(i)*

Mental Health Act 1983 section 4—emergency application by nearest relative for admission for **2–144**
assessment

THIS FORM IS TO BE USED ONLY FOR AN EMERGENCY APPLICATION

To the managers of [name and address of hospital]

I [PRINT your full name and address] apply for the admission of [PRINT full name and address of patient] for assessment in accordance with Part 2 of the Mental Health Act 1983.

Complete (a) or (b) as applicable and delete the other.

   (a) To the best of my knowledge and belief I am the patient's nearest relative within the meaning of the Act.

       I am the patient's [state your relationship with the patient].

   (b) I have been authorised to exercise the functions under the Act of the patient's nearest relative by a county court/the patient's nearest relative *<delete the phrase which does not apply>*, and a copy of the authority is attached to this application.

I last saw the patient on [date] [at time]], which was within the last 24 hours.

In my opinion it is of urgent necessity for the patient to be admitted and detained under section 2 of the Act and compliance with the provisions of Part 2 of the Act relating to applications under that section would involve undesirable delay.

This application is founded on a medical recommendation in the prescribed form.

If the medical practitioner did not have previous acquaintance with the patient before making the recommendation, please explain why you could not get a recommendation from a medical practitioner who did have previous acquaintance with the patient—

. . . .
. . . .
. . . .

[If you need to continue on a separate sheet please indicate here [ ] and attach that sheet to this form]

                       Signed . . . .

                       Date . . . .

                       Time . . . .

2–145 **Mental Health Act 1983 section 4—emergency application by an approved mental health professional for admission for assessment**
THIS FORM IS TO BE USED ONLY FOR AN EMERGENCY APPLICATION

To the managers of [name and address of hospital]

I [PRINT your full name and address] apply for the admission of [PRINT full name and address of patient] for assessment in accordance with Part 2 of the Mental Health Act 1983.

I am acting on behalf of [name of local social services authority] and am approved to act as an approved mental health professional for the purposes of the Act by *<delete as appropriate>*

    that authority
    [name of local social services authority that approved you, if different].

I last saw the patient on [date] at [time], which was within the last 24 hours.

I have interviewed the patient and I am satisfied that detention in a hospital is in all the circumstances of the case the most appropriate way of providing the care and medical treatment of which the patient stands in need.

In my opinion it is of urgent necessity for the patient to be admitted and detained under section 2 of the Act and compliance with the provisions of Part 2 of the Act relating to applications under that section would involve undesirable delay.

This application is founded on a medical recommendation in the prescribed form.

If the medical practitioner did not have previous acquaintance with the patient before making the recommendation, please explain why you could not get a recommendation from a medical practitioner who did have previous acquaintance with the patient—

. . . .
. . . .
. . . .

[If you need to continue on a separate sheet please indicate here [ ] and attach that sheet to this form]

Signed . . . .

Date . . . .

Time . . . .

Form A11 *Regulation 4(1)(f)*

Mental Health Act 1983 section 4—medical recommendation for emergency admission for assessment

2–146

THIS FORM IS TO BE USED ONLY FOR AN EMERGENCY APPLICATION

I [PRINT name and address of medical practitioner], a registered medical practitioner, recommend that [PRINT full name and address of patient] be admitted to a hospital for assessment in accordance with Part 2 of the Mental Health Act 1983.

I last examined this patient on [date] at [time].

*I had previous acquaintance with the patient before I conducted that examination.

*I am approved under section 12 of the Act as having special experience in the diagnosis or treatment of mental disorder.

<*Delete if not applicable>

I am of the opinion,

    (a) this patient is suffering from mental disorder of a nature or degree which warrants the detention of the patient in hospital for assessment (or for assessment followed by medical treatment) for at least a limited period,

AND

    (b) this patient ought to be so detained
        (i) in the interests of the patient's own health
        (ii) in the interests of the patient's own safety
        (iii) with a view to the protection of other persons,
        <delete the indents not applicable>

AND

    (c) it is of urgent necessity for the patient to be admitted and detained under section 2 of the Act.

My reasons for these opinions are: [Your reasons should cover (a), (b) and (c) above. As part of them: describe the patient's symptoms and behaviour and explain how those symptoms and behaviour lead you to your opinion; and explain why the patient ought to be admitted to hospital urgently and why informal admission is not appropriate.]

. . . .
. . . .
. . . .

[If you need to continue on a separate sheet please indicate here [ ] and attach that sheet to this form]

Compliance with the provisions of Part 2 of the Act relating to applications under section 2 would involve undesirable delay, because— [Say approximately how long you think it would take to obtain a second medical recommendation and what risk such a delay would pose to the patient or to other people.]

. . . .
. . . .

[If you need to continue on a separate sheet please indicate here [ ] and attach that sheet to this

Signed . . . .

Date . . . .

Time . . . .

695

2–147   **Mental Health Act 1983 section 5(2)—report on hospital in-patient**
Part 1

(To be completed by a medical practitioner or an approved clinician qualified to do so under section 5(2) of the Act)
To the managers of [name and address of hospital]

I am [PRINT full name]

and I am *<Delete (a) or (b) as appropriate>*

  (a)   the registered medical practitioner/the approved clinician (who is not a registered medical practitioner) *<delete the phrase which does not apply>*

  (b)   a registered medical practitioner/an approved clinician (who is not a registered medical practitioner)* who is the nominee of the registered medical practitioner or approved clinician (who is not a registered medical practitioner) *<*delete the phrase which does not apply>*

in charge of the treatment of [PRINT full name of patient], who is an in-patient in this hospital and not at present liable to be detained under the Mental Health Act 1983.

It appears to me that an application ought to be made under Part 2 of the Act for this patient's admission to hospital for the following reasons—

. . . .
. . . .
. . . .

[The full reasons why informal treatment is no longer appropriate must be given. If you need to continue on a separate sheet please indicate here [ ] and attach that sheet to this form.]

I am furnishing this report by: *<Delete the phrase which does not apply>*

consigning it to the hospital managers' internal mail system today at [time]

delivering it (or having it delivered) by hand to a person authorised by the hospital managers to receive it.

Signed . . . .

Date . . . .

Mental Health (Hospital) (England) Regs 2008, Form H1

PART 2

(To be completed on behalf of the hospital managers)

This report was <*Delete the phrase which does not apply*>

furnished to the hospital managers through their internal mail system

delivered to me in person as someone authorised by the hospital managers to receive this report at [time] on [date]

Signed ....
on behalf of the hospital managers

PRINT NAME ....
Date ....

2–148 **Mental Health Act 1983 section 5(4)—record of hospital in-patient**
To the managers of [name and address of hospital]

[PRINT full name of the patient]

It appears to me that—

    (a) this patient, who is receiving treatment for mental disorder as an in-patient of this hospital, is suffering from mental disorder to such a degree that it is necessary for the patient's health or safety or for the protection of others for this patient to be immediately restrained from leaving the hospital;

AND

    (b) it is not practicable to secure the immediate attendance of a registered medical practitioner or an approved clinician [(who is not a registered medical practitioner)] for the purpose of furnishing a report under section 5(2) of the Mental Health Act 1983.

I am [PRINT full name], a nurse registered—
<*Delete whichever do not apply*>

    (a) in Sub-Part 1 of the register, whose entry includes an entry to indicate the nurse's field of practice is mental health nursing;

    (b) in Sub-Part 2 of the register, whose entry includes an entry to indicate the nurse's field of practice is mental health nursing;

    (c) in Sub-Part 1 of the register, whose entry includes an entry to indicate the nurse's field of practice is learning disabilities nursing;

    (d) in Sub-Part 2 of the register, whose entry includes an entry to indicate the nurse's field of practice is [learning disabilities nursing].

Signed ....

Date ....

Time ....

Form H3   *Regulation 4(4) and (5)*

Mental Health Act 1983 sections 2, 3 and 4—record of detention in hospital   **2–149**

(To be attached to the application for admission)

PART 1

[Name and address of hospital]

[PRINT full name of patient]

Complete (a) if the patient is not already an in-patient in the hospital.
Complete (b) if the patient is already an in-patient.

Delete the one which does not apply.

(a) The above named patient was admitted to this hospital on [date of admission to hospital] at [time] in pursuance of an application for admission under section [state section] of the Mental Health Act 1983.

(b) An application for the admission of the above named patient (who had already been admitted to this hospital) under section [state section] of the Mental Health Act 1983 was received by me on behalf of the hospital managers on [date] at [time] and the patient was accordingly treated as admitted for the purposes of the Act from that time.

Signed . . . .
on behalf of the hospital managers

PRINT NAME . . . .
Date . . . .

PART 2

(To be completed only if the patient was admitted in pursuance of an emergency application under section 4 of the Act)

On [date] at [time] I received, on behalf of the hospital managers, the second medical recommendation in support of the application for the admission of the above named patient.

Signed . . . .
on behalf of the hospital managers

PRINT NAME . . . .
Date . . . .

NOTE: IF THE PATIENT IS BEING DETAINED AS A RESULT OF A TRANSFER FROM GUARDIANSHIP, THE PATIENT'S ADMISSION SHOULD BE RECORDED IN PART 2 OF THE FORM G8 WHICH AUTHORISED THE TRANSFER.

2–150 **Mental Health Act 1983 section 19—authority for transfer from one hospital to another under different managers**

PART 1

(To be completed on behalf of the managers of the hospital where the patient is detained)

Authority is given for the transfer of [PRINT full name of patient] from [name and address of hospital in which the patient is liable to be detained] to [name and address of hospital to which patient is to be transferred] in accordance with the Mental Health (Hospital, Guardianship and Treatment) (England) Regulations 2008 within 28 days beginning with the date of this authority.

Signed ....
on behalf of the managers of the first named hospital

PRINT NAME ....
Date ....

PART 2

RECORD OF ADMISSION

(This is not part of the authority for transfer but is to be completed at the hospital to which the patient is transferred)

This patient was transferred to [name of hospital] in pursuance of this authority for transfer and admitted to that hospital on [date of admission to receiving hospital] at [time].

Signed ....
on behalf of the managers of the receiving hospital

PRINT NAME ....
Date ....

Form H5   *Regulation 13(1), (2) and (3)*

Mental Health Act 1983 section 20—renewal of authority for detention   **2–151**

PART 1

(To be completed by the responsible clinician)

To the managers of [name and address of hospital in which the patient is liable to be detained]

I examined [PRINT full name of patient] on [date of examination].

The patient is liable to be detained for a period ending on [date authority for detention is due to expire].

I have consulted [PRINT full name and profession of person consulted] who has been professionally concerned with the patient's treatment.

In my opinion,

(a) this patient is suffering from mental disorder of a nature or degree which makes it appropriate for the patient to receive medical treatment in a hospital,

AND

(b) it is necessary
  (i) for the patient's own health
  (ii) for the patient's own safety
  (iii) for the protection of other persons
  <delete the indents not applicable>

that this patient should receive treatment in hospital,

because— [Your reasons should cover both (a) and (b) above. As part of them: describe the patient's symptoms and behaviour and explain how those symptoms and behaviour lead you to your opinion; say whether other methods of treatment or care (eg out-patient treatment or social services) are available and, if so, why they are not appropriate.]

. . . .
. . . .
. . . .

[If you need to continue on a separate sheet please indicate here [ ] and attach that sheet to this form]

Such treatment cannot be provided unless the patient continues to be detained under the Act, for the following reasons — [Reasons should indicate why informal admission is not appropriate.]

. . . .
. . . .
. . . .

[If you need to continue on a separate sheet please indicate here [ ] and attach that sheet to this form.]

I am also of the opinion that, taking into account the nature and degree of the mental disorder from which the patient is suffering and all the other circumstances of the case, appropriate medical treatment is available to the patient.

Signed . . . .

PRINT NAME . . . .

Profession . . . .

Date . . . .

Delegated Legislation

(To be completed by a professional who has been professionally concerned with the patient's medical treatment and who is of a different profession from the responsible clinician)

I agree with the responsible clinician that: this patient is suffering from mental disorder of a nature or degree which makes it appropriate for the patient to receive medical treatment in a hospital; it is necessary for the patient's own health or safety or for the protection of other persons that the patient should receive treatment and it cannot be provided unless the patient continues to be detained under the Act; and that, taking into account the nature and degree of the mental disorder from which the patient is suffering and all other circumstances of the case, appropriate medical treatment is available to the patient.

Signed ....

PRINT NAME ....

Profession ....

Date ....

PART 3

(To be completed by the responsible clinician)

I am furnishing this report by: *<Delete the phrase which does not apply>*

today consigning it to the hospital managers' internal mail system.

sending or delivering it without using the hospital managers' internal mail system.

Signed ....

PRINT NAME ....

Date ....

PART 4

(To be completed on behalf of the hospital managers)

This report was *<Delete the phrase which does not apply>*

furnished to the hospital managers through their internal mail system.

received by me on behalf of the hospital managers on [date].

Signed ....
on behalf of the hospital managers

PRINT NAME ....
Date ....

702

Form H6 Regulation 14(1)(a) and (b)

Mental Health Act 1983 section 21B—authority for detention after absence without leave for more than 28 days 2–152

PART 1

(To be completed by the responsible clinician)

To the managers of [name and address of hospital in which the patient is liable to be detained]

I examined [PRINT full name of patient] on [date of examination] who:

(a) was absent without leave from hospital or the place where the patient ought to have been beginning on [date absence without leave began];

(b) was/is* liable to be detained for a period ending on [date authority for detention would have expired, apart from any extension under section 21, or date on which it will expire]; <*delete the phrase which does not apply*> and

(c) returned to the hospital or place on [date].

I have consulted [PRINT full name of approved mental health professional] who is an approved mental health professional.

I have also consulted [PRINT full name and profession of person consulted] who has been professionally concerned with the patient's treatment.

In my opinion,

(a) this patient is suffering from mental disorder of a nature or degree which makes it appropriate for the patient to receive medical treatment in a hospital,

AND

(b) it is necessary
(i) for the patient's own health
(ii) for the patient's own safety
(iii) for the protection of other persons
<*delete the indents not applicable*>

that this patient should receive treatment in hospital,

because— [Your reasons should cover both (a) and (b) above. As part of them: describe the patient's symptoms and behaviour and explain how those symptoms and behaviour lead you to your opinion; say whether other methods of treatment or care (eg out-patient treatment or social services) are available and, if so, why they are not appropriate.]

....
....
....

[If you need to continue on a separate sheet please indicate here [ ] and attach that sheet to this form]

Such treatment cannot be provided unless the patient continues to be detained under the Act, for the following reasons— [Reasons should indicate why informal admission is not appropriate.]

....
....
....

[If you need to continue on a separate sheet please indicate here [ ] and attach that sheet to this form]

I am also of the opinion that, taking into account the nature and degree of the mental disorder from which the patient is suffering and all other circumstances of the case, appropriate medical treatment is available to the patient.

The authority for the detention of the patient is/is not* due to expire within a period of two months beginning with the date on which this report is to be furnished to the hospital managers. *<*Delete the phrase which does not apply>*

Complete the following only if the authority for detention is due to expire within that period of two months.

This report shall/shall not* have effect as a report duly furnished under section 20(3) for the renewal of the authority for the detention of the patient. *<*Delete the phrase which does not apply>*

Complete the following in all cases.

I am furnishing this report by: *<Delete the phrase which does not apply>*

today consigning it to the hospital managers' internal mail system.

sending or delivering it without using the hospital managers' internal mail system.

Signed . . . .

PRINT NAME . . . .

Date . . . .

PART 2

(To be completed on behalf of the hospital managers)

This report was *<Delete the phrase which does not apply>*

furnished to the hospital managers through their internal mail system

received by me on behalf of the hospital managers on [date]

Signed . . . .
on behalf of the hospital managers

PRINT NAME . . . .
Date . . . .

Form G1   *Regulation 5(1)(a)(i) and (1)(b)*

Mental Health Act 1983 section 7—guardianship application by nearest relative

PART 1

(To be completed by the nearest relative)

To the [name of local social services authority]   **2–153**

I [PRINT your full name and address] apply for the reception of [PRINT full name and address of patient] into the guardianship of [PRINT full name and address of proposed guardian] in accordance with Part 2 of the Mental Health Act 1983.

Complete (a) or (b) as applicable and delete the other.

    (a) To the best of my knowledge and belief I am the patient's nearest relative within the meaning of the Act.

        I am the patient's [state your relationship with the patient].

    (b) I have been authorised to exercise the functions under the Act of the patient's nearest relative by a county court/the patient's nearest relative *<delete the phrase which does not apply>*, and a copy of the authority is attached to this application.

*The patient's date of birth is [date]

OR

*I believe the patient is aged 16 years or over.
*<*Delete the phrase which does not apply.>*

I last saw the patient on [date], which was within the period of 14 days ending on the day this application is completed.

This application is founded on two medical recommendations in the prescribed form.

If neither of the medical practitioners had previous acquaintance with the patient before making their recommendations, please explain why you could not get a recommendation from a medical practitioner who did have previous acquaintance with the patient—

....
....

[If you need to continue on a separate sheet please indicate here [ ] and attach that sheet to this form]

Signed ....

Date ....

PART 2*

*<*Complete only if proposed guardian is not a local social services authority>*
(To be completed by the proposed guardian)

My full name and address is as entered in Part 1 of this form and I am willing to act as the guardian of the above named patient in accordance with Part 2 of the Mental Health Act 1983.

Signed ....

Date ....

705

Mental Health Act 1983 section 7—guardianship application by an approved mental health professional

PART 1

(To be completed by the approved mental health professional)

2–154 To the [name of local social services authority]

I [PRINT your full name and address] apply for the reception of [PRINT full name and address of patient] into the guardianship of [PRINT full name and address of proposed guardian] in accordance with Part 2 of the Mental Health Act 1983.

I am acting on behalf of [name of local social services authority] and am approved to act as an approved mental health professional for the purposes of the Act by *<delete as appropriate>*

that authority
[name of local social services authority that approved you, if different.]

Complete the following where consultation with the nearest relative has taken place.

Complete (a) or (b) as applicable and delete the other.

    (a) I have consulted [PRINT full name and address] who to the best of my knowledge and belief is the patient's nearest relative within the meaning of the Act;

    (b) I have consulted [PRINT full name and address] who I understand has been authorised by a county court/ the patient's nearest relative to exercise the functions under the Act of the patient's nearest relative. *<Delete the phrase which does not apply>*

That person has not notified me or the local social services authority on whose behalf I am acting that he or she objects to this application being made.

Complete the following where the nearest relative has not been consulted. Delete whichever two of (a), (b) and (c) do not apply.

    (a) I have been unable to ascertain who is this patient's nearest relative within the meaning of the Act,

OR

    (b) to the best of my knowledge and belief this patient has no nearest relative within the meaning of the Act,

OR

    (c) [PRINT full name and address] is
        (i) this patient's nearest relative within the meaning of the Act,
        (ii) authorised to exercise the functions of this patient's nearest relative under the Act,

<Delete either (i) or (ii)>

but in my opinion it is not reasonably practicable/would involve unreasonable delay *<delete as appropriate>* to consult that person before making this application, because—

. . . .
. . . .

[If you need to continue on a separate sheet please indicate here [ ] and attach that sheet to this form]

The remainder of Part 1 of this form must be completed in all cases.

I last saw the patient on [date], which was within the period of 14 days ending on the day this application is completed.

*The patient's date of birth is [date]

OR

*I believe the patient is aged 16 years or over.
<*Delete the phrase which does not apply.>

This application is founded on two medical recommendations in the prescribed form.

If neither of the medical practitioners had previous acquaintance with the patient before making their recommendations, please explain why you could not get a recommendation from a medical practitioner who did have previous acquaintance with the patient—

. . . .
. . . .

[If you need to continue on a separate sheet please indicate here [ ] and attach that sheet to this form]

Signed . . . .

Date . . . .

PART 2*

<*Complete only if proposed guardian is not a local social services authority>

(To be completed by the proposed guardian)

My full name and address is as entered in Part 1 of this form and I am willing to act as the guardian of the above named patient in accordance with Part 2 of the Mental Health Act 1983.

Signed . . . .

Date . . . .

Mental Health Act 1983 section 7—joint medical recommendation for reception into guardianship

2–155 We, registered medical practitioners, recommend that [PRINT full name and address of patient] be received into guardianship in accordance with Part 2 of the Mental Health Act 1983.

I [PRINT full name and address of first practitioner] last examined this patient on [date], and

< **delete if not applicable*>

* I had previous acquaintance with the patient before I conducted that examination.

* I am approved under section 12 of the Act as having special experience in the diagnosis or treatment of mental disorder.

I [PRINT full name and address of second practitioner] last examined this patient on [date], and

< **delete if not applicable*>

* I had previous acquaintance with the patient before I conducted that examination.

* I am approved under section 12 of the Act as having special experience in the diagnosis or treatment of mental disorder.

In our opinion,

    (a)   this patient is suffering from mental disorder of a nature or degree which warrants the patient's reception into guardianship under the Act,

AND

    (b)   it is necessary
         (i)   in the interests of the welfare of the patient
        (ii)   for the protection of other persons
       <delete (i) or (ii) unless both apply>

that the patient should be so received.

Our reasons for these opinions are:

[Your reasons should cover both (a) and (b) above. As part of them: describe the patient's symptoms and behaviour and explain how those symptoms and behaviour lead you to your opinion; and explain why the patient cannot appropriately be cared for without powers of guardianship.]

....
....
....

[If you need to continue on a separate sheet please indicate here [ ] and attach that sheet to this form]

                         Signed ....
                         Date ....

                         Signed ....
                         Date ....

NOTE: AT LEAST ONE OF THE PRACTITIONERS SIGNING THIS FORM MUST BE APPROVED UNDER SECTION 12 OF THE ACT.

Form G4   *Regulation 5(1)(c)(ii)*

Mental Health Act 1983 section 7—medical recommendation for reception into guardianship

I [PRINT full name and address of practitioner], a registered medical practitioner recommend that **2–156**
[PRINT full name and address of patient] be received into guardianship in accordance with Part 2
of the Mental Health Act 1983.

I last examined this patient on [date].

*I had previous acquaintance with the patient before I conducted that examination.

*I am approved under section 12 of the Act as having special experience in the diagnosis or treatment
of mental disorder. *<*Delete if not applicable>*

In my opinion,

    (a) this patient is suffering from mental disorder of a nature or degree which warrants the patient's
         reception into guardianship under the Act,

AND

    (b) it is necessary
         (i) in the interests of the welfare of the patient
         (ii) for the protection of other persons
         <delete (i) or (ii) unless both apply>

that the patient should be so received.

My reasons for these opinions are:

[Your reasons should cover both (a) and (b) above. As part of them: describe the patient's symptoms
and behaviour and explain how those symptoms and behaviour lead you to your opinion; and explain
why the patient cannot appropriately be cared for without powers of guardianship.]

. . . .
. . . .
. . . .

[If you need to continue on a separate sheet please indicate here [ ] and attach that sheet to this form]

                          Signed . . . .
                          Date . . . .

Mental Health Act 1983 section 7—record of acceptance of guardianship application

(To be attached to the guardianship application)

2–157   [PRINT full name and address of patient]

This application was accepted by/on behalf* of the local social services authority on [date].
<*Delete the phrase that does not apply*>

Signed ....
on behalf of the responsible local social services authority
PRINT NAME ....
Date ....

Form G6   *Regulation 7(4)(a),(d) and (e)*

Mental Health Act 1983 section 19—authority for transfer from hospital to guardianship

PART 1

(To be completed on behalf of the managers of the hospital where the patient is detained)

Authority is given for the transfer of [PRINT full name of patient] who is at present liable to be detained **2–158** in [name and address of hospital] to the guardianship of [PRINT full name and address of proposed guardian] in accordance with the Mental Health (Hospital, Guardianship and Treatment) (England) Regulations 2008.

This transfer was agreed by the [name of local social services authority] on [date of confirmation].

The transfer is to take place on [date].

Signed ....
on behalf of the hospital managers
PRINT NAME ....
Date ....

PART 2*

<*Complete only if proposed guardian is not a local social services authority>

(To be completed by the proposed private guardian)

My full name and address is as entered in Part 1 of this form and I am willing to act as the guardian of the above named patient in accordance with Part 2 of the Mental Health Act 1983.

Signed ....
Date ....

IF THE GUARDIAN IS TO BE A PRIVATE GUARDIAN, THE TRANSFER MAY NOT TAKE PLACE UNTIL BOTH PARTS OF THIS FORM ARE COMPLETED

Form G7   *Regulation 8(1)(a), (d) and (e)*

Mental Health Act 1983 section 19— authority for transfer of a patient from the guardianship of one guardian to another

PART 1

(*To be completed by the present guardian*)

2–159   Authority is given for the transfer of [PRINT full name and address of patient] from the guardianship of [PRINT full name and address of the present guardian] to the guardianship of [PRINT full name and address of the proposed guardian] in accordance with the Mental Health (Hospital, Guardianship and Treatment) (England) Regulations 2008.

This transfer was agreed by the [name of local social services authority] on [date of confirmation].

The transfer is to take place on [date].

Signed . . . .
the guardian/on behalf of the local social services
authority which is the guardian
<Delete whichever does not apply>
PRINT NAME . . . .
Date . . . .

PART 2*
<*Complete only if proposed guardian is not a local social services authority>

(*To be completed by the proposed private guardian*)

My full name and address is as entered in Part 1 of this form and I am willing to act as the guardian of the above named patient in accordance with Part 2 of the Mental Health Act 1983.

Signed . . . .
Date . . . .

IF THE NEW GUARDIAN IS TO BE A PRIVATE GUARDIAN, THE TRANSFER MAY NOT TAKE PLACE UNTIL BOTH PARTS OF THIS FORM ARE COMPLETED

Form G8	*Regulation 8(2) and (4)*

Mental Health Act 1983 section 19— authority for transfer from guardianship to hospital

PART 1

(To be completed on behalf of the local social services authority)

Authority is given for the transfer of [PRINT full name and address of patient] who is at present under **2–160** the guardianship of [name and address of guardian] to [name and address of hospital] in accordance with the Mental Health (Hospital, Guardianship and Treatment) (England) Regulations 2008.

Signed . . . .
on behalf of the local social services authority
PRINT NAME . . . .
Date . . . .

PART 2
RECORD OF ADMISSION

(This is not part of the authority for transfer but is to be completed at the hospital to which the patient is transferred)

This patient was admitted to the above named hospital in pursuance of this authority for transfer on [date of admission to receiving hospital] at [time].

Signed . . . .
on behalf of the managers of the receiving hospital
PRINT NAME . . . .
Date . . . .

Mental Health Act 1983 section 20 — renewal of authority for guardianship

PART 1

2–161   (*To be completed by the responsible clinician or nominated medical attendant*)

To   [name of guardian]
[name of responsible local social services authority if it is not the guardian]

I examined [PRINT full name and address of patient] on [date].

The patient is subject to guardianship for a period ending on [date authority for guardianship is due to expire].

In my opinion,

  (a) this patient is suffering from mental disorder of a nature or degree which warrants the patient's reception into guardianship under the Act,

AND

  (b) it is necessary

      (i) in the interests of the welfare of the patient
      (ii) for the protection of other persons

      <*delete (i) or (ii) unless both apply*>

that the patient should remain under guardianship under the Act.

My reasons for these opinions are:

[Your reasons should cover both (a) and (b) above. As part of them: describe the patient's symptoms and behaviour and explain how those symptoms and behaviour lead you to your opinion; and explain why the patient cannot appropriately be cared for without powers of guardianship.]
. . . .
. . . .
. . . .

[If you need to continue on a separate sheet please indicate here [ ] and attach that sheet to this form]

Signed . . . .
*Responsible clinician
*Nominated medical attendant
<*Delete whichever does not apply*>
PRINT NAME . . . .
Date . . . .

Mental Health (Hospital) (England) Regs 2008, Form G9

(To be completed on behalf of the responsible local social services authority)

This report was received by me on behalf of the local social services authority on [date].

Signed ....
on behalf of the local social services authority
PRINT NAME ....
Date ....

Mental Health Act 1983 section 21B — authority for guardianship after absence without leave for more than 28 days

PART 1

2–162   (*To be completed by the responsible clinician or nominated medical attendant*)

To   [name of guardian]
      [name of responsible local social services authority if it is not the guardian]

I examined [PRINT full name and address of patient] on [date of examination] who:

  (a) was absent without leave from the place where the patient is required to reside beginning on [date absence without leave began];

  (b) was/is* subject to guardianship for a period ending on [date authority for guardianship would have expired, apart from any extension under section 21, or date on which it will expire]; <*delete phrase which does not apply*> and

  (c) returned to that place on [date].

In my opinion,

  (a) this patient is suffering from mental disorder of a nature or degree which warrants the patient's reception into guardianship under the Act,

AND

  (b) it is necessary

        (i) in the interests of the welfare of the patient
        (ii) for the protection of other persons

        <*delete (i) or (ii) unless both apply*>

that the patient should remain under guardianship under the Act.

My reasons for these opinions are:

[Your reasons should cover both (a) and (b) above. As part of them: describe the patient's symptoms and behaviour and explain how those symptoms and behaviour lead you to your opinion; and explain why the patient cannot appropriately be cared for without powers of guardianship.]
. . . .
. . . .
. . . .

[If you need to continue on a separate sheet please indicate here [ ] and attach that sheet to this form]

The authority for the guardianship of the patient is/is not* due to expire within a period of two months beginning with the date on which this report is to be furnished. *<*Delete the phrase which does not apply>*

Complete the following only if the authority for guardianship is due to expire within that period of two months.

This report shall/shall not* have effect as a report duly furnished under section 20(6) for the renewal of the authority for the guardianship of the patient. *<*Delete the phrase which does not apply>*

Signed ....
*Responsible clinician
*Nominated medical attendant
<*Delete whichever does not apply>
PRINT NAME ....
Date ....

PART 2

(To be completed on behalf of the responsible local social services authority)

This report was received by me on behalf of the local social services authority on [date].

Signed ....
on behalf of the local social services authority
PRINT NAME ....
Date ....

Mental Health Act 1983 Part 6—date of reception of a patient in England

2–163 [PRINT full name of patient]

*was admitted to [name and address of hospital] at [time] on [date]

*was received into the guardianship of [name and address of guardian] on [date]

*became a community patient as if discharged from [name and address of responsible hospital], on [date].
< *Complete as appropriate and delete the others>*

Signed ....
on behalf of the hospital managers/
on behalf of the local social services authority/
the private guardian
<Delete whichever do not apply>
PRINT NAME ....
Date ....

Form M2   *Regulation 25(1)(a) and (b)*

Mental Health Act 1983 section 25—report barring discharge by nearest relative

PART 1

(To be completed by the responsible clinician)

To the managers of [name and address of hospital]   **2–164**

[Name of nearest relative] gave notice at [time] on [date] of an intention to discharge [PRINT full name of patient].

I am of the opinion that the patient, if discharged, would be likely to act in a manner dangerous to other persons or to himself or herself.

The reasons for my opinion are—

. . . .
. . . .
. . . .

[If you need to continue on a separate sheet please indicate here [ ] and attach that sheet to this form]

I am furnishing this report by: *<Delete the phrase which does not apply>*

consigning it to the hospital managers' internal mail system today at [time].

sending or delivering it without using the hospital managers' internal mail system.

Signed . . . .
Responsible clinician

PRINT NAME . . . .
Date . . . .
Time . . . .

PART 2

(To be completed on behalf of the hospital managers)

This report was: *<Delete the phrase which does not apply>*

furnished to the hospital managers through their internal mail system.

received by me on behalf of the hospital managers at [time] on [date].

Signed . . . .
on behalf of the hospital managers

PRINT NAME . . . .
Date . . . .

Mental Health Act 1983 section 57—certificate of consent to treatment and second opinion

(*Both parts of this certificate must be completed*)

PART 1

2–165 I [PRINT full name and address], a registered medical practitioner appointed for the purposes of Part 4 of the Act (a SOAD), and we [PRINT full name, address and profession], being two persons appointed for the purposes of section 57(2)(a) of the Act, certify that [PRINT full name and address of patient]

   (a) is capable of understanding the nature, purpose and likely effects of: [Give description of treatment or plan of treatment. Indicate clearly if the certificate is only to apply to any or all of the treatment for a specific period.]

. . . .
. . . .
. . . .

[If you need to continue on a separate sheet please indicate here [ ] and attach that sheet to this form]

AND

   (b) has consented to that treatment.

                                        Signed . . . .
                                        Date . . . .

                                        Signed . . . .
                                        Date . . . .

                                        Signed . . . .
                                        Date . . . .

PART 2

(*To be completed by SOAD only*)

I, the above named registered medical practitioner appointed for the purposes of Part 4 of the Act have consulted [PRINT full name of nurse] a nurse and [PRINT full name and profession] who have been professionally concerned with the medical treatment of the patient named above and certify that it is appropriate for the treatment to be given.

My reasons are as below/I will provide a statement of my reasons separately. <*Delete as appropriate*> [When giving reasons please indicate if, in your opinion, disclosure of the reasons to the patient would be likely to cause serious harm to the physical or mental health of the patient or to that of any other person.]

. . . .
. . . .
. . . .

If you need to continue on a separate sheet please indicate here [ ] and attach that sheet to this form.]

Signed . . . .
Date . . . .

Mental Health Act 1983 section 58(3)(a)—certificate of consent to treatment

2–166 I [PRINT full name and address], the approved clinician in charge of the treatment described below/a registered medical practitioner appointed for the purposes of Part 4 of the Act (a SOAD) *<delete the phrase which does not apply>* certify that [PRINT full name and address of patient]

  (a) is capable of understanding the nature, purpose and likely effects of: [Give description of treatment or plan of treatment. Indicate clearly if the certificate is only to apply to any or all of the treatment for a specific period.]

. . . .
. . . .
. . . .

[If you need to continue on a separate sheet please indicate here [ ] and attach that sheet to this form.]

AND

  (b) has consented to that treatment.

Signed . . . .
Date . . . .

Form T3   *Regulation 27(2)*

Mental Health Act 1983 section 58(3)(b)—certificate of second opinion

I [PRINT full name and address], a registered medical practitioner appointed for the purposes of Part 4 **2–167**
of the Act (a SOAD), have consulted [PRINT full name of nurse], a nurse and [PRINT full name and
profession] who have been professionally concerned with the medical treatment of [PRINT full name
and address of patient].

I certify that the patient— *<Delete the phrase which does not apply>*

    (a) is not capable of understanding the nature, purpose and likely effects of

    (b) has not consented to

the following treatment: [Give description of treatment or plan of treatment. Indicate clearly if the certificate is only to apply to any or all of the treatment for a specific period.]
. . . .
. . . .
. . . .

[If you need to continue on a separate sheet please indicate here [ ] and attach that sheet to this form]

but that it is appropriate for the treatment to be given.

My reasons are as below/I will provide a statement of my reasons separately. *<Delete as appropriate>*
[When giving reasons please indicate if, in your opinion, disclosure of the reasons to the patient would
be likely to cause serious harm to the physical or mental health of the patient, or to that of any other
person.]

. . . .
. . . .
. . . .

[If you need to continue on a separate sheet please indicate here [ ] and attach that sheet to this form.]

Signed . . . .
Date . . . .

Mental Health Act 1983 section 58A(3)—certificate of consent to treatment (patients at least 18 years old)

THIS FORM IS NOT TO BE USED FOR PATIENTS UNDER 18 YEARS OF AGE

2–168 I [PRINT full name and address], the approved clinician in charge of the treatment described below/a registered medical practitioner appointed for the purposes of Part 4 of the Act (a SOAD) *<delete as appropriate>* certify that [PRINT full name and address of patient] who has attained the age of 18 years,

(a) is capable of understanding the nature, purpose and likely effects of: [Give description of treatment or plan of treatment. Indicate clearly if the certificate is only to apply to any or all of the treatment for a specific period.]

. . . .
. . . .
. . . .

[If you need to continue on a separate sheet please indicate here [ ] and attach that sheet to this form]

AND

(b) has consented to that treatment.

Signed . . . .
Date . . . .

Mental Health Act 1983 section 58A(4)—certificate of consent to treatment and second opinion (patients under 18)

THIS FORM IS ONLY TO BE USED FOR PATIENTS UNDER 18 YEARS OF AGE

I [PRINT full name and address], a registered medical practitioner appointed for the purposes of Part 4 **2–169** of the Act (a SOAD) certify that [PRINT full name and address of patient] who has not yet attained the age of 18 years,

(a) is capable of understanding the nature, purpose and likely effects of: [Give description of treatment or plan of treatment. Indicate clearly if the certificate is only to apply to any or all of the treatment for a specific period.]

. . . .
. . . .
. . . .

[If you need to continue on a separate sheet please indicate here [ ] and attach that sheet to this form]

AND

(b) has consented to that treatment.

In my opinion it is appropriate for that treatment to be given.

My reasons are as below/I will provide a statement of my reasons separately. *<Delete as appropriate>* [When giving reasons please indicate if, in your opinion, disclosure of the reasons to the patient would be likely to cause serious harm to the physical or mental health of the patient, or to that of any other person.]

. . . .
. . . .
. . . .

[If you need to continue on a separate sheet please indicate here [ ] and attach that sheet to this form.]

Signed . . . .
Date . . . .

Mental Health Act 1983 section 58A(5)—certificate of second opinion (patients who are not capable of understanding the nature, purpose and likely effects of the treatment)

2–170 I [PRINT full name and address], a registered medical practitioner appointed for the purposes of Part 4 of the Act (a SOAD), have consulted [PRINT full name of nurse] a nurse and [PRINT full name and profession] who have been professionally concerned with the medical treatment of [PRINT full name and address of patient].

I certify that the patient is not capable of understanding the nature, purpose and likely effects of: [Give description of treatment or plan of treatment. Indicate clearly if the certificate is only to apply to any or all of the treatment for a specific period.]

. . . .
. . . .
. . . .

[If you need to continue on a separate sheet please indicate here [ ] and attach that sheet to this form]

but that it is appropriate for the treatment to be given.

My reasons are as below/I will provide a statement of my reasons separately. *<Delete as appropriate>* [When giving reasons please indicate if, in your opinion, disclosure of the reasons to the patient would be likely to cause serious harm to the physical or mental health of the patient or to that of any other person.]

. . . .
. . . .
. . . .

[If you need to continue on a separate sheet please indicate here [ ] and attach that sheet to this form.]

I further certify that giving the treatment described above to the patient would not conflict with—

  (i) any decision of an attorney appointed under a Lasting Power of Attorney or deputy (appointed by the Court of Protection) of the patient as provided for by the Mental Capacity Act 2005

  (ii) any decision of the Court of Protection, or

  (iii) any advance decision to refuse treatment that is valid and applicable under the Mental Capacity Act 2005.

          Signed . . . .
          Date . . . .

Form CTO1   *Regulation 6(1)(a), (b) and 6(2)(a)*

Mental Health Act 1983 section 17A—community treatment order   **2–171**
(Parts 1 and 3 of this form are to be completed by the responsible clinician and Part 2 by an approved mental health professional)

PART 1

I [PRINT full name and address of the responsible clinician] am the responsible clinician for [PRINT full name and address of patient].

In my opinion,

   (a) this patient is suffering from mental disorder of a nature or degree which makes it appropriate for the patient to receive medical treatment,

   (b) it is necessary for
         (i) the patient's health
         (ii) the patient's safety
         (iii) the protection of other persons
         <delete any phrase which is not applicable>

      that the patient should receive such treatment;

   (c) such treatment can be provided without the patient continuing to be detained in a hospital provided the patient is liable to being recalled to hospital for medical treatment;

   (d) it is necessary that the responsible clinician should be able to exercise the power under section 17E(1) to recall the patient to hospital;

   (e) taking into account the nature and degree of the mental disorder from which the patient is suffering and all other circumstances of the case, appropriate medical treatment is available to the patient.

My opinion is founded on the following grounds—

. . . .
. . . .
. . . .

[If you need to continue on a separate sheet please indicate here [ ] and attach that sheet to this form]

I confirm that in determining whether the criterion at (d) above is met, I have considered what risk there would be of deterioration of the patient's condition if the patient were not detained in hospital, with regard to the patient's history of mental disorder and any other relevant factors.

Conditions to which the patient is to be subject by virtue of this community treatment order

The patient is to make himself or herself available for examination under section 20A, as requested.

If it is proposed to give a certificate under Part 4A of the Act in the patient's case, the patient is to make himself or herself available for examination to enable the certificate to be given, as requested.

The patient is also to be subject to the following conditions (if any) under section 17B(2) of the Act:

. . . .
. . . .
. . . .

[If you need to continue on a separate sheet please indicate here [ ] and attach that sheet to this form]

I confirm that I consider the above conditions to be made under section 17B(2) of the Act are necessary or appropriate for one or more of the following purposes:

- to ensure that the patient receives medical treatment
- to prevent risk of harm to the patient's health or safety
- to protect other persons.

Signed ....

Date ....

PART 2

I [PRINT full name and address] am acting on behalf of [name of local social services authority] and am approved to act as an approved mental health professional for the purposes of the Act by *<delete as appropriate>*

that authority
[name of local social services authority that approved you, if different].

I agree that:

(i) the above patient meets the criteria for a community treatment order to be made
(ii) it is appropriate to make a community treatment order, and
(iii) the conditions made above under section 17B(2) are necessary or appropriate for one or more of the purposes specified.

Signed ....
Approved mental health professional

Date ....

PART 3

I exercise my power under section 17A of the Mental Health Act 1983 to make a community treatment order in respect of the patient named in Part 1 of this Form.

This community treatment order is to be effective from [date] at [time].

Signed ....
Responsible clinician

Date ....

THIS COMMUNITY TREATMENT ORDER IS NOT VALID UNLESS ALL THREE PARTS ARE COMPLETED AND SIGNED

IT MUST BE FURNISHED AS SOON AS PRACTICABLE TO THE MANAGERS OF THE HOSPITAL IN WHICH THE PATIENT WAS LIABLE TO BE DETAINED BEFORE THE ORDER WAS MADE

Mental Health Act 1983 section 17B—variation of conditions of a community treatment order   **2–172**

I [PRINT full name and address of the responsible clinician] am the responsible clinician for [PRINT full name and address of the community patient].

I am varying the conditions attaching to the community treatment order for the above named patient.

The conditions made under section 17B(2), as varied, are: [List the conditions as varied in full (including any which are not being varied) or state that there are no longer to be any such conditions.]

. . . .
. . . .
. . . .

[If you need to continue on a separate sheet please indicate here [ ] and attach that sheet to this form]

The variation is to take effect from [date].

I confirm that I consider the above conditions to be necessary or appropriate for one or more of the following purposes:

- to ensure that the patient receives medical treatment
- to prevent risk of harm to the patient's health or safety
- to protect other persons.

Signed . . . .
Responsible clinician

Date . . . .

THIS FORM MUST BE FURNISHED AS SOON AS PRACTICABLE TO THE MANAGERS OF THE RESPONSIBLE HOSPITAL

2–173 Mental Health Act 1983 section 17E—community treatment order: notice of recall to hospital
(To be completed by the responsible clinician)

I notify you, [PRINT name of community patient], that you are recalled to [PRINT full name and address of the hospital] under section 17E of the Mental Health Act 1983.

Complete either (a) or (b) below and delete the one which does not apply.

    (a) In my opinion,

        (i) you require treatment in hospital for mental disorder, AND
        (ii) there would be a risk of harm to your health or safety or to other persons if you were not recalled to hospital for that purpose.

This opinion is founded on the following grounds—

. . . .
. . . .
. . . .

[If you need to continue on a separate sheet please indicate here [ ] and attach that sheet to this form]

    (b) You have failed to comply with the condition imposed under section 17B of the Mental Health Act 1983 that you make yourself available for examination for the purpose of: *<delete as appropriate>*
        (i) consideration of extension of the community treatment period under section 20A
        (ii) enabling a Part 4A certificate to be given.

                       Signed . . . .
                       Responsible clinician

                       PRINT NAME . . . .
                       Date . . . .
                       Time . . . .

A COPY OF THIS NOTICE IS TO BE FORWARDED TO THE MANAGERS OF THE HOSPITAL TO WHICH THE PATIENT IS RECALLED AS SOON AS POSSIBLE AFTER IT IS SERVED ON THE PATIENT. IF THAT HOSPITAL IS NOT THE RESPONSIBLE HOSPITAL, YOU SHOULD INFORM THE HOSPITAL MANAGERS THE NAME AND ADDRESS OF THE RESPONSIBLE HOSPITAL.

This notice is sufficient authority for the managers of the named hospital to detain the patient there in accordance with the provisions of section 17E of the Mental Health Act 1983.

Mental Health Act 1983 section 17E — community treatment order: record of patient's detention **2–174**
in hospital after recall

[PRINT full name and address of patient] ('the patient') is currently a community patient.

In pursuance of a notice recalling the patient to hospital under section 17E of the Act, the patient was detained in [full name and address of hospital] on [enter date and time at which the patient's detention in the hospital as a result of the recall notice began].

Signed . . . .
on behalf of the hospital managers

PRINT NAME . . . .
Date . . . .
Time . . . .

2–175　**Mental Health Act 1983 section 17F(4)—revocation of community treatment order**

(Parts 1 and 3 of this form are to be completed by the responsible clinician and Part 2 by an approved mental health professional)

PART 1

I [PRINT full name and address of the responsible clinician] am the responsible clinician for [PRINT full name and address of community patient] who is detained in [name and address of hospital] having been recalled to hospital under section 17E(1) of the Act.

In my opinion,

    (a) this patient is suffering from mental disorder of a nature or degree which makes it appropriate for the patient to receive medical treatment in a hospital,

AND

    (b) it is necessary for
        (i) the patient's own health
       (ii) the patient's own safety
      (iii) the protection of other persons
      <delete the indents not applicable>

that this patient should receive treatment in hospital,

AND

    (c) such treatment cannot be provided unless the patient is detained for medical treatment under the Act,

because— [Your reasons should cover (a), (b) and (c) above. As part of them: describe the patient's symptoms and behaviour and explain how those symptoms and behaviour lead you to your opinion; say whether other methods of treatment or care (eg out-patient treatment or social services) are available and, if so, why they are not appropriate; indicate why informal admission is not appropriate.]

. . . .
. . . .
. . . .

[If you need to continue on a separate sheet please indicate here [ ] and attach that sheet to this form]

I am also of the opinion that taking into account the nature and degree of the mental disorder from which the patient is suffering and all other circumstances of the case, appropriate medical treatment is available to the patient at the hospital named above.

Signed . . . .
Responsible clinician

Date . . . .

PART 2

I [PRINT full name and address] am acting on behalf of [name of local social services authority] and am approved to act as an approved mental health professional for the purposes of the Act by *<delete as appropriate>*

    that authority

[name of local social services authority that approved you, if different].

I agree that:

    (i) the patient meets the criteria for detention in hospital set out above and

    (ii) it is appropriate to revoke the community treatment order.

Signed ....
Approved mental health professional

Date ....

PART 3

I exercise my power under section 17F(4) to revoke the community treatment order in respect of the patient named in Part 1 who has been detained in hospital since [time] on [date], having been recalled under section 17E(1).

Signed ....
Responsible clinician

Date ....

THIS REVOCATION ORDER IS NOT VALID UNLESS ALL THREE PARTS ARE COMPLETED AND SIGNED

IT MUST BE SENT AS SOON AS PRACTICABLE TO THE MANAGERS OF THE HOSPITAL IN WHICH THE PATIENT IS DETAINED

2–176 Mental Health Act 1983 section 17F(2)—authority for transfer of recalled community patient to a hospital under different managers
(*To be completed on behalf of the managers of the hospital in which the patient is detained by virtue of recall*)

PART 1

This form authorises the transfer of [PRINT full name of patient] from [name and address of hospital in which the patient is detained] to [name and address of hospital to which patient is to be transferred] in accordance with the Mental Health (Hospital, Guardianship and Treatment) (England) Regulations 2008.

I attach a copy of Form CTO4 recording the patient's detention in hospital after recall.

*The hospital in which the patient is currently detained is the patient's responsible hospital.

*The hospital to which the patient is to be transferred is the patient's responsible hospital.

*The patient's responsible hospital is [name and address of responsible hospital].
<*Delete the phrases which do not apply>

Signed . . . .
on behalf of managers of the first named hospital

PRINT NAME . . . .
Date . . . .

PART 2

RECORD OF ADMISSION

(*This is not part of the authority for transfer but is to be completed at the hospital to which the patient is transferred*)

This patient was admitted to [name of hospital] in pursuance of this authority for transfer on [date of admission to receiving hospital] at [time].

Signed . . . .
on behalf of managers of the receiving hospital

PRINT NAME . . . .
Date . . . .

Form CTO7   Regulation 13(6)(a) and (b), and 13(7)

Mental Health Act 1983 section 20A — community treatment order: report extending the community treatment period

Parts 1 and 3 of this form are to be completed by the responsible clinician and Part 2 by an approved **2–177** *mental health professional. Part 4 is to be completed by or on behalf of the managers of the responsible hospital.*

PART 1

To the managers of [name and address of the responsible hospital]

I am [PRINT full name and address of the responsible clinician] the responsible clinician for [PRINT full name and address of patient].

The patient is currently subject to a community treatment order made on [enter date].

I examined the patient on [date].

In my opinion,

(a) this patient is suffering from mental disorder of a nature or degree which makes it appropriate for the patient to receive medical treatment;

(b) it is necessary for
    (i) the patient's health
    (ii) the patient's safety
    (iii) the protection of other persons
    <delete any indent which is not applicable>

that the patient should receive such treatment;

(c) such treatment can be provided without the patient continuing to be detained in a hospital provided the patient is liable to being recalled to hospital for medical treatment;

(d) it is necessary that the responsible clinician should continue to be able to exercise the power under section 17E(1) to recall the patient to hospital;

(e) taking into account the nature and degree of the mental disorder from which the patient is suffering and all other circumstances of the case, appropriate medical treatment is available to the patient.

My opinion is founded on the following grounds—

. . . .
. . . .

[If you need to continue on a separate sheet please indicate here [ ] and attach that sheet to this form]

I confirm that in determining whether the criterion at (d) above is met, I have considered what risk there would be of deterioration of the patient's condition if the patient were to continue not to be detained in hospital, with regard to the patient's history of mental disorder and any other relevant factors.

Signed . . . .
Responsible clinician
Date . . . .

PART 2

I [PRINT full name and address] am acting on behalf of [name of local social services authority] and am approved to act as an approved mental health professional for the purposes of the Act by *<delete as appropriate>*

that authority

[name of local social services authority that approved you, if different].

I agree that:

(i) the patient meets the criteria for the extension of the community treatment period and

(ii) it is appropriate to extend the community treatment period.

Signed . . . .
Approved mental health professional
Date . . . .

PART 3

Before furnishing this report, I consulted [PRINT full name and profession of person consulted] who has been professionally concerned with the patient's treatment.

I am furnishing this report by: *<Delete the phrase which does not apply>*

today consigning it to the hospital managers' internal mail system.

sending or delivering it without using the hospital managers' internal mail system.

Signed . . . .
Responsible clinician
Date . . . .

THIS REPORT IS NOT VALID UNLESS PARTS 1, 2 & 3 ARE COMPLETED AND SIGNED

PART 4

This report was *<Delete the phrase which does not apply>*

furnished to the hospital managers through their internal mail system.

received by me on behalf of the hospital managers on [date].

Signed . . . .
on behalf of the managers of the
responsible hospital
PRINT NAME . . . .
Date . . . .

Form CTO8   *Regulation 14(3)(a) and (b)*

Mental Health Act 1983 section 21B—authority for extension of community treatment period after absence without leave for more than 28 days

PART 1

(To be completed by the responsible clinician)

To the managers of [enter name and address of responsible hospital]   **2–178**

I am [PRINT full name and address of the responsible clinician] the responsible clinician for [PRINT full name and address of patient].

I examined the patient on [date of examination] who:

(a) was recalled to hospital on [date] under section 17E of the Mental Health Act 1983;

(b) was absent without leave from hospital beginning on [date absence without leave began];

(c) was/is <*delete as appropriate*> subject to a community treatment order for a period ending on [date community treatment order would have expired, apart from any extension under section 21, or date on which it will expire]; and

(d) returned to the hospital on [date].

I have consulted [PRINT full name of approved mental health professional] who is an approved mental health professional.

I have also consulted [PRINT full name and profession of person consulted] who has been professionally concerned with the patient's treatment.

In my opinion,

(a) this patient is suffering from mental disorder of a nature or degree which makes it appropriate for the patient to receive medical treatment;

(b) it is necessary for

  (i) the patient's health
  (ii) the patient's safety
  (iii) the protection of other persons
  <*delete any indent which is not applicable*>

  that the patient should receive such treatment;

(c) such treatment can be provided without the patient continuing to be detained in a hospital provided the patient is liable to being recalled to hospital for medical treatment;

(d) it is necessary that the responsible clinician should continue to be able to exercise the power under section 17E(1) to recall the patient to hospital;

(e) taking into account the nature and degree of the mental disorder from which the patient is suffering and all other circumstances of the case, appropriate medical treatment is available to the patient.

I confirm that in determining whether the criterion at (d) above is met, I have considered what risk there would be of deterioration of the patient's condition if the patient were to continue not to be detained in hospital, with regard to the patient's history of mental disorder and any other relevant factors.

My opinion is founded on the following grounds—

. . . .
. . . .

Delegated Legislation

[If you need to continue on a separate sheet please indicate here [ ] and attach that sheet to this form]

The community treatment order is/is not* due to expire within a period of two months beginning with the date on which this report is to be furnished to the managers of the responsible hospital. *<*Delete the phrase which does not apply>*

[*Complete the following only if the community treatment order is due to expire within that period of two months*]

This report shall/shall not* have effect as a report duly furnished under section 20A(4) for the extension of the community treatment period for this patient. *<*Delete the phrase which does not apply>*

Complete the following in all cases.

I am furnishing this report by: *<Delete the phrase which does not apply>*

today consigning it to the hospital managers' internal mail system.

sending or delivering it without using the hospital managers' internal mail system.

Signed . . . .

Date . . . .

PART 2

(To be completed on behalf of the managers of the responsible hospital)

This report was *<Delete the phrase which does not apply>*

furnished to the hospital managers through their internal mail system. received by me on behalf of the hospital managers on [date].

Signed . . . .

on behalf of the hospital managers

PRINT NAME. . . . .

Date . . . .

Form CTO9	*Regulation 16(4) and (5)*

Mental Health Act 1983 Part 6—community patients transferred to England

PART 1

(To be completed by the responsible clinician)

I [PRINT full name and address of the responsible clinician] am the responsible clinician for [PRINT **2–179** full name and address of patient] who is treated as if subject to a community treatment order having been transferred to England.

The patient is to be subject to the following conditions by virtue of that community treatment order:

The patient is to make himself or herself available for examination under section 20A, as requested.

If it is proposed to give a certificate under Part 4A of the Act in the patient's case, the patient is to make himself or herself available for examination to enable the certificate to be given, as requested.

The patient is also to be subject to the following conditions (if any) under section 17B(2) of the Act:

. . . .
. . . .

[If you need to continue on a separate sheet please indicate here [ ] and attach that sheet to this form]

I confirm that I consider the above conditions to be made under section 17B(2) of the Act are necessary or appropriate for one or more of the following purposes:

- to ensure that the patient receives medical treatment
- to prevent risk of harm to the patient's health or safety
- to protect other persons.

Signed . . . .
Responsible clinician
Date . . . .

PART 2

(To be completed by the approved mental health professional)

I [PRINT full name and address] am acting on behalf of [name of local social services authority] and am approved to act as an approved mental health professional for the purposes of the Act by *<Delete as appropriate>*

that authority
[name of local social services authority that approved you, if different].

I agree that the conditions made above under section 17B(2) are necessary or appropriate for one or more of the purposes specified.

Signed . . . .
Approved mental health professional
Date . . . .

THE PATIENT IS NOT SUBJECT TO THE CONDITIONS SET OUT IN THIS FORM UNLESS BOTH PARTS OF THE FORM ARE COMPLETED.

Form CTO10   *Regulation 17(3)(a) and (d)(i) and (ii)*

Mental Health Act 1983 section 19A—authority for assignment of responsibility for community patient to hospital under different managers

(To be completed on behalf of the responsible hospital)

This form gives authority for the assignment of responsibility for [PRINT full name and address of **2–180** patient] from [name and address of responsible hospital] to [name and address of hospital to which responsibility is to be assigned in accordance with the Mental Health (Hospital, Guardianship and Treatment) (England) Regulations 2008.

This assignment was agreed by the managers of the hospital to which the responsibility is to be assigned on [date of confirmation]

The assignment is to take place on [date].

Signed ....
on behalf of managers of first named hospital
PRINT NAME....................
Date ....

Mental Health Act 1983 section 64C(4) — certificate of appropriateness of treatment to be given to community patient (Part 4A certificate)

[. . .]

2–181   I [PRINT full name and address] am a registered medical practitioner appointed for the purposes of Part 4 of the Act (a SOAD).

I have consulted [PRINT full name and profession] and [full name and profession] who have been professionally concerned with the medical treatment of [PRINT full name and address of patient] who is subject to a community treatment order.

I certify that it is appropriate for the following treatment to be given to this patient while the patient is not recalled to hospital, subject to any conditions specified below. The treatment is: [Give description of treatment or plan of treatment.]

. . . .
. . . .
. . . .

I specify the following conditions (if any) to apply: [Conditions may include time-limits on the approval of any or all of the treatment.]

. . . .
. . . .
. . . .

I certify that it is appropriate for the following treatment (if any) to be given to this patient following any recall to hospital under section 17E of the Act, subject to any conditions specified below. The treatment is: [Give description of treatment or plan of treatment].

. . . .
. . . .
. . . .

I specify the following conditions (if any) to apply to the treatment which may be given to the patient following any recall to hospital under section 17E: [Conditions may include time-limits on the approval of any or all of the treatment.]

. . . .
. . . .
. . . .

My reasons are as below/I will provide a statement of my reasons separately. *<Delete as appropriate>* [When giving reasons please indicate if, in your opinion, disclosure of the reasons to the patient would be likely to cause serious harm to the physical or mental health of the patient, or to that of any other person.]

. . . .
. . . .
. . . .

[If you need to continue on a separate sheet for any of the above please indicate here [ ] and attach that sheet to this form.]

Signed . . . .
Date . . . .

Mental Health Act 1983 section 64C(4A)–certificate that community patient has capacity to consent (or if under 16 is competent to consent) to treatment and has done so (Part 4A consent certificate)

(To be completed on behalf of the responsible hospital)

I [PRINT full name and address] am the approved clinician in charge of the treatment of [PRINT full **2–182** name and address of patient] who is subject to a community treatmen order.

I certify that this patient has the capacity/is competent to consent [*delete the one that is not appropriate*] and has consented to the following treatment. The treatment is: [Give description of treatment or plan of treatment.]

Signed . . . .

Date . . . .]

AMENDMENT

This Form was inserted by SI 2012/1118 reg.2(3).

2–183 Regulations 32

SCHEDULE 2

REVOCATIONS

[Not reproduced]

THE MENTAL HEALTH ACT 1983 (INDEPENDENT MENTAL HEALTH ADVOCATES) (ENGLAND) REGULATIONS 2008

(SI 2008/3166)

Dated December 9, 2008, and made by the Secretary of State under the Mental Health Act 1983, section 130A, and the National Health Service Act 2006, sections 7, 8, 14, 19, 75, 272(7) and (8) and 233(4).

GENERAL NOTE

Section 130A of the Act provides that local authorities shall make arrangements to **2–184** enable Independent Mental Health Advocates (IMHAs) to be available to help qualifying patients. These Regulations contain provisions about the arrangements for the appointment of IMHAs and as to who can be appointed to act as an IMHA.

Citation, commencement and extent

1.—(1) These Regulations may be cited as the Mental Health Act 1983 **2–185** (Independent Mental Health Advocates) (England) Regulations 2008.

(2) These Regulations shall come into force on 1st April 2009.

(3) These Regulations apply in relation to England only.

Interpretation

2. In these Regulations—   **2–186**

"the Act" means the Mental Health Act 1983;

["commissioning body" means a local social services authority whose area is in England;]

"IMHA" means an independent mental health advocate;

"provider of advocacy services" means a person (including a voluntary organisation) that employs or engages individuals who may be made available to act as an IMHA but does not include a commissioning body;

["section 130A functions" means the functions under section 130A of the Act of a local social services authority whose area is in England.]

AMENDMENTS

The amendments to this regulation were made by SI 2013/261 reg.16(2).

[Circumstances in which a person may be appointed to be an Independent Mental Health Advocate

3.—(1) A commissioning body, in exercising section 130A functions, may **2–187** enter into arrangements to appoint an individual to act as an IMHA only if the commissioning body is satisfied that the conditions set out in regulation 6 are satisfied.

(2) A commissioning body, in exercising section 130A functions, may enter into arrangements with a provider of advocacy services only if such arrangements include a term that the provider is satisfied that the conditions set out in regulation 6 are satisfied in respect of an individual made available by the provider to act as an IMHA.

(3) A commissioning body may only enter into the arrangements described in paragraphs (1) or (2) above where it has had due regard to the diverse

circumstances (including but not limited to the ethnic, cultural and demographic needs) of qualifying patients.]

AMENDMENT
This regulation was substituted by SI 2013/261 reg.16(3).

2–188   **4.** [*Repealed by SI 2013/261 reg.16(4)*]

2–189   **5.** [*Repealed by SI 2013/261 reg.16(5)*]

Independent Mental Health Advocates: conditions

2–190   **6.**— (1) A person may not act as an IMHA unless the conditions specified in paragraph (2) are satisfied.

(2) Those conditions are that the person referred to in paragraph (1)—

(a) has appropriate experience or training or an appropriate combination of experience and training;

(b) is a person of integrity and good character;

(c) is able to act independently of any person who is professionally concerned with the qualifying patient's medical treatment; and

(d) is able to act independently of any person who requests that person to visit or interview the qualifying patient.

(3) For the purposes of the condition referred to in paragraph (2)(a) regard must be had to standards in guidance that may be issued from time to time by the Secretary of State.

(4) The standards referred to in paragraph (3) may include any qualification that the Secretary of State may determine as appropriate.

[(5) For the purposes of the condition referred to in paragraph (2)(b) there must be obtained, in respect of that person, an enhanced criminal record certificate issued pursuant to section 113B of the Police Act 1997 which includes—

(a) where the qualifying patient has not attained the age of 18, suitability information relating to children (within the meaning of section 113BA of the Police Act 1997);

(b) where the qualifying patient has attained the age of 18, suitability information relating to vulnerable adults (within the meaning of section 113BB of that Act).]

AMENDMENT
Paragraph (5) was substituted by SI 2009/2376 reg.3.

GENERAL NOTE

2–191   The Department of Health has published the following guidance under Gateway reference: 10593:

"This is guidance on what constitutes appropriate experience and training for Independent Mental Health Advocates (IMHAs), including an appropriate qualification, referred to in regulation 6 of the Mental Health Act 1983 (Independent Mental Health Advocates) (England) Regulations 2008.

In deciding whether a person has appropriate experience and training, the person or organisation appointing the IMHA should in particular consider:

– Previous experience working in advocacy, particularly mental health advocacy
– Previous experience working with people with mental health needs

– Successful completion of an advocacy qualification, in particular the IMHA module of the National Advocacy Qualification (see below).

National Advocacy Qualification

To achieve national consistency in the way IMHA services are delivered by multiple independent advocacy providers, a national advocacy qualification is being developed. The qualification is to be modular in structure, consisting of four core modules on generic advocacy, and several specialist modules, including an IMHA module. Learners will be able to take any unit in any order, and there will be no requirement to complete the core units before completing a specialist unit.

As it is a competency-based qualification and reliant on practical experience, not all potential IMHAs will be able to complete the IMHA module before starting to practise. However, to ensure that IMHAs are appropriately trained to meet the needs of patients, IMHAs should be expected to have successfully completed the IMHA module by the end of their first year of practice (making necessary adjustments for any maternity leave, long term sickness or other similar absences)."

Persons not professionally concerned with a patient's medical treatment

7. For the purposes of section 130A(5) of the Act a person is not to be regarded **2–192** as professionally concerned with a qualifying patient's medical treatment if that person—

  (a) is representing the patient in accordance with—
      (i) arrangements made for the purposes of section 130A functions;
      (ii) arrangements made other than for the purposes of that section;
  (b) has in the past represented the qualifying patient in accordance with arrangements referred to in sub-paragraph (a) and in doing so was not otherwise professionally concerned in that patient's treatment.

PART 3

PRACTICE AND PROCEDURE

CIVIL PROCEDURE RULES 1998

(SI 1998/3132)

PART 8

ALTERNATIVE PROCEDURE FOR CLAIMS

Types of claims in which Part 8 procedure may be followed

3–001

. . .

8.1(6) A rule or practice direction may, in relation to a specified type of proceedings—

(a) require or permit the use of the Part 8 procedure; and

(b) disapply or modify any of the rules set out in this Part as they apply to those proceedings.

(Rule 8.9 provides for other modifications to the general rules where the Part 8 procedure is being used)

. . .

Practice Direction 8A – Alternative Procedure for Claims

. . .

Section C

Special Provisions

10.1 The following special provisions apply to the applications indicated.

. . .

Applications under Mental Health Act 1983

18.1 In this paragraph—

3–002

(1) a section referred to by a number refers to the section so numbered in the Mental Health Act 1983 and 'Part II' means Part II of that Act;

(2) 'hospital manager' means the manager of a hospital as defined in section 145(1) of the Act; and

(3) 'place of residence' means, in relation to a patient who is receiving treatment as an in-patient in a hospital or other institution, that hospital or institution.

18.2 The claim form must be filed—

(1) in the court for the district in which the patient's place of residence is situated; or

(2) in the case of an application under section 30, in the court that made the order under section 29 which the application seeks to discharge or vary.

18.3 Where an application is made under section 29 for an order that the functions of the nearest relative of the patient are to be exercisable by some other person—

(1) the nearest relative must be made a respondent, unless—

(a) the application is made on the grounds that the patient has no nearest relative or that it is not reasonably practicable to ascertain whether he has a nearest relative; or

(b) the court orders otherwise; and

(2) the court may order that any other person shall be made a respondent.

18.4 Subject to paragraph 18.5, the court may accept as evidence of the facts relied upon in support of the application, any report made—

(1) by a medical practitioner; or

(a) a probation officer;

(b) an officer of a local authority;

(c) an officer of a voluntary body exercising statutory functions on behalf of a local authority; or

(d) an officer of a hospital manager.

18.5 The respondent must be informed of the substance of any part of the report dealing with his fitness or conduct that the court considers to be material to the determination of the claim.

18.6 An application under Part II shall be heard in private unless the court orders otherwise.

18.7 The judge may, for the purpose of determining the application, interview the patient. The interview may take place in the presence of, or separately from, the parties. The interview may be conducted elsewhere than at the court. Alternatively, the judge may direct the district judge to interview the patient and report to the judge in writing.

GENERAL NOTE

3–003   This provision is concerned with applications to the County Court under ss.29 and 30 of the Act. The court, on hearing an application under s.29, has the power to make an interim order: see the General Note to s.29.

A district judge does not have jurisdiction to hear a case under this provision (CPR Practice Direction 2B: Allocation of Cases to Levels of Judiciary, para.11.1(a)(vii)).

In order to achieve judicial continuity, in *Northamptonshire Healthcare NHS Foundation Trust v ML* [2014] EWCOP 2, Hayden J. reserved to himself any application to displace the nearest of the patient by constituting himself as a judge of the County Court.

Paragraph 18.3

3–004   Neither the wording of this paragraph nor the judgment of the Court of Appeal in *Lewis v Gibson* [2007] EWCA Civ 587; [2005] M.H.L.R. 309, preclude an application for an interim displacement being made without notice being given to the nearest relative: see *R. (on the application of Holloway) v Oxfordshire County Council* [2007] EWHC 776 (Admin) which is considered in the General Note to s.29. In *Lewis v Gibson*, the Court of Appeal endorsed the Official Solicitor's proposal for the implementation of this paragraph, as it appeared in CCR, Ord.49 r.12, in such a way as to ensure compliance with the patient's rights under the European Convention on Human Rights (ECHR). Thorpe L.J. said at para.40:

"Although [this paragraph] does not require it, I support the Official Solicitor's conclusion that the patient must be served with the proceedings and notified of the right to be joined. Second the County Court Judge must at the earliest stage enquire whether the patient has been so served and ensure that appropriate steps are taken to secure the patient's Article 6 and 8 rights. Third he should extend his enquiry into the patient's capacity in order to ensure that a person willing to act as litigation friend has been identified and served. These precautions must be taken even in cases where urgent relief is sought. I accept the Official Solicitor's submission that it is difficult to conceive of circumstances in which a patient could lawfully be deprived of any opportunity to participate in proceedings. Any justification would have to address the patient's Article 6 and 8 rights."

Paragraph 18.5

3–005   To comply with the requirement of this paragraph, it is sufficient if a report is handed to the respondent's legal adviser in circumstances where the legal adviser can give advice and take instructions (*B(A) v B(L) (Mental Health: Patient)* [1980] 1 W.L.R. 116). This case was considered by Hale L.J. in *R. (on the application of S) v Plymouth City Council* [2002] EWCA Civ 388, paras 36 to 38, where her Ladyship held that:

(i) this paragraph, as it appeared in CCR Ord.49, r.12, imposes a minimum obligation;

(ii) the court has to comply with the rules of natural justice, which normally require that anything relevant to the court's decision be seen by both parties to the dispute;

(iii) the right to see all the documents in a case may be outweighed by other considerations, but there must be a clear and proper public objective and the limitation must be proportionate to that objective;

(iv) in general one would expect disclosure of all the information put before the court in proceedings under s.29 for the purposes of establishing that the nearest relative has "exercised without due regard to the welfare of the patient or the interests of the public his power to discharge the patient from guardianship, or is likely to do so", unless there was a demonstrable risk of harm to the patient or others in so doing; and

(v) in principle, the approach of a court in a s.29 application should be no less open than that of a Mental Health Review Tribunal.

Paragraph 18.6
The publication of information relating to proceedings before any court sitting in private **3–006** shall be a contempt of a court where the proceedings are brought under the Act authorising an application or reference to be made to the First-tier Tribunal, the Mental Health Review Tribunal for Wales or to a county court (Administration of Justice Act 1960 s.12(1)(b)).

Paragraph 18.7
In using this power, the judge will act in accordance with s.6(1) of the Human Rights Act **3–007** 1998 and will not act in a way which is incompatible with the patient's rights under Art.5 of the ECHR (*R. (on the application of MH) v Secretary of State for Health* [2004] EWHC 56 (Admin); [2004] M.H.L.R. 155 at para.45).

TRIBUNAL PROCEDURE (FIRST-TIER TRIBUNAL) (HEALTH, EDUCATION AND SOCIAL CARE CHAMBER) RULES 2008

SI 2008/2699

Made - - - - - - - - -	*9th October 2008*
Laid before Parliament - -	*15th October 2008*
Coming into force - - - -	*3rd November 2008*

CONTENTS

PART 1

INTRODUCTION

1. Citation, commencement, application and interpretation
2. Overriding, objective and parties' obligation to co-operate with the Tribunal
3. Alternative dispute resolution and arbitration

PART 2

GENERAL POWERS AND PROVISIONS

4. Delegation to staff
5. Case management powers
6. Procedure for applying for and giving directions
7. Failure to comply with rules etc
8. Striking out a party's case
9. Substitution and addition of parties
10. Orders for costs
11. Representatives
12. Calculating time
13. Sending and delivery of documents
14. Use of documents and information
15. Evidence and submissions
16. Summoning of witnesses and orders to answer questions or produce documents
17. Withdrawal

PART 3

PROCEEDINGS BEFORE THE TRIBUNAL OTHER THAN IN MENTAL HEALTH CASES

[Not reproduced]

Practice and Procedure

PART 4

Proceedings before the Tribunal in mental health cases

CHAPTER 1

Before the hearing

31. Application of Part 4
32 Procedure in mental health cases
33. Notice of proceedings to interested persons
34. Medical examination of the patient

CHAPTER 2

Hearings

35. No disposal of proceedings without a hearing
36. Entitlement to attend a hearing
37. Time and place of hearings
38. Public and private hearings
39. Hearings in a party's absence
40. Power to pay allowances

CHAPTER 3

Decisions

41. Decisions
42. Provisional decisions

PART 5

Correcting, setting aside, reviewing and appeal Tribunal decisions

43. Interpretation
44. Clerical mistakes and accidental slips or omissions
45. Setting aside a decision which disposes of proceedings
46. Application for permission to appeal
47. Tribunal's consideration of application for permission to appeal
48. Application for review in special educational needs cases
49. Review of a decision
50. Power to treat an application as a different type of application

SCHEDULE—[*Not reproduced*]

After consulting in accordance with paragraph 28(1) of the Tribunals, Courts and Enforcement Act 2007, the Tribunal Procedure Committee has made the following Rules in exercise of the power conferred by sections 9(3), 22 and 29(3) and (4) of, and Schedule 5 to, that Act.

The Lord Chancellor has allowed the Rules in accordance with paragraph 28(3) of Schedule 5 to the Tribunals, Courts and Enforcement Act 2007.

GENERAL NOTE

An account of the genesis of the First-tier Tribunal (Mental Health) and of rights of **3–009** appeal from decisions of the tribunal to the Upper Tribunal can be found in the General Note to s.65 of the Act.

These Rules are concerned with the conduct of proceedings before the First-tier Tribunal in mental health cases. A failure to comply with the Rules does not render the tribunal proceedings void (r.7).

Under para.4 of the Practice Statement "Composition of Tribunals in relation to matters that fall to be decided by the Health, Education and Social Care Chamber on or after 18 January 2010", issued by the Senior President of Tribunals on December 16, 2009, a "decision that disposes of proceedings or determines a preliminary issue made at, or following, a hearing [in respect of a mental health case] must be made by:

    (a) One judge; and
    (b) One other member who is a registered medical practitioner; and
    (c) One other member who has substantial experience of health, or social care matters".

Tribunal jurisdiction

The function of a tribunal is limited to reviewing the justification for the patient's con- **3–010** tinued detention, guardianship or supervised community treatment by considering evidence relating to the relevant statutory grounds for discharge. It has no power to consider the validity of the original decision to bring the patient within the scope of the Act (*R. v East London and The City Mental Health Trust Ex p. Brandenburg* [2003] UKHL 58; [2004] 1 All E.R. 400 at para.9(3)). Neither has it jurisdiction to determine whether a patient had been detained under the appropriate section of the Act nor to investigate the circumstances that led to the powers of the Act being invoked. However, such circumstances would need to be taken account of when the tribunal considers the patient's condition at the time of the hearing.

Although the tribunal will receive a significant amount of evidence on the medical and other treatment that the patient is receiving, the tribunal's task is confined to considering such evidence only in so far as it relates to the statutory grounds. In particular, the tribunal's jurisdiction does not extend to issues relating to the operation of either Part IV or Part IVA of the Act (*R. (on the application of B) v Dr SS* [2005] EWCA Civ 28; [2006] M.H.L.R. 131, per Phillips L.C.J. at para.65; also see *SH v Cornwall Partnership NHS Trust* [2012] UKUT 290 (AAC); [2012] M.H.L.R. 383 and *GA v Betsi Cadwaladr University LHB* [2013] 280 (AAC; [2014] M.H.L.R. 27)).

Tribunal procedure and the rules of natural justice

As it is a creature of statute, a tribunal has no inherent jurisdiction; its jurisdiction is con- **3–011** fined to that conferred on it by statute. It is obliged to follow the procedure laid down in these Rules and where the Rules are silent on a point of procedure the tribunal must follow the rules of natural justice, i.e. it should act in a fair and unbiased way and should provide an opportunity for each party to adequately state his case (*Secretary of State for the Home Department v Oxford Regional Mental Health Review Tribunal* [1987] 3 All E.R. 8 HL). The forming and expression of a provisional opinion by a member of the tribunal does not give rise to unfairness: see the General Note to r.34 and *Re Application for Judicial Review* [2008] NIQB 75, at para.24.

In *MB v BEH MH NHS Trust* [2011] UKUT 328 (AAC): [2011] M.H.L.R. 246, the presiding Judge at the tribunal hearing had "clearly indicated that the application for discharge had no prospect of success" (para.15; see also para.8 where the judge was reported as having invited the patient to withdraw his application). On those facts, UT Judge Levenson held that there had been a breach of natural justice, agreeing with counsel for the appellant that the presiding Judge had:

"... 'expressed himself in such a way as to give rise to reasonable apprehension that he had formed a preconceived concluded opinion ... [the appellant] was effectively told that he should give up. It was an indication by the tribunal that he had no possibility of success'."

The role of the tribunal

3–012   In *AMA v Greater Manchester West Mental Health NHS Foundation Trust* [2015] UKUT 36 (AAC), Charles J. said at para.35:

"(i) The main purpose of Article 5 [of the European Convention on Human Rights] is to provide that no one should be deprived of their liberty in an arbitrary manner.

(ii) The reviewing body, and so the [First-tier Tribunal], must consider whether the reasons that initially justified detention continue and review the substantive and procedural conditions that are essential for the deprivation of liberty to be lawful.

(iii) Article 5(4) applies to those reviews and is directed to ensuring that there is a fair procedure for reviewing the lawfulness of a detention.

(iv) To my mind the most important principles to take into account in the decision making process of the [First-tier Tribunal] are: (a) the underlying purpose and importance of the review and so the need to fairly and thoroughly assess the reasons for the detention, (b) the vulnerability of the person who is its subject and what is at stake for that person (i.e. a continuation of a detention for an identified purpose), (c) the need for flexibility and appropriate speed, (d) whether, without representation (but with all other available assistance and the prospect of further reviews), the patient will practically and effectively be able to conduct their case, and if not whether nonetheless (e) the tribunal is likely to be properly and sufficiently informed of the competing factors relating to the case before it and so able to carry out an effective review. (As to this the tribunal should when deciding the case review this prediction).

(v) The presumption of capacity and the requirement for it to be assessed by reference to the relevant decision, issue or activity must be remembered but care needs to be taken not to embark on unnecessary assessments and to maintain flexibility to achieve the underlying purpose, namely a practical and effective review of a deprivation of liberty in an appropriate timescale."

Concessions

3–013   In *NL v Hampshire County Council* [2014] UKUT 475 (AAC), UT Judge Jacobs said at para.24:

"[T]ribunals are not required to accept concessions unless they are satisfied that they are correct. That applies to matters of fact and law. Tribunals are entitled to require the parties to satisfy them by evidence and argument that concessions are sound and, if they fail to do so, tribunals are not obliged to accept them."

Bias of tribunal members

3–014   In *Equilibrium Health Care v AK* [2013] UKUT 543 (AAC); [2014] M.H.L.R. 268, para.11, UT Judge Jacobs said:

"Bias comes in different forms. Two are relevant in this case: actual bias and the real possibility of bias. The test for actual bias is whether the tribunal member is partial in the sense of favouring one side or being hostile to another. The test for the real possibility of bias is 'whether the fair-minded and informed observer, having considered the facts, would conclude that there was a real possibility that the tribunal was biased': Lord Hope in *Porter v Magill* [2002] 2 AC 357 at [103]."

The attributes of a fair-minded and informed observer were examined by the House of Lords in *Helow v Secretary of State for the Home Department* [2009] 2 All E.R. 1031 at paras 2 and 3.

The question whether the tribunal was biased because the consultant psychiatrist who sat as a member of the tribunal was an employee of the detaining NHS Trust was addressed in *R. (on the application of PD) v West Midlands and North West Mental Health Review Tribunal* [2004] EWCA Civ 311; [2004] M.H.L.R 174, which is considered in the General Note to r.34. *PD* was applied in *R. (on the application of M) v Mental Health Review Tribunal* [2005] EWHC 2791 (Admin); [2006] M.H.L.R. 46, where Bennett J. confirmed that cases involving a consideration of bias are fact-sensitive and that an examination of case precedent was of limited value (also see *PD* at para.8). His Lordship found that the fair-minded and informed observer, having taken account of the facts of the case, would not say that there was a real possibility of bias on the part of a judge when sitting as a legal member of the tribunal in November 2004 on the ground that he had imposed a hospital order and a restriction order on the patient in September 2003.

Every application for the recusal of a tribunal member on the ground of bias must be decided on the facts and circumstances of the individual case. If in any case there is real ground for doubt, that doubt should be resolved in favour of recusal (*Locabail (UK) Ltd v Bayfield Properties Ltd* [2000] 1 All E.R. 65 at para.25).

In the *Equilibrium Health Care* case, Judge Jacobs said that "decisions on recusal are best challenged, if at all, after the proceedings are concluded" (para.34).

Tribunal hearings

In *W v Egdell* [1989] 1 All E.R. 1089 at 1095, Scott J. described the nature of a hearing **3–015** before a tribunal as inquisitorial, not adversarial. Tribunal procedure was said by Stanley Burnton J. to be "to a significant extent inquisitorial" in *R. (on the application of Ashworth Hospital Authority) v Mental Health Review Tribunal for the West Midlands and North West Regions* [2001] EWHC Admin 901; [2002] M.H.L.R. 13, para.16. In the opinion of Collins J., "it is not particularly helpful to label the proceedings one way or the other" (*R. (on the application of X) v Mental Health Review Tribunal* [2003] EWHC 1272 (Admin); [2003] M.H.L.R. 299, para.24).

There is nothing to prevent the chairman of a tribunal from presiding over more than one hearing involving the same patient (*R. v Oxford Regional Mental Health Review Tribunal Ex p. Mackman, The Times*, June 2, 1986). This ruling would undoubtedly apply to other members of the tribunal.

Accommodation for hearings

In November 2012, the Tribunal issued guidance to Responsible Authorities on "Room **3–016** and facilities requirements for tribunal hearings". Also see the *Code of Practice* at paras 12.36 to 12.38.

Contempt of Court

Although a tribunal has no powers itself to deal with the contempt of its proceedings, the **3–017** ruling of the House of Lords in *Pickering v Liverpool Daily Post and Echo Newspapers Plc* [1991] 1 All E.R. 622 that the Mental Health Review Tribunal was a court for the purposes of the law of contempt means that it is open to a party of the proceedings before the tribunal to apply to the High Court for the committal of any party who is in contempt of the tribunal.

Victims

The Chamber President has published "Practice guidance on proceedings concerning **3–018** handling representations from victims in the First-tier Tribunal (Mental Health)", 2011, which can be accessed at: *www.judiciary.gov.uk/wp-content/uploads/2014/10/practice-direction-handling-representations-from-victims.pdf*. The definition of "victim" in the guidance "is taken to include any person in relation to the patient's index offence or offences who appears to the relevant local probation board to be the victim of the offence or offences. This includes a victim's family in a case where the offence has resulted in the victim's death or incapacity and in other cases where the victim's age or circumstances make it more sensible to approach a family member" (para.(2)).

The Ministry of Justice has published "Duties to victims under the Domestic Violence, Crime and Victims Act 2004: Guidance for clinicians" which can be accessed at: *www.justice.gov.uk/offenders/types-of-offender/mentally-disordered-offenders*. Also see Ch.40 of the *Code of Practice*.

Independent Mental Health Advocates

3–019   The Courts and Tribunals Service has published a guidance note on the "Role of the Independent Mental Health Advocate (IMHA) in First-tier Tribunal (Mental Health) hearings" (2012) which can be accessed at the Mental Health Law Online website. Paragraph 3.2 of the guidance note states:

> "The role that the IMHA plays in a tribunal hearing should . . . be informed by the statutory provisions and the Code of Practice, but the role should also take account of the requirements of The Tribunal Procedure (First-tier Tribunal) (Health, Education and Social Care Chamber) Rules 2008. The overriding objective in Rule 2 refers to '(c) ensuring, so far as practicable, that the parties are able to participate fully in the proceedings' and the tribunal must, of course, give effect to the overriding objective in exercising its powers. In general, therefore, the tribunal should enable and support the IMHA in the discharge of his or her legitimate functions before the tribunal."

Information for patients

3–020   The *Code of Practice* states:

> "4.22 Hospital managers should ensure that patients are offered assistance to request a hospital managers' hearing or make an application to the Tribunal, and that the applications are transmitted to the Tribunal without delay. They should also be told:
>
> • how to contact a suitably qualified legal representative (and should be given assistance to do so if required)
>
> • that free legal aid may be available, and
>
> • how to contact any other organisation which may be able to help them make an application to the Tribunal.
>
> 4.23 It is particularly important that patients are well-informed and supported to make an application to the Tribunal if they are on a CTO, do not otherwise have regular contact with their nearest relative or people who could help them make an application, or lack capacity. If a patient lacks capacity to decide whether to seek a review of detention or a CTO, an IMHA should be introduced to the patient so that the IMHA can explain what help they can offer.
>
> 4.24 Patients whose CTOs are revoked, and conditionally discharged patients recalled to hospital, should be told that their cases will be referred automatically to the Tribunal."

Interpretation services

3–021   See the *Code of Practice* at para.12.40.

Human Rights Act 1998

3–022   As a "public authority" for the purposes of the 1998 Act, the tribunal is required to act in a way which is compatible with the rights contained in the European Convention on Human Rights (ECHR) and these Rules must be read and given effect in a way which is compatible with such rights: see ss.3 and 6 of the 1998 Act. Articles 5(4) and 6(1) of the ECHR are particularly relevant to the operation of the tribunal: see Pt 5. In *MD v Nottinghamshire Health Care NHS Trust* [2010] UKUT 59 (AAC); [2010] M.H.L.R. 93, para.47, UT Judge Jacobs said:

"[T]he tribunal, like all judicial bodies, is under a duty to comply with the Convention right to a hearing. As part of that duty, it must ensure an equality of arms as that is understood in the Strasbourg jurisprudence. It is relevant that the tribunal is not merely a body that hears evidence, finds facts and decides on arguments. It is, as I have said, a body with its own expertise. Its use of that expertise is an important contribution to ensuring an equality of arms. The psychiatrist on the panel makes an examination of the patient and the panel uses its collective knowledge, experience and expertise to assess the evidence. Both those tasks are performed independently. They reduce the need, which may exist in the court system, for the parties to have their own expert evidence. Patients are, of course, entitled to produce evidence on their own behalf. My point is simply that greater access to experts is not a necessary, or the only, way to ensure the equality of arms that the law requires."

Article 5 of the ECHR does not enable a patient who has failed before a tribunal and who had a favourable medical opinion which had not been accepted by the tribunal, to be bound to be granted leave to bring judicial review proceedings to challenge the tribunal's decision (*R. (on the application of MacDonald) v Mental Health Review Tribunal* [2001] EWHC Admin 1032, at para.18).

Skeleton Arguments

3–023

The First-tier Tribunal (Mental Health) has stated on its website that for "complex cases, legal representatives are encouraged to supply skeleton arguments especially where a Human Rights Act issue is raised. With Human Rights Act issues the Civil Procedure Rules Practice Direction Part 39[A] (Hearings) 8.1 applies". Paragraph 8.1 states:

"If it is necessary for a party to give evidence at a hearing of an authority referred to in section 2 of the Human Rights Act 1998—

(1) the authority to be cited should be an authoritative and complete report; and

(2) the party must give to the court and any other party a list of the authorities he intends to cite and copies of the reports not less than three days before the hearing. (Section 2(1) of the Human Rights Act 1998 requires the court to take into account the authorities listed there)

(3) Copies of the complete original texts issued by the European Court and Commission either paper based or from the Court's judgment database (HUDOC), which is available on the Internet, may be used."

Legal Aid

3–024

Paragraph 6.21 of the Reference Guide states:

"Legal Aid is available through the Legal Aid Agency to fund legal advice and representation for patients before the First-tier Tribunal, without requiring any assessment of the patients' means. Legal Aid for appeals to the Upper Tribunal is means-tested and subject to a merits test."

Code of Practice

3–025

Guidance on the role of the tribunal is given in Ch.12.

Wales

3–026   Separate rules, which are not reproduced in this Manual, have been made to govern the practice and procedure to be followed in proceedings before the Mental Health Review Tribunal for Wales: see the Mental Health Review Tribunal for Wales Rules 2008 (SI 2008/2705 (L.17) (the "Welsh Rules")). The Mental Health Review Tribunal for Wales has not issued any Practice Directions.

PART 1

INTRODUCTION

Citation, commencement, application and interpretation

3–027   **1.**—(1) These Rules may be cited as the Tribunal Procedure (First-tier Tribunal) (Health, Education and Social Care Chamber) Rules 2008 and come into force on 3rd November 2008.

[(2) These Rules apply to proceedings before the Health, Education and Social Care Chamber of the First-tier Tribunal.]

(3) In these Rules—

"the 2007 Act" means the Tribunals, Courts and Enforcement Act 2007;

"applicant" means a person who—

(a) starts Tribunal proceedings, whether by making an application, an appeal, a claim or a reference;

(b) makes an application to the Tribunal for leave to start such proceedings; or

(c) is substituted as an applicant under rule 9(1) (substitution and addition of parties);

"childcare provider" means a person who is a childminder or provides day care as defined in [section 19 of the Children and Families (Wales) Measure 2010], or a person who provides childcare as defined in section 18 of the Childcare Act 2006;

"disability discrimination in schools case" means proceedings concerning disability discrimination in the education of a child [or young person] or related matters;

"dispose of proceedings" includes, unless indicated otherwise, disposing of a part of the proceedings;

"document" means anything in which information is recorded in any form, and an obligation under these Rules or any practice direction or direction to provide or allow access to a document or a copy of a document for any purpose means, unless the Tribunal directs otherwise, an obligation to provide or allow access to such document or copy in a legible form or in a form which can be readily made into a legible form;

[. . .]

["health service case" means a case under the National Health Service Act 2006, the National Health Service (Wales) Act 2006, regulations made under either of those Acts, or regulations having effect as if made under either of those Acts by reason of section 4 of and Schedule 2 to the National Health Service (Consequential Provisions) Act 2006;]

"hearing" means an oral hearing and includes a hearing conducted in whole or in part by video link, telephone or other means of instantaneous two-way electronic communication;

"legal representative" means [a person who, for the purposes of the Legal Services Act 2007, is an authorised person in relation to an activity which constitutes the exercise of a right of audience or the conduct of litigation within the meaning of that Act];

"mental health case" means proceedings brought under the Mental Health Act 1983 or paragraph 5(2) of the Schedule to the Repatriation of Prisoners Act 1984;

"nearest relative" has the meaning set out in section 26 of the Mental Health Act 1983;

"party" means—

    (a) in a mental health case, the patient, the responsible authority, the Secretary of State (if the patient is a restricted patient or in a reference under rule 32(8) (seeking approval under section 86 of the Mental Health Act 1983)), and any other person who starts a mental health case by making an application;

    (b) in any other case, a person who is an applicant or respondent in proceedings before the Tribunal or, if the proceedings have been concluded, a person who was an applicant or respondent when the Tribunal finally disposed of all issues in the proceedings;

"patient" means the person who is the subject of a mental health case;

"practice direction" means a direction given under section 23 of the 2007 Act;

"respondent" means—

    (a) in an appeal against an order made by a justice of the peace under [section 34 of the Children and Families (Wales) Measure 2010], section 20 of the Care Standards Act 2000 or section 72 of the Childcare Act 2006, the person who applied to the justice of the peace for the order;

    (b) in an appeal against any other decision, the person who made the decision;

    (c) in proceedings on a claim under section 28I of the Disability Discrimination Act 1995, the body responsible for the school as determined in accordance with paragraph 1 of Schedule 4A to that Act or, if the claim concerns the residual duties of a local education authority under section 28F of that Act, that local education authority;

    (d) in proceedings on an application under section 4(2) of the Protection of Children Act 1999 or section 86(2) of the Care Standards Act 2000, the Secretary of State;

    [(da) in an application for, or for a review of, a stop order under the National Health Service (Optical Charges and Payments) Regulations 1997—

        (i) the supplier, where the Secretary of State is the applicant;

        (ii) the Secretary of State, where the supplier is the applicant;

    (db) in any other [health service case] —

        (i) the practitioner, performer or person against whom the application is made, where [the National Health Service Commissioning Board] [or Local Health Board] is, or is deemed to be, the applicant;

       (ii) [the National Health Service Commissioning Board] [or Local Health Board] that served the notice, obtained the order or confirmation of the order, where any other person is the applicant; or]

  (e) a person substituted or added as a respondent under rule 9 (substitution and addition of parties);

"responsible authority" means—

  (a) in relation to a patient detained under the Mental Health Act 1983 in a hospital within the meaning of Part 2 of that Act, the managers (as defined in section 145 of that Act);

  (b) in relation to a patient subject to guardianship, the responsible local social services authority (as defined in section 34(3) of the Mental Health Act 1983);

  (c) in relation to a community patient, the managers of the responsible hospital (as defined in section 145 of the Mental Health Act 1983);

  (d) [. . .]

"restricted patient" has the meaning set out in section 79(1) of the Mental Health Act 1983;

["special educational needs case" means proceedings concerning—

  (a) an EHC needs assessment within the meaning of section 36(2) of the Children and Families Act 2014, or

  (b) an EHC plan within the meaning of section 37(2) of that Act,

of a child or young person who has or may have special educational needs;]

"Suspension Regulations" means regulations which provide for a right of appeal against a decision to suspend, or not to lift the suspension of, a person's registration as a childcare provider;

"Tribunal" means the First-tier Tribunal;

"working day" means any day except a Saturday or Sunday, Christmas Day, Good Friday or a bank holiday under section 1 of the Banking and Financial Dealings Act 1971.

["young person" means, in relation to a special educational needs case or a disability discrimination in schools case, a person over compulsory school age but under 25].

AMENDMENTS

The amendments to this rule were made by SI 2010/15 r.15, SI 2010/2653 r.3, SI 2011/651 r.3(2), SI 2013/477 r.11 and SI 2014/2128 r.20.

GENERAL NOTE

Paragraph (3)

3–028   PARTY. The identity of the responsible authority in para.(a) can change if the patient is subject to a transfer under s.19 of the Act after the decision under challenge has been made. An independent mental health advocate for the patient is not a party to the proceedings.

    RESPONDENT. The tribunal can give a direction adding a person to the proceedings as a respondent (r.9(2)).

Overriding objective and parties' obligation to co-operate with the Tribunal

3–029   **2.**—(1) The overriding objective of these Rules is to enable the Tribunal to deal with cases fairly and justly.

(2) Dealing with a case fairly and justly includes—

(a) dealing with the case in ways which are proportionate to the importance of the case, the complexity of the issues, the anticipated costs and the resources of the parties;

(b) avoiding unnecessary formality and seeking flexibility in the proceedings;

(c) ensuring, so far as practicable, that the parties are able to participate fully in the proceedings;

(d) using any special expertise of the Tribunal effectively; and

(e) avoiding delay, so far as compatible with proper consideration of the issues.

(3) The Tribunal must seek to give effect to the overriding objective when it—

(a) exercises any power under these Rules; or

(b) interprets any rule or practice direction.

(4) Parties must—

(a) help the Tribunal to further the overriding objective; and

(b) co-operate with the Tribunal generally.

DEFINITIONS   **3–030**
    Tribunal: r.1(3).
    party: r.1(3).
    practice direction: r.1(3).

GENERAL NOTE
    This rule establishes that the tribunal's overriding objective when performing functions **3–031** under these Rules is to deal with cases fairly and justly. It also requires parties to help the tribunal to further this objective and to co-operate with the tribunal. It cannot be taken into account when interpreting the Act (para.3).
    The objective of dealing with cases fairly and justly:

> "includes the avoidance of unnecessary applications and unnecessary delay. That requires parties to cooperate and liaise with each other concerning procedural matters, with a view to agreeing a procedural course promptly where they are able to do so, before making any application to the tribunal. This is particularly to be expected where parties have legal representation. Parties should endeavour to agree disclosure issues without the need for the tribunal to make a ruling. However, even where a direction from the tribunal may be required (for example, where a responsible authority holding medical records requires an order for the disclosure of medical records to overcome issues of confidentiality or arising from the Data Protection Act, or where there are genuine issues as to how most appropriately to proceed), it will assist the tribunal to further the overriding objective if the parties can identify any directions they are able to agree, subject to the approval of the tribunal. Where they are unable to agree every aspect, this liaison will at least have the advantage of crystallising their positions, and more clearly identifying the issue(s) upon which the tribunal will have to rule. We stress that, in the context of an urgent application in the mental health jurisdiction, this liaison between the parties must not lead to any unavoidable delay" (*Dorset Healthcare NHS Foundation Trust v MH* [2009] UKUT 4 (AAC); [2009] M.H.L.R. 102 at para.13).

According to UT Judge Jacobs, the objective also "includes ensuring full participation, so far as practicable. Rule 14(2) requires the tribunal to have regard to the interests of justice. Justice and fairness generally require openness. Sometimes, they are not compatible and a compromise is possible": see *RM v St Andrew's Healthcare* at para.31. *RM* is noted under r.14(2).

Paragraph (2)
3–032   INCLUDES.   The list is not exclusive.

Paragraph (4)
3–033   This paragraph was not included in the Welsh Rules because it was felt that placing an obligation on the patient to co-operate with the tribunal was undesirable.

In *MD v Nottinghamshire Health Care NHS Trust* [2010] UKUT 59 (AAC); [2010] M.H.L.R. 93, para.46, UT Judge Jacobs said that the duties placed on the parties under this paragraph "must include making their experts available to comply with any directions that are given by the tribunal".

Alternative dispute resolution and arbitration
3–034   **3.**—(1) The Tribunal should seek, where appropriate—

(a) to bring to the attention of the parties the availability of any appropriate alternative procedure for the resolution of the dispute; and

(b) if the parties wish and provided that it is compatible with the overriding objective, to facilitate the use of the procedure.

(2) Part 1 of the Arbitration Act 1996 does not apply to proceedings before the Tribunal.

3–035   DEFINITIONS
Tribunal: r.1(3).
party: r.1(3).

GENERAL NOTE
3–036   Although this rule is not applicable to mental health cases, the tribunal could draw the attention of a patient to the availability of relevant complaint procedures.

PART 2

GENERAL POWERS AND PROVISIONS

Delegation to staff
3–037   **4.**—(1) Staff appointed under section 40(1) of the 2007 Act (tribunal staff and services) may, with the approval of the Senior President of Tribunals, carry out functions of a judicial nature permitted or required to be done by the Tribunal.

(2) The approval referred to at paragraph (1) may apply generally to the carrying out of specified functions by members of staff of a specified description in specified circumstances.

(3) Within 14 days after the date on which the Tribunal sends notice of a decision made by a member of staff under paragraph (1) to a party, that party may apply in writing to the Tribunal for that decision to be considered afresh by a judge.

3–038   DEFINITIONS
the 2007 Act: r.1(3).
Tribunal: r.1(3).
party: r.1(3).

GENERAL NOTE
3–039   This rule enables judicial functions, such as case management, to be undertaken by tribunal staff if this is authorised by the Senior President of Tribunals.

A Practice Statement on "Delegation of functions to staff and to registrars on or after 27 April 2015" was issued by the Senior President of Tribunals. It is reproduced below.

Case management powers

5.—(1) Subject to the provisions of the 2007 Act and any other enactment, the **3–040** Tribunal may regulate its own procedure.

(2) The Tribunal may give a direction in relation to the conduct or disposal of proceedings at any time, including a direction amending, suspending or setting aside an earlier direction.

(3) In particular, and without restricting the general powers in paragraphs (1) and (2), the Tribunal may—

(a) extend or shorten the time for complying with any rule, practice direction or direction, unless such extension or shortening would conflict with a provision of another enactment containing a time limit;

(b) consolidate or hear together two or more sets of proceedings or parts of proceedings raising common issues, or treat a case as a lead case;

(c) permit or require a party to amend a document;

(d) permit or require a party or another person to provide documents, information or submissions to the Tribunal or a party;

(e) deal with an issue in the proceedings as a preliminary issue;

(f) hold a hearing to consider any matter, including a case management issue;

(g) decide the form of any hearing;

(h) adjourn or postpone a hearing;

(i) require a party to produce a bundle for a hearing;

(j) stay proceedings;

(k) transfer proceedings to another court or tribunal if that other court or tribunal has jurisdiction in relation to the proceedings and—

    (i) because of a change of circumstances since the proceedings were started, the Tribunal no longer has jurisdiction in relation to the proceedings; or

    (ii) the Tribunal considers that the other court or tribunal is a more appropriate forum for the determination of the case; or

(l) suspend the effect of its own decision pending the determination by the Tribunal or the Upper Tribunal of an application for permission to appeal against, and any appeal or review of, that decision.

DEFINITIONS

    the 2007 Act: r.1(3).   **3–041**

    Tribunal: r.1(3).

    practice direction: r.1(3).

    party: r.1(3).

    document: r.1(3).

    hearing: r.1(3).

GENERAL NOTE

    This rule, which states that a direction under this rule can be given on the application of **3–042** one or more of the parties or by the tribunal on its own initiative, should be read with r.6. It enables the tribunal to give case management directions so as to facilitate: (1) the speedy determination of the case in compliance with the art.5(4) of the European Convention on Human Rights (ECHR); and (2) the overriding objective of dealing with cases fairly and justly under r.2. It is supplemented by r.15. The tribunal and the Upper Tribunal are reluctant to grant permission to appeal against case management decisions: see the notes to r.46.

Under paras 9 and 10 of the Practice Statement "Composition of Tribunals in relation to matters that fall to be decided by the Health, Education and Social Care Chamber on or after 18 January 2010", issued by the Senior President of Tribunals on December 16, 2009, where the tribunal:

> "has given a decision that disposes of proceedings ('the substantive decision'), any matter decided under, or in accordance with, Rule 5(3)(l) or Part 5 of [these] Rules or section 9 of the Tribunals, Courts and Enforcement Act 2007 must be decided by one judge, unless the Chamber President considers it appropriate that it is decided either by:—

> (a) the same members of the Tribunal as gave the substantive decision; or
> (b) a Tribunal . . . comprised of different members of the Tribunal to that which gave the substantive decision.

> Any other decision, including striking out a case under Rule 8 . . . (except at, or following, a hearing) or giving directions under Rule 5 . . . (whether or not at a hearing) must be made by:—

> (a) One judge."

A Case Management Request Form (CMR 1) is available as a means of ensuring that applicants provide the necessary information under the Rules when applying for directions and other interlocutory matters.

In *B v Mental Health Review Tribunal and the Secretary of State for the Home Department* [2002] EWHC Admin 1553; [2003] M.H.L.R. 19, Scott Baker J. said at para.49:

> "At each stage the tribunal should have had in mind the delay that has occurred until then and given directions against that background. The longer the delay that has occurred the more aggressive the directions will need to be to ensure early disposal of the case. There comes a time when the convenience of expert witnesses must cede to the need for the tribunal to conclude a substantive hearing".

A tribunal does not have the power to make a direction after it has determined an application. It is therefore not possible for a tribunal to incorporate a direction into the reasons that it gives for a decision not to discharge the patient, unless the case has not been fully determined because the tribunal has reserved to itself the possibility of reconvening by virtue of s.72(3)(b) or s.72(3A)(b).

The tribunal cannot use its power under this provision either to circumvent its obligations under the Act or to direct a party to do something which it is prevented from doing by legislation. Neither can it require a party to undertake a task which it is not otherwise legally obliged to perform under the Act, e.g. to direct the after-care bodies to provide the tribunal with a fully developed after-care plan prior to the hearing: see *W v Doncaster MBC* [2004] EWCA Civ.378; [2004] M.H.L.R. 201 which is noted under s.117.

It is advisable for a without notice direction to include a reference to the right to make an application under r.(6)(5) if there is an objection to the direction (*Dorset Healthcare NHS Foundation Trust v MH* [2009] UKUT 4 (AAC); [2009] M.H.L.R. 102 at para.35).

Paragraph (3)

3–043   The list of powers is not exclusive.

Paragraph (3)(a)

The following provisions of the Act contain time limits which relate to tribunal applica- **3–044** tions or references which cannot be altered by the tribunal under this provision: ss.66(1),(2), 68(2), 69(1),(2),(4), 70, 71(2), and 75(1).

Paragraph (3)(d)

This provision enables tribunals to direct those who are late in producing reports to do so **3–045** forthwith. It also enables the tribunal to direct a party or other person to produce a document that the party or person had no intention of submitting to the tribunal. A failure to comply with such a requirement could result in the tribunal using its power under r.16.

Where a nearest relative makes an application under s.66(1)(g) of the Act and applies for the disclosure of the patient's medical records, the tribunal must apply the balancing exercise identified by Hale L.J. in *R. (on the application of S) v Plymouth City Council* [2002] EWCA Civ 388; [2002] M.H.L.R. 118, at para.48. The interests that need to be considered include the confidentiality of the information sought; the proper administration of justice; the rights of both the patient and the nearest relative to respect for their family life and adequate involvement in decision-making processes about it; the patient's right to respect for his private life; and the protection of the patient's health and welfare and/or the protection of other people. In *TR v Ludlow Street Healthcare Ltd* [2011] UKUT (AAC); [2011] M.H.L.R. 190, UT Judge Jacobs considered *S* and said that "the consent of the patient, and the patient's capacity to give consent, are not decisive and have to be balanced along with other factors" (para.14).

A patient's victim could be invited to make written submissions to the tribunal under this provision.

Paragraph (3)(h)

In *Mental Health Tribunals: Law, Policy and Practice* (2013), Philip Fennel et al state **3–046** that these Rules "do not define postponement or adjournment, but an adjournment is generally understood to be a decision made at the tribunal hearing, whereas a postponement decision is made before the hearing commences" (p.217).

ADJOURN. When exercising this power, the tribunal should bear in mind the overriding objective in r.2 and the requirement in art.5(4) of the ECHR for a speedy decision. The power to adjourn "must be exercised judicially and in accordance with the overriding objective in rule 2. As a procedural power, it cannot be exercised to override the provisions of the substantive legislation. In particular, a tribunal cannot adjourn if it is obliged to give a decision under section 73 of the 1983 Act" (*DC v Nottinghamshire Healthcare NHS Trust* [2012] UKUT 92 (AAC); [2012] M.H.L.R. 238, per UT Judge Jacobs at para.23). In *RC v NHS Islington* [2013] UKUT 0167 (AAC), para.11, UT Judge Bano held that the power to adjourn had to be exercised judicially on the facts of each case and that a fixed rule of policy by a tribunal in relation to the grant of postponements or adjournments would constitute an unlawful fetter of its discretionary powers. In this case, the UT held that the tribunal's policy of only allowing an adjournment to a fixed date was unlawful.

A decision not to adjourn a hearing can be appealed, but entertaining such interlocutory appeals is not to be encouraged because it is usually better to wait until the substantive appeal has been decided to determine whether the interlocutory decision had any material bearing on the lawfulness of the substantive decision arrived at by the First-tier Tribunal on the appeal: see *AF v Nottinghamshire NHS Trust* [2015] UKUT 216 (AAC), para.39, and the cases noted in the General Note to r.46.

In *B v Mental Health Review Tribunal* [2002] EWHC Admin 1533, Scott Baker J. held that:

1. It is not good practice to adjourn a hearing without any indication of when it will be resumed. If for some reason it is impossible to identify a specific date at the moment

of adjournment, it is perfectly in order to say that the adjourned hearing will take place no later than a certain date.

2. What is required is not only a return date when the case could be heard but also some clear directions to ensure that all the expert evidence was available for the adjourned hearing. To provide for expert evidence to be obtained sequentially is a recipe for delay.

3. There is no reason why experts should not meet at an early stage to try and identify, and if possible narrow, any differences of opinion.

4. An adjournment should not be granted without giving the patient's representatives an opportunity to be heard.

5. Brief reasons should be given for a decision to adjourn.

B was applied in *R. (on the application of X) v Mental Health Review Tribunal* [2003] EWHC 1272 (Admin); [2003] M.H.L.R. 299, where Collins J. held that:

1. Although the tribunal will normally rely upon the material that is put before it by the parties, the tribunal has power of its own motion to adjourn for the purposes of obtaining information, even though the parties have decided not to put that information before it.

2. The tribunal should not adjourn a case unless it regards it as necessary for the purpose of doing justice and of reaching the right result in a given case, and in deciding whether it is necessary, it will have to balance the need which it perceives for the extra information against any delay that that will occasion to the determination of the application before it.

A tribunal should give serious consideration to an adjournment if the tribunal considers that the absence of a doctor from a hearing "is likely to affect materially the weight they feel able to give to the opinions expressed in their written reports, and if that is likely to be critical to their ultimate decision", or if it has concerns about the availability of the after-care services that will be available for the patient (*R. (on the application of H) v Ashworth Hospital Authority* [2000] EWCA Civ 923; [2002] M.H.L.R. 314 at paras 68, 85).

In *AM v West London MH NHS Trust & Secretary of State for Justice* [2012] UKUT 382; [2012] M.H.L.R. 399, the patient had not progressed to the point where the issue of after-care that was actually available would arise. UT Judge Jacobs said at para.16:

"The tribunal's decision, including its approach to adjournments for further information, should be informed by its knowledge, expertise and assessment of the possibilities. In that context, I do not accept that it is essential for the tribunal to have specific information about aftercare in every case. It is an individual judgment to be made in the circumstances of the particular case."

On refusing permission to appeal in this case, Richards L.J. said:

"[It] seems to me . . . that it must, as a matter of principle, be open to a Tribunal to conclude in the circumstances of a particular case that information or better information of aftercare is incapable of affecting the decision, and that an adjournment to secure its provision could achieve nothing beyond additional expense and delay and would therefore be inappropriate" ([2013] EWCA Civ 1010; [2014] M.H.L.R. 174, para.9).

The power to adjourn can only be exercised in relation to a function which the Act either permits or requires the tribunal to do. In the case of a restricted patient, the tribunal cannot therefore adjourn for the sole purpose of assisting its determination of whether to exercise its non-statutory discretion to recommend the patient's transfer to another hospital; it can only adjourn for the purpose of assisting it in determining whether the patient should be discharged or not and, if a discharge is being considered, what conditions should be attached to it (*R. (on the application of the Secretary of State for the Home Department v Mental Health Review Tribunal* [2000] M.H.L.R. 209).

As the tribunal has no power to consider the validity of the admission which gave rise to the patient's liability to be detained (*R. v East London and The City Mental Health Trust Ex p. Brandenburg* [2003] UKHL 58; [2004] 1 All E.R. 400), it is submitted that the tribunal has no power to adjourn an application to enable the parties to consider an alleged defect in the admission papers. Any concerns that the patient's legal representative might have about the contents of the statutory documentation should be raised with the hospital prior to the hearing.

It is unlawful to adjourn the proceedings so as to monitor the patient's progress in the hope that a projected course of treatment would eventually permit the tribunal to discharge the patient (*R. v Nottinghamshire Mental Health Review Tribunal Ex p. Secretary of State for the Home Department, The Times,* October 12, 1988 CA). It is submitted that any adjournment that purports to exercise a general supervisory function over the patient's progress would be unlawful.

In *R. v Mental Health Review Tribunal Ex p.Cleveland* (1989) CO/819/88, unreported, Popplewell J. upheld the decision of a tribunal not to adjourn the proceedings to enable the applicant to submit further evidence on the ground that even if the evidence sought had been available it would not have effected the tribunal's decision.

HEARING.   This term embraces the proceedings before the tribunal until it reaches its formal decision (*R. (on the application of X) v Mental Health Review Tribunal*, above at para.20).

Paragraph (3)(k)
The provision enables a case to be transferred to the Mental Health Review Tribunal for **3–047** Wales if a patient is transferred to a Welsh hospital. Rule 23(2) of the Welsh Rules provides the MHRT for Wales with an equivalent power.

Procedure for applying for and giving directions
6.—(1) The Tribunal may give a direction on the application of one or more of **3–048** the parties or on its own initiative.

(2) An application for a direction may be made—

(a) by sending or delivering a written application to the Tribunal; or

(b) orally during the course of a hearing.

(3) An application for a direction must include the reason for making that application.

(4) Unless the Tribunal considers that there is good reason not to do so, the Tribunal must send written notice of any direction to every party and to any other person affected by the direction.

(5) If a party, or any other person given notice of the direction under paragraph (4), wishes to challenge a direction which the Tribunal has given, they may do so by applying for another direction which amends, suspends or sets aside the first direction.

DEFINITIONS
  Tribunal: r.1(3).
  party: r.1(3).
  hearing: r.1(3).

3–049

GENERAL NOTE
3–050   This rule enables the tribunal to make a direction on the application of a party or on its own initiative and provides a mechanism to enable a party to challenge a direction made by the tribunal.

Failure to comply with rules etc.

3–051   **7.**—(1) An irregularity resulting from a failure to comply with any requirement in these Rules, a practice direction or a direction, does not of itself render void the proceedings or any step taken in the proceedings.

(2) If a party has failed to comply with a requirement in these Rules, a practice direction or a direction, the Tribunal may take such action as it considers just, which may include—

(a) waiving the requirement;

(b) requiring the failure to be remedied;

(c) exercising its power under rule 8 (striking out a party's case);

(d) exercising its power under paragraph (3); or

(e) except in mental health cases, restricting a party's participation in the proceedings.

(3) The Tribunal may refer to the Upper Tribunal, and ask the Upper Tribunal to exercise its power under section 25 of the 2007 Act in relation to, any failure by a person to comply with a requirement imposed by the Tribunal—

(a) to attend at any place for the purpose of giving evidence;

(b) otherwise to make themselves available to give evidence;

(c) to swear an oath in connection with the giving of evidence;

(d) to give evidence as a witness;

(e) to produce a document; or

(f) to facilitate the inspection of a document or any other thing (including any premises).

DEFINITIONS
3–052   practice direction: r.1(3).
party: r.1(3).
Tribunal: r.1(3).
mental health case: r.1(3).
document: r.1(3).

GENERAL NOTE
3–053   This rule identifies the options open to the tribunal should a party fail to comply with these Rules, a practice direction or a direction. The tribunal also has the option of using its power under r.16 to summons witnesses and to order the production of documents.

Paragraph (3)
3–054   Section 25 of the 2007 Act vests the Upper Tribunal with the powers of the High Court to require the attendance and examination of witnesses and the production and inspection of documents, together with such other matters as are incidental to its functions.

Striking out a party's case

3–055   **8.**—(1) With the exception of paragraph (3), this rule does not apply to mental health cases.

(2) [*Not reproduced*].

(3) The Tribunal must strike out the whole or a part of the proceedings if the Tribunal—

(a) does not have jurisdiction in relation to the proceedings or that part of them; and

(b) does not exercise its power under rule 5(3)(k)(i) (transfer to another court or tribunal) in relation to the proceedings or that part of them.

(4)–(9) [*Not reproduced*]

DEFINITIONS **3–056**
    mental health case: r.1(3).
    Tribunal: r.1(3)

GENERAL NOTE
    A decision made under this rule must be made by a judge: see the General Note to r.5. **3–057**
Also see the notes on r.35(4).

Substitution and addition of parties
    9.—(1) The Tribunal may give a direction substituting a party if— **3–058**

(a) the wrong person has been named as a party; or

(b) the substitution has become necessary because of a change in circumstances since the start of proceedings.

(2) The Tribunal may give a direction adding a person to the proceedings as a respondent.

(3) If the Tribunal gives a direction under paragraph (1) or (2) it may give such consequential directions as it considers appropriate.

DEFINITIONS **3–059**
    Tribunal: r.1(3).
    party: r.1(3).
    respondent: r.1(3).

GENERAL NOTE
Paragraph (1)
    Where the responsible hospital for a patient made subject to a community treatment **3–060**
order is not the same as the hospital where the patient was formerly detained, this provision
can be used to substitute the managers of the responsible hospital as a party in place of the
managers of the other hospital.

Orders for costs
    10.—(1) Subject to paragraph (2), the Tribunal may make an order in respect of **3–061**
costs only—

(a) under section 29(4) of the 2007 Act (wasted costs) [and costs incurred in applying for such costs]; or

(b) if the Tribunal considers that a party or its representative has acted unreasonably in bringing, defending or conducting the proceedings.

(2) The Tribunal may not make an order under paragraph (1)(b) in mental health cases.

(3) The Tribunal may make an order in respect of costs on an application or on its own initiative.

(4) A person making an application for an order under this rule must—

(a) send or deliver a written application to the Tribunal and to the person against whom it is proposed that the order be made; and

(b) send or deliver a schedule of the costs claimed with the application.

(5) An application for an order under paragraph (1) may be made at any time during the proceedings but may not be made later than 14 days after the date on which the Tribunal [sends—

(a) a decision notice recording the decision which finally disposes of all issues in the proceedings; or

(b) notice under rule 17(6) that a withdrawal which ends the proceedings has taken effect].

(6) The Tribunal may not make an order under paragraph (1) against a person (the "paying person") without first—

(a) giving that person an opportunity to make representations; and

(b) if the paying person is an individual, considering that person's financial means.

(7) The amount of costs to be paid under an order under paragraph (1) may be ascertained by—

(a) summary assessment by the Tribunal;

(b) agreement of a specified sum by the paying person and the person entitled to receive the costs ("the receiving person"); or

(c) assessment of the whole or a specified part of the costs [, including the costs of the assessment,] incurred by the receiving person, if not agreed.

(8) Following an order for assessment under paragraph (7)(c), the paying person or the receiving person may apply to a county court for a detailed assessment of costs in accordance with the Civil Procedure Rules 1998 on the standard basis or, if specified in the order, on the indemnity basis.

[(9) Upon making an order for the assessment of costs, the Tribunal may order an amount to be paid on account before the costs or expenses are assessed.]

AMENDMENTS

The amendments to this rule were made by SI 2013/477 rr.12,13,14 and 15.

DEFINITIONS

3–062   Tribunal: r.1(3).
party: r.1(3).
mental health case: r.1(3).

GENERAL NOTE

3–063   In *RB v Nottinghamshire Healthcare NHS Trust* [2011] UKUT 135 (AAC); [2011] M.H.L.R. 299, UT Judge Jacobs reviewed the powers to make a costs order and concluded that "(i) the Upper Tribunal has power only to award costs where the First-tier Tribunal could do so; (ii) in a mental health case, that tribunal has power only to make a wasted costs order; (iii) a wasted costs order may only be made against a legal or other representative. There is no statutory authority to make an order for costs against the First-tier Tribunal" (para.6).

Paragraph (1)(b)

3–064   This paragraph does not apply to mental health cases (para.(2)).

Representatives

11.—(1) A party may appoint a representative (whether a legal representative **3–065** or not) to represent that party in the proceedings.

[(1A) Where a child or young person is a party to proceedings, that child or young person may appoint a representative under paragraph (1).]

(2) If a party appoints a representative, that party (or the representative if the representative is a legal representative) must send or deliver to the Tribunal and to each other party written notice of the representative's name and address.

(3) Anything permitted or required to be done by a party under these Rules, a practice direction or a direction may be done by the representative of that party, except—

(a) signing a witness statement; or

(b) signing an application notice under rule 20 (the application notice) if the representative is not a legal representative.

(4) A person who receives due notice of the appointment of a representative—

(a) must provide to the representative any document which is required to be provided to the represented party, and need not provide that document to the represented party; and

(b) may assume that the representative is and remains authorised as such until they receive written notification that this is not so from the representative or the represented party.

(5) At a hearing a party may be accompanied by another person whose name and address has not been notified under paragraph (2) but who, subject to paragraph (8) and with the permission of the Tribunal, may act as a representative or otherwise assist in presenting the party's case at the hearing.

(6) Paragraphs (2) to (4) do not apply to a person who accompanies a party under paragraph (5).

(7) In a mental health case, if the patient has not appointed a representative, the Tribunal may appoint a legal representative for the patient where—

(a) the patient has stated that they do not wish to conduct their own case or that they wish to be represented; or

(b) the patient lacks the capacity to appoint a representative but the Tribunal believes that it is in the patient's best interests for the patient to be represented.

(8) In a mental health case a party may not appoint as a representative, or be represented or assisted at a hearing by—

(a) a person liable to be detained or subject to guardianship [. . .], or who is a community patient, under the Mental Health Act 1983; or

(b) a person receiving treatment for mental disorder at the same hospital as the patient.

AMENDMENTS

The amendments to this rule was made by SI 2013/477 r.16 and SI 2014/2128 r.21.

DEFINITIONS   **3–066**
   party: r.1(3).
   legal representative: r.1(3).
   Tribunal: r.1(3).
   practice direction: r.1(3).
   document: r.1(3).
   patient: r.1(3).

GENERAL NOTE

3–067   This rule enables a party, including a child or young person (para.(1A)), to appoint a representative to represent that party in the proceedings. The representative need not be legally qualified (para.(1)). A representative is entitled to question witnesses and to make submissions to the tribunal *(R. (on the application of Mersey Care NHS Trust) v Mental Health Review Tribunal* [2003] EWHC 1182 (Admin); [2003] M.H.L.R. 354). Subject to para.(8), a patient is entitled to have anyone, including an independent mental health advocate, to act as a representative. In *AMA v Greater Manchester West Mental Health NHS Foundation Trust* [2015] UKUT 36 (AAC), Charles J. said at para.50 that unless an order of the Court of Protection appointing a welfare deputy expressly so provides it does not appoint the deputy to act as the patient's representative in proceedings under this Act.

Apart from the exceptions noted in para.(3), the representative can act on behalf of the party. Written notice of the appointment must be given to the tribunal and to other parties (para.(2)). Documents which are provided to the representative need not be provided to the represented party (para.(4)(a)). Provision is made in para.(5) for a party to be represented or otherwise assisted by a person who has not given prior notice to the tribunal. Paragraph (7), which enables the tribunal to appoint a legal representative for the patient, applies where the patient has said that he either does not wish to conduct the case or does not wish to be represented, or the patient lacks the capacity to appoint a representative. Paragraph (8) disqualifies certain persons from acting as a representative. Neither these Rules nor the Act provide for a litigation friend to represent a mentally incapacitated patient before the tribunal.

Although the patient's responsible clinician is usually seen as the appropriate person to represent the responsible authority, there is nothing to prevent another member of staff, such as a nurse or a Mental Health Act administrator, from performing this role: also see the *Code of Practice* at paras 12.31 and 12.32. Being identified as the responsible authority's representative does not require the representative to perform all of the tasks usually associated with the role. A major advantage of being identified as the representative is that it provides the person concerned with the opportunity of question witnesses should the need arise. It is submitted that a representative who is a member of the clinical team which is treating the patient cannot be excluded from the hearing at the request of the patient while the patient gives evidence by virtue of the decision in *R. (on the application of Mersey Care NHS Trust v Mental Health Review Tribunal*, above. If the tribunal did decide to interview the patient in the absence of the representative, the requirements of art.6 of the European Convention on Human Rights and the rules of natural justice would require that any salient facts that were divulged by the patient during the interview be communicated to the representative. A note of caution about the responsible authority being represented by the patient's responsible clinician has been expressed by C. Jones et al in "Mental health tribunals in England and Wales: a representative's guide", Advances in Psychiatric Treatment 2013; 19, 40–47.

The Law Society has published a Practice Note on "Representation before mental health tribunals", January 2015, which is reproduced at Appendix E.

The role of the legal representative

3–068   This was considered by Charles J. in the "Overview" section of his judgment in *YA v Central and North West London NHS Trust* [2015] UKUT 37 (AAC).

A. Patients with the capacity to provide instructions on all relevant matters relating to the conduct of the proceedings

His Lordship said:

"(11) The position of a solicitor acting for a patient with capacity to instruct him to conduct the proceedings whether appointed by the patient or the tribunal is effectively the same as that under any other retainer for the purposes of proceedings, including the consideration of the capacity of the client to give and terminate instructions for that purpose. Generally, in such a case the appointment by the tribunal would have been under Rule 11(7)(a) and so based on the wish or request of the patient and so the patient effectively has the right to terminate the appointment even if formally the tribunal has to end it. Exceptionally, after an appointment under Rule 11(7)(b) it may be found as a result of change or an initial error that the patient has capacity to instruct the solicitor to conduct the proceedings and in such a case the patient would also effectively have a right of termination because the original basis for the appointment would have gone even if formally the tribunal has to end it.

(12) Such a retainer would be to advise on and conduct the tribunal proceedings pursuant to the patient's instructions and subject to the solicitor's professional obligations and duties."

B. Patients who do not have the capacity to provide instructions on all relevant matters relating to the conduct of the proceedings

His Lordship said:

"(15) The main problems are likely to arise when (a) the legal representative's views on what is in the patient's best interests and those of the patient diverge in respect of issues where factors that the patient does not have capacity to give instructions on are relevant, (b) the patient wants the legal representative to advance an unarguable point and/or (c) the patient maintains that he does not want to be represented. In all of those situations it is to be noted that as approved by the Court of Appeal and found by the ECtHR in *RP* [2012] ECHR 1796, [2013] 2 FCR 77:

- withdrawal of representation or the advancement of unreasoned or hopeless argument may well not promote (a) the patient's best interests, or (b) an effective and practical review of a deprivation of liberty, and thus the underlying purposes of Article 5 and its procedural safeguards,

- representation of a patient by another against the patient's wishes as to any representation, or parts of it, is not contrary to Article 6 or in my view Article 5(4), although the departure from the views and wishes of the patient should only be when this is necessary, and

- the failure to provide assistance to a litigant who lacks capacity may itself result in a breach of procedural safeguards.

(16) The points that:

- the grounds for the detention and its continuation should be tested and reviewed as effectively as is practicable, and

- in many cases this can be done effectively by reference to the relevant statutory provisions and existing reports (and evidence from their authors and others)

strongly support the view that the appointment of the legal representative should continue and that the legal representative should act as follows:

(i) so far as is practicable do what a competent legal representative would do for a patient who has capacity to instruct him to represent him in the proceedings and thus for example (a) read the available material and seek such other relevant material as is likely to be or should be available, (b) discuss the proceedings with the patient and in so doing take all practicable steps to explain to the patient the issues, the nature of the proceedings, the possible results and what the legal representative proposes to do,

(ii) seek to ascertain the views, wishes, feelings, beliefs and values of the patient,

(iii) identify where and the extent to which there is disagreement between the patient and the legal representative,

(iv) form a view on whether the patient has capacity to give instructions on all the relevant factors to the decisions that found the disagreement(s),

 (v) if the legal representative considers that the patient has capacity on all those factors and so to instruct the representative on the areas of disagreement the legal representative must follow those instructions or seek a discharge of his appointment,

(vi) if the legal representative considers that the patient does not have or may not have capacity on all those issues, and the disagreements or other problems do not cause him to seek a discharge of his appointment, the legal representative should inform the patient and the tribunal that he intends to act as the patient's appointed representative in the following way:

- he will provide the tribunal with an account of the patient's views, wishes, feelings, beliefs and values (including the fact but not the detail of any wish that the legal representative should act in a different way to the way in which he proposes to act, or should be discharged),

- he will invite the tribunal to hear evidence from the patient and/or to allow the patient to address the tribunal (issues on competence to give evidence are in my view unlikely to arise but if they did they should be addressed before the tribunal),

- he will draw the tribunal's attention to such matters and advance such arguments as he properly can in support of the patient's expressed views, wishes, feelings, beliefs and values, and

- he will not advance any other arguments.

(17) In such circumstances, the tribunal should not in my view delve into the areas of disagreement or why the legal representative is of the view he cannot properly draw matters to the attention of the tribunal or advance argument. These may be apparent from the account of the patient's wishes or what they say directly to the tribunal but in my view the decisions on what the legal representative can and cannot argue are matters for the legal representative and not the tribunal who are charged with deciding whether the legal representative it has appointed should continue to act and not with how he should do so.

(18) Where there is no conflict between the wishes of the patient and his views the legal representative should still consider whether or not the patient has capacity to instruct him on all relevant factors and act on the patient's instructions if he concludes that the patient has that capacity. But if the legal representative concludes that the patient does not or may not have such capacity generally he should advance all arguable points to test the bases for the detention in hospital. In those circumstances it may or may not be appropriate to invite the tribunal to hear directly from the patient.

(19) Having determined the capacity test set by Rule 11(7)(b) the most important guiding principles to be applied under the best interests test (and so in deciding whether to exercise the power) are:

- the underlying purpose and importance of the review and so the need to fairly and thoroughly assess the reasons for the detention,

- the vulnerability of the person who is its subject and what is at stake for that person (i.e. a continuation of a detention for an identified purpose),

- the need for flexibility and appropriate speed,

- whether, without representation (but with all other available assistance and the prospect of further reviews), the patient will practically and effectively be able to conduct their case, and if not whether nonetheless

- the tribunal is likely to be properly and sufficiently informed of the competing factors relating to the case before it and so be able to carry out an effective review. (As to this the tribunal should when deciding the case review this prediction).

(20) To those I add (a) the nature and degree of the objections and of the distress caused to a patient if his or her wishes are not followed, (b) the likely impact of that distress on his or her well being generally and (c) the prospects that if a legal representative is appointed or not discharged that legal representative will seek a discharge of the appointment."

The role of the legal representative is also considered in the Law Society's Practice Note "Representation before mental health tribunals", see above, and by UT Judge Rowland in *AA v Cheshire and Wirral Partnership NHS Foundation Trust* [2009] UKUT 195 (AAC); [2009] M.H.L.R. 308. In *YA,* Charles J. said at para.71:

"The Law Society submits (as it asserts in its Practice Note) that paragraph 20 of the decision in *AA* is incorrect in suggesting that even when the patient has full capacity and despite their instructions a solicitor may be under a duty to draw the tribunal's attention to particular matters that appear to be in the patient's best interests. I agree that that is incorrect and is inconsistent with the judge's correct comment at paragraph 15 that:

'A patient may be capable of giving valid instructions and, where valid instructions are given, a solicitor must act in accordance with them.'"

Human Rights Act 1998
See the notes on art.5(4) of the ECHR in Part 5. **3–069**

An IMHA's relationship with the patient's legal representative
Paragraphs 5.1.1 to 5.1.3 of the guidance note on the "Role of the Independent Mental **3–070** Health Advocate (IMHA) in First-tier Tribunal (Mental Health) hearings", noted in the General Note to these Rules, state:

"It is to be hoped that there will have been a discussion before the start of the hearing as to the role to be played by the IMHA. It would be appropriate for the tribunal judge to make a few opening remarks emphasising that the legal representative has the formal representational role, that the IMHA is there to assist the patient, the legal representative and the tribunal to understand each other–and that, if they need any time to consult in private, they should just ask.

If an IMHA infringes the proper role of the legal representative (for example starts to give unprompted evidence or asks questions or addresses the tribunal), the judge should politely ask them to stop, and clarify with the IMHA what it is they want to do, and why. The judge should then ask the legal representative whether they are content for this to happen. If the IMHA is seeking to open up something that the legal representative has not pursued, it may be appropriate for the IMHA and the legal representative to have a private discussion so that the IMHA does not unwittingly introduce an argument that may weaken the patient's case, or pursue irrelevant issues.

It should be recognised, of course, that tribunals are not purely adversarial and that the tribunal's inquisitorial role might be engaged by the introduction by the IMHA of fresh issues. However, it is also important to recognise that the overall conduct of the patient's case is in the hands of the legal representative, not the IMHA, and that the tribunal needs to be sensitive to the legal representative's wishes. For example, it is likely to be inappropriate for an IMHA to send a written statement from a patient to the tribunal in advance of the hearing, without prior discussion with the legal representative."

Paragraph (3)

3–071 This power includes the power to give a notice of withdrawal under r.17 (*AMA*, above, para.48).

Paragraph (7)

3–072 This provision enables the tribunal to appoint a legal representative for the patient where the patient has not appointed a representative (who need not be a legal representative). The role of the legal representative is considered above. For "sensible pragmatic reasons the appointment . . . is regularly made by a member of the tribunal staff pursuant to Rule 4" (*AMA v Greater Manchester West Mental Health NHS Foundation Trust* above, para.28).

It is submitted that the tribunal cannot avoid using its power under this provision by utilising its case management powers to direct that the responsible authority appoints a legal representative for the patient on the ground that a direction cannot be used to require a party to undertake a task which it is not otherwise legally obliged to perform under the Act. In any event, such a direction would lead to the responsible authority being faced with a clear conflict of interest.

The Official Solicitor will not agree to act as the patient's legal representative: see *AA* at para.11.

Paragraph (b)

3–073 In *YA v Central and North West London NHS Trust* [2015] UKUT 37 (AAC), Charles J. identified the factors that the tribunal should take into account in determining whether to exercise the power under this paragraph to appoint or to discharge the appointment of a legal representative when the patient is objecting to the appointment. The power only arises if the patient lacks capacity to make the appointment. His Lordship said:

"118. Having determined that the patient lacks capacity to appoint a representative the best interests test has to be applied.

119. In my view, the most important guiding principles on the application of that test are set out in paragraph 45 above, namely:

(i) the underlying purpose and importance of the review and so the need to fairly and thoroughly assess the reasons for the detention,

(ii) the vulnerability of the person who is its subject and what is at stake for that person (i.e. a continuation of a detention for an identified purpose),

(iii) the need for flexibility and appropriate speed,

(iv) whether, without representation (but with all other available assistance and the prospect of further reviews), the patient will practically and effectively be able to conduct their case, and if not whether nonetheless

(v) the tribunal is likely to be properly and sufficiently informed of the competing factors relating to the case before it and so be able to carry out an effective review. (As to this the tribunal should when deciding the case review this prediction).

120. To those I add (a) the nature and degree of the objections and of the distress caused to a patient if his or her wishes are not followed, (b) the likely impact of that distress on his or her well being generally and (c) the prospects that if a legal representative is appointed or not discharged that legal representative will seek a discharge of the appointment."

BEST INTERESTS. In *YA*, above, Charles J. said at para.10 of his "Overview":

"[I]t is clear from the best interests test in Rule 11(7)(b) and the general requirement to act in the best interests of a person who lacks relevant capacity that the legal representative is not only appointed in the patient's best interests but must act in them (having regard to the relevant issues of fact and law that are relevant in the proceedings)."

LACKS THE CAPACITY. The principles and approach set out in the Mental Capacity Act 2005 (see in particular ss.1 to 3) and its associated statutory guidance in the Code of Practice: Mental Capacity Act 2005 (see in particular Ch.4) should be applied (*YA*, above, para.30). In *YA*, Charles J. said at para.58 that the "factors that the patient will have to be able to sufficiently understand, retain, use and weigh will be likely to include the following:

(i) the detention, and so the reasons for it, can be challenged in proceedings before the tribunal who, on that challenge, will consider whether the detention in justified by the provisions of the MHA,

(ii) in doing that, the tribunal will investigate and invite and consider questions and argument on the issues, the medical and other evidence and the legal issues,

(iii) the tribunal can discharge the section and so bring the detention to an end,

(iv) representation would be free,

(v) discussion can take place with the patient and the representative before and so without the pressure of a hearing,

(vi) having regard to that discussion a representative would be able to question witnesses and argue the case on the facts and the law, and thereby assist in ensuring that the tribunal took all relevant factual and legal issues into account,

(vii) he or she may not be able to do this so well because of their personal involvement and the nature and complication of some of the issues (e.g. when they are finely balanced or depend on the likelihood of the patient's compliance with assessment or treatment or relate to what is the least restrictive available way of best achieving the proposed assessment or treatment),

(viii) having regard to the issues of fact and law his or her ability to conduct the proceedings without help, and so

(ix) the impact of these factors on the choice to be made".

Calculating time
12.—(1) An act required by these Rules, a practice direction or a direction to be **3–074** done on or by a particular day must be done by 5pm on that day.

(2) If the time specified by these Rules, a practice direction or a direction for doing any act ends on a day other than a working day, the act is done in time if it is done on the next working day.

(3)–(4) [*These paragraphs do not apply to mental health cases*]

DEFINITIONS **3–075**
    practice direction: r.1(3).
    working day: r.1(3).
    Tribunal: r.1(3).

Sending and delivery of documents
13.—(1) Any document to be provided to the Tribunal under these Rules, a **3–076** practice direction or a direction must be—

(a) sent by pre-paid post or delivered by hand to the address specified for the proceedings;

(b) sent by fax to the number specified for the proceedings; or

(c) sent or delivered by such other method as the Tribunal may permit or direct.

[(1A) If the Tribunal permits or directs documents to be provided to it by email, the requirement for a signature on applications or references under rules 20(2), 22(4)(a) or 32(1)(b) may be satisfied by a typed instead of a handwritten signature.]

(2) Subject to paragraph (3), if a party provides a fax number, email address or other details for the electronic transmission of documents to them, that party must accept delivery of documents by that method.

(3) If a party informs the Tribunal and all other parties that a particular form of communication, other than pre-paid post or delivery by hand, should not be used to provide documents to that party, that form of communication must not be so used.

(4) If the Tribunal or a party sends a document to a party or the Tribunal by email or any other electronic means of communication, the recipient may request that the sender provide a hard copy of the document to the recipient. The recipient must make such a request as soon as reasonably practicable after receiving the document electronically.

(5) The Tribunal and each party may assume that the address provided by a party or its representative is and remains the address to which documents should be sent or delivered until receiving written notification to the contrary.

AMENDMENT
Paragraph (1A) was inserted by SI 2011/651, reg.4(3).

DEFINITIONS
3–077   document: r.1(3).
Tribunal: r.1(3).
practice direction: r.1(3).
party: r.1(4).

Use of documents and information
3–078   **14.**—(1) The Tribunal may make an order prohibiting the disclosure or publication of—

(a) specified documents or information relating to the proceedings; or

(b) any matter likely to lead members of the public to identify any person whom the Tribunal considers should not be identified.

(2) The Tribunal may give a direction prohibiting the disclosure of a document or information to a person if—

(a) the Tribunal is satisfied that such disclosure would be likely to cause that person or some other person serious harm; and

(b) the Tribunal is satisfied, having regard to the interests of justice, that it is proportionate to give such a direction.

(3) If a party ("the first party") considers that the Tribunal should give a direction under paragraph (2) prohibiting the disclosure of a document or information to another party ("the second party"), the first party must—

(a) exclude the relevant document or information from any documents that will be provided to the second party; and

(b) provide to the Tribunal the excluded document or information, and the reason for its exclusion, so that the Tribunal may decide whether the document or information should be disclosed to the second party or should be the subject of a direction under paragraph (2).

(4) The Tribunal must conduct proceedings as appropriate in order to give effect to a direction given under paragraph (2).

(5) If the Tribunal gives a direction under paragraph (2) which prevents disclosure to a party who has appointed a representative, the Tribunal may give a direction that the documents or information be disclosed to that representative if the Tribunal is satisfied that—

(a) disclosure to the representative would be in the interests of the party; and

(b) the representative will act in accordance with paragraph (6).

(6) Documents or information disclosed to a representative in accordance with a direction under paragraph (5) must not be disclosed either directly or indirectly to any other person without the Tribunal's consent.

(7) Unless the Tribunal gives a direction to the contrary, information about mental health cases and the names of any persons concerned in such cases must not be made public.

DEFINITIONS

Tribunal: r.1(3).　　　　　　　　　　　　　　　　　　　　　　　　　　　**3–079**

document: r.1(3).

party: r.1(3).

mental health case: r.1(3).

GENERAL NOTE

This rule enables the tribunal to make an order prohibiting the disclosure or publication **3–080** of material relating to the proceedings to a person (para.(1)). Such an order can only be made if the tribunal is satisfied that the disclosure would be likely to cause serious harm to that person or another, and that it is proportionate, having regard to the interests of justice, to make such an order (para.(2)). Reasons for requesting the tribunal to exclude a document or information must be provided (para.(3)). An excluded document or information can be disclosed to the patient's representative (not necessarily a legal representative) as long as the representative does not disclose it further without the tribunal's consent (paras (5), (6)). Unless the tribunal directs otherwise, information about mental health cases must not be made public (para.(7)).

Although the tribunal is not explicitly required to give reasons for its decision on non-disclosure, a brief statement of reasons which avoids identifying the nature of the material under consideration should be given because the time limit for appealing the decision on a point of law is determined by the date when the person was sent "written reasons for the decision" (r.46(2)(a)).

The tribunal can decide to exclude the patient while the issue of non-disclosure is discussed (r.38(4)(b) and can direct that a person be excluded from the hearing in order to give effect to a direction made under para.(2) (r.38(4)(c)).

In *Dorset Healthcare NHS Foundation Trust v MH* [2009] UKUT 4 (AAC); [2009] M.H.L.R. 102 at paras 23–34, the Upper Tribunal, after stating that the "starting point is that full disclosure of all relevant material should generally be given" (para.20), provided the following obiter guidance to assist parties who seek the disclosure of the patient's medical records (note that the published transcript has two paragraphs numbered 29):

"23. However, rule 14 does not provide the only procedure by which disclosure of documents can be withheld. The medical records of many patients contain documents from third parties which, irrespective of any harm to the patient that may ensure from their disclosure, may be sensitive. For example, a relative of a patient may provide details of his/her own medical condition which may be relevant to that person's ability to look after the patient if the patient were returned home: or simply set out reasons why, if the patient were returned home, relatives or potential carers would be unable to cope. Sometimes such documents are submitted to the responsible authority holding the medical records with an express requirement that they be kept confidential from the patient (and sometimes also from even the patient's solicitors). In any event, that authority often considers, rightly, that it owes a duty of confidence to the relevant third-parties and is unwilling to disclose documents to the patient (and occasionally even to the patient's solicitors) without an order. If the documents are relevant to the issues in an application made by the patient (as they usually will be), leaving aside the various common law and statutory obligations that fall on the responsible authority holding the medical records, there is an obvious potential tension between the Article 6 rights of the patient and the Article 8 rights of the third parties, and it is important that all of these rights are properly considered and maintained (see *R (B) v Crown Court at Stafford* [2007] 1 WLR 1524, especially at [23]). What is the correct approach in these circumstances?

24. As we have already observed, in dealing with such a situation the parties should first do all they can to agree the approach to be adopted and avoid applying to the tribunal unless it is essential. Disclosure does not and should not present a problem in the vast majority of cases.

25. Given the general rule in favour of full disclosure the burden will be on the responsible authority to demonstrate that it is appropriate to withhold disclosure of any particular documents.

26. Where there are third-party documents which the responsible authority considers may be confidential to the third-party, then, where this is practical, the authority may seek the relevant third parties' consent to disclosure. However, this may not be practical because of the delay that would be involved in identifying and locating the third parties.

27. In most cases where there are confidential third-party documents, it should be possible for the responsible authority to disclose all such documents to the patient's solicitors subject to an undertaking from the solicitors not to disclose to the patient third-party documents specifically identified by the authority. The solicitors can then take a view as to whether the third-party rights override the rights of the patient, or vice versa. Where they consider the documents ought to be disclosed to the patient, then they must make an application to the tribunal for disclosure.

28. In other circumstances, the responsible authority may take the view that the documents are so sensitive that they should not be disclosed even to the solicitors or they are unable to rely on an undertaking that the representative will not disclose to the patient documents received. However, an undertaking from a solicitor (who owes a duty to the tribunal) will only not be acceptable in quite exceptional circumstances.

29. Where a responsible authority seeks to avoid disclosure of documents even to the patient's representative, then it should submit a skeleton argument setting out the reasons for resisting disclosure and should identify the documents in question. The skeleton argument, but not the documents, should be served on the patient's solicitors who will be given an opportunity to respond in writing.

29. In circumstances in which the responsible authority has served all of the documents on the solicitors subject to an undertaking, and the solicitor then wishes to disclose the documents (or some of them) to the patient, the procedure will be reversed; and the patient's solicitor should submit a skeleton argument setting out why it is considered appropriate to disclose the documents to the patient and the authority will be given the opportunity to respond in writing.

30. Where the exchange of skeleton arguments does not resolve the issue, then an application to the tribunal will be necessary. Where a patient's solicitor is seeking permission to disclose documents to a patient, then the application should be made by that solicitor: if a responsible authority is seeking to deny disclosure to even the patient's solicitor then the application should be made by the authority.

31. In most cases, any application should be capable of being determined by the tribunal on the day of the substantive hearing. However, there may be circumstances where the issue is more complicated, when it would be appropriate for the matter to be considered and determined by a single judge in advance of the substantive hearing. Depending on the circumstances and complexity this could be either on written submissions or by holding an oral hearing.

32. We can also envisage circumstances in which the tribunal will need to obtain information as to the third-party's views on the issue of disclosure. Where this occurs, the tribunal should notify the responsible authority which should then obtain this information and submit it to the tribunal, thus avoiding where possible any direct involvement by the third-party in the tribunal's procedures.

33. All of these steps can be taken under the general case management powers of the tribunal, particularly under rule 5(3)(d). The steps are all consistent with the specific provisions set out in rule 14, to which we have already made reference: and the parties should adopt a similar procedure in circumstances in which rule 14 might apply. Again in most instances those applications should be dealt with on the day of the substantive hearing and only exceptionally should it be necessary for a single judge to determine the issue on written submissions or by a separate hearing prior to the substantive hearing.

34. This guidance is intended to assist all parties who seek disclosure of medical records, and face requests for disclosure of medical records; and hopefully there will be few cases where the procedures suggested above will not suffice. However, this is only guidance and is not prescriptive for all cases. In cases where there are idiosyncratic features or complexities, it is always open to either party to make an application to the tribunal for specific directions or for a tribunal of its own motion to give appropriate directions."

The Data Protection Act 1998 provides patients with a right of access to their medical records. The patient's representative should obtain the written authority of the patient to apply for such access. In *NR's Application* [2015] NIQB 35, the following declaration was made by the High Court of Northern Ireland:

"The legal advisors of patients detained under the Mental Health (Northern Ireland) Order 1986 have a right, pursuant to Articles 5 and 6 of the European Convention on Human Rights to view their client's medical notes and records, in a practice and manner which safeguards the confidential and sensitive information therein, in advance of a Mental Health Review Tribunal Hearing as soon as reasonably practicable after reasonable notice has been given to the detaining trust accompanied by a properly executed written form of authority signed and dated by the detained patient."

The following guidance is provided by the Courts and Tribunal Service in *Reports for Mental Health Tribunals* (2012) at pp.5, 6:

"If the Responsible Authority, or the source or author of the information, statement, report or document considers that the tribunal should give a direction prohibiting the disclosure of the material to the patient, they must:

a. separate and exclude the relevant information, statement, report or document from any other material submitted;

b. separately provide to the tribunal copies of the excluded information, statement, report or document, ensuring that the excluded material is clearly marked:

c. provide the tribunal with full written reasons for the proposed exclusion, so that the tribunal may decide for itself whether the grounds for exclusion have been made out and whether the information, statement, report or document should be disclosed to the patient, or whether it should be excluded."

Human Rights Act 1998

3–081   A decision by the tribunal not to disclose a document or information to the patient under para.(1) would constitute an interference with the patient's right to respect for his private and family life under art.8(1) of the European Convention on Human Rights (ECHR). Article 8(2) provides a justification for such an interference on the ground of either protecting the patient's "health or morals" or the prevention of "disorder or crime". An interference on the general ground of protecting the "welfare of the patient" is not allowed for.

In *Winterwerp v Netherlands* (App.No.6301/73), the European Commission of Human Rights said that the patient's lawyer had the right to examine the patient's file, but that it was not necessary for the patient to be informed of all the evidence or that he be allowed access to all of the information in his medical file. This approach was confirmed by the European Court of Human Rights in *Nikolova v Bulgaria* (2001) E.H.R.R. 3 at para.58, where it was said that "[e]quality of arms is not ensured if counsel is denied access to those documents in the investigation file which are essential in order effectively to challenge the lawfulness of his client's detention".

In *Roberts v Nottinghamshire Healthcare NHS Trust* [2008] EWHC 1934 (QB); [2008] M.H.L.R. 294, at para.25, Cranston J. said that although a party has a right to a fair trial under art.6 "that does not mean that he or she has an absolute or unqualified right to see every document".

Although there has been no reported case which has considered the compatibility of this rule with art.5(4) of the ECHR, in *McGrady's application for Judicial Review* [2003] NIQB 15, Kerr J. considered a similar provision in r.12(2) of the Mental Health Review Tribunal Rules (Northern Ireland) 1986 (SI 1986/193). His Lordship said at paras 20 to 22:

"Where . . . disclosure may cause harm to the applicant or to the informant, the tribunal must balance the right of the applicant under Art.5(4) with the interests that may be adversely affected if the material is disclosed. In this context the tribunal will want to consider carefully whether the convention rights of the informant would be infringed if the material that that person has provided in confidence is revealed to the applicant.

It appears to me that the tribunal will also take into account that the applicant's legal representatives have seen the material in question. While they may not disclose that material to the applicant, they may nevertheless take his instructions on the themes with which the material is concerned. There is no reason that the applicant should not be at liberty to present material to the tribunal on the matters raised in the addendum even if he remains unaware of its contents.

If the tribunal concludes that the addendum's contents should not be disclosed to the applicant it should approach the assessment with care. It must keep in mind that details of the information have not been revealed to the applicant. Its duty is to ensure that the proceedings are conducted fairly. This duty arises under pre-incorporation law as well as under the convention. But the applicant is not denied fairness simply because the material is withheld from him. As I have said, a balance must be struck between, on the one hand, the requirement that an applicant applying for discharge should generally have the opportunity to see and comment on all material adverse to him and, on the other, that the safety of the informant should not be imperilled. Unfairness would arise if the tribunal failed to acknowledge that the applicant has not been able to see and answer specifically the details of the allegations made against him. Provided they are conscious of this and cater for it in their approach to the assessment of the addendum, the proceedings will not be unfair to the applicant".

Disclosure of the Victim's Evidence to the Patient in cases covered by the Domestic Violence, Crime and Victims Act 2004
See the note to r.15 under this heading.   **3–082**

Paragraph (2)
The criterion of "serious harm" is not the exclusive rationale for non-disclosure, as   **3–083**
issues of third party confidentiality may arise: see *Dorset Healthcare NHS Foundation Trust v MH*, above, and Kris Gledhill, "The First Flight of the Fledgling: the Upper Tribunal's Substantive Debut", J.M.H.L., Spring 2009, at 89–91.
  When considering the "interests of justice" criterion in para.(b), the test to be applied is: does the non-disclosure allow the patient to make an effective challenge to the decision to detain him?: see *RM v St Andrew's Healthcare* [2010] UKUT 119 (AAC); [2010] M.H.L.R. 176 at para.23. UT Judge Jacobs said at para.31:

> "The Convention right under Article 6 guarantees a fair hearing. [*Secretary of State for the Home Department v AF (No.3)* [2009] UKHL 28; [2009] 3 All E.R. 643] shows how highly a fair hearing is rated in the balance with non-disclosure. . . . The overriding objective in r.2 requires that the rules of procedure be applied so that cases are dealt with fairly and justly. This includes ensuring full participation, so far as practicable. Rule 14(2) requires the tribunal to have regard to the interests of justice. Justice and fairness generally require openness. Sometimes, they are not compatible and a compromise is possible. It may, for example, be possible and necessary to conduct proceedings while concealing that the true prognosis is worse than the patient realises. In this case, I have set out the full implications of the tribunal's order. They involve more than a compromise between justice and openness. They involve the sacrifice of the patient's right to challenge his detention effectively."

In *RM*, which was a case where "a patient's best interests medically [clashed] with his best interests legally" (per Judge Jacobs at para.1), the non-disclosure order made by the First-tier tribunal referred to documents relating to the fact that the patient was being covertly medicated. Prior to being covertly medicated, the patient had been refusing medication and, as a consequence, had become very ill to the point where he was at risk of sudden, unexpected death (para.3). The question that had to be answered by the Upper Tribunal was: can the patient effectively challenge his detention without knowing that he was being covertly medicated? (para.26). The non-disclosure order was set aside on the ground that it would "exclude [the patient] completely from knowing the real process that was being followed and allow him to participate only in a pretence of a process" and "would severely hamper his legal team in participating effectively in that process" (para.32). The finding in this case is troubling in that a consequence of enabling the patient to fully participate in the tribunal hearing could have been his death.
  Judge Jacobs said that a tribunal should draft non-disclosure orders in terms of information rather that documents. Although the terms of such an order would depend upon the facts of the individual case, the following was offered, at para.36, as "a useful starting point":

> "'The Tribunal prohibits disclosure to the patient of:
>
>   (a) information relating to . . .;
>   (b) any document containing or referring to that information, in particular—
>   (i) the reports of . . .;
>   (ii) any other report prepared in connection with these proceedings; and
>   (iii) this order.'

Paragraph (a) deals with the key issue of the information that must not be disclosed. It needs to be precise, clear and exhaustive. Paragraph (b) deals with the means by which disclosure might be made, directly or indirectly. It is supportive of paragraph (a) and need not be exhaustive.

The tribunal also needs to consider the patient's access to medical records. The order did not prohibit disclosure of the patient's medical records that, no doubt, contain details of his medication. A patient is entitled to access to medical records under section 7 of the Data Protection Act 1998. This is subject to the Data Protection (Subject Access Modification) (Health) Order 2000 (SI No 413). Article 5(1) contains an exemption from section 7 'to the extent to which the application of that section would be likely to cause serious harm to the physical or mental health or condition of the data subject or any other person.' That condition is effectively the same as rule 14(2)(a). The decision whether the exemption applies is made by the data controller."

In *AF (No.3)* above, para.105, Baroness Hale said obiter:

"These days, a . . . Tribunal would be unlikely to uphold a non-disclosure claim on the general ground that disclosure would be damaging to the doctor patient relationship. They would want to know precisely what it was in this doctor's evidence that might cause serious harm to this patient or to some other person and to weigh that damage against the interests of fairness. It will be an individualised balancing act carried out after discussion with the patient's own advocate and in the light of the opinions of the patient's own independent medical adviser."

DOCUMENT. The natural limit of this provision is on documents that are relevant to the proceedings (*RM v St Andrew's Healthcare*, above, para.15).

WOULD BE LIKLELY TO CAUSE . . . SERIOUS HARM. A similar phrase is found in the Data Protection (Subject Access Modification) (Health) Order 2000 (SI 2000/413) para.5. In *Roberts v Nottinghamshire Healthcare NHS Trust* [2008] EWHC 1934 (QB); [2008] M.H.L.R. 294 at para.9, Cranston J. interpreted the phrase contained in the 2000 Order as follows:

"The question is whether there may very well be a risk of harm to health even if the risk falls short of being more probable that not. Harm to health could arise in various ways. In the context of mental health, it could be self harm or harm to others. The issue demands a factual enquiry: taking all matters into account such as the personality of the applicant, his past history, the care regime to which he is subject and so on, might there very well be a risk of harm to health on release of the data?"

His Lordship applied the judgment of Munby J. in *R (on the application of Lord) v Secretary of State for the Home Department* [2004] Prison Law Reports 65, where it was said that the term "likely . . . connotes a degree of probability where there would be a significant and weighty chance of prejudice to the identified public interest. The degree of risk must be such that there 'may very well' be prejudice to those interests, even if the risk falls short of being more probable than not".

Paragraph (5)

3–084   Paragraphs 5.1.5 of the guidance note on the "Role of the Independent Mental Health Advocate (IMHA) in First-tier Tribunal (Mental Health) hearings" (see the General Note to these Rules) states that if an IMHA is appointed as the patient's representative, this "is likely to create considerable difficulty since, if the IMHA receives a document which is not to be disclosed to the patient, they will have had to undertake under Rule 14(5) not to disclose it or its contents to the patient. The IMHA might well consider that this undertaking conflicts with their general duty to the patient and, if so, the tribunal will be unable to disclose information to the IMHA because they will not be satisfied that the representative will act in accordance with Rule 14(6). This situation should be avoided to protect the patient's rights to effective legal representation".

Paragraph (7)
This paragraph should be considered in the context of the requirement under r.38(1) that **3–085** all hearings must be held in private unless the tribunal considers that it is in the necessary in the interests of justice for the hearing to be held in private.

Evidence and submissions
15.—(1) Without restriction on the general powers in rule 5(1) and (2) (case **3–086** management powers), the Tribunal may give directions as to—
(a) issues on which it requires evidence or submissions;
(b) the nature of the evidence or submissions it requires;
(c) whether the parties are permitted or required to provide expert evidence, and if so whether the parties must jointly appoint a single expert to provide such evidence;
(d) any limit on the number of witnesses whose evidence a party may put forward, whether in relation to a particular issue or generally;
(e) the manner in which any evidence or submissions are to be provided, which may include a direction for them to be given—
   (i) orally at a hearing; or
   (ii) by written submissions or witness statement; and
(f) the time at which any evidence or submissions are to be provided.
(2) The Tribunal may—
(a) admit evidence whether or not—
   (i) the evidence would be admissible in a civil trial in England and Wales; or
   (ii) the evidence was available to a previous decision maker; or
(b) exclude evidence that would otherwise be admissible where—
   (i) the evidence was not provided within the time allowed by a direction or a practice direction;
   (ii) the evidence was otherwise provided in a manner that did not comply with a direction or a practice direction; or
   (iii) it would otherwise be unfair to admit the evidence.
(3) The Tribunal may consent to a witness giving, or require any witness to give, evidence on oath, and may administer an oath for that purpose.
(4)–(5) [*These paragraphs do not apply to mental health cases*]

DEFINITIONS
    Tribunal: r.1(3).   **3–087**
    party: r.1(3).
    practice direction: r.1(3).

GENERAL NOTE
The evidence of the patient's responsible clinician (RC) is likely to be of "particular cen- **3–088** trality" in any hearing before the tribunal (*R. (on the application of Nottingham Healthcare NHS Trust) v Mental Health Review Tribunal* [2008] EWHC 2445 (Admin); [2008] M.H.L.R. 326 para.19). However, in *AC v Partnerships in Care Ltd and Secretary of State for Justice* [2012] UKUT 450 (AAC), UT Judge Jacobs said at para.11:

"[I]t does not always follow that greater knowledge means greater insight. The tribunal should have explained what it was in the RC's experience that made her view preferable."

The significance of the RC's evidence, and the way in which a tribunal should approach it, was touched upon in a different context by Dyson L.J in *R. (on the application of K) v West London Mental Health NHS Trust* [2006] EWCA Civ 118; [2006] M.H.L.R. 89 at para.70:

"The weight to be given to opinion of [RCs] must be a matter for the decision-maker having regard to all relevant circumstances. It is not appropriate to attempt an exhaustive definition of what these might be. But they will include how long the [RC] has been in charge of the treatment of the patient, the strength of conviction with which the [RC's] clinical judgment has been expressed, the weight of other clinical opinion and the reasons given by other medical practitioners for their disagreement with the opinion expressed by the [RC]."

The medical evidence that is given on behalf of the responsible authority need not come from the patient's RC. However, the medical evidence must be up to date (*R. v Mental Health Review Tribunal, London and North East Ex p. Manns* [1999] M.H.L.R. 101 at para.28). If the tribunal concludes that it should hear evidence from the RC and the RC is not available, it could consider using its power to adjourn the hearing under r.5(3)(h).

Oral evidence given by the authors of clinical reports can only address the position as it is at the time of the hearing (*BB v South London & Maudsley NHS Trust* [2009] UKUT 157 (AAC); [2009] M.H.L.R. 302, para.10).

Evidence given by an Independent Mental Health Advocate

3–089   Paragraphs 6.1 and 6.2 of the guidance note on the "Role of the Independent Mental Health Advocate (IMHA) in First-tier Tribunal (Mental Health) hearings" (see the General Note to these Rules) state:

"It will not usually be appropriate for the IMHA to give evidence to the tribunal, as this is not their general role. However, there are occasions when the IMHA knows all about an issue that has arisen in the past in respect of the patient and will ask (or just begin) to give evidence to the tribunal.

It is suggested that, if these circumstances arise without warning, the judge should stop the IMHA, and remind him or her that neither of the parties (patient or Responsible Authority) may wish them to give evidence, and if the panel is to seek evidence on its own initiative, it must have cogent reasons for doing so. Moreover, the giving of evidence may well result in the IMHA being cross-examined by the patient's legal representative and by any person representing the Responsible Authority, and being questioned by the panel. Should the IMHA still wish to give evidence, or remain undecided, the legal representative may then wish to have a private consultation with the IMHA in order to ensure that the representative understands the nature of any evidence the IMHA wishes to give, and to enable the representative to decide how they wish to proceed–for example, whether they wish to call the IMHA to give evidence, or whether there may be a better way to place the relevant information before the panel. The tribunal may regulate its own procedure [Rule 5(1)] and may give directions as to the admission and exclusion of evidence [Rule 15]."

Inference to be drawn from the fact that an independent psychiatrist who had visited a patient did not submit a report to the tribunal

3–090   In *MM v Nottinghamshire Healthcare NHS Trust* [2013] UKUT 107 (AAC), UT Judge Jacobs said at para.10:

"The First-tier Tribunal always has medical evidence from the clinical team. The medical member of the panel will have interviewed the patient. And the patient may have produced medical evidence in support of the application. I cannot imagine any realistic circumstances in which a tribunal, having such evidence, could properly rely on the failure by a patient to produce a report as a basis for drawing inferences that would affect the outcome. The tribunal's duty, and the only proper course, would be to decide on the evidence available rather than speculate on possible explanations of why the report was not produced."

Should a panel recuse themselves on account of having adjudicated on the admissibility of evidence at a preliminary hearing?
In *MM*, above, Judge Jacobs said at paras 12 to 14: **3–091**

"I begin with the proposition that it is a judicial skill that judges should be able to disregard things that they have heard. . . .

This ability is recognised by the rules of procedure that apply in the First-tier Tribunal. Rule 15 of the Tribunal Procedure (First-tier Tribunal) (Health, Education and Social Care) Chamber 2008 allows tribunals to rule on the admissibility of evidence and on issues that may be presented. That will almost certainly involve the panel knowing at least something of that evidence or those issues. And the circumstances in which the panel has to make its ruling means that it may well have to be made by the same panel that hears the substantive case.

My reasoning so far relates only to the judge. The other panel members come from different professional backgrounds and may be less experienced in putting matters out of their minds. Even if that is so, there is always a judge present and it is one of the duties of that judge to ensure that the other members of the panel disregard evidence that is not properly before them."

Disclosure of the Victim's Evidence to the Patient in cases covered by the Domestic Violence, Crime and Victims Act 2004
Paragraphs 24 and 25 of "Practice guidance on proceedings concerning handling repre- **3–092** sentations from victims in the First-tier Tribunal (Mental Health)", noted in the General Note to these Rules, read:

"Rule 15 (2) provides that the tribunal may admit in evidence any document or written material, whether or not that such document or material would be admissible in a civil trial. However, the tribunal will generally wish to copy such information or written material to the patient, unless it is satisfied that there are grounds to prohibit disclosure under Rule 14. If the tribunal decides to prohibit disclosure to the patient, it will usually send a copy of the material to the patient's legal representatives. In such circumstances, the representatives will not be permitted to disclose material, or the information contained within it, to the patient.

Victims should be made aware that no guarantees can be given that any representations they make will not be disclosed to the patient. The expectation is that all documents will be disclosed to the patient, and the circumstances in which documents can be withheld are very limited. Rule 14 allows the tribunal to withhold any document from the patient if they are satisfied that:

a) disclosure would be likely to cause that person or some other person serious harm, and
b) having regard to the interests of justice, it is proportionate not to disclose."

Paragraph (2)

3–093   This paragraph was considered in *LN v Surrey NHS Primary Care Trust* [2011] UKUT 76 (AAC) where UT Judge Rowland said, at paras 22, 23, that the issue for the tribunal "is not whether evidence is admissible, i.e. whether it *can* be admitted, but is whether it *should* be admitted. Relevance is the key consideration. Irrelevant evidence should not be admitted".

With regard to the use of hearsay evidence, Munby J. said in *R. (on the application of DJ) v Mental Health Review Tribunal* [2005] EWHC 587 (Admin); [2005] M.H.L.R. 56 at para.129:

> "If the tribunal is relying on hearsay evidence it must take into account the fact that it is hearsay and must have regard to the particular dangers involved in relying upon second, third or fourth hand hearsay. The tribunal must be appropriately cautious of relying upon assertions as to past events which are not securely recorded in contemporaneous notes, particularly if the only evidence is hearsay. The tribunal must be alert to the well-known problem that constant repetition in 'official' reports or statements may, in the 'official' mind, turn into established fact something which rigorous forensic investigation shows is in truth nothing more than 'institutional folklore' with no secure foundation in either recorded or provable fact. The tribunal must guard against too quickly jumping to conclusions adverse to the patient in relation to past events where the only direct evidence is that of the patient himself, particularly where there is no clear account in contemporaneous notes of what is alleged to have happened. In relation to past incidents which are centrally important to the decision it has to take the tribunal must bear in mind the need for proof to the civil standard of proof; it must bear in mind the potential difficulties of relying upon second or third hand hearsay; and, if the incident is really fundamental to its decision, it must bear in mind fairness may require the patient to be given the opportunity to cross-examine the relevant witness(es) if their evidence is to be relied on at all."

On appeal, the Court of Appeal said that it saw "no reason to disagree" with this guidance ([2005] EWCA Civ 1605; [2006] 4 All E.R. 194 at para.77).

Summoning of witnesses and orders to answer questions or produce documents

3–094   **16.**—(1) On the application of a party or on its own initiative, the Tribunal may—

(a) by summons require any person to attend as a witness at a hearing at the time and place specified in the summons; or

(b) order any person to answer any questions or produce any documents in that person's possession or control which relate to any issue in the proceedings.

(2) A summons under paragraph (1)(a) must—

(a) give the person required to attend 14 days' notice of the hearing, or such shorter period as the Tribunal may direct; and

(b) where the person is not a party, make provision for the person's necessary expenses of attendance to be paid, and state who is to pay them.

(3) No person may be compelled to give any evidence or produce any document that the person could not be compelled to give or produce on a trial of an action in a court of law.

(4) A summons or order under this rule must—

(a) state that the person on whom the requirement is imposed may apply to the Tribunal to vary or set aside the summons or order, if they have not had an opportunity to object to it; and

(b) state the consequences of failure to comply with the summons or order.

DEFINITIONS **3–095**
  party: r.1(3).
  Tribunal: r.1(3).
  hearing: r.1(3).

GENERAL NOTE
  The Senior President of Tribunals has issued a Practice Direction on "Child, Vulnerable **3–096**
Adult and Sensitive Witnesses" which is reproduced below.
  The tribunal can refer a person's failure to comply with a requirement imposed by it to
the Upper Tribunal (r.7(3)). Provision is made in r.7 of the Tribunal Procedure (Upper
Tribunal) Rules 2008 (SI 2008/2698) and s.25 of the Tribunals, Courts and Enforcement
Act 2007 regarding the Upper Tribunal's options on such a reference being made.

Paragraph (1)
  Although the summonsed person can be required to attend the hearing, he or she cannot **3–097**
be compelled to give evidence or to produce a document if para.(3) applies.
  In *CB v Suffolk CC* [2010] UKUT 413 (AAC), a case involving a witness's failure to
respond to a witness summons, the Upper Tribunal said, at para.29, that while it would
not wish to suggest that every last avenue must always be explored to avoid issuing a witness summons, tribunals "should always consider alternatives to personal attendance
available to them under relevant Tribunal Procedure Rules, including the power under
r.16(1)(b) to order a person to answer any questions or produce any documents in that person's possession or control which relate to any issue in the proceedings". In this case, a fine
of £500, with imprisonment in default, was imposed for failure to comply. In a letter to
Mental Health Act administrators dated April 17, 2015, the Deputy Chamber President
said that the tribunal "will keep records of witnesses who have failed to comply so that,
if relevant, we can consider the witness's previous record of non-compliance when considering making a referral".

Withdrawal

  17.—(1) Subject to paragraphs (2) and (3), a party may give notice of the with- **3–098**
drawal of its case, or any part of it—
  (a) [. . .] by sending or delivering to the Tribunal a written notice of with-
      drawal; or
  (b) orally at a hearing.
  (2) Notice of withdrawal will not take effect unless the Tribunal consents to the
withdrawal except—
  (a) in proceedings concerning the suitability of a person to work with children
      or vulnerable adults; [. . .]
  (b) in proceedings started by a reference under section 67 or 71(1) of the Mental
      Health Act 1983[; or
  (c) where a local authority notifies the Tribunal before the expiry of the time
      limit for submitting a response that it will not oppose the appeal in a special
      educational needs case].
  (3) A party which started a mental health case by making a reference to the
Tribunal under section 68, 71(2) or 75(1) of the Mental Health Act 1983 may
not withdraw its case.
  (4) A party which has withdrawn its case may apply to the Tribunal for the case
to be reinstated.
  (5) An application under paragraph (4) must be made in writing and be received
by the Tribunal within 28 days after—

(a) the date on which the Tribunal received the notice under paragraph (1)(a); or

(b) the date of the hearing at which the case was withdrawn orally under paragraph (1)(b).

(6) The Tribunal must notify each party in writing [that a withdrawal has taken place under this rule] under this rule.

[(7) Where a local authority has notified the Tribunal before the expiry of the time limit for submitting a response that it will not oppose the appeal in a special educational needs case, the notice under paragraph (6) must state the date on which the Tribunal was so notified.]

AMENDMENTS
The amendments to this rule were made by SI 2013/477 r.17 and SI 2014/2128 r.22.

DEFINITIONS
3–099 party: r.1(3).
Tribunal: r.1(3).
hearing: r.1(3).

GENERAL NOTE
3–100 This rule, which enables an applicant to apply to the tribunal in writing to withdraw a case, does not apply to mandatory references (para.(3)). A discretionary reference may be withdrawn (para.(2)(b)). A withdrawal cannot take effect without the consent of the tribunal (para.(2)). If an application is withdrawn, the applicant can make a further application to the tribunal during the relevant period (s.77(2)). Provision is made for the reinstatement of a withdrawn case in paras (4) and (5).

The approach that the tribunal should adopt when considering an application to withdraw was identified by Charles J. in *AMA v Greater Manchester West Mental Health NHS Foundation Trust* [2015] UKUT 36 (AAC) at para.37:

"(i) the FtT must always ask for and consider who made the application to withdraw, how it was made, and perhaps most importantly the reasons for it and thus the continuation of a detention,

(ii) the FtT must always make its own mind up on whether it should agree to it or conduct a review of the detention and give reasons for its decision, and

(iii) if it is in doubt it should refuse consent and as a consequence carry out the review itself.

In effect the decision to give consent has to be based on a conclusion of the tribunal that continued detention under the MHA is justified for the reasons founding the application to withdraw (or other reasons)."

In the light of the judgment in *AMA* and para.12.24 of the *Code of Practice*, which states that the "Tribunal is not bound to agree [to a withdrawal], especially if the withdrawal is merely tactical or is sought within 48 hours of the hearing", Judge Mark Hinchliffe, Deputy Chamber President, wrote to the Chairman of the Mental Health Lawyers Association as follows:

"I have decided that a withdrawal should not be agreed by staff with delegated powers if the withdrawal request was received less than 48 hours (not counting weekends etc) before the tribunal hearing, or if the withdrawal appears to be merely tactical—such as where the case is part-heard, or if there are two cases that ought to be heard together and an attempt is made to withdraw one of them, or if an application for a postponement

792

or adjournment has been made and refused and the withdrawal appears to be an attempt to get round the refusal. Such withdrawals will be referred either to a Registrar, Salaried Judge, or Panel—who will apply the principles set out in *AMA*.

It follows, that for requests received less than 48 hours before the scheduled start of the hearing (not counting non-working days):

(1) the tribunal should always be provided with full reasons why the patient wants to withdraw the application (and thus agrees to the continuation of detention or a MHA order); and

(2) the tribunal must always make its own mind up on whether it should agree or, instead, proceed; and

(3) the tribunal will bear in mind that the need for, and right to, a periodic review of a patient's detention is an important safeguard and is necessary for Article 5 ECHR purposes. It should not be abandoned lightly, especially if the hearing may achieve some good; and

(4) if in doubt, the tribunal should (as Charles J suggests) refuse consent and, as a consequence, carry on with the hearing.

If the request is received after 4.30pm on the working day before the hearing, it will not be considered in advance, the panel will convene, and the decision whether or not to consent will be made by the panel, again applying the *AMA* principles."

In *MB v BEH MH NHS Trust* (2011) UKUT 328 (AAC); [2011] M.H.L.R. 246, UT Judge Levenson held that:

1. A decision of the tribunal to consent to a withdrawal is a judicial act which is appealable.

2. It is a breech of the rules of natural justice and fair procedure for a presiding judge to invite a patient to withdraw his application in such a way as to give rise to reasonable apprehension that he had formed a preconceived concluded opinion that the patient had no possibility of succeeding in his application.

With regard to point 2, it is permissible for the tribunal to express a preliminary view: see the General Note to r.32.

Paragraph (1)
BEFORE A HEARING TO CONSIDER THE DISPOSAL OF THE PROCEEDINGS. An application to **3–101** withdraw the case can be made after a recommendation has been made by the tribunal but before it reconvened to consider the case when the recommendation was not followed (*R. (on the application of O) v Mental Health Review Tribunal* [2006] EWHC 2659 (Admin); [2006] M.H.L.R. 326).

Paragraph (2)
UNLESS THE TRIBUNAL CONSENTS. The tribunal should not consent "if it takes the view **3–102** that [the application for withdrawal] is merely a tactical ploy and is not in the interests of the patient" (*R. (on the application of O) v Mental Health Review Tribunal*, above at para.41, Collins J.). An example of a tactical ploy was encountered by the author in a case where the tribunal agreed to a withdrawal where the application was made after all of the evidence has been heard, but before the tribunal had reached its decision.

O was considered by the Upper Tribunal in *KF v Birmingham and Solihull Mental Health NHS Foundation Trust* [2010] UKUT 185 (AAC); [2010] M.H.L.R. 176 at paras 37–38:

"In our view a First-tier Tribunal would certainly be justified in refusing consent to a withdrawal where it is no more than such a tactical ploy. However, that should not be taken as meaning that a tribunal should *only* refuse its agreement in such a scenario. There is plainly no automatic right to withdraw, and we agree with both counsel that the case for accepting a withdrawal will depend very much on the particular circumstances of the case (or cases). The 1983 rules did not contain either the overriding objective or the extensive case management powers to which we have already made reference and the First-tier Tribunal should always have regard to those provisions when considering whether or not it is appropriate to consent to a withdrawal.

[Counsel] submitted that a patient's desire to make an application whenever legitimately possible within the terms of the Act can hardly amount to a 'tactical ploy'. In most cases we doubt whether it is helpful to use the terminology of 'tactical ploy'. The question is whether a patient who has both an outstanding s.2 application and a subsequent s.3 application in hand near the start of a six month period may be justified in seeking to withdraw the latter application in order to preserve the possibility of making such an application later in that period of treatment. There may be a number of relevant factors, for example the initial s.3 application may have been taken without the benefit of legal advice, and an individual's mental health may well change considerably over time. The danger of an unduly broad approach to the notion of a 'tactical ploy' is that a patient might be denied what would otherwise be a legitimate opportunity to question their continued detention."

PART 3

PROCEEDINGS BEFORE THE TRIBUNAL OTHER THAN IN MENTAL HEALTH CASES

[Not reproduced]

PART 4

PROCEEDINGS BEFORE THE TRIBUNAL IN MENTAL HEALTH CASES

CHAPTER 1

Before the hearing

Application of Part 4

3–103   **31.** This Part applies only to mental health cases.

DEFINITION

3–104   mental health case: r.1(3).

Procedure in mental health cases

3–105   **32.**—(1) An application or reference must be—

(a)   made in writing;

(b)   signed (in the case of an application, by the applicant or any person authorised by the applicant to do so); and

(c)   sent or delivered to the Tribunal so that it is received within the time specified in the Mental Health Act 1983 or the Repatriation of Prisoners Act 1984.

(2) An application must, if possible, include—

(a)   [name, address and date of birth] of the patient;

(b) if the application is made by the patient's nearest relative, the name, address and relationship to the patient of the patient's nearest relative;

(c) the provision under which the patient is detained, liable to be detained, subject to guardianship, [or] a community patient [. . .];

(d) whether the person making the application has appointed a representative or intends to do so, and the name and address of any representative appointed;

(e) the name and address of the responsible authority in relation to the patient.

[(2A) A reference must, if possible, include—

(a) the name and address of the person or body making the reference;

(b) the name, address and date of birth of the patient;

(c) the name and address of any representative of the patient;

(d) the provision under which the patient is detained, liable to be detained, subject to guardianship or a community patient (as the case may be);

(e) whether the person or body making the reference has appointed a representative or intends to do so, and the name and address of any representative appointed;

(f) if the reference is made by the Secretary of State, the name and address of the responsible authority in relation to the patient, or, in the case of a conditionally discharged patient, the name and address of the responsible clinician and any social supervisor in relation to the patient.]

(3) Subject to rule 14(2) (withholding evidence likely to cause harm), when the Tribunal receives a document from any party it must send a copy of that document to each other party.

[(4) If the patient is a conditionally discharged patient—

(a) upon being notified by the Tribunal of an application, the Secretary of State must immediately provide to the Tribunal the names and addresses of the responsible clinician and any social supervisor in relation to the patient; and

(b) upon being notified by the Tribunal of an application or reference, the responsible clinician and any social supervisor named by the Secretary of State under this rule must send or deliver the documents specified in the relevant practice direction to the Tribunal so that they are received by the Tribunal as soon as practicable and in any event within 3 weeks after the notification.

(5) In proceedings under section 66(1)(a) of the Mental Health Act 1983 (application in respect of an admission for assessment), on the earlier of receipt of the copy of the application or a request from the Tribunal, the responsible authority must immediately send or deliver to the Tribunal a copy of—

(a) the application for admission; and

(b) the written medical recommendations on which that application was founded; and must as soon as practicable send or deliver to the Tribunal the documents specified in the relevant practice direction.

(6) If neither paragraph (4) nor (5) applies, the responsible authority must send or deliver the documents specified in the relevant practice direction to the Tribunal so that they are received by the Tribunal as soon as practicable and in any event within 3 weeks after the responsible authority made the reference or received a copy of the application or reference.

(7) If the patient is a restricted patient, a person or body providing a document to the Tribunal in accordance with paragraph (4)(b) or (6) must also send or deliver a copy of the document to the Secretary of State.

(7A) The Secretary of State must send the information specified in paragraph (7B) and any observations the Secretary of State wishes to make to the Tribunal as soon as practicable and in any event—

(a) in proceedings under section 75(1) of the Mental Health Act 1983 (reference concerning a conditionally discharged restricted patient who has been recalled to hospital), within 2 weeks after the Secretary of State received the documents sent or delivered in accordance with paragraph (7);

(b) otherwise, within 3 weeks after the Secretary of State received the documents sent or delivered in accordance with paragraph (7).

(7B) The information specified in this paragraph is—

(a) a summary of the offence or alleged offence that resulted in the patient being detained in hospital subject to a restriction order or, in the case of a patient subject to a restriction or limitation direction, that resulted in the patient being remanded in custody, kept in custody or sentenced to imprisonment;

(b) a record of any other criminal convictions or findings recorded against the patient;

(c) full details of the history of the patient's liability to detention under the Mental Health Act 1983 since the restrictions were imposed;

(d) any further information in the Secretary of State's possession that the Secretary of State considers relevant to the proceedings.]

(8) If the Secretary of State wishes to seek the approval of the Tribunal under section 86(3) of the Mental Health Act 1983 [(removal of alien patients)], the Secretary of State must refer the patient's case to the Tribunal and the provisions of these Rules applicable to references under that Act apply to the proceedings.

[(9) The responsible authority must make records relating to the detention or treatment of the patient and any after-care services available to the Tribunal on request and the Tribunal or an appropriate member of the Tribunal may, before or at the hearing, examine and take notes and copies of such records for use in connection with the proceedings.]

AMENDMENTS

The amendments to this rule were made by SI 2012/500 r.3 and SI 2014/514 r.17.

DEFINITIONS

3–106   applicant: r.1(3).
Tribunal: r.1(3).
patient: r.1(3).
nearest relative: r.1(3).
party: r.1(3).
responsible authority: r.1(3).
practice direction: r.1(3).

GENERAL NOTE

3–107   This Rule deals with applications and references to tribunals in mental health cases (paras (1), (2) and (2A)) and the submission of information to the tribunal by the responsible authority and the Secretary of State (paras (4)–(9)). Subject to r.14(2), a copy of every document received by the tribunal must be sent to each other party (para.(3)). An application may be withdrawn under r.17.

With s.2 cases, the information set out in para.(5) must be sent to the tribunal prior to the hearing date. In other cases, the responsible authority must ensure that the tribunal receives the information required by the practice direction on mental health cases within three weeks of the authority making the reference or receiving a copy of the application or reference (para.(6)). If the patient is a restricted patient, the authority must also send the statement to the Secretary of State (para.(7)), and the Secretary of State must send the information specified in para.(7B) to the tribunal within the time limits set out in para.(7A). If the patient is a conditionally discharged patient, the patient's responsible clinician and any social supervisor named by the Secretary of State must send a statement containing the information required by the practice direction so that it is received by the tribunal within three weeks of them being notified by the tribunal of the application or reference (para.(4)).

The tribunal can remedy any defects in a report that it has received by exercising its power under r.7(2)(b).

Where the tribunal receives the information required by paras (4), (5) or (6) it must give notice of the proceedings to the persons and/or bodies specified in r.33.

There is provision for the time limits in this rule to be extended (r.5(3)(a)). See rr.12 and 13 for the calculation of time and methods of service.

The references in this Rule to "the relevant practice direction" are to "Practice Direction—First-Tier Tribunal, Health Education and Social Care Chamber, Statements and Reports in Mental Health Cases", which was issued on October 28, 2013, and is reproduced below. The Tribunal Service has published *Reports for Mental Health Tribunals* (2012) which provides guidance, based on a previous edition of the Practice Direction, for those who have to prepare reports for the tribunal. It can be accessed on the Mental Health Law Online website.

The authors of reports and their attendance at Tribunal hearings
In *AF v Nottinghamshire NHS Trust* [2015] UKUT 216 (AAC), UT Judge Wright **3–108** observed obiter that:

1. The law does not require that the social circumstances report must "be prepared by a social worker or CPN and not a nurse, or that that report writer must be a different person to the person who prepares the nursing report. The important issue is not the professional title of the report writer but the relevance and quality of the information provided in the report and thus the report writer's position of knowledge in respect of that information" (para.45).

2. Neither does the law dictate "that the report writer, and that person alone, must attend the First-tier Tribunal hearing to speak to their report". It was therefore "not unlawful for a different person to attend before [the] tribunal" (para.49).

Also see the note on this case in the General Note to s.117 under the heading *Applications to the First-tier Tribunal (Mental Health) and to the Hospital Managers*.

Paper reviews
The CQC's "Monitoring the Mental Health Act in 2013/2014" reports, at p.41, that in **3–109** 2012–13, "the Tribunal introduced a system of 'paper reviews' for automatic referrals of CTO cases. This means that the Tribunal will not meet with the patient, but will carry out a review of the patient's records and reports. Since it was introduced, the Tribunal has reviewed 884 cases in this way. Patients are given the opportunity to object to having their case determined through a paper review, and will have a full hearing if they do so. In 2013/14, paper reviews accounted for 17% (516) of CTO cases considered by the Tribunal."

Paragraph (1)(b)
An application can only be made if the applicant either has the mental capacity to make it **3–110** or to authorise a person to sign the application on his behalf. Only a "very limited capacity" is required for either purpose (*R. (on the application of H) v Secretary of State for Health* [2005] UKHL 60; [2005] 4 All E.R. 1311 per Lady Hale at para.4).

Under the Mental Capacity Act 2005, a mentally capable person (the donor) can execute a legal document called a lasting power of attorney (LPA) which empowers another person (the donee) to act in his or her stead, either generally or for specific purposes. An act done by a donee can be treated as an act done by the donor. A LPA which confers on the donee (or donees) power to make decisions about the donor's personal welfare matters could cover the making of an application to a tribunal. A personal welfare LPA can only take effect after the donor has lost the mental capacity to make the decision in question. A donee could therefore make an application to a tribunal on the patient's behalf if:

(i) the welfare LPA either gives a general power to the donee or the power to make such an application has been specified by the donor; and

(ii) the patient does not possess the mental capacity to make the application.

A deputy appointed by the Court of Protection under the 2005 Act to make personal welfare decisions on behalf of the patient can also make an application to the tribunal on the patient's behalf if such a power has been conferred on the deputy by the court and the patient does not have the mental capacity to make the application.

Paragraph (2)

3–111 There are no statutory forms. Application and referral forms produced by HM Courts and Tribunals Service can be accessed at the Mental Health Law Online website.

Paragraph (3)

3–112 A failure to comply with this provision could give rise to a right to challenge the tribunal's decision under r.45. A failure to give notice to the Secretary of State in the case of a restricted patient would inevitably lead to the tribunal setting aside its decision under that rule as there would have been a breach of the most fundamental rule of natural justice in that the Secretary of State, as a vitally interested party whose role was to safeguard the public interest, was denied a hearing (*Secretary of State for the Home Department v Oxford Regional Mental Health Review Tribunal* [1987] 3 All E.R. 8, HL and *R. (on the application of the Secretary of State for the Home Department) v Mental Health Review Tribunal* [2004] EWHC 650 (Admin)).

Although this paragraph and the practice direction are mandatory, they are qualified by r.7: see *AM v West London MH NHS Trust & Secretary of State for Justice* [2012] UKUT 382 where UT Judge Jacobs said at para.12:

"The generalities of the rules, the practice direction and the code of practice give way to the practicalities and realities of the individual patient and the evidence. To take an obvious example, the patient's representative may tell the tribunal that detention is not disputed, but the tribunal is being invited to make a non-statutory recommendation. In those circumstances, it does not matter whether or not the practice direction has been complied with. Rule 7 provides the powers that a tribunal may need once the transition has taken place from case management to decision-making. In the example I have just given, it allows the tribunal to waive any failure to comply with the practice direction."

Paragraph (8)

3–113 SECTION 86(3). Which states that the Secretary of State or the Welsh Ministers must not exercise their power to remove a patient from the UK under that section without the approval of the tribunal.

Paragraph (9)

3–114 HH Judge Sycamore, the Chamber President, issued the following guidance on this paragraph on March 11, 2014:

"As in all other types of legal proceedings, it is for the parties to draw the panel's attention to any salient records or notes where there is sufficient time to do so. Therefore, if there are any aspects of the records or notes that any party considers the tribunal should consider, then they should prepare an extract and submit it to the tribunal, in advance.

It follows that, in all those cases where there is no pre-hearing examination or where the pre-hearing examination only arises because a patient fails to attend their hearing, tribunal doctors are not expected to routinely inspect the patient's records.

However, with a Section 2 pre-hearing examination or an examination properly requested or directed well in advance, the tribunal doctor should also inspect the patient's records as has previously been the case. This Rule provides the authority for the tribunal doctor (or the panel as a whole) to have access to records upon request.

Finally, where a pre-hearing interview is not required, panels may consider giving patients an opportunity of speaking first and, again, at the end of the hearing. Many patients have things they want to say at the outset and, of course, much time will be saved by not having to feedback the tribunal doctor's preliminary opinion in such cases."

Notice of proceedings to interested persons

33. When the Tribunal receives the information required by rule 32(4), (5) or **3–115** (6) (procedure in mental health cases) the Tribunal must give notice of the proceedings—

(a) where the patient is subject to the guardianship of a private guardian, to the guardian;

(b) where there is an extant order of the Court of Protection, to that court;

(c) subject to a patient with capacity to do so requesting otherwise, where any person other than the applicant is named by the authority as exercising the functions of the nearest relative, to that person;

(d) [. . .] and

(e) to any other person who, in the opinion of the Tribunal, should have an opportunity of being heard.

AMENDMENT
The amendment to this rule was made by SI 2013/477 r.19.

DEFINITIONS **3–116**
Tribunal: r.1(3).
mental health case: r.1(3).
patient: r.1(3).
nearest relative: r.1(3).

GENERAL NOTE
A person who is notified under this rule may either attend and take part in the proceed- **3–117** ings to such extent as the tribunal considers proper, or provide written submissions to the tribunal (r.36).

Applications to Attend the Hearing by Victims covered by the Domestic Violence, Crime and Victims Act 2004
Paragraphs 18 to 23 of "Practice guidance on proceedings concerning handling repre- **3–118** sentations from victims in the First-tier Tribunal (Mental Health)", noted in the General Note to these Rules, read:

"Rule 33(e) of the Tribunal Procedure (First-tier Tribunal) (Health, Education and Social Care Chamber) Rules 2008 ("the Rules") compels the tribunal to give notice of the proceedings (i.e. date, time and place) to any person who in the opinion of the tribunal: 'should have an opportunity of *being heard*'.

Representations made by a victim can only cover only a limited range of issues (see above) and the victim is not a party to the proceedings. In most cases, therefore, a written statement will be the most satisfactory way for the victim to express his/her views because direct involvement in the proceedings, or a procedure that brings the victim into direct conflict with the patient, is unlikely to be helpful to the victim, to the patient, or to the tribunal. However there may be some cases in which the victim believes that this is not sufficient and may decide to ask to attend the hearing. Any such requests will be treated on a case by case basis applying the principles in the overriding objective as set out in Rule 2. The victim will have to demonstrate that the opportunity to make written representations is insufficient and that he or she needs an opportunity to *be heard* in relation to relevant matters (see paragraphs 4 & 15 above).

If a victim wishes to contend that he or she needs an opportunity to give oral evidence in relation to relevant matters, they must make a written application to the tribunal in advance of the hearing. The application must explain why the right to provide relevant documents, or relevant information or submissions in writing is not sufficient to enable the tribunal to deal with the case fairly and justly.

The victim should understand that the tribunal will be required to consider a large amount of information from different sources, including confidential medical reports which the victim will not be permitted to see. A victim's representations, whilst potentially relevant and helpful, are only part of a constellation of factors that will inform the tribunal's final decision.

If the tribunal determines that a victim should have an opportunity of being heard, then the tribunal will advise the victim of the date, time and place of the hearing. Rule 36(2) then permits such a person to attend and take part in the hearing to such extent as the tribunal considers proper. This gives the tribunal a wide discretion to regulate its own procedure, taking account of all the relevant circumstances.

Rule 38(4) and (5) may be particularly helpful when a tribunal is deciding what approach to take when dealing with the oral evidence of a victim who is permitted to attend a hearing. In particular, the tribunal has power under Rule 38(5) to exclude a victim from a hearing until the time comes for the victim to give his or her evidence. However, notwithstanding Rule 38(4), the tribunal will be reluctant to exclude a patient from a hearing relating to that patient's liberty, unless there are strong and evidentially supported reasons for doing so. Rule 5 empowers a tribunal judge to consider these matters at any time up to the hearing. Consequently, the manner and format in which the victim's oral evidence is presented to the tribunal (e.g. whether it is in the presence or absence of the other parties to the hearing) can be determined either by the judge dealing with the management of the case in advance of the hearing, or by the panel at the hearing itself."

Paragraph (c)

3–119   The responsible authority should inform the tribunal of a capacious patient's objection to his nearest relative being given notice of the proceedings.

Paragraph (e)

3–120   ANY OTHER PERSON.   Including the victim of the patient. Victims need to be advised that any written representations that are made under r.36(2)(b) will be disclosed to the patient unless r.14(2) applies.

Medical examination of the patient

[**34.**—(1) Where paragraph (2) applies, an appropriate member of the Tribunal **3–121** must, so far as practicable, examine the patient in order to form an opinion of the patient's mental condition, and may do so in private.

(2) This paragraph applies—

(a) in proceedings under section 66(1)(a) of the Mental Health Act 1983(d) (application in respect of an admission for assessment), unless the Tribunal is satisfied that the patient does not want such an examination;

(b) in any other case, if the patient or the patient's representative has informed the Tribunal in writing, not less than 14 days before the hearing, that—

(i) the patient; or

(ii) if the patient lacks the capacity to make such a decision, the patient's representative, wishes there to be such an examination; or

(c) if the Tribunal has directed that there be such an examination.]

AMENDMENT

This rule was substituted by SI 2014/514 r.18.

DEFINITIONS **3–122**

hearing: r.1(3).

mental health case: r.1(3).

Tribunal: r.1(3).

patient: r.1(3).

GENERAL NOTE

Under this rule, the medical member of the tribunal will conduct a pre-hearing examin- **3–123** ation of the patient in all s.2 cases unless the patient does not want such an examination. In any other case, the tribunal doctor will not conduct such an examination unless:

- the tribunal is informed in writing by or on behalf of the patient, not less than 14 days before the hearing, that a pre-hearing examination is wanted, or

- the tribunal has directed that there must be such an examination. This will either be a direction by a salaried judge or Registrar in advance of the hearing, or a direction made by the panel because the patient has failed to attend the hearing.

HH Judge Sycamore, the Chamber President, issued the following guidance on this rule (as substituted) on March 11, 2014:

"The jurisdiction has drafted a leaflet, which the office will send at an early stage to all Section 2 and unrepresented patients, that advises patients of their rights to legal representation and/or to see the tribunal doctor in advance – and that provides a clear and easy method to promptly inform the tribunal of any wishes.

I expect legally represented patients to receive appropriate and timely advice from their lawyers, and the office will be vigilant in seeking capacity assessments for unrepresented patients to make sure that legal representatives are promptly appointed for patients who do not have the capacity to decide for themselves whether or not to appoint a representative.

Timely requests for a pre-hearing examination will be processed quickly so that tribunal doctors have time to make arrangements to see patients a day or two before the hearing.

In addition, there are two other situations when a pre-hearing examination may arise:

First, a salaried tribunal judge or Registrar can direct that an examination take place in advance of the hearing, as part of their case-management powers. Late requests from or on behalf of patients will be referred for case-management decision (although granting a late request may involve a postponement to give the tribunal doctor time to arrange a visit). Additionally, there may be other cases where, either upon the request of a party or the panel, or on their own initiative, a salaried tribunal judge or Registrar considers whether a pre-hearing examination is required. The test for all such decisions will be whether such an examination is necessary to enable the tribunal to deal with the case fairly and justly.

Second, if the patient completely fails to attend the hearing, the panel itself should direct the tribunal doctor to interview the patient on the ward before proceeding with the hearing unless such an interview is impractical or unnecessary – which it may be if, for example, the patient is too unwell, does not wish to see the tribunal doctor, has gone absent without leave, or lives in the community and has chosen not to attend a hearing. It may also be that the patient's representative agrees that a pre-hearing interview is unnecessary."

All requests for pre-hearing medical examinations must be made on either Form T129 (for patients) or Form CMR1 (for lawyers).

Under para.5 of the Practice Statement "Composition of Tribunals in relation to matters that fall to be decided by the Health, Education and Social Care Chamber on or after 18 January 2010", issued by the Senior President of Tribunals on December 16, 2009, the "appropriate member" is the member of the tribunal who is a registered medical practitioner. The medical member must be a fully registered person within the meaning of the Medical Act 1983 whether or not he or she holds a licence to practise under that Act (SI 2008/2692 r.1(2), as amended by SI 2009/1592 art.3). The position is different in Wales: see the General Note to s.65.

Although the tribunal will doubtless be guided by the medical member, it is the tribunal as a whole which determines issues relating to the patient's mental condition in the light of their own experience and examination of the patient (*R. v Trent Mental Health Review Tribunal Ex p. Ryan* [1992] C.O.D. 15 DC). In *MD v Nottinghamshire Health Care NHS Trust* [2010] UKUT 59 (AAC); [2010] M.H.L.R. 93, para.47, UT Judge Jacobs said that the presence of a psychiatrist on the tribunal panel reduces the need for parties to have their own expert evidence: see further the note on "Human Rights Act 1998" in the General Note to these Rules. The tribunal may not proceed with a hearing in the absence of the patient unless the requirements of this rule have been satisfied (r.39(2)(a)).

The question whether the tribunal was biased because the consultant psychiatrist who sat as a member of the tribunal was a consultant who was employed by the detaining NHS Trust was considered in *R. (on the application of PD) v West Midlands and North West Mental Health Review Tribunal* [2004] EWCA Civ 311; [2004] M.H.L.R 174, where it was alleged that the involvement of the psychiatrist in the decision was incompatible with art.6 of the European Convention on Human Rights (ECHR) and with natural justice and, in particular, the common law test of bias. The Court of Appeal held that the test of apparent bias under the ECHR and under public law is the same and that the court had to consider the case by applying the following test which had been established by the House of Lords in *Lawal v Northern Spirit Ltd* [2003] UKHL 35: would a fair minded and informed observer who is neither complacent nor unduly sensitive or suspicious conclude that there was a real possibility that the tribunal was biased when it made the decision under challenge. Applying this test to the facts of the case, the question was whether the reasonable and informed member of the public might suspect that someone in the position of the psychiatrist would be so concerned at the potential reaction of the managers of the trust if the patient were to be discharged, and the implications of such reaction for his own position, that this might consciously or unconsciously affect his decision. The court answered this question by rejecting the contention that an appearance of bias arises simply from the fact that the psychiatrist was employed by the detaining trust. The court said that an appearance of bias could have arisen if the psychiatrist had been employed at the hospital where the patient was detained. Also see the General Note to these Rules under the heading *Bias of tribunal members*.

In *DN v Switzerland* (2003) 37 E.H.R.R. 21; [2001] M.H.L.R. 117 the European Court of Human Rights held that the fact that a psychiatrist member of a court who, in his role as judge rapporteur, had previously prepared an expert opinion on the patient and had communicated his opinion on whether the patient's application should succeed to the court, constituted a violation of art.5(4) of the ECHR. The court said, at para.54, that the psychiatrist's position in the proceedings gave rise to legitimate fears in the applicant that "he had a preconceived opinion as to her request for release from detention and that he was not, therefore, approaching her case with due impartiality". *DN* was applied in *R. (on the application of S) v Mental Health Review Tribunal* [2002] EWHC (Admin) 2522; [2003] M.H.L.R. 118, where Stanley Burnton J. held that:

1. This rule does not expressly require the medical member to form an opinion of the patient's mental condition: it requires him to take the steps necessary to form an opinion.

2. The medical member must not form a concluded opinion on the patient's mental condition until the conclusion of the hearing, since otherwise the outcome of the hearing would be prejudiced.

3. The forming and expression of a provisional opinion by the medical member does not give rise to unfairness.

4. As a matter of domestic law, there can be no objection to the expression of a provisional opinion by a medical member to his tribunal colleagues prior to the hearing, provided the other members are aware that is only a provisional opinion and treat it as such, and provided that they understand that they are free to disagree with it if the evidence and submissions before them lead them to a different conclusion.

5. The phrase "due impartiality" used by the court in *DN* requires a member of a tribunal not to have a preconceived concluded opinion on the merits of the patient's case. The court did not suggest that a provisional view formed before the commencement of the hearing is objectionable. If an otherwise impartial and independent member of a tribunal has a preconceived concluded opinion, or if he expresses himself in such a way as to give rise to reasonable apprehension that he has a preconceived concluded opinion, he lacks the necessary impartiality, but not otherwise.

6. It follows that this rule [as it appeared in the MHRT Rules 1983] is not inconsistent with the requirements of art.5(4) as interpreted in *DN*.

S was applied in *R. (on the application of RD) v Mental Health Review Tribunal* [2007] EWHC 781 (Admin) where Munby J. held that the power to express preliminary views was not confined to the medical member and that such views could relate to all aspects of the case.

Paragraph (1)
AN APPROPRIATE MEMBER OF THE TRIBUNAL.   See the General Note, above.

MUST, SO FAR AS PRACTICABLE.   This covers the situation where the patient refuses to **3–124** see the medical member, is too disturbed to be examined, or is absent without leave. The member will be protected by s.139 of the Act when acting under this rule.

AN OPINION OF THE PATIENT'S MENTAL CONDITION. The opinion must be provisional: see above. The tribunal is entitled to rely on the evidence of the medical member regarding the nature of the patient's mental disorder even if it conflicts with the evidence of the patient's responsible clinician (RC) and the patient's independent psychiatrist. However, any evidence or information which has only been made available to the member must be shown at least to the patient's representative so that he or she can have the opportunity to present countervailing arguments (*R. v Mental Health Review Tribunal Ex p. Clatworthy* [1985] 3 All E.R. 699 DC). In *R. (on the application of H) v Ashworth Hospital Authority* [2002] EWCA Civ 923; [2002] M.H.L.R. 314 at para.84 Dyson L.J. said:

"It seems to me both fair and sensible that, if the medical member of the tribunal has formed any views on the basis of his or her interview with the patient, the substance of those views should be communicated to the patient and/or those who are representing him. I cannot think of any good reason why this should not be a requirement, although I would not wish to rule out the possibility of exceptional cases where such a course may not be practicable."

This passage was cited by Stanley Burnton J. in *R. (on the application of S) v Mental Health Review Tribunal,* above, where his Lordship said, at para.34, that the following guidance taken from para.7 of "The Members' Handbook of the Mental Health Review Tribunals in England and Wales" must be followed:

"[The medical member] must appreciate that he performs a dual role at the tribunal as a fact finder and as a decision-maker and it is therefore essential that his opinion of the patient's mental condition, if it differs significantly from that of the [RC], should have been disclosed to the patient and the representative at the outset of the hearing. Thus, a situation will be avoided where the members of the tribunal are acting on the basis of evidence known only to themselves which would, of course, be a breach both of fundamental principle, and likely to invalidate the decision."

Further guidance on this point was provided in *R. (on the application of KW) v Avon and Wiltshire Mental Health Partnership NHS Trust and Bristol City Council* [2003] EWHC 919 (Admin); [2003] M.H.L.R. 315 (Admin) at para.25, where it was held that if the medical member makes a finding relevant to the existence of the patient's mental disorder, or forms a provisional opinion as to the existence or otherwise of a mental disorder, that view should be shared with the patient's RC in the course of the hearing.

CHAPTER 2

Hearings

[Restrictions on disposal of proceedings without a hearing]

3–125   **35.**—[(1) Subject to the following paragraphs, the Tribunal must hold a hearing before making a decision which disposes of proceedings.]

(2) This rule does not apply to a decision under Part 5.

[(3) The Tribunal may make a decision on a reference under section 68 of the Mental Health Act 1983 (duty of managers of hospitals to refer cases to tribunal) without a hearing if the patient is a community patient aged 18 or over and either—

(a) the patient has stated in writing that the patient does not wish to attend or be represented at a hearing of the reference and the Tribunal is satisfied that the patient has the capacity to decide whether or not to make that decision; or

(b) the patient's representative has stated in writing that the patient does not wish to attend or be represented at a hearing of the reference.

(4) The Tribunal may dispose of proceedings without a hearing under rule 8(3) (striking out a party's case).]

AMENDMENTS
The amendments to this rule were made by SI 2012/500 r.3.

DEFINITIONS **3–126**
    Tribunal: r.1(3).
    dispose of proceedings: r.1(3).
    hearing: r.1(3).

GENERAL NOTE
This rule states that, apart from the exceptions provided for in paragraphs (3) and (4), a **3–127** tribunal must not make a decision which disposes of proceedings without holding a hearing.

Paragraph (3)
This paragraph allows the tribunal to dispose of a reference under s.68 in respect of a **3–128** community patient without a hearing in specified circumstances.

STATED IN WRITING. The Courts and Tribunal Service has produced an explanatory leaflet (T128) which includes a form which enables the patient to indicate a preference with regard to attendance and representation.

THE PATIENT HAS THE CAPACITY TO DECIDE. An assessment of capacity must be made by the patient's responsible clinician: see para.15(a) of the Practice Direction on Statements and Reports in Mental Health Cases, which is reproduced below.

Paragraph (4)
This paragraph allows mental health cases to be struck out without a hearing where the **3–129** tribunal has no jurisdiction. Although it has been said in a communication with the author that this paragraph has been invoked to strike out a case on the ground that the tribunal considered that the documentation relating to the "sectioning" of the patient revealed an error which rendered the patient's detention unlawful, it is submitted that such action would be ultra vires as the tribunal has no jurisdiction to consider the legal validity of the statutory documentation. In this case, the patient lost her opportunity to have her application considered by the tribunal, yet remained a detained patient because the detaining hospital did not agree with the opinion expressed by the tribunal.

Entitlement to attend a hearing

36.—(1) Subject to rule 38(4) (exclusion of a person from a hearing), each party **3–130** to proceedings is entitled to attend a hearing.

(2) Any person notified of the proceedings under rule 33 (notice of proceedings to interested persons) may—
    (a) attend and take part in a hearing to such extent as the Tribunal considers proper; or
    (b) provide written submissions to the Tribunal.

DEFINITIONS **3–131**
    party: r.1(3).
    hearing: r.1(3).

Tribunal: r.1(3).

GENERAL NOTE
3–132 Subject to the power of the tribunal in r.38(4) to exclude a person from a hearing, this rule states that a party is entitled to attend a tribunal hearing, and that an interested party may either attend and take part in a hearing to such extent as the tribunal considers proper or provide written submissions to the tribunal. A hearing can take place in the absence of a party if r.39 applies.

Paragraph (1)
3–133 PARTY. Note r.11(5).

Time and place of hearings
3–134 **37.**—(1) In proceedings under section 66(1)(a) of the Mental Health Act 1983 the hearing of the case must start within 7 days after the date on which the Tribunal received the application notice.

(2) In proceedings under section 75(1) of that Act, the hearing of the case must start at least 5 weeks but no more than 8 weeks after the date on which the Tribunal received the reference.

(3) The Tribunal must give reasonable notice of the time and place of the hearing (including any adjourned or postponed hearing), and any changes to the time and place of the hearing, to—

(a) each party entitled to attend a hearing; and

(b) any person who has been notified of the proceedings under rule 33 (notice of proceedings to interested persons).

(4) The period of notice under paragraph (3) must be at least [21 days], except that—

(a) in proceedings under section 66(1)(a) of the Mental Health Act 1983 the period must be at least 3 working days; and

(b) the Tribunal may give shorter notice—

(i) with the parties' consent; or

(ii) in urgent or exceptional circumstances.

AMENDMENT
The amendment to para.4 was made by SI 2014/514 r.19.

DEFINITIONS
3–135 Tribunal: r.1(3).
party: r.1(3).
hearing: r.1(3).
working day: r.1(3).

GENERAL NOTE
3–136 In *R. (on the application of C) v Mental Health Review Tribunal London South and South West Region* [2001] EWCA Civ 1110; [2001] M.H.L.R. 110, the Court of Appeal held that:

1. A uniform policy that tribunal hearings requested by patients who had been detained under s.3 of the Act would be fixed eight weeks after the date of the application did not comply with art.5(4) of the European Convention on Human Rights (ECHR), which requires the lawfulness of the patient's detention to be decided speedily. Each application had to be heard as soon as reasonably practicable.

2. However urgent the patient's demand for a hearing, such time could properly be allowed for preparation as was reasonably necessary to ensure that the tribunal was in a position adequately and fairly to adjudicate on the issues before it.

3. There was nothing inconsistent with art.5(4) in having a target date of eight weeks maximum for the listing of hearings. In cases requiring eight weeks' preparation, that period would not conflict with the requirement that a decision on the application had to be reached speedily.

Lord Phillips M.R. said at para.60:

"It seems to me that the [appropriate] stage at which to fix a [hearing] date would be after receipt of the statement required by rule 6 [now see r.32], when the scope of the remaining activities that would need to take place before the hearing would be clear".

C was applied by Stanley Burnton J. in *R. (on the application of KB) v The Mental Health Review Tribunal and the Secretary of State for Health* [2002] EWHC 639 (Admin); [2003] M.H.L.R. 1 at para.31, where his Lordship said:

"What is a speedy decision in any case will depend on a number of factors, including the nature and importance of the subject matter of the case, the complexity of the issues, the preparation required before the hearing, and the evidence to be considered. Factors extraneous to the particular case may also be relevant, such as a sudden increase in similar applications, or the intervention of a holiday period. However, in my judgment the fact that a patient's case is perceived to be unmeritorious does not deprive him of his right to a speedy hearing; and similarly, if there is unjustified delay before the hearing, the fact that his case is belatedly held to be unmeritorious does not excuse the infringement of that right."

Having considered the causes of the delays involved in the cases before him, his Lordship said that:

1. In the ordinary way it should be practicable for tribunal hearings in s.3 cases to take place within eight weeks of the application.

2. Central government should ensure that tribunals are provided with the resources and administrative systems that would enable them to satisfy this expectation.

3. In any sensibly managed judicial system there are bound to be adjournments and cancelled hearings for a number of reasons: the illness of a judge or the unavailability of a necessary witness, the over-running of an earlier hearing, or the need to accommodate an urgent case. The postponement of a hearing for such reasons does not necessarily involve any infringement of a ECHR right. The correct approach to adopt in a case where there has been a delay in arranging a tribunal hearing is to consider whether the delay in question is, on the face of it, inconsistent with the requirement for a speedy hearing. If it is, the onus is on the state to excuse the delay. It may do so by establishing, for example, that the delay has been caused by a sudden and unpredictable increase in the workload of the tribunal, and it has taken effective and sufficient measures to remedy the problem. But if the state fails to satisfy that onus, the claimant will have established a breach of his right under art.5(4).

Paragraph (4)
Where notice is unavoidably given late, the tribunal has the power to waive the irregularity under r.7. **3–137**

Public and private hearings

3–138   **38.**—(1) All hearings must be held in private unless the Tribunal considers that it is in the interests of justice for the hearing to be held in public.

(2) If a hearing is held in public, the Tribunal may give a direction that part of the hearing is to be held in private.

(3) Where a hearing, or part of it, is to be held in private, the Tribunal may determine who is permitted to attend the hearing or part of it.

(4) The Tribunal may give a direction excluding from any hearing, or part of it—

(a) any person whose conduct the Tribunal considers is disrupting or is likely to disrupt the hearing;

(b) any person whose presence the Tribunal considers is likely to prevent another person from giving evidence or making submissions freely;

(c) any person who the Tribunal considers should be excluded in order to give effect to a direction under rule 14(2) (withholding information likely to cause harm); or

(d) any person where the purpose of the hearing would be defeated by the attendance of that person.

(5) The Tribunal may give a direction excluding a witness from a hearing until that witness gives evidence.

DEFINITIONS
3–139   hearing: r.1(3).
Tribunal: r.1(3).

GENERAL NOTE
3–140   Tribunal hearings are to be held in private unless the tribunal considers that the interests of justice require a public hearing (para.(1)). The hearing can be part public and part private (para.(2)). The overwhelming majority of hearings are held in private. The tribunal has the power to give directions excluding various categories of persons from both public and private hearings (paras (4), (5)).

In *AH v West London Mental Health Trust* [2010] UKUT 264 (AAC); [2010] M.H.L.R. 326, at para.44, the Upper Tribunal considered that the relevant factors in deciding whether to direct a hearing in public are:

• Is it consistent with the subjective and informed wishes of the applicant (assuming he is competent to make an informed choice)?

• Will it have an adverse effect on his mental health in the short or long term, taking account of the views of those treating him and any other expert views?

• Are there any other special factors for or against a public hearing?

• Can practical arrangements be made for an open hearing without disproportionate burden on the authority?

The Upper Tribunal said, at para.25, that although the underlying assumption in this rule is that the interests of justice will normally require a hearing in private, having regard to the reasons for the exception to the right to a public hearing under art.6 of the European Convention of Human Rights (ECHR) the principal consideration remains the protection of the interests of the patient.

At a further hearing ([2011] UKUT 74 (AAC); [2011] M.H.L.R. 85), the Upper Tribunal directed that the tribunal must accede to the patient's request by holding a public hearing of his application. The UT said at para.22:

"It seems to us that once the threshold tests [set out in the four bullet points] above for establishing a right to a public hearing have been satisfied, art.6 of the ECHR (re-enforced by art.13 of the Convention on the Rights of Persons with Disabilities) requires that a patient should have the same or substantially equivalent right of access to a public hearing as a non-disabled person who has been deprived of his or her liberty, if this art.6 right to a public hearing is to be given proper effect. Such a right can only be denied a patient if enabling that right imposes a truly disproportionate burden on the state. The European Court of Human Rights has emphasised the need for special consideration to be given to the rights of particularly vulnerable groups such as the mentally disabled (see eg *Kiss v Hungary* [2010] M.H.L.R. 245, para 42)."

The UT made the following comments on the conduct of public hearings at para.23:

"How the right to a public hearing can practically and proportionately be achieved will depend on the facts of each individual case, including the facilities available in the hospital in question. On the evidence provided to us by the Broadmoor Hospital Clinical Director, it seems likely that if similar cases arise in the future, it should be possible for arrangements to be made between the hospital and the Tribunals Service for a hearing at the hospital with a video-link to suitable premises off-site where any interested members of the press or public can view the proceedings."

In *R. (on the application of Mersey Care NHS Trust) v Mental Health Review Tribunal* [2004] EWHC 1749 (Admin); [2005] 2 All E.R. 820, Beatson J. held that:

1. Rule 21 of the Mental Health Review Tribunal Rules 1983, which dealt with the privacy of proceedings, created a presumption that hearings before tribunals are private [A similar presumption is made by para.(1) of this rule]. Such a presumption can be justified under art.6 of the ECHR where it is considered necessary in the interests of morals, public order or national security or where required by the interests of juveniles or the protection of the private life of the parties (*B and P v United Kingdom* (2002) 34 E.H.R.R. 19 at para.39). In *AH v West London Mental Health Trust*, above, para.20, the Upper Tribunal said mental health cases can be added to this list.

2. The High Court has jurisdiction to commit for the contempt of an order of a tribunal: see *Pickering v Liverpool Daily Post and Echo Newspapers Plc* [1991] 1 All E.R. 622, where the House of Lords held that a tribunal is, by virtue of s.19 of the Contempt of Court Act 1981 and s.12 of the Administration of Justice Act 1960, a "court" whose proceedings are subject to the law of contempt.

3. Although the general rule in s.12 of the 1960 Act is that the publication of information relating to proceedings before any court sitting in private shall not of itself be a contempt of court, proceedings in mental health tribunals are one of the exceptions so that publication of such information is itself a contempt: s.12(1)(b) of the 1960 Act.

4. Where a tribunal holds a public hearing, the control over publicity is by means of the "strict liability" rule in s.2 of the Contempt of Court Act 1981. The fact that the protection afforded by the strict liability rule would be only for a limited period coupled with the difficulty of determining in advance what kind of public comment about proceedings will create "a substantial risk that the course of justice . . . will be seriously impeded or prejudiced" (s.2(2)) of the 1981 Act) mean that the tribunal's powers if the hearing is in public are significantly more limited than they are if it is in private.

5. Any restrictions on the right to "impart information and ideas" gained by attendance at a public hearing held by a mental health tribunal would prima facie require justification under art.10(2) of the ECHR.

It would be a contempt of court under the 1981 Act for sound recording equipment, including a mobile phone which is capable of recording sound, to be used at a tribunal hearing without permission.

Observers

3–141   "Guidance for the observation of tribunal hearings" has been issued by the Courts and Tribunal Service. It can be accessed at the Mental Health Law Online website.

Paragraph (3)

3–142   The tribunal can authorise a member of the clinical team to be present to hear the evidence of the patient contrary to the wishes of the patient *(R. (on the application of B) v South Region Mental Health Review Tribunal* [2008] EWHC 2356 (Admin); [2008] M.H.L.R. 312).

The guidance note on the "Role of the Independent Mental Health Advocate (IMHA) in First-tier Tribunal (Mental Health) hearings" (see the General Note to these Rules) states at para.4.1.1 that it "is not suggested that an IMHA needs to apply to the tribunal in advance for permission to attend a hearing".

Paragraph 4(b)

3–143   A representative has a right to question witnesses *(R. (on the application of Mersey Care NHS Trust v Mental Health Review Tribunal* [2003] EWHC 1182 (Admin): [2003] M.H.L.R. 354). It is therefore submitted that the responsible authority's representative, including a representative who is a member of the clinical team that is treating the patient, cannot be excluded under this provision. If the tribunal did decide to interview the patient in the absence of the representative, the requirements of art.6 of the ECHR and the rules of natural justice would require that any salient facts that were divulged by the patient during the interview be communicated to the representative.

Hearings in a party's absence

3–144   **39.**—(1) Subject to paragraph (2), if a party fails to attend a hearing the Tribunal may proceed with the hearing if the Tribunal—

    (a) is satisfied that the party has been notified of the hearing or that reasonable steps have been taken to notify the party of the hearing; and

    (b) considers that it is in the interests of justice to proceed with the hearing.

    [(2) The Tribunal may not proceed with a hearing that the patient has failed to attend unless the Tribunal is satisfied that—

    (a) the patient—

        (i) has decided not to attend the hearing; or

        (ii) is unable to attend the hearing for reasons of ill health; and

    (b) an examination under rule 34 (medical examination of the patient)—

        (i) has been carried out; or

        (ii) is impractical or unnecessary.]

AMENDMENT
Paragraph (2) was substituted by SI 2014/514 r.20.

DEFINITIONS

3–145   party: r.1(3).
hearing: r.1(3).
Tribunal: r.1(3).
patient: r.1(3).

GENERAL NOTE
This rule establishes when a tribunal hearing may proceed in the absence of a party or the **3–146** patient.

Paragraph (2)
HH Judge Sycamore, the Chamber President, issued the following guidance on this para- **3–147** graph (as substituted) on March 11, 2014:

"I do not expect that this interview will take too long and, in any event, it should shorten the hearing because the patient will not be giving evidence to the panel as a whole.

If the patient on the ward fails to attend the hearing then a pre-hearing interview provides an opportunity for the patient to be heard. However, all other evidence must be made available to the panel in the usual way. Thus, if the patient has decided not to attend or is unable to attend the hearing, it should not also be necessary to review the patient's records.

Apart from a patient failing to attend, I do not expect panels at the hearing to direct pre-hearing examinations. I recognise that the desirability of a pre-hearing examination may become clear only when the members of a panel read the reports. But it will then be poss-ible for the panel to ask a salaried judge to consider whether or not to direct a pre-hearing examination. Moreover (except in Section 2 cases) if the patient is going to attend at the hearing, even if they have chosen to be unrepresented, there will rarely be time or necess-ity on the hearing day for a pre-hearing examination as well."

Power to pay allowances

40. The Tribunal may pay allowances in respect of travelling expenses, subsist- **3–148** ence and loss of earnings to—
  (a) any person who attends a hearing as an applicant or a witness;
  (b) a patient who attends a hearing otherwise than as the applicant or a witness; and
  (c) any person (other than a legal representative) who attends as the represen-tative of an applicant.

DEFINITIONS
3–149
  Tribunal: r.1(3).
  hearing: r.1(3).
  applicant: r.1(3).
  legal representative: r.1(3).

CHAPTER 3

Decisions

Decisions

41.—(1) The Tribunal may give a decision orally at a hearing. **3–150**
  (2) Subject to rule 14(2) (withholding information likely to cause harm), the Tribunal must provide to each party as soon as reasonably practicable after mak-ing [a decision (except a decision under Part 5) which finally disposes of all issues in the proceedings or of a preliminary issue dealt with following a direction under rule 5(3)(e)]—
  (a) a decision notice stating the Tribunal's decision;
  (b) written reasons for the decision; and

(c) notification of any right of appeal against the decision and the time within which, and the manner in which, such right of appeal may be exercised.

(3) The documents and information referred to in paragraph (2) must—

(a) in proceedings under section 66(1)(a) of the Mental Health Act 1983, be provided at the hearing or sent within 3 working days after the hearing; and

(b) in other cases, be provided at the hearing or sent within 7 days after the hearing.

(4) The Tribunal may provide written reasons for any decision to which paragraph (2) does not apply.

AMENDMENT
The amendment to this rule was made by SI 2013/477 r.20.

DEFINITIONS
3–151   Tribunal: r.1(3).
hearing: r.1(3).
respondent: r.1(4).

GENERAL NOTE
3–152   Although the tribunal may give its decision orally at the hearing (para.(1)), it is required to provide its written decision, the reasons for it, and information about any rights of appeal, to each party (para.(2)) within the time limits set out in para.(3).

A First-tier Tribunal consisting of more than one member is allowed to reach a decision by a majority by virtue of art.8 of the First-tier Tribunal and Upper Tribunal (Composition of Tribunal) Order 2008 (SI 2008/2835). There is no obligation placed upon the tribunal to state that a decision was given by a majority. If the tribunal chooses to state that a decision was given by a majority, the statement of reasons should provide "at least a brief statement of reasons for the dissent of the minority member" (*Secretary of State for Work and Pensions v SS* [2010] UKUT 384 (AAC), para.10).

A tribunal has its statutory duty to perform and could not avoid that by accepting a submission that it is bound to follow another tribunal's decision, even though there had been no change of circumstances. There could be no res judicata (the legal principle that a matter which has been settled by a court cannot be reopened or challenged as to the matter decided) (*R. v South-West Thames Mental Health Review Tribunal Ex p. Demetri (No.1)* [1997] C.O.D. 44 CA). However, there is nothing to prevent a previous tribunal decision being placed before the tribunal hearing the patient's case. The weight to be given to the decision will be a matter for that tribunal (*RH v South London and Maudsley NHS Foundation Trust* [2010] EWCA Civ 1273; [2010] M.H.L.R. 341, para.35).

If a decision of a tribunal which appears to have been made without jurisdiction has not been quashed by proceedings which were properly commenced within time, the decision must be treated as being a valid decision (*Bath and North East Somerset Council v AJC* [1999] M.H.L.R. 184).

Paragraph (2)
3–153   FINALLY DISPOSES.   See r.42.

WRITTEN REASONS FOR THE DECISION.   Excluding reasons which would be likely to cause serious harm to the patient or another (r.14(2)). The reasons must contain numbered paragraphs (Practice Statement on Form of Decisions and Neutral Citation, issued by the Senior President on October 31, 2008).

The importance of the requirement for a decision-maker to give reasons was emphasised by Sedley J. in *R. v Solihull Metropolitan Borough Council Housing Benefits Review Board Ex p. Simpson* (1993) 26 H.L.R. 370 at 377:

"A statutory duty imposed on a named decision maker to give reasons . . . is not simply a bureaucratic chore or an opportunity for lawyers to find fault. It is, and is increasingly recognised as being, a fundamental aspect of good public administration (underpinned increasingly by law) because it focuses the decision maker's mind on exactly what it is that has to be decided, within what legal framework, and according to what relevant evidence and material. Experience shows that it will sometimes produce an opposite conclusion to that which was initially in the decision-makers mind before the rigour of formulating acceptable reasons was applied."

In *MS v North East London Foundation Trust* [2013] UKUT 092 (AAC) at para.15, UT Judge Jacobs said that the written reasons should:

- state what facts the tribunal found;
- explain how and why the tribunal made them;
- show how the tribunal applied the law to those facts.

The following aide memoire of matters which may assist in the production of adequate and intelligible reasons was provided by UT Judge Knowles in *HK v Llanarth Court Hospital* [2014] UKUT 410 (AAC); [2015] M.H.L.R. 88:

"12. First, it would be helpful if tribunals were to set out their reasons by reference to the relevant criteria for detention. As Upper Tribunal Judge Jacobs observed in para.9 of *JL v Managers of Llanarth Court and SOS for Justice* [2011] UKUT 62 (AAC), it might be better if tribunals were to set out their reasons under the headings provided by the legal questions they have to determine. I agree. Using headings within the statement of reasons makes it easier to show that the tribunal has dealt with each of the legal criteria it has to address. I note that the First-tier Tribunal (Mental Health) in England has made template decisions using appropriate headings available to tribunal judges to assist them in reason writing.

13. Second, the tribunal's reasons should address how the tribunal dealt with any disputes as to either the law or the evidence. If this is not done, the unsuccessful party might believe that the tribunal has ignored important issues. In particular, failing to address explicitly any applications made by one or other of the parties may render a set of reasons inadequate. Such an omission certainly makes it more difficult for a party to know why they have been unsuccessful and additionally raises doubt as to whether the tribunal has dealt fairly with that party's case. However, it is not necessary for a set of reasons to resolve evidential matters which are irrelevant to the legal issues that the tribunal has to determine; a prudent tribunal though may wish to explain briefly why it has not resolved a factual dispute.

14. Third, the reasons themselves must be clear and unambiguous. It is not for a party to deduce the reasons for a decision.

15. Fourth, rehearsing what each witness told the tribunal is, without more liable to render a set of reasons erroneous in law. What is required is to explain (i) what facts the tribunal found as a result of that evidence and (ii) what conclusions on those facts the tribunal reached.

16. Fifth, it is not necessary for the tribunal's reasons to mention all of the evidence in a case. It is entitled to be selective in its references to evidence in its reasons though it should, as I have indicated in paragraph 13 above, identify and resolve evidence and applications which are in dispute."

The following notes of caution need to be made when considering the adequacy of reasons given to justify the decision of a tribunal: (1) the decision of a tribunal "is not required to be an elaborate formalistic product of refined legal draftsmanship" (*Meek v Birmingham City Council* [1987] I.R.L.R. 250, para.8, per Sir Thomas Bingham M.R.); (2) tribunal reasons "are not intended to include a comprehensive and detailed analysis of the case, either in terms of fact or in law . . . their purpose remains what it has always been, which is to tell the parties in broad terms why they lose or, as the case may be, win. I think it would be a thousand pities if these reasons began to be subjected to a detailed analysis and appeals were to be brought based upon any such analysis. This, to my mind, is to misuse the purpose for which the reasons are given" (*UCATT v Brain* [1981] I.R.L.R. 225, 227 per Donaldson L.J.); (3); "it is probable that in understanding and applying the law in their specialised field the tribunal will have got it right . . . Their decisions should be respected unless it is quite clear that they have misdirected themselves in law" (*Secretary of State for the Home Department v AH (Sudan)* [2007] UKHL 49; [2008] 4 All E.R. 190, para.30, per Lady Hale: see also *R. (on the application of W) v Mental health Review Tribunal* [2004] EWHC 3266 (Admin); [2005] M.H.L.R. 134 at para.18); and (4) there is a danger of "elevating into general principles what are statements by judges made by reference to the facts and circumstances of particular cases but taken out of context" (*H v East Sussex County Council* [2009] EWCA Civ 249, para.15, per Waller L.J.).

The duty to give reasons under this provision (as it appeared in r.23 of the MHRT Rules 1983) was considered by the Court of Appeal in *R. (on the application of H) v Ashworth Hospital Authority* [2002] EWCA Civ 923; [2002] M.H.L.R. 314. The leading judgment was given by Dyson L.J. who adopted the approach taken by the Court of Appeal in *English v Emery Reimbold & Strick Ltd* [2002] EWCA Civ 605; [2002] 3 All E.R. 385 where Lord Phillips M.R. summarised the present state of the law regarding appeals from lower to higher courts. Lord Phillips said that, putting the matter at its simplest, "justice will not be done if it is not apparent to the parties why one has won and the other lost" (para.16). A judge should:

> "provide an explanation as to why he has accepted the evidence of one expert and rejected that of another. It may be that the evidence of one or the other accorded more satisfactorily with facts found by the Judge. It may be that the explanation of one was more inherently credible than that of the other. It may simply be that one was better qualified, or manifestly more objective, than the other. Whatever the explanation may be, it should be apparent from the judgment" (para.20).

Dyson L.J. rejected a submission that inadequate reasons may be treated as adequate on the ground that inadequate resources were made available to the tribunal (para.76). His Lordship said that "it is at least arguable" that the "informed audience point" (see *R. v Mental Health Review Tribunal Ex p. Booth,* noted below) "has less force in relation to a tribunal decision than to a decision by a lower court in the civil justice system". This is because, in the light of *R. v East London and City Mental Health NHS Trust Ex p. Brandenburg* [2003] UKHL 58; [2004] 1 All E.R. 400, it is essential that an approved mental health professional who is contemplating re-sectioning a patient subsequent to a tribunal discharge should know the facts and circumstances which a tribunal took into account when deciding to discharge a patient, and the reasons for its decision.

In *H*, the Court of Appeal found the tribunal's reasons to be inadequate for two principal reasons:

1. The tribunal had failed to indicate the reasoning process by which they decided to accept the minority medical evidence and reject the majority medical evidence. Dyson L.J. said, at para.80, that the following passage from the judgment of Henry L.J. in *Flannery v Halifax Estate Agencies Ltd* [2001] 1 W.L.R. 377 at 381–382, is "as apt in relation to the decisions of tribunals as it is to lower courts generally":

"Where there is a straightforward factual dispute whose resolution depends simply on which witness is telling the truth about events which he claims to recall, it is likely to be enough for the judge (having no doubt, summarised the evidence) to indicate simply that he believes X rather than Y; indeed there may be nothing else to say. But where the dispute involves something in the nature of an intellectual exchange, with reasons and analysis advanced on either side, the judge must enter into issues canvassed before him and explain why he prefers one case over another. This is likely to apply particularly in litigation where as here there is disputed expert evidence; but it is not necessarily limited to such cases."

2. The tribunal failed to give any reasons for not adjourning in order to see whether suitable after-care would be made available for the patient, or whether an order for deferred discharge would be appropriate. In this case, the question of what after-care arrangements would be available in the community was relevant to the issue of whether the statutory criteria were met.

With regard to point 1, if the tribunal has accepted the evidence of the patient as to the risk or lack of risk of him accepting medication if discharged into the community, and implicitly rejected the views of his responsible clinician and nurse, it is particularly important for the tribunal to explain the basis of its decision and the reasons for its preferring one witness to another (*R. (on the application of the Secretary of State for the Home Department) v Mental Health Review Tribunal and CH* [2005] EWHC 746 (Admin); [2005] M.H.L.R. 199 at para.35).

The reasons "must be read as a whole, in a common sense way, not as a legal treatise"; per Sullivan J. in *R. (on the application of Epsom & St Helier NHS Trust v The Mental Health Review Tribunal* [2001] M.H.L.R. 8 at para.49. They must be "adequate and intelligible . . . and must grapple with the important issues raised" *(R. v Mental Health Review Tribunal Ex p. Pickering* [1986] 1 All E.R. 99 at 102 per Forbes J.). It is therefore not sufficient for the tribunal's reasons merely to (1) recite the evidence or submissions (*J v Devon County Council* [2001] EWHC 958 (Admin)); or (2) recite the statutory criteria for discharge (*Bone v Mental Health Review Tribunal* [1985] 3 All E.R. 330). In *AS v First-tier Tribunal*, Upper Tribunal Case No.JR/3048/2012, at para.17, UT Judge Jacobs said that the basic principle that can be distilled from the "vast number of authorities on the standard that reasons have to attain" is that "reasons must be adequate to ensure that:

- the parties, especially the party whose case has not been accepted, know why the tribunal made the decision it did; and

- an appeal court can judge whether the tribunal has made an error of law".

The fact that the responsible clinician had more experience of the patient than did another doctor is not of itself a reason for preferring her evidence. It does not always follow that greater knowledge means greater insight. The tribunal should explain what it was in the responsible clinician's experience that made her view preferable (*AC v Partnerships in Care Ltd and Secretary of State for Justice* [2012] UKUT 450 (AAC); [2013] M.H.L.R. 52).

In *RH v South London and Maudsley NHS Foundation Trust* [2010] UKUT 32 (AAC) [2010] M.H.L.R. 118, para.17, UT Judge Rowland said that where the tribunal merely disagreed with the conclusion to be drawn from the professional assessments when it came to considering whether a restriction order should cease to have effect, it was difficult to "give reasons beyond those required to show that the tribunal has directed itself correctly as to the law and to show to what matters the tribunal has had regard".

On a reconsideration of a decision that had been deferred under s.73(7) of the Act, it is impermissible for the tribunal in its reasons for not discharging the patient to take into account matters, such as risk factors, to which it had not referred in its original decision even though they must have been relevant then (*LC v DHIC* [2010] UKUT 319 (AAC); [2010] M.H.L.R. 337).

In *R. v Mental Health Review Tribunal Ex p. Booth* [1998] C.O.D. 203, Laws J. said:

"It has to be remembered . . . that the quality of reasons required of a Mental Health Review Tribunal has to be looked at in light of the fact that the decision is addressed to an informed audience. Those who receive it and who are concerned with it will be familiar with the essential documents in the case . . . They will be familiar with what has been said at the tribunal by way of oral evidence and what the issues there were which had been argued. Given that necessary familiarity, if there was a case in which it could still be said that the parties simply were not told why the tribunal arrived at the decision it did, then no doubt there would be a sound basis for a legal challenge."

This passage must be read subject to the caveat expressed by Dyson L.J. in *R. (on the Application of H) v Ashworth Hospital Authority*, above.

If the tribunal provides reasons that are considered to be inadequate, the review procedure should be invoked: see rr.47(1) and 49.

Paragraph (3)(b)

3–154   7 DAYS.   Not 7 working days.

Paragraph (4)

3–155   It is submitted that the overriding objective (r.2) requires the tribunal to provide reasons for all disputed decisions.

Provisional decisions

3–156   **42.** For the purposes of this Part and Parts 1, 2 and 5, a decision with recommendations under section 72(3)(a) or (3A)(a) of the Mental Health Act 1983 or a deferred direction for conditional discharge under section 73(7) of that Act is a decision which disposes of the proceedings.

DEFINITION

3–157   dispose of proceedings: r.1(3).

PART 5

CORRECTING, SETTING ASIDE, REVIEWING AND APPEALING TRIBUNAL DECISIONS

Interpretation

3–158   **43.** In this Part—

"appeal" means the exercise of a right of appeal on a point of law under section 11 of the 2007 Act; and

"review" means the review of a decision by the Tribunal under section 9 of the 2007 Act.

DEFINITION

3–159   Tribunal: r.1(3).

Clerical mistakes and accidental slips or omissions

3–160   **44.** The Tribunal may at any time correct any clerical mistake or other accidental slip or omission in a decision, direction or any document produced by it, by—

(a) sending notification of the amended decision or direction, or a copy of the amended document, to all parties; and

(b) making any necessary amendment to any information published in relation to the decision, direction or document.

DEFINITIONS

    Tribunal: r.1(3).   **3–161**

    document: r.1(3).

    party: r.1(3).

Setting aside a decision which disposes of proceedings

45.—(1) The Tribunal may set aside a decision which disposes of proceedings, **3–162** or part of such a decision, and re-make the decision or the relevant part of it, if—

(a) the Tribunal considers that it is in the interests of justice to do so; and

(b) one or more of the conditions in paragraph (2) are satisfied.

(2) The conditions are—

(a) a document relating to the proceedings was not sent to, or was not received at an appropriate time by, a party or a party's representative;

(b) a document relating to the proceedings was not sent to the Tribunal at an appropriate time;

(c) a party, or a party's representative, was not present at a hearing related to the proceedings; or

(d) there has been some other procedural irregularity in the proceedings.

(3) A party applying for a decision, or part of a decision, to be set aside under paragraph (1) must make a written application to the Tribunal so that it is received no later than 28 days after the date on which the Tribunal sent notice of the decision to the party.

DEFINITIONS

    Tribunal: r.1(3).   **3–163**

    dispose of proceedings: r.1(3).

    document: r.1(3).

    party: r.1(3).

    hearing: r.1(3).

GENERAL NOTE

    This rule, which deals with matters of procedure, not jurisdiction (Decision HM/0339/ **3–164** 2015, July 6, 2015, UT Judge Jacobs at para.26), enables the tribunal to set aside a decision, or part of a decision, which disposes of proceedings (see r.42) and to remake the decision or the relevant part of it on the ground of procedural irregularity if such action is in the interests of justice. An application form for this purpose (Form P9), together with a guidance note has been published by the Courts and Tribunal Service.

    A decision by the tribunal to set aside a decision cannot be appealed to the Upper Tribunal (Tribunals, Courts and Enforcement Act 2007 s.11(1), (5)(d)(iii)).

    A procedure for challenging a direction is contained in r.6(5).

Paragraph (3)

    28 DAYS.   See rr.12 and 13 for the calculation of time and methods of service. There is **3–165** provision for this time limit to be extended (r.5(3)(a)).

Application for permission to appeal

3–166   **46.**—(1) A person seeking permission to appeal must make a written application to the Tribunal for permission to appeal.

(2) An application under paragraph (1) must be sent or delivered to the Tribunal so that it is received no later than 28 days after the latest of the dates that the Tribunal sends to the person making the application—

[(za)] the relevant decision notice;]

(a) written reasons for the decision[, if the decision disposes of—

    (i) all issues in the proceedings; or

    (ii) subject to paragraph (2A), a preliminary issue dealt with following a direction under rule 5(3)(e);]

(b) notification of amended reasons for, or correction of, the decision following a review; or

(c) notification that an application for the decision to be set aside has been unsuccessful.

[(2A) The Tribunal may direct that the 28 days within which a party may send or deliver to the Tribunal an application for permission to appeal against a decision that disposes of a preliminary issue shall run from the date of the decision that disposes of all issues in the proceedings.]

(3) The date in paragraph (2)(c) applies only if the application for the decision to be set aside was made within the time stipulated in rule 45 (setting aside a decision which disposes of proceedings) or any extension of that time granted by the Tribunal.

(4) If the person seeking permission to appeal sends or delivers the application to the Tribunal later than the time required by paragraph (2) or by any extension of time under rule 5(3)(a) (power to extend time)—

(a) the application must include a request for an extension of time and the reason why the application was not provided in time; and

(b) unless the Tribunal extends time for the application under rule 5(3)(a) (power to extend time) the Tribunal must not admit the application.

(5) An application under paragraph (1) must—

(a) identify the decision of the Tribunal to which it relates;

(b) identify the alleged error or errors of law in the decision; and

(c) state the result the party making the application is seeking.

AMENDMENTS
The amendments to this rule were made by SI 2013/477 r.21.

DEFINITIONS
3–167   appeal: r.43.
Tribunal: r.1(3).
review: r.43.
dispose of proceedings: r.43.
party: r.1(3).

GENERAL NOTE
3–168   For a consideration of appeals generally, see the General Note to s.65. Under s.11 of the Tribunals, Courts and Enforcement Act 2007, an appeal lies to the Upper Tribunal "on any point of law arising from a decision made by the First-tier Tribunal". The Upper Tribunal can set aside the decision if it involves "an error on a point of law" (ibid., s.12(1)). In *JLG v*

Managers of Llanarth Court [2011] UKUT 62 (AAC); [2011] M.H.L.R. 74, para.3, UT Judge Jacobs provided guidance on the nature of an error of law:

"The essence of the legal requirement for a tribunal's decision is that: (i) the tribunal asked itself the correct legal questions; (ii) it made findings of fact that were rationally based in the evidence; and (iii) it answered the legal questions appropriately given its findings of fact. Additionally, the tribunal must: (iv) give the parties a fair hearing; and (v) provide adequate reasons. In simple terms, the issue is whether the tribunal did its job properly."

Judge Jacobs further stated that when identifying whether an error of law exists, tribunals "are assumed to know the essentials of what their work involves". They therefore do not need to "spell out" fundamental matters such as the burden and standard of proof. The task of the Upper Tribunal is to examine whether "there is anything to indicate that [the tribunal] have exceptionally failed to apply the basic tools of their craft" (paras 5 and 6). See also the notes on r.41(2).

In *CNWL NHS Foundation Trust v H-JH* [2012] UKUT 210 (AAC); [2012] M.H.L.R. 305, para.12, Judge Jacobs described the Upper Tribunal's appellate role as follows:

"In deciding whether the First-tier Tribunal made an error of law, the Upper Tribunal has no power to undertake its own assessment of the evidence or to make its own findings of fact in substitution for those of the First-tier Tribunal. It must respect the fact-finding role, provided that the First-tier Tribunal carried out that task rationally and explained why it made its findings. To do otherwise would subvert the statutory limit of its jurisdiction."

The scope of this rule is not confined to appeals against the tribunal's decision which disposes of proceedings; an appeal lies against an interlocutory decision (*LS v London Borough of Lambeth* [2010] UKUT 461 (AAC)) In *RM v St Andrew's Healthcare* [2010] UKUT 119 (AAC), Judge Jacobs considered the approach that should be taken with regard to appeals against case management decisions. He said that although appellate courts are supportive of such decisions and "discourage appeals against them" as they "often have to be made with little time for analysis or reflection" (para.7), this "does not mean that [they] are immune from scrutiny" (para.8). It was suggested in *Dorset Healthcare NHS Foundation Trust v MH* [2009] UKUT 4 (AAC) at para.19, that where case-management decisions are being challenged, the First-tier Tribunal can treat an application for permission to appeal as an application for a new direction if it is satisfied that the challenged direction is not appropriate.

An application form for permission to appeal (Form P10), together with a guidance note has been published by the Courts and Tribunal Service. On receiving the application, the tribunal must first consider whether to review the decision in accordance with r.49 (r.47(1)). If permission to appeal is refused, reasons must be given (r.47(4)).

There is nothing unfair in an initial application for permission to appeal being made to the judge who made the decision being challenged: see *AA v Cheshire and Wirral Partnership NHS Foundation Trust* [2009] UKUT 195 (AAC); [2009] M.H.L.R. 308, where Judge Rowland said at para.27:

"The advantage to a superior court or tribunal of having this kind of procedure is that it gives the judge whose decision is being challenged, who will have the relevant issues in mind, an opportunity to comment on the grounds of appeal and indicate whether he or she thinks there is anything in them."

Encouragement to respondents, especially public authority respondents, to take part in proceedings before the Upper Tribunal was given by Judge Rowland in *RH v South London and Maudsley NHS Foundation Trust* [2010] UKUT 32 (AAC); [2010] M.H.L.R. 118 at para.29 et seq. Public authorities will doubtless remain reluctant to take part in such proceedings when the decision under challenge is that of the tribunal, not the authority.

Paragraph (2)

3–169   28 Days.   See rr.2 and 13 for the calculation of time and methods of service. There is provision for this time limit to be extended (r.5(3)(a)).

Tribunal's consideration of application for permission to appeal

3–170   **47.**—(1) On receiving an application for permission to appeal the Tribunal must first consider, taking into account the overriding objective in rule 2, whether to review the decision in accordance with rule 49 (review of a decision).

(2) If the Tribunal decides not to review the decision, or reviews the decision and decides to take no action in relation to the decision, or part of it, the Tribunal must consider whether to give permission to appeal in relation to the decision or that part of it.

(3) The Tribunal must send a record of its decision to the parties as soon as practicable.

(4) If the Tribunal refuses permission to appeal it must send with the record of its decision—

(a) a statement of its reasons for such refusal; and

(b) notification of the right to make an application to the Upper Tribunal for permission to appeal and the time within which, and the method by which, such application must be made.

(5) The Tribunal may give permission to appeal on limited grounds, but must comply with paragraph (4) in relation to any grounds on which it has refused permission.

DEFINITIONS

3–171   appeal: r.43.
Tribunal: r.1(3).
party: r.1(3).

GENERAL NOTE

3–172   In *KF v Birmingham and Solihull Mental Health NHS Foundation Trust* [2010] UKUT 185 (AAC), para.19, the Upper Tribunal accepted the following analysis of the relevant legislative provisions that had been prepared by counsel:

"On receipt of an application for permission to appeal, the First-tier Tribunal has a *discretion* as to whether to undertake a review (r.47(1)). If there is no review, the First-tier Tribunal has a *duty* to consider whether to give permission to appeal but a *discretion* as to whether or not to grant permission (r.47(2)). If permission is refused and the application is renewed before the Upper Tribunal, the Upper Tribunal also has a *discretion* as to whether to give permission (Tribunal Procedure (Upper Tribunal) Rules 2008, SI 2008/2698, r.21(2)). If permission is granted and the Upper Tribunal finds an error of law, it has a *discretion* as to whether to set aside the First-tier Tribunal decision (s.12(2)(a) of the 2007 Act), but if that tribunal decision is set aside, then the Upper Tribunal has a *duty* either to re-make the decision or to remit it to the First-tier Tribunal for a re-hearing (s.12(2)(b) of the 2007 Act)."

In *KF*, the UT said, at para.41, that there may be circumstances in which it is appropriate to grant either a review or permission to appeal notwithstanding the fact that the patient has been discharged:

"In many cases where the patient has since been released, there will be no individual or wider public interest in continuing proceedings, even where the decision of the First-tier Tribunal under challenge may well be suspect. To that extent we would agree that there may well be a presumption in practice against granting either a review or permission to appeal or against setting aside on appeal in such cases. However, we do not accept that it will *never* be appropriate to exercise such a procedural discretion in the patient's favour where he or she has already been released. We recognise that these are cases involving fundamental issues about the liberty of the subject. There may well be circumstances in which it remains appropriate for there to be further scrutiny of the initial tribunal decision, notwithstanding the individual's subsequent discharge. There may be a danger that a future decision-maker may give inappropriate weight to a flawed decision. Moreover, there may be an urgent need for the legal principles at stake to be clarified."

Application for review in special educational needs cases
48. [*Applies to special educational needs cases*]   **3–173**

Review of a decision
49.—(1) The Tribunal may only undertake a review of a decision—   **3–174**
  (a) pursuant to rule 47(1) (review on an application for permission to appeal) if it is satisfied that there was an error of law in the decision; or
  (b) pursuant to rule 48 (application for review in special educational needs cases).

(2) The Tribunal must notify the parties in writing of the outcome of any review, and of any right of appeal in relation to the outcome.

(3) If the Tribunal takes any action in relation to a decision following a review without first giving every party an opportunity to make representations, the notice under paragraph (2) must state that any party that did not have an opportunity to make representations may apply for such action to be set aside and for the decision to be reviewed again.

DEFINITIONS   **3–175**
  Tribunal: r.1(3).
  review: r.43.
  appeal: r.43.
  party: r.1(3).

GENERAL NOTE
  This power is intended to capture decisions that are clearly wrong in that there is an error **3–176** of law in the decision, so avoiding the need for an appeal. As the propensity to fall into error is not confined to the English, it is unfortunate that this useful power has no equivalent in the Welsh Rules. The tribunal has the power to review a decision on its own initiative under s.9(2)(a) of the Tribunals, Courts and Enforcement Act 2007. The powers of the tribunal on undertaking a review are set out in s.9(4) to (6) of that Act:

"(4) Where the First-tier Tribunal has under subsection (1) reviewed a decision, the First-tier Tribunal may in the light of the review do any of the following—

(a) correct accidental errors in the decision or in a record of the decision;
(b) amend reasons given for the decision;
(c) set the decision aside.

(5) Where under subsection (4)(c) the First-tier Tribunal sets a decision aside, the First-tier Tribunal must either—

(a) re-decide the matter concerned, or

(b) refer that matter to the Upper Tribunal.

(6) Where a matter is referred to the Upper Tribunal under subsection (5)(b), the Upper Tribunal must re-decide the matter."

A decision by the tribunal either to review, or not to review a decision cannot be appealed to the Upper Tribunal as it is an "excluded decision" (s.11(1),(5)(d)(i) of the 2007 Act). Although such a decision is not appealable, an application for the judicial review of the decision may be made to the Upper Tribunal by virtue of ss.15 to 18 of the 2007 Act where it does not seek a declaration of incompatibility under the Human Rights Act 1998 and it is within the scope of *Practice Direction (Upper Tribunal: Judicial Review Jurisdiction)* [2009] 1 W.L.R. 327 made by the Lord Chief Justice under s.18(6) of the 2007 Act. The Practice Direction specifies, with immaterial exceptions, "[a]ny decision of the First-tier Tribunal made under Tribunal Procedure Rules or section 9 of the 2007 Act where there is no right of appeal . . .": see *RB*, below at para.11.

In *R (RB) v First-tier Tribunal (Review)* [2010] UKUT 160 (AAC); [2010] M.H.L.R. 192 the Upper Tribunal held that:

1. This Rule cannot be used to usurp the Upper Tribunal's function of determining appeals on contentious points of law. If the power is to be exercised to set aside the original decision because of a perceived error of law, this should only be done in clear cases ((para.24). It should be possible to give brief reasons for the decision; it will be seldom be necessary to set out the facts or the background legislation or to cite at length from authorities (para.32).

2. Even if there is a clear error of law, the tribunal may decide not to review a decision but instead to give permission to appeal if it would be helpful to have an authoritative decision of the Upper Tribunal on the point (para.27).

3. Paragraph (3) of this Rule enables the First-tier Tribunal to take a robust approach when it first receives an application for permission to appeal because it enables it to take a decision without calling for representations by the other side, on the basis that if the other side objects there can be an application to set aside. However, in many cases it will be preferable to invite representations before concluding that an original decision should be set aside (para.26).

4. There may be occasions when it is desirable for a case to be reconsidered by the First-tier Tribunal so that further findings may be made even if it is likely to go to the Upper Tribunal eventually (para.28).

5. Where the First-tier Tribunal is to re-decide a case, the composition of the tribunal must be the same as was required for the original decision, although the particular judge and members may be different (para.29). [In *AA v Cheshire and Wirral Partnership NHS Foundation Trust* [2009] UKUT 195 (AAC); [2009] M.H.L.R. 308, the UT said that there is nothing unfair in a review being undertaken by the judge who made the decision being challenged].

6. The substantial element of judgment or discretion is no doubt a reason for review decisions not being appealable and it is also a reason for expecting that the Upper Tribunal will seldom interfere with review decisions when judicial review proceedings are brought (para.30).

RB was applied by UT Judge Wikeley in *R. (on the application of MP) v First-tier Tribunal* [2012] UKUT 231 (AAC) who said, at para.19, that there will need to be a "compelling case" to give permission to apply for the judicial review of a review decision.

When deciding whether to set aside a decision, it is relevant to consider whether such action could be of practical benefit to any of the parties. This is unlikely to be this case where a further hearing was due to take place which would consider the up-to-date position and would proceed on the basis that the previous decision would be erroneous in law (*BB v South London and Maudsley NHS Trust* [2009] UKUT 157 (AAC); [2009] M.H.L.R. 302).

In general, unless there is good reason why not, if the tribunal is asked to review a tribunal decision on a s.2 application where the patient has been subsequently detained under s.3, and concludes that it involves an error of law, then the appropriate way forward is for the tribunal to set aside the substantive decision and to re-list the case for hearing together with any existing s.3 application. The patient has the right to apply to withdraw that application under r.17. This approach has a number of practical ramifications. Some of the issues that may arise are as follows: (i) time limits; (ii) case management and consolidation; (iii) withdrawal; and (iv) provision of reports (*KF v Birmingham and Solihull Mental Health NHS Foundation Trust* [2010] UKUT 185 (AAC); [2010] M.H.L.R. 201 para.30).

A review decision cannot be used to criticise a decision that is under appeal (*RM v St Andrew's Healthcare* [2010] UKUT 119 (AAC); [2010] M.H.L.R. 176, para.5).

Power to treat an application as a different type of application

50. The Tribunal may treat an application for a decision to be corrected, set **3–177** aside or reviewed, or for permission to appeal against a decision, as an application for any other one of those things.

DEFINITIONS
    Tribunal: r.1(3). **3–178**
    review: r.43.
    appeal: r.43.

                SCHEDULE   Rules 20(1)(a) and 21(1)(a) **3–179**

[*The Schedule does not apply to mental health cases*]

PRACTICE DIRECTION
FIRST-TIER TRIBUNAL
HEALTH EDUCATION AND SOCIAL CARE CHAMBER
STATEMENTS AND REPORTS IN MENTAL HEALTH CASES

GENERAL NOTE
An overview of this Practice Direction is provided by C. Curran and B. Leason in "A **3–180** Brief Guide to the 2013 Practice Direction for Mental Health Tribunals in England", *Legal Action*, January 2014, pp.40–41.

1. This Practice Direction is made by the Senior President of Tribunals with the agree- **3–181** ment of the Lord Chancellor in the exercise of powers conferred by Section 23 of the Tribunals, Courts and Enforcement Act 2007. It applies to a "mental health case" as defined in Rule 1(3) the Tribunal Procedure (First-tier Tribunal) (Health, Education and Social Care Chamber) Rules 2008. Rule 32 requires that certain statements and reports must be sent or delivered to the tribunal (and, in restricted cases, to the Secretary of State) by the Responsible Authority, the Responsible Clinician and any Social Supervisor (as the case may be). This Practice Direction specifies the contents of such documents. It replaces the previous Practice Directions on mental health cases dated 30 October 2008 and 6 April 2012, with effect from 28 October 2013.

2. In this Practice Direction "the Act" refers to the Mental Health Act 1983 (as amended by the Mental Health Act 2007).

3. This Practice Direction contains five separate parts for the following categories of patient:

A. IN-PATIENTS (NON-RESTRICTED AND RESTRICTED)
B. COMMUNITY PATIENTS
C. GUARDIANSHIP PATIENTS
D. CONDITIONALLY DISCHARGED PATIENTS
E. PATIENTS UNDER THE AGE OF 18.

4. Responsible Authorities and authors of reports should refer to the relevant part of this Practice Direction, depending on the status of the patient under the Act.

SIR JEREMY SULLIVAN
SENIOR PRESIDENT OF TRIBUNALS
28 OCTOBER 2013

A. IN-PATIENTS (NON-RESTRICTED AND RESTRICTED)

3–182 5. For the purposes of this Practice Direction, a patient is an in-patient if they are detained in hospital to be assessed or treated for a mental disorder, whether admitted through civil or criminal justice processes, including a restricted patient (i.e. subject to special restrictions under the Act), and including a patient transferred to hospital from custody. A patient is to be regarded as an in-patient detained in a hospital even if they have been permitted leave of absence, or have gone absent without leave.

6. In the case of a restricted patient detained in hospital, the tribunal may make a provisional decision to order a Conditional Discharge. However, before it finally decides to grant a Conditional Discharge, the tribunal may defer its decision so that satisfactory arrangements can be made. The patient will remain an in-patient unless and until the tribunal finally grants a Conditional Discharge, so this part of the Practice Direction applies.

7. If the patient is an in-patient, the Responsible Authority must send or deliver to the tribunal the following documents containing the specified information in accordance with the relevant paragraphs below:

- *Statement of Information about the Patient.*

- *Responsible Clinician's Report, including any relevant forensic history.*

- *Nursing Report, with the patient's current nursing plan attached.*

- *Social Circumstances Report including details of any Care Pathway Approach (CPA) and/or Section 117 aftercare plan in full or in embryo and, where appropriate, the additional information required for patients under the age of 18, and any input from a Multi Agency Public Protection Arrangements (MAPPA) agency or meeting.*

8. In all in-patient cases, except where a patient is detained under Section 2 of the Act, the Responsible Authority must send to the tribunal the required documents containing the specified information, so that they are received by the tribunal as soon as practicable and in any event within 3 weeks after the Authority made or received the application or reference. If the patient is a restricted patient, the Authority must also, at the same time, send copies of the documents to the Secretary of State (Ministry of Justice).

9. Where a patient is detained under Section 2 of the Act, the Responsible Authority must prepare the required documents as soon as practicable after receipt of a copy of the application or a request from the tribunal. If specified information has to be omitted because it is not available, then this should be mentioned in the statement or report. These documents must be made available to the tribunal panel and the patient's representative at least one hour before the hearing is due to start.

10. The authors of reports should have personally met and be familiar with the patient. If an existing report becomes out-of-date, or if the status or the circumstances of the patient change after the reports have been written but before the tribunal hearing takes place (e.g. if

a patient is discharged, or is recalled), the author of the report should then send to the tribunal an addendum addressing the up-to-date situation and, where necessary, the new applicable statutory criteria.

Statement of Information about the Patient – In-Patients

11. The statement provided to the tribunal must be up-to-date, specifically prepared for **3–183** the tribunal, signed and dated, and must include:

a) the patient's full name, date of birth, and usual place of residence;

b) the full official name of the Responsible Authority;

c) the patient's first language/dialect and, if it is not English, whether an interpreter is required and, if so, in which language/dialect;

d) if the patient is deaf, whether the patient will require the services of British Sign Language Interpreters and/or a Relay Interpreter;

e) a chronological table listing:

- the dates of any previous admissions to, discharge from, or recall to hospital, stating whether the admissions were compulsory or voluntary;

- the date when the current period of detention in hospital originally commenced, stating the nature of the application, order or direction that is the authority for the detention of the patient;

- the dates of any subsequent renewal of, or change in, the authority for the patient's detention, and any changes in the patient's status under the Act;

- dates and details of any hospital transfers since the patient's original detention;

- the date of admission or transfer to the hospital where the patient now is;

- the dates and outcomes of any tribunal hearings over the last three years;

f) the name of the patient's Responsible Clinician and the date when the patient came under the care of that clinician;

g) the name and contact details of the patient's Care Co-ordinator, Community Psychiatric Nurse, Social Worker/AMHP or Social Supervisor;

h) where the patient is detained in an independent hospital, details of any NHS body that funds, or will fund, the placement;

i) the name and address of the local social services authority which, were the patient to leave hospital, would have a duty to provide Section 117 after-care services;

j) the name and address of the NHS body which, were the patient to leave hospital, would have a duty to provide Section 117 after-care services;

k) the name and address of any legal representative acting for the patient;

l) except in the case of a restricted patient, the name and address of the patient's Nearest Relative or of the person exercising that function, whether the patient has made any request that their Nearest Relative should not be consulted or should not be kept informed about the patient's care or treatment and, if so, the details of any such request, whether the Responsible Authority believes that the patient has capacity to make such a request and the reasons for that belief;

m) the name and address of any other person who plays a significant part in the care of the patient but who is not professionally involved;

n) details of any legal proceedings or other arrangements relating to the patient's mental capacity, or their ability to make decisions or handle their own affairs.

GENERAL NOTE

3–184   Guidance on drafting a Responsible Authority statement of information about the patient is provided by C. Curran, P. Fennell and S. Burrows in "Responsible Authority Statements for Mental Health Tribunals in England under the 2013 Practice Direction" *Legal Action*, September 2014, pp.17–22.

Responsible Clinician's Report – In-Patients

3–185   12. The report must be up-to-date, specifically prepared for the tribunal and have numbered paragraphs and pages. It should be signed and dated. The report should be written or counter-signed by the patient's Responsible Clinician. The sources of information for the events and incidents described must be made clear. This report should not be an addendum to (or reproduce extensive details from) previous reports, or recite medical records, but must briefly describe the patient's recent relevant medical history and current mental health presentation, and must include:

a) whether there are any factors that may affect the patient's understanding or ability to cope with a hearing and whether there are any adjustments that the tribunal may consider in order to deal with the case fairly and justly;

b) details of any index offence(s) and other relevant forensic history;

c) a chronology listing the patient's previous involvement with mental health services including any admissions to, discharge from and recall to hospital;

d) reasons for any previous admission or recall to hospital;

e) the circumstances leading up to the patient's current admission to hospital;

f) whether the patient is now suffering from a mental disorder and, if so, whether a diagnosis has been made, what the diagnosis is, and why;

g) whether the patient has a learning disability and, if so, whether that disability is associated with abnormally aggressive or seriously irresponsible conduct;

h) depending upon the statutory criteria, whether any mental disorder present is of a nature or degree to warrant, or make appropriate, liability to be detained in a hospital for assessment and/or medical treatment;

i) details of any appropriate and available medical treatment prescribed, provided, offered or planned for the patient's mental disorder;

j) the strengths or positive factors relating to the patient;

k) a summary of the patient's current progress, behaviour, capacity and insight;

l) the patient's understanding of, compliance with, and likely future willingness to accept any prescribed medication or comply with any appropriate medical treatment for mental disorder that is or might be made available;

m) in the case of an eligible compliant patient who lacks capacity to agree or object to their detention or treatment, whether or not deprivation of liberty under the Mental Capacity Act 2005 (as amended) would be appropriate and less restrictive;

n) details of any incidents where the patient has harmed themselves or others, or threatened harm, or damaged property, or threatened damage;

o) whether (in Section 2 cases) detention in hospital, or (in all other cases) the provision of medical treatment in hospital, is justified or necessary in the interests of the patient's health or safety, or for the protection of others;

p) whether the patient, if discharged from hospital, would be likely to act in a manner dangerous to themselves or others;

q) whether, and if so how, any risks could be managed effectively in the community, including the use of any lawful conditions or recall powers;

r) any recommendations to the tribunal, with reasons.

Nursing Report – In-Patients

13. The report must be up-to-date, specifically prepared for the tribunal and have numbered paragraphs and pages. It should be signed and dated. The sources of information for the events and incidents described must be made clear. This report should not recite the details of medical records, or be an addendum to (or reproduce extensive details from) previous reports, although the patient's current nursing plan should be attached. In relation to the patient's current in-patient episode, the report must briefly describe the patient's current mental health presentation, and must include: **3–186**

a) whether there are any factors that might affect the patient's understanding or ability to cope with a hearing, and whether there are any adjustments that the tribunal may consider in order to deal with the case fairly and justly;

b) the nature of nursing care and medication currently being made available;

c) the level of observation to which the patient is currently subject;

d) whether the patient has contact with relatives, friends or other patients, the nature of the interaction, and what community support the patient has;

e) strengths or positive factors relating to the patient;

f) a summary of the patient's current progress, engagement with nursing staff, behaviour, cooperation, activities, self-care and insight;

g) any occasions on which the patient has been absent without leave whilst liable to be detained, or occasions when the patient has failed to return as and when required, after having been granted leave;

h) the patient's understanding of, compliance with, and likely future willingness to accept any prescribed medication or treatment for mental disorder that is or might be made available;

i) details of any incidents in hospital where the patient has harmed themselves or others, or threatened harm, or damaged property, or threatened damage;

j) any occasions on which the patient has been secluded or restrained, including the reasons why such seclusion or restraint was necessary;

k) whether (in Section 2 cases) detention in hospital, or (in all other cases) the provision of medical treatment in hospital, is justified or necessary in the interests of the patient's health or safety, or for the protection of others;

l) whether the patient, if discharged from hospital, would be likely to act in a manner dangerous to themselves or others;

m) whether, and if so how, any risks could be managed effectively in the community, including the use of any lawful conditions or recall powers;

n) any recommendations to the tribunal, with reasons.

GENERAL NOTE

Guidance on drafting an in-patient nursing report is provided by C. Curran, B. Leason and A. Deery in "Inpatient Nursing Reports and Current Nursing Plans for Mental **3–187**

Health Tribunals in England under the 2013 Practice Direction" *Legal Action*, November 2014, pp.30–36.

Social Circumstances Report – In-Patients

3–188   14. The report must be up-to-date, specifically prepared for the tribunal and have numbered paragraphs and pages. It should be signed and dated. The sources of information for the events and incidents described must be made clear. This report should not be an addendum to (or reproduce extensive details from) previous reports, but must briefly describe the patient's recent relevant history and current presentation, and must include:

a) whether there are any factors that might affect the patient's understanding or ability to cope with a hearing, and whether there are any adjustments that the tribunal may consider in order to deal with the case fairly and justly;

b) details of any index offence(s) and other relevant forensic history;

c) a chronology listing the patient's previous involvement with mental health services including any admissions to, discharge from and recall to hospital;

d) the patient's home and family circumstances;

e) the housing or accommodation available to the patient if discharged;

f) the patient's financial position (including benefit entitlements);

g) any available opportunities for employment;

h) the patient's previous response to community support or Section 117 aftercare;

i) so far as is known, details of the care pathway and Section 117 after-care to be made available to the patient, together with details of the proposed care plan;

j) the likely adequacy and effectiveness of the proposed care plan;

k) whether there are any issues as to funding the proposed care plan and, if so, the date by which those issues will be resolved;

l) the strengths or positive factors relating to the patient;

m) a summary of the patient's current progress, behaviour, compliance and insight;

n) details of any incidents where the patient has harmed themselves or others, or threatened harm, or damaged property, or threatened damage;

o) the patient's views, wishes, beliefs, opinions, hopes and concerns;

p) except in restricted cases, the views of the patient's Nearest Relative unless (having consulted the patient) it would inappropriate or impractical to consult the Nearest Relative, in which case give reasons for this view and describe any attempts to rectify matters;

q) the views of any other person who takes a lead role in the care and support of the patient but who is not professionally involved;

r) whether the patient is known to any MAPPA meeting or agency and, if so, in which area, for what reason, and at what level – together with the name of the Chair of any MAPPA meeting concerned with the patient, and the name of the representative of the lead agency;

s) in the event that a MAPPA meeting or agency wishes to put forward evidence of its views in relation to the level and management of risk, a summary of those views (or an Executive Summary may be attached to the report); and where relevant, a copy of the Police National Computer record of previous convictions should be attached;

t) in the case of an eligible compliant patient who lacks capacity to agree or object to their detention or treatment, whether or not deprivation of liberty under the Mental Capacity Act 2005 (as amended) would be appropriate and less restrictive;

u) whether (in Section 2 cases) detention in hospital, or (in all other cases) the provision of medical treatment in hospital, is justified or necessary in the interests of the patient's health or safety, or for the protection of others;

v) whether the patient, if discharged from hospital, would be likely to act in a manner dangerous to themselves or others;

w) whether, and if so how, any risks could be managed effectively in the community, including the use of any lawful conditions or recall powers;

x) any recommendations to the tribunal, with reasons.

GENERAL NOTE

Guidance on drafting a social circumstances report is provided by C. Curran, M. **3–189** Golightley and P. Fennell in "Social Circumstances Reports for Mental Health Tribunals under the 2013 Practice Direction – Part 1", *Legal Action*, April 2014, pp.37–42. Part 2 of this article is published at *Legal Action*, June 2014, pp.39–44. Also see *The authors of reports and their attendance at Tribunal hearings* in the General Note to r.32.

B. COMMUNITY PATIENTS

15. The Responsible Authority must send to the tribunal the following documents, con- **3–190** taining the specified information, so that the documents are received by the tribunal as soon as practicable and in any event within 3 weeks after the Authority made or received the application or reference:

- *Statement of Information about the Patient*

- *Responsible Clinician's Report, including any relevant forensic history.*

- *Social Circumstances Report including details of any Section 117 aftercare plan and, where appropriate, the additional information required for patients under the age of 18, and any input from a Multi Agency Public Protection Arrangements (MAPPA) agency or meeting.*

16. The authors of reports should have personally met and be familiar with the patient. If an existing report becomes out-of-date, or if the status or the circumstances of the patient change after the reports have been written but before the tribunal hearing takes place (e.g. if a patient is recalled, or again discharged into the community), the author of the report should then send to the tribunal an addendum addressing the up-to-date situation and, where necessary, the new applicable statutory criteria.

Statement of Information about the Patient – Community Patients

17. The statement provided to the tribunal should be up-to-date, signed and dated, **3–191** specifically prepared for the tribunal, and must include:

a) the patient's full name, date of birth, and current place of residence;

b) the full official name of the Responsible Authority;

c) the patient's first language/dialect and, if it is not English, whether an interpreter is required and, if so, in which language/dialect;

d) if the patient is deaf, whether the patient will require the services of British Sign Language Interpreters and/or a Relay Interpreter;

e) a chronological table listing:

- the dates of any previous admissions to, discharge from, or recall to hospital, stating whether the admissions were compulsory or voluntary, and including any previous instances of discharge on to a Community Treatment Order (CTO);

- the date of the underlying order or direction for detention in hospital prior to the patient's discharge onto the current CTO;

- the date of the current CTO;

- the dates of any subsequent renewal of, or change in, the authority for the patient's CTO, and any changes in the patient's status under the Act;

- the dates and outcomes of any tribunal hearings over the last three years;

f) the name of the patient's Responsible Clinician and the date when the patient came under the care of that clinician;

g) the name and contact details of the patient's Care Co-ordinator, Community Psychiatric Nurse, and/or Social Worker/AMHP;

h) the name and address of the local social services authority which has the duty to provide Section 117 after-care services;

i) the name and address of the NHS body which has the duty to provide Section 117 after-care services;

j) the name and address of any legal representative acting for the patient;

k) the name and address of the patient's Nearest Relative or of the person exercising that function, whether the patient has made any request that their Nearest Relative should not be consulted or should not be kept informed about the patient's care or treatment and, if so, the details of any such request, whether the Responsible Authority believes that the patient has capacity to make such a request and the reasons for that belief;

l) the name and address of any other person who plays a significant part in the care of the patient but who is not professionally involved;

m) details of any legal proceedings or other arrangements relating to the patient's mental capacity, or their ability to make decisions or handle their own affairs.

Responsible Clinician's Report – Community Patients

3–192   18. The report must be up-to-date, specifically prepared for the tribunal and have numbered paragraphs and pages. It should be signed and dated. This report should be written or counter-signed by the patient's Responsible Clinician. The sources of information for the events and incidents described must be made clear. The report should not be an addendum to (or reproduce extensive details from) previous reports, or recite medical records, but must briefly describe the patient's recent relevant medical history and current mental health presentation, and must include:

a) where the patient is aged 18 or over and the case is a reference to the tribunal, whether the patient has capacity to decide whether or not to attend or be represented at a tribunal hearing;

b) whether, if there is a hearing, there are any factors that may affect the patient's understanding or ability to cope with it, and whether there are any adjustments that the tribunal may consider in order to deal with the case fairly and justly;

c) details of any index offence(s) and other relevant forensic history;

d) a chronology listing the patient's previous involvement with mental health services including any admissions to, discharge from and recall to hospital;

e) reasons for any previous admission or recall to hospital;

f) the circumstances leading up to the patient's most recent admission to hospital;

g) the circumstances leading up to the patient's discharge onto a CTO;

h) any conditions to which the patient is subject under Section 17B, and details of the patient's compliance;

i) whether the patient is now suffering from a mental disorder and, if so, what the diagnosis is and why;

j) whether the patient has a learning disability and, if so, whether that disability is associated with abnormally aggressive or seriously irresponsible conduct;

k) whether the patient has a mental disorder of a nature or degree such as to make it appropriate for the patient to receive medical treatment;

l) details of any appropriate and available medical treatment prescribed, provided, offered or planned for the patient's mental disorder;

m) the strengths or positive factors relating to the patient;

n) a summary of the patient's current progress, behaviour, capacity and insight;

o) the patient's understanding of, compliance with, and likely future willingness to accept any prescribed medication or comply with any appropriate medical treatment for mental disorder that is or might be made available;

p) details of any incidents where the patient has harmed themselves or others, or threatened harm, or damaged property, or threatened damage;

s) whether it is necessary for the patient's health or safety, or for the protection of others, that the patient should receive medical treatment and, if so, why;

t) whether the patient, if discharged from the CTO, would be likely to act in a manner dangerous to themselves or others;

u) whether, and if so how, any risks could be managed effectively in the community;

v) whether it continues to be necessary that the Responsible Clinician should be able to exercise the power of recall and, if so, why;

w) any recommendations to the tribunal, with reasons.

Social Circumstances Report – Community Patients

19. The report must be up-to-date, specifically prepared for the tribunal and have num- **3–193** bered paragraphs and pages. It should be signed and dated. The sources of information for the events and incidents described must be made clear. This report should not be an addendum to (or reproduce extensive details from) previous reports, but must briefly describe the patient's recent relevant history and current presentation, and must include:

a) whether there are any factors that might affect the patient's understanding or ability to cope with a hearing, and whether there are any adjustments that the tribunal may consider in order to deal with the case fairly and justly;

b) details of any index offence(s), and other relevant forensic history;

c) a chronology listing the patient's previous involvement with mental health services including any admissions to, discharge from and recall to hospital;

d) the patient's home and family circumstances;

e) the housing or accommodation currently available to the patient;

f) the patient's financial position (including benefit entitlements);

g) any employment or available opportunities for employment;

h) any conditions to which the patient is subject under Section 17B, and details of the patient's compliance;

i) the patient's previous response to community support or Section 117 aftercare;

j) details of the community support or Section 117 after-care that is being, or could be made available to the patient, together with details of the current care plan;

k) whether there are any issues as to funding the current or future care plan and, if so, the date by which those issues will be resolved;

l) the current adequacy and effectiveness of the care plan;

m) the strengths or positive factors relating to the patient;

n) a summary of the patient's current progress, behaviour, compliance and insight;

o) details of any incidents where the patient has harmed themselves or others, or threatened harm, or damaged property, or threatened damage;

p) the patient's views, wishes, beliefs, opinions, hopes and concerns;

q) the views of the patient's Nearest Relative unless (having consulted the patient) it would inappropriate or impractical to consult the Nearest Relative, in which case give reasons for this view and describe any attempts to rectify matters;

r) the views of any other person who takes a lead role in the care and support of the patient but who is not professionally involved;

s) whether the patient is known to any Multi Agency Public Protection Arrangements (MAPPA) meeting or agency and, if so, in which area, for what reason, and at what level – together with the name of the Chair of any MAPPA meeting concerned with the patient, and the name of the representative of the lead agency;

t) in the event that a MAPPA meeting or agency wishes to put forward evidence of its views in relation to the level and management of risk, a summary of those views (or an Executive Summary may be attached to the report); and where relevant, a copy of the Police National Computer record of previous convictions should be attached;

u) whether it is necessary for the patient's health or safety, or for the protection of others, that the patient should receive medical treatment and, if so, why;

v) whether the patient, if discharged from the CTO, would be likely to act in a manner dangerous to themselves or others;

w) whether, and if so how, any risks could be managed effectively in the community;

x) whether it continues to be necessary that the Responsible Clinician should be able to exercise the power of recall and, if so, why;

y) any recommendations to the tribunal, with reasons.

C. GUARDIANSHIP PATIENTS

3–194   20. If the patient has been received into guardianship the Responsible Authority must send to the tribunal the following documents, containing the specified information, so that they are received by the tribunal as soon as practicable and in any event within 3 weeks after the Authority made or received a copy of the application or reference:

- *Statement of Information about the Patient*
- *Responsible Clinician's Report, including any relevant forensic history.*

- *Social Circumstances Report including details of any Care Pathway Approach (CPA) and, where appropriate, the additional information required for patients under the age of 18, and any input from a Multi Agency Public Protection Arrangements (MAPPA) agency or meeting.*

21. The authors of reports should have personally met and be familiar with the patient. If an existing report becomes out-of-date, or if the status or the circumstances of the patient change after the reports have been written but before the tribunal hearing takes place, the author of the report should then send to the tribunal an addendum addressing the up-to-date situation and, where necessary, the new applicable statutory criteria.

Statement of Information about the Patient – Guardianship Patients
22. The statement provided to the tribunal should be up-to-date, signed and dated, **3–195** specifically prepared for the tribunal, and must include:

a) the patient's full name, date of birth, and current place of residence;

b) the full official name of the Responsible Authority;

c) the patient's first language/dialect and, if it is not English, whether an interpreter is required and, if so, in which language/dialect;

d) if the patient is deaf, whether the patient will require the services of British Sign Language Interpreters and/or a Relay Interpreter;

e) a chronological table listing:

- the dates of any previous admissions to, discharge from or recall to hospital, stating whether the admissions were compulsory or voluntary;

- the dates of any previous instances of reception into guardianship;

- the date of reception into current guardianship, stating the nature of the application, order or direction that constitutes the original authority for the guardianship of the patient;

- the dates and outcomes of any tribunal hearings over the last three years;

f) the name and address of any private guardian;

g) the name of the patient's Responsible Clinician and the date when the patient came under the care of that clinician;

h) the name and contact details of the patient's Care Co-ordinator, Community Psychiatric Nurse, and/or Social Worker/AMHP;

i) the name and address of any legal representative acting for the patient;

j) the name and address of the patient's Nearest Relative or of the person exercising that function, whether the patient has made any request that their Nearest Relative should not be consulted or should not be kept informed about the patient's care or treatment and, if so, the details of any such request, whether the Responsible Authority believes that the patient has capacity to make such a request and the reasons for that belief;

k) the name and address of any other person who plays a significant part in the care of the patient but who is not professionally involved;

l) details of any legal proceedings or other arrangements relating to the patient's mental capacity, or their ability to make decisions or handle their own affairs.

Responsible Clinician's Report – Guardianship patients

3–196   23. The report must be up-to-date, specifically prepared for the tribunal and have numbered paragraphs and pages. It should be signed and dated. The report should be written or counter-signed by the patient's Responsible Clinician. The sources of nformation for the events and incidents described must be made clear. This report should not be an addendum to (or reproduce extensive details from) previous reports, or recite medical records, but must briefly describe the patient's recent relevant medical history and current mental health presentation, and must include:

a) whether there are any factors that may affect the patient's understanding or ability to cope with a hearing, and whether there are any adjustments that the tribunal may consider in order to deal with the case fairly and justly;

b) details of any index offence(s), and other relevant forensic history;

c) a chronology listing the patient's previous involvement with mental health services including any admissions to, discharge from and recall to hospital, and any previous instances of reception into guardianship;

d) the circumstances leading up to the patient's reception into guardianship;

e) any requirements to which the patient is subject under Section 8(1), and details of the patient's compliance,

f) whether the patient is now suffering from a mental disorder and, if so, what the diagnosis is and why;

g) whether the patient has a learning disability and, if so, whether that disability is associated with abnormally aggressive or seriously irresponsible conduct;

h) details of any appropriate and available medical treatment prescribed, provided offered or planned for the patient's mental disorder;

i) the strengths or positive factors relating to the patient;

j) a summary of the patient's current progress, behaviour, capacity and insight;

k) the patient's understanding of, compliance with, and likely future willingness to accept any prescribed medication or comply with any appropriate medical treatment for mental disorder that is, or might be, made available;

l) details of any incidents where the patient has harmed themselves or others, or threatened harm, or damaged property, or threatened damage;

m) whether, and if so how, any risks could be managed effectively in the community;

n) whether it is necessary for the welfare of the patient, or for the protection of others, that the patient should remain under guardianship and, if so, why;

o) any recommendations to the tribunal, with reasons.

Social Circumstances Report – Guardianship Patients

3–197   24. The report must be up-to-date, specifically prepared for the tribunal and have numbered paragraphs and pages. It should be signed and dated. The sources of information for the events and incidents described should be made clear. This report should not be an addendum to (or reproduce extensive details from) previous reports, but must briefly describe the patient's recent relevant history and current presentation, and must include:

a) whether there are any factors that might affect the patient's understanding or ability to cope with a hearing, and whether there are any adjustments that the tribunal may consider in order to deal with the case fairly and justly;

b) details of any index offence(s), and other relevant forensic history;

c) a chronology listing the patient's previous involvement with mental health services including any admissions to, discharge from and recall to hospital, and any previous instances of reception into guardianship;

d) the patient's home and family circumstances;

e) the housing or accommodation currently available to the patient;

f) the patient's financial position (including benefit entitlements);

g) any employment or available opportunities for employment;

h) any requirements to which the patient is subject under Section 8(1), and details of the patient's compliance,

i) the patient's previous response to community support;

j) details of the community support that is being, or could be, made available to the patient, together with details of the current care plan;

k) the current adequacy and effectiveness of the care plan;

l) whether there are any issues as to funding the current or future care plan and, if so, the date by which those issues will be resolved;

m) the strengths or positive factors relating to the patient;

n) a summary of the patient's current progress, behaviour, compliance and insight;

o) details of any incidents where the patient has harmed themselves or others, or threatened harm, or damaged property, or threatened damage;

p) the patient's views, wishes, beliefs, opinions, hopes and concerns;

q) the views of the guardian;

r) the views of the patient's Nearest Relative unless (having consulted the patient) it would inappropriate or impractical to consult the Nearest Relative, in which case give reasons for this view and describe any attempts to rectify matters;

s) the views of any other person who takes a lead role in the care and support of the patient but who is not professionally involved;

t) whether the patient is known to any MAPPA meeting or agency and, if so, in which area, for what reason, and at what level – together with the name of the Chair of any MAPPA meeting concerned with the patient, and the name of the representative of the lead agency;

u) in the event that a MAPPA meeting or agency wishes to put forward evidence of its views in relation to the level and management of risk, a summary of those views (or an Executive Summary may be attached to the report); and where relevant, a copy of the Police National Computer record of previous convictions should be attached;

v) whether, and if so how, any risks could be managed effectively in the community;

w) whether it is necessary for the welfare of the patient, or for the protection of others, that the patient should remain under guardianship and, if so, why;

x) any recommendations to the tribunal, with reasons.

D. CONDITIONALLY DISCHARGED PATIENTS

25. A conditionally discharged patient is a restricted patient who has been discharged **3–198** from hospital into the community, subject to a condition that the patient will remain liable to be recalled to hospital for further treatment, should it become necessary. Other

conditions may, in addition, be imposed by the tribunal, or by the Secretary of State (Ministry of Justice).

26. This part only applies to restricted patients who have actually been granted a Conditional Discharge and who are living in the community. In the case of a restricted patient detained in hospital, the tribunal may make a provisional decision to order a Conditional Discharge. Before it finally grants a Conditional Discharge, the tribunal may defer its decision so that satisfactory arrangements can be put in place. Unless and until the tribunal finally grants a Conditional Discharge, the patient remains an in-patient, and so the in-patient part of this Practice Direction (and not this part) applies.

27. Upon being notified by the tribunal of an application or reference, the Responsible Clinician must send or deliver the Responsible Clinician's Report, and any Social Supervisor must send or deliver the Social Circumstances Report. If there is no Social Supervisor, the Responsible Clinician's report should also provide the required social circumstances information.

28. The required reports, which must contain the specified information, are:

- *Responsible Clinician's Report, including any relevant forensic history.*

- *Social Circumstances Report from the patient's Social Supervisor, including details of any Section 117 aftercare plan and, where appropriate, the additional information required for patients under the age of 18, and any input from a Multi Agency Public Protection Arrangements (MAPPA) agency or meeting.*

29. The reports must be sent or delivered to the tribunal so that they are received by the tribunal as soon as practicable and in any event within 3 weeks after the Responsible Clinician or Social Supervisor (as the case may be) received the notification.

30. The Responsible Clinician and any Social Supervisor must also, at the same time, send copies of their reports to the Secretary of State (Ministry of Justice).

31. The authors of reports should have personally met and be familiar with the patient. If an existing report is more than six weeks old, or if the status or the circumstances of the patient change after the reports have been written but before the tribunal hearing takes place (e.g. if a patient is recalled), the author of the report should then send to the tribunal an addendum addressing the up-to-date situation and, where necessary, the new applicable statutory criteria.

Responsible Clinician's Report – Conditionally Discharged Patients

3–199

32. The report must be up-to-date, specifically prepared for the tribunal and have numbered paragraphs and pages. It should be signed and dated. The report should be written or counter-signed by the patient's Responsible Clinician. If there is no Social Supervisor, the Responsible Clinician's report should also provide the required social circumstances information. The sources of information for the events and incidents described must be made clear. This report should not be an addendum to (or reproduce extensive details from) previous reports, or recite medical records, but must briefly describe the patient's recent relevant medical history and current mental health presentation, and must include:

a) whether there are any factors that might affect the patient's understanding or ability to cope with a hearing, and whether there are any adjustments that the tribunal may consider in order to deal with the case fairly and justly;

b) details of the patient's index offence(s), and any other relevant forensic history;

c) details and details of the patient's relevant forensic history;

d) a chronology listing the patient's involvement with mental health services including any admissions to, discharge from and recall to hospital;

e) reasons for any previous recall following a Conditional Discharge and details of any previous failure to comply with conditions;

f) the circumstances leading up to the current Conditional Discharge;

g) any conditions currently imposed (whether by the tribunal or the Secretary of State), and the reasons why the conditions were imposed;

h) details of the patient's compliance with any current conditions;

i) whether the patient is now suffering from a mental disorder and, if so, what the diagnosis is and why;

j) whether the patient has a learning disability and, if so, whether that disability is associated with abnormally aggressive or seriously irresponsible conduct;

k) details of any legal proceedings or other arrangements relating to the patient's mental capacity, or their ability to make decisions or handle their own affairs;

l) details of any appropriate and available medical treatment prescribed, provided, offered or planned for the patient's mental disorder;

m) the strengths or positive factors relating to the patient;

n) a summary of the patient's current progress, behaviour, capacity and insight;

o) the patient's understanding of, compliance with, and likely future willingness to accept any prescribed medication or comply with any appropriate medical treatment for mental disorder;

p) details of any incidents where the patient has harmed themselves or others, or threatened harm, or damaged property, or threatened damage;

q) an assessment of the patient's prognosis, including the risk and likelihood of a recurrence or exacerbation of any mental disorder;

r) the risk and likelihood of the patient re-offending and the degree of harm to which others may be exposed if the patient does re-offend;

s) whether it is necessary for the patient's health or safety, or for the protection of others, that the patient should receive medical treatment and, if so, why;

t) whether the patient, if absolutely discharged, would be likely to act in a manner harmful to themselves or others, whether any such risks could be managed effectively in the community and, if so, how;

u) whether it continues to be appropriate for the patient to remain liable to be recalled for further medical treatment in hospital and, if so, why;

v) whether, and if so the extent to which, it is desirable to continue, vary and/or add to any conditions currently imposed;

w) any recommendations to the tribunal, with reasons.

Social Circumstances Report – Conditionally Discharged Patients
33. The report must be up-to-date, specifically prepared for the tribunal and have num- **3–200** bered paragraphs and pages. It should be signed and dated. The sources of information for the events and incidents described should be made clear. This report should not be an addendum to (or reproduce extensive details from) previous reports, but must briefly describe the patient's recent relevant history and current presentation, and must include:

a) the patient's full name, date of birth, and current address;

b) the full official name of the Responsible Authority;

c) whether there are any factors that might affect the patient's understanding or ability to cope with a hearing, and whether there are any adjustments that the tribunal may consider in order to deal with the case fairly and justly;

d) details of the patient's index offence(s), and any other relevant forensic history;

e) a chronology listing the patient's involvement with mental health services including any admissions to, discharge from and recall to hospital;

f) any conditions currently imposed (whether by the tribunal or the Secretary of State), and the reasons why the conditions were imposed;

g) details of the patient's compliance with any past or current conditions;

h) the patient's home and family circumstances;

i) the housing or accommodation currently available to the patient;

j) the patient's financial position (including benefit entitlements);

k) any employment or available opportunities for employment;

l) details of the community support or Section 117 after-care that is being, or could be made available to the patient, together with details of the current care plan;

m) whether there are any issues as to funding the current or future care plan and, if so, the date by which those issues will be resolved;

n) the current adequacy and effectiveness of the care plan;

o) the strengths or positive factors relating to the patient;

p) a summary of the patient's current progress, compliance, behaviour and insight;

q) details of any incidents where the patient has harmed themselves or others, or threatened harm, or damaged property, or threatened damage;

r) the patient's views, wishes, beliefs, opinions, hopes and concerns;

s) the views of any partner, family member or close friend who takes a lead role in the care and support of the patient but who is not professionally involved;

t) whether the patient is known to any Multi Agency Public Protection Arrangements (MAPPA) meeting or agency and, if so, in which area, for what reason, and at what level – together with the name of the Chair of any MAPPA meeting concerned with the patient, and the name of the representative of the lead agency;

u) in the event that a MAPPA meeting or agency wishes to put forward evidence of its views in relation to the level and management of risk, a summary of those views (or an Executive Summary may be attached to the report); and where relevant, a copy of the Police National Computer record of previous convictions should be attached;

v) in the case of an eligible compliant patient who lacks capacity to agree or object to their placement or treatment, whether or not deprivation of liberty under the Mental Capacity Act 2005 (as amended) would be more appropriate;

w) whether the patient, if absolutely discharged, would be likely to act in a manner harmful to themselves or others, whether any such risks could be managed effectively in the community and, if so, how;

x) whether it continues to be appropriate for the patient to remain liable to be recalled for further medical treatment in hospital and, if so, why;

y) whether, and if so the extent to which, it is desirable to continue, vary and/or add to any conditions currently imposed;

z) any recommendations to the tribunal, with reasons.

E. PATIENTS UNDER THE AGE OF 18

34. All the above requirements in respect of statements and reports apply, as appropriate, **3–201** depending upon the type of case.

35. In addition, *for all patients under the age of 18*, the **Social Circumstances Report** must also state:

a) the names and addresses of any people with parental responsibility, and how they acquired parental responsibility;

b) which public bodies either have worked together or need to liaise in relation to after-care services that may be provided under Section 117 of the Act;

c) the outcome of any liaison that has taken place;

d) if liaison has not taken place, why not and when liaison will take place;

e) the details of any multi-agency care plan in place or proposed;

f) whether there are any issues as to funding the care plan and, if so, the date by which those issues will be resolved;

g) the name and contact details of the patient's Care Co-ordinator, Community Psychiatric Nurse, Social Worker/AMHP or Social Supervisor;

h) whether the patient's needs have been assessed under the Children Act 1989 or the Chronically Sick and Disabled Persons Act 1970 and, if not, the reasons why such an assessment has not been carried out and whether it is proposed to carry out such an assessment;

i) if there has been such an assessment, what needs or requirements have been identified and how those needs or requirements will be met;

j) if the patient is subject to or has been the subject of a Care Order or an Interim Care Order:

- the date and duration of any such order;
- the identity of the relevant local authority;
- the identity of any person(s) with whom the local authority shares parental responsibility;
- whether there are any proceedings which have yet to conclude and, if so, the court in which proceedings are taking place and the date of the next hearing;
- whether the patient comes under the Children (Leaving Care) Act 2000;
- whether there has been any liaison between, on the one hand, social workers responsible for mental health services to children and adolescents and, on the other hand, those responsible for such services to adults;
- the name of the social worker within the relevant local authority who is discharging the function of the Nearest Relative under Section 27 of the Act;

k) if the patient is subject to guardianship under Section 7 of the Act, whether any orders have been made under the Children Act 1989 in respect of the patient, and what consultation there has been with the guardian;

l) if the patient is a Ward of Court, when the patient was made a ward of court and what steps have been taken to notify the court that made the order of any significant steps taken, or to be taken, in respect of the patient;

m) whether any other orders under the Children Act 1989 are in existence in respect of the patient and, if so, the details of those orders, together with the date on which such orders were made, and whether they are final or interim orders;

n) if a patient has been or is a looked after child under Section 20 of the Children Act 1989, when the child became looked after, why the child became looked after, what steps have been taken to discharge the obligations of the local authority under Paragraph 17(1) of Schedule 2 of the Children Act 1989, and what steps are being taken (if required) to discharge the obligations of the local authority under Paragraph 10 (b) of Schedule 2 of the Children Act 1989;

o) if a patient has been treated by a local authority as a child in need (which includes a child who has a mental disorder) under Section 17(11) of the Children Act 1989, the period or periods for which the child has been so treated, why they were considered to be a child in need, what services were or are being made available to the child by virtue of that status, and details of any assessment of the child;

p) if a patient has been the subject of a secure accommodation order under Section 25 of the Children Act 1989, the date on which the order was made, the reasons it was made, and the date it expired;

q) if a patient is a child provided with accommodation under Sections 85 and 86 of the Children Act 1989, what steps have been taken by the accommodating authority or the person carrying on the establishment in question to discharge their notification responsibilities, and what steps have been taken by the local authority to discharge their obligations under Sections 85, 86 and 86A of the Children Act 1989.

PRACTICE DIRECTION
FIRST TIER AND UPPER TRIBUNAL
CHILD, VULNERABLE ADULT AND SENSITIVE WITNESSES

1. In this Practice Direction:

a. "child" means a person who has not attained the age of 18;

b. "vulnerable adult" has the same meaning as in the Safeguarding Vulnerable Groups Act 2006;

c. "sensitive witness" means an adult witness where the quality of evidence given by the witness is likely to be diminished by reason of fear or distress on the part of the witness in connection with giving evidence in the case.

CIRCUMSTANCES UNDER WHICH A CHILD, VULNERABLE ADULT OR SENSITVE WITNESS MAY GIVE EVIDENCE

2. A child, vulnerable adult or sensitive witness will only be required to attend as a witness and give evidence at a hearing where the Tribunal determines that the evidence is necessary to enable the fair hearing of the case and their welfare would not be prejudiced by doing so.

3. In determining whether it is necessary for a child, vulnerable adult or sensitive witness to give evidence to enable the fair hearing of a case the Tribunal should have regard to all the available evidence and any representations made by the parties.

4. In determining whether the welfare of the child, vulnerable adult or sensitive witness would be prejudiced it may be appropriate for the Tribunal to invite submissions from interested persons, such as a child's parents.

5. The Tribunal may decline to issue a witness summons under the Tribunal Procedure Rules or to permit a child, vulnerable adult or sensitive witness to give evidence where it is satisfied that the evidence is not necessary to enable the fair hearing of the case and must decline to do so where the witness's welfare would be prejudiced by them giving evidence.

MANNER IN WHICH EVIDENCE IS GIVEN

6. The Tribunal must consider how to facilitate the giving of any evidence by a child, vulnerable adult or sensitive witness.

7. It may be appropriate for the Tribunal to direct that the evidence should be given by telephone, video link or other means directed by the Tribunal, or to direct that a person be appointed for the purpose of the hearing who has the appropriate skills or experience in facilitating the giving of evidence by a child, vulnerable adult or sensitive witness.

8. This Practice Direction is made by the Senior President of Tribunals with the agreement of the Lord Chancellor. It is made in the exercise of powers conferred by the Tribunals, Courts and Enforcement Act 2007.

LORD JUSTICE CARNWATH
SENIOR PRESIDENT OF TRIBUNALS
30 October 2008

PRACTICE STATEMENT
DELEGATION OF FUNCTIONS TO STAFF AND TO REGISTRARS ON OR AFTER 27 APRIL 2015
FIRST-TIER TRIBUNAL
HEALTH, EDUCATION & SOCIAL CARE CHAMBER
(MENTAL HEALTH)

3–205   1. This Practice Statement replaces the previous Practice Statement for mental health cases dated 10th June 2014 in respect of authorised tribunal staff and approved Registrars.

2. In accordance with rule 4(1) of The Tribunal Procedure (First-tier Tribunal) (Health, Education and Social Care Chamber) Rules 2008 the Senior President of Tribunals hereby approves that, in relation to mental health cases (as defined in rule 1(3)), the following specified functions of the Health, Education & Social Care Chamber of the First-tier Tribunal may be carried out by those members of staff appointed under section 40(1) of the Tribunals, Courts and Enforcement Act 2007 where those members of tribunal staff have been authorised by an Operations Manager (B and C) of the First-tier Tribunal Mental Health in relation to each specified function.

(a) The issue of standard non-compliance directions by authorised tribunal staff for information and reports required under rule 32. The non-compliance directions are to be in standard form (as approved, from time to time, by the relevant Deputy Chamber President) and, in the absence of an application under rule 5(3)(a), are to be sent to the defaulting person following non-compliance with rule 32 and the most recent Senior President's Practice Direction on the Contents of Reports in Mental Health Cases;

(b) The giving of consent by authorised tribunal staff under rule 5(3)(a) to an application made in writing by the Responsible Authority (or, in the case of a conditionally discharged patient, by the Responsible Clinician or the Social Supervisor) to extend time for compliance with rule 32(4)(b) and rule 32(6) obligations subject to the application being made on or prior to the original date for compliance and subject to the maximum extension for compliance being 7 days;

(c) The giving of consent by authorised tribunal staff under rule 17(2) to a notice of withdrawal lodged by or on behalf of a patient by a representative under rule 17(1)(a), by those tribunal staff responsible for receiving and processing notices of withdrawal, subject to the notice of withdrawal being received by the tribunal 48 hours or more before the scheduled start time of the hearing of the application to the tribunal; and subject to the case not being part-heard, there being in existence no concurrent application or reference, and no other reason for tribunal staff to believe that consent to the withdrawal should be refused, such as it appearing that the withdrawal is merely tactical;

(d) The issue of an order to any person in standard form (as approved, from time to time, by the relevant Deputy Chamber President) to answer questions or produce any documents in that person's control which relate to any issue in the proceedings pursuant to rule 16(1)(b) following non-compliance with a request made under rule 5(3)(d) including a standard non-compliance direction;

(e) The issue of an order appointing a representative under rule 11(7)(a) and (b) and the issue of a direction in standard form (as approved, from time to time, by the relevant Deputy Chamber President) in order to obtain sufficient information from the parties to make such an order;

(f) The issue of an order under rule 5 (3)(b) for two or more sets of proceedings in relation to the same patient and involving identical parties to be heard together;

(g) The correction, by those tribunal staff responsible for checking and promulgating decisions, of a clear and obvious clerical mistake, or other clear and obvious accidental slips or omissions, in any document recording a decision or direction of the tribunal.

3. The Senior President of Tribunals hereby approves that a legally qualified member of staff appointed under section 40(1) of the Tribunals, Courts and Enforcement Act 2007 may carry out the following functions of the Health, Education and Social Care Chamber of the First-tier Tribunal under the Tribunal Procedure (First-tier Tribunal) (Health, Education and Social Care Chamber) Rules 2008 where that legally qualified member of staff, who for the purpose of exercising those functions shall be known as a Registrar, has been authorised by the Chamber President or a Deputy Chamber President of the Health, Education and Social Care Chamber to exercise those functions in respect of Mental Health cases—

(a) Exercising any case management powers under rule 5 except under rule 5(3)(l);

(b) Dealing with irregularities under rule 7(2)(a) or (b);

(c) Striking out if the tribunal does not have jurisdiction under rule 8(3)(a);

(d) Giving directions to substitute or add a party or parties under rule 9;

(e) Appointing a legal representative for the patient under rule 11(7);

(f) Making orders prohibiting disclosure or publication of documents or information under rule 14;

(g) Giving directions in relation to evidence and submissions under rule 15(1);

(h) Summoning witnesses and issuing orders to persons to answer questions or produce documents under rule 16;

(i) Consenting to withdrawal of a case, or directing reinstatement of a case, under rule 17;

(j) Deciding to whom notice of proceedings should be sent under rule 33;

(k) Correcting clerical mistakes or other accidental slips or omissions in decisions or records of decisions under rule 44;

(l) Exercising the powers of a judge under rule 4(3) where an authorised member of tribunal staff has made the initial decision under the delegated powers set out in paragraph 2 of this Practice Statement.

4. In accordance with rule 4(3) of the Tribunal Procedure (First Tier Tribunal) (Health Education and Social Care Chamber) Rules 2008, within 14 days after the date that the Tribunal sends notice of a decision made by an authorised member of tribunal staff or a Registrar (pursuant to an approval under paragraph 3 above) to a party, that party may apply in writing to the Tribunal for the decision to be considered afresh by a judge (if the decision was made under paragraph 3 above) or by a Judge or Registrar if made under paragraph 2 above).

SIR JEREMY SULLIVAN
SENIOR PRESIDENT OF TRIBUNALS
27 April 2015

PART 4

GOVERNMENT GUIDANCE

EXTRACTS FROM THE MENTAL HEALTH ACT 1983
CODE OF PRACTICE

PUBLISHED 2015, PURSUANT TO SECTION 118 OF THE ACT

DEPARTMENT OF HEALTH

ARRANGEMENT OF EXTRACTS

Guiding principles (Ch.1)

Privacy, safety and dignity (Ch.8)

Confidentiality and information sharing (Ch.10)

The Tribunal (Ch.12)

Detention under the Act or deprivation of liberty under a DoLS authorisation? (Ch.13, paras 13.49–13.62)

Applications for detention in hospital (Ch.14)

Police powers and places of safety (Ch.16)

Transport of patients (Ch.17)

Children and young people under the age of 18 (Ch.19)

The appropriate medical treatment test (Ch.23)

Medical treatment (Ch.24)

Treatments subject to special rules and procedures (Ch.25)

Procedures for the safe use of restrictive interventions (Ch.26, paras 26.62–26.172)

Guardianship (Ch.30)

Guardianship, leave of absence or CTO (Ch.31)

After-care (Ch.33)

Hospital managers' discharge power (Ch.38)

Information for victims (Ch.40)

1. GUIDING PRINCIPLES

Why read this chapter?

4–001   1.1 It is essential that all those undertaking functions under the Act understand the five sets of overarching principles which should always be considered when making decisions in relation to care, support or treatment provided under the Act. This chapter provides an explanation of the overarching principles and stresses that they should be considered when making decisions under the Act. Although all are of equal importance the weight given to each principle in reaching a particular decision will depend on context and the nature of the decision being made.

The five overarching principles are:

Least restrictive option and maximising independence

Where it is possible to treat a patient safely and lawfully without detaining them under the Act, the patient should not be detained. Wherever possible a patient's independence should be encouraged and supported with a focus on promoting recovery wherever possible.

Empowerment and involvement

Patients should be fully involved in decisions about care, support and treatment. The views of families, carers and others, if appropriate, should be fully considered when taking decisions. Where decisions are taken which are contradictory to views expressed, professionals should explain the reasons for this.

Respect and dignity

Patients, their families and carers should be treated with respect and dignity and listened to by professionals.

Purpose and effectiveness

Decisions about care and treatment should be appropriate to the patient, with clear therapeutic aims, promote recovery and should be performed to current national guidelines and/or current, available best practice guidelines.

Efficiency and equity

Providers, commissioners and other relevant organisations should work together to ensure that the quality of commissioning and provision of mental healthcare services are of high quality and are given equal priority to physical health and social care services. All relevant services should work together to facilitate timely, safe and supportive discharge from detention.

LEAST RESTRICTIVE OPTION AND MAXIMISING INDEPENDENCE

4–002   1.2 Where it is possible to treat a patient safely and lawfully without detaining them under the Act, the patient should not be detained.

1.3 Commissioners, providers and other relevant agencies should work together to prevent mental health crises and, where possible, reduce the use of detention through prevention and early intervention by commissioning a range of services that are accessible, responsive and as high quality as other health emergency services.

1.4 If the Act is used, detention should be used for the shortest time necessary in the least restrictive hospital setting available, and be delivered as close as reasonably possible to a location that the patient identifies they would like to be close to (eg their home or close to a family member or carer). In cases where the patient lacks capacity to make a decision about the location they would like to be close to, a best interests decision on the location should be taken. This will promote recovery and enable the patient to maintain contact with family, friends, and their community.

1.5 Any restrictions should be the minimum necessary to safely provide the care or treatment required having regard to whether the purpose for the restriction can be achieved in a way that is less restrictive of the person's rights and freedom of action.

1.6 Restrictions that apply to all patients in a particular setting (blanket or global restrictions) should be avoided. There may be settings where there will be restrictions on all patients that are necessary for their safety or for that of others. Any such restrictions should have a clear justification for the particular hospital, group or ward to which they apply. Blanket restrictions should never be for the convenience of the provider. Any such restrictions, should be agreed by hospital managers, be documented with the reasons for such restrictions clearly described and subject to governance procedures that exist in the relevant organisation.

EMPOWERMENT AND INVOLVEMENT

1.7 Patients should be given the opportunity to be involved in planning, developing and reviewing their own care and treatment to help ensure that it is delivered in a way that is as appropriate and effective for them as possible. Wherever possible, care plans should be produced in consultation with the patient. **4–003**

1.8 A patient's views, past and present wishes and feelings (whether expressed at the time or in advance), should be considered so far as they are reasonably ascertainable. Patients should be encouraged and supported to develop advance statements of wishes and feeling and express their views about future care and treatment when they are well.

1.9 The patient's choices and views should be fully recorded. Where a decision in the care plan is contrary to the wishes of the patient or others the reasons for this should be transparent, explained to them and fully documented.

1.10 Patients should be enabled to participate in decision-making as far as they are capable of doing so. Consideration should be given to what assistance or support a patient may need to participate in decision-making and any such assistance or support should be provided, to ensure maximum involvement possible. This includes being given sufficient information about their care and treatment in a format that is easily understandable to them.

1.11 Patients should be encouraged and supported in involving carers (unless there are particular reasons to the contrary). Professionals should fully consider their views when making decisions.

1.12 Patients should be informed of the support that an advocate can provide, including carers or, if they are eligible, an independent mental health advocate (IMHA) (or an independent mental capacity advocate (IMCA) where relevant). Local authorities should ensure that timely access to IMHAs is available and that IMHAs have appropriate training and skills to support the patient effectively including where a patient has particular needs.

RESPECT AND DIGNITY

4–004   1.13 Patients and carers should be treated with respect and dignity. Practitioners performing functions under the Act should respect the rights and dignity of patients and their carers, while also ensuring their safety and that of others.

1.14 People taking decisions under the Act must recognise and respect the diverse needs, values and circumstances of each patient, including their age, disability, gender reassignment, marriage and civil partnership, pregnancy and maternity, race, religion or belief, sex and sexual orientation, and culture. There must be no unlawful discrimination.

PURPOSE AND EFFECTIVENESS

4–005   1.15 Care, support and treatment given under the Act should be given in accordance with up-to-date national guidance and/or current best practice from professional bodies, where this is available. Treatment should address an individual patient's needs, taking account of their circumstances and preferences where appropriate.

1.16 Patients should be offered treatment and care in environments that are safe for them, staff and any visitors and are supportive and, therapeutic. Practitioners should deliver a range of treatments which focus on positive clinical and personal outcomes, where appropriate. Care plans for detained patients should focus on maximising recovery and ending detention as soon as possible. Commissioners, providers and professionals should consider the broad range of interventions and services needed to promote recovery not only in hospital but after a patient leaves hospital, including maintaining relationships, housing, opportunities for meaningful daytime activity and employment opportunities,

1.17 Physical healthcare needs should be assessed and addressed including promotion of healthy living and steps taken to reduce any potential side effects associated with treatments.

EFFICIENCY AND EQUITY

4–006   1.18 Commissioners and providers, including their staff, should give equal priority to mental health as they do to physical health conditions.

1.19 Where patients are subject to compulsory detention, health and social care agencies should work together to deliver a programme of care that, as far as practicable, minimises the duration of detention, facilitates safe discharge from hospital and takes into account the patient's wishes.

1.20 Commissioners, providers and other relevant organisations should establish effective relationships to ensure efficient working with accountability defined through joint governance arrangements. Joint working should be used to minimise delay in care planning needed to facilitate discharge.

1.21 Commissioners, providers and other relevant organisations should ensure that their staff have sufficient skills, information and knowledge about the Act and provision of services to support all their patients. There should be clear mechanisms for accessing specialist support for those with additional needs.

USING THE PRINCIPLES

4–007   1.22 All decisions must be lawful and informed by good professional practice. Lawfulness necessarily includes compliance with the Human Rights Act 1998 (HRA) and Equality Act 2010.

1.23 All five sets of principles are of equal importance, and should inform any decision made under the Act. The weight given to each principle in reaching a particular decision will need to be balanced in different ways according to the circumstances and nature of each particular decision. The guidance in the Code is based on these principles and reference is made to them throughout the Code.

1.24 Commissioners, providers, professionals and others providing care under the Act should document, and justify, any decision to depart from the Code or a particular guiding principle. The Care Quality Commission will look for evidence of this during their inspections and commissioners can use it as part of their contract monitoring.

8. PRIVACY, SAFETY AND DIGNITY

Why read this chapter?

8.1 This chapter deals with privacy, safety and dignity in hospitals where **4–008** patients are detained under the Act, including access to telephones and other mobile computing devices, access to the internet, and the use of searches.

8.2 Privacy, safety and dignity are important constituents of a therapeutic environment and hospital staff should respect a patient's privacy as far as possible, while maintaining safety. Patients should have every opportunity to maintain contact with family and friends by telephone, and hospitals should ensure they have policies for the use of mobile phones and computing devices.

8.3 Sleeping and bathroom areas should be segregated to protect the needs of patients of different genders and transgender patients. The nature of engagement with patients and of therapeutic environments and the structure and quality of life on a ward are important in encouraging patients to remain in the ward and minimising a culture of containment. The chapter also includes guidance on conducting personal and other searches, enhanced security, physical security and blanket locked door policy.[1]

RESPECT FOR PRIVACY

8.4 Article 8 of the European Convention on Human Rights (ECHR) requires **4–009** public authorities to respect a person's right to a private life. Article 8 has particular importance for people detained under the Act. Privacy, safety and dignity are important constituents of a therapeutic environment. Hospital staff should make conscious efforts to respect the privacy and dignity of patients as far as possible, while maintaining safety, including enabling a patient to wash and dress in private, and to send and receive mail, including in electronic formats, without restriction. Respecting patients' privacy encompasses the circumstances in which patients may meet or communicate with people of their choosing in private, including in their own rooms, and the protection of their private property.

BLANKET RESTRICTIONS

8.5 In this chapter, the term 'blanket restrictions' refers to rules or policies that **4–010** restrict a patient's liberty and other rights, which are routinely applied to all

---

[1] For patients in high security hospitals, this chapter should be read in conjunction with The High Security Psychiatric Services (Arrangements for Safety and Security) Directions 2013 and associated guidance. https://www.gov.uk/government/publications/high-security-psychiatric-services-directions.

patients, or to classes of patients, or within a service, without individual risk assessments to justify their application. Blanket restrictions should be avoided unless they can be justified as necessary and proportionate responses to risks identified for particular individuals. The impact of a blanket restriction on each patient should be considered and documented in the patient's records.

8.6 Restrictions should never be introduced or applied in order to punish or humiliate, but only ever as a proportionate and measured response to an individually identified risk; they should be applied for no longer than can be shown to be necessary.

8.7 Blanket restrictions include restrictions concerning: access to the outside world, access to the internet, access to (or banning) mobile phones and chargers, incoming or outgoing mail, visiting hours, access to money or the ability to make personal purchases, or taking part in preferred activities. Such practices have no basis in national guidance or best practice; they promote neither independence nor recovery, and may breach a patient's human rights.

8.8 Within secure service settings some restrictions may form part of a broader package of physical, procedural and relational security measures associated with an individual's identified need for enhanced security in order to manage high levels of risk to other patients, staff and members of the public. The individual's need for such security measures should be justified to meet the admission criteria for any secure service. In any event, the application of security measures should be based on the needs of and identified risks for individual patients, and impose the least restriction possible. Where individual patients in secure services are assessed as not requiring certain security measures, consideration should be given to relaxing their application, where this will not compromise the overall security of the service. Where this is not possible, consideration should also be given as to whether the patient should more appropriately be managed in a service that operates under conditions of lesser security.

8.9 No form of blanket restriction should be implemented unless expressly authorised by the hospital managers on the basis of the organisation's policy and subject to local accountability and governance arrangements.

BLANKET LOCKED DOOR POLICY

4–011   8.10 A blanket locked door policy which affects all patients in a hospital or on a ward could, depending on its implementation, amount to a restriction or a deprivation of liberty.

8.11 It is unlikely that there will be a deprivation of liberty if an informal patient, who has capacity to consent to being admitted and has done so, is informed of the locked door policy and consents to being informally admitted and remaining on the ward under these conditions. The patient should be told who they can speak to if they wish to leave and must be able to leave at any time they wish to, unless they are being detained using the holding powers under section 5 of the Act (chapter 18) or an application for detention (chapters 14 and 15).

8.12 A patient's article 8 rights should be protected by ensuring a locked door policy only imposes proportionate restrictions on their contact with family and friends which can be justified as being in the interests of the health and safety of the patient or others. The impact of a locked door policy on each patient should be considered and documented in the patient's records. The policy should conform to the 'empowerment and involvement' guiding principle (paragraphs 1.7–1.12).

8.13 Hospitals should not lock patients in clinical areas simply because of inadequate staffing levels. Local policies for locking clinical areas should be clearly displayed and explained to each patient on admission.

8.14 The safety of informal patients, who would be at risk of harm if they wandered out of a clinical environment at will, should be ensured by adequate staffing levels, positive therapeutic engagement and good observation, not simply by locking the doors of the unit or ward.

8.15 Services should consider how to reduce the negative psychological and behavioural effects of having locked doors, whether or not patients are formally detained.

PRIVATE TELEPHONE CALLS AND E-MAIL AND INTERNET ACCESS

8.16 Communication with family and friends is integral to a patient's care and **4–012** hospitals should make every effort to support the patient in making and maintaining contact with family and friends by telephone, mobile, e-mail or social media. Providers should, however, provide patients access to a coin or card operated phone.

8.17 Mobile phones and other electronic devices commonly have functions including cameras and video and voice recording capability. There is therefore the potential for patients and visitors to use such equipment in a way that interferes with the confidentiality, dignity and privacy of other patients, staff and visitors. Staff should be mindful of enabling patients and visitors to maintain communication and contact while protecting others against the misuse of such technology.

8.18 When patients are admitted, staff should assess the risk and appropriateness of patients having access to mobile phones and other electronic devices and this should be detailed in the patient's care plan. Particular consideration should be given to people who are deaf who will have special communication needs. Patients should be able to use such devices if deemed appropriate and safe for them to do so and access should only be limited or restricted in certain risk-assessed situations.

8.19 Hospital managers should have a policy for the possession and use of mobile phones and other mobile devices (such as laptops and tablets). These should be proportionate to risk and not seek to impose blanket restrictions on patients.

8.20 When drawing up their policy on the use of mobile phones and mobile devices, hospital managers should bear in mind the following points.

- Mobile phones and mobile computing devices provide a readily available means of communication with family and friends and are in widespread use. Most detained patients are therefore likely to have one. It is unlikely to be appropriate to impose a blanket restriction banning their use except in units specifically designed to provide enhanced levels of security in order to protect the public. Blanket restrictions may breach article 8.

- Different considerations will apply to different locations within the hospital. There may be valid reasons for banning or limiting the use of mobile phones or mobile computing devices in some parts of the premises to which detained patients have access or certain types of mobile phone or mobile computing device, eg because of the potential risk of interference with medical and other electronic equipment which could adversely affect the health of patients or because of the risk of intrusion into the privacy of other patients or others.

- Each patient should expect a peaceful environment, and that constant interruptions from ringing telephones have a potentially anti-therapeutic effect.

- It may be reasonable to require mobile phones and mobile computing devices to be switched off except where their use is permitted and to restrict their use to designated areas to which detained patients have access.

- Many mobile phones and mobile computing devices have cameras and give access to the internet and can be used as sound recorders. This creates a potential for the violation of the privacy and dignity of other patients, staff and visitors to the ward and may constitute a security risk. It would therefore be appropriate to stipulate the circumstances in which photographs, videos and sound recordings can be taken, eg only with specific permission from hospital staff and the patients involved.

- The difficulty in identifying when camera functions are being used may be an additional reason for restricting the areas in which mobile phones and computing devices may be used.

- It is important to ensure that the hospital's policy on the use of mobile phones and mobile computing devices can be enforced effectively, eg it may be appropriate in certain circumstances to confiscate mobile phones or mobile computing devices from patients who consistently refuse to comply with the rules.

- Any decision to prevent the use of cameras or to confiscate a mobile phone or mobile computing device should be fully documented and be subject to periodic review.

- There should be rules on when staff and visitors can bring mobile phones and mobile computing devices into a secure setting.

- The normal rules governing the use of the hospital's power supply to charge mobile phones or mobile computing devices may need to be varied for detained patients (given the restrictions with which such patients are faced).

- Staff should be fully informed of the hospital's policy, and steps should be taken to communicate it to all patients, carers, families and visitors, eg by displaying it clearly in each unit and providing it in a format and language that a patient can understand.

- The policy will need to be reviewed regularly, and updated where necessary, in the light of experience. It is good practice to involve patients, former patients and their carers in drawing up the policy.

8.21 Managers should develop policies on access by patients to e-mail and internet facilities by means of the hospital's IT infrastructure. This guidance should cover the availability of such facilities and rules prohibiting access to illegal or what would otherwise be considered inappropriate material, eg pornography, gambling or websites promoting violence, abuse or hate. Additionally, the guidance should cover the appropriate use of social media such as Skype. A blanket restriction on access to the internet could breach article 8 if it cannot be justified as necessary and proportionate. For further details about not applying blanket restrictions see paragraphs 8.5–8.9.

8.22 Managers should also develop guidance on the use of social media. As in paragraph 8.21 above, a blanket restriction on the use of social media could breach article 8 if it cannot be justified as necessary and proportionate. Staff should remind patients of confidentiality requirements, and the implications of breaching patient and staff confidentiality, and encourage patients to consider what they post on social media. Where wards contain coin-operated and card-operated telephones, hospital managers should ensure that patients are able use them without being overheard. Installing booths or hoods around them may help to provide the necessary level of privacy. Some patients may need help to make a phone call, but should still be given privacy during the call.

8.23 The principle that should underpin hospital or ward policies on all telephone use is that detained patients are not free to leave the premises but that their freedom to communicate with family and friends should be maintained as far as possible and restricted to the minimum extent necessary.

PRIVATE PROPERTY

8.24 Hospitals should provide adequate storage in lockable facilities (with staff **4–013** override) for the clothing and other personal possessions which patients may keep with them on the ward and for the secure central storage of anything of value or items which may pose a risk to the patient or to others, eg razors. Information about arrangements for storage should be easily accessible to patients on the ward. Hospitals should compile an inventory of what has been allowed to be kept on the ward and what has been stored and give a copy to the patient. The inventory should be updated when necessary. Patients should always be able to access their private property on request if it is safe to do so.

SEPARATE FACILITIES FOR MEN AND WOMEN

8.25 All sleeping and bathroom areas should be segregated, and patients should **4–013** not have to walk through an area occupied by another sex to reach toilets or bathrooms. Separate male and female toilets and bathrooms should be provided, as should women-only day rooms. Women-only environments are important because of the increased risk of sexual and physical abuse and risk of trauma for women who have had prior experience of such abuse. Consideration should be given to the particular needs of transgender patients.[2]

8.26 A patient should not be admitted to mixed-sex accommodation. It may be acceptable, in a clinical emergency, to admit a patient temporarily to a single, ensuite room in the opposite-gender area of a ward. In such cases, a full risk-assessment should be carried out and the patient's safety, privacy and dignity maintained. Steps should be taken to rectify the situation as soon as possible. For more information see NHS guidance on eliminating the use of mixed-sex accommodation in relation to mental health patients. This includes information

---

[2] Eliminating Mixed Sex Accommodation. Department of Health. 2009. PL/CNO/2009/2. https://www.gov.uk/government/uploads/system/uploads/attachment_data/file/200215/CNO_note_dh_098893.pdf.

on temporary admissions in exceptional circumstances and the required reporting to the NHS Commissioning Board on mental health patients.[3]

SEPARATE FACILITIES FOR OTHER REASONS

4–015 8.27 Arrangements for the patient's accommodation should also consider the patient's history and personal circumstances, including:

- history and personal circumstances where known, including history of sexual or physical abuse and risks of trauma

- the particular needs of transgender patients

- cultural or religious preferences

- mothers and babies during and after pregnancy, or

- other health conditions (physical disabilities, learning disabilities or sensory impairments.

8.28 If, in an emergency, it is necessary to treat a patient in an environment that does not fully meet their needs, then senior management should be informed, steps should be taken to rectify the situation as soon as possible, and staff should protect the patient's privacy and dignity against intrusions—particularly in sleeping accommodation, toilets and bathrooms.

PERSONAL AND OTHER SEARCHES

4–016 8.29 Hospital managers should ensure that there is an operational policy for searching patients detained under the Act, their belongings and surroundings and their visitors. When preparing the policy, hospital managers should consider the position of informal patients. The policy should be clearly displayed and communicated to patients in a format and language they understand.

8.30 The policy should be based on the following clear principles:

- the intention is to create and maintain a therapeutic environment in which treatment may take place and to ensure the security of the premises and the safety of patients, staff and the public

- the authority to conduct a search of a person or their property is controlled by law, and it is important that hospital staff are aware of whether they have legal authority to carry out any such search

- searching should be proportionate to the identified risk and should involve the minimum possible intrusion into the individual's privacy, and

- all searches will be undertaken with due regard to and respect for the person's dignity and privacy.

8.31 The policy may extend to the routine and random searching without cause of detained patients, if necessary without their consent, but only in exceptional circumstances. For example, such searches may be necessary if the patients

---

[3] Eliminating Mixed Sex Accommodation. Department of Health. 2010. PL/CNO/2010/3. https://www.gov.uk/government/uploads/system/uploads/attachment_data/file/215932/dh_121860.pdf.

detained in a particular unit tend to have dangerous or violent propensities which means they create a self-evident pressing need for additional security.

8.32 Patients, staff and visitors should be informed that there is a policy on searching. Information about searches should be provided in a variety of formats to meet patients' and visitors' needs and should be readily available.

Conducting personal and other searches

8.33 The consent of the person should always be sought before a personal **4–017** search of them or a search of their possessions is attempted. If consent is given, the search should be carried out with regard to ensuring the maximum dignity and privacy of the person. Undertaking a personal search in a public area will only be justified in exceptional circumstances.

8.34 Consent obtained by means of a threat, intimidation or inducement is likely to render the search illegal. Any person who is to be searched personally or whose possessions are to be searched should be informed that they do not have to consent.

8.35 A person being searched or whose possessions are the subject of a search should be kept informed of what is happening and why. If they do not understand or are not fluent in English, the services of an interpreter should be sought, if practicable. The specific needs of people with impaired hearing or a learning disability and those of children and young people should be considered.

8.36 A personal search should be carried out by a member of the same sex, unless necessity dictates otherwise. The search should be carried out in a way that maintains the person's privacy and dignity and respects issues of gender, culture and faith. It is always advisable to have another member of the hospital staff present during a search, especially if it is not possible to conduct a same-sex search.

8.37 A comprehensive record of every search, including the reasons for it and details of any consequent risk assessment, should be made.

8.38 Staff involved in undertaking searches should receive appropriate instruction and refresher training.

8.39 In certain circumstances, it may be necessary to search a detained patient or their possessions without their consent.

8.40 If a detained patient refuses consent or lacks capacity to decide whether or not to consent to the search, their responsible clinician (or, failing that, another senior clinician with knowledge of the patient's case) should be contacted without delay in the first instance, if practicable, so that any clinical objection to searching by force may be raised. The patient should be kept separated and under close observation, while being informed of what is happening and why, in terms appropriate to their understanding. This is particularly important for individuals who may lack capacity to decide whether or not to consent to the search.[4] Searches should not be delayed if there is reason to think that the person is in possession of anything that may pose an immediate risk to their own safety or that of anyone else.

8.41 If a search is considered necessary, despite the patient's objections, and there is no clinical objection to one being conducted, the search should be carried out. If force has to be used, it should be the minimum necessary.

---

[4] Separation of a patient under close observation in order to await the arrival of the responsible clinician is different to seclusion (which is defined at paragraph 26.103).

8.42 The policy should set out the steps to be taken to resolve any disagreement or dispute where there is a clinical objection to a search.

8.43 Where a patient physically resists being personally searched, physical intervention should normally only proceed on the basis of a multi-disciplinary assessment, unless it is urgently required. A post-incident review should follow every search undertaken where consent has been withheld.

8.44 There should be support for patients and for staff who are affected by the process of searching. This may be particularly necessary where a personal search has had to proceed without consent or has involved physical intervention (see paragraphs 8.40–8.43 and chapter 26 on use of physical interventions).

8.45 Where a patient's belongings are removed during a search, the patient should be told why they have been removed, given a receipt for them, told where the items will be stored, and when they will be returned.

8.46 The exercise of powers of search should be audited regularly and the outcomes reported to the hospital managers.

HOSPITAL ACCOMMODATION OFFERING CONDITIONS OF ENHANCED SECURITY

4–018   8.47 Some detained patients may be liable to present a particular danger to themselves or to others and therefore need to be accommodated in wards or units specifically designed to offer enhanced levels of physical security. For patients detained under part 3 of the Act, this may be a requirement of a court or of the Secretary of State for Justice, but in many cases the decision will lie primarily with the patient's responsible clinician.

8.48 When considering whether patients should be placed in, moved to or remain in such a ward or unit, responsible clinicians should, in consultation with the multi-disciplinary team, ensure that:

- they have carefully weighed the patient's individual circumstances and the degree of risk involved, and

- they have assessed the relative clinical considerations of placing the patient in an environment with enhanced physical security, in addition to or as opposed to providing care by way of intensive staffing.

8.49 Treatment in conditions of enhanced security should last for the minimum period necessary. Where responsible clinicians have taken the decision to transfer a patient within a hospital to a ward with enhanced security, they should ensure that arrangements are made to facilitate the patient's prompt return to a less secure ward when that enhanced security is no longer required.

8.50 Where responsible clinicians believe that patients no longer require conditions of enhanced security (or the current level of security), they should take steps to arrange their transfer to more appropriate accommodation. Where necessary, this may involve identifying another hospital that is willing and able to offer the patient suitable accommodation.

8.51 In the case of restricted patients, it will be necessary to seek the consent of the Secretary of State for Justice for a transfer to another hospital or, where the patient's detention is restricted to a particular unit, for a move within the same hospital.

8.52 Managers of hospitals offering accommodation with enhanced levels of security should ensure that:

- accommodation specifically designated for this purpose has adequate staffing levels, and

- written guidelines are drawn up, setting out the categories of patient for whom it is appropriate to use physically secure conditions and those for whom it is not appropriate.

PHYSICAL SECURITY IN OTHER HOSPITAL ACCOMMODATION

8.53 Hospital managers will need to consider what arrangements should be put **4–019** in place to protect the safety of patients who are not subject to enhanced security.

8.54 Patients admitted to acute wards, whether or not they are formally detained there, will have complex and specific needs. In such an environment, ward staff will need to balance competing priorities and interests when determining what safety measures are necessary. This should not amount to a blanket locked door policy (see paragraphs 8.10–8.15 above).

8.55 The intention should be to protect patients, in particular those who are at risk of suicide, self-harm, accidents or inflicting harm on others unless they are prevented from leaving the ward. Arrangements should also aim not to impose any unnecessary or disproportionate restrictions on patients or to make them feel as though they are subject to such restrictions. It may also be necessary to have in place arrangements for protecting patients and others from people whose mere presence on a ward may pose a risk to their health or safety.

8.56 It should be borne in mind that the nature of engagement with patients and of therapeutic interventions and the structure and quality of life on the ward are important factors in encouraging patients to remain in the ward and in minimising a culture of containment.

8.57 All patients should have regular access to outside space. Locking doors, placing staff on reception to control entry to particular areas, and the use of electronic swipe cards, electronic key fobs and other technological innovations of this sort are all methods that providers should consider to manage entry to and exit from clinical areas to ensure the safety of their patients and of others.

8.58 If providers are to manage entry to and exit from the ward effectively, they will need to have a policy for doing so. A written policy that sets out precisely what the ward arrangements are and how patients can exit from the ward, if they are legally free to leave, should be drawn up and given to all patients in the ward. The policy should be explained to patients on admission and to their visitors. In addition to producing the policy in English, providers may need to consider drawing it up it in other languages if these are in common use in the local area, as well as in accessible formats.

8.59 If managing entry and exit by means of locked external doors (or other physical barriers) is considered to be an appropriate way to maintain safety, the practice adopted should be reviewed regularly to ensure that there are clear benefits for patients and that it is not being used for the convenience of staff. It is never acceptable to lock patients and others in clinical areas simply because of inadequate staffing levels. In conjunction with clinical staff, managers should regularly review and evaluate the mix of patients (there may, for example, be some patients who ought to be in a more secure environment), staffing levels and the skills mix and training needs of staff.

10. CONFIDENTIALITY AND INFORMATION SHARING

Why read this chapter?

4–020   10.1 This chapter deals with issues about confidentiality and information sharing which arise in connection with the Act.

10.2 The law on confidentiality is the same for patients subject to the Act as it is for any other patients, except where the Act says otherwise. Under the Act, there are some situations where confidential information about a patient is legally authorised to be disclosed, even if the patient does not consent. Guidance is given on the sharing of information by professionals and agencies to manage serious risks which certain patients pose to others.

SHARING INFORMATION

4–021   10.3 Except where the Act itself says otherwise, the law on confidentiality is the same for patients subject to the Act as it is for any other patients. The box below gives a brief summary of the most fundamental points of the general law. These points are relevant to patients of all ages, although there are some additional considerations in relation to children and young people (see chapter 19).

CONFIDENTIALITY—A BRIEF SUMMARY

There will be specific considerations for healthcare professionals such as doctors and nurses to whom the common law duty of confidentiality applies. The duty arises when one person discloses information to another in circumstances where it is reasonable to expect that the information will be held in confidence. Certain situations, such as discussions with a health professional or social worker, are generally presumed to be confidential.

There are circumstances in which it is both justifiable and important to share otherwise confidential patient information with people outside the immediate team treating a patient. Before considering such disclosure of confidential patient information, the individual's consent should normally be sought.

If a person lacks the capacity to consent to the disclosure, it may be acceptable and appropriate to disclose the information in the person's best interests. Healthcare professionals should use their professional judgement to determine what is in the patient's best interest. This should include consultation with colleagues, and the organisation's Caldicott Guardian[5] and take into account the patient's previously expressed wishes and views. It is also good practice for independent sector providers of NHS-funded services to have a Caldicott Guardian.

---

[5] A Caldicott Guardian is the senior person in the organisation responsible for protecting the confidentiality of patient and service-user information and enabling appropriate information-sharing. Each NHS commissioner, NHS provider and local authority with social services responsibilities is required to have a Caldicott Guardian. It is also good practice for independent sector providers of NHS-funded services to have a Caldicott Guardian.

Otherwise, confidential patient information should be disclosed outside the team only:

- with the patient's consent (where the patient has capacity to consent)
- if there is a specific legal obligation or authority to do so, or
- where there is an overriding public interest in disclosing the information.

The 'public interest' is not the same as what might be of interest to the public. Where confidential patient information is involved, public interest justifications for overriding confidentiality could include (but are not limited to) protecting other people from serious harm and preventing serious crime.

The common law does not normally permit disclosure of confidential patient information solely in the patient's own interests, if they have capacity to consent to the disclosure but refuse to do so.

A person's right to have their privacy respected is protected by article 8 of the European Convention on Human Rights (ECHR). The disclosure of confidential information may be a breach of that right unless it is a necessary and proportionate response to the situation.

10.4 Information sharing between professionals can contribute to and support the care and treatment of patients and help to protect people from harm. This includes information sharing as part of the care programme approach (CPA) (or its equivalent) or the Welsh Measure (see paragraphs 34.24–34.27 for information on the Welsh Measure).

10.5 A range of public agencies is involved in the provision of services to patients who are subject to compulsory measures under the Act, including housing and social services. Patients must be consulted about what information it may be helpful to share with these services and when. Professionals should be clear about how the sharing of such information could benefit the patient or help to prevent serious harm to others and whether there are any potential negative consequences. Advocates and advice services can support patients in helping them decide what information should be shared.

10.6 Sharing information with carers and other people with a valid interest in the care and wellbeing of the patient can contribute to and support their care and treatment. Where patients have capacity to agree and are willing to do so, carers and other people with a valid interest should be given information about the patient's progress to help them form and offer views about the patient's care and provide effective care and support to the patient, especially if the individual is a community patient, subject to guardianship, or on leave. A patient's agreement to such disclosure must be freely given. In the case of patients detained under part 3 of the Act, people with a valid interest may include victims and the families of victims (see chapter 40).

DISCLOSURE OF CONFIDENTIAL PATIENT INFORMATION FOR THE PURPOSES OF THE ACT

4–022   10.7 The Act creates a number of situations where confidential information about patients is legally authorised to be disclosed, even if the patient does not consent. These include:

- reports to the Tribunal when a patient's case is to be considered

- reports to the Care Quality Commission (CQC) in relation to patients who have been treated on the basis of a certificate issued by a second opinion appointed doctor (SOAD), and

- reports to the Secretary of State for Justice on restricted patients.

10.8 The Act also gives certain people and bodies—including the CQC, SOADs and (in certain circumstances) independent mental health advocates (IMHAs)—the right to access records relating to patients.

10.9 In addition, where the Act allows steps to be taken in relation to patients without their consent, it is implicit that confidential patient information may be disclosed only to the extent that it is necessary to take those steps. For example, confidential patient information may be shared to the extent that it is necessary for:

- medical treatment which may be given without a patient's consent under the Act

- safely and securely transport a patient to hospital (or anywhere else) under the Act

- finding and returning a patient who has absconded from legal custody or who is absent without leave, or

- transferring responsibility for a patient who is subject to the Act from one set of people to another (eg where a detained patient is to be transferred from one hospital to another, or where responsibility for a patient is to be transferred between England and another jurisdiction).

10.10 Even though information may be disclosed in these cases, it is still necessary for people proposing to disclose the information to be confident that it is necessary in the circumstances, that the aim of disclosure cannot reasonably be achieved without it, and that any breach of the patient's confidentiality is a proportionate response given the purpose for which the disclosure is being considered. Care must also always be taken to ensure that any information disclosed is accurate.

LIMITATIONS ON SHARING INFORMATION WITH CARERS

4–023   10.11 Simply asking for information from carers, relatives, friends or other people about a patient without that patient's consent need not involve any breach of confidentiality, provided the person requesting the information does not reveal any personal confidential information about the patient which the carer, relative, friend or other person being asked would not legitimately know.

10.12 Apart from information which must be given to nearest relatives, the Act does not create any exceptions to the general law about disclosing confidential patient information to carers, relatives or friends.

10.13 Carers cannot be told a patient's particular diagnosis or be given any other confidential personal information about the patient unless the patient consents or there is another basis on which to disclose it in accordance with the law. Carers, including young carers, should always be offered information which may help them understand the nature of mental disorder generally, the ways it is treated and the operation of the Act.

10.14 Carers, relatives, friends and other people have a right to expect that any personal information about themselves, or any information about the patient which they pass on to professionals in confidence, will be treated as confidential. Unless there is an overriding reason that makes it necessary and there is legal authority to do so, information they provide about patients should not be repeated to patients in a way that might reveal its source, unless the carer, relative, friend or other person was made aware that that could happen and had not objected to it.

SHARING INFORMATION TO MANAGE RISK

10.15 Although information may be disclosed only in line with the law, professionals and agencies may need to share information to manage any serious risks which certain patients pose to others. **4–024**

10.16 Where the issue is the management of the risk of serious harm, the judgement required is normally a balance between the public interest in disclosure, including the need to prevent harm to others, and both the rights of the individual concerned and the public interest in maintaining trust in a confidential service.

10.17 Whether there is an overriding public interest in disclosing confidential patient information may vary according to the type of information. Even in cases where there is no overriding public interest in disclosing detailed clinical information about a patient's state of health there may, nonetheless, be an overriding public interest in sharing more limited information about the patient's current, and past status under the Act, if that will help ensure properly informed risk management by the relevant authorities, families and carers.

RECORDING DISCLOSURE WITHOUT CONSENT

10.18 Any decision to disclose confidential information about patients should be fully documented. The relevant facts should be recorded, with the reasons for the decision and the identity of all those involved in the decision-making. Reasons should be given by reference to the grounds on which the disclosure is to be justified. **4–025**

INFORMATION FOR VICTIMS OF CRIMES

10.19 As set out in chapter 40, the victims of certain part 3 patients (mentally disordered offenders) detained in hospital have rights to make representations and receive information about that patient's discharge under the Domestic Violence, Crime and Victims Act 2004 (DVCVA).[6] **4–026**

10.20 In other circumstances, professionals should encourage (but may not require) mentally disordered offender patients to agree to share information that

---

[6] Domestic Violence, Crime and Victims Act 2004. http://www.legislation.gov.uk/ukpga/2004/28/contents.

will enable victims and victims' families to be informed about their progress. Among other benefits, disclosure of such information can sometimes serve to reduce the danger of harmful confrontations after a discharge of which victims were unaware.

10.21 Professionals should be ready to discuss with patients the benefits of enabling some information to be given by professionals to victims, within the spirit of the Code of Practice for Victims of Crime issued under the DVCVA.[7]

12. THE TRIBUNAL

Why read this chapter?

4–027   12.1 This chapter provides guidance on the role of the Tribunal and related duties on hospital managers and others.

12.2 The Tribunal is an independent judicial body which reviews cases of detained and conditionally discharged patients and patients subject to community treatment orders under the Act. Hospital managers and the local authority have a duty to ensure that patients understand their rights to apply for a Tribunal hearing. Managers have duties to refer patients to the Tribunal. Guidance is given about the reports to be prepared for the Tribunal, medical examinations, withdrawing an application, and representation.[8]

PURPOSE OF THE TRIBUNAL

4–028   12.3 The First-tier Tribunal (Mental Health) ('the Tribunal') is an independent judicial body. Its main purpose is to review the cases of detained and conditionally discharged patients and patients subject to community treatment orders (CTOs) under the Act ('community patients') and to direct the discharge of any patients where it thinks it appropriate. It also considers applications for discharge from guardianship.

12.4 The Tribunal provides a significant safeguard for patients who have had their liberty curtailed under the Act. Those giving evidence at hearings should do what they can to help enable tribunal hearings to be conducted in a professional manner, which includes having regard to the patient's wishes and feelings and medical condition and ensuring that the patient feels as comfortable as possible with the proceedings.

12.5 It is for those who believe that a patient should continue to be detained or remain a community patient to prove their case, not for the patient to disprove it. They will therefore need to present the Tribunal with sufficient evidence to support continuing liability to detention or a CTO. Clinical and social reports form the backbone of this evidence. Care should be given to ensure that all information is as up-to-date as possible to avoid adjournment. In order to support the Tribunal in making its decision, all information should be clear and concise.

---

[7] The code of practice for victims of crime and supporting public information materials. Ministry of Justice. 2013. https://www.gov.uk/government/publications/the-code-of-practice-for-victims-of-crime.

[8] The First-tier Tribunal established under the Tribunals, Courts and Enforcement Act 2007. There is a right of appeal, on a point of law, from that Tribunal to the Upper Tribunal. http://www.legislation.gov.uk/ukpga/2007/15/contents.

INFORMING THE PATIENT AND NEAREST RELATIVE OF RIGHTS TO APPLY TO THE TRIBUNAL

12.6 Hospital managers and the local authority are under a duty to take steps to **4–029** ensure that patients understand their rights to apply for a Tribunal hearing. Hospital managers and the local authority should also advise patients of their entitlement to free legal advice and representation. They should do both whenever:

- patients are first detained in hospital, received into guardianship or discharged onto a CTO

- whenever their detention or guardianship is renewed or CTO is extended, and

- whenever their status under the Act changes—eg if they move from detention under section 2 to detention under section 3 or if their CTO is revoked.

12.7 Unless the patient requests otherwise, and the patient should be asked, the information should normally also be given to their nearest relative (subject to the normal considerations about involving nearest relatives—see chapter 5).

12.8 Hospital managers and professionals should enable detained patients to be visited by their legal representatives at any reasonable time. This is particularly important where visits are necessary to discuss a Tribunal application. Where the patient consents, legal representatives and independent doctors should be given prompt access to the patient's medical records. Delays in providing access can hold up Tribunal proceedings and should be avoided.

12.9 In connection with an application (or a reference) to a Tribunal, an independent doctor or approved clinician authorised by (or on behalf of) a patient has a right to visit and examine the patient in private (see paragraph 12.23). Those doctors and approved clinicians also have a right to inspect any records relating to the patient's detention, treatment and (where relevant) after-care under section 117. Where nearest relatives have a right to apply to the Tribunal, they too may authorise independent doctors or approved clinicians in the same way. The patient's consent is not required for authorised doctors or approved clinicians to see their records, and they should be given prompt access to the records they wish to see.

HOSPITAL MANAGERS' DUTY TO REFER CASES TO THE TRIBUNAL

12.10 Hospital managers have various duties to refer patients to the Tribunal **4–030** (see paragraphs 37.39–37.43). They may also request the Secretary of State to refer a patient, and there are certain circumstances where they should always consider doing so (see paragraphs 37.44–37.46 and for children and young people, paragraphs 19.107–19.110).

REPORTS FOR THE TRIBUNAL

12.11 Responsible authorities (ie the managers of the relevant hospital or the **4–031** local authority responsible for a guardianship patient) should be familiar with the Tribunal's rules and procedures. The rules place a statutory duty on the responsible authority to provide the Tribunal with a statement of relevant facts together with certain reports.

12.12 It is important that documents and information are provided in accordance with the Tribunal's rules and procedures in good time for any Tribunal hearing. Missing, out-of-date or inadequate reports can lead to adjournments or unnecessarily long hearings. Where responsible clinicians, social workers or other professionals are required to provide reports, they should do this promptly and within the statutory timescale. For more information refer to the Practice Direction First-tier Tribunal Health Education and Social Care Chamber: Statements and Reports in Mental Health Cases.[9]

12.13 In the case of a restricted patient, if the opinion of the responsible clinician or other professional changes from what was recorded in the original Tribunal report(s), it is vital that this is communicated in writing as soon as possible, prior to the hearing, to the Tribunal office and the Mental Health Unit of the Ministry of Justice to allow them the opportunity to prepare a supplementary statement. Information about the Tribunal can be found at: *https://www.gov.uk/ mental-health-tribunal*

12.14 If a Tribunal panel feels that it needs more information on any report, it may request it, either in the form of a supplementary report or by questioning a witness at the hearing itself if the witness or their representative judge that it would not be detrimental to the patient's health or wellbeing.

12.15 In some circumstances, the Tribunal will not sit immediately after receiving the report. In these cases, the report writers should consider whether anything in the patient's circumstances have changed and should produce a concise update to the report. This is especially important if the patient's status changes—eg if a patient becomes a community patient or moves from detention under section 2 to section 3.

12.16 In those cases, the application will need to be considered under the new circumstances of the case, and the report will need to provide a justification for continued detention or liability to recall under the new circumstances. The Tribunal may ask the author of the reports to talk through their report, so it is good practice for the authors to re-familiarise themselves with the content of any report before the hearing. If the author of the report is unable to attend, it is important that anyone attending in their place should wherever possible also have a good knowledge of the patient's case.

12.17 Hospital managers (or local authorities in guardianship cases) should ensure that the Tribunal is notified immediately of any events or changes that might have a bearing on Tribunal proceedings—eg where a patient is discharged or one of the parties is unavailable.

12.18 If the author of a report prepared for the Tribunal is aware of information they do not think the patient should see, they should follow the Tribunal's procedure for the submission of such information. Ultimately, it is for the Tribunal to decide what should be disclosed to the patient.

12.19 Reports should be sent to the Tribunal office, preferably by secure e-mail, otherwise by post.

12.20 The responsible authority must ensure that up-to-date reports prepared specifically for the Tribunal are provided in accordance with the Tribunal's rules and procedures. In practice, this will normally include a report completed by the patient's responsible clinician.

---

[9] At the time of publication this was detailed in Annex E of Practice Direction. First-tier Tribunal, Health, Education and Social Care Chamber: statements and reports in mental health cases. Tribunals Judiciary. 2013. http://www.judiciary.gov.uk/wp-content/uploads/JCO/Documents/ Practice+Directions/Tribunals/statements-in-mental-health-cases-hesc-28102013.pdf.

12.21 Where possible, reports should be written by the professionals with the best overall knowledge of the patient's situation.

12.22 The reports should be submitted in good time to enable all parties, including the Secretary of State in restricted cases, to fulfil their responsibilities.

MEDICAL EXAMINATION

12.23 In certain categories of case, a medical member of the Tribunal may be **4–032** asked to examine the patient, sometime before the hearing. Hospital managers must ensure that the medical member can see patients who are in hospital in private, where this is safe and practicable, and make provision for the member and the Tribunal panel at the hearing to be able to examine the patient's medical records, if necessary. It is important that the patient is told of any visit in advance, so that they can be available when the medical member visits.

WITHDRAWING THE APPLICATION

12.24 A request to withdraw an application may be made by the applicant in **4–033** accordance with the Tribunal rules. The Tribunal is not bound to agree, especially if the withdrawal is merely tactical or is sought within 48 hours of the hearing. The applicant may not withdraw a reference made by a hospital manager or the Secretary of State.

12.25 An application will be considered to be withdrawn if the patient is discharged. If this happens outside office hours, someone acting on behalf of the hospital managers (or the local authority, if it is a guardianship case) should contact the Tribunal office as soon as possible, to inform them. For detained patients, this could be done by a member of the ward staff.

REPRESENTATION

12.26 Hospital managers (or local authorities, as the case may be) should **4–034** inform patients of their right to present their own case to the Tribunal and their right to be represented by someone else (whether legally qualified or not) and of any free legal advice and representation available. Staff should be available to help patients make an application and prepare them for the Tribunal. This is especially important for community patients who may not have daily contact with professionals.

12.27 If a patient has not appointed a representative and they do not wish to present their own case, or the patient lacks capacity to decide whether they want a representative and the Tribunal considers it is in the patient's best interests to be represented, then the Tribunal can appoint a person before the hearing, or permit a person who has accompanied the patient to the hearing, to be a representative for the patient. A patient's family member, carer or advocate could be their representative.

THE HEARING

Attendance at hearings

12.28 Normally patients will be present throughout hearings. Patients and **4–035** carers do not need to attend the Tribunal hearing, but professionals should encourage and support them to attend unless they judge that it would be detrimental to the patient's health or wellbeing.

12.29 A carer or advocate will only be able to present the patient's case if they are appointed, or given permission, by the Tribunal as a representative under the Tribunal's procedural rules (see paragraph 12.26 above). If the patient is not well enough to attend the hearing or speak on their own behalf then an advocate or carer should be given the opportunity to attend and speak on their behalf.

12.30 It is important that the patient's responsible clinician/s attend the Tribunal, supported by other staff involved in the patient's care, where appropriate, as their evidence is crucial for making the case for a patient's continued detention or CTO under the Act. Wherever possible the responsible clinician, and other relevant staff, should attend for the full hearing so that they are aware of all the evidence made available to the Tribunal and the Tribunal's decision and reasons.

12.31 Responsible clinicians can attend the hearing solely as a witness or as the nominated representative of the responsible authority. As a representative of the responsible authority, the responsible clinician has the ability to call and cross-examine witnesses and to make submissions to the Tribunal. This may not always be desirable where it is envisaged that the responsible clinician will have to continue working closely with a patient.

12.32 Responsible authorities should therefore consider whether they want to send an additional person to represent their interests, allowing the responsible clinician to appear solely as a witness. Responsible clinicians should be clear in what capacity they are attending the Tribunal, as they may well be asked this by the panel.

12.33 It is important that other people who prepare reports submitted by the responsible authority attend the hearing to provide further up-to-date information about the patient, including (where relevant) their home circumstances and the aftercare available in the event of a decision to discharge the patient.

12.34 Increasingly, Tribunal hearings find it helpful to speak to a nurse, particularly a nurse who knows the patient. It is often helpful for a nurse who knows the patient to accompany them to the hearing.

12.35 Hospital managers should ensure that all professionals who attend Tribunal hearings are adequately prepared. They should provide patients and their carers with sufficient information to understand the matters the Tribunal is considering in a format and language that patients and their carers understand. This could include pictorial or video formats outlining what the patient can expect.

ACCOMMODATION FOR HEARINGS

4–036   12.36 The managers of a hospital in which a Tribunal hearing is to be held should provide suitable accommodation for that purpose. The hearing room should be private, quiet, clean and adequately sized and furnished. It should not contain confidential information about other patients. If the room is used for other purposes, care should be taken to ensure that any equipment (such as a video camera or a two-way mirror) would not have a disturbing effect on the patient.

12.37 The patient should have access to a separate room in which to hold any private discussions that are necessary—eg with their representative—as should the Tribunal members, so that they can discuss their decision.

12.38 Where a patient is being treated in the community, the hospital managers should consider whether a hospital venue is appropriate. They may wish to discuss alternatives with the Tribunal office.

INTERPRETATION

12.39 The Tribunal should ensure that Tribunal panel members understand **4–037** equality issues and that there are sufficient numbers of panel members with a specialised understanding of the specific needs of particular groups including those listed below, and that panel members can communicate effectively with them:

- patients from minority cultural or ethnic backgrounds

- patients with physical impairments and/or sensory impairments, and/or

- patients with learning disabilities and/or autistic spectrum disorders.

12.40 It is important that patients and their representatives are able to understand and participate in the Tribunal hearing. This includes providing information in formats that they understand and, if required, providing interpretation services free of charge, including sign language. Hospital managers and local authorities should inform the Tribunal well in advance if they think any such services might be necessary.

COMMUNICATION OF THE DECISION

12.41 The Tribunal will normally communicate its decision to all parties orally **4–038** at the end of the hearing. Provided it is feasible to do so, and the patient wishes it, the Tribunal will speak to them personally. Otherwise, the decision will be given to the patient's representative (if they have one). If the patient is unrepresented, and it is not feasible to discuss matters with them after the hearing, the hospital managers or local authority should ensure that they are told the decision as soon as possible. All parties to the hearing should receive a written copy of the reasons for the decision.

COMPLAINTS

12.42 Complaints from users about the Tribunal should be sent to the Tribunal **4–039** offices. The Tribunal has procedures in places to deal with complaints promptly. This information is available at: *https://www.gov.uk/mental-health-tribunal*.

FURTHER INFORMATION ON THE TRIBUNAL

12.43 The Tribunal itself publishes further information and guidance about its **4–040** procedures and operations.

DETENTION UNDER THE ACT OR DEPRIVATION OF LIBERTY UNDER A DOLS AUTHORISATION? (Ch.13, paras 13.49–13.62)

13.49 If an individual: **4–041**

a. is suffering from a mental disorder (within the meaning of the Act)
b. needs to be assessed and/or treated in a hospital setting for that disorder or for physical conditions related to that disorder (and meets the criteria for an application for admission under sections 2 or 3 of the Act)

c. has a care treatment package that may or will amount to a deprivation of liberty

d. lacks capacity to consent to being accommodated in the relevant hospital for the purpose of treatment, and

e. does not object to being admitted to hospital, or to some or all the treatment they will receive there for mental disorder.

Then in principle a DoLS authorisation (or potentially a Court of Protection order) and detention under the Act would both be available (subject to the assessments required for a DoLS authorisation, including the eligibility assessment). This is the one situation where the option of using either the Act or DoLS exists. It is important to note that a person cannot be detained under the Act at the same time as being subject to a DoLS authorisation or a Court of Protection order.

13.50 Below is an options grid summarising the availability of the Act and of DoLS where a deprivation of liberty has been identified for a mental health patient, accommodated in hospital for the purpose of treatment for a mental disorder.

13.51 Whether a patient is objecting has to be considered in the round, taking into account all the circumstances, so far as they are reasonably ascertainable. The decision to be made is whether the patient objects, the reasonableness of that objection is not the issue. In many cases the patient will be perfectly able to state their objection. In other cases the relevant person will need to consider the patient's behaviour, wishes, feelings, views, beliefs and values, both present and past, so far as they can be ascertained. In deciding whether a patient objects to being admitted to hospital, or to some or all of the treatment they will receive there for mental disorder, decision-makers should err on the side of caution and, where in doubt, take the position that a patient is objecting.

Figure 5: Options grid summarising the availability of the Act and of DoLS

	Individual **objects** to the proposed accommodation in a hospital for care and/ or treatment; or to any of the treatment they will receive there for mental disorder	Individual **does not object** to the proposed accommodation in a hospital for care and/or treatment; or to any of the treatment they will receive there for mental disorder
Individual has the capacity to consent to being accommodated in a hospital for care and/or treatment	Only the Act is available	The Act is available. Informal admission might also be appropriate. Neither DoLS authorisation nor Court of Protection order available
Individual lacks the capacity to consent to being accommodated in a hospital for care and/or treatment	Only the Act is available	The Act is available. DoLS authorisation is available, or potentially a Court of Protection order

Important points for consideration

13.52 Figure 5 above reveals a number of important points in addition to those **4–042** discussed earlier in this chapter.

13.53 First, a person who lacks capacity to consent to being accommodated in a hospital for care and/or treatment for mental disorder and who is likely to be deprived of their liberty should never be informally admitted to hospital (whether they are content to be admitted or not.

13.54 Decision-makers should also consider whether an individual deprived of their liberty may regain capacity or may have fluctuating capacity. Such a situation is likely to indicate use of the Act to authorise a deprivation of liberty should be preferred over use of a DoLS authorisation or Court of Protection order.

13.55 An individual will be ineligible for a DoLS authorisation or a Court of Protection order if they fall within Schedule 1A to the MCA, which should be considered carefully.

13.56 Individuals who are ineligible include the following:

- those persons detained in a hospital under sections 2, 3, 4, 35–38, 44, 45A, 47, 48 or 51 of the Act

- those persons liable to be detained under one of the above mentioned sections of the Act but who are not detained in a hospital under that regime; AND (i) proposed care and treatment in a hospital or care home would conflict with a requirement imposed on them in connection with their liability to detention under the Act (eg as a condition of a leave of absence) OR (ii) the relevant care and treatment consists in whole or in part of treatment for mental disorder in a hospital

- those persons on a community treatment order (CTO) under the Act AND (i) proposed care and treatment in a hospital or care home would conflict with a condition of their CTO OR (ii) the relevant care and treatment consists in whole or in part of treatment for mental disorder in a hospital

- those persons subject to guardianship under the Act AND (i) proposed detention or care and treatment would conflict with a requirement imposed on them by the guardianship regime (eg a requirement that they should reside elsewhere) OR (ii) it is proposed that the person will be detained in a hospital for treatment for mental disorder and they object, or are likely to object (and the person's attorney or deputy has not consented), and

- those persons who would meet the criteria for being detained under section 2 or 3 of the Act, but who is not liable to be detained under sections 4, 35–38, 44, 45A, 47, 48 or 51 or subject to a CTO or guardianship, AND it is proposed that the person will be detained in a hospital for treatment for mental disorder, AND the person objects to being accommodated in hospital for that treatment, or to being given some or all of that treatment (and the person's attorney or deputy has not consented where the person objects)

13.57 For those individuals detailed in paragraph 13.49 where both detention under the Act and a DoLS authorisation or a Court of Protection order are available, decision-makers should determine which regime is the more appropriate. The following paragraphs detail factors that should feature in this decision-making process.

13.58 The choice of legal regime should never be based on a general preference for one regime or the other, or because one regime is more familiar to the decision-maker than the other. Such considerations are not legally relevant and lead to arbitrary decision-making. In addition decision-makers should not proceed on the basis that one regime is generally less restrictive than the other. Both regimes are based on the need to impose as few restrictions on the liberty and autonomy of patients as possible. In the particular circumstances of an individual case, it may be apparent that one regime is likely to prove less restrictive. If so, this should be balanced against any potential benefits associated with the other regime.

13.59 Both regimes provide appropriate procedural safeguards to ensure the rights of the person concerned are protected during their detention. Decision-makers should not therefore proceed on the basis that one regime generally provides greater safeguards than the other. However, the nature of the safeguards provided under the two regimes are different and decision-makers will wish to exercise their professional judgement in determining which safeguards are more likely to best protect the interests of the patient in the particular circumstances of each individual case.

13.60 In the relatively small number of cases where detention under the Act and a DoLS authorisation or Court of Protection order are available, this Code of Practice does not seek to preferentially orientate the decision-maker in any given direction. Such a decision should always be made depending on the unique circumstances of each case. Clearly recording the reasons for the final decision made will be important. The most pressing concern should always be that if an individual lacks capacity to consent to the matter in question and is deprived of their liberty they should receive the safeguards afforded under either the Act or through a DoLS authorisation or a Court of Protection order.

13.61 Part 9 of the DoLS Code of Practice details steps to be taken if someone thinks a person is being deprived of their liberty without authorisation. These steps include raising the matter with the responsible person at the managing authority (the provider) and if necessary with the supervisory body (the local authority). Hospitals should have policies in place to deal with circumstances where disagreement results in an inability to take a decision as to whether the Act or DoLS should be used to give legal authorisation to a deprivation of liberty—to ensure that one is selected.

DECIDING WHETHER THE ACT AND/OR MCA WILL BE AVAILABLE TO BE USED

4–042   13.62 The flowchart opposite describes the key decision-making steps when determining whether the Act and/or the MCA including the DoLS will be available to be used. The flowchart does not replace careful consideration by decision-makers of all relevant circumstances in individual cases. Decision-makers should use their professional judgment within the framework of the legislation. Annex D provides a written description of figure 6.

Figure 6: Deciding whether the Act and/or MCA will be available to be used

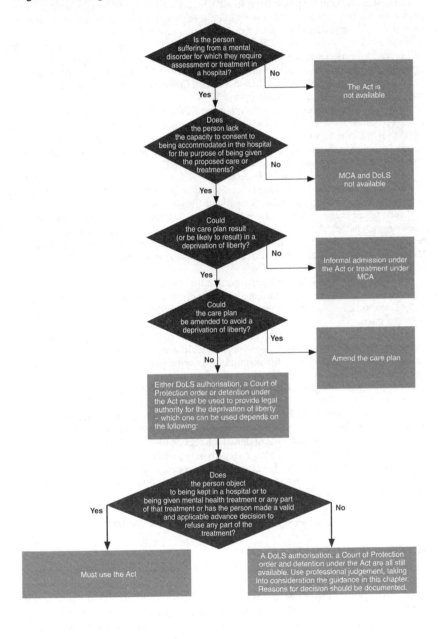

Is the person suffering from a mental disorder for which they require assessment or treatment in a hospital?

No → The Act is not available

Yes

Does the person lack the capacity to consent to being accommodated in the hospital for the purpose of being given the proposed care or treatments?

No → MCA and DoLS not available

Yes

Could the care plan result (or be likely to result) in a deprivation of liberty?

No → Informal admission under the Act or treatment under MCA

Yes

Could the care plan be amended to avoid a deprivation of liberty?

Yes → Amend the care plan

No

Either DoLS authorisation, a Court of Protection order or detention under the Act must be used to provide legal authority for the deprivation of liberty – which one can be used depends on the following:

Does the person object to being kept in a hospital or to being given mental health treatment or any part of that treatment or has the person made a valid and applicable advance decision to refuse any part of the treatment?

Yes → Must use the Act

No → A DoLS authorisation, a Court of Protection order and detention under the Act are all still available. Use professional judgement, taking into consideration the guidance in this chapter. Reasons for decision should be documented.

GENERAL NOTE

The first question in the flowchart is to ask whether the individual in question is suffering from a mental disorder for which they require assessment or treatment in a hospital. If the answer is 'no', then detention under the Act is not an available option.

If the answer is 'yes' then the decision-maker should consider a second question. The second question is: Does the individual in question lack the mental capacity to consent to being accommodated in the hospital for the purpose of being given the proposed care or treatment? If the answer is 'no' then the Mental Capacity Act and the deprivation of liberty safeguards are not an available option.

However, if the answer is 'yes' (in other words the individual in question is suffering from a mental disorder for which they require assessment and treatment in hospital AND they lack the capacity to consent to consent to being accommodated in the hospital for the proposed care or treatment) then the next question to be asked is: Could the care plan result, or be likely to result, in a deprivation of liberty?

If the answer is 'no', then the individual could be admitted to the hospital on an informal basis (ie not detained under the Act) or treated under the provisions of the Mental Capacity Act (without the need to use the deprivation of liberty safeguards).

If the answer is 'yes' (there is, or is likely to be, a deprivation of liberty) then the next question is whether the care and or treatment plan could be amended to reduce any restraints or restrictions in place—thereby preventing a deprivation of liberty from arising. If the answer is 'yes', the care and treatment plan should be amended so that there is no deprivation of liberty.

If the care plan cannot be amended—so that there is (or is likely to be) an unavoidable deprivation of liberty, then the individual in question must either be detained under the Act, a DoLS authorisation or Court of Protection order. The individual cannot be admitted on an informal basis.

In determining whether the MHA or the DoLS is the most appropriate way of authorising the deprivation of liberty the decision-maker should consider the question: does the individual object to being kept in the hospital or to being given mental health treatment or any part of that treatment, or has the individual made a valid and applicable advance decision to refuse any part of the treatment? If the answer to this question is 'yes' then use of the Act is indicated—use of the DoLS would be inappropriate.

However, if the answer is 'no' (in other words, the individual is not objecting) then both detention under the Act and a DOLS authorisation or Court of Protection order are available. Decision-makers must decide under which regime the individual will be detained; the individual cannot be detained under both regimes. Guidance for decision makers regarding this decision is to be found elsewhere in this chapter but it is important to remember that the choice of which regime to use should be made in the best interests of the individual—not because of the personal preference of the decision-maker.

14. APPLICATIONS FOR DETENTION IN HOSPITAL

Why read this chapter?

4–043   14.1 This chapter gives guidance on making applications for detention in hospital under Part 2 of the Act.

14.2 An application for detention may only be made where the grounds in either section 2 or section 3 of the Act are met. An application for detention may be made by an approved mental health professional (AMHP) or the patient's nearest relative, and they should understand the criteria for detention and their responsibilities under the Act.

GROUNDS FOR MAKING AN APPLICATION FOR DETENTION

14.3 An application for detention may only be made where the grounds in either **4–044** section 2 or section 3 of the Act are met (see below).

Criteria for applications

14.4 A person can be detained for assessment under section 2 only if both the **4–045** following criteria apply:

- the person is suffering from a mental disorder of a nature or degree which warrants their detention in hospital for assessment (or for assessment followed by treatment) for at least a limited period, and

- the person ought to be so detained in the interests of their own health or safety or with a view to the protection of others.

14.5 A person can be detained for treatment under section 3 only if all the following criteria apply:

- the person is suffering from a mental disorder of a nature or degree which makes it appropriate for them to receive medical treatment in hospital

- it is necessary for the health or safety of the person or for the protection of other persons that they should receive such treatment and it cannot be provided unless the patient is detained under this section, and

- appropriate medical treatment is available.

14.6 The criteria require consideration of both the nature and degree of a patient's mental disorder. Nature refers to the particular mental disorder from which the patient is suffering, its chronicity, its prognosis, and the patient's previous response to receiving treatment for the disorder. Degree refers to the current manifestation of the patient's disorder.

14.7 Before it is decided that admission to hospital is necessary, consideration must be given to whether there are alternative means of providing the care and treatment which the patient requires. This includes consideration of whether there might be other effective forms of care or treatment which the patient would be willing to accept and of whether guardianship would be appropriate instead.

14.8 In all cases, consideration should be given to:

- the patient's wishes and view of their own needs

- the patient's age and physical health

- any past wishes or feelings expressed by the patient

- the patient's cultural background

- the patient's social and family circumstances

- the impact that any future deterioration or lack of improvement in the patient's condition would have on their children, other relatives or carers, especially those living with the patient, including an assessment of their ability and willingness to cope, and

- the effect on the patient, and those close to the patient, of a decision to admit or not to admit under the Act.

Factors to consider—the health or safety of the patient

4-046   14.9 Factors to be considered in deciding whether patients should be detained for their own health or safety include:

- the evidence suggesting that patients are at risk of:
  - suicide
  - self-harm
  - self-neglect or being unable to look after their own health or safety
  - jeopardising their own health or safety accidentally, recklessly or unintentionally, or
  - that their mental disorder is otherwise putting their health or safety at risk
- any evidence suggesting that the patient's mental health will deteriorate if they do not receive treatment, including the views of the patient or carers, relatives or close friends (especially those living with the patient) about the likely course of the disorder
- the patient's own skills and experience in managing their condition
- the patient's capacity to consent to or refuse admission and treatment (and the availability of the deprivation of liberty safeguards (DoLS))
- whether the patient objects to treatment for mental disorder—or is likely to
- the reliability of such evidence, including what is known of the history of the patient's mental disorder and the possibility of their condition improving
- the potential benefits of treatment, which should be weighed against any adverse effects that being detained might have on the patient's wellbeing, and
- whether other methods of managing the risk are available.

Factors to consider—protection of others

4-047   14.10 In considering whether detention is necessary for the protection of other people, the factors to consider are the nature of the risk to other people arising from the patient's mental disorder, the likelihood that harm will result and the severity of any potential harm, taking into account:

- that it is not always possible to differentiate risk of harm to the patient from the risk of harm to others
- the reliability of the available evidence, including any relevant details of the patient's clinical history and past behaviour, such as contact with other agencies and (where relevant) criminal convictions and cautions
- the willingness and ability of those who live with the patient and those who provide care and support to the patient to cope with and manage the risk

- whether other methods of managing the risk are available, and
- harm to other people including psychological as well as physical harm.

Alternatives to detention under the Act

14.11 In deciding whether it is necessary to detain patients, doctors and AMHPs **4–048** must always consider the alternative ways of providing the treatment or care they need. Decision-makers should always consider whether there are less restrictive alternatives to detention under the Act, which may include:

- informal admission to hospital of a patient based on that person's consent (see chapter 19 for guidance on consent to informal admission for children and young people)
- treatment under the Mental Capacity Act (MCA) if the person lacks capacity to consent to admission and treatment. If a deprivation of liberty occurs, or is likely to occur, either the Act, a DoLS authorisation or a deprivation of liberty order by the Court of Protection must be in place (see chapter 13)
- management in the community—eg by a crisis and support team, in a crisis house or with a host family (see chapter 29 on community patients), or
- guardianship (see chapter 30 and 31).

14.12 In considering whether it is necessary for the person to be detained under the Act, decision-makers must consider whether the person has capacity to consent to or refuse admission and treatment. This should be assessed in accordance with the MCA, which makes clear that a person must be assumed to have capacity unless it is established that they do not.

14.13 Professionals must consider available alternatives, having regard to all the relevant circumstances, to identify the least restrictive way of best achieving the proposed assessment or treatment. This will include considering what is the person's best interests (if the person lacks capacity, this will be determined in accordance with the MCA).

Patients with capacity to give or to refuse consent to admission

14.14 When a patient needs to be in hospital, informal admission is usually **4–049** appropriate when a patient who has the capacity to give or to refuse consent is consenting to admission. (See chapter 19 for guidance on when parents might consent to admission on behalf of children and young people.)

14.15 This should not be regarded as an absolute rule, especially if the reason for considering admission is that the patient presents a clear risk to themselves or others because of their mental disorder.

14.16 Compulsory admission should, in particular, be considered where a patient's current mental state, together with reliable evidence of past experience, indicates a strong likelihood that they will have a change of mind about informal admission, either before or after they are admitted, with a resulting risk to their health or safety or to the safety of other people.

14.17 The threat of detention must not be used to coerce a patient to consent to admission to hospital or to treatment (and is likely to invalidate any apparent consent).

14.18 If consideration is being given to the informal admission of a patient who is subject to Secretary of State for Justice restrictions, the Mental Health Casework Section (MHCS) of the Ministry of Justice should be contacted. Further advice is provided in chapter 22 and on the Ministry of Justice website.[10]

Patients who lack capacity to give or to refuse consent to admission or treatment

4–050 14.19 Where the criteria for detention under the Act are met, the situations where an application for detention should be made under the Act instead of relying on the DoLS include where:

- the patient has made a valid and applicable advance decision to refuse treatment which includes a necessary element of the treatment for which they are to be admitted to hospital (see chapter 9)

- the use of the DoLS would conflict with a decision of the person's attorney, deputy, guardian or the Court of Protection, or

- the patient is objecting to being admitted to (or remaining in) hospital for mental health treatment.[11]

14.20 In that last case, whether a patient is objecting has to be considered in the round, taking into account all the circumstances, so far as they are reasonably ascertainable. The decision to be made is whether the patient objects to treatment—the reasonableness of that objection is not the issue. In many cases the patient will be perfectly able to state their objection. In other cases doctors and AMHPs will need to consider the patient's behaviour, wishes, feelings, views, beliefs and values, both present and past, so far as they can be ascertained. If there is reason to think that a patient would object, if able to do so, then the patient should be taken to be objecting.

14.21 Even if providing appropriate care or treatment will not unavoidably involve a deprivation of liberty, in some cases it may be necessary to detain a patient under the Act rather than rely on the MCA. For example, where the patient:

- has, by means of a valid and applicable advance decision, refused a necessary element of the treatment required, or

- lacks capacity to make decisions on some elements of the care and treatment they need, but has capacity to decide about a vital element—eg admission to hospital—and has either already refused it or is likely to do so.

---

[10] At the time of publication, contact details are available at www.justice.gov.uk/contacts/noms/mental-health-unit, and the Ministry of Justice switchboard is contactable on 020 3334 3555. For urgent queries out of office hours the telephone number (operated by the Home Office) is 020 7035 4848: select option 5.

[11] The patient would be ineligible to be deprived of their liberty under the MCA: see paragraphs 1, 2 (Case E), 5 and 12 of Schedule 1A to the MCA. This means they are ineligible to be deprived of their liberty under an authorisation under Schedule A1 (see section 4A(5) read with paragraphs 12(1)(e) and 17 of Schedule A1) or a Court of Protection order (see section 16A).

14.22 Whether or not the DoLS could be used, other reasons why it may be necessary to detain a patient under the Act and not rely on the MCA alone include the following:

- the patient's lack of capacity to consent or refuse is fluctuating or temporary and the patient is not expected to consent to admission or treatment when they regain capacity. This may be particularly relevant to patients having acute psychotic, manic or depressive episodes

- a degree of restraint may need to be used which is justified by the risk to other people but which is not permissible under the MCA[12] because, exceptionally, it cannot be said to be proportionate to the risk to the patient personally, and

- there is some other specific identifiable risk that the person might not receive the treatment they need if the MCA is relied on and either the person or others might potentially suffer harm as a result.

14.23 Otherwise, if the MCA can be used safely and effectively to assess or treat a patient, it is likely to be difficult to demonstrate that the criteria for detaining the patient under the Act are met.

14.24 For further information on the DoLS, see chapter 13, the MCA Code of Practice and its supplementary DoLS Code.[13]

14.25 For the different considerations which apply to children and young people under the age of 18, see chapter 19.

USE OF SECTION 2 OR SECTION 3 OF THE ACT

14.26 An application for detention can be made under either section 2 or section **4–051** 3 of the Act.

14.27 Section 2 should only be used if:

- the full extent of the nature and degree of a patient's condition is unclear

- there is a need to carry out an initial in-patient assessment in order to formulate a treatment plan, or to reach a judgement about whether the patient will accept treatment on a voluntary basis following admission, or

- there is a need to carry out a new in-patient assessment in order to re-formulate a treatment plan, or to reach a judgement about whether the patient will accept treatment on a voluntary basis.

14.28 Section 3 should be used if:

- the patient is already detained under section 2 (detention under section 2 cannot be renewed by a new section 2 application), or

---

[12] Mental Capacity Act 2005: Code of Practice. Department for Constitutional Affairs (now Ministry of Justice). 2007. https://www.gov.uk/government/publications/mental-capacity-act-code-of-practice.
[13] Mental Capacity Act 2005: Code of Practice. Department for Constitutional Affairs (now Ministry of Justice). 2007. https://www.gov.uk/government/publications/mental-capacity-act-code-of-practice.

- the nature and current degree of the patient's mental disorder, the essential elements of the treatment plan to be followed and the likelihood of the patient accepting treatment as an informal patient are already sufficiently established to make it unnecessary to undertake a new assessment under section 2.

14.29 The rationale for decisions to use section 2 or section 3 should be clearly recorded.

THE ASSESSMENT PROCESS

4–052   14.30 An application for detention may be made by an AMHP or the patient's nearest relative (for information on the nearest relative see Chapters 4 and 5). An AMHP is usually a more appropriate applicant than a patient's nearest relative, given their professional training and knowledge of the legislation and local resources. This also removes the risk that an application by the nearest relative might have an adverse effect on their relationship with the patient.

14.31 An application must be supported by two medical recommendations given in accordance with the Act.

14.32 Doctors who are approached directly by a nearest relative about the possibility of an application being made should advise the nearest relative of their right to require a local authority to arrange for an AMHP to consider the patient's case.

Objective of the assessment

4–053   14.33 The objective of the assessment is to determine whether the criteria for detention are met and, if so, whether an application for detention should be made.

14.34 Because a proper assessment cannot be done without considering alternative means of providing care and treatment, AMHPs and doctors should, as far as possible in the circumstances, identify and liaise with services which may potentially be able to provide alternatives to admission to hospital, such as crisis and home treatment teams.

Responsibilities of local authorities

4–054   14.35 Local authorities are responsible for ensuring that sufficient AMHPs are available to carry out their roles under the Act, including assessing patients to decide whether an application for detention should be made. To fulfil their statutory duty, local authorities should have arrangements in place in their area to provide a 24-hour service that can respond to patients' needs.

14.36 Section 13 of the Act places a specific duty on local authorities to arrange for an AMHP to consider the case of any patient who is within their area if they have reason to believe that an application for detention in hospital may need to be made in respect of the patient. Local authorities must make such arrangements if asked to do so by (or on behalf of) the nearest relative.

14.37 If a patient is already detained under section 2 as the result of an application made by an AMHP, the local authority on whose behalf that AMHP was acting is responsible for arranging for an AMHP to consider the patient's case again if the local authority has reason to believe that an application under section 3 may be necessary. This applies even if the patient has been detained outside that local authority's area. These duties do not prevent any other local authority from arranging for an AMHP to consider a patient's case if that is more appropriate.

Setting up the assessment

14.38 Local arrangements should, as far as possible, ensure that assessments **4–055** are carried out by the most appropriate AMHP and doctors in the particular circumstances.

14.39 Where a patient is known to belong to a group for which particular expertise is desirable (eg they are aged under 18 or have a learning disability), at least one of the professionals involved in their assessment should have expertise in working with people from that group, wherever possible.

14.40 If this is not possible, at least one of the professionals involved in the person's assessment should consult with one or more professionals who do have relevant expertise at the earliest opportunity and involve them as closely as the circumstances of the case allow.

14.41 Unless different arrangements have been agreed locally between the relevant authorities, AMHPs who assess patients for possible detention under the Act have overall responsibility for co-ordinating the process of assessment. In doing so, they should be sensitive to the patient's age, sex, gender identity, social, cultural or ethnic background, religion or belief, and/or sexual orientation (see chapter 3 for more information). They should also consider how any disability the patient has may affect the way the assessment needs to be carried out.

14.42 Given the importance of good communication, it is essential that those professionals who assess patients are able to communicate with the patient effectively and reliably to prevent potential misunderstandings. AMHPs should establish, as far as possible, whether patients have particular communication needs or difficulties and take steps to meet these, by arranging, for example a signer or a professional interpreter. AMHPs should also be in a position, where appropriate, to supply appropriate equipment to make communication easier with patients who have impaired hearing, but who do not have their own hearing aid.

14.43 See paragraphs 14.115–14.119 for specific guidance in relation to the assessment of people who are deaf and paragraphs 14.120–14.125 for people with dementia. For further guidance on specific issues that may arise when assessing people who have a learning disability or an autistic spectrum disorder, or who have a personality disorder, see chapter 20 and chapter 21 respectively.

14.44 Doctors and AMHPs undertaking assessments need to apply professional judgement and reach decisions independently of each other, but in a framework of co-operation and mutual support.

14.45 Unless there is good reason for undertaking separate assessments, patients should, where possible, be seen jointly by the AMHP and at least one of the two doctors involved in the assessment.

14.46 While it may not always be feasible for the patient to be examined by both doctors at the same time, they should both discuss the patient's case with the person considering making an application for the patient's detention.

14.47 Everyone involved in an assessment should be alert to the need to provide support to colleagues, especially where there is a risk of the patient causing physical harm. People carrying out assessments should be aware of circumstances in which the police should be asked to provide assistance, in accordance with arrangements agreed locally with the police (see paragraph 14.48), and how to use that assistance to maximise the safety of everyone involved in the assessment.[14]

14.48 Commissioners, providers, local authorities and the police should have joint locally agreed arrangements on the involvement of the police. These should include a joint risk assessment tool to help determine the level of risk and what (if any) police assistance may be required and how quickly it is needed. In cases where no warrant for the police to enter premises under section 135 is being applied for (see chapter 16), the risk assessment should indicate the reasons and why police assistance is nonetheless necessary.

THE ROLE OF APPROVED AMHPS

4–056   14.49 AMHPs may make an application for detention only if they:

- have interviewed the patient in a suitable manner

- are satisfied that the statutory criteria for detention are met, and

- are satisfied that, in all the circumstances of the case, detention in hospital is the most appropriate way of providing the care and medical treatment the patient needs.

14.50 Once an AMHP has decided that an application should be made, they must then decide whether it is necessary or proper for them (rather than the nearest relative) to make the application. If, having considered any views expressed by the patient's relatives and all the other relevant circumstances, they decide that it is, the AMHP must make the application.

14.51 At the start of an assessment, AMHPs should identify themselves to the person being assessed, members of the family, carers or friends and the other professionals present. AMHPs should ensure that the purpose of the visit, their role and that of the other professionals is explained. They should carry documents with them at all times which identify them as AMHPs and which specify both the local authority which approved them and the local authority on whose behalf they are acting.

14.52 Although AMHPs act on behalf of a local authority, they cannot be told by the local authority or anyone else whether or not to make an application. They must exercise their own judgement, based on social and medical evidence, when deciding whether to apply for a patient to be detained under the Act. The role of AMHPs is to provide an independent decision about whether or not there are alternatives to detention under the Act, bringing a social perspective to bear on their decision, and taking account of the least restrictive option and maximising independence guiding principle.

14.53 If a patient wants someone else (eg a familiar person or an advocate) to be present during the assessment and any subsequent action that may be taken, then ordinarily AMHPs should assist in securing that person's attendance, unless the urgency of the case makes it inappropriate to do so. Patients may feel safer or more confident with a friend or other person they know well in attendance. Equally, an advocate can help to reassure patients. Some patients may already

---

[14] Local policies should already be in place between partner agencies in line with the Crisis Care Concordat. Mental Health Crisis Care Concordat: Improving outcomes for people experiencing mental health crisis. Department of Health and Concordat signatories. 2014. https://www.gov.uk/government/uploads/system/uploads/attachment_data/file/281242/36353_Mental_Health_Crisis_accessible.pdf.

be receiving help from an advocate and, if this is the case, the advocate should also be present.

14.54 Patients should usually be given the opportunity of speaking to the AMHP alone. If an AMHP has reason to fear physical harm, they should insist that another professional is present.

14.55 It is not desirable for patients to be interviewed through a closed door or window, and this should be considered only where other people are at serious risk. Where direct access to the patient is not possible, but there is no immediate risk of physical danger to the patient or to anyone else, AMHPs should consider applying for a warrant under section 135 of the Act allowing the police to enter the premises (see chapter 16).

14.56 Where patients are subject to the short-term effects of alcohol or drugs (whether prescribed or self-administered) which make interviewing them diffi- cult, the AMHP should either wait until the effects have abated before interviewing the patient or arrange to return later. If it is not realistic to wait because of the patient's disturbed behaviour and the urgency of the case, the assessment will have to be based on whatever information the AMHP can obtain from reliable sources. This should be made clear in the AMHP's record of the assessment.

The AMHP and the nearest relative

14.57 AMHPs are required by the Act to attempt to identify the patient's nearest **4–057** relative as defined in section 26 of the Act (See chapter 5).

14.58 When AMHPs make an application for admission under section 2, they must take such steps as are practicable to inform the nearest relative and, if differ- ent, carer, that the application is to be (or has been) made and of the nearest relative's power to discharge the patient.

14.59 Before making an application for admission under section 3, AMHPs must consult the nearest relative, unless it is not reasonably practicable or would involve unreasonable delay.

14.60 Circumstances in which the nearest relative need not be informed or con- sulted include those where:

- it is not practicable for the AMHP to obtain sufficient information to estab- lish the identity or location of the nearest relative or where to do so would require an excessive amount of investigation involving unreasonable delay, and

- consultation is not possible because of the nearest relative's own health or mental incapacity.

14.61 There may also be cases where, although physically possible, it would not be reasonably practicable to inform or consult the nearest relative because the detrimental impact of this on the patient would interfere with the patient's right to respect for their privacy and family life under article 8 of the European Convention on Human Rights to an extent that would not be justified and propor- tionate in the particular circumstances of the case. Detrimental impact may include cases where patients are likely to suffer emotional distress, deterioration in their mental health, physical harm, or financial or other exploitation as a result of the consultation. Consultation with the nearest relative that interferes with the patient's Article 8 rights may be justified to protect the patient's article 5 right to liberty.[15]

14.62 Consulting and notifying the nearest relative is a significant safeguard for patients. Therefore decisions not to do so on these grounds should not be taken lightly. AMHPs should consider all the circumstances of the case, including:

- the benefit to the patient of the involvement of their nearest relative, including to protect the patient's article 5 rights

- the patient's wishes including taking into account whether they have the capacity to decide whether they would want their nearest relative involved and any statement of their wishes they have made in advance. However, a patient's wishes will not be determinative of whether it is reasonably practicable to consult the nearest relative

- any detrimental effect that involving the nearest relative would have on the patient's health and wellbeing, and

- whether there is any good reason to think that the patient's objection may be intended to prevent information relevant to the assessment being discovered.

14.63 If they do not consult or inform the nearest relative, AMHPs should record their reasons. Consultation must not be avoided purely because it is thought that the nearest relative might object to the application.

14.64 When consulting nearest relatives AMHPs should, where possible:

- ascertain the nearest relative's views about both the patient's needs and the nearest relative's own needs in relation to the patient

- inform the nearest relative of the reasons for considering an application for detention and what the effects of such an application would be, and

- inform the nearest relative of their role and rights under the Act.

14.65 If the nearest relative objects to an application being made for admission for treatment under section 3, the application cannot be made. If it is thought necessary to proceed with the application to ensure the patient's safety or that of others and the nearest relative cannot be persuaded to agree, the AMHP will need to consider applying to the county court for the nearest relative's displacement under section 29 of the Act (see paragraphs 5.7 and 5.11–5.24).

Consultation with other people

4–058　14.66 Although there are specific requirements to consult the nearest relative, it is important to recognise the value of involving other people in the decision-making process, particularly the patient's carers, family members and advocates, who are often able to provide a particular perspective on the patient's circumstances. In so far as the urgency of the case allows, AMHPs should consider consulting with other relevant relatives, carers or friends and should take their views into account.

---

[15] See TW v Enfield Borough Council. 2014. EWCA Civ 362. http://www.bailii.org/ew/cases/EWCA/Civ/2014/362.html.

14.67 Where patients are under 18, AMHPs should in particular consider consulting with the patient's parents (or other people who have parental responsibility for the patient—see chapter 19), assuming they are not the patient's nearest relative anyway.

14.68 In deciding whether it is appropriate to consult carers and other family members, AMHPs should consider:

- the patient's wishes

- the nature of the relationship between the patient and the person in question, including how long the relationship has existed, and

- whether the patient has referred to any hostility between them and the person in question, or there is other evidence of hostility, abuse or exploitation.

14.69 AMHPs should also consult wherever possible with other people who have been involved with the patient's care, including their care co-ordinator if they are supported on the care programme approach (see chapter 34). This could include people working for statutory, voluntary or independent services and other service providers who do not specialise in mental health services but have contact with the patient. For example, the patient may be known to services for older people or substance misuse services.

14.70 Some patients may have an attorney or deputy appointed under the MCA who has authority to make decisions about their personal welfare. Where such a person is known to exist, AMHPs should take reasonable steps to contact them and seek their opinion. Where attorneys or deputies have the power to consent or refuse treatment for mental disorder on the patient's behalf, they should also be given the opportunity to talk directly to the doctors assessing the patient, where practicable.

Medical examination by doctors as part of the assessment

14.71 A medical examination must involve: **4–059**

- direct personal examination of the patient and their mental state, and

- consideration of all available relevant clinical information, including that in the possession of others, professional or non-professional.

14.72 If direct physical access to the patient is not immediately possible and it is not desirable to postpone the examination in order to negotiate access, consideration should be given to requesting that an AMHP apply for a warrant under section 135 of the Act (see paragraph 14.55 and chapter 16).

14.73 Where practicable, at least one of the medical recommendations must be provided by a doctor with previous acquaintance with the patient. Preferably, this should be a doctor who has personally treated the patient. It is sufficient for the doctor to have had some previous knowledge of the patient's case.

14.74 It is preferable that a doctor who does not have previous acquaintance with the patient be approved under section 12 of the Act. The Act requires that at least one of the doctors must be so approved.

14.75 Doctors must give reasons for the opinions stated in their recommendations. When giving a clinical description of the patient's mental disorder as part of these reasons, doctors should include a description of the patient's symptoms and behaviour, not merely a diagnostic classification.

14.76 When making recommendations for detention under section 3, doctors are required to state that appropriate medical treatment is available for the patient (see chapter 23). Preferably, they should know in advance of making the recommendation the name of the hospital to which the patient is to be admitted. If that is not possible, their recommendation may state that appropriate medical treatment will be available if the patient is admitted to one or more specific hospitals (or units within a hospital).

COMMISSIONING AND SECTION 140 OF THE ACT

4–060   14.77 If the doctors reach the opinion that the patient needs to be admitted to hospital, it is their responsibility to take the necessary steps to secure a suitable hospital bed; it is not the responsibility of the applicant. In some cases, it could be agreed locally between the local authority and the relevant NHS bodies and communicated to the AMHP that this will be done by any AMHP involved in the assessment.

14.78 Clinical commissioning groups (CCGs) are responsible for commissioning mental health services to meet the needs of their areas. Under section 140 of the Act, CCGs have a duty to notify local authorities in their areas of arrangements which are in force for the reception of patients in cases of special urgency or the provision of appropriate accommodation or facilities specifically designed for patients under the age of 18. The arrangements should include details of which providers in their area can receive patients in cases of special urgency and provide accommodation or facilities designed to be specifically suitable for patients under the age of 18. CCGs should provide a list of hospitals and their specialisms to local authorities which will help inform AMHPs as to where these hospitals are. This should in turn help inform AMHPs as to where beds are available in these circumstances if they are needed.

14.79 The NHS Commissioning Board (known as NHS England) is responsible for the commissioning of secure mental health services and other specialist services. NHS commissioners should work with providers to ensure that procedures are in place through which beds can be identified whenever required.

14.80 Local authorities, providers, NHS commissioners, police forces and ambulance services should ensure that they have in place a clear joint policy for the safe and appropriate admission of people in their local area agreed at board or board-equivalent level by each party and each party should appoint a named senior lead ('senior lead'). It is good practice for the parties to the local policy to meet regularly to discuss its effectiveness in the light of experience and review the policy where necessary, and to decide when information about specific cases can be shared between relevant parties for the purposes of protecting the person or others, in line with the law. Persons carrying out functions for these parties should understand the policies and their purpose, the roles and responsibilities of other agencies involved, and follow the local policy and receive the necessary training to be able to carry out fully their functions.[16]

---

[16] Local crisis care policies and agreements should already in place through the Mental Health Crisis Care Concordat: Improving outcomes for people experiencing mental health crisis. Department of Health and Concordat signatories. 2014. https://www.gov.uk/government/uploads/system/uploads/attachment_data/file/281242/36353_Mental_ Health_Crisis_accessible.pd.

14.81 In order to promote a patient's recovery, NHS commissioners and providers should work together to take steps, with appropriate input from section 12 doctors and AMHPs, to place individuals as close as is reasonably possible to a location that the patient identifies they would like to be close to (eg their home or close to a family member or carer). This should take account of any risk assessment undertaken, the availability of services which can meet the patient's individual needs, any assessment in respect of the likely duration of the patient's stay, and any other factors raised by the patient and their family. The location of the placement, and considerations relevant to that decision, should be monitored and reviewed regularly. Where secure care is needed further issues become relevant (see paragraph 14.82). This will help to facilitate effective discharge and after-care planning (see chapters 32 and 33).

14.82 For individuals who require low and medium secure mental health services, consideration should be given, through clinical and risk assessment, to the type of care required, especially where this includes specialist care. Steps should be taken to place individuals as close as is reasonably possible to a location that the patient identifies they would like to be close to that is suitable for their needs. If an individual is assessed as requiring high secure mental health services, they will be placed in a high security hospital according to the defined catchment areas of these hospitals. Rampton Hospital is the provider of national services for women, deaf people and people with learning disabilities who require high secure mental health services. Decisions regarding the location and type of facility where restricted patients are placed will be determined by appropriate clinical and risk assessment of the type of care required to meet the needs of the patient and to protect public safety.

14.83 In cases where the patient lacks capacity to make a decision about the location they would like to be close to, a best interests decision on the location should be taken.

14.84 Having regard to the empowerment and involvement principle, commissioners should ensure as far as is possible that carers are involved in the decision about where to locate an individual, and are informed of the reasons for the decision taken. Commissioners should have in place a policy so that the patient and/or the patient's carers are able to challenge a decision.8

14.85 When a patient's carer informs the commissioner of difficulties in visiting the patient because of the distance that they need to travel, the commissioner should consider whether they can provide any assistance to support the patient's carer to visit and maintain contact with the patient. The commissioner should inform the carer that they can request a carer's assessment from the local authority. CCGs should work with the relevant NHS Commissioning Board regional team under these circumstances to seek to move the patient closer to their preferred location.

14.86 Local recording and reporting mechanisms should be in place to ensure the details of any delays in placing patients, and the impacts on patients, their carers, provider staff and other professionals are reported to commissioning and local authority senior leads. These details should feed into local demand planning. AMHPs should be supported by their local authority in these circumstances and should not be expected by commissioners and providers to address the delay themselves. In the meantime, commissioners should, in partnership with providers, ensure that alternative arrangements to meet the person's needs pending the availability of a bed are accessible, eg crisis houses, and should communicate those arrangements to the local authority. The local authority should ensure that AMHPs are aware of these arrangements.

ACTION WHEN IT IS DECIDED TO MAKE AN APPLICATION

4-061   14.87 Most compulsory admissions require prompt action. Applicants have up to 14 days (depending on when the patient was last examined by a doctor as part of the assessment) in which to decide whether to make the application, starting with the day they personally last saw the patient. There may be cases where AMHPs conclude that they should delay taking a final decision in order to see whether the patient's condition changes, or whether successful alternatives to detention can be put in place in the interim.

14.88 Before making an application, AMHPs should ensure that appropriate arrangements are in place for the immediate care of any dependent children the patient may have and any adults who rely on the patient for care. Their needs should already have been considered as part of the assessment. Where relevant, AMHPs should also ensure that practical arrangements are made for the care of any pets and for the local authority to carry out its other duties under the Care Act 2014 to secure the patient's home and protect their property.

14.89 Applications for detention must be addressed to the managers of the hospital where the patient is to be detained. An application must state a specific hospital. An application cannot, for example, be made to a multi-site provider without specifying which of the provider's sites the patient is to be admitted to. Providers should identify a bed manager or other single point of contact who will be responsible for finding a suitable bed as soon as possible and telling the applicant the name of the site at which it is situated. Effective systems of bed management including discharge planning, possible alternatives to admission and demand planning should be in place. The bed manager should work closely with commissioners to proactively identify local need, and with assessing doctors and AMHPs to secure a bed. AMHPs should be adequately supported by their local authority in establishing working partnerships with other local agencies listed at paragraph 14.80.

14.90 Where units under the management of different bodies exist on the same site (or even in the same building), they will be separate hospitals for the purposes of the Act, because one hospital cannot be under the control of two sets of managers. Where there is potential for confusion, the respective hospital managers should ensure that there are distinct names for the units. In collaboration with local authorities, they should take steps to ensure that information is available to AMHPs who are likely to be making relevant applications to enable them effectively to distinguish the different hospitals on the site and to describe them correctly in applications.

14.91 Once an application has been completed, the patient should be transported to hospital as soon as possible, if they are not already in the hospital. However, patients should not be moved until it is known that the hospital is willing to accept them.

14.92 A properly completed application supported by the necessary medical recommendations provides the applicant with the authority to transport the patient to hospital even if the patient does not wish to go. That authority lasts for 14 days from the date when the patient was last examined by one of the doctors with a view to making a recommendation to support the application. See chapter 17 for further guidance on transport.

14.93 The AMHP should provide an outline report for the hospital at the time the patient is first admitted or detained, giving reasons for the application and any practical matters about the patient's circumstances which the hospital should know. Where possible, the report should include the name and telephone number of the AMHP or a care co-ordinator who can give further information. Local authorities should use a standard form on which AMHPs can make this outline report.

14.94 Where it is not realistic for the AMHP to accompany the patient to the hospital, it is acceptable for them to provide the information outlined above by telephone, fax or other electronic means compatible with transferring confidential information. If providing the information by telephone, the AMHP should ensure that a written report is sent to the admitting hospital as soon as possible.

14.95 An outline report does not take the place of the full report which AMHPs are expected to complete for their employer (or the local authority on whose behalf they are acting—if different).

14.96 If the patient is a restricted patient, the AMHP should ensure that the MHCS of the Ministry of Justice is notified of the detention as soon as possible. This information should be left during office hours, although a duty officer is available at all times for urgent queries.[17]

14.97 If the patient is a looked after child under the Children Act 1989, AMHPs should inform the local authority's children's services as soon as possible. If this patient is placed out of the area of the local authority that looks after the child ('responsible authority'), AMHPs should inform the children's services in both the responsible authority and the local authority in which the child is placed.

14.98 An application cannot be used to admit a patient to any hospital other than the one stated in the application (although once admitted a patient may be transferred to another hospital—see paragraphs 37.16–37.27).

14.99 In exceptional circumstances, if patients are transported to a hospital which has agreed to accept them, but there is no longer a bed available, the managers and staff of that hospital should assist in finding a suitable alternative for the patient. This may involve making a new application to a different hospital. If the application is under section 3, new medical recommendations will be required, unless the original recommendations already state that appropriate medical treatment is available in the proposed new hospital. The hospital to which the original application was made should assist in securing new medical recommendations if they are needed. A situation of this sort should be considered a serious failure and should be recorded and investigated accordingly.

COMMUNICATING THE OUTCOME OF THE ASSESSMENT

14.100 Having decided whether or not to make an application for admission, **4–062** AMHPs should inform the patient, giving their reasons. Subject to the normal considerations of patient confidentiality, AMHPs should also give their decision and the reasons for it to:

- the patient's nearest relative
- the doctors involved in the assessment

---

[17] At the time of publication, contact details are available at www.justice.gov.uk/contacts/noms/mental-health-unit, and the Ministry of Justice switchboard is contactable on 020 3334 3555. For urgent queries out of office hours the telephone number (operated by the Home Office) is 020 7035 4848: select option 5.

- the patient's care co-ordinator (if they have one), and

- the patient's GP, if they were not one of the doctors involved in the assessment.

14.101 An AMHP should, when informing the nearest relative that they not do intend to make an application, advise the nearest relative of their right to do so instead. If the nearest relative wishes to pursue this, the AMHP should suggest that they consult with the doctors to see if they would be prepared to provide recommendations.

14.102 Where the AMHP has considered a patient's case at the request of the nearest relative, the reasons for not applying for the patient's admission must be given to the nearest relative in writing. Such a letter should contain, as far as possible, sufficient details to enable the nearest relative to understand the decision while at the same time preserving the patient's right to confidentiality.

ACTION WHEN IT IS DECIDED NOT TO APPLY FOR ADMISSION

4–063   14.103 There is no obligation on an AMHP or nearest relative to make an application for admission just because the statutory criteria are met.

14.104 Where AMHPs decide not to apply for a patient's detention they should record the reasons for their decision. The decision should be supported, where necessary, by an alternative framework of care or treatment (or both). AMHPs should decide how to pursue any actions which their assessment indicates are necessary to meet the needs of the patient. That might include, for example, referring the patient to social, health or other services.

14.105 The steps to be taken to put in place any new arrangements for the patient's care and treatment, and any plans for reviewing them, should be recorded in writing and copies made available to all those who need them (subject to the normal considerations of patient confidentiality).

14.106 It is particularly important that the patient's care co-ordinator (where they require support under the care programme approach (CPA)—see chapter 34) is fully involved in decisions about meeting the patient's needs.

14.107 Arrangements should be made to ensure that information about assessments and their outcome is passed to professional colleagues where appropriate, eg where an application for admission is not immediately necessary but might be in the future. This information will need to be available at short notice at any time of day or night.

14.108 More generally, making out-of-hours services aware of situations that are ongoing—such as when there is concern for an individual but no assessment has begun or when a person has absconded before an assessment could start or be completed—assists out-of-hours services in responding accordingly.

RESOLVING DISAGREEMENTS

4–064   14.109 Sometimes there will be differences of opinion between professionals involved in the assessment. There is nothing wrong with disagreements: handled properly these offer an opportunity to safeguard the interests of the patient by widening the discussion about the best way of meeting their needs. Doctors and AMHPs should be ready to consult other professionals, especially care co-ordinators and others involved with the patient's current care, and to consult carers and family, while retaining for themselves the final responsibility for their decision.

Where disagreements do occur, professionals should ensure that they discuss these with each other.

14.110 Where there is an unresolved dispute about an application for detention, it is essential that the professionals do not abandon the patient. Instead, they should explore and agree an alternative plan—if necessary on a temporary basis. Such a plan should include a risk assessment and identification of the arrangements for managing the risks. The alternative plan should be recorded in writing, as should the arrangements for reviewing it. Copies should be made available to all those who need it (subject to the normal considerations of patient confidentiality).

RESPONSIBILITIES OF APPROVING BODIES FOR DOCTORS APPROVED UNDER SECTION 12

14.111 The Secretary of State for Health's functions of approving medical prac- **4–065** titioners under section 12(2) of the Act are exercised by the approving bodies listed on the gov.uk website. Medical practitioners who are approved clinicians under the Act are automatically treated as being approved under section 12 as well.

14.112 Approving bodies should:

- take active steps to encourage doctors, including GPs and those working in prison health services and police services, to apply for approval, and

- ensure that the up-to-date list of approved doctors and details of their availability are available to all those who may need them, including GPs, providers of hospital and community mental health services and social services. There is now an online national Section 12/Approved Clinician register in England available to providers, AMHPs and others.[18]

CO-OPERATION BETWEEN LOCAL AGENCIES

14.113 NHS commissioners, NHS-funded providers and local authorities **4–066** should co-operate in ensuring that there are opportunities for regular communication between professionals involved in mental health assessments, in order to promote understanding and to provide a forum for clarification of their respective roles and responsibilities. NHS commissioners, NHS-funded providers and local authorities should also keep in mind the interface with the criminal justice agencies, including the probation service and the police.

14.114 Opportunities should also be sought to involve and learn directly from people with experience of being assessed (patients and former patients), their carers, family and advocates.

PATIENTS WHO ARE DEAF

14.115 AMHPs and doctors assessing a deaf person should, wherever possible, **4–067** have had deaf awareness training, including basic training in issues relating to mental health and deafness. Where required, they should also seek assistance from specialists with appropriate expertise in mental health and deafness. This may be available from one of the specialist hospital units for deafness and mental

---

[18] Instructions for Approving Doctors and Clinicians under the Mental Health Act 1983. Department of Health. 2013. https://www.gov.uk/government/ publications/mental-health-act-exercise-of-approval-instructions-2013.

health. Contact with such units may, in particular, help to prevent deaf people being wrongly assessed as having a learning disability or another mental disorder.

14.116 Unless different arrangements have been agreed locally, the AMHP involved in the assessment should be responsible for booking and using registered qualified interpreters with expertise in mental health interpreting, bearing in mind that the interpretation of thought-disordered language requires particular expertise. Relay interpreters (interpreters who relay British Sign Language (BSL) to hands-on BSL or visual frame signing or close signing) may be necessary, such as when the deaf person has a visual impairment, does not use BSL to sign or has minimal language skills or a learning disability.

14.117 Reliance on unqualified interpreters or health professionals with only limited signing skills should be avoided. Subject to the normal considerations about patient confidentiality, family members may occasionally be able to assist a professional interpreter in understanding a patient's idiosyncratic use of language. Family members should not be relied upon in place of a professional interpreter, even if the patient is willing for them to be involved.

14.118 Pre-lingual deafness may cause delayed language acquisition, which may in turn influence social behaviour. People carrying out assessments under the Act should have an awareness and knowledge of how mental health problems present in pre-lingually deaf people.

14.119 Cultural issues need to be taken into account, for instance in people who are pre-lingually deaf, as they have a visual perspective of the world and may consider themselves to be part of a cultural and linguistic minority. This means that they may behave in ways which are misperceived as evidence of mental disorder. For example, animated signing may be misunderstood as aggression, while touching a hearing person to talk to them may be misunderstood as an assault. A deaf person's spoken or written English may be poor, giving rise to a false assumption of thought disorder.

PATIENTS WITH DEMENTIA

4–068   14.120 Individuals who are presenting signs and symptoms of dementia as well as those with a confirmed diagnosis of dementia can fall within the Act's definition of mental disorder. Dementia can pose particular challenges and understanding of the condition is essential to delivery of quality care.

14.121 Generally, people who have dementia present a range of behaviours:

- dementia is generally progressive, meaning symptoms gradually get worse over time. How quickly it progresses varies from person to person

- people with dementia experience memory loss, have problems recalling things that happened recently and can sometimes repeat themselves

- people with dementia often have difficulty communicating, including through speech; many have difficulty reading and understanding written material

- some people with dementia experience problems concentrating, are confused about time or place, and/or have difficulty problem solving and sequencing tasks

- some people experience sight or visual difficulties, for example judging distances or misinterpreting reflections in mirrors, and/or

- people with dementia can have problems controlling their emotions, experience mood changes and lose interest in things; they can for example become unusually sad or frightened, angry or upset or withdrawn.

14.122 People with dementia may present and behave in very different ways from those with other kinds of mental disorder. It is important that such behaviours are understood properly if the Act is to be used appropriately. Effective communication is key to supporting people to understand the assessment process, eg giving people time to answer questions and using non-verbal aids where appropriate.

14.123 Where possible, professionals with specialist skills and knowledge to support people who have dementia should be involved in any decision to use the Act. Professionals working in hospital or the community to support patients who have dementia should have appropriate skills, knowledge and expertise, or be able to acquire these, to support patients with dementia effectively.

14.124 Especially in times of crisis, decisions about the use of the Act for people with dementia may have to be made by professionals who are not specialists in the field. It is important that AMHPs and doctors assessing the person have a sufficient understanding of signs and symptoms of dementia as well as other forms of mental disorder.

14.125 Individuals identified by various local agencies as having dementia may never have had a thorough clinical assessment and diagnosis. Professionals should use validated assessment tools, eg Mini Mental State Examinations, to conduct such an assessment and diagnosis.

PATIENTS DETAINED UNDER THE IMMIGRATION ACT 1971 OR NATIONALITY, IMMIGRATION AND ASYLUM ACT 2002

14.126 Section 48 of the Act empowers the Secretary of State for Justice to **4–069** direct the removal from custody to hospital of individuals who are detained under particular provisions of the Immigration Act 1971 or under section 62 of the Nationality Immigration and Asylum Act 2002,[19] who are suffering from a mental disorder of a nature or degree which makes it appropriate for them to be detained in a hospital, are in need of urgent medical treatment and where appropriate medical treatment is available. Section 53 makes further provision in relation to such detainees and their transfer to hospital or back to custody, and when a transfer direction ceases to have effect.[20]

14.127 Providers should ensure that in supporting individuals in immigration removal centres they are alert to the need to identify individuals' mental health needs as early as possible. Where transfers to hospital for assessment and treatment have been deemed appropriate, they should be made in a timely manner to the most suitable location based on clinical need.

14.128 Professionals should be aware that immigration detainees may be particularly vulnerable patients—for example, they may be victims of violence, war or torture; they may have limited access to friends or relatives to support them and

---

[19] Immigration Act 1971. http://www.legislation.gov.uk/ukpga/1971/77/contents Section 62 of the Nationality Immigration and Asylum Act 2002. http://www.legislation.gov.uk/ukpga/2002/41/section/62.

[20] See Reference Guide to the Mental Health Act 1983. Department of Health. 2015. https://www.gov.uk/government/publications/reference-guide-to-the-mental-health-act-1983.

they may need additional support, eg interpretation services. Consideration should be given to any special support they might require as a result of their background, including their culture, ethnicity or religion. Consideration should also be given to why they may behave in certain ways (eg why they might be unwilling to disclose mental health problems).

14.129 Due consideration should be given to appropriate discharge planning and care following the discharge of a patient from an in-patient setting, including if they are returning to an immigration removal centre.

16. POLICE POWERS AND PLACES OF SAFETY

Why read this chapter?

4–070 16.1 Under the Act, police officers have a power to enter private premises with a warrant and temporarily remove people to a place of safety, and a power to remove persons from public places to a place of safety, provided that specified criteria are met. This chapter gives guidance on obtaining a warrant, the need for agreed local policies, the definition of a place of safety, transfer of patients between places of safety, and assessment.

16.2 Approved mental health professionals (AMHPs), doctors and police officers should, in particular, be aware of the guidance given in this chapter.

SECTION 135: WARRANT TO SEARCH FOR AND REMOVE PATIENTS

Section 135(1) warrant

4–071 16.3 The purpose of a section 135(1) warrant is to provide police officers with a power of entry to private premises, for the purposes of removing the person to a place of safety for a mental health assessment or for other arrangements to be made for their treatment or care. The warrant must be applied for by an AMHP and can be granted by a magistrate when the person is believed to be suffering from mental disorder and is being ill-treated, neglected or kept otherwise than under proper control, or is living alone and unable to care for themselves.

16.4 The warrant gives any police officer the right to enter the premises, by force if necessary. The police officer may remain even if asked to leave, and may also search the premises for the person believed to be suffering from a mental disorder. When acting on the warrant, the officer must be accompanied by an AMHP and a doctor. It may be helpful if the doctor who accompanies the police officer is approved for the purposes of section 12(2) of the Act. A person should be told the reasons for the removal before they are removed. The police officer may then remove the person to a place of safety, where they can be detained for up to 72 hours from the time of their arrival.

16.5 Where it is reasonably practicable, the intended place of safety should be identified, and the necessary arrangements made, before a warrant is applied for under section 135(1). Proper planning should ensure that it is not necessary to use a police station as a place of safety for people removed under section 135(1), other than in the exceptional circumstances described in paragraph 16.38.

16.6 Before the execution of the warrant, the AMHP should contribute to any assessment of the risk presented by the person that is carried out by the police, in order to plan to mitigate the risks identified and to help to keep that person safe during the process of their assessment or removal.

16.7 Following entry under section 135(1), the AMHP and doctor between them should determine whether the person needs to be taken to a place of safety for further assessment or for arrangements to be made for their treatment or care. The power to detain a person under section 135(1) ceases once an application for further detention has been made under the Act, other arrangements have been made for their treatment or care, or it has been decided that no further action is to be taken in respect of the person.

16.8 The AMHP and the doctor may convene a mental health assessment in the person's home if it is safe and appropriate to do so and the person consents to this. In taking this decision, consideration should be given as to who else is present, particularly if a person might be distressed by the assessment taking place in these circumstances.

16.9 Local authorities should ensure that guidance to AMHPs on how and when to apply for a warrant is also available to the relevant partner agencies (including the relevant local authority and police force).

16.10 Local authorities and hospital managers should ensure that there are procedures in place for obtaining warrants, both during and outside court hours. These procedures should describe the necessary processes, the evidence which individuals may be reasonably expected to produce, and the documents that should be prepared to help the process run smoothly and quickly.

16.11 Magistrates have to be satisfied that it is appropriate to issue a warrant. They are likely to ask applicants why they are applying for a warrant, whether reasonable attempts to enter without a warrant have been made and, if not, why not. Although it is not necessary for permission to enter to have been refused in order for a section 135(1) warrant to be granted, applicants should provide documented reasons for seeking a warrant if they have not already tried to gain access.

16.12 Magistrates should ensure that section 135 warrants can be granted in a timely way, taking into account that situations can be very urgent and that it should be possible to grant a warrant outside of normal business hours.

16.13 Reliance upon section 135 to gain entry in an emergency situation may be inappropriate due to the time it can take to obtain the necessary warrant. The police may use their power of entry under Section 17(1)(e) of the Police and Criminal Evidence Act 1984 (PACE)[21] for the purposes of saving life or limb or preventing serious damage to property: however this does not confer on the police any power to remove the person to a place of safety or to detain them.

Section 135(2) warrant

16.14 The purpose of a section 135(2) warrant is to provide police officers with **4–072** a power of entry to private premises for the purposes of removing a patient who is liable to be taken or returned to hospital or any other place or into custody under the Act. The warrant must be granted by a magistrate. It enables a police officer to enter the premises, search for, and remove the patient so they can be taken to, or returned to, where they ought to be. Such a warrant may be used, for example to help return a patient who has absconded, or who needs to be transported to hospital, if access to the premises where they are staying has been refused or is likely to be refused. (See chapter 28 for detailed guidance on patients who are absent from hospital without leave.)

---

[21] Section 17(1)(e) of the Police and Criminal Evidence Act 1984. http://www.legislation.gov.uk/ukpga/1984/60/section/17.

16.15 When a warrant issued under section 135(2) is being used, it is good practice for the police officer to be accompanied by a person with authority from the managers of the relevant hospital (or local authority, if applicable) to detain the patient and to take or return them to where they ought to be. For patients on a community treatment order (CTO) it is good practice for this person to be a member of the multi-disciplinary team responsible for the patient's care. The patient should be told why they are being detained, taken or retaken, before this happens. See chapters 29 and 31 for further information on CTOs.

16.16 When taking the person to a place of safety on a section 135 warrant, the AMHP, hospital managers or the local authority (as appropriate) should ensure that an ambulance or other transport is available to take the person to the place of safety or to the place where they ought to be, in accordance with a locally agreed policy on the transport of patients under the Act (see chapter 17). It may be helpful for the AMHP to escort the person or meet them on arrival at the place of safety, in order to ensure continuity of care and to provide information for the hand-over. The police should not normally be needed to transport the person or to escort them for a section 135 warrant.

SECTION 136: MENTALLY DISORDERED PEOPLE FOUND IN PUBLIC PLACES

4–073 16.17 Section 136 is an emergency power which allows for the removal of a person who is in a place to which the public have access, to a place of safety, if the person appears to a police officer to be suffering from mental disorder and to be in immediate need of care or control, if the police officer believes it necessary in the interests of that person, or for the protection of others. The person should then receive a mental health assessment, and any necessary arrangements should be made for their on-going care.

16.18 'A place to which the public have access' includes places to which members of the public have open access, access if a payment is made, or access at certain times of the day. It does not include private premises, such as the person's own place of residence or private homes belonging to others, in which case a section 135 warrant is needed. It is not appropriate to encourage a person outside in order to use section 136 powers. Section 135 should be used if the person is in private premises.

16.19 A police officer may use section 136 if they encounter the person in a public place, including if they are already on scene, responding to a call, are approached, or otherwise come into contact with the person.

16.20 The police should not be called to a hospital ward to use their section 136 powers. If the person is already an in-patient in hospital, a nurse, doctor or approved clinician should instead use their holding powers under section 5 if it is considered necessary to detain the person (see chapter 18). It may be appropriate for the police to attend a hospital if the person is in the grounds, or another public part of the hospital, such as a part of the accident and emergency department to which the public have access, in which case they may use section 136.

16.21 Section 136 is not intended to be used as a way to gain access to mental health services and the person should be encouraged to take a route via primary care services, or to contact local mental health community services. A police officer may, without the use of section 136 powers, decide to escort a person who is voluntarily seeking urgent mental healthcare to an appropriate service.

16.22 When considering the use of police powers to detain people under the Act, less restrictive alternatives to detention should be considered. Health and/ or social care professionals may be able to identify alternative options. For example, with the person's consent, the police, or any other qualified person may convene a mental health assessment without using section 135 or section 136 powers, by requesting that a section 12-approved doctor attend in order to assess the person and make any arrangements for their on-going care. Where appropriate, and depending on specific circumstances, consultation with carers may help, particularly in the case of children and young people. Health and social care professionals, and the police, should have regard to the principles of the Mental Capacity Act 2005 (see chapter 13 for more information).

16.23 When deciding that detention may be necessary, the police may also benefit from seeking advice before using section 136 powers in cases where they are unsure that the circumstances are sufficiently serious for using these powers. Local protocols should set out how this advice can be provided and who the police should contact, including outside of normal business hours.

16.24 The use of physical restraint or force may be required when removing a person, or in a place of safety, for the protection of the person or others (such as the public, staff or patients). If physical restraint is used, it should be necessary and unavoidable to prevent harm to the person or others, and be proportionate to the risk of harm if restraint was not used. The least restrictive type of restraint should be used. There should be a clear local protocol about the circumstances when, very exceptionally, police may be asked to use physical restraint in a health-based place of safety. For definitions of restraint and guidance on the use of restraint in hospital see chapter 26.

16.25 The purpose of removing a person to a place of safety in these circumstances is only to enable the person to be examined by a doctor and interviewed by an AMHP, so that the necessary arrangements can be made for the person's care and treatment. It is not a substitute for an application for detention under the Act, even if it is thought that the person will need to be detained in hospital only for a short time. It should not be used as a substitute for, or affect the use of, other police powers.

16.26 The maximum period a person may be detained under section 136 is 72 hours. In practice, detentions should not need to be this long. The imposition of consecutive periods of detention under section 136 is unlawful. The maximum 72-hour period begins at the time of arrival at the first place of safety (including if the person needs to be transferred between places of safety).

16.27 The person should be assessed by a doctor and interviewed by an AMHP as soon as possible after the person is brought to the place of safety. As soon as practicable after the assessment and interview, the person should either be discharged, informally admitted, further detained under the Act, or other arrangements made for the person's treatment or care in the community. The person may continue to be detained while these arrangements are being made, provided that the maximum period of detention is not exceeded.

16.28 People detained under section 136 are sometimes far from home. Arrangements should be in place so that the police can take a patient to the nearest available health-based place of safety, which should admit the person even when the person resides in another area. Local authorities should also have arrangements in place so that the nearest AMHP can attend, although consideration should always be given to whether an AMHP from the person's home authority, with the benefit of local knowledge and understanding of any relevant history, could reasonably travel to assess the person. These arrangements should also ensure that, when a place of safety serves an area that includes more than one local authority, the relevant AMHP services work together to ensure continuity of care and timely attendance.

16.29 Police should generally use section 135 or 136, rather than their common law power of arrest for breach of the peace, when the person appears to be suffering from mental disorder which makes it necessary for them to be taken to a place of safety.

LOCAL POLICIES ON USE OF POLICE POWERS AND PLACES OF SAFETY

4–074   16.30 Local authorities, NHS commissioners, hospitals, police forces and ambulance services should have local partnership arrangements in place to deal with people experiencing mental health crises. The objective of local partnership arrangements is to ensure that people experiencing mental health crises receive the right medical care from the most appropriate health agencies as soon as possible. The police will often, due to the nature of their role, be the first point of contact for individuals in crisis, but it is crucial that people experiencing mental health crises access appropriate health services at the earliest opportunity.

16.31 It is also important to ensure that a jointly agreed local policy is in place governing all aspects of the use of section 135 and section 136. Good practice depends on a number of factors. For example:

- local authorities, hospitals, NHS commissioners, police forces and ambulance services should ensure that they have a clear and jointly agreed policy for use of the powers under sections 135 and 136, as well as the operation of agreed places of safety within their localities

- all professionals involved in implementation of the powers should understand them and their purpose, the roles and responsibilities of other agencies involved, and follow the local policy

- professionals involved in implementation of the powers should receive the necessary training to be able to carry out fully the role ascribed to their agency

- the parties to the local policy should meet regularly to discuss its effectiveness in the light of experience and review the policy where necessary, and

- partner agencies should decide when relevant information about specific cases can be shared between them for the purposes of safeguarding the person and the protection of others, if there is thought to be a risk of harm.

16.32 The policy should define responsibilities for:

- commissioning and providing sufficient safe and secure health-based places of safety, including for people under the age of 18

- identifying and agreeing the most appropriate places of safety in local areas, including contingency arrangements for those cases where the preferred place of safety is not available. This should ensure that local agency boundaries are not an overriding constraint, and that there are arrangements to ensure children and young people can access a place of safety in their local area

- escalating and reviewing decisions, particularly in the event of disagreement

- providing prompt assessment (including how soon the doctor and AMHP should attend) and, where appropriate, admission to hospital for further assessment or treatment

- securing the attendance of police officers at health-based places of safety, where appropriate, for the patient's health or safety or the protection of others

- the safe, timely and appropriate transport of the person to and between places of safety (bearing in mind that hospital or ambulance transport will usually be preferable to police transport, which should only be used exceptionally, such as in cases of extreme urgency or where there is an immediate risk of violence)

- deciding whether it is appropriate to transfer the person from the place of safety to which they have been taken to another place of safety (see paragraphs 16.53—16.58)

- ensuring that people who are intoxicated can be safely managed in any place of safety or an emergency department, and receive an assessment of both their physical and mental health needs. Intoxication should not be used as a basis for excluding people from particular places of safety, except in the circumstances outlined in the policy such as where the patient's current behaviour clearly indicates that there may be a risk to their own safety, or that of the staff, which cannot be safely managed in the health-based place of safety.

- ensuring that people who are behaving, or have behaved, violently can be safely managed in a place of safety taking into account the needs of the person and the safety of staff and others

- arranging access to a hospital emergency department for assessment for people who need it, and having an agreed list of circumstances when this will be necessary, such as where a person is self-harming, has a high body temperature or physical injury

- record keeping (see paragraphs 16.59–16.62) and monitoring (see paragraphs 16.63–16.65) and audit of practice against policy

- the release, transport and follow-up of people assessed under section 135 or 136 who are not then admitted to hospital or immediately accommodated elsewhere, and

- preparing multi-agency care plans for people who are repeatedly detained under section 136.

16.33 Responsibilities should be allocated to those who are best placed to discharge them, bearing in mind the different purposes for which health and social services and the police service exist. Local policies should ensure that police officers know who to contact prior to the removal of a person to a place of safety under section 136, in order to help secure their acceptance into a health-based place of safety.

16.34 Such policies should cover arrangements for police officers to remain in attendance when a person arrives at a health-based place of safety. Healthcare staff, including ambulance staff, should take responsibility for the person as soon as possible, including preventing the person from absconding before the assessment can be carried out. The police officer should not be expected to remain until the assessment is completed; the officer should be able to leave when the situation is agreed to be safe for the patient and healthcare staff.

16.35 Such policies may be best maintained by the establishment of a liaison committee, which might also take responsibility for examining the processes in place for other multi-agency tasks, such as transport of persons under the Act and policies in respect of patients who go absent without leave.

PLACES OF SAFETY

4–075 16.36 The locally agreed policy should contain a list of identified places of safety. The process for identifying the most appropriate place of safety to which a particular person is to be removed should be clearly outlined in the local policy. This should be a hospital or other health-based place of safety where mental health services are provided. Health-based places of safety should ensure that they have arrangements in place to cope with periods of peak demand, for example using other suitable parts of a hospital, neighbouring health-based places of safety, or alternative places of safety.

16.37 Other options which might be appropriate to the individual's needs should be considered, for example a residential care home or the home of a relative or friend of the person who is willing to accept them temporarily. There is nothing that precludes other areas of a psychiatric hospital (such as a ward) being used as a temporary place of safety, provided that it is a suitable place and it is appropriate to use that place in the individual case.

16.38 A police station should not be used as a place of safety except in exceptional circumstances, for example it may be necessary to do so because the person's behaviour would pose an unmanageably high risk to other patients, staff or other users if the person were to be detained in a healthcare setting. A police station should not be used as the automatic second choice if there is no local health-based place of safety immediately available.

16.39 If, exceptionally, a police station is used, the locally agreed policy should set out the time within which the appropriate health and social care professionals will attend the police station to assess the person or to assist in arranging to transfer them to a more suitable place of safety.

16.40 Although the Act provides a limit of 72 hours for detention under section 136, when a police station is used as a place of safety in the absence of a health-based place of safety being available, an assessment should be made as quickly as possible and made a priority by the doctor and AMHP (see paragraphs 16.47 and 16.49 below). Alternatively, a transfer to a more appropriate place of safety should be made as soon as one becomes available unless it is clearly in the best interests of the person not to move them. Wherever practicable, detention in a police station under section 136 should not exceed a maximum period of 24 hours.

16.41 People taken to a health-based place of safety should be transported there by an ambulance or other health transport arranged by the police who should, in the case of section 136, also escort them in order to facilitate hand-over to health-care staff.

16.42 If, in exceptional circumstances, a police officer needs to take a person to an emergency department after detaining that person under section 136, for example because emergency medical assessment or treatment is required, the emergency department should provide a safe and suitable place for immediate care for that person.

16.43 In identifying the most appropriate place of safety for an individual, consideration should be given to the impact that the proposed place of safety (and the journey to it) may have on the person and on their examination and interview. It should always be borne in mind that the use of a police station can give the impression that the person detained is suspected of having committed a crime. This may cause distress and anxiety to the person concerned and may affect their co-operation with, and therefore the effectiveness of, the assessment process. In the event that a person is taken to a police station, it should be clearly explained to them that they are not suspected of any crime or other wrongdoing, and they are being kept there until they can be assessed to see if they need any care or treatment.

16.44 Where an individual is removed to a place of safety by the police, the following apply:

- where the place of safety is a hospital, the police should make contact as soon as is practicable with the hospital and local authority (or the people arranging AMHP services on its behalf) before the person's arrival at the place of safety. This will allow arrangements to be made for the person to be interviewed and examined as soon as possible. Where a warrant has been issued under section 135, these arrangements should, wherever possible, have been made in advance by the AMHP, the hospital or any other organisation responsible for the person

- where a hospital is used as a place of safety, it is a local decision whether the person is admitted to a bed on arrival or whether that happens only after they have been interviewed and examined

- where a police station is to be used as the place of safety, the police should make contact quickly with the local authority (or its AMHP service) and with an appropriate doctor. This will enable the examination and interview to be conducted as quickly as possible, thus ensuring that the person spends no longer than necessary in police custody before being allowed to leave or taken to hospital. Early assessment will also allow consideration to be given to the possibility of a transfer to an alternative place of safety as soon as this is considered to be safe and appropriate in all of the circumstances

- intoxication (whether through drugs or alcohol) should not be used as a basis for exclusion from places of safety, except in circumstances set out in the local policy, where there may be too high a risk to the safety of the individual or staff. Health-based places of safety should not be conducting tests to determine intoxication as a reason for exclusion, and

- a child or young person should not be taken to a place of safety in a police station unless, having regard to the best interests of the child or young person, there is no suitable alternative available. If this occurs, consideration should also be given to using a different part of a police station or other place under the supervision of a police officer and not a police custody suite.

ASSESSMENT AT A PLACE OF SAFETY

4–076   16.45 The same care should be taken in examining and interviewing people in places of safety as in any other assessment. No assumptions should be made about them simply because the police have been involved, nor should they be assumed to be in any less need of support and assistance during the assessment. Guidance in chapters 14 and 15 on assessment applies in these circumstances as in any others.

16.46 Doctors examining patients should, wherever possible, be approved under section 12 of the Act. Where the examination has to be conducted by a doctor who is not approved under section 12, the doctor concerned should record the reasons for that.

16.47 Assessment by the doctor and AMHP should begin as soon as possible after the arrival of the individual at the place of safety. In cases where there are no clinical grounds to delay assessment, it is good practice for the doctor and AMHP to attend within three hours; this is in accordance with best practice recommendations made by the Royal College of Psychiatrists. Where possible, the assessment should be undertaken jointly by the doctor and the AMHP.

16.48 If possible, either a consultant psychiatrist in learning disabilities or an AMHP with knowledge and experience of working with people with learning disabilities should be available to make the assessment where it appears that the detained person has a learning disability.

16.49 Where the person detained is under the age of 18, or is known to have moved recently to adult mental health services, they should be taken to an appropriate place of safety (see paragraph 19.105), where either a child and adolescent mental health services (CAMHS) consultant or an AMHP with knowledge and experience of caring for this age group should undertake the assessment. If arranging for a CAMHS specialist to assess the person would result in a substantial delay, then those assessing the person should at least discuss the case with an appropriately qualified person. Where there is no local place of safety specifically for under 18s, the local health-based place of safety should be used.

16.50 The authority to detain a person under section 135(1) or 136 ends as soon as the assessment has been completed and suitable arrangements have been made. This may include detention under part 2 of the Act, informal admission, an offer of community treatment or other arrangements necessary for a safe discharge including necessary social arrangements. If a doctor assesses the person and concludes that the person is not suffering from a mental disorder then the person must be discharged, even if not seen by an AMHP.

16.51 If the doctor sees the person first and concludes that they have a mental disorder and that compulsory admission to hospital is not necessary, but that they may still need treatment or care (whether in or out of hospital), the person should still be seen by an AMHP. The AMHP should consult the doctor about any arrangements that might need to be made for the person's treatment or care.

16.52 It is important to remember that the definition of mental disorder is wide and includes personality disorder (see chapter 2). If the assessment by a doctor reveals that the person is not suffering from a mental disorder, but there are physical symptoms which require treatment, then the person should be released and appropriate steps taken to manage the physical condition.

TRANSFER BETWEEN PLACES OF SAFETY

16.53 A person removed to a place of safety under section 135(1) or section 136 **4–077** may be moved to a different place of safety within the maximum 72-hour period for which they may be detained. Transfers should take place only when it is in the person's best interests. The maximum period of detention begins from the time of the person's arrival at the first place of safety to which they are taken and cannot be extended if the person is transferred to another place of safety.

16.54 The person may be taken to the second or subsequent place of safety by transport arranged by a police officer, the AMHP or a person authorised by either a police officer or the AMHP.

16.55 A person may be transferred before their assessment has begun, while it is in progress, or after it is completed and they are waiting for any necessary arrangements for their care or treatment to be put in place. If it is unavoidable, or it is in the person's interests, an assessment begun by one AMHP or doctor may be taken over and completed by another, either in the same location or at another place to which the person is transferred.

16.56 Although it may be helpful for local policies to outline circumstances in which a person is usually to be transferred between places of safety, the decision in each case should reflect the individual circumstances, including the person's needs and the level of risk. For example, where the purpose of the transfer would be to move a person from a police station to a more appropriate health-based place of safety, the benefit of that move needs to be weighed against any delay it might cause in the person's assessment and any distress that the journey might cause them. Any delays resulting from transferring the person cannot result in an overall period of detention which exceeds 72 hours.

16.57 Unless it is an emergency, a person should not be transferred without the agreement of an AMHP, a doctor or another healthcare professional who is competent to assess whether the transfer would put the person's health or safety (or that of other people) at risk. Someone with the authority to effect a transfer should proceed by agreement wherever possible. It is for those professionals to decide whether they first need to see the person personally.

16.58 A person should never be moved from one place of safety to another unless it has been confirmed that the new place of safety is willing and able to accept them.

RECORD KEEPING

16.59 A record of the person's time of arrival must be made immediately when **4–078** they reach the place of safety. As soon as detention in a place of safety under section 135(1) or 136 ends, the individual must be told that they are free to leave by those who are detaining them. The organisation responsible for the place of safety should ensure that proper records are kept of the end of the person's detention under these sections. In cases where alternative places of safety are used (such as the home of a relative or friend), local policies should define responsibilities to ensure that proper records are kept of the time of arrival, and the time the detention ends.

16.60 Given that the maximum period of detention at a place of safety is not affected by any subsequent transfer to a different place of safety (see paragraph 16.26 above), it is very important to ensure that the time of arrival at the first place of safety is recorded clearly. This information should be shared between the transferring and receiving place of safety in the event of a transfer.

16.61 When admitted to a place of safety in a hospital, a record of the admission, and of the outcome of the assessment, should be made by the hospital. Where persons who do not work for the hospital undertake the assessment, local procedures should be in place to ensure good record keeping.

16.62 If a person is excluded from a place of safety in a hospital and taken to a police station as a place of safety a record should be made of the decision, of who made the decision, and the reason it was made.

MONITORING USE OF THE ACT TO REMOVE PEOPLE

4–079   16.63 The locally agreed policy should include arrangements for the use of section 136 (in particular) to be monitored effectively so that:

- a check can be made of the circumstances and outcomes of its use, including in relation to people from black and minority ethnic communities, children and young people, and with people with protected characteristics as defined under the Equality Act 2010 (see chapter 3), and

- the parties to the policy can consider any changes to the mental health services or police operations or any other matters that might result in a reduction of its use.

16.64 The local policy should address who is responsible for collecting, analysing, and disseminating the information required for monitoring purposes. Although information systems (and definitions) may differ between organisations, efforts should be made to ensure that the most important data for monitoring purposes is collected in a way that allows it to be analysed so that it is of use to all the parties to the policy.

16.65 It should also set the expected time limits within which the assessment at a place of safety should commence, and the relevant NHS bodies and local authorities should review local practice against these targets.

RIGHTS OF PEOPLE DETAINED IN PLACES OF SAFETY

4–080   16.66 The PACE Code of Practice C applies to persons removed to a police station as a place of safety under sections 135 and 136 (with the exception of section 15 of Code C). This provides the benefit of many of the safeguards applicable to any person who is in police detention. A person should expect to receive a copy of the Notice of Rights and Entitlements, which states that an individual can tell the police if they want access to a solicitor, if they want someone to be told that they are at the police station, and if they want medical help. It also states that an individual can tell the police that they want to look at the PACE Codes of Practice.[22]

16.67 PACE Code of Practice C also requires an appropriate adult to be available for a person who appears to be mentally disordered or mentally vulnerable, who can be a relative, guardian or other person responsible for their care or custody, someone experienced in dealing with mentally disordered or mentally vulnerable people but who is not a police officer or employed by the police or, failing these, some other responsible adult aged 18 or over who is not a police

---

[22] Revised code of practice for the detention, treatment and question of persons by Police officers. Police and Criminal Evidence Act 1984 (PACE)—Code C. Home Office. 2014. https://www.gov.uk/government/publications/pace-code-c-2014.

officer or employed by the police. Although an appropriate adult should be available, they have no role in the doctor's assessment or AMHP's interview of the patient and their presence is not required for these to be undertaken.

16.68 A person detained under section 136 may be searched by the constable to ascertain what they have on them which could be used to harm themselves or others, damage property, or assist them to escape. The constable can hold on to anything found in the search, including clothes and personal effects, which the constable believes the person may use to cause such harm or damage or escape.

16.69 Where a hospital is used as a place of safety, the managers must ensure that the provisions of section 132 (giving of information) are complied with. In addition, access to legal advice should be facilitated whenever it is requested.

16.70 In all cases, the person detained should be told that the maximum period of detention is 72 hours.

16.71 Police and healthcare services should have regard to the Equality Act 2010 when using section 135 and 136 (see chapter 3).

PLACES OF SAFETY AND CONSENT TO TREATMENT

16.72 Detaining a patient in a place of safety under sections 135 or 136 does not **4–081** confer any power under the Act to treat them without their consent. In other words, they are in exactly the same position in respect of consent to treatment as patients who are not detained under the Act.

MAKING NECESSARY ARRANGEMENTS FOLLOWING ASSESSMENT

16.73 Once the assessment has been concluded, it is the responsibility of the **4–082** doctors and AMHPs involved to make any necessary further arrangements for the person's treatment or care.

16.74 Where compulsory admission is indicated, the AMHP should arrange for a second doctor to examine the patient in accordance with the Act (unless it has been agreed locally that someone else should make such arrangements).

16.75 It is unlikely that an emergency application would be justified in these circumstances. If there was an urgent need to secure the transfer of the patient to hospital, the power of transfer between places of safety could be used.

16.76 A person who is detained under section 135 or 136 in hospital pending completion of their assessment cannot have their detention extended by use of section 5(2) or section 5(4).

19. CHILDREN AND YOUNG PEOPLE UNDER THE AGE OF 18

Why read this chapter?

19.1 Particular issues arise in relation to children (under 16 years of age) and **4–083** young people (16 or 17 years old). In addition to the Act, other relevant legislation includes the Children Acts 1989 and 2004, the Mental Capacity Act (MCA) 2005 and the Human Rights Act (HRA) 1998. Professionals, practitioners and others responsible for the care of children and young people should be familiar with this legislation.

19.2 This chapter provides guidance on the role of those with parental responsibility for a child or young person; confidentiality and sharing information; how children and young people should be safeguarded where admission to hospital is not appropriate and on decisions related to admission and treatment. It should be read in conjunction with other chapters in this Code.

19.3 This chapter sets out some of the key factors including:

- some of the main concepts to be considered when providing care and treatment to children and young people, such as 'parental responsibility' and decisions within the 'scope of parental responsibility'[23]

- assessing the competence of children and the capacity of young people to make decisions about their admission and/or treatment

- when informal admission might be appropriate and when the Mental Health Act 1983 (the Act) should be used

- specific provisions relating to the treatment of children and young people under the Act

- the duty to provide age appropriate services

- applications and references to the Tribunal, and

- general duties of local authorities in relation to children and young people in hospital.

GENERAL CONSIDERATIONS

4-084   19.4 In addition to the Act, those responsible for the care of children and young people in hospital should be familiar with other relevant legislation, including the Children Acts 1989 and 2004, the MCA and the HRA. They should also be aware of the United Nations Convention on the Rights of the Child (UNCRC), and keep up-to-date with relevant case law and guidance.

19.5 When making decisions in relation to the care and treatment of children and young people, practitioners should keep the following points in mind:

- the best interests of the child or young person must always be a significant consideration

- everyone who works with children has a responsibility for keeping them safe and to take prompt action if welfare needs or safeguarding concerns are identified

- all practitioners and agencies are expected to contribute to whatever actions are needed to safeguard and promote a child or young person's welfare

- the developmental process from childhood to adulthood, particularly during adolescence, involves significant changes in a wide range of areas, such as physical, emotional and cognitive development—these factors need to be taken into account, in addition to the child and young person's personal circumstances, when assessing whether a child or young person has a mental disorder

- children and young people should always be kept as fully informed as possible and should receive clear and detailed information concerning their care

---

[23] The term 'scope of parental responsibility' replaces the term 'zone of parental control' used in the Mental Health Act 1983: Code of Practice. Department of Health. 2008. http://webarchive.nationalarchives.gov.uk/20130107105354/http:/www.dh.gov.uk/en/Publicationsandstatistics/Publications/PublicationsPolicyAndGuidance/DH_084597.

and treatment, explained in a way they can understand and in a format that is appropriate to their age

- the child or young person's views, wishes and feelings should always be sought, their views taken seriously and professionals should work with them collaboratively in deciding on how to support that child or young person's needs

- any intervention in the life of a child or young person that is considered necessary by reason of their mental disorder should be the least restrictive option and the least likely to expose them to the risk of any stigmatisation, consistent with effective care and treatment, and it should also result in the least possible separation from family, carers, friends and community or interruption of their education

- where hospital admission is necessary, the child or young person should be placed as near to their home as reasonably practicable, recognising that placement further away from home increases the separation between the child or young person and their family, carers, friends, community and school

- all children and young people should receive the same access to educational provision as their peers

- children and young people have as much right to expect their dignity to be respected as anyone else, and

- children and young people have as much right to privacy and confidentiality as anyone else.

PEOPLE WITH PARENTAL RESPONSIBILITY

19.6 Those with parental responsibility have a central role in relation to **4–085** decisions about the admission and treatment of their child (see paragraphs 19.38–19.43 below). It is therefore essential that those proposing the admission and/or treatment identify who has parental responsibility.

19.7 Those with parental responsibility will usually, but not always, be the parents of the child or young person. Other people may also acquire parental responsibility. Where the parents are not married, it will be necessary to ascertain whether the father has gained parental responsibility (this might be by a court order, parental responsibility agreement, or (since 1st December 2003) as a result of the father registering his child's birth jointly with the child's mother).[24] The question whether the father has acquired parental responsibility will also be relevant when ascertaining who is the nearest relative under the Act[25] (see paragraph 5.3 above in chapter 5).

19.8 Those taking decisions under the Act must be clear about who has parental responsibility. When seeking to identify who has parental responsibility for the child or young person, practitioners should always check whether the child or young person's medical and/or social service files include any relevant court

---

[24] For a list of persons who may have parental responsibility see Reference guide to consent for examination or treatment. Department of Health. 2009. https://www.gov.uk/government/publications/reference-guide-to-consent-for-examination-or-treatment-second-edition.

[25] Section 26(2)(b) of the Mental Health Act 1983. http://www.legislation.gov.uk/ukpga/1983/20/section/26.

orders, and request copies of any such orders. These orders may include care orders, child arrangements orders (which replace residence orders and contact orders),[26] special guardianship orders, evidence of appointment as the child or young person's guardian, parental responsibility agreements or orders under section 4 of the Children Act 1989 and any order under wardship. Practitioners should always check with those caring for the child or young person whether any child arrangements orders, parental responsibility agreements or orders, or special guardianship orders have been obtained.

19.9 Where the parents of a child or young person (both of whom have parental responsibility), are separated and the child or young person is living with one parent in accordance with a child arrangements order (formerly known as a residence order), practitioners should be aware that the parents continue to share parental responsibility and both should be involved in making decisions about their child.

19.10 Where a special guardianship order is in place, the special guardian will share parental responsibility with the child or young person's parents. However, except for certain purposes specified in the Children Act 1989, the special guardian is entitled to exercise parental responsibility to the exclusion of any other person with parental responsibility for the child (apart from another special guardian) (see section 14C of the Children Act 1989).

CHILDREN LOOKED AFTER BY THE LOCAL AUTHORITY

4–086   19.11 Where children or young people are looked after by the local authority (see section 22 of the Children Act 1989), it will be important to establish whether they are subject to a care order (or interim care order) or are being voluntarily accommodated by the local authority.

19.12 If a child or young person is voluntarily accommodated by the local authority, parents or others with parental responsibility have the same rights and responsibilities in relation to treatment as they would otherwise. Admission and/or treatment decisions should therefore be discussed with the parent or other person with parental responsibility who continues to have parental responsibility for the child.

19.13 If the child or young person is subject to a care order, the parents (and any others with parental responsibility) share parental responsibility with the local authority. The local authority and those with parental responsibility should negotiate and agree who should be consulted about admission and/or treatment decisions. However, where the local authority is satisfied that it is necessary to do so in order to safeguard or promote the child or young person's welfare, they can limit the extent to which parents (or others) may exercise their parental responsibility (see section 33(3)(b) of the Children Act 1989).

CONFIDENTIALITY AND SHARING INFORMATION

4–087   19.14 As with adults, children and young people have a right to confidentiality (see chapter 10). Where children are competent, and young people have the capacity, to make decisions about the use and disclosure of information they have provided in confidence, their views should be respected. (Paragraphs 19.24–19.37 below provide guidance on assessing a child's competence and a

---

[26] Section 12 of the Children and Families Act 2014 amends section 8(1) of the Children Act 1989. http://www.legislation.gov.uk/ukpga/2014/6/section/12/enacted.

young person's capacity to decide.) However, as with adults, in certain circumstances confidential information may be disclosed without the child or young person's consent; for example if there is reasonable cause to believe that the child or young person is suffering, or is at risk of suffering, significant harm. Practitioners should be familiar with the Department of Health's Information Sharing: guidance for practitioners and managers 2008, which includes guidance on assessing a child or young person's ability to make decisions about sharing information.

19.15 The same principles of confidentiality apply if a child who is competent, or a young person who has capacity, to make a decision regarding the information does not wish their parent (or others with parental responsibility) to be involved in decision-making about their care and treatment. Their decision should be respected unless the disclosure can be justified; for example, if there is cause to suspect that the child or young person is suffering or is likely to suffer, serious harm. Practitioners should encourage the child or young person to involve their parents (unless it is considered that to do so would not be the best interests of the child or young person). They should also be proactive in discussing with the child or young person the consequences of their parent(s) not being involved.

19.16 Where a child or young person does not wish their parent(s) to be involved, every effort should be made to understand the child or young person's reasons with a view to establishing whether the child or young person's concerns can be addressed. For example, the child or young person may be receiving counselling that they do not want their parents to know about, but would be happy for their parents to be informed about more general aspects of their care and treatment. See also paragraph 10.6 on sharing information with carers, relatives and friends, which also applies to people with parental responsibility.

SAFEGUARDING CHILDREN AND YOUNG PEOPLE WHERE ADMISSION TO HOSPITAL IS NOT APPROPRIATE

19.17 There is no minimum age limit for detention in hospital under the Act. It **4–088** may be used to detain children or young people who need to be admitted to hospital for assessment and/or treatment of their mental disorder, when they cannot be admitted and/or treated on an informal basis (see paragraphs 19.49–19.70 below), and where the criteria for detention under the Act are met.

19.18 Where practitioners conclude that admission to hospital is not the appropriate course of action, consideration must be given to alternative means of care and support that will meet the needs of the child or young person. The appropriate action will usually be to refer the child or young person's case to the relevant local authority's children's services, in accordance with local protocols for interagency working to safeguard and promote the welfare of children and young people.

19.19 In cases where admission to hospital under the Act is not appropriate, but the child or young person has significant needs which mean that the level and type of intervention is likely to amount to a deprivation of liberty, their placement in secure accommodation under section 25 of the Children Act 1989 may be required.[27] This will be a matter for the local authority children's services to

---

[27] Note that section 25 of the Children Act 1989 refers to 'restricting liberty'. The court held in Re K (A Child (Secure Accommodation Order: Right to Liberty). 2001. Fam 377 that a secure accommodation order is a deprivation of liberty within the meaning of article 5 of the European Convention on Human Rights.

consider in the light of the provisions of section 25 of the Children Act 1989, and relevant Children Act 1989 guidance.[28] Children who are not Gillick competent (see paragraphs 19.34–19.37) or young people who lack capacity (see paragraphs 19.26–19.30) whose needs are severe and long-term, and where deprivation of liberty is one necessary element of their education or care, may also be accommodated in other placements.[29]

DECISIONS ON ADMISSION AND TREATMENT OF UNDER 18S

4–089   19.20 The decision to admit a child or young person to hospital is inextricably linked to the decision to treat them once they have been admitted. They are, however, different decisions and need to be considered separately. In addition, the law about admission and treatment of young people aged 16 and 17 differs from that applicable to children under 16. The following four concepts will be relevant to admission and treatment decisions of both children and young people:

- consent

- assessing capacity (young people) or competence (children) to make decisions

- the role of those with parental responsibility and the 'scope of parental responsibility', and

- deprivation of liberty (DoL).

These four concepts are discussed below.

Children and young people and consent

4–090   19.21 The valid consent of a child or young person will be sufficient authority for their admission to hospital and/or treatment for mental disorder; additional consent by a person with parental responsibility will not be required. It is good practice to involve the child or young person's parents and/or others involved in their care in the decision-making process, if the child or young person consents to information about their care and treatment being shared.

19.22 Consent should be sought for each aspect of the child or young person's admission, care and treatment as it arises. 'Blanket' consent forms (ie forms that purport to give consent to any proposed treatment) are not acceptable and should not be used.

19.23 A young person must have the capacity, or a child must have competence, to make the particular decision in question (see paragraph 19.24 below). They must have sufficient information to make that decision (see chapter 4) and not be subject to any undue influence when doing so (see paragraph 24.34). Unlike adults, the refusal by a competent child or young person with capacity under the age of 18 may in certain circumstances, be overridden by a court.[30] In the

---

[28] Court orders and pre-proceedings for local authorities. Department of Education. 2014. https://www.gov.uk/government/publications/children-act-1989-court-orders–2.

[29] See by way of example: P v Cheshire West and Chester Council and another and P and Q v Surrey County Council ('Cheshire West'). 2014. WLR 2. https://www.supremecourt.uk/decided-cases/docs/UKSC_2012_0068_Judgment.pdf and Barnsley Metropolitan Borough Council vs GS and ES. 2014. EWCOP 46. http://www.bailii.org/ew/cases/EWCOP/2014/46.html.

[30] See paragraph 19.53 in relation to section 131 of the Act and informal admission of those aged 16 and 17.

case of Re W (a minor) (medical treatment: court's jurisdiction), the court decided that it has jurisdiction to override the refusal of a child or young person of treatment in circumstances that will, in all probability, lead to the death of the child or young person or to severe permanent injury; or where there is a serious and imminent risk that the child or young person will suffer grave and irreversible mental or physical harm.[31] However, the court also emphasised that the child or young person's refusal is a very important consideration when deciding whether treatment should be given, despite the child or young person's refusal, noting that its importance increases with their age and maturity. Guidance on the action that can be taken in cases requiring emergency life-saving treatment is set out below at paragraphs 19.71–19.72.

Assessing a young person's capacity and a child's competence to make decisions

19.24 Before relying on the consent of a child or young person it is necessary to **4–091** ascertain whether they can give valid consent. The test for assessing whether a child under 16 can give valid consent differs from that of a young person aged 16 or 17. The capacity of a young person aged 16 or 17 to consent is assessed in accordance with the MCA, while the test for children under 16 is determined by considering whether they are 'Gillick competent'.[32] Practitioners with expertise in working with children and young people should be consulted in relation to these assessments. The different tests are explained in more detail below.

19.25 Practitioners should consider the following three questions which should be read in conjunction with the paragraphs below:

- has the child or young person been given the relevant information in an appropriate manner (such as age appropriate language)?

- have all practicable steps been taken to help the child or young person make the decision? The kind of support that might help the decision-making will vary, depending on the child or young person's circumstances. Examples include:

- steps to help the child or young person feel at ease

- ensuring that those with parental responsibility are available to support their child (if that is what the child or young person would like)

- giving the child or young person time to absorb information at their own pace, and

- considering whether the child or young person has any specific communication needs (and if so, adapting accordingly).

- can the child or young person decide whether to consent, or not to consent, to the proposed intervention?

---

[31] Re W (a minor) (medical treatment: court's jurisdiction). 1992. 3 WLR 758.
[32] See Gillick v West Norfolk and Wisbech Area Health Authority. 1986. AC 112. http://www.bailii.org/uk/cases/UKHL/1985/7.html.

Decision-making and young people

4–091   19.26 The MCA applies to people aged 16 or over, so young people must be assumed to have capacity to make the decision about a proposed admission to hospital and/or treatment unless it is established that they lack capacity, as is the case with adults (paragraphs 13.17–13.22).

19.27 Section 2 of the MCA states that a person lacks capacity in relation to a matter if at the relevant time they are unable to make a decision for themselves in relation to the matter 'because of an impairment of, or a disturbance in the functioning of, the mind or brain'. It does not matter whether the impairment is permanent or temporary (see section 2(2)). Section 3 of the MCA then states that a person is unable to make a decision if they are unable to:

- understand the information relevant to the decision

- retain that information

- use or weigh that information as part of the decision-making process, or

- communicate their decision (whether by talking, sign language or any other means).

19.28 The MCA also states that a person must not be regarded as unable to understand the information relevant to the decision if they are able to understand an explanation of it given in a way that is appropriate to their circumstances. It is therefore essential that steps are taken to enable a person to understand information, such as using simple language and visual aids (see section 3(2) MCA).

19.29 Where there are concerns that the young person is unable to make the particular decision, the young person's capacity should be assessed by a professional with expertise in working with children and young people. Wherever possible, consideration should be given to whether the decision could be delayed to a time when the young person might be able to make the decision.

19.30 If the young person is unable to decide about the proposed action at the relevant time 'because of an impairment of, or disturbance in the functioning of, the mind or brain', they will lack capacity as defined in section 2 of the MCA. The reason for the young person's inability to decide about the proposed admission or treatment may be because of their mental disorder. Alternatively, the young person's inability to decide might arise from a temporary 'impairment of, or disturbance in, the functioning of, their mind or brain' that does not amount to a mental disorder (eg an impairment or disturbance caused by the distress related to the proposed admission or treatment). In either case, the young person will lack capacity within the meaning of the MCA and the MCA will apply in the same way as it does for adults. It may therefore be possible for the particular decision to be made in accordance with the MCA for, and in the best interests of, the young person.

19.31 When assessing a young person's capacity to make the decision in question, practitioners should be aware that in some cases a young person may be unable to make a decision for reasons other than an impairment of, or a disturbance in the functioning of, their mind or brain (even if that is only temporary). In such cases, the person will not lack capacity within the meaning of the MCA. For example, a young person who is informed that they need to be admitted into hospital may, in the particular circumstances of the case, be unable to make a decision. This might be because they find themselves in an unfamiliar and novel situation, having never before been asked to absorb that type and quantity of information, or they are worrying about the implications of deciding one way or the other.

19.32 In such cases (which are likely to be rare) every effort should be made to ensure that the young person is supported in making the decision (eg by involving those with parental responsibility and/or advocates). Steps should also be taken to explain fully and clearly why admission is thought necessary, what the alternatives to the admission are and why they are considered not to be the best option. Save where the case requires urgent action, the young person should be given the time that they need to think things over and ask for clarification.

19.33 It is important that practitioners are aware of the distinction between those cases that fall within the MCA and those that do not. If it is not clear whether the young person's inability to decide is because of an 'impairment of, or a disturbance in the functioning of, the mind or brain' or whether due to some other reason, a specialist opinion should be sought from a professional with expertise in working with children and young people. The relevance of this distinction to admission and treatment is explained below at paragraphs 19.53–19.64.

Decision-making and children under 16

19.34 Children under 16 should be assessed to establish whether they have **4–092** competence to make a particular decision at the time it needs to be made. This is because in the case of Gillick,[33] the court held that children who have sufficient understanding and intelligence to enable them to understand fully what is involved in a proposed intervention will also have the competence to consent to that intervention. In such cases, the child is sometimes described as being 'Gillick competent'.[34] A child may be Gillick competent to consent to admission to hospital, medical treatment, research, or any other activity that requires their consent.

19.35 The concept of Gillick competence reflects the child's increasing development to maturity. The understanding required to make decisions about different interventions will vary considerably. A child may have the competence to consent to some interventions but not others. The child's competence to consent should be assessed carefully in relation to each decision that needs to be made.

19.36 When considering whether a child has the competence to decide about the proposed intervention, practitioners may find it helpful to consider the following questions.

- Does the child understand the information that is relevant to the decision that needs to be made?

---

[33] Gillick v West Norfolk and Wisbech Area Health Authority. 1986. AC 112. http://www.bailii.org/uk/cases/UKHL/1985/7.html.

[34] This term is used by the courts to refer to a child who has been assessed as having sufficient maturity and understanding to be able to consent to the decision in question (see Re R (a minor) (wardship: consent to treatment) [1992] Fam 11). It should not be confused with 'Lord Fraser's Guidelines' which concern the conditions which must be met before advising a child on sexual matters without parental consent (see R(Axon) v Secretary of State for Health and the Family Planning Association. 2006. EWHC 37 (Admin). http://www.bailii.org/ew/cases/EWHC/Admin/2006/37.html).

- Can the child hold the information in their mind long enough so that they can use it to make the decision?

- Is the child able to weigh up that information and use it to arrive at a decision?

- Is the child able to communicate their decision (by talking, using sign language or any other means)?

19.37 A child may lack the competence to make the decision in question either because they have not as yet developed the necessary intelligence and understanding to make that particular decision; or for another reason, such as because their mental disorder adversely affects their ability to make the decision. In either case, the child will be considered to lack Gillick competence.

The role of those with parental responsibility and decisions within the scope of parental responsibility

4–093
19.38 Those who have parental responsibility for the child or young person, who may be able to provide parental consent to the proposed admission and/or treatment, should be identified. This is because, subject to the child or young person's right to confidentiality (see paragraphs 19.14–19.16), they should be consulted about the proposed decision concerning their child. In relation to 16 and 17 year olds, if decisions are to be made in accordance with the MCA (on the basis that the young person lacks capacity within the meaning of the MCA) those with parental responsibility should be consulted about the best interests of the young person (see section 4 of the MCA).

19.39 Parental consent should not be relied upon when the child is competent or the young person has capacity to make the particular decision. The effect of section 131(4) of the Act in relation to the informal admission to hospital of a 16 or 17 year old, who has capacity, is that parental consent cannot be relied upon to override that young person's decision about their admission. In relation to decisions about such a young person's treatment, it is inadvisable to rely on the consent of a person with parental responsibility to treat a young person who has capacity to make the decision and has refused the treatment. Similarly, in relation to children, it is not advisable to rely on the consent of a parent with parental responsibility to admit or treat a child who is competent to make the decision and does not consent to it. Although in the past the courts have found that a person with parental responsibility can overrule their child's refusal, such decisions were made before the introduction of the HRA and since then court decisions concerning children and young people have given greater weight to their views.[35]

19.40 In some circumstances, it will be possible for children lacking competence and young people lacking capacity to be admitted to hospital and/or treated on the basis of parental consent (see paragraphs 19.53–19.70). However, practitioners must be satisfied that it is appropriate to rely on parental consent. This is important because court decisions relating to parental consent

---

[35] See for example R (on the application of Axon) v Secretary of State for Health and the Family Planning Association. 2006. EWHC 37 (Admin), in which the court expressed doubt as to why a parent should retain a right to parental authority relating to a medical decision where the young person concerned understood the advice provided by the medical professional and its implications. http://www.bailii.org/ew/cases/EWHC/Admin/2006/37.html.

have emphasised that there are limits to both the types of decisions that can be made by those with parental responsibility on behalf of their child, and the circumstances in which these decisions can be made.[36] For example, when making decisions on behalf of their child, parents must act in their child's best interests. The limits to what a parent can consent to on behalf of their child is relevant to whether a deprivation of liberty has arisen (see paragraphs 19.44–19.48). This guidance uses the term 'scope of parental responsibility' to highlight the need to establish whether the particular decision can be authorised by parental consent or not. Those cases in which parental consent is sufficient are described as falling within the scope of parental responsibility.

19.41 Whether the particular intervention can be undertaken on the basis of parental consent will need to be assessed in the light of the particular circumstances of the case. Practitioners will need to consider a range of factors. These are set out below, under the two key questions that must be addressed (the term 'parent' is used to cover all people with parental responsibility):

- **First, is this a decision that a parent should reasonably be expected to make?** If the decision goes beyond the kind of decisions parents routinely make in relation to the medical care of their child, clear reasons as to why it is acceptable to rely on parental consent to authorise this particular decision will be required. When considering this question, any relevant human rights decisions made by the courts should be taken into account. Significant factors in determining this question are likely to include:

  - the type and invasiveness of the proposed intervention—the more extreme the intervention, the greater the justification that will be required. Relying on parental consent to authorise an intrusive form of treatment might be justified because it is necessary to prevent a serious deterioration of the child or young person's health, but this would need to be balanced against other factors such as whether the child or young person is resisting the treatment; whether the specific form of treatment is particularly invasive and/or controversial (eg careful consideration should be given to the appropriateness of relying on parental consent to authorise electro-convulsive therapy (ECT)[37]

  - the age, maturity and understanding of the child or young person: the role of parents in decision-making should diminish as their child develops greater independence, with accordingly greater weight given to the views of the child or young person

  - the extent to which the decision accords with the wishes of the child or young person, and whether the child or young person is resisting the decision, and

  - whether the child or young person had expressed any views about the proposed intervention when they had the competence or capacity to make such decisions; for example, if they had expressed a willingness to receive one

---

[36] See for example, RK v BCC. 2011. EWCA Civ 1305; Nielsen v Denmark. 1989. 11 EHRR (paragraph 72) Gillick v West Norfolk and Wisbech Area Health Authority. 1986. A.C. 112; and Hewer v Bryant. 1970. 1 QB 357.

[37] Section 58A of the Act includes specific safeguards for all children and young people for whom ECT is proposed, whether or not they are detained under the Act—see paragraphs 19.80–19.88.

form of treatment but not another, it might not be appropriate to rely on parental consent to give the treatment that they had previously refused.

- **Secondly are there any factors that might undermine the validity of parental consent?** Irrespective of the nature of the decision being proposed, there may be reasons why relying on the consent of a person with parental responsibility may be inappropriate; for example:

  - where the parent is not able to make the relevant decision; for example, this may arise, if the parent lacks capacity as defined in the MCA, because of their own mental health problems or learning disabilities. In cases of doubt, the parent's capacity will need to be assessed in accordance with the MCA

  - where the parent is not able to focus on what course of action is in the best interests of their child; for example, where the parents have gone through a particularly acrimonious divorce, they may find it difficult to separate the decision whether to consent to their child's admission to hospital from their own hostilities

  - where the poor mental health of the child or young person has led to significant distress and/or conflict between the parents, so that they feel unable to decide on what is best for their child and/or cannot agree on what action should be taken, and

  - where one parent agrees with the proposed decision but the other is opposed to it. Although parental consent is usually needed from only one person with parental responsibility,[38] it may not be appropriate to rely on parental consent if another person with parental responsibility disagrees strongly with the decision to admit and/or treat their child, and is likely to take action to prevent the intervention, such as removing the child from hospital or challenging the decision in court.

19.42 If the decision is not one that a parent would reasonably be expected to make, or there are concerns about the validity of the consent of the person with parental responsibility, it will not be appropriate to rely on parental consent. In such cases, the proposed intervention must be lawfully authorised by other means. In cases where the proposed intervention relates to the assessment and/or treatment of the child or young person's mental disorder, they could be admitted and treated under the Act if the criteria are met. This is discussed below. If the Act is not applicable, legal advice should be sought on the need to seek authorisation from a court before further action is taken. If there is doubt as to whether or not parental consent can be relied upon to authorise the particular intervention, professionals should take legal advice so that account may be taken of the most recent case law.

19.43 Whether persons with parental responsibility can consent to restrictions that would otherwise amount to a deprivation of liberty is considered below.

---

[38] See section 2(7) of the Children Act 1989. http://www.legislation.gov.uk/ukpga/1989/41/section/2.

Deprivation of liberty

19.44 Determining whether the admission to hospital and assessment and/or the **4–094** treatment proposed amounts to a deprivation of liberty is as important for admission and treatment decisions concerning children and young people as it is for adults. Article 5 (the right to liberty) of the European Convention on Human Rights (ECHR) applies to individuals of all ages.

19.45 In establishing whether there is a deprivation of liberty the circumstances of each case should be considered, looking at a range of factors, such as the type and duration of the restrictions imposed on the person and the impact of such restrictions on that person. Paragraphs 13.44–13.47 provide guidance on assessing whether the particular circumstances give rise to a deprivation of liberty.

19.46 Decisions as to whether the child or young person's admission and/or treatment amounts to a deprivation of liberty must be considered on a case by case basis. Where children and young people are admitted informally, the question of whether the care regime amounts to a deprivation of liberty must be kept under regular review. This is because although initially informal admission might be appropriate because the child or young person's care plan involves only restrictions of liberty, a change in circumstances may mean that the restrictions placed upon the child or young person amount to a deprivation of liberty for which lawful authority will be needed.

19.47 An additional and significant factor when considering whether the proposed intervention in relation to a child or young person is a restriction of liberty or amounts to a deprivation of liberty is the role of parental control and supervision. Practitioners will need to determine whether the care regime for, and restrictions placed on, the child or young person accord with the degree of parenting control and supervision that would be expected for a child or young person of that age. For example, whereas it is usual for a child of under 12 years not to be allowed out unaccompanied without their parent's permission, this would not usually be an acceptable restriction on a 17 year old. Account also needs to be taken of the particular experience of the child or young person. For example, a younger child who has been caring for their parent, including shopping for the household and/or accompanying their parent to medical appointments, might not be used to being prevented from going out unaccompanied.

19.48 Prior to the Supreme Court's judgment in Cheshire West,[39] case law had established that persons with parental responsibility cannot authorise a deprivation of liberty.[40] Cheshire West clarified the elements establishing a deprivation of liberty, but did not expressly decide whether a person with parental responsibility could, and if so in what circumstances, consent to restrictions that would, without their consent, amount to a deprivation of liberty. In determining whether a person with parental responsibility can consent to the arrangements which would, without their consent, amount to a deprivation of liberty, practitioners will need to consider and apply developments in case law following Cheshire West. In determining the limits of parental responsibility, decision-makers must carefully consider and balance: (i) the child's right to liberty

---

[39] P v Cheshire West and Chester Council and another and P and Q v Surrey County Council ('Cheshire West'). 2014. AC 896. https://www.supremecourt.uk/decided-cases/docs/UKSC_2012_0068_Judgment.pdf.

[40] See RK (by her litigation friend and the official Solicitor) v BCC, YK and AK. 2011. EWCA Civ 1305. http://www.bailii.org/ew/cases/EWCA/Civ/2011/1305.html.

under article 5, which should be informed by article 37 of the UNCRC, (ii) the parent's right to respect for the right to family life under article 8, which includes the concept of parental responsibility for the care and custody of minor children, and (iii) the child's right to autonomy which is also protected under article 8. Decision makers should seek their own legal advice in respect of cases before them. (Chapter 26 provides guidance on the use of restrictive interventions.)

INFORMAL ADMISSION AND TREATMENT

4–095   19.49 The law about admission to hospital and treatment for mental disorder of young people aged 16 and 17 differs from that of children under 16. In both cases, whether they are competent (in the case of children) or have capacity (in the case of young people) to decide about their admission and/or treatment is of central importance. (See paragraphs 19.24–19.37 for assessing the competence of children and the capacity of young people to make decisions.)

19.50 In relation to admission, children and young people may be admitted to hospital for treatment for mental disorder informally, on the basis of their consent (see section 131 of the Act (informal admission of patients). Where they lack capacity as defined in the MCA (16 or 17 year olds) or competence ('Gillick competence' in respect of under 16s) they can be admitted informally in the circumstances outlined below.

19.51 In all cases concerning admission and/or treatment, practitioners must determine whether the proposed intervention can be undertaken on an informal basis. Informal admission and treatment can be authorised by either the child or young person's consent, parental consent (where the child lacks competence or the young person lacks capacity) or in relation to young people who lack capacity, in accordance with the MCA. The following paragraphs provide guidance on how to determine whether such routes to informal admission and/or treatment are applicable. These should be considered in the light of the particular circumstances of each case. Where the proposed admission and/or treatment cannot be authorised on an informal basis, the criteria for detention under the Act must be met for the child or young person to be admitted under the Act or (where the Act is not applicable), the admission can be authorised by the High Court. The only exception to this is where a life-threatening emergency has arisen (see paragraphs 19.71–19.72).

19.52 In cases where a child or young person cannot be admitted and/or treated informally, and the criteria for detention under the Act are not met, legal advice should be obtained on whether to seek the assistance of the High Court. The court's authorisation may be sought by way of an order or declaration, under its inherent jurisdiction, or for a section 8 order under the Children Act 1989. Whether the court is prepared to assist will depend on the facts of the particular case. It should also be noted that the Court of Protection can make a deprivation of liberty order in respect of young people aged 16 and 17.

16 and 17 year olds

Informal admission of 16 and 17 year olds with capacity to consent

4–097   19.53 The effect of section 131 of the Act is that where a young person aged 16 or 17 has capacity (as defined in the MCA) to consent to being admitted to hospital for treatment for mental disorder, they may either consent, or refuse to consent, to the proposed informal admission. If a young person has the capacity to consent to informal admission and gives such consent, they can be admitted, irrespective of the views of a person with parental responsibility (who cannot prevent the admission). If the young person with capacity does not consent to the admission, then a person with parental responsibility cannot consent on their behalf.

19.54 In some cases, the young person may be unable to decide whether or not to agree to their admission to hospital, but not because they lack capacity within the meaning of the MCA. For example, this might be because, despite every effort in helping the young person to make this decision, the young person finds the decision too difficult to make (see paragraphs 19.31–19.33 above). In such cases, it will not be possible for a person with parental responsibility to consent on their behalf. This is because section 131 of the Act only allows informal admission on the basis of parental consent if the young person lacks capacity within the meaning of the MCA.

19.55 Where the young person does not consent to their admission to hospital, but the admission is thought to be necessary, consideration should be given to whether the criteria for admission under the Act are met. If the Act is not applicable, legal advice should be sought on the need to seek authorisation from the court before further action is taken.

19.56 If the young person is admitted informally, the considerations set out in paragraphs 19.58–19.64 will apply to their treatment.

Informal admission of 16 and 17 year olds who lack capacity to consent

19.57 Where a young person aged 16 or 17 lacks capacity it may be possible for **4–098** them to be admitted informally, in accordance with the MCA, unless the admission and treatment amounts to a deprivation of liberty. In cases where the MCA cannot authorise informal admission, but the admission is thought to be necessary, consideration should be given to as whether the criteria for admission under the Act are met. If the Act is not applicable, legal advice should be sought on the need to seek authorisation from the court before further action is taken.

Informal treatment of 16 and 17 year olds with capacity to consent

19.58 Section 8 of the Family Law Reform Act 1969[41] means that young people **4–099** aged 16 or 17 can consent to their medical treatment and to any ancillary procedures involved in that treatment, such as an anaesthetic. Accordingly, treatment can be given if the young person, who has capacity, gives valid consent.

19.59 Where a young person has the capacity to consent to proposed medical treatment but refuses to consent, it would be inadvisable to rely on the consent of a person with parental responsibility in order to treat the young person (see above, paragraph 19.39). In such cases, consideration should be given to whether admission under the Act for the purposes of treatment is necessary, and if so, whether the criteria are met. If the Act is not applicable, legal advice should be sought on the need to seek authorisation from the court before further action is taken.

---

[41] Section 8 of the Family Law Reform Act 1969. http://www.legislation.gov.uk/ukpga/1969/46/section/8.

Informal treatment of 16 and 17 year olds who lack capacity to consent

4–100   19.60 Different considerations apply to a decision to treat a young person aged 16 or 17 informally where the young person lacks capacity or is otherwise not able to decide whether or not to consent to the proposed treatment.

19.61 Where the young person lacks capacity, the MCA will apply in the same way as it does to those aged 18 and over, and treatment may be given in accordance with the MCA, unless it amounts to a deprivation of liberty.

19.62 A person with parental responsibility may also be able to consent on behalf of the young person who lacks capacity to make decisions about their treatment. Factors to consider in deciding whether it is possible to rely on parental consent are in paragraph 19.41. The guidance at paragraphs 19.44–19.48 should be considered in relation to whether persons with parental responsibility can consent to restrictions that would otherwise amount to a deprivation of liberty.

19.63 A person with parental responsibility may be able to consent to the treatment on behalf of a young person who although unable to decide about the proposed treatment, does not lack capacity within the meaning of the MCA (the circumstances when this might occur is explained at paragraph 19.31). In such cases every effort must be made to help the young person in making the decision for themselves (see paragraph 19.32).

19.64 If it is not possible to provide treatment relying on the MCA or parental consent, consideration should be given to whether admission under the Act for the purposes of treatment is necessary, and if so, whether the criteria are met. If the Act is not applicable, legal advice should be sought on the need to seek authorisation from the court before further action is taken.

Under 16s

Informal admission and treatment of under 16s who are Gillick competent

4–101   19.65 Where a child who is Gillick competent to decide about their admission to hospital for assessment and/or treatment of their mental disorder consents to this, they may be admitted to hospital as an informal patient. A child who is Gillick competent and has consented to being admitted informally, may also be given treatment if they are competent to consent to the proposed treatment, and do consent. Consent will be required for each aspect of the child's care and treatment as it arises. This will involve an assessment of the child's competence to make the particular decision and, where the child is competent to do so, confirmation that they have given their consent.

19.66 Where a child who is Gillick competent refuses to be admitted for treatment it may be inadvisable to rely on the consent of a person with parental responsibility (see paragraph 19.39). In such cases, consideration should be given to whether admission under the Act is necessary, and if so, whether the criteria are met. If the Act is not applicable, legal advice should be sought on the need to seek authorisation from the court before further action is taken.

Informal admission and treatment of under 16s who are not Gillick competent

4–102   19.67 Where a child is not Gillick competent then it may be possible for a person with parental responsibility to consent, on their behalf, to their informal admission to hospital for treatment for mental disorder.

19.68 If parental consent can be relied upon and consent is given by a person with parental responsibility, then the child may be admitted and treated as an informal patient.

19.69 Consent will be required for each aspect of the child's care and treatment as it arises. This will involve consideration as to whether the child is competent to make decisions about their treatment, and if not whether such treatment can be authorised by parental consent.

19.70 If it is not considered appropriate to rely on parental consent for the proposed admission and/or treatment, for example because the consent of a person with parental responsibility is not given or the matter is outside the scope of parental responsibility (see paragraphs 19.38–19.43), the child cannot be admitted and treated informally. In such cases, consideration should be given to whether admission under the Act is necessary, and if so, whether the criteria are met. If the Act is not applicable, legal advice should be sought on the need to seek authorisation from the court before further action is taken.

EMERGENCY TREATMENT

19.71 A life-threatening emergency may arise when treatment needs to be **4–103** given but it is not possible to rely on the consent of the child, young person or person with parental responsibility and there is no time to seek authorisation from the court or (where applicable) to detain and treat under the Act. If the failure to treat the child or young person would be likely to lead to their death or to severe permanent injury, treatment may be given without their consent, even if this means overriding their refusal when they have the competence (children) or the capacity (young people and those with parental responsibility), to make this treatment decision. In such cases, the courts have stated that doubt should be resolved in favour of the preservation of life, and it will be acceptable to undertake treatment to preserve life or prevent irreversible serious deterioration of the child or young person's condition.

19.72 The treatment given must be no more than necessary and in the best interests of the child or young person. Once the child or young person's condition is stabilised, legal authority for on-going treatment must be established; this might be on an informal basis (see paragraphs 19.49–19.70) or in accordance with either a court order or, if the child or young person is detained, under part 4 of the Act (see paragraphs 19.78–19.89).

ASSESSING WHETHER TO MAKE AN APPLICATION UNDER THE ACT

19.73 At least one of the people involved in assessing whether a child or young **4–104** person should be admitted to hospital, and if so whether they should be detained under the Act (ie one of the two medical practitioners or the approved mental health professional (AMHP)), should be a child and adolescent mental health services (CAMHS) professional. Where this is not possible, and admission to hospital is considered necessary, the AMHP should have access to an AMHP with experience of working in CAMHS, and the medical practitioners should consult a CAMHS clinician as soon as possible and involve them as closely as the circumstances of the case allow. In cases where the child or young person has complex or multiple needs, other clinicians may need to be involved, for example, a learning disability CAMHS consultant where the child or young person has a learning disability. (See chapter 14 for fuller information on the assessment process, and chapter 20.)

19.74 As part of their role in setting up an assessment (see paragraphs 14.49–14.56) AMHPs should consider whether to inform the relevant local authority children's services that an assessment is being arranged and request that any relevant information about the child or young person is provided prior to the assessment. The AMHP should consider with children's services whether a representative from children's services should attend the assessment. The AMHP should employ their best efforts to identify those who have parental responsibility, and who would be the nearest relative (see chapter 5).

INFORMATION TO UNDER 18S DETAINED

4–105 19.75 Chapter 4 provides guidance on the provision of information to people detained under the Act and chapter 6 provides guidance on the role of independent mental health advocates. Both these chapters apply to children and young people.

19.76 Hospital managers should ensure that staff providing children and young people with information about their rights in accordance with section 132 of the Act have sufficient knowledge and experience to be able to provide information to children and young people and determine whether the information has been understood. Written information must always be made available. Such information should be age appropriate and include an explanation about when they have the right to see an independent mental health advocate (IMHA) under the Act and an explanation of how one can be made available.

19.77 IMHAs have an important role in ensuring that children and young people understand, and are able to exercise, their rights under the Act, such as applying to a Tribunal (see paragraph 19.107), and to the hospital managers for discharge from detention (see chapter 38 for further guidance). It is therefore essential that the IMHAs working in CAMHS (or providing assistance to under 18s who are admitted to adult psychiatric wards—see paragraph 19.94 below) have experience of working with children and young people and an understanding of children's services and relevant law and policy, as well as an in-depth knowledge of the Act.

TREATMENTS FOR UNDER 18S REGULATED BY THE ACT

4–106 19.78 As with adults, treatment for mental disorder for under 18s is regulated by part 4 and part 4A of the Act. Chapters 24 and 25 provide general guidance and the following paragraphs highlight issues of relevance to children and young people under 18. Although in some cases the Act provides that treatment can be given to a child or young person without their consent, their consent should still be sought, wherever practicable. This will necessitate an assessment of the child's competence or young person's capacity to decide about the treatment proposed.

Treatments requiring the patient's consent (section 57)

4–107 19.79 Treatment covered by section 57 of the Act (primarily neurosurgery for mental disorder) cannot be given to a child or young person who does not personally consent to it, whether they are detained or not. These treatments cannot, therefore, be given to any young person or child who does not have the competence or capacity to consent, even if a person with parental responsibility consents. If such treatment is proposed in respect of a child or young person who has the competence or capacity to consent (such cases are likely to be rare), the requirements set out under section 57 of the Act must be met before the treatment can be given and these are explained in chapter 25 (paragraphs 25.7–25.10). The child or young person is eligible for help from an IMHA and must be informed of this right.

Electro-convulsive therapy (ECT) (section 58A)

19.80 The Act provides specific safeguards in relation to ECT for patients who **4–108** are under 18.

19.81 As with adults, children and young people who are detained under the Act cannot be given ECT without their consent, if they are capable of consenting to the treatment, unless it is emergency treatment (see section 62 of the Act ('emergency treatment'). If they are not capable of consenting, or if it is emergency treatment, they may be given ECT without their consent in accordance with the rules described in chapter 25.

19.82 Children and young people on a community treatment order (CTO) who are competent (children) or who have capacity (young people) to make such treatment decisions cannot be given ECT without their consent, even in emergencies. If they are recalled to hospital ECT can be given in accordance with the treatment provisions under part 4 of the Act. Part 4A sets out the circumstances in which children who are not competent, and young people who lack capacity, to consent can be given treatment, including ECT when on a CTO. Part 4A is explained in chapter 25.

19.83 Whether or not they are detained under the Act, except where emergency treatment is given under section 62 of the Act, no child or young person under the age of 18 can be given ECT without the approval of a second opinion appointed doctor (SOAD). This means:

- for children and young people who are 'capable of understanding the nature, purpose and likely effects' of ECT and consent to it, the SOAD must certify, in writing, that the child or young person is capable of consenting, they have consented to ECT, and it is appropriate for ECT to be given, and

- for children and young people who are not capable of consenting to ECT, the SOAD must certify that the child or young person is not capable of understanding the nature, purpose and likely effects of ECT, but it is appropriate for ECT to be given. In addition, in relation to a young person who lacks capacity to consent to ECT, the SOAD must certify that giving the treatment would not conflict with a decision made by a deputy appointed by the Court of Protection, or the Court of Protection.

19.84 The legal authority to give ECT to children and young people who are neither detained under the Act, nor subject to a CTO and who lack the capacity (young people) or the competence (children) to consent to ECT will need to be clarified. (The approval of a SOAD is not in itself sufficient authorisation for ECT to be given.) This means that in the case of young people who lack capacity, the MCA could provide the necessary authority to give ECT, so long as this would not involve a deprivation of liberty.

19.85 Although the Act does not prevent a person with parental responsibility from consenting to ECT on behalf of a child who lacks competence, or young person who lacks capacity, to consent and who is neither detained under the Act nor a patient subject to a CTO, careful consideration should be given as to whether to rely on parental consent. This is because although there is no case law at present directly on this point, given the nature and invasiveness of ECT, it may lie outside the types of decision that parents can make on behalf of their child. The factors to consider whether it is possible to rely on parental consent are set out in paragraph 19.41 above.

19.86 In cases where ECT cannot be given on the basis of either the child or young person's consent, or parental consent, or the MCA, consideration should be given to whether the child or young person should be admitted under the Act for ECT, if the criteria are met (or recalled to hospital, in case of a community patient).

19.87 In cases where the Act is not applicable, court authorisation should be sought. Although the application to the court should be made before a SOAD is asked to approve the treatment the views of a SOAD should be sought before making the application as the court is likely to wish to consider a SOAD's opinion before determining whether to authorise ECT. In practice, the issues the court is likely to address will mirror those that the SOAD is required to consider.

19.88 All children and young people, whether or not they are detained under the Act, are eligible for help from IMHAs if ECT is proposed and must be informed of this right.

Other treatments under the Act in respect of patients who are liable to be detained and CTO patients who have been recalled

4–109 19.89 Part 4 of the Act sets out when people of all ages who are liable to be detained, or have been recalled to hospital from a CTO, can be given other types of treatment for mental disorder (see chapters 24 and 25).

AGE-APPROPRIATE SERVICES

4–110 19.90 Section 131A of the Act says that children and young people admitted to hospital for the treatment of mental disorder should be accommodated in an environment that is suitable for their age (subject to their needs). This duty applies to the admission of all under 18s, whether or not they are detained under the Act and includes children and young people who are subject to a CTO, who are recalled to hospital, or who agree to informal admission.

19.91 This means that children and young people should have:

- appropriate physical facilities

- staff with the right training, skills and knowledge to understand and address their specific needs

- a hospital routine that will allow their personal, social and educational development to continue as normally as possible, and

- equal access to educational opportunities as their peers, in so far as that is consistent with their ability to make use of them, considering their mental state.

19.92 The duty requires hospital managers to ensure that the environment in the hospital is suitable. When determining the suitability of the environment, they must consult a person whom they consider to have knowledge or experience in working with children and young people receiving in-patient mental healthcare and who are able to make this assessment (this will usually be a CAMHS professional). The duty applies to all in-patient mental health services, including highly specialised services such as eating disorder units, and learning disability services.

19.93 The Care Quality Commission (CQC) must be notified without delay if an under 18-year old is placed on an adult psychiatric ward for longer than a continuous period of 48 hours.[42] Section 140 of the Act requires clinical commissioning groups to notify local authorities in their area of the hospitals that are designed to be specifically suitable for patients under the age of 18.

19.94 Section 131A does not prohibit all admissions of individuals aged under 18 to adult wards. Such admissions are permissible only in exceptional circumstances, where this is considered to be the most suitable place for an under 18 year old. These exceptional circumstances generally fall into two distinct categories, referred to in this guidance as 'emergency situations' and 'atypical cases' (see paragraphs 19.98–19.101).

19.95 In all cases, to be lawful, the admission of a person aged under 18 to an adult ward must be suitable for that particular individual at the time that the admission is being considered.

19.96 In all cases where an under 18 year old is admitted to an adult ward, the reasons for the admission should be recorded, including an explanation as to why this is considered to be suitable having regard to their age and why other options were not available and/or suitable. Details of whether action will be necessary to rectify the situation, and what action taken by whom, and when, should also be recorded.

19.97 In the case of children aged under 16, it is Government policy that they should not be admitted to an adult ward. If this occurs or if the child is treated in any other inappropriate setting due to lack of appropriate CAMHS beds, the commissioner of the CAMHS inpatient services should be notified. The commissioner should report it as a serious incident and investigate it in accordance with the NHS Serious Incident Framework.

19.98 In a small number of cases the child or young person's need to be accommodated in a safe environment could, in the short term, take precedence over the suitability of that environment for their age (referred to as an 'emergency situation'). Such situations will arise where the child or young person needs to be admitted urgently to hospital and accordingly waiting for a bed to become available on a CAMHS unit is not considered to be an acceptable option. An 'emergency situation' should be a rare and unusual case. It is not unusual for children or young people to require unplanned admissions and accordingly local policies should be in place to ensure that such admissions are to age appropriate environments.

19.99 There is a clear difference between what is a suitable environment for a child or young person in an emergency situation, and what is a suitable environment for a child or young person on a longer-term basis. In an emergency, such as when the patient is in crisis, the first imperative is to ensure that the child or young person is in a safe environment. Once the initial emergency situation is over,

---

[42] Care Quality Commission (Registration) Regulations. 2009. SI 2009/3112. Regulation 18.2(h): Any placement of an individual under the age of eighteen in a psychiatric unit whose services are intended for persons over that age where that placement has lasted for longer than a continuous period of 48 hours.

hospital managers must ensure that action is taken to transfer the child or young person to more appropriate accommodation unless they have determined that the adult ward is the most appropriate environment for the child or young person. In determining whether the environment is suitable beyond the initial crisis, in addition to the appropriateness of the mental healthcare that can be provided on the adult ward, the hospital managers would need to consider issues such as whether the child or young person can mix with individuals of their own age, can receive visitors of all ages, and has access to education.

19.100 An 'atypical case' describes a situation where those arranging a young person's admission conclude that the best option for that young person is to be admitted to an adult ward even if a CAMHS bed were available. While likely to be rare, such cases may arise from time to time when the young person is very close to their 18th birthday and placing them on a CAMHS ward for a matter of weeks or days before transferring them to an adult ward would be counter-therapeutic and:

- the young person may express a preference to be on an adult ward, such as when they are under the care of the early intervention psychosis (EIP) team which has beds on an adult ward. The young person may prefer to have continuity of care from the EIP team rather than be admitted to a unit with different clinicians, or

- if a young mother requires admission for post-natal depression, admission to an adult mother and baby unit would allow the young mother to remain with her child, whereas admission to a CAMHS unit would not.

19.101 Where, whether owing to an emergency or because the admission is an 'atypical' case, it is considered appropriate for the child or young person to be admitted to an adult ward, it will still be necessary to ensure that appropriate steps have been taken to safeguard the young person. Discrete accommodation in an adult ward, with facilities, security and staffing appropriate to the needs of that young person, might provide the most satisfactory solution; for example, young female patients should be placed in single sex accommodation. Wherever possible all those involved in the care and treatment of children and young people should be CAMHS specialists. Anyone who looks after them must always have enhanced disclosure clearance from the disclosure and barring service (DBS), including a barred list check, and that clearance must be kept up-to-date.

19.102 Where the placement of a child or young person on a CAMHS unit might have a detrimental effect on the other children and young people, hospital managers need to ensure that the interests of other patients are protected. However, the needs of other children and young people should not override the need to provide accommodation in an environment that is suitable for the patient's age (subject to their needs) for an individual patient aged under 18. This means that the detrimental impact on other young patients is not an acceptable reason for transferring a child or young person to an adult ward.

19.103 Children and young people aged under 18 should also have access to age-appropriate leisure activities and facilities for visits from parents, guardians, siblings, or carers.

19.104 Section 131A of the Act applies to under 18s who are detained in hospital, as a place of safety under sections 135 or 136 of the Act, but not to other places of safety. People under 18 may be admitted to adult hospital facilities in 'emergency situations'. A child or young person may be detained in a place of safety that is not specifically designated for under 18s if this is assessed to be a suitable environment for the child or young person at that time, given the particular circumstances. If, subsequently, the child or young person is assessed as requiring admission to hospital, the admission must be to an age-appropriate (and otherwise suitable) environment and this should be arranged as soon as possible. Section 131A should never be relied upon as a reason for detaining a child or youngperson under the age of 18 in a police cell rather than a hospital. The safety of the child or young person should always be central to the decision-making process.

UNDER 18S DETENTION IN A PLACE OF SAFETY

19.105 As chapter 16 states, the process for identifying the most appropriate **4–111** place of safety to which a particular person is to be removed should be clearly outlined in the local place of safety policy. This applies to children and young people as much as adults. Unless there are specific arrangements in place with CAMHS, the healthcare setting identified by local policies as the place of safety should be used, and the fact that this is attached to an adult ward should not preclude its use for this purpose. In addition, the policies should make clear that a person under 18 should not be removed to a police station as a place of safety unless there are exceptional circumstances, and clear reasons (which should be recorded according to the local policy and shared with relevant local authority children's services), why this is the most appropriate place in which to safeguard that child or young person (see paragraphs 16.43–16.52).

THE RESPONSIBLE CLINICIAN AND OTHERS CARING FOR AND TREATING UNDER 18S

19.106 Wherever possible, those responsible for the care and treatment of chil- **4–112** dren and young people should be CAMHS specialists. Chapter 36 provides guidance in relation to identifying responsible clinicians. In the exceptional cases where a young person is admitted to an adult psychiatric ward, the hospital managers should ensure that the clinical staff have regular access to, and make use of, a CAMHS specialist for advice and consultation.

The Tribunal

19.107 Children and young people who are detained under the Act have the **4–113** same rights as other patients to apply to the Tribunal (see chapter 12). It is important that children and young people are informed of their right to apply to the Tribunal and are assisted in obtaining legal representation at an early stage. IMHAs have an important role in ensuring that children and young people understand, and are able to exercise, their rights under the Act. The IMHA's help in relation to applications to Tribunal will be particularly important, such as helping the child or young person contact a lawyer and understanding the role of the Tribunal, and what to expect at the Tribunal hearing.

19.108 A CAMHS panel of the Tribunal has been established so that, wherever possible, at least one member of the panel considering a child or young person's case will have experience of working with under 18s.

19.109 Professionals preparing social circumstances reports for the Tribunal must ensure that such reports include any information required in the Tribunal's Practice Directions.[43]

19.110 Hospital managers should ensure that systems are in place to identify cases requiring referral to a Tribunal in accordance with section 68 of the Act. They have a duty to refer patients to the Tribunal under section 68(6) of the Act after a one-year period without a Tribunal hearing in relation to under 18s. Hospital managers should also consider asking that the Secretary of State refers a child or young person's case to a Tribunal under section 67 of the Act in cases where that child or young person is unable to have their case considered speedily by the Tribunal (see paragraphs 37.44–37.46).

AFTER-CARE

4–114   19.111 Prior to their discharge from hospital all children and young people should have an assessment of their needs, on which a care plan for their after-care is based. Guidance on the duty to provide after-care under section 117 of the Act, is set out in chapter 33. Such guidance is applicable to individuals of all ages, but in relation to children and young people additional factors will need to be considered. This may include ensuring that the after-care integrates with any existing provision made for looked after children and those with special educational needs or disabilities, as well as safeguarding vulnerable children. Whether or not section 117 of the Act applies, a child or young person who has been admitted to hospital for assessment and/or treatment of their mental disorder may be 'a child in need' for the purpose of section 17 of the Children Act 1989. See also paragraph 19.118 below in relation to children and young people with special educational needs.

19.112 For information about after-care payments, see chapter 33 for relevant details covering children and young people.

COMMUNITY TREATMENT ORDER (CTO) AND GUARDIANSHIP

4–115   19.113 There is no lower age limit for a CTO. The number of children and young people whose clinical and family circumstances make them suitable to move from being detained to being a community patient is likely to be small, but it should be used where appropriate (see chapters 29 and 31).

19.114 Parents (or other people with parental responsibility) cannot consent (or refuse consent) to treatment for mental disorder on a child or young person's behalf while the child or young person is on a CTO. If community patients under the age of 18 are living with one or both parents, the responsible clinician should consult with the parent(s) about the particular treatment (subject to the normal considerations of patient confidentiality). This dialogue should continue throughout the period of the CTO. If a parent is unhappy with the particular treatment or conditions attached to the CTO, and the child is not competent to consent (or young person lacks capacity to consent), a review by the child or young person's team should take place. This will be to consider whether the treatment and care plan, and CTO in general, are still appropriate for them.

---

[43] At the time of publication this was detailed in Annex E of Practice Direction. First-tier Tribunal, Health, Education and Social Care Chamber: statements and reports in mental health cases. Tribunals Judiciary. 2013. http://www.judiciary.gov.uk/wp-content/uploads/JCO/Documents/Practice+Directions/Tribunals/statements-in-mental-health-cases-hesc-28102013.pdf.

19.115 The powers of guardianship under the Act apply to individuals aged 16 and over andmay be appropriate for young people aged 16 and 17 (see chapter 30).

EDUCATION

19.116 Local authorities must make arrangements to provide suitable education **4–116** for all children of compulsory school age. Suitable education means education suitable to their age, ability and aptitude and to any special educational needs (SEN) they may have. This education must be full-time, unless the local authority determines that, for reasons relating to the physical or mental health of the child, a reduced level of education would be in the child's best interests. Children and young people admitted to hospital under the Act should have access to education that is on a par with that of mainstream provision, including appropriate support for those with SEN. Practitioners and local authorities should work together to minimise any disruption to education, and in order to ensure that local authorities can meet their duty to provide suitable education, when a child or young person is admitted under the Act, they should be notified as soon as possible, ideally in advance of the placement. The duty on local authorities to ensure suitable education also applies when a child or young person is receiving treatment in an area where they are not normally resident.

19.117 Young people over the school leaving age should also be encouraged to continue learning. Under Raising the Participation Age legislation (part of the Education and Skills Act 2008),[44] local authorities have duties to promote effective participation in education or training for 16 and 17 year olds including those admitted to hospital.

19.118 When a child or young person with a statement SEN, a learning difficulty assessment (LDA) or an education, health and care plan (EHC plan) is admitted to hospital under the Act the local authority who maintains the plan should be informed, so that they can ensure that educational support continues to be provided. If necessary, the plan may be reviewed and amended to ensure targets and provisions remain appropriate. The local authority should also be involved in creating the discharge plan, so that the statement, LDA or EHC plan is revised as necessary to continue to reflect the child or young people educational, health and social care needs.

TRANSITION FROM CAMHS

19.119 Young people's transition from CAMHS requires careful planning, **4–117** which should start at least six months before the young person is due to leave CAMHS. The planning process should ensure the full involvement of the child or young person and (subject to issues of confidentiality) those who will be involved in their care, including those with parental responsibility. The young person should be listened to and helped to improve their self-sufficiency; they should be provided with appropriate and accessible information so they can exercise choice effectively and participate in decisions about which adult and other services they receive.

19.120 Where a young person has an EHC plan that includes agreed provision to support mental health then health commissioners must put arrangements in place to secure that provision. Commissioners should be aware that where appropriate, local authorities may maintain EHC plans up to the age of 25.

---

[44] Education and Skills Act 2008. http://www.legislation.gov.uk/ukpga/2008/25/contents.

DUTIES OF LOCAL AUTHORITIES IN RELATION TO CHILDREN AND YOUNG PEOPLE IN HOSPITAL

4–118   19.121 Local authorities should ensure that they arrange for visits to be made to:

- children and young people looked after by them who are in hospital, whether or not they are under a care order, and

- children and young people accommodated or intended to be accommodated for three months or more by NHS-funded providers. Such visits must be undertaken in accordance with the relevant regulations.[45]

19.122 Local authorities should consider whether it would be appropriate to provide financial support to enable families to visit children and young people placed in hospital, taking into account their duties to promote contact between children and young people and their families. Such duties arise when children and young people are being looked after by local authorities as well as when they are accommodated in hospital for three months or more. The provision of financial support to cover the travel costs of visiting might be essential for some families on low incomes, especially if their child has been placed out of area (see paragraphs 8A and 16 of schedule 2 of the Children Act 1989).

19.123 Section 116 of the Act also places duties on local authorities in respect of children and young people in their care by virtue of a care order and who are admitted to a hospital, independent hospital or care home in England and Wales. In such cases, local authorities are required to arrange for the child or young person to be visited and to take such other steps in relation to the child or young person while they are in a hospital, independent hospital or care home as would be expected to be taken by their parent(s).

19.123 Local authorities are under a duty in the Children Act 1989 to:

- promote contact between children and young people who are children in need, or looked after children, and their families, if they live away from home, and to help them get back together (paragraphs 10 and 15 of Schedule 2 to the Children Act 1989), and

- arrange for people (independent visitors) to visit, advise and befriend children and young people looked after by the authority wherever they are, if they have not been regularly visited by their parents (paragraph 17 of Schedule 2 to the Children Act 1989).

19.125 Local authorities should be alerted if the whereabouts of the person with parental responsibility is not known or if that person has not visited the child or young person for a significant period of time. When alerted to this situation the local authority should consider whether visits should be arranged.

19.126 Hospital managers should set up systems to ensure that directors of children's services are notified of cases in which their duty to visit and consider the welfare of children and young people in hospital arises (see chapter 37 for further details on the functions of hospital managers).

---

[45] See Visits to Children in Long-term Residential Care Regulations. SI 2011/1010. 2011. http://www.legislation.gov.uk/uksi/2011/1010/contents/made.

23. THE APPROPRIATE MEDICAL TREATMENT TEST

Why read this chapter?
23.1 This chapter provides guidance on the application of the appropriate medi-   **4–119**
cal treatment test and the criteria for detention or a community treatment order
(CTO) under the Act. It includes guidance on appropriate treatment for people
with dementia.

PURPOSE OF MEDICAL TREATMENT FOR MENTAL DISORDER
23.2 For the purposes of the Act, medical treatment includes nursing, psycho-   **4–120**
logical intervention and specialist mental health habilitation, rehabilitation and
care. Habilitation means equipping someone with skills and abilities they have
never had, whereas rehabilitation means helping them recover skills and abilities
they have lost.

23.3 In the Act, medical treatment for mental disorder means medical treatment
which is for the purpose of alleviating, or preventing a worsening of, a mental disorder or one or more of its symptoms or manifestations.

23.4 Purpose is not the same as likelihood. Medical treatment must be for the
purpose of alleviating or preventing a worsening of mental disorder even if it cannot be shown, in advance, that a particular effect is likely to be achieved.

23.5 Symptoms and manifestations include the way a disorder is experienced
by the individual concerned and the way in which the disorder manifests itself
in the person's thoughts, emotions, communication, behaviour and actions. It
should be remembered that not every thought or emotion or every aspect of the
behaviour, of a patient suffering from mental disorder will be a manifestation
of that disorder.

23.6 Even if particular mental disorders are likely to persist or get worse despite
treatment, there may well be a range of interventions which would represent
appropriate medical treatment. It should never be assumed that any disorders,
or any patients, are inherently or inevitably untreatable. Nor should it be assumed
that likely difficulties in achieving long-term and sustainable change in a person's
underlying disorder make medical treatment to help manage their condition and
the behaviours arising from it either inappropriate or unnecessary.

APPROPRIATE MEDICAL TREATMENT TEST
23.7 The Act requires appropriate medical treatment to be available to a patient   **4–121**
in order to meet the criteria for section 3 detention or a CTO. Where the appropriate medical treatment test forms part of the criteria for detention, the medical
treatment in question is treatment for mental disorder in the hospital in which
the patient is to be detained. Where it is part of the criteria for a CTO it refers
to the treatment for mental disorder that the person will be offered while on a
CTO.

23.8 The appropriate medical treatment test must be applied to ensure that no
one is detained (or remains detained) for treatment, or is on a CTO, unless medical
treatment for their mental disorder is both appropriate and available.

23.9 In order to be deemed appropriate, medical treatment must be for the purpose of alleviating or preventing a worsening of the patient's mental disorder or its
symptoms or manifestations. It must also be appropriate, having taken account of
the nature and degree of the patient's mental disorder and all their particular circumstances, including cultural, ethnic and religious or belief considerations.

23.10 The appropriate medical treatment test requires a judgement about whether an appropriate treatment or package of treatment for mental disorder is available for the individual in question. It is not consistent with the least 'restrictive option and maximising independence' and 'purpose and effectiveness' guiding principles' to detain someone for treatment that is not actually available or may not become available until some future point in time.

Applying the appropriate medical treatment test

4–123   23.11 The test requires a balanced and holistic judgement as to whether, medical treatment to available to the patient is appropriate, given:

- the nature and degree of the patient's mental disorder, and
- all the other circumstances of the patient's case. In other words, both the clinical appropriateness of the treatment and its appropriateness more generally must be considered.

23.12 The other circumstances of a patient's case might, for example, include factors such as:

- the patient's physical health—how this might impact on the effectiveness of the available medical treatment for the patient's mental disorder and the impact that the treatment might have in return
- the patient's age
- any physical disabilities or sensory impairments the patient has
- the patient's culture and ethnicity
- the patient's gender, gender identity, sexual identity and sexual orientation
- the patient's religion or beliefs
- the location of the available treatment
- the implications of the treatment for the patient's family and social relationships, including their role as a parent (where applicable)
- its implications for the patient's education or work
- the consequences for the patient, and other people, if the patient does not receive the treatment available (for mentally disordered offenders about to be sentenced for an offence, the consequence will sometimes be a prison sentence), and
- the patient's views and wishes about what treatment works for them and what doesn't.

23.13 Medical treatment must always be an appropriate response to the patient's condition and situation and indeed wherever possible should be the most appropriate treatment available. It may be that a single medical treatment does not address every aspect of a patient's mental disorder.

23.14 Medical treatment must actually be available to the patient. It is not sufficient that appropriate treatment could theoretically be provided.

23.15 What is appropriate will vary greatly between patients. It will depend, in part, on what might reasonably be expected to be achieved given the nature and degree of the patient's disorder.

23.16 Medical treatment which aims merely to prevent a disorder worsening is unlikely, in general, to be appropriate in cases where normal treatment approaches would aim (and be expected) to alleviate the patient's condition significantly. However, for some patients with persistent and severe mental disorders, management of the undesirable effects of their disorder may be the most that can realistically be hoped for.

23.17 Appropriate medical treatment does not have to involve medication or psychological therapy—although it very often will. There may be patients whose particular circumstances mean that treatment may be appropriate even though it consists only of nursing and specialist day-to-day care under the clinical supervision of an approved clinician in a safe and secure therapeutic environment with a structured regime.

23.18 Simply detaining someone, even in a hospital, does not constitute medical treatment.

23.19 A patient's attitude towards the proposed treatment may be relevant in determining whether the appropriate medical treatment test is met. An indication of unwillingness to co-operate with treatment generally, or with a specific aspect of treatment, does not make such treatment inappropriate.

23.20 In particular, psychological therapies and other forms of medical treatments which, to be effective, require the patient's co-operation are not automatically inappropriate simply because a patient does not currently wish to engage with them. Such treatments can potentially remain appropriate and available as long as it continues to be clinically suitable to offer them and they would be provided if the patient agreed to engage.

23.21 In determining whether the appropriate medical treatment test is met, those making the judgement must satisfy themselves that appropriate medical treatment is available for the time being, given the patient's condition and circumstances as they are currently understood. Determinations are time specific and may need to be reconsidered as the patient's condition changes or clinicians obtain a greater understanding of the patient's case.

Patients with dementia

23.22 Generally, treatment approaches for dementia differ according to the type **4–124** of dementia the person has. People with dementia may take time to engage and develop motivation for treatment. People with dementia can benefit from approaches that do not involve drugs, eg reminiscence therapy or cognitive stimulation therapy. People with dementia may experience depression or anxiety and it may be appropriate to offer them antidepressant drugs and/or offered talking therapies.

23.23 Some people with dementia may display challenging behaviour (see chapter 20) because they are distressed, confused or in pain. The use of sedation or antipsychotic medication may not be appropriate in these circumstances and alternative intervention or treatment could be deemed more appropriate.

24. MEDICAL TREATMENT

Why read this chapter?

4–125 24.1 This chapter gives guidance on medical treatment for mental disorder under the Act, especially treatment given without patients' consent. It also gives guidance on promoting good physical healthcare for patients subject to the Act.

24.2 Treatment under the Act must be appropriate to the patient's mental health condition and take account of the person's wishes or feelings and advance decisions. The chapter provides guidance about appropriate treatment; treatments to which special rules and procedures apply; the treatment of detained patients and patients under community treatment orders (CTOs); and on issues of capacity and consent. It gives guidance on treatment plans, explaining their importance, and provides a summary of the treatment of incapacitated patients and the interface between the Act and the Mental Capacity Act (MCA).

DEFINITIONS

4–126 24.3 In the Act, 'medical treatment' includes nursing, psychological intervention and specialist mental health habilitation, rehabilitation and care.

24.4 The Act defines medical treatment for mental disorder as medical treatment which is for the purpose of alleviating or preventing a worsening of a mental disorder or one or more of its symptoms or manifestations.

24.5 This includes treatment of physical health problems only to the extent that such treatment is part of, or ancillary to, treatment for mental disorder (eg treating wounds self-inflicted as a result of mental disorder). Otherwise, the Act does not regulate medical treatment for physical health problems.

APPROPRIATE TREATMENT

4–127 24.6 All treatment provided should be appropriate to the patient's mental health condition and take account of any advance decisions made by the person and any wishes or feelings they have expressed in advance of treatment. The practicalities of how the treatment is to be delivered, and how outcomes will be monitored should be considered.

24.7 Where reasonably practicable, treatment should be based on a strong evidence-base. Professionals should ensure that any treatment is compliant with the current guidelines and standards about what is appropriate treatment. Examples include, National Institute for Health and Care Excellence (NICE)/Social Care Institute for Excellence (SCIE) guidelines, NICE quality standards and Department of Health Care Programme Approach (CPA) guidance. In the case of medications that are used to treat mental disorder, particular care is required when prescribing medications that exceed the maximum dosage listed in the British National Formulary (BNF) or where multiple medications are used to treat a patient.[46]

---

[46] The British National Formulary is available at: https://www.medicinescomplete.com/about/subscribe.htm See also CR190. Consensus statement on high-dose antipsychotic medication. Royal College of Psychiatrists. 2014. http://www.rcpsych.ac.uk/usefulresources/publications/collegereports/cr/cr190.aspx.

TREATMENTS TO WHICH SPECIAL RULES AND PROCEDURES APPLY

24.8 Section 57 (treatments requiring consent or a second opinion), section 58 **4–128** (treatments requiring consent or a second opinion) and section 58A of the Act electro-convulsive therapy (ECT) set out types of medical treatment for mental disorder to which special rules and procedures apply, including, in many cases, the need for a certificate from a second opinion appointed doctor (SOAD) approving the treatment.

24.9 Guidance on sections 57, 58 and 58A is given in chapter 25, but in summary the treatments involved are as in the figure below.

Figure 10: Summary of treatments covered by sections 57, 58 and 58A

Section	Forms of treatment covered
Section 57	Neurosurgery for mental disorder Surgical implantation of hormones to reduce male sex drive
Section 58	Medication after an initial three-month period, except medication administered as part of ECT
Section 58A	ECT and medication administered as part of ECT

Note: it is possible that other forms of treatment may be added to any of these sections by regulations.

Treatment of detained patients and CTO patients recalled to hospital (part 4 of the Act)

24.10 Part 4 of the Act deals mainly with the treatment of people who are liable **4–129** to be detained in hospital, including patients who have been recalled to hospital from CTOs and conditional discharge. They are referred to in this chapter as 'detained patients'.

24.11 Some patients detained in hospital, as set out below, are not covered by these rules. When this chapter talks about detained patients, these patients are not included. There are no special rules about treatment for these patients—they are in the same position as patients who are not subject to the Act at all, and they have exactly the same rights to consent to and refuse treatment.

Figure 11: Meaning of detained patients in this chapter

In this chapter 'detained patients' means:	Exceptions
Patients who are liable to be detained in hospital under any section of the Act (including those who are not actually detained, such as patients who are on leave of absence or absent without leave).	• Patients detained on the basis of an emergency application under section 4 unless or until the second medical recommendation is received • Patients held in hospital under the holding powers in section 5 • Patients remanded to hospital for a report on their mental condition under section 35 • Patients detained in hospital as a place of safety under section 135 or 136

	• Patients temporarily detained in hospital as a place of safety under section 37 or 45A, pending admission to the hospital named in their hospital order or hospital direction • Restricted patients who have been conditionally discharged (unless or until they are recalled to hospital) • Qualifying patients within the meaning of section 22 who have remained in custody for six months or longer in total.
Patients on CTOs who have been recalled to hospital	
Restricted patients who have been conditionally discharged and recalled to hospital	

24.12 Unless section 57, section 58 or 58A apply, section 63 of the Act (treatment not requiring consent) means that detained patients may be given medical treatment for any kind for mental disorder, whether they:

- consent to it, or

- have not consented to it,
  but the treatment must be given by or under the direction of the approved clinician in charge of the treatment in question.

24.13 If sections 57, 58 or 58A apply, detained patients may be given the treatment only if the rules in those sections are followed (see chapter 25).

TREATMENT OF CTO PATIENTS NOT RECALLED TO HOSPITAL (PART 4A PATIENTS)

4–130   24.14 Part 4A of the Act sets out different rules for treatment for patients on CTOs who have not been recalled to hospital by their responsible clinician. This includes patients on CTOs who are in hospital without having been recalled (eg if they have been admitted to hospital voluntarily).

24.15 For convenience, this chapter refers to patients on CTOs who have not been recalled to hospital (ie admitted to hospital voluntarily) as 'part 4A patients'.

24.16 The rules for part 4A patients differ depending on whether or not they have the capacity to consent to or refuse the treatment in question. Except where otherwise stated, references in the paragraphs below to a person who lacks capacity to consent to or refuse treatment includes patients aged under 16 who lack the competence to consent to or refuse treatment (see paragraph 24.18 and chapter 19).

24.17 Part 4A patients, who have the capacity to consent to or refuse a treatment, may not be given that treatment unless they consent. There are no exceptions to this rule, even in emergencies. The effect is that treatment can be given without their consent only if they are recalled to hospital.

24.18 For part 4A patients, aged 18 and over, who lack the capacity to consent to or refuse a treatment, it may be given if someone who has lasting power of attorney (an attorney) or a Court of Protection appointed deputy consents on their behalf. Similarly it may be given in the case of those aged 16 and over if a deputy consents to the treatment on their behalf.

24.19 Part 4A patients who lack capacity to consent to or refuse a treatment may also be given it, without anyone's consent by or under the direction of the approved clinician in charge of the treatment, unless:

- in the case of a patient aged 18 or over, the treatment would be contrary to a valid and applicable advance decision made by the patient (see chapter 9)

- in the case of a patient aged 18 or over, the treatment would be against the decision of someone with the authority under the MCA 2005 to refuse it on the patient's behalf (an attorney, a deputy or the Court of Protection), or

- in the case of a patient aged 16 or over, the treatment would be against the decision of a deputy who has authority to refuse it on the patient's behalf, or force needs to be used in order to administer the treatment and the patient objects to the treatment.

24.20 In this last case, force means the actual use of physical force on the patient. Where force needs to be used, it is up to the person proposing to give the treatment to decide whether a patient objects to the treatment. The question is simply whether the patient objects—the reasonableness (or unreasonableness) of the objection is irrelevant. In any situation where force is used, if it amounts to a restrictive intervention then the provisions within chapter 26 apply and particular note should be taken of paragraphs 26.36–26.44.

24.21 In deciding whether patients object to treatment, all the relevant evidence should be taken into account, so far as it reasonably can be. In many cases, patients will be perfectly able to state their objection, either verbally or by their dissenting behaviour. In other cases, especially where patients are unable to communicate (or only able to communicate to a limited extent), clinicians will need to consider the patient's behaviour, wishes, feelings, views, beliefs and values, both present and past, so far as they can be ascertained.

24.22 If there is reason to think that a patient would object, if able to do so, then the patient should be taken to be objecting. Occasionally, it may be that the patient's behaviour initially suggests an objection to being treated, but is in fact not directed at the treatment at all. In that case the patient would not be taken to be objecting.

24.23 In addition to the requirements described in paragraphs 24.17–24.22 (the Act calls these the 'authority' to give treatment), the Act also refers to the 'certificate requirement' that applies to certain treatments that can only be given if they have either been: approved by a SOAD on a 'part 4A certificate'; or certified by the approved clinician in charge of the patient's treatment on a 'part 4A consent certificate', if the patient has capacity (or competence, for patients under 16) to consent to the treatment and has done so. Broadly speaking, the certificate requirement applies to any treatment for which a certificate would be necessary under section 58 or 58A of the Act were the patient detained instead (see chapter 25).

EMERGENCY TREATMENT UNDER SECTION 64G FOR CTO PATIENTS NOT RECALLED TO HOSPITAL (PART 4A PATIENTS)

4–131   24.24 In an emergency, treatment can also be given to part 4A patients who lack capacity to consent to or refuse a treatment (and who have not been recalled to hospital) by anyone, whether or not they are acting under the direction of an approved clinician.

24.25 It is an emergency only if the treatment is immediately necessary to:

- save the patient's life

- prevent a serious deterioration of the patient's condition and the treatment does not have unfavourable physical or psychological consequences which cannot be reversed

- alleviate serious suffering by the patient and the treatment does not have unfavourable physical or psychological consequences which cannot be reversed and does not entail significant physical hazard, or

- prevent patients behaving violently or being a danger to themselves or others and the treatment represents the minimum interference necessary for that purpose, does not have unfavourable physical or psychological consequences which cannot be reversed and does not entail significant physical hazard.

If the treatment is ECT (or medication administered as part of ECT), only the first two categories above apply.

24.26 Where treatment is immediately necessary in these terms, it can be given even though it conflicts with an advance decision or the decision of someone who has the authority under the MCA to refuse it on the patient's behalf.

24.27 In addition, force may be used (whether or not the patient objects), provided that:

- the treatment is necessary to prevent harm to the patient, and

- the force used is proportionate to the likelihood of the patient suffering harm and to the seriousness of that harm.

24.28 These are the only circumstances in which force may be used to treat patients on CTOs who object, without recalling them to hospital. This exception is for situations where the patient's interests would be better served by being given urgently needed treatment by force outside hospital rather than being recalled to hospital. This might, for example, be where the situation is so urgent that recall is not realistic, or where taking patients to hospital would exacerbate their condition, damage their recovery or cause them unnecessary anxiety or suffering. Situations like this should be exceptional.

TREATMENT OF OTHER PATIENTS

4–133   24.29 The Act does not regulate treatment for any other patients, except that:

- the special rules and procedures in section 57 apply to all patients, and
- the special rules and procedures in section 58A apply to all patients under the age of 18. See chapters 25 and 19.

CAPACITY AND CONSENT

24.30 The Act frequently requires healthcare professionals to determine: **4–134**

- whether a patient has the capacity to consent to or refuse a particular form of medical treatment, and
- if so, whether the patient does in fact consent.

The rules for answering these questions are the same as for any other patients.

Capacity to consent: people aged 16 or over

24.31 For people aged 16 or over, capacity to consent is defined by the MCA **4–135** (see chapter 13). The principles of the MCA state (among other things) that:

- people must be assumed to have capacity unless it is established that they lack capacity
- people are not to be treated as unable to make a decision unless all practicable steps to help them do so have been taken without success
- people are not to be treated as unable to make a decision merely because they make an unwise decision.

24.32 When taking decisions about patients under the Act, it should be remembered that:

- mental disorder does not necessarily mean that a patient lacks capacity to give or refuse consent, or to take any other decision
- any assessment of an individual's capacity has to be made in relation to the particular decision being made—a person may, for example, have the capacity to consent to or refuse one form of treatment but not to another
- capacity in an individual with a mental disorder can vary over time and should be assessed at the time the decision in question needs to be taken
- where a patient's capacity fluctuates in this way, consideration should be given, if a decision is not urgently required, to delaying the decision until the patient has capacity again to make it for themselves
- not everyone is equally capable of understanding the same explanation— explanations should be appropriate to the level of the patient's assessed ability, and
- all assessments of an individual's capacity should be fully recorded in the patient's notes.

Competence to consent to treatment—children under 16

4–136   24.33 The MCA does not apply to medical treatment for children under 16. Children who have sufficient understanding and intelligence to enable them fully to understand what is involved in a proposed treatment are considered to be competent (or 'Gillick competent') to consent to it. Further information on assessing a child's competence to make treatment decisions is provided in chapter 19.

Consent

4–137   24.34 Consent is the voluntary and continuing permission of a patient to be given a particular treatment, based on a sufficient knowledge of the purpose, nature, likely effects and risks of that treatment, including the likelihood of its success and any alternatives to it. Permission given under any unfair or undue pressure is not consent.

24.35 By definition, a person who lacks capacity is unable to consent or refuse treatment, even if they co-operate with the treatment or actively seek it.

24.36 It is the duty of everyone seeking consent to use reasonable care and skill, not only in giving information prior to seeking consent, but also in meeting the continuing obligation to provide the patient with sufficient information about the proposed treatment and alternatives to it.

24.37 The information which should be given should be related to the particular patient, the particular treatment and relevant clinical knowledge and practice. In every case, sufficient information should be given to the patient to ensure that they understand in broad terms the nature, likely effects and all significant possible adverse outcomes of that treatment, including the likelihood of its success and any alternatives to it. A record should be kept of information provided to patients.

24.38 Patients should be invited to ask questions and professionals should answer fully, frankly and truthfully. If a patient asks about a risk, they should always be given an honest answer. There may sometimes be a compelling reason, in the patient's interests, for not disclosing certain information. A professional who chooses not to disclose information should be prepared to justify the decision. A professional who chooses not to answer a patient's question should make this clear to the patient so that the patient knows where they stand. A record should be kept of any decision not to disclose information, and the reasons for that decision.

24.39 Patients should be told that their consent to treatment can be withdrawn at any time. Where patients withdraw their consent (or are considering withdrawing it), they should be given a clear explanation of the likely consequences of not receiving the treatment and (where relevant) the circumstances in which the treatment may be given without their consent under the Act. A record should be kept of the information provided to patients.

Treatment without consent—general points

4–138   24.40 To give time to develop a treatment programme suitable for the patient's needs, the Act allows treatment to be given in the initial three month period starting the day on which any form of medication for mental disorder was first administered to the patient during the current period in which the patient is liable to be detained under the Act.

24.41 During this time, the patient's consent should still be sought before any medication is administered, wherever practicable. The patient's consent, refusal to consent, or a lack of capacity to give consent should be recorded in the case notes. If a person has capacity to consent, but such consent is not forthcoming or is withdrawn during this period, the clinician in charge of the treatment must consider carefully whether to proceed in the absence of consent, to give alternative treatment or stop treatment.

24.42 Clinicians authorising or administering treatment without consent under the Act are performing a function of a public nature and must therefore comply with the Human Rights Act (HRA) 1998, which gives effect in the UK to certain rights and freedoms guaranteed under the European Convention on Human Rights (ECHR).

24.43 In particular, the following should be noted:

- compulsory administration of treatment which would otherwise require consent is invariably an infringement of article 8 of the ECHR (respect for family and private life). However, it may be justified where it is in accordance with law (in this case the procedures in the Act) and where it is proportionate to a legitimate aim (in this case, the reduction of the risk posed by a person's mental disorder and the improvement of their health)

- compulsory treatment is capable of being inhuman treatment (or in extreme cases even torture) contrary to article 3 of the ECHR, if its effect on the person concerned reaches a sufficient level of severity. But the European Court of Human Rights has said that a measure which is convincingly shown to be of medical necessity from the point of view of established principles of medicine cannot in principle be regarded as inhuman and degrading.

24.44 Scrupulous adherence to the requirements of the legislation and good clinical practice should ensure that there is no such incompatibility. If clinicians have concerns about a potential breach of a person's human rights they should seek senior clinical and, if necessary, legal advice.

TREATMENT PLANS

24.45 Treatment plans are essential for patients being treated for mental dis- **4–139** order under the Act. A patient's responsible clinician is responsible for ensuring that a treatment plan is in place for that patient.

24.46 A treatment plan should include a description of the immediate and long-term goals for the patient and should give a clear indication of the treatments proposed and the methods of treatment.

24.47 The treatment plan should form part of a coherent care plan under the CPA (or its equivalent), and be recorded in the patient's notes (see chapter 34).

24.48 Psychological therapies should be considered as a routine treatment option at all stages, including the initial formulation of a treatment plan and each subsequent review of that plan. Any programme of psychological intervention should form part of the agreed treatment plan and be recorded in the patient's notes as such.

24.49 Wherever possible, the whole treatment plan should be discussed with the patient. Patients should be encouraged and assisted to make use of advocacy support available to them, if they want it. This includes, but need not be restricted to, independent mental health advocacy services under the Act. Where patients cannot (or do not wish to) participate in discussion about their treatment plan, any views they have expressed previously should be taken into consideration (see chapter 9).

24.50 Subject to the normal considerations of patient confidentiality, the treatment plan should also be discussed with their carers, with a view to enabling them to contribute to it and express agreement or disagreement.

24.51 Discussion with carers is particularly important where carers will themselves be providing care to the patient while the plan is in force. Plans should not be based on any assumptions about the willingness or ability of carers to support patients, unless those assumptions have been discussed and agreed with the carers. Carers have an important role to play in maintaining the patient's contact with home and community life and providing emotional support when the patient is detained. In some cases carers' willingness and ability to contribute to the provision of care may be dependent on additional support and they should be reminded of possible sources of such support and their entitlement to a carer's assessment by the local authority.

24.52 For children and young people, subject to the normal considerations of patient confidentiality, the plan should similarly be discussed with the people who have parental responsibility for them. For further information on confidentiality and sharing information concerning children and young people, paragraphs 19.14–19.16.

24.53 Treatment plans should be regularly reviewed and the results of reviews recorded in the patient's notes.

TREATMENT OF INCAPACITATED PATIENTS—INTERFACE BETWEEN PARTS 4 AND 4A OF THE ACT AND THE MCA (SECTION 28)

4–140 24.54 In so far as it deals with decisions about medical treatment for people aged 16 or above who lack capacity to consent to or refuse such treatment, the MCA applies to patients subject to the Act in the same way as to anyone else, with exceptions set out in the following table. These exceptions apply only to medical treatment for mental disorder.

Figure 12: Medical treatment of patients subject to the Mental Health Act— exceptions to the normal rules on treatment and consent in the MCA

Situation	Exceptions
Section 57 treatment (neurosurgery for mental disorder etc)	The MCA may not be used to give anyone treatment to which section 57 applies (see chapter 25 for guidance on section 57).
Section 58 treatment (medication after an initial three month period, except ECT-related medication)	The MCA may not be used to give anyone treatment to which section 58 applies (see chapter 25 for guidance on section 58).
Section 58A treatment (ECT and related medication)	The MCA may not be used to give detained patients (as defined in paragraphs 24.10–24.11) ECT and any other treatment to which section 58A applies.

Treatment regulated by part 4 of the Act for detained patients	he MCA may not be used to give detained patients (as defined in this chapter) any other medical treatment for mental disorder. Treatment regulated by part 4 of the Act at the time of the proposed treatment must be given in accordance with part 4 of the Act instead (see paragraphs 24.10–24.13).
Treatment for patients on CTOs who have not been recalled to hospital (part 4A patients)	The MCA may not generally be used to give these CTO patients any medical treatment for mental disorder, but attorneys, deputies and the Court of Protection may consent to such treatment on behalf of these CTO patients.
Advance decisions to refuse treatment (as defined in the MCA)	Where the Act allows treatment to be given against the wishes of a patient who has capacity to consent, it also allows treatment to be given despite the existence of a valid and applicable advance decision made under the MCA (see chapter 9). But note that, except in emergencies: • treatment to which section 58A applies cannot be given contrary to a valid and applicable advance decision, and • treatment cannot be given to CTO patients who have not been recalled to hospital (part 4A patients) contrary to a valid and applicable advance decision.
Patients who have attorneys or court-appointed deputies under the MCA with authority to take decisions on their behalf about their medical treatment	Attorneys and deputies (acting within the scope of their authority under the MCA) may not: • consent to treatment to which section 57 or 58 applies on behalf of any patient • consent to treatment to which section 58A applies—but note that (except in emergencies) they may refuse it on a patient's behalf, or • consent to or refuse any other treatment on behalf of detained patients (as defined in paragraphs 24.10–24.11). But note that attorneys and deputies may: • consent to treatment on behalf of CTO patients who have not been recalled to hospital (part 4A patients), even if treatment is to be given forcibly, and • except in emergencies, refuse treatment on behalf of those patients.

24.55 See chapter 13 for guidance on the interface between detention under the Act and the deprivation of liberty safeguards under the MCA. See chapter 30 for the interface between the powers of guardians under the Act and the MCA.

COURT OF PROTECTION AND OTHER COURTS

4–141 24.56 The Court of Protection, as well as other courts may, in certain circumstances, have the power to order that the treatment must not be given. Should such an order be made, legal advice should be sought on the legal authority for continuing or starting any such treatment.

Figure 13: Summary of when medical treatment for mental disorder may be given under the Act

Type of patient (and relevant part of the Act	When treatment can be given	Notes (for further detail see chapter 24
Detained patients (part 4)—see definition in paragraphs 24.10–24.13	If sections 57, 58 or 58A apply, treatment may be given only in accordance with those sections. Otherwise, treatment may be given: • with the patient's consent, and • without the patient's consent under section 63, if the treatment is by or under the direction of the approved clinician in charge.	Neurosurgery for mental disorder and other treatments to which section 57 applies cannot be given without the patient's consent and must always be approved by a SOAD. ECT and other treatments to which section 58A applies cannot be given to a patient who has capacity to consent but refuses to do so. They can only be given to patients who lack capacity (or who are under 18) if approved by a SOAD. Medication to which section 58 apply can be given without the patient's consent, but only with the approval of a SOAD. Sections 57, 58 and 58A do not apply in emergencies, where treatment is defined in section 62 as immediately necessary (see paragraphs 25.37–25.42).
CTO patients who have not been recalled to hospital (part 4A patients)	If section 57 applies, treatment can be given only with the patient's consent and if the other rules in section 57 are followed.	Unless it is an emergency, if treatment is one to which section 58 or 58A would apply if the person was liable to be detained, the treatment

	Otherwise, if the patient has capacity to consent to or refuse treatment, treatment may be given only with the patient's consent. Or, if the patient lacks capacity to consent, treatment may be given: • with the consent of an attorney, deputy or the Court of Protection • without anyone's consent, provided that (i) the treatment is given by or under the direction of the approved clinician in charge of the patient's case, (ii) it is not inconsistent with a valid and applicable advance decision, or a decision of an attorney, deputy or Court of Protection, and either (iii) no force needs to be used, or (iv) force does need to be used but the patient does not object, or • in an emergency only, if the treatment is (i) immediately necessary and (ii) if force is to be used, the treatment is needed to protect the patient from harm and any force used is proportionate to the risk of harm.	has to either be: approved by a SOAD on a part 4A certificate; or certified by the approved clinician in charge of the patient's treatment on a part 4A consent certificate, if the patient has capacity (or competence, for patients under 16) to consent to the treatment and has done so.
Other patients	Treatment is not regulated by the Act, except that: • where section 57 applies, patients can be given treatment only if they consent • and the other rules in section 57 are followed, and • patients under 18 cannot be given ECT or other treatments to which section 58A applies, unless they consent and the treatment is approved by a SOAD. (Sections 57 and 58A do not apply in emergencies.)	

PROMOTING GOOD PHYSICAL HEALTH

24.57 Commissioners and providers should ensure that patients with a mental **4–142** disorder receive physical healthcare that is equivalent to that received by people without a mental disorder. The physical needs of patients should be assessed routinely alongside their psychological needs. Commissioners need to ensure that long term physical health conditions are not undiagnosed or untreated, and that patients receive regular oral health and sensory assessments and, as required, referral.

24.58 Patients detained under the Act are at particular risk of comorbidities.[47] Commissioners should build into their procurement outcomes the requirement for physical health checks, physical healthcare planning and reporting arrangements that include evidence that physical health issues have been routinely considered for every individual patient they have commissioned a service for. Providers should deliver services that consider and address the physical health needs of their population. This would include practices in place to routinely screen for and provide interventions for high risk health conditions such as heart disease and diabetes and attention to care planning that had a focus on reducing common risk factors (eg smoking, poor diet and physical inactivity).

24.59 Good nutrition and access to dietary advice is essential for healthy outcomes. Providers should ensure that they are compliant with current requirements on food, diet and nutrition, as set out in the NHS Standard Contract and compliance monitored via annual patient-led assessments of the care environment (PLACE) assessments.

24.60 Every provider should have a food and drink strategy (see annex B) that covers:

- the nutrition and hydration needs of patients

- healthier eating for the whole hospital community, and

- sustainable procurement of food and catering services.

24.61 Patients should have their nutritional state assessed on admission and at regular intervals thereafter, using an accredited screening tool. Providers should offer food and drink that meets the needs of all their patients (eg high density food for frail and underweight patients, and healthier food for those whose needs are more akin to the general population). Where necessary, support should be given to patients who need help to eat, or who wish to take action to improve their diet. Food that meets religious, cultural or personal preference should be available.[48]

24.62 Providers should ensure that all patients have sufficient opportunities to undertake sufficient physical and other meaningful activity to support their physical and mental health.

25. TREATMENTS SUJECT TO SPECIAL RULES AND PROCEDURES

Why read this chapter?

4–143 25.1 This chapter gives guidance on the special rules and procedures in the Act for certain types of medical treatment for mental disorder.

25.2 This chapter provides guidance on the 'clinician in charge of treatment' and the treatments under section 57, or 58, or 58A of the Act. Guidance is

---

[47] Comorbidities Framework: a framework of principles for system-wide action. Department of Health, Public Health England and NHS England. 2014. https://www.gov.uk/government/uploads/system/uploads/attachment_data/file/307143/Comorbidities_framework.pdf

[48] The Hospital Food Standards Panel's report on standards for food and drink in NHS hospitals. Department of Health. 2014. https://www.gov.uk/government/publications/establishing-food-standards-for-nhs-hospitals.

given on second opinion approved doctor (SOAD) certificates and a summary of the circumstances in which certificates cease to authorise treatment, even though they have not been withdrawn is provided, is provided.

DEFINITIONS

25.3 In this chapter: **4–144**

- 'detained patients' means the same as in chapter 24 (see paragraphs 24.10–24.13)

- 'SOAD' means a second opinion approved doctor appointed by the care quality commission (CQC) to approve certain forms of treatment

- 'SOAD certificate' means a certificate issued by a SOAD approving treatment for a particular patient

- 'part 4A patient' means a patient on a community treatment order (CTO) who has not been recalled to hospital

- 'part 4A certificate' means a SOAD certificate issued under part 4A of the Act in respect of the treatment of a patient on a CTO

- 'part 4A consent certificate' means a certificate issued by the approved 'clinician in charge of treatment' in respect of a patient on a CTO who has capacity (or competence, if under 16) to consent to or refuse a treatment, and consents to the treatment.

CLINICIAN IN CHARGE OF TREATMENT

25.4 This chapter frequently refers to the 'clinician in charge of treatment'. This **4–145** means the clinician in charge of the particular treatment in question for a patient, who need not be the same as the responsible clinician who is in charge of a patient's case overall.

25.5 In many cases, for detained patients and patients on a CTO the clinician in charge of treatment must be an approved clinician, as set out in the following table.

Figure 14: Summary of when the person in charge of treatment under the Act must be an approved clinician

Type of patient	When the clinician in charge of the treatment must be an approved clinician
Detained patients	When the treatment is being: • given without the patient's consent • given with the patient's consent, on the basis of a certificate issued under section 58 or, in relation to a patient over 18 a certificate issued under section 58A, by an approved clinician (rather than a SOAD)—see paragraphs 25.14 and 25.21 below, or

	● continued with the consent of a community patient who has been recalled to hospital (including one whose CTO has then been revoked) to avoid serious suffering to the patient, pending compliance with section 58—see paragraph 25.33.
Part 4A patients	When the treatment is being: ● given by that clinician or under the direction of that clinician to a patient who lacks capacity to consent to or refuse it and without the consent of an attorney, deputy or the Court of Protection—see paragraph 25.27 below. (Unless it is immediately necessary and being given under section 64G—see paragraphs 24.24–24.25), or ● given to a patient who has capacity to consent and has done so, on the basis of a part 4A consent certificate issued by the approved clinician in charge of the person's treatment—see paragraph 25.33 below.

25.6 Hospital managers should keep a record of approved clinicians who are available to treat patients for whom they are responsible and should ensure that approved clinicians are in charge of treatment where the Act requires it.

Treatments requiring consent and a second opinion under section 57

4–146   25.7 Section 57 applies to neurosurgery for mental disorder, to surgical implantation of hormones to reduce male sex drive and other treatments as specified by the Secretary of State. It applies to all patients, whether or not they are otherwise subject to the Act.

25.8 Where section 57 applies, these treatments can be given only if all three of the following requirements are met:

● the patient consents to the treatment

● a SOAD (and two other people appointed by the CQC) certify that the patient has the capacity to consent[49] to the treatment and has done so, and

● the SOAD also certifies that it is appropriate for the treatment to be given to the patient.

25.9 A decision to administer treatments to which section 57 applies requires particularly careful consideration, given their significance and sensitivity. Hospitals proposing to offer such treatments are strongly encouraged to agree with the CQC the procedures which will be followed to implement the requirements of section 57.

25.10 Before asking the CQC to put in hand the process of issuing a certificate, referring professionals should personally satisfy themselves that the patient is capable of giving valid consent and is willing to consent. The restrictions and

---

[49] Here and in section 58 and 58A, the Act refers to the patient being 'capable of understanding the nature, purpose and likely effects' of the treatment. For all practical purposes this can be understood to mean the same as the test of whether the patient has the capacity to consent (or, if under 16, the competence to do so).

procedures imposed by section 57 should be explained to the patient, and it should be made clear to the patient that their willingness to receive treatment does not necessarily mean that the treatment will be given.

TREATMENTS REQUIRING CONSENT OR A SECOND OPINION UNDER SECTION 58

25.11 Section 58 applies to the administration of medication for mental dis- **4–147** order. But it only applies once three months ('the three-month period') have passed from the day on which any form of medication for mental disorder was first administered to the patient during the current period in which the patient is liable to be detained under the Act.

25.12 For these purposes, the three-month period continues even if the section under which the patient is detained changes or if the patient has withdrawn consent for the treatment. It also includes any time the patient has spent on a CTO. The three-month period is broken if a part 2 patient is discharged without becoming a CTO patient or if the patient is placed under guardianship, or upon the conditional discharge of a restricted patient.

25.13 Section 58 does not apply to medication administered as part of electro-convulsive therapy (ECT). That is covered by section 58A instead (see paragraphs 25.19–25.25).

25.14 Section 58 applies only to detained patients. They cannot be given medication to which section 58 applies unless:

- the approved clinician in charge of the treatment, or a SOAD, certifies that the patient has the capacity to consent and has done so, or
- a SOAD certifies that the treatment is appropriate and either that:
- the patient does not have the capacity to consent, or
- the patient has the capacity to consent but has refused to do so.

25.15 Hospital managers should ensure that systems are in place to remind both the clinician in charge of the medication and the patient at least four weeks before the expiry of the three-month period.

25.16 Warning systems must be capable of dealing with the possibility that a patient may become a CTO patient, and may also have their CTO revoked, during the three-month period. A patient's move between detention and CTO does not change the date on which the three-month period expires.

25.17 Where approved clinicians certify the treatment of a patient who consents, they should not rely on the certificate as the only record of their reasons for believing that the patient has consented to the treatment. A record of their discussion with the patient including any capacity assessment, should be made in the patient's notes as normal.

25.18 Certificates under this section must clearly set out the specific forms of treatment to which they apply. All the relevant drugs should be listed, including medication to be given 'as required' (prn), either by name or by the classes described in the British National Formulary (BNF). If drugs are specified by class, the certificate should state clearly the number of drugs authorised in each class, and whether any drugs within the class are excluded. The maximum dosage and route of administration should be clearly indicated for each drug or category of drugs proposed. This can exceed the dosages listed in the BNF, but particular care is required in these cases.[50]

ELECTRO-CONVULSIVE THERAPY UNDER SECTION 58A

4–148 25.19 Section 58A applies to ECT and to medication administered as part of ECT. It applies to detained patients and to all patients aged under 18 (whether or not they are detained).

25.20 The key differences from section 58 are that:

- patients who have the capacity to consent to or refuse treatment may not be given treatment under section 58A unless they do in fact consent

- no patient aged under 18 can be given treatment under section 58A unless a SOAD has certified that the treatment is appropriate, and

- there is no initial three-month period during which a certificate is not needed (even for the medication administered as part of the ECT).

25.21 A patient who is consenting may not be given treatment under section 58A unless the clinician in charge, or a SOAD, has certified that the patient has the capacity to consent and has done so. If the patient is under 18, only a SOAD may give the certificate, and the SOAD must also certify that the treatment is appropriate.

25.22 A patient who lacks the capacity to consent may not be given treatment under section 58A unless a SOAD certifies that the patient lacks capacity to consent and that:

- the treatment is appropriate

- no valid and applicable advance decision has been made by the patient under the Mental Capacity Act 2005 (MCA) refusing the treatment in question

- no suitably authorised attorney or deputy objects to the treatment on the patient's behalf, and

- the treatment would not conflict with a decision of the Court of Protection which prevents the treatment being given.

25.23 In all cases, SOADs should indicate on the certificate the maximum number of administrations of ECT which it approves.

25.24 For children and young people under 18, a SOAD certificate by itself is not sufficient to authorise the treatment, unless they are detained. Clinicians must also have the patient's own consent or some other legal authority, just as they would if section 58A did not exist (see paragraphs 19.80–19.88).

25.25 Whether or not section 58A applies, patients of all ages who are to be treated with ECT should be given written information before their treatment starts

---

[50] The British National Formulary is available at: https://www.medicinescomplete.com/about/subscribe.htm; See also CR190. Consensus statement on high-dose antipsychotic medication. Royal College of Psychiatrists. 2014. http://www.rcpsych.ac.uk/usefulresources/publications/collegereports/cr/cr190.aspx.

which helps them to understand and remember, both during and after the course of ECT, the advice given about its nature, purpose and likely effects.

CTO PATIENTS NOT RECALLED TO HOSPITAL—PART 4A CERTIFICATES AND PART 4A CONSENT CERTIFICATES FOR SECTION 58 AND 58A TYPE TREATMENT

25.26 Compulsory treatment cannot be given to a patient on a CTO who has not **4–149** been recalled (referred to in this chapter as a 'part 4A patient') and who has capacity (or competence, for patients under 16) to consent to or refuse a treatment, and who refuses the treatment (unless it is immediately necessary and being given under section 64G—see paragraphs 25.24–25.25). Refusal to consent to treatment in itself does not justify a recall to hospital and fuller consideration of the patient's presentation and circumstances is required when considering whether a recall to hospital is warranted (see chapter 29).

25.27 In addition to rules governing treatment of CTO patients described in chapter 29, there are specific rules regarding the certification of certain treatment given to part 4A patients:

- 'section 58 type treatment'—treatment to which section 58 would apply if the patient were detained. Ie medication after an initial three-month period, and

- 'section 58A type treatment'—ECT and other types of treatment to which section 58A applies.

25.28 In the case of a part 4A patient who lacks capacity (or competence, if under 16) to consent to treatment, a SOAD must certify that the treatment is appropriate (a part 4A certificate).

25.29 In the case of a part 4A patient who has capacity (or, if under 16, is competent) to consent to the treatment and has consented, the approved clinician in charge of the patient's treatment must certify that the patient has capacity/competence and has consented (a part 4A consent certificate).

25.30 In the case of patients aged under 18, regardless of capacity to consent, ECT can only be authorised by a part 4A certificate (ie not by a part 4A consent certificate).

25.31 Neither a part 4A certificate nor a part 4A consent certificate is required for section 58 type treatment to be given:

- where less than three months have passed since the patient was first given the treatment during an unbroken period of detention and discharge onto a CTO (or an unbroken succession of periods of detention and CTO), or

- during the first month following a patient's discharge from detention onto a CTO (even if the three-month period referred to in section 58 has already expired or expires during that first month)

- if the criteria under section 64G are met for emergency treatment in the community of patients lacking capacity or competence, or

- it is immediately necessary and the patient has capacity to consent to it and has consented, or their donee or deputy or the Court of Protection has consented on the patient's behalf (see chapter 7).

25.32 When giving part 4A certificates, SOADs do not have to certify whether a patient has, or lacks, capacity to consent to the treatments in question, nor whether a patient with capacity is consenting or refusing. They may make it a condition of their approval that particular treatments are given only in certain circumstances. For example, they might specify that a particular treatment is to be given only with the patient's consent. Similarly, they might specify that a medication may be given up to a certain dosage if the patient lacks capacity to consent, but that a higher dosage may be given with the patient's consent.

CTO PATIENTS RECALLED TO HOSPITAL—EXCEPTIONS TO THE NEED FOR CERTIFICATES UNDER SECTION 58 OR 58

4–150   25.33 In general, CTO patients recalled to hospital are subject to sections 58 and 58A in the same way as other detained patients. But there are exceptions, as follows:

- a certificate under section 58 is not needed for medication if less than one month has passed since the patient was discharged from hospital and became a CTO patient (see paragraph 25.31 above)

- a certificate is not needed under either section 58 or 58A if a part 4A certificate or part 4A consent certificate has been issued

- a certificate is not needed under either section 58 or 58A if the treatment in question is explicitly authorised for administration on recall on the patient's SOAD issued part 4A certificate, and

- treatment that was already being given on the basis of a part 4A certificate may be continued, even though it is not authorised for administration on recall, if the approved clinician in charge of the treatment considers that discontinuing it would cause the patient serious suffering. It may only be continued pending compliance with section 58 or 58A (as applicable)—in other words while steps are taken to obtain a new certificate.

25.34 As a result, SOADs giving part 4A certificates need to consider what (if any) treatments to approve should the patient be recalled to hospital. They must decide whether to impose any conditions on that approval. Unless they specify otherwise, the certificate will authorise the treatment even if the patient has capacity to refuse it (unless it is a section 58A type treatment).

25.35 The potential advantage of authorising treatments to be given on recall to hospital is that it will enable such treatments to be given quickly without the need to obtain a new certificate. SOADs should do so only where they believe they have sufficient information on which properly to make such a judgement.

25.36 The exceptions to the requirement to have a certificate under section 58 or 58A set out in paragraph 25.31 continue to apply if the patient's CTO is revoked, but only while steps are taken to comply with section 58 (where relevant). Responsible clinicians should ensure that steps are in hand to obtain a new SOAD certificate under section 58 or 58A, if one is needed, as soon as they revoke a CTO.

URGENT CASES WHERE CERTIFICATES ARE NOT REQUIRED
(SECTIONS 62, 64B, 64C AND 64E)

25.37 Sections 57, 58 and 58A do not apply in urgent cases where treatment is **4–151** immediately necessary (section 62). Similarly, a part 4A certificate is not required in urgent cases where the treatment is immediately necessary (sections 64B, 64C and 64E).

25.38 This applies only if the treatment in question is immediately necessary to:

- save the patient's life

- prevent a serious deterioration of the patient's condition, and the treatment does not have unfavourable physical or psychological consequences which cannot be reversed

- alleviate serious suffering by the patient, and the treatment does not have unfavourable physical or psychological consequences which cannot be reversed and does not entail significant physical hazard, or

- prevent patients behaving violently or being a danger to themselves or others, and the treatment represents the minimum interference necessary for that purpose, does not have unfavourable physical or psychological consequences which cannot be reversed and does not entail significant physical hazard.

25.39 If the treatment is ECT (or medication administered as part of ECT) only the first two categories above apply.

25.40 These are strict tests. It is not enough for there to be an urgent need for treatment or that the clinicians involved believe the treatment is necessary or beneficial.

25.41 Urgent treatment under these sections can continue only for as long as it remains immediately necessary. If it is no longer immediately necessary, the normal requirements for certificates apply. Although certificates are not required where treatment is immediately necessary, the other requirements of parts 4 and 4A of the Act still apply. The treatment is not necessarily allowed just because no certificate is required.

25.42 Hospital managers should monitor the use of these exceptions to the certificate requirements to ensure that they are not used inappropriately or excessively. They are advised to provide a form (or other method) by which the clinician in charge of the treatment in question can record details of:

- the proposed treatment

- why it is immediately necessity to give the treatment, and

- the length of time for which the treatment was given.

SOAD CERTIFICATES

25.43 If a SOAD certificate is required, the clinician in charge of the treatment **4–152** in question has the personal responsibility of ensuring that a request is made to the CQC for a SOAD to visit.

25.44 Clinicians should not normally request a visit from a SOAD in order to obtain a certificate which they could issue themselves confirming that a patient has consented to treatment. They should request a visit for that purpose only if they are genuinely unable to determine for themselves whether the patient has the capacity to consent or whether the patient is in fact consenting.

Arranging and preparing for SOAD visits

4–153   25.45 SOADs will visit detained patients in hospital. For CTO patients, hospital managers should ensure that arrangements are made for the SOAD to see the patient at a mutually agreed place, eg at an outpatient clinic or somewhere that the patient might visit regularly.

25.46 Attending hospital for examination by a SOAD is a condition of all CTOs. If CTO patients fail to attend when asked to do so, they may be recalled to hospital for the examination, if necessary, but this should only ever be a last resort (see paragraph 29.45).

25.47 The treatment proposal for the patient, together with notes of any relevant multi-disciplinary discussion on which it was based, must be given to the SOAD before or at the time of the visit. If a part 4A certificate is being requested, the proposal should clearly indicate which (if any) treatments it is proposed should be authorised in the case of the patient's recall to hospital.

25.48 During a visit, SOADs should interview the patient in private if possible. Others may attend if the patient and the SOAD wish, or if it is thought that the SOAD would be at significant risk of physical harm from the patient (and the SOAD agrees).

25.49 Hospital managers are responsible for ensuring that people whom the SOAD wishes to meet (including the clinician in charge of the treatment) are available in person at the time the SOAD visits.

25.50 SOADs have a right of access to records, without the patient's consent if necessary, and may ask hospital managers to provide the clinical notes to help inform their decision. Managers are responsible for ensuring that such requests can be fulfilled promptly.

25.51 Where the proposed treatment includes medication, the SOAD's attention should be drawn specifically to any recent review of the patient's treatment, including the rationale for using medication, and what other forms of treatment have been tried or considered. Clinicians should consider seeking a review by a specialist mental health pharmacist before seeking a SOAD certificate, particularly if the patient's medication regimen is complex or unusual.

25.52 Approved clinicians should ensure that SOADs are informed if the hospital knows that the patient has an attorney or deputy who is authorised under the MCA to make decisions on the patient's behalf about medical treatment. Details of any relevant advance decisions, or advance statements of views, wishes or feelings, should already be recorded in the patient's notes. If they are not, they should be drawn to the SOAD's attention.

Statutory consultees

4–154   25.53 SOADs are required to consult two people ('statutory consultees') before issuing certificates approving treatment.[51] Where section 57, 58 or 58A applies, one of the statutory consultees must be a nurse; the other must not be either a nurse or a medical doctor. Both must have been professionally concerned with the patient's medical treatment, and neither may be the clinician in charge of the

---

[51] For part 4 certificates, see sections 57(3), 58(4), 58A(6) and 64H(3).

proposed treatment or the responsible clinician. Where a SOAD is considering giving a part 4A certificate, at least one of the statutory consultees must not be a medical doctor (but need not be a nurse), and neither may be the clinician in charge of the proposed treatment or the responsible clinician (if the patient has one).

25.54 The Act does not specify who the statutory consultees should be, but they should be people whose knowledge of the patient and the patient's treatment can inform the SOAD when making decisions as to the patient's capacity to consent to or refuse treatment and the appropriateness of the proposed treatment, and will commonly be members of the wider multi-disciplinary team. People who may be particularly well placed to act as statutory consultees are those who have detailed and/or up-to-date knowledge of the patient. For part 4A certificates, it is permissible for one of the two consultees to be a medical doctor, but that person cannot be the responsible clinician; typically a general practitioner (GP) may be consulted.

25.55 The statutory consultees whom the SOAD proposes to consult should consider whether they are sufficiently concerned professionally with the patient's care to fulfil the function. If not, or if a consultee feels that someone else is better placed to fulfil the function, they should make this known to the clinician in charge of the treatment and to the SOAD in good time.

25.56 Statutory consultees may expect a private discussion with the SOAD and to be listened to with consideration. Issues that the consultees may be asked about include, but are not limited to:

- the proposed treatment and the patient's ability to consent to it

- their understanding of the past and present views and wishes of the patient

- other treatment options and the way in which the decision on the treatment proposal was arrived at

- the patient's progress and the views of the patient's carers, and

- where relevant, the implications of imposing treatment on a patient who does not want it and the reasons why the patient is refusing treatment.

25.57 If the SOAD wishes to speak to the statutory consultees face-to-face, the hospital managers should ensure that the SOAD is able to do so.

25.58 SOADs should make a record of their consultation with statutory consultees, which will become part of the patient notes.

25.59 SOADs should, where appropriate, consult a wider range of people who are concerned with the patient's care than those required by the Act. That might include the patient's GP, nearest relative, family and carers, and any independent mental health advocate or other advocate representing the patient.

The SOAD's decision and reasons

25.60 The SOAD's role is to provide an additional safeguard to protect the **4–155** patient's rights, primarily by deciding whether certain treatments are appropriate and issuing certificates accordingly. Although appointed by the commission, SOADs act as independent professionals and must reach their own judgement about whether the proposed treatment is appropriate.

25.61 When deciding whether it is appropriate for treatment to be given to a patient, SOADs are required to consider both the clinical appropriateness of the treatment to the patient's mental disorder and its appropriateness in the light of all the other circumstances of the patient's case.

25.62 SOADs should, in particular:

- seek to understand the patient's views on the proposed treatment, and the reasons for them. This includes involving an advocate, carers or making any reasonable adjustments, as appropriate

- give due weight to the patient's views, including any objection to the proposed treatment and any preference for an alternative

- consider the appropriateness of alternative forms of treatment, not just that proposed

- balance the potential therapeutic efficacy of the proposed treatment against the side effects and any other potential disadvantages to the patient;

- take into account any previous experience of comparable treatment for a similar episode of disorder, and

- give due weight to the opinions, knowledge, experience and skills of those consulted.

25.63 SOADs must provide written reasons in support of their decisions to approve specific treatments for patients. SOADs do not have to give an exhaustive explanation, but should provide their reasons for what they consider to be the substantive points on which they made their clinical judgement. These reasons can be recorded on the certificate itself when it is given, or can be provided to the clinician in charge of the treatment separately as soon as possible afterwards.

25.64 A certificate may be acted on even though the SOAD's reasons have yet to be received. If there is no pressing need for treatment to begin immediately, it is preferable to wait until the reasons are received, especially if the patient is likely to be unhappy with the decision.

25.65 When giving reasons, SOADs will need to indicate whether, in their view, disclosure of the reasons to the patient would be likely to cause serious harm to the patient's physical or mental health or to that of any other person. The responsible clinician should take into account this view when deciding whether or not to disclose the reasons to the patient. The expectation is that in the overwhelming majority of cases the patient should be able to see the SOAD's reasons.

25.66 It is the personal responsibility of the clinician in charge of the treatment to communicate the results of the SOAD visit to the patient. This need not wait until any separate statement of reasons has been received from the SOAD. But when a separate statement is received from the SOAD, the patient should be given the opportunity to see it as soon as possible, unless the clinician in charge of the treatment (or the SOAD) thinks that it would be likely to cause serious harm to the physical or mental health of the patient or any other person.

25.67 Documents provided by SOADs are a part of, and should be kept in, the patient's notes. The clinician in charge of the treatment should record their actions in providing patients with (or withholding) the reasons supplied by a SOAD.

25.68 Every attempt should be made by the clinician in charge of the treatment and the SOAD to reach agreement. A generally sound plan need not be rejected as a whole because of a minor disagreement about one aspect of it.

25.69 If SOADs are unable to agree with the clinician in charge of the treatment, they should inform the clinician personally as soon as possible. It is good practice for SOADs to give reasons for their disagreement.

25.70 Neither the SOAD nor the approved clinician should allow a disagreement in any way to prejudice the interests of the patient. If agreement cannot be reached, the position should be recorded in the patient's notes by the clinician in charge of the treatment in question, and the patient's responsible clinician (if different) should be informed.

25.71 The opinion given by the SOAD is the SOAD's personal responsibility. There can be no appeal to the CQC against the opinion.

Status of certificates under part 4 and part 4A

25.72 A certificate issued by an approved clinician or by a SOAD is not an **4–156** instruction to administer treatment.

25.73 The fact that the SOAD has authorised a particular treatment does not mean that it will always be appropriate to administer it on any given occasion, or even at all. People administering the treatment (or directing its administration) must still satisfy themselves that it is an appropriate treatment in the circumstances.

25.74 People administering the treatment (or directing its administration) should take reasonable steps to assure themselves that the treatment is, in fact, authorised by the certificate, given what is said in the certificate about the patient's capacity and willingness to consent (see paragraph 25.76).

25.75 Original signed certificates should be kept with the documents which authorise the patient's detention or CTO, and copies should be kept in the patient's notes. As a matter of good practice, a copy of the certificate relating to medication should be kept with the patient's medicine chart (if there is one) to minimise the risk of the patient being given treatment in contravention of the provisions of the Act.

Review of treatment and withdrawal of approval (sections 61 and 64H)

25.76 Although the Act does not require the validity of certificates to be **4–157** reviewed after any particular period, it is good practice for the clinician in charge of the treatment to review them (in consultation with the responsible clinician, if different) at regular intervals.

25.77 The clinician in charge of any treatment given in accordance with a SOAD certificate must provide a written report on that treatment and the relevant patient's condition at any time if requested to do so by the CQC under sections 61 or 64H of the Act. This is in addition to the reports they are automatically required to provide periodically under those sections.[52] Copies of reports should be given to patients.

25.78 Under sections 61 and 64H, the CQC may also, at any time, direct that a certificate is no longer to approve either some or all of the treatments specified in it from a particular date.

---

[52] At the time of publication, the Care Quality Commission expects these reports to be submitted on form MHAC1 which it provides for this purpose.

25.79 However, where the CQC revokes approval in that way, treatment (or a course of treatment) which is already in progress may continue, pending a new certificate, if the clinician in charge of it considers that discontinuing it would cause the patient serious suffering (section 62 (2)).

25.80 This exception only applies pending compliance with the relevant requirement to have a certificate—in other words, while steps are taken to obtain a new certificate. It cannot be used to continue treatment under section 57 or section 58A against the wishes of a patient who has the capacity to refuse the treatment, because in those cases there is no prospect of obtaining a new certificate.

Action where treatment is continued pending a new certificate

4–158 25.81 Where treatment is continued to avoid serious suffering pending compliance with a certificate requirement, the clinician in charge of the treatment should immediately take steps to ask for a SOAD visit. This applies both to cases where certificates have been withdrawn by the CQC and to cases where the treatment of CTO patients is being continued pending a new certificate following their recall to hospital (see paragraphs 25.33 and 25.36). If the SOAD visits and decides not to give a certificate for treatment which requires one, the treatment must end immediately.

25.82 As with immediately necessary treatment, hospital managers should monitor the use of these exceptions. They should require clinicians to record details of why it was necessary to continue treatment without a certificate and how long it took to obtain a new certificate.

Other circumstances when certificates cease to be effective

4–159 25.83 There are a number of other circumstances in which a certificate will cease to authorise treatment (or a particular treatment). These are summarised in the following figure. People administering treatment on the basis of a certificate should always take reasonable steps to satisfy themselves that the certificate remains applicable to the circumstances.

Figure 15: Circumstances in which certificates cease to authorise treatment, even though they have not been withdrawn

Type of certificate	Circumstances in which the certificate ceases to authorise treatment
Certificate issued by approved clinician under section 58 or 58A	The patient no longer consents to the treatment. The patient no longer has capacity to consent to the treatment. The patient stops (even if only temporarily) being either a detained patient (as defined in chapter 24) or a community patient who is not recalled to hospital. There is a permanent change in the approved clinician in charge of the patient's treatment.

SOAD certificate under section 57	The patient no longer consents to the treatment. The patient no longer has capacity to consent to the treatment. The SOAD specified a time limit on the approval of treatment, and the time limit has expired.
SOAD certificate under section 58 or 58A	The patient stops (even if only temporarily) being either a detained patient (as defined in chapter 24 or a community patient who is not recalled to hospital—except in the case of section 58A certificates for patients aged under 18. The SOAD specified a time limit on the approval of a course of treatment, and the time limit has expired. The certificate was given on the basis that the patient consented, but the patient no longer consents or has lost the capacity to consent. The certificate was given on the basis that the patient lacked capacity to consent, but the patient now has that capacity. Section 58 only: The certificate was given on the basis that the patient had capacity to consent but was refusing, and the patient is now either consenting or has lost the capacity to consent. Section 58A only: The certificate was given on the understanding that the treatment would not conflict with an advance decision to refuse treatment, but the person giving the treatment has since become aware that there is such a conflict. Section 58A only: The certificate was given on the understanding that the treatment would not conflict with a decision of an attorney, deputy or the Court of Protection, but the person giving the treatment has since become aware that there is such a conflict, or an attorney, deputy or the Court of Protection makes a new decision that the treatment should not be given.
Part 4A certificate	The patient stops (even if only temporarily) being either a detained patient (as defined in chapter 24) or patient on a CTO. (But note that a part 4A certificate authorises section 58 type treatment for a patient whose CTO has been revoked only pending compliance with section 58 itself.) The certificate was given on the basis that the patient lacked capacity to consent to or refuse the treatment, but the patient now has that capacity and consents to the treatment. The SOAD specified a time limit on the approval of a course of treatment, and the time limit has expired.

Part 4A consent certificate	The patient stops (even if only temporarily) being either a detained patient (as defined in chapter 24) or patient on a CTO. (But note that a part 4A consent certificate authorises section 58 type treatment for a patient whose CTO has been revoked only pending compliance with section 58 itself.)
	There is a permanent change in the approved clinician in charge of the patient's treatment.
	The certificate was given on the basis that the patient consented, but the patient no longer consents or has lost the capacity to consent.

25.84 In all the circumstances listed in the table, treatment cannot be continued while a new certificate is obtained, unless no certificate is needed because the treatment is immediately necessary (see paragraphs 25.37–25.42) and, in respect of CTO patients not recalled to hospital, the treatment is given under section 64G.

25.85 It is not good practice to use a certificate that was issued to a patient when detained and who has since been discharged onto a CTO to authorise treatment if the patient is then recalled to hospital, even if the certificate remains technically valid. A new certificate should be obtained as necessary.

25.86 Hospital managers should make sure that arrangements are in place so that certificates which no longer authorise treatment (or particular treatments) are clearly marked as such, as are all copies of those certificates kept with the patient's notes and medication chart.

Procedures for the safe use of restrictive interventions (Ch.26, paras 26.62–26.166)

4–160 26.62 Provider polices concerning the use of restrictive interventions and their implementation should be kept under ongoing review in order to ensure consistency with current national policy, best practice guidance and evidence. Restrictive interventions should never be employed to deliberately punish or humiliate, and staff should not cause deliberate pain to a person in an attempt to force compliance with their instructions except in the most exceptional circumstances to mitigate an immediate risk to life.

26.63 Any initial attempt to manage an acute behavioural disturbance should, as far as the situation allows, be non-restrictive. For example, assistance might be sought using an emergency alarm system or by verbally summoning assistance. A single member of staff should assume control of the incident. Where possible, the patient should be asked to stop the behaviour. An individual's communication needs should be taken into account including those arising from sensory impairments, learning disability, autism spectrum disorders, or an individual for whom English is not their first language. Where possible, an explanation should be given of the consequences of refusing the request from staff to stop the behaviour. The explanation should be provided calmly and every attempt should be made to avoid the explanation being perceived by the patient as a threat.

26.64 The nature and manner of application of any restrictive intervention, the reason(s) for its use and the consequences or outcome, should be recorded in an open and transparent manner.

26.65 Staff should only use methods of restrictive interventions for which they have received training. Training records should record precisely the techniques for which a member of staff has received training.

26.66 Verbal de-escalation should continue throughout a restrictive intervention. Negotiations should focus on establishing rapport, demonstrating concern, helping the patient to relax, and reducing the patient's level of agitation.

26.67 Whenever restrictive interventions are being used, provider's policies should make provision for the timely attendance of a doctor in response to staff requests concerning a psychiatric emergency whether in relation to medication, restraint or seclusion.

26.68 Where a behavioural disturbance occurs and a restrictive intervention has been used, family members should be informed in accordance with any prior agreements (see paragraph 26.16).

PHYSICAL RESTRAINT

26.69 Physical restraint refers to any direct physical contact where the intention **4–161** is to prevent, restrict, or subdue movement of the body (or part of the body) of another person.

26.70 Patients should not be deliberately restrained in a way that impacts on their airway, breathing or circulation. The mouth and/or nose should never be covered and there should be no pressure to the neck region, rib cage and/or abdomen. Unless there are cogent reasons for doing so, there must be no planned or intentional restraint of a person in a prone position (whereby they are forcibly laid on their front) on any surface, not just the floor.

26.71 Full account should be taken of the individual's age, physical and emotional maturity, health status, cognitive functioning and any disability or sensory impairment, which may confer additional risks to the individual's health, safety and wellbeing in the face of exposure to physical restraint. Throughout any period of physical restraint:

- a member of staff should monitor the individual's airway and physical condition to minimise the potential of harm or injury. Observations, including vital clinical indicators such as pulse, respiration and complexion (with special attention for pallor/discolouration), should be conducted and recorded. Staff should be trained so that they are competent to interpret these vital signs

- emergency resuscitation devices should be readily available in the area where restraint is taking place, and

- a member of staff should take the lead in caring for other patients and moving them away from the area of disturbance.

26.72 Where physical restraint has been used, staff should record the decision and the reasons for it, including details about how the intervention was implemented and the patient's response.

26.73 If an individual is not detained under the Act, but physical restraint of any form is necessary, consideration should be given to whether the criteria in sections 5 and 6 of the MCA apply (restraint to be used in respect of people aged 16 and over who lack capacity) and/or whether detention under the Act is appropriate (subject to the criteria being met).

26.74 Provider policies concerning the use of physical restraint should be kept under ongoing review in order to ensure consistency with national policy and best practice.

MECHANICAL RESTRAINT

4–162   26.75 Mechanical restraint is a form of restrictive intervention that refers to the use of a device to prevent, restrict or subdue movement of a person's body, or part of the body, for the primary purpose of behavioural control.

26.76 Mechanical restraint should only be used exceptionally, where other forms of restriction cannot be safely employed. It should be used in line with the principle of least restrictive option and should not be an unplanned response to an emergency situation. Mechanical restraint should never be used instead of adequate staffing.

26.77 The use of mechanical restraint should be approved following multi-disciplinary consultation (which should include an IMHA where the patient has one—see chapter 6). The nature of the multi-disciplinary team should be defined in a provider's policies. Provision for the use of mechanical restraint should be recorded as a tertiary strategy in the positive behaviour support plan (or equivalent). This plan should detail the circumstances which might warrant mechanical restraint, the type of device to be applied, how continued attempts should be made to de-escalate the situation and any special measures that are required to reduce the likelihood of physical or emotional trauma resulting.

26.78 Where the agreed provisions for the use of mechanical restraint in positive behaviour support plans (or equivalent) allow a nurse or other professional to authorise the actual use of mechanical restraint, then that professional should notify, without delay, the responsible clinician or duty doctor (or equivalent).

26.79 Staff applying mechanical restraint devices should have appropriate training in their application and use.

26.80 An individual who is mechanically restrained should remain under continuous observation throughout. It may be necessary for the individual to remain at arm's length.

26.81 The individual should be reviewed by a nurse every fifteen minutes for the duration of the period of mechanical restraint.

26.82 The individual should have a medical review by a registered medical practitioner at least one hour after the beginning of mechanical restraint. Subsequently there should be ongoing medical reviews at least every four hours by a registered medical practitioner. Local policies should determine which of their registered medical practitioners should undertake medical reviews. Reviews should be undertaken more frequently if requested by nursing staff. Reviews should ensure that the individual is as comfortable as possible and should include a full evaluation of the patient's physical and mental health condition.

26.83 Procedures should be in place to enable nursing staff to summon a doctor to conduct a medical review ahead of the next scheduled review if they have concerns about the patient's condition.

26.84 The patient's clinical record should provide details of the rationale for the decision to mechanically restrain them, the medical and psychiatric assessment, the patient's condition at the beginning of mechanical restraint, the response to mechanical restraint and the outcomes of the medical reviews.

26.85 Mechanical restraint which involves tying an individual (using tape or a part of the individual's garments) to some part of a building or its fixtures should never be used.

26.86 If, exceptionally, a belt (or similar device) is applied to an individual's body to secure their arms or wrists and the resulting degree of immobility prevents their ability to leave an area (such as where they are unable to reach or operate door handles), this will amount to either seclusion or long-term segregation. The individual should be afforded safeguards regarding associated observation and monitoring, review procedures and care plans to ensure that their privacy and dignity are preserved. Such devices should never be used as an alternative to (or in addition to) seclusion because a suitable safe environment in which to undertake seclusion is not available.

26.87 There may be circumstances where mechanical restraint devices need to be used on a long-term basis, such as to limit self-injurious frequent and intense behaviour (in which case the requirement for post-incident review in paragraph 26.167 does not apply). This will be rare and encountered with small numbers of patients who have severe cognitive impairments, where devices such as arm splints or cushioned helmets may be required to safeguard an individual from the hazardous consequences of their behaviour. In such cases, tertiary strategies within positive behaviour support plans (or equivalent) should aim to provide brief recurrent periods when restraints can be removed. The positive behaviour support plan (or equivalent) may also allow for less frequent medical and nursing reviews provided that the whole clinical team, the patient's family, carers and advocates are in agreement.

Patients subject to a Ministry of Justice Order

26.88 There may be occasions when the use of mechanical restraint (including **4–163** handcuffs) is required for security purposes when transferring prisoners into a healthcare setting. Guidance for prison and health staff to develop local procedures for the safe management of prisoners at hospital was agreed in a concordat between the National Offender Management Service (NOMS) and the NHS Counter Fraud and Security Service, which forms part of the National Security Framework (Note: Since 2011 NHS Counter Fraud and Security Management Services have been under the auspices of NHS Protect).

26.89 Similarly, there may be occasions where mechanical restraint (including handcuffs) may be used for security purposes for the transfer of restricted patients in secure settings to non-secure settings. The use of mechanical restraint in these circumstances should be informed by an assessment of the risks posed by the patient, as well as their presenting physical and mental condition and the need to maximise their dignity. Escorting staff should alert medical staff to any identified risks if restraints were to be removed; however, if requested by medical staff, they should be removed whilst medical treatment is carried out.

26.90 On occasion, in high-risk cases, the Secretary of State for Justice will make permission for a restricted patient to leave hospital conditional on the use of restraint. Staff should discuss any concerns about this with Mental Health Casework Section (see paragraph 22.86 for contact details).

RAPID TRANQUILLISATION
26.91 Rapid tranquillisation refers to the use of medication to calm or lightly **4–164** sedate an individual to reduce the risk of harm to self or others and to reduce

agitation and aggression. This may provide an important opportunity for a thorough psychiatric examination to take place. Prescribers should aim to ensure that the degree of sedation arising from rapid tranquillisation does not compromise the patient's capacity to understand and respond to what is said to them.

26.92 Rapid tranquillisation may also be used to manage acute behavioural disturbance, though this should be a very short-term strategy designed solely to reduce immediate risk and is distinct from treating any underlying mental illness.

26.93 Rapid tranquillisation should only be used where a patient is highly aroused, agitated, overactive and aggressive, or is making serious threats or gestures towards others, or is being destructive to their surroundings, when other therapeutic interventions have failed to contain the behaviour.

26.94 Rapid tranquillisation includes the use of both intra-muscular injections and oral medication. Oral medication should always be considered before any injections.

26.95 Rapid tranquillisation should be prescribed in accordance with evidence-based practice guidelines such as those published by NICE 3 and in a manner that is consistent with General Medical Council's good practice in prescribing and managing medicines. It must be in line with legal requirements (in respect of patients subject to the Act, the rules concerning treatment and emergency treatment powers under the Act) (see chapter 24).

26.96 Staff prescribing rapid tranquilisation should note any physical observations and monitoring needed following administration and make that clear to staff caring for the patient.

26.97 Where a prescription indicates a choice of administration routes for rapid tranquillisation (eg oral or intramuscular injection), the person prescribing the medication should list factors which should be considered in deciding which route to use under any reasonably foreseeable circumstances.

26.98 Where rapid tranquilisation in the form of an intramuscular injection is needed, the person prescribing the injection should state the preferred injection site, having taken full account of the need to avoid prone restraint (ie where the person is forcibly laid on their front).

26.99 Physical restraint may, on occasion, need to be used to administer rapid tranquillisation by intramuscular injection to an unwilling patient, where the patient may lawfully be treated without consent. It must not be used unless there is such legal authority, whether under the Act (see provisions for treatment in chapter 24), the MCA or otherwise. Rapid tranquillisation must not be used to treat an informal patient who has the capacity to refuse treatment and who has done so.

26.100 The use of restraint to administer treatment in non-emergency circumstances should be avoided wherever possible, but may sometimes be necessary, especially if an emergency situation would be likely to occur if the treatment were not administered. The decision to use restraint should be discussed first with the clinical team and should be properly documented and justified in the patient's notes.

26.101 Following the administration of rapid tranquillisation, the patient's condition and progress should be closely monitored. Subsequent records should indicate the reason for the use of rapid tranquillisation and provide a full account of both its efficacy and any adverse effects observed or reported by the patient.

26.102 Rapid tranquillisation should never be used to manage patients as a substitute for adequate staffing.

SECLUSION

26.103 Seclusion refers to the supervised confinement and isolation of a **4–165** patient, away from other patients, in an area from which the patient is prevented from leaving, where it is of immediate necessity for the purpose of the containment of severe behavioural disturbance which is likely to cause harm to others.

26.104 If a patient is confined in any way that meets the definition above, even if they have agreed to or requested such confinement, they have been secluded and the use of any local or alternative terms (such as 'therapeutic isolation') or the conditions of the immediate environment do not change the fact that the patient has been secluded. It is essential that they are afforded the procedural safeguards of the Code.

26.105 Seclusion should only be undertaken in a room or suite of rooms that have been specifically designed and designated for the purposes of seclusion and which serves no other function on the ward. Seclusion does not include locking people in their rooms at night in accordance with the High Security Psychiatric Services (Arrangements for Safety and Security) Directions 2013.

26.106 Seclusion should only be used in hospitals and in relation to patients detained under the Act. If an emergency situation arises involving an informal patient and, as a last resort, seclusion is necessary to prevent harm to others, then an assessment for an emergency application for detention under the Act should be undertaken immediately.

26.107 Seclusion should not be used as a punishment or a threat, or because of a shortage of staff. It should not form part of a treatment programme.

26.108 Seclusion should never be used solely as a means of managing self-harming behaviour. Where the patient poses a risk of self-harm as well as harm to others, seclusion should be used only when the professionals involved are satisfied that the need to protect other people outweighs any increased risk to the patient's health or safety arising from their own self-harm and that any such risk can be properly managed.

26.109 The following factors should be taken into account in the design of rooms or areas where seclusion is to be carried out:

- the room should allow for communication with the patient when the patient is in the room and the door is locked, eg via an intercom
- rooms should include limited furnishings which should include a bed, pillow, mattress and blanket or covering
- there should be no apparent safety hazards
- rooms should have robust, reinforced window(s) that provide natural light (where possible the window should be positioned to enable a view outside)
- rooms should have externally controlled lighting, including a main light and subdued lighting for night time
- rooms should have robust door(s) which open outwards
- rooms should have externally controlled heating and/or air conditioning, which enables those observing the patient to monitor the room temperature
- rooms should not have blind spots and alternate viewing panels should be available where required

- a clock should always be visible to the patient from within the room, and

- rooms should have access to toilet and washing facilities.

26.110 Provider policies should include detailed guidance on the use of seclusion and should be consistent with the guiding principles of the Code. (See chapter 1.) The policy should:

- ensure the physical and emotional safety and wellbeing of the patient

- ensure that the patient receives the care and support rendered necessary by their seclusion both during and after it has taken place

- designate a suitable environment that takes account of the patient's dignity and physical wellbeing

- set out the roles and responsibilities of staff, and

- set requirements for recording, monitoring and reviewing the use of seclusion and any follow-up action.

26.111 In order to ensure that seclusion measures have a minimal impact on a patient's autonomy, seclusion should be applied flexibly and in the least restrictive manner possible, considering the patient's circumstances. Where seclusion is used for prolonged periods then, subject to suitable risk assessments, flexibility may include allowing patients to receive visitors, facilitating brief periods of access to secure outside areas or allowing meals to be taken in general areas of the ward. The possibility of facilitating such flexibility should be considered during any review of the ongoing need for seclusion. Particularly with prolonged seclusion, it can be difficult to judge when the need for seclusion has ended. This flexibility can provide a means of evaluating the patient's mood and degree of agitation under a lesser degree of restriction, without terminating the seclusion episode.

Procedure for seclusion

4–166   26.112 The following procedure should be incorporated into the provider's policy on seclusion.

Figure 16: Procedure for seclusion

Overview of seclusion and monitoring process	
• If not authorised by a psychiatrist, there must be a medical review within one hour or without delay if the individual is not known or there is a significant change from their usual presentation	Paragraphs 26.116 and 26.127
• Seclusion area to be within constant sight and sound of staff member	Paragraphs 26.118–26.121
• Documented report by person monitoring every 15 minutes	Paragraphs 26.123–26.124

• Nursing reviews by two nurses every two hours throughout seclusion	Paragraphs 26.132–26.134
• Continuing medical reviews every four hours until the first [internal] multi-disciplinary team	Paragraphs 26.129
• First (internal) multi-disciplinary team as soon as is practicable	Paragraphs 26.135–26.138
• Independent multi-disciplinary team after eight hours consecutive or 12 hours intermittent seclusion (within a 48 hour period)	Paragraphs 26.139–26.141
• Following first (internal) multi-disciplinary team continuing medical reviews at least twice daily (one by the responsible clinician)	Paragraph 26.130

Authorising seclusion   **4–167**

Figure 17: Authorising seclusion

Seclusion may be ordered by either:	Additional considerations
A psychiatrist	if the psychiatrist who authorises seclusion is neither the patient's responsible clinician (RC) nor an approved clinician (AC), the RC or duty doctor (or equivalent) should be informed of seclusion as soon as practicable.
An approved clinician who is not a doctor	provider policies should determine the appropriateness of using ACs who are not doctors to authorise seclusion the patient's RC or duty doctor (or equivalent) should be informed of seclusion as soon as practicable.
The professional in charge (eg a nurse) of a ward	the patient's RC or duty doctor (or equivalent) must be informed of seclusion as soon as practicable.

Commencing seclusion

26.113 Staff may decide what a patient can take into the seclusion area. The **4–168**
patient should never be deprived of clothing when in seclusion (see paragraphs
26.161–26.166).

26.114 The person authorising seclusion (see Authorising seclusion table)
should have seen the patient immediately prior to the commencement of
seclusion.

26.115 When a patient is placed in seclusion, the start time of the seclusion
should be recorded in the seclusion record (see paragraph 26.149).

26.116 If seclusion was authorised by an approved clinician who is not a doctor,
or by the professional in charge of the ward, the responsible clinician or duty

doctor (or equivalent) should attend to undertake the first medical review (see paragraph 26.128) within one hour of the beginning of seclusion. If the patient is newly admitted, not well known to the staff, or there has been a significant change in the patient's physical, mental state and/or behavioural presentation, this medical review should take place without delay. Where seclusion has been authorised by a psychiatrist, whether or not they are the patient's responsible clinician or an approved clinician, the first medical review will be the review that they undertook immediately before authorising seclusion (meaning that a medical review within one hour of seclusion is not necessary).

26.117 Where it has been agreed in a positive behaviour support plan (or equivalent) that family members will be notified of significant behavioural disturbances and the use of restrictive interventions, this should take place as agreed in the plan (see paragraph 26.15).

Observation during seclusion

4–169 26.118 A suitably skilled professional should as a minimum be readily available within sight and sound of the seclusion area at all times throughout the patient's period of seclusion.

26.119 The professional should have the means to summon urgent assistance from other staff at any point.

26.120 Consideration should be given to whether a male or female person should carry out ongoing observations; this may be informed by consideration of a patient's trauma history.

26.121 The aim of observation is to safeguard the patient, monitor their condition and behaviour and to identify the earliest time at which seclusion can end.

26.122 For patients who have received sedation, a skilled professional will need to be outside the door at all times.

26.123 A record of the patient's behaviour should be made at least every 15 minutes (see paragraph 26.149).

26.124 The record made should include, where applicable: the patient's appearance, what they are doing and saying, their mood, their level of awareness and any evidence of physical ill health especially with regard to their breathing, pallor or cyanosis.

26.125 Where a patient appears to be asleep in seclusion, the person observing the patient should be alert to and assess the level of consciousness and respirations of the patient as appropriate.

Seclusion reviews

4–170 26.126 A series of review processes should be instigated when a patient is secluded. These include the multi-disciplinary team (MDT), nursing, medical and independent MDT reviews. All reviews provide an opportunity to determine whether seclusion needs to continue or should be stopped, as well as to review the patient's mental and physical state. Where agreed (see paragraph 26.16), family members should be advised of the outcomes of reviews.

Medical reviews

4–171 26.127 For the purposes of medical reviews, where the responsible clinician is not immediately available, eg outside of normal working hours, local policies should make provision for a 'duty doctor' to deputise for the responsible clinician. The policy should also identify which of their doctors are competent to carry out a medical review (see paragraph 26.133). Whenever the duty doctor is not an approved clinician, they should at all times have access to an on-call docter who is an approved clinician.

26.128 The first medical review should:

- if seclusion was authorised either by an approved clinician, who is not a doctor or the professional in charge of the ward, be undertaken by the responsible clinician or duty doctor (or equivalent) within one hour of the commencement of seclusion, or

- if seclusion was authorised by a consultant psychiatrist (whether or not they are the patient's responsible clinician or an approved clinician), be the review that they undertook immediately before seclusion was authorised.

26.129 If it is agreed that seclusion needs to continue, a seclusion care plan (see paragraph 26.147) should be agreed and prepared, which should identify how the patient's presenting and ongoing needs whilst in seclusion can continue to be met.

26.130 Subsequent medical reviews should be undertaken by either the responsible clinician, a doctor who is an approved clinician, or a duty doctor (see paragraph 26.127).

26.131 Continuing four-hourly medical reviews of secluded patients should be carried out until the first (internal) MDT has taken place including in the evenings, night time, on weekends and bank holidays. A provider's policy may allow different review arrangements to be applied when patients in seclusion are asleep.

26.132 Following the first internal MDT review, further medical reviews should continue at least twice in every 24-hour period. At least one of these should be carried out by the patient's responsible clinician (local arrangements for out-of-hours cover may provide for an alternative approved clinician to cover these responsible clinician reviews.

26.133 Medical reviews provide the opportunity to evaluate and amend seclusion care plans, as appropriate (see paragraph 26.147). They should be carried out in person and should include, where appropriate:

- a review of the patient's physical and psychiatric health

- an assessment of adverse effects of medication

- a review of the observations required

- a reassessment of medication prescribed

- an assessment of the risk posed by the patient to others

- an assessment of any risk to the patient from deliberate or accidental self-harm, and

- an assessment of the need for continuing seclusion, and whether it is possible for seclusion measures to be applied more flexibly or in a less restrictive manner.

Nursing reviews

26.134 Nursing reviews of the secluded patient should take place at least every **4–172** two hours following the commencement of seclusion. These should be undertaken by two individuals who are registered nurses, and at least one of whom should not have been involved directly in the decision to seclude.

26.135 In the event of concerns regarding the patient's condition, this should be immediately brought to the attention of the patient's responsible clinician or duty doctor.

26.136 When patients in seclusion are asleep, provider policies may allow reviews to be undertaken in accordance with a revised schedule which should be recorded in the seclusion care plan (see paragraph 26.147) in order to avoid waking the patient.

MDT reviews

4–173   26.137 The first internal MDT seclusion review should be held as soon as is practicable.

26.138 Appropriate membership of the MDT review meetings should be determined by provider policies. Membership would likely include the responsible clinician, a doctor who is an approved clinician, or an approved clinician who is not a doctor but who has appropriate expertise, the senior nurse on the ward, and staff from other disciplines who would normally be involved in patient reviews.

26.139 At weekends and overnight, membership of the initial MDT review may be limited to medical and nursing staff, in which case the on-call senior site manager (or equivalent) should also be involved. Further MDT reviews should take place once in every 24-hour period of continuous seclusion.

26.140 Where seclusion continues, these reviews should evaluate and make amendments, as appropriate, to the seclusion care plan (see paragraph 26.147).

Independent MDT review

4–174   26.141 An independent MDT review should be promptly undertaken where a patient has either been secluded for eight hours consecutively or for 12 hours intermittently during a 48-hour period.

26.142 Appropriate membership of the meeting should be determined by provider policies, but as a minimum they should include a doctor who is an approved clinician, or an approved clinician who is not a doctor a nurse and other professionals who were not involved in the incident which led to the seclusion and an IMHA (in cases where the patient has one). It is good practice for the independent MDT to consult those involved in the original decision.

26.143 If it is agreed that seclusion needs to continue, the review should evaluate and make recommendations, as appropriate, for amendments to the seclusion care plan (see paragraph 26.147).

Ending seclusion

4–175   26.144 Seclusion should immediately end when a MDT review, a medical review or the independent MDT review determines it is no longer warranted. Alternatively where the professional in charge of the ward feels that seclusion is no longer warranted, seclusion may end following consultation with the patient's responsible clinician or duty doctor. This consultation may take place in person or by telephone.

26.145 Seclusion ends when a patient is allowed free and unrestricted access to the normal ward environment or transfers or returns to conditions of long-term segregation.

26.146 Opening a door for toilet and food breaks or medical review does not constitute the end of a period of seclusion.

Further guidance on seclusion

26.147 A seclusion care plan should set out how the individual care needs of the **4–176** patient will be met whilst the patient is in seclusion and record the steps that should be taken in order to bring the need for seclusion to an end as quickly as possible. As a minimum the seclusion care plan should include:

- a statement of clinical needs (including any physical or mental health problems), risks and treatment objectives

- a plan as to how needs are to be met, how de-escalation attempts will continue and how risks will be managed

- details of bedding and clothing to be provided

- details as to how the patient's dietary needs are to be provided for, and

- details of any family or carer contact/communication which will maintained during the period of seclusion in accordance with paragraph 26.16.

26.148 Wherever possible, the patient should be supported to contribute to the seclusion care plan and steps should be taken to ensure that the patient is aware of what they need to do for the seclusion to come to an end. In view of the potentially traumatising effect of seclusion, care plans should provide details of the support that will be provided when the seclusion comes to an end.

26.149 The seclusion record format should be determined by providers' policies on seclusion. Different providers may use different systems, which may be electronic or paper-based (or a combination of both); in any case they should meet recognised professional record keeping standards. The seclusion record should provide the following details:

- who authorised the seclusion

- the date and time of commencement of seclusion

- the reason(s) for seclusion

- what the patient took into the seclusion room

- if and when a family member, carer and/or advocate was informed of the use of seclusion

- 15 minute recordings by the person undertaking continuous direct observation

- details of who undertook scheduled nursing reviews, their assessment, and a record of the patient's condition and recommendations

- details of who undertook scheduled medical reviews, their assessment and a record of the patient's condition and recommendations

- details of who undertook the independent MDT review, their assessment and a record of the patient's condition and recommendations

- details of who undertook the scheduled MDT reviews, their assessment and a record of the patient's condition and recommendations

- the date and time seclusion ended, and

- details of who determined that seclusion should come to an end.

LONG-TERM SEGREGATION

4–177   26.150 Long-term segregation refers to a situation where, in order to reduce a sustained risk of harm posed by the patient to others, which is a constant feature of their presentation, a multi-disciplinary review and a representative from the responsible commissioning authority determines that a patient should not be allowed to mix freely with other patients on the ward or unit on a long-term basis. In such cases, it should have been determined that the risk of harm to others would not be ameliorated by a short period of seclusion combined with any other form of treatment. The clinical judgement is that, if the patient were allowed to mix freely in the general ward environment, other patients or staff would continue to be exposed to a high likelihood of serious injury or harm over a prolonged period of time. Where consideration is being given to long-term segregation, wherever appropriate, the views of the person's family and carers should be elicited and taken into account. The multi-disciplinary review should include an IMHA in cases where a patient has one.

26.151 It is permissible to manage this small number of patients by ensuring that their contact with the general ward population is limited. The environment should be no more restrictive than is necessary. This means it should be as homely and personalised as risk considerations allow. Facilities which are used to accommodate patients in conditions of long-term segregation should be configured to allow the patient to access a number of areas including, as a minimum, bathroom facilities, a bedroom and relaxing lounge area. Patients should also be able to access secure outdoor areas and a range activities of interest and relevance to the person.

26.152 Patients should not be isolated from contact with staff (indeed it is highly likely they should be supported through enhanced observation) or deprived of access to therapeutic interventions. Treatment plans should aim to end long-term segregation.

26.153 The local safeguarding team should be made aware of any patient being supported in longer term segregation.

26.154 Staff supporting patients who are long-term segregated should make written records on their condition on at least an hourly basis.

26.155 The patient's situation should be formally reviewed by an approved clinician who may or not be a doctor at least once in any 24-hour period and at least weekly by the full MDT. The composition of the MDT should be decided by the provider's policy on long-term segregation, but should include the patient's responsible clinician and an IMHA where appropriate. Provider's policies should provide for periodic reviews by a senior professional who is not involved with the case. The outcome of all reviews and the reasons for continued segregation should be recorded and the responsible commissioning authority should be informed of the outcome).

26.156 Where long-term segregation continues for three months or longer, regular three monthly reviews of the patient's circumstances and care should be undertaken by an external hospital. This should include discussion with the patient's IMHA (where appropriate) and commissioner.

26.157 The patient's treatment plan should clearly state the reasons why long-term segregation is required. In these cases, the way that the patient's situation is reviewed needs to reflect the specific nature of their management plan. The purpose of a review is to determine whether the ongoing risks have reduced sufficiently to allow the patient to be integrated into the wider ward community and to check on their general health and welfare. The decision to end long-term segregation should be taken by the MDT (including consultation with the patient's IMHA where appropriate), following a thorough risk assessment and observations from staff of the patient's presentation during close monitoring of the patient in the company of others.

26.158 The patient's care plan should outline how they are to be made aware of what is required of them so that the period of long-term segregation can be brought to an end.

26.159 Where successive MDT reviews determine that segregation continues to be required, more information should be available to demonstrate its necessity and explain why the patient cannot be supported in a less restrictive manner.

26.160 At times of acute behavioural disturbance where there is a need to contain an immediate risk of harm to others, there may be a need to transfer the person, for a short period of time, to a physical area that is more secure and restrictive and which has been designed for the purpose of seclusion. In such a situation, the procedure for seclusion in the Code should be followed with regards to authorising and commencing seclusion, observation, seclusion reviews and ending seclusion.

DEPRIVATION OF ACCESS TO NORMAL DAYTIME CLOTHING

26.161 Individuals should never be deprived of appropriate clothing with the **4–178** intention of restricting their freedom of movement, neither should they be deprived of other aids necessary for their daily living.

26.162 It may be appropriate, in a small number of instances, for individuals to be asked to wear special tear-proof clothing, such a decision should be authorised by the patient's responsible clinician. An MDT should undertake an individualised risk assessment before this decision is taken. (Local policy should determine the appropriate complexion of the MDT.) This is particularly likely to be the case where the risk of shredded clothing being used to self-harm or attempt suicide has been assessed and is considered to be very high.

26.163 Tear-proof clothing should never be a first-line response to such risks and should never be used as a substitute for enhanced levels of support and observation. The requirement to wear tear-proof clothing should never be a blanket rule within a service.

26.164 Any tear-proof clothing should fit the person so as to preserve their dignity. It should not be demeaning or stigmatising, and should, where possible, meet any specific cultural or religious requirements.

26.165 Any requirement that an individual should wear tear-proof clothing should be proportionate to the assessed risk and documented evidence should show that it is used only as long as absolutely necessary. As soon as the risk is assessed to have diminished, consideration should be given by nursing staff or the MDT team to a return to usual clothing. This will require ongoing dynamic risk assessment.

26.166 Positive behaviour support plans (or equivalents) should detail primary preventative strategies that will aim to avoid the ongoing need for such restrictions. The patients should be told what they need to do so that they can wear their usual and preferred clothing.

30. GUARDIANSHIP

Why read this chapter?

4–179 30.1 Guardianship enables patients to receive care outside hospital where it cannot be provide without the use of compulsory powers. This chapter provides guidance on guardianship, in particular, on the purpose of guardianship, assessing a patient for guardianship, the responsibilities of local authorities and the components of effective guardianship.

PURPOSE OF GUARDIANSHIP

4–180 30.2 The purpose of guardianship is to enable patients to receive care outside hospital where it cannot be provided without the use of compulsory powers. Such care may, or may not, include specialist medical treatment for mental disorder.

30.3 A guardian may be a local authority or someone else approved by a local authority (a 'private guardian'). Guardians have three specific powers as follows:

- they have the exclusive right to decide where a patient should live, taking precedence even over an attorney or deputy appointed under the Mental Capacity Act 2005 (MCA). The Court of Protection also lacks jurisdiction to determine a place of residence of a patient whilst that patient is subject to guardianship and there is a residence requirement in effect[53]

- they can require the patient to attend for treatment, work, training or education at specific times and places (but they cannot use force to take the patient there), and

- they can demand that a doctor, approved mental health professional (AMHP) or another relevant person has access to the patient at the place where the patient lives.

30.4 Guardianship therefore provides an authoritative framework for working with a patient, with a minimum of constraint, to achieve as independent a life as possible within the community. Where it is used, it should be part of the patient's overall care plan.

30.5 Guardianship must not be used to impose restrictions that amount to a deprivation of liberty.

30.6 Guardianship does not give anyone the right to treat the patient without their permission or to consent to treatment on their behalf.

30.7 While the reception of a patient into guardianship does not affect the continued authority of an attorney or deputy appointed under the MCA, such attorneys and deputies will not be able to take decisions about where a

---

[53] C v Blackburn and Darwen Borough Council. 2011. EWHC 2231. http://www.bailii.org/ew/cases/EWHC/COP/2011/3321.html.

guardianship patient is to reside, or take any other decisions which conflict with decisions made by the guardian.

ASSESSMENT FOR GUARDIANSHIP

30.8 An application for guardianship may be made, in relation to a person who **4–181** is aged 16 or over and who is not a ward of court, on the grounds that:

- the patient is suffering from mental disorder of a nature or degree which warrants their reception into guardianship, and
- it is necessary, in the interests of the welfare of the patient or for the protection of other persons, that the patient should be so received.

30.9 Guardianship is most likely to be appropriate where:

- the patient is thought to be likely to respond well to the authority and attention of a guardian and so be more willing to comply with necessary treatment and care for their mental disorder, and
- there is a particular need for someone to have the authority to decide where the patient should live or to insist that doctors, AMHPs or other people be given access to the patient.

30.10 As with applications for detention in hospital (see chapter 14), AMHPs and doctors making recommendations should consider whether the objectives of the proposed application could be achieved in another, less restrictive, way, without the use of guardianship.

30.11 Where patients lack capacity to make some or all important decisions concerning their own welfare, one potential alternative to guardianship will be to rely solely on the MCA—especially the protection from liability for actions taken in connection with care or treatment provided by section 5 of the MCA. While this is a factor to be taken into account, it will not by itself determine whether guardianship is necessary or unnecessary. AMHPs and doctors need to consider all the circumstances of the particular case.

30.12 Where an patient aged 16 or over is assessed as requiring residential care but lacks the capacity to make a decision about whether they wish to be placed there, guardianship is unlikely to be necessary where the move can properly, quickly and efficiently be carried out on the basis of:

- section 5 of the MCA or the decision of an attorney or deputy, and
- (where relevant) a deprivation of liberty authorisation (a DoL authorisation) (in relation to a patient aged 18 or over) or deprivation of liberty order (Court of Protection order) under the MCA.

30.13 But guardianship may still be appropriate in such cases if:

- there are other reasons—unconnected to the move to residential care—to think that the patient might benefit from the attention and authority of a guardian

- there is a particular need to have explicit statutory authority for the patient to be returned to the place where the patient is to live should they go absent, or

- it is thought to be important that decisions about where the patient is to live are placed in the hands of a single person or authority—eg where there have been long-running or particularly difficult disputes about where the person should live.

30.14 It will not always be best to use guardianship as the way of deciding where patients who lack capacity to decide for themselves must live. In cases which raise unusual issues, or where guardianship is being considered in the interests of the patient's welfare and there are finely balanced arguments about where the patient should live, it may be preferable instead to seek a best interests decision from the Court of Protection under the MCA.

30.15 Where the relevant criteria are met, guardianship may be considered in respect of a patient who is to be discharged from detention under the Act. However, if it is thought that the patient needs to remain liable to be recalled to hospital (and the patient is eligible), a community treatment order (CTO) may be appropriate (see chapter 29).

Responsibilities of local authorities

4–182   30.16 Each local authority should establish a policy setting out the arrangements for:

- receiving, scrutinising and accepting or refusing applications for guardianship. Such arrangements should ensure that applications are properly but quickly dealt with

- monitoring the progress of each patient's guardianship, including steps to be taken to fulfil the authority's statutory obligations in relation to private guardians and to arrange visits to the patient

- ensuring the suitability of any proposed private guardian, and that they are able to understand and carry out their duties under the Act

- ensuring that patients under guardianship receive, both orally and in writing, information in accordance with regulations under the Act, including their right to have access to an independent mental health advocate (IMHA)

- ensuring that patients are aware of their right to apply to a Tribunal and that patients are given the name of someone who will give them necessary assistance, on behalf of the local authority, in making such an application

- authorising an approved clinician to be the patient's responsible clinician

- maintaining detailed records relating to guardianship patients

- ensuring that the need to continue guardianship is reviewed in the last two months of each period of guardianship in accordance with the Act, and

- discharging patients from guardianship as soon as it is no longer required.

30.17 Patients may be discharged from guardianship at any time by the local authority, the responsible clinician authorised by the local authority, or (in most cases) the patient's nearest relative.

30.18 Discharge decisions by local authorities may be taken only by:

- the local authority itself, or

- three or more members of the local authority, or

- a committee or subcommittee of the local authority authorised for that purpose.

Where decisions are taken by three or more local authority members (or a committee or sub-committee), all three people (or at least three of them, if there are more) must agree.

30.19 Local authorities may consider discharging patients from guardianship at any time, but must consider doing so when they receive a report from the patient's nominated medical attendant or responsible clinician renewing their guardianship under section 20 of the Act.

COMPONENTS OF EFFECTIVE GUARDIANSHIP

Care planning

30.20 An application for guardianship should be accompanied by a comprehen- **4–183** sive care plan established on the basis of multi-disciplinary discussions in accordance with the care programme approach (or its equivalent).

30.21 The plan should identify the services needed by the patient and who will provide them. It should also indicate which of the powers that guardians have under the Act are necessary to achieve the plan. If none of the powers are required, guardianship should not be used.

30.22 Key elements of the plan are likely to be:

- suitable accommodation to help meet the patient's needs

- access to day care, education and training facilities, as appropriate

- effective co-operation and communication between all persons concerned in implementing the care plan

- (if there is to be a private guardian) support from the local authority for the guardian.

30.23 A private guardian should be prepared to advocate on behalf of the patient in relation to those agencies whose services are needed to carry out the care plan. So should a local authority which is itself the guardian.

30.24 A private guardian should be a person who can appreciate any special disabilities and needs of a mentally disordered person and who will look after the patient in an appropriate and sympathetic way. The guardian should display an interest in promoting the patient's physical and mental health and in providing for their occupation, training, employment, recreation and general welfare in a suitable way. The local authority must satisfy itself that a proposed private guardian is capable of carrying out their functions and it should assist them with advice and other forms of support.

30.25 Regulations require private guardians to appoint a doctor as the patient's nominated medical attendant. It is the nominated medical attendant who must examine the patient during the last two months of each period of guardianship and decide whether to make a report extending the patient's guardianship. (Where the patient's guardian is the local authority itself, this is done by the responsible clinician authorised by the local authority.)

30.26 It is for private guardians themselves to decide whom to appoint as the nominated medical attendant, but they should first consult the local authority. The nominated medical attendant may be the patient's GP, if the GP agrees.

Power to require a patient to live in a particular place

4–184   30.27 Guardians have the power to decide where patients should live. If patients leave the place they are required to live without the guardian's permission, they can be taken into legal custody and brought back there (see chapter 28).

30.28 This power can also be used to take patients for the first time to the place they are required to live, if patients do not (or, in practice, cannot) go there by themselves.

30.29 Patients should always be consulted first about where they are to be required to live, unless their mental state makes that impossible. Guardians should not use this power to make a patient move without warning.

30.30 The power to take or return patients to the place they are required to live may be used, eg to discourage them from:

- living somewhere the guardian considers unsuitable
- breaking off contact with services
- leaving the area before proper arrangements can be made, and
- sleeping rough.

But it may not be used to restrict their freedom to come and go so much that they are effectively being detained.

30.31 The power to require patients to reside in a particular place may not be used to require them to live in a situation in which they are deprived of liberty. Guardianship will not be appropriate for a person who has the capacity to decide where to live and will not reside in the place they are required to live by their guardian, unless they were to be deprived of their liberty under the Act.

30.32 If the person lacks the capacity to decide where to live, they may be deprived of their liberty if this is authorised separately by either (a) a DoL authorisation in respect of a hospital or care home placement if they are 18 or over; or (b) by a Court of Protection order made by the Court of Protection under the MCA in respect of other community settings if they are 16 or over. If it is appropriate for deprivation of liberty to be authorised under the MCA, the local authority should consider whether guardianship remains appropriate, bearing in mind the need to apply the least restrictive option and maximising independence principle (see paragraphs 1.2–1.6 and paragraphs 30.2–30.7).

GUARDIANSHIP AND HOSPITAL CARE

30.33 Guardianship does not restrict patients' access to hospital services on an **4–185** informal basis. Patients who require treatment but do not need to be detained may be admitted informally in the same way as any other patient. This applies both to physical and mental healthcare.

30.34 Nor does guardianship prevent the deprivation of a person's liberty being authorised under the MCA, if the person needs to be detained in a hospital in their best interests in order to receive care and treatment. A DoL authorisation or Court of Protection order can be sought so long as:

- it would not be inconsistent with the guardian's decision about where the patient should live, and

- the person does not object to being kept in hospital for treatment for mental disorder or to receiving that treatment.[54]

30.35 Otherwise, guardianship should not be used to require a patient to reside in a hospital except where it is necessary for a very short time in order to provide shelter while accommodation in the community is being arranged.

30.36 Guardianship can remain in force if the patient is detained in hospital under section 2 or 4 of the Act for assessment, but it ends automatically if a patient is detained for treatment as a result of an application under section 3. Regulations also allow a patient to be transferred from guardianship to detention in hospital under section 3. The normal requirements for an application and medical recommendations must be met, and the transfer must be agreed by the local authority.

PATIENTS WHO RESIST THE AUTHORITY OF THE GUARDIAN

30.37 If a patient consistently resists exercise by the guardian of any of their **4–186** powers, it can normally be concluded that guardianship is not the most appropriate form of care for that person, and the guardianship should be discharged. The local authority should first consider whether a change of guardian—or change in the person who, in practice, exercises the local authority's powers as guardian— might be appropriate instead.

GUARDIANSHIP ORDERS UNDER SECTION 37

30.38 Guardianship may be used by courts as an alternative to hospital orders **4–187** for offenders with mental disorders where the criteria set out in the Act are met. The court must first be satisfied that the local authority or named person is willing to act as guardian. In considering the appropriateness of the patient being received into their guardianship, local authorities should be guided by the same considerations as apply to applications for guardianship under part 2 of the Act.

30.39 The guidance in this chapter on components of effective guardianship applies to guardianship order patients in the same way as it applies to other guardianship patients. The main difference between applications for guardianship under part 2 of the Act and guardianship orders is that nearest relatives may not

---

[54] In these circumstances, a DoL authorisation or Court of Protection order cannot be made because the person will be ineligible to be deprived of their liberty by the MCA: see paragraphs 12 and 17 of Schedule A1, read with paragraphs 2 (Case D), 3 and 5 of Schedule 1A, to the Mental Capacity Act 2005.

discharge patients from guardianship orders. Nearest relatives have rights to apply to the Tribunal instead (see paragraphs 12.6–12.9).

31. GUARDIANSHIP, LEAVE OF ABSENCE OR CTO?

Why read this chapter?

4–188   31.1 An unrestricted patient may be subject to the powers of the Act while living in the community by one of three ways: guardianship, leave of absence or a community treatment order (CTO). This chapter provides guidance on deciding between these three options.

DECIDING BETWEEN GUARDIANSHIP, LEAVE OF ABSENCE AND CTO

4–189   31.2 There are three ways in which an unrestricted patient may be subject to the powers of the Act while living in the community: guardianship, leave of absence and CTO.

31.3 Guardianship (section 7 of the Act) is social care-led and is primarily focused on patients with welfare needs. Its purpose is to enable patients to receive care in the community where it cannot be provided without the use of compulsory powers (see chapter 30).

31.4 Leave of absence (section 17) is primarily intended to allow a patient detained under the Act to be temporarily absent from hospital where further in-patient treatment as a detained patient is still thought to be necessary. It is clearly suitable for short-term absences for a fixed period or specific purpose eg to allow visits to family and to trial living more independently (see also chapter 27).

31.5 Leave of absence may be useful in the longer term (more than seven consecutive days) where the clinical team wish to see how the patient manages outside hospital before making the decision to discharge. Leave for a longer period should also be for a specific purpose or a fixed period, and not normally more than one month. For most patients who are able to live in the community, a CTO should be considered a better option than longer-term leave for the ongoing management of their care. Reflecting this, whenever considering longer-term leave for a patient (that is, for more than seven consecutive days), the responsible clinician must first consider whether the patient should be discharged onto a CTO instead. Any decision to authorise section 17 leave for more than seven days on a second occasion should be fully documented, including why a CTO or discharge is not appropriate (see paragraph 27.14).

31.6 A CTO (section 17A) is used where it is necessary for the patient's health or safety or for the protection of others to continue to receive treatment after their discharge from hospital. It seeks to prevent the 'revolving door' scenario and the harm which could arise from relapse. It is a more structured system than leave of absence and has more safeguards for patients. A key feature of the CTO framework is that it is suitable only where there is no reason to think that the patient will need further treatment as a detained in-patient for the time being, but where the responsible clinician needs to be able to recall the patient to hospital if necessary (see chapter 29).

31.7 Some pointers to the use of the three options are given in the following figures:

Figure 18: CTO or longer-term leave of absence: relevant factors to consider

Factors suggesting longer-term leave	Factors suggesting a CTO
• Discharge from hospital is for a specific purpose or a fixed period. • The patient's discharge from hospital is deliberately on a 'trial' basis. • The patient is likely to need further in-patient treatment without their consent or compliance. • There is a serious risk of arrangements in the community breaking down or being unsatisfactory—more so than for a CTO.	There is confidence that the patient is ready for discharge from hospital on an indefinite basis. • There are good reasons to expect that the patient will not need to be detained for the treatment they need to be given. • The patient appears prepared to consent or comply with the treatment they need—but risks as below mean that recall may be necessary. • The risk of arrangements in the community breaking down, or of the patient needing to be recalled to hospital for treatment, is sufficiently serious to justify a CTO, but not to the extent that it is very likely to happen.

Figure 19: CTO or guardianship: relevant factors to consider

Factors suggesting guardianship	Factors suggesting a CTO
• The focus is on the patient's general welfare, rather than specifically on medical treatment. • There is little risk of the patient needing to be admitted compulsorily and quickly to hospital. • There is a need for an enforceable power to require the patient to reside at a particular place.	• The main focus is on ensuring that the patient continues to receive necessary medical treatment for mental disorder, without having to be detained again. • Compulsory recall to hospital for treatment may well be necessary, and a speedy recall is likely to be important.

DEPRIVATION OF LIBERTY WHILE ON A CTO, LEAVE OR SUBJECT TO GUARDIANSHIP

31.8 Patients who are on a CTO or on leave, and who lack capacity to decide **4–190** whether or not to consent to the arrangements required for their care or treatment, may occasionally need to be detained for further care or treatment for their mental disorder in circumstances in which recall to hospital for this purpose is not considered necessary. They might also need to be admitted to a care home or hospital because of physical health problems.

31.9 If they will be detained in a care home, a deprivation of liberty authorisation (DoL authorisation) or Court of Protection order under the Mental Capacity Act 2005 (MCA) must be obtained. Deprivation of liberty under the MCA can exist alongside a CTO or leave of absence, provided that there is no conflict with the conditions of the CTO or leave set by the patient's responsible clinician.[55]

31.10 If they will be detained in a hospital for further treatment for mental disorder (whether or not they will also receive treatment for physical health problems), they should be recalled to be treated under the Act. The MCA cannot be used to authorise the deprivation of their liberty.[56]

31.11 For guidance on the use of a DoL authorisation or Court of Protection order in relation to a patient who is subject to guardianship, see chapter 30 on guardianship.

33. AFTER-CARE

Why read this chapter?

4–191 33.1 Section 117 of the Act requires clinical commissioning groups and local authorities, in co-operation with voluntary agencies, to provide or arrange for the provision of after-care to particular patients detained in hospital for treatment who then cease to be detained. This chapter provides guidance on this duty of after-care. It should be read in conjunction with chapter 34 on the care programme approach. The guidance covers after-care planning and direct payments.

MENTAL HEALTH AFTER-CARE

4–192 33.2 Section 117 of the Act requires clinical commissioning groups (CCGs) and local authorities, in co-operation with voluntary agencies, to provide or arrange for the provision of after-care to patients detained in hospital for treatment under section 3, 37, 45A, 47 or 48 of the Act who then cease to be detained. This includes patients granted leave of absence under section 17 and patients going on community treatment orders (CTOs). It applies to people of all ages, including children and young people.

33.3 After-care services mean services which have the purposes of meeting a need arising from or related to the patient's mental disorder and reducing the risk of a deterioration of the patient's mental condition (and, accordingly, reducing the risk of the patient requiring admission to hospital again for treatment for mental disorder.[57] Their ultimate aim is to maintain patients in the community, with as few restrictions as are necessary, wherever possible.

33.4 CCGs and local authorities should interpret the definition of after-care services broadly. For example, after-care can encompass healthcare, social care and employment services, supported accommodation and services to meet the person's wider social, cultural and spiritual needs, if these services meet a need that arises directly from or is related to the particular patient's mental disorder, and help to reduce the risk of a deterioration in the patient's mental condition.

33.5 After-care is a vital component in patients' overall treatment and care. As well as meeting their immediate needs for health and social care, after-care should aim to support them in regaining or enhancing their skills, or learning new skills, in order to cope with life outside hospital.

---

[55] If it would conflict with the conditions of their CTO or leave, the person would be ineligible to be deprived of their liberty under the MCA: see paragraphs 12 and 17 of Schedule A1, read with paragraphs 2 (Cases B and C), 3 and 4 of Schedule 1A to the MCA.

[56] Patients who are on a CTO or on leave are ineligible to be deprived of their liberty under the MCA for the purpose of being detained in a hospital to receive medical treatment for mental disorder: see paragraphs 12 and 17 of Schedule A1, read with paragraphs 2 (Cases B and C) and 4 of Schedule 1A to the MCA.

[57] The definition of 'after-care services' was inserted into section 117 by the Care Act 2014. http://www.legislation.gov.uk/ukpga/2014/23/contents/enacted.

33.6 The duty to provide after-care services continues as long as the patient is in need of such services. In the case of a patient on a CTO, after-care must be provided for the entire period they are on the CTO, but this does not mean that the patient's need for after-care will necessarily cease as soon as they are no longer on a CTO.

33.7 Mental health after-care services must be jointly provided or commissioned by local authorities and CCGs. They should maintain a record of people for whom they provide or commission after-care and what after-care services are provided. Services provided under section 117 can include services provided directly by local authorities or which local authorities commission from other providers. CCGs will commission (rather than provide) these services.

33.8 The NHS Commissioning Board (NHS England) is responsible for a patient's after-care if the after-care services required are of the type that the NHS Commissioning Board would be responsible for commissioning rather than a CCG. In these circumstances local authorities and CCGs should liaise with the NHS Commissioning Board to ensure these services are commissioned promptly.

33.9 Where eligible patients have remained in hospital informally after ceasing to be detained under the Act, they are still entitled to after-care under section 117 once they leave hospital. This also applies when patients are released from prison, having spent part of their sentence detained in hospital under a relevant section of the Act.

AFTER-CARE PLANNING

33.10 Although the duty to provide after-care begins when the patient leaves **4–193** hospital, the planning of after-care needs to start as soon as the patient is admitted to hospital. CCGs and local authorities should take reasonable steps, in consultation with the care programme approach care co-ordinator and other members of the multi-disciplinary team to identify appropriate after-care services for patients in good time for their eventual discharge from hospital or prison.

33.11 When considering relevant patients' cases, the Tribunal and hospital managers will expect to be provided with information from the professionals concerned on what after-care arrangements might be made if they were to be discharged. Some discussion of after-care arrangements involving local authorities, other relevant agencies and families or carers (where appropriate) should take place in advance of the Tribunal hearing.

33.12 Where a Tribunal or hospital managers' hearing has been arranged for a patient who might be entitled to after-care under section 117 of the Act, the hospital managers should ensure that the relevant CCG and local authority have been informed. The CCG and local authority should consider putting practical preparations in hand for after-care in every case, but should in particular consider doing so where there is a strong possibility that the patient will be discharged if appropriate after-care can be arranged. Where the Tribunal has provisionally decided to give a restricted patient a conditional discharge, the CCG and local authority should do their best to put after-care in place which would allow that discharge to take place.

33.13 Before deciding to discharge or grant more than very short-term leave of absence to a patient or to place a patient onto a CTO, the responsible clinician should ensure that the patient's needs for after-care have been fully assessed, discussed with the patient (and their carers, where appropriate) and addressed in their care plan. If the patient is being given leave for only a short period, a less comprehensive review may be sufficient, but the arrangements for the patient's care should still be properly recorded.

33.14 After-care for all patients admitted to hospital for treatment for mental disorder should be planned within the framework of the care programme approach (see chapter 34). This applies whether or not they are detained or will be entitled to receive after-care under section 117 of the Act. But because of the specific statutory obligation it is important that all patients who are entitled to after-care under section 117 are identified and that records are kept of what is provided to them under that section.

33.15 In order to ensure that the after-care plan reflects the full range of needs of each patient, it is important to consider who needs to be involved, in addition to patients themselves. This may involve carers and a wide range of professionals (see the list in paragraph 34.12).

33.16 The issues likely to be covered by a thorough assessment are set out in paragraph 34.19.

After-care payments
4–194   33.17 A local authority may make direct payments to pay for after-care services under section 117 of the Act.[58] An adult who is eligible for after-care can request the local authority to make direct payments to them, if they have capacity to do this. If the adult lacks capacity to do so, the local authority can make direct payments to an authorised person or suitable person if certain conditions are met. A key condition is that the local authority must consider that making the direct payments to the 'authorised person' is an appropriate way to discharge their section 117 duty, and that they must be satisfied the 'authorised person' will act in the adult's best interests in arranging for the after-care.

33.18 If a local authority is providing or arranging accommodation as part of a patient's after-care, the patient and/or friends or relatives identified in regulations may make top-up payments to enable the patient to live in their preferred accommodation if certain conditions are met.[59]

33.19 A CCG or the NHS Commissioning Board may also make direct payments in respect of after-care to the patient or, where the patient is a child or a person who lacks capacity, to a representative who consents to the making of direct payments in respect of the patient. A payment can only be made if valid consent has been given. In determining whether a direct payment should be made, a CCG or the NHS Commissioning Board is required to have regard to whether it is appropriate for a person with that person's condition, the impact of that condition on the person's life and whether a direct payment represents value for money. A payment can also, in certain circumstances, be made to a nominee.[60]

---

[58] Care and Support Statutory Guidance Issued under the Care Act 2014. Department of Health. 2014. http://www.gov.uk/government/uploads/system/uploads/attachment_data/file/315993/Care-Act-Guidance.pdf.

[59] Care and Support Statutory Guidance Issued under the Care Act 2014. Department of Health. 2014. http://www.gov.uk/government/uploads/system/uploads/attachment_data/file/315993/Care-Act-Guidance.pdf.

ENDING SECTION 117 AFTER-CARE SERVICES

33.20 The duty to provide after-care services exists until both the CCG and the **4–195**
local authority are satisfied that the patient no longer requires them. The circumstances in which it is appropriate to end section 117 after-care will vary from
person to person and according to the nature of the services being provided.
The most clear-cut circumstance in which after-care would end is where the person's mental health improved to a point where they no longer needed services to
meet needs arising from or related to their mental disorder. If these services
included, for example, care in a specialist residential setting, the arrangements
for their move to more appropriate accommodation would need to be in place
before support under section 117 is finally withdrawn. Fully involving the patient
and (if indicated) their carer and/or advocate in the decision-making process will
play an important part in the successful ending of after-care.

33.21 After-care services under section 117 should not be withdrawn solely on
the grounds that:

- the patient has been discharged from the care of specialist mental health
  services
- an arbitrary period has passed since the care was first provided
- the patient is deprived of their liberty under the MCA
- the patient has returned to hospital informally or under section 2, or
- the patient is no longer on a CTO or section 17 leave.

33.22 After-care services may be reinstated if it becomes obvious that they have
been withdrawn prematurely, eg where a patient's mental condition begins to
deteriorate immediately after services are withdrawn.

33.23 Even when the provision of after-care has been successful in that the
patient is now well-settled in the community, the patient may still continue to
need after-care services, eg to prevent a relapse or further deterioration in their
condition.

33.24 Patients are under no obligation to accept the after-care services they are
offered, but any decisions they may make to decline them should be fully
informed. An unwillingness to accept services does not mean that patients have
no need to receive services, nor should it preclude them from receiving them
under section 117 should they change their minds.

38. HOSPITAL MANAGERS' DISCHARGE POWERS

Why read this chapter?

38.1 Hospital managers have the power to discharge most detained patients and **4–196**
all patients subject to a community treatment order (CTO). This chapter provides
guidance on the exercise of these powers. It includes matters relating to when to
review detention or a CTO, the criteria to be applied, the procedure for reviewing

---

[60] The National Health Service (Direct Payments) Regulations. 2013. SI 2013/1617, as amended by
the National Health Service (Direct Payments) (Amendment) Regulations. 2013. SI 2013/2354 prescribe the conditions for making a direct payment. http://www.legislation.gov.uk/uksi/2013/2354/
pdfs/uksi_20132354_en.pdf.

detention or a CTO, how to conduct reviews where the detention or CTO is contested, uncontested renewals, and recording the reasons for a decision.

THE POWER TO DISCHARGE

4–197   38.2 Section 23 of the Act gives hospital managers the power to discharge most detained patients and all CTO patients. They may not discharge patients who are held under the section 5 holding powers or in a place of safety under sections 135 or 136 or those remanded to hospital under sections 35 or 36 of the Act or subject to interim hospital orders under section 38, and they may not discharge restricted patients without the consent of the Secretary of State for Justice.

EXERCISE OF POWER OF DISCHARGE

4–198   38.3 The hospital managers—meaning the organisation or individual in charge of the hospital—must either consider discharge themselves or arrange for their power to be exercised on their behalf by a 'managers' panel'.

38.4 A managers' panel may consist of three or more people who are:

- members of the organisation in charge of the provider (eg the chair or non-executive directors), or

- members of a committee or sub-committee which is authorised for the purpose.

38.5 In the case of an NHS foundation trust, a panel can consist of any three or more people appointed for the purpose by the trust whether or not they are members of the trust itself or any of its committees or sub-committees.

38.6 In NHS trusts and NHS foundation trusts none of the people on managers' panels may be employees of the body concerned (or executive directors of the boards of NHS foundation trusts). People do not become employees or officers simply because they are paid a fee for serving on managers' panels.

38.7 In independent hospitals, managers' panels should not include people who are on the staff of the hospital or who have a financial interest in it.

38.8 In all cases, the board (or the equivalent) of the organisation concerned should ensure that the people appointed properly understand their role and the working of the Act. The organisation should ensure that people appointed to a managers' panel receive suitable training to understand the law, work with patients and professionals, to be able to reach sound judgements and properly record their decisions. This should include training or development in understanding risk assessment and risk management reports, and the need to consider the views of patients, and if the patient agrees, their nearest relative, and if different, carer.

38.9 Appointments to managers' panels should be made for a fixed period. Reappointment (if permitted) should not be automatic and should be preceded by a review of the person's continuing suitability.

38.10 Hospital managers should ensure that they and the hospital managers' panel understand equality issues and that there are sufficient numbers of panel members with a specialised understanding of the specific needs of particular groups including those listed below, and that panel members can communicate effectively with them:

- patients from minority cultural or ethnic backgrounds
- patients with physical impairments and/or sensory impairments, and/or
- patients with learning disabilities and/or autistic spectrum disorders.

Reviewing detention or a CTO

38.11 Hospital managers should ensure that all relevant patients, and their near- **4–199** est relative and, if different carer, are aware that the patient may ask to be discharged by the hospital managers and of the distinction between this and their right to apply for a Tribunal hearing (see chapter 12). Hospital managers should ensure that the appropriate level of support is provided to help the patient understand this right and distinction. This is particularly important if the patient is a child or young person or an individual who has communication difficulties or limited capacity.

38.12 Hospital managers:

- may undertake a review of whether or not a patient should be discharged at any time at their discretion
- must undertake a review if the patient's responsible clinician submits a report to them under section 20 of the Act renewing detention or under section 20A extending the CTO
- should consider holding a review when they receive a request from a patient (who may be supported by their independent mental health advocate (IMHA) (see chapter 6), independent mental capacity advocate (IMCA), attorney or deputy (see chapter 7) or a carer, and
- should consider holding a review when the responsible clinician makes a report to them under section 25 barring an order by the nearest relative to discharge a patient.

38.13 In the last two cases, when deciding whether to consider the case, hospital managers are entitled to take into account whether the Tribunal has recently considered the patient's case or is due to do so in the near future. The decision should be recorded in writing and if the decision is taken not to consider the case the reasons documented.

38.14 Before the current period of detention or the CTO ends, it is desirable that a managers' panel considers a report made under section 20 or section 20A and decides whether to exercise its discharge power. However, the responsible clinician's report itself provides authority for the patient's continued detention or period on a CTO, even if a managers' panel has not yet considered the case or reached a decision.

Criteria to be applied

38.15 The Act does not define specific criteria to be used by hospital managers **4–200** when considering discharge. The essential consideration is whether the grounds for continued detention or continued CTO under the Act are satisfied. To ensure that this is done in a systematic and consistent way, managers' panels should consider the questions set out below, in the order stated.

38.16 For patients detained for assessment under sections 2 or 4 of the Act:

- Is the patient still suffering from mental disorder?

  - If so, is the disorder of a nature or degree that warrants the continued detention of the patient in hospital?

  - Ought the detention to continue in the interests of the patient's health or safety or for the protection of other people?

38.17 For other detained patients:

- Is the patient still suffering from mental disorder?
- If so, is the disorder of a nature or degree that makes treatment in a hospital appropriate?
- Is continued detention for medical treatment necessary for the patient's health or safety or for the protection of other people?
- Is appropriate medical treatment available for the patient?
- Consideration should also be given to whether the Mental Capacity Act 2005 can be used to treat the patient safely and effectively.

38.18 For patients on a CTO:

- Is the patient still suffering from mental disorder?
- If so, is the disorder of a nature or degree that makes it appropriate for the patient to receive medical treatment?
- If so, is it necessary in the interests of the patient's health or safety or the protection of other persons that the patient should receive such treatment?
- Is it still necessary for the responsible clinician to be able to exercise the power to recall the patient to hospital, if that is needed? (For example, if a patient has been on a CTO for an extended period without the need to exercise the power to recall, it may not be appropriate to continue on a CTO)
- Is appropriate medical treatment available for the patient?

38.19 If three or more members of the panel (who between them make up a majority) are satisfied from the evidence presented to them that the answer to any of the questions set out above is 'no', the patient should be discharged. If so, where a patient lacks capacity to decide where to live, the hospital managers may request that consideration be given to making a deprivation of liberty authorisation or a deprivation of liberty order.

38.20 Where the answer to all the relevant questions above is 'yes', but the responsible clinician has made a report under section 25 barring a nearest relative's attempt to discharge the patient, the panel should also consider the following question:

- Would the patient, if discharged, be likely to act in a manner that is dangerous to other persons or to themselves?

38.21 This last question provides a more stringent test for continuing the detention or the CTO (see chapter 29).

38.22 If three or more members of the panel (being a majority) disagree with the responsible clinician and decide that the answer to this question is 'no', the panel should usually discharge the patient. The hospital managers retain a residual discretion not to discharge in these cases, so panels should always consider whether there are exceptional reasons why the patient should not be discharged.

38.23 In all cases, hospital managers have discretion to discharge patients even if the criteria for continued detention or a CTO are met. Managers' panels should always consider whether there are other reasons why the patient should be discharged despite the answers to the questions set out above; regard should be had to the principle of least restrictive option and maximising independence (see paragraphs 1.2–1.6).

Procedure for reviewing detention or a CTO

38.24 The Act does not define the procedure for reviewing a patient's detention **4–201** or a CTO. However, the exercise of this power is subject to the general law and to public law duties that arise from it. Hospital managers' conduct of reviews must satisfy the fundamental legal requirements of fairness, reasonableness and lawfulness. Hospital managers' panels should:

- adopt and apply a procedure which is fair and reasonable

- not make irrational decisions—that is, decisions which no managers' panel, properly directing itself as to the law and on the available information, could have made, and

- not act unlawfully—that is, contrary to the provisions of the Act and any other legislation (including the Human Rights Act 1998 (HRA) and the Equality Act 2010—for further details see chapter 3).

38.25 Hospital managers should have a process in place that seeks to involve the patient, their nearest relative and, if different, carer, including at the hearing, and in doing so, should have regard to the empowerment and involvement principle. This should include offering the patient information and advice on the review process, supporting them to fully participate and ensuring that, wherever practicable, hearings are scheduled in consultation with the patient so that any representative of the patient and others supporting them may attend. Patients and their representatives should be given reasonable notice of when a hearing will take place and arrangements put in place to enable them to be fully involved.

Conduct of reviews where detention or CTO is contested

38.26 Reviews should be conducted in such a way as to ensure that the case for **4–202** continuing the patient's detention or CTO is properly considered against the questions set out above and in the light of all the relevant evidence. This means that managers' panels need to have before them sufficient information about the patient's past history of care and treatment, and details of any future plans. The main source of this is likely to be the patient's documentation and care plan under the care programme approach (CPA) (or its equivalent) (see paragraphs 34.13–34.16). It is essential that panels are fully informed about any history of violence or self-harm and that a recent risk assessment and/or risk management plan is provided to the panel.

38.27 Hospital managers should ensure that mechanisms are in place so that, in advance of the hearing, managers' panels are provided with written reports from the patient's responsible clinician and from other key individuals directly involved in the patient's care as appropriate, such as the patient's care co-ordinator, named nurse, social worker, occupational therapist or clinical psychologist.

38.28 The patient should be provided with copies of the reports as soon as they are available, unless (in the light of any recommendation made by their authors) panels are of the opinion that disclosing the information would be likely to cause serious harm to the physical or mental health of the patient or any other individual. The patient's legal or other representative (such as their donee or deputy), including their IMHA, and, if the patient agrees, their nearest relative and, if different, carer should receive copies of these reports.

38.29 Reports should be provided in good time so that patients and their representatives can consider them and, where relevant, draw the panel's attention to any apparent inaccuracies. Any decision to withhold a report (in whole or part) should be recorded, with reasons.

38.30 The nearest relative should normally be informed when managers' panels are to consider a patient's case, unless the patient objects, subject to the normal considerations about involving nearest relatives (see paragraphs 4.31–4.36).

38.31 Panels should be prepared to consider the views of the patient's relatives and carers, and other people who know the patient well, either at the patient's request or where such people offer their views on their own initiative. Carers and any other relevant people may be invited to put their views to the managers' panel in person or in writing. If the patient objects to this, a suitable member of the professional care team should be asked to include the person's views in their report.

38.32 The report submitted by the responsible clinician should be in a similar format to those provided for Tribunals and cover the history of the patient's care and treatment and details of their care plan, including all risk assessments. Where the review is being held because the responsible clinician has made a report under section 20, 20A or 21B renewing detention or extending the CTO, panels should also have a copy of the report itself before them. This should be supplemented by a record of the consultation undertaken by the responsible clinician in accordance with those sections before making the report. The written reports should be considered by the panel alongside documentation compiled under the CPA (or its equivalent).

38.33 Where relevant, panels should also have in front of them any order made by the responsible clinician under section 25 barring a patient's discharge by their nearest relative.

38.34 The procedure for the conduct of any hearing is for managers' panels themselves to decide, but generally it needs to balance informality against the rigour demanded by the importance of the task, as this promotes the empowerment and involvement principle (see paragraphs 1.7–1.12). Key points are:

- the patient should be given a full opportunity, and any necessary help, eg from an IMHA, to explain why they should no longer be detained or on a CTO

- the patient should be allowed to be accompanied by a representative of their own choosing to help in putting their point of view to the panel. If the patient lacks capacity to put their point of view, their deputy, attorney or other representative of their choosing should be allowed to represent them

- the patient should also be allowed to have a relative, friend, carer, deputy, attorney or advocate attend to support them, and

- the responsible clinician and other professionals should be asked to give their views on whether the patient's continued detention or a CTO is justified and to explain the grounds on which those views are based.

38.35 It is for hospital managers themselves to decide where hearings should take place, but that decisions should take into account what is in the best interests of the patient. For CTO patients, and patients currently on leave of absence from hospital, the hospital itself may not be the most convenient or acceptable place for the patient. Hospital managers should be prepared to consider whether there are more appropriate locations it would be feasible to use.

38.36 The patient and the other people giving views to the panel should, if the patient wishes, be able to hear each other's statements to the panel and to put questions to each other, unless the panel believes that would be likely to cause serious harm to the physical or mental health of the patient or any other individual. Unless, exceptionally, it is considered too unsafe, patients should always be offered the opportunity of speaking to the panel alone (with or without their representative and anyone else they have asked to attend to support them at the hearing).

38.37 Member of managers' panels will not normally be qualified to form clinical assessments of their own. They should give full weight to all the evidence in relation to the patient's care. If there is a divergence of views among the professionals about whether the patient meets the clinical grounds for continued detention or CTO, managers' panels should reach an independent judgement based on the evidence that they hear. Regard should be had to the least restrictive option and maximising independence principle (see paragraphs 1.2–1.6). In some cases, it might be necessary to consider adjourning to seek further medical or other professional advice.

38.38 In considering the questions set out earlier in this chapter and in the light of them deciding whether or not to discharge the patient from detention, managers' panels need to consider very carefully the implications for the patient's subsequent care. Before a managers' panel considers a case, the responsible clinician, in consultation with the multi-disciplinary team, should have considered what services and other arrangements might be put in place for the patient if discharged and whether those arrangements would be sufficient to make it no longer necessary to continue detention or the CTO (as the case may be).

38.39 The presence or absence of adequate community care arrangements, including a deprivation of liberty authorisation or Court of Protection order may be critical in deciding whether continued detention (in particular) is necessary. If managers' panels believe they have not been provided with sufficient information about arrangements that could be made were the patient discharged, they should consider adjourning and request further information.

38.40 If panels conclude that the patient ought to be discharged, but practical steps to put after-care in place (chapter 33), or obtain a deprivation of liberty authorisation or a Court of Protection order, need to be taken first, they may adjourn the panel for a brief period to enable that to happen before formally discharging the patient. Professionals should work together to minimise the time it takes to do this.

Uncontested renewals

4–203   38.41 If a patient's detention is renewed or their CTO is extended by their responsible clinician, the hospital managers must always decide whether the patient should be discharged anyway, even if the patient has indicated that they do not wish to challenge the renewal or extension. This applies in all cases, but particularly where the patient lacks capacity.

38.42 Hospital mangers and managers' panels should apply as much rigour to considering uncontested cases as to contested ones to ensure that the least restrictive option and maximising independence principle is being applied and those decisions are only being made on the basis of the statutory criteria.

38.43 It is good practice to follow the same procedures to conduct reviews in uncontested cases as in contested cases. If hospital managers decide to adopt a different procedure (eg a paper based review) in a particular uncontested case this should be documented with the reasons for this recorded.

38.44 Where a different procedure is used patients should be offered the opportunity to be interviewed by at least one member of the managers' panel considering their case.

38.45 Hospital managers may consider the case based on the papers, if they wish (sometimes referred to as a 'paper review'). They should hold a full hearing if they have reason to suspect that the patient may, in fact, want to contest, or there are prima facie grounds to think that the statutory grounds to renew detention or extend the CTO are not met. This is particularly important if the patient lacks capacity. The fact that patients have not said they object to the renewal or extension should not be taken as evidence that they agree with it, or that it is the correct decision.

38.46 In deciding whether or not to review the case on the papers, hospital managers should consider if previous reviews during the current period of compulsory powers have been 'paper reviews'.

DECISIONS

4–204   38.47 Hospital managers have a common law duty to give reasons for their decisions. The decisions of managers' panels, and the reasons for them, should be fully recorded at the end of each review. The decision should be communicated as soon as practicable, both orally and in writing, to the patient and their representative, to the nearest relative and, if different, carer (where relevant), and to the professionals concerned.

38.48 If the patient is not to be discharged, where practicable at least one member of the panel should offer to see the patient (or their representative) to explain in person the reasons for the decision. The formal record of the decision and reasons should be shared with the patient, and copies of the papers relating to the review should be kept in the patient's notes.

38.49 Following the hearing, hospital managers should ensure that patients are offered an opportunity to discuss the hearing and informed of their rights to be considered for discharge by the Tribunal (paragraphs 4.21–4.24).

NOT HOLDING A REVIEW BEFORE DETENTION EXPIRES

38.50 If a responsible clinician or the hospital manager, as appropriate, does not **4–205** hold a review before the period of detention or CTO expires, this should be considered a very serious matter that should be urgently reviewed (see paragraphs 32.10). The hospital managers should have processes in place to ensure that this does not happen. The reasons for the review not having been taken place and the actions put in place to stop this happening again should be fully documented.

40. INFORMATION FOR VICTIMS

Why read this chapter?

40.1 This chapter provides information about the rights of victims of serious **4–206** violent and sexual offences with regard to a part 3 patient's (mentally disordered offender) treatment and discharge. Under the Domestic Violence, Crime and Victims Act 2004, and the Mental Health Act (the Act) victims of serious violent and sexual offences have the right to receive certain information about key stages in a part 3 patient's progress and treatment. Victims may also engage with the Victim Contact Scheme (VCS). This chapter provides further guidance about the statutory rights of victims to information and the obligations placed on Secretaries of State for Justice and Health and professionals with regard to victims. It also provides guidance on the Victims' Code.

THE VICTIM CONTACT SCHEME (VCS) AND THE VICTIMS' CODE

40.2 The concerns of victims must be given appropriate weight and fully con- **4–207** sidered by staff responsible for the treatment of part 3 patients. The offence may have been committed by someone with a mental disorder, but the impact on the victim will be the same as if the part 3 patient had been well. Victims' concerns and fears, including those of bereaved victims, must be given appropriate weight and consideration at all key points of the part 3 patient's treatment, including community leave and discharge.

40.3 Under the Domestic Violence, Crime and Victims Act 2004 (DVCVA), where the part 3 patient was sentenced on or after 1 July 2005, victims of serious violent and sexual offences have the right to information from the National Probation Service (NPS) under the VCS. Under the VCS, these victims ('statutory victims') have a right to be informed of key developments in the part 3 patient's progress and to make representations about conditions that should be in place on discharge.

40.4 The Code of Practice for Victims of Crime[61] ('the Victims' Code') sets out the information, support and services, that victims of relevant crimes can expect to receive from criminal justice agencies in England and Wales. The Victims' Code also summarises the information victims are entitled to under the VCS, as set out in the DVCVA 2004.

40.5 The Victims' Code and the VCS apply to victims in respect of restricted and unrestricted part 3 patients. Where victims of part 3 restricted patients do not fall within the scope of the DVCVA 2004 for statutory contact under the VCS (ie non-statutory victims), it is good practice for the National Probation

---

[61] The Code of Practice for Victims of Crime. Ministry of Justice. 2013. https://www.gov.uk/government/publications/the-code-of-practice-for-victims-of-crime.

Service (NPS) to consider providing VCS services to any victim of a restricted patient who requests information. Examples include:

- where the conviction occurred prior to the DVCVA 2004, but the victim has now made contact
- the victim of a non-qualifying offence or sentence length (for prisoners transferred under sections 47 who are subject to restriction directions made under section 49) where the victim has expressed concerns about their safety, or
- to the victims of co-defendants convicted in connection with the same incident.

40.6 Once the discretion has been exercised to offer such a non-statutory victim contact under the VCS, they should be offered the same service as statutory victims. This means that, once the NPS has decided to offer the VCS to these non-statutory victims, they should be assigned a victim liaison officer (VLO), provided with the opportunity to make representations about discharge conditions, and provided with information which the NPS considers to be appropriate in all the circumstances of the case, in the same way as statutory victims.

40.7 Each provider organisation should have a nominated individual who is responsible for understanding the Victims Code, VCS, promoting the rights of victims and developing, overseeing and reporting on policy and initiatives in the organisation to support all victims (including those of restricted and unrestricted patients). Details of who this individual is should be available so that victims, professionals and patients can identify them and obtain the required information and, if required, raise any concerns or complaints.

THE NPS VICTIM CONTACT SCHEME

Specified offences

4–208   40.8 For relevant offences committed on or after 1 July 2005, the police or joint police and Crown Prosecution Service Witness Care Unit should send details of statutory victims to the appropriate NPS Victim Liaison Unit (VLU). The VLU should offer victims the opportunity to engage with the VCS if the part 3 patient is:

- convicted of a specified sexual or violent offence and made the subject of a hospital order with a restriction order (section 37 and section 41 of the Act)
- found unfit to plead in respect of a specified sexual or violent offence, but has committed and been charged with the offence
- found not guilty by reason of insanity under the Criminal Procedure (Insanity) Act 1964 in respect of a specified sexual or violent offence, and made subject to a hospital order with special restrictions (section 37 and section 41 of the Act)
- convicted of a specified sexual or violent offence and then made the subject of a hospital direction and limitation direction (section 45A and section 45B of the Act), or

- sentenced to 12 months imprisonment or more for a specified sexual or violent offence, and transferred to hospital under a transfer direction and restriction direction (section 47 and section 49 of the Act).

40.9 For the purpose of this chapter, 'relevant offences', or 'specified offences', are those set out in section 45(2) of the DVCVA 2004:

- murder or an offence specified in Schedule 15 to the Criminal Justice Act 2003[62]

- an offence in respect of which the patient is subject to the notification requirements of part 2 of the Sexual Offences Act 2003,[63] or

- an offence against a child within the meaning of part 2 of the Criminal Justice and Court Services Act 2000.[64]

The NPS Victim Contact Scheme (restricted patients)

40.10 Under the VCS, victims must, as a minimum, be: **4–209**

- offered the opportunity to engage with the VCS by the VLU

- assigned a VLO (for restricted patients and prisoners transferred under section 47 who are subject to restriction directions made under section 49 who have not passed their licence expiry date)

- offered the right to make representations to whoever is responsible for making the decision on the patient's discharge, either the Secretary of State for Justice or the Tribunal, about the patient's discharge conditions—victims typically request geographic exclusion zones or 'no contact' conditions

- informed of discharge conditions which relate to them, and

- informed about any other key information about the patient's progress, which it is appropriate to share in all the circumstances of the case.

40.11 Victims can choose to opt in or out of the VCS at any time. If a victim was not identified at the time of sentencing or did not take up contact when it was offered, they may contact or be referred to the VLU at any time during the patient's treatment and rehabilitation. From 22 April 2014 victims of restricted part 3 patients, who have opted in to the VCS, will be told if permission for community leave, whether escorted or unescorted, is granted by the Mental Health Casework Section (MHCS) of the Ministry of Justice, unless there are exceptional reasons why they should not be told. This followed a Ministerial commitment and means that the scope of information provided to victims of part 3 patients granted leave from the detaining authority is the same as the information given to victims

---

[62] The full list of offences can be found at: http://www.legislation.gov.uk/ukpga/2003/44/schedule/15. This list can change as new offences can be added. Practitioners can contact the Victims Team in the Ministry of Justice at VCSpolicy@noms.gsi.gov.uk if they wish to check if a new offence has been included in the Schedule.

[63] Sexual Offences Act 2003. http://www.legislation.gov.uk/ukpga/2003/42/contents.

[64] A full list of offences can be found at Schedule 4 of the Criminal Justice and Court Services Act 2000: http://webarchive.nationalarchives.gov.uk/20100416132449/http://opsi.gov.uk/acts/acts2000/ukpga_20000043_en_10

of prisoners who are granted temporary licence from prison (eg Release on Temporary Licence (ROTL) and Home Detention Curfew (HDC)).

40.12 Information about restricted patients will be provided by the VLO to the victim whereas information about unrestricted patients will come directly to the victim from hospital managers or clinicians once any relevant licence period has expired.

MENTAL HEALTH CASEWORK SECTION REQUIREMENTS

Victims of part 3 restricted patients

4–210   40.13 The MHCS will, through the VLO, contact victims who are in the VCS. Information will be shared on certain key stages of the patient's progress, including:

- when the patient is transferred to hospital thus becoming a restricted patient
- if the prisoner is transferred to hospital under section 47 of the Act
- when the Secretary of State for Justice is considering a proposal for discharge, to request representations from the victim
- if the Secretary of State for Justice decides to discharge the patient
- the conditions of discharge relating to the victim or their family
- any variation of conditions of discharge relating to the victim or their family
- if the restricted patient is recalled for further treatment under the Act
- if the part 3 patient is absolutely discharged, resulting in the cessation of conditions and the removal of the part 3 patient's liability to be recalled to hospital
- when the patient's restrictions are lifted or expire
- if a patient previously found unfit to plead is remitted back to court to continue legal proceedings
- if a patient is to be remitted to prison
- if the MHCS has approved or rescinded escorted or unescorted leave.

40.14 The MHCS may pass on additional information, for example about a hospital transfer, to VLOs or directly to the victim (in the small number of cases where the victim is in direct contact with MHCS). Similarly the probation VLO may provide victims with more information only if appropriate in all the circumstances of the case, and whilst being mindful of patient confidentiality including in respect of confidential medical information.

40.15 When considering requests for community leave or transfer, MHCS will take into account victim concerns. MHCS also expects that, where the responsible clinician knows of VLO involvement, he or she will contact them to ensure that victim concerns are addressed in any application. This can include ensuring patients are not allowed leave or to be placed in a hospital in the vicinity of the victim.

DUTIES OF HOSPITALS IN RESPECT OF UNRESTRICTED PATIENTS

Unrestricted part 3 patients

40.16 The VLU should offer victims the opportunity to engage with the VCS if **4–211** the part 3 patient has been made subject to a hospital order without a restriction order (section 37 of the Act). Victims who want to engage with the VCS will have their details passed to the hospital. The hospital manager or responsible clinician then becomes responsible for providing information to the victim.

40.17 Where a part 3 patient is transferred from prison to hospital with a restriction order (section 47 and section 49 of the Act), or is transferred without a restriction order as the custodial part of their sentence was about to end (ie they are a 'notional section 37 patient'), they will be treated as an unrestricted patient when they reach their sentence end date (see paragraphs 22.75-22.77 on 'Notional section 37 patients'). At this time, if there is a victim identified in the NPS VCS, the VLU will send the victim's details to the hospital. The hospital manager or responsible clinician then becomes responsible for providing information to the victim. The VLO should continue to provide updates to the victim until the end of the licence period, even if the patient remains in hospital, and, in particular if they are released on licence.

40.18 The probation VLO will pass details of victims who wish to receive information to the hospital, and liaison should then take place between the hospital and the victim. The VLO has no further role so clinical teams and hospital managers should be fully aware of their obligations with respect to the victims of unrestricted patients.

40.19 Hospital managers must ensure that the statutory minimum of information is communicated to victims. Statutory information consists of:

- whether the patient is to be discharged
- whether a community treatment order (CTO) is to be made, including allowing the victim to make representations about the conditions attached to the CTO
- what conditions of the CTO relate to the victim
- when the CTO ceases
- when authority to detain the patient expires
- when the part 3 patient is discharged, including allowing the victim to make representations about discharge conditions, and
- what conditions of discharge relate to the victim, and when these cease.

The decision about whether to pass more information to victims than the statutory minimum will be for the relevant hospital manager to decide. The information that can be provided to a victim will be limited if it relates to medical treatment, as this information will be confidential medical information. The usual rules under the Data Protection Act 2004 and guidance in the Code on confidentiality apply (see chapter 10 on confidentiality and information sharing).

Information for victims of part 3 unrestricted patients

4–212   40.20 The Mental Health Act 20075 included amendments to the DVCVA 2004 to the extent that victims of part 3 unrestricted patients should be provided with the same level of information as restricted patients in terms of consideration for discharge and the victim's right to make representations with regard to discharge conditions and to be informed of these conditions.

ADDITIONAL SUPPORT FOR VICTIMS WHO ARE FAMILY, CARERS OR FRIENDS

4–213   40.21 Professionals should be particularly mindful that some victims of mental disordered patients may also be the patient's family member, carer, friend, or their nearest relative, and may wish to maintain contact with the patient, including visiting them in hospital. The guidance in relation to enabling contact and visits should be applied equally to these individuals as to other family, friends and carers (see chapter 11). Professionals may need to balance the needs and rights of victims who are also family, friends or carers with their needs and rights as victims and/or to reduce the risk of harm arising from contact with the patient. Such victims may require additional support in order for them to maintain contact, and keep them safe, especially if the victim is a child or young person, lacks capacity or has a learning disability or autism.

40.22 Hospital managers must ensure that they fulfil the terms specified in the European directive on minimum standards on rights, support and protection of victims of crime in any of their interactions with victims of a part 3 patient.6

40.23 There may be a family member, friend and carer who is a victim or for other reasons does not wish to maintain contact or visit, despite a part 3 patient's wish for them to do so. The rights of the individual victim should be protected and maintained in this and, if appropriate, this should be explained to the patient (see for example paragraph 4.27 on withholding patient correspondence).

PART 5

HUMAN RIGHTS ACT 1998

(1998 c.42)

An Act to give further effect to rights and freedoms guaranteed under the **5–001**
European Convention on Human Rights; to make provision with respect to
holders of certain judicial offices who become judges of the European
Court of Human Rights; and for connected purposes.

[9th November 1998]

$$* \quad * \quad * \quad *$$

GENERAL NOTE

This Part examines the Human Rights Act 1998 as it applies to the care and treatment of
mentally disordered people.

Introduction

The Second World War and its associated horrors caused an upsurge in international con- **5–002**
cern for human rights. The European Convention for the Protection of Human Rights and
Fundamental Freedoms, commonly known as the European Convention on Human Rights
("the Convention"), emerged out of that concern. It was concluded under the auspices of
the Council of Europe in 1950, was ratified by the UK in 1951 and entered into force in
1953. In *Pretty v United Kingdom* (2002) 35 E.H.R.R. 1, para.65, the European Court of
Human Rights said that the "very essence of the Convention is respect for human dignity
and human freedom".

The Commission and the Court

One of the most distinctive features of the Convention has been the role played by two **5–003**
organs, the European Commission on Human Rights ("the Commission") and the
European Court on Human Rights ("the Court"), in building up a substantial body of
case law in the course of deciding petitions brought by individuals. In 1998 the
Commission was abolished and there are now only two European institutions, the Court
(which can sit in Chambers and in a Grand Chamber) and the Committee of Ministers of
the Council of Europe, that administer the Convention. Under art.35 of the Convention,
the Court will only deal with an application after all domestic remedies have been
exhausted.

In exceptional circumstances, it is possible for a non-governmental organisation to lodge
an application with the Court on behalf of a victim (*Centre for Legal Resources on behalf of
Valentin Campeanu v Romania,* App.No. 47848/08).

Human Rights Act 1998

This Act is one of the most significant pieces of constitutional legislation enacted in the **5–004**
UK. It incorporates provisions from the Convention into UK law. The relevant provisions
of the Convention are reproduced in Sch.1 to the Act, which is set out below. The Act is
ultimately subject to the sovereignty of Parliament, in that:

1. It does not provide the courts with a power to strike down primary legislation that is inconsistent with the Convention.

2. It leaves Parliament free, if it chooses to do so, to enact and maintain legislation that is incompatible with the Convention.

3. The Act is not entrenched against repeal.

Within these constraints, the Act attempts to achieve the Government's aim to "bring rights home" (*Rights Brought Home: the Human Rights Bill*, Cm.3782 (1997)) by operating through three mechanisms:

1. Courts and tribunals are required to construe all legislation (past and future) "so far as it is possible to do so . . . in a way which is compatible with Convention rights" (s.3). When doing so the court or tribunal must take account of the case law of the Court and the Commission. This requirement means that domestic courts must search for a construction that would prevent the making of a "declaration of incompatibility": see point 3, below.

2. All public authorities, including all courts and tribunals, and private providers who are exercising "functions of a public nature", are required to act in accordance with the Convention, within the scope permitted by primary legislation (s.6) and to have regard to European jurisprudence (s.2). An "act" includes a failure to act (s.6(6)). Approved mental health professionals, responsible clinicians, approved clinicians and nurses are public authorities for the purposes of the Convention when they perform functions under the Mental Health Act. Decisions made by a private hospital relating to the care or treatment of detained patients are decisions of a public nature. The hospital therefore becomes a public authority for the purposes of s.6 and its decisions are susceptible to judicial review (*R. (on the application of A) v Partnership in Care Ltd* [2002] EWHC 529; [2002] 1 W.L.R. 261).

3. The higher courts are able to make a "declaration of incompatibility" in respect of a provision of primary legislation, which the court considers to be incompatible with a Convention right (s.4). Such a declaration does not affect the validity, continued operation or enforcement of the provision in respect of which it is made (s.4(6)(a)) but it may lead to the correction of the legislation by Parliament making a "remedial order" which has the effect of bypassing the full legislative process (s.10).

Where it is not possible to interpret subordinate legislation so as to be compatible with the Convention, the courts have power to disapply it unless the primary legislation prevents removal of the incompatibility (s.4(4)(b)).

SCHEDULE 1

THE ARTICLES

PART I

THE CONVENTION

RIGHTS AND FREEDOMS

ARTICLE 2

RIGHT TO LIFE

1. Everyone's right to life shall be protected by law. No one shall be deprived of his life intentionally **5–005** save in the execution of a sentence of a court following his conviction of a crime for which this penalty is provided by law.

2. Deprivation of life shall not be regarded as inflicted in contravention of this Article when it results from the use of force which is no more than absolutely necessary:

(a) in defence of any person from unlawful violence;

(b) in order to effect a lawful arrest or to prevent the escape of a person lawfully detained;

(c) in action lawfully taken for the purpose of quelling a riot or insurrection.

GENERAL NOTE

The European Court of Human Rights (the Court) has stated that this article "ranks as **5–006** one of the most fundamental provisions in the Convention and, together with Article 3, enshrines one of the basic values of the democratic societies making up the Council of Europe" (*Cakici v Turkey* (2001) 31 E.H.R.R. 5 para.86). The object and purpose of the Convention requires that this Article be interpreted and applied so as to make its safeguards practical and effective (*McCann v United Kingdom* (1996) 21 E.H.R.R. 97, paras 146–147).

This article is unconcerned with issues to do with the quality of living or what a person chooses to do with his or her life. It cannot be interpreted as conferring the diametrically opposite right, namely a right to die; nor can it create a right to self-determination in the sense of conferring on an individual the entitlement to choose death rather than life (*Pretty v United Kingdom* (2002) 35 E.H.R.R. 1 para.39). However, the right of an individual to decide how and when to end his life is one aspect of the right to respect for private life within the meaning of art.8: see *Haas v Switzerland* (2011) 53 E.H.R.R. 33, noted under art.8 under "private life".

In *Osman v United Kingdom* (2000) 29 E.H.R.R. 245 para.115, the Court said that it was common ground that the State's obligation under this article:

"extends beyond its primary duty to secure the right to life by putting in place effective criminal law provisions to deter the commission of offences against the person backed up by law-enforcement machinery for the prevention, suppression and sanctioning of such provisions. It is thus accepted by those appearing before the Court that Article 2 of the Convention may also imply in certain well-defined circumstances a positive obligation on the authorities to take preventive operational measures to protect an individual whose life is at risk from the criminal acts of another individual".

The Court said that for this positive obligation to be breached it must be established to the Court's satisfaction "that the authorities knew or ought to have known at the time of the existence of a real and immediate risk to the life of an identified individual or individuals from criminal acts of a third party and that they failed to take measures within the scope of their powers which, judged reasonably, might have been expected to take to avoid that risk" (para.116). Note, however, that in *Sarjantson v The Chief Constable of Humberside Police* [2013] EWCA Civ 1252, the Court of Appeal reviewed subsequent Strasbourg authorities and held that the scope of this article is not limited to circumstances where there is a risk to *identified* individuals. In *Osman*, the Court also said that, given the reality of resource allocation and the operational choices that have to be made, not every claimed risk to life can entail for the authorities a Convention requirement to take operational measures to prevent the risk from materialising and that the positive obligation "must be interpreted in a way which does not impose an impossible or disproportionate burden on the authorities" (para.116). The positive obligation applies in the public-health sphere (*Dodov v Bulgaria* (2008) 47 E.H.R.R. 41 para.80). However, "where a Contracting State had made adequate provision for securing high professional standards among health professionals and the protection of the lives of patients, it cannot accept that matters such as error of judgment on the part of a health professional or negligent co-ordination among health professionals in the treatment of a particular patient are sufficient of themselves to call a Contracting State to account from the standpoint of its positive obligations under art.2 of the Convention to protect life" (*Powell v UK* (2000) 30 E.H.R.R. CD 362).

5–007 The *Osman* case places professionals who are performing functions under the Mental Health Act under a positive obligation to take appropriate preventative measures in respect of patients whom they know (or ought to have known) to be so dangerous as to be a threat to the lives of identified others. A positive obligation to save the life of a detained patient who is on hunger strike could also arise (see *X v Germany*, noted in art.3 under "degrading"). The *Osman* principle has been extended to self harm by people for whose welfare the state is responsible (*Keenan v United Kingdom* (2001) 33 E.H.R.R. 38; also see *Renolde v France* [2008] M.H.L.R. 331). The application of the positive obligation to hospital patients who are detained under the Mental Health Act was examined by the House of Lords in *Savage v South Essex Partnership NHS Foundation Trust* [2008] UKHL 74; [2009] 1 All E.R. 1053 where it was held that it was not necessary for a claimant alleging a breach of this article to establish either gross negligence or anything more serious. The obligations of health authorities under this article were summarised by Lord Rodger at paras 68 to 72 of his speech:

"In terms of Art 2, health authorities are under an over-arching obligation to protect the lives of patients in their hospitals. In order to fulfil that obligation, and depending on the circumstances, they may require to fulfil a number of complementary obligations.

In the first place, the duty to protect the lives of patients requires health authorities to ensure that the hospitals for which they are responsible employ competent staff and that they are trained to a high professional standard. In addition, the authorities must ensure that the hospitals adopt systems of work which will protect the lives of patients. Failure to perform these general obligations may result in a violation of Art 2. If, for example, a health authority fails to ensure that a hospital puts in place a proper system for supervising mentally ill patients and, as a result, a patient is able to commit suicide, the health authority will have violated the patient's right to life under Art 2.

Even though a health authority employed competent staff and ensured that they were trained to a high professional standard, a doctor, for example, might still treat a patient negligently and the patient might die as a result. In that situation, there would be no violation of Art 2 since the health authority would have done all that the article required of it to protect the patient's life. Nevertheless, the doctor would be personally liable in damages for the death and the health authority would be vicariously liable for her negligence. This is the situation envisaged by *Powell* [*Powell v United Kingdom* (2000) 30 E.H.R.R.

CD 362].

The same approach would apply if a mental hospital had established an appropriate system for supervising patients and all that happened was that, on a particular occasion, a nurse negligently left his post and a patient took the opportunity to commit suicide. There would be no violation of any obligation under Art 2, since the health authority would have done all that the article required of it. But, again, the nurse would be personally liable in damages for the death and the health authority would be vicariously liable too. Again, this is just an application of *Powell*.

Finally, Art 2 imposes a further 'operational' obligation on health authorities and their hospital staff. This obligation is distinct from, and additional to, the authorities' more general obligations. The operational obligation arises only if members of staff know or ought to know that a particular patient presents a 'real and immediate' risk of suicide. In these circumstances Art 2 requires them to do all that can reasonably be expected to prevent the patient from committing suicide. If they fail to do this, not only will they and the health authorities be liable in negligence, but there will also be a violation of the operational obligation under art 2 to protect the patient's life. This is comparable to the position in *Osman* and *Keenan*. As the present case shows, if no other remedy is available, proceedings for an alleged breach of the obligation can be taken under the Human Rights Act 1998." [NB Identifying whether a person is at "real and immediate" risk of suicide is problematic: see G. Szmukler et al., "'Rabone' and four unresolved problems in mental health law", *The Psychiatrist* (2013), 37, 297–301.]

In *Rabone v Pennine Care NHS Trust* [2012] UKSC 2; [2012] 2 All E.R. 381, the Supreme Court held that the "operational obligation" identified in *Savage* also applied to an informal patient in a situation where the patient was admitted to hospital as a real suicide risk, was extremely vulnerable and the NHS Trust had assumed responsibility for her; she was under its control. If she had tried to leave the hospital voluntarily, the Trust could and should have sought her detention under the 1983 Act as a means of preventing her leaving. The difference between the patient's position and that of a hypothetical detained psychiatric patient was one of form not substance.

In both *Savage* and *Rabone*, the court identified close relatives of the patients as victims for the purposes of s.7(7) of the 1998 Act and awarded them damages of £10,000 (*Savage* [2012] EWHC 865 (QB)) and £5000 *(Rabone)* for non-pecuniary loss.

There is authority for the proposition that this article would only be engaged by failure of process or systemic failures on the part of a hospital and would not be engaged by one-off or "casual" acts by hospital staff: see *Powell v UK*, above, *Savage v South Essex NHS Trust*, above at paras 45 and 5758 per Lord Rodger and para.91 per Lady Hale, and *Rabone v Pennine Care NHS Trust*, above, at paras 19 and 119 per Lord Dyson and Lord Mance.

The provision of care to a detainee who is at risk of self harm could also give rise to issues under art.8.

The procedural element contained in this article:

5–008

"imposes the minimum requirement that where a state or its agents potentially bear responsibility for loss of life the events in question should be subject to an effective investigation or scrutiny which enables the facts to become known to the public, and in particular to the relatives of any victim" (*Taylor, Campton and Gibson families v United Kingdom (Admissibility)* (1994) 18 E.H.R.R. CD15; also see *McCann v United Kingdom* (1996) 21 E.H.R.R. 97, para.161).

Whatever form of investigation is employed, the authorities must act of their own motion, once the matter has come to their attention. They cannot leave it to the initiative of the next of kin either to lodge a formal complaint or to take responsibility for the conduct of any investigative procedures (*Edwards v United Kingdom* (2002) 35 E.H.R.R. 19, para.69). The Court has said that the investigation must be independent, effective, and reasonably prompt, must have a sufficient element of public scrutiny, and the next of kin must be involved to the appropriate extent (*Jordan v United Kingdom* (2003) 37 E.H.R.R. 2 paras 106 to 109). In the *Edwards* case, the Court said at para.105:

"The essential purpose of such investigation is to secure the effective implementation of the domestic laws which protect the right to life and, in those cases involving State agents or bodies, to ensure accountability for deaths occurring under their responsibility. What form of investigation will achieve those purposes may vary in different circumstances".

In *R. (on the application of Antoniou) v Central and North West London NHS Foundation Trust* [2013] EWHC 3055 (Admin); [2014] M.H.L.R. 212, the Divisional Court held that where a detained patient takes their own life, the procedural obligation imposed by this article is fulfilled by a coroner's inquest and that, unlike prison or police station deaths, there is no additional requirement for an immediate and independent investigation prior to the inquest.

Paragraph 1

5–009   EVERYONE'S LIFE SHALL BE PROTECTED BY LAW.   Apart from the law relating to abortion, the extent to which this article can be invoked to protect the life of an unborn child is uncertain: see the note on "Human Rights Act 1998" under s.3 of the Act.

INTENTIONALLY.   This word should be given its natural and ordinary meaning, and applies only to cases where the purpose of the prohibited action is to cause death (*Re A (Children) (Conjoined Twins: Surgical Separation)* [2004] 4 All E.R. 961 CA; also see *Association X v United Kingdom* (1978) 14 D. & R. 31).

Paragraph 2

5–010   USE OF FORCE.   The force used must be strictly proportionate to the achievement of the permitted aims (*McKerr v United Kingdom* (2002) 34 E.H.R.R. 20 para.110). In *Saoud v France*, App.No.9375/02, October 9, 2007, the Court said that the authorities had a positive obligation to protect the health of persons who were in detention or police custody or who had just been arrested. A breach of this article was found in this case where an arrested person who suffered from schizophrenia and was very dangerous died from slow asphyxia after being held on the ground by the police for 35 minutes. The Court deplored the fact that no precise instructions had been issued to the police regarding this type of immobilisation technique.

ARTICLE 3

PROHIBITION OF TORTURE

No one shall be subjected to torture or to inhuman or degrading treatment or punishment.

GENERAL NOTE

5–011   In *Stanev v Bulgaria* (2012) 55 E.H.R.R.; [2012] M.H.L.R. 23 at paras 201 to 205, the Court summarised the approach that it takes to claims based on this article:

"Article 3 enshrines one of the most fundamental values of democratic society. It prohibits in absolute terms torture or inhuman or degrading treatment or punishment, irrespective of the circumstances and the victim's behaviour (see, among other authorities, *Kudła v. Poland* [GC], no. 30210/96, § 90, ECHR 2000-XI, and *Poltoratskiy v. Ukraine*, no. 38812/97, § 130, ECHR 2003-V).

Ill-treatment must attain a minimum level of severity if it is to fall within the scope of Article 3. The assessment of this minimum is, in the nature of things, relative; it depends on all the circumstances of the case, such as the nature and context of the treatment, the manner and method of its execution, its duration, its physical or mental effects and, in some instances, the sex, age and state of health of the victim (see *Kud?a*, cited above, § 91, and *Poltoratskiy*, cited above, § 131).

Treatment has been held by the Court to be "inhuman" because, inter alia, it was pre-meditated, was applied for hours at a stretch and caused either actual bodily injury or intense physical or mental suffering (see *Labita v. Italy* [GC], no. 26772/95, § 120, ECHR 2000-IV). Treatment has been considered "degrading" when it was such as to arouse in its victims feelings of fear, anguish and inferiority capable of humiliating and debasing them and possibly breaking their physical or moral resistance or driving them to act against their will or conscience (see *Jalloh v. Germany* [GC], no. 54810/00, § 68, ECHR 2006-IX). In this connection, the question whether such treatment was intended to humiliate or debase the victim is a factor to be taken into account, although the absence of any such purpose does not inevitably lead to a finding that there has been no violation of Article 3 (see *Peers v. Greece*, no. 28524/95, §§ 67, 68 and 74, ECHR 2001-III, and *Kalashnikov v. Russia*, no. 47095/99, § 95, ECHR 2002-VI).

The suffering and humiliation involved must in any event go beyond that inevitable element of suffering or humiliation connected with a given form of legitimate treatment or punishment. Measures depriving a person of his liberty may often involve such an element. Yet it cannot be said that deprivation of liberty in itself raises an issue under Article 3 of the Convention. Nevertheless, under that Article the State must ensure that a person is detained in conditions which are compatible with respect for his human dignity, that the manner and method of the execution of the measure do not subject him to distress or hardship of an intensity exceeding the unavoidable level of suffering inherent in detention and that, given the practical demands of imprisonment, his health and well-being are adequately secured by, among other things, providing him with the requisite medical assistance (see *Kudła*, cited above, §§ 92–94).

When assessing the conditions of a deprivation of liberty under Article 3 of the Convention, account has to be taken of their cumulative effects and the duration of the measure in question (see *Kalashnikov*, cited above, §§ 95 and 102; *Kehayov v. Bulgaria*, no. 41035/98, § 64, 18 January 2005; and *Iovchev v. Bulgaria*, no. 41211/98, § 127, 2 February 2006). In this connection an important factor to take into account, besides the material conditions, is the detention regime. In assessing whether a restrictive regime may amount to treatment contrary to Article 3 in a given case, regard must be had to the particular conditions, the stringency of the regime, its duration, the objective pursued and its effects on the person concerned (see *Kehayov*, cited above, § 65)."

Provided it is sufficiently real and immediate, a mere threat of conduct prohibited by this article may itself constitute a violation (*Campbell v Cosans v United Kingdom* (1982) 4 E.H.R.R. 293 para.26). In assessing evidence, the Court has adopted the standard of proof "beyond reasonable doubt". However, as applied by the Court, this term has an autonomous meaning. The role of the Court is not to rule on criminal guilt or civil liability, but on the responsibility of Contracting States under the Convention (*Mathew v Netherlands* (2006) 43 E.H.R.R. 23 para.156).

Although this article admits of no exceptions, logically the prohibition of inhuman and degrading treatment ought to have the same exceptions as those contained in art.2(2). The Court has acted on the assumption that this article is subject to such exceptions as long as any force used is strictly necessary and proportionate: see, for example, *RIVAS v France*, April 1, 2004, at paras 41, 42.

In *A v United Kingdom* (1999) 27 E.H.R.R. 611, the Court held that this article requires "States to take measures designed to ensure that individuals within their jurisdiction are not subjected to torture or inhuman or degrading treatment or punishment, including such ill-treatment administered by private individuals" (para.22). There is a particular need for states to take such measures in the context of psychiatric hospitals, where patients are typically in a position of inferiority and helplessness (*Wilkinson v United Kingdom* (1998) 26

E.H.R.R. CD131). A failure to take reasonably available measures which could have had a real prospect of altering the outcome or mitigating the harm is sufficient to engage the responsibility of the state (*E v United Kingdom* (2003) 36 E.H.R.R. 31 para.99). These measures "should provide effective protection, in particular, of children and other vulnerable persons and include reasonable steps to prevent ill-treatment of which the authorities had or ought to have had knowledge" (*Z v United Kingdom* (2002) 34 E.H.R.R. 3 para.73). Also see *ZH v Hungary* [2014] M.H.L.R. 1 at para.29, where the Court said that any "interference with the rights of persons belonging to particularly vulnerable groups—such as those with mental disorders—is required to be subject to strict scrutiny, and only very weighty reasons could justify any restriction". In *Dordevic v Croatia* [2013] M.H.L.R. 89, the Court held that the failure of the Croatian State to prevent the persistent harassment of a severely disabled young man was a breach of this article.

Where an individual raised an arguable claim that, in breach of this article, he had been seriously ill-treated by state agents, this article read with art.1 required by implication that there should be an effective official investigation (*Kucheruk v Ukraine* (2011) 52 E.H.R.R. 28, para.155). The investigation "should be capable of leading to the identification and punishment of those responsible" (*Assenov v Bulgaria* (1999) 28 E.H.R.R. 652, para.102). A failure to find state agents guilty of a crime of violence against a detainee under their control cannot absolve the state of its responsibilities under the Convention (*Afanasyev v Ukraine* (2006) 42 E.H.R.R. 52 para.64). In *M.S. v Croatia (No.2)*, February 19, 2015, the Court said at para.74 that a state's domestic legal system, and in particular the criminal law applicable in the circumstances of the case, must provide practical and effective protection of the rights guaranteed by this article.

The duration of the ill-treatment can be short. In *ZH v Metropolitan Police Commissioner* [2013] EWCA Civ 69; [2013] 3 All E.R. 113, the duration of the episode which constituted ill-treatment was 40 minutes.

In *O'Rourke v United Kingdom*, June 26, 2001, para.60, the Court said that "it is quite impossible by a simple definition to embrace all human conditions that will engage Article 3". The Court provided the following guidance in *Pretty v United Kingdom* (2002) 35 E.H.R.R. 1 at para.52:

"As regards the types of 'treatment' which falls within the scope of Article 3 of the Convention, the court's case law refers to 'ill-treatment' that attains a minimum level of severity and involves actual bodily injury or intense physical or mental suffering. Where treatment humiliates or debases an individual showing lack of respect for, or diminishing, his or her human dignity or arouses feelings of fear, anguish or inferiority capable of breaking an individual's moral and physical resistance, it may be characterised as degrading and also fall within the prohibition of Article 3. The suffering which flows from naturally occurring illnesses, physical or mental, may be covered by Article 3, where it is, or risks being, exacerbated by treatment, whether flowing from conditions of detention, expulsion or other measures, for which the authorities can be held responsible".

This paragraph was cited in *R.(on the application of S) v Secretary of State for the Home Department* [2011] EWHC 2120 (Admin) at paras 191,192 as support for the proposition that "in a sufficiently extreme case", the adverse effects of detention on an existing mental illness could breach this article.

In *Selmouni v France* (2000) 29 E.H.R.R. 403 at para.101, the Court said that it:

"has previously examined cases in which it concluded that there had been treatment which could only be described as torture. However, having regard to the fact that the Convention is a 'living instrument which must be interpreted in the light of present-day conditions', the Court considers that certain acts which were classified in the past as 'inhuman and degrading treatment' as opposed to 'torture' could be classified differently in future. It takes the view that the increasingly high standard being required in the area of the protection of human rights and fundamental liberties correspondingly and inevitably requires greater firmness in assessing breaches of the fundamental values in a democratic society".

This significant statement means that the concept of inhuman or degrading treatment will inevitably expand to encompass conduct that was previously outside the scope of this article. Note, however, that in *R. (on the application of DB) v Secretary of State for the Home Department* [2006] EWHC 659 (Admin) at para.45. Davis J. said that over-ready assertions of reliance on this article, "if not kept under proper restraint, can only operate to debase in the public perception what ought to be regarded as one of the most fundamental of rights enshrined in the Convention".

The assessment of whether a particular treatment or punishment is incompatible with the **5–012** standards of this article has, in the case of mentally ill persons, to take into consideration their vulnerability and their inability, in some cases, to complain coherently or at all about how they are being affected by any particular treatment (*Keenan v United Kingdom*, above, para.110). In *Keenan*, the Court said at para.112 that:

"in respect of a person deprived of his liberty, recourse to physical force which has not been made strictly necessary by his own conduct diminishes human dignity and is in principle an infringement of the right set out in Article 3. Similarly, treatment of a mentally ill person may be incompatible with the standards imposed by Article 3 in the protection of fundamental human dignity, even though that person may not be able, or capable of, pointing to any specific ill-effects".

Case law on this article indicates that medical treatment only engages the article if the free and informed consent of the patient has not been forthcoming (*X v Denmark* (1983) 32 D. & R. 282). The Court has been reluctant to categorise either psychiatric treatment (no matter how disagreeable (*Naumenko v Ukraine*, February 10, 2004)) or institutional conditions as "inhuman or degrading treatment". In *Herczegfalvy v Austria* (1993) 15 E.H.R.R. 437, the patient had been handcuffed to a security bed with a belt placed around his ankles. The Court, in holding that medical treatment could, in principle reach a level of severity sufficient to amount to "inhuman or degrading treatment" contrary to this article, said at paras 82, 83:

"The Court considers that the position of inferiority and powerlessness which is typical of patients confined in psychiatric hospitals calls for increased vigilance in reviewing whether the Convention has been complied with. While it is for the medical authorities to decide, on the basis of recognised rules of medical science, on the therapeutic methods to be used, if necessary by force, to preserve the physical and mental health of patients who are entirely incapable of deciding for themselves and for whom they are therefore responsible, such patients nevertheless remain under the protection of Article 3, the requirements of which permit no derogation . . . [H]owever, the evidence before the Court is not sufficient to disprove the Government's argument that, according to the psychiatric principles generally accepted as the time, medical necessity justified the treatment in issue".

Although these principles were advanced in relation to a patient who lacked capacity, in *Nevmerzhitsky v Ukraine* (2006) 43 E.H.R.R. 32, the Court applied them to a mentally capable applicant, who was not mentally ill, who complained that he had been force-fed while in criminal detention and that this had infringed this article. The Court held at para.94:

"[A] measure which is of therapeutic necessity from the point of view of established principles of medicine cannot in principle be regarded as inhuman or degrading. The same can be said about force-feeding that is aimed at saving the life of a particular detainee who consciously refuses to take food. The Convention organs must nevertheless satisfy themselves that the medical necessity has been convincingly shown to exist."

The *Bolam* test (see *Bolam v Friern Barnet Hospital* [1957] 1 W.L.R. 582) does not apply to the question of "medical necessity" under this article (*R. (on the application of N) v M and others* [2002] EWHC Admin 1911). The onus of justifying medical necessity is placed on the patient's approved clinician (*Bolam* above). This approach was approved by the Court of Appeal ([2002] EWCA Civ 1789; [2003] M.H.L.R. 157 at paras 17, 18) where the court said that the phrase "convincingly shown" is easily understood. Although the standard is a high one, it does not need "elaboration or further explanation". The factors that need to be addressed when forming a judgment as to whether the proposed treatment has been convincingly shown to be a medical necessity include:

"(a) how certain is it that the patient does suffer from a treatable mental disorder; (b) how serious a disorder is it; (c) how serious a risk is presented to others; (d) how likely is it that, if the patient does suffer from such a disorder, the proposed treatment will alleviate the condition; (e) how much alleviation is there likely to be; (f) how likely is it that the treatment will have adverse consequences for the patient; and (g) how severe may they be" (para.19).

5–013 The court rejected a submission that, in a case where there is a responsible body of opinion that a patient is not suffering from a treatable condition, that the treatment is not in the patient's best interests and is not medically necessary, then it cannot be convincingly shown that the treatment proposed is in the patient's best interests or medically necessary (para.29).

The conclusion from *Herczegfalvy* is that forcible measures inflicted upon either an incapacitated or a capacitated patient which are not a medical necessity may constitute inhuman or degrading treatment. Conversely, a denial of treatment which has been found to be a medical necessity could also be claimed to be a violation of this article (*D v United Kingdom* (1997) 24 E.H.R.R. 423). *Herczegfalvy* was applied in *Bures v Czech Republic* [2013] M.H.L.R. 126, where the Court said that "using restraints is a serious measure which must always be justified by preventing imminent harm to the patient or the surroundings and must be proportionate to such an aim" (para.96).

An admissibility decision of the Commission in *Grare v France* (1992) 15 E.H.R.R. CD 100, suggests that psychiatric treatment in the form of medication with unpleasant side-effects could involve a breach of this article if the side-effects were sufficiently serious: see O. Thorold "The Implications of the European Convention on Human Rights for United Kingdom Mental Health Legislation" [1996] E.H.R.L. 619–636, at 620. If the medication is therapeutically justified, an application on this ground would have little prospect of success unless it could be shown that there was alternative medication available which was equally efficacious and gave rise to significantly less serious side effects.

Although the courts will doubtless be reluctant to interfere in matters of pure clinical judgment, the Commission, in *Tanko v Finland*, App.No.23634/94, said that it "does not exclude that a lack of proper care in a case where someone is suffering from a serious illness could be certain circumstances amount to treatment contrary to Article 3". In *X v Denmark* (1983) 32 D. & R. 282 at 283, the Commission held that "medical treatment of an experimental character and without the consent of the person involved may under certain circumstances be prohibited by Article 3" (cited in E. Wicks, "The Right to Refuse Medical Treatment under the European Convention on Human Rights" (2001) 9 Med. L.R. 17 at 22).

Although this article cannot be interpreted as laying down a general obligation to release a detainee on health grounds or to place him in a civil hospital to enable him to receive specific medical treatment (*Kalashnikov v Russia* (2003) 36 E.H.R.R. 34 para.95), the detention of persons of unsound mind in an unsatisfactory or non-therapeutic environment could amount to a violation of this article if the ill-treatment of the patient attains a minimum level of severity (*Aerts v Belgium* (2000) 29 E.H.R.R. 50). In *Aerts* the Court held that, where the sole basis of detention is unsoundness of mind, an anti-therapeutic environment may contravene art.5(1), even if it is not severe enough to amount to inhuman and degrading treatment under this article. When assessing conditions of detention, account has to be taken of the cumulative effect of those conditions, as well as the specific allegations made by the applicant (*Dougoz v Greece* (2002) 34 E.H.R.R. 61 para.46). The effect of the decision in *Aerts* was explained by the Court in *Kudla v Poland* (2002) 35 E.H.R.R. 11 at para.94:

"[Under Article 3] the State must ensure that a person is detained in conditions which are compatible with respect for his human dignity, that the matter and method of the execution of the measure do not subject him to distress or hardship of an intensity exceeding the unavoidable level of suffering inherent in detention and that, given the practical demands of imprisonment, his health and well-being are adequately secured by, among other things, providing him with the requisite medical assistance".

There are three particular elements to be considered in relation to the compatibility of an applicant's health with his stay in detention: (a) the medical condition of the prisoner, (b) the adequacy of the medical assistance and care provided in detention, and (c) the advisability of maintaining the detention measure in view of the state of health of an applicant (*Dybeku v Albania* (App.No.41153/06) December 18, 2007, para.42.) In this case, the Court said at para.50 that "a lack of resources cannot in principle justify detention conditions which are so poor as to reach the threshold of severity for Art.3 to apply". In *Parascineti v Romania* (App.No.32060/05), March 13, 2012, the Court found that a combination of severe overcrowding, unhygienic conditions, and low staffing levels in a psychiatric hospital violated this article.

The lack of appropriate medical treatment for a prison detainee may amount to treatment contrary to this article (*Keenan v United Kingdom* (2001) 33 E.H.R.R. 38, para.110). *Keenan* was a case where the threshold of this article was reached where a serious disciplinary punishment involving segregation and additional detention was imposed on a mentally ill prisoner known to be a suicide risk without any effective monitoring or psychiatric care. A similar finding was made in *Renolde v France* (2009) 48 E.H.R.R. 42. The threshold was not reached in *Drew v United Kingdom* (2006) 43 E.H.R.R. SE2, where a prisoner was detained on a prison medical wing for eight days without access to effective psychiatric medication prior to his transfer to hospital. In *Brand v Netherlands* [2001] M.H.L.R. 275, the Court declared inadmissible an application that a lengthy detention of a mentally disordered person in prison pending a place being found in a secure psychiatric institution constituted a breach of this article on the ground that there was no evidence that the applicant's mental health or the possibilities of treatment had suffered on account of the time spent in prison.

In *M.S. v Croatia (No.2)*, February 19, 2015, the Court said at para.97:

"In respect of persons deprived of their liberty, recourse to physical force which has not been made strictly necessary by their own conduct diminishes human dignity and is in principle an infringement of the right set forth in Article 3 of the Convention (see *Krastanov v. Bulgaria*, no. 50222/99, § 53, 30 September 2004)".

With respect to the use of physical restraint and seclusion, the Court said at paras 104 and 105:

"In respect of the use of measures of physical restraint on patients in psychiatric hospitals, the Court sees no reason to disagree in principle with the Government's submission that medical standards in psychiatry allow for a recourse to such measures when no other measures could produce the desired result of calming an agitated individual down and to prevent him or her from harming himself or herself or others . . .. It notes, however, that the developments in contemporary legal standards on seclusion and other forms of coercive and non-consensual measures against patients with psychological or intellectual disabilities in hospitals and all other places of deprivation of liberty require that such measures be employed as a matter of last resort and when their application is the only means available to prevent immediate or imminent harm to the patient or others . . . .

Furthermore, the use of such measures must be commensurate with adequate safeguards from any abuse, providing sufficient procedural protection, and capable of demonstrating sufficient justification that the requirements of ultimate necessity and proportionality have been complied with and that all other reasonable options failed to satisfactorily contain the risk of harm to the patient or others. It must also be shown that the coercive measure at issue was not prolonged beyond the period which was strictly necessary for that purpose . . . ."

5–014 Removal from association, such as the seclusion of a mentally disordered patient, does not normally amount to inhuman or degrading treatment, but it will depend upon the conditions, duration, purpose and the effects on the person concerned (*Koskinen v Finland* (1994) 18 E.H.R.R. CD 146 and *A v United Kingdom*, App.No.6840/74). In *Dhoest v Belgium* (1987) 12 E.H.R.R. 97 at para.117, the Commission said that it had stated that:

"complete sensory deprivation, coupled with total social isolation, can destroy the personality and constitutes a form of treatment which cannot be justified by the requirements of security or for any other reason. It has moreover drawn a distinction between this and removal from association with other prisoners for security, disciplinary or protective reasons, and would not normally consider that this form of segregation from the prison community amounts to inhuman or degrading treatment. The same reasoning applies *mutatis mutandis* to persons who have been committed to a mental hospital in the framework of criminal proceedings".

A strip and intimate body search carried out in an appropriate manner with due respect for human dignity and for a legitimate purpose may be compatible with this article. However, where the manner in which a search is carried out has debasing elements which significantly aggravate the inevitable humiliation of the procedure, this article will be engaged. The requirement to submit to a strip search will generally constitute an interference under art.8(1) and require to be justified under art.8(2) (*Wainwright v United Kingdom* (2007) 44 E.H.R.R. 40 at paras 42, 43). Also see *Hellig v Germany* (2012) 55 E.H.R.R. 3, para.56, where it was said that depriving a person of their clothing is capable of giving rise to feelings of fear, anguish and humiliation capable of humiliating and debasing him.

In *D v United Kingdom* (1997) 24 E.H.R.R. 423 the Court said, at para.54, that "aliens . . . who are subject to expulsion cannot in principle claim any entitlement to remain on the territory of a contracting state in order to continue to benefit from medical, social or other forms of assistance provided by the expelling state during their stay". *D* was applied in *N v United Kingdom* (2008) 47 E.H.R.R. 39 where the Court said, at para.42, that the:

"decision to remove an alien who is suffering from a serious mental or physical illness to a country where the facilities for the treatment of that illness are inferior to those available in the Contracting State may raise an issue under Article 3, but only in a very exceptional case, where the humanitarian grounds against the removal are compelling. In the *D.* case the very exceptional circumstances were that the applicant was critically ill and appeared to be close to death, could not be guaranteed any nursing or medical care in his country of origin and had no family there willing or able to care for him or provide him with even a basic level of food, shelter or social support".

5–015 The Court observed, at para.45:

"that, although the present application . . . is concerned with the expulsion of a person with an HIV and AIDS-related condition, the same principles must apply in relation to the expulsion of any person afflicted with any serious, naturally occurring physical or mental illness which may cause suffering, pain and reduced life expectancy and require specialised medical treatment which may not be so readily available in the applicant's country of origin or which may be available only at substantial cost".

D and *N* were applied in *GS (India) v Secretary of State for the Home Department* [2015] EWCA Civ 40 where the Court of Appeal confirmed that foreign nationals may be removed from the UK even where their lives will be significantly shortened due to a lack of appropriate healthcare in their home states.

A breach of this article was found in *Aswat v United Kingdom* [2014] M.H.L.R. 130, where the Court held that there was a real risk that the mentally ill "applicant's extradition to different country and to a different, and potentially more hostile, prison environment would result in a significant deterioration in his mental and physical health" (para.57). In this case, the applicant was receiving treatment for schizophrenia at Broadmoor hospital.

In expulsion cases involving a risk of suicide, the steps taken by the authorities to mitigate against the risk would be considered when determining whether the high threshold of this article has been reached (*Balogun v United Kingdom* (2013) 56 E.H.R.R. 3, para.31). In *J v Secretary of State for the Home Department* [2005] EWCA Civ 629, the court held that, in deciding whether there was a real risk of a breach of this article in a case involving a risk of suicide on a person's enforced return to his country of origin, one question that had to be addressed was whether the fear of ill-treatment upon which the risk of suicide was said to be based, was objectively well founded. *J* was applied in *Y and Z (Sri Lanka) v Secretary of State for the Home Department* [2009] EWCA Civ 362, the first reported art.3 "foreign" claim based on the risk of suicide that has succeeded, where Sedley L.J., at para.15, said that a question of equal importance was whether any genuine fear, albeit without an objective foundation, is such as to create a risk of suicide if there is an enforced return. Also see *Lacki v Poland* [2012] EWHC 1747 (Admin) where it was held that L's extradition to Poland should proceed as his suicide risk could be treated appropriately by the Polish health service.

The Court's case law does not exclude that treatment which does not reach the severity of treatment under this article may nonetheless breach art.8 in its private life aspect where there are sufficiently adverse effects on physical and moral integrity (*Costello-Roberts v United Kingdom* (1995) 19 E.H.R.R. 112). However it would be difficult, although not necessarily impossible, for a claimant who relies on health grounds to resist removal from the UK to fail under this article but succeed under art.8 (*R. (on the application of Razgar) v Secretary of State for the Home Department* [2004] UKHL 27; [2004] 3 All E.R. 821 para.59). Also see *Maslov v Austria*, noted under s.86.

Aspects of mental health practice that could be challenged under this article include:

(a) the placing of female patients with a history of sexual abuse by men in a mixed sex environment;

(b) the automatic handcuffing of patients. In *Mouisel v France* [2004] 38 E.H.R.R. 34 at para.48, the Court held that handcuffing did not normally give rise to an issue under art.3 where it was imposed in connection with lawful detention and did not entail use of force or public exposure exceeding what was reasonably considered necessary. It was important to consider whether there was a risk that the person might abscond or cause injury or damage. The case law on this issue was considered in *R. (on the application of Faizovas) v Secretary of State for Justice* [2009] EWCA Civ 373, where the Court of Appeal considered *Unyan v Turkey*, January 8, 2009, and said, at para.22, that *Unyan* highlights the importance of separate consideration of the necessity for security measures at the treatment stage and that at that stage the authorities had to take account of not only the security risk but also the type of treatment which the prisoner had to undergo.

(c) the unjustified use of CS spray;

(d) the imposition of control and restraint techniques on a patient where neither the patient's history nor a current assessment justifies their use;

(e) forcible measures inflicted upon a patient which are not a medical necessity; and

(f) the forced feeding of a patient: see the note on "degrading" below.

TORTURE. The Court has defined torture as "deliberate inhuman treatment causing very serious and cruel suffering" (*Ireland v United Kingdom* (1978) 2 E.H.R.R. 25 para.167).

INHUMAN. See *Stanev v Bulgaria*, above.

5–016   DEGRADING. In *X v Germany* (1984) 7 E.H.R.R. 152, the Commission said that:

"the forced feeding of a person does involve degrading elements which in certain circumstances may be regarded as prohibited by Article 3 . . . Under the Convention the High Contracting parties are, however, also obliged to secure to everyone the right to life as set out in Article 2. Such an obligation should in certain circumstances call for positive action on the part of the Contracting Parties, in particular an active measure to save lives when the authorities have taken the person in question into their custody. When, as in the present case, a detained person maintains a hunger strike this may inevitably lead to a conflict between an individual's right to physical integrity and the High Contracting Party's obligation under Article 2 . . . a conflict which is not solved by the Convention itself".

X was applied in *Nevmerzhitsky v Ukraine* (2006) 43 E.H.R.R. 32, where the Court held, at para.94, that force-feeding that was aimed at saving the life of a detainee who consciously refused to take food could not in principle be regarded as inhuman and degrading. However, the medical necessity for such a procedure had to be convincingly shown to exist and the Court had to ascertain that the procedural guarantees for the decision to force feed had been complied with. Moreover, the manner in which an individual was subjected to force-feeding could not trespass the threshold of minimum severity envisaged by the case law on this article. Force feeding which was not a medical necessity was found to have breached this article in *Ciorap v Moldova*, App.No.12066/02, June 19, 2007. It is clear from these cases that a State may on occasions be justified in inflicting treatment which would otherwise be in breach of this article in order to serve the ends of art.2 (*R. (on the application of Pretty) v Director of Public Prosecutions* [2001] UKHL 61; [2002] 1 All E.R.1, per Lord Bingham at para.13).

In *NHS Trust A v NHS Trust B v H* [2001] 1 All E.R. 801, Butler-Sloss P. held that this Article "requires the victim to be aware of the inhuman and degrading treatment which he or she is experiencing or at least be in a state of physical or mental suffering" (para.49). This surprising finding, which has the effect of removing the protection afforded by this article from a group of extremely vulnerable citizens, i.e. insensate patients, was criticised by Munby J. in *R. (on the application of Burke) v General Medical Council* [2004] EWHC 1879 (Admin); [2004] 2 F.L.R. 1121, who said at para.149:

"In my judgment treatment is capable of being 'degrading' within the meaning of Article 3, whether or not it arouses feelings of fear, anguish or inferiority in the victim. It is enough if judged by the standard of right thinking bystanders—human rights violations obviously cannot be judged by the standards of the perpetrators—it would be viewed as humiliating or debasing the victim, showing a lack of respect for, or diminishing, his or her human dignity."

It is submitted that Munby J.'s obiter statement is to be preferred as it is consistent with Convention caselaw: see *Keenan v United Kingdom* (2001) 33 E.H.R.R. 913 para.112.

ARTICLE 4

PROHIBITION OF SLAVERY AND FORCED LABOUR

5–017

1. No one shall be held in slavery or servitude.
2. No one shall be required to perform forced or compulsory labour.
3. For the purpose of this Article the term "forced or compulsory labour" shall not include:

(a) any work required to be done in the ordinary course of detention imposed according to the provisions of Article 5 of this Convention or during conditional release from such detention;

(b) any service of a military character or, in case of conscientious objectors in countries where they are recognised, service exacted instead of compulsory military service;

(c) any service exacted in case of an emergency or calamity threatening the life or well-being of the community;

(d) any work or service which forms part of normal civic obligations.

ARTICLE 5

RIGHT TO LIBERTY AND SECURITY

1. Everyone has the right to liberty and security of person. No one shall be deprived of his liberty **5–018** save in the following cases and in accordance with a procedure prescribed by law:

(a) the lawful detention of a person after conviction by a competent court;

(b) the lawful arrest or detention of a person for non-compliance with the lawful order of a court or in order to secure the fulfilment of any obligation prescribed by law;

(c) the lawful arrest of detention of a person effected for the purpose of bringing him before the competent legal authority on reasonable suspicion of having committed an offence or when it is reasonably considered necessary to prevent his committing an offence or fleeing after having done so;

(d) the detention of a minor by lawful order for the purpose of educational supervision or his lawful detention for the purpose of bringing him before the competent legal authority;

(e) the lawful detention of persons for the prevention of the spreading of infectious diseases, of persons of unsound mind, alcoholics or drug addicts or vagrants;

(f) the lawful arrest or detention of a person to prevent his effecting an unauthorised entry into the country or of a person against whom action is being taken with a view to deportation or extradition.

2. Everyone who is arrested shall be informed promptly, in a language which he understands, of the reasons for his arrest and of any charge against him.

3. Everyone arrested or detained in accordance with the provisions of paragraph 1(c) of this Article shall be brought promptly before a judge or other officer authorised by law to exercise judicial power and shall be entitled to trial within a reasonable time or to release pending trial. Release may be conditioned by guarantees to appear for trial.

4. Everyone who is deprived of his liberty by arrest or detention shall be entitled to take proceedings by which the lawfulness of his detention shall be decided speedily by a court and his release ordered if the detention is not lawful.

5. Everyone who has been the victim of arrest or detention in contravention of the provisions of this Article shall have an enforceable right to compensation.

GENERAL NOTE

5–019 In *McKay v United Kingdom* (2007) 44 E.H.R.R. 41 at para.20, the Court said:

"Article 5 of the Convention is, together with Articles 2, 3 and 4, in the first rank of the fundamental rights that protect the physical security of an individual and as such its importance is paramount. Its key purpose is to prevent arbitrary or unjustified deprivations of liberty."

The protection that art.5(1) provides against a deprivation of liberty is absolute, subject only to the cases listed in sub-paragraphs (a) to (f). A person who is deprived of his liberty continues to enjoy all the fundamental rights and freedoms guaranteed under the Convention save for the right to liberty; see *Munjaz v United Kingdom* [2012] M.H.L.R. 351 which is noted in the General Note to art.8.

In *Storck v Germany* (2006) 43 E.H.R.R. 6; [2005] M.H.L.R. 211, the Court held that:

1. The State has a positive obligation to protect the liberty of its citizens, and the State was therefore obliged to take measures providing effective protection of vulnerable persons, including reasonable steps to prevent a deprivation of liberty of which the authorities had or ought to have had knowledge (para.100).

2. The State could not completely absolve itself from its responsibility by delegating its obligations in this sphere to private bodies or individuals. Private psychiatric institutions, in particular those able to hold persons without a court order, need not only a licence, but a competent supervision on a regular basis of the justification of the confinement and medical treatment (para.103).

3. Detention in a private institution could engage the State's responsibility under the Convention in three ways; by the direct involvement of public authorities, such as police officers, in the applicant's detention; by the courts' failure to interpret the provisions of the civil law relating to her claim in the spirit of art.5; and by the violation of its positive obligations to protect the applicant against interferences with her liberty carried out by private persons (para.89).

This Article embraces the detention and release of the mentally disordered, but not the conditions of detention or a right to treatment (*Winterwerp v Netherlands* (1979) 2 E.H.R.R. 387 at para.51 and *Ashingdane v United Kingdom* (1985) 7 E.H.R.R. 528, at para.44). In *A (A Mental Patient) v The Scottish Ministers* [2001] UKPC D5; [2002] H.R.L.R. 6 PC at para.29, Lord Hope said that it followed from these cases that "the fact that [the patient's] mental disorder is not susceptible to treatment does not mean that, in Convention terms, his continued detention in a hospital is arbitrary or disproportionate".

Paragraph 1

5–020 The Court has said that:

". . . the list of exceptions to the right to liberty secured by Article 5(1) is an exhaustive one and only a narrow interpretation of those exceptions is consistent with the aim and purpose of that provision, namely to ensure that no one is arbitrarily deprived of his or her liberty" (*Quinn v France* (1996) 21 E.H.R.R. 529 at para.42).

Detention pursuant to this paragraph inevitably brings with it a restriction for the detained person of his private and family life. The Court has held that it is essential that the detaining authority helps that person to maintain contact with his close family (*Messina v Italy (No.2)*, September 28, 2000, para.41).

EVERYONE. Including children (*Nielsen v Denmark* (1989) 11 E.H.R.R. 175 para.58).

SECURITY OF PERSON. This phrase is to be understood in the context of physical liberty rather than physical safety. The inclusion of the word "security" simply serves to emphasise the requirement that detention could not be arbitrary (*Hajdova v Slovakia* (2001) 53 E.H.R.R. 8, para.54).

DEPRIVED OF HIS LIBERTY. The nature of a deprivation of liberty is considered in Part 6.

PROCEDURE PRESCRIBED BY LAW. As this expression and the expression "in accordance with the law" in art.8(2) are to be understood as bearing the same meaning (*R. (on the application Gillan) v Metropolitan Police Commissioner* [2006] UKHL 12; [2006] 4 All E.R. 1041 para.31) reference should be made to the note on that phrase in art.8(2).

Although it is generally useful to keep detailed records of what happens at hearings, neither this article nor any other provision of the Convention contains a requirement that an official record of a hearing be kept, whether verbatim or in summary form (*Nakach v Netherlands* [2006] M.H.L.R. 22 paras 35, 36). However, a failure to draw up an official record of a hearing as required by domestic law would breach para.1 of this article (*Schenkel v Netherlands* [2006] M.H.L.R. 27).

Paragraph 1(a)

CONVICTION. A mentally disordered offender who is convicted of a criminal offence **5–021** and ordered to be detained in a psychiatric hospital will be detained under both art.5(1)(a) and 5(1)(e) (*X v United Kingdom* (1982) 4 E.H.R.R. 188 para.39).

Sentencing decisions concerning placement or treatment for mental disorder should be made by courts on the basis of valid and reliable standards of medical expertise and after taking into consideration the need for persons with a mental disorder to be treated in a place appropriate for their health needs (*Proshkin v Russia* (App.No.28869/03), February 7, 2012, para.104).

Paragraph 1(e)

In *Witold Litwa v Poland* (2001) 33 E.H.R.R. 53, the Court identified a link between all **5–022** of the categories of people noted in this sub-paragraph. The link is that all those persons:

"may be deprived of their liberty either in order to be given medical treatment or because of considerations dictated by social policy, or on both medical and social grounds . . . [A] predominant reason why the Convention allows the persons mentioned in paragraph 1(e) of Article 5 to be deprived of their liberty is not only that they are dangerous for public safety but also that their own interests may necessitate their detention" (para.60).

In *Stanev v Bulgaria* (2012) 55 E.H.R.R.; [2012] M.H.L.R. 23 at paras 143 to 147, the Court summarised the principles relating to the detention of persons of unsound mind as follows:

"The Court reiterates that in order to comply with Article 5 § 1, the detention in issue must first of all be 'lawful', including the observance of a procedure prescribed by law; in this respect the Convention refers back essentially to national law and lays down the obligation to conform to the substantive and procedural rules thereof. It requires in addition, however, that any deprivation of liberty should be consistent with the purpose of Article 5, namely to protect individuals from arbitrariness (see *Herczegfalvy v. Austria*, 24 September 1992, § 63, Series A no. 244). Furthermore, the detention of an individual is such a serious measure that it is only justified where other, less severe measures have been considered and found to be insufficient to safeguard the individual or public interest which might require that the person concerned be detained. That means that it does not suffice that the deprivation of liberty is in conformity with national law; it must also be necessary in the circumstances (see *Witold Litwa v. Poland*, no. 26629/95, § 78, ECHR 2000-III).

In addition, sub-paragraphs (a) to (f) of Article 5 § 1 contain an exhaustive list of permissible grounds of deprivation of liberty; such a measure will not be lawful unless it falls within one of those grounds (ibid., § 49; see also, in particular, *Saadi v. the United Kingdom* [GC], no. 13229/03, § 43, ECHR 2008, and *Jendrowiak v. Germany*, no. 30060/04, § 31, 14 April 2011).

As regards the deprivation of liberty of mentally disordered persons, an individual cannot be deprived of his liberty as being of 'unsound mind' unless the following three minimum conditions are satisfied: firstly, he must reliably be shown to be of unsound mind; secondly, the mental disorder must be of a kind or degree warranting compulsory confinement; thirdly, the validity of continued confinement depends upon the persistence of such a disorder (see *Winterwerp v. the Netherlands*, 24 October 1979, § 39, Series A no. 33; *Shtukaturov*, cited above, § 114; and *Varbanov*, cited above, § 45).

As to the second of the above conditions, the detention of a mentally disordered person may be necessary not only where the person needs therapy, medication or other clinical treatment to cure or alleviate his condition, but also where the person needs control and supervision to prevent him, for example, causing harm to himself or other persons (see *Hutchison Reid v. the United Kingdom*, no. 50272/99, § 52, ECHR 2003-IV).

The Court further reiterates that there must be some relationship between the ground of permitted deprivation of liberty relied on and the place and conditions of detention. In principle, the 'detention' of a person as a mental-health patient will be 'lawful' for the purposes of Article 5 § 1 (e) only if effected in a hospital, clinic or other appropriate institution authorised for that purpose (see *Ashingdane*, cited above, § 44, and *Pankiewicz v. Poland*, no. 34151/04, § 42–45, 12 February 2008). However, subject to the foregoing, Article 5 § 1 (e) is not in principle concerned with suitable treatment or conditions (see *Ashingdane*, cited above, § 44, and *Hutchison Reid*, cited above, § 49)."

Taking the three *Winterwerp* requirements in turn:

(i) The Court held that the term "persons of unsound mind" is "not one that can be given a definitive interpretation it is a term whose meaning is constantly evolving as research in psychiatry progresses, an increasing flexibility in treatment is developing and society's attitude to mental illness changes, in particular so that a greater understanding of the problems of mental patients is becoming wide-spread. In any event, Art.5(1)(e) obviously cannot be taken as permitting the detention of a person simply because his views or behaviour deviate from the norms prevailing in a particular society" (para.37). In *X v Federal Republic of Germany*, 6 D. & R. 182, the Commission found that the term "unsound mind" did not just mean mental illness, but must be understood in a wider sense to include abnormal personality disorder. The test under this paragraph has been described in the domestic courts as one of "whether it can 'reliably be shown' that [the patient] suffers from a mental disorder sufficiently serious to warrant detention" (*R. (on the application of H) v Mental Health Review Tribunal, North and East London Region* [2001] EWCA Civ 415, at para.29 per Lord Phillips M.R. at para.29).

The medical assessment must be based on the actual state of mental health of the person concerned and not solely on past events. A medical opinion cannot be seen as sufficient to justify deprivation of liberty if a significant period of time has elapsed between the deprivation and the provision of the opinion (*Varbanov v Bulgaria* [2000] M.H.L.R. 263, para.47). In *Winterwerp*, the Court said that a period of emergency detention which lasted for six weeks before a medical opinion was obtained from a general practitioner did not violate this article.

In *Stanev v Bulgaria*, above, para.153, the Court said that, "in certain circumstances, the welfare of a person with mental disorders might be a further factor to be taken into account, in addition to medical evidence, in assessing whether it is necessary to place the person in an institution".

The national authorities have a certain margin of appreciation regarding the merits of clinical diagnoses since it is in the first place for them to evaluate the evidence in a particular case (*S v Estonia* [2011] M.H.L.R. 396, para.38). The Commission has held that the medical evidence may come from a general practitioner rather than a psychiatrist (*Schuurs v The Netherlands* 41 D. & R. 186, 188–9). In *G v E* [2010] EWCA Civ 822, para.60, the Court of Appeal said that evidence from a psychologist was appropriate if the person concerned had learning difficulties.

(ii) In *Kolanis v United Kingdom* (2006) 42 E.H.R.R. 12, para.70, the Court rejected a submission that the decision of the Mental Health Review Tribunal that the patient could be discharged subject to conditions was tantamount to a finding that the second *Winterwerp* criterion was no longer fulfilled, with the result that any subsequent undue delay in release was in breach of art.5; see further the notes on s.73(7).

(iii) The requirement relating to the persistence of the mental disorder links to the review procedure provided for under para.4 of this article. In *Johnson v United Kingdom* (1999) 27 E.H.R.R. 296, the Court rejected the submission of the applicant, a restricted patient, that once there had been a finding by an expert authority, in this case the Mental Health Review Tribunal, that the mental disorder had ceased, he should as a consequence have been immediately and unconditionally released.

In *Aerts v Belgium* (2000) 25 E.H.R.R. 50, the applicant, who was an offender patient, was placed in provisional detention in the psychiatric wing of a prison for seven months before a place became available in a psychiatric institution. The Court heard evidence that the wing was not regarded as an appropriate institution for persons of unsound mind, as there was no regular medical attention and it was not a therapeutic environment. The Court held that, in principle, the detention of a person of unsound mind will only be lawful for the purposes of this paragraph "if effected in a hospital, clinic or other appropriate institution authorised for that purpose" (para.44). In this context "for that purpose" must mean purpose of caring for the mentally disordered. The detention of the applicant violated this paragraph because the "proper relationship between the aim of the detention and the conditions in which it took place was deficient" (para.49). This implies that there must be some therapeutic involvement with the patient. The Court further found that the conditions in which the applicant was detained were not sufficiently severe to lead to a finding of inhuman or degrading treatment under art.3. It follows that where detention is justified under this paragraph, complaints about the conditions in the patient's place of detention are better brought under this article rather than art.3. It is likely that the Court would need evidence that standards relating to the provision of services and/or the quality of conditions in the place of detention had fallen very low for it to be satisfied that this article had been violated; also see the note on s.47 under the heading "Human Rights Act 1998".

LAWFUL. This paragraph does not require the initial detention to be authorised by a court or tribunal. The lawfulness under domestic law of a person's detention is not of itself decisive: it must also be established that the detention was in conformity with para.1, which is to prevent persons from being deprived of their liberty in an arbitrary fashion (*Withold Litwa v Poland*, above, paras 72, 73). A detention will be arbitrary where, despite complying with the letter of national law, there has been an element of bad faith or deception on behalf of the authorities or where the domestic authorities neglected to attempt to apply the relevant legislation correctly or where there was an excessive delay in renewing the patient's detention (*Mooren v Germany* (2010) 50 E.H.R.R. 23, paras 78 to 81)). Lawfulness implies "that the deprivation of liberty is in keeping with the purpose of the restrictions permissible under Article 5(1)" (*Bouamar v Belgium* (1989) 11 E.H.R.R. 1 para.50). A subsequent finding that a court erred under domestic law in making the

order depriving a person of their liberty will not necessarily affect the validity of the intervening period of detention (*Benham v United Kingdom* (1996) 22 E.H.R.R. 293 para.42).
Benham was applied in *R. (on the application of A) v Harrow Crown Court* [2003] EWHC
2020 (Admin) where Stanley Burton J. held that the detention of a patient on the authority
of an irregular order did not infringe this article because the detention was not arbitrary.
However, there will be a breach of this article if the defect in the order amounts to "a
gross and irregular irregularity" (*Mooren v Germany*, above, para.75).

A significant delay in the transfer of a mentally disordered person who needs psychiatric
treatment from a penal establishment to a psychiatric hospital can constitute a violation of
this paragraph (*Mocarska v Poland* [2007] M.H.L.R. 228; also see *Pankiewicz v Poland*
[2008] M.H.L.R. 233). In the absence of an exceptional and unforeseeable situation, a
delay of six months is impermissible (*Proshkin v Russia* (App.No.28869/03), February
7, 2012, para.81).

DETENTION. Whether a person's situation constitutes a "deprivation of liberty" for the
purposes of para.1 is considered in Part 6.

In *Munjaz v United Kingdom* [2012] M.H.L.R. 351, the Court did not consider that there
was a general rule that either solitary confinement or seclusion *per se* can amount to a
further deprivation of the liberty of a person who was already lawfully detained.
Whether or not there has been a further deprivation of liberty in respect of such a person
must depend on the circumstances of case, including the type, duration, effects and manner
of implementation of the measure in question (paras 65–66). The Court held that the
secluded detained patient had not been the subject of a further deprivation of liberty
because:

(i) he was a long-term patient in a high security hospital: even when he was not in seclusion, he was already subjected to greater restrictions on his liberty than would
normally be the case for a mental health patient;

(ii) seclusion, though coercive, was not imposed as a punishment but to contain severely
disturbed behaviour likely to cause harm to others;

(iii) while its duration, notably of 9, 14 and 18 days, would point towards a further deprivation of liberty, duration alone was not determinative; the length of seclusion was
foremost a matter of clinical judgment; and

(iv) the manner of implementing the hospital's seclusion policy carried the greatest
weight: the hospital's approach was to allow secluded patients the most liberal
regime that was compatible with their presentation, and seclusion was being flexibly
applied (paras 69–72).

The Convention does not guarantee "for a person who has been ordered to undergo compulsory psychiatric treatment, the right to choose the place of his detention" (*Valle v
Finland* [2000] M.H.L.R. 255).

PERSONS OF UNSOUND MIND. See the note on the first of the *Winterwerp* requirements,
above.

ALCOHOLICS. Persons who are not medically diagnosed as "alcoholics", but whose
conduct and behaviour under the influence of alcohol pose a threat to public order or themselves, can be taken into custody for the protection of the public or their own interests, such
as their health or personal safety (*Withold Litwa v Poland* (2001) 33 E.H.R.R. 35). This
finding would equally apply to persons who were not medically diagnosed as drug addicts,
but whose conduct and behaviour under the influence of drugs give rise to similar concerns.

Paragraph 2

In *X v United Kingdom* (1982) 4 E.H.R.R. 188, para.66, the Court found it unnecessary to **5–023** decide whether this paragraph applies to patients detained under mental health legislation.

Paragraph 4

Article 5.4 "is first and foremost a guarantee of a fair procedure for reviewing the law- **5–024** fulness of detention—an applicant is not required, as a precondition to enjoying that protection, to show that on the facts of his case he stands any particular chance of success in obtaining his release. In matters of such crucial importance as the deprivation of liberty and where questions arise involving, for example, an assessment of the applicant's character or mental state, the Court's case-law indicates that it may be essential to the fairness of the proceedings that the applicant be present at an oral hearing" (*Waite v United Kingdom* (2003) 36 E.H.R.R. 54, para.59). The applicant's legal representative must meet the patient before the hearing. At the hearing he or she must not just act as a passive observer (*M.S. v Croatia (No.2),* February 19, 2015, para.156).

The role of the reviewing body is to identify whether the reasons which initially justified the detention continue to subsist, not to review the decision to detain (*X v UK* (1992) 14 E.H.R.R. 188 para.58). This paragraph does not require the reviewing body to have any other control of the detention process, such as decisions regarding leave of absence (*Roux v UK* (1986) 48 D. & R. 263 at 268). Where a court initially orders detention, the review required by this paragraph is incorporated in that decision (*Winterwerp v Netherlands* (1979) 2 E.H.R.R. 387, para.55).

This paragraph and para.1 are "separate provisions and observance of the former does not necessarily entail observance of the latter" (*Douiyeb v Netherlands* (2000) 30 E.H.R.R. 790, para.57). It is not concerned with the details of detention, such as the place and conditions of the patient's detention (*Ashingdane v UK* (1985) 7 E.H.R.R. 528 paras 43, 49) and it cannot be invoked by a person who is lawfully released (*Stephens v Malta* (2010) 50 E.H.R.R. 8, para.102).

The principles which emerge from the Court's case law on this paragraph as they apply to the detention of person of unsound mind were summarised in *Megyeri v Germany* (1993) 15 E.H.R.R. 584, at para.22. They include the following:

(i) A person of unsound mind who is compulsorily confined in a psychiatric institution for an indefinite or lengthy period is in principle entitled, at any rate where there is no automatic periodic review of a judicial character, to take proceedings "at reasonable intervals" before a court to put in issue the "lawfulness"—within the meaning of the Convention—of his detention (see *X v United Kingdom*, above, at para.52).

(ii) Article 5(4) requires that the procedures followed have a judicial character and give to the individual concerned guarantees appropriate to the kind of deprivation of liberty in question; in order to determine whether a proceeding provides adequate guarantees, regard must be had to the particular nature of the circumstances in which such proceedings takes place (see *Wassink v Netherlands*, September 27, 1990, Series A, No. 185–A, p.13, para.30).

(iii) The judicial proceedings referred to in art.5(4) need not always be attended by the same guarantees as those required under art.6(1) for civil or criminal litigation. None the less, it is essential that the person concerned should have access to a court and the opportunity to be heard either in person or, where necessary, some form of representation. Special procedural safeguards may prove called for in order to protect the interests of persons who, on account of their mental disabilities, are not fully capable of acting for themselves (see *Winterwerp v Netherlands*, above, at para.60).

(iv) Article 5(4) does not require that persons committed to care under the head of "unsound mind" should themselves take the initiative in obtaining legal representation before having recourse to a court (*Winterwerp*, above, para.60)

The Court went on to say at para.23 that it:

"follows from the foregoing that where a person is confined in a psychiatric institution on the ground of the commission of acts which constituted criminal offences but for which he could not be held responsible on account of mental illness, he should—unless there are special circumstances—receive legal assistance in subsequent proceedings relating to the continuation, suspension or termination of his detention. The importance of what is at stake for him—personal liberty—taken together with the very nature of his affliction—diminished mental capacity—compel this conclusion".

The legal assistance must be "effective" (*Pereira v Portugal* (2003) 36 E.H.R.R. 49, para.61).

5–025   In *MH v United Kingdom* (2014) 58 E.M.R.R. 965; [2014] M.H.L.R. 249 at para.77(a), the Court identified an additional principle arising from the Court's case law concerning persons of unsound mind:

"[A]n initial period of detention may be authorised by an administrative authority as an emergency measure provided that it is of short duration and the individual is able to bring judicial proceedings 'speedily' to challenge the lawfulness of any such detention including, where appropriate, its lawful justification as an emergency measure (*Winterwerp v Netherlands*, above, paras.57–61 and *X v. the United Kingdom*, above, para.58)".

Where a tribunal finds that a patient's detention in hospital is no longer necessary and that she is eligible for release on conditions, new issues of lawfulness may arise where detention nonetheless continues, due, for example, to difficulties in fulfilling the conditions. It follows that such patients are entitled under this paragraph to have the lawfulness of that continued detention determined by a court with requisite promptness (*Kolanis v United Kingdom* (2006) 42 E.H.R.R. 12, para.80).

In the *Winterwerp* case, the Commission said that the patient's lawyer had the right to examine the patient's file, but that it was not necessary for the patient to be informed of all the evidence or that he be allowed access to all of the information in his medical file. This approach was confirmed by the Court in *Nikolova v Bulgaria* [2001] E.H.R.R. 3 at para.58 where it was said that "[e]quality of arms is not ensured if counsel is denied access to those documents in the investigation file which are essential in order effectively to challenge the lawfulness of his client's detention".

EVERYONE.   Either personally or through some form of representation (*De Wilde, Ooms and Versyp v Belgium* (1971) 1 E.H.R.R. 373, paras 73–76).

TO TAKE PROCEEDINGS.   Until relatively recently, the Court accepted that an automatic review of the patient's case would satisfy this paragraph; see, for example, *X v United Kingdom* [1981] 4 E.H.R.R. 188. However a study of the Strasbourg jurisdiction reveal a shift of emphasis in recent years towards a greater stress on the requirement that a detained person should be able to take the initiative himself to start proceedings to challenge the lawfulness of his detention; see, for example, *Rakevich v Russia* [2004] M.H.L.R. 37. This shift is considered by Keene L.J. in *Secretary of State for Justice v Rayner* [2008] EWCA Civ 176; [2008] M.H.L.R. 115.

LAWFULNESS OF HIS DETENTION.   It is for the authorities to prove that an individual satisfies the conditions for compulsory detention, rather than the converse (*Reid v United Kingdom*, (2003) 37 E.H.R.R. 9 para.70). The review must encompass the lawfulness of the detention under this article as well as its lawfulness under domestic law (*Johnson v*

United Kingdom (1999) E.H.R.R. 296 para.60). Detention lasts from the time when the detention is authorised to the time when it is officially lifted, even if the patient is not physically detained during the whole of this period, i.e. it covers periods of leave of absence and absence without leave (*Van der Leer v Netherlands* (1990) 12 E.H.R.R. 567, para.35).

DECIDED. It is not sufficient for the court to have merely advisory functions, it must have the power to order release if it finds the detention to be unlawful (*Benjamin and Wilson v United Kingdom* (2003) 36 E.H.R.R. 1, para.34).

SPEEDILY. Which is a less stringent requirement than arises with the tem "promptly" in para.3 (*E v Norway*, below, para.64). In the Court's view, "this concept cannot be defined in the abstract; the matter must . . . be determined in the light of the circumstances of each case" (*Sanchez-Reisse v Switzerland* (1987) 9 E.H.R.R. 71 at para.55). In practice, the Court has dealt with this issue on a case-by-case basis. It is the obligation of the state to organise its legal system to enable it to comply with convention requirements (*Bezicheri v Italy* (1989) 12 E.H.R.R. 210 para.25). The "excessive workload" of the judge assigned to a particular case cannot be prayed in aid. Nor can the fact that the judge is on holiday (*E v Norway* (1990) 17 E.H.R.R. 30, para.64). There is no general principle that "administrative necessity" excuses delay (*R. (on the application of Noorkoiv) v Secretary of State for the Home Department* [2002] EWCA Civ 770; [2002] 4 All E.R. 515 para.26). Where there has been a delay in undertaking a review, the Court must determine whether the delay can be attributed to the authorities (*Luberti v Italy* (1984) 6 E.H.R.R. 440 para.34). In proceedings concerning a review of a psychiatric detention, the complexity of the medical issues involved in a case is a factor which may be taken into account when assessing compliance with the requirements of this paragraph (*Musial v Poland* (2001) 31 E.H.R.R. 29 para.47). Where there are complex issues to be determined "the primary responsibility for delays resulting from the provision of expert opinions rests ultimately with the state" (*Musial* at para.46).

In *Cottenham v United Kingdom* [1999] M.H.L.R. 97, the Court, in an admissibility **5–026** decision, found that the tribunal could not be criticised for a delay of 10 months which had been caused by the patient's solicitor's request for an adjournment to obtain an independent psychiatric report. The Court said that it:

"does not rule out that, given the particular problems of detained patients, where it appears that the legal representatives of such a person are acting negligently or in some way causing unjustified delay in the presentation of an application to a MHRT, the tribunal would be under a duty to make enquiries and to ensure that the application is proceeded with expeditiously".

Less urgency is required when the patient makes a further application in pursuance of his right to a periodic review of his detention. A delay of over four months in these circumstances has been held by the Court to be incompatible with this paragraph (*Koendjbiharie v Netherlands* (1990) 13 E.H.R.R. 820). It is also the case that the standard of "speediness" is less stringent when it comes to proceedings before a court of appeal (*Dzhurayev v Russia* (2013) 57 E.H.R.R. 22, para.224).

In *R. (on the application of C) v Mental Health Review Tribunal London South and West Region* [2001] EWCA Civ 1110; [2002] 1 W.L.R. 176, the Court of Appeal said that decisions of the Court such as *E v Norway*, above, where a delay of eight weeks between application and hearing was held to violate this paragraph, were not attempts to decide as of principle whether a particular practice or policy of setting a specified time for a hearing was in breach of this paragraph. What the Court made clear is that each case has to be decided upon its own particular circumstances. The Court of Appeal held that this approach was not compatible with a policy of automatically listing cases for hearing eight weeks after the application had been made: see the note on r.37 of the Tribunal Procedure (First-tier Tribunal) (Health, Education and Social Care Chamber) Rules 2008.

COURT. A body can be a court if it is independent of the executive and of the parties to the case and has a judicial character (*De Wilde, Ooms and Versp* (1971) 1 E.H.R.R. 373 para.76). The court must also be impartial (*DN v Switzerland* (2003) 37 E.H.R.R. 21 para.42). In *DN*, the Court said that "impartiality must be determined by a subjective test, that is on the basis of the personal conviction of a particular judge in a given case, and also by an objective test, that is ascertaining whether the judge offered guarantees sufficient to exclude any legitimate doubt in this respect" (para.44). The Court also said that:

> "any judge in respect of whom there is legitimate reason to fear a lack of impartiality must withdraw. In deciding whether in a given case there is a legitimate reason to fear that a particular judge lacks impartiality, the standpoint of the parties concerned is important but not decisive. What is decisive is whether this fear can be held to be objectively justified" (para.46).

A tribunal clearly qualifies as a court for the purposes of the Convention (*X v United Kingdom* (1982) 4 E.H.R.R. 188). Hospital managers, when exercising their power to review the detention of a patient, are not a court because the managers are a party to the review (*De Wilde, Ooms and Versp*, above).

Paragraph 5

5–027   This paragraph requires an enforceable claim for compensation before a national court if a breach of any of the other paragraphs in this article has occurred. The Court has held that ". . . there can be no question of 'compensation' where there is no pecuniary or non-pecuniary damage to compensate" (*Wassink v Netherlands*, September 27, 1990, para.38). In *R. (on the application of Wright) v Secretary of State for the Home Department* [2006] EWCA Civ 67; [2006] H.R.L.R. 23, the Court of Appeal held that the right under this paragraph is a domestic right and, as a matter of construction, a person could only be the victim of a detention in contravention of the provisions of this paragraph if there were a breach of paras 1 and/or 4 recognised by domestic law.

The current trend of authority in the Court is not to award pecuniary damages on a finding of a violation of this paragraph: see the cases cited in *Niedbala v Poland* ((2001) 33 E.H.R.R. 48 at para.88. Modest pecuniary damages have been awarded where the applicant has suffered damage resulting from a deprivation of liberty that he would not have suffered had this paragraph not been violated (*Niedbala* above).

Damages under this paragraph should be calculated in accordance with the guidance given by the House of Lords in *R. (on the application of Greenfield) v Secretary of State for the Home Department* [2005] UKHL 14; [2005] 2 All E.R. 240, an art.6 case, and by the Supreme Court in *R (on the application of Faulkner) v Secretary of State for Justice* [2013] UKSC 23; [2013] 2 All E.R. 1013: see the General Note to s.6 of the Act under the heading "Damages for an unlawful detention".

ARTICLE 6

RIGHT TO FAIR TRIAL

5–028   1. In the determination of his civil rights and obligations or of any criminal charge against him, everyone is entitled to a fair and public hearing within a reasonable time by an independent and impartial tribunal established by law. Judgment shall be pronounced publicly but the press and public may be excluded from all or part of the trial in the interest of morals, public order or national security in a democratic society, where the interests of juveniles or the protection of the private life of the parties so require, or to the extent strictly necessary in the opinion of the court in special circumstances where publicity would prejudice the interests of justice.

2. Everyone charged with a criminal offence shall be presumed innocent until proved guilty according to law.

3. Everyone charged with a criminal offence has the following minimum rights:

(a) to be informed promptly, in a language which he understands and in detail, of the nature and cause of the accusation against him;

(b) to have adequate time and facilities for the preparation of his defence;

(c) to defend himself in person or through legal assistance of his own choosing or, if he has not sufficient means to pay for legal assistance, to be given it free when the interests of justice so require;

(d) to examine or have examined witnesses against him and to obtain the attendance and examination of witnesses on his behalf under the same conditions as witnesses against him;

(e) to have the free assistance of an interpreter if he cannot understand or speak the language used in court.

GENERAL NOTE

This article, which provides for the right to a fair hearing in civil or criminal proceedings **5–029** in domestic law, "is concerned with standards of justice, the separation of powers and the rule of law" (*Matthews v Ministry of Defence* [2003] UKHL 4; [2003] 1 All E.R. 689 at para.25 per Lord Hoffmann). The Court in *Aerts v Belgium* (1998) 29 E.H.R.R. 50, para.59, held that "the right to liberty . . . is a civil right". This article is therefore engaged when a tribunal reviews the detention of a patient. The lawfulness of the detention of patients can be challenged under art.5(4) and the Court, in its interpretation of that paragraph, has been prepared to borrow some of the concepts of fairness in judicial proceedings from this article: see *Shtukaturov v Russia* (2012) 54 E.H.R.R. 27; [2008] M.H.L.R. 238 para.66.

In *RP v UK* (App.No.38245/08), October 9, 2012, para.65, the Court, when deciding that the appointment of the Official Solicitor to act for a mentally incapacitated litigant did not violate this article, recalled that, with regard to those with disabilities, it had permitted domestic courts

"a certain margin of appreciation to enable them to make the relevant procedural arrangements to secure the good administration of justice and protect the health of the person concerned (see, for example, *Shtukaturov v. Russia*, [above, para.68]). This is in keeping with the United Nations Convention on the Rights of Persons with Disabilities, which requires States to provide appropriate accommodation to facilitate the role of disabled persons in legal proceedings. However, the Court has held that such measures should not affect the very essence of an applicant's right to a fair trial as guaranteed by Article 6.1 of the Convention. In assessing whether or not a particular measure was necessary, the Court will take into account all relevant factors, including the nature and complexity of the issue before the domestic courts and what was at stake for the applicant (see, for example, *Shtukaturov v. Russia*, [above])".

As Wachenfeld has stated: "Guardianship proceedings must comply with the standards of Article 6(1) because it involes the determination of a civil right. See for example, Commission Admissibility Decision *X, Y and Z v Switzerland*, App.No.6916/76, 6 D. & R. 107, 112, 12 March 1976" (Margaret G. Wachenfeld, "The Human Rights of the Mentally Ill in Europe" (1991) 60 *Nordic Journal of International Law*, 109–292, at 224).

Paragraph 1

The right of access to a court guaranteed by this Article is "practical and effective", not **5–030** "theoretical or illusory" (*Del Sol v France* (2002) 35 E.H.R.R. 38 at para.21).

In *Ashingdane v UK* (1985) 7 E.H.R.R. 528, the Court found that the restrictions on bringing legal proceedings placed on patients by s.141 of the Mental Health Act 1959 (now see s.139 of the 1983 Act) did not transgress the patient's "right to a court" under this paragraph. The Court said at para.57:

"Certainly, the right of access to the courts is not absolute but may be subject to limitations; these are permitted by implication since the right of access 'by its very nature calls for regulation by the State, regulation which may vary in time and in place according to the needs and resources of the community and of individuals' (*Golder v UK* (1979) 1 E.H.R.R. 524, paragraph 38). In laying down such regulation, the Contracting States enjoy a certain margin of appreciation. Whilst the final decision as to observance of the Convention's requirements rests with the Court, it is no part of the Court's function to substitute for the assessment of the national authorities any other assessment of what might be the best policy in this field".

CIVIL RIGHTS AND OBLIGATIONS. In *(R. (on the application of Wilkinson) v The Responsible Medical Officer Broadmoor Hospital* [2001] EWCA Civ 1545; [2002] 1 W.L.R. 419 at para.35, Simon Brown L.J. said that a decision to treat a patient forcibly will inevitably determine his civil rights. However, the right to state medical treatment is not a civil right falling within this article (*L v Sweden* (App.No.10801/84)). Neither is the provision of services, such as social care services, which are dependent upon a series of evaluative judgments by the provider as to whether the statutory criteria are satisfied and how the need for it ought to be met (*Ali v Birmingham City Council* [2010] UKSC 8).

A decision to place a patient in seclusion does not engage this article (*R. (on the application of King) v Secretary of State for Justice* [2012] EWCA Civ 376).

FAIR . . . HEARING. Among the rights that the Court and the Commission have identified as comprising the right to a fair hearing are: the right to adversarial proceedings, the right to have a hearing within a reasonable time, the right to equality of arms, the right to know the grounds on which a decision is based and access to information necessary to bring the case effectively: see further S. Grosz et al., *Human Rights: The 1998 Act and the European Convention* (2000), pp.244 et seq. Whilst domestic courts enjoy a certain margin of appreciation when dealing with mentally ill persons, that should not be at the expense of a fair trial (*Shtukaturov v Russia*, above, para.68).

The right to have access to information can engage the art.8 rights of the subject of the information (*McMichael v United Kingdom* (1995) 20 E.H.R.R. 205). Although a party has a right to a fair trial under this article, that does not mean that he or she necessarily has an absolute and unqualified right to see all the documents (*Doorson v Netherlands* (1996) 22 E.H.R.R. 330 para.70; also see *Re B (Disclosure to Parties)* [2001] 2 F.L.R. 1017).

Although there is no automatic right under the Convention for legal aid or legal representation to be available for an applicant who is involved in proceedings which determine his or her civil rights and obligations, this article may be engaged under two interrelated aspects. Firstly, para.(1) embodies the right of access to a court. A failure to provide the applicant with the assistance of a lawyer may breach this provision where such assistance is indispensable for effective access to court. Secondly, the key principle governed by the application of this article is fairness. In cases where an applicant appears in court notwithstanding lack of assistance of a lawyer and manages to conduct his or her case, the question may nonetheless arise as to whether the procedure was fair (*P, C and S v UK* (2002) 35 E.H.R.R. 31).

INDEPENDENT AND IMPARTIAL TRIBUNAL. In order to establish whether a tribunal is "independent" for the purposes of this paragraph, regard must be had, inter alia, to the manner of appointment of its members and their terms of office, the existence of safeguards against outside pressures and the question whether it presents an appearance of independence (*Incal v Turkey* (2000) 29 E.H.R.R. 449, para.65). As to "impartiality", in *Pullar v United Kingdom* (1996) 22 E.H.R.R. 391 at para.30, the Court said that there are two tests for assessing whether a tribunal is impartial within the meaning of this paragraph: the first consists in seeking to determine the personal conviction of a particular judge in a given case and the second in ascertaining whether the judge offered guarantees sufficient to exclude any legitimate doubt in this respect. The House of Lords has explained that "there is now no difference between the common law test of bias and the requirements under Article 6 of the Convention of an independent and impartial tribunal" (*Lawal v Northern Spirit Ltd* [2003] I.C.R. 856 at 862 para.14 per Lord Steyn); see further the notes on r.34 of the Tribunal Procedure (First-tier Tribunal) (Health, Education and Social Care Chamber) Rules 2008.

In *R. (on the application of PD) v West Midlands and North West London Mental Health Review Tribunal* [2004] EWCA Civ 311, the Court of Appeal made reference to *Piersack v Belgium* (1982) 5 E.H.R.R. 169 where "the Court appears to have contemplated that the practical problems of finding properly qualified members of a Tribunal may be relevant when considering whether a member is disqualified on account of bias". The Court of Appeal said, at para.11, that it "would not exclude the possibility that such considerations might be relevant in an extreme case where it was impossible, or virtually impossible, to assemble a Tribunal free of connections that might give rise to apprehension of apparent bias".

ARTICLE 7

NO PUNISHMENT WITHOUT LAW

1. No one shall be held guilty of any criminal offence on account of any act or omission which did **5–031** not constitute a criminal offence under national or international law at the time when it was committed. Nor shall a heavier penalty be imposed than the one that was applicable at the time the criminal offence was committed.

2. This Article shall not prejudice the trial and punishment of any person for any act or omission which, at the time when it was committed, was criminal according to the general principles of law recognised by civilised nations.

ARTICLE 8

RIGHT TO RESPECT FOR PRIVATE AND FAMILY LIFE

1. Everyone has the right to respect for his private and family life, his home and his correspondence. **5–032**

2. There shall be no interference by a public authority with the exercise of this right except such as is in accordance with the law and is necessary in a democratic society in the interests of national security, public safety or the economic well-being of the country, for the prevention of disorder or crime, for the protection of health or morals, or for the protection of the rights and freedoms of others.

GENERAL NOTE

The purpose of this article "is to protect the individual against intrusion by agents of the **5–033** state, unless for good reason, into the private sphere within which individuals expect to be left alone to conduct their personal affairs and live their persona lives as they choose" (*R. (on the application of the Countryside Alliance) v Attorney General* [2007] UKHL 52 at para.10). It was described by Stanley Burnton J. as "the least defined and most unruly of the rights enshrined in the Convention" in *R. (on the application of Wright) v Secretary of State for Health* [2006] EWHC 2886 (Admin) at para.60. A person can consent to acts which would otherwise involve an infringement of his rights, whether at common law or under this article (*Millar v Dickson* [2001] UKPC D4).

The "Strasbourg institutions have analysed Article 8 issues by asking the following questions: (1) does the subject matter fall within the scope of Article 8? (2) if so, has there been an interference by a public authority? (3) if so, was it 'in accordance with the law'? (4) if so, did it pursue a legitimate aim, i.e. one of those set out in Article 8(2)? (5) if so, was it 'necessary', i.e. did the interference correspond to a 'pressing social need' and was it proportionate to that need?" (S. Grosz, J. Beatson, P. Duffy, *Human Rights: The 1998 Act and the European Convention*, (2000), p.265).

In *Glaser v United Kingdom* (2001) 33 E.H.R.R. 1, the Court said at para.63:

"The essential object of Article 8 is to protect the individual against arbitrary interference by public authorities. There may however be positive obligations inherent in an effective 'respect' for family life. These obligations may involve the adoption of measures designed to secure respect for family life even in the sphere of relations between individuals, including both the provision of a regulatory framework of adjudicatory and enforcement machinery protecting individuals' rights and the implementation, where appropriate, of specific steps (see among other authorities, *X and Y v Netherlands* (1986) 8 E.H.R.R. 235, and, mutatis mutandis, *Osman v United Kingdom* (2000) 29 E.H.R.R. 245). In both the negative and positive contexts, regard must be had to the fair balance which has to be struck between the competing interests of the individual and the community, including other concerned third parties, and of the state's margin of appreciation (see, among other authorities, *Keegan v Ireland* ((1994) 18 E.H.R.R. 342)".

The reference to "relations between individuals" in *Glaser* demonstrates the link between the right to private life and the right to family life. If members of a family are prevented from sharing family life together, art.8(1) is likely to be infringed (*Anufrijeva v London Borough of Southwark* [2003] EWCA Civ 1406; [2004] 1 All E.R. 833 at para.12).

Positive obligations may exceptionally arise in the case of the handicapped in order to ensure that they are not deprived of the possibility of developing social relations with others and therefore developing their own personalities. In the case of the physically handicapped, positive obligations require appropriate measures to be taken, to the greatest extent feasible, to ensure that they have access to essential economic and social activities and to an appropriate range of recreational and cultural activities. A positive obligation will only be imposed where there is both (i) a direct and immediate link between the measures sought and the applicant's private life (*Botta v Italy* (1998) 26 E.H.R.R. 241, paras 34,35) and (ii) a special link between the situation complained of and the particular needs of the applicants private life (*Sentges v Netherlands* (2004) 7 C.C.L.R. 400, 405).

The Court has applied the concept of positive obligation in a number of areas including requiring a state to enable the guardians of a mentally defective girl to lodge a complaint with a view to instituting criminal proceedings against a man who had sexually abused her (*X and Y v Netherlands*, above); to establish a fair system whereby the question of access to the personal files of a child in public care will be determined (*Gaskin v United Kingdom* (1990) 12 E.H.R.R. 36); and to take all reasonable steps to facilitate reunion between a child in public care and his parents (*Hokkanen v Finland* (1995) 19 E.H.R.R. 139). Positive obligations are not absolute. Before inaction can amount to a lack of respect for private and family life, there must be some ground for criticising the failure to act. There must be an element of culpability. Where the complaint is that there has been culpable delay in the administrative process necessary to determine and to give effect to an art.8 right, there will be no infringement of the article unless substantial prejudice has been caused to the applicant. There is a need to have regard to resources when considering the obligations imposed by a State by this article (*Anufrijeva v London Borough of Southwark*, above, paras 45–47).

With regard to medical treatment and care, this article cannot be considered applicable every time an individual's everyday life was disrupted but only in exceptional circumstances where the State's failure to adopt measures interfered with an art.8 right because of a special link between the inaction and the needs of the individual. Even then a fair balance has to be struck between the competing demands of the community as a whole and those of the individual (see *Glaser*, above). A particularly wide margin of appreciation was due where the issues involved an assessment of competing priorities for a limited state resource (*Sentges v Netherlands* (2004) 7 C.C.L.R. 400). In *R. (on the application of Condliff) v North Staffordshire Primary Care Trust* [2011] EWCA Civ 010; [2012] 1 All E.R. 689, the Court of Appeal held that this article did not make it unlawful for the PCT to adopt an individual funding request policy by which all such requests are to be considered and determined exclusively by reference to clinical factors.

In *Passannante v Italy* (1998) 26 E.H.R.R. CD 153, a case where the applicant had waited five months to see a hospital specialist, the Commission stated that:

"where the State has an obligation to provide medical care, an excessive delay of the public health service in providing a medical service to which the patient is entitled and the fact that such a delay has, or is likely to have, a serious impact on the patient's health could raise an issue under Article 8(1) of the Convention."

Under this Article the authorities:

5–034

"must strike a fair balance between the interests of a person of unsound mind and the other legitimate interests concerned. However, as a rule, in such a complex matter as determining somebody's mental capacity, the authorities should enjoy a wide margin of appreciation. This is mostly explained by the fact that the national authorities have the benefit of direct contact with the persons concerned and are therefore particularly well placed to determine such issues" (*Shtukaturov v Russia* (2012) 54 E.H.R.R. 27; [2008] M.H.L.R. 238 at para.87).

The Commission recognised that public authorities might have to take particular steps to protect the mentally disordered in order to fulfil their obligations under this article:

". . . The impossibility for the above category of persons [the mentally disabled] to form or express their will calls for protective measures on behalf of the authorities which go beyond what is required with regard to persons who are in full possession of their physical and mental capacities" (*X and Y v Netherlands* (1983) 6 E.H.R.R. CD311 at para.81).

In *Munjaz v United Kingdom* [2012] M.H.L.R. 351, the Court said at paras 79 and 80:

"In assessing the proper scope of private life for those who are deprived of their liberty, the Court reiterates that, under the Convention system, the presumption is that detained persons 'continue to enjoy all the fundamental rights and freedoms guaranteed under the Convention save for the right to liberty, where lawfully imposed detention expressly falls within the scope of Article 5 of the Convention' ([*Hirst v.United Kingdom* (2006) 42 E.H.R.R. 41, para.69]). Any restriction on those rights must be justified in each individual case ([*Dickson v.United Kingdom* (2008) 46 E.H.R.R. 41, para.68]).

In applying those principles to the present case, the Court agrees that the compulsory seclusion of the applicant interfered with his physical and psychological integrity and even a minor such interference must be regarded as an interference with the right to respect for private life under Article 8 if it is carried out against the individual's will ([*Storck v Germany* (2006) 43 E.H.R.R. 6, para.143]) Moreover, the importance of the notion of personal autonomy to Article 8 and the need for a practical and effective interpretation of private life demand that, when a person's personal autonomy is already restricted, greater scrutiny be given to measures which remove the little personal autonomy that is left."

Where a public authority commits acts which it knows are likely to cause psychiatric harm to an individual, those acts are capable of constituting an infringement of this article. Maladministration will not, however, cause such an infringement simply because it causes stress that leads to a particularly susceptible individual to suffer such harm in circumstances where this was not reasonably to be anticipated. No lack of respect for family life is manifested in such circumstances (*Anufrijeva v London Borough of Southwark*, above, para.143).

In "Protecting the Rights of People with Mental Disabilities: The European Convention on Human Rights", Oliver Lewis states that in the psychiatric setting, this article will be engaged by issues as diverse as:

"freedom of correspondence, right not to be in a crowded living space, access to non-pharmacological therapy, access to fresh air and exercise, privacy in washing and toileting, privacy of visits, confidentiality of medical records, rights to sexuality, right to be free from unwanted sexual advances, freedom from surveillance of daily life and searches of living space and of person" (E.J.H.L. (2002) 9: 293–320, 308).

In *Ciliz v Netherlands* [2000] 2 F.L.R. 469 at 482, the Court said that whilst this article contains no explicit procedural requirements, the decision-making process leading to measures of interference must be fair and such as to afford due respect to the interests safeguarded by the article; see also *H and L v A City Council* [2011] EWCA Civ 403, per Munby L.J. at para.51. It is therefore the case that a violation of this article is likely to occur if an application is made to detain a child under the Mental Health Act in circumstances where the parents of the child have not been offered the opportunity of being involved in the decision-making process. In *Glass v United Kingdom* (2004) 39 E.H.R.R. 15, the Court held that a failure to obtain the authority of the High Court to authorise the treatment of a child in a non-emergency situation where the child's parents objected to the treatment in question constituted a violation of this article.

Treatment that does reach the level of severity required by art.3 may nevertheless breach this article in its private life aspects where there are sufficiently adverse effects on a person's physical and moral integrity (*Costello-Roberts v United Kingdom* (1995) 19 E.H.R.R. 112). However it would be difficult, although not necessarily impossible, for a claimant who relies on health grounds to resist removal from the UK to fail under art.3 but succeed under this article (*R. (on the application of Razgar) v Secretary of State for the Home Department* [2004] UKHL 27; [2004] 3 All E.R. 821 at para.59).

In *Storck v Germany* (2006) 43 E.H.R.R. 6; [2005] M.H.L.R. 211, the Court held that the state's obligations under this article in respect of a person who has been detained in a private psychiatric clinic arises for the same reasons to those relevant to art.5.

Paragraph 1

5–035   EVERYONE. Including a person who lacks mental capacity (*A Local Authority v E* [2012] EWHC 1639 (COP), para.124).

RESPECT. "'Respect' means more than 'acknowledge' or 'take into account', it implies some positive obligations on the part of the public authorities (*Campbell and Cosans v United Kingdom* (1982) 4 E.H.R.R. 293; *Valsamis v Greece* (1997) 24 E.H.R.R. 294)" (*Anufrijeva v Southwalk London Borough Council* [2002] EWHC 3136 (QB) at para.104 per Newman J.). In *Sheffield and Horsham v United Kingdom* (1998) 27 E.H.R.R. 163, the Court said at para.52:

"The Court reiterates that the notion of 'respect' is not clear cut, especially as far as the positive obligations inherent in that concept are concerned: having regard to the diversity of the practices followed and the situation obtaining in the Contracting States, the notion's requirements will vary considerably from case to case".

PRIVATE . . . LIFE. In *Bensaid v United Kingdom* (2001) 33 E.H.R.R. 10, the Court said at para.47:

"Private life is a broad term not susceptible to exhaustive definition. The Court has already held that elements such as gender identification, name and sexual orientation and sexual life are important elements of the personal sphere protected by Article 8. Mental health must be regarded as a crucial part of private life associated with the aspect of moral integrity. Article 8 protects a right to identity and personal development, and the right to establish and develop relationships with other human beings and the outside world. The preservation of mental stability is in that context an indispensable precondition to effective enjoyment of the right to respect for private life".

But, not "every act or measure which adversely affects moral or physical integrity will interfere with the right to respect to private life" (*Bensaid*, above, para.46). However, even a minor interference with the physical integrity of an individual must be regarded as an interference with the right to respect for private life if it is carried out against the individual's will (*Storck v Germany* (2006) 43 E.H.R.R. 6, para.168).

In *Botta v Italy* (1998) 26 E.H.R.R. 241, the Court said that "the guarantee afforded Art.8 is primarily intended to ensure the development, without outside interference, of the personality of each individual in his relations with other human beings" (para.32). In this case the Court's case law on the concept of private life was described being "based on a pragmatic, common-sense approach rather than a formalistic or purely legal one" (para.27). The rights invoked must not be "too wide and indeterminate" (*Zehnalova and Zehnal v Czech Republic*, May 14, 2002). In *Niemietz v Germany* (1992) 16 E.H.R.R. 97 at para.29, the Court said that

> "it would be too restrictive to limit the notion to an 'inner circle' in which the individual may live his own personal life as he chooses and to exclude therefrom entirely the outside world encompassed within that circle. Respect for private life must also comprise, to a certain degree, the right to establish and develop relationships with human beings".

The right of an individual to decide how and when to end his life, provided he was in a position to make up his own mind in that respect and to take appropriate action, is one aspect of the right to respect for private life within the meaning of this article. The state's positive obligation to take steps to allow for a dignified suicide is subject to a certain margin of appreciation which varies in accordance with the issues and the importance of the interests at stake (*Haas v Switzerland* (2011) 53 E.H.R.R. 33).

A person's private life may be concerned in measures effected outside his or her home or private property. It can include the publication of a person's photograph (*Sciacca v Italy* (2006) 43 E.H.R.R. 20). A person's reasonable expectation of privacy is a significant though not necessarily conclusive factor (*Perry v United Kingdom* (2004) 39 E.H.R.R. 3 para.37). The "ability to conduct one's life in a manner of one's own choosing may also include the opportunity to pursue activities perceived to be of a physically or morally harmful or dangerous nature for the individual concerned" (*Pretty v United Kingdom* (2002) 35 E.H.R.R. 1, at para.62).

In *Raninen v Finland* (1998) 26 E.H.R.R. 563 para.63, the Court acknowledged that the **5–036** notion of physical and moral integrity of the person extends to situations of deprivation of liberty (which can involve the seclusion of a patient (*Munjaz v United Kingdom* [2012] M.H.L.R. 351)). It also includes information about a person's mental condition (*Gaskin v United Kingdom* (1990) 12 E.H.R.R. 36 para.37).

In *R. (on the application of H) v Ashworth Hospital Authority* [2001] EWHC Admin 872; [2001] M.H.L.R. 241, Sir Christopher Bellamy QC said, citing *Guerra v Italy* (1998) 26 E.H.R.R. 357 and *Lopez Ostra v Spain* (1995) 20 E.H.R.R. 277, that there was support for the proposition that the notion of physical integrity identified in *X and Y v Netherlands* (1986) 8 E.H.R.R. 235, extends to the protection of a person's health (para.124). In order to succeed under this article the claimant would have to show that there was a real and immediate risk to his health from which the defendant has failed to protect him, and that the defendant had not taken such steps as were reasonably to be expected of it to obviate that risk (para.128).

The "imposition of medical treatment, without consent of a mentally competent adult patient, would interfere with a person's physical integrity in a manner capable of engaging the rights protected by [this article]" (*Pretty v United Kingdom*, above, para.63; also see

Wilkinson v UK [2006] M.H.L.R. 142). Mentally competent patients have a right to make choices about medical treatment "that accord with their own views and values, regardless of how irrational, unwise or imprudent such choices may appear to others" (*Jehovah's Witnesses of Moscow v Russia* [2011] 53 E.H.R.R. 4, para.136). This article would not be breached if forcible treatment is given to a mentally incompetent detained patient in a situation where, "according to the psychiatric principles generally accepted at the time, medical necessity justified the treatment in issue": see *Herczegfalvy v Austria* (1993) 15 E.H.R.R. 437, paras 83, 86, noted under art.3. However, in the context of the forced administration of medication, safeguards must be in place to protect all patients against arbitrary interference with their rights under this article: see *X v Finland* [2012] M.H.L.R. 318, which is considered in the note to s.63 of the Act under the heading "Human Rights Act 1998". Where the patient is a child, any medical treatment (including the taking of a medical photograph) must be authorised by the person with parental responsibility for that child (*Glass v United Kingdom* (2004) 39 E.H.R.R. 15, para.75).

With regard to action taken to prevent detainees harming themselves, the authorities:

> ". . . must discharge their duties in a manner compatible with the rights and freedoms of the individual concerned. There are general measures and precautions which will be available to diminish the opportunities for self-harm, without infringing personal autonomy. Whether any more stringent measures are necessary in respect of a prisoner and whether it is reasonable to apply them will depend on the circumstances of the case" (*Keenan v United Kingdom* (2001) 33 E.H.R.R 38, para.91).

A decision that a person lacks mental capacity may amount to an interference with his private life. Such a decision should be made in the personal presence of the person concerned and departure from this rule is only possible where the domestic court has carefully examined the issue (*Lashin v Russia* [2014] M.H.L.R. 109, paras 77 and 82). The forcible medical examination of a person in order to determine whether his mental capacity could be restored was found to be an interference with his private life in *Matter v Slovakia* (2001) 31 E.H.R.R. 32.

In *R (on the application of N) v Secretary of State for Health* [2009] EWCA Civ 795; [2009] M.H.L.R. 266, the Court of Appeal held that this article did not protect the right for patients to smoke at Rampton Hospital: the prohibition of smoking in such an institution did not have a sufficiently adverse effect on a patient's physical or moral integrity. The Court found that the hospital's policy which banned smoking on its premises, but allowed for individual exceptions on clinical grounds, was lawful. Reservations about the approach adopted by the Court of Appeal in this case were expressed by Lord Stewart in the Scottish Court of Session in *Re CM* [2013] CSOH 143.

In *Goodwin v United Kingdom* (2002) 35 E.H.R.R. 18, the issue before the Court was whether or not the UK government had failed to comply with a positive obligation to ensure the right of the applicant, a post-operative male to female transsexual, to respect for her private life, in particular through the lack of legal recognition given to her gender reassignment. In finding that there had been a breach of this article, the Court made reference to *Dudgeon v United Kingdom* (1982) 4 E.H.R.R. 149 at para.41, where the Court had said that it must be recognised that serious interference with private life can arise where the state of domestic law conflicts with an important aspect of personal identity.

5–037   Restrictions placed on a male psychiatric patient's freedom to dress as a woman and to assume the appearance of a woman constitutes an interference with his private life: see *R. (on the application of E) v Ashworth Hospital Authority* [2001] EWHC Admin 1089 para.40, where Richards J. held that the interference was justified under para.2 by virtue of therapeutic and security concerns that had been put forward in support of the hospital's approach. As a matter of domestic law, a hospital is entitled to give precedence to the interests of the patients as a whole over the interests of individual patients (*R. v Broadmoor Special Hospital Ex p. S, H and D* [1998] C.O.D. 199).

A person has a right under this article to have access to files concerning his own life. Any restriction on this right in domestic law must meet the requirements of para.2. In cases involving the disclosure of personal data, the Court has recognised that a margin of appreciation should be left to national authorities in striking a fair balance between the relevant public and private interests. The scope of this margin depends on such factors as the nature and seriousness of the interests at stake and the gravity of the interference (*Peck v United Kingdom*, (2003) 36 E.H.R.R. 41 para.77). The data subject is not required to specifically justify a request to be provided with a copy of their personal files; rather, it is for the authorities to show that there existed compelling reasons for refusing that facility (*KH v Slovakia* (2009) 49 E.H.R.R. 34, para.48). If a public authority is not able to secure the consent of a person who has contributed to the file to have that material disclosed, there must be an independent authority that can decide whether the material should be disclosed (*Gaskin v United Kingdom*, above and *MG v United Kingdom* (2003) 36 E.H.R.R. 3).

In *Z v Finland* (1997) 25 E.H.R.R. 371 at paras 95–97, the Court said that:

> "the protection of personal data, not least medical data, is of fundamental importance to a person's enjoyment of his or her right to respect for private and family life . . . Respecting the confidentiality of health data . . . is crucial not only to respect the sense of privacy of a patient but also to preserve his or her confidence in the medical profession and in health services in general. [Disclosure must be justified by] an overriding requirement in the public interest".

At the same time, the Court accepted that "the interests of a patient and the community as a whole in protecting the confidentiality of medical data may be outweighed by the interest in investigation and prosecution of crime and in the publicity of court proceedings . . . where such interests are shown to be of even greater importance".

The confidentiality of a patient's medical records belongs to the patient. For the particular importance of confidentiality in psychiatric medical notes, see *Ashworth Hospital Authority v MGN Ltd* [2002] UKHL 29; [2002] 4 All E.R. 193 para.63; also see the note on the "rights and freedoms of others", below and Fenella Morris, "Confidentiality and the Sharing of Information" (2003) *Journal of Mental Health Law*, 9, 38–50.

Where the report of an independent inquiry into homicides committed by a mentally disordered person contains citations from his medical and other records, a claim that the publication of the report to the world at large would breach this article in that it was not necessary in the public interest must be the subject of a "very high intensity" review by a court. It is not enough to assert that the decision to taken was a reasonable one: a compelling case needs to exist to justify publication. In such a situation art.10 also comes into play if only because of the general corresponding right of the public to be free to *receive* information where it is sought to be published (*R. (on the application of Stone) v South East Coast Strategic Health Authority* [2006] EWHC 1668 (Admin); [2006] M.H.L.R. 288 at paras 31–33).

An enquiry by a patient's doctor addressed to a third party which is aimed at obtaining information about the patient rather than communicating it does not infringe this article (*R. (on the application of O'Reilly) v Blenheim Healthcare Ltd* [2005] EWHC 241 (Admin)).

The appointment of a guardian for a mentally disordered patient is an interference with that person's private life because the guardian is given power to make personal decisions on behalf of that person (*X v Federal Republic of Germany* (1980) 20 D. & R. 193). Although the Convention does not place any restrictions on the guardian's powers, the exercise of such powers must fall within one of the limitations set out in para.2.

The searching of a mentally disordered detained patient would violate this article in the **5–038** absence of a justification under para.2. It has been stated that the Court:

> "has exercised particular judicial vigilance where the authorities are empowered under national law to order and effect searches without a judicial warrant. Very strict limits on such powers are called for in such cases in order to protect individuals from arbitrary

interference by the authorities with the rights guaranteed under [this article (*Camenzind v Switzerland* (1999) 28 E.H.R.R. 458)]" (S. Grosz et al., above, at p.285).

However, in *R. (on the application Gillan) v Metropolitan Police Commissioner* [2006] UKHL 12; [2006] 4 All E.R. 1041 at para.28, Lord Bingham said that he was:

"doubtful whether an ordinary superficial search of the person can be said to show a lack of respect for private life. It is true that 'private life' has been generously construed to embrace wide rights to personal autonomy. But it is clear Convention jurisprudence that intrusions must reach a certain level of seriousness to engage the operation of the Convention which is, after all, concerned with human rights and fundamental freedoms, and I incline to the view that an ordinary superficial search of the person and an opening of bags, of the kind which passengers uncomplainingly submit at airports, for example, can scarcely be said to reach that level."

In *Wainwright v United Kingdom* (2007) 44 E.H.R.R. 40 para.43, the Court held that the requirement to submit to a strip search will generally constitute interference under this paragraph that would require justification under para.2.

The use of surveillance techniques, such as CCTV in hospitals and care homes may well involve art.8 rights. In *Khan v UK* (2001) 31 E.H.R.R. 45, a case involving the use of a covert listening device by the police, the Court said at para.26:

"The Court recalls, with the Commission in the case of *Govell*, that the phrase 'in accordance with the law' not only requires compliance with domestic law but also relates to the quality of that law, requiring it to be compatible with the rule of law. In the context of covert surveillance by public authorities, in this instance the police, domestic law must provide protection against arbitrary interference with an individual's right under Article 8. Moreover, the law must be sufficiently clear in its terms to give individuals an adequate indication as to the circumstances in which and the conditions on which public authorities are entitled to resort to such covert measures."

Surveillance operations conducted by local authorities and NHS trusts must comply with the provisions of Pt II of the Regulations of Investigatory Powers Act 2000 which was passed partly as a result of the decision in *Khan*. The normal use of security cameras per se, whether in the public street or on premises, do not raise issues under this article as long as they serve a legitimate and foreseeable purpose (*Perry v United Kingdom* (2004) 39 E.H.R.R. 3 para.40).

5–039   FAMILY . . . LIFE.   The state must act in a manner calculated to allow those concerned to lead a normal family life (*Z and E v Austria* (1986) 49 D. & R. 67). The existence or non-existence of "family life" is essentially a question of fact depending upon the reality in practice of close personal ties (*K v Finland* (No.1); *T v Finland* (No.1) (2001) 31 E.H.R.R. 18 para.150). It is therefore the case that it is actual family life, rather than family life in the abstract that needs to be considered (*R. (on the application of Ahmadi) v Secretary of State for the Home Department* [2005] EWHC 687 (Admin) para.25). This article "makes no distinction between the 'legitimate and the illegitimate' family" (*Marckx v Belgium* (1979) 2 E.H.R.R. 330 para.31). The concept of family life embraces, even where there is no co-habitation, the tie between a parent and his or her child (*Boughanemi v France* (1996) 22 E.H.R.R. 228) including adoptive parent/child relationships (*X v Belgium and Netherlands* (1975) D.R. 75). When deciding whether a relationship between a couple can be said to amount to "family life", a number of factors may be relevant, including whether the couple live together, the length of their relationship and whether they have demonstrated their commitment to each other by having children together or by any other means (*Al-Nashif v Bulgaria* (2003) 36 E.H.R.R. 37 para.112). In *R. (on the application of L) v Secretary of State for Health* [2001] 1 F.L.R. 406, Scott Baker J. considered the jurisprudence on this article. He said:

"Family life it seems to me, is an elastic concept that depends very much on the facts of the individual case. In some cases the existence of family life will be immediately obvious; in others the reverse will be true. But the onus of establishing family life in each case is in my judgment on the applicant".

There must be extraordinarily compelling reasons before a baby can be physically removed from its mother, against her will, immediately after birth as a consequence of a procedure in which neither she nor her partner has been involved (*P, C and S v United Kingdom* (2002) 35 E.H.R.R. 31). In "judicial decisions where the rights under Article 8 of parents and of a child are at stake, the child's rights must be the paramount consideration" (*Yousef v Netherlands* (2003) 36 E.H.R.R. 20 at para.73).

There is no Convention duty to provide support to foreign nationals who are in a position freely to return home (*R. (on the application of Kimani) v Lambeth LBC* [2003] EWCA Civ 1150; [2004] 1 W.L.R. 272), and the right to family life is not infringed because it must be conducted outside the United Kingdom in a country with a lower standard of living (*R. (on the application of Mahmood) v Secretary of State for the Home Department* [2001] 1 W.L.R. 840). However deportation cases can raise issues under this article: see *Maslov v Austria* (1638/03) (2008) 47 E.H.R.R. 20 noted under s.86 of the Act.

HOME. For the purposes of this article, a home is "will usually be the place, the phy- **5–040** sically defined area, where private and family life develops" (*Gomez v Spain* (2005) 41 E.H.R.R. 40 at para.53). Neither this article nor any other provision of the Convention guarantees housing of a particular standard or at all (*Chapman v United Kingdom* (2001) 33 E.H.R.R. 399, para.99). However, a refusal of the authorities to solve a housing problem of an individual suffering from a severe disease might in certain circumstances raise an issue under this article because of the impact of such refusal on the private life of the individual (*Marzari v Italy* (1999) 28 E.H.R.R. CD 175). Although not every breach of a local authority's duty to provide residential accommodation under s.21 of the National Assistance Act 1948 [now see s.18 of the Care Act 2014] will result in a breach of this article, those entitled to care under s.21 are a particularly vulnerable group. Positive measures have to be taken, by way of community care facilities, to enable them to enjoy, so far as possible, a normal and family life. The question that needs to be asked is what was the effect of the breach in practical terms on the claimant's family and private life? (*R. (on the application of Bernard) v London Borough of Enfield* [2002] EWHC 2282 (Admin); (2002) 5 C.C.L.R. 577). In *Anufrijeva v Southwalk London Borough Council* [2003] EWCA Civ 1406; [2004] 1 All E.R. 833, the Court of Appeal, in confirming the correctness of the approach adopted in *Bernard*, said at para.43:

"We find it hard to conceive, however, of a situation in which the predicament of an individual will be such that Article 8 requires him to be provided with welfare support, where his predicament is not sufficiently severe to engage Article 3. Article 8 may more readily engaged where a family unit is involved. Where the welfare of children is at stake, Article 8 may require the provision of welfare support in a manner which enables family life to continue."

In *R (on the application of N) v Secretary of State for Health* [2009] EWCA Civ 795, the Court of Appeal held that although Rampton Hospital was the patient's home, it was not the same as a private home in that it was a public institution operated as a hospital where supervision was intense for safety and security reasons. The degree to which a person could expect freedom to do as he pleased, and engage in personal and private activity, would vary according to the nature of the accommodation in which he lived. A patient in a high security hospital did not lose all rights to a private life but the nature of that life and the activities he may pursue were seriously restricted, and always supervised.

In *R. v North and East Devon Health Authority Ex p. Coughlan* [2000] 3 All E.R. 850, the Court of Appeal held that the enforced move of a patient by an NHS Trust from accommodation that had been promised as her home for life, a move that would be both emotionally devastating and seriously anti-therapeutic, was a breach of this article that was not justified by para.2.

CORRESPONDENCE. A law which allows for state interference with correspondence must not leave the authorities too much latitude. It must "indicate with reasonable clarity the scope and manner of the exercise of the relevant discretion conferred on the public authorities" (*Domenichini v Italy* (2001) 32 E.H.R.R. 4 para.33).

In *Klass v Germany* (1979) 2 E.H.R.R. 214, the Court held that this article protects telephone conversations as well as written correspondence. A similar finding would almost certainly be made on other forms of communication, such as email.

Paragraph 2

5–041   The exceptions provided for in this paragraph must be interpreted narrowly, and the need for them in any given case must be convincingly established (*Societe Colas Est v France* (2004) 39 E.H.R.R. 17 para.47). In *Re L (Care: Threshold Criteria)* [2007] 1 F.L.R. 2050 at para.51, Hedley J. said that "Art.8(2) . . . contemplate[s] the exceptional rather than the commonplace".

The principles which govern the court's approach in determining whether an interference with an art.8 right can be justified under this paragraph were identified by Newman J. in *R. (on the application of N) v Ashworth Special Hospital Authority and the Secretary of State for Health* [2001] EWHC Admin 339; [2001] M.H.L.R. 77 at para.9:

"(i) When considering whether an interference with a Convention right is proportionate the burden lies on the state to justify its actions.
(ii) The interference must go no further than is strictly necessary to achieve its permitted purpose.
(iii) The more substantial the interference the more that is required to justify it.
(iv) The court should anxiously scrutinise a decision of the executive which interferes with human rights and should consider applying an objective test 'whether the decision maker could reasonably have concluded that the interference was necessary to achieve one or more of the legitimate aims recognised by the Convention'.
(v) The mode of such objective review is more intrusive, or it could be said, more demanding than the convention *Wednesbury* test.
(vi) The court should give due deference or allow a margin of appreciation to the decision maker".

Where the interference is with an intimate part of an individual's private life, there must be particularly serious reasons to justify the interference (*Smith v United Kingdom* (2000) 29 E.H.R.R. 493 at para.89). However, the state is entitled to control even seemingly consensual sexual acts in private where it is necessary to "safeguard . . . against exploitation and corruption . . . those who are specially vulnerable because they are young, weak in body or mind, inexperienced, or in a state of special physical, official or economic dependence" (*Dudgeon v United Kingdom* (1982) 4 E.H.R.R. 149 at para.49).

IN ACCORDANCE WITH THE LAW.   The Court's case law on the meaning of this phrase was summarised in *Munjaz v United Kingdom* [2012] M.H.L.R. 351, at para.88:

"[T]he wording 'in accordance with the law' requires the impugned measure both to have some basis in domestic law and to be compatible with the rule of law, which is expressly mentioned in the preamble to the Convention and inherent in the object and purpose of Article 8. The law must thus be adequately accessible and foreseeable, that is, formulated with sufficient precision to enable the individual—if need be with appropriate advice—to regulate his conduct ([*S. v the United Kingdom* (2009) 48 E.H.R.R. 50, para.95]). It is also well-established in its case-law that the Court recognises the impossibility of attaining absolute certainty in the framing of laws and the risk that the search for certainty may entail excessive rigidity ([*Silver v the United Kingdom* (1983) 5 E.H.R.R. 247, para.88]). Instead, the level of precision required of the domestic legislation depends to a considerable degree on the content of the instrument considered, the field it is designed to cover and the number and status of those to whom it is addressed ([*Hasan v Bulgaria* (2002) 34 E.H.R.R. 55, para.84]). With respect to the need for foreseeability, what is required is that, where discretionary powers are conferred on authorities, the law must indicate the scope of any such discretion conferred on the competent authorities and the manner of its exercise with sufficient clarity to give the individual adequate protection against arbitrary interference (see, among many authorities, [*Liberty v the United Kingdom* (2009) 48 E.H.R.R. 1, paras 66–69])".

In applying these requirements to the seclusion policy adopted by Ashworth Hospital, the Court held that the discretion conferred on Ashworth to depart from the guidance in the *Code of Practice* and to formulate its own seclusion policy met the requirement of foreseeability because there was sufficient indication of the scope of discretion that Ashworth enjoyed and the manner of exercise of that discretion was indicated with sufficient clarity such as to protect the applicant against arbitrary interference with his art.8 rights (paras 89–90).

NECESSARY IN A DEMOCRATIC SOCIETY. The: **5–042**

"notion of necessity implies that the interference corresponds to a pressing social need and, in particular, that it is proportionate to the legitimate aims pursued. In determining whether an interference was 'necessary in a democratic society' the Court will take into account that a margin of appreciation is left to Contracting States. Furthermore the Court cannot confine itself to considering the impugned facts in isolation but must apply an objective standard and look at them in the light of the case as a whole" (*Matter v Slovakia* (2001) 31 E.H.R.R. 32, para.66).

The criteria used to determine whether an interference with private or family life in an expulsion case is "necessary in a democratic society" have been summarised by the Grand Chamber in *Uner v Netherlands* (2007) 45 E.H.R.R. 14 at paras 57 and 58.

ECONOMIC WELL-BEING. A court should be slow to interfere with decisions which involve a balance of competing claims on the public purse in the allocation of economic resources (*R. v Criminal Injuries Compensation Board Ex p. P* [1995] 1 All E.R. 870 per Neill L.J. at 881). This approach has been reaffirmed in home closure cases since the coming into force of the 1998 Act. For example, in *R. (on the application of Phillips and Rowe) v Walsall MBC* [2001] EWHC 789 (Admin), Lightman J. said at para.11:

"I may add that if (contrary to my view) a move such as is presently contemplated could possibly constitute an interference with a fundamental right under Article 8, it could surely be justified as required for the economic well-being of the Council and of those in need of its services. Resources of public authorities are notoriously limited and it must be a matter for elected authorities such as the Council to have leeway in how they are husbanded and applied."

PROTECTION OF HEALTH. The Court has not developed an equivalent test of "medical **5–043** necessity" in relation to this article, as it has in the context of art.3.

In *R. (on the application of Razgar) v Secretary of State for the Home Department* [2004] UKHL 27; [2004] 3 All E.R. 821 at para.59, Baroness Hale made the following comments in a case where the applicant's health needs were being properly or at least adequately met in this country and the complaint was that they would not be adequately met in the county to which he is to be expelled:

> "Although the possibility cannot be excluded, it is not easy to think of a foreign health care case which would fail under Art.3 but succeed under Art.8. There clearly must be a strong case before the Article is even engaged and then a fair balance must be struck under Art.8(2). In striking that balance, only the most compelling humanitarian considerations are likely to prevail over the legitimate aims of immigration control or public safety."

In *L v Sweden*, 45 D. & R. 181, the Commission held that a decision provisionally to release a patient who had been detained in a psychiatric hospital constituted an interference with his right to respect for family life under this article. However, the Commission went onto declare the application manifestly ill-founded as the decision was justified in the interests of the patient's health. The reason for not discharging the patient absolutely was that there were reasons to believe that she would stop taking her medication if this happened, and that this would lead to a deterioration in her health. This decision sanctions both the granting of leave to, and the conditional discharge of, a detained patient on condition that the patient continues to accept medication, as long as the terms of this paragraph are satisfied.

RIGHTS OF FREEDOM OF OTHERS. "Article 8.2 could have been, but is not, expressly limited to Convention rights and liberties"; per Stanley Burnton J. in *Craven v Secretary of State for the Home Department and the Parole Board* [2001] EWHC Admin 850 at para.35. In this case an exclusion zone attached to a prisoner's parole was upheld partly because "the respect for private life protected by Article 8 should include a victim's family right to go about their business with a minimum of anxiety, and without undue restriction on their own movements". Also note the statement of Hale L.J. in *Re W & B (Children)* [2001] EWCA Civ 757 at para.54, that the rights of the child to be taken into account in this paragraph are not confined to his Convention rights, and include his interests.

In *TV v Finland* (1994) 18 E.H.R.R. CD 179, the Commission held that the disclosure that a prisoner was HIV positive to prison staff directly involved in his custody and who themselves were subject to obligations of confidentiality was justified as being necessary "for the protection of the rights and freedoms of others". Similar considerations would apply to a patient who had been assessed as being a danger to other patients or to staff.

ARTICLE 9

FREEDOM OF THOUGHT, CONSCIENCE AND RELIGION

5–044
1. Everyone has the right to freedom of thought, conscience and religion; this right includes freedom to change his religion or belief and freedom, either alone or in community with others and in public or private, to manifest his religion or belief, in worship, teaching, practice and observance.

2. Freedom to manifest one's religion or beliefs shall be subject only to such limitations as are prescribed by law and are necessary in a democratic society in the interests of public safety, for the protection of public order, health or morals, or for the protection of the rights and freedoms of others.

GENERAL NOTE

5–045
In *JP v South London and Maudsley NHS Foundation Trust* [2012] UKUT 486 (AAC); [2013] M.H.L.R. 148, UT Judge Lane said at para.46:

> "Detention under s.2 of the Mental Health Act 1983 is not aimed at controlling political, religious or other thoughts or beliefs but at ensuring that any underlying mental disorder of the appropriate degree is assessed and (if possible) treated (*inter alia*) for the safety or

health of the patient or others. To those ends alone, he may be detained. But that is the subject matter of Article 5 of the ECHR. The jurisprudence of the European Court of Human Rights on art 9 shows that the 'Strasbourg institutions have resisted the attempts of applicants to raise issues under article 9 when they may be considered as falling under some other article of the Convention' (Lester & Pannick, *Human Rights Law and Practice* [4.9.2], LexisNexus 2009). It would, therefore, be surprising if Article 9 was engaged in relation to a decision that a patient had a mental disorder which warranted detention for assessment for a limited period justified in the interests of his own health, where such detention is lawful under Article 5."

ARTICLE 10

FREEDOM OF EXPRESSION

1. Everyone has the right to freedom of expression. This right shall include freedom to hold opinions **5–046** and to receive and impart information and ideas without interference by public authority and regardless of frontiers. This Article shall not prevent States from requiring the licensing of broadcasting, television or cinema enterprises.

2. The exercise of these freedoms, since it carries with it duties and responsibilities, may be subject to such formalities, conditions, restrictions or penalties as are prescribed by law and are necessary in a democratic society, in the interests of national security, territorial integrity or public safety, for the prevention of disorder or crime, for the protection of health or morals, for the protection of the reputation or rights of others, for preventing the disclosure of information received in confidence, or for maintaining the authority and impartiality of the judiciary.

GENERAL NOTE

The courts "have frequently stated that in the field of freedom of speech there is no dif- **5–047** ference in principle between English law and [this Article]" (*Ashworth Security Hospital v MGN Ltd* [2001] 1 All E.R. 991 at para.71 CA, per Lord Phillips M.R.). Paragraph 1 of this article guarantees the right to freedom of expression. An interference with this right entails a violation of the article if it does not fall within one of the exceptions provided for in para.2.

This Article will often overlap with an art.8 claim, especially with regard to a claim concerning access to information.

Paragraph 2

In *Kelly v BBC* [2001] 1 All E.R. 323, Munby J. said at 335:   **5–048**

"Well-known jurisprudence of the European Court on Human Rights establishes: (i) that the exceptions in paragraph 2 must be narrowly interpreted; (ii) that if a restraint is to be justified under paragraph 2 it must be 'necessary in a democratic society'—that is to say, the necessity for any such restriction must be 'convincingly established' by reference to the existence of a 'pressing social need', and the restriction must be 'proportionate to the legitimate aim pursued'; and (iii) that the restriction must be 'prescribed by law'—that is, the law must be 'adequately accessible to the citizen' and must be 'formulated with sufficient precision to enable a citizen to regulate his conduct': see *Rantzen v Mirror Group Newspapers (1986) Ltd* [1993] 4 All E.R. 975 at 990, citing *Sunday Times v United Kingdom (No.1)* (1979) 2 E.H.R.R. 245 and *Sunday Times v United Kingdom (No.2)* (1992) 14 E.H.R.R. 229".

With regard to the question whether a detained patient should be allowed to have in his possession hardcore pornographic magazines, it is likely that the courts will adopt the reasoning of Scott Baker L.J. in *R. (on the application of Morton) v The Governor of Long Lartin Prison* [2003] EWCA Civ 644, in respect of hospitals that detain patients whose mental disorder might be adversely affected if they had access to such material. His Lordship said at para.22:

"Because the prisoner lives in a small and enclosed community, the interests of others are concerned as well as those of the prisoner himself. That is why Article 10(2) bites in this case. It seems to me obvious that once material of the kind prohibited in this case is allowed in the hands of a prisoner, there is an obvious risk that it will reach the eyes and hands of others, with the consequential risk of abuse, exploitation, assault and so forth".

The interviewing of detained patients by journalists can be monitored without contravening this article. Permission for the interview need not be forthcoming if it would place the patient's well-being at risk or would have an adverse effect on other patients or on good order or security in the hospital. Where national security is involved, the interview can take place within the earshot of an official and tape-recorded (*R. (on the application of A) v Home Secretary* [2003] EWHC 2846 (Admin)).

The provisions of s.134 of the Act, under which a patient's correspondence can be with-held, are likely to be held to be in accordance with this paragraph in that the restrictions in the section "are necessary in a democratic society, in the interests of . . . public safety, . . . for the protection of health or morals, [or] for the protection of the reputation or rights of others . . . ".

ARTICLE 11

FREEDOM OF ASSEMBLY AND ASSOCIATION

5–049   1. Everyone has the right to freedom of peaceful assembly and to freedom of association with others, including the right to form and to join trade unions for the protection of his interests.

2. No restrictions shall be placed on the exercise of these rights other than such as are prescribed by law and are necessary in a democratic society in the interests of national security or public safety, for the prevention of disorder or crime, for the protection of health or morals or for the protection of the rights and freedoms of others. This Article shall not prevent the imposition of lawful restrictions on the exercise of these rights by members of the armed forces, of the police or of the administration of the State.

ARTICLE 12

RIGHT TO MARRY

5–050   Men and women of marriageable age have the right to marry and to found a family, according to the national laws governing the exercise of this right.

GENERAL NOTE

5–051   This article "secures the fundamental right of a man and a woman to marry and to found a family. The second aspect is not however a condition of the first and the inability of any couple to conceive or parent a child cannot be regarded as *per se* removing their right to enjoy the first limb of this provision" (*Goodwin v United Kingdom* (2002) 35 E.H.R.R. 18 at para.98).

While this article is confined to legally formalised heterosexual relationships (as defined by gender, see *Goodwin*, above), art.8 is far broader in its scope. An interference with fam-ily life which is justified under art.8(2) cannot at the same time constitute a violation of this article (*X & Y v Switzerland* (1978) 13 D. & R. 105).

The Marriage Act 1983 places no restrictions on mentally disordered patients, whether detained or not, from marrying as long as they have sufficient mental capacity to contract a marriage (see the General Note to the Act under the heading "Marriage"). Any substantial interference with this right would violate this article. However, the Commission in *Hamer v United Kingdom* ((1982) 4 E.H.R.R. 139) left open whether it might, exceptionally, be possible to prohibit a patient's marriage on the grounds of special dangerousness, and the consequential risk posed to the partner: see O. Thorold, "The Implications of the

European Convention on Human Rights for United Kingdom Mental Health Legislation" [1996] E.H.R.L.R. 619–636 at 634.

Although the Court has declined to require the provision of conjugal visits to prisoners by their partners, it has left open the possibility that the position might change. In *Aliev v Ukraine*, App.No.41220/98, July 29, 2003, para.188, the Court said:

> "Whilst noting with approval the reform movements in several European countries to improve prison conditions by facilitating conjugal visits, the Court considers that the refusal of such visits may for the present time be regarded as justified for the prevention of disorder and crime within the meaning of the second paragraph of Article 8 of the Convention . . . ."

Different considerations would apply to the position of mentally disordered detained patients because the justification of the "prevention of disorder and crime" will not be applicable in the majority of cases. Thorold argues that conjugal visits:

> "can help to preserve a patient's marital relationship and thereby improve longer-term mental health prognosis. Any limitation on sexual relationships between patients, or a patient and a spouse, would have to be strictly justified. A prohibition which was expressed in general terms would be in grave danger of breaching Art.12. It may therefore be necessary for a policy to be formulated which permits sexual relations subject to well-defined exceptions, of which danger to another person would clearly be one" (op. cit., at 635).

In *Secretary of State for the Home Department Ex p. Mellor* [2001] EWCA Civ 472, the Court of Appeal concluded that the qualifications on the right to respect for family life that are recognised by art.8(2) apply equally to rights under this article (per Lord Phillips M.R. at para.39). This means that justification for the exceptions referred to by Thorold must be found in art.8(2).

RIGHT TO MARRY. Even if there is no prospect of cohabitation (*Hamer v United Kingdom*, above).

ARTICLE 14

PROHIBITION OF DISCRIMINATION

5–052 The enjoyment of the rights and freedoms set forth in this Convention shall be secured without discrimination on any ground such as sex, race, colour, language, religion, political or other opinion, national or social origin, association with a national minority, property, birth or other status.

GENERAL NOTE

5–053 This article does not provide a free-standing prohibition on discrimination. It prohibits discrimination only in relation to enjoyment of rights and freedoms guaranteed by the Convention (*R. (on the application of Carson) v Secretary of State for Work and Pensions* [2005] UKHL 37; [2005] 4 All E.R. 545). In *Botta v Italy* (1998) 26 E.H.R.R. 241, the Court said at para.39:

> "Article 14 complements the other substantive provisions of the Convention and its protocols. It has no independent existence, since it has effect solely in relation to 'the enjoyment of the rights and freedoms' safeguarded by those provisions. Although the application of Article 14 does not presuppose a breach of one or more of those provisions—and to this extent it is autonomous—there can be no room for its application unless the facts of the case fall within the ambit of one or more of the latter."

A tenuous link with another provision of the Convention is not sufficient to bring this article into play (*M v Secretary of State for Work and Pensions* [2006] UKHL 11; [2006] 4 All E.R. 929).

In *Pretty v UK* (2002) 35 E.H.R.R. 1, the Court said at para.88:

"For the purpose of Article 14 a difference in treatment between persons in analogous or relevantly similar positions is discriminatory if it has no objective and reasonable justification, that is if it does not pursue a legitimate aim or if there is not a reasonable relationship of proportionality between the means employed and the aim sought to be realised. Moreover, the Contracting States enjoy a margin of appreciation in assessing whether and to what extent differences in otherwise similar situations justify a different treatment. Discrimination may also arise where States without an objective and reasonable justification fail to treat differently persons whose situations are significantly different."

Abdulaziz v UK (1985) 7 E.H.R.R. 471 is authority for the proposition that there may be a violation of this article considered together with another article (in that case art.8) in a case where there would be no violation of that other article taken alone.

ANY GROUND SUCH AS. The list that follows is illustrative, not exhaustive. In *R. (on the application of Pretty) v Director of Public Prosecutions* [2001] UKHL 61; [2002] 1 All E.R. 1 at para.105, Lord Hope held this article is capable of extending to discrimination in the enjoyment of Convention rights on the grounds of physical or mental capacity. Also note that in *B v Secretary of State for Work and Pensions* [2005] EWCA Civ 929 at para.25, Sedley L.J. said that mental capacity, "although not listed in [this article], is arguably at least as sensitive a personal characteristic, in relation to discrimination, as race or sex".

SEX. Very weighty reasons are generally required for differences of treatment based solely on gender (*Abdulaziz, Cabales and Balkandali v United Kingdom* (1985) 7 E.H.R.R. 471 at para.78).

OTHER STATUS. Which could include the status of a patient detained under the 1983 Act and a prisoner (*R (on the application of N) v Secretary of State for Health* [2009] EWCA Civ 795). This term has been held to include a personal characteristic (*Kjeldsen v Denmark* (1976) 1 E.H.R.R. 711), sexual orientation (*Salgueiro v Portugal* (2001) 31 E.H.R.R. 47), family status (*R. (on the application of L) v Manchester City Council* [2001] EWHC Admin 707 at para.91), disability (*Glor v Switzerland* (App.No.13444/04, April 30, 2009)) and "a patient's status when detained in an institution which is not a hospital following their conditional discharge" (*Secretary of State for Justice v RB* [2011] EWCA Civ 1608; [2012] M.H.L.R. 131, at para.64). In *R (RJM) v Secretary of State for Work and Pensions* [2009] 1 A.C. 311 the House of Lords held that this phrase should be given a "generous meaning", and that on that basis homelessness was a personal characteristic which fell within the ambit of this article.

ARTICLE 16

RESTRICTIONS ON POLITICAL ACTIVITY OF ALIENS

5–054 Nothing in Article 10, 11 and 14 shall be regarded as preventing the High Contracting Parties from imposing restrictions on the political activity of aliens.

ARTICLE 17

PROHIBITION OF ABUSE OF RIGHTS

Nothing in this Convention may be interpreted as implying for any State, group or person any right to **5–055** engage in any activity or perform any act aimed at the destruction of any of the rights and freedoms set forth herein or at their limitation to a greater extent than is provided for in the Convention.

ARTICLE 18

LIMITATION OF USE OF RESTRICTIONS ON RIGHTS

The restrictions permitted under this Convention to the said rights and freedoms shall not be applied **5–056** for any purpose other than those for which they have been prescribed.

PART II

THE FIRST PROTOCOL

ARTICLE 1

PROTECTION OF PROPERTY

Every natural or legal person is entitled to the peaceful enjoyment of his possessions. No one shall be **5–057** deprived of his possessions except in the public interest and subject to the conditions provided for by law and by the general principles of international law.

The preceding provisions shall not, however, in any way impair the right of a State to enforce such laws as it deems necessary to control the use of property in accordance with the general interest or to secure the payment of taxes or other contributions or penalties.

ARTICLE 2

RIGHT TO EDUCATION

No person shall be denied the right to education. In the exercise of any functions which it assumes in **5–058** relation to education and to teaching, the State shall respect the right of parents to ensure such education and teaching in conformity with their own religious and philosophical convictions.

ARTICLE 3

RIGHT TO FREE ELECTIONS

The High Contracting Parties undertake to hold free elections at reasonable intervals by secret ballot, **5–059** under conditions which will ensure the free expression of the opinion of the people in the choice of the legislature.

GENERAL NOTE

While this article is phrased in terms of the obligation to hold elections, the case law of **5–060** the Court establishes that it guarantees individual rights, including the right to vote and to stand for election. In *Hirst v United Kingdom (No.2)* (2006) 42 E.H.R.R. 41, the Court held that although states enjoy a wide margin of appreciation in determining whether restrictions on prisoners' right to vote can be justified, it could not accept that s.3 of the Representation of the People Act 1983, which provides for absolute bar on voting by any serving prisoner in any circumstances, falls within an acceptable margin of appreciation. The Court said, at para.71, that there must be a discernable link "between the sanction and the conduct and circumstances of the individual concerned". This ruling has required the Government to review the position of patients who are detained under the Mental Health Act and who are disenfranchised by virtue of the operation of s.3A of the 1983 Act: see the General Note to the Act under the heading "Voting".

PART III

THE SIXTH PROTOCOL

ARTICLE 1

ABOLITION OF THE DEATH PENALTY

5–061   The death penalty shall be abolished. No one shall be condemned to such penalty or executed.

ARTICLE 2

DEATH PENALTY IN TIME OF WAR

5–062   A state may make provision in its law for the death penalty in respect of acts committed in time of war or of imminent threat of war; such penalty shall be applied only in the instances laid down in the law and in accordance with its provisions. The State shall communicate to the Secretary General of the Council of Europe the relevant provisions of that law.

PART 6

DEPRIVATIONS OF LIBERTY—MENTAL HEALTH ACT 1983 OR MENTAL CAPACITY ACT 2005?

This Part considers the following question: if action taken, or about to be taken, **6–001** with respect to a mentally incapacitated person constitutes a deprivation of that person's liberty which Act should be invoked, the Mental Health Act ("the 1983 Act") or the Mental Capacity Act ("the 2005 Act")? This choice exists as a result of the Government's response to the finding of the European Court of Human Rights ("the ECtHR") in *HL v United Kingdom* (2005) 40 E.H.R.R. 32.

HL v United Kingdom (the *"Bournewood case"*)

In *HL,* Mr L alleged that he had been detained at the Bournewood Hospital as an **6–002** informal patient in violation of art.5(1) of the European Convention on Human Rights ("the Convention") which is designed to ensure that no one should be arbitrarily deprived of his liberty. He also claimed that the procedures available to him for a review of the legality of his detention did not satisfy the requirements of art.5(4), which provides a person who has been deprived of his liberty with a right to a speedy independent legal review of the detention. The facts of the case are remarkable. From the age of 13, for a period of over 30 years, Mr L, who had a profound learning disability, was autistic and lacked the capacity to consent or dissent from being in hospital, was a patient at the Bournewood Hospital. He was eventually discharged into the community to live with carers, Mr and Mrs E. Under their care Mr L flourished for three years until an incident occurred that led to his readmission to hospital. While attending a day centre, Mr L became particularly agitated and he could not be calmed. Mr and Mrs E, who had been able to deal with such incidents successfully, could not be contacted. A doctor attended the day centre and administered a sedative to Mr L. On the advice of Mr L's social worker, he was taken to the Bournewood Hospital by which time the effect of the sedative was beginning to wear off and he was becoming increasingly agitated. Mr L was assessed by a psychiatrist as requiring inpatient treatment. On Mr L's admission, his consultant psychiatrist considered whether it was necessary to detain him under the provisions of the 1983 Act but decided that this was not necessary because he appeared to be fully compliant and had not resisted admission to the hospital. He was therefore admitted informally. Mr and Mrs E made it plain that they wanted to take Mr L back into their care. Mr L's consultant psychiatrist was not prepared to countenance this and he remained in the hospital. Proceedings were commenced in the name of Mr L against the Bournewood NHS Trust for judicial review of the trust's decision to detain him and for a writ of habeas corpus to release him from detention. It was claimed that Mr L's detention was unlawful on the ground that the 1983 Act, which had not been invoked, was the only basis for the hospital's right to detain him. The hospital claimed that Mr L was not being detained, but if he was, the detention was authorised under the common law doctrine of necessity.

Subsequent to the decision of the House of Lords ([1998] 3 All E.R. 289) to dismiss Mr L's claim, an application was made to the ECtHR.

The decision of the ECtHR focused on the finding of the House of Lords that the detention of a compliant mentally incapacitated patient could be justified under the doctrine of necessity. The court held that:

1. In order to determine whether a person has been deprived of his liberty for the purposes of art.5(1) of the Convention, the starting point must be the specific situation of the individual concerned and account must be taken of a whole range of factors arising in a particular case such as the type, duration, effects and manner of implementation of the measure in question. The distinction between a deprivation of, and a restriction upon, liberty is merely one of degree or intensity and not one of nature or substance (para.89).

2. The correspondence between HL's carers and his psychiatrist reflected both the carers' wish to have HL immediately released to their care and, equally, the clear intention of the health care professionals to exercise strict control over his assessment, treatment, contacts and, notably, movement and residence: HL would only be released from the hospital to the care of his carers as and when the professionals considered it appropriate. It followed that HL was being deprived of his liberty because "professionals treating and managing [HL] exercised complete and effective control over his movements" in that he "was under continuous supervision and control and was not free to leave [to return to his carers]" (para.91). The fact that HL might have been on a ward which was not "locked" or "lockable" was not determinative (para.92). With regard to HL's compliance to his admission, the court observed that:

   "the right to liberty is too important in a democratic society for a person to lose the benefit of Convention protection for the single reason that he may have given himself up to be taken into detention, especially when it is not disputed that that person is legally incapable of consenting to, or disagreeing with, the proposed action" (para.90).

3. The court found "striking the lack of any fixed procedural rules by which the admission and detention of compliant incapacitated patients is conducted" when contrasted with "the extensive network of safeguards applicable to psychiatric committals covered by the 1983 Act" (para.120). This absence of procedural safeguards in the doctrine of necessity failed to protect HL against arbitrary deprivations of his liberty. His detention therefore violated art.5(1).

4. There had also been a violation of art.5(4) as HL did not have the opportunity to have the lawfulness of his detention reviewed by a court as neither judicial review nor other judicial remedies cited by the Government satisfied the requirements of art.5(4) (para.141).

What constitutes a "deprivation of liberty"?

6–003 Restrictions on a person's movements and freedom to chose his residence which do not constitute a deprivation of liberty and which are necessary "for the prevention of crime, for the protection of health or morals, or for the protection of the rights and freedom of others" are allowed for under art.2 of Protocol 4 of the Convention, which has not been ratified by the United Kingdom. According to Lord Hope, "art.2 of Protocol 4 helps to put the ambit of [art.5] into its proper perspective" (*Austin v Commissioner of Police of the Metropolis* [2009] UKHL 5 at para.15).

In *Secretary of State for the Home Department v JJ* [2007] UKHL 45, Lady Hale said at para.57:

> "My Lords, what does it mean to be deprived of one's liberty? Not, we are all agreed, to be deprived of the freedom to live one's life as one pleases. It means to be deprived of one's physical liberty . . . And what does this mean? It must mean being forced or obliged to be at a particular place where one does not choose to be . . . But even that is not always enough because merely being required to live at a particular place or to keep within a particular geographical area does not, without more, amount to a deprivation of liberty. There must be a greater degree of control over one's physical ability than that. But how much?"

The Supreme Court addressed this question in *P v Cheshire West and Chester Council; P and Q v Surrey County Council* [2014] UKSC 19; [2014] 2 All E.R. 585 ("*Cheshire West*") which are cases about the criteria for judging whether the living arrangements made for a mentally incapacitated person amount to a deprivation of liberty. If they do, then the deprivation has to be authorised, either by the Court of Protection or by the deprivation of liberty safeguards: see below. The following description of the situation of the individuals who were the focus of the hearing is taken from the press summary prepared by the court:

> "P and Q (otherwise known as MIG and MEG) are sisters who became the subject of care proceedings in 2007 when they were respectively 16 and 15. Both have learning disabilities. MIG was placed with a foster mother to whom she was devoted and went to a further education unit daily. She never attempted to leave the foster home by herself but would have been restrained from doing so had she tried. MEG was moved from foster care to a residential home for learning disabled adolescents with complex needs. She sometimes required physical restraint and received tranquillising medication. When the care proceedings were transferred to the Court of Protection in 2009, the judge held that these living arrangements were in the sisters' best interests and did not amount to a deprivation of liberty. This finding was upheld by the Court of Appeal.

> P is an adult born with cerebral palsy and Down's syndrome who requires 24 hour care. Until he was 37 he lived with his mother but when her health deteriorated the local social services authority obtained orders from the Court of Protection that it was in P's best interests to live in accommodation arranged by the authority. Since November 2009 he has lived in a staffed bungalow with other residents near his home and has one to one support to enable him to leave the house frequently for activities and visits. Intervention is sometimes required when he exhibits challenging behaviour. The judge held that these arrangements did deprive him of his liberty but that it was in P's best interests for them to continue. The Court of Appeal substituted a declaration that the arrangements did not involve a deprivation of liberty, after comparing his circumstances with another person of the same age and disabilities as P."

The scope of article 5 of the ECHR

6–004 The "first and most fundamental question" before the court in *Cheshire West* was "whether the concept of physical liberty protected by art.5 is the same for everyone, regardless of whether or not they are mentally or physically disabled" (per Lady Hale at para.33). Lady Hale, who gave the lead judgment, provided a forthright answer:

> "45. [I]t is axiomatic that people with disabilities, both mental and physical, have the same human rights as the rest of the human race. It may be that those rights have sometimes to be limited or restricted because of their disabilities, but the starting point should be the same as that for everyone else. This flows inexorably from the universal character of human rights, founded on the inherent dignity of all human beings, and is confirmed in the United Nations Convention on the Rights of Persons with Disabilities. Far from disability entitling the state to deny such people human rights: rather it places upon the state (and upon others) the duty to make reasonable accommodation to cater for the special needs of those with disabilities.

> 46. Those rights include the right to physical liberty, which is guaranteed by article 5 of the European Convention. This is not a right to do or to go where one pleases. It is a more focussed right, not to be deprived of that physical liberty. But, as it seems to me, what it means to be deprived of liberty must be the same for everyone, whether or not they have physical or mental disabilities. If it would be a deprivation of my liberty to be obliged to live in a particular place, subject to constant monitoring and control, only allowed out with close supervision, and unable to move away without permission even if such an opportunity became available, then it must also be a deprivation of the liberty of a disabled person. The fact that my living arrangements are comfortable, and indeed make my life as enjoyable as it could possibly be, should make no difference. A gilded cage is still a cage."

Although a minority of the justices could "see the attractions of a universal test, applicable to all regardless of any physical or mental disabilities", as Lady Hale proposed, they considered that "it is not a concept which we can find reflected in the Strasbourg cases" and that the ECtHR "has remained wedded to a case-specific test" (per Lord Carnwarth and Lord Hodge at para.94).

How to identify a deprivation of liberty?

6–005 Lord Kerr defined liberty at para.76:

> "Liberty means the state or condition of being free from external constraint. It is predominantly an objective state. It does not depend on one's disposition to exploit one's freedom. Nor is it diminished by one's lack of capacity."

Lady Hale examined the relevant case law of the ECtHR to identify the essential character of a deprivation of liberty. Three components were identified:
  (i) the objective component of confinement in a particular restricted place for a not negligible length of time;
  (ii) the subjective component of lack of valid consent; and
  (iii) the attribution of responsibility to the state.

Components (ii) and (iii), which are considered below, were not in issue before the court, but component (i) was. With regard to component (i), Lady Hale said at para.38:

> "Simply asking whether a person is 'confined' is not enough except in obvious cases. The 'starting point' is always upon the 'concrete situation' of the particular person concerned and 'account must be taken of a whole range of criteria such as the type, duration, effects and manner of implementation of the measures in question'. The presence or absence of coercion is also relevant. Thus there is no single 'touchstone' of what constitutes a deprivation of liberty in this or any other context."

The "starting point" identified by Lady Hale is taken from the case of *Guzzardi v Italy* (1980) 3 E.H.R.R. 33. In *Guzzardi* it was said that the difference between "deprivation of and restriction upon liberty is . . . merely one of degree or intensity, and not one of nature or substance" (para.93). Lady Hale said that the cases before the court were not about this distinction (para.48), although it is difficult to see why this was the case.

Rather than attempt to lay down a prescriptive list of criteria for a deprivation of liberty, Lady Hale identified, at para.50, the factors that are *not* relevant to the determination. They are:
  (i)   the person's compliance or lack of objection;
  (ii) the relative normality of the placement (whatever the comparison made); and
  (iii) the reason or purpose behind a particular placement.
With regard to factor (ii), Lord Kerr said at para.77:

> "The question whether one is restricted (as a matter of actuality) is determined by comparing the extent of your actual freedom with someone of your age and station whose freedom is not limited. Thus a teenager of the same age and familial background as MIG and MEG is the relevant comparator for them. If one compares their state with a person of similar age and full capacity it is clear that their liberty is in fact circumscribed. They may not be conscious, much less resentful, of the constraint but, objectively, limitations on their freedom are in place."

The attribution of responsibility to the state

In *A (child), Re and C (adult), Re* [2010] EWHC 978 (Fam) Munby J. agreed with counsel's submission that such responsibility may happen in one of three ways:
  (i)   First, by the "direct involvement" of public authorities in the person's deprivation of liberty. If it takes place in a hospital or care home that is run by a public authority then the State will be directly involved. But even where the place of detention is privately owned, the State may be, or become, directly involved in the deprivation of liberty.
  (ii) Secondly, the State can violate art.5(1) if its courts, in domestic proceedings brought by a detainee, fail to interpret the provisions of domestic law in the spirit of art.5.
  (iii) Thirdly, the State can violate its positive obligations to protect the detainee against interferences with his liberty carried out by private persons.

In this case, his Lordship said at para.106 said that a local authority will only be responsible for a deprivation of liberty in a domestic setting so as to engage the state's responsibility for the deprivation under art.5 if it is "directly or actively involved in the domestic, family regime" and that the mere provision of support services for the family would not be sufficient to trigger such responsibility.

The close involvement of P's family in her care at her home led Bodey J. to reach the following conclusion in *W City Council v Mrs L* [2015] EWCOP 20 at para.27:

> "This is a shared arrangement set up by agreement with a caring and pro-active family: and the responsibility of the State is, it seems to me, diluted by the strong role which the family has played and continues to play. I do not consider in such circumstances that the mischief of State interference at which Article 5 was and is directed, sufficiently exists."

The lack of valid consent to the deprivation of liberty
If a person has validly consented to his confinement, there can be no deprivation of liberty (*Stanev v Bulgaria* (2012) 55 E.H.R.R. 22, para.117).

The information that must be provided to a patient before he makes a decision whether to consent to a placement in a hospital which amounts to a deprivation of liberty was identified by Baker J., in *A Primary Care Trust v LDV* [2013] EWHC 272 (Fam) which is considered in the General Note to s.131 of the 1983 Act.

Whether an adult in the exercise of parental responsibility may lawfully detain or authorise the deprivation of liberty of a child was considered by Keehan J. in *Trust A v X* [2015] EWHC 922 (Fam): see the General Note to s.131.

The "acid test"

6–006 In *Cheshire West* at para.49, Lady Hale identified the "acid test" for a deprivation of liberty as being the fact that the person concerned "was under continuous supervision and control and was not free to leave" (*HL v United Kingdom,* above, para. 91). It is important to appreciate that to be deprived of his liberty the person must be under continuous supervision *and* control *and* must not be free to leave. Lord Neuberger added "area and period of confinement" to the test at para.63. The significance of the term "area" is not clear. With regard to the period of confinement, in *Storck v Germany* (2006) 43 E.H.R.R. 6 at para.74, the ECtHR held that will be no deprivation of liberty if the confinement in question is for a negligible length of time. Neither is there a deprivation of liberty if the deprivation is required for a short period in order to respond to an emergency (*X v United Kingdom* (1982) 4 E.H.R.R. 188, para.41). However, cases are very fact sensitive and in *ZH v Commissioner of the Police for the Metropolis* [2013] EWCA Civ 69 a deprivation of liberty was found to have occurred in a situation where P had been subjected to intense restraint for approximately 40 minutes. This was a case where "the restraint of ZH was closely analogous to the classic or paradigm case of detention in prison or a police cell" (per Lord Dyson MR at para.83).

Lady Hale said the supervision and control is not relevant only insofar as it demonstrates that the person is not free to leave as a "person might be under constant supervision and control but still be free to leave should he express the desire so to do. Conversely, it is possible to imagine situations in which a person is not free to leave but is not under such continuous supervision and control as to lead to the conclusion that he was deprived of his liberty". For an example of the latter situation, see *W City Council v Mrs L* [2015] EWCOP 20 where, although Mrs L was prevented from leaving her home, the restrictions placed on her were not "continuous or complete" (para.26).

Continuous supervision and control

What constitutes continuous supervision and control? Although it is clearly some- **6–007** thing more substantial that occasional supervision and control, no guidance was provided by the court on the nature or extent of the supervision and control that must be present. This is regrettable, given that a court has to consider "the degree of supervision and control over the person's movements" (*Chosta v Ukraine*, App.No. 35807/05, January 14, 2014). In *Guzzardi v Italy* (1981) 3 E.H.R.R. 333 at para.95, the ECtHR said that the supervision was carried out "strictly and on an almost constant basis". Lady Hale used the phrase "constant monitoring and control" at para.46 of her judgment. Given that "continuous" means "without a break" (Shorter OED), it is suggested that a significant degree of supervision and control which is exercised on an almost constant basis has to be present before this component of the "acid test" can be satisfied.

It is important to recognise that control, which involves the exercise of power to ensure that something happens to a person even if he does not want it to happen, is not the same as support, which is to help and/or encourage a person to do something for himself. It is not entirely clear what "supervision" means in this context. It probably involves both the monitoring (see Lady Hale, above) and observation of individuals. It is submitted that all mentally incapacitated hospital in-patients should be subject to continuous supervision, but that not all such patients would be the subject of continuous control. The point at which "supervision" becomes "control" was not addressed by the court.

It is important for those who are assessing whether a deprivation of liberty exists to take account of the cumulative effect of the restrictions imposed on a person (*Guzzardi v Italy*, above, para.95), bearing in mind that the exercise of restraint which does not constitute a deprivation of liberty is authorised under s.6 of the 2005 Act.

Not free to leave

No analysis of this component of the "acid test" was provided, although in the **6–008** cases before the court not free to leave meant "not free to go anywhere without permission and close supervision" (per Lady Hale at para.48). It is not a precondition of the test that the person must have expressed a desire to leave; it is sufficient for those in control to have formed the opinion that the person would be prevented from leaving if he made an attempt to leave. The vast majority of people who have a significant degree of mental incapacity are likely to come into this category. It is suggested that if the person lacks the physical ability to leave, the test would be satisfied if those in control would have prevented him from leaving if he had that ability. It seems that the absence of an alternative place of residence for P is not a relevant factor.

Deprivation of liberty in domestic settings

With regard to the situation of MIG and MEG in *Cheshire West*, Lady Hale said at **6–009** para.54:

"If the acid test is whether a person is under the complete supervision and control of those caring for her and is not free to leave the place where she lives, then the truth is that both MIG and MEG are being deprived of their liberty. Furthermore, that deprivation is the responsibility of the state. Similar constraints would not necessarily amount to a deprivation of liberty for the purpose of article 5 if imposed by parents in the exercise of their ordinary parental responsibilities and outside the legal framework governing state intervention in the lives of children or people who lack the capacity to make their own decisions."

Lord Neuberger said at para.72:

"In the case of children living at home, what might otherwise be a deprivation of liberty would normally not give rise to an infringement of article 5 because it will have been imposed not by the state, but by virtue of what the Strasbourg court has called 'the rights of the holder of parental authority', which are extensive albeit that they 'cannot be unlimited' (see *Nielsen v Denmark* (1988) 11 EHRR 175, para 72, a decision which, at least on its facts, is controversial, as evidenced by the strength of the dissenting opinions). However, it is fair to say that, while this point would apply to adoptive parents, I doubt that it would include foster parents (unless, perhaps, they had the benefit of a residence order). But in the great majority of cases of people other than young children living in ordinary domestic circumstances, the degree of supervision and control and the freedom to leave would take the situation out of article 5.4. And, where article 5.4 did apply, no doubt the benignly intimate circumstances of a domestic home would frequently help to render any deprivation of liberty easier to justify" [NB It is suggested that the references to art 5.4 should be references to art.5.1].

A minority of the Justices did not agree that MIG and MEG were deprived of their liberty on the ground "that nobody using ordinary language would describe people living happily in a domestic setting as being deprived of their liberty" (per Lord Carnwath and Lord Hodge at para.99).

In *W City Council v Mrs L* [2015] EWCOP 20 at para.24, Bodey J. said that the fact that Mrs L who was living in her own home was "capable of expressing her wishes and feelings in such things as for example her choice of clothes, the choice of what she does around the property, and in her going in and out of the garden at will" was "relevant" in the evaluation of whether Mrs L is being deprived of her liberty. His Lordship also made reference at para.28 to Lady Hale's statement in *Cheshire West* that "the presence or absence of coercion" is a relevant consideration.

The case law of the European Court of Human Rights

6–010 The effect of s.64(5) of the 2005 Act is that the interpretation of the meaning of a "deprivation of liberty" will evolve with successive decisions of the ECtHR. Lady Hale described the case law of the ECtHR on the meaning of a deprivation of liberty as being "clear in some respects but not in others" (para.32).

When examining decisions of the ECtHR on the meaning of "continuous supervision and control" and "not free to leave", it should be noted that in *R. (on the application of Gillan) v Metropolitan Police Commissioner* [2006]

UKHL 12, Lord Bingham said that the jurisprudence of the ECtHR on what constitutes a deprivation of liberty "is closely focused on the facts of particular cases, and this makes it perilous to transpose the outcome of one case to another where the facts are different" (para.23).

Policy

Lady Hale made the following comments at para.57 under this heading. They contain a thinly veiled plea for legislative reform: **6–011**

> "Because of the extreme vulnerability of people like P, MIG and MEG, I believe that we should err on the side of caution in deciding what constitutes a deprivation of liberty in their case. They need a periodic independent check on whether the arrangements made for them are in their best interests. Such checks need not be as elaborate as those currently provided for in the Court of Protection or in the Deprivation of Liberty safeguards (which could in due course be simplified and extended to placements outside hospitals and care homes). Nor should we regard the need for such checks as in any way stigmatising of them or of their carers. Rather, they are a recognition of their equal dignity and status as human beings like the rest of us."

Implications of the judgement

Although the judgment clarified the law by identifying the factors that are to be **6–012** disregarded when determining whether a deprivation of liberty exists, practitioners will continue to be faced with the task of deciding whether a person is subject to continuous supervision and control and is free to leave the place where he is. This will not always be an easy task in the light of the Supreme Court's failure to provide guidance on the components of the "acid test".

Of particular significance are the findings of the court that (i) a deprivation of liberty can occur in a situation where P and his family are perfectly happy with the placement, (ii) the deprivation of liberty can occur in a placement which comprises living arrangements of relative normality, (iii) P does not have to try to leave in order to found to be not free to leave, (iv) the absence of an objection to the placement by P cannot be equated with consent, and (v) the fact that all that can be done for P is being done is not relevant to the existence of a deprivation of liberty. These findings have resulted in a very significant increase in the number of individuals who are assessed as being deprived of their liberty.

As "account must be taken of a whole range of criteria such as the type, duration, effects and manner of implementation of the measures in question" (Lady Hale at para.38) before a determination is made as to whether a person is deprived of his liberty and as this formulation enables a court "to have regard to the specific context and circumstances surrounding types of restriction other than the paradigm of confinement in a cell" (*Austin v United Kingdom* (App.No.39692/09), March 15, 2012, para.59), consideration should be given to whether a degree of pragmatism should be adopted when making the determination. For example, it is suggested that mentally incapacitated patients who are receiving life sustaining treatments in an intensive care unit of a hospital would not be the subject of a deprivation of liberty due to the type and manner of the restrictions that are being imposed. The contention that a degree of pragmatism may be adopted when making such determinations is supported by the following comment of

Lord Hope in *Austin v Commissioner of Police of the Metropolis* [2009] UKHL 16, at para.34:

> "I would hold therefore that there is room, even in a case of fundamental rights as to whose application no restriction or limitation is permitted by the Convention, for a pragmatic approach to be taken which takes full account of all the circumstances."

It is also noteworthy that Lord Neuberger said that the "acid test" proposed by Lady Hale "should be adopted unless there is good reason not to do so" (para.61).

The Law Society has published "Identifying a deprivation of liberty: a practical guide" (2015). This comprehensive guide can be accessed at the Society's website.

The response of the Government to the judgment in *HL v United Kingdom*

6–013 In order to remedy the breaches of art.5 identified by the ECtHR in *HL v United Kingdom*, the Government undertook to provide additional procedural safeguards for incapacitated people who were not subject to the 1983 Act, but whose care and treatment involved a deprivation of liberty. Accordingly, a consultative document ("'Bournewood' Consultation: The approach to be taken in response to the judgment of the European Court of Human Rights in the 'Bournewood' case" (March 2005)) was issued by the Government. The following options were identified:

1. A new form of "protective care" which would consist of a new system to govern admission/detention procedures, reviews of detention and appeals.
2. Extending the use of detention under the 1983 Act to the *Bournewood* group of patients.
3. Using existing arrangements for guardianship under the 1983 Act (modified as necessary).

A report of the outcome of the consultation was published in June 2006. At the same time the Government announced its decision to proceed with the protective care option, which had been favoured by the majority of respondents to the consultation, with a view to new deprivation of liberty safeguards being introduced into the Mental Capacity Act 2005. The Mental Health Bill (now the Mental Health Act 2007) was identified as a suitable vehicle through which to amend the 2005 Act for this purpose.

Deprivations of Liberty under the Mental Capacity Act 2005

6–014 Section 4A of the 2005 Act prohibits the deprivation of the liberty of a person under that Act other than in the following situations:

(i) where, in an order made under s.16(2)(a), the Court of Protection has authorised the deprivation;
(ii) where the deprivation is authorised for life-sustaining or other emergency treatment while a decision is awaited from the Court (s.4B); or
(iii) where the deprivation is authorised by Sch.A1.

As an authorisation under Sch.A1 can only apply to the deprivation of a person's liberty in a hospital or a care home, an application must be made to the Court of Protection if the deprivation takes place elsewhere. A deprivation of liberty authorised under the 2005 Act does not entitle the institution to do anything other than detain the patient or resident for the purposes of the order or authorisation.

The authorisation procedures, which are set out in Sch.A1 (and the associated Sch.1A), are considered in Pt 2 of the author's *Mental Capacity Act Manual* (2014). There are two types of authorisation: standard and urgent. A "managing authority" must request a standard authorisation when it appears likely that at some time during the next 28 days someone will be accommodated in its hospital or care home in circumstances that amount to a deprivation of liberty within the meaning of art.5. The request must be made to the "supervisory body". Whenever possible, authorisation should be obtained in advance of the deprivation occurring. Where this is not possible, and the managing authority believes it is necessary to deprive someone of their liberty in their best interests before the standard authorisation process can be completed, the managing authority must itself give an urgent authorisation and then apply for a standard authorisation.

Schedule 1A—persons ineligible to be deprived of liberty by the Mental Capacity Act

The 2005 Act cannot be used to deprive P of his liberty if P is "ineligible": see **6–015** s.16A of the 2005 Act for the Court of Protection and Sch.A1 paras 12(e) and 17 for the authorisation procedure. P is ineligible if he falls within Cases A to E of Sch.1A.

In *GJ v Foundation Trust* [2009] EWHC 2972 (Fam); [2010] M.H.L.R. 13 and *AM v South London & Maudsley NHS Foundation Trust* [2013] UKUT 365 (AAC); [2014] M.H.L.R. 181, Charles J. analysed the circumstances under which the 1983 Act has primacy over the 2005 Act. These cases are considered in the notes to Case E and under the heading "The 1983 Act or the 2005 Act", below.

In the following notes, "P" is used to denote a person who would otherwise satisfy the authorisation eligibility criteria set out in Sch.A1, and references to paragraph numbers are references to the paragraphs in Sch.1A.

Case A (Patients detained under the Mental Health Act 1983)
P is ineligible if he is subject to the "hospital treatment regime" and is detained **6–016** under that regime in either an independent or NHS hospital by virtue of being subject to a "hospital treatment obligation", i.e. he is detained under ss.2, 4, 3, 35, 36, 37, 38, 44, 45A, 47, 48 or 51 of the 1983 Act or under "another England and Wales enactment which has the same effect as a hospital treatment obligation", such as the Criminal Procedure (Insanity) Act 1964 (paras 2, 8). The consequence of this is that if P is detained under the 1983 Act he is ineligible for detention under the 2005 Act for any purpose (*A NHS Trust v Dr A* [2013] EWHC 2442 (COP)). However, P could be treated for a physical disorder under that Act.

Case B (Patients on Leave of Absence or Conditional Discharge)
This Case applies if P is subject to the "hospital treatment regime" (i.e. he is sub- **6–017** ject to a "hospital treatment obligation": see above) but is not detained in hospital under that regime. This covers patients who have been granted leave of absence under s.17 of the 1983 Act or who have been granted a conditional discharge under either s.42 or s.73 of that Act. P will be ineligible if:

(i) the proposed course of action under the 2005 Act is "not in accordance with a requirement" which the 1983 Act imposes, such as a requirement as to where P is, or is not, to reside (para.3). This means that P would be ineligible if, for example, there is a conflict between where P is required to reside under the conditions of a conditional discharge and where he would be required to reside under a standard authorisation; or

   (ii) the proposed care and treatment to be administered under the 2005 Act "consists in whole or in part of medical treatment for mental disorder in a hospital" (para.4). This means that an authorisation cannot be used as an alternative to the procedures for a patient's recall to hospital under the 1983 Act. However, the patient would be eligible if he required treatment in hospital for a physical disorder: see, for example, *Re P* [2014] EWHC 119 (COP).

Case C (Patients on a Community Treatment Order)

6–018 P is ineligible if:

   (i) he is subject to a "community treatment regime", i.e. a community treatment order under s.17A of the 1983 Act, or "an obligation under another England and Wales enactment which has the same effect as a community treatment order" (para.9); and

   (ii) either of the situations set out in paras (i) or (ii) of Case B, above, apply.

Case D (Patients subject to Guardianship)

6–019 If P is subject to a guardianship application under s.7 of the 1983 Act, a guardianship order under s.37 of that Act, or an obligation under another England and Wales enactment which has similar effect (para.10), he will be ineligible if:

   (i) the proposed course of action under the 2005 Act is not in accordance with a requirement imposed by the guardian, including any requirement where P is to reside (para.3). This means that P would be ineligible if, for example, there is a conflict between where P is required to reside by the guardian and where he would be required to reside under a standard authorisation; or

   (ii) the standard authorisation would authorise P to be a mental health patient (i.e. a person accommodated in a hospital for the purpose of being given medical treatment for mental disorder (para.16)), P objects (or would be likely to object if he was in a position to do so) to being a mental patient or to being given some or all of the mental health treatment, and no valid consent has been given by a donee of a lasting power of attorney or a court deputy to each matter to which P objects: see the notes on Case E. If such consent is forthcoming, P becomes eligible. The donee and the deputy will be required to act in P's best interests when making their decision (s.4 of the 2005 Act). In determining whether P would be likely to object, regard must be had to all the circumstances, including P's behaviour, his wishes and feelings and his views values and beliefs, although circumstances from the past only need to be considered insofar as it is appropriate to consider them (para.5).

Case E (Patients who are "within the scope" of the 1983 Act but are not subject to it)

6–020 P is "within the scope" of the 1983 Act if an application under s.2 or s.3 of that Act "could be made in respect of him" and P could be detained in a hospital in pursuance of such an application, were one made (para.12(1)). Note that the reference is to "a hospital"; the assessor cannot restrict his or her consideration to the hospital where the patient might be receiving treatment for a physical condition.

A patient will not come within the scope of the 1983 Act if it is not possible to make an application under either s.2 or 3 in respect of him by virtue of the ruling in *R. v East London and The City Mental Health Trust Ex p. Brandenburg* [2003] UKHL 58 where it was held that a patient who had been discharged from the 1983 Act by a Mental Health Review Tribunal could not be re-detained under that Act in the absence of a "new information" test being satisfied.

When assessing whether P comes within the scope of the 1983 Act, it is to be assumed that the necessary medical recommendations are in place (para.12(3),(4)) and that the treatment referred to in s.3(2)(c) of that Act cannot be provided under the 2005 Act (para.12(5)).

If P comes within the scope of the 1983 Act, he would be ineligible if the situation set out in para.(ii) of Case D, above, applies, i.e. he objects (or would be likely to object if he was in a position to do so) to being admitted to hospital or to being treated for his mental disorder there and no valid consent has been given by a donee or a deputy. If a donee or deputy consents, P will be eligible. In determining whether P would be likely to object, regard must be had to all the circumstances, including P's behaviour, his wishes and feelings and his views, values and beliefs, although circumstances from the past only need to be considered insofar as it is appropriate to consider them (para.5, and see below).

In *GJ v Foundation Trust* [2009] EWHC 2972 (Fam); [2010] M.H.L.R. 13, Charles J. said that as the test in s.3(2)(c) relates to treatment rather than assessment, "an assessment can be said to be outside paragraph 5(3) of Sch.1A to the MCA [para.5 of Sch.1A is set out below]. But, as the focus of this aspect of the authorisation scheme concerning eligibility is (a) on P being detained in a hospital or in a care home for the purpose of being given care or treatment (see paras 1(2) and 2 of Sch.A1 to the MCA), and (b) arises when an application under s.2 or s.3 MHA could be made in respect of P, in my judgment the provisions looked at as a whole have the result that the assessor under the MCA should also proceed on the assumption that assessment and treatment under s.2 MHA 1983 cannot be provided under the MCA" (para.44).

In determining whether the first condition of the objection test (see below) is satisfied i.e. the relevant instrument "authorises P to be a mental health patient", his Lordship held in *GJ* that the decision maker should adopt a "but for" test if P suffers from both a mental and a physical disorder (para.87). This means that the decision maker should ask (i) what treatment would P receive for his physical disorder which is unconnected to his mental disorder, and (ii) what treatment would P receive for his mental disorder (including treatment for a physical disorder or illness that is connected to his mental disorder and/or which is likely to directly affect his mental disorder). The decision maker should then ask whether, "but for" the need for P to have treatment for his physical disorder, should P be detained in hospital. If the answer is in the negative, P does not satisfy the test. Put another way, the test is not satisfied if the need for treatment for his physical disorder is "the only effective reason" for P's detention (para.89).

His Lordship said that the "objection" condition has to be looked at "without taking any fine distinctions between the potential reasons for the objection to treatment of different types, or to simply being in a hospital. As is recognised and provided for by para.5(6), this is because it is often going to be the case that the relevant person (P) does not have the capacity to make a properly informed and balanced decision. So what matters, applying the approach set out in paragraph 5(6), is whether P will or does object to what is proposed" (para.83). This statement establishes a low threshold for establishing whether P objects in that any non compliant behaviour by P is likely to constitute evidence of an objection.

The Code of Practice on the Deprivation of Liberty Safeguards, para.4.46, states that if there is reason to think that P would object if able to do so, then P "should be assumed to be objecting". It is not the role of the assessor to consider whether an objection is reasonable.

Paragraph 5 of Sch.1A reads:

"P objects to being a mental health patient etc

5.—(1) This paragraph applies in cases D and E in the table in paragraph 2.

(2) P is ineligible if the following conditions are met.

(3) The first condition is that the relevant instrument authorises P to be a mental health patient.

(4) The second condition is that P objects—

(a) to being a mental health patient, or

(b) to being given some or all of the mental health treatment.

(5) The third condition is that a donee or deputy has not made a valid decision to consent to each matter to which P objects.

(6) In determining whether or not P objects to something, regard must be had to all the circumstances (so far as they are reasonably ascertainable), including the following—

(a) P's behaviour;

(b) P's wishes and feelings;

(c) P's views, beliefs and values.

(7) But regard is to be had to circumstances from the past only so far as it is still appropriate to have regard to them."

The 1983 Act or the 2005 Act?

Deprivations of liberty in hospitals

6–021 The *Code of Practice* guidance on "Detention under the Act or deprivation of liberty under a DoLS authorisation?" is reproduced in Part 4. Paragraph 13.69 of the *Code* states:

> "In the rare cases where neither the Act nor a DoLS authorisation nor a Court of Protection order is appropriate, then to avoid an unlawful deprivation of liberty it may be necessary to make an application to the High Court to use its inherent jurisdiction to authorise the deprivation of liberty."

Schedule 1A sets out the circumstances that prevent a person who is being deprived of his liberty from being the subject of a standard authorisation under the 2005 Act. If Sch.1A applies, the 1983 Act must be used. In *AM v South London & Maudsley NHS Foundation Trust* [2013] UKUT 365 (AAC); [2014] M.H.L.R. 181, para.28, Charles J. reached the following conclusions:

"(i) in the circumstances defined therein the DOLS were intended to and do provide an alternative basis to that provided by the MHA to authorise the deprivation of the liberty of an incapacitated person for a range of purposes including his or her assessment or treatment for mental or physical disorders in hospital, and so

(ii) a decision maker under the MHA has to consider whether that alternative is available and, if it is, whether it should be used when he or she applies the 'necessity test' set by the MHA.

The qualification 'in the circumstances defined thereby' in sub-paragraph (i) is important and means that the relevant decision maker has to consider the application of those provisions to the circumstances of the particular case."

His Lordship held at para.75 that the fact that a choice has to be made between the two statutory schemes leads to the following results:

"(i) the First-tier Tribunal (and earlier decision makers under the MHA) have to apply the statutory tests imposed by the MHA and the possible application of the MCA and its DOLS are relevant to that exercise,

(ii) the First-tier Tribunal (and the earlier decision makers under the MHA) have to assess whether as a result of the identified risks the relevant person ought to be detained, or kept in hospital in circumstances which on a objective assessment give rise to a risk that cannot be ignored that they amount to a deprivation of liberty (see for example paragraph 22 of Upper Tribunal Judge Jacobs decision in *DN v Northumberland & Wear NHS Foundation Trust* [see below]),

(iii) if the answer is 'yes', this triggers a value judgment applying the 'necessity test' as between the choices that are or will or may become available,

(iv) the search applying the MHA 'necessity test' is for the alternative that best achieves the objective of assessment or treatment of the type described in ss. 2 and 3 MHA in the least restrictive way. This potentially introduces tensions and so a need to balance the impact of detention under the MCA and an authorisation under the DOLS as the means of ensuring that a deprivation of liberty to best achieve the desired objective is lawful and governed by a statutory regime, and

(v) the theoretical and practical availability of the MCA regime and its DOLS is one of the factors that needs to be considered by the MHA decision maker in carrying out that search, as are their overall impact in best achieving the desired objective when compared with other available choices and so detention under ss. 2 or 3 MHA".

Among the factors that must be considered when applying the "necessity test" are: "consideration of what is in the best interests of the incapacitated person in line with the best interests assessment in the DOLS process, and so for example conditions that can be imposed under the DOLS, fluctuating capacity and the comparative impact of both the independent scrutiny and review and the enforcement provisions relating to the MHA scheme on the one hand and the MCA scheme and its DOLS on the other, and possibly . . . a consideration of the likelihood of continued compliance and triggers to possible non-compliance and their effect on the suitability of the regimes . . ." (para.73).

It is likely that the practical effect of this analysis will be largely confined to the situation of an incapacitated patient who, subsequent to being detained under the 1983 Act, becomes compliant to both detention and treatment but who continues to be detained because he satisfies the "acid test" established by the Supreme Court in *Cheshire West*. The question of whether compliant mentally incapable patients should be detained under the 1983 Act or be made the subject of a DOL authorisation is considered in the General Note to Part 2 of the 1983 Act under the heading *The detention of compliant mentally incapable patients*.

If the patient has been discharged from detention under the 1983 Act by the tribunal in anticipation of an authorisation being granted under the 2005 Act but the DOL assessor concludes that the patient is ineligible for an authorisation, a fresh application for the detention of the patient under the 1983 Act might have to be made. The justification for making such an application would be that the decision of the assessor satisfies the new information test established by the House of Lords in *R. v East London and The City Mental Health Trust Ex p. Brandenburg* [2003] UKHL 58. The *Brandenburg* case is discussed in the General note to s.3 of the Act under the heading *The re-sectioning of a patient subsequent to a discharge by the First-tier Tribunal (Mental Health) or the Mental Health Review Tribunal for Wales*.

A request for a standard authorisation under Sch.A1 of the 2005 Act can be made in respect of a patient who is detained under the 1983 Act in anticipation of the patient being discharged from detention and being placed in a care home if (i) he would be subject to a deprivation of liberty in the care home and (ii) the provisions of para.12 of Sch.A1 would be satisfied: see *DN v Northumberland Tyne and Wear NHS Foundation Trust* [2011] UKHT 327 (AAC); [2011] M.H.L.R. 249, para.22. This decision follows the approach set out by the Department of Health in a letter to the tribunal about the relationship between the two Acts. The letter is reproduced in Part 2 of the author's *Mental Capacity Act Manual* (2014).

Deprivations of liberty in care homes

6–022   In the *Cheshire West* case, the Supreme Court held that in order to be deprived of his liberty for the purposes of the 2005 Act a mentally incapacitated person must be under "continuous supervision and control and . . . not free to leave". It follows that although the guardianship provisions of the 1983 Act provide authority to convey P to a care home, to require him to remain there, and to return him if he absconds, an authorisation under Sch.A1 will be required if P is subject to a continuous supervision and control within the care home and is assessed as meeting the qualifying requirements (*C v Blackburn and Darwen Borough Council* [2011] EWHC 3321; [2012] M.H.L.R. 202, para.30, where Peter Jackson J. incorrectly states that guardianship does not provide a power to prevent the person from leaving: see *KD v A Borough Council*, noted under s.8(1)(a)).

Although it was held in *DCC v KH* (2009) COP, Case No. 11729380, that a standard authorisation provides an implied authority to use restraint on P, amounting if necessary to a deprivation of liberty, if P refused to return to the care home where the deprivation of liberty was authorised, professionals might prefer to rely on the explicit power contained in s.18(3) of the 1983 Act.

APPENDIX A

FURTHER POWERS TO RESTRAIN AND/OR DETAIN MENTALLY DISORDERED PATIENTS

Where a patient has been detained under the Mental Health Act (the Act), there is an **A–001** implied power for staff to exercise a degree of control over the activities of the patient: see the note on "the power to control the activities of detained patients" in s.139. Both statute and the common law provide further powers that can be used to restrain and/or detain patients. They are:

1. In *R. (on the application of Munjaz) v Mersey Care NHS Trust* [2003] EWCA Civ 1036; [2003] M.H.L.R. 362 at para.46 Hale L.J. said:

   "There is a general [common law] power to take such steps as are reasonably necessary and proportionate to protect others from the immediate risk of significant harm. This applies whether or not the patient lacks the capacity to make decisions for himself".

   It is submitted that this power extends to the use of sedation on a person in an emergency if the sedation is used to restrain that person from causing harm to others.

2. If the patient is mentally incapacitated, s.6 of the Mental Capacity Act 2005 enables the patient to be restrained when: (1) the person using the restraint reasonably believes that its use is necessary to prevent harm to the patient; and (2) its use is proportionate both to the likelihood and seriousness of the harm and is in the patient's best interests; see further, the author's *Mental Capacity Act Manual* (2014), pp.65–69.

3. Under s.3(1) of the Criminal Law Act 1967 "a person may use such force as is reasonable in the circumstances in the prevention of crime, or in effecting or assisting the lawful arrest of offenders or suspected offenders or persons unlawfully at large". This provision, which could apply to any patient, enables a member of staff to use reasonable force to either restrain the patient or to place him in seclusion in self-defence or in the defence of others or to protect property. It does not apply where the patient is insane within the meaning of the M'Naghten rules because such a person is deemed not capable of committing a crime. The test of insanity established by the House of Lords in the *M'Naghten* case [1843–60] All E.R. 229, is that:

   "it must be clearly proved that, at the time of the committing of the act, the party accused was labouring under such a defect of reason, from disease of the mind, as not to know the nature and quality of the act he was doing was wrong, or, if he did know it, that he did not know he was doing what was wrong".

Caselaw has established that "disease of the mind": (i) covers diseases of the body affecting the operation of the mind (*R. v Kemp* [1957] 1 Q.B. 399); and (ii) includes patients who suffer from epilepsy (*R. v Sullivan* [1983] 2 All E.R. 673) and diabetic patients who suffer from hyper-glycaemia because of a failure to take insulin (*R. v Hennessy* [1989] 2 All E.R. 9). "Defect of reason" does not cover patients who retain the power of reasoning but who in moments of confusion or absentmindedness either fail to use their powers to the full (*R. v Clarke* [1972] 1 All E.R. 219) or know that their actions are unlawful (*R. v Windle* [1952] 2 Q.B. 826).

4. The common law power to prevent a breach of the peace was summarised by Lord Bingham in *R. (on the application of the Laporte) v Chief Constable of Gloucestershire Constabulary* [2006] UKHL 55; [2007] 2 All E.R. 529 at para.29:

> "Every constable, and also every citizen, enjoys the power and is subject to the duty to seek to prevent, by arrest or other action short of arrest, any breach of the peace occuring in his presence, or any breach of the peace which (having occurred) is likely to be renewed, or any breach of the peace which is about to occur."

A breach, which can take place in public or on private property, involves "actual harm done either to a person or to a person's property in his presence or some other form of violent disorder or disturbance and itself necessarily involves a criminal offence" (ibid., per Lord Brown at para.111). Harm to property will constitute a breach only if done or threatened in the owner's presence because the natural consequence of such harm is likely to be a violent retaliation (*Percy v Director of Public Prosecutions* [1995] 3 All E.R. 124 DC). The power to prevent a breach of the peace would enable a nurse physically to restrain a patient whose words or behaviour are such that imminent violence is expected on a hospital ward. Detention under this power can only be justified for a short period. Prolonged detention must be authorised either by the Act or by arresting the person concerned and bringing him or her before a magistrate.

A–002

With regard to the use of this power, the Court of Appeal has held that: (i) there has to be a sufficiently real and present threat to the peace to justify the extreme step of depriving a citizen of his liberty when that citizen is not at that time acting unlawfully (*Foulkes v Chief Constable of Merseyside Police* [1998] 3 All E.R. 705); and (ii) a breach can occur on private premises even if the only persons likely to be affected by the breach are inside the premises and no member of the public outside the premises is involved (*McConnell v Chief Constable of the Greater Manchester Police* [1990] 1 All E.R. 423).

5. In *Black v Forsey*, 1987 S.L.T. 681, a case under the Mental Health (Scotland) Act 1984, the House of Lords held that although the powers of detention conferred on hospital authorities by the 1984 Act were exhaustive and that any common law power of detention which a hospital authority might otherwise have possessed had been impliedly removed, the common law continues to confer upon a private individual power to detain, in a situation of necessity, a person of unsound mind who is a danger to him or herself or others. A person exercising the power must be able to justify his or her action, if challenged, by proving the mental disorder of the detainee and the necessity of detention. In the opinion of Lord Griffiths, the power is:

> "confined to imposing temporary restraint on a lunatic who has run amok and is a manifest danger either to himself or to others—a state of affairs as obvious to a layman as to a doctor. Such a common law power is confined to the short period of confinement necessary before the lunatic can be handed over to a proper authority".

The existence of this power was confirmed by Lord Goff in *R. v Bournewood NHS Trust, Ex p. L* [1998] 3 All E.R. 289, at 302:

> "[T]he common law permit[s] the detention of those who were a danger, or potential danger, to themselves or others, in so far as this was shown to be necessary."

The combination of powers set out above provide sufficient authority for a mental health **A–003** professional or member of the public to act swiftly to prevent a mentally disordered person from causing harm to himself, to another person or to property as long as the force used is both necessary and proportionate to the harm threatened. They cannot be used as an *alternative* to the powers of detention contained in the Act: if the Act provides for the detention of a person in a particular situation, neither the common law nor the Mental Capacity Act 2005 apply (*R. (on the application of Sessay) v South London and Maudsley NHS Foundation Trust* [2011] EWHC 2617 (QB); [2012] M.H.L.R. 94). However, the powers can be invoked for a short period in emergency situations where the persons who have the authority to invoke the appropriate Mental Health Act power are not immediately available. This was implicitly accepted in *Sessay* where Supperstone J. said at para.39:

> "[I]f a patient evidences an intention to leave the hospital before the s.4 application is completed, hospital staff may contact the police who have the power to detain the patient under s.136. We do not accept that there should be any problem with the use of s.136 in these circumstances. The Accident & Emergency Department of a hospital is a place to which the public have access and accordingly it is a public place for the purposes of s.136."

The detention of a patient by staff while awaiting the attendance of the police is governed by the common law. A similar justification obtains if a patient needs to be restrained during the course of an assessment under the Mental Health Act. Supperstone J. said at para.57:

> "[I]n our view it is unlikely in the ordinary case that there will be a false imprisonment at common law or deprivation of liberty for the purposes of Article 5(1) ECHR if there is no undue delay during the processing of an application under ss.2 or 4 MHA for admission."

The European Court of Human Rights has confirmed that the detention of a person for a short period in an emergency does not involve a violation of art.5 of the European Convention on Human Rights (*Winterwerp v Netherlands* (1979-80) 2 E.H.R.R. 387, para.39 and *X v United Kingdom* (1982) 4 E.H.R.R. 188, para.45).

Apart from the powers noted above, the extent to which common law powers enable informal patients to be subject to the control of staff is unclear. In *Pountney v Griffiths* [1976] A.C. 314, the House of Lords noted that it had been conceded by counsel for a Broadmoor Hospital patient that hospital staff have "powers of control over all mentally disordered patients, whether admitted voluntarily or compulsorily, though the nature and duration of control varies with the category to which the patient belongs". The Report of the Committee of Inquiry into Complaints about Ashworth Hospital (Cm. 2028–1) considered, at p.196, that this statement "would be likely to receive the endorsement of the courts today ... see *R. v Deputy Governor of Parkhurst Prison and others Ex p. Hague*; sub nom. *Hague v Deputy Governor of Parkhurst Prison; Weldon v Home Office* [1992] 1 A.C. 58". The powers to control informal patients are clearly far less extensive that those that apply to detained patients. If a mentally capable informal patient is unable to accept the control and discipline that is considered by staff to be in his best interests and/or conducive to the good administration of the hospital, he should either be asked to leave or consideration should be given to using the powers of detention under the Act.

THE HIGH SECURITY PSYCHIATRIC SERVICES (ARRANGEMENTS FOR VISITS BY CHILDREN) DIRECTIONS 2013

GENERAL NOTE

A previous version of these Directions was found to be lawful and not in breach of the **B–001** European Convention on Human Rights *in R. (on the application of L) v Secretary of State for Health* [2001] 1 F.L.R. 406 where Scott Baker J. said:

"If there are special circumstances in which the patient has good reason for being visited by a child who is not within the permitted category relationship the remedy is to apply to the court for an order under the Children Act 1989."

Guidance
Guidance on these Directions, which was published by the Department of Health in **B–002** December, 2013, can be accessed at: *https://www.gov.uk/government/publications/high-security-psychiatric-services-directions.*

The Secretary of State gives the following Directions in exercise of the powers conferred by ss.4(3A)(a), 8 and 273(1) and (4) of the National Health Service Act 2006.

Citation, commencement and interpretation

1.—These Directions may be cited as the High Security Psychiatric Services **B–003** (Arrangements for Visits by Children) Directions 2013 and come into force on 15th July 2013.

(2) In these Directions—

"the 1983 Act" means the Mental Health Act 1983;

"the 2006 Act" means the National Health Service Act 2006;

"chief executive" means, in relation to a hospital, the chief executive of the Trust which is responsible for that hospital or that person's deputy;

"child" means a person under the age of eighteen;

"clinical team" means the multi-disciplinary team responsible for a patient's treatment, including the responsible clinician;

"executive director" means a member of the provider's senior management team with executive responsibilities for a hospital at which high security psychiatric services are provided;

"hospital" means a hospital or any part of a hospital which is treated as a separate unit as covered by the definition of "hospital premises" in section 4(4) of the 2006 Act;

"nominated officer" means the officer nominated pursuant to paragraph 3(1)(a) of these Directions;

"parental responsibility" has the same meaning as in the Children Act 1989;

"patient" means a patient liable to be detained at a hospital under—

    (a) the 1983 Act;
    (b) an order of the Crown Court under section 5 of the Criminal Procedure (Insanity) Act 1964; or
    (c) an order of the Court of Appeal under section 6 or 14 of the Criminal Appeal Act 1968;

"provider" means any person who is approved to provide high security psychiatric services under section 4(3)(b) of the 2006 Act;

"relevant local authority" means the local authority in which the child resides;

"responsible clinician" has the meaning given in sections 34 and 55 of the 1983 Act;

"Trust" means an NHS trust established under section 25 of the 2006 Act or an NHS foundation trust authorised under section 35 of the 2006 Act;

"ward area" means the day rooms, patients' bedrooms, corridors, toilets, bathrooms, ward kitchens and any other rooms or garden area in the residential parts of the hospital to which the patients have access as a matter of course.

Visits by children

B–004   2.—A provider must only permit a patient in a hospital to receive a visit from a child in accordance with these Directions.

(2) Subject to paragraph (4), a hospital must not permit a patient to receive a visit from a child unless—

(a) the nominated officer has approved the child's visit in accordance with these Directions; and

(b) in the case of a patient who is assessed as posing a risk or potential risk of harm to the child, that patient—

   (i) is the parent or relative of that child; or
   (ii) has parental responsibility of that child; or
   (iii) was cohabiting with the parent of that child immediately prior to their detention under the 1983 Act and the child was treated as a member of their household.

(3) In paragraph (2) "parent" means the mother or father, the adoptive mother or father or the stepmother or stepfather of the child, and "relative" means a grandparent, brother, sister, uncle or aunt or cousin related to the child by blood (including half-blood), marriage or adoption.

(4) Paragraph (2) does not apply where an order made under the Children Act 1989 specifies that the child may visit the patient in the hospital.

Procedure for deciding on requests for visits

B–005   3.— A hospital must—

(a) nominate a senior manager to act as the nominated officer to be responsible for overseeing the process of dealing with any request for permission for a child to visit a patient and for deciding whether to approve the visit;

(b) set up a multi-disciplinary panel to assist and advise the nominated officer in carrying out their responsibilities and reaching decisions on applications; and

(c) ensure that the nominated officer discharges their responsibilities in accordance with these Directions.

(2) Any request for permission for a child to visit a patient in a hospital must be made in writing by the patient and must be forwarded to the nominated officer.

(3) Except in a case to which paragraphs (11) to (14) or direction 6 applies, the procedure set out in paragraphs (4) to (10) will apply.

(4) The nominated officer must arrange for the patient's clinical team to carry out the assessment—

(a) as to whether, in their view, it would be appropriate for the visit to take place having regard to the patient's offending history (if any), their clinical history and present mental state; and

(b) in the event that a visit is recommended, of any particular arrangements which would need to be made for a visit by that child to take place.

(5) Where following the assessment referred to in paragraph (4)—

(a) the nominated officer is satisfied that it would not be appropriate for the child to visit the patient, they must refuse the request for a visit, or

(b) in any other case, the nominated officer must seek the advice of the relevant local authority as to whether it is in the best interests of the child to visit the patient and must send with that request for advice, a copy of the assessment referred to in paragraph (4).

(6) Subject to paragraph (8), on receipt of the advice from the relevant local authority, the nominated officer must decide whether to approve the visit having regard to—

(a) that advice;

(b) the assessment referred to in paragraph (4); and

(c) any other relevant information.

(7) When deciding whether to approve the visit, if the advice from the relevant local authority has been received within the last 12 months, the nominated officer does not need to seek advice again, but should obtain confirmation from the local authority that there has not been any new contact with or concerns raised with the local authority which may affect the nominated officer's decision.

(8) The nominated officer must not approve a visit in any case where the advice from the relevant local authority is that it is not or may not be in the best interests of the child to visit the patient.

(9) If no decision has been reached within eight weeks of the date on which a request for a visit is received from a patient the nominated officer must inform the patient in writing of the reasons for the delay and refer the matter to the executive director of the hospital.

(10) The nominated officer must notify—

(a) the patient;

(b) the parent of the child and any other person with parental responsibility for the child or caring for the child;

(c) the child if they are of sufficient age and understanding; and

(d) any relevant local authority,

of the decision and the reasons for that decision in writing.

(11) Subject to paragraph (14), where the patient is assessed as posing a risk or potential risk of harm to the child and that child is not within the categories of relationship set out in direction 2(2)(b), paragraphs (4) to (10) shall not apply and the nominated officer must refuse the request for a visit and notify the patient accordingly.

(12) Subject to paragraphs (13) and (14), where the person with parental responsibility for the child, or in the case of a child subject to a care order the designated local authority in whose care the child is placed under section 31(1)(a) of the Children Act 1989, has not agreed the child may visit the patient, paragraphs (4) to (10) shall not apply and the nominated officer must refuse the request for the visit and notify the patient accordingly.

(13) Save in the case of a child subject to a care order, where there is more than one person with parental responsibility for the child, it is the person with parental responsibility with whom the child is living who must agree to the visit.

(14) In any case where an order made under the Children Act 1989 specifies that the child may visit the patient in the hospital the nominated officer must allow the visit to take place.

Validity of approval of visit and withdrawal of such approval

B–006   4.— Subject to paragraph (3), any approval for the child to visit the patient must be valid for a period of 12 months from the date on which it is given and may only be withdrawn in that period if the nominated officer is satisfied that there has been a relevant change of circumstances.

(2) If, after that period of 12 months referred to in paragraph (1) has elapsed, the patient wishes to continue to have visits from the child, the nominated officer must—

   (a) review the permission in accordance with paragraphs (3) to (9) of direction 3; and

   (b) must notify the persons mentioned in paragraph (9) of direction 3 of their decision and the reasons for that decision in writing.

(3) Notwithstanding paragraph (1), the nominated officer may at any time refuse to allow a visit to take place if there are concerns about the patient's mental state at the time of the proposed visit.

Complaints

B–007   5. A provider must set up a procedure to enable a patient to make representations against any decision of the nominated officer not to approve a visit other than a refusal on the grounds set on in direction 3, paragraphs (10) or (11).

Visits in exceptional circumstances

B–008   6.— In exceptional circumstances and subject to any guidance given by the Secretary of State, the chief executive or the executive director may give their written authority for a patient to receive a visit from a child without an assessment in accordance with direction 3.

(2) The chief executive or the executive director must consult the nominated officer before approving a visit in such circumstances.

(3) Paragraph (1) does not apply where the patient is a person described in sub-paragraph (2)(b) of direction 2 and the child is not within the permitted categories of relationship set out in that sub-paragraph.

Arrangements to be put in place for visits

B–009   7.— A hospital must ensure that—

   (a) during a visit the child has direct contact only with the patient for whom permission has been given for that child to visit,

   (b) subject to paragraph (2), the child is accompanied by—

      (i) a person with parental responsibility for that child and with whom the child is living, or

      (ii) another person who is caring for the child,

   (c) a visit takes place in an appropriate setting designated for visits by children and not in the ward area,

   (d) if in exceptional circumstances, a visit takes place in an area or place other than an appropriate setting designated for visits by children as set out in sub-paragraph (c), it must be appropriate, not be detrimental to the child and approved by the nominated officer, and

(e) that there are sufficient staff of any appropriate grade and with requisite knowledge and understanding present to supervise a child's visit at all times.

(2) Sub-paragraph (1)(b) does not apply in the case of a child aged 16 or 17 where the nominated officer, having regard to the information they have received under direction 3, is satisfied that an unaccompanied visit is unlikely to prejudice the child's welfare.

Annual report to the Provider's Board of Directors

8. The chief executive must submit an annual report to the provider's board at the end of each financial year providing details of— **B–010**

(a) the number of patients visited by children in that year;

(b) any special arrangements put in place to ensure that safety of those children whilst visiting patients, together with the chief executive's assessment of the appropriateness of such arrangements; and

(c) the chief executive's assessment of the continuing adequacy of the arrangements put in place by the hospital to ensure the safety of children whilst visiting patients.

Revocation

9. The Visits by Children to Ashworth, Broadmoor and Rampton Hospitals Directions that came into force on 1st September 1999 are revoked. **B–011**

THE HIGH SECURITY PSYCHIATRIC SERVICES (ARRANGEMENTS FOR SAFETY AND SECURITY) DIRECTIONS 2013

GENERAL NOTE

In *Buck v Nottinghamshire Healthcare NHS Trust* [2006] EWCA Civ 1576, the Court of **C–001** Appeal held that the existence of a previous version of these Directions and the failure to implement them could inform the court as to the content of the duty of care owned by Rampton Hospital to its nursing staff. *Buck* was applied in *Watson v Nottinghamshire NHS Trust*, Lincoln County Court, September 26, 2008, a case where a nurse at Rampton Hospital was subjected to a prolonged and violent attack by a patient. In a trial on the issue of liability under, inter alia, the Directions, Recorder Beale held that the hospital was under a duty, in considering whether some precaution needed to be taken against a foreseeable risk, to weigh, on the one hand, the magnitude of the risk, the likelihood of an accident happening and the possible serious consequences if an accident were to happen, and, on the other hand, the difficulty and expense and any other disadvantage of taking the precaution.

The National Health Service Commissioning Board has been directed to assess compliance with the requirements of the Directions (High Security Psychiatric Services (National Health Service Commissioning Board) Directions 2013, para.5).

Guidance

Guidance on these Directions, which was published by the Department of Health in **C–002** December, 2013, can be accessed at: *https://www.gov.uk/government/publications/high-security-psychiatric-services-directions*.

The Secretary of State gives the following Directions in exercise of the powers conferred by ss.4(3A)(a), 8 and 273(1) and (4) of the National Health Service Act 2006.

Application, citation and commencement

1.—(1) These Directions apply to any person who is approved by the Secretary of State **C–003** for the purposes of section 4(3)(b) of the 2006 Act to provide high security psychiatric services.

(2) These Directions may be cited as the High Security Psychiatric Services (Arrangements for Safety and Security) Directions 2013.

(3) The Directions come into force on 15th July 2013.

Interpretation

C–004

2. In these Directions—

"abscond" means where a patient unlawfully gains liberty outside of the perimeter of the hospital by breaking away from the custody and supervision of staff;

"authorised member of staff" means a person appointed under section 134(7) of the 1983 Act;

"the 1983 Act" means the Mental Health Act 1983;

"the 2006 Act" means the National Health Service Act 2006;

"the Additional Functions Regulations 2011" means the Care Quality Commission (Additional Functions) Regulations 2011;

"chief executive" means, in relation to a hospital, the chief executive of the Trust which is responsible for that hospital or that person's deputy;

"clinical team" means the multi-disciplinary team responsible for a patient's treatment, including the responsible clinician;

"contractor" means a person, other than a member of staff or a member of the emergency services, who provides services to a hospital;

"grounds access" means unescorted access to areas of a hospital other than the ward area;

"hospital" means a hospital or any part of a hospital which is treated as a separate unit as covered by the definition of "hospital premises" in section 4(4) of the 2006 Act;

"illicit substance" means—

(a) any drug which is a controlled drug for the purposes of the Misuse of Drugs Act 1971; or
(b) alcohol;

"key-holder" means, in relation to a hospital, a person who is authorised by the provider to hold keys to the secure area of the hospital;

"leave of absence" means leave granted under section 17 of the 1983 Act;

"medical director" means, in relation to a hospital, the medical director of the hospital appointed by the provider which is responsible for that hospital or a deputy medical director;

"member of staff" means, in relation to a hospital—

(a) any person employed by the provider responsible for the hospital in connection with the provision of high security psychiatric services at the hospital, or any other person who provides services under contract and is treated as being an employee by the provider; and
(b) the chairman and any non-executive director of the provider;

"patient" means a patient liable to be detained at a hospital under—

(a) the 1983 Act;
(b) an order of the Crown Court under section 5 of the Criminal Procedure (Insanity) Act 1964; or
(c) an order of the Court of Appeal under section 6 or 14 of the Criminal Appeal Act 1968;

"postal packet" has the same meaning as in the Postal Services Act 2000;

"provider" means any person who is approved to provide high security psychiatric services for the purposes of section 4(3)(b) of the 2006 Act;

"the 2008 Regulations" means the Mental Health (Hospital, Guardianship and Treatment) (England) Regulations 2008;

"responsible clinician" has the meaning given in sections 34 and 55 of the 1983 Act;

"risk assessment" means a risk assessment carried out under direction 33;

"rub-down search" means a search of a person, and the contents of that person's pockets, but does not include a search that involves the removal of any item of clothing other than an outer layer of clothing;

"secure area" means the part of the hospital that is inside the secure perimeter;

"security department" means the members of staff of a hospital responsible for advising on, monitoring and, where relevant, implementing security policy at that hospital;

"security director" means, in relation to a hospital, the member of staff with responsibility for the security department at the hospital;

"security information" means any information about the safety and security of the hospital;

"senior member of the Royal Family" means those carrying the style His or Her Majesty (HM) or His or Her Royal Highness (HRH);

"Trust" means an NHS trust established under section 25 of the 2006 Act or an NHS foundation trust authorised under section 30 of the 2006 Act;

"visiting child" means any person visiting a hospital who is under the age of 18;

"visitor" means any person, other than a member of staff, visiting a hospital who is 18 or over;

"ward area" means the day rooms, patients' bedrooms, corridors, toilets, bathrooms, ward kitchens and any other rooms or garden area in the residential parts of the hospital to which patients have access as a matter of course.

Promotion of safety and security

3.—(1) For the purpose of promoting safety and security in the hospital for which it is **C–005** responsible, each provider must exercise its functions in connection with the provision of high security psychiatric services in accordance with these Directions.

(2) In exercising those functions, each provider must have regard to any guidance issued by the Secretary of State on arrangements for safety and security at the hospital.

(3) If a provider—

(a) intends to perform its functions other than in accordance with guidance issued by the Secretary of State under paragraph (2) of this direction; or

(b) performs its functions other than in accordance with such guidance,

it must notify the Board and the NHS Trust Development Authority without delay and give reasons for the decision or act.

Duty to co-operate

4. Each provider must co-operate with other providers for the purpose of making **C–006** arrangements in respect of safety and security in the hospital for which it is responsible.

Requirements for conducting a rub-down search of a patient

5.—(1) Each provider must ensure in respect of the hospital for which it is responsible **C–007** that any rub-down search of a patient in the hospital is carried out in accordance with this direction.

(2) Subject to paragraph (15), a rub-down search may only be carried out—

(a) with the patient's consent; or

(b) where authorised by the responsible clinician or the medical director in accordance with the provisions of this direction.

(3) If a patient does not consent to a rub-down search, the matter must be referred to the patient's responsible clinician.

(4) Where there has been a referral under paragraph (3), the responsible clinician must consider whether the proposed search would be detrimental to the patient's wellbeing.

(5) The responsible clinician may authorise a rub-down search if the clinician considers that the proposed search would not be detrimental to the patient's wellbeing.

(6) If the responsible clinician considers that the proposed search would be detrimental to the patient's wellbeing, that clinician must consult a member of the security department.

(7) Following consultation with a member of the security department, the responsible clinician may authorise, or refuse to authorise, a rub-down search.

(8) In making a decision under paragraph (7) the responsible clinician must take into account—

(a) the interests of the patient;

(b) the opinion of the member of the security department consulted under paragraph (6);

(c) the safety of staff, patients, visitors and visiting children; and

(d) the security of the hospital.

(9) If the responsible clinician refuses to authorise a search under paragraph (7), the member of the security department consulted under paragraph (6) may refer the matter to the medical director.

(10) Where a matter is referred under paragraph (9), the medical director may authorise, or refuse to authorise, the search.

(11) In making a decision under paragraph (10), the medical director must take into account—

(a) the opinion of the responsible clinician;

(b) the opinion of the member of the security department consulted under paragraph (6);

(c) the interests of the patient;

(d) the safety of staff, patients, visitors and visiting children to the hospital; and

(e) the security of the hospital.

(12) Any patient who has refused to consent to a rub-down search must be—

(a) kept under observation;

(b) isolated from other patients; and

(c) kept informed of what is happening and why in terms appropriate to their understanding,

until such time as a search has been authorised, or refused, under paragraph (5), (7) or (10).

(13) In all cases a rub-down search must be carried out with due regard for the patient's dignity and privacy.

(14) Unless there are exceptional circumstances, a rub-down search must be carried out by members of staff who are of the same sex as the patient.

(15) This direction does not apply to the search of a patient if a member of staff has reason to believe that the patient possesses an item which causes an immediate risk to the patient's own safety or the safety of any other person.

Searches of patients that involve the removal of clothing other than outer clothing

C–008   6.—(1) Each provider must ensure in respect of the hospital for which it is responsible that any search of a patient in the hospital, other than a rub down search under direction 5 of these Directions, is carried out in accordance with this direction.

(2) A search that involves the removal of clothing may only be carried out—

(a) on the patient's admission to the hospital;

(b) if, before that patient goes on leave of absence, the provider requires a search to be carried out;

(c) where there is reason to believe that the patient may be in possession of—

(i) illicit substances, or

(ii) a weapon; or

(d) if the patient is considered by a member of staff to pose a risk—

(i) of harm to themselves,

(ii) to the safety of any person, or

(iii) to the security of the hospital.

(3) Subject to paragraph (19), a search involving the removal of clothing may only be carried out—

(a) with the patient's consent; or

(b) where authorised by the responsible clinician or the medical director in accordance with this direction.

(4) If a patient does not consent to a search involving the removal of clothing, the matter must be referred to the patient's responsible clinician.

(5) Where there is a referral under paragraph (4), the responsible clinician must consider whether the proposed search would be detrimental to the patient's wellbeing.

(6) The responsible clinician may authorise the search if the clinician considers that the proposed search would not be detrimental to the patient's wellbeing.

(7) If the responsible clinician considers that the proposed search would be detrimental to the patient's wellbeing, that clinician must consult a member of the security department.

(8) Following consultation with a member of the security department, the responsible clinician may authorise, or refuse to authorise, the search.

(9) In making a decision under paragraph (8), the responsible clinician must take into account—

(a) the opinion of the member of the security department consulted under paragraph (7);

(b) the interests of the patient;

(c) the safety of staff, patients, visitors and visiting children; and

(d) the security of the hospital.

(10) If the responsible clinician refuses to authorise a search under paragraph (8), the member of the security department consulted under paragraph (7) may refer the matter to the medical director.

(11) Where a matter is referred under paragraph (10), the medical director may authorise, or refuse to authorise, the search.

(12) In making a decision under paragraph (11), the medical director must take into account—

(a) the opinion of the responsible clinician;

(b) the opinion of the member of the security department consulted under paragraph (7);

(c) the interests of the patient;

(d) the safety of staff, patients, visitors and visiting children to the hospital; and

(e) the security of the hospital.

(13) Any patient who has refused to consent to a search involving the removal of clothing must be—

(a) kept under observation;

(b) isolated from other patients; and

(c) kept informed of what is happening and why in terms appropriate to their understanding,

until such time as a search has been authorised, or refused, under paragraph (6), (8) or (11).

(14) A search under this direction must take place on the patient's ward or in the hospital's admission facility which is a facility designed for carrying out administrative and security checks associated with the admission of patients.

(15) A search under this direction must be carried out by two members of staff, at least one of whom must be a registered nurse.

(16) A search under this direction may only be undertaken by members of staff who are the same sex as the patient.

(17) In all cases a search under this direction must be carried out with due regard for the patient's dignity and privacy.

(18) Nothing in this direction should be taken as allowing an intimate body search of a patient.

(19) This direction does not apply to the search of a patient if a member of staff has reason to believe that the patient possesses an item which causes an immediate risk to the patient's own safety or the safety of any other person.

(20) In this direction "intimate body search" means a search which consists of the physical examination of a person's body orifices other than the mouth.

Searches of patients, rooms and lockers

C–009   7.—(1) Each provider must in respect of the hospital for which it is responsible make arrangements for the routine searching of patients, their rooms and lockers in the hospital, in accordance with this direction.

(2) Each patient's room, its contents and any locker used by that patient must be searched at least once each calendar month at any day or time on a random basis.

(3) Subject to paragraph (4), each patient's locker located on a ward must be searched on one further occasion each month at any day or time on a random basis.

(4) Paragraph (3) does not apply where there is more than one search of that locker under paragraph (2) in any calendar month.

(5) On each occasion that a search is undertaken under paragraph (2) or (3), a rub-down search of the patient must be carried out if the requirements for carrying out such a search set out in direction 5 are met.

(6) Any patient who receives a visitor who is not a key-holder must be subject to a rub-down search immediately before, and immediately after, that visit.

(7) Any patient who goes on leave of absence must be subject to a rub-down search both on leaving, and on re-entering, the secure area.

(8) On each occasion that a search is undertaken under paragraph (6) or (7), a rub-down search of the patient must be carried out if the requirements for carrying out such a search set out in direction 5 are met.

(9) A search under paragraph (7) must not be undertaken by a member of staff who is responsible for that patient during the leave of absence.

(10) The requirement for a rub-down search under paragraph (5) does not apply where the medical director and the security director have agreed that—

(a) a rub-down search would present a significant risk to the member of staff undertaking the search; and

(b) the requirements for the patient's management are such that any risk that the patient is concealing an object have been minimised.

Searches when patients move around in the secure area

8.—(1) Each provider must in respect of the hospital for which it is responsible make **C–010** arrangements for searching patients who move between different parts of the hospital in accordance with this direction.

(2) Subject to paragraph (4) a member of staff shall carry out a rub-down search of—

(a) where there is only one patient moving, that patient;

(b) where there is a group of no more than 10 patients moving together, at least one patient selected on a random basis; or

(c) where there is a group of more than 10 patients moving together, at least 10% of those patients, selected on a random basis.

(3) On each occasion that a search is undertaken under paragraph (2), a rub-down search of the patient must be carried out if the requirements for carrying out such a search set out in direction 5 are met.

(4) A patient shall not be searched under paragraph (2)(a) if both the medical director and the security director have agreed that—

(a) a rub-down search of that patient would present a significant risk to the member of staff undertaking the search; and

(b) the requirements for the patient's management are such that any risk that the patient is concealing an object have been minimised.

Searches of ward areas and other areas

9. Each provider must in respect of the hospital for which it is responsible make arrange- **C–011** ments to ensure that—

(a) all ward areas, other than patients' rooms, of the hospital are searched not less than once a week; and

(b) all therapy, workshop, recreation and leisure facility areas, and any other areas (other than wards) of that hospital which a patient may visit within the secure area, are searched not less than once every three months.

Security of tools, equipment and materials

10.—(1) Each provider must issue written instructions to members of staff at the hospital **C–012** for which it is responsible on the control of tools, equipment and materials in the secure area of the hospital.

(2) Each provider must make arrangements to ensure that where, prior to the end of an activity or session, a patient leaves an area in which a tool or other equipment is or has been in use, that patient is subject to a rub-down search before leaving that area if the requirements for carrying out such a search set out in direction 5 are met.

Searches of members of staff

11.—(1) Each provider must in respect of the hospital for which it is responsible, make **C–013** arrangements to ensure that—

(a) at least 10% of occasions when members of staff enter the secure area and 5% of occasions when members of staff leave the secure area, will result in a rub-down search of members of staff who are chosen randomly;

(b) members of staff pass through a staffed metal detection portal immediately prior to entry into the secure area;

(c) all bags, packages or similar possessions of members of staff are x-rayed and (where appropriate) physically inspected prior to entry into the secure area;

(d) any member of staff escorting a patient on leave of absence is subject to a rub-down search on entry to or departure from the secure area; and

(e) where a member of staff is escorting a patient on leave of absence, any bags, packages or similar possessions of that member of staff are x-rayed and, where appropriate, physically inspected on entry to or departure from the secure area.

(2) The provider must x-ray and, where appropriate, physically inspect any bags, packages or similar possessions of a member of staff who is subject to a rub-down search under paragraph (1)(a) on leaving the secure area.

(3) A rub-down search under paragraphs (1)(a) and (d) must be carried out—

(a) by a person of the same sex as the member of staff, unless there are exceptional circumstances; and

(b) with due regard for the dignity of the member of staff.

(4) Each provider must determine whether a visitor who is a key-holder should be treated as a member of staff for the purposes of this direction.

Arrangements in respect of visitors and visiting children

C–014   **12.**—(1) Each provider must in respect of the hospital for which it is responsible make arrangements in respect of any visitor or visiting children in accordance with this direction.

(2) All patient visits must be arranged with the provider in advance.

(3) Tobacco or tobacco products must not be brought into the secure area unless they are being supplied to the provider.

(4) The provider must provide facilities within the secure area for the purpose of enabling visitors to acquire, in accordance with such rules as the provider may determine from time to time, food for consumption by themselves, by any visiting child accompanying them or by a patient whom they are visiting.

(5) Visitors and visiting children must not bring food into the secure area unless—

(a) that food is being supplied to the hospital under contract with the provider; or

(b) following consultation with the patient's clinical team and the medical director, the responsible clinician gives permission for the visitor to bring food into the secure area and for the patient to consume that food during the visit as part of the patient's care treatment plan.

(6) Subject to paragraphs (9), (10) and (11), a visitor or a visiting child must—

(a) be subject to a rub-down search; and

(b) have their possessions inspected,

before they are permitted to enter the secure area.

(7) Subject to paragraphs (9), (10) and (11), a visitor must be refused entry to the secure area unless the visitor—

(a) consents to a rub-down search and an inspection of their possessions; or

(b) in the case where the visitor is accompanied by a visiting child for whom the visitor is responsible, consents to a rub-down search of that child and an inspection of that child's possessions.

(8) Subject to paragraphs (9), and (11), any visiting child shall not be permitted to enter the secure area unless—

(a) the visitor responsible for that child consents to a rub-down search of that child and an inspection of the child's possessions; or

(b) if the child is of sufficient understanding to make an informed decision about any search or inspection, that child consents to a rub-down search and an inspection of their possessions.

(9) A visiting child must be permitted access to the secure area if a contact order has been made under section 8 of the Children Act 1989 in respect of that child and a patient in that hospital.

(10) Where a visitor is a member of the First-tier Tribunal (Mental Health) and needs to enter the secure area in connection with performing their judicial function, they shall not be subject to a rub-down search on entering or leaving the secure area on that occasion unless—

(a) they will be carrying out an examination of a patient in accordance with Rule 34 of the Tribunal Procedure (First-tier Tribunal) (Health, Education and Social Care Chamber) Rules 2008 whilst in the secure area;

(b) they activate the metal detection portal on passing through it and the reason for the activation cannot be established by other means; or

(c) the chief executive considers that there is an exceptional reason why they should be subject to a rub-down search.

(11) Where a visitor, or a visiting child, is not permitted access to the secure area, the chief executive of the hospital shall, if so requested, review that decision and may permit entry subject to such conditions as the chief executive may require.

(12) Where there is a contact order in place in respect of a visiting child and the child and any accompanying visitor is permitted to enter the secure area without being searched or their possessions being inspected, entry to the secure area may be subject to such conditions as the director of security may require.

(13) Paragraphs (6) to (12) do not apply to—

(a) a senior member of the Royal Family; or

(b) a member of the emergency services who is attending to an emergency.

(14) This direction does not apply to any visitor who is a key holder and who is treated as a member of staff for the purposes of direction 11.

(15) In this direction "tobacco products" means a product consisting wholly or partly of tobacco and intended to be smoked, sniffed, sucked or chewed.

Searches of visitors and inspection of possessions

13.—(1) Each provider must ensure that in respect of the hospital for which it is respon- **C–015** sible, any search of any visitor, or visiting child, and the inspection of any possessions of that person, is carried out in accordance with this direction.

(2) Any rub-down search must be carried out—

(a) subject to paragraph (5),

(i) with the consent of the person searched or, in the case of a visiting child, the consent of the responsible adult in respect of that child; and

(ii) by a person of the same sex as the person being searched, unless there are exceptional circumstances and the person to be searched, or the responsible adult in respect of any visiting child, consents to the search on that basis; and

(b) with due regard for the dignity of the person being searched.

(3) All visitors must pass through a metal detection portal on entry to the secure area.

(4) All bags, packages and other possessions to be taken into the secure area— (a) must, where possible, be inspected by x-ray equipment;

(b) may, following x-ray, be physically inspected; and

(c) must be physically inspected if inspection by x-ray is not possible.

(5) Where a visiting child is of sufficient understanding to make an informed decision about any search, that child must consent to the search, before it takes place.

(6) Paragraphs (3) and (4) do not apply to—

(a) a senior member of the Royal Family; or

(b) a member of the emergency services who is attending to an emergency.

Supply of food by staff to patients

C–016   **14.**—(1) Subject to paragraph (2), each provider must ensure that in respect of the hospital for which it is responsible, any member of staff does not bring food into the secure area for consumption by a patient.

(2) The chief executive of the hospital may authorise members of catering staff or staff, including porters, employed in the supplies department of the hospital to bring food for a patient into the secure area of the hospital where it is not practicable for a contractor to do so.

Checks of vehicles

C–017   **15.**—(1) Each provider must in respect of the hospital for which it is responsible, issue written instructions to all members of staff on the management and escorting of vehicles in the secure area.

(2) Subject to paragraph (3), each provider must make arrangements to ensure that before any vehicle enters or leaves the secure area it is checked by a member of staff for the presence of any unauthorised persons or items.

(3) Paragraph (2) does not apply to any vehicle belonging to the emergency services that is attending to an emergency.

Contractors' vehicles in the secure area

C–018   **16.**—(1) Each provider must make arrangements in respect of the hospital for which it is responsible for the control of vehicles in the secure area of the hospital in accordance with this direction.

(2) Subject to paragraph (5), each provider must ensure that any vehicle owned or controlled by a contractor shall not be located in the secure area unless the contractor is present in the secure area and—

(a) the contractor is loading or unloading tools or supplies; or

(b) the vehicle needs to be located within the secure area to give the contractor access to tools or supplies.

(3) Where the vehicle is—

(a) moving, or

(b) left unlocked,

a member of staff must be present in the immediate vicinity of the vehicle at all times.

(4) Where the vehicle is locked and immobilised, a member of staff must have possession of any keys to the vehicle held within the secure area.

(5) Paragraph (2) does not apply where—

(a) the security director has given permission for the vehicle to be located in the secure area;

(b) the contractor has left the secure area; and

(c) the vehicle is locked and immobilised.

Testing for illicit substances

17.—(1) Each provider must, in respect of the hospital for which it is responsible, make **C–019** arrangements for testing patients for the use of illicit substances in accordance with this direction.

(2) Provided that the patient consents, samples must be collected from—

(a) each patient on admission to the hospital;

(b) any patient suspected of using illicit substances; and

(c) at least 5% of the total number of patients at the hospital each month, selected randomly.

(3) Any patient required to provide a sample shall be afforded such privacy as is compatible with the need to prevent or detect adulteration or falsification of the sample.

(4) In no circumstances shall a patient be required to provide a sample of urine in the sight of a person of the opposite sex.

(5) In this direction "sample" means—

(a) a sample of urine;

(b) a breath test for alcohol;

(c) a swab taken from a patient's mouth; or

(d) a sample of hair, other than pubic hair.

Control of prescribed drugs

18.—(1) Each provider must, in respect of the hospital for which it is responsible, issue **C–020** written instructions to members of staff on the control of prescribed drugs.

(2) Instructions issued under paragraph (1) shall include instructions on—

(a) the transportation of prescribed drugs between the hospital pharmacy and a ward;

(b) the security of medication storage units and the location of those units;

(c) arrangements for distributing prescribed drugs to patients; and

(d) arrangements for ensuring that patients take prescribed drugs at the point at which they are dispensed, or at such other times as may be authorised by the clinical team.

Written records of certain searches and tests

C–021   **19.** Each provider must, in respect of the hospital for which it is responsible, make arrangements to ensure that a written record is kept of—

(a) any search of persons or possessions undertaken under these Directions;

(b) any refusal to consent to a search;

(c) any refusal of entry under direction 12 of these Directions (arrangements in respect of visitors and visiting children);

(d) any test undertaken in accordance with arrangements made under direction 17 (testing for illicit substances), and the outcome of that test; and

(e) any refusal by a patient to give a sample in accordance with arrangements made under direction 17.

Security information

C–022   **20.**—(1) Each provider must ensure that, in respect of the hospital for which it is responsible, information concerning the safety and security of the hospital is gathered and maintained in accordance with this direction.

(2) The security director for the hospital must establish and maintain electronic security records having regard to any guidance issued, on this issue, by the Secretary of State.

(3) For the purposes of this direction "security records" means records concerning possible threats to safety or security and includes information on—

(a) plans for escape;

(b) potential disturbances at the hospital;

(c) attempts to bring unauthorised items into the hospital; and

(d) any other matters which could threaten the well-being of a patient, visitor, visiting children or a member of staff.

(4) The security director must ensure that—

(a) security reports are given to members of the patients' clinical teams and the board of directors of the provider on a regular basis;

(b) instructions are given to the security department on the collection, collation, evaluation and assessment of the reliability of security information;

(c) instructions are given to members of staff on what, and how, security information should be reported to the security department; and

(d) instructions are given to members of staff on sharing security information and on data protection.

Patients' possessions

C–023   **21.**—(1) Each provider must make arrangements, in respect of the hospital for which it is responsible to ensure that—

(a) the number, type and volume of a patient's possessions, and access to those possessions, is consistent with the requirements of safety and security in the hospital;

  (b) the number, type and volume of possessions that are located in a patient's room is limited to that consistent with the requirements of safety and security;

  (c) the possessions of a patient are identified in an inventory to be compiled and kept up to date jointly by the patient and a member of staff; and

  (d) that inventory is signed and dated on each occasion when it is compiled or updated by—

      (i) the patient and the member of staff; or

     (ii) if the patient does not agree to sign by the member of staff and another member of staff.

(2) Where a patient requests access to any possessions—

  (a) which are stored on the ward, access must be provided within 24 hours of the request;

  (b) which are stored elsewhere, access must be provided within 48 hours, not including weekends or public holidays.

(3) A provider may refuse a patient's request for access under paragraph (2) if access to those possessions is not consistent with the safety and security requirements of these Directions or the provider's general policy in respect of the arrangements referred to in paragraph (1)(a).

(4) In this direction "public holiday" means any day that is specified or proclaimed as a bank holiday in England and Wales pursuant to section 1 of the Banking and Financial Dealings Act 1971.

Items delivered or brought to hospital premises for patients

22.—(1) Each provider must make arrangements in respect of the hospital for which it is **C–024** responsible, to ensure that any item which is delivered or brought to the hospital for delivery to a patient is examined in accordance with the provisions of this direction.

(2) The item must be—

  (a) x-rayed, and

  (b) opened and inspected,

by a member of staff.

(3) Any item brought to the hospital for a patient may be withheld on the grounds that the item—

  (a) is one which the patient has asked to be withheld;

  (b) is likely to cause distress to the person to whom it is addressed or to any other person;

  (c) may cause a danger to any person;

  (d) may prejudice the safety of any person; or

  (e) may prejudice security in the hospital.

(4) Where an item is withheld—

  (a) that decision must be recorded;

  (b) the patient must be given notice of the decision and told why the item has been withheld; and

(c) the patient must be given notice that the decision may be reviewed by the Care Quality Commission if a written application for review is made within six months beginning with the day on which the information set out in this sub-paragraph is received.

(5) The provider shall comply with any direction given by the Care Quality Commission under regulation 2(2) of the Additional Functions Regulations 2011.

(6) This direction does not apply to incoming postal packets addressed to a patient.

GENERAL NOTE

Paragraph (3)

C–025   Regulation 2 of the Care Quality Commission (Additional Functions) Regulations 2011 (SI 2011/1551) (as amended) reads:

"Review of decision to withhold an item delivered or brought to a high security hospital for a patient

2.—(1) The Care Quality Commission shall review a decision made under direction 22(3) of [the 2013 Directions] (items delivered or brought to hospital premises for patients) to withhold an item if an application to review that decision is made by the intended recipient of the item within six months beginning with the day on which that person receives the information set out in direction 22(4)(c) of those Directions.

(2) On an application under paragraph (1) the Care Quality Commission may direct that the item which is the subject of the application shall not be withheld."

Patients' access to computer equipment and games consoles

C–026   **23.**—(1) Each provider must make arrangements in respect of the hospital for which it is responsible, for the control of patients' access to computer equipment and games consoles in accordance with the provisions of this direction. A "games console", in this direction, means a video games console which can be used or adapted for use as a personal computer or connected to the internet, or any telephone or any wireless communication system.

(2) Each provider must prepare, maintain and make available to patients a statement setting out its policy in respect of—

(a) access to, and usage of, computer equipment and games consoles;

(b) any conditions of use or access; and

(c) the circumstances in which access may be withdrawn.

(3) A patient may only have access to computer equipment or a games console that is owned and controlled by the provider, or hired to the provider, and on such terms as the provider considers appropriate.

(4) Each provider must make arrangements for the monitoring and supervision of patient access to, and use of, computer equipment and any games console.

Location of patients' shops

C–027   **24.**—(1) Subject to paragraph (2), each provider must ensure that a patients' shop is not located in a ward area of a hospital for which it is responsible.

(2) Subject to the prior approval of the security director, a mobile patients' shop may visit a ward area from time to time.

Role of patients in managing or working in patients' shops and other specified employment

C–028   **25.**—(1) Each provider must ensure that in respect of the hospital for which it is responsible a patient is not allowed to—

(a) manage a patients' shop; or

(b) work in a patients' shop or in other specified employment unless—

(i) the Grounds Access Committee has given permission under direction 38 or the medical director has given permission under direction 39; and

(ii) a member of staff monitors and supervises any such work at all times.

(2) In paragraph (1) "other specified employment" means employment where the nature or location of the work, or the proposed level of supervision, generates a significant level of risk.

Patients' incoming post

26.—(1) Each provider must make arrangements in respect of the hospital for which it is **C–029** responsible for incoming postal packets addressed to a patient to be x-rayed.

(2) Subject to—

(a) sections 134 (correspondence of patients) and 134A (review of decisions to withhold correspondence) of the 1983 Act; and

(b) regulations 29 and 30 of the 2008 Regulations (inspection and opening of postal packets: review of decisions to withhold),

each provider must make arrangements for incoming postal packets addressed to a patient at a hospital for which it is responsible to be opened and inspected by an authorised member of staff in accordance with this direction.

(3) Paragraphs (1) and (2) shall not apply where a postal packet has been sent by or on behalf of any person or body identified in section 134(3) of the 1983 Act.

(4) Where paragraph (3) applies the postal packet may only be opened and inspected by an authorised member of staff in so far as it is necessary to confirm its origin.

(5) A postal packet opened and inspected in accordance with paragraph (4) must be delivered to the patient without further inspection if the packet has been sent by a person or body listed in section 134(3) of the 1983 Act.

Internal post

27.—(1) Each provider must make arrangements in respect of the hospital for which it is **C–030** responsible for the inspection of internal postal packets in accordance with this direction.

(2) An authorised member of staff may open and inspect any item of internal post.

(3) The provider may withhold delivery of internal post, or an item included in such post if—

(a) the recipient has asked for internal post from another patient to be withheld;

(b) it is likely in the opinion of the provider to cause distress to any person (not being a member of staff);

(c) it is likely in the opinion of the provider to cause danger to any person; or

(d) it is necessary to do so in the interests of the safety of the patient or for the protection of any other person.

(4) If any post, or an item included in such post, is withheld under paragraph (3) the provider must ensure that—

(a) a record is made of the decision; and

(b) both the sender and the recipient are informed—

(i) that the post or item has been withheld;

(ii) the reason why; and

(iii) that they have a right to a review of that decision by the Care Quality Commission if a written application is made within six months beginning with the day on which the information set out in this sub-paragraph is received.

(5) For the purposes of this paragraph "internal post" means post—

(a) between patients within the same hospital; or

(b) from a patient to a member of staff of the hospital where the patient is detained.

(6) The provider shall comply with any direction given by the Care Quality Commission under regulation 3(2) of the Additional Functions Regulations 2011.

GENERAL NOTE

Paragraph (3)

C–031   Regulation 3 of the Care Quality Commission (Additional Functions) Regulations 2011 (SI 2011/1551) (as amended) reads:

"Review of decision to withhold internal post in high security hospitals

3.—(1) The Care Quality Commission shall review a decision made under direction 27(3) of [the 2013 Directions] (internal post) to withhold internal post, or an item included in such post, if an application to review that decision is made by the sender or the intended recipient of the post or item within six months beginning with the day on which that person receives the information set out in direction 27(4)(b) of those Directions.

(2) On an application under paragraph (1) the Care Quality Commission may direct that the post or item which is the subject of the application shall not be withheld."

Patients' outgoing post

C–032   **28.**—(1) Subject to—

(a) section 134 and 134A(1) to (3) of the 1983 Act; and

(b) regulations 29 and 30 of the 2008 Regulations,

each provider must make arrangements for the inspection of patients' outgoing postal packets at a hospital for which it is responsible in accordance with this direction.

(2) Any outgoing postal packet from a patient, other than a letter or card, shall be packaged and sealed by the patient on their ward and in the presence of an authorised member of staff.

(3) Subject to paragraph (4) an authorised member of staff may open and inspect any outgoing letter or card.

(4) Where a letter or card is addressed to any person or body identified in section 134(3) of the 1983 Act, the letter or card may only be opened where it is necessary to confirm its destination and must not be further inspected if the intended recipient is a person or body identified in that section.

Incoming post addressed to members of staff

C–033   **29.**—(1) Each provider must make arrangements in respect of the hospital for which it is responsible for the examination of postal packets addressed to a member of staff in accordance with this direction.

(2) A postal packet addressed to a member of staff must be x-rayed before delivery of it to that person within the secure area.

(3) An authorised member of staff may open and inspect a postal packet under paragraph (1) with the consent of the member of staff to whom it is addressed.

(4) A postal packet shall not be delivered to a member of staff within the secure area if, following a request, that person refuses to allow it to be opened and inspected.

Mobile telephones

30.—(1) Each provider must make arrangements in respect of the hospital for which it is **C–034** responsible for the control of mobile telephones in the hospital in accordance with this direction.

(2) Patients must not have possession of, or access to, a mobile telephone in the secure area.

(3) Subject to paragraph (5), visitors and visiting children must not have possession of, or access to, a mobile telephone in the secure area.

(4) Members of staff must not have possession of a mobile telephone in the secure area unless—

    (a) that telephone is owned, or hired, by the provider; and

    (b) the security director has authorised possession on the ground that there are exceptional circumstances.

(5) Members of the emergency services may carry mobile telephones where—

    (a) they are responding to an emergency; or

    (b) the security director has so authorised.

Patients' outgoing telephone calls

31.—(1) Each provider must make arrangements in respect of the hospital for which it is **C–035** responsible for the control of patients' outgoing telephone calls in accordance with the provisions of this direction.

(2) If the provider allows a patient to telephone the Samaritans it must provide a telephone dedicated solely for that purpose.

(3) A patient may not make a telephone call to another patient in the same hospital.

(4) Subject to paragraph (2), a patient may only make a telephone call—

    (a) to a telephone number pre-programmed by a member of staff using the pre-programmed system; or

    (b) if access to the pre-programmed system is temporarily unavailable, to any number that has been pre-programmed subject to paragraph (7) of this direction.

(5) For the purposes of paragraph (4), pre-programmed telephone numbers must—

    (a) include the telephone number of any person or organisation identified in section 134(3) of the 1983 Act where the patient has asked for that number to be pre-programmed ; or

    (b) otherwise be approved by the responsible clinician, having consulted with the clinical team.

(6) Except for a dedicated telephone provided under paragraph (2), a patient may only have access to a telephone in any area where the patient normally has access, including a ward or therapeutic area—

    (a) at such times as the provider may determine between 8.00am and 10.00pm; and

(b) at other times, where access is specifically authorised by a member of staff.

(7) Where paragraph (4)(b) applies, a member of staff—

(a) must dial the telephone number and establish the identity of the person or organisation called; and

(b) observe the patient at all times during the call.

Patients' incoming telephone calls

C–036   32.—(1) Each provider must make arrangements in respect of the hospital for which it is responsible for the control of patients' incoming telephone calls in accordance with the provisions of this direction.

(2) Subject to paragraph (4), a patient may not receive an incoming telephone call.

(3) Where there is an incoming telephone call for a patient, a member of staff must—

(a) answer that call; and

(b) inform the patient that a call has been received and the main points of the conversation between the caller and the member of staff.

(4) A patient may receive a telephone call, other than a call from another patient in the same hospital, where—

(a) the call has been pre-arranged by a member of staff and authorised by the director of security; or

(b) in the opinion of a member of staff—

(i) the urgency of the case is such that the patient should receive the call; or
(ii) there are compassionate grounds for allowing the patient to receive the call.

(5) Where a patient receives a telephone call under paragraph (4), a member of staff—

(a) must observe the patient at all times during the telephone call; and

(b) may monitor the telephone call in accordance with direction 34.

Risk assessments

C–037   33.—(1) Each provider must make arrangements for risk assessments to be carried out in the hospital for which it is responsible in accordance with this direction.

(2) Subject to paragraph (3), a risk assessment must be carried out by the clinical team prior to the admission of a patient.

(3) Where it is not practicable to carry out a risk assessment prior to the admission of a patient, a risk assessment must be carried out by the clinical team within 6 hours of admission of the patient.

(4) The risk assessment must include an assessment of whether a patient presents a high risk of—

(a) immediately harming others;

(b) committing suicide or self harming;

(c) being assaulted;

(d) escaping or absconding; or

(e) subverting safety and security, or organising action to subvert safety or security.

(5) Following a risk assessment the clinical team must prepare a risk management plan.

(6) Any risk management plan must include details of any decision to—

(a) monitor the patient's telephone calls in accordance with direction 34; or

(b) lock the room of the patient at night in accordance with direction 35.

(7) Where there is a high risk of the patient undertaking one or more of the actions identified in paragraph (4), the clinical team must consult a member of the security department before finalising the risk management plan.

(8) The risk management plan must—

(a) if the clinical team decides that a patient presents a high risk in accordance with sub-paragraph (4), record the reasons;

(b) specify the date on which any decision to—

(i) monitor the telephone calls of the patient, or

(ii) lock the patient's room at night,

must be reviewed; and

(c) specify when the risk management plan must be reviewed.

(9) The clinical team must review each risk assessment, and each risk management plan—

(a) following any significant incident or change of circumstances which could impact on a patient's risk assessment, including—

(i) where a patient commits or threatens to commit an act of self harm,

(ii) where a patient is the victim of actual or threatened violence,

(iii) where a patient has used or threatened violence towards another patient or a member of staff,

(iv) any act, or the receipt of any intelligence, relating to escape or unauthorised absence of the patient, or

(v) any action, or threat of action, by the patient which would subvert security;

(b) in relation to a risk management plan, by the dates specified in the plan; and

(c) at least once every six months.

Monitoring telephone calls

34.—(1) Each provider must make arrangements in respect of the hospital for which it is **C–038** responsible for the monitoring of patients' telephone calls in accordance with the provisions of this paragraph.

(2) A telephone call between a patient and any person or body identified in section 134(3) of the 1983 Act (persons or bodies to whom section 134(1)(b) or (2) do not apply) may not be monitored or recorded.

(3) A telephone call between a patient and the Samaritans may not be monitored or recorded.

(4) Before an incoming or outgoing telephone call is monitored or recorded in accordance with this direction the patient and any other person making or receiving the call must be informed if the call—

(a) is being monitored and recorded; or

(b) may be monitored and recorded.

(5) Subject to paragraphs (2) and (3) if, following a risk assessment, the patient's clinical team decide that—

(a) a patient presents a high risk of escaping or organising action to subvert safety and security; or

(b) there is a need to protect the safety and security of the patient or of others,

it must consider including in the risk management plan for that patient arrangements for an authorised member of staff to monitor and record the patient's incoming and outgoing telephone calls.

(6) Where the risk management plan requires a patient's telephone calls to be monitored and recorded—

(a) that patient's telephone calls may be monitored and recorded;

(b) each telephone call must be monitored at the time at which it is made or received; and

(c) the patient must be informed of the reasons for the decision to monitor and record telephone calls and of the right to have that decision reviewed by the Care Quality Commission, if a written application for review is made within six months beginning with the day on which the information set out in this sub-paragraph is received.

(7) In addition to any recording made under arrangements included in a risk management plan under paragraph (5), an authorised member of staff—

(a) may record up to 10 per cent of incoming or outgoing patient telephone calls over a seven day period; and

(b) must listen to any recording made under sub-paragraph (a).

(8) A recording of a telephone conversation made under this direction may—

(a) be retained for such initial period and such subsequent extension of that period as the provider considers necessary; and

(b) at the end of that period, including any extension where relevant, must be destroyed.

(9) The provider shall comply with any direction given by the Care Quality Commission under regulation 4(2) of the Additional Functions Regulations 2011.

GENERAL NOTE

Paragraph (5)

C–039   Regulation 4 of the Care Quality Commission (Additional Functions) Regulations 2011 (SI 2011/1551) (as amended) reads:

"Review of decisions to record and monitor telephone calls in high security hospitals
4.—(1) The Care Quality Commission shall review a decision made in accordance with direction 34(5) of [the 2013 Directions] (monitoring telephone calls) that a patient's telephone calls will be monitored and recorded if an application to review that decision is made by the patient within six months beginning with the day on which that person receives the information set out in direction 34(6)(c) of those Directions.

(2) On an application under paragraph (1) the Care Quality Commission may direct that the recording and monitoring of the patient's telephone calls [pursuant to direction 34(5) and (6) of [the 2013 Directions]] shall cease."

Paragraph (7)
In *R. (on the application of N) v Ashworth Special Hospital Authority* [2001] EWHC 339 **C–040**
(Admin), a patient challenged the legality of the equivalent to para.(7) in the High Security Psychiatric Services (Arrangements for Safety and Security at Ashworth, Broadmoor and Rampton Hospitals) Directions 2011. In dismissing the application for judicial review, Newman J. held that the provision of random monitoring of telephone calls, whilst constituting an interference with patient's rights under art.8 of the European Convention on Human Rights, is directed at a legitimate aim, namely the Secretary of State's duty under s.4 of the National Health Service Act 1977 (now the NHS Act 2006), and that the direction was a proportionate response to the permitted purpose of reducing the security risks at the three high security hospitals.

Security at night
35.—(1) Each provider in respect of the hospital for which it is responsible may, having **C–041**
regard to guidance issued by the Secretary of State, make arrangements for patients' rooms to be locked at night in accordance with this direction.

(2) The provider may only lock a patient's room at night if—

(a) the room has integral sanitation facilities and a staff call system; or

(b) the patient is subject to continuous observation by a member of staff.

Grounds Access
36.—(1) Each provider must ensure that a patient is not granted grounds access at the **C–042**
hospital for which it is responsible otherwise than in accordance with this direction.

(2) Grounds access may be granted only by the provider's Grounds Access Committee in accordance with direction 38 or by the medical director in accordance with direction 39.

(3) A member of the clinical team may request that a patient be granted grounds access only after the patient's clinical team has—

(a) undertaken a risk assessment; and

(b) proposed that grounds access is granted as part of that patient's treatment plan.

Grounds Access Committee
37.—(1) Each provider must continue to maintain a Grounds Access Committee at the **C–043**
hospital for which it is responsible.

(2) A Grounds Access Committee must be chaired by—

(a) the security director; or

(b) a person nominated by the security director.

Functions of the Grounds Access Committee

C–044 **38.**—(1) Each provider must ensure that the Grounds Access Committee for the hospital for which it is responsible performs its functions in accordance with this direction.

(2) The Grounds Access Committee must—

(a) consider any request by a member of the clinical team for a patient to be granted grounds access; and

(b) consider any proposal by a member of the clinical team concerning the proposed employment of a patient under direction 25 (role of patients in managing or working in patients' shops and other specified employment).

(3) When considering a proposal referred to in paragraph (2)(b), the Grounds Access Committee must consider any recommendations made by a member of the patient's clinical team.

(4) The Grounds Access Committee may—

(a) grant grounds access or a request concerning the employment of a patient unconditionally;

(b) grant such access or such a request with conditions; or

(c) refuse such access or such a request.

(5) Where the Grounds Access Committee grants grounds access, it must specify the areas of the hospital to which access is granted.

(6) In performing its functions the Grounds Access Committee must take into account—

(a) the safety and security of the patients, staff and visitors; and

(b) the security of the hospital.

Review of decision of the Grounds Access Committee

C–045 **39.**—(1) Each provider must ensure that, where a patient's responsible clinician considers that a decision made by the Grounds Access Committee under direction 38 would impede the treatment of a patient, the decision is referred to the medical director.

(2) In reviewing a decision the medical director must consult the security director and take into account—

(a) the views of the responsible clinician;

(b) the safety and security of the patients, staff and visitors; and

(c) the security of the hospital.

(3) The medical director may—

(a) confirm the decision of the Grounds Access Committee;

(b) vary the decision of the Grounds Access Committee; or

(c) overturn the decision of the Grounds Access Committee.

(4) Where the medical director grants grounds access, they must specify the areas of the hospital to which access is granted.

Leave of absence

40.—(1) Each provider must ensure that, before a patient in a hospital for which it is **C–046** responsible is granted leave of absence—

(a) the responsible clinician, having consulted the patient's clinical team, produces a risk assessment;

(b) the clinical team develop a management plan addressing any risks that are identified in that assessment; and

(c) the security director, or a member of the security department who is authorised by the security director to act on his behalf, considers and approves that management plan.

(2) For the purposes of paragraph (1) the clinical team must include a member of the security department.

Escorting patients

41. Each provider must— **C–047**

(a) provide training for members of staff who are responsible for escorting patients outside the secure area of the hospital for which it is responsible; and

(b) issue written instructions to those members of staff on escorting patients outside the secure area, including instructions on the use of handcuffs and escorting chains.

Security of keys and locks

42. Each provider must ensure that the security director of the hospital for which it is **C–048** responsible issues written instructions to—

(a) members of staff; and

(b) any other key-holders,

on the use and control of locks and keys.

Security Audits

43.—(1) Each provider must provide such assistance as is necessary for the purpose of **C–049** facilitating a yearly security audit of the hospital for which it is responsible.

(2) In paragraph (1) "security audit" means an audit undertaken by the prison service audit team.

Provision of training

44.—(1) Each provider must make arrangements for the provision of safety and security **C–050** training to—

(a) all members of staff at the hospital for which it is responsible; and

(b) any other key holders at that hospital.

(2) For the purposes of paragraph (1) training must include—

(a) security induction training;

(b) training on the control of keys and locks;

(c) training on the management of violence and aggression;

(d) an annual security update; and

(e) such other training as the provider considers appropriate.

(3) Each provider must ensure that any person to whom keys are to be allocated receives—

(a) security induction training; and

(b) training on the control of keys and locks,

before keys are allocated.

Revocation

C–051 **45.** The High Security Psychiatric Services (Arrangements for Safety and Security at Ashworth, Broadmoor and Rampton Hospitals) Directions 2011 and the High Security Psychiatric Services (Arrangements for Safety and Security at Ashworth, Broadmoor and Rampton Hospitals) Amendment Directions 2012 are revoked.

APPENDIX D

MENTAL HEALTH ACT 1983 INSTRUCTIONS WITH RESPECT TO THE EXERCISE OF APPROVAL FUNCTIONS 2014

The Secretary of State for Health, in exercise of the powers conferred by section 12ZA(5) of the Mental Health Act 1983, gives the following Instructions:

PART 1

Application, etc.

Application, commencement and interpretation

1.—(1) These Instructions apply to a body with whom the Secretary of State has made an **D–001** agreement under section 12ZA of the Mental Health Act 1983.

(2) These Instructions apply in relation to England.

(3) These Instructions come into force on 17th February 2014.

(4) The Mental Health Act 1983 Instructions with respect to the Exercise of Approval Functions 2013, which were signed on 27th March 2013 and effective from 1st April 2013, are revoked from 17th February 2014.

(5) In these Instructions —

"the 1983 Act" means the Mental Health Act 1983;

"approval functions" means the function of approving a registered medical practitioner under section 12(2) of the 1983 Act and the function of approving a person to act as an approved clinician under section 145(1) of the 1983 Act;

"approve" and "approval" includes "re-approve" and "re-approval";

"approved clinician" has the meaning given by section 145(1) of the 1983 Act;

"approved mental health professional" has the meaning given by section 114 of the 1983 Act;

"approving body" means a body that is or becomes responsible for the approval of a person to act as a section 12 doctor or an approved clinician (as the case may be) in relation to an area specified in an agreement made under section 12ZA or 12ZB of the 1983 Act;

"clinical director" means a person the approving body considers to be a clinical director or a person the approving body considers to be equivalent to a clinical director;

"consultant" means a person who has been appointed to a medical consultant post with a health service provider;

"forensic physician" means a person the approving body considers is a forensic physician or a person the approving body considers is a forensic medical examiner;

"induction training course" means a course approved by an approving body for the purpose of the induction of a prospective section 12 doctor or an approved clinician;

"medical director" means a person the approving body considers to be a medical director or a person the approving body considers to be equivalent to a medical director;

"medical treatment" has the meaning given by section 145(1) and (4) of the 1983 Act;

"mental disorder" has the meaning given by section 1(2) of the 1983 Act;

"performers list" means a list of medical practitioners prepared, maintained and published under regulations made under section 91 of the National Health Service Act 2006(**c**) or section 28 of the National Health Service (Wales) Act 2006;

"period of approval" means the period of time for which the approval is granted in accordance with instruction 6;

"professional requirements" means the requirements set out in the relevant Part of Schedule 1 to these Instructions;

"refresher training course" means a course approved by an approving body for the purpose of refreshing the skills and competencies of a person who has previously been approved to act as a section 12 doctor or an approved clinician;

"relevant competencies" means the skills and competencies set out in Schedule 2 to these Instructions;

"responsible clinician" has the meaning given by section 34(1) of the 1983 Act;

"second opinion appointed doctor" means a registered medical practitioner appointed for the purposes of Part 4 of the 1983 Act;

"section 12 doctor" means a person who is approved under section 12(2) of the 1983 Act for the purposes of section 12 of that Act;

"specialist register" means the specialist register kept by the General Medical Council under section 34D of the Medical Act 1983;

"specialist in psychiatry" means a person kept on the specialist register as a—

(a) a specialist in psychiatry or
(b) specialist in an area that the approving body considers to be equivalent to psychiatry; and

"treatment" means medical treatment for mental disorder.

PART 2

Approvals: General

Function of approval

D–002   2. The Secretary of State instructs the approving body to exercise the approval functions in accordance with these Instructions and any agreement made under section 12ZA or 12ZB of the 1983 Act which is in force between the Secretary of State and the approving body.

Approval under section 12(2) of the 1983 Act

D–003   3. An approving body must only approve a person under section 12(2) of the 1983 Act (approval of doctors providing medical recommendations) to act as a section 12 doctor in England ("the section 12 applicant") where the approving body is satisfied that the section 12 applicant—

(a) fulfils the professional requirements in Part 1 of Schedule 1 to these Instructions;

(b) can provide an enhanced criminal record certificate under section 113B of the Police Act 1997 (enhanced criminal record certificates) including suitability information relating to children under section 113BA and vulnerable adults under section 113BB of that Act, unless the section 12 applicant is—

(i) a person who is, or is a partner in a partnership that is, registered under Chapter 2 of the Health and Social Care Act 2008; or

(ii) currently employed by a person so registered;

(c) has—

    (i) completed an induction training course for section 12 doctors within the twelve month period immediately preceding the date of the application; or

    (ii) been approved (or is treated as having been approved) to act as a section 12 doctor in relation to England or Wales and has completed a relevant refresher training course within the twelve month period immediately preceding the date on which the person's approval expires (if applicable) or the approving body considers the person's application, whichever is later;

(d) has provided evidence which the approving body considers shows satisfactory participation in continuing professional development, which must—

    (i) in the case of a psychiatrist, include evidence by way of a certificate from the Royal College of Psychiatrists stating that the section 12 applicant is in good professional standing for continuing professional development or must include any other evidence which the approving body considers demonstrates sufficient and suitable continuing professional development;

    (ii) in the case of a psychiatrist in a training programme recognised by the Royal College of Psychiatrists, include evidence from the section 12 applicant's programme director that the applicant has made satisfactory progress in their continuing professional development for the purposes of being approved to act as a section 12 doctor;

    (iii) in the case of a general practitioner on the performers list, include evidence of participation in an annual appraisal process required as a condition of continued inclusion in the relevant performers list and evidence of continued inclusion in that list;

    (iv) in the case of a general practitioner who has been but is not currently on the performers list and who has previously been approved to act as a section 12 doctor, include evidence of participation in an annual appraisal process which is satisfactory to the General Medical Council; or

    (v) in the case of a forensic physician who is neither a psychiatrist nor a general practitioner on the performers list, include evidence of participation in an annual professional appraisal and evidence of completing continuing professional development appropriate for a role as a section 12(2) approved doctor;

(e) has provided written evidence—

    (i) of any relevant professional qualification; and

    (ii) if the section 12 applicant completed all of their training, or a part of training which the approving body considers substantial, in another jurisdiction and has not previously been approved, of the steps they have taken to familiarise themselves with psychiatric practice and the organisation of psychiatric services in England or Wales, including the practical application of the 1983; and

(f) has provided an up to date curriculum vitae and the contact details of two referees who meet the following requirements and can provide references to the satisfaction of the approving body—

    (i) each referee must have known the section 12 applicant for a period of time that the approving body considers to be reasonable and be able to provide a reference concerning the applicant's ability to understand and implement the 1983 Act;

    (ii) at least one referee must have worked with the section 12 applicant in England or Wales for a period of time which the approving body considers reasonable in the twelve month period immediately preceding the date of the application;

   (iii) one referee must be a consultant psychiatrist who is a section 12 doctor and the
          other referee must be one of the following—
          (aa) an approved clinician;
          (bb) a consultant psychiatrist who is a section 12 doctor;
          (cc) a person who is currently responsible for undertaking the section 12 appli-
                cant's professional appraisal;
          (dd) an approved mental health professional with whom the section 12 appli-
                cant has worked for a period of time which the approving body considers
                reasonable in the twelve months preceding the date of the application; or
          (ee) the section 12 applicant's current medical director or clinical director.

D–004   **4.** An approving body must only approve a section 12 applicant for a period following
that applicant's current period of approval if it is satisfied that the applicant has provided
satisfactory evidence of ongoing involvement in the diagnosis or treatment of mental disorder, which may be shown by undertaking one or more of the following activities in the
twelve month period preceding the date of the application—

   (a) acting as a medical member of the Health, Education and Social Care Chamber of
        the First-tier Tribunal or the Mental Health Review Tribunal for Wales;

   (b) assessments as a second opinion appointed doctor for the Care Quality Commission
        or the Healthcare Inspectorate Wales;

   (c) giving evidence to, or preparing reports or assessments for, a court for the purposes
        of—

        (i) Part 3 of the 1983 Act (patients concerned in criminal proceedings or under
             sentence);
        (ii) the Mental Capacity Act 2005; or
        (iii) the Children Act 1989;

   (d) at least two assessments under the 1983 Act;

   (e) acting as a responsible clinician or an approved clinician in charge of the treatment
        of a patient; or

   (f) being employed in a clinical post and having a level of responsibility for the diag-
        nosis or treatment of mental disorder which the approving body considers to be
        substantial.

Approval to act as an approved clinician
D–005   **5.** An approving body must only approve a person to act as an approved clinician in
England ("the applicant") where it is satisfied that the applicant—

   (a) fulfils at least one of the professional requirements in Part 2 of Schedule 1;

   (b) has the relevant competencies;

   (c) has an enhanced criminal record certificate under section 113B of the Police Act
        1997 including suitability information relating to children under section 113BA
        and vulnerable adults under section 113BB of that Act unless the applicant is:

        (i) a person who is, or is a partner in a partnership that is, registered under Chapter
             2 of the Health and Social Care Act 2008; or
        (ii) currently employed by a person so registered;

   (d) has—

        (i) completed a course for the initial training of approved clinicians within the two
             year period immediately preceding the date of the application; or

(ii) been approved to act as an approved clinician in England within the five year period immediately preceding the date of the application and has completed a relevant refresher training course within the two year period immediately preceding the date on which the person's approval expires (if applicable) or the approving body considers the person's application, whichever is later;

(e) has provided evidence which the approving body considers shows satisfactory participation in continuing professional development;

(f) has provided an up to date curriculum vitae and the contact details of two referees who meet the following requirements and can provide references to the satisfaction of the approving body—

    (i) each referee must have known the applicant for a period of time that the approving body considers to be reasonable and be able to provide a reference concerning the applicant's ability to understand and implement the 1983 Act;

    (ii) one of the referees must have worked with the applicant in England or Wales for a period of time which the approving body considers reasonable within the twelve month period immediately preceding the date of the application;

    (iii) one of the referees must be the applicant's current or most recent medical director or clinical director, but where an applicant is on a training programme recognised by the Royal College of Psychiatrists, the referee may be the programme director or a person the approving body considers to be equivalent to a programme director;

    (iv) one of the referees must be an approved clinician and the other referee must be one of the following—

        (aa) an approved clinician;

        (bb) a consultant psychiatrist who is a section 12 doctor;

        (cc) an approved mental health professional with whom the applicant has worked for a period of time which the approving body considers reasonable within the twelve month period preceding the date of application; or

        (dd) the applicant's current or most recent clinical director or medical director or, where the applicant is in the last year of a training programme recognised by the Royal College of Psychiatrists, their programme director.

Period of approval
D–006

6.—(1) An approving body may approve a person to act as—

(a) a section 12 doctor for a period of up to five years; and

(b) an approved clinician for five years;

commencing from the date of the approval.

(2) Subject to instructions 7, 8 and 9, the approval, including the period of approval which is specified by the approving body, is not affected if another approving body becomes responsible for the approved person's approval as a result of the approved person taking up employment in another area.

Conditions of approval
D–007

7.—(1) An approval granted by an approving body must be subject to the following conditions—

(a) the person must immediately cease to act as a section 12 doctor or an approved clinician (as the case may be) and immediately notify the approving body if—

    (i) the person no longer meets any of the requirements set out in instruction 3 or 5 (as the case may be); or

(ii) the person is suspended from any of the registers or lists referred to in the professional requirements;

(b) the person must notify the approving body immediately if the person becomes subject to fitness to practice proceedings;

(c) the person must notify the approving body as soon as practicable of any change in the person's home or work address, telephone numbers, email address or other contact information;

(d) the person must inform the approving body of any employment move to an area for which a different approving body is responsible which is anticipated to be longer than six months, at least one month before such a move;

(e) the person must cease to act as a section 12 doctor or an approved clinician if the person's approval is suspended or has lapsed;

(f) the person must comply with the Data Protection Act 1998;

(g) if the person is in specialist training and is to be employed as a consultant psychiatrist before they have finished their specialist training, the person must provide evidence to the approving body within 12 months of the date of the approval that they have been included on the specialist register as a specialist in psychiatry;

(h) if the person is in specialist training and is not to be employed in a consultant psychiatrist post before they have finished their specialist training, the approval must only be effective from the date on which the person notifies the approving body that the person has been included on the specialist register as a specialist in psychiatry; and

(i) such other conditions that the approving body considers are reasonable and appropriate.

(2) An approving body may vary an existing condition or impose a new condition under instruction 7(1)(i) in circumstances including but not limited to where the approving body is considering suspending, or has suspended, a person's approval under instruction 8.

(3) Where an approving body (A) has granted an approval to a person for whom another approving body (B) then becomes responsible, B may vary or remove any conditions imposed by A under instruction 7(1)(g), (h) or (i).

(4) An approving body must take reasonable steps to confirm whether or not a person has met the conditions to which the person's approval is subject.

Suspension of approval

D–008 **8.**—(1) If, at any time after a person is approved as a section 12 doctor or as an approved clinician, the body responsible for the person's professional registration or listing suspends that registration or listing, the approving body must suspend that person's approval for as long as the registration or listing is suspended.

(2) Where the approving body is notified that the suspension of the registration or listing has ended, the approving body must end the suspension of approval unless paragraph (3) applies.

(3) The approving body may suspend a person's approval for a period which is reasonably necessary for the approving body to determine whether to end the suspension under paragraph (1) or to end the approval under instruction 9, if the approving body is not satisfied that the person—

(a) meets any condition to which that person's approval is subject; or

(b) in the case of an approved clinician, has the relevant competencies.

(4) Before an approving body suspends a person's approval under paragraph (3), it must—

(a) give the person its reasons for considering suspending the approval;

(b) give the person a period of time which the approving body considers reasonable to make representations in respect of the proposed action; and

(c) consider representations submitted by the person to the approving body.

(5) When the approving body suspends a person's approval, the approving body must inform the person and the body responsible for regulating the person's professional registration or listing of its reasons for the decision.

(6) If a person's approval is suspended, that person may not act in that capacity unless and until the suspension of approval is ended by the approving body.

(7) The period of a person's approval continues to run during any period during which the approval is suspended.

(8) Where the suspension of approval has ended, the approval is to continue to run for any unexpired period of approval, unless the approving body ends it earlier in accordance with instruction 9.

End of approval

9.—(1) Except where paragraph (2) applies, the approval of a person to act as a section **D–009** 12 doctor or an approved clinician must end at the end of the day on which the person's period of approval expires.

(2) The approving body must end the approval before the expiry of the period of approval—

(a) in accordance with a request in writing by that person; or

(b) except where paragraph (1) of instruction 8 applies, if it is not satisfied that the person—

    (i) fulfils at least one of the professional requirements;
    (ii) meets any condition attached to that person's approval; or
    (iii) in the case of an approved clinician, has the relevant competencies.

(3) Before an approving body ends a person's approval under paragraph (2)(b), the approving body must—

(a) give the person its reasons for considering ending the approval;

(b) give the person a period of time which the approving body considers reasonable to make representations in respect of the proposed action; and

(c) consider representations submitted by the person to the approving body.

(4) When the approving body ends the person's approval under paragraph (2)(b), the approving body must inform the person of its reasons for the decision and inform the body responsible for regulating the person's professional registration or listing.

Records

10.—(1)The approving body must keep a record in respect of each person it approves as **D–010** a section 12 doctor or an approved clinician and the record must include—

(a) the person's application for approval;

(b) the date of approval;

(c) the conditions attached to the person's approval, any variations to those conditions, and any evidence provided to the approving body that the person has met or continues to meet such conditions;

(d) details of any period of suspension of approval under instruction 8;

(e) details of the completion of any training referred to in instruction 3(c)(i) or 5(d)(i);

(f) details of any previous approvals referred to in instruction 3(c)(ii) or 5(d)(ii); and

(g) the date of the end of approval and, if applicable, the reason for ending the approval.

(2) The record referred to in paragraph (1) must be retained by the approving body for a period of six years beginning on the day on which the person's latest approval ended.

SCHEDULE 1

PROFESSIONAL REQUIREMENTS

PART 1

Section 12 Doctors

D–011 1. The professional requirements in relation to a section 12 doctor are that the person is—

(a) a registered medical practitioner with special experience in the diagnosis or treatment of mental disorder;

(b) holds a full registration with a licence to practice from the General Medical Council; and

(c) meets one of the requirements in paragraph 2.

D–012 2. The person must—

(1) be a member or fellow of the Royal College of Psychiatrists;

(2) be a member of the Royal College of General Practitioners and have a minimum of three years of experience, whether gained in consecutive years or not, which meets the following requirements—

(a) is in a salaried or principal post, which is not a temporary post, in which the person gained experience that the approving body considers to be substantial experience in the diagnosis or treatment of mental disorder, which may have been recognised by the award of a higher degree or diploma relevant to mental health work; and

(b) four months or more of that experience must have been in a supervised psychiatric training post within a training programme recognised by the Royal College of Psychiatrists or one that satisfies the criteria for accreditation by the Royal College of General Practitioners as a general practitioner with a special interest in mental health;

(3) have four years of experience, whether gained in consecutive years or not, in a psychiatric training post, a non-consultant career grade post which includes training or supervision which is equivalent to the training or supervision in a training programme recognised by the Royal College of Psychiatrists, or a salaried or principal psychiatrist post which is not a temporary post and this experience must—

(a) have provided experience that the approving body considers to be substantial experience in the diagnosis and treatment of mental disorder, which may have been recognised by the award of a higher degree or diploma relevant to mental health work;

(b) in the case of a general practitioner on the performers list, include at least four months of experience in a supervised psychiatric training post within a training programme recognised by the Royal College of Psychiatrists or one that satisfies the criteria for accreditation by the Royal College of General Practitioners as a general practitioner with a special interest in mental health; and

(c) include two assessments under the 1983 Act, which have been supervised by a person who was approved at that time to act as a section 12 doctor and who is also either a member of the Royal College of Psychiatrists or a person on the specialist register as a specialist in psychiatry, and evidence that it was carried out competently;

(4) be on the specialist register as a specialist in psychiatry and must—

(a) have a minimum of three months of experience of psychiatric practice in England or Wales; and

(b) be able to provide evidence of having competently undertaken two assessments under the 1983 Act supervised by a person who was approved at that time to act as a section 12 doctor and who is either a member or fellow of the Royal College of Psychiatrists or a person on the specialist register as a specialist in psychiatry; or

(5) be a member of the Faculty of Forensic and Legal Medicine of the Royal College of Physicians and must supply the name and address of the local lead forensic physician who can provide a reference (including evidence with respect to training) to the approving body and must have experience which includes—

(a) at least four years of post-registration clinical experience in areas relevant to the assessment of mental disorder, whether gained in consecutive years or not, at least four months of which must be in a supervised psychiatric training post;

(b) a minimum of six months' full time or twelve months' part time employment as a forensic physician, whether gained in consecutive years or not; and

(c) two assessments under the 1983 Act supervised by a section 12 doctor, including evidence that these were competently undertaken.

PART 2

Approved Clinicians

3. The professional requirements in relation to an approved clinician are that the person **D–013** is—

(a) a registered medical practitioner;

(b) a practitioner psychologist listed in the register maintained by the Health and Care Professions Council;

(c) a first level nurse, registered in Sub-Part 1 of the Nurses' Part of the register maintained under article 5 of the Nursing and Midwifery Order 2001, with the inclusion of an entry indicating their field of practice is mental health or learning disabilities nursing;

(d) an occupational therapist listed in the register maintained by the Health and Care Professions Council; or

(e) a social worker listed in the register maintained by the Health and Care Professions Council.

SCHEDULE 2

RELEVANT COMPETENCIES: APPROVED CLINICIANS

Relevant competencies for approved clinicians

D–014   **1.** A person must have the skills and competencies set out in paragraphs 2 to 9 below.

The role of the approved clinician and responsible clinician

D–015   **2.** A comprehensive understanding of the role, legal responsibilities and key functions of the approved clinician and the responsible clinician.

Legal and policy framework

D–016   **3.**—(1) Applied knowledge of—

     (a) mental health legislation, related codes of practice and national and local policy and guidance;

     (b) other relevant legislation, codes of practice and national and local policy guidance, in particular, relevant parts of the Human Rights Act 1998, the Mental Capacity Act 2005, the Children Act 1989 and the Children Act 2004, and

     (c) relevant guidance issued by the National Institute for Health and Clinical Excellence (NICE).

   (2) In the above paragraph "relevant" means relevant to the decisions likely to be taken by an approved clinician or responsible clinician.

Assessment

D–017   **4.**—(1) Ability to—

     (a) identify the presence of mental disorder;

     (b) identify the severity of the disorder; and

     (c) determine whether the disorder is of a kind or degree warranting compulsory detention.

   (2) Ability to assess all levels of clinical risk, including risks to the safety of the patient and others within an evidence-based framework for risk assessment and management.

   (3) Ability to undertake mental health assessments incorporating biological, psychological, cultural and social perspectives.

Treatment

D–018   **5.**—(1) Understanding of—

     (a) mental health related treatments, which include physical, psychological and social interventions;

     (b) different evidence based treatment approaches and their applicability to different patients; and

     (c) the range of appropriate treatments and treatment settings which can be provided in the least restrictive environment and will deliver the necessary health and social outcomes.

(2) High level of skill in determining whether a patient has capacity to consent to treatment.

(3) Ability to formulate, review appropriately and lead on treatment in relation to which the clinician is appropriately qualified in the context of a multi-disciplinary team.

(4) Ability to communicate clearly the aims of the treatment to patients, carers and the team.

Care Planning   D–019

6. Ability to manage and develop care plans which combine health (including measures relating to physical and psychological health and medication), social services (including housing and employment) and other resources, preferably within the context of the Care Programme Approach.

Leadership and Multi-Disciplinary Team Working   D–020

7.—(1) Ability to effectively lead a multi-disciplinary team.

(2) Ability to assimilate the (potentially diverse) views and opinions of other professionals, patients and carers, whilst maintaining an independent view.

(3) Ability to manage and take responsibility for making decisions in complex cases without the need to refer to supervision in each individual case.

(4) Understanding and recognition of the limits of the person's own skills and an ability to seek professional views from others to inform a decision, for example through peer review and appraisal.

Equality and Cultural Diversity   D–021

8.—(1) Up-to-date knowledge and understanding of relevant equality issues.

(2) Ability to identify, challenge, and where possible and appropriate redress discrimination and inequality in relation to approved clinician practice.

(3) Understanding of the need to sensitively and actively promote equality and diversity.

(4) Understanding of how cultural factors and personal values can affect practitioners' judgements and decisions concerning the application of mental health legislation and policy.

Communication   D–022

9.—(1) Ability to communicate effectively with professionals, patients, carers and others, particularly in relation to decisions taken and the underlying reasons for these.

(2) Ability to keep appropriate records and an awareness of the legal requirements in relation to record keeping, including the processing of all personal data or sensitive personal data (as both terms are defined in the Data Protection Act 1998) in accordance with that Act.

(3) Understanding of, and ability to manage, the competing requirements of confidentiality and effective information sharing, to the benefit of the patient and other stakeholders.

(4) Ability to compile and complete statutory documentation and to provide written reports as required of an approved clinician.

(5) Ability to present evidence to courts and tribunals.

APPENDIX E

REPRESENTATION BEFORE MENTAL HEALTH TRIBUNALS

Appendix E is reproduced with kind permission of The Law Society
and may also be found at the Society's website.

22 January 2015

This practice note includes detailed advice on:

- communicating with and taking instructions from your client;
- your duties of confidentiality and disclosure;
- the representation of children and young people;
- good tribunal practice.

References to professional rules are based on the SRA Code 2011.

Legal status

This practice note is the Law Society's view of good practice in this area. It is not legal advice.

Practice notes are issued by the Law Society for the use and benefit of its members. They represent the Law Society's view of good practice in a particular area. They are not intended to be the only standard of good practice that solicitors can follow. You are not required to follow them, but doing so will make it easier to account to oversight bodies for your actions.

Practice notes are not legal advice, nor do they necessarily provide a defence to complaints of misconduct or of inadequate professional service. While care has been taken to ensure that they are accurate, up to date and useful, the Law Society will not accept any legal liability in relation to them.

For queries or comments on this practice note contact the Law Society's Practice Advice Service.

Professional conduct

The following sections of the SRA Code of Conduct 2011 are relevant to the issues covered in this practice note:

- Chapter 1—client care.
- Chapter 2—client confidentiality and disclosure.

SRA Principles

There are 10 mandatory principles which apply to all those the SRA regulates and to all aspects of practice. The principles can be found in the SRA Handbook.

The principles apply to solicitors or managers of authorised bodies who are practising from an office outside the UK. They also apply if you are a lawyer-controlled body practising from an office outside the UK.

Update notes

This practice note updates the version published on 30 September 2011.

It has been updated to clarify aspects of the advice contained in the previous version, as well as reflect changes in:

- procedural and other rules;
- case law; and
- the SRA Code of Conduct.

1. Introduction

E–001

1.1 Who should read this practice note?

All lawyers who represent clients before the First-tier Tribunal (Mental Health) in England and the Mental Health Review Tribunal for Wales.

Unless otherwise specified, references to 'the tribunal' includes both tribunals.

Appendix E

E–002 **2. The right to legal advice and representation before the tribunal**

The right of access to a court is a fundamental right at common law under the European Convention on Human Rights (ECHR) and is guaranteed by Article 6 of the Convention.

Article 5(4) of the convention (PDF) further guarantees the right to legal representation.

When an individual is detained on the grounds of mental disorder, Article 5(4) requires that effective legal representation is provided by the state, free of charge, unless there are 'special circumstances'.

To comply with the state's obligations under Article 5(4) any legal representation that is provided must be 'effective'. That means the legal representative must be suitably qualified and experienced (although not necessarily a qualified lawyer) and must have adequate time and facilities to prepare the case, including sufficient opportunity to visit the client and take instructions.

'Special circumstances' do not include the fact that the detainee's prospects of release are poor or that the detainee has the means to instruct his own lawyers. Even if representation is available (whether at the detainee's or the state's expense) the state must still ensure the detainee is represented unless satisfied that he or she has capacity and has made an informed choice not to be represented. See for example *Megyeri v Germany* (1992) 15 EHRR 584.

In England and Wales, public authorities have duties under the Human Rights Act to ensure that detained patients are represented. In practical terms this will mean that a tribunal should consider appointing a legal representative for an unrepresented patient under rule 11(7) of the First-Tier Tribunal Rules in England or Rule 30 in Wales, even where the detainee has chosen not to be represented, unless satisfied that the individual has capacity to make that choice.

See 8.1 Legal and other requirements for further details.

E–003 **2.1 The role of the hospital**

Under the English and Welsh codes of practice, hospital managers must ensure that patients are told how to contact a suitably experienced representative (para 2.18 and para 26.5, respectively). The way in which hospitals assist clients to obtain legal representation varies widely.

Under Section 132 of the MHA 1983, hospital managers must ensure that a patient understands 'what rights of applying to a tribunal are available to him in respect of his detention', which would include advice on the right to be legally represented. This information is contained in a leaflet which should be given to patients upon admission.

A list of mental health legal practitioners can be provided by the ward or the Mental Health Act administrator to patients. The tribunal in both England and Wales also holds a list of accredited practitioners as does the Law Society.

You are advised to contact the Mental Health Act administrator at hospitals to check if you or your firm have been included in the list of representatives available to represent detained patients. Details of firms that employ a qualified practitioner in England and Wales can be found using the Law Society's online Find a Solicitor service.

See also a list of Law Society accredited representatives, which is updated monthly.

E–004 **2.2 Independent mental health advocates**

The role of an independent mental health advocate (IMHA) is to help qualifying patients understand the legal provisions to which they are subject under the Mental Health Act 1983 (MHA 1983), and the rights and safeguards to which they are entitled. IMHAs can accompany patients to tribunal and hospital managers' hearings and may speak on their behalf if they are not legally represented. The IMHA may also assist patients to exercise their rights (for example, helping them complete an application to the tribunal).

IMHAs are not the same as legal representatives and are not expected to take over duties currently undertaken by solicitors or other legal practitioners. The following patients are entitled to have access to an IMHA:

- patients detained under the MHA 1983, even if they are currently on leave of absence from hospital, apart from those patients detained under sections 4, 5(2), 5(4), 135 or 136;
- patients subject to guardianship under the act; or
- a community patient.

A patient will also qualify for the assistance of an IMHA if:

(i) they discuss with a registered medical practitioner or approved clinician the possibility of being given a form of treatment to which section 57 applies; or

(ii) not having attained the age of 18 years and not being a qualifying patient they discuss with a registered medical practitioner or approved clinician the possibility of being given a form of treatment to which section 58A applies.

In England the tribunal has issued guidance on the role of IMHAs.

You should note that in Wales all psychiatric in-patients have the right of access to an IMHA following implementation of the Mental Health (Wales) Measure 2010.

2.3 Receiving referrals

E–005

You must comply with SRA principles when seeking to obtain new instructions. You should also read and abide by any code of conduct issued by the relevant trust or hospital.

If you are a member of the Mental Health Lawyers Association (MHLA) you should look at clause 3 of the MHLA Code of Conduct, which deals with facilitating referrals.

You may:

- contact the Mental Health Act administrator of the hospitals in your area to express willingness to accept referrals for tribunal representation;
- contact IMHA service providers in your area to express willingness to accept referrals for tribunal representation.

You must not approach clients on hospital wards without prior appointments to obtain referrals. You should also be mindful of the potential for a conflict of interest to arise should you provide gifts or incentives to members of hospital staff.

If you are in doubt as to how to resolve any issue relating to referrals or gifts you should contact the SRA Professional Ethics Helpline.

If a patient approaches you on a ward seeking representation then you should check with the Mental Health Act administrator to ascertain whether that patient is already legally represented.

If the patient is not already represented, or the Mental Health Act administrator does not know whether or not the patient is legally represented, you can leave your details and invite the patient to contact you for an appointment.

You can take instructions immediately in emergency situations after first checking that no other legal practitioner has been approached. Examples of emergency situations include Section 2 patients where a date has already been set for a hearing or the time limit for appealing is very close.

2.4 Change of solicitor

E–006

Under the Civil Legal Aid (Procedure) Regulations 2013, you must not provide legal help to a client who has received legal help for the same matter from another supplier within the preceding six months. The exceptions to this are:

- there has been a material change in relevant circumstances since the initial determination;
- the individual has reasonable cause to be dissatisfied with the services provided under the initial determination;
- the individual's usual residence has changed since the initial determination and, as a result, effective communication between the individual and the provider is not practicable; or the provider named in the initial determination has confirmed in writing that no remuneration will be claimed under arrangements made by the Lord Chancellor under section 2(1) of the Act in respect of any services provided under the initial determination.

Where a patient requests a change of solicitor, you should record brief reasons in a file note as to why the patient is seeking to change their legal representative to you. You should write to the firm currently instructed and ask if they object to the change of solicitor.

2.5 Appointing a representative

E–007

The tribunal can exercise its power to appoint a representative:

- in England under Rule 11(7) of the Tribunal Procedure (First-tier Tribunal) (Health, Education and Social Care Chamber) Rules 2008 (the FTT Procedure Rules 2008);
- in Wales under Rule 13(5) of the Mental Health Review Tribunal for Wales Rules 2008 (the Tribunal (Wales) Rules 2008).

See 8.2 Legal and other requirements.

The tribunal may exercise this power when a patient either:

- states they want to be represented or does not want to conduct their own case;

- lacks the capacity to appoint a representative but the tribunal believes that being represented is in the patient's best interests.

A refusal of representation from a client with capacity to make that decision cannot be overridden. See 4.1 Clients with capacity.

The Upper Tribunal has the power to appoint a representative for the patient under rule 11(7) of the Tribunal Procedure (Upper Tribunal) Rules 2008 (the UT Rules 2008) in the same circumstances as the Tribunal.

The MHA 1983 does not provide for a litigation friend to be appointed for a person who lacks capacity to give instructions to a representative.

For more information, see 4.2 Clients without capacity.

E–008 3 Communication with the client

Tailoring the way in which you communicate with clients who have mental health problems is crucial in providing effective representation. The tribunal process can be a daunting process for patients who will often require increased levels of client care, including attendance time, well ahead of significant milestones in their case.

A report by the Administrative Justice and Tribunals Council (PDF) provides useful analysis and information for you to consider when preparing for and undertaking hearings before the tribunal. You should:

- be alert to, and seek to overcome, communication challenges which the client faces, including those arising from:
  - lack of capacity or use of medication;
    - hearing difficulties;
    - learning difficulties;
    - language barriers or other cross-cultural issues;

present information in a clear and straightforward manner, avoiding complicated forms and overly legalistic language

- allow extra time to explain issues in the case to clients and, if necessary attend clients well ahead of a hearing to minimise confusion on the day of the hearing;
- ensure clients have timely access to necessary information on their case for example, expert reports where necessary.

E–009 3.1 Initial contact with the client

You should make initial contact with the client in a timely manner, to take instructions and give initial advice. You should advise clients on:

- their rights as a detained patient;
- the issue of consent to treatment;
- entitlement to legal aid;
- the strengths and weaknesses of their case;
- hearing procedures;
- tribunal powers;
- timescales;
- their right to independent advocacy assistance.

You may not be able to communicate all the information above in one meeting—it depends on the unique circumstances of each client. You should refer a client to another specialist legal adviser if you lack expertise on other significant issues for which they might need legal advice. Importantly, this is a requirement of legal aid contracts (see section 2.40 of the 2014 Standard Civil Contract Specification General Rules). Examples of common significant issues include:

- family;
- welfare benefits;
- debt;
- housing;

- crime;
- public law;
- discrimination;
- human rights;
- community care;
- clinical negligence.

Legal aid changes have severely restricted or terminated funding in many of these areas. In some cases it may be appropriate to refer clients to the Citizens Advice Bureau.

You should maintain regular contact with the client, and be willing to adjust the level of contact depending on the client's mental health condition. The client's clarity may change during the case as a result of changing mental health or medication.

You should aim to make contact with clients in person as much as possible, rather than relying on telephone or written communication. If your first referral is from a member of staff at the hospital or an IMHA you should try and speak to the client before your first attendance to reassure them that you will be coming to see them. If your client is not detained but lives in the community then you should offer them an appointment at your office. If they are unable to attend your office you should consider what arrangements can be made to meet your client in private at a venue that is appropriate to your client's needs and is safe for you both.

You should be aware that your correspondence, although addressed to the client, may find its way on to the client's medical notes, thereby breaching solicitor/client confidentiality. It will sometimes be appropriate to visit the client rather than send correspondence by post. If you do so, you should read out the correspondence, offer the client a copy to keep and make a note on your file accordingly. If you find that your correspondence has been put into your client's records, you should check with your client whether they object to this and if so raise it with staff on the ward.

You must not disclose to the client any documents sent to you by the Tribunal Service or the Tribunal Secretariat in Wales which is marked 'not for disclosure'. You may only disclose such documents to your client if the tribunal authorises you to do so. For more information on disclosure issues see section 5.3.

E–010

3.2 Client care letters

Client care letters are especially important when working with clients who have mental health problems. The general rules (set out below) apply but special care and attention may be required.

Chapter 1 of the SRA Code of Conduct 2011 (Client Care) outlines client care requirements.

Chapter 1 provides that solicitors must provide a proper standard of service, which takes into account the individual needs and circumstances of each client. This includes providing clients with the information they need to make informed decisions about the services they need, how these will be delivered and how much they will cost.

Chapter 1 should be interpreted in reference to the 10 mandatory principles in the SRA Handbook.

Your initial letter to the client explaining terms of business is often called the client care letter. It acts as:

- a clear record for you and the client of the instructions given and what will happen next;
- a useful guide for your client on your role and responsibilities;
- evidence against complaints of insufficient information or inadequate professional service.

You should tailor client care letters to the individual needs of the client, reflecting their communication needs. You should use clear, simple and jargon-free language.

In some cases it may be inappropriate to send a letter, for example if the likelihood of distress to your client is significant. If for any reason you consider it inappropriate to send the client a client care letter you should retain the letter on file and go through the letter in person with the client when appropriate and as far as their comprehension allows.

You should always record the reason for taking this approach. If an IMHA or independent mental capacity advocate (IMCA) is involved, you may wish to make them aware of the contents of the letter, subject to client confidentiality (see below).

For more information see the practice note on client care letters.

4. Taking instructions

E–011 **4.1 Clients with capacity**

The following guidance applies where:

- a patient with capacity has instructed you directly;

- you have been appointed to represent them under r 11(7) (a) FTT Rules 2008 or rule 13(5) (a) of the Tribunal (Wales) Rules or r 11(7) (a) Upper Tribunal Rules 2008; namely where the patient 'states they want to be represented or does not want to conduct their own case'.

You must assume that your client has capacity unless the contrary is established (section 1(2) MCA). The test of litigation capacity is set out in *Masterman-Lister v Brutton & Co* [2003] 1 WLR 1511, namely 'whether the party to legal proceedings is capable of understanding, with the assistance of proper explanation from legal advisers and experts in other disciplines as the case may require, the issues on which his consent or decision is likely to be necessary in the course of those proceedings'. This is sometimes referred to as the client having capacity to instruct a solicitor. It is important to note, as the Supreme Court made clear in Dunhill v Burgin [2014] 1 WLR 993, that the test must be applied to the claim that the party in fact has, not to the claim as formulated by their lawyers.

The information that a patient is required to understand to instruct a solicitor in the context of an application to a tribunal is not complex and people severely affected by a mental disorder may still be able to provide instructions if you explain matters simply and clearly.

The question of whether the person is able to provide instructions is a judgment that in many cases an experienced mental health advocate will be able to make themselves. In the rare cases where you are unable to form an opinion you should obtain the opinion of the responsible clinician (RC)—either directly or via the Mental Health Act Administrator—as to the client's litigation capacity by reference to the test in *Masterman-Lister*. You should also ask the RC for his or her opinion of the client's capacity to appoint you.

If you conclude that your client has the capacity to instruct you, you must take instructions from them and must act in accordance with those instructions, even where they are inconsistent, unhelpful to the case or vary during the preparation of the case, or during the hearing itself. However, the fact that the client's instructions are contrary to their best interests may be evidence that they lack capacity.

You must refuse to advance an argument which is not 'properly arguable', despite instructions to do so, see *Buxton v Mills-Owen* [2010] EWCA Civ 122, para 45. However, a submission may be 'properly arguable' even if it has few, if any, prospects of success (para 43). It will depend upon the context and your judgment. It is highly unlikely that to seek a client's discharge in accordance with his or her express wishes would not be 'properly arguable', even if it is unlikely to succeed.

If you consider that an argument that your client instructs you to advance is properly arguable, you must advance it without reservation. In other words, you should not advance a submission at the same time as signaling to the judge that you may think that it is weak or hopeless, for example by using coded language such as 'I am instructed that'. Such coded language is well understood as conveying that the advocate expects it to be rejected: *Buxton v Mills-Owen* at para 44.

Where you believe your client's instructions are unrealistic or contrary to their interests you should discuss with the client an alternative and more realistic line of challenge.

You may pursue this alternative line only if the client agrees. Your duty to act in accordance with the client's instructions takes precedence over your duty to act in what you perceive to be their best clinical interests. Therefore if your client wishes you to argue for their discharge you should do this, even if in your view your client needs hospital treatment.

The duty to follow the client's instructions is subject to an exception. This is where you believe the client's instructions are affected by either duress or undue influence: see SRA Handbook IB (25)—acting for a client when there are reasonable grounds for believing that the instructions are affected by duress or undue influence.

In those circumstances you must not act on those instructions until you have satisfied yourself that they represent the client's wishes.

As an advocate, you are responsible for decisions about the manner in which you put your client's case to the tribunal, and you must bear in mind your professional responsibilities to the court—in this case the tribunal—as well as to the client. See [*R v Farooqi and others* [2013] EWCA Crim 1649].

E–012 **4.2 Clients without capacity**

You must assume that your client has capacity to give you instructions unless the contrary is established. Nevertheless, there will be occasions on which you will not be able to accept instructions directly, or by way of a referral, because the client lacks capacity to instruct you. You may form this view if, for example, the client is profoundly learning disabled and cannot appreciate that they are detained under the Mental Health Act.

If you think that your client lacks capacity to instruct you then you cannot act for this client unless either:

- you are instructed by a properly authorised third party, such as a court-appointed deputy or the donee of a power of property and affairs power of attorney; or

- the relevant tribunal has appointed you to act under the First-tier Tribunal Rules, Tribunal (Wales) Rules or the Upper Tribunal Rules.

See above: 2.5 Appointing a representative.

As set out at paragraph 2.5, the tribunal can appoint a solicitor for a patient if satisfied that the patient lacks capacity to appoint a representative. This is not the same as 'capacity to litigate'. There will be a few patients who lack capacity to litigate at a tribunal but who have capacity to appoint a representative.

The appointment by the tribunal operates as a retainer for the client.

An appointment by the tribunal does not mean that you are also appointed to act as the client's litigation friend: there is no provision for such an appointment within the rules. You should not automatically assume that guidance that may have been prepared for the use of a litigation friend in other court proceedings applies to you as a representative.

Once appointed by the tribunal you have a heightened responsibility to identify and then to act in the interests of the client. The duty to act in the client's best interests is set out in Principle 1 of the SRA Code 2011 and applies to clients with or without litigation capacity.

In our view the client's interest in a fair hearing to determine the lawfulness of their detention is paramount. When your client lacks litigation capacity, you will not take instructions in the same way that you would in respect of a client with capacity. Instead you must do your best to ascertain their wishes and feelings. You must give weight to the wishes that your client expresses.

The closer the patient is to having capacity, the greater the weight you must give to their wishes in seeking to formulate and advance submissions on their behalf. Nonetheless, you remain under the same duty to the tribunal to advance only submissions which are properly arguable as if your client had capacity (see *Buxton v Mills-Owen* and section 4.1 Clients with capacity).

There are likely to be few cases where a client who is able to express their wish to be discharged by a tribunal will be assessed as lacking capacity to instruct you. Similarly, where a client without litigation capacity tells you they wish to be discharged from hospital, there will be few cases it will not be appropriate to argue for their discharge. This is because of the over-riding importance of the client's right under Article 5(4) to challenge the lawfulness of their detention—a right that exists without the detained individual needing to show that they have any particular chance of success in obtaining their release—see *Waite v UK* (2003) 36 EHRR 54.

Where the client lacks the ability to express their wishes you should:

- ensure that the tribunal receives all relevant material so that it can determine whether the criteria for continued detention are satisfied;

- test the criteria for continued detention;

- remember your client's right to treatment in the least restrictive setting and alert the tribunal to possible alternatives to detention under the MHA 1983 such as Community Treatment Orders (CTOs) and guardianship;

- In the case of a patient who is unable to consent to be detained for purposes of assessment or treatment in hospital but appears to be compliant, you may wish to consider whether the DoLS regime under Schedule A1 to the MCA 2005 might provide a better and less restrictive way of ensuring that your client receives treatment or assessment in hospital: see *AM v SLAM NHS Foundation Trust* [2013] UKUT 365 (AAC).

You should not automatically argue for discharge if you are unable to ascertain the patient's wishes, but you are obliged to test the criteria for detention.

Separate considerations arise if the client is adamant that they do not wish to be represented by you, notwithstanding your appointment by the tribunal under Rule 11(7) (b), the tribunal having assessed the client as lacking capacity to appoint a representative.

If on meeting the client you think that he or she has capacity to appoint you then you should alert the tribunal and ask for the appointment to be discharged. It is then the client's decision whether to instruct you or not.

If you consider that the client lacks capacity to instruct you but think the client is hostile to being represented by you, then in some cases you should consider informing the tribunal and requesting the appointment to be discharged. This may be appropriate where:

- attempting to represent the client would cause them distress or interfere with their ability to participate in proceedings;

- the client's hostility is such that you cannot fulfil your professional obligations to them; or

- continuing to attempt to represent the client puts your safety at risk and the risk cannot be managed using local policies at the unit where the client is detained.

For further guidance on obtaining copies of the medical records of a client lacking capacity see section 6.2 Access to medical records.

5. Your duties towards your client

E–013 **5.1 Duty to act in the best interests of clients**

Solicitors must act in the best interests of the client under Principle 4 of the SRA Principles. This duty arises whether the client has litigation capacity or not. It is important to note that the term 'best interests' here does not necessarily mean the same as 'best interests' for the purposes of the MCA 2005. As set out below, you will need to draw a distinction between what has been termed the client's 'legal best interests' and their 'clinical interests.'

See Professional conduct in the Legal status box above and 8.1 Legal and other requirements Aspects of the duty to act in the client's best legal interests will include:

- advising clients of the likelihood of being discharged;

- advising clients on possible steps towards discharge;

- advising clients in respect of disclosure issues;

- following the instructions of a client with capacity to instruct you or advocating the views or wishes of a client without capacity to instruct you;

- advising on aftercare;

- advising on other related issues, for example compulsory treatment provisions, alternatives to detention such as CTOs and Guardianship;

- advising on the possibility and consequences of the patient withdrawing the application to the tribunal.

E–014 **5.2 Situations where legal and clinical interests may conflict**

Conflicts may arise because of the nature of the information that you have access to as a representative (regardless of your client's capacity to give you instructions). For example, in *RM v St. Andrew's Healthcare* [2010] UKUT 119 (AAC) the Upper Tier Tribunal ruled that documents revealing the patient was being covertly medicated should be disclosed to the patient because his fair trial rights (which the Upper Tier Tribunal referred to as his best legal interests) required it, even though it was accepted it was likely to affect his health adversely (which the Upper Tier Tribunal referred to as the patient's best clinical interests).

There may be other situations not covered by this practice note. If you are in doubt you should seek guidance from the Solicitor's Regulation Authority's Professional Ethics helpline.

E–015 **5.3 Duty of confidentiality**

5.3.1 Confidential information

This duty is covered in Chapter 4 of the SRA Code of Conduct. You must achieve Outcome 4.1 which requires solicitors to keep the affairs of clients and former clients confidential except where disclosure is required or permitted by law or the client consents.

Practitioners should be aware that the previous version of the code provided for specific exceptions to the absolute duty of confidentiality. These do not appear in the current version of the code and we recognise that this may give rise to difficult questions for practitioners. For example, you are speaking to a client on the ward and as you are about to leave they tell you they have been saving up their medication. They know the ward will be short-staffed tonight and intend to take an overdose and end their life. You know that they have attempted to take their own life before. You suggest that the two of you speak to one of the nurses to tell them this but they will not agree.

In this situation, as the client has refused consent to disclose their intentions, any subsequent disclosure by you would appear to be a technical breach of Outcome 4.1 yet not to do so could also potentially be said to conflict with your duty to act in the best interests of your client.

For guidance as to how you should approach situations such as this you should contact the SRA Ethics Helpline.

5.3.2 Privileged information

E–016

You should not disclose information passed to you in circumstances giving rise to a duty of legal professional privilege, which is absolute: see *R v Derby Magistrates ex p B* [1996] A.C. 487, *L (a minor)* [1997] A.C. 17 (see 24B-G) and *B v Auckland Law Society* [2003] 2 A.C. 736.

If you found yourself in this situation—for example, if disclosure of privileged information has been made mistakenly—you should contact the SRA's Professional Ethics Helpline for advice (0370 606 2577).

5.3.3 Duties of disclosure and circumstances where non-disclosure may be appropriate

E–017

Chapter 4 of the SRA Code of Conduct 2011 deals with the issue of disclosure.

The relevant outcomes which you must achieve are:

Outcome 4.2: any individual who is advising a client makes that client aware of all information material to that retainer of which the individual has personal knowledge;

Outcome 4.3: you ensure that where your duty of confidentiality to one client comes into conflict with your duty of disclosure to another client, your duty of confidentiality takes precedence.

The relevant indicative behaviours are:

IB 4.4:

where you are an individual who has responsibility for acting for a client or supervising a client's matter, you disclose to the client all information material to the client's matter of which you are personally aware, except when:

(a) the client gives specific informed consent to non-disclosure or a different standard of disclosure arises;

(b) there is evidence that serious physical or mental injury will be caused to a person(s) if the information is disclosed to the client;

(c) legal restrictions effectively prohibit you from passing the information to the client, such as the provisions in the money-laundering and anti-terrorism legislation.

The tribunal can withhold disclosure of documents from a patient if disclosure is likely to cause serious harm to the patient or another person and it is proportionate to do so. In England, this is possible under Rule 14, Tribunal Procedure (First-tier Tribunal) (Health, Education and Social Care Chamber) Rules 2008. In Wales, this is possible under Rule 17, Mental Health Review Tribunal for Wales Rules 2008.

Under these rules, the information can be disclosed to the solicitor on the basis that they do not disclose it to anyone else, including the client. Rule 14(6) prohibits the representative from disclosing documents or the information they contain either directly or indirectly to anyone else, including the representative's client. The rule does not prohibit the representative from informing the client that the representative has a document or information that cannot be disclosed to the client, provided that the representative does not thereby indirectly disclose to the client the information which is being withheld.

If the tribunal has made such a direction then your duty to disclose the information to the client is over-ridden by this legal restriction: see IB4.4. This can be a difficult situation for you to manage—if documents are disclosed to you on this basis you should either:

- consider requesting an earlier hearing which the client does not attend;
- consider dealing with disclosure as a preliminary issue without the client on the day of the hearing;
- consider making an application for the issue to be considered by a salaried tribunal judge on the papers before the hearing.

Dorset Healthcare NHS Foundation Trust v MHRT (2009) UKUT 4 (AAC) gives guidance on when a responsible authority can resist disclosure of confidential third-party information or when a solicitor wishes to disclose such information to their client.

If you request full access to your client's medical records, the responsible authority should disclose all documents to you subject to an undertaking, if necessary, not to disclose certain specific third-party documents to the patient.

If in 'exceptional circumstances' the responsible authority refuses even to disclose documents to the solicitor, they must show that it is appropriate to do so by serving a skeleton argument to the tribunal office and the tribunal must make a ruling.

You should seek permission from the tribunal to disclose to your client any documents disclosed to you if you consider that it may improve the prospects of a successful outcome. In other words, if the documents are 'material to the client's matter' for the purpose of IB4.4.

You should set out your reasons for disclosure by way of a skeleton argument. In *RM v St Andrew's Healthcare* [2010] UKUT 119 (AAC), also referred to in paragraph 5.2.1 above. In this case the Upper Tribunal ruled that in deciding whether disclosure should be ordered the overriding consideration must be to ensure that the patient has a fair hearing, and that this must take precedence over any concerns that disclosure will harm the patient's health. It would follow that the requirement of a fair hearing can often override considerations of third party confidentiality.

Where a request or refusal of request is not resolved, either party can apply to the tribunal, for an order under Rule 5(d). This can be heard as a preliminary issue on the day of the hearing or a decision can be taken before the hearing following written or oral submissions.

The Upper Tribunal has stressed the desirability of dealing with disclosure issues between the parties without the need to involve the tribunal.

Please note that the guidance above with regard to disclosure which arises from the Dorset case is limited to those cases where there are ongoing proceedings in the tribunal. In other circumstances, if a trust or other body holding data on your client provides you with material that is relevant to your client's case then you must disclose it to the client unless any of the circumstances in IB 4.4 apply.

6. Good tribunal practice

E–018   **6.1 Avoiding delay**

The tribunal's overriding objective is to deal with cases fairly and justly. This includes avoiding delay, so far as compatible with proper consideration of the issues.

Often delay can be caused by late reports from the responsible authority. In this situation it is the responsibility of the Mental Health Act Administrator to secure reports and submit them to the tribunal within the time limit. The tribunal in turn is responsible for issuing directions where reports are late. You should keep an eye on time limits for the submission of reports and ensure that the tribunal issue appropriate directions when it is necessary.

Once statutory reports are received you should ensure they comply with the President's Practice Direction (PDF).

These objectives are stated in Rule 2, the Tribunal Procedure (First-tier Tribunal) (Health, Education and Social Care Chamber) Rules 2008 and Rule 3 of the Mental Health Review Tribunal for Wales Rules 2008. This is also the case in the Upper Tribunal as stated in Rule 2, The Tribunal Procedure (Upper Tribunal) Rules 2008.

See 8.1 Legal and other requirements.

You should take all appropriate steps to ensure that tribunal hearings are not delayed.

E–019   **6.2 Access to medical records**

You should examine the section papers as soon as possible after your appointment as this will enable you to scrutinise the legality of your client's detention. For this you will require your client's signed consent authorising you to have access to your client's medical records. This requires the approval of the RC. In some hospitals this will be arranged via the MHAA but practice varies across hospitals.

You must read your client's medical records. These include documents such as progress notes, prescription charts, minutes of ward or CPA meetings, and records held in the community. Again, the means by which you can obtain access will vary across hospitals.

If your client lacks capacity to consent to your access to their section papers or records then you should ask the RC to agree to disclosure on the basis that it is in their best interests to have their case properly prepared. If you cannot resolve this issue with the RC you should apply to the tribunal using CMR1 for an order for disclosure under Rule 5(d). In Wales you should apply for an order under rule 5(c).

E–020   **6.3 Independent reports**

You should always consider whether it is appropriate to obtain independent evidence. Expert evidence may cover a range of issues such as diagnosis, treatment, placement and activities of daily living. You should also maintain an approved list of experts. Prompt instruction of an expert may reduce the need for adjournments and will ensure that your client has a fair hearing. Further guidance is available in the Mental Health Peer Review guidance.

You should request independent reports as soon as possible and in restricted cases send them to the tribunal office and the Ministry of Justice no later than 21 days before the hearing so that the secretary of state can comment on the report.

E–021

6.4 Witnesses

You should confirm in advance the availability of all witnesses, including experts, who are expected to attend the tribunal. You should be aware of IB 5.6 which provides that you should not appear as an advocate if you or anyone in your firm will be called as a witness.

E–022

6.5 Interpreters

In England Form T110 (Application to the FTT (Mental Health) and the listing form HQ1, you must indicate whether your client will require an interpreter. If you need an interpreter, you should notify the tribunal as early as possible in proceedings. In Wales you should notify the tribunal by email or letter.

E–023

6.6 Documents

You should send all relevant documents to the tribunal office no later than seven days before the hearing.

E–024

6.7 Pre hearing medical examination

A pre-hearing examination is indicated in all section 2 cases. In all other cases you should always consider whether it is appropriate to request a pre-hearing medical examination by the medical member of the tribunal. You must make such a request on form CMR1 within the prescribed period ie 14 days before the date fixed for the hearing. If your client lacks capacity to make the decision you must consider whether or not it would benefit your client's case for there to be such an examination.

E–025

6.8 Applications for postponements

You should avoid applications for postponements wherever possible. The tribunal frequently refuses applications for postponement, especially those made at the last minute. An application for a postponement should be made to the tribunal using Form CMR1. You must use this form where a request is made for any of the following:

- directions;
- postponement;
- prohibition of disclosure of information;
- wasted costs;
- permission to withdraw an application;
- other applications.

If you consider that a postponement is in the interests of the client, you should advise the client accordingly, but leave the final decision to the client if the client has capacity to litigate.

If a postponement appears unavoidable, you should apply as early as possible, setting out the reasons.

Where delay is caused by late reports from the responsible authority, if the tribunal has not already issued directions, solicitors should request directions immediately after the breach of the time limits on submission of statutory reports.

E–026

6.9 Withdrawing an application to the tribunal

An application can be withdrawn at any time by the client if the tribunal accepts the withdrawal. A reference cannot be withdrawn.

If the client wants to withdraw the application, you should notify the tribunal office using Form CMR1, giving the reasons.

Early notification allows for other cases to be rescheduled and maximises the use of the tribunal's time.

Where the withdrawal is received directly from the patient and that patient is represented, the solicitor will be approached by the tribunal and encouraged to make contact with the client to discuss the request to ensure the patient has not been put under pressure to withdraw.

The patient may make a fresh application for a tribunal within the same period of eligibility.

6.10 Other codes of conduct

6.10.1 Mental Health Lawyers Association (MHLA) code of conduct

E–027

The MHLA has adopted a Code of Conduct. It covers:

- quality of service;
- making appointments;
- behaviour on the wards;
- disputes over representation;
- seeking clients;
- gifts;
- hospital procedures.

E–028 **6.10.2 NHS mental health trusts—codes of conduct**

Some NHS mental health trusts and private hospitals have developed voluntary codes of conduct for solicitors. These codes ask solicitors to:

- contact the ward in advance to inform them of their intention to visit;
- produce identification when visiting;
- report to the ward office when visiting;
- inform a member of staff if they wish to hold an informal meeting with another client whom they are visiting;
- respect the operational needs of the unit/ward;
- leave the ward following the completion of their appointment with a client.

Solicitors are asked not to:

- make unsolicited visits or telephone calls;
- talk to or approach other patients;
- hand out publicity materials;
- offer gifts or money to service users other than existing clients;
- offer gifts to staff.

You should find out whether there is such a code in place at the relevant hospital. If you have any concerns about the code, you should contact the relevant trust.

E–029 **7 Representing children and young people before the tribunal**

The tribunal has established a Child and Adolescent Mental Health Service (CAMHS) panel. Its purpose is to ensure that at least one of the tribunal members has special expertise in dealing with cases where a child is either detained under the Mental Health Act 1983 or subject to another order under the act. For the purposes of the CAMHS panel a child is treated as any person under the age of 18 at the time of the application or reference.

Although the Tribunal Rules do not make any specific provision in relation to child patients, the solicitor representing a child should always consider the following:

- the wishes and feelings of the child;
- the need to ensure that the child is able to participate fully in the proceedings by, for example, requesting that the proceedings are dealt with in as informal manner as appropriate;
- any legal issues that are specific to the child, for example the impact of the Children Act 1989 on decision making in relation to the child and the need to identify the child's entitlement to aftercare services under children's legislation and mental health legislation.

8 More information

E–030 **8.1 Legal and other requirements**

- The Mental Health Act 1983 as amended by Mental Health Act 2007.
- The Tribunal Procedure (First-tier Tribunal) (Health, Education and Social Care Chamber) Rules 2008.
- The Practice Direction issued 30/10/08 (for England).
- The Mental Health Review Tribunal for Wales Rules 2008 (for Wales).

- The MHA codes of practice (different for England and Wales).
- Mental Capacity Act 2005.
- Tribunal Procedure (Upper Tribunal) Rules 2008.
- The Equality Act 2010.
- Mental Health (Wales) Measure 2010.

8.2 Mental Health Accreditation Scheme

E–031

The Law Society operates the Mental Health Accreditation Scheme.

If you are a member of the scheme you are authorised to advise and represent clients who have been detained under the Mental Health Act 1983 (the MHA 1983), before the relevant tribunal.

Since 1 August 2014 membership of the scheme is mandatory for advocates appearing before the tribunal other than self-employed counsel, and that all legal aid providers must comply with this (see 7.6(b) Category Specific Rules, 2014 Standard Civil Contract Mental Health Specification). Requirements for membership of the scheme include a good working knowledge of this practice note. The provisions of the Mental Health Act 1983 (the MHA 1983) have been qualified by the following legislation, statutory instruments and Codes of Practice:

- The Mental Health Act 2007.
- The Tribunal Procedure (First-tier Tribunal) (Health, Education and Social Care Chamber) Rules 2008 (for England).
- The Mental Health Review Tribunal for Wales Rules 2008 (for Wales).
- The Mental Health Act codes of practice (different for England and Wales).
- Mental Health (Wales) Measure 2010.
- Code of Practice to Parts 2 and 3 of Mental Health (Wales) Measure 2010.

You should familiarise yourself with all of the above and know which provisions apply, depending on whether you practise in England or Wales.

You should also have knowledge of:

- 2014 Standard Civil Contract Mental Health Specification
- Peer review guidance, Mental Health—3rd Edition, 2011.

Read copies of the relevant practice directions and updates (PDF), which all practitioners should be familiar with.

See 8.1 Legal and other requirements for further details.

Find out more about eligibility and membership.

8.3 Other products and services

E–032

8.3.1 Practice Advice Service

The Law Society's Practice Advice Service can be contacted on 020 7320 5675 from 09:00 to 17:00 on weekdays.

E–033

8.3.2 Solicitors Regulation Authority's Professional Ethics Helpline

Solicitors may obtain further help on matters relating to professional ethics from the Solicitors Regulation Authority's Professional Ethics Helpline (0370 606 2577) from 09:00 to 17:00 on weekdays.

E–034

8.3.3 Law Society publications

- Assessment of Mental Capacity, 3rd ed.
- Mental Health Tribunals.
- Mental Capacity, 2nd ed.
- Advising Mentally Disordered Offenders, 2nd ed.

E–035

8.4 Terminology in this practice note

Must

- A specific requirement in legislation or of a principle, rule, outcome or other mandatory provision in the SRA Handbook. You must comply, unless there are specific exemptions or defences provided for in relevant legislation or the SRA Handbook.

Should

- Outside of a regulatory context, good practice for most situations in the Law Society's view.
- In the case of the SRA Handbook, an indicative behaviour or other non-mandatory provision (such as may be set out in notes or guidance).

These may not be the only means of complying with legislative or regulatory requirements and there may be situations where the suggested route is not the best possible route to meet the needs of your client. However, if you do not follow the suggested route, you should be able to justify to oversight bodies why the alternative approach you have taken is appropriate, either for your practice, or in the particular retainer.

May

- A non-exhaustive list of options for meeting your obligations or running your practice. Which option you choose is determined by the profile of the individual practice, client or retainer. You may be required to justify why this was an appropriate option to oversight bodies.

SRA Code—SRA Code, 2011
OFR—Outcomes-Focused regulation
SRA—Solicitors Regulation Authority
IB—Indicative Behaviour

E–036 8.5 Acknowledgements

This practice note has been prepared and updated by the Law Society's Mental Health and Disability Committee. The committee would like to thank the SRA and the Mental Health Lawyers Association for their input into the practice note.

INDEX

LEGAL TAXONOMY
FROM SWEET & MAXWELL

This index has been prepared using Sweet and Maxwell's Legal Taxonomy. Main index entries conform to keywords provided by the Legal Taxonomy except where references to specific documents or non-standard terms (denoted by quotation marks) have been included. These keywords provide a means of identifying similar concepts in other Sweet & Maxwell publications and online services to which keywords from the Legal Taxonomy have been applied. Readers may find some minor differences between terms used in the text and those which appear in the index. Suggestions to *sweet&maxwell.taxonomy@thomson.com*.

A & E DEPARTMENTS
  see **Accident and emergency departments**
ABORTION
  consent, 1–133
  human rights, 1–059, 5–009
ABSENCE WITHOUT LEAVE
  Act provisions, 1–276
  assisting patients, 1–1208—1–1212, 2–004
  detained patients, 2–005, 2–087
  extension of authority
    1–341—1–346
    human rights, 1–358
    return after 28 days, 1–354—1–366
    return within 28 days, 1–348—1–353
  guardianship patients, 2–086, 2–087
  human rights, 1–281
  introduction, 1–278
  patients who abscond from Scotland, 1–280
  patients who abscond to Scotland, 1–279
  patients who have gone abroad, 1–563
  prisoners, 1–676
  Regulations, 2–087
  return of patients
    Channel Islands, 1–1073, 1–1081—1–1083
    England and Wales, 1–1078—1–1080
    generally, 1–341—1–346
    Isle of Man, 1–1081—1–1083
    Northern Ireland, 1–1074—1–1077
    return after 28 days, 1–354—1–366
    return within 28 days, 1–348—1–353
    Scotland, from, 2–088—2–091
    Scotland, to, 1–1073
  Scotland, 2–003
  time limits, 1–287—1–289
  transfer directions, 1–676, 2–005
ABSOLUTE DISCHARGE
  effect, 1–587
  generally, 1–373—1–386
  guardianship, 1–382
  human rights, 1–376, 1–935
  nearest relative, 1–381
  responsible local social services authority, 1–382

ABSOLUTE DISCHARGE—*cont.*
  restricted patients, 1–936
  restriction orders, 1–578, 1–587
ABUSE OF RIGHTS
  see also **Human rights**; **Ill treatment of mental patients**
  human rights, 1–1204, 1–1205, 1–1271, 5–055
ACCIDENT AND EMERGENCY DEPARTMENTS
  mentally disordered person found in public place, 1–1336
  remands to hospital, 1–483
ACCIDENTAL SLIPS AND OMISSIONS
  see **Clerical errors**
ADDITION OF PARTIES
  tribunal procedure, 3–058—3–060
ADMISSION ARRANGEMENTS
  see **Admissions for assessment; Compulsory admissions**
ADMISSIONS FOR ASSESSMENT
  see also **Compulsory admissions**
  Act provisions, 1–036
  applicants, 1–045
  applications, 1–043, 1–045
  classification of mental disorder, 1–047
  Code of Practice
    action when decision made not to proceed, 4–063
    action when decision made to proceed, 4–061
    communication of outcome, 4–062
    consultation with nearest relative, 4–057
    consultation with other people, 4–058
    dispute resolution, 4–064
    medical examination, 4–059
    responsibilities of approved bodies, 4–065
    role of AMHPs, 4–056—4–060
  compliant mentally incapable patients, 1–039, 1–054
  definition, 1–047
  detention routes, 1–041
  detention, 1–038
  deteriorating patient, 1–042
  health of patients, 1–048
  human rights, 1–040

ADMISSIONS FOR ASSESSMENT—*cont.*
  initial detention, 1–041
  introduction, 1–038
  medical recommendations, 1–049
  medical treatment, 1–045
  mental disorder, 1–045
  protection of others, 1–048
  risk assessment, 1–048
  safety of patients, 1–048
  suffering, 1–047
  time limits, 1–050
ADULT COMMUNITY PATIENTS
  see also **Child community patients**
  definition, 1–1376
  medical treatment
    certificates, 1–847—1–853
    certified in writing, 1–811
    conditions, 1–811
    emergency treatment, 1–838—1–846
    generally, 1–799—1–806
    patients lacking capacity, 1–817—1–823
    supplemental, 1–807—1–816
    withdrawal of consent, 1–835—1–837
  provision of information, 1–1292—1–1295
AFTER-CARE
  Act provisions, 1–1120
  applications to Tribunal and Hospital Managers,
    1–1133
  charges, 1–1127
  clinical commissioning groups, 1–1142—1–1147
  Code of Practice
    generally, 4–192
    introduction, 1–1155, 4–191
    planning, 4–193
    payments, 4–194
    Reference Guide, 1–1158
    termination, 4–195
  community treatment orders, 1–399
  contracting out, 1–1132
  discharge by Tribunal, 1–916
  duty, 1–1136
  exception for provision of nursing care, 1–1152—
    1–1154
  hospital order patients, 1–1135
  human rights, 1–1126
  independent mental capacity advocates, 1–1129
  introduction, 1–1122—1–1124
  leave of absence
    generally, 1–214
  local social services authorities' duties
    Act provisions, 1–1120
    generally, 1–1134—1–1142
  NHS Continuing Healthcare, 1–1128
  partnership arrangements, 1–1131
  planning, 4–193
  preference for particular accommodation, 1–1148—
    1–1151
  termination, 4–195
  transitional provisions, 1–1121
  transitory provisions, 1–1120
  Wales, 1–1125

"AGE-APPROPRIATE SERVICES"
  Code of Practice, 4–110
AGGRESSIVE BEHAVIOUR
  abnormally aggressive conduct, **1–030**
  severe mental impairment, 1–030
ALCOHOL DEPENDENCE
  see **Alcoholism**
ALCOHOLISM
  mental disorder, 1–031
ALIENS
  human rights
    generally, 1–1068
    restriction on political activities, 5–054
  removal of patients
    Act provisions, 1–1061
    generally, 1–1063
    human rights, 1–1068
    travel restriction orders, 1–1067
  travel restriction orders, 1–1067
ALTERNATIVE DISPUTE RESOLUTION
  tribunal procedure, 3–034—3–036
ALTERNATIVE PROCEDURE
  see **Part 8 claims**
ANOREXIA NERVOSA
  see **Eating disorders**
ANTECEDENTS
  restriction orders, 1–573
APPEALS
  guardianship orders, 1–518
  hospital directions, 1–613
  hospital orders, 1–518
  interim hospital orders, 1–539
  limitation directions, 1–613
  magistrates' courts, 1–607—1–609
  Mental Health Review Tribunal for Wales, from
    generally, 1–975—1–976
    introduction, 1–865
  restriction orders
    Crown Court, from, 1–593—1–599
    generally, 1–570
  Upper Tribunal, to
    generally, 1–975—1–976
    introduction, 1–865
APPLICATIONS
  assessment
    action when decision made not to proceed, 4–063
    action when decision made to proceed, 4–061
    communication of outcome, 4–062
    consultation with nearest relative, 4–057
    consultation with other people, 4–058
    dispute resolution, 4–064
    medical examination, 4–059
    responsibilities of approved bodies, 4–065
    role of AMHPs, 4–056—4–060
  choice between s 2 and s 3, 4–051
  Code of Practice
    alternatives to detention, 4–048
    assessment, 4–052—4–055
    choice between s 2 and s 3, 4–051
    co-operation between local agencies, 4–066
    commissioning, 4–060

APPLICATIONS—*cont.*
Code of Practice—*cont.*
criteria, 4–045
deaf patients, 4–067
dementia patients, 4–068
factors to consider, 4–046—4–047
foreign nationals, 4–069
grounds, 4–044—4–050
health of patient, 4–046
introduction, 4–043
patients with capacity, 4–049
patients without capacity, 4–050
protection of others, 4–047
responsibilities of local authorities, 4–054
role of approved mental health professionals, 4–056—4–060
safety of patient, 4–046
compulsory admissions
Act provisions, 1–147
Code of Practice, 1–151
consultation with nearest relatives, 1–158—1–159
court applications, 1–451—1–453
defective, 1–202—1–210
generally, 1–149—1–160
human rights, 1–150
interview of patients, 1–160
objections, 1–157
co-operation between local agencies, 4–066
county court, 1–451—1–453
deaf patients, 4–067
defective applications
Act provisions, 1–202
Code of Practice, 1–206
defects, 1–207
emergency applications, 1–210
general note, 1–197
impossibility of rectification, 1–204
medical recommendations, insufficient, 1–208
guardianship
Act provisions, 1–112
children, 1–115
cleansing of filthy or verminous premises, 1–119
Code of Practice, 1–118
defective, 1–202—1–210
effect of applications, 1–125—1–137
general note, 1–114
LSSA, 1–114
medical recommendations, 1–120
persons in custody, 1–114
procedure, 1–147—1–160
provision of information, 1–114
rectification, 1–202—1–210
time limits, 1–120
hospital admissions
Act provisions, 1–147
Code of Practice, 1–151
consultation with nearest relatives, 1–158—1–159
court applications, 1–451—1–453
defective, 1–202—1–210

APPLICATIONS—*cont.*
hospital admissions—*cont.*
generally, 1–152—1–160
human rights, 1–150
interview of patients, 1–160
objections, 1–157
procedure, 2–055—2–060
reclassification of patients, 1–869—1–874
Tribunal applications, 1–869—1–874
APPROPRIATE ADULTS
arrest of mentally disordered persons, 1–1333
APPROPRIATE PRACTITIONERS
see **Nominated medical attendants**
APPROPRIATE TREATMENT TEST
application, 4–123
appropriate treatment, 1–066—1–067
dementia patients, 4–124
generally, 4–121
purpose of medical treatment, 4–120
APPROVED CLINICIANS
see also **Responsible clinicians**
administration of medication, 1–740
approval functions, D–001—D–022
consent to treatment and, 1–789—1–793
definition, 1–1376
generally, 1–1376
legal detention, 1–056
mutual recognition
generally, 1–1368—1–1370
Regulations, 2–007—2–012
APPROVED MENTAL HEALTH PROFESSIONALS
applications for compulsory admissions
Act provisions, 1–186
applications outside local authority areas, 1–196
change of circumstances, 1–188
Code of Practice, 1–191
duty of care, 1–192
human rights, 1–190
interview of patients, 1–195
initial applications, 1–041
introduction, 1–188
legal detention, 1–056
relatives requests, 1–197
statutory documentation, 1–189
applications for guardianship
Act provisions, 1–186
applications outside local authority areas, 1–196
change of circumstances, 1–188
Code of Practice, 1–191
duty of care, 1–192
human rights, 1–190
interview of patients, 1–195
introduction, 1–188
legal detention, 1–056
relatives requests, 1–197
statutory documentation, 1–189
approval
cessation, 2–036—2–037
competence determination, 2–041
conditions, 2–034
definitions, 2–031

APPROVED MENTAL HEALTH PROFESSIONALS—*cont.*
approval—*cont.*
  duration, 2–033
  grant, 2–032
  introduction, 2–027
  local social services authorities, by, 1–1094—
    1–1102
  professional requirements, 2–039—2–040
  records, 2–038
  suspension, 2–035
  termination, 2–036—2–037
  transitional provisions, 2–029
  Wales, 2–028
approval functions, D–001—D–022
competence
  generally, 1–1100
  Regulations, 2–041
conflict of interest
  business reasons, 2–021—2–022
  definitions, 2–016
  financial reasons, 2–018—2–020
  introduction, 2–012—2–014
  personal relationship, 2–026
  professional reasons, 2–023—2–025
  Wales, 2–014
courses
  England, 1–1103—1–1105
  Wales, 1–1106—1–1108
definition, 1–1376
human rights and, 1–1097
mutual recognition
  generally, 1–1368—1–1370
  Regulations, 2–010
professional requirements, 2–039—2–040
Regulations
  approval, 2–041
  conflict of interest, 2–026
role, 4–056—4–060
transfer of guardianship, 1–143
APPROVED SOCIAL WORKERS
generally, 1–1096
ARBITRATION
tribunal procedure, 3–034—3–036
ARREST
mentally disordered persons found in public places,
  1–1333
police powers, 1–283, 1–499, 1–546
ASYLUM SEEKERS
after-care, 1–1122
BAD FAITH
applications for detention, 1–190
duty of care, 1–193, 1–1096, 1–1352
ill treatment of patients, 1–1204
immunity from liability, 1–1355, 1–1356, 2–006
BEHAVIOUR
see also **Aggressive behaviour; Conduct;**
  Disturbed behaviour
mental disorder, 1–029
BREACH OF THE PEACE
mentally disordered persons found in public places,
  1–1336

BREACH OF THE PEACE—*cont.*
warrant to search for and remove patients, 1–1317—
  1–1321, 1–1325
CAPACITY
acting nearest relatives, 1–436
contempt of court and, 1–008
court orders and, 1–008
guardians, 1–145
incapacity
  acting nearest relatives, 1–436
  contempt of court, 1–008
  guardians, 1–145
injunctions, 1–008
marriage, 1–010
medical treatment
  consent and second opinion, 1–726—1–743
medical treatment for community patients lacking
  adults, 1–817—1–823
  children, 1–830—1–834
  emergency treatment, 1–838—1–846
  withdrawal of consent, 1–835—1–837
relatives, 1–436
voting, 1–009
CARE
see **Looked-after children**
CARE HOMES
definition, 1–1376
guardianship, 1–119
generally, 1–1376
ill treatment of patients, 1–1206
leave of absence, 1–224
patient welfare, 1–1115, 1–1117
place of residence, 1–132
CARE PROGRAMME APPROACH
after-care
  preference for particular accommodation, 1–1150
appropriate treatment, 1–705
guardianship, 1–114
Independent Mental Health Advocates
  joint assessments, 1–129
CARE QUALITY COMMISSION
action statements, 1–1179—1–1181
annual reports, 1–1185—1–1187
investigation reports, 1–1175—1–1177
protection of relevant patients
  action statements, 1–1179—1–1181
  investigation reports, 1–1175—1–1177
  provision of information, 1–1182—1–1184
provision of information, 1–1182—1–1184
remuneration of practitioners, 1–1165—1–1168
review of decisions to withhold correspondence,
  1–1314—1–1316
CARERS
nearest relatives, 1–409
offences, 1–1096
CASE MANAGEMENT
tribunal procedure, 3–040—3–047
CELEBRITIES
threats to, 1–014
CENSORSHIP
correspondence, 1–1304

CERTIFICATES
  barring reports, 1–380
  consent to treatment
    consent and second opinion, 1–726—1–743
    medical treatment for community patients, 1–847—
      1–853
CHANNEL ISLANDS
  guardianship, 1–1034
  removal of offenders found insane from, 1–1042—
    1–1046
  removal of patients absent without leave to, 1–1073,
    1–1081—1–1083
  removal of patients detained or subject to guar-
    dianship from, 1–1047—1–1051
  removal of patients detained or subject to guar-
    dianship to, 1–1032—1–1034
  transfer of community patients from, 1–1052—
    1–1055
  transfer of community patients to, 1–1035—1–1037
  transfer of conditionally discharged patients from,
    1–1056—1–1060
  transfer of conditionally discharged patients to,
    1–1038—1–1041
CHILD ARRANGEMENT ORDERS
  generally, 1–418
CHILD COMMUNITY PATIENTS
  see also **Community patients**
  Code of Practice, 1–827
  definition, 1–1376
  medical treatment
    certificates, 1–847—1–853
    emergency treatment, 1–838—1–846
    generally, 1–824—1–829
    patients lacking competence, 1–830—1–834
    withdrawal of consent, 1–835—1–837
CHILDREN
  accommodation, 1–1279—1–1282
  age-appropriate services, 4–110
  applications to the Tribunal, 4–113
  Code of Practice
    after care, 4–114
    age-appropriate services, 4–110
    applications to the Tribunal, 4–113
    assessing competence, 4–091
    capacity, 4–091, 4–097—4–100
    community treatment orders, 4–115
    confidentiality, 4–087
    consent, 4–090, 4–107
    decisions on admission and treatment, 4–089—
      4–102
    deprivation of liberty, 4–094
    duties of local authorities as to hospital patients,
      4–118
    education, 4–116
    electro-convulsive therapy, 4–108
    emergency medical treatment, 4–103
    general considerations, 4–084
    Gillick competence, 4–101—4–102
    informal admissions, 4–095—4–102
    introduction, 4–083
    looked-after child, 4–086

CHILDREN—*cont.*
  Code of Practice—*cont.*
    parental responsibility, 4–085
    place of safety, 4–111
    provision of information to, 4–105
    regulated treatments, 4–106—4–109
    responsible clinician, 4–112
    role of those with parental responsibility, 4–093
    safeguarding when admission is not appropriate,
      4–088
    sharing information, 4–087
    transition from CAMHS, 4–117
    whether to make an application, 4–104
  community treatment orders, 4–115
  confidentiality, 4–087
  consent to treatment
    aged 16 or 17, 1–1275
    under the age of 16, 1–1276
  Convention on the Rights of the Child, 1–018
  decisions on admission and treatment, 4–089—
    4–102
  definition, 1–700
  detention, 1–1278
  duties of local authorities as to hospital patients,
    4–118
  education, 4–116
  electro-convulsive therapy, 4–108
  emergency medical treatment
    Code of Practice, 4–103
    generally, 1–838—1–846
  Gillick competence, 4–101—4–102
  independent mental health advocates, 1–749
  informal admissions
    accommodation, 1–1279—1–1282
    Code of Practice, 4–095—4–102
    detention, 1–1278
    secure accommodation, 1–1277
  looked-after children
    Code of Practice, 4–086
    generally, 1–413—1–415
  medical treatment for community patients
    certificates, 1–847—1–853
    Code of Practice, 1–827, 1–833
    emergency treatment, 1–838—1–846
    generally, 1–824—1–829
    patients lacking competence, 1–830—1–834
    withdrawal of consent, 1–835—1–837
  nearest relative, as, 1–410
  nearest relatives, 1–416—1–422
  parental responsibility, 4–085
  provision of information to, 4–105
  regulated treatments, 4–106—4–109
  responsible clinician, 4–112
  secure accommodation, 1–1277
  visits to high security psychiatric services, B–001—
    B–011
  welfare visits, 1–1115—1–1119
CIVIL PARTNERSHIPS
  generally, 1–011
  nearest relatives, 1–411

Civil prisoners
  definition, 1–700
  transfer directions, 1–690—1–692
Civil procedure
  appointment of acting nearest relatives, 1–431
  Civil Procedure Rules
    generally, 3–001
    practice direction, 3–001—3–007
  compulsory admissions
    Act provisions, 1–147
    Code of Practice, 1–151
    consultation with nearest relatives, 1–158—1–159
    court applications, 1–451—1–453
    defective, 1–202—1–210
    generally, 1–149—1–160
    human rights, 1–150
    interview of patients, 1–160
    objections, 1–157
  guardianship
    Act provisions, 1–147
    Code of Practice, 1–151
    consultation with nearest relatives, 1–158—1–159
    court applications, 1–451—1–453
    defective, 1–202—1–210
    generally, 1–149—1–160
    human rights, 1–150
    interview of patients, 1–160
    objections, 1–157
  Part 8 claims
    generally, 3–001
    practice direction, 3–001—3–007
Civil Procedure Rules
  see Part 8 claims
Civil proceedings
  immunity from liability, 1–1355
Clerical errors
  tribunal procedure, 3–160—3–161
Clothing
  deprivation of daytime clothing, 4–178
Codes of practice
  after-care
    generally, 4–192
    introduction, 1–1155, 4–191
    planning, 4–193
    payments, 4–194
    Reference Guide, 1–1158
    termination, 4–195
  applications for detention
    alternatives to detention, 4–048
    assessment, 4–052—4–055
    choice between s 2 and s 3, 4–051
    co-operation between local agencies, 4–066
    commissioning, 4–060
    criteria, 4–045
    deaf patients, 4–067
    dementia patients, 4–068
    factors to consider, 4–046—4–047
    foreign nationals, 4–069
    grounds, 4–044—4–050

Codes of practice—cont.
  applications for detention—cont.
    health of patient, 4–046
    introduction, 4–043
    patients with capacity, 4–049
    patients without capacity, 4–050
    protection of others, 4–047
    responsibilities of local authorities, 4–054
    role of approved mental health professionals, 4–056—4–060
    safety of patient, 4–046
  appropriate medical treatment test
    application, 4–123
    dementia patients, 4–124
    generally, 4–121
    purpose of medical treatment, 4–120
  approved mental health professionals
    role, 4–056—4–060
  assessment
    action when decision made not to proceed, 4–063
    action when decision made to proceed, 4–061
    communication of outcome, 4–062
    consultation with nearest relative, 4–057
    consultation with other people, 4–058
    dispute resolution, 4–064
    medical examination, 4–059
    responsibilities of approved bodies, 4–065
    role of AMHPs, 4–056—4–060
  children
    after care, 4–114
    age-appropriate services, 4–110
    applications to the Tribunal, 4–113
    assessing competence, 4–091
    capacity, 4–091, 4–097—4–100
    community treatment orders, 4–115
    confidentiality, 4–087
    consent, 4–090, 4–107
    decisions on admission and treatment, 4–089—4–102
    deprivation of liberty, 4–094
    duties of local authorities as to hospital patients, 4–118
    education, 4–116
    electro-convulsive therapy, 4–108
    emergency medical treatment, 4–103
    general considerations, 4–084
    Gillick competence, 4–101—4–102
    informal admissions, 4–095—4–102
    introduction, 4–083
    looked-after child, 4–086
    parental responsibility, 4–085
    place of safety, 4–111
    provision of information to, 4–105
    regulated treatments, 4–106—4–109
    responsible clinician, 4–112
    role of those with parental responsibility, 4–093
    safeguarding when admission is not appropriate, 4–088
    sharing information, 4–087
    transition from CAMHS, 4–117
    whether to make an application, 4–104

CODES OF PRACTICE—*cont.*
community treatment orders
  deprivation of liberty, 4–190
  factors determining choice, 4–189
confidentiality
  children, 4–087
  disclosure of patient information, 4–022
  information for victims of crimes, 4–026
  introduction, 4–020
  recording disclosure without consent, 4–025
  sharing information, 4–021, 4–023, 4–024
deaf patients, 4–067
dementia patients, 4–068
discharge by hospital managers
  decisions, 4–204
  exercise of power, 4–198
  introduction, 4–196
  power, 4–197
  review of detention or CTO, 4–199—4–203, 4–205
  uncontested renewals, 4–203
First-tier Tribunal (mental health)
  accommodation, 4–036
  communication of decision, 4–038
  complaints, 4–039
  detention under the Act, 4–041—4–042
  DoLS authorisations, 4–041—4–042
  further information, 4–040
  hearings, 4–035
  interpretation services, 4–037
  introduction, 4–027
  medical examination, 4–032
  provision of information about rights, 4–029
  purpose, 4–028
  referral by hospital managers, 4–030
  reports, 4–031
  representation, 4–034
  right to apply, 4–029
  withdrawal of application, 4–033
guardianship
  assessment, 4–181
  care planning, 4–183
  components, 4–183—4–184
  deprivation of liberty, 4–190
  factors determining choice, 4–189
  hospital care, 4–185
  introduction, 4–180
  leave of absence or, 4–189
  patients resisting authority of guardian, 4–186
  residence in particular place, 4–184
  responsibilities of local authorities, 4–182
guardianship orders and, 4–187
guiding principles
  effectiveness principle, 4–005
  efficiency and equity principle, 4–006
  empowerment and involvement, 4–003
  introduction, 4–001
  least restriction principle, 4–002
  purpose principle, 4–005
  respect principle, 4–004
  use of, 4–007

CODES OF PRACTICE—*cont.*
informal admissions, 1–1279—1–1282
leave of absence
  deprivation of liberty, 4–190
  factors determining choice, 4–189
  guardianship or, 4–189
  introduction, 4–188
medical treatment
  appropriate treatment, 4–127
  capacity to consent, 4–134—4–138
  competence to consent, 4–135—4–136
  courts, 4–141
  CTO patients not recalled, of, 4–130, 4–131
  CTO patients recalled, of, 4–129
  decisions of other courts, 4–141
  definition, 4–126
  emergencies, in, 4–131
  incapacitated patients, 4–140
  interface with MCA 2005, 4–140
  introduction, 1–794, 4–125
  other patients, of, 4–133
  promoting good physical health, 4–142
  special rules and procedures, 4–128—4–129, 4–143—4–159
  treatment plans, 4–139
  without consent, 4–138
mental disorder
  generally, 1–025
mentally disordered persons found in public places, 1–1336
place of safety
  arrangements following assessment, 4–082
  assessment at, 4–076
  consent to treatment, 4–081
  generally, 4–074, 4–075
  local policies, 4–074
  minors, 4–111
  record keeping, 4–078
  rights of persons detained, 4–080
  transfer between, 4–077
police powers and duties
  introduction, 4–070
  mentally disordered found in public places, 4–073
  monitoring use, 4–079
  record keeping, 4–078
  removal to place of safety, 4–074—4–077
  rights of persons detained, 4–080
  use policies, 4–074
  warrant to search for and remove patients, 4–071, 4–072
principles
  effectiveness principle, 4–005
  efficiency and equity principle, 4–006
  empowerment and involvement, 4–003
  introduction, 4–001
  least restriction principle, 4–002
  purpose principle, 4–005
  respect principle, 4–004
  use of, 4–007

CODES OF PRACTICE—*cont.*
privacy
blanket locked door policy, 4–011
blanket restrictions, 4–010
electronic mail, 4–012
generally, 4–008
Internet access, 4–012
personal searches, 4–016—4–017
private property, 4–013
respect for, 4–009
searches, 4–016—4–017
separate facilities for men and women, 4–014
telephone calls, 4–012
provision of information
generally, 1–1286
provision of information for victims
additional support, 4–213
duties of hospitals, 4–211, 4–212
introduction, 4–206
mental health casework section requirements, 4–210
NPS victim contact scheme, 4–208, 4–209
victim contact scheme, 4–207
victims' code, 4–207
safety of patients
enhanced security accommodation, 4–018
other accommodation, 4–019
search warrants, 1–1324
seclusion
authorisation, 4–167
commencing, 4–168
conditions, 4–141
further guidance, 4–176
generally, 4–165
introduction, 4–132
observation during, 4–169
procedure, 4–166
reviews, 4–170—4–174
terminating, 4–175
special rules and procedures
clinician in charge of treatment, 4–145
CTO patients not recalled to hospital, 4–149
CTO patients recalled to hospital, 4–150
definitions, 4–144
deprivation of access to normal clothing, 4–178
electro-convulsive therapy, 4–148
introduction, 4–143
long-term segregation, 4–177
mechanical restraint, 4–162, 4–163
Part 4A certificates, 4–149—4–151
patients subject to Ministry of Justice order, 4–163
physical restraint, 4–161
rapid tranquilisation, 4–164
seclusion, 4–165—4–176
SOAD certificates, 4–152—4–160
treatments requiring consent, 4–146, 4–147
treatments requiring second opinion, 4–147
tribunals
accommodation, 4–036
communication of decision, 4–038

CODES OF PRACTICE—*cont.*
tribunals—*cont.*
complaints, 4–039
detention under the Act, 4–041—4–042
DoLS authorisations, 4–041—4–042
further information, 4–040
hearings, 4–035
interpretation services, 4–037
introduction, 4–027
medical examination, 4–032
provision of information about rights, 4–029
purpose, 4–028
referral by hospital managers, 4–030
reports, 4–031
representation, 4–034
right to apply, 4–029
withdrawal of application, 4–033
victims
additional support, 4–213
duties of hospitals, 4–211, 4–212
introduction, 4–206
mental health casework section requirements, 4–210
NPS victim contact scheme. 4–208, 4–209
victim contact scheme, 4–207
victims' code, 4–207
young people
decisions on admission and treatment, 4–089—4–102
general considerations, 4–084
informal admissions, 4–095—4–102
introduction, 4–083
looked-after child, 4–086
parental responsibility, 4–085
COHABITEES
see **Unmarried couples**
COMMON LAW
consent, 1–705
duty of care, 1–1204
generally, 1–072
insanity defence, 1–530
refusing treatment, 1–081
secure hospitals, 1–1277
COMMUNICATIONS
see **Letters**
COMMUNITY CARE
assessment, 1–1339
services, 1–114
COMMUNITY PATIENTS
adult community patients, 1–799—1–823, 1–847—1–853
assignment of responsibility, 2–095—2–098
child community patients, 1–847—1–853
community treatment orders and
Act provisions, 1–228
applications, 1–233
background, 1–230
Code of Practice, 1–234
conditions, 1–241—1–247
Domestic Violence, Crime and Victims Act, 1–231

COMMUNITY PATIENTS—*cont.*
community treatment orders and—*cont.*
duration, 1–248—1–252
effect, 1–253—1–255
human rights, 1–232
introduction, 1–230
powers over recalled patient, 1–265—1–272
recall power, 1–256—1–264
revocation, 1–273—1–275
definition, 1–1376
medical treatment
adult community patients, 1–799—1–823
certificates, 1–847—1–853
child community patients, 1–847—1–853
community patients, 1–838—1–846
Code of Practice, 1–795, 4–125—4–178
definitions, 1–858—1–860
introduction, 1–794
liability for negligence, 1–854
objection to treatment, 1–855—1–857
Part 4A certificates, 1–847—1–853
patients lacking capacity, 1–817—1–823,
1–838—1–846
"relevant treatment", 1–796—1–798
provision of information, 1–1292—1–1295
Regulations
generally, 2–124—2–125
transfer of patients, 2–081
transfer of responsibility for
Channel Islands, from, 1–1052—1–1055
Channel Islands, to, 1–1035—1–1037
Isle of Man, from, 1–1052—1–1055
Isle of Man, to, 1–1035—1–1037
Northern Ireland, to, 1–1013—1–1015
Scotland, to, 1–987—1–989
transfer of responsibility to another hospital,
1–306—1–309
COMMUNITY RESPONSIBLE MEDICAL OFFICERS
see **Responsible clinicians**
COMMUNITY TREATMENT ORDERS
Act provisions, 1–228
applications, 1–233
background, 1–230
community treatment period
definition, 1–1376
generally, 1–325—1–337
introduction, 1–254
conditions
Code of Practice, 1–245
generally, 1–241—1–247
victim representations, 1–244
consent to treatment, 1–778—1–782
definition, 1–1376
Domestic Violence, Crime and Victims Act 2004
conditions, 1–244
duration, 1–251
generally, 1–231
duration
community treatment period, 1–325—1–337
effect of expiry, 1–338—1–340
generally, 1–248—1–252

COMMUNITY TREATMENT ORDERS—*cont.*
duration—*cont.*
victim representations, 1–244
effect, 1–253—1–255
expiry, 1–338—1–340
generally, 1–235—1–240
human rights, 1–232
introduction, 1–230
leave of absence and, 1–223
procedures for, 2–062—2–065
powers over recalled patient, 1–265—1–272
recall to hospital, 1–256—1–264
Regulations, 2–062—2–065
revocation of order, 1–273—1–275
COMPULSORY ADMISSIONS
absence without leave
Act provisions, 1–276
assisting patients and, 1–1208—1–1212
Code of Practice, 1–282
duration, 1–310—1–340
expiry of detention period, 1–289
extension of authority, 1–341—1–346
generally, 1–283—1–290
human rights, 1–281
introduction, 1–278
offences, 1–1208—1–1212
patients who abscond from Scotland, 1–280
patients who abscond to Scotland, 1–279
time limits, 1–287—1–289
applications
Act provisions, 1–147
Code of Practice, 1–151
consultation with nearest relatives, 1–158—
1–159
county court, to, 1–451—1–453
defective, 1–202—1–210
due completion of applications, 1–104
generally, 1–152—1–160
human rights, 1–150
interview of patients, 1–160
introduction, 1–147
objections, 1–157
appropriate medical treatment test
application, 4–123
dementia patients, 4–124
generally, 4–121
introduction, 4–119
purpose of medical treatment, 4–120
assessment, for
Act provisions, 1–036
applications, 1–043, 1–045
classification of mental disorder, 1–047
Code of Practice, 1–044
definition, 1–047
discharge, 1–038
discretion to admit, 1–045
generally, 1–041—1–050
human rights, 1–040
introduction, 1–038
leave of absence, 1–045
medical recommendations, 1–049

Compulsory admissions—*cont.*
  assessment, for—*cont.*
    medical treatment, 1–047
    protection of others, 1–048
    risk assessment, 1–048
    safety of patients, 1–048
    time limits, 1–050
  asymptomatic patients, 1–059
  authority to act, 1–110
  compliant patients, 1–034
  conflict of interest, , 1–182—1–185
  criminal proceedings, and
    courts' powers, 1–511—1–534
    effect, 1–555—1–563
    extension, 1–367—1–372
    information from social services, 1–551—1–554
    interim orders, 1–535—1–546
  defective applications
    Act provisions, 1–202
    Code of Practice, 1–206
    defects, 1–207
    emergency applications, 1–210
    impossibility of rectification, 1–204
    introduction, 1–204
    medical recommendations, 1–208
  deteriorating patient, 1–057
  discharge
    Act provisions, 1–373
    admission for assessment, 1–038
    admission for treatment, 1–053—1–056
    Code of Practice, 1–377
    dangerousness, 1–380
    delegation of powers, 1–386
    discretion, 1–380
    examination of patients, 1–387—1–391
    generally, 1–378—1–386
    hospital managers, 1–381
    human rights, 1–376
    in-patients, 1–086
    introduction, 1–375
    nearest relatives, 1–381
    provision of information, 1–1296—1–1299
    readmission, 1–053—1–056
    Tribunal, by, 1–904—1–931
    visiting of patients, 1–387—1–391
  discharge by tribunals
    Act provisions, 1–904
    after-care, 1–917
    conditionally discharged patients, 1–951—1–958
    dangerousness, 1–916
    deferral, 1–927
    guardianship, 1–929—1–931
    human rights, 1–914
    introduction, 1–904
    limitation directions, 1–943—1–950
    nearest relatives applications, 1–921
    public protection, 1–919
    restricted patients, 1–932—1–942
    restriction directions, 1–943—1–950
    safety of patients, 1–919

Compulsory admissions—*cont.*
  duration
    absence without leave, 1–341—1–346
    Act provisions, 1–310
    applications, 1–314
    appropriate practitioner, 1–317
    Code of Practice, 1–315
    examination of patients, 1–317
    generally, 1–316—1–324
    human rights, 1–313
    introduction, 1–312
    renewal, 1–318—1–324
    reports, 1–317
    sentenced patients, 1–367—1–372
    time limits, 1–316
  duty of AMHP to apply
    Act provisions, 1–186
    applications outside local authority areas, 1–196
    change of circumstances, 1–188
    Code of Practice, 1–191
    consultation, 1–184
    duty of care, 1–192
    human rights, 1–190
    interview of patients, 1–195
    introduction, 1–188
    legal detention, 1–056
    relatives requests, 1–197
    statutory documentation, 1–189
  effect
    Act provisions, 1–095
    authorised persons, 1–104
    authority to act provisions, 1–110
    Code of practice, 1–103
    conveyance of patients, 1–104
    detention, 1–109
    due completion of applications, 1–104
    human rights, 1–102
    introduction, 1–097—1–101
    prior applications, 1–111
    time limits, 1–107—1–108
  emergencies
    Act provisions, 1–070
    applications, 1–075
    Code of Practice, 1–074
    delay, 1–076
    introduction, 1–072
    medical recommendations, 1–077
    time limits, 1–078
    urgent necessity, 1–076
  extension of authority
    absence without leave, 1–341—1–346
    sentenced patients, 1–367—1–372
  extension of authority (absence of leave)
    generally, 1–341—1–346
    human rights, 1–358
    return after 28 days, 1–354—1–366
    return within 28 days, 1–348—1–353
  generally, 1–033
  guardianship
    generally, 1–127
    guardians powers, 1–130

COMPULSORY ADMISSIONS—*cont.*
  habeas corpus, 1–867—1–868
  human rights, 1–040, 1–059, 1–465
  in-patients
    Act provisions, 1–079
    applications, 1–086
    Code of Practice, 1–083, 1–087, 1–092
    definition, 1–087
    detention, 1–089
    discharge, 1–086
    effect of provisions, 1–085
    human rights, 1–084
    informal patients, 1–085—1–087
    introduction, 1–081
    medical practitioners in charge, 1–088
    medical treatment, 1–053
    nominated deputies, 1–090—1–091
    nurses powers, 1–092—1–094
    powers of detention, 1–081
    reports, 1–088
    risk assessment, 1–086
    time limits, 1–089
    transfer of patients, 1–082
  leave of absence
    Act provisions, 1–212
    after-care, 1–214
    another hospital, to, 1–216
    applications to tribunals, 1–219
    assessment, for, 1–044
    Code of Practice, 1–220, 4–188—4–190
    community treatment orders, 1–223
    conditions, 1–221
    custody, 1–224
    "from the hospital", 1–221
    hospitals, between, 1–216
    human rights, 1–218
    introduction, 1–214
    recall to hospital, 1–226
    "responsible clinician may grant", 1–221
    restricted patients, 1–221
    revocation, 1–225
    Scotland, to, 1–217
    secure hospitals, 1–214
    specified occasions, 1–222
    trial hospital, to, 1–216
  medical recommendations
    acquaintance with patients, 1–168
    Act provisions, 1–161
    approval of medical practitioners, 1–169
    defective recommendations, 1–167
    duty of care, 1–166
    examination of patients, 1–167
    generally, 1–163—1–170
    guidance for medical practitioners, 1–166
    human rights, 1–165
    introduction, 1–163
    joint recommendations, 1–167
    rectification, 1–202—1–210
    time limits, 1–167
    Wales, 1–167
    withdrawal of recommendations, 1–166

COMPULSORY ADMISSIONS—*cont.*
  medical treatment, for
    Act provisions, 1–051
    applications, 1–060, 1–062
    appropriate treatment, 1–066—1–067
    classification of mental disorder, 1–064
    Code of Practice, 1–061
    deterioration of patient's condition, 1–057
    discharge, 1–054—1–056
    generally, 1–051—1–069
    health of patients, 1–066—1–067
    human rights, 1–059
    in-patient treatment, 1–053
    introduction, 1–053
    medical recommendations, 1–066—1–067
    mental disorder classification, 1–064
    necessary treatment, 1–065
    out-patient treatment, 1–053
    protection of others, 1–066—1–067
    readmission, 1–055—1–056
    risk assessment, 1–066—1–067
    safety of patients, 1–066—1–067
    time limits, 1–062
    treatability, 1–065
  nearest relatives
    definition, 1–400—1–412
    human rights, 1–404
  power to control activities, 1–473
  procedural applications
    Act provisions, 1–147
    Code of Practice, 1–151
    consultation with nearest relatives, 1–158—
      1–159
    county court, to, 1–451—1–453
    defective, 1–202—1–210
    due completion of applications, 1–104
    formalities, 1–147
    generally, 1–152—1–160
    human rights, 1–150
    interview of patients, 1–160
    introduction, 1–147
    objections, 1–157
  readmission, 1–055—1–056
  reassessment, 1–038
  reclassification of patients, 1–211
  references by hospital managers
    generally, 1–879—1–885
    power to reduce periods, 1–886—1–889
  references by Secretary of State, 1–875—1–878
  Regulations, 1–454—1–457
  relatives
    definition, 1–400—1–412
    human rights, 1–404
  renewal
    conditions, 1–318—1–321
    consultation, 1–322
    generally, 1–324
    guardianship, 1–324
    supporting opinion, 1–323
  sentenced patients, 1–367—1–372
  social reports, 1–199—1–201

COMPULSORY ADMISSIONS—*cont.*
transfer of patients
another hospital, to, 1–306—1–309
generally, 1–291—1–305
Tribunal applications
generally, 1–869—1–874
wards of court, 1–458—1–461
COMPULSORY MEDICAL TREATMENT
generally, 1–783—1–788
human rights, 1–786
CONDITIONAL DISCHARGE
deferral, 1–941
generally, 1–937
recall to hospital, 1–938—1–940
restricted patients
generally, 1–951—1–958
human rights, 1–954
restriction orders, 1–587
CONDITIONAL LEAVE OF ABSENCE
see **Leave of absence**
CONDUCT
see also **Aggressive Behaviour**
seriously irresponsible conduct, 1–030
CONFIDENTIALITY
Code of Practice
children, 4–087
disclosure of patient information, 4–022
information for victims of crimes, 4–026
introduction, 4–020
recording disclosure without consent, 4–025
sharing information, 4–021, 4–023, 4–024
CONFLICT OF INTEREST
business reasons, 2–021—2–022
definitions, 2–016
financial reasons, 2–018—2–020
generally, 1–182—1–185
introduction, 2–012—2–014
personal relationship, 2–026
professional reasons, 2–023—2–025
Regulations
application, 2–015
citation, 2–015
commencement, 2–015
definitions, 2–016
general note, 2–012—2–014
general provisions, 2–017—2–026
Wales, 2–014
CONSENT
see also **Consent to treatment**
guardianship orders, 1–533
lack of valid consent to deprivation of liberty, 6–005
CONSENT TO TREATMENT
"Androcur", 1–720
ancillary treatment, 1–787
birth
treatment without consent, 1–787
children
aged 16 or 17, 1–1275
under the age of 16, 1–1276
Code of Practice, 1–709, 4–134—4–138
common law, 1–705

CONSENT TO TREATMENT—*cont.*
covert administration of medication, 1–738
Cyproterone acetate, 1–720
delegated legislation, 2–121—2–123
disguised administration of medication, 1–738
electroconvulsive therapy, 1–744—1–754
Goserelin, 1–720
human rights, 1–707, 1–708
informal admissions
children aged 16 or 17, 1–1275
children under the age of 16, 1–1276
generally, 1–1281
secure accommodation, 1–1277
introduction, 1–705
irreversible treatment, 1–777
medical necessity, 1–713
Mental Capacity Act 2005 and, 1–706
patients liable to detention, 1–710—1–715
placebo medication, 1–739
plans of treatment, 1–755—1–758
provision of information to patients, 1–722
recall of community patient, 1–778—1–782
Regulations, 2–121—2–123
remands to hospital for reports, 1–483
review of treatment, 1–764—1–770
second opinions and
Act provisions, 1–716
certification, 1–723
consent, 1–722—1–723
generally, 1–720
hormone implantation for reduction of sex drive,
1–720
introduction, 1–718
surgical operations, 1–720
second opinion or
Act provisions, 1–726
covert administration of medication, 1–738
generally, 1–726—1–743
human rights, 1–729—1–733
introduction, 1–726
medication, 1–738—1–739
placebo medication, 1–739
time limits, 1–736
use of forms, 1–737
sex drive, 1–720
surgical procedures, 1–720
treatment plans, 1–755—1–758
treatment with consent and second opinion,
1–716—1–725
treatment with consent or second opinion
generally, 1–726—1–743
human rights, 1–729—1–733
treatment without consent
ancillary treatment, 1–787
Caesarean sections, 1–787
core treatment, 1–787
covert administration of medication, 1–738
deep-brain stimulation, 1–787
diagnosis, 1–787
disguised administration of medication, 1–738
generally, 1–783—1–788

CONSENT TO TREATMENT—*cont.*
  treatment without consent—*cont.*
    human rights, 1–786
    poisoning, 1–787
    pregnancy, 1–787
    suicide, 1–787
  understanding treatment, 1–722—1–723
  urgent treatment, 1–771—1–777
  withdrawal, 1–759—1–763
  young people
    aged 16 or 17, 1–1275
    under the age of 16, 1–1276
CONSULTATION
  medical treatment
    consent and second opinion, 1–716—1–725
    consent or second opinion, 1–726—1–743
CONTEMPT OF COURT
  guardianship orders, 1–522
  hospital orders, 1–522
  interim hospital orders, 1–540
  remands to hospital for reports, 1–486
CONVENTION ON THE RIGHTS OF THE CHILD
  generally, 1–018
CONVEYANCE OF PATIENTS
  compulsory admissions, 1–103
  generally, 1–1341—1–1343
  remands to hospital for reports, 1–498
  restriction orders, 1–591
CO-OPERATION
  tribunal procedure, 3–029—3–033
CORRESPONDENCE
  see **Letters**
COSTS ORDERS
  tribunal procedure, 3–061—3–064
CPA
  see **Care Programme Approach**
CPR
  see **Civil Procedure Rules**
CRC
  see **Convention on the Rights of the Child**
CRIMINAL PROCEEDINGS
  Code of Practice, 1–480
  defective court orders, 1–474
  detention at Her Majesty's pleasure, 1–630
  DNA profiling, 1–477
  extension of detention in hospital, 1–367—1–372
  extension of guardianship, 1–367—1–372
  generally, 1–468
  guardianship orders
    courts' powers, 1–511—1–534
    effect, 1–555—1–563
    extension, 1–367—1–372
    information from social services, 1–551—1–554
    interim orders, 1–535—1–546
  hospital directions
    courts' powers, 1–610—1–625
    effect, 1–626—1–629
  hospital orders
    courts' powers, 1–511—1–534
    effect, 1–555—1–563
    information from hospitals, 1–547—1–550

CRIMINAL PROCEEDINGS—*cont.*
  hospital orders—*cont.*
    interim orders, 1–535—1–546
    time limits, 1–698—1–699
  immunity from liability, 1–1355
  insanity
    generally, 1–475
  interim hospital orders
    Act provisions, 1–535
    appeals, 1–539
    applications, 1–538
    contempt of court, 1–540
    effect, 1–560
    family law orders, 1–540
    generally, 1–542—1–545
    introduction, 1–536
    return of patients to court, 1–541
  limitation directions
    courts' powers, 1–610—1–625
    effect, 1–626—1–629
  medical evidence, 1–693—1–697
  medical reports prior to disposal, 1–471
  mental health treatment requirements, 1–476
  multi-agency public protection arrangements,
    1–479
  remands to hospital for reports
    Act provisions, 1–481
    applications, 1–485
    consent to treatment, 1–483
    contempt of court, 1–486
    conveyance to hospital, 1–498
    evidence of mental disorder, 1–493
    family law orders, 1–486
    further remands, 1–495
    generally, 1–481—1–499
    housing, 1–486, 1–487
    insanity, 1–484
    introduction, 1–483
    orders made in other proceedings, 1–486
    offences punishable with imprisonment, 1–491—
      1–492
    time limits, 1–496
    transport to and from court, 1–489
    variation or rescission of sentence, 1–488
  remands to hospital for treatment
    Act provisions, 1–500
    applications, 1–503
    further remands, 1–509
    generally, 1–506—1–510
    introduction, 1–502
    offences punishable with imprisonment, 1–507
    orders made in other proceedings, 1–504
    transport to and from court, 1–505
  restriction orders
    appeals from magistrates' courts, 1–607—1–609
    courts' powers, 1–564—1–580
    magistrates' courts' powers, 1–593—1–599
    Secretary of State's powers, 1–581—1–592
  Secretary of State's functions
    generally, 1–469
    Wales, for, 1–470

CRIMINAL PROCEEDINGS—*cont.*
  sex offenders register, 1–478
  transfer directions
    civil prisoners, 1–690—1–692
    discharge of patients, 1–654—1–666
    immigration offences, 1–690—1–692
    release from prison, 1–667—1–676
    remand in custody by magistrates' courts,
      1–685—1–689
    return to prison, 1–676
    sentenced patients, 1–631—1–645
    unsentenced patients, 1–646—1–653, 1–677—
      1–684
  transporting patients, 1–472
  unfitness for trial, 1–475
CUSTODIAL SENTENCES
  Armed Forces Act 2006 and, 1–522
  contempt of court, 1–522
  defective court orders, 1–521
  generally, 1–519
  human rights, 1–524
  life imprisonment, 1–525
  magistrates' courts, 1–525
  mandatory sentences, 1–526
  named hospital units, 1–520
  sentencing options, 1–519
CUSTODY
  escape from, 1–1344—1–1348
  generally, 1–1341—1–1343
  guardianship, 1–116
  leave of absence, 1–214
  power to control activities, 1–1354
  retaking of patients, 1–1344—1–1348
  Damages
  unlawful detention, 1–100, 1–1353
DANGEROUSNESS
  discharge from compulsory admissions
    generally, 1–380
    nearest relatives, by, 1–397
  discharge from guardianship
    generally, 1–380
    nearest relatives, by, 1–397
  restriction orders, 1–574
DEAF PERSONS
  see **Hearing impaired persons**
DEATH
  guardians, 1–141—1–146
DEATH PENALTY
  abolition, 5–061
  wartime, in, 5–062
DEFAULT POWERS
  Secretary of State and, 1–1094
DEGRADING TREATMENT
  see **Human rights**
DELAY
  emergency admission to hospital, 1–076
DELEGATION
  consent to treatment, 1–721
  discharge, 1–386
  managers of NHS foundation trusts, 1–1371—
    1–1372

DELEGATION—*cont.*
  Regulations, 2–102—2–107
  tribunal procedure, 3–037—3–039
DEMENTIA
  Code of Practice
    applications, 4–068
    appropriate treatement test, 4–124
DETENTION
  see also **Compulsory admissions**
  "acid test", 6–006
  additional powers, A–001—A–003
  attribution of responsibility to the state, 6–005
  Bournewood case
    generally, 1–1242, 6–002—6–019
  children, 6–009
  compliant mentally incapable patients, 1–039,
    1–054
  continuous supervision and control, 6–007
  definition, 6–003, 6–005
  detention at Her Majesty's pleasure
    generally, 1–630
    transfer directions, 1–646
  detention by police
    escape from, 1–1344—1–1348
    generally, 1–1341—1–1343
    mentally disordered persons found in public
      places, 1–1336
  detention in hospital
    absence without leave, 1–289
    duration, 1–310—1–324
    effect of admission, 1–109
    in-patients, 1–086
    legality, 1–097—1–099
  European Convention on Human Rights
    Art. 5, 6–004
  European Court of Human Rights
    case law, 6–010—6–012
  not free to leave, 6–008
  policy, 6–011
  unlawful detention
    damages, 1–100
  use of statutory procedures, 6–001—6–019
DETENTION AT HER MAJESTY'S PLEASURE
  generally, 1–630
  transfer directions, 1–645
DETENTION IN HOSPITAL
  absence without leave, 1–289
  choice of statutory procedure, 6–001—6–019
  duration
    Act provisions, 1–310
    applications, 1–314
    Code of Practice, 1–315
    extension, 1–440
    generally, 1–316—1–324
    human rights, 1–313
    introduction, 1–312
  effect of admission, 1–109
  in-patients, 1–086—1–094
  legality, 1–098—1–099
DIPLOMATIC IMMUNITY
  generally, 1–015

DIRECTIONS
  generally, 3–048—3–050
DIRECTOR OF PUBLIC PROSECUTIONS
  ill treatment of patients, 1–1202, 1–1204
  prosecutions by local authorities, 1–1217, 1–1349
DISCHARGE
  absolute discharge
    effect, 1–587
    generally, 1–380—1–386
    guardianship, 1–382
    human rights, 1–376, 1–935
    nearest relative, 1–381
    responsible local social services authority, 1–382
    restricted patients, 1–936
    restriction orders, 1–578, 1–587
  acting nearest relatives, 1–443—1–450
  compulsory admission
    Act provisions, 1–373
    admission for assessment, 1–038
    admission for treatment, 1–054—1–056
    Code of Practice, 1–377
    dangerousness, 1–380, 1–397
    delegation of powers, 1–386
    discretion, 1–380—1–381
    examination of patients, 1–387—1–391
    generally, 1–373—1–386
    hospital managers, 1–381
    human rights, 1–376
    in-patients, 1–086
    introduction, 1–375
    nearest relatives, 1–381, 1–392—1–398, 1–438
    provision of information, 1–1296—1–1299
    readmission, 1–055—1–056
    restrictions on nearest relatives, 1–392—1–398
    Tribunal, by, 1–904—1–931
    visiting of patients, 1–387—1–391
  guardianship
    Act provisions, 1–373
    admission for assessment, 1–038
    admission for treatment, 1–054—1–056
    Code of Practice, 1–377, 4–180—4–190
    dangerousness, 1–397
    delegation of powers, 1–386
    discretion, 1–380—1–381
    examination of patients, 1–387—1–391
    generally, 1–373—1–386
    hospital managers, 1–381
    human rights, 1–376
    in-patients, 1–086
    introduction, 1–375
    nearest relatives, 1–381, 1–392—1–398, 1–438
    provision of information, 1–1296—1–1299
    readmission, 1–055—1–056
    restrictions on nearest relatives, 1–392—1–398
    visiting of patients, 1–387—1–391
  hospital managers
    decisions, 4–204
    exercise of power, 4–198
    introduction, 4–196
    power, 4–197

DISCHARGE—*cont.*
  hospital managers—*cont.*
    review of detention or CTO, 4–199—4–203,
      4–205
    uncontested renewals, 4–203
  nearest relatives
    generally, 1–381
    Regulations, 2–117—2–118
    restrictions, 1–392—1–398
    without due regard, 1–438
  Regulations
    generally, 2–099—2–101
    nearest relatives, 2–117—2–118
  responsible clinician, 2–099—2–101
  restricted patients
    conditionally discharged patients, 1–951—1–958
    generally, 1–932—1–942
    limitation directions, 1–943—1–950
    restriction directions, 1–943—1–950
  restriction orders, 1–587
  restrictions on nearest relatives
    Act provisions, 1–392
    applications, 1–395
    Code of Practice, 1–396
    generally, 1–397—1–398
    introduction, 1–394
  transfer directions
    generally, 1–654—1–666
    human rights, 1–662
    "technical lifers", 1–663
  tribunals
    Act provisions, 1–904
    after-care, 1–917
    conditionally discharged patients, 1–951—1–958
    dangerousness, 1–916
    deferral, 1–927
    discretion, 1–915
    guardianship, 1–929—1–931
    human rights, 1–914
    introduction, 1–913
    limitation directions, 1–943—1–950
    nearest relatives applications, 1–921
    public protection, 1–919
    restricted patients, 1–932—1–942
    restriction directions, 1–943—1–950
    safety of patients, 1–919
DISCRIMINATION
  failure to provide treatment, 1–059
  human rights, 5–052—5–053
DISTURBED BEHAVIOUR
  restraint
    administration of medication, for, 4–164
    mechanical restraint, 4–162, 4–163
    physical restraint, 4–161
  seclusion
    authorisation, 4–167
    commencing, 4–168
    conditions, 4–141
    further guidance, 4–176
    generally, 4–165
    introduction, 4–132

DISTURBED BEHAVIOUR—*cont.*
  seclusion—*cont.*
    observation during, 4–169
    procedure, 4–166
    reviews, 4–170—4–174
    terminating, 4–175
DNA PROFILING
  criminal proceedings, 1–477
DOCTORS
  compulsory admissions
    generally, 1–088
    nominated deputies, 1–090—1–091
    reports, 1–088
  remuneration, 1–1165—1–1168
DOMESTIC VIOLENCE, CRIME AND VICTIMS ACT 2004
  community treatment orders, and
    conditions, 1–244
    duration, 1–251
    generally, 1–231
  disclosure of victim's evidence to patient and, 3–092
DPP
  see **Director of Public Prosecutions**
DRUG ADDICTION
  mental disorder, 1–031
DRUG TRAFFICKING
  travel restriction orders, 1–1067
DRUGS (MEDICATION)
  see **Pharmaceuticals**
DURATION
  compulsory admissions
    absence without leave, 1–341—1–366
    Act provisions, 1–310
    applications, 1–314
    applications for extension, 1–869—1–874
    appropriate practitioner, 1–317
    Code of Practice, 1–315
    examination of patients, 1–317
    extension of, 1–341—1–346, 1–367—1–372,
      1–869—1–874
    generally, 1–316—1–324
    human rights, 1–313, 1–358
    introduction, 1–312
    renewal, 1–316—1–324
    reports, 1–317
    sentenced patients, 1–367—1–372
    time limits, 1–316
  guardianship
    absence without leave, 1–341—1–366
    Act provisions, 1–310
    applications, 1–314
    applications for extension, 1–869—1–874
    Code of Practice, 1–315
    examination of patients, 1–317
    extension of, 1–341—1–346, 1–367—1–372,
      1–869—1–874
    generally, 1–316—1–324
    human rights, 1–313, 1–358
    introduction, 1–312
    renewal, 1–318—1–324
    reports, 1–317
    sentenced patients, 1–367—1–372

DURATION—*cont.*
  guardianship—*cont.*
    time limits, 1–316
  renewal
    conditions, 1–318—1–321
    consultation, 1–322
    generally, 1–324
    guardianship, 1–324
    supporting opinion, 1–323
DUTY OF CARE
  approved mental health professionals
    duty to apply for guardianship, 1–192
    generally, 1–041
  bad faith, 1–193, 1–1352
  common law, 1–1204
  medical recommendations, 1–166
EATING DISORDERS
  mental disorder, 1–029
ECT
  see **Electroconvulsive therapy**
EDUCATION
  see Human rights
ELECTIONS
  human rights, 5–059—5–060
ELECTROCONVULSIVE THERAPY
  Code of Practice
    children, 4–108
  compliant patients, 1–034
  generally, 1–744—1–754
ELECTRONIC MAIL
  privacy, 4–012
EMERGENCIES
  children's medical treatment
    generally, 1–838—1–846
  compulsory admissions
    Act provisions, 1–070
    applications, 1–075
    Code of Practice, 1–074
    delay, 1–076
    introduction, 1–072
    medical recommendations, 1–077
    risk assessment, 1–076
    time limits, 1–078
    urgent necessity, 1–076
  guardianship, 1–210
  immunity from liability, 1–1355
ENCEPHALITIS
  mental disorder, 1–029
ESCAPING
  custody, 1–1344—1–1348
EUROPEAN COMMISSION ON HUMAN RIGHTS
  generally, 5–003
EUROPEAN CONVENTION ON HUMAN RIGHTS
  generally, 1–018—1–019, 5–002
  incorporation, 5–004
EUROPEAN COURT OF HUMAN RIGHTS
  generally, 5–003
EVIDENCE
  see **Medical evidence**
EXPENSES
  Tribunal powers, 1–974

FALSE STATEMENTS
  generally, 1–1198—1–1201
FAMILY LAW ACT 1996
  guardianship orders, 1–522
  hospital orders, 1–522
  interim hospital orders, 1–540
  remands to hospital for reports, 1–486
FAMILY RELATIONSHIPS
  see **Nearest relatives**
FEES
  after-care, 1–1127
FIRST-TIER TRIBUNAL (MENTAL HEALTH)
  accidental slips and omissions, 3–160—3–161
  accommodation, 3–016, 4–036
  addition of parties, 3–058—3–060
  allowances, 3–148—3–149
  alternative dispute resolution, 3–034—3–036
  appeals to Upper Tribunal
    generally, 1–975—1–976
    introduction, 1–865
  applications
    compulsory admissions, 1–869—1–874
    generally, 1–963—1–967
    guardianship, 1–869—1–874
    guardianship orders, 1–890—1–894
    hospital orders, 1–890—1–894
    permission to appeal, for, 3–166—3–169
    procedure, 3–105—3–114
    restriction orders, 1–895—1–897
    venue, 1–963—1–967
    withdrawal, 1–966
  arbitration, 3–034—3–036
  authors of reports, 3–108
  bias of members, 3–014
  calculation of time, 3–074—3–075
  case management, 3–040—3–047
  clerical errors, 3–160—3–161
  Code of Practice
    accommodation, 4–036
    communication of decision, 4–038
    complaints, 4–039
    detention under the Act, 4–041—4–042
    DoLS authorisations, 4–041—4–042
    further information, 4–040
    hearings, 4–035
    interpretation services, 4–037
    introduction, 4–027
    medical examination, 4–032
    provision of information about rights, 4–029
    purpose, 4–028
    referral by hospital managers, 4–030
    reports, 4–031
    representation, 4–034
    right to apply, 4–029
    withdrawal of application, 4–033
  communication of decision, 4–038
  complaints, 4–039
  concessions, 3–013
  conduct of proceedings
    before hearings, 3–103—3–124
    decisions, 3–150—3–157

FIRST-TIER TRIBUNAL (MENTAL HEALTH)—*cont.*
  conduct of proceedings—*cont.*
    hearings, 3–125—3–149
  constitution
    Act provisions, 1–861
    habeas corpus, 1–867—1–868
    introduction, 1–863—1–866
    judicial review, 1–867—1–868
  contempt of court, 3–017
  co-operation of parties, 3–029—3–033
  costs orders, 3–061—3–064
  decisions
    clerical errors, 3–160—3–161
    generally, 3–150—3–155
    provisional, 3–156—3–157
    review, 3–174—3–176
    setting aside, 3–162—3–165
  delegation of functions, 3–037—3–039
  delivery of documents, 3–076—3–077
  directions, 3–048—3–050
  discharge
    generally, 1–904—1–931
    restricted patients, 1–932—1–942
  evidence, 3–086—3–093
  examination of patients, 1–959—1–962
  failure to comply with rules or directions, 3–051—3–054
  habeas corpus, 1–867—1–868
  hearings
    accommodation, 3–016
    absence of party, in, 3–144—3–147
    Code of Practice, 4–035
    entitlement to attend, 3–130—3–133
    generally, 3–015, 3–125—3–129
    place, 3–134—3–137
    private, in, 3–138—3–143
    public, in, 3–138—3–143
    restrictions on disposal of proceedings without hearing, 3–125—3–129
    time, 3–134—3–137
  hospital directions, 1–616
  independent mental health advocates
    role, 3–022
  information for patients, 3–020
  interpretation services, 3–021, 4–037
  introduction, 1–863—1–866
  judicial review, 1–867—1–868
  jurisdiction, 1–863—1–866, 3–010
  lay representatives
    Rules, 3–065—3–073
  legal aid, 3–024
  legal representatives
    Rules, 3–065—3–073
  limitation directions, 1–616, 1–620
  medical examinations
    generally, 3–121—3–124
  natural justice, 3–011
  notice of proceedings to interested persons, 3–115—3–120
  overriding objective, 3–029—3–033
  paper reviews, 3–109

First-Tier Tribunal (mental health)—*cont.*
parties' obligations, 3–029—3–033
permission to appeal, 3–166—3–169
practice directions
child, vulnerable adult and sensitive witnesses, 3–202—3–204
statements and reports in mental health cases, 3–181—3–201
procedure, 3–011
production of documents, 3–094—3–097
provision of information about rights, 4–029
references by hospital managers
generally, 1–879—1–885
power to reduce periods, 1–886—1–889
references by Secretary of State
guardianship, 1–875—1–878
compulsory admissions, 1–875—1–878
restriction orders, 1–898—1–903
representation
generally, E–001—E–036
Rules, 3–065—3–073
review of decision
applications in SEN cases, 3–173
power, 3–177—3–179
role, 3–012
Rules
application, 3–027
citation, 3–027
commencement, 3–027
contents, 3–008
definitions, 3–027
general note, 3–009—3–026
introduction, 3–009
legal aid, 3–024
natural justice, 3–011
Wales, 3–026
sending documents, 3–076—3–077
setting aside, 3–162—3–165
skeleton arguments, 3–023
striking out, 3–055—3–057
substitution of parties, 3–058—3–060
submissions, 3–086—3–093
summoning witnesses, 3–094—3–097
time, 3–074—3–075
use of documents, 3–078—3–085
victims
generally, 3–018
use of documents, 3–082
visiting of patients, 1–959—1–962
Wales, 3–026
withdrawal of case
Code of Practice, 4–033
generally, 3–098—3–102
statutory provision, 1–966
witness expenses and allowances, 3–148—3–149
witness summonses, 3–094—3–097
Fitness to plead
generally, 1–475, 1–572, 1–1135
Forced labour
human rights, 5–017

Force feeding
treatment without consent, 1–787
Forcible treatment
see **Compulsory medical treatment**
Foreign travel
generally, 1–016
Forgery
generally, 1–1198—1–1201
Forms
certificates of second opinions, 1–737
certification of consent to treatment, 1–737
Form T2/Form T3, 1–737
loss, 2–133
precedents, 2–136—2–183
retention of forms, 2–135
scanned documents, 2–134
Freedom of assembly and association
human rights, 5–049
Freedom of thought, conscience and religion
human rights, 5–044—5–045
Gillick competence
Code of Practice, 4–101—4–102
informal admission of patients
generally, 1–1270
minors, 1–1276
Guardians
Code of Practice
factors determining choice, 4–189
introduction, 4–180
consent to guardianship orders, 1–533
death, 1–141—1–146
definition, 1–700
duties, 2–108—2–110
factors determining choice, 4–189
generally, 4–180—4–190
incapacity, 1–145
powers
accommodation, 1–132
Act provisions, 1–125
compulsory admissions, 1–130
introduction, 1–127
medical treatment, 1–130
residence, 1–132
relinquishment, 1–141—1–146
Guardianship
see also **Guardianship orders**
absence without leave
Act provisions, 1–276
assisting patients and, 1–1208—1–1212
Code of Practice, 1–282
expiry of detention period, 1–289
extension of authority, 1–341—1–346
generally, 1–283—1–290
human rights, 1–281
introduction, 1–278
patients who abscond from Scotland, 1–280
patients who abscond to Scotland, 1–279
Regulations, 2–086, 2–087
time limits, 1–287—1–289
applications
Act provisions, 1–112

GUARDIANSHIP—*cont.*
applications—*cont.*
children, 1–115
cleansing of filthy or verminous premises, 1–119
Code of Practice, 1–118
defective, 1–202—1–210
effect of applications, 1–125—1–137
general note, 1–114
LSSA, 1–114
medical recommendations, 1–120
persons in custody, 1–114
procedure, 1–147—1–160
protection of others, 1–114
provision of information, 1–114
rectification, 1–202—1–210
time limits, 1–120
welfare of patients, 1–119
applications procedure
Act provisions, 1–147
Code of Practice, 1–151
consultation with nearest relatives, 1–158—1–159
county court, to, 1–451—1–453
defective, 1–202—1–210
generally, 1–152—1–160
human rights, 1–150
interview of patients, 1–160
introduction, 1–147
objections, 1–157
assessment, 4–181
authorising deprivation of a person's liberty, 1–129
care planning, 4–183
Channel Islands, 1–1034
children, 1–115
Code of Practice
assessment, 4–181
care planning, 4–183
components, 4–183—4–184
deprivation of liberty, 4–190
factors determining choice, 4–189
guardianship orders and, 4–187
hospital care, 1–151, 4–185
introduction, 4–180
leave of absence or, 4–189
patients resisting authority of guardian, 4–186
residence in particular place, 4–184
responsibilities of local authorities, 4–182
components
care planning, 4–183
hospital care, 4–185
residence in particular place, 4–184
compulsory admissions, 1–127
conflict of interest, 1–182—1–185
criminal proceedings, and
courts' powers, 1–511—1–534
effect, 1–555—1–563
information from social services, 1–551—1–554
interim orders, 1–535—1–546
death of guardian, 1–145
defective applications
Act provisions, 1–202

GUARDIANSHIP—*cont.*
defective applications—*cont.*
Code of Practice, 1–206
defects, 1–207
emergency applications, 1–210
general note, 1–197
impossibility of rectification, 1–204
medical recommendations, insufficient, 1–208
discharge
Act provisions, 1–373
admission for assessment, 1–038
admission for treatment, 1–054—1–056
Code of Practice, 1–377
dangerousness, 1–380, 1–397
delegation of powers, 1–386
discretion, 1–380—1–381
examination of patients, 1–387—1–391
generally, 1–378—1–386
hospital managers, 1–381
human rights, 1–376
in-patients, 1–086
introduction, 1–375
nearest relatives, 1–381, 1–392—1–398, 1–438
provision of information, 1–1296—1–1299
readmission, 1–055—1–056
restrictions on nearest relatives, 1–392—1–398
visiting of patients, 1–387—1–391
Tribunal, by, 1–904—1–931
duration
absence without leave, 1–341—1–366
Act provisions, 1–310
applications, 1–314
applications for extension, 1–869—1–874
appropriate practitioner, 1–317
Code of Practice, 1–315
examination of patients, 1–317
extension of, 1–341—1–346, 1–367—1–372, 1–869—1–874
generally, 1–316—1–324
human rights, 1–313, 1–358
introduction, 1–312
renewal, 1–318—1–324
reports, 1–317
sentenced patients, 1–367—1–372
time limits, 1–316
duty of AMHP to apply
Act provisions, 1–186
applications outside local authority areas, 1–196
change of circumstances, 1–188
Code of Practice, 1–191
consultation, 1–184
duty of care, 1–192
human rights, 1–190
interview of patients, 1–195
introduction, 1–188
legal detention, 1–056
relatives requests, 1–197
statutory documentation, 1–189
effect of applications
Act provisions, 1–125

GUARDIANSHIP—*cont.*
effect of applications—*cont.*
authorising the deprivation of a person's liberty, 1–129
confidentiality, 1–127
compulsory admissions, 1–130
human rights, 1–128
introduction, 1–127
powers of guardians, 1–130—1–131
extension
absence without leave, 1–341—1–346
sentenced patients, 1–367—1–372
extension of authority (absence of leave)
generally, 1–341—1–346
human rights, 1–358
return after 28 days, 1–354—1–366
return within 28 days, 1–348—1–353
factors determining choice, 4–189
hospital admissions, 1–127
hospital care, 4–185
human rights, 1–128
Isle of Man, 1–1034
incapacity of guardian, 1–145
leave of absence
Act provisions, 1–212
after-care, 1–214
another hospital, to, 1–216
applications to tribunals, 1–219
Code of Practice, 1–220, 4–189
community treatment orders, 1–223
conditions, 1–221
custody, 1–224
"from the hospital", 1–221
hospitals, between, 1–216
human rights, 1–218
introduction, 1–214
recall to hospital, 1–226
"responsible clinician may grant", 1–221
restricted patients, 1–221
revocation, 1–225
Scotland, to, 1–217
secure hospitals, 1–214
specified occasions, 1–222
trial hospital, to, 1–216
medical recommendations
acquaintance with patients, 1–168
Act provisions, 1–161
approval of medical practitioners, 1–169
defective recommendations, 1–167
duty of care, 1–166
examination of patients, 1–167
generally, 1–163—1–170
guidance for medical practitioners, 1–166
human rights, 1–165
introduction, 1–163
joint recommendations, 1–167
rectification, 1–202—1–210
time limits, 1–167
Wales, 1–167
withdrawal of recommendations, 1–166
mutual recognition, 2–007—2–012

GUARDIANSHIP—*cont.*
nearest relatives
definition, 1–400—1–412
human rights, 1–404
Northern Ireland, 1–1010
powers of guardians
accommodation, 1–132
Act provisions, 1–125
compulsory admissions, 1–130
introduction, 1–127
medical treatment, 1–130
residence, 1–132
procedure
court applications, 1–451—1–453, 2–061
generally, 1–147—1–160
human rights, 1–150
reclassification of patients, 1–211
rectification
Act provisions, 1–202
Code of Practice, 1–206
defects, 1–205
emergency applications, 1–210
human rights, 1–204
introduction, 1–204
medical recommendations, insufficient, 1–208
references to tribunal
hospital managers, by, 1–879—1–885
human rights, 1–882
Secretary of State, by, 1–875—1–878
Regulations, 1–138—1–140, 1–454—1–457, 2–072—2–077
relatives
definition, 1–400—1–412
human rights, 1–404
renewal
conditions, 1–318—1–321
consultation, 1–322
generally, 1–324
guardianship, 1–324
supporting opinion, 1–323
relinquishment, 1–141
residence in particular place, 4–184
sentenced patients, 1–367—1–372
social reports, 1–199—1–201
transfer
Act provisions, 1–141
death, 1–141—1–146
generally, 1–141—1–142
incapacity, 1–145
introduction, 1–141
relinquishment, 1–141
transfer of patients
another hospital, to, 1–306—1–309
generally, 1–291—1–305
Tribunal applications
generally, 1–869—1–874
wards of court, 1–458—1–461
GUARDIANSHIP ORDERS
Act provisions, 1–511
admission arrangements, 1–516
appeals, 1–518

GUARDIANSHIP ORDERS—*cont.*
application of statutory provisions
generally, 1–1393—1–1394
applications, 1–515, 1–517
Armed Forces Act 2006 and, 1–522
consent of guardians, 1–533
contempt of court, 1–522
conviction, without, 1–522
courts' power
Act provisions, 1–511
generally, 1–511—1–534
human rights, 1–524
introduction, 1–513
custodial sentences, 1–519
defective orders, 1–474
effect, 1–555—1–563
evidence, 1–528
family law orders, 1–522
generally, 1–516
human rights, 1–524
information from social services, 1–551—1–554
introduction, 1–513
life imprisonment, 1–525
magistrates' courts, 1–525
mandatory custodial sentences, 1–526
named hospital units, 1–520
other orders, 1–534
place of safety, 1–531
sentencing options, 1–519
suitability of orders, 1–529
time limits, 1–698—1–699
transport to and from courts, 1–523
Tribunal applications, 1–890—1–894
Habeas corpus
compulsory admissions, 1–867—1–868
HEALTH (PATIENTS)
assessment, 1–047
treatment, 1–066—1–067
HEALTH POLICY
NHS Continuing Healthcare, 1–1128
HEALTH RECORDS
retention of mental health records, 2–135
HEARING IMPAIRED PERSONS
assessment for detention, 4–067
HEARINGS
legal representation, 1–1288
tribunals
absence of party, in, 3–144—3–147
definitions, 3–126
entitlement to attend, 3–130—3–133
generally, 3–125—3–129
place, 3–134—3–137
private, in, 3–138—3–143
public, in, 3–138—3–143
restrictions on disposal of proceedings without
hearing, 3–125—3–129
time, 3–134—3–137
HER MAJESTY'S PLEASURE
see **Detention**
HIGH SECURITY PSYCHIATRIC HOSPITALS
absolute discharge, 1–587

HIGH SECURITY PSYCHIATRIC HOSPITALS—*cont.*
correspondence
incoming, 1–1305
outgoing, 1–1304
definition, 1–1376
directions
safety and security, C–001—C–051
visits by children, B–001—B–011
generally, 1–1376
leave of absence, 1–214, 1–221
transfer to/from, 1–293, 1–1193—1–1194
visits by children, B–001—B–011
HOLDING POWERS
see **Powers of detention**
HOSPITAL ADMISSIONS
see also **Compulsory admissions; Hospital
orders; Informal admissions**
criminal proceedings and
courts' powers, 1–511—1–534
effect, 1–555—1–563
extension, 1–367—1–372
information from social services, 1–551—1–554
interim orders, 1–535—1–546
emergency admission to hospital, 1–076
informal admissions
generally, 1–1279—1–1282
magistrates' courts' powers, 1–593—1–599
remands to hospital
reports, for, 1–490
treatment, for, 1–506
restriction orders, 1–593—1–599
Tribunal applications
generally, 1–869—1–874
urgent necessity, 1–076
HOSPITAL ADMISSIONS
see also **Admissions for assessment, Medical
treatment (compulsory admissions)**
assessment
Act provisions, 1–036
applications, 1–043, 1–045
classification of mental disorder, 1–047
Code of Practice, 1–061, 4–056—4–065
definition, 1–047
discharge, 1–038
discretion to admit, 1–045
generally, 1–041—1–050
health of patients, 1–048
human rights, 1–040
introduction, 1–038
leave of absence, 1–045
medical recommendations, 1–049
medical treatment, 1–047
protection of others, 1–048
risk assessment, 1–048
safety of patients, 1–048
time limits, 1–050
Tribunal applications, 1–869—1–874
Code of Practice
action when decision made not to proceed, 4–063
action when decision made to proceed, 4–061
communication of outcome, 4–062

HOSPITAL ADMISSIONS—*cont.*
  Code of Practice—*cont.*
    consultation with nearest relative, 4–057
    consultation with other people, 4–058
    dispute resolution, 4–064
    medical examination, 4–059
    responsibilities of approved bodies, 4–065
    role of AMHPs, 4–056—4–060
  compliant mentally incapable patients, 1–039,
    1–054
  medical treatment
    Act provisions, 1–051
    admissions for assessment, 1–047
HOSPITAL AND LIMITATION DIRECTIONS
  appeals, 1–613
  applications to Tribunal, 1–616
  courts' powers, 1–610—1–625
  discharge by Tribunal, 1–943—1–950
  domestic violence, 1–617
  effect, 1–626—1–629
  generally, 1–620
  leave of absence, 1–615
  named hospital units, 1–614
HOSPITAL BEDS
  availability, 1–104
HOSPITAL DIRECTIONS
  see **Hospital and limitation directions**
HOSPITAL MANAGERS
  Code of Practice
    decisions, 4–204
    discharge and, 4–196—4–205
    exercise of functions, 4–198
    functions, 4–198—4–205
    reviewing detention or CTO, 4–199—4–203,
      4–205
    specific powers and duties, 4–198—4–205
  definition, 1–1376
  discharge
    overview, 1–381
    powers, 4–197, 4–198
  functions
    exercise, 4–198
    generally, 2–102—2–105, 4–198—4–205
  generally, 1–1376, 4–196
  provision of information
    community patients, to, 1–1292—1–1295
    discharge, about, 1–1296—1–1299
    generally, 1–1283—1–1291
    nearest relatives, to, 1–1296—1–1299
  review of detention or CTO, 4–199—4–203
  Tribunal references
    Code of Practice, 4–196—4–205
    generally, 1–879—1–885
    power to reduce periods, 1–886—1–889
  uncontested renewals, 4–203
HOSPITAL ORDERS
  Act provisions, 1–511
  admission arrangements, 1–516
  appeals, 1–518
  application of statutory provisions
    generally, 1–1393—1–1394

HOSPITAL ORDERS—*cont.*
  application of statutory provisions—*cont.*
    applications, 1–515, 1–517
  Armed Forces Act 2006 and, 1–522
  connection between offence and mental disorder,
    1–525
  consent of guardians, 1–533
  contempt of court, 1–522
  conviction, without, 1–522
  courts' power
    Act provisions, 1–511
    generally, 1–511—1–534
    human rights, 1–524
    introduction, 1–513
  custodial sentences, 1–519
  defective orders, 1–474
  effect, 1–555—1–563
  evidence, 1–528
  family law orders, 1–522
  generally, 1–514
  human rights, 1–524
  information from hospitals, 1–547—1–550
  interim hospital orders
    Act provisions, 1–535
    appeals, 1–539
    applications, 1–538
    contempt of court, 1–540
    effect, 1–560
    family law orders, 1–540
    generally, 1–542—1–545
    introduction, 1–536
    return of patients to court, 1–541
  introduction, 1–513
  life imprisonment, 1–525
  magistrates' courts, 1–525
  mandatory custodial sentences, 1–526
  named hospital units, 1–520
  other orders, 1–534
  place of safety, 1–531
  restriction orders, 1–573, 1–578
  sentencing options, 1–519
  suitability of orders, 1–529
  time limits, 1–698—1–699
  transport to and from courts, 1–523
  Tribunal applications, 1–890—1–894
HOSPITALS
  definition, 1–1376
  generally, 1–1376
  notification of provision of urgent treatment,
    1–1359—1–1361
HUMAN RIGHTS
  abortion, 5–009
  abuse of rights, 5–055
  acting nearest relatives, 1–427
  after-care, 1–1126
  aliens
    political activities, 5–054
    removal of patients, 1–1068
  approved mental health professionals and, 1–1097
  compulsory admissions
    absence without leave, 1–281

Index

HUMAN RIGHTS—*cont.*
  compulsory admissions—*cont.*
    assessment, 1–040
    duration, 1–313
    extension, 1–358
    generally, 1–102
    in-patients, 1–084
    leave of absence, 1–218
    treatment, 1–059
  correspondence
    Code of Practice, 1–1304
    interference, 5–040
    withholding, 1–1303
  death penalty
    abolition, 5–061
    wartime, in, 5–062
  discharge
    generally, 1–376
    Tribunal, by, 1–914
  discharge of restricted patients by Tribunal, 1–935
  discrimination, 5–052—5–053
  European Commission on Human Rights, 5–003
  European Convention on Human Rights
    generally, 1–018—1–019, 5–002
    incorporation, 5–004
  European Court of Human Rights, 5–003
  forced labour, 5–017
  freedom of assembly and association, 5–049
  freedom of expression, 5–046—5–048
  freedom of thought, conscience and religion,
    5–044—5–045
  guardianship
    absence without leave, 1–281
    authorising deprivation of a person's liberty,
      1–129
    duration, 1–313
    duty to apply for, 1–190
    extension, 1–358
    generally, 1–128
    leave of absence, 1–218
    medical recommendations, 1–165
    procedure, 1–147—1–160
  guardianship orders, 1–524
  hospital decisions, 1–465
  hospital orders, 1–524
  Human Rights Act 1998
    introduction, 5–001—5–002
    proceedings, 5–004
  immunity from prosecution, 1–1353
  informal admissions, 1–1281
  inhuman or degrading treatment or punishment
    degrading, 5–016
    generally, 5–011—5–015
    meaning, 5–015
  international aspects, 1–018—1–019
  limitation of use of restriction on rights, 5–056
  mental disorder, 1–027
  mentally disordered persons found in public places,
    1–1334
  nearest relatives
    acting, 1–415

HUMAN RIGHTS—*cont.*
  nearest relatives—*cont.*
    generally, 1–404
  no punishment without law, 5–031
  postal packets, 1–1303
  privacy and, 4–009
  protection of property, 5–057
  relatives
    acting, 1–427
    generally, 1–404
  removal to hospital, 1–637
  restriction orders, 1–584
  restrictions on political activities of aliens
    generally, 5–054
    removal of patients, 1–1068
  right to education, 5–058
  right to fair trial
    civil rights and obligations, 5–030
    fair hearing, 5–030
    generally, 5–028—5–030
    independent and impartial tribunal, 5–030
  right to free elections, 5–059—5–060
  right to liberty and security
    alcoholics, 5–022
    children, 5–020
    conviction, 5–021
    generally, 5–018—5–027
    lawful, 5–022
    lawfulness of detention, 5–025
    persons of unsound mind, 5–022
    procedure prescribed by law, 5–020
    security of person, 5–020
  right to life
    abortion, 5–009
    generally, 5–005—5–008
    use of force, 5–010
  right to marry
    generally, 1–010, 5–050—5–051
  right to respect for correspondence
    interference, 5–040
    withholding, 1–1303
  right to respect for private and family life
    correspondence, 5–040
    economic well-being, 5–042
    family life, 5–039
    generally, 5–032—5–044
    home, 5–040
    in accordance with the law, 5–041
    necessary in democratic society, 5–042
    private life, 5–035—5–038
    protection of health, 5–043
    public authority, 5–041
    respect, 5–035
  search warrants, 1–1323
  slavery, 5–017
  torture
    degrading, 5–016
    generally, 5–011—5–015
    meaning, 5–015
  transfer directions
    generally, 1–662

HUMAN RIGHTS—*cont.*
  transfer directions—*cont.*
    release from prison, 1–670
    return to prison, 1–670
    treatment
      consent or second opinion, 1–729—1–733
      without consent, 1–786
    tribunals
      "public authority", 3–022
  UN Convention on the Rights of Persons with
    Disabilities, 1–019, 1–708
  Universal Declaration of Human Rights, 1–018—
    1–019
  use of force, 5–010
  warrants for search for and removal of patients,
    1–1323
ICCPR
  see **International Covenant on Civil and Political
    Rights**
ICESR
  see **International Covenant on Economic, Social
    and Cultural Rights**
ILL TREATMENT OF MENTAL PATIENTS
  Act provisions, 1–1202
  care home, 1–1206
  carers, 1–1205, 1–1207
  criminal offence, 1–1205
  custodians, 1–1207
  definition, 1–1206
  hospital and care home staff, 1–1206
  ill-treat, 1–1206
  introduction, 1–1204
  officers, 1–1206
IMMIGRATION OFFENCES
  detention, 1–690—1–692
IMMUNITY FROM PROSECUTION
  absence of reasonable care, 1–1355, 2–006
  Act provisions, 1–1349
  acts, 2–006
  bad faith, 1–1355, 2–006
  civil proceedings, 1–1355
  control of patients, 1–1354
  criminal proceedings, 1–1355
  Director of Public Prosecutions, 1–1357
  disapplication, 1–1358
  discipline of patients, 1–1354
  human rights, 1–1353
  introduction, 1–1349—1–1352
  permission for commencement of proceedings,
    1–1356—1–1357
  reasonable care and, 1–1355, 2–006
  Scotland, 2–003
IMPAIRMENT
  see **Mental impairment**
INCAPACITY
  see **Capacity**
INDEPENDENT HOSPITALS
  definition, 1–1376
  duty to inform nearest relatives, 1–1298
  generally, 1–1376
  transfer of patients, 1–305

INDEPENDENT HOSPITALS—*cont.*
  visiting patients, 1–1117
INDEPENDENT MENTAL CAPACITY ADVOCATES
  after-care, 1–1129
  Regulations, 2–129
INDEPENDENT MENTAL HEALTH ADVOCATES
  after-care, 1–1129
  appointment
    generally, 1–1222—1–1226
    Regulations, 2–184—2–192
  conditions of appointment
    generally, 1–1222—1–1226
    Regulations, 2–190—2–191
  experience, training and qualifications, 2–190—
    2–191
  evidence and submissions, 3–089
  generally, 1–1222—1–1226
  hospital managers' obligations, 1–1242
  patients' legal representatives and, 3–070
  provision of information
    generally, 1–1242—1–1244
    Regulations, 2–184—2–192
  responsible person, 1–1242
  role, 3–084, 4–056
  supplemental provisions, 1–1235—1–1241
INDEPENDENT MENTAL HEALTH ADVOCATES (WALES)
  arrangements
    qualifying compulsory patients, for, 1–1247—
      1–1249
    qualifying informal patients, for, 1–1250—
      1–1251
  duty to give information about IMHAs
    qualifying compulsory patients, to, 1–1262—
      1–1264
    qualifying informal patients, for, 1–1265—
      1–1266
  evidence and submissions, 3–089
  generally, 1–1245—1–1246
  supplementary powers and duties, 1–1253—1–1255
  Welsh qualifying compulsory patients
    arrangements for, 1–1247—1–1249
    duty to give information about IMHAs, 1–1262—
      1–1264
    generally, 1–1256—1–1258
  Welsh qualifying informal patients
    arrangements for, 1–1250—1–1251
    duty to give information about IMHAs, 1–1265—
      1–1266
    generally, 1–1259—1–1261
INFORMAL ADMISSIONS
  see also **Detention**
  Act provisions, 1–1268
  Bournewood detention, 1–1242, 6–002
  children
    accommodation, 1–1279—1–1282
    Code of Practice, 4–095—4–102
    detention, 1–1278
    secure accommodation, 1–1277
  Code of Practice
    children, 4–095—4–102
    generally, 1–1282

INFORMAL ADMISSIONS—*cont.*
consent to treatment
children aged 16 or 17, 1–1275
children under the age of 16, 1–1276
generally, 1–1281
secure accommodation, 1–1277
human rights, 1–1281
informal patients, 1–1281
introduction, 1–1281
overview, 1–086
voluntary patients, 1–1281
INFORMATION
see **Provision of information**
INHUMAN OR DEGRADING TREATMENT OR PUNISHMENT
degrading, 5–016
generally, 5–011—5–015
meaning, 5–015
INJUNCTIONS
authorities performance of duties, in aid of, 1–007
correspondence, 1–1302
mentally incapable persons, against, 1–008
INJURIES
see **Personal injury**
IN-PATIENTS
compulsory admissions
Act provisions, 1–079
applications, 1–086
Code of Practice, 1–083, 1–087, 1–092
definition, 1–087
detention, 1–089
discharge, 1–086
effect of provisions, 1–085
human rights, 1–084
informal patients, 1–085—1–087
introduction, 1–081
medical practitioners in charge, 1–090—1–091
medical treatment, 1–053
nurses powers, 1–092—1–094
powers of detention, 1–081, 1–086
reports, 1–088
risk assessment, 1–086
time limits, 1–089
transfer of patients, 1–082
detained patients, 1–105
emergency departments, 1–106
general hospitals, 1–105
INSANITY
generally, 1–475
remands to hospital for reports, 1–484
Tribunal applications, 1–892
INSPECTION
correspondence, 1–1302, 1–1308
powers, 1–1109—1–1114
premises, 1–1213
records, 1–1235
Wales, 1–1112
INTERIM HOSPITAL ORDERS
Act provisions, 1–535
appeals, 1–539
applications, 1–538
contempt of court, 1–540

INTERIM HOSPITAL ORDERS—*cont.*
effect, 1–560
family law orders, 1–540
generally, 1–542—1–545
introduction, 1–536
return of patients to court, 1–541
INTERIM ORDERS
appointment of acting nearest relatives, 1–426
INTERNATIONAL BILL OF HUMAN RIGHTS
generally, 1–018
INTERNATIONAL COVENANT ON CIVIL AND POLITICAL
RIGHTS
generally, 1–018
INTERNATIONAL COVENANT ON ECONOMIC, SOCIAL AND
CULTURAL RIGHTS
generally, 1–018
INTERNET
privacy, 4–012
INTERVIEWS
compulsory admissions
duty to make, 1–192—1–195
social reports, 1–201
guardianship
duty to make, 1–192—1–195
social reports, 1–201
ISLE OF MAN
guardianship, 1–1034
removal of offenders found insane from, 1–1042—
1–1046
removal of patients absent without leave to,
1–1081—1–1083
removal of patients detained or subject to guardianship from, 1–1047—1–1051
removal of patients detained or subject to guardianship to, 1–1032—1–1034
transfer of community patients from, 1–1052—
1–1055
transfer of community patients to, 1–1035—1–1037
transfer of conditionally discharged patients from,
1–1056—1–1060
transfer of conditionally discharged patients to,
1–1038—1–1041
JUDICIAL REVIEW
compulsory admissions, 1–867—1–868
LAY REPRESENTATIVES
tribunal procedure
Rules, 3–065—3–073
LEARNING DISABILITIES
definition, 1–032
generally, 1–030
LEAVE OF ABSENCE
Act provisions, 1–212
after-care, 1–214
another hospital, to, 1–216
assessment, for, 1–045
Code of Practice
deprivation of liberty, 4–190
factors determining choice, 4–189
guardianship or, 4–189
introduction, 4–188
community treatment orders, 1–223

LEAVE OF ABSENCE—*cont.*
  compulsory admissions
    Act provisions, 1–212
    after-care, 1–214
    another hospital, to, 1–216
    applications to tribunals, 1–219
    assessment, for, 1–045
    Code of Practice, 1–220
    community treatment orders, 1–223
    conditions, 1–221
    custody, 1–224
    from the hospital, 1–221
    hospitals, between, 1–216
    human rights, 1–218
    introduction, 1–214
    recall to hospital, 1–226
    responsible clinician may grant, 1–221
    restricted patients, 1–221
    revocation, 1–225
    Scotland, to, 1–217
    secure hospitals, 1–214
    specified occasions, 1–222
    within hospital site, 1–221
  conditional leave, 1–221
  conditions, 1–221
  courts' powers, 1–615
  custody, 1–224
  guardianship, and
    Act provisions, 1–212
    after-care, 1–214
    another hospital, to, 1–216
    applications to tribunals, 1–219
    assessment, for, 1–045
    Code of Practice, 1–220
    community treatment orders, 1–223
    conditions, 1–221
    custody, 1–224
    from the hospital, 1–221
    hospitals, between, 1–216
    human rights, 1–218
    introduction, 1–214
    recall to hospital, 1–226
    responsible clinician may grant, 1–221
    restricted patients, 1–221
    revocation, 1–225
    Scotland, to, 1–217
    secure hospitals, 1–214
    specified occasions, 1–222
    treatment, for, 1–058
    trial hospital, to, 1–209
    within hospital site, 1–221
  high security hospitals, 1–214
LEGAL AID
  tribunal procedure, 3–024
LEGAL REPRESENTATION
  generally, 3–065, E–001—E–036
  hospital orders, 1–514
  information about, 1–1288
  tribunal procedure
    Code of Practice, E–001—E–036
    Rules, 3–065—3–073

LEGAL REPRESENTATION—*cont.*
  role, 3–068, 3–069
LETTERS
  Act provisions, 1–1300
  censoring of correspondence, 1–1304
  delegation of powers, 1–1311
  exceptions, 1–1306
  high security hospitals
    incoming correspondence, 1–1305
    outgoing correspondence, 1–1304
  human rights
    Code of Practice, 1–1304
    generally, 5–040
    introduction, 1–1303
  incoming, 1–1305
  introduction, 1–1302
  notice, 1–1310
  opening and inspection
    generally, 1–1308
    Regulations, 2–126
  outgoing, 1–1304
  postal operators, 1–1313
  privacy, 4–012
  record-keeping requirements, 1–1309
  Regulations, 2–126—2–129
  review of decision to withhold correspondence
    Act provisions, 1–1314
    Regulations, 2–127—2–128
  right to respect for private and family life, 5–040
LIABILITIES
  detention for treatment, 1–710—1–715
  liability for negligence, 1–854
LIFE IMPRISONMENT
  guardianship orders, 1–525
  hospital directions, 1–612
  hospital orders, 1–525
  limitation directions, 1–612
  transfer directions
    generally, 1–672—1–673
    "technical lifers", 1–663
LIMITATION DIRECTIONS
  see **Hospital and limitation directions**
LOCAL HEALTH BOARDS
  definition, 1–1376
LOCAL SOCIAL SERVICES AUTHORITIES
  after-care
    Act provisions, 1–1120
    applications to Tribunal and Hospital Managers, 1–1133
    charges, 1–1127
    contracting out, 1–1132
    generally, 1–1134—1–1142
    human rights, 1–1126
    independent mental capacity advocates, 1–1129
    introduction, 1–1122—1–1124
    NHS Continuing Healthcare, 1–1128
    partnership arrangements, 1–1131
  applications outside, 1–196
  approved mental health professionals and, 1–1094—1–1102
  definition, 1–1376

LOCAL SOCIAL SERVICES AUTHORITIES—*cont.*
  delegation, 2–106—2–107
  generally, 1–1224
  prosecutions, 1–1217—1–1219
  welfare visits, 1–1115—1–1119
LOOKED-AFTER CHILDREN
  generally, 1–413—1–415
LOSS OF EARNINGS
  Tribunal powers to award, 1–974
MAGISTRATES' COURTS
  guardianship orders, 1–525
  hospital orders, 1–525
  remand in custody, 1–685—1–689
  restriction orders
    Act provisions, 1–593
    committal to Crown Court, 1–598
    committal to hospital, 1–600—1–606
    introduction, 1–595
MAIL INTERCEPTION
  Act provisions, 1–1300
  censoring of correspondence, 1–1304
  Code of Practice, 1–1304
  delegation of powers, 1–1311
  exceptions, 1–1306
  high security hospitals
    incoming correspondence, 1–1305
    outgoing correspondence, 1–1304
  human rights
    Code of Practice, 1–1304
    generally, 5–040
    introduction, 1–1303
  incoming, 1–1305
  introduction, 1–1302
  notice, 1–1310
  opening and inspection
    generally, 1–1308
    Regulations, 2–126
  outgoing, 1–1304
  postal operators, 1–1313
  record-keeping requirements, 1–1309
  Regulations, 2–126—2–129
  review of decision to withhold correspondence
    Act provisions, 1–1314
    Regulations, 2–127—2–129
  right to respect for private and family life, 5–040
MANAGERS (HOSPITALS)
  see **Hospital managers**
MANDATORY CUSTODIAL SENTENCES
  see **Custodial sentences**
MANDATORY LIFE IMPRISONMENT
  hospital directions, 1–612
  limitation directions, 1–612
MAPPA
  see **Multi-agency public protection arrangements**
MARRIAGE
  generally, 1–010
  human rights, 5–050—5–051
MEDICAL EVIDENCE
  guardianship/hospital orders
    appeals, 1–518
    generally, 1–528

MEDICAL EVIDENCE—*cont.*
  restriction orders, 1–574
MEDICAL EXAMINATIONS
  discharge, 1–387—1–391
  joint recommendations, 1–167
  medical recommendations, 1–167
  mentally disordered persons found in public places, 1–1336
  Tribunal powers, 1–959—1–962
  tribunal procedure
    Code of Practice, 4–032
    generally, 3–121—3–124
  Wales, 1–167
MEDICAL PRACTITIONERS
  see **Doctors**
MEDICAL RECOMMENDATIONS
  acquaintance with patients, 1–168
  Act provisions, 1–161
  approval of medical practitioners, 1–056, 1–169
  compulsory admissions, and
    assessment, 1–049
    emergencies, 1–077
    treatment, 1–066—1–067
  defective recommendations, 1–167
  duty of care, 1–166
  examination of patients, 1–167
  fresh medical recommendations
    compulsory admissions, 1–208
    hospital orders, 1–518
  guidance for medical practitioners, 1–166
  human rights, 1–165
  introduction, 1–163
  joint recommendations, 1–167
  rectification
    Act provisions, 1–202
    Code of Practice, 1–206
    defects, 1–207
    emergency applications, 1–210
    impossibility of, 1–204
    insufficient recommendations, 1–209
    introduction, 1–204
  time limits, 1–167
  Wales, 1–167
  withdrawal of recommendations, 1–166
MEDICAL TREATMENT
  see also **Medical treatment (community patients); Medical treatment (compulsory admissions)**
  Code of Practice
    appropriate treatment, 4–127
    capacity to consent, 4–134—4–138
    competence to consent, 4–135—4–136
    courts, 4–141
    CTO patients not recalled, of, 4–130, 4–131
    CTO patients recalled, of, 4–129
    decisions of other courts, 4–141
    definition, 4–126
    emergencies, in, 4–131
    incapacitated patients, 4–140
    interface with MCA 2005, 4–140
    introduction, 1–794, 4–125

MEDICAL TREATMENT—*cont.*
Code of Practice—*cont.*
other patients, of, 4–133
promoting good physical health, 4–142
special rules and procedures, 4–128—4–129,
4–143—4–159
treatment plans, 4–139
without consent, 4–138
Community patients
generally, 1–794
compulsory admissions, 1–051—1–069
definition, 1–1376
generally, 1–1397
guardians powers, 1–130
informal admissions, 1–1268
remands to hospital
Act provisions, 1–500
applications, 1–503
further remands, 1–509
generally, 1–500—1–510
introduction, 1–502
offences punishable with imprisonment, 1–507
orders made in other proceedings, 1–504
transport to and from court, 1–505
MEDICAL TREATMENT (COMMUNITY PATIENTS)
adult community patients
certificates, 1–847—1–853
certified in writing, 1–811
conditions, 1–811
emergency treatment, 1–838—1–846
generally, 1–799—1–806
patients lacking capacity, 1–817—1–823
supplemental, 1–807—1–816
withdrawal of consent, 1–835—1–837
certificates, 1–847—1–853
child community patients
certificates, 1–847—1–853
Code of Practice, 1–827
emergency treatment, 1–838—1–846
generally, 1–824—1–829
patients lacking competence, 1–830—1–834
withdrawal of consent, 1–835—1–837
community patients
adults, 1–799—1–823
children, 1–830—1–834
emergency treatment, 1–838—1–846
withdrawal of consent, 1–835—1–837
Code of Practice, 1–795
definitions, 1–858—1–860
introduction, 1–794
liability for negligence, 1–854
objection to treatment, 1–855—1–857
Part 4A certificates, 1–847—1–853
patients lacking capacity
adults, 1–817—1–823
children, 1–830—1–834
emergency treatment, 1–838—1–846
withdrawal of consent, 1–835—1–837
relevant treatment, 1–796—1–798
withdrawal of consent, 1–835—1–837

MEDICAL TREATMENT (COMPULSORY ADMISSIONS)
Act provisions, 1–051
applications, 1–060, 1–062
appropriate treatment, 1–066—1–067
classification of mental disorder, 1–064
Code of Practice, 1–061
deterioration of patient's condition, 1–057
discharge
generally, 1–053
readmission, 1–055—1–056
discretion to admit, 1–058
health of patients, 1–066—1–067
human rights, 1–059
in-patient treatment, 1–053
introduction, 1–053
medical recommendations, 1–066—1–067
out-patient treatment, 1–053
protection of others, 1–066—1–067
readmission, 1–055—1–056
risk assessment, 1–066—1–067
safety of patients, 1–066—1–067
time limits, 1–062
treatability, 1–065
Tribunal applications, 1–869—1–874
MEMBERS OF PARLIAMENT
mental illness, 1–1362—1–1363
MENTAL CAPACITY ACT 2005
Code of Practice, 1–017
consent to treatment, 1–706
"nearest relative", 1–403
"relative", 1–403
MENTAL DISORDER
abnormally aggressive conduct
generally, 1–030
Act provisions, 1–023
alcohol dependency
generally, 1–031
arrested development of mind, 1–029
Code of Practice, 1–026
compulsory admissions
assessment, 1–047
treatment, 1–064
definition, 1–029
disability of mind, 1–029
disorder of the mind, 1–029
drug dependency
generally, 1–031
generally, 1–028—1–032
human rights, 1–027
incomplete development of mind, 1–032
introduction, 1–025
learning disabilities
definition, 1–032
generally, 1–030
mental illness, 1–029
mental impairment, 1–029
neuroses, 1–029
paraphilias, 1–029
psychopathic disorders,
generally, 1–029
persistent psychopathic disorders, 1–031

MENTAL DISORDER—*cont.*
remands to hospital for reports, 1–477
seriously irresponsible conduct, 1–030
severe mental impairment, 1–029
sexual deviancy, 1–029
transient mental disturbances, 1–029
treatment without consent, 1–787
MENTAL HEALTH ACT 1983
abbreviations, 1–022
allocation of resources to detained patients, 1–006
amendments
consequential, 1–1400
local Acts, 1–1375
application
Act provisions, 1–023
Code of Practice, 1–026
generally, 1–028—1–032
introduction, 1–025
Northern Ireland, 1–1387—1–1389
Scilly Isles, 1–1391—1–1392
Scotland, 1–1384—1–1386
commencement, 1–1391—1–1392
consequential amendments, 1–1400
consequential provisions, 1–1390
diplomatic immunity, 1–015
extent, 1–021
generally, 1–001—1–002
injunctions
authorities performance of duties, in aid of, 1–007
mentally incapable persons, against, 1–008
international aspects, 1–018—1–019
interpretation
generally, 1–1377—1–1383
Part II, 1–462—1–467
Part III, 1–700—1–704
Part IV, 1–789—1–793
Part IVA, 1–858—1–860
Part V, 1–977—1–978
Part VI, 1–1090—1–1092
local Act amendments, 1–1375
marriage, 1–010
Northern Ireland, 1–1387—1–1389
orders, 1–1373
policy of the Act, 1–004
regulations, 1–1373
repeals, 1–1390
rules, 1–1373
savings, 1–1401—1–1408
schedules
consequential amendments, 1–1400
Mental Health Review Tribunal for Wales, 1–1395—1–1398
patients subject to orders, 1–1393—1–1394
savings, 1–1401—1–1408
transitional provisions, 1–1401—1–1408
Scilly Isles, 1–1391—1–1392
Scotland, 1–1384—1–1386
short title, 1–1391—1–1392
transfer of functions, 1–003
transitional provisions
generally, 1–020, 1–1390

MENTAL HEALTH ACT 1983—*cont.*
transitional provisions—*cont.*
supplementary, 1–1401—1–1408
voting rights, 1–009
Wales, 1–003
MENTAL HEALTH ACT COMMISSION
see also **Care Quality Commission**
abolition, 1–1188
MENTAL HEALTH REVIEW TRIBUNAL FOR WALES
appeals to Upper Tribunal
generally, 1–975—1–976
introduction, 1–865
applications
compulsory admissions, 1–869—1–874
generally, 1–963—1–967
guardianship, 1–869—1–874
guardianship orders, 1–890—1–894
hospital orders, 1–890—1–894
permission to appeal, for, 3–166—3–169
procedure, 1 – 968 – 1 – 973
restriction orders, 1–895—1–897
venue, 1–963—1–967
withdrawal, 1–966
constitution
generally, 1 – 861
habeas corpus, 1–867—1–868
introduction, 1–863—1–866
judicial review, 1–867—1–868
discharge
generally, 1–904—1–931
restricted patients, 1–932—1–942
evidence, 3–086—3–093
examination of patients, 1–959—1–962
habeas corpus, 1–867—1–868
hospital directions, 1–616
introduction, 1–863—1–866
judicial review, 1–867—1–868
jurisdiction, 1–863—1–866
limitation directions, 1–620
references by hospital managers
generally, 1–879—1–885
power to reduce periods, 1–886—1–889
references by Secretary of State
compulsory admissions, 1–875—1–878
guardianship, 1–875—1–878
restriction orders, 1–898—1–903
visiting of patients, 1–959—1–962
withdrawal of case
statutory provision, 1–966
MENTAL HEALTH TREATMENT REQUIREMENTS
criminal proceedings and, 1–476
MENTAL ILLNESS
generally, 1–029
Members of Parliament, 1–1362—1–1363
MENTAL IMPAIRMENT
generally, 1–030
MENTALLY DISORDERED OFFENDERS
see also **Criminal proceedings**
detention at Her Majesty's pleasure, 1–630
generally, 1–471—1–472

MENTALLY DISORDERED OFFENDERS—*cont.*
guardianship
  courts' powers, 1–511—1–534
  effect, 1–555—1–563
  extension, 1–367—1–372
  information from social services, 1–551—1–554
  interim orders, 1–535—1–546
hospital detention, 1–367—1–372
hospital directions
  courts' powers, 1–610—1–625
  effect, 1–626—1–629
hospital orders
  courts' powers, 1–511—1–534
  effect, 1–555—1–563
  information from hospitals, 1–547—1–550
  interim, 1–535—1–546
  time limits, 1–698—1–699
interim hospital orders
  Act provisions, 1–535
  appeals, 1–539
  applications, 1–538
  contempt of court, 1–540
  effect, 1–560
  family law orders, 1–540
  generally, 1–542—1–545
  introduction, 1–536
  return of patients to court, 1–541
limitation directions
  effect, 1–626—1–629
medical evidence, 1–682
medical reports prior to disposal, 1–471
payment for treatment, 1–012
restriction orders
  appeals from magistrates' courts, 1–607—1–609
  courts' powers, 1–564—1–580
  magistrates' courts' powers, 1–593—1–599
  Secretary of State's powers, 1–581—1–592
return of patients, 1–367—1–372
right to choose and pay for treatment, 1–012
rights of victims, 1–013
transfer directions
  civil prisoners, 1–690—1–692
  discharge of patients, 1–654—1–666
  immigration offences, 1–690—1–692
  release from prison, 1–667—1–676
  remand in custody by magistrates' courts,
    1–685—1–689
  return to prison, 1–667—1–676
  sentenced patients, 1–631—1–645
  "technical lifers", 1–663
  unsentenced patients, 1–646—1–653, 1–677—
    1–684
transporting patients, 1–472
MENTALLY DISORDERED PERSONS
absence without leave, 1–1339
powers of detention, 1–1338
public places
  appropriate adults, 1–1333
  arrest, 1–1333
  breach of the peace, 1–1334
  Code of Practice, 1–1335

MENTALLY DISORDERED PERSONS—*cont.*
public places—*cont.*
  detention, 1–1337
  generally, 1–1331—1–1333
  human rights, 1–1334
  introduction, 1–1331—1–1333
  nuisance, 1–1333
  patients' rights, 1–1333—1–1331
  place of safety, 1–1337
  police powers and duties, 1–1336
  prevention of breach of the peace, 1–1334
  prevention of nuisance, 1–1333
  "public place", 1–1336
  registered medical practitioners, 1–1339
  removal to place of safety, 1–1337
MINORS
see **Children; Young persons**
MISREPRESENTATION
consent to treatment, 1–721
MISTAKE
consent to treatment, 1–721
MPs
see **Members of Parliament**
MULTI-AGENCY PUBLIC PROTECTION ARRANGEMENTS
communications with mental health service provi-
    ders, 1–479
responsibilities, 1–479
MUTUAL RECOGNITION PRINCIPLE
approved clinicians
  generally, 1–1368—1–1370
  Regulations, 2–010—2–012
approved practitioners
  generally, 1–1368—1–1370
  Regulations, 2–010
definitions, 2–008
guardianship, 2–011
Regulations
  citation, 2–008
  commencement, 2–008
  definitions, 2–008
  general note, 2–007
  general provisions, 2–007—2–012
"NAMED HOSPITAL UNITS"
guardianship orders, 1–520
hospital directions, 1–614
hospital orders, 1–520
limitation directions, 1–614
restriction orders, 1–568
transfer directions, 1–636
NEAREST RELATIVE ORDERS
Act provisions, 1–423
appeals, 1–428
applications, 1–429
Code of Practice, 1–430
discharge, 1–443—1–450
duration, 1–441
extension of detention pending applications, 1–440
functions of nearest relatives, 1–442
generally, 1–431—1–442
grounds
  absence of nearest relatives, 1–435

NEAREST RELATIVE ORDERS—*cont.*
  grounds—*cont.*
    discharge by nearest relatives without due regard,
      1–438
    generally, 1–434
    incapability of nearest relatives, 1–436
    unreasonable objections of nearest relatives,
      1–437
  human rights, 1–427, 1–439
  introduction, 1–425
  nomination of person, 1–432
  procedure, 1–431
  standing, 1–425
  variation, 1–443—1–450
NEAREST RELATIVES
  Act provisions, 1–400
  appointment by court
    appeals, 1–428
    applications, 1–429
    Code of Practice, 1–430
    discharge, 1–443—1–450
    duration, 1–441
    extension of detention pending applications,
      1–440
    functions of nearest relatives, 1–442
    grounds, 1–434—1–437
    human rights, 1–427
    interim orders, 1–426
    introduction, 1–425
    nomination of person, 1–432
    procedure, 1–431
    standing, 1–425
    variation of orders, 1–443—1–450
    without notice applications, 1–426
  care providers, 1–409
  care home patients, 1–412
  children under guardianship and, 1–416—1–422
  Code of Practice, 1–430
  cohabitees of patients, 1–411
  communal living arrangements, 1–412
  consultation, 1–158—1–160
  daughters, 1–406
  definition
    generally, 1–400—1–412
    human rights, 1–404
  deserting partners, 1–410
  discharge by
    generally, 1–381
    Regulations, 2–117—2–118
    restrictions, 1–392—1–398
  discharge by Tribunal, 1–921
  disqualification, 1–410
  duty to inform
    Wales, 2–079
  elder/eldest of class, 1–419
  fathers, 1–406
  five-year rule, 1–412
  guardians, 1–416—1–422
  guardianship
    duty to consider requests, 1–197
    regard to wishes, 1–193

NEAREST RELATIVES—*cont.*
  half-blood, 1–407
  human rights, 1–404
  husbands, 1–406
  introduction, 1–402
  leaflets, 1–1287
  looked-after children, 1–413—1–415
  Mental Capacity Act 2005, 1–403
  mother, 1–406
  parental responsibility, 1–406
  performance of functions, 2–113—2–116
  provision of information
    Act provisions, 1–1283
    Code of Practice, 1–1286, 4–029
    discharge, as to, 1–1296—1–1299
    generally, 1–1283—1–1291
    introduction, 1–1285
    leaflets, 1–1287
  Regulations
    discharge, 2–117—2–118
    performance of functions, 2–113—2–116
  residence with patients
    carers, 1–409
    generally, 1–412
  restrictions on discharge by
    Act provisions, 1–392
    applications, 1–395
    Code of Practice, 1–396
    introduction, 1–394
  separated partners, 1–410
  sons, 1–406
  spouses, 1–406
  Tribunal applications, 1–869—1–874
  wives, 1–406
NEGLECT OF PATIENTS
  see **Ill treatment of mental patients**
NEGLIGENCE
  actions, 1–166
  community patients, 1–854
  covert administration of medication, 1–738
  duty of care, 1–166
  liabilities resulting from, 1–819, 1–832, 1–840,
    1–854
NHS CONTINUING HEALTHCARE
  after-care, 1–1128
NHS FOUNDATION TRUSTS
  delegation of powers of managers, 1–1371—
    1–1372
NOMINATED MEDICAL ATTENDANTS
  background, 1–462
  definition, 1–462
  generally, 1–466
  human rights, 1–465
NON-COMPLIANCE
  community treatment orders, 1–230
  dispute resolution, 1–101
  mental disorder, 1–918
NORTHERN IRELAND
  guardianship, 1–1010
  removal of community patients to, 1–1013—
    1–1015

NORTHERN IRELAND—*cont.*
  removal of patients detained or subject to guardianship from, 1–1022—1–1027
  removal of patients detained or subject to guardianship to, 1–1006—1–1012
  return of patients absence without leave to, 1–1074—1–1077
  transfer of conditionally discharged restricted patient from, 1–1028—1–1031
  transfer of conditionally discharged restricted patient to, 1–1016—1–1021
NOTIFICATION (HOSPITALS)
  urgent treatment, 1–1359—1–1361
NUISANCE
  mentally disordered persons found in public places, 1–1333
NURSES
  reviews of secluded patient, 4–172
OBJECTIONS
  nearest relatives
    procedure, 1–157
    unreasonable, 1–437
  treatment for community patients, 1–855—1–857
OBSTRUCTION
  generally, 1–1213—1–1216
OFFENCES
  assisting in absence without leave, 1–1208—1–1212
  care workers, 1–1197
  false statements, 1–1198—1–1201
  forgery of documents, 1–1198—1–1201
  ill treatment of patients, 1–1202—1–1207
  introduction, 1–1197
  obstruction, 1–1213—1–1216
  patients, against, 1–1197
  prosecutions, 1–1217—1–1219
  remands to hospital
    reports, 1–490
    treatment, 1–493
  sexual offences, 1–1197
OFFENDERS (MENTALLY DISORDERED PERSONS)
  see **Mentally disordered offenders**
OVERRIDING OBJECTIVE
  tribunal procedure, 3–029—3–033
PALS
  see **Patient advocacy and liaison services**
PARENTAL RESPONSIBILITY
  nearest relatives, 1–407
PARENTS
  nearest relatives, 1–406
"PART 4A CERTIFICATES"
  community patients, 1–847—1–853
PART 8 CLAIMS
  generally, 3–001
  practice direction, 3–001—3–007
PATIENT ADVOCACY AND LIAISON SERVICES
  generally, 1–1307
  Regulations, 2–129
PATIENTS
  definition, 1–1376
  generally, 1–1379

PATIENTS—*cont.*
  legal representatives, 3–070
  liability for detention for treatment, 1–710—1–715
  right to choose and pay for treatment, 1–012
  rights of victims of serious, violent or sexual offences, 1–013
PENSION INCOME
  mentally disordered persons, 1–1364—1–1367
PERSONAL INJURY
  mental disorder and, 1–029
PERSONAL SEARCHES
  arresting officers, 1–283, 1–499, 1–546
  privacy, 4–016—4–017
PERSONAL WELFARE
  patients
    guardianship, 1–119
PERSONALITY DISORDERS
  generally, 1–029
PHARMACEUTICALS
  failure to take, 1–057
  treatment with consent or second opinion, 1–736
PHYSICAL DISABILITIES
  treatment without consent, 1–787
PHYSICAL INJURIES
  see **Personal injury**
PLACE OF SAFETY
  Code of Practice
    arrangements following assessment, 4–082
    assessment at, 4–076
    consent to treatment, 4–081
    generally, 4–074, 4–075
    local policies, 4–074
    minors, 4–111
    record keeping, 4–078
    rights of persons detained, 4–080
    transfer between, 4–077
  definition, 1–700
  guardianship orders, 1–531
  hospital orders, 1–531
  mentally disordered persons found in public places
    Code of Practice, 4–073
    removal to place of safety, 1–1337
  remands to hospital, 1–495
  warrants for removal, 1–1325
POLICE DETENTION
  see also **Detention**
  escape from, 1–1344—1–1348
  generally, 1–1341—1–1343
  mentally disordered persons found in public places
    removal to place of safety, 1–1337
POLICE POWERS AND DUTIES
  Code of Practice
    introduction, 4–070
    mentally disordered found in public places, 4–073
    monitoring use, 4–079
    record keeping, 4–078
    removal to place of safety, 4–074—4–077
    rights of persons detained, 4–080
    use policies, 4–074

POLICE POWERS AND DUTIES—*cont.*
  Code of Practice—*cont.*
    warrant to search for and remove patients, 4–071,
      4–072
  custody of patients, 1–1341—1–1343
  detention
    escape from, 1–1344—1–1348
    generally, 1–1341—1–1343
    mentally disordered persons found in public
      places, 1–1336
  escape from custody, 1–1344—1–1348
  mentally disordered persons found in public places,
    1–1336
  warrants for search for and removal of patients,
    1–1317—1–1321
POSTAL PACKETS
  see also **Letters**
  Act provisions, 1–1300
POWERS OF ENTRY
  police powers and duties, 4–071—4–072
  warrants for search for and removal of patients,
    1–1325
  Wales, 1–1112
PRACTICE AND PROCEDURE
  see **Procedure**
PRACTICE DIRECTIONS
  child, vulnerable adult and sensitive witnesses,
    3–202—3–204
  delegation of functions to staff and registrars, 3–205
  statements and reports in mental health cases
    community patients, 3–190—3–193
    conditionally discharged patients, 3–198—3–200
    guardianship patients, 3–194—3–197
    in-patients, 3–182—3–189
    minors, 3–201
  Part 8 claims, 3–001—3–007
PREGNANCY
  treatment without consent, 1–787
PREMISES
  dangerous premises, 1–119
  police powers and duties
    search warrants, 1–325
  warrants for search for and removal of patients,
    1–1325
PRISONS
  release from/return to
    absence without leave, 1–676
    Act provisions, 1–667, 1–677
    generally, 1–667—1–676
    human rights, 1–670
    introduction, 1–669
    life imprisonment, 1–672—1–673
    treatability, 1–671
PRIVACY
  blanket locked door policy, 4–011
  blanket restrictions, 4–010
  electronic mail, 4–012
  generally, 4–008
  human rights and, 4–009
  Internet access, 4–012
  introduction, 4–008

PRIVACY—*cont.*
  personal searches, 4–016—4–017
  private property, 4–013
  respect for, 4–009
  searches, 4–016—4–017
  separate facilities for men and women, 4–014
  telephone calls, 4–012
PRIVILEGED COMMUNICATIONS
  withholding of correspondence, 1–1306
PROCEDURE
  appointment of acting nearest relatives, 1–432
  Civil Procedure Rules
    generally, 3–001
    practice direction, 3–001—3–007
  compulsory admissions
    Act provisions, 1–147
    Code of Practice, 1–151
    consultation with nearest relatives, 1–158—
      1–159
    court applications, 1–451—1–453
    defective, 1–202—1–210
    generally, 1–152—1–160
    human rights, 1–150
    interview of patients, 1–160
    introduction, 1–147
    objections, 1–157
  county court applications, 1–451—1–453
  First-tier Tribunal Rules, 3–008—3–179
  guardianship
    Act provisions, 1–147
    Code of Practice, 1–151
    consultation with nearest relatives, 1–158—
      1–159
    court applications, 1–451—1–453
    defective, 1–202—1–210
    generally, 1–152—1–160
    human rights, 1–150
    interview of patients, 1–160
    introduction, 1–147
    objections, 1–157
  Part 8 claims
    generally, 3–001
    practice direction, 3–001—3–007
  tribunals
    procedure, 3–008—3–179
    Wales, 1–968—1–976
PRODUCTION OF DOCUMENTS
  see **Disclosure**
PROPERTY
  see **Human rights**
PROSECUTIONS
  generally, 1–1217—1–1219
  immunity from liability, 1–1355
PROTECTION FROM LIABILITY
  see **Immunity from prosecution**
PROTECTION OF OTHERS
  see **Public protection**
PROTECTION OF PATIENTS
  see **Mental patients' rights**
PROTECTION OF PROPERTY
  human rights, 5–057

Index

PROTECTION OF PUBLIC
see **Public protection**
PROVISION OF INFORMATION
children, to, 1–1286
Code of Practice
nearest relatives, to, 4–029
patients, for, 4–029
community patients, to, 1–1292—1–1295
consent and, 1–722
discharge, as to, 1–1296—1–1299
legal representation, about, 1–1288
nearest relatives
Act provisions, 1–1296
Code of Practice, 1–1286, 4–029
discharge, as to, 1–1296—1–1299
generally, 1–1283—1–1291
introduction, 1–1285
leaflets, 1–1287
patients
Act provisions, 1–1283, 1–1292
Code of Practice, 1–1286, 4–020—4–026
generally, 1–1283—1–1291
introduction, 1–1285
Regulations, 2–119—2–120
young people, to, 1–1286
PSYCHOPATHIC DISORDER
mental disorder, 1–029
PSYCHOSURGERY
consent to treatment, 1–718
PUBLIC PROTECTION
compulsory admissions
assessment, 1–048
treatment, 1–066—1–067
discharge by Tribunal, 1–919
guardianship, 1–119
restriction orders, 1–573
REASONABLE CARE
immunity from liability, 1–1355, 2–006
RECALL TO HOSPITAL
absence without leave
Channel Islands, 1–1073, 1–1081—1–1083
England and Wales, 1–1078—1–1080
generally, 1–341—1–346
Isle of Man, 1–1081—1–1083
Northern Ireland, 1–1074—1–1077
return after 28 days, 1–354—1–366
return within 28 days, 1–348—1–353
Scotland, to, 1–1073
community treatment orders and, 1–256—1–264
consent to treatment, 1–778—1–782
discharge of restricted patients by Tribunal, 1–937
escape from custody, 1–1344—1–1348
interim hospital orders, 1–540
sentenced patients, 1–367—1–372
leave of absence, 1–226
restriction orders, 1–588—1–589
RECTIFICATION
applications
Act provisions, 1–202
Code of Practice, 1–206
defects, 1–207

RECTIFICATION—*cont.*
applications—*cont.*
emergency applications, 1–210
impossibility of, 1–204
introduction, 1–204
medical recommendations, insufficient, 1–209
REFERENCES
compulsory admissions, 1–875—1–878
guardianship, 1–875—1–878
hospital managers, by
generally, 1–879—1–885
power to reduce periods, 1–886—1–889
restriction orders, 1–898—1–903
Secretary of State, by
compulsory admissions, 1–875—1–878
guardianship, 1–875—1–878
restriction orders, 1–898—1–903
REFUGEES
after-care, 1–1122
"REGISTERED ESTABLISHMENTS"
definition, 1–462
human rights, 1–465
REGISTERED MEDICAL PRACTITIONERS
see **Doctors**
REGULATIONS
generally, 1–454—1–457
guardianship, 1–138—1–140
REGULATORY AUTHORITY
see **Care Quality Commission**
RELATIVES
see also **Nearest relatives**
definition, 1–400—1–412
RELEASE FROM CUSTODY
absence without leave, 1–676
Act provisions, 1–667, 1–677
generally, 1–667—1–676
human rights, 1–670
introduction, 1–669
life imprisonment, 1–672—1–673
treatability, 1–671
REMAND
custody
magistrates' courts, 1–685—1–689
REMANDS TO HOSPITAL
medical treatment, for
Act provisions, 1–500
applications, 1–503
further remands, 1–509
generally, 1–506—1–510
insanity, 1–491
introduction, 1–502
offences punishable with imprisonment, 1–507
orders made in other proceedings, 1–504
transport to and from court, 1–505
reports on condition, for
Act provisions, 1–481
applications, 1–485
consent to treatment, 1–483
contempt of court, 1–486
conveyance to hospital, 1–498
evidence of mental disorder, 1–493

REMANDS TO HOSPITAL—*cont.*
reports on condition, for—*cont.*
  family law orders, 1–486
  further remands, 1–495
  generally, 1–481—1–499
  housing, 1–486, 1–487
  insanity, 1–484
  introduction, 1–483
  orders made in other proceedings, 1–486
  offences punishable with imprisonment, 1–491—1–492
  time limits, 1–496
  transport to and from court, 1–489
  variation or rescission of sentence, 1–488
REMOVAL
see also **Transfer of patients**
place of safety, to
  guardianship orders, 1–531
  hospital orders, 1–531
  mentally disordered persons found in public
    places, 1–1336
  warrants, 1–1324—1–1328
REMOVAL TO HOSPITAL
see **Transfer directions**
REMOVAL OF PATIENTS
see **Transfer of patients**
REMUNERATION
mentally disordered persons, 1–1364—1–1367
registered medical practitioners, 1–1165—1–1168
REPATRIATION
patients, of, 1–1061, 1–1065
REPORTS
compulsory admission of in-patients, 1–088
remands to hospital
  Act provisions, 1–481
  applications, 1–485
  consent to treatment, 1–483
  contempt of court, 1–486
  conveyance to hospital, 1–498
  evidence of mental disorder, 1–493
  family law orders, 1–486
  further remands, 1–495
  generally, 1–481—1–499
  housing, 1–486, 1–487
  insanity, 1–484
  introduction, 1–483
  orders made in other proceedings, 1–486
  offences punishable with imprisonment, 1–491—1–492
  time limits, 1–496
  transport to and from court, 1–489
  variation or rescission of sentence, 1–488
  restriction orders, 1–580
RESIDENCE
carers, 1–409
Code of Practice, 1–132
designated place of residence, 1–132
nearest relatives, 1–412
RESIDENTIAL ACCOMMODATION
children, 1–1279—1–1282
informal admissions, 1–1279—1–1282

RESIDENTIAL CARE
nearest relatives, 1–412
RESPONSIBLE CLINICIANS
administration of medication, 1–740
background, 1–462
definition, 1–462, 1–700
generally, 1–466
human rights, 1–465
RESPONSIBLE MEDICAL OFFICERS
see **Responsible clinicians**
RESTRAINT
additional powers, A–001—A–003
Code of Practice
  administration of medication, for, 4–164
  mechanical restraint, 4–162, 4–163
  physical restraint, 4–161
treatment without consent, 1–787
RESTRICTED PATIENTS
absolute discharge
  generally, 1–934—1–936
Act provisions, 1–932
conditional discharge
  deferral, 1–941
  generally, 1–937
  recall to hospital, 1–938—1–940
conditionally discharged patients
  Act provisions, 1–951
  generally, 1–953
  human rights, 1–954
  introduction, 1–953
foreign nationals, 1–1064
human rights
  conditional discharge, 1–941
  generally, 1–935
  introduction, 1–934
  leave of absence, 1–214
  limitation directions, 1–943—1–950
  recall to hospital, 1–938—1–940
  restriction directions, 1–943—1–950
  Secretary of State's powers, 1–221, 1–942
RESTRICTION DIRECTIONS
generally, 1–943—1–950
leave of absence, 1–658
RESTRICTION ORDERS
antecedents, 1–573
appeals
  Crown Court, from, 1–596
  introduction, 1–570
  magistrates' courts, from, 1–607—1–609
applications by restricted patients, 1–569
conveyance of patients to hospital, 1–590
courts' powers
  Act provisions, 1–564
  generally, 1–564—1–580
  introduction, 1–566
dangerousness, 1–574
discharge by Secretary of State, 1–587
discharge by Tribunal
  conditionally discharged patients, 1–951—1–958
  generally, 1–932—1–942
  limitation directions, 1–943—1–950

Index

RESTRICTION ORDERS—*cont.*
discharge by Tribunal—*cont.*
restriction directions, 1–943—1–950
Domestic Violence, Crime and Victims Act 2004 and, 1–571
end of restrictions
generally, 1–579
Secretary of State's powers, 1–591
evidence, 1–574
hospital orders, 1–573
human rights, 1–584
introduction, 1–566—1–567
jurisdiction, 1–573
magistrates' courts' powers
Act provisions, 1–593
appeals, 1–596
committal to Crown Court, 1–593—1–599
committal to hospital, 1–600—1–606
introduction, 1–595
nature, 1–566
medical evidence, 1–574
named hospital units, 1–568
public protection, 1–573
recall to hospital, 1–588—1–590
reports, 1–580
restrictions, 1–575—1–577
review, 1–580
Secretary of State's powers
Act provisions, 1–581
applications, 1–585
attendance requirements, 1–591
community leave, 1–577
discharge of patients, 1–587
end of restriction orders, 1–590
generally, 1–581—1–592
human rights, 1–584
introduction, 1–583
lifting of restrictions, 1–586
recall to hospital, 1–588—1–589
taking and conveyance of patients to hospital, 1–590
serious harm to public, 1–573
taking patients to hospital, 1–590
transfer of patients, 1–577
Tribunal applications, 1–895—1–897
Tribunal references, 1–898—1–903
RESTRICTIONS ON POLITICAL ACTIVITY OF ALIENS
generally, 5–054
RETURN TO CUSTODY
absence without leave, 1–676
Act provisions, 1–667, 1–677
generally, 1–667—1–676, 1–685—1–689
human rights, 1–670, 1–680
introduction, 1–669, 1–679
life imprisonment, 1–673
treatability, 1–671
REVIEWS
consent to treatment, 1–740
informal admissions, 1–1281
medical treatment
consent, 1–740

REVIEWS—*cont.*
medical treatment—*cont.*
generally, 1–764—1–770
restriction orders, 1–580
tribunal decisions
applications in SEN cases, 3–173
power, 3–177—3–179
withholding correspondence
Act provisions, 1–1314
REVOCATION
leave of absence, 1–225
Regulations, 2–130—2–135
RIGHT TO EDUCATION
see also **Human Rights**
generally, 5–058
RIGHT TO FAIR TRIAL
see also **Human Rights**
civil rights and obligations, 5–030
fair hearing, 5–030
generally, 5–028—5–030
independent and impartial tribunal, 5–030
RIGHT TO FREE ELECTIONS
see also **Human Rights**
generally, 5–059—5–060
RIGHT TO LIBERTY AND SECURITY
see also **Human Rights**
alcoholics, 5–022
children, 5–020
conviction, 5–021
generally, 5–018—5–027
lawful, 5–022
lawfulness of detention, 5–025
persons of unsound mind, 5–022
procedure prescribed by law, 5–020
security of person, 5–020
speedily, 5–025
RIGHT TO LIFE
see also **Human Rights**
abortion, 5–009
generally, 5–005—5–008
use of force, 5–010
RIGHT TO MARRY
see also **Human Rights**
generally, 1–010, 5–050—5–051
RIGHT TO RESPECT FOR CORRESPONDENCE
see also **Human Rights; Withholding correspondence**
Code of Practice, 1–1304
interference, 5–040
withholding correspondence, 1–1303
RIGHT TO RESPECT FOR HOME
see also **Human Rights**
generally, 5–033—5–043
home, 5–040
RIGHT TO RESPECT FOR PRIVATE AND FAMILY LIFE
see also **Human Rights**
correspondence
Code of Practice, 1–1304
interference, 5–040
withholding, 1–1303
economic well-being, 5–042

RIGHT TO RESPECT FOR PRIVATE AND FAMILY LIFE—*cont.*
family life, 5–039
generally, 5–033—5–043
home, 5–040
in accordance with the law, 5–041
necessary in democratic society, 042
private life, 5–035—5–038
protection of health, 5–043
public authority, 5–041
respect, 5–035
RISK ASSESSMENT
compulsory admissions
assessment, 1–048
emergencies, 1–076
in-patients, 1–086
treatment, 1–066—1–067
restriction orders, 1–566—1–567
SAFETY (PATIENTS)
assessment
Code of Practice, 4–008
generally, 1–048
Code of Practice
enhanced security accommodation, 4–018
other accommodation, 4–019
compulsory admissions
assessment, 1–048
treatment, 1–066—1–067
discharge by Tribunal, 1–919
guardianship, 1–119
treatment, 1–066—1–067
SCILLY ISLES
application of Act provisions, 1–1391—1–1392
SCOTLAND
absence without leave, 1–279, 1–280
application of Act provisions, 1–1384
Mental Health (Care and Treatment) Scotland Act
2003 (Consequential Provisions Order 2005
absent without leave, 2–003
assisting patients, 2–004
detention, 2–005
interpretation, 2–002
removal of patients detained from
generally, 1–994—1–998
requesting a transfer warrant, 1–997
removal of patients detained to, 1–983—1–986
removal of patients subject to compulsion in the
community from, 1–999—1–1002
return of patients absence without leave to, 1–1073
transfer of community patients to, 1–987—1–989
transfer of conditionally discharged patients from,
1–1003—1–1005
transfer of conditionally discharged patients to,
1–990—1–998
SEARCH WARRANTS
Act provisions, 1–1317
applications, 1–1325
Code of Practice, 1–1324
entry onto premises, 1–1325
grounds, 1–1325
human rights, 1–1323
introduction, 1–1319—1–1321

SEARCH WARRANTS—*cont.*
police powers and duties, 1–1320—1–1321
SEARCHES
privacy, 4–016—4–017
SECLUSION
authorisation, 4–167
commencing, 4–168
conditions, 4–141
further guidance, 4–176
generally, 4–165
introduction, 4–132
observation during, 4–169
procedure, 4–166
reviews, 4–170—4–174
terminating, 4–175
SECOND OPINIONS
treatment with consent and
Act provisions, 1–716
certification, 1–723
consent, 1–722—1–723
generally, 1–720
hormone implantation for reduction of sex drive,
1–720
introduction, 1–718
surgical operations, 1–720
treatment with consent or
Act provisions, 1–726
consent, 1–740
covert administration of medication, 1–738
generally, 1–726—1–743
human rights, 1–729—1–733
introduction, 1–726
medication, 1–738—1–739
placebo medication, 1–739
time limits, 1–736
use of forms, 1–737
SECRETARIES OF STATE
agreement for exercise of approval function,
1–171—1–176
Code of Practice
Act provisions, 1–1155
criminal proceedings
generally, 1–469
Wales, for, 1–470
default powers, 1–1094
discharge of restricted patients by Tribunal, 1–941
Mental Health Act Commission, 1–1188
pocket-money for hospital patients, 1–1189—
1–1192
references to Tribunal
compulsory admissions, 1–875—1–878
guardianship, 1–875—1–878
restriction orders, 1–898—1–903
registered medical practitioners, 1–1165—1–1168
restriction orders
Act provisions, 1–581
applications, 1–585
attendance requirements, 1–591
discharge of patients, 1–587
end of restriction orders, 1–590
generally, 1–581—1–592

SECRETARIES OF STATE—*cont.*
  restriction orders—*cont.*
    human rights, 1–584
    introduction, 1–583
    lifting of restrictions, 1–586
    recall to hospital, 1–588—1–589
    taking and conveyance of patients to hospital,
      1–590
    transfer to/from special hospitals, 1–1193—1–1194
SECTIONING
  see **Compulsory admissions**
SECURE ACCOMMODATION
  informal admissions, 1–1277
SECURE HOSPITALS
  leave of absence, 1–214
SELF-HARM
  treatment without consent, 1–787
SENTENCED PATIENTS
  see **Mentally disordered offenders**
SENTENCING
  guardianship orders, 1–519
  hospital orders, 1–519
SETTING ASIDE
  tribunal decisions, 3–158—3–179
SEVERE MENTAL IMPAIRMENT
  mental disorder, 1–029
SEX OFFENDERS REGISTER
  generally, 1–478
SEXUAL DYSFUNCTION
  mental disorder, 1–029
SEXUAL OFFENCES
  generally, 1–1096
  rights of victims, 1–013
SKELETON ARGUMENTS
  tribunal procedure, 3–023
SLAVERY
  human rights, 5–017
SOCIAL SERVICES
  see **Local social services authorities**
SPECIAL HOSPITALS
  correspondence
    incoming, 1–1305
    outgoing, 1–1304
  transfer to/from, 1–1193—1–1194
SPOUSES
  nearest relatives, 1–406
STRIKING OUT
  tribunal procedure, 3–055—3–057
SUBSTITUTION OF PARTIES
  tribunal procedure, 3–058—3–060
SUICIDE
  predicting risk, 1–048
  treatment without consent, 1–787
SUPERVISED COMMUNITY TREATMENT
  See **Community treatment orders**
SUPERVISED DISCHARGE
  see **After-care**
SUPERVISION
  after-care, 1–399
SURGICAL PROCEDURES
  consent to treatment, 1–720

"TECHNICAL LIFERS"
  generally, 1–663
TELEPHONE CALLS
  privacy, 4–012
  withholding of correspondence, 1–1306
TIME
  tribunal procedure, 3–074—3–075
TIME LIMITS
  guardianship
    absence without leave, 1–287—1–288
    applications, 1–120
    medical recommendations, 1–167
  guardianship orders, 1–698—1–699
  compulsory admissions
    absence without leave, 1–287—1–288
    assessment, 1–050
    emergencies, 1–078
    generally, 1–107—1–108
  hospital orders, 1–698—1–699
  remands to hospital
    reports, 1–496
  return to hospital, 1–287—1–288
  treatment with consent or second opinion, 1–736
  Tribunal applications, 1–874
TORTURE
  degrading, 5–016
  generally, 5–011—5–015
  meaning, 5–015
TRANSFER DIRECTIONS
  civil prisoners, 1–690—1–692
  discharge of patients
    Act provisions, 1–654
    generally, 1–654—1–666
    human rights, 1–662
    "technical lifers", 1–663
  immigration offences, 1–690—1–692
  leave of absence, 1–650
  release from prison
    absence without leave, 1–676
    Act provisions, 1–667, 1–677
    generally, 1–667—1–676
    human rights, 1–670
    introduction, 1–669
    life imprisonment, 1–672—1–673
    treatability, 1–671
  remand in custody by magistrates' courts, 1–685—
    1–689
  return to prison
    absence without leave, 1–676
    Act provisions, 1–667, 1–677
    generally, 1–667—1–676
    human rights, 1–670
    introduction, 1–669
    life imprisonment, 1–672—1–673
    treatability, 1–671
  sentenced patients
    Act provisions, 1–631
    emergency, 1–635
    generally, 1–639—1–645
    human rights, 1–637
    introduction, 1–633—1–635

TRANSFER DIRECTIONS—*cont.*
  sentenced patients—*cont.*
    leave of absence, 1–650
    medical treatment, 1–642
    named hospital units, 1–636
    out-of-hours, 1–635
    sentences, 1–645
    start dates, 1–643
  unsentenced patients
    end of transfer directions, 1–674
    generally, 1–646—1–653
"TRANSFER OF GUARDIANSHIP"
  Act provisions, 1–141
  death, 1–141—1–146
  generally, 1–141—1–142
  incapacity, 1–145
  introduction, 1–141
  relinquishment, 1–141
"TRANSFER OF PATIENTS"
  absence without leave
    Channel Islands, 1–1073, 1–1081—1–1083
    England and Wales, 1–1078—1–1080
    generally, 1–341—1–346
    Isle of Man, 1–1081—1–1083
    Northern Ireland, 1–1074—1–1077
    return after 28 days, 1–354—1–366
    return within 28 days, 1–348—1–353
    Scotland, to, 1–1073
  Act provisions, 1–981
  aliens
    Act provisions, 1–1061
    generally, 1–1061—1–1072
    human rights, 1–1068
    travel restriction orders, 1–1067
  Channel Islands, from
    generally, 1–1047—1–1051
    offenders found insane, 1–1042—1–1046
  Channel Islands, to
    absence without leave, 1–1073, 1–1081—1–1083
    Act provisions, 1–981
    generally, 1–1032—1–1034
  Community patients
    another responsible hospital, to, 1–306—1–309,
      2–066—2–071
    Channel Islands, from, 1–1052—1–1055
    Channel Islands, to, 1–1035—1–1037
    Isle of Man, from, 1–1052—1–1055
    Isle of Man, to, 1–1035—1–1037
    Northern Ireland, to, 1–1013—1–1015
    recalled to hospital, 2–078—2–080
    Scotland, to, 1–987—1–989
  conditionally discharged patients, and
    Channel Islands, from, 1–1056—1–1060
    Channel Islands, to, 1–1042—1–1046
    Isle of Man, from, 1–1056—1–1060
    Isle of Man, to, 1–1042—1–1046
    Northern Ireland, from, 1–1028—1–1031
    Northern Ireland, to, 1–1016—1–1021
    Scotland, from, 1–1003—1–1005
    Scotland, to, 1–990—1–998
  guardianship, from, 2–072—2–077

"TRANSFER OF PATIENTS"—*cont.*
  hospitals, between
    community patients, of, 1–306—1–309
    generally, 1–291—1–305, 2–066—2–071
  human rights, 1–294
  in-patients and, 1–088
  introduction, 1–980
  Isle of Man, from
    generally, 1–1047—1–1051
    offenders found insane, 1–1042—1–1046
  Isle of Man, to
    absence without leave, 1–1081—1–1083
    Act provisions, 1–981
    generally, 1–1032—1–1034
  leave of absence, 1–217
  Northern Ireland, from, 1–1022—1–1027
  Northern Ireland, to
    absence without leave, 1–1074—1–1077
    Act provisions, 1–981
    generally, 1–1006—1–1012
  Regulations, 1–1084
  repatriation of prisoners, 1–1065, 1–1066
  restriction orders, 1–577
  Scotland, from
    generally, 1–994—1–998
    requesting a transfer warrant, 1–997
    subject to compulsion in the community, 1–999—
      1–1002
  Scotland, to
    absence without leave, 1–1073
    Act provisions, 1–981
    generally, 1–983—1–986
  Secretary of State's consent, 1–297, 1–299
TRAVEL RESTRICTION ORDERS
  removal of aliens, 1–1067
TREATABILITY
  compulsory admissions, 1–065
  release from/return to prison, 1–671
TREATMENT
  see **Medical treatment**
TREATMENT WITHOUT CONSENT
  see **Consent to treatment**
TRESPASS
  taking of patients to hospital, 1–104
TRIBUNAL APPLICATIONS
  see **Applications**
  Tribunals
  see **First-tier Tribunal (mental health); Upper
    Tribunal**
UN DECLARATION OF THE RIGHTS OF PERSONS WITH
  DISABILITIES
  generally, 1–019, 1–708
UNBORN CHILDREN
  compulsory admissions for assessment, 1–049
  compulsory admissions for treatment, 1–059
UNFITNESS FOR TRIAL
  see **Fitness to plead**
UNIVERSAL DECLARATION OF HUMAN RIGHTS
  generally, 1–018—1–019
UNMARRIED COUPLES
  nearest relatives, 1–411

Index

UNMARRIED PARENTS
nearest relatives, 1–407
UPPER TRIBUNAL
appeals from Mental Health Review Tribunal for
Wales
generally, 1–975—1–976
introduction, 1–865
URGENT TREATMENT
Act provisions, 1–771
continuation, 1–776
electro-convulsive therapy, 1–773
generally, 1–771—1–777
hazardous, 1–777
immediate necessity, 1–774
introduction, 1–773
irreversible, 1–777
unfavourable consequences, 1–777
USE OF FORCE
compliant patients, 1–034
human rights and, 5–010
taking of patients, 1–104
VENUES
Tribunal hearings, 1–963—1–967
VICTIMS
disclosure of evidence to patient, 3–092
rights of victims of serious, violent and sexual
offences, 1–013
tribunal procedure, 3–018
VISITORS
children
high security facilities, B–001—B–011
discharge, 1–387—1–391
local social services authorities duties, 1–1115—
1–1119
Regulations, 2–111—2–112
Tribunal powers, 1–959—1–962
VOLUNTARY PATIENTS
see Informal in-patients
VOTING RIGHTS
patients in psychiatric hospitals, 1–009
WAGES
mentally disordered persons, 1–1364—1–1367
registered medical practitioners, 1–1165—1–1168
WALES
see also Independent mental health advocates
(Wales); Mental Health Review Tribunal for
Wales
after-care, 1–1125
approved mental health professionals
conflict of interest, 2–014
courses, 1–1106—1–1108
generally, 2–028
statutory documentation, 1–189
Code of Practice, 1–1158
community treatment orders, 1–233, 1–1262—
1–1264
courses, 1–1106—1–1108
emergency treatment, 1–073
functions of the Secretary of State, 1–470
guardianship
applications, 1–116

WALES—cont.
guardianship—cont.
human rights, 1–128
statutory documentation, 1–189
independent mental health advocates, 1–1220,
1–1245—1–1267
medical recommendations, 1–167
mentally disordered persons found in public places,
1–1336
powers of entry and inspection, 1–1112
re-sectioning of a patient, 1–055
removal to Wales of patients from Channel Islands,
1–1042—1–1046
removal to Wales of patients from Isle of Man,
1–1042—1–1046
removal to Wales of patients from Northern Ireland,
1–1022—1–1027
responsibility to inform patients nearest relative,
2–079
transfer of functions under the Act, 1–003
transfer of responsibility to Wales of patients from
Northern Ireland, 1–1028—1–1031
WARDS OF COURT
generally, 1–458—1–461
WARRANTS
recall to hospital under restriction orders, 1–589
removal to place of safety, 1–1324—1–1328
search for patients
Act provisions, 1–1317
applications, 1–1325
Code of Practice, 1–1324, 4–071, 4–072
entry onto premises, 1–1325
grounds, 1–1325
human rights, 1–1323
introduction, 1–1319—1–1321
police powers and duties, 1–1320—1–1321
WITHDRAWAL
consent to treatment, 1–759—1–763
medical recommendations, 1–167
Tribunal applications
Code of Practice, 4–033
generally, 3–098—3–102
statutory provision, 1–966
WITHHOLDING CORRESPONDENCE
Act provisions, 1–1300
censoring of correspondence, 1–1304
Code of Practice, 1–1304
delegation of powers, 1–1311
exceptions, 1–1306
high security hospitals
incoming correspondence, 1–1305
outgoing correspondence, 1–1304
human rights
generally, 5–040
introduction, 1–1303
incoming, 1–1305
introduction, 1–1302
notice, 1–1310
opening and inspection
generally, 1–1308
Regulations, 2–126

WITHHOLDING CORRESPONDENCE—*cont.*
  outgoing, 1–1304
  postal operators, 1–1313
  record-keeping requirements, 1–1309
  Regulations, 2–126—2–129
  review of decision to withhold correspondence
    Act provisions, 1–1314
    Regulations, 2–127—2–128
  right to respect for private and family life, 5–040
WITNESS EXPENSES AND ALLOWANCES
  see **Expenses**
WITNESS SUMMONSES
  tribunal procedure, 3–094—3–097
YOUNG PERSONS
  accommodation, 1–1279—1–1282
  age-appropriate services, 4–410
  applications to the Tribunal, 4–413
  Code of Practice
    after care, 4–114
    age-appropriate services, 4–110
    applications to the Tribunal, 4–113
    assessing competence, 4–091
    capacity, 4–091, 4–097—4–100
    community treatment orders, 4–115
    confidentiality, 4–087
    consent, 4–090, 4–107
    decisions on admission and treatment, 4–089—
      4–102
    deprivation of liberty, 4–094
    duties of local authorities as to hospital patients,
      4–118
    education, 4–116
    electro-convulsive therapy, 4–108
    emergency medical treatment, 4–103
    general considerations, 4–084
    Gillick competence, 4–101—4–102
    informal admissions, 4–095—4–102
    introduction, 4–083
    looked-after child, 4–086
    parental responsibility, 4–085
    place of safety, 4–111
    provision of information to, 4–105
    regulated treatments, 4–106—4–109
    responsible clinician, 4–112
    role of those with parental responsibility, 4–093
    safeguarding when admission is not appropriate,
      4–088
    sharing information, 4–087
    transition from CAMHS, 4–117
    whether to make an application, 4–104
  community treatment orders, 4–115
  confidentiality, 4–087
  consent to treatment
    aged 16 or 17, 1–1275
    under the age of 16, 1–1276
  Convention on the Rights of the Child, 1–018
  decisions on admission and treatment, 4–089—
    4–102
  definition, 1–700
  detention, 1–1278

YOUNG PERSONS—*cont.*
  duties of local authorities as to hospital patients,
    4–118
  education, 4–116
  electro-convulsive therapy, 4–108
  emergency medical treatment
    Code of Practice, 4–103
    generally, 1–838—1–846
  Gillick competence, 4–101—4–102
  independent mental health advocates, 1–749
  informal admissions
    accommodation, 1–1279—1–1282
    Code of Practice, 4–095—4–102
    detention, 1–1278
    secure accommodation, 1–1277
  looked-after children
    Code of Practice, 4–086
    generally, 1–413—1–415
  medical treatment for community patients
    certificates, 1–847—1–853
    Code of Practice, 1–827, 1–833
    emergency treatment, 1–838—1–846
    generally, 1–824—1–829
    patients lacking competence, 1–830—1–834
    withdrawal of consent, 1–835—1–837
  nearest relative, as, 1–399
  nearest relatives, 1–416—1–422
  parental responsibility, 4–085
  provision of information, 4–105
  regulated treatments, 4–106—4–109
  secure accommodation, 1–1277
  unborn child, 1–048
  welfare visits, 1–1115—1–1119
YOUTH COURTS
  remand in custody, 1–685—1–689
  restriction orders
    Act provisions, 1–593
    committal to Crown Court, 1–525, 1–593—
      1–599
    committal to hospital, 1–600—1–606